Significant Dates and Events in the History of Clinical Psychology

1879   Wilhelm Wundt establishes first formal psychology laboratory at the University of Leipzig.

1885   Sir Francis Galton establishes first mental testing center at the South Kensington Museum, London.

1890   James McKeen Cattell coins the term *mental test*.

1892   American Psychological Association (APA) founded.

1895   Breuer and Freud publish *Studies in Hysteria*.

1896   Lightner Witmer founds first psychological clinic, University of Pennsylvania.

1905   Binet-Simon Intelligence Scale published in France.

1907   Witmer founds first clinical journal, *The Psychological Clinic*.

1908   First clinical internship offered at Vineland Training School.

1909   William Healy founds first child-guidance center, the Juvenile Psychopathic Institute, Chicago.
Freud lectures at Clark University.

1910   Goddard's English translation of the 1908 revision of the Binet-Simon Intelligence Scale published.

1912   J.B. Watson publishes *Psychology as a Behaviorist Views It*.

1916   Terman's Stanford-Binet Intelligence Test published.

1917   Clinicians break away from APA to form American Association of Clinical Psychology (AACP).

1919   AACP rejoins APA as its clinical section.

1920   Watson and Rayner demonstrate that a child's fear can be learned.

1921   James McKeen Cattell forms Psychological Corporation.

1924   Mary Cover Jones employs learning principles to remove children's fears.

1931   Clinical section of APA appoints committee on training standards.

1935   Thematic Apperception Test (TAT) published.

1937   Clinical section of APA breaks away to form American Association for Applied Psychology (AAAP).

1938   First Buros *Mental Measurement Yearbook* published.

1939   Wechsler-Bellevue Intelligence Test published.

1942   Carl Rogers publishes *Counseling and Psychotherapy*, outlining an alternative to psychodynamic therapy.

1943   Minnesota Multiphasic Personality Inventory (MMPI) published.

1945   AAAP rejoins APA.
Journal of Clinical Psychology published.
Connecticut State Board of Examiners in Psychology issues first certificate to practice psychology.

1946   Veterans Administration and National Institute of Mental Health begin support for training of clinical psychologists.

1947   American Board of Examiners in Professional Psychology organized.
Shakow Report recommends clinical training standards to APA.

1949   Colorado conference on training in clinical psychology convenes, recommends "Boulder Model."

1950   APA publishes first standards for approved internships in clinical psychology.

1952   American Psychiatric Association's *Diagnostic and Statistical Manual (DSM-I)* published.

1953   APA's *Ethical Standards for Psychologists* published.

1955   Wechsler Adult Intelligence Test published.

1956   Stanford Training Conference.

1958   Miami Training Conference.
Clinical Division of APA holds NIMH-sponsored conference about research on psychotherapy.

1959   The first psychotherapy benefit in a prepaid insurance plan appears.

1965   Chicago Training Conference.

1968   Psy.D. training program begins at the University of Illinois, Urbana-Champaign.
Second edition of *DSM (DSM-II)* published.
Committee on Health Insurance begins campaign to allow payment of clinical psychologists' services by health insurance plans without requiring medical supervision.

1969   California School of Professional Psychology founded.
APA begins publication of the journal, *Professional Psychology*.

1970   Department of Defense health insurance program authorizes payment of clinical psychologists' services without medical referral.
Classes begin at California School of Professional Psychology, the first independent clinical psychology training program in the United States

1971   Council for the Advancement of Psychological Professions and Sciences, a political advocacy group for clinical psychology, is organized.
Journal of Clinical Child Psychology published.

1972   Menninger Conference on Postdoctoral Education in Clinical Psychology.

1973   Vail, Colorado, Training Conference.

1974   National Register of Health Service Providers in Psychology established.
Federal government allows payment for clinical psychologists' services to its employees without medical supervision or referral.
APA establishes *Standards for Providers of Psychological Services*.
First Inter-American Congress of Clinical Psychology held in Porto Alegre, Brazil.

1977   All fifty U.S. states have certification or licensing laws for clinical psychologists.

1980   Third edition of *DSM (DSM-III)* published.
Smith, Glass, and Miller publish *The Benefits of Psychotherapy*.
Blue Shield health insurance companies in Virginia successfully sued for refusing to pay for clinical psychologists' services to people covered by their plans.

1981   APA publishes its revised *Ethical Principles of Psychologists*.

1983	Joint Commission for the Accreditation of Hospitals allows clinical psychologists to become members of hospital medical staffs.
1987	*DSM-III-R* published.
	Conference on graduate education in psychology, Salt Lake City, Utah.
1988	American Psychological Society formed.
1990	California Supreme Court affirms right of clinical psychologists to independently admit, diagnose, treat, and release mental patients without medical supervision.
	Dick McFall publishes "Manifesto for a Science of Clinical Psychology."
1993	Commander John L. Sexton and Lt. Commander Morgan T. Sammons complete psychopharmacology program at Walter Reed Army Medical Center, becoming first psychologists legally permitted to prescribe psychoactive drugs.
1994	*DSM-IV* published.
	Amendment to Social Security Act guarantees psychologists the right to independent practice and payment for hospital services under Medicare.
	Academy of Psychological Clinical Science is established.

1995	APA task force of clinical psychologists publishes list of empirically validated psychological therapies and calls for students to be trained to use them.
1996	Dorothy W. Cantor becomes first president of APA to hold the Psy.D. rather than the Ph.D.
2000	*DSM-IV-TR* published.
2002	New Mexico grants prescription privileges to specially trained clinical psychologists.
2005	APA sponsors a Presidential Task Force on evidencebased practice.
2006	Psychologists win a second settlement in two years in federal court alleging that managed care companies conspired to reduce and delay provider payments in violation of federal law.
2008	*The U.S. House of Representatives passes legislation requiring mental health parity: The Paul Wellstone Mental Health and Addiction Equity Act of 2007.*
2009	University of Illinois becomes the first PCSAS accredited program.
2013	DSM-5 published.

Eighth Edition

INTRODUCTION TO CLINICAL PSYCHOLOGY

Geoffrey P. Kramer

Douglas A. Bernstein

Vicky Phares

PEARSON

Boston   Columbus   Indianapolis   New York   San Francisco   Upper Saddle River
Amsterdam   Cape Town   Dubai   London   Madrid   Milan   Munich   Paris   Montréal   Toronto
Delhi   Mexico City   São Paulo   Sydney   Hong Kong   Seoul   Singapore   Taipei   Tokyo

Editor in Chief: Ashley Dodge
Executive Editor: Susan Hartman
Editorial Project Manager: Reena Dalal
Vice President/Director of Marketing: Brandy Dawson
Executive Marketing Manager: Wendy Albert
Marketing Assistant: Frank Alarcon
Digital Media Editor: Rachel Comerford

Managing Editor: Denise Forlow
Project Manager, Production: Annemarie Franklin
Manufacturing Buyer: Diane Peirano
Art Director: Jayne Conte
Cover Designer: Karen Noferi
Composition: Laserwords Pvt Ltd, India

Credits and acknowledgments borrowed from other sources and reproduced, with permission, in this textbook appear on appropriate page within text (or on page 517).

Library of Congress Cataloging-in-Publication Data

Kramer, Geoffrey P.
  Introduction to clinical psychology / Geoffrey P. Kramer, Douglas A. Bernstein, Vicky Phares. — Eighth edition.
    pages cm
Includes bibliographical references and indexes.
ISBN 0-205-87185-2 (alk. paper)
1. Clinical psychology. I. Bernstein, Douglas A. II. Phares, Vicky. III. Title.
RC467.N54 2014
616.89—dc23
                                                        2013012895

16   17

ISBN-10: 0-205-87185-2
ISBN-13: 978-0-205-87185-8

CONTENTS

PREFACE

In the seven previous editions of this book, we tried to accomplish three goals. First, we wanted a book that, while appropriate for graduate students, was written especially with sophisticated undergraduates in mind. Many undergraduate psychology majors express an interest in clinical psychology without having a clear understanding of what the field involves and requires. An even larger number of nonmajors also wish to know more about clinical psychology. We felt that both groups would benefit from a thorough survey of the field which does not go into all the details typically found in graduate study only texts.

Second, we wanted to present a scholarly portrayal of the history of clinical psychology, its scope, functions, and future that reviewed a full range of theoretical perspectives. Our goal is to present approaches to clinical psychology—psychodynamic, relational, humanistic, cognitive-behavioral, systems, group, etc.—fairly, highlighting the strengths and weaknesses of the empirical evidence supporting each of them. We do champion the empirical research tradition of clinical psychology throughout the book because we believe it is a necessary and useful perspective for all clinicians to follow, regardless of their theoretical orientation.

Third, we wanted our book to be interesting and enjoyable to read. Because we like being clinical psychologists and because we enjoy teaching, we tried to create a book that communicates our enthusiasm for its content.

Though we are still guided by the above goals, we sought to make some significant changes in the eighth edition. Since our last edition, numerous changes have occurred in clinical psychology and in the health care delivery system, both in the United States and internationally. Accordingly, we have undertaken a comprehensive updating of research and other material in all chapters. With over 900 new references, we have described how research has led to new ways to conceptualize, assess, and treat psychological dysfunction. Some of the other significant changes are listed below.

NEW TO THIS EDITION

- New pedagogical features. In addition to the updated study/discussion questions, and updated websites, the new features include suggestions for movies and memoirs, and bibliographical references at the end of each chapter.
- New case material. Cases have been updated and their number increased in order to make the material more compelling for students.
- Updated diagnostic criteria. The new edition discusses changes made in the **DSM-5** and the controversies that continue to surround diagnostic classification.
- Greater integration of research and practice. Rather than presenting these topics pitted against one another, we stress the importance of both and highlight the growing consensus created by focusing on clinical utility; we synthesize the Common Factors and Evidence-Based approaches to effectiveness research and update discussion of treatment planning.
- Discussion of new mental health delivery models. We discuss how technologies have affected the options for delivering mental health services, including going well beyond the traditional individual psychotherapy model.
- Revised presentation of several assessment instruments. We have included discussion of the PAI, MMPI-2, and MMPI-2 Restructured Clinical Scales and others; expanded discussion of cultural fairness and bias in psychological testing; revised and integrated our presentation of clinical versus actuarial prediction.
- Updated topics of relevance to students. Many topics that are of particular interest to students have been updated, including the evolving roles of technology and social media, information on careers within clinical psychology, the use of evidence-based practices; new techniques such as mindfulness which have become integral to the field; the status of complementary and alternative medicine.

- Updated information on getting into graduate school. This edition informs students about the new GRE scoring system and provides updated information on how to apply to graduate school, with special focus on new hardcopy and on-line resources.
- Updated discussion of clinical psychology training. We've added information on the new PCSAS accreditation system, the current internship crisis in clinical psychology, new choices in graduate training, and the increasing importance of multicultural competence.
- Updated discussion of popular therapies such as relational psychodynamic approaches, motivatinal interviewing, and emotion-focused therapy.

This text is available in a variety of formats—digital and print. To learn more about our programs, pricing options, and customization, visit www.pearsonhighered.com.

ACKNOWLEDGMENTS

We want to thank several people for their valuable contributions to this book. We wish to express our appreciation to Catherine Stoney for her help in updating the health psychology chapter, to Joel Shenker for his help in updating the neuropsychology chapter, and to Elaine Cassel for her help in updating the chapter on forensic psychology. We would also like to thank Lauren Snoeyink for her comments on chapter drafts.

Countless undergraduate and graduate students asked the questions, raised the issues, and explored multiple perspectives that have found their way into the text; they are really the people who stimulated the creation of this book, and who continue to make us want to revise and update its content. We thank them all. We would also like to thank Susan Hartman, Jeff Marshall, Reena Dalal, and Lindsay Bethoney at Pearson Prentice Hall and Haseen Khan at Laserwords for their help and patience in guiding the creation of this latest edition. Finally, we thank our families, loved ones, and friends for their support throughout this project. Your infinite patience and kind encouragement is a debt we can never repay.

Geoffrey P. Kramer
Douglas A. Bernstein
Vicky Phares

1 | WHAT IS CLINICAL PSYCHOLOGY?

Chapter Preview

In this chapter we introduce the field of clinical psychology. We first outline the requirements for becoming a clinical psychologist and discuss the profession's popularity. Next we describe how clinical psychology relates to other mental health professions. We describe the work activities of most clinical psychologists and the rewards of the profession, financial and otherwise. Finally, we introduce some of the key issues shaping the field today. These issues include how to (a) strike a balance between science and practice, (b) train new clinicians, (c) combine divergent theoretical approaches, and (d) adapt clinical practice to a changing health care environment.

A Clinical Case

Bonnie, a 15-year-old European American girl in 9th grade, asked her parents to get her some help to deal with her fear and anxiety. They did so, and as part of the intake evaluation at her first appointment, Bonnie was interviewed by a clinical psychologist specializing in treatment of childhood anxiety disorders. At the beginning of the interview, Bonnie said her problem was that she would "get nervous about everything," particularly about things at school and doing anything new. When asked to give an example, Bonnie mentioned that her father wanted her to go to camp during the coming summer, but she did not want to go to camp because of her "nerves." It soon became clear that Bonnie's anxiety stemmed from a persistent fear of social situations in which she might be the focus of other people's attention. She said she felt very self-conscious in the local mall and constantly worried about what others might be thinking of her. She was also fearful of eating in public, using public restrooms, being in crowded places, and meeting new people. She almost always tried to avoid such situations. She experienced anxiety when talking to her teachers and was even more afraid of talking to store clerks and other unfamiliar adults. Bonnie would not even answer the telephone in her own home.

In most of these situations, Bonnie said that her fear and avoidance related to worry about possibly saying the wrong thing or not knowing what to say or do, which would lead others to think badly of her. Quite often, her fear in these situations became so intense that she experienced a full-blown panic attack, complete with rapid heart rate, chest pain, shortness of breath, hot flashes, sweating, trembling, dizziness, and difficulty swallowing.

To get a clearer picture of the nature of Bonnie's difficulties, the psychologist conducted a separate interview with Bonnie's parents. While confirming what their daughter had said, they reported that Bonnie's social anxiety was even more severe than she had described it. (Based on Brown & Barlow, 2001, pp. 37–38.)

How can we best understand Bonnie's fears and anxieties? How did her problems develop, and what can be done to help her overcome them? These questions are important to Bonnie, her loved ones, and anyone interested in her condition, but the questions are especially important to clinical psychologists.

In this book you will learn how clinical psychologists address problems such as those faced by Bonnie. You will learn how clinicians assess and treat persons with psychological problems, how they conduct research into the causes and treatments for psychological disorders, and how they are trained. You will learn how clinical psychologists have become key providers of health care in the United States and in other countries, and how clinical psychology continues to evolve and adapt to the social, political, and cultural climate in which it is practiced.

AN OVERVIEW OF CLINICAL PSYCHOLOGY

SECTION PREVIEW

Here we define clinical psychology and identify the essential requirements satisfied by its practitioners. We also discuss the continued appeal of clinical psychology, popular conceptions of clinical psychologists, and how clinical psychology overlaps with, and differs from, other mental health professions.

As its name implies, clinical psychology is a subfield of the larger discipline of psychology. Like all psychologists, clinical psychologists are interested in *behavior and mental processes*. Like some other psychologists, clinical psychologists generate research about human behavior, seek to apply the results of that research, and engage in individual assessment. Like the members of some other professions, clinical psychologists provide assistance to those who need help with psychological problems. It is difficult to capture in a sentence or two the ever-expanding scope and shifting directions of clinical psychology. Nevertheless, we can outline the central features of the discipline as well as its many variations.

Definition of Clinical Psychology

The definition of clinical psychology adopted by the American Psychological Association's Division of Clinical Psychology reads as follows: "The field of Clinical Psychology integrates science, theory, and practice to understand, predict, and alleviate maladjustment, disability, and discomfort as well to promote human adaptation, adjustment, and personal development. Clinical Psychology focuses on the intellectual, emotional, biological, social, and behavioral aspects of human functioning across the life span, in varying cultures, and at all socioeconomic levels" (American Psychological Association, Division 12, 2012). As you can see, the definition focuses on the *integration* of science and practice, the *application* of this integrated knowledge across diverse human populations, and the *purpose* of alleviating human suffering and promoting health. But what are the requirements to become a clinical psychologist?

Personal Requirements to Be a Clinical Psychologist

Certain requirements for those wishing to be clinical psychologists have more to do with attitudes and character than with training and credentialing. Perhaps the most notable distinguishing feature of clinical psychologists has been called the *clinical attitude* or the *clinical approach* (Korchin, 1976), which is the tendency to combine knowledge from research on human behavior and mental processes with efforts at individual assessment in order to understand and help a particular

Clinical psychology's purpose is to alleviate human suffering and promote health. Those wishing to become clinical psychologists must satisfy rigorous personal, legal, and educational requirements. *Source*: Alina Solovyova-Vincent/E+/Getty Images.

person. The clinical attitude sets clinicians apart from other psychologists who search for general principles that apply to human behavior problems in general. Clinical psychologists are interested in research of this kind, but they also want to know how general principles shape lives, problems, and treatments on an individual level.

Because clinical psychology is both rigorously scientific and deeply personal, it requires that people entering the field have a strong and compassionate interest in human beings. Clinical training programs' admissions committees look for a number of characteristics as they make decisions about which applicants to admit to graduate study in clinical psychology. Personality variables such as an interest in people, integrity in dealing with others, emotional stability, and intellectual curiosity are of particular importance in selecting candidates (Johnson & Campbell, 2004; Prideaux et al., 2011; Swaminathan, 2012). These traits are important in many jobs, but they are crucial in clinical psychology because clinicians regularly work in situations that can have significant and lasting personal and interpersonal consequences. Even those clinical researchers who don't themselves offer psychotherapy may still make decisions about matters of personal consequence to participants, so integrity, emotional stability, and sound judgment are required for them, too.

The potential impact that clinical psychologists can have helps explain why, when considering candidates for admission to graduate training in clinical psychology, many psychology departments tend to rank letters of recommendations, personal statements, and interviews as slightly more important than more standardized academic indicators such as grade point averages or Graduate Record Exam (GRE) scores (Norcross, Kohout, & Wicherski, 2005). Nevertheless, as noted in Chapter 16, "Getting into Graduate School in Clinical Psychology," those standardized academic admission requirements for clinical psychology programs are typically quite high and predictive of success on the national licensing examination required to practice as a clinical psychologist (Sharpless & Barber, 2013).

Legal, Educational, and Ethical Requirements to Be a Clinical Psychologist

As one of psychology's *health service provider* subfields, clinical psychology requires its practitioners to receive specific training. In addition to having a degree from an accredited institution, those who practice clinical psychology must be licensed or certified to do so by state and national agencies. In the United States and Canada, each state or province establishes the requirements for licensure in clinical psychology, awards licenses to those who qualify, and retains the power to penalize or revoke the licenses of those who violate licensing laws. In other words, clinical psychology, like medicine, pharmacy, law, and dentistry, is a legally regulated profession.

Legal requirements vary not only by state but also by levels of training. For instance, in most states a *full license* in clinical psychology allows one to practice independently, to "hang out a shingle." Fully licensed clinicians can rent or own their own offices, set fees, establish work hours, bill insurance companies or other third parties, consult, testify in court, and engage in a number of other activities characteristic of independent private practice. These privileges usually come after a trainee has completed a doctoral-level degree that includes course work, research training, and the additional requirements listed below.

EDUCATION How much additional education beyond the bachelor's is required? An earned doctorate from an accredited program is the basic educational requirement for clinical psychology licensure (American Psychological Association, Division 12, 2012). Students complete substantial advanced coursework in psychopathology, assessment, and intervention strategies, and they become involved in conducting clinical research. Most states also require continuing education training for the periodic renewal of licenses.

Doctoral-level degrees for fully licensed clinical psychologists are typically either the *PhD* or the *PsyD*, though they occasionally include others (e.g., the EdD, or Doctor of Education). The PhD and PsyD degrees both stress intensive clinical training in preparation for clinical practice, but they differ in the extent to which science and research are stressed. Later in this chapter and in subsequent chapters, we explain the differences in these two models of training and describe the debates about the advantages and disadvantages of each. For now, just be aware that the number of doctoral-level psychologists produced by the two models has shifted; PsyD programs now accept and graduate more doctoral-level clinical psychologists than PhD programs do (Sayette, Norcross, & Dimoff, 2011).

At the subdoctoral level, practitioners have titles such as *limited license psychologist, marriage and family therapist, psychological assistant, mental health counselor,* and similar terms. To obtain a limited license, one usually needs a master's degree and a specific period of postgraduate supervised experience. Some states regulate the limited license much as they regulate the doctoral-level license, but other states provide less oversight, or no oversight, for subdoctoral practitioners (Sales, Miller, & Hall, 2005). Many states place limits on the practice of clinicians who are not fully licensed. An example would be requiring that the subdoctoral-level clinician always practices under the supervision of a fully licensed psychologist. Unfortunately, subdoctoral degrees are too often accompanied by restricted or lesser levels of reimbursement from insurance companies, lower salaries, and higher job turnover (Rajecki & Borden, 2011). This is not to say that qualified master's-level clinicians provide inferior services—well-trained masters level clinicians have helped millions of people—but rather, as in medicine, law, or any other profession, higher levels of training are usually associated with higher levels of skill in those areas and greater financial rewards. Given that clinical psychology is such a popular and competitive field, the best advice for students contemplating entry into this field is to resolve to work very hard and to seek the highest levels of training available.

EXPERIENCE   Some term of supervised practice in the field, often embodied in successful completion of an approved practicum, internship, or period of supervision is also a critical part of a clinical psychologist's required training. The duration of supervised practice varies, but one-year and two-year internships are common. Students are typically paid a modest stipend during their internships. As the number of persons applying for internships has recently outpaced the number available in a given year, internship placement has become more competitive (Vasquez, 2011). The APA annually publishes a list of accredited clinical psychology programs and approved internship sites in its flagship journal, the *American Psychologist.*

TESTING OF COMPETENCE   To be licensed as a clinical psychologist, candidates must declare to licensing boards their areas of competence, and they must pass a comprehensive examination, often called a *licensing board exam,* which may include both written and oral components. The written national licensing test used in the United States and Canada is called the *Examination for Professional Practice in Psychology* (EPPP). Passing this examination also makes it easier for clinicians to have their licenses recognized in a state other than the one where they were first licensed, a process called *reciprocity.* Some states require other examinations, particularly if candidates want to declare certain areas of competency.

GOOD CHARACTER   Prospective clinical psychologists must show the physical, mental, and moral capability to engage in the competent practice of the profession. This characteristic is often denoted by letters of recommendations and by the absence of ethical or legal violations. Practitioners of clinical psychology should also know the *ethical codes* that guide practice: the American Psychological Association's *Ethical Principles of Psychologists and Code of Conduct* (2010). Referred to hereafter as the *Ethics Code,* this publication offers guidance on ethical concerns related to competence, human relations, privacy and confidentiality, record keeping, education and training, therapy, and many other situations. It is especially useful in navigating the gray areas that invariably come up in the practice of clinical psychology. Of course, all practitioners should know the obligations, freedoms, and limitations that go with practice under their level of licensure and in their state. Familiarity with the Ethics Code, as well as with state and federal laws, is necessary for these psychologists to be effective and to avoid professional mistakes that could have serious consequences.

Most clinical psychologists hold professional licenses and provide psychotherapy treatment, but as suggested earlier, not all do. Rather than specialize in assessment and treatment, some choose to engage primarily in some combination of teaching, research, consulting, or administration, while doing little or no direct service delivery. But non practicing clinical psychologists, too, must complete formal educational requirements and follow professional codes of conduct and regulations. For instance, clinical researchers must follow sections of the Ethics Code dealing with research in psychology, and their studies are overseen by *Institutional Review Boards,* which are established under federal guidelines to protect the rights and well-being of human participants in research.

Popularity of Clinical Psychology

Clinical psychology is the largest subfield of psychology. Graduate programs in clinical psychology attract more applicants than do graduate programs in any other area of psychology (see Figure 1.1), and far more doctoral-level degrees are awarded in clinical and related health service provider areas than in other areas of psychology (Kohout & Wicherski, 2011). The prominence of clinical psychology helps explain why the terms *psychologist* and *clinical psychologist* are practically synonymous in public discourse.

The appeal of clinical psychology is also reflected in the composition of the largest organization of psychologists in the United States: the American Psychological Association. Of the 56 divisions in APA, the largest divisions relate to clinical psychology (Division 12—Clinical Psychology, Division 40—Clinical Neuropsychology, and Division 42—Psychologists in Independent Practice). Of course, for students interested in clinical psychology, popularity means competition, especially for spots in graduate schools. Indeed, the stronger, research-oriented PhD programs, whose students typically score the highest on the Examination for Professional Practice in Psychology, accept as few as 7% of applicants, while some freestanding PsyD programs accept closer to 50% (Norcross, Ellis, & Sayette, 2010). Despite the competition, the outlook for clinical psychologists looks promising. The U.S. Department of Labor's Occupational Outlook Handbook (2011) projects that job prospects for doctoral-level applied psychologists are best, while master's degree holders will face keen competition and bachelor's degree holders will find limited opportunities. CNN's Money.com (2012) rates clinical psychologist as 23rd among the top 50 jobs in America, with personal satisfaction, job security, future growth, and benefit to society at high levels.

The field's popularity is also shown by the numerous portrayals of clinical psychologists and their distressed clients in movies, television, and other media. This kind of popularity is a double-edged sword. On the one hand, accurate portrayals can contribute to the public's *mental health literacy*—accurate understanding of psychological disorders and their treatments (Jorm, 2000). On the other hand, inaccurate portrayals can decrease mental health literacy and create inaccurate, stereotyped views of the profession. Unfortunately, the latter outcome seems to be more common. Clinical psychologists are often portrayed as oracles, agents of social compliance, or wounded healers, and the techniques by which they help clients are seldom portrayed accurately (Orchowski, Spickard, & McNamara, 2006). Inaccurate portrayals might make for good drama, but they don't reveal what clinical psychology is really like. We hope that this book does a much better job.

Clinical Psychology and the Related Mental Health Professions

As noted earlier, clinical psychologists are considered *health service providers*. Other subfields within psychology belonging to this category include behavioral and cognitive psychology, clinical psychology, clinical child psychology, clinical health psychology, clinical neuropsychology, counseling psychology, family psychology, forensic psychology, professional geropsychology, psychoanalytic psychology, and school psychology (Nelson, 2013). Clinical services are also offered by professionals trained outside psychology in professions such as social work, psychiatry, and nursing. Like clinical

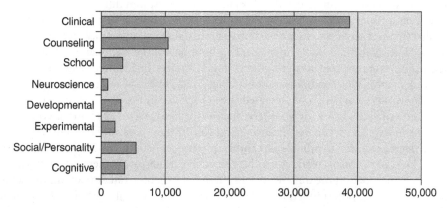

FIGURE 1.1 Applicants to U.S. Psychology Programs, 2009–2010. *Source:* Adapted from Kohout and Wicherski (2011).

psychology, each of the professions mentioned above has one or more national or international organizations, networks of accredited training programs, well-established research traditions, and specific licensing or certification requirements. Each group also has its own unique history and traditions. Practitioners from each group offer mental health services in one form or another. How then are clinical psychologists similar to, and different from, these other professionals?

COUNSELING PSYCHOLOGY Counseling psychologists are the most similar to clinical psychologists in their training and in the types of services that they offer. Much of their course work and supervised training overlaps with that of clinical psychologists—practitioners are trained in psychopathology, interviewing, assessment, counseling and psychotherapy, research, and the like. Students in the two fields apply to the same list of accredited internship sites, and graduates from the two subfields are eligible for the same licensure, practice opportunities, and insurance reimbursement. These two subfields are similar enough in their training, research interests, professional activities, and licensure requirements that calls to merge the two fields are often heard (Norcross, 2011). Nevertheless, there are a few salient differences between clinical and counseling psychology.

Clinical psychology programs are invariably housed in psychology departments, while counseling psychology programs are sometimes housed in psychology departments, but are often located in education departments or other departments or divisions. Counseling psychologists can earn a PhD, PsyD, or EdD degree, all doctoral-level degrees but differing in emphasis (discussed later in this chapter and in Chapter 15).

Counseling psychology was founded to promote personal, educational, vocational, and group adjustment (American Psychological Association Division 17, 2012). Accordingly, counseling psychologists are more likely to deal also with normal transitions and adjustments that people may face. Besides offering psychotherapy, counseling psychologists might, for instance, do career counseling or other forms of counseling related to life changes or developmental problems. Clinical psychology, on the other hand, was founded primarily to assess and treat persons with psychological disorders (see Chapter 2). Therefore, clinical psychologists focus more specifically on prevention, diagnosis, and treatment of psychological problems and on research related to these issues, and they generally deal with more severe pathology than counseling psychologists do. So the differences between clinical psychology and counseling psychology are largely a matter of emphasis. Despite these differences, there is considerable overlap between the professions.

SCHOOL PSYCHOLOGY School psychologists also have much in common with clinical and counseling psychologists: they generally share a scientist-practitioner model of training, move through similar internship and licensure requirements, conduct assessments, design interventions at the individual and system levels, and evaluate programs. The obvious difference is that school psychologists typically receive more training in education and child development, and they focus their interventions on children, adolescents, adults, and their families in school and other educational settings. Despite the differences in emphasis, the similarities to clinical, especially to clinical child psychology, and to counseling psychology are greater than the differences (American Psychological Association Division 16, 2012; Cobb et al., 2004).

SOCIAL WORK As the nation's largest group of mental health service providers, social workers are employed in a variety of settings, including hospitals, businesses, community mental health centers, courts, schools, prisons, and family service agencies. Students in social work programs may choose to specialize in direct services to clients, or they may specialize in community services (Ambrosino, Heffernan, Shuttlesworth, & Ambrosino, 2012). About half of the National Association of Social Workers members are engaged in offering direct clinical services, including various forms of therapy; the rest work in areas such as administration, public policy, research, and community organizing.

Social workers can earn a bachelor's degree (Bachelor of Social Work, or BSW), master's degree (Master of Social Work, or MSW), or doctoral degree (Doctorate in Social Work, or DSW or PhD). As in clinical psychology, licensing and certification laws vary by state. Typically, the minimum degree required to provide psychotherapy services is an MSW (National Association of Social Workers, 2012). Social workers may be trained in various psychotherapy techniques, but as a general rule, they focus more on how social/situational variables, rather than intrapersonal and interpersonal variables, affect functioning. Social workers, like clinical psychologists, spend much of their time in direct client contact, helping clients cope with problems and navigate a world that has become complex and difficult because of those problems.

PSYCHIATRY One of the first questions students ask when they begin studying psychology is "What's the difference between a psychologist and a psychiatrist?" The most entertaining answer is: "about $80,000 per year," but the more comprehensive answer involves the differences in training and practice between the two professions. Psychiatry is a specialty within the medical field. So, just as pediatrics focuses on children, ophthalmologists specialize in eyes, and neurologists focus on the brain and nervous system, psychiatrists are medical doctors who specialize in treating psychological disorders. Persons training to be psychiatrists typically complete a psychiatric residency in which they take course work in psychology and undergo supervision by qualified psychiatrists as they work with patients. This residency often occurs in a hospital setting and therefore generally involves exposure to more serious psychopathology, but it may also occur in outpatient settings. Many psychiatrists offer psychotherapy, but not all do. According to recent surveys, the majority see patients for less than 25 minutes at a time, often for medication reviews (Kane, 2011). In addition to doing therapy and prescribing medication, psychiatrists order or conduct other medical tests, teach, do research, work in administration, and perform other tasks commensurate with their level of training. Though psychiatrists generally have more medical training than clinical psychologists, clinical psychologists typically have more formal training in psychological assessment and a broader exposure to a variety of approaches to psychology.

The historical distinction between psychiatrists and clinical psychologists has been understood as reflecting the difference between a more biological (psychiatrists) and a more psychological (clinical psychologists) view of the causes of mental disorders. Recent years, however, have seen increased collaboration between the professions. Much of the change can be attributed to the growing realization that psychological disorders are seldom *either* biological or psychological in origin but typically a complex interaction of both. As a result, clinical psychologists are increasingly employed in medical settings, where their psychological and research expertise are valued. Psychiatrists and psychologists often work cooperatively on task forces devoted to issues of valid diagnoses and effective treatments. This is consistent with a broader shift toward psychology becoming a health profession rather than strictly a mental health profession (Rozensky, 2011).

OTHER SPECIALTIES RELATED TO CLINICAL PSYCHOLOGY Mental health services are also offered by a variety of other *specialists* and *caregivers*. We have already mentioned counseling psychology and school psychology as two subfields that are closely related to clinical psychology. In Chapters 11–14, we detail four other specialties related to clinical psychology: clinical child psychology, health psychology, clinical neuropsychology, and forensic psychology. Other psychology programs that train *health service providers* include sport psychology, rehabilitation psychology, marriage and family therapy, humanistic psychology, and community counseling.

Still other specialists are trained outside psychology in programs specifically devoted to that specialty. For instance, as specialists within the nursing profession, psychiatric nurses usually work in hospital settings and operate as part of a treatment team that is headed by a psychiatrist and includes one or more clinical psychologists. They may be trained in some forms of therapy, often those specific to the populations they encounter. Pastoral counselors typically get training in counseling from a faith-based perspective. For clients whose religious faith is central to their identity and outlook on life, the availability of a counselor who affirms this faith can be important.

Paraprofessionals, psychological assistants, and others who go by similar names, are usually bachelor's-level or associate-level personnel trained to administer a specific form of treatment to a specific population. They generally work as part of a treatment team, and their activities are supervised by professionals. Their training varies, but many come from disciplines that have some or all of the following indicators of professional quality: well-articulated standards of practice, national organizations that promote and oversee the profession, course offerings in colleges and universities, empirical research traditions, and peer-reviewed journals.

Others specialties, such as aromatherapy, reflexology, homeopathy, and spiritual healing techniques, have few or none of the indicators of professional quality just listed and might be described as further from the mainstream of mental health treatment. Often classified as *alternative treatments* or *alternative medicine*, many of these further-from-the-mainstream treatments combine somatic or sensual experiences with variants on psychological, social, or spiritual intervention. Some of these practices derive from ancient traditions; some are new inventions. Persons who practice alternative treatments often describe their work as falling within a *holistic* tradition that emphasizes the integration of mind, body, and spirit (Feltham, 2000).

SECTION SUMMARY

Clinical psychology involves the application of principles, methods, and procedures to reduce or alleviate maladjustment, disability, and discomfort in a wide range of client populations. Its title and practices are regulated by professional organizations and by state licensing boards. Specific kinds of training are required for the different types of licensure, and certain personal traits, such as a clinical attitude, sound judgment, and emotional stability, are needed to practice the profession effectively. As one of the health service provider professions, clinical psychology overlaps with other mental health professions but is distinguished by psychological training that is both research oriented and practical. It remains the most popular specialty within psychology, one of the most popular majors among undergraduates, and a profession, the practice of which is a source of considerable curiosity and interest in the public.

CLINICAL PSYCHOLOGISTS AT WORK

SECTION PREVIEW

Here we describe the various professional activities of clinical psychologists and how clinicians distribute their work time among those activities. We also describe the various employment settings and general salary ranges of clinical psychologists.

Activities of Clinical Psychologists

Let's consider in more detail some of the activities that clinical psychologists pursue, the variety of places in which they are employed, the array of clients and problems on which they focus their attention, and the rewards of the job. Not all clinicians are equally involved with all the activities we will describe, but our review should provide a better understanding of the wide range of options open to those who enter the field. It might also help explain why the field remains attractive to so many students.

About 95% of all clinical psychologists spend their working lives engaged in some combination of six activities: assessment, treatment, research, teaching (including supervision), consultation, and administration. Figure 1.2 shows the results of surveys taken over the last few decades examining how clinical psychologists spend their time. Keep in mind that the percentages vary considerably across work settings—psychologists in university settings will spend more time engaged in teaching and research, and those in private practice will spend more time conducting psychotherapy and assessment.

ASSESSMENT   Assessment involves collecting information about people: their behavior, problems, unique characteristics, abilities, and intellectual functioning. This information may be used to diagnose problematic behavior, to guide a client toward an optimal vocational choice, to facilitate selection of job candidates, to describe a client's personality characteristics, to select treatment techniques, to guide legal decisions regarding the commitment of individuals to institutions, to provide a more complete picture of a client's problems, to screen potential participants

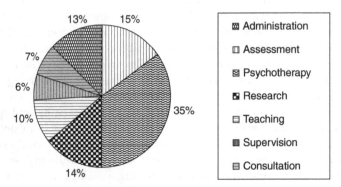

FIGURE 1.2   Percentage of Time Licensed Psychologists Spend in Professional Activities.   *Source:* Based on Norcross, J. C., Karpiak, C. P., & Santoro, S. O. (2005). Clinical psychologists across the years: The Division of Clinical Psychology from 1960 to 2003. *Journal of Clinical Psychology, 61,* 1467–1483.

in psychological research projects, to establish pretreatment baseline levels of behavior against which to measure posttreatment improvement, and for literally hundreds of other purposes. Most clinical assessment instruments fall into one of three categories: tests, interviews, and observations. We cover each of these in detail in the chapters devoted to assessment.

Clinicians today have an array of assessment options not formerly available to them. For instance, computers can administer assessment items, analyze results, and generate entire written reports. Another frontier of psychological assessment is developing from research on a variety of biological factors associated with human functioning. During the last two decades, research focusing on genetic, neurochemical, hormonal, and neurological factors in the brain has led to the development of new neurobiological assessments. These changes, too, have the potential to greatly enhance the assessment efforts of clinicians, but as with computer-based assessment, they raise a number of procedural, practical, and ethical questions (Gazzaniga, 2011; Popma & Raine, 2006).

TREATMENT   Clinical psychologists offer treatments designed to help people better understand and solve distressing psychological problems. These interventions are known as psychotherapy, behavior modification, psychological counseling, or other terms, depending on the theoretical orientation of the clinician. Treatment sessions may include client or therapist monologues, painstaking construction of new behavioral skills, episodes of intense emotional drama, or many other activities that range from the highly structured to the utterly spontaneous.

Individual psychotherapy has long been the single most frequent activity of clinicians (Kazdin, 2011), but psychologists may also treat two or more clients together in couple, family, or group therapy. Sometimes, two or more clinicians work in therapy teams to help their clients. Treatment may be as brief as one session or may extend over several years. Some psychologists, known as community psychologists, focus on preventing psychological problems by altering the institutions, environmental stressors, or behavioral skills of people at risk for disorder (e.g., teenage parents) or of an entire community. The results of psychological treatments are usually positive, though in some cases the change may be small, nonexistent, or even negative (Castonguay, Boswell, Constantino, Goldfried, & Hill, 2010; Lilienfeld, 2007). Of course, increasing the effectiveness of treatments offered to the public is a key goal of research. (Treatment outcomes are discussed in several later chapters, especially Chapter 10, "Research on Clinical Intervention.")

RESEARCH   By training and by tradition, clinical psychologists are research oriented. For most of the first half of its existence, the field was strongly dominated by research rather than by application (see Chapter 2). Although that balance has changed, research continues to play a vital role in clinical psychology.

Research activity makes clinicians stand out among other helping professions, and we believe it is in this area that they may make their greatest contribution. In the realm of psychotherapy, for example, theory and practice were once based mainly on case study evidence, subjective impressions of treatment efficacy, and rather poorly designed research. This "prescientific" era (Paul, 1969) in the history of psychotherapy research has evolved into an "experimental" era in which the quality of research has improved greatly and the conclusions we can draw about the effects of therapy are much stronger. This development is due in large measure to the research of clinical psychologists.

Clinical research varies greatly with respect to its setting and scope. Some studies are conducted in research laboratories, while others are conducted in the more natural, but less controllable, conditions outside the lab. Some projects are supported by governmental or private grants that pay for research assistants, computers and other costs, but a great deal of clinical research is performed by investigators whose budgets are limited and who depend on volunteer help and their own ability to obtain space, equipment, and participants.

Clinical psychology's tradition of research is reflected in graduate school admission criteria, which often emphasize applicants' grades in statistics or research methods over grades in abnormal psychology or personality theory. Many graduate departments in psychology in the United States regard research experience as among the three most important criteria for admission, and graduates of research-oriented clinical psychology programs typically outperform graduates of programs that don't emphasize research as much (Norcross, Ellis, & Sayette, 2010; Pate, 2001). Even though most clinical psychologists do not end up pursuing a research career—many never publish a single piece of research—most graduate programs in clinical psychology still devote a significant amount of time to training in empirical research. Why?

There are at least four reasons. First, it is important that all clinicians be able to critically evaluate published research so that they can determine which assessment procedures and therapeutic interventions are likely to be effective. Second, clinicians who work in academia must often supervise and evaluate research projects conducted by their students. Third, when psychologists who work in community mental health centers or other service agencies are asked to assist administrators in evaluating the effectiveness of the agency's programs, their research training can be very valuable. Finally, research training can help clinicians objectively evaluate the effectiveness of their own clinical work. Tracking client change can signal the need to change treatment plans, reveal the need for additional clinical training, and contribute to third party (e.g., insurance companies, clinical researchers) efforts to document and understand factors affecting clinical effectiveness (Hatfield & Ogles, 2004).

TEACHING   A considerable portion of many clinical psychologists' time is spent in educational activities. Clinicians who hold full- or part-time academic positions typically teach undergraduate and graduate courses in areas such as personality, abnormal psychology, introductory clinical psychology, psychotherapy, behavior modification, interviewing, psychological testing, research design, and clinical assessment. They conduct specialized graduate seminars on advanced topics, and they supervise the work of graduate students who are learning assessment and therapy skills in practicum courses.

A good deal of clinical psychologists' teaching takes the form of research supervision. This kind of teaching begins when students and professors discuss research topics of mutual interest that are within the professor's area of expertise. Most research supervisors help the student frame appropriate research questions, apply basic principles of research design to address those questions, and introduce the student to the research skills relevant to the problem at hand.

Clinical psychologists also do a lot of teaching in the context of in-service (i.e., on-the-job) training of psychological, medical, or other interns, social workers, nurses, institutional aides, ministers, police officers, prison guards, teachers, administrators, business executives, day-care workers, lawyers, probation officers, and many other groups whose vocational skills might be enhanced by increased psychological sophistication. Clinicians even teach while doing therapy—particularly if they adopt a behavioral approach in which treatment includes helping people learn more adaptive ways of behaving (see Chapter 8). Finally, many full-time clinicians teach part time in colleges, universities, and professional schools. Working as an adjunct faculty member provides another source of income, but clinicians often teach because it offers an enjoyable way to share their professional expertise and to remain abreast of new developments in their field.

CONSULTATION   Clinical psychologists often provide advice to organizations about a variety of problems. This activity, known as consultation, combines aspects of research, assessment, treatment, and teaching. Perhaps this combination of activities is why some clinicians find consultation satisfying and lucrative enough that they engage in it full time. Organizations that benefit from consultants' expertise range in size and scope from one-person medical or law practices to huge government agencies and multinational corporations. The consultant may also work with neighborhood associations, walk-in treatment centers, and many other community-based organizations. Consultants perform many kinds of tasks, including education (e.g., familiarizing staff with research relevant to their work), advice (e.g., about cases or programs), direct service (e.g., assessment, treatment, and evaluation), and reduction of intraorganizational conflict (e.g., eliminating sources of trouble by altering personnel assignments).

When consulting is *case* oriented, the clinician focuses attention on a particular client or organizational problem and either deals with it directly or offers advice on how it might best be handled. When consultation is *program* or *administration* oriented, the clinician focuses on those aspects of organizational function or structure that are causing trouble. For example, the consultant may suggest and develop new procedures for screening candidates for various jobs within an organization, set up criteria for identifying promotable personnel, or reduce staff turnover rates by increasing administrators' awareness of the psychological impact of their decisions on employees.

ADMINISTRATION   Many clinical psychologists find themselves engaged in managing or running the daily operations of organizations. Examples of the administrative posts held by clinical psychologists include head of a college or university psychology department, director of a graduate training program in clinical psychology, director of a student counseling center, head of a consulting firm or testing center, superintendent of a school system, chief psychologist at a hospital or clinic, director of a mental hospital, director of a community mental health center, manager of a government agency, and director of the psychology service at a Veterans Administration (VA) hospital. Administrative duties tend to become more common as clinicians move through their professional careers.

Although some clinical psychologists spend their time at only one or two of the six activities we have described, most engage in more, and some perform all six. To many clinicians, the potential for distributing their time among several functions is one of the most attractive aspects of their field.

Employment Settings of Clinical Psychologists

At one time, most clinical psychologists worked in a single type of facility: child clinics or guidance centers. Today, however, the settings in which clinicians function are much more diverse. You will find clinical psychologists in the following as well as many other settings:

college and university psychology departments
law schools
public and private medical and
    psychiatric hospitals
city, county, and private mental
    health clinics
community mental health centers
student health and counseling centers
medical schools
the military
university psychological clinics
child treatment centers
public and private schools

institutions for the intellectually disabled
police departments
prisons
juvenile offender facilities
business and industrial firms probation
    departments
rehabilitation centers for the
    handicapped
nursing homes and other geriatric facilities
orphanages
alcoholism treatment centers
health maintenance
    organizations (HMOs)

The work settings that clinical psychologists choose strongly influence how they distribute their time across professional activities. But so do their training, individual interests, and areas of expertise. Work activities are also influenced by larger social factors. For example, a clinician could not work in a Veterans Administration hospital today if federal legislation had not been passed in the 1940s creating such hospitals. (The role played by sociocultural forces in shaping clinical psychology is more fully detailed in Chapter 2.) In short, what clinicians do and where they do it has always depended—and always will depend—on situational demands, cultural values, changing political climates, and the pressing needs of the society in which they function. Table 1.1 shows the primary and secondary work settings of health service providers in psychology, the majority of which are clinical psychologists.

TABLE 1.1 Primary and Secondary Work Settings of APA-Affiliated Health Service Providers

Setting	Primary Setting (%)	Secondary Setting (%)
Independent private practice		
Individual	36	37
Group	10	9
Hospitals	12	6
Other human service settings	11	11
Managed care	5	3
Business and government	7	9
Academic	19	25

Source: Michalski and Kahout (2011).

Salaries of Clinical Psychologists

The financial rewards for employment as a clinical psychologist are significant. A 2010 report by the APA Center for Workforce Studies showed that the overall 11–12-month median salary for licensed doctoral-level clinical psychologists was $87,015. As you no doubt have guessed, salary levels vary according to employment setting, years of experience, and economic conditions. Table 1.2 presents the median as well as the 25th and 75th percentile (Q1 and Q3, respectively) salaries for clinical psychologists in a variety of settings. These figures should give you an idea of salary ranges for clinical psychologists.

The APA periodically surveys its members concerning salaries, demographics, practice concerns, and many other topics, and then makes the results public. Much of that information can be accessed at APA's Web site: http://www.apa.org (though some information is available only to APA members).

TABLE 1.2 Salaries of Licensed Doctoral-Level Clinical Psychologists in Direct Human Service Positions

| Setting and Years of Experience | Median, 25th, and 75th Percentile Salaries | | |
	Median	Q1	Q3
Individual Private Practice			
10–14 years	82,733	64,028	125,000
20–24 years	89,000	65,000	120,000
Group Psychological Practice			
10–14 years	90,000	68,000	120,000
20–24 years	95,000	75,000	130,000
Primary Care Group Practice			
15–19 years	88,000	40,000	159,000
20–24 years	96,500	79,900	129,715
VA Medical Center			
15–19 years	102,000	91,000	112,228
20–24 years	104,000	85,500	114,500
Public General Hospital			
10–14 years	80,500	65,000	87,125
20–24 years	85,000	65,000	97,000
University Student Counseling Center			
10–14 years	58,900	50,000	67,250
20–24 years	63,500	52,145	79,000
Elementary or Secondary School			
10–14 years	NA	NA	NA
20–24 years	94,278	74,250	128,639
Community Mental Health Center			
15–19 years	69,950	60,500	90,750
25–29 years	72,500	69,196	103,250
Criminal Justice System			
15–19 years	80,000	51,000	107,160
20–24 years	80,500	75,000	103,000
Federal Government Agency			
10–14 years	99,000	94,750	99,833
15–19 years	99,050	82,375	112,500

Note: NA = not available.

Source: Finno, Michalski, Hart, Wicherski, and Kohout (2010)

Diversity Among Clinical Psychologists

The workforce in clinical psychology has become more diverse over the years. In 1950, for instance, women earned only 15% of the doctoral degrees awarded in psychology, but since that time, there has been a dramatic reversal in the gender distribution. As illustrated in Figure 1.3, women made up a third of new clinical doctoral degrees in 1976, but by 2010 they made up over 70% of earned clinical doctorates (Michalski, 2009; National Center for Education Statistics, 2000; Pate, 2001; Rozell et al., 2011; Sayette et al. 2011). This percentage is quite similar in both more practice-oriented and more research-oriented programs. A survey of student gender distribution in clinical psychology programs showed that in European countries, too, women outnumber men, often by wide margins (Olos & Hoff, 2006).

Of course, there is a lag of several years between enrollment in a degree program and the attainment of senior status within a profession. As a result, there are still more men than women among senior clinical psychology faculty in colleges and universities and more men than women among the higher-salary private practitioners of clinical psychology. But at all levels, there is a clear trend toward greater representation of women, and there are now more women than men in the health service provider workforce (58% versus 42%; Michalski & Kohout, 2011).

Ethnic minorities currently make up approximately 20% of the new doctoral degrees in clinical psychology, up from about 8% in 1977. While this is a positive trend, the overall pace of change in minority representation has been slow, with percentages of minorities hovering around 20% for nearly a decade (Michalski, 2009; Rozell et al., 2011). African Americans represent the highest percentage of minorities in all psychology graduate programs, followed by persons of Hispanic and Asian origin and Native Americans. Many colleges and universities have specific recruitment plans for targeting persons of color, and many psychology departments have their own department-level strategies for recruiting minorities. Examples of such efforts include outreach programs to "feeder" undergraduate schools, financial assistance to minorities, brochures or other materials geared toward persons of color, and involvement of more persons of color in the recruitment and screening process.

The median age of recent doctorates in clinical psychology is 32. That may seem old (or perhaps "mature" is a better word) to students approaching or just finishing their bachelor's degrees, but it can be accounted for by a couple of factors. First, many people enter doctoral programs after having worked in the field for several years with a master's or bachelor's degree. Second, it takes years to complete a doctoral degree. While most students complete a clinical doctorate in 5–6 years, some take 7 or 8 years or more. Keep in mind that during a significant portion of this time, most students are working, at least part time, and earning a wage, and this invariably slows down progress toward completion (but it helps to pay the bills).

Finally, clinical psychologists vary in terms of their sexual orientation. In the most recent survey of the workforce, about 91% of health service providers identified themselves as heterosexual, while 7% identified themselves as gay, lesbian, bisexual, or transgendered (a small percent did not respond to this part of the survey). These percentages are close to the percentages researchers typically find in surveys of sexual orientation in the general population (Weiten, 2011), though

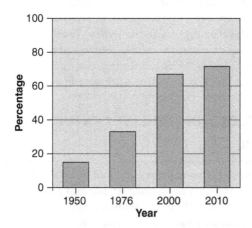

FIGURE 1.3 Percent of Women Earning Doctorates in Clinical Psychology. *Sources:* National Center for Education Statistics, 2000; Pate, 2001; Rozell, Berke, Norcross, and Karpiak, 2011; Sayette, Norcross, and Dimoff, 2011.

such percentages vary according to how questions are asked and whether responses are simply categorized or measured on a scale that allows variation across a continuum (see Epstein, 2007).

Diversity Among Clients

Clinical psychologists in the United States and Canada can expect to see increasing diversity in their clients too. By 2050, non-Hispanic whites are expected to be 50% of the U.S. population with ethnic minorities making up the other half. A greater proportion of Americans will have been born in other countries, or will have parents who were, than has been the case for decades. How does this diversity affect clinical psychology?

For one thing, persons from different backgrounds often have different ways of expressing psychological distress, so clinicians have become increasingly sensitive to cultural variations in symptoms (Hays & Iwamasa, 2006). Responses to treatments can also vary depending on clients' backgrounds. Even willingness to seek psychological help varies by cultural and ethnic background. Clinicians will therefore need additional training in order to provide culturally sensitive services to diverse groups (Hall, 2005).

Clients will be diverse not only in their demographics, but also in the types of problems they bring to clinical psychologists. Which are the most common problems? The National Comorbidity Survey (1990–1992) and National Comorbidity Survey Replication (2001–2003) are among the largest studies to try to examine the general population prevalence and severity of psychological disorders. They show that anxiety disorders (e.g., panic disorders, social phobia), mood disorders (e.g., depression), impulse-control disorders (e.g., intermittent explosive disorder), and substance disorders (e.g., alcohol abuse, drug abuse) are among the most common. Yet only about half of those who receive treatment actually meet the criteria for a diagnosable mental disorder (Kessler et al., 2005). The remainder have symptoms that do not quite fit the current diagnostic criteria (discussed in Chapter 3). Such problems include difficulties in interpersonal relationships, marital problems, school difficulties, psychosomatic and physical symptoms, job-related difficulties, and so on. The prevalence and types of problems for which people seek help have remained similar over the years, suggesting that the need for clinical psychologists has not declined, even though the cultural backgrounds of clients who experience those problems have become more diverse. The bottom line is that cultural competence has become a requirement for clinical psychologists (Sehgal et al., 2011). In numerous places throughout this book, we describe how personal, ethnic, and cultural diversity affects clinical practice.

SECTION SUMMARY

Clinical psychologists spend most of their professional time engaged in assessment, psychotherapy, research, teaching, consultation, and administration. The activities in which they engage, and the clients they see, are strongly affected by employment settings, personal preferences, training, and broader social factors. Clinicians are employed in a variety of settings, including individual and group practices, hospitals of various types, community mental health centers, college and university psychology departments and medical schools, government agencies, private corporations, and others. In those settings, they see clients from a variety of cultural backgrounds and with a variety of problems. Clinicians' salaries vary by level of training, employment setting, and regional factors but are on par with many other professions with similar levels of training. Once dominated by white males, the field now has a higher percentage of women and ethnic minorities than in the past.

CLINICAL PSYCHOLOGY IN THE 21ST CENTURY

SECTION PREVIEW

Here we outline some of the more prominent issues shaping clinical psychology today. The first of these relates to the need to balance science and practice within the field. Other key issues concern how clinicians should be trained, how the traditionally separate "schools" or theoretical orientations within clinical psychology might be brought together, and how the practice of clinical psychology has been affected by the social and cultural environment, particularly by the way managed care and legislation have changed health care delivery.

Science and Practice

Some of the liveliest discussions within clinical psychology involve the extent to which the field should reflect the concerns of its scientists and its practitioners. If scientists/researchers hold one viewpoint but practitioners hold another, whose view should prevail? There is a long history to this topic, and here we introduce only the broad outlines and suggest some of its major implications. Later, especially in Chapters 2, 10, and 15, we detail the various positions and work through their implications for the field.

We have already noted that the official definition of clinical psychology incorporates both science and practice. The question is: *how* should science and practice be combined? This seemingly simple question goes well beyond mere philosophical or academic debate. It affects how clinicians are trained, how clients are treated, how research is conducted, and how others view psychological interventions.

EVIDENCE-BASED PRACTICE   Imagine going to a physician who was unaware of, or who chose to disregard, the last two decades of medical research results and relied instead on intuition, outdated training, and folklore to decide what treatments to provide. If you wanted state-of-the-art treatment, you probably would not go back to that doctor. Basing professional practice on solid, up-to-date research is referred to as *evidence-based practice* (EBP). The idea is that rather than rely on the best guesses of individuals or on "the way it's always been done," practitioners should use those diagnostic and therapeutic practices that the best scientific evidence finds most effective.

Clearly, evidence-based practice is an idea whose time has come, and no reasonable person doubts that clinical psychologists should base their practice on the results of high-quality scientific research. The problem is that the field lacks a clear consensus on which research is of the highest quality, what it shows, and exactly how it should guide practice. In short, different groups within the APA have different understandings of what evidence-based practice means. Our own perspective, which we detail in Chapter 10, is that both empirical evidence and clinical experience are crucial for evaluating the usefulness of different psychological interventions. Clinical experience is invaluable as a starting point for generating hypotheses about what makes psychotherapy effective, but if certain therapy techniques underperform in repeated clinical trials, those techniques should be abandoned in favor of techniques that perform better.

There is some urgency in the field's reaching consensus about what constitutes the best evidence and how to train and update clinicians in the best practices. Some local and state agencies and some insurance providers have constructed lists of the psychotherapies for which they will provide reimbursement to patients (Norcross, Beutler, & Levant, 2006). They do so on the basis of *their* understanding of the research and of their needs, not on the basis of official positions taken by clinical psychologists. Presumably, clinical researchers and practitioners should have more expertise in these matters, and many believe that they and their official organizations should be more active in listing which psychotherapies are most effective.

Fortunately, the urgency of establishing best practices (while recognizing that research and practice are continually evolving) is being recognized. Indeed, the term "evidence-based" has become a rallying cry that is widely shared, even among people who may disagree about exactly what it means. Consider, for example, that a search of APA's PsychScan clinical psychology database (which surveys journals related to clinical psychology) from the years 1990 to 2000 yielded a total of eight articles with the term "evidence-based" in the titles. Between 2000 and 2011 there were 206 hits. Lately, numerous authors have suggested ways to better align research and practice (see Goodheart, 2011; Kazdin, 2011). And in 2010, the American Psychological Association initiated a process to develop evidence-based treatment guidelines, the first time that organization has sought to develop recommendations for treatments for specific disorders (Kurtzman & Bufka, 2011).

CLINICAL PSYCHOLOGY TRAINING   Decisions about the most desirable mix of science and practice also affect how students are trained in clinical psychology (and how textbooks such as this one are written!). There are two general models upon which clinical psychology training is based. Both are named after Colorado cities that hosted conferences where those models were developed. The *Boulder model* came out of clinical psychology's first major training conference, held in 1949 (Raimy, 1950). Often referred to as the *scientist-practitioner* model, the Boulder model recommended that clinical psychologists be proficient in research and professional practice, earn a PhD in psychology from a university-based graduate program, and complete a supervised, year-long internship.

In 1973, the National Conference on Levels and Patterns of Professional Training in Psychology was held at Vail, Colorado. The resulting *Vail model* recommended alternative training that placed proportionately less emphasis on scientific training and more on preparation for the delivery of clinical services (Korman, 1976). The Vail delegates also proposed that when training emphasis is on the delivery and evaluation of professional services, the PsyD would be the appropriate degree. They suggested, too, that clinical psychology training programs could be housed not only in universities but also in medical schools or in free-standing schools of professional psychology (such as those in California, Illinois, and other states), and that these independent schools should have status equal to that of more traditional scientist-professional training venues. We discuss these models of clinical training in more detail in Chapter 15. For now, perhaps the most important thing to remember about the differences among the various types of clinical psychology training is that programs vary widely in their application processes, costs, training orientations, and outcomes (Ameen & El-Ghoroury, 2013; Norcross, Ellis, & Sayette, 2010; Sayette Norcross, & Dimoff, 2011). We do not yet know for certain which of these, if any, affect outcomes for clients, but it is vital that we learn.

Eclecticism and Integration

Most of the clinical psychologists engaged in practice, research, and teaching today were trained in programs that emphasized one main theoretical orientation, such as psychodynamic, cognitive-behavioral, humanistic, family/systems, and the like. Is this the best way to organize clinical psychology training? Some have expressed concerns that a theory-based approach to clinical education has created such divisiveness within the field that those who have pledged allegiance to one orientation too often reflexively dismiss research and theory supporting other approaches (Gold & Strickler, 2006). This reaction is problematic because there is seldom a compelling empirical reason to adhere to only one theoretical approach; they all have their strengths and weaknesses. As a result, many clinical psychologists now favor *eclecticism*, an approach in which it is acceptable, and even desirable, to employ techniques from a variety of "schools" rather than sticking to just one.

Eclecticism is closely related to the idea of *psychotherapy integration*, the systematic combining of elements of various clinical psychology theories. In our view, it makes sense to combine approaches in reasonable ways rather than to strictly segregate them. If assessment and therapy techniques are tools, it is easy to see that possessing a wide range of tools, and knowledge of when and how to use them makes for an effective psychotherapist. Indeed, most therapists now identify themselves as *eclectic* (Santoro, Kister, Karpiak, & Norcross, 2004), and there is now a journal—the *Journal of Psychotherapy Integration*—devoted to integrating various therapy approaches.

But integration and eclecticism are not as easy to achieve in practice as they are in theory. How should theories and practices be combined? Might clinicians be better off trying to understand clients' problems within one reasonably coherent theoretical orientation rather than with a multitude of orientations, some of which may feature conflicting assumptions? Chapter 9 describes some of the answers to these questions.

The Health Care Environment

Like all other professions, clinical psychology is shaped partly by the culture in which it operates. Popular beliefs and attitudes affect how mental health concerns are perceived, how problems are treated, and how treatment is funded. The last few years have seen significant changes in the health care laws affecting clinical psychology practice.

MENTAL HEALTH PARITY In 2008, the Mental Health Parity and Addiction Act (MHPAA) became law. Mental health parity requires that health insurers provide the same level of coverage for mental illness as they do for physical illness. Prior to 2008, parity had been the exception rather than the norm in U.S. health care. In other words, mental health problems have been regarded as less deserving than other health problems, and people were seen as more responsible for their psychological problems than for their medical problems.

This belief might have been easier to maintain a century ago when the most severe physical ailments were infectious diseases—smallpox, typhoid, diphtheria, for example—and when theories about the causes of mental illness did not incorporate interactions of biological, psychological, and social factors. But few people knowledgeable about psychological disorders today argue that persons simply choose to have a psychological problem. At the same time, many of today's most urgent physical problems—heart disease, obesity, diabetes, for example—are related to lifestyle choices that people make. In short, people probably do not choose to be psychologically ill any more, or any less, than they choose to be physically ill, but disparities in health coverage can suggest that they do. Fortunately, there are signs that this pattern is changing, though negative attitudes toward mental health treatment have certainly not disappeared.

MANAGED CARE   Clinical psychology training, practice, and research are all affected by how health care is structured. Whereas clients once paid providers directly for services, now most health care, including mental health care, involves three parties: client, clinician, and an insurance company, HMO, or similar organization. When the third-party organization influences who provides service, which treatments are used, how long treatments last, how much providers are paid, what records are kept, and so on, it is called *managed care*. Managed care systems use business principles, not just clinicians' judgments, to make decisions about treatment.

As managed care systems in the United States have grown and exerted their influence over psychological treatments, clinicians have had to adapt. In one study, clinicians reported a culture clash between themselves and the managed care companies, complaining that they sometimes had to violate standards of care or ethical standards in order to be paid (Cohen, Marecek, & Gillham, 2006). Managed care's influence helps explain why the salary discrepancy between private practice and other areas of clinical work is now smaller than it used to be. No wonder, then, that in general, clinicians dislike managed care.

Although the relationship between managed care and clinical psychology has sometimes been rocky, as it has between managed care and other health professions, it is not entirely negative (Bobbitt, 2006; Wilson, 2011). One positive effect of health care changes has been to stimulate research into which treatments are most effective for which problems; another is to put more emphasis on prevention (Silverman, 2013). It is in the interest of clients, clinicians, *and* insurers to know which interventions have the most positive and lasting impact on health, because that information, correctly applied, will ultimately lower costs and improve client well-being. The influence of managed care is also partly responsible for the pressure on clinicians to more precisely measure the outcome of the treatments they provide.

Clinical psychologists are continuing to adapt, often changing services to better match those for which managed care systems will pay. This adaptability makes sense, but it can lead to problems if psychologists simply allow managed care personnel to make decisions about clinical practice. Those with the most training and expertise should be in the best position to provide empirical evidence about what works best and what should be reimbursed.

PRESCRIPTION PRIVILEGES FOR CLINICAL PSYCHOLOGISTS   A final aspect of the health care environment is the movement for clinical psychologists to be able to prescribe drugs. In 2002, New Mexico became the first state to pass legislation that permitted licensed psychologists with specialized training to prescribe psychotropic medications. In 2004, Louisiana followed, and prescription privileges now exist and in the military and Indian Health Services. There are several reasons that many think this trend will continue. One is the increasing public acceptance of medications for psychological problems, fueled in part by pervasive television and print advertising by drug companies. Another is that clinical psychologists deal extensively with persons taking certain medications. As a result, those psychologists are sometimes as knowledgeable, if not more so, about the effects of these drugs as the general practice physicians who referred the clients. Prescription privileges make sense also because psychologists see clients regularly, so they are often in a better position to monitor the effectiveness of the medications.

However, there are also arguments against prescription privileges, some coming from clinical psychologists themselves. One concern is that as prescription privileges expand, clinicians may prescribe drugs more and offer psychotherapy less. If this happens, and there is some evidence that it might, then clients would receive less of the services for which clinical psychology is best known, services that help clients develop coping and problem-solving skills that they can apply in the future (Nordal, 2010). Suffice it to say that the prescription privileges debate continues, and we discuss the pros and cons in Chapter 15.

MODELS OF TREATMENT DELIVERY   As the previous discussion indicates, clinical psychologists have worked hard to identify the most effective treatments, and they have promoted the preferential use of these evidence-based treatments, for instance, via publication of practice guidelines.

Compared with a decade ago, the evidence base for psychological interventions is much stronger. However, the primary method of delivering psychological services to clients is still individual, face-to-face psychotherapy. Some have questioned whether this should change. For example, Kazdin (2011) argues that in-person one-on-one psychotherapy may not be the most effective model. He advocates models of treatment delivery that optimize the benefits of psychological interventions across broader segments of the population. This is especially pressing because in any given year, approximately 25% of the population meets the criteria for one or more psychological disorders and the majority of people in need of psychological services still do not receive them (Kessler & Wang, 2008).

More effective treatment delivery would still include one-on-one psychotherapy, but also other approaches. Those less likely to use in-person one-on-one psychotherapy would especially benefit from interventions delivered via technologies. For instance, television and telephone-based interventions, interactive computer-based or cellphone-based interactions, computer-based virtual reality treatments, and social media interventions have all been used to expand how clinical psychologists provide services (Harwood et al., 2011; Kazdin, 2011; Miller, 2013). Greater attention to supply and demand could also improve public psychological health. For example, psychological services are typically clustered in metropolitan areas, so greater attention to the needs of rural areas might also help underserved populations (Jameson, Blank, & Chambliss, 2009). We discuss alternate modes of clinical intervention, along with their ethical and clinical implications, more in Chapter 9.

SECTION SUMMARY

Clinical psychology combines science and practice, but the appropriate mix of the two is a matter of a debate that has intensified as the need to establish clear evidence-based practices in clinical psychology has grown. That need comes both from within the profession and from outside organizations that fund and pay for clinical services. In light of changes within the profession and within the broader society, clinical psychologists continue to examine their training models, particularly the dominant models that lead to PhD and PsyD degrees. They have also had to think more carefully about ways to integrate and combine various approaches to psychotherapy and assessment, as well as ways to deliver services. It has become clear that the turf wars among adherents of different approaches do not benefit the profession. Managed care organizations have influenced clinical practice and will continue to do so. Cultural and legal factors affect the field as well, as exemplified by the fate of legislation requiring mental health parity and that permitting prescription privileges for clinicians.

Chapter Summary

Clinical psychology is the largest single subfield within the larger discipline of psychology. It involves research, teaching, and other services designed to understand, predict, and alleviate maladjustment and disability. To become a licensed clinical psychologist, one must meet certain educational, legal, and personal qualifications. As one of the core health service provider professions, clinical psychology is distinguished from other helping professions by the clinical attitude: the tendency to use the results of research on human behavior in general to assess, understand, and assist particular individuals. The discipline is also distinguished by its emphasis on empirical research and by its diversity in training and practice.

That diversity can be seen in how clinicians distribute their time among six main functions: assessment, treatment, research, teaching, consultation, and administration. It can also be seen in

the increasing diversity of clinical psychologists themselves, and in the diversity of the population in need of mental health care. Clinical psychologists are employed in many different settings, from university psychology departments and medical clinics to community mental health centers and prisons. Many are self-employed private practitioners.

Clinical psychology faces numerous challenges, not the least of which is that most people with psychological problems still do not receive treatment. Other factors shaping the discipline involve, among other issues, decisions about how science and practice should be combined, how training of new psychologists should be conducted, how the various theoretical approaches can be integrated, and how the current (and future) systems of health care delivery affect the practice of clinical psychology.

Study Questions

1. Define clinical psychology.
2. What are the general licensure or certification requirements to be a clinical psychologist?
3. What educational and degree options are available for someone who wants to go into clinical psychology?
4. What personal and ethical criteria are needed to be a good clinical psychologist?
5. How are clinical psychologists similar to and different from counseling psychologists, school psychologists, psychiatrists, social workers, and other mental health professionals?
6. How do clinical psychologists spend most of their work time?
7. How does their work setting influence the way clinicians spend their time?
8. What are the salary ranges for clinical psychologists?
9. How have differing opinions about the balance of science and practice influenced the way psychotherapists operate and how graduate schools educate?
10. What is the eclectic approach to psychopathology and treatment?
11. How might integration of different theoretical approaches be possible?
12. How does cultural diversity influence approaches to psychological treatment?
13. How has managed care influenced clinical psychology research, training, and practice?
14. What is mental health parity?
15. What are the pros and cons associated with specially trained clinical psychologists being able to prescribe certain kinds of drugs?

Web Sites

- American Psychological Association (APA): http://www.apa.org
- Division 12 of the APA, the Society for Clinical Psychology: http://www.div12.org/
- Division 16 of the APA, School Psychology: http://www.apa.org/about/division/div16.html
- Division 17 of the APA, the Society for Counseling Psychology: http://www.apa.org/about/division/div17.html
- American Psychiatric Association: http://www.psych.org
- National Association of Social Workers: http://www.socialworkers.org
- American Psychiatric Nurses Association: http://www.apna.org

MOVIES

Shrink (2009): Somber film about a troubled therapist who has a best-selling self-help book and a growing drug addition, with limited abilities to help his troubled clients.

What about Bob? (1991): Amusing and apocryphal film of a client who seeks to be close to his therapist and his therapist's family, while the therapist seeks to be rich and famous.

MEMOIRS

A Piece of Cake: A Memoir by Cupcake Brown (2006; Three Rivers Press). This memoir describes many of the issues that clinical psychologists deal with, including child abuse, sexual assault, substance abuse, forensic issues, poverty, and eventual resilience to overcome these challenges.

Undercurrents: A Therapist's Reckoning With Her Own Depression (1995; New York: Harper Collins). Through her own actual diary entries, this clinical psychologist shows her own personal descent into severe depression—including a moment when she was assessing a client for depression and realized that she met the criteria herself.

References

Ambrosino, R., Heffernan, J., Shuttlesworth, G., & Ambrosino, R. (2012). *Social work and social welfare: An introduction*. Belmont, CA: Brooks/Cole.

Ameen, E., & El-Ghoroury, N. (2013). Are you prepared for graduate school? *Psychology Student Network*. Retrieved Mar 19, 2013 from http://www.apa.org/ed/precollege/psn/2013/01/graduate-school.aspx.

American Psychological Association (2010). *Ethical principles of psychologists and code of conduct*. American Psychological Association.

American Psychological Association, Division 12 (2012). *About clinical psychology*. Retrieved Jan 1, 2012 from http://www.apa.org/divisions/div12/aboutcp.html.

American Psychological Association, Division 16 (2012). *About school psychology*. Retrieved Jan 1, 2012 from http://www.apa.org/divisions/div12/aboutcp.html.

American Psychological Association, Division 17 (2012). *About counseling psychology*. Retrieved Jan 1, 2012 from http://www.apa.org/divisions/div17/aboutcp.html.

Bobbitt, B. L. (2006). The importance of professional psychology: A view from managed care. *Professional Psychology: Research and Practice, 37*, 590–597.

Brown, T. A, & Barlow, D. H. (2001). *Casebook in abnormal psychology* (2nd ed.). Belmont, CA: Wadsworth.

Castonguay, L. G., Boswell, J. F., Constantino, M. J., Goldfried, M. R., & Hill, C. E. (2010). Training implications of the harmful effects of psychological treatments. *American Psychologist, 65*, 34–39.

CNNMoney (2012). *Best jobs in America*. Retrieved from http://money.cnn.com/magazines/moneymag/bestjobs/2009/snapshots/23.html.

Cobb, H. C., Reeve, R. E., Shealy, C. N., Norcross, J. C., Schare, M. L., et al. (2004). Overlap among clinical, counseling, and school psychology: Implications for the profession and combined-integrated training. *Journal of Clinical Psychology, 60*, 939–955.

Cohen, J., Marecek, J., & Gillham, J. (2006). Is three a crowd? Clients, clinicians, and managed care. *American Journal of Orthopsychiatry, 76*, 251–259.

Epstein, R. (2007). Sexual orientation lies smoothly on a continuum: Verification and extension of Kinsey's hypothesis in a large-scale internet study. *Scientific American*, October, 6.

Feltham, C. (2000). What are counselling and psychotherapy? In C. Feltham & I. Horton (Eds.), *Handbook of counselling and psychotherapy*. London, United Kingdom: Sage.

Finno, A. A., Michalski, M., Hart, B., Wicherski, M., & Kohout, J. L. (2010). Report of the 2009 APA Salary Survey. Retrieved Dec, 28, 2011 from http://www.apa.org/workforce/publications/09-salaries/index.aspx?tab=4.

Gazzaniga, M. (2011) *Who's in charge: Free will and the science of brain*. New York, NY: Harper Collins.

Gold, J., & Strickler, G. (2006). Introduction: An overview of psychotherapy integration. In G. Strickler & J. Gold (Eds.), *A casebook of psychotherapy integration*. Washington, DC: American Psychological Association.

Goodheart, C. D. (2011). Design for tomorrow. *American Psychologist, 66*, 339–347.

Hall, G. C. N. (2005). Introduction to the special section on multicultural and community psychology: Clinical psychology in context. *Journal of Consulting and Clinical Psychology, 73*, 787–789.

Harwood, T. M., Pratt, D., Beutler, L. E., Bongar, B. M., Lenore, S., & Forrester, B. T. (2011). Technology, telehealth, treatment enhancement, and selection. *Professional Psychology: Research and Practice, 42*, 448–454.

Hatfield, D. R., & Ogles, B. M. (2004). The use of outcome measures by psychologists in clinical practice. *Professional Psychology: Research and Practice, 35*, 485–491.

Hays, P. A., & Iwamasa, G. Y. (Eds.). (2006). *Culturally responsive cognitive-behavioral therapy*. Washington, DC: American Psychological Association.

Jameson, J. P., Blank, M. B., & Chambless, D. L. (2009). If we built it, they will come: An empirical investigation of supply and demand in the recruitment of rural psychologists. *Journal of Clinical Psychology, 65*, 723–735.

Johnson, B. W., & Campbell, C. D. (2004). Character and fitness requirements for professional psychologists: Training directors' perspectives. *Professional Psychology: Research and Practice, 35*, 405–411.

Jorm, A. F. (2000). Mental health literacy: Public knowledge and beliefs about mental disorders. *The British Journal of Psychiatry, 177*, 396–401.

Kane, L. (2011). Medscape psychiatry compensation report: 2011 results. Retrieved Dec 27, 2011 from http://www.medscape.com/features/slideshow/compensation/2011/psychiatry.

Kazdin, A. E. (2011). Evidence-based treatment research: Advancements, limitations, and next steps. *American Psychologist, 66*, 685–698.

Kessler, R. C., Demler, O., Frank, R. G., Olfson, M., Pincus, H. A., et al. (2005). Prevalence and treatment of mental disorders 1990 to 2003. *New England Journal of Medicine, 352*, 2515–2523.

Kessler, R. C., & Wang, P. S. (2008). The descriptive epidemiology of commonly occurring mental disorders in the United States. *Annual Review of Public Health, 29*, 115–129.

Kohout, J., & Wicherski, M. (2011). 2011 Graduate Study in Psychology: Applications, acceptances, enrollments, and degrees awarded to master's- and doctoral-level students in the U.S. and Canadian graduate departments of psychology: 2009–2010. *APA Center for Workforce Studies*. Retrieved Dec 21, 2011 from http://www.apa.org/workforce/publications/11-grad-study/applications.aspx.

Korchin, S. J. (1976). *Modern clinical psychology: Principles of intervention in the clinic and community*. New York, NY: Basic Books.

Korman, M. (Ed.). (1976). *Levels and patterns of professional training in psychology*. Washington, DC: American Psychological Association.

Kurtzman, H., & Bufka, L. (2011). APA moves forward on developing clinical treatment guidelines. Practice update retrieved December 21, 2011 from http://www.apapracticecentral.org/update/2011/07-14/clinical-treatment.aspx.

Lilienfeld, S. O. (2007). Psychological treatments that cause harm. *Perspectives on Psychological Science, 2*, 53–70.

Michalski, D. (2009). Clinical workforce in psychology: Pipeline, employment, challenges, and opportunities. Presentation given at the American Psychological Association Conference, August 6, Toronto, Ontario, Canada.

Michalski, D. S., & Kohout, J. L. (2011). The state of the psychology health service provider workforce. *American Psychologist, 66*, 825–843.

Miller, A. (2013). Phone therapy works for mild to moderate disorders, study suggests. *Monitor on Psychology*, January, 2013, 10.

National Association of Social Workers website (2012).

National Center for Education Statistics (2000). Digest of Education Statistics, 1999. Retrieved Dec 13, 2001 from http://nces.ed.gov/pubs2000/Digest99/d99t298.htm.

Nelson, P. D. (2013). Psychology: A science with many applications and a profession with many specialties. Retrieved March 20, 2013 from American Psychological Association Psychology Teacher Network at http://www.apa.org/ed/precollege/ptn/2013/02/psychology-specialties.aspx.

Norcross, J. C. (2011). Clinical versus counseling psychology: What's the diff? Eye on Psi Chi: Fall, 2000 Retrieved Dec 27, 2011 from http://www.psichi.org/pubs/articles/article_73.aspx.

Norcross, J. C., Beutler, L. E., & Levant, R. F. (2006). *Evidence-based practices in mental health*. Washington, DC: American Psychological Association.

Norcross, J. C., Ellis, J. L., & Sayette, M. A. (2010). Getting in and getting money: A comparative analysis of admission standards, acceptance rates, and financial assistance across the research-practice continuum in clinical psychology programs. *Training and Education in Professional Psychology, 42*, 99–104.

Norcross, J. C., Karpiak, C. P., & Santoro, S. O. (2005). Clinical psychologists across the years: The Division of Clinical Psychology from 1960 to 2003. *Journal of Clinical Psychology, 61*, 1467–1483.

Norcross, J. C., Kohout, J. L., & Wicherski, M. (2005). Graduate study in psychology: 1971 to 2004. *American Psychologist, 60*, 959–975.

Nordal, K. C. (2010). Where has all the psychotherapy gone? *Monitor on Psychology, 41*, 10.

Occupational Outlook Handbook, 2010–2011 Edition. U.S. Department of Labor Bureau of Labor Statistics. Retrieved Jan 1, 2012 from http://www.bls.gov/oco/ocos056.htm.

Olos, L., & Hoff, E. H. (2006). Gender ratios in European psychology. *European Psychologist, 11*, 1–11.

Orchowski, L. M., Spickard, B. A., & McNamara, J. R. (2006). Cinema and the valuing of psychotherapy: Implications for clinical practice. *Professional Psychology: Research and Practice, 37*, 506–514.

Pate, W. E., II. (2001). Analyses of data from graduate study in psychology: 1999–2000. Retrieved Dec 12, 2001 from APA Research office, http://research.apa.org/grad00contents.html.

Paul, G. L. (1969). Behavior modification research: Design and tactics. In C. M. Franks (Ed.), *Behavior therapy: Appraisal and status* (pp. 29–62). New York: McGraw-Hill.

Popma, A., & Raine, A. (2006). Will future forensic assessment be neurobiologic? *Child and Adolescent Psychiatric clinics of North America, 15*, 429–444.

Prideaux, D., Roberts, C., Eva, K., Centeno, A., Maccrorie, P., et al. (2011). Assessment for selection for the health care professionals and specialty training: Consensus statement and recommendations from the Ottawa 2010 conference. *Medical Teacher, 33*, 215–223.

Raimy, V. C. (1950). *Training in clinical psychology*. New York NY: Prentice-Hall.

Rajecki, D. W., & Borden, V. M. H. (2011). Psychology degrees: Employment, wage, and career trajectory consequences. *Perspectives on Psychological Science, 6*, 321–335.

Rozell, C. A., Berke, D. M., Norcross, J. C., & Karpiak, C. P. (2011). *Clinical psychologists in the 2010s: Fifty-year trends in Division 12 membership*. Presentation given at 2011 American Psychological Association Convention, August 4, 2011, Washington, DC.

Rozensky, R. H. (2011). The institution of the institutional practice of psychology: Health care reform and psychology's future workforce. *American Psychologist, 66* , 797–808.

Sales, B. D., Miller, M. O., & Hall, S. R. (2005). Legal credentialing and privileges to practice. In B. D. Sales, M. O. Miller, & S. R. Hall (Eds.), *Laws affecting clinical practice* (pp. 13–22). Washington, DC: American Psychological Association.

Santoro, S. O., Kister, K. M., Karpiak, C. P., & Norcross, J. C. (2004, April). Clinical psychologists in the 2000s: A national study. Paper presented at the annual meeting of the Eastern Psychological Association, Washington, DC.

Sayette, M. A., Norcross, J. C., & Dimoff, J. D. (2011). The heterogeneity of clinical psychology Ph.D. programs and the distinctiveness of APCS programs. *Clinical Psychology: Science and Practice, 18*, 4–11.

Sehgal, R., Saules, K., Young, A., Grey, M. J., Gillem, A. R., Nabors, N. A., et al. (2011). Practicing what we know: Multicultural counseling competence among clinical psychology trainees and experienced multicultural psychologists. *Cultural Diversity and Ethnic Minority Psychology, 17*, 1–10.

Sharpless, B. A., & Barber, J. P. (2013). Predictors of program performance on the Examination for Professional Practice in Psychology. *Professional Psychology: Research and Practice*, Advance online publication. doi: 10.1037/a0031689.

Silverman, W. H. (2013). The future of psychotherapy: One editor's perspective. *Psychotherapy*. Advance online publication. doi: 10.1037/a0030573.

Swaminathan, N. (2012). What predicts grad school success? American Psychological Association gradPSYCH Magazine. Retrieved Mar 20, 2013 from http://www.apa.org/gradpsych/2012/09/cover-success.aspx.

Vasquez, M. J. T. (2011). The internship crisis: Strategies and solutions. *Monitor on Psychology, 42*, 4.

Weiten, W. (2011). *Psychology: Themes and variations*. New York, NY: Wadsworth/Cengage.

Wilson, G. T. (2011). Clinical psychology. In P. R. Martin, F. M. Cheung, M. C., Knowles, et al. (Eds.), *IAPP handbook of applied psychology*. Oxford, United Kingdom: Wiley-Blackwell.

2 | CLINICAL PSYCHOLOGY'S PAST AND PRESENT

Chapter Preview

In this chapter, we explain the events that gave birth to clinical psychology as a profession. We describe the slow but steady growth of the field during the first half of the 20th century, followed by the explosive growth that gave rise to the major approaches to clinical psychology: psychodynamic, humanistic, behavioral, cognitive, systems, and biological. We tell the story of how these approaches came into being, and we outline how the different approaches might be applied to an individual case. (In subsequent chapters, we consider in detail the specific assessment and treatment tactics used by clinicians who adopt these and other approaches.)

Anyone born in the United States after World War II might assume that the field of clinical psychology has always existed. However, clinical psychology did not emerge as a discipline until the beginning of the 20th century and did not begin rapid development until World War II ended. Between its initial and its current form, the field of clinical psychology changed significantly (Benjamin, 2005; L'Abate, 2013 discussed in detail; Resnick, 1997; Routh, 1994; Taylor, 2000). It was often a struggle for psychologists to become clinical psychologists.

THE ROOTS OF CLINICAL PSYCHOLOGY

SECTION PREVIEW

Three sets of social and historical factors initially shaped clinical psychology and continue to influence it. These factors include (a) the use of scientific research methods—the empirical tradition, (b) the measurement of individual differences—the psychometric tradition, and (c) the classification and treatment of behavior disorders—the clinical tradition.

The roots of clinical psychology extend back to before the field of psychology was ever named, back to developments in philosophy, medicine, and several of the sciences. A few of these roots are especially important because they converged and created the field of clinical psychology, though only in embryonic form.

The Empirical Tradition

Historians typically mark the beginning of modern psychology as 1879, the year that Wilhelm Wundt established the first laboratory devoted to studying mental processes in Leipzig, Germany. Wundt was convinced that psychology—like biology, physics, and other sciences—should seek knowledge through the application of empirical research methods. He and others who came after him were determined to study human behavior by employing the two most powerful tools of science: observation and experimentation.

The founding of Wundt's laboratory was not the only beginning point for the new discipline. Others in physiology and medicine had been working on problems that were essentially psychological in nature. For instance, Johannes Müller and his student Herman Helmholtz identified and explored the neural pathways for vision and hearing, discoveries that addressed the question of how physical energy became mental experiences. Ernst Weber and Gustav Fechner showed that people's perceptual experiences changed in mathematically predictable ways as stimuli (e.g., weight or brightness) changed, suggesting that mind and body were fundamentally connected (Hunt, 1993). Still, Wundt is regarded as the founder of psychology because the advent of his laboratory so clearly proclaimed psychology as a science and because he trained many students who went on to establish psychology programs in European and U.S. universities.

One of Wundt's students was an American named Lightner Witmer. Following his graduation from the University of Pennsylvania in 1888, Witmer worked on his PhD in psychology with Wundt at the University of Leipzig. After completing his doctorate in 1892, Witmer was appointed director of the University of Pennsylvania psychology laboratory. In March 1896, a local schoolteacher named Margaret Maguire asked Witmer to help one of her students, Charles Gilman, whom she described as a "chronic bad speller." Once a schoolteacher himself, Witmer "took the case," thus becoming the first clinical psychologist and simultaneously beginning an enterprise that became the world's first psychological clinic (Benjamin, 2005; Routh, 1994).

Witmer's approach was to assess Charles's problem and then arrange for appropriate remedial procedures. His assessment showed that Charles had a visual impairment, as well as reading and memory problems that Witmer termed "visual verbal amnesia." Today, these difficulties would probably be diagnosed as a reading disorder. Witmer recommended intensive tutoring to help the boy recognize words without having to spell them first. This procedure successfully brought Charles to the point that he could read normally (McReynolds, 1987).

By 1900, three children a day were being served by a clinic staff that had grown to 11 members, and in 1907, Witmer set up a residential school for training children with intellectual disability. That same year, he founded and edited the first clinical journal, *The Psychological Clinic*, and wrote the lead article, which he titled simply "Clinical Psychology." By 1909, over 450 cases had been seen in Witmer's facilities. Under Witmer's influence, the University of Pennsylvania began offering formal courses in clinical psychology during the 1904–1905 academic year. Clinical psychology was on its way.

The initial reception for this new endeavor was not enthusiastic, however. In a talk at the 1896 meeting of the 4-year-old American Psychological Association, Witmer described his new brand of psychology. His friend Joseph Collins recounted the scene as follows:

> [Witmer said] that clinical psychology is derived from the results of an examination of many human beings, one at a time, and that the analytic method of discriminating mental abilities and defects develops an ordered classification of observed behavior, by means of postanalytic generalizations. He put forth the claim that the psychological clinic is an institution for social and public service, for original research, and for the instruction of students in psychological orthogenics which includes vocational, educational, correctional, hygienic, industrial, and social guidance. The only reaction he got from his audience was a slight elevation of the eyebrows on the part of a few of the older members. (Quoted in Brotemarkle, 1947, p. 65)

This lead-balloon reception is understandable given the following four facts prevalent at the time: First, most psychologists considered themselves to be laboratory scientists and probably did not regard the role described by Witmer as appropriate for them. Second, even if they had considered his suggestions admirable, few psychologists were prepared by training or experience to perform the functions he proposed. Third, they were not about to jeopardize their identification as scientists, which was tenuous enough in those early years, by plunging their profession into what they felt were premature applications. Fourth, Witmer had an unfortunate talent for antagonizing his colleagues (Reisman, 1976, p. 46). The responses to Witmer's talk provided the first clues that conflicts would arise between psychology as a science and psychology as an applied profession, conflicts which remain to this day.

Several aspects of Witmer's new clinic came to characterize subsequent clinical work for many years:

1. Most of his clients were children, a natural development since Witmer had been offering a course on child psychology, had published his first papers in the journal *Pediatrics*, and had attracted the attention of teachers concerned about their students.
2. His recommendations for helping clients were preceded by diagnostic assessment.
3. He did not work alone but in a team approach that saw members of various professions consulting and collaborating on cases.
4. He emphasized prevention of future problems through early diagnosis and remediation.
5. He emphasized that clinical psychology should be built on the principles being discovered in scientific psychology as a whole.

The last one in particular, that clinical practice should be built on solid scientific evidence, has remained a core of clinical psychology. Following Witmer's lead, other empirically trained psychologists became interested in applying their knowledge to problems outside the laboratory.

TABLE 2.1 Landmarks of the Empirical Tradition in Clinical Psychology

Dates	Key Figures	Contributions
Mid-1800s	Müller, Helmholtz, Weber, Fechner	Studied sensory discrimination and perception; explored and measured nerve impulses; sought explanations of mental events in terms of physical processes
1879	Wundt	Established first laboratory designed specifically to study mental processes; trained many students who went on to establish psychology programs at universities in Europe and the United States
1896–1900	Witmer	Student of Wundt; established the first psychology clinic and the first journal devoted to psychology clinics; founded clinical psychology in the United States

Thus, the earliest history of clinical psychology, like the early history of psychology in general, is largely one of experimental psychology (Boring, 1950) (see Table 2.1).

Witmer got clinical psychology rolling, but he had little to do with steering it. He lost influence largely because he ignored developments that would later become central to the field. For instance, Witmer used the psychological tests available to him at the time, but he largely ignored the development of new intelligence tests. This decision was costly because intelligence testing came to characterize applied psychology perhaps more than any other activity during the first half of the 20th century (Benjamin, 2005). Witmer also ignored early forms of adult psychotherapy that would come to dominate the field and virtually define psychology in the eyes of the public. Witmer remained active, of course, but mainly with functions and clients that have since become more strongly associated with school psychology, vocational counseling, speech therapy, and remedial education than with clinical psychology (Fagan, 1996). In short, Witmer's contributions were significant, but they cannot account for the diversity and growth that clinical psychology experienced after him. For that, we must look to other sources.

The Psychometric Tradition

A second source from which clinical psychology developed was the practice of measuring people's physical and mental abilities. The importance of measuring individual differences has been recognized for centuries. In his *Republic*, Plato suggested that prospective soldiers be tested for military ability before their acceptance in the army. In the 6th century B.C., Pythagoras selected members of his brotherhood on the basis of facial characteristics, intelligence, and emotionality, and 4,000 years ago, prospective government employees in China were given individual ability tests before being hired (DuBois, 1970; McReynolds, 1975).

Surprisingly, the earliest developments in the scientific measurement of individual differences came in the fields of astronomy, anatomy, and biology. The astronomical story began in 1796, when Nevil Maskelyne was Astronomer Royal at the Greenwich (England) Observatory. He recorded the moment at which various stars and planets crossed a certain point in the sky. His assistant, David Kinnebrook, made the same recordings, but Kinnebrook's recordings consistently differed from those of his boss by five- to eight-tenths of a second. Maskelyne assumed that his readings were correct and that Kinnebrook was in error. As a result, Kinnebrook lost his job.

This incident drew the attention of F. W. Bessel, an astronomer at the University of Konigsberg (Germany) observatory. Bessel wondered whether Kinnebrook's "error" might reflect something about the characteristics of various observers, and over the next several years, he compared his own observations with those of other experienced astronomers. Bessel found that discrepancies appeared regularly and that the size of the differences depended upon the person with whom he compared notes. The differences associated with each observer became known as the "personal equation," because they allowed calculations to be corrected for personal characteristics. Bessel's work led to later research by psychologists on the speed of, and individual differences in, reaction time.

Interest in individual differences can also be seen in the early 19th-century work of German anatomist Franz Gall and his pupil Johann Spurzheim. Gall thought he saw a relationship between his schoolmates' mental characteristics and the shapes of their heads. This notion later led Gall to espouse *phrenology* (see Figure 2.1), an alleged science based on the assumptions that (1) each area of the brain is associated with a different faculty or function (e.g., self-esteem, language, or reverence); (2) the better developed each of these areas is, the more strongly that faculty or function is manifested in behavior; and (3) the pattern of over- or underdevelopment of each faculty is reflected in corresponding bumps or depressions in the skull. Gall traveled throughout Europe measuring the bumps on people's heads, beginning with prisoners and mental patients whose behavioral characteristics seemed well established (he thought the "acquisitiveness" bump was especially strong among pickpockets), and later on more respectable segments of society. Eventually, a map of the brain's 37 "powers" or "organs" was drawn. Many people paid phrenologists to "have their head examined," after which they received a profile allegedly describing their mental makeup. Although certain brain areas are associated with certain functions such as vision, movement, and language, Gall's claims about the locations of functions and about the meaning of irregularities in the skull were recognized—even by the scientists of his day—as spectacularly wrong.

Individual differences were also central to Charles Darwin's momentous work, *Origin of Species*, published in 1859. In it, Darwin proposed two important ideas: that (1) variation of individual characteristics occurs within and between species (including humans), and (2) natural selection takes place in part on the basis of those characteristics. Darwin's cousin, Sir Francis Galton, was fascinated by these ideas, and he quickly applied Darwin's notions to the inheritance of individual differences—especially in mental abilities. For example, Galton (1883) sought to measure people's ability to make fine discriminations between objects of differing weight and between varying intensities of heat, cold, and pain. He also developed the word-association test to explore associative processes. Eventually, Galton set up the world's first mental testing center, where, for a small fee, anyone could take a battery of tests and receive a copy of the results.

The person usually credited with merging individual mental measurement with the new science of psychology is James McKeen Cattell, also a former student of Wundt. Cattell was one of the first psychologists to appreciate the practical uses of tests in the selection and diagnosis of people. Cattell's experience in Wundt's laboratory taught him that "psychology cannot attain

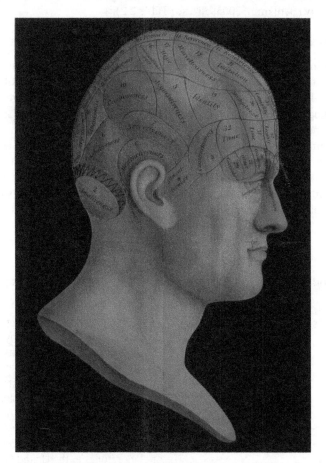

FIGURE 2.1   Phrenology, an Early Form of Psychological Testing, Involved the Practice of Assessing Personality by Reading Bumps or Variations in the Skull.   *Source*: Courtesy of the Library of Congress, LC-USZC4-4556.

the certainty and exactness of the physical sciences unless it rests on a foundation of experiment and measurement" (Dennis, 1948, p. 347). Consequently, one of his first tasks was to construct a standard battery of mental tests for use by researchers interested in individual differences. He chose 10 tests that reflected the then-prevalent tendency to use sensorimotor functioning as an index of mental capacity, and he tested people's performance under varying conditions. He also collected less systematic information about people's dreams, diseases, preferences, recreational activities, and future plans (Shaffer & Lazarus, 1952). So Galton's method of systematically collecting samples of behavior from large groups of people launched what came to be called the mental testing movement.

Alfred Binet, a French lawyer, scientist, and former student of Wilhem Wundt, was another key figure in this movement. In 1896, Binet and his colleague Victor Henri described a battery of tests that measured not just "simple part processes," such as space judgment, motor skills, muscular effort, and memory, but also comprehension, attention, suggestibility, aesthetic appreciation, and moral values in both normal and "defective" children. Binet's new intelligence test, the Binet–Simon scale, was introduced in the United States where, in 1916, it was revised by Lewis Terman of Stanford University. This *Stanford–Binet Intelligence Test* grew so rapidly in the United States that it overshadowed all other tests of intelligence, including those used by Witmer. In spite of Binet's warning that it did not provide a wholly objective measure of intelligence, new university psychological clinics and institutions for the intellectually disabled (formerly called retarded) began adopting the Binet approach.

Thus, by the early 1900s, psychology was involved in measuring individual differences in mental functioning, and it hosted two overlapping approaches to the task: (1) the Galton–Cattell sensorimotor tests, aimed at assessing inherited, relatively fixed mental *structures*, and (2) the instruments of Binet and others, which emphasized complex mental *functions* that could be taught to some degree. Each approach was important to the development of clinical psychology, the former because it influenced Witmer and helped foster the appearance of the first psychological clinic, and the latter because it provided mental tests that gave the new field of clinical psychology its first clear identity (Benjamin, 2005; also see Table 2.2).

The Clinical Tradition

From the beginning of recorded history, human beings have tried to explain behavior that is bizarre or apparently irrational. Early explanations of disordered behavior involved possession by demons or spirits. Treatments for such supernaturally induced maladies involved various forms of exorcism, including *trephining*, the boring of holes in the skull to provide evil spirits with an exit.

In early monotheistic cultures, God was seen as a possible source of behavior problems. In the Old Testament, for example, we are told that "the Lord shall smite thee with madness, and blindness, and astonishment of heart" (Deuteronomy 28:28). Where supernatural approaches to behavior disorders were prevalent, philosophy and religion were dominant in explaining and dealing with them. Although they are not prominent in Western cultures today, supernatural—and especially demonological—explanations remain influential in other cultures around the world and in some ethnic and religious subcultures in North America.

TABLE 2.2 Landmarks of the Psychometric Tradition in Clinical Psychology

Dates	Key Figures	Contributions
Late 1700s–1880s	Bessell, Gall, Galton	Noted individual differences in recording observations; measured physical and physiological reactions to assess personality and mental functioning
1896	Binet	Developed a battery of tests to assess mental processes in children; administered tests to large numbers to develop norms
1890s–early 1900s	Goddard, Terman, Cattell	Helped to popularize Binet-style tests in the United States; founded psychology laboratories in the United States that emphasized measurement

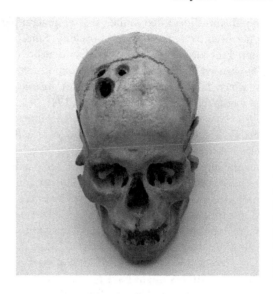

Trephining (also called trephination or trepanning) involved drilling holes into the skulls of persons suffering from severe mental illness in the belief that demons causing their illness could then escape.   *Source*: Science and Society/Superstock.

Supernatural explanations of behavior disorders were still highly influential when, in about the 4th century B.C., the Greek physician Hippocrates suggested that these aberrations stem from natural rather than supernatural causes. Hippocrates argued that behavior disorders, like other behaviors, are a function of the distribution of four bodily fluids, or humors: blood, black bile, yellow bile, and phlegm. This theory, generally acknowledged as the first medical model of disordered behavior, paved the way for the concept of *mental illness* and legitimized the involvement of the medical profession in its treatment. From Hippocrates until the fall of Rome in 476 A.D., physicians supported and reinforced a physical, or medical, model of behavior disorder.

In the Middle Ages, the medical model was swept away as the church became the primary social and legal institution in Europe. Demonological explanations of behavior disorders regained prominence, and religious personnel again took over responsibility for dealing with cases of deviance. Ever resourceful, many physicians soon became priests and began "treating" the insane by exorcizing the spirits presumed to possess them.

With the Renaissance, the pendulum gradually swung back to naturalistic explanations of mental illness. At first, the treatment of deviant individuals took the form of confinement in newly established hospitals and asylums, such as London's St. Mary of Bethlehem, organized in 1547 and referred to by locals as "bedlam." Feared and misunderstood by the general public— many undoubtedly still believed the mentally ill to be possessed—residents were little more than prisoners who lived under abominable conditions and received grossly inadequate care. Fortunately, changing conceptions of mental illness led European and North American reformers of the 18th and early 19th centuries to push for more humane living conditions and treatments in mental institutions. In France, Philippe Pinel ushered in this era of more humane treatment with the following comment: "It is my conviction that these mentally ill are intractable only because they are deprived of fresh air and liberty" (quoted in Ullmann & Krasner, 1975, p. 135). In the United States and Great Britain, movements to improve the treatment of persons with severe disorders paralleled those in France. Benjamin Rush, often regarded as the father of American psychiatry (Schneck, 1975), was instrumental in changing the way institutionalized mental patients were treated in the United States. In Great Britain, William Tuke played a similar role. Both men had one foot in the past—Rush, for instance, advocated the antiquated treatments of bloodletting and a tranquilizer chair for immobilization while Tuke favored the whirling chair and plunge baths. But both men also anticipated the future—they favored removing restraints (as Pinel had in France), they sought to study mental illness scientifically, and they argued that suffering persons were worthy of respect, kindness, and treatment. Reformers such as Dorothea Lynde Dix, a New England schoolteacher, campaigned to improve conditions for the mentally ill, launched public information campaigns, lobbied legislative groups, and eventually played a role in founding more than 30 state institutions for the mentally ill (Schneck, 1975).

Thus began a new awareness of the possibility that mental patients could be helped rather than simply hidden, and physicians assumed the responsibility for helping them. The role of physicians in treating mental disorders was further solidified when, later in the 19th century, syphilis was identified as the cause of general paresis, a deteriorative brain syndrome that had once been treated as a form of insanity. Finding an organic cause for this mental disorder bolstered the view that all behavior disorders are organically based. The notion that there could be "no twisted thought without a twisted molecule" (Abood, 1960) triggered a psychiatric revolution in which doctors searched feverishly for organic causes of—and physical treatments for—all forms of mental illness (Zilboorg & Henry, 1941).

New ways of thinking about mental illness required new ways of categorizing it. Emil Kraepelin was a German psychiatrist who, over a 40-year period, wrote and revised the first formal classifications of psychological disorders. Kraepelin's main interest was in a careful classification of mental illness, but his career also included participation in the formation of the first state mental hygiene committee in the United States, attending Wundt's summer course, giving expert testimony in murder trials, screening soldiers in World War I, writing poetry, and studying Buddhism (Carlson, 1981). Kraepelin's classification system is no longer used, but his approach—classifying mental illnesses in terms of observable symptoms—is still evident in the current system of classification, the *Diagnostic and Statistical Manual of Mental Disorders (DSM)*.

Ironically, the revolution that viewed mental illness as disease also led to the idea that mental disorders might have *psychological* causes, too. In the mid-1800s, a French physician named Jean-Martin Charcot found that hypnosis could alleviate certain behavior disorders, particularly hysteria (today known as conversion disorder). Charcot's lectures were well attended—among the regulars were Alfred Binet, William James, Sigmund Freud, and a French neurologist named Pierre Janet. Janet believed that some parts of the personality could become split off or *dissociated* from the conscious self and produce symptoms such as paralysis. Janet's views anticipated those of Sigmund Freud, the young Viennese neurologist who, by 1896, had already proposed the first stage of a theory in which behavior disorders were seen not as the result of organic problems but as a consequence of the dynamic struggle of the human mind to satisfy instinctual (mainly sexual) desires while also coping with the rules and restrictions of the outside world. Dispute arose over whether Janet's or Freud's work came first, but there is little doubt that Freud did more to develop the theory (Watson, 1978), and thus he became far better known than Janet.

Freud's theories were first introduced to American psychologists during the 1890s, mostly in journal reviews by William James and James Baldwin (Taylor, 2000), psychologists with strong interests in the self, the ego, and "dissociated" states of consciousness such as trance, hypnosis, and unexplained memory loss. These theories at first drew a less-than-enthusiastic reaction both in Europe and in the United States. One doctor called Freud's ideas "a scientific fairy tale" (Krafft-Ebing, quoted in Reisman, 1976, p. 41). Nevertheless, those ideas eventually grew to become a comprehensive theory of the dynamic nature of behavior and behavior disorder and a detailed description of psychological treatments for such disorders. So it was that ideas from the clinical (medical) tradition ultimately redirected the entire course of the mental health professions, including clinical psychology (see Table 2.3).

TABLE 2.3 Landmarks of the Clinical Tradition in Clinical Psychology

Dates	Key Figures	Contributions
1880–1890s	Kraepelin, Charcot, Janet	Classified psychological disorders; studied and treated patients with atypical neurological symptoms ("dissociations"); used case studies of pathology to reveal general principles about healthy and unhealthy workings of the mind
1890	James	Psychologist/physician who participated in both empirical and clinical traditions; introduced European psychology and psychiatry to U.S. audiences; wrote *The Principles of Psychology*, which some still regard as the most influential psychology book ever written
1895–1939	Freud	Advanced psychoanalytic view of personality and psychotherapy in numerous writings; his approach came to dominate psychiatry and clinical psychology in the United States during the first half of the 20th century

SECTION SUMMARY

Although the seeds of clinical psychology were planted centuries ago by philosophers and by pioneers in the physical sciences, the roots of clinical psychology did not appear until the middle and late 1800s. The most prominent roots were the empirical research tradition, begun in Germany with Wundt, the psychometric tradition, begun in Great Britain and France with Galton and Binet, and the clinical/therapeutic tradition, begun in France and Austria with Charcot, Freud, and others. Each of these traditions found expression in the United States, and in the U.S. melting pot tradition, eventually combined to form a new specialty in psychology. The three traditions provided a stable base for clinical psychology, much as three legs provide a stable base for a stool. Without any one of them, the discipline would have collapsed. With all three, it could grow and support future developments—which is exactly what happened.

CLINICAL PSYCHOLOGY BEGINS TO GROW

SECTION PREVIEW

With its roots well established, clinical psychology began to grow during the first four decades of the 20th century. Opportunities for application expanded, initially in psychological testing and later in psychotherapy. Psychologists created professional organizations to support practitioners and establish guidelines for the discipline. Much of the accelerating growth of clinical psychology can be traced to societal needs made evident during and following World Wars I and II.

By the early 1900s, psychology departments had been established at many U.S. and European universities, and persons associated with these departments had begun to apply their discipline. There were 20 psychological clinics on university campuses by 1914 (Watson, 1953). Many of them were created in the image of Witmer's clinic, but the emphasis gradually shifted from testing and treating children with academic difficulties to testing and treating children with other problems, and then to testing and treating adolescents and adults with problems.

Psychological Testing Expands

Because of its emphasis on careful measurement and standardized administration, psychological testing had the respect of many early empirical psychologists. Compared to psychotherapy, testing was considered a more rigorous, "hardheaded" application of psychology. And as psychologists were employed in mental hospitals, clinics, and specialized settings for the physically and mentally handicapped, their testing contributions were accepted by medical coworkers (usually psychiatrists). Those contributions often came during staff meetings to discuss individual cases (Benjamin, 2005).

During World War I, the need for "mental testers" became acute. When the United States entered the War, large numbers of military recruits had to be classified in terms of intellectual prowess and psychological stability. No techniques existed for such testing, so the Army asked Robert Yerkes (then president of the American Psychological Association) to head a committee of assessment-oriented experimental psychologists who were to develop appropriate measures. To measure mental abilities, the committee produced the Army Alpha and Army Beta intelligence tests (for group administration to literate and nonliterate adults respectively). To help detect behavior disorders, the committee recommended Robert Woodworth's Psychoneurotic Inventory (discreetly retitled "Personal Data Sheet"; Yerkes, 1921, in Dennis, 1948). By 1918, psychologists had conducted evaluations of nearly 2 million men.

For much of the first two decades of the 20th century, intelligence testing and psychological testing were synonymous. However, as psychologists found more employment opportunities in child guidance clinics, mental hospitals, and other adult facilities, it became clear that tests of intelligence were not enough. The foreword to Raymond Cattell's 1936 *A Guide to Mental Testing* described the situation:

> For some time there has been a lull in the progress of mental testing as a practical procedure. After the first wave of enthusiasm in the so-called Intelligence Tests, and their indiscriminate

and often unintelligent application, this was bound to happen. It became evident that the results of these tests were influenced by factors other than intelligence, which seemed to elude measurement even if they were taken into account at all . . . . The psychotherapist, faced with problems of behaviour dependent on forces much more instinctive than intellectual, found the estimation of mental endowment alone of only limited value, especially since variations in mental capacity were always complicated by disturbances of the personality. (Moodie, 1936, p.vii)

The need for measures of personality, interests, specific abilities, emotions, and traits led to the development of many new tests during the 1920s and 1930s. Some of the more familiar instruments of this period include Jung's Word Association Test (1919), the Rorschach Inkblot Test (1921), the Miller Analogies Test (1926), the Goodenough Draw-A-Man Test (1926), the Strong Vocational Interest Test (1927), the Thematic Apperception Test (TAT) (1935), the Bender–Gestalt Test (1938), and the Wechsler-Bellevue Intelligence Scale (1939). Testing was so popular during the first few decades of the 1900s that there were complaints from some quarters that professional meetings were being overrun with psychologists describing their newest mental tests (Benjamin, 1997, 2005). In fact, so many psychological tests appeared (over 500 by 1940) that a Mental Measurements Yearbook was needed to catalog them (Buros, 1938). For most clinicians of the day, treatment appeared a natural extension of the diagnostic and remedial services they were already providing, and discussing test results gave psychologists and psychiatrists a shared clinical language and brought clinical psychologists that much closer to the treatment role.

Clinicians Pursue Roles as Psychotherapists

Clinical psychologists added psychotherapy to their assessment role, but not without some opposition. Because psychology began as an academic, laboratory-based discipline, relatively few early psychologists sought to conduct psychotherapy with adults, and many, including Witmer, were quite skeptical about such activities (Benjamin, 2005; Taylor, 2000). Change occurred slowly as a natural outcome of at least three factors: (a) as already noted, psychological testing expanded to include measures of personality and psychopathology; (b) child guidance clinics, where clinical psychologists worked since the time of Witmer, broadened their client base to include treatment of social as well as educational maladjustment; and (c) psychologists of the early 20th century became eager to learn psychoanalysis, the dominant approach to psychotherapy among psychiatrists.

Sigmund Freud, seated at left, was introduced to an American audience in 1909 at a conference of psychologists held at Clark University in Worcester, Massachusetts. *Source*: Bettmann/Corbis.

Recall that Witmer's psychology clinic focused on children with academic difficulties. In contrast, the child guidance clinic founded in Chicago in 1909 by William Healy, an English-born psychiatrist, was heavily influenced by Freud's psychoanalytic theories. Healy focused on cases of child misbehavior that drew the attention of school authorities, the police, or the courts. Healy's clinic operated on the assumption that juvenile offenders suffered from mental illness that should be dealt with before it caused more serious problems. In the same year Healy opened his clinic, psychologist G. Stanley Hall arranged for Sigmund Freud and two of his followers, Carl Jung and Sandor Ferenczi, to speak at a conference celebrating the 20th anniversary of Clark University in Worcester, Massachusetts. In retrospect, this conference was special because it brought together many of the most influential American and European founders of clinical psychology and because it introduced psychoanalysis to American psychologists. Photographs taken during this event have an iconic quality.

The United States was fertile ground for Freud's ideas, but their growth among psychologists was slow at first. Few psychologists of the day engaged in any form of treatment, and many remained quite skeptical; Witmer did not attend the Clark University conference (Routh, 1994). Even if early clinical psychologists had been interested in learning and practicing psychoanalysis, training was difficult to obtain. University psychology departments, dominated by those trained in Wundt's empirical tradition, were reluctant to develop graduate programs in clinical psychology because their faculties questioned the appropriateness of "applied" psychology and worried about the cost of clinical training. Many also criticized the imprecise nature of Freud's concepts. With few exceptions, formal training in psychoanalysis was available only from psychoanalytic institutes and medical schools, and these were typically run by psychiatrists who sought to assure that treatment would remain the province of psychiatrists (Abt 1992; Schneck, 1975). In 1917, for example, a New York psychiatric organization issued a report calling for an end to clinical psychologists' involvement in the diagnosis and treatment of patients with mental disorders (Benjamin, 2005).

Nevertheless, by 1911, the first U.S. psychoanalytic association had formed in New York, and over the next 20 years, psychiatrists and psychologists in increasing numbers identified themselves with Freud's theories (Watson, 1953). To many it became clear that growth in clinical psychology would be in the practice of psychotherapy, and the foundations of psychotherapy would be in psychoanalysis. At the Clark University conference, William James famously said to Freud, "The future of psychology belongs to your work" (Jones, 1955, p. 27).

Despite growing popularity, psychoanalytic and other forms of psychotherapy did not become a mainstay of clinical psychologists' activities until after World War II. As in World War I, there was a great need for psychological assessment in World War II, and a corresponding need to treat not only military personnel who had experienced trauma, but also their family members and others in their communities whose lives had been disrupted by the war. Psychologists with clinical training were recruited in large numbers and worked shoulder to shoulder with psychiatrists and social workers. It was in this arena that many clinical psychologists began to learn and apply psychoanalysis and other variations of Freud's "talking cure" (Cautin, 2011). After the War, many psychologists sought to continue their work as psychotherapists, and a series of U.S. government initiatives dramatically increased their ability to do so.

One of these was the Veteran's Administration's (VA for short; now the U.S. Department of Veteran's Affairs) new program to support training in the mental health disciplines. In 1946, the VA made clinical internships available in VA hospitals and mental hygiene clinics. Prior to this, internships for clinical psychologists—typically involving a year of practical experience—had existed mainly in child guidance clinics and mental hospitals (Routh, 2000). With the VA's blessing, however, formal internship training became available for clinicians interested in providing psychotherapy to adult clients who suffered from a variety of disorders.

A second initiative was the national effort, beginning in 1955, to create *community mental health clinics* throughout the United States. Sponsored by the U.S. Public Health Services and the newly formed National Institute of Mental Health, the initiative was a broad response to concerns about mental health. To this day, it remains as one of the largest government-led mental health efforts. Some of these Community Mental Health (CMH) centers also established internships for psychologists in training, expanding the training opportunities for clinicians. By now, mental hospitals and psychiatric facilities, long the training ground for psychiatrists, had begun to open their doors to clinical psychologists, if only in small numbers (Abt, 1992).

Clinical psychologists now had training internships and job opportunities. Some universities and a few psychoanalytic institutes had created training programs for them. But there was no standard set of educational and training experiences that defined what a clinical psychologist was. These standards would come from professional organizations.

Clinicians Form Professional Organizations

In most professions, decisions about the training and experience that their members need in order to qualify to practice are made by the leadership of their national and state organizations. These organizations usually then publish guidelines for training, establish codes of conduct for practice, define professional boundaries, and work with state legislators to establish laws governing licensing. It did not work this way for the profession of clinical psychology. At the beginning of World War II, there were still no official university training programs for clinicians, so there were no clearly articulated requirements for training and no such thing as a license to practice clinical psychology. To get a job as a clinical psychologist, all a person needed was a few courses in testing, abnormal psychology, and child development, along with an "interest in people."

There certainly was an organization of psychologists, the *American Psychological Association*, which had been established in 1892, but it was dominated by researchers who had doubts about the wisdom of a clinical psychology profession. The APA did appoint committees on clinical training at various times during the 1920s and 1930s (and had even set up a short-lived clinical certification program), but its involvement was half hearted. For example, in 1935 the APA Committee on Standards of Training in Clinical Psychology suggested that a PhD plus 1 year of supervised experience was necessary to become a clinical psychologist, but after issuing its report, the committee disbanded and little came of its efforts.

As more psychologists became interested in applying their knowledge beyond the laboratory, conflicts arose among APA members who wanted the discipline to be a pure science and those who wanted it to be an applied science, too (Benjamin, 1997).

Those favoring an applied approach to psychology—mainly the practitioners of mental testing and psychotherapy—decided to form organizations that would be more responsive to their concerns. The first such organization, the *American Association of Clinical Psychologists* (AACP), was cofounded in 1917 by Leta Hollingworth, a member of the Columbia University psychology faculty. Hollingworth was also the first to suggest a more practice-oriented form of training for clinical psychologists—leading, more than half a century later, to a PsyD, or doctor of psychology degree—as an alternative to the research-based PhD. She also suggested that a national examining board be created to identify and grant licenses to qualified clinicians (Benjamin, 2005; Donn, Routh, & Lunt, 2000). Although the AACP did not survive, it foreshadowed things to come.

As World War II approached, the American Psychological Association had begun to recognize that psychology was developing into an applied discipline. Members of APA, many of whom were now also members of alternative state and national professional psychology associations, decided to reorganize to make room for the practice concerns of applied psychologists (Benjamin, 1997). When they reorganized APA and allowed members to affiliate with particular special interest groups called divisions, about twice as many chose to be in the division of clinical psychology (Division 12) as in any other (Benjamin, 1997). The rapid rise in APA memberships beginning around 1950 was driven largely by the rapid rise of clinical psychology over the same time period (see Figure 2.2).

Clinical psychology, firmly rooted and organized as a professional discipline by the mid-20th century, was poised for strong growth. Between the mid-1940s and the mid-1950s, a series of actions by APA and its members defined clinical psychology with a clarity that it had not known before. For example, beginning with Connecticut in 1945, states began passing certification laws for psychologists. A year later, the *American Board of Examiners in Professional Psychology* (ABPP) was established to certify that clinicians holding a PhD were qualified. The *American Psychologist*, the flagship journal of APA, was first published in 1946. Three years later, a conference was held in Boulder, Colorado, to discuss the various training models for clinical psychologists, and as discussed in detail in Chapter 15, this landmark *Boulder Conference* established a model of clinical training that would dominate university graduate programs

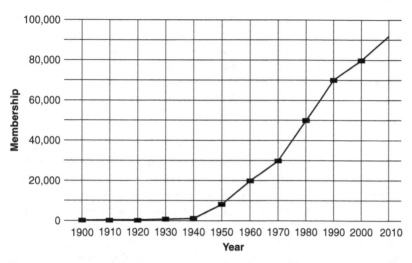

FIGURE 2.2 Total APA Membership (Associates, Members, and Fellows), 1900–2010. *Source*: American Psychological Association (2012).

for decades. In 1953, the APA published its first ethical guidelines for clinical psychologists. These and other events launched clinical psychology into a period of rapid expansion. We discuss them, and their impact, in more detail in later chapters.

SECTION SUMMARY

By the early 1900s, psychology departments had been established at many U.S. and European universities, and persons associated with these departments had begun to apply their discipline. Psychological testing was the most accepted area of application, but clinical psychologists increasingly saw the value of treating psychological problems in adult clients. At first, they had difficulty finding training to do so because university programs were often dominated by faculty skeptical of psychotherapy and because psychiatrists were reluctant to admit psychologists into psychoanalytic training institutes. But advances in testing, the expanding need for treatment created by two world wars, the establishment of new university-based training programs and community mental health centers, and the establishment of strong professional organizations, eventually opened up the field of psychotherapy to clinical psychologists.

THE MAJOR APPROACHES DEVELOP

SECTION PREVIEW

After World War II, clinical psychology grew rapidly, branching out into the major theoretical approaches that came to define the field: psychodynamic, humanistic, behavioral, cognitive, systems, and biological. Each of these approaches is best thought of as a broad school of thought rather than a single theory. We assume that most students reading this book will have already had a course in personality and/or abnormal psychology, so our goal here is to describe the basic assumptions and general application of various approaches to psychological problems. In subsequent chapters, we show how clinicians adopting these approaches apply them to cases.

The Psychodynamic Approach

As already noted, Sigmund Freud's psychoanalysis became a dominant force in early clinical psychology. Subsequent modifications and variations on psychoanalytic theory are known collectively as *psychodynamic*. All psychodynamic approaches have a common origin and all share certain assumptions about personality, psychopathology, and psychotherapy.

Freud's psychodynamic theory was founded on the idea that human behavior is derived from the constant struggle between the individual's desire to satisfy inborn sexual and aggressive instincts and the need to respect the rules and realities imposed by the outside world (Funder, 2001). To Freud, the human mind is an arena in which what the person *wants* to do (instincts, impulses) must be reconciled with the controlling requirements of what can or *should* be done (reason, social norms, morality). This conflict often leads to anxiety against which the person tries to build defenses. If the anxiety gets too strong, or if the defenses become ineffective, a variety of psychological symptoms can appear.

Freud employed the terms id, ego, and superego to represent the aspects of the mind that are often in conflict. Those conflicts, as well as their historical origins (often in childhood), lie outside the person's awareness, in the unconscious. What clients are aware of, and what others see, are the clients' symptoms—maladaptive ways of behaving, feeling, and thinking adopted (also unconsciously) as a way to defend against the anxiety associated with historically rooted conflicts.

Treatment in the psychoanalytic approach is aimed at unearthing the sources of the clients' symptoms. Freud compared his method with archeology: the therapist searches for deeper meaning, uncovering forgotten or repressed memories and unexpressed emotions that lie beneath the overt symptoms. With the therapist's help, the client gradually becomes aware of how historically rooted conflicts, pushed (not quite successfully) into the unconscious, have come to be expressed in current experience. This awareness, called *insight*, is a central goal in psychoanalytic treatment.

As the psychoanalytic approach developed, others expanded upon, challenged, and changed some of Freud's original concepts. We detail these variations on classical psychoanalysis in Chapter 7, "Psychodynamic and Humanistic Psychotherapies." For now, suffice it to say that later theorists expanded the role of the ego (i.e., beyond being a "referee" between the id and superego), placed more emphasis on social and cultural variables (i.e., less on sexual and aggressive impulses), and explored forms of psychodynamic treatment that were less restrictive than classical psychoanalysis (i.e., briefer in duration, greater flexibility in the therapist's role). Despite these modifications, however, all psychodynamic psychotherapies share certain basic assumptions (see Table 2.4).

The Humanistic Approach

The humanistic approach to psychotherapy developed as an alternative to the psychodynamic approach that dominated personality theory and clinical practice during the early 20th century. The humanistic approach views persons as creative, growthful beings who, if all goes well, consciously guide their own behavior toward realization of their fullest potential as unique individuals. When behavior disorders arise, they are usually seen as stemming from disturbances in awareness or restrictions on existence that can be eliminated through various therapeutic experiences (Fischer, 1989; Greenberg, Elliott, & Lietaer, 1994). Treatment approaches aimed at addressing and correcting these problems are also known as *phenomenological* or *experiential therapies*.

The roots of humanistic therapies are in the clinical tradition, but they also grow from the philosophical position of *phenomenology*, which states that behavior is determined by the

---

TABLE 2.4 Basic Concepts of the Psychoanalytic Approach

1. Human behavior is determined by impulses, desires, motives, and conflicts that are often out of awareness.	3. Clinical assessment, treatment, and research should emphasize the aspects of intrapsychic activity that must be uncovered if behavior is to be understood and behavior problems are to be alleviated.
2. Psychological problems typically occur because clients unsuccessfully defend against, and unconsciously replay, internal (or intrapsychic) internal (or intrapsychic) conflicts that were originally experienced in childhood relationships with family, peers, and authority figures.	4. The goals of psychotherapy are to improve ego functioning and to help clients recognize and change the ways they inappropriately repeat the past.

FIGURE 2.3 What Is "Reality"? Your shifting perceptions of this fixed stimulus allow you to see it as either a young woman in a feathered hat or an old woman in a shawl

perceptions and experiences of the behaving person. Phenomenology puts the client's perceptions and experiences at the center of therapy—what the client perceives, feels, and thinks in the here-and-now takes center stage. Childhood history buried in the unconscious may have played a formative role, but the client's current experiences of reality (including experiences of the self) are what matter most (see Figure 2.3).

Perhaps the most prominent advocate of humanistic psychology was Carl Rogers, a psychologist who was initially trained in psychoanalysis. In Rogers's view, as the developing child begins to differentiate between the self and the rest of the world, there is a growing awareness of this self—a recognition of the "I" or "me." According to Rogers, all of a person's experiences, including "self" experiences, are evaluated as positive or negative, depending on whether they are consistent or inconsistent with the child's self-actualizing tendency. However, these evaluations are not made on the basis of direct or *organismic* feelings alone, as when a child evaluates the taste of candy as positive. They are also influenced by the judgments of other people. Thus, a young boy may end up negatively evaluating the experience of fondling his genitals (even though the direct feelings are positive) because his parents tell him that he is a bad boy to do so.

Rogers noted, however, that most people value the positive regard of others so highly that they will seek it even if it means thinking and acting in ways that are *incongruent* with organismic experience and the self-actualizing motive. This tendency is encouraged by what Rogers called *conditions of worth*—circumstances in which a person receives positive regard from others (and, ultimately, from the self) only for certain approved behaviors, attitudes, and beliefs. Conditions of worth are usually first created by parents, family, and other societal agents, but they are later maintained internally by the individual. People who face extreme or excessive conditions of worth are likely to be uncomfortable. If they behave primarily to please others, it may be at the expense of personal growth.

Perhaps Rogers's most important contributions have been his emphasis on empathic listening on the part of the therapist and on the quality of the therapist–client relationship (Cain, 1990). He described the role of the therapist as follows:

> The therapist must lay aside his preoccupation with diagnosis and his diagnostic shrewdness, must discard his tendency to make professional evaluations, must cease his endeavors to formulate an accurate prognosis, must give up the temptation subtly to guide the individual and must concentrate on one purpose only: that of providing deep understanding and acceptance of the attitudes consciously held at this moment by the client as he explores step by step into the dangerous areas which he has been denying to consciousness. (Rogers, 1946, pp. 420–421)

TABLE 2.5 Basic Concepts of the Humanistic Approach

1. Humanistic psychologists view human nature as essentially positive and believe that their clients' lives can be understood only when seen from the point of view of those clients.	3. Therapists treat clients as responsible individuals who are experts on their own experiences and who must ultimately be the ones to make decisions about their lives.
2. Humanistic psychologists believe problems develop when a person tries to avoid experiencing emotions that are confusing or painful—such avoidance causes the person to become alienated from, and unaccepting of, his or her true self.	4. Humanistic therapists view the therapeutic relationship as the primary vehicle by which therapy achieves its benefits. Focusing on the immediate, moment-to-moment experiences in an atmosphere of honesty and acceptance is what helps clients perceive themselves more positively.

This quote illustrates the similarities and differences between the psychodynamic and humanistic approaches. Both trace psychological problems to painful experiences that are prevented from fully entering consciousness. Unlike psychoanalysts, however, humanistic therapists do not look for deep historical roots of this problem. Rather, they attempt to help clients identify the phenomenal (here-and-now) experience of avoidance as they occur in perceptions, feelings, and thoughts. The idea is that if the therapist does this with compassion and empathy, the client can more accurately understand and accept the *self* (see Table 2.5).

The Behavioral Approach

The behavioral approach to psychotherapy grew more from the empirical tradition in psychology than from the clinical or psychometric tradition. This orientation makes behavioral psychologists inclined to see the causes and treatment of disorders somewhat differently than psychodynamic or humanistic therapists do. In general, behaviorists are more inclined to focus on specific, learned behaviors and environmental conditions associated with those behaviors. They are also inclined to seek evidence of treatment outcomes that are objectively measurable. Although clinical observations are relevant, experimental findings form the basis of the theory and application of behavior therapy.

Groundwork for the emergence of behavior therapy occurred in the 1920s, when psychologists became interested in studying the role of conditioning and learning in the development of anxiety. The discovery of "experimental neuroses" in animals led to research on similar problems in humans. The most famous of these studies was an experiment in 1920 by John B. Watson and his graduate student, Rosalie Rayner. A 9-month-old infant, Albert B., was presented with several stimuli such as a white rat, a dog, a rabbit, a monkey, masks, and a burning newspaper. He showed no fear toward any of these objects, but he did become upset when a loud noise was sounded by striking a steel bar with a hammer. To see whether Albert's fear could be conditioned to a harmless object, Watson and Rayner associated the loud noise with a tame white rat. Albert was shown the rat, and as soon as he began to reach for it, the noise was sounded. After several pairings, the rat alone elicited a strong emotional reaction in the child. This conditioned fear also generalized to some extent to other, previously neutral, furry objects including a rabbit, a fur coat, Watson's own hair, and even a Santa Claus mask. Albert's fear persisted in less extreme form during assessments conducted over a 1-month period.

A few years later, Mary Cover Jones, another of Watson's students, investigated several techniques for *reducing* children's fears (Jones, 1924a, b). For example, she used social *imitation* to help a 3-year-old named Peter conquer his fear of rabbits. "Each day Peter and three other children were brought to the laboratory for a play period. The other children were selected carefully because of their entirely fearless attitude toward the rabbit" (Jones, 1924b, p. 310). The fearless examples set by the other children helped Peter become more comfortable with the rabbit, but his treatment was interrupted by a bout of scarlet fever, and his progress was jeopardized by a frightening encounter with a big dog. When treatment resumed, it included *direct conditioning*, a procedure in which Peter was fed his favorite food in a room with a caged rabbit. At each session, some of which were attended by Peter's fearless friends, the bunny was placed a little closer to him.

Mary Cover Jones helped pioneer the behavioral treatment of psychological disorders in children.   *Source*: G. Paul Bishop.

This procedure eliminated Peter's fear of rabbits; Peter summed up the results of the treatment by announcing, "I like the rabbit."

The cases of Albert and Peter encouraged the application of conditioning principles to the treatment of fear and many other disorders; the 1920s and 1930s saw learning-based treatments for sexual disorders, substance abuse, and various anxiety-related conditions.

The term *behavior therapy* first appeared in a 1953 paper that described the use of operant conditioning to improve the functioning of people with chronic schizophrenia (Lindsley, Skinner, & Solomon, 1953). In the years since, numerous behavioral techniques have been developed for the treatment of psychological disorders. It is interesting that many of the people advocating behavioral approaches were not trained in clinical psychology, but rather in experimental or developmental psychology (Routh, 2011). However, the applicability of behavioral methods for treating disorders was gradually recognized, and behavior therapy ultimately achieved its status as a major treatment approach (see Table 2.6).

The Cognitive Approach

Cognitively oriented researchers and therapists view certain cognitions, particularly thoughts about the self, as especially important in the development of psychological disorders. Because these thoughts are usually connected to emotions, they affect how persons feel about themselves and their relationships with others. Cognitive therapists attempt to modify maladaptive behavior by influencing a client's cognitions: beliefs, schemas, self-statements, assumptions, expectations, and problem-solving strategies.

The cognitive approach to clinical psychology grew from the more general "cognitive revolution" that has influenced all of psychology. This revolution can be traced to developments both inside and outside of psychology. The outside influences include advances in mathematics, biology, and artificial intelligence, and especially the development of the computer. Inside

---

TABLE 2.6 Basic Concepts of the Behavioral Approach

1. Behavioral psychologists view human behavior as learned through conditioning and observation.	**3.** Behavior therapy focuses on changing variables that maintain situation-specific learned maladaptive responses.
2. Psychological problems are assumed to be learned and specific to situations or classes of situations.	**4.** Behavior therapy is derived from empirical research and stresses collection of data to evaluate treatment effectiveness.

influences were those that focused on how habitual cognitive routines (people's "programming") were related to behavior and emotional experiences.

Practicing clinicians welcomed the expanded consideration of mental events. Behavioral clinicians had not adopted the concepts of psychoanalysis, preferring instead to remain closer to empirical psychology's emphasis on observable events and laboratory research. Yet it was inconvenient for behavioral clinicians to avoid references to the client's understanding of their conditions. The client's beliefs about the causes of events, called *attributions* or *appraisals*, seemed to play an important role in their problems.

George Kelly was arguably the first cognitive clinical psychologist (Reinecke & Freeman, 2003). He developed a theory based on the fundamental assumption that human behavior is determined by *personal constructs*, or ways of anticipating the world (Kelly, 1955). According to Kelly, individuals act in accordance with their unique set of expectations about the consequences of behavior, and their major goal is to validate their personal constructs and thus make sense of the world as they perceive it.

According to Kelly's theory, disordered behavior results when a person develops inaccurate, oversimplified, or otherwise faulty constructs about social experiences. Much as a scientist will make incorrect predictions from faulty constructs, people are likely to behave inappropriately if their personal constructs do not allow them to correctly anticipate and comprehend daily events. Thus, a man who construes everything in life as either "good" or "bad" is going to have problems, because not all events and people can be classified this way without distorting them. He may decide that all college students, political activists, and foreigners are bad and that all children, doctors, and clergy are good, but he will be wrong—at least part of the time. He will also be seen by others as close-minded, prejudiced, and a poor judge of character. His interpersonal relationships will likely be stormy.

Another influential figure in the cognitive approach was Albert Ellis (1962, 1973, 1993, 2011). The core principle of his *rational-emotive therapy* is evident in this quote:

> When a highly charged emotional Consequence (C) follows a significant Activating Event (A), A may seem to but actually does not cause C. Instead, emotional Consequences are largely created by B—the individual's Belief System. When, therefore, an undesirable Consequence occurs, such as severe anxiety, this can usually be quickly traced to the person's irrational Beliefs, and when these Beliefs are effectively Disputed (at point D), by challenging them rationally, the disturbed Consequences disappear and eventually cease to reoccur. (Ellis, 1973, p. 167)

According to Ellis, the therapist's task is to attack these irrational, unrealistic, self-defeating beliefs and to instruct clients in more rational or logical thinking patterns that will not upset them (Ellis, 1962; Ellis & Dryden, 1987; Ellis & Grieger, 1977). For example, clients who believe that they are unlovable are likely to claim that "nobody likes me". The belief that they cannot tolerate rejection and may break down emotionally is revealed by the comment, "I can't ask them for that—what if they say no?". Ellis advocated use of strong, direct communication in order to persuade clients to give up the irrational ideas with which they indoctrinate themselves into misery. Other versions of cognitive therapy, like that of Aaron Beck (1976), provided detailed accounts of how specific types of thoughts influence specific disorders, such as depression. They are all related to theories that describe the connections between cognitive processes and social behavior (see Table 2.7).

The Cognitive-Behavioral Approach

Initially, the behavioral and cognitive approaches were conceptual adversaries: strict behaviorists abhorred "mentalism," and cognitive psychologists were convinced that strict behaviorism was too one dimensional. But as early as the 1960s and 1970s, there were signs of a truce between the behavioral and cognitive camps (Mahoney, 1977). Behaviorally oriented therapists recognized the importance of cognitions in various disorders, and cognitively oriented therapists recognized the importance of translating cognitive change into behavior change. Albert Ellis, for instance, understood the importance of focusing on specific behaviors (in addition to irrational beliefs); he

TABLE 2.7 Basic Concepts of the Cognitive Approach

1. Behavior develops not only from learned connections between stimuli and responses but also from how individuals *construe* or think about events.

2. Individuals develop their own idiosyncratic ways of understanding events that affect them, and those explanations affect how they feel and behave.

3. Psychological problems can develop when people's beliefs (assumptions, explanations, attributions) contribute to the things they most fear—for instance, when a depressed person's belief that she is not liked causes her to be uncommunicative which in turn causes others to see her as unapproachable (a faulty feedback loop).

4. Therapists engage clients in a rational examination of their beliefs, encouraging them to test their hypotheses, explore alternate beliefs, and practice applying alternate beliefs.

eventually changed the name of his treatment approach from rational-emotive therapy to *rational-emotive behavior therapy* (Ellis, 1993).

There were other reasons for combining behavioral and cognitive approaches to therapy. Both of them are focused on treating specific aspects of functioning, both had come from the empirical tradition in clinical psychology, and both emphasized well-controlled research to test their underlying theories, assessment techniques, and psychotherapy outcomes.

The result was that the two forms of therapy, originally distinct, are now typically taught and practiced together as *cognitive-behavioral therapy*, or *CBT*. Cognitive-behavioral therapy refers to a family of therapy techniques and approaches originally developed as either behavioral or cognitive. It now also includes refinements and integrations that were developed using both behavioral and cognitive principles (Beck, 2011). The fact that behavior therapy associations around the world have added the term cognitive to their names (Reinecke & Freeman, 2003) and that psychology textbooks now typically present the two systems together testify the popularity of CBT (see Figure 2.4).

Group, Family, Marital, Couples, and Systems Approaches

A number of alternatives to the psychodynamic, humanistic, and cognitive-behavioral approaches developed during the latter half of the 20th century. Many of these alternatives shared the view that people's behavior develops in, and is a reflection of, the relationship systems in which they live. These approaches, which we call *group* or *systems* approaches, are quite diverse in terms of their theoretical foundations and methods, but they all emphasize interventions directed at a group or pair of interacting people rather than just at an individual (see Table 2.8).

One of the earliest of these approaches is embodied in *group therapy*, which was first practiced at the beginning of the 20th century in Boston by Joseph Pratt (Dies, 2003). Later, stimulated by the shortage of professional personnel around the time of World War II, group therapy became

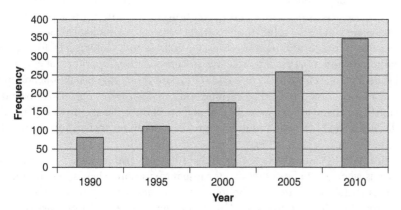

FIGURE 2.4 Frequency with Which the Term *Cognitive-Behavioral* Appeared in APA PsychNETTitles, 1990–2010

TABLE 2.8 Basic Concepts of the Group, Family, Marital, and Related Systems Approaches	
1. Human behavior develops in, and is maintained by, social contexts. **2.** The interlocking system of roles, beliefs, behaviors, and feedback mechanisms can function well or poorly.	**3.** Group, family, and marital therapists focus on and attempt to influence specific patterns of interaction and exchange that have significance for individuals in the system.

a practical answer to a surplus of clients (typically soldiers and veterans) and a shortage of clinicians. Group therapy grew in popularity especially in the 1960s and 1970s and has since progressed to the point that it is now regarded as a valuable intervention in its own right.

Every major approach to clinical psychology developed group treatments: there are analytic groups, client-centered and gestalt groups, and cognitive behavioral groups. As you might expect, groups are conducted somewhat differently depending on the theoretical approach employed.

Around the middle of the last century, *family therapy* developed as clinical child psychologists realized they could treat children's behavior problems more effectively if parents were involved. Some therapists began to look at children's disorders as symptoms of family dysfunctions rather than as the individual child's problem. In *Family Diagnosis: An Approach to the Preschool Child*, Nathan Ackerman and Raymond Sobel (1950) argued that the focus of diagnosis and treatment should be the family rather than the child. The focus was on the family as a system.

Closely allied with the family therapy movement was the *marital therapy* movement. The first marital therapists were often obstetricians, gynecologists, clergy, social workers, and educators. Conjoint marital therapy (treating both partners at the same time) by clinical psychologists did not become commonplace until well into the 1970s. Initially, clinical work focused mostly on helping couples adjust to culturally accepted marital roles and giving advice about practical aspects of marriage such as sexuality and parenting (Gurman, 2003).

As psychologists became involved in studying and treating marital conflicts, the theories supporting marital therapy expanded. Therapists like Jay Haley and Don Jackson of California's Mental Research Institute adopted many of the "family system" ideas from family therapy and applied them to marital therapy (Gurman, 2003). Predictably, humanistically oriented therapists also developed marital therapy approaches (e.g., Satir, 1967), as did behaviorists (e.g., Stuart, 1969) and cognitive-behaviorists (e.g., Baucom & Epstein, 1990). This type of therapy is now often called *couple therapy*, in recognition that many unmarried straight and gay or lesbian couples also seek professional help for their relationships (Wetchler, 2011).

Biological Influences on Clinical Psychology

Approaches to clinical psychology traditionally emphasize psychological variables such as unconscious conflicts, learned associations, and perceptions of the self, but few would disagree that disordered behavior can be most fully understood by also taking biological factors into account. Early psychiatrists in the clinical tradition took for granted that biological factors were involved in psychopathology, and more recently research in neuroscience, experimental psychopathology, behavioral genetics, and related areas has made clinicians aware that behavioral and mental processes rest on a foundation provided by each person's biological makeup. This makeup includes genetically inherited characteristics as well as the activity of the brain and other organs and systems that underlie all kinds of behavior and mental processes, both normal and abnormal (Bernstein, Penner, Clarke-Stewart, & Roy, 2011).

Biological factors can influence mental disorders in various ways. Sometimes, the influence is direct, as when alcohol or other drugs cause intoxication, when degeneration of neurons in certain areas of the brain causes Alzheimer's disease, and when genetic abnormalities cause particular forms of intellectual disability. Other disorders can result from more than one cause, only some of which involve biological factors. Such multiple pathways to disorder are suspected in the appearance of various subtypes of depressive disorders, anxiety disorders, schizophrenia, and personality disorders.

Clinicians also recognize that finding biological contributions to disorders does not automatically negate the value of psychological treatments. Thus, even if a child's hyperactivity is traced to a neurological defect, a solution might be provided by cognitive-behavioral therapy instead of, or in addition to, drugs. Clinicians are also becoming more interested in biological causes of mental disorders because it appears that those factors can often be modified by psychological interventions. You will see in Chapter 12, "Health Psychology," and Chapter 13, "Clinical Neuropsychology," for example, that researchers in health psychology and neuroscience are finding that the mind and body influence each other in ways we are just beginning to understand. In short, recognizing the importance of biological variables in psychopathology does not render traditional approaches to clinical psychology irrelevant; indeed, it deepens and expands their range of inquiry.

Clinical researchers today are focusing special attention on the diathesis–stress view of psychopathology in which biological factors are seen as one of three causal components. The first, known as a *diathesis*, is the presence of some kind of biological defect, usually a biochemical or anatomical problem in the brain, the autonomic nervous system, or the endocrine system. This defect or set of defects is often inherited but can also result from physical trauma, infection, or other disease processes. The second is known as *vulnerability* to developing a psychological disorder. People who carry certain diatheses are said to be at risk for or predisposed to developing the disorders with which those diatheses have been associated. The third causal component is the presence of *pathogenic (disease-causing) stressors*. If at-risk persons are exposed to such stressors, their predisposition to a disorder may actually evolve into that disorder. However, if those same at-risk individuals encounter less stressful environmental experiences, their predisposition may never express itself as a clinically significant disturbance.

The diathesis–stress view has been employed in the construction of a vulnerability model of schizophrenia that includes and integrates biological, psychological, and environmental causes (Cornblatt & Erlenmeyer-Kimling, 1985; Ingram & Price, 2010; Zubin & Spring, 1977). This model suggests that (a) vulnerability to schizophrenia is mainly biological; (b) different people have differing degrees of vulnerability; (c) vulnerability is transmitted partly through genetics and partly through neurodevelopmental abnormalities associated with prenatal risk factors, birth complications, and other problems; and (d) psychological components, such as exposure to poor environments and failure to develop adequate coping skills, may play a role in whether schizophrenia appears and in how severe it will be (Beaton & Simon, 2011; Wearden et al., 2000).

As shown in Figure 2.5, many different blends of vulnerability and stress can lead to schizophrenia. And, in accordance with the diathesis–stress perspective, people vulnerable to schizophrenia will be especially likely to actually display it if they are exposed to environmental demands and other stressors that elicit and maintain schizophrenic patterns of thought and action. Those same stressors would not be expected to lead to schizophrenia in people who are less vulnerable to it.

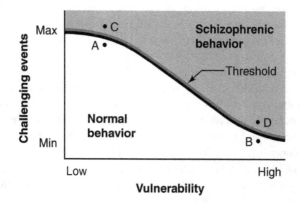

FIGURE 2.5 The Vulnerability Model of Schizophrenia. According to this model, a strong predisposition to schizophrenia and little environmental stress (point D), a weak predisposition and a lot of stress (point C), or any other sufficiently potent combination can lead a person to cross the threshold into schizophrenia

Numerous textbooks on abnormal psychology provide more detailed coverage of biological factors in mental disorders and of the use of diathesis–stress perspectives in explanatory theories. We address biological influences at various points throughout the remaining chapters.

Comparing Approaches: An Illustrative Case

How might the various treatment approaches be applied by clinical psychologists? Let's consider a case in point:

> Anna B., a 17-year-old high school junior, was referred by her physician to a psychology clinic because of a suspected eating disorder and possible depression. She is underweight, has stopped menstruating, and complains of a sore throat along with other physical ailments. She also reports that she has difficulty sleeping. Her mother states that Anna's affluent, upper-middle-class family is loving and supportive and that Anna has seemed moody and depressed for the past several months. During an initial interview, Anna admitted that she had contemplated suicide and had been restricting her intake of food and occasionally inducing vomiting to avoid gaining weight. There are cut marks on her wrist, which Anna says she made on two occasions. She reports having two close friends with whom she talks intimately. Since a break up with a boyfriend 4 months earlier, she has not been dating, but she is active in the school choir and hopes to pursue singing in college. Her grades in school, normally As, have begun to slip to Bs and one C, which deeply concerns her. Anna is reluctant to agree that she has an eating disorder, but she agrees that she may be depressed—she reports feeling constant pressure to succeed, has doubts about her ability to do so, and has begun to wonder if life is worth living that way.

Clinicians representing all theoretical approaches would consult with Anna's physician to ensure that she had all necessary medical treatment, including any indicated medications. In the few states where it is permitted, some psychologists with special training might prescribe medications themselves, though still in collaboration with Anna's physician. Most psychologists would seek input and involvement of Anna's family as well, though the degree of family involvement sought and used in treatment could vary widely depending on how the clinician understands Anna's problems and their treatment. In short, clinicians from different approaches would likely focus on different causal explanations, diagnostic and assessment procedures, and treatment techniques. You might get some ideas about applying different approaches by examining Table 2.9.

Psychoanalytic therapists would likely speculate about unconscious conflicts that motivate Anna's behavior. They would use techniques designed to help Anna become aware of the anxiety-provoking conflicts she defends against, perhaps symbolically with self-starvation. They might also help her to understand how past and current relationships have contributed to these defenses.

Humanistic psychologists would likely focus on Anna's self-concept, on how she understands and experiences her symptoms, and what they mean to her. They would help her become more accepting of aspects of herself that she has likely become critical of—perhaps her desire to be perfect, to be in control, to be liked.

Behavioral psychologists might help Anna learn to recognize the situations in which she restricts her food intake and the situations in which she feels most depressed. They would help her examine her behavior in those situations as well as the potential rewards she might receive for those behaviors. They would probably help Anna develop a step-by-step plan for food intake that would maintain a weight she was comfortable with (and that was reasonable) and help her set up suitable ways to reward herself to maintain her gains. They may help Anna set up similar programs for behaviors related to her feelings of depression. They would also likely involve the family in these plans, as family members are a critical component of the situation in which the behavior occurs.

Cognitive clinicians would likely add to the behavioral approach by also exploring and challenging Anna's beliefs and assumptions, which would come out directly or indirectly in the course of talking with her (e.g., "I can't ever allow myself to fail," "My social worth depends on my appearance," "No one likes me"). Through practice, Anna might learn to recognize the situations in which she makes these statements to herself, and she might learn to counter them with more reasonable and adaptive self-statements.

Family therapists would likely focus on how family dynamics influence Anna's eating disorder and depression. Are there conflicts within the family that are overt or festering unexpressed, and if so, are Anna's symptoms reactions to these broader problems she cannot fully understand or fix? How do other family members interact with Anna, and she with them? Can roles, expectations, or

TABLE 2.9 Basic Assumptions of the Major Psychological Approaches to Psychotherapy

	Psychodynamic	Humanistic	Behavioral	Cognitive	Systems
View of Human Nature	Much of mental life is hidden from awareness and embroiled in conflict	Human nature is generally growth oriented; perception is reality	Human behavior is learned primarily via conditioning, reinforcement, and similar processes	Cognitions are learned and mediate between events (stimuli) and actions (responses)	Human behavior emanates from, and must be understood in, social contexts
Basic Assumption About the Causes of Pathology	Unconscious conflicts rooted in the past and unconsciously replayed in the present	Alienation from the true self caused by avoidance of threatening emotions	Learned maladaptive responses to situations	Learned maladaptive cognitions, particularly about the self	Dysfunctional systems
Focus of Therapeutic Intervention	Unconscious conflicts and historically based maladaptive patterns	Immediate experiences	Specific overt behaviors, their triggering antecedents, and their reinforcing consequences	Maladaptive cognitions (attributions, beliefs, etc.) that mediate between antecedents and consequences	Group, family roles, and interaction patterns
Role of the Therapist	"Archeologist": guide the client to an understanding of roots and current manifestations of intrapsychic conflicts	"Mirror": create a supportive emotional climate in which the client feels understood, accepted, and valued	"Coach": help the client identify, plan, and execute specific behavioral changes and the conditions for maintaining them	"Scientist": help the client learn to identify, challenge, and replace habitual maladaptive thoughts	"Social planner": help group members to make changes in roles, intergroup relations, and communication patterns

communication patterns be altered to relieve Anna or others in the family of burdens or help create more supportive relationships? Systems theorists, and likely therapists from the other orientations, would also help Anna to understand some of the cultural and gender issues that tend to make some achievement-oriented young women from affluent families feel such pressure.

A full treatment of the diagnostic and treatment stages of each approach is well beyond the scope of this chapter, but in subsequent chapters we cover therapeutic approaches in much more detail.

SECTION SUMMARY

The foundations of psychodynamic and behavioral approaches to clinical psychology developed well before World War II, but after the war, when treatment became a central activity for clinicians, these approaches surged. Other approaches to treatment soon developed: humanistic, cognitive, group/systems, and hybrid approaches such as cognitive-behavioral. These "schools" dominated clinical psychology, shaping theory and practice during the field's most rapid period of development. They continue to exert strong influence today.

THE PROS AND CONS OF TAKING A SPECIFIC APPROACH

SECTION PREVIEW

A single theoretical approach to clinical psychology can help organize a vast amount of confusing information about human behavior. It can also help direct clinicians in their assessment and treatment activities. However, adopting a single approach can produce myopia and impede the development of the discipline, especially if clinicians are rigid or dogmatic in their championing of one approach.

An approach to clinical psychology provides clinicians with a framework to guide thinking and practice. It helps them narrow the vast range of variables to a few manageable ones. By doing so, clinicians can then more easily note relationships among those variables. They can propose and test explanations for how behavior develops and becomes problematic. An approach is also like a region of the world that develops its own dialect. That dialect eases communication among those who share it; so the terms used by a particular approach become a kind of professional shorthand, making communication among like-minded professionals more efficient. Based on their shared language and explanations, clinicians adopting the same approach can then develop assessment methods that efficiently provide data about the variables of interest, develop treatment techniques targeted for specific problems or persons, and conduct research to discover the level of effectiveness of those interventions. A clinician's approach guides all these activities.

Ironically, a specific approach to clinical psychology can act not only as a compass and guide but also as a set of blinders. Some clinicians allow their favorite approach to so completely organize their thinking about behavior and mental processes that their views become fossilized, leaving them rigid and closed to potentially valuable ideas associated with other approaches (Gold & Strickler, 2006). The approaches themselves are partly to blame. Many of the newer clinical approaches appearing over the years have defined themselves partly by their rejection of assumptions held dear by other approaches (e.g., behavioral approaches rejected unconscious and unobservable mental events in favor of observable behavior; humanistic approaches rejected deterministic assumptions of psychoanalysis and behaviorism in favor of self-determination in the here-and-now). Clinical training often compounds perceived differences among approaches. Through the influence of professors and supervisors, graduates of programs that favor one particular theoretical orientation may come to advocate for that approach over all others more or less automatically. In short, taking a consistent perspective can evolve from an asset to a liability if it produces such a narrow focus that other points of view are overlooked. When this happens, clients are poorly served and the profession is diminished.

Fortunately, most problems associated with taking a specific approach to clinical psychology can be reduced by (a) avoiding the overzealous commitment to it that fosters conceptual rigidity, behavioral inflexibility, and semantic narrowness, and (b) evaluating that approach according to rigorous scientific methods, and revising the approach when the data demand it. Understanding and appreciating other points of view can act as insurance against a narrow-mindedness that could be detrimental to clinicians and clients alike. We hope that the material in this chapter helps you remain open-minded.

How do clinicians choose their approach to clinical psychology? There are no universally agreed-upon criteria available to guide the choice; even the advice offered in this chapter about the value of scientifically testable approaches is based on the authors' personal biases, which, though shared by many, are biases nonetheless. Freudians might suggest that unconscious motivation influences clinicians' choices, behaviorists might argue that we tend to choose the approach modeled for us by our mentors, while humanistic psychologists might seek the answer in the perceived congruity between a particular approach and the self-concepts of its adherents. Research suggests that trainees' personality characteristics, world view, and general cognitive style influence their choices (Buckman & Barker, 2010; Kaplan, 1964; Poznanski & McLellan, 2003), but the truth is that no one really knows exactly why particular clinicians choose particular approaches. We only know which ones are most popular. Among clinicians expressing a specific choice, cognitive and cognitive-behavioral approaches are most often selected (Andersson & Asmundson, 2008; Hollon & DiGiuseppe, 2010). Psychodynamic approaches remain popular as well, though certainly not to the extent that they were a few decades ago. Systems and biological approaches also remain attractive to many clinicians. But not all clinicians make only one choice. When asked about their theoretical orientation, many clinicians say that they do not confine themselves to a single approach (Norcross, Hedges, & Castle, 2002). Instead, they tend to adopt aspects of two or more approaches that they find valuable and personally satisfying, a position described in Chapter 1 as *eclecticism*. Estimates of clinicians identifying themselves as eclectic range from near one-third (Norcross, Hedges, & Castle, 2002; Norcross, Karg, & Prochaska, 1997) to two-thirds or more (Hollanders & McLeod, 1999; Slife & Reber, 2001). Whatever the percentage, it is clear that eclecticism is a favored approach among practicing clinicians (L'Abate, 2013).

The advantages of eclecticism are clear—people open to a variety of approaches avoid the conceptual blinders created by allegiance to one theoretical model. They are also in a better position to adopt changes in thinking or practice when research shows that they should. But being eclectic might be easier in theory than in practice because approaches in clinical psychology are so varied that it is difficult for trainees to gain in-depth knowledge of multiple approaches, and the effort to do so might be more confusing than enlightening. A recent article addressing this question was titled "Is that an unconscious fantasy or an automatic thought? Challenges of learning multiple psychotherapies simultaneously" (Gastelum et al., 2011). Even the time required to develop solid conceptual grounding in several theories can be prohibitive, meaning that few, if any, practicing clinicians or researchers have an encyclopedic knowledge of the field.

So today, clinical psychologists and clinical psychology training programs are looking for new and better ways to integrate what the various theoretical approaches have to offer, searching anew for common elements in the causes of disorders and in the effectiveness of treatments (Nolen-Hoeksema & Watkins, 2011). Some have even suggested that the era of traditional theoretical orientations is at its end, that a new unified, integrative approach is at hand (Melchert, 2011). But change is not easy, and integrative approaches are very much works in progress (Goldfried, Glass, & Arnkoff, 2010; Wampold, Hollon, & Hill, 2010). But the same is true of any scientific field—it is often difficult to recognize the shortcomings of our most beloved theories and to look beyond them to find better ways to understand and apply what others have learned. However, true clinical scientists wouldn't want it any other way.

SECTION SUMMARY

There are a variety of approaches to clinical psychology. An approach is necessary for clinical psychologists to limit the number of variables they attend to and study. Yet, an approach can do as much harm as good if clinicians become overzealous in their allegiances. Common sense and empirical research suggest that each major approach has contributed to clinical psychology. When viewed from the perspective of several decades, the three most noticeable trends in therapists' selection of approaches are (a) the decline in popularity of the psychodynamic approach from its dominance in the mid-20th century to its leveling off in the last two to three decades, (b) the increase in the percentage of clinicians selecting cognitive and cognitive-behavioral approaches, and (c) the increase in the percentage of clinicians favoring eclectic and integrative approaches.

Chapter Summary

Clinical psychology has grown rapidly since its birth in the late 19th and early 20th centuries. Although it began primarily as a laboratory-based research discipline, clinical psychology soon grew into an applied one, first in Witmer's psychology clinic, then in psychological testing, and later in psychotherapy. World events, particularly the two world wars, were especially important in contributing to the development of the field.

Each of several theoretical approaches to clinical psychology that developed before, and especially after, World War II emphasizes different explanations of how behavior develops and becomes problematic. The psychodynamic approach is based on Sigmund Freud's psychoanalysis, which sees both normal and abnormal behavior as determined by intrapsychic processes, especially conflicts among id, ego, and superego, that have roots in childhood. The humanistic approach sees behavior as determined primarily by unique perceptions of the world as experienced by humans who are responsible for themselves and capable of changing themselves. Clinicians taking this approach try to see the world through their clients' eyes and help them reach self-actualization by encouraging their awareness of genuine feelings, wishes, and goals. The behavioral approach focuses on measurable behavior, not inferred personality constructs, and emphasizes the principles of operant learning, classical conditioning, and observational learning in understanding the causes and treatments of problems. In recent years, the behavioral approach has blended with cognitive theories, which focus on habitual, learned ways of thinking about events. The combined cognitive-behavioral approach has become one of the most popular in clinical psychology, particularly for those who favor a more focused, empirically based perspective. Group, marital, family, and related systems approaches developed during the latter half of the 20th century. What these approaches have in common is the recognition that interpersonal environments exert a powerful influence on behavior; treatments are therefore often built around changing some interpersonal system rather than changing a single individual.

Research in neuroscience has made clinicians from all approaches more aware of the important roles played by genetics, the nervous system, and other biological factors in behavior and behavior disorders. The value of integrating psychological and biological factors can be seen in diathesis–stress explanations of various forms of mental disorder and in the growth of fields such as health psychology and neuropsychology.

Although some approaches to clinical psychology are more popular than others, none has a monopoly on describing and explaining behavior. Many clinicians therefore adopt elements of more than one approach in their daily work. Among the most prominent recent trends are those toward eclecticism and integration. Both of these emphasize the need to determine, through empirical evidence, which models of abnormality are the most useful, and which forms of therapy are most effective. Of course, as mentioned in Chapter 1, all this is taking place in the changing climate of health care delivery in the United States and elsewhere.

Study Questions

1. How did the field of clinical psychology come into being?
2. What are the empirical, psychometric, and clinical roots of clinical psychology?
3. What applications of clinical psychology developed during the first half of the 20th century?
4. How did historical events, especially the two world wars, influence the development of clinical psychology?
5. What major approaches to clinical psychology developed during the second half of the 20th century?
6. How do the major approaches to clinical psychology differ in their basic assumptions about causes of psychopathology and recommendations for treatment?
7. How might the different clinical approaches be applied to specific cases?
8. What are the pros and cons of taking a specific approach to clinical psychology?
9. What are the challenges and major areas of transition facing clinical psychology today?

Web Sites

- APA's Society for the History of Psychology: http://www.apa.org/about/division/div26.html
- APA's Division 29, Psychotherapy: http://www.apa.org/about/division/div29.html
- The Association for Psychological Science: http://www.psychologicalscience.org
- A Web site for the Freud Museum in London, where Freud spent the last year of his life after fleeing Vienna from the Nazis in 1938: http://www.freud.org.uk

MOVIES

Frances (1982): Loosely based on the life of actress, Frances Farmer, this film portrays a part of the history of mental health services (including lobotomy and involuntary hospitalization in harsh conditions) that most of us would rather forget.

One Flew Over the Cuckoo's Nest (1975): Classic film of some of the worst conditions of inpatient mental health treatment, and the enduring spirit of individuals struggling to overcome those conditions and their own psychological challenges.

MEMOIRS

All Out: An Autobiography by Albert Ellis (2010; Amherst, NY: Prometheus). The founder of Rational Emotive Behavior Therapy provides an inside look at his life and the history of clinical psychology in this amusing and insightful book.

My Lobotomy: A Memoir by Howard Dully (2008; New York: Three Rivers Press). Painful memoir describing the history of unnecessary psychosurgery that the author endured when he was 12, and the social, emotional, and cognitive challenges that he faced into his adult years.

References

Abood, L. G. (1960). A chemical approach to the problem of mental illness. In D. D. Jackson (Ed.), *The etiology of schizophrenia* (pp. 91–119). New York, NY: Basic Books.

Abt, L. E. (1992). Clinical psychology and the emergence of psychotherapy. *Professional Psychology: Research and Practice, 23*, 176–178.

Ackerman, N., & Sobel, R. (1950). Family diagnosis: An approach to the preschool child. *American Journal of Orthopsychiatry, 20*, 744–753.

American Psychological Association History and Archives, (2012). APA membership statistics. Retrieved January 5, 2012 from http://www.apa.org/about/archives/membership/index.aspx.

Andersson, G., & Asmundson, G. J. G. (2008). Editorial: Should CBT rest on its success? *Cognitive Behavior Therapy, 37*, 1–4.

Baucom, D. H., & Epstein, N. (1990). *Cognitive-behavioral marital therapy*. New York, NY: Bruner/Mazel.

Beaton, E. A., & Simon, T. J. (2011). How might stress contribute to increased risk for schizophrenia in children with chromosome 22q11.2 deletion syndrome? *Journal of Neurodevelopmental Disorders, 31*, 68–75.

Beck, A. T. (1976). *Cognitive therapy and the emotional disorders*. New York: International Universities Press.

Beck, J. S. (2011). *Cognitive behavior therapy*. New York, NY: Guilford Press.

Benjamin, L. S. (1997). The origins of psychological species: A history of the beginnings of the divisions of the American Psychological Association. *American Psychologist, 52*, 725–732.

Benjamin, L. T. (2005). A history of clinical psychology as a profession in America (and a glimpse at the future). *Annual Review of Clinical Psychology, 1*, 1–30.

Bernstein, D., Penner, L. A., Clarke-Stewart, A., & Roy, E. (2011). *Psychology* (9th ed.). Belmont, CA: Wadsworth.

Boring, E. G. (1950). *A history of experimental psychology* (2nd ed.). New York, NY: Appleton-Century-Crofts.

Brotemarkle, B. A. (1947). Fifty years of clinical psychology: Clinical psychology 1896–1946. *Journal of Consulting Psychology, 11*, 1–4.

Buckman, J. R., & Barker, C. (2010). Therapeutic orientation preferences in trainee clinical psychologists: Personality or training? *Psychotherapy Research, 20*, 247–258. doi: 10.1080/10503300903352693.

Buros, O. K. (Ed.). (1938). *The 1940 mental measurements yearbook*. Highland Park, NJ: Gryphon Press.

Cain, D. J. (1990). Celebration, reflection, and renewal: 50 years of client-centered therapy and beyond. *Person-Centered Review, 5*, 357–363.

Carlson, E. T. (1981). Introduction. In R. I. Watson (Ed.), *Clinical psychiatry [Facsimile reproduction of the 1907 volume, History of Psychology Series.* Delmar, NY: Scholars' Facsimiles & Reprints.

Cautin, R. L. (2011). A century of psychotherapy, 1860–1960. In J. C. Norcross, G. R. VandenBos, & D. K. Freedheim (Eds.), *History of psycotherapy* (2nd ed., pp. 3–38). Washington, DC: American Psychological Association

Cornblatt, B., & Erlenmeyer-Kimling, L. E. (1985). Global attentional deviance in children at risk for schizophrenia: Specificity and predictive validity. *Journal of Abnormal Psychology, 94*, 470–486.

Dennis, W. (1948). *Readings in the history of psychology*. New York, NY: Appleton-Century-Crofts.

Dies, R. (2003). Group psychotherapies. In A. S. Gurman & S. B. Messer (Eds.),. *Essential psychotherapies* (2nd ed., pp. 515–550). New York, NY: Guilford.

Donn, J. E., Routh, D. K., & Lunt, I. T. I. (2000). From Leipzig to Luxembourg (via Boulder and Vail): A history of clinical psychology training in Europe and the United States. *Professional Psychology: Research and Practice, 31*, 423–428.

DuBois, P. H. (1970). *A history of psychological testing*. Boston, MA: Allyn & Bacon.

Ellis, A. (1962). *Reason and emotion in psychotherapy*. New York, NY: Lyle Stuart.

Ellis, A. (1973). Rational-emotive therapy. In R. Corsini (Ed.), *Current psychotherapies* (pp. 167–206). Ithaca, IL: F. E. Peacock.

Ellis, A. (1993). Changing rational-emotive therapy (RET) to rational-emotive behavior therapy (REBT). *The Behavior Therapist, 16*, 257–258.

Ellis, A. (2011). *Rational emotive behavior therapy*. Washington, American Psychological Association.

Ellis, A. & Dryden, W. (1987). *The practice of rational-emotive therapy*. New York, NY: Springer.

Ellis, A., & Grieger, R. (Eds.). (1977). *Handbook of rational-emotive therapy*. New York, NY: Springer.

Fagan, T. K. (1996). Witmer's contribution to school psychological services. *American Psychologist, 51*, 241–243.

Fischer, C. T. (1989). A life-centered approach to psychodiagnostics: Attending to lifeworld, ambiguity, and possibility. *Person-Centered Review, 4*, 163–170.

Funder, D. (2001). *The personality puzzle* (2nd ed.). New York, NY: W. W. Norton.

Galton, F. (1883). *Inquiries into the human faculty and its development*. London, United Kingdom: Macmillan.

Gastelum, E. D., Hyun, A. M., Goldberg, D. A., Stanley, B., Sudak, D. M., et al. (2011). Is that an unconscious fantasy or an automatic thought? Challenges of learning multiple psychotherapies simultaneously. *Journal of the American Academy of Psychoanalysis & Dynamic Psychiatry, 39*, 111–132.

Gold, J., & Strickler, G. (2006). Introduction: An overview of psychotherapy integration. In G. Strickler & J. Gold (Eds.), *A casebook of psychotherapy integration*. Washington, DC: American Psychological Association.

Goldfried, M. R., Glass, C. R., & Arnkoff, D. B. (2010). Integrative approaches to psychotherapy. In J. C. Norcross, G. R. VandenBos,

& D. K. Freedheim (Eds.), *History of psychotherapy: Continuity and change* (2nd ed.). Washington, DC: American Psychological Association.

Greenberg, L. S., Elliot, R. K., & Lietaer, G. (1994). Research on experiential psychotherapies. In A. E. Bergin & S. L. Garfield (Eds.), *Handbook of psychotherapy and behavior change* (pp. 509–512). New York, NY: Wiley.

Gurman, A. S. (2003). Marital therapy. In A. S. Gurman & S. B. Messer (Eds.), *Essential psychotherapies*, (2nd ed., pp. 463–514). New York, NY: Guilford.

Hollanders, H., & McLeod, J. (1999). Theoretical orientation and reported practice: A survey of eclecticism among counselors in Britain. *British Journal of Guidance and Counseling, 27*, 405–414.

Hollon, S. D., & DiGiuseppe, R. (2010). Cognitive theories of psychotherapy. In J. C. Norcross, G. R. VandenBos, & D. K. Freedheim (Eds.), *History of psychotherapy: Continuity and change* (2nd ed.). Washington, DC: American Psychological Association.

Hunt, M. (1993). *The story of psychology.* New York, NY: Anchor Books.

Ingram, R. E., & Price, J. M. (Eds.). (2010). *Vulnerability to psychopathology: Risk across the lifespan* (2nd ed). New York, NY: Guilford Press.

Jones, E. E. (1955). *The life and work of Sigmund Freud* (Vol. 2). New York, NY: Basic Books.

Jones, M. C. (1924a). The elimination of children's fears. *Journal of Experimental Psychology, 7*, 382–390.

Jones, M. C. (1924b). A laboratory study of fear: The case of Peter. *Pedagogical Seminary and Journal of Genetic Psychology, 31*, 308–315.

Kaplan, A. (1964). *The conduct of inquiry.* San Francisco, CA: Chandler.

Kelly, G. A. (1955). *The psychology of personal constructs.* New York, NY: W. W. Norton.

L'Abate, L. (2013). *Clinical psychology and psychotherapy as a science.* New York, NY: Springer.

Lindsley, O. R., Skinner, B. F., & Solomon, H. C. (1953). *Study of psychotic behavior.* Studies in Behavior Therapy, Harvard Medical School, Department of Psychiatry, Metropolitan State Hospital, Waltham, MA, Office of Naval Research Contract N5-ori-07662, Status Report I, 1 June 1953–31 December 1953.

Mahoney, M. J. (1977). Reflections on the cognitive-learning trend in psychotherapy. *American Psychologist, 32*, 5–13.

McReynolds, P. (1975). Historical antecedents of personality assessment. In P. McReynolds (Ed.), *Advances in psychological assessment* (Vol. 3, pp. 477–532). San Francisco, CA: Jossey-Bass.

McReynolds, P. (1987). Lightner Witmer: Little-known founder of clinical psychology. *American Psychologist, 42*, 849–858.

Melchert, T. P. (2011). *Foundations of professional psychology: The end of theoretical orientations and the emergence of the biopsychosocial approach.* New York, NY: Elsevier Insights.

Moodie, W. (1936). Foreward In R. B. Cattell,. *A guide to mental testing* (pp. vii–viii). London, United Kingdom: University of London Press.

Nolen-Hoeksema, S., & Watkins, E. R. (2011). A heuristic for developing transdiagnostic models of psychopathology: Explaining multifinality and divergent trajectories. *Perspectives on Psychological Science, 6*, 589–609.

Norcross, J. C., Hedges, M., & Castle, P. H. (2002). Psychologists conducting psychotherapy in 2001: A study of the Division 29 membership. *Psychotherapy: Theory, Research, Practice, Training, 39*, 97–102.

Norcross, J. C., Karg, R. S., & Prochaska, J. O. (1997). Clinical psychologists in the 1990s: Part I. *Clinical Psychologist, 50*, 4–9.

Poznanski, J. J., & McLennan, J. (2003). Becoming a psychologist with a particular theoretical orientation to counseling practice. *Australian Psychologist, 38*, 223–226.

Reinecke, M. A. & Freeman, A. (2003). Cognitive therapy. In A. S. Gurman & S. B. Messer (Eds.), *Essential psychotherapies* (2nd ed., pp. 224–271). New York, NY: Guilford.

Reisman, J. M. (1976). *A history of clinical psychology.* New York, NY: Irvington.

Resnick, R. J. (1997). A brief history of practice—Expanded. *American Psychologist, 52*, 463–468.

Rogers, C. R. (1946). Significant aspects of client-centered therapy. *American Psychologist, 1*, 415–422.

Routh, D. K. (1994). *Clinical psychology since 1917: Science, practice, organization.* New York, NY: Plenum.

Routh, D. K. (2000). Clinical psychology training: A history of ideas and practices prior to 1946. *American Psychologist, 55*, 236–241.

Routh, D. K. (2011). How clinical psychology linked up with applied behavior analysis. *The Clinical Psychologist, 64*, 10–11.

Satir, V. (1967). *Conjoint family therapy* (rev. ed.). Palo Alto, CA: Science and Behavior Books.

Schneck, J. M. (1975). United States of America in J. G. Howells (Ed.), *World history of psychiatry.* New York, NY: Brunner/Mazel, 432–475.

Shaffer, G. W., & Lazarus, R. S. (1952). *Fundamental concepts in clinical psychology.* New York, NY: McGraw-Hill.

Slife, B. D., & Reber, J. S. (2001). Eclecticism in psychotherapy: Is it really the best substitute for traditional theories? In B. D. Slife, R. N. Williams, & S. H. Barlow (Eds.), *Critical issues in psychotherapy* (pp. 213–234). Thousand Oaks, CA: Sage.

Stuart, R. B. (1969). Operant-interpersonal treatment of marital discord. *Journal of Consulting and Clinical Psychology, 33*, 675–682.

Taylor, E. (2000). Psychotherapeutics and the problematic origins of clinical psychology in America. *American Psychologist, 55*, 1029–1033.

Ullmann, L. P., & Krasner, L. (1975). *A psychological approach to abnormal behavior.* Englewood Cliffs, NJ: Prentice-Hall.

Wampold, B. E., Hollon, S. D., & Hill, C. E. (2010). Unresolved questions and future direction in psychotherapy research. In J. C. Norcross, G. R. VandenBos, & D. K. Freedheim (Eds.), *History of psychotherapy: Continuity and change* (2nd ed.). Washington, DC: American Psychological Association.

Watson, R. I. (1953). A brief history of clinical psychology. *Psychological Bulletin, 50*, 321–346.

Watson, R. I. (1978). *The great psychologists* (2nd ed.). Philadelphia, PA: Lippincott.

Wearden, A. J., Tarrier, N., Barrowclough, C., Zastowny, T. R., & Rahill, A. A. (2000). A review of expressed emotion research in health care. *Clinical Psychology Review, 20*, 633–666.

Wetchler, J. L. (Ed.). (2011). *Handbook of clinical issues in couple therapy* (2nd ed). New York, NY: Routledge/Taylor & Francis Group.

Yerkes, R. M. (1921). Psychological examining in the United States army. *Memoirs of the National Academy of Sciences. 15*, 1–890.

Zilboorg, G., & Henry, G. W. (1941). *A history of medical psychology.* New York, NY: W. W. Norton.

Zubin, J., & Spring, B. (1977). Vulnerability—A new view of schizophrenia. *Journal of Abnormal Psychology, 86*, 103–126.

3

BASIC FEATURES OF CLINICAL ASSESSMENT

Chapter Preview

In this chapter we offer an overview of the clinical assessment process. We outline the range of assessment options available to clinicians, then describe the typical goals of assessment: diagnosis, description, treatment planning, and prediction. We also introduce factors affecting a clinician's choices about how to conduct an assessment, including the purpose of the assessment, the clinician's theoretical views, the psychometric properties of assessment instruments, and other contextual factors. We discuss the use of clinical judgment, focusing especially on errors that clinicians try to avoid. Assessments ultimately must be communicated to clients and third parties, so we conclude by discussing factors associated with reporting assessment results.

A Clinical Case

Dr. T was asked to take the case of Jessie, a 17-year-old male whose school counselor had become concerned that Jessie was showing signs of depression and rebellion. In addition to missing school because of alleged illnesses (his counselor does not believe him), Jessie has frequently been belligerent with some of his teachers. Jessie's parents drove him to the appointment, but they declined to meet with the therapist, saying only that they wanted to know what was wrong with their son and that they wanted him to get whatever treatment the insurance would cover. In the intake interview, Jessie expressed a strong dislike of school, saying it was a waste of time. He said that no one understands him there, and most of his classmates only ignore him or make fun of him. In school, he was mostly silent and sullen and did not speak with classmates. Outside of school, he spent most of his time with a 20-year-old friend who worked as a dishwasher at a local diner. Last week, the two young men had been caught in possession of alcohol. He admitted that he had been depressed and that for at least the last 3 weeks had "no interest in anything." He said that during this time he had slept for longer periods, sometimes as much as 14 to 16 hours per day. He also claimed to have had "some pretty bizarre thoughts about leaving this life and living in another dimension." Elaborating further, Jesse admitted to beliefs that he was not meant for this world, that he was being told (he could not or would not say by whom) that he might be better off dead. He also informed the therapist that his parents were in the process of getting a divorce.

How can the therapist best understand Jessie's problems? Which of the problems are the most pressing? What diagnosis most accurately describes those problems? Is Jessie suicidal or dangerous to others? What role do the parents play in his difficulties? How can an effective treatment be designed? In order to answer these questions, the psychologist must conduct an assessment.

Assessment is the collection and synthesis of information to reach a judgment. Almost everyone engages in some type of assessment at one time or another. For example, whether we realize it or not, we collect, process, and interpret information about the background, attitudes, behaviors, and characteristics of the people we meet. Then, in light of our experiences, expectations, and sociocultural frame of reference, we form impressions that guide decisions to seek out some people and avoid others.

Clinical psychologists collect and process assessment information that is more formal and systematic than that available to nonprofessionals. As discussed in Chapter 2, "Clinical

Psychology's Past and Present," before psychotherapy became a major role for clinicians, assessment was their most common applied activity. Although no longer the dominant activity of clinical psychologists, assessment remains a critical part of their training and practice. After all, assessment is required in order to delineate a client's problems, plan treatments, measure treatment effectiveness, conduct other kinds of research, and answer a multitude of questions asked of clinicians (Antony & Barlow, 2010). In this chapter, we consider what clinical psychologists have learned about the challenge of clinical assessment. In the following two chapters, we discuss specific types of assessments.

AN OUTLINE OF THE ASSESSMENT PROCESS

SECTION PREVIEW

Assessment involves a series of steps, beginning with a problem or referral and ending with the psychologist's communicating the results of the assessment to appropriate parties. In between, the clinician must make a number of judgments, such as which instruments to use and how best to convert clinical assessment data into a clinical judgment. At each step, the clinician must engage in activities to ensure that the most relevant data are gathered and analyzed.

Clinical assessment has been described in various ways (Tallent, 1992), but all of them portray it as a process of gathering information to solve a problem. All of them recognize that to be most effective, assessment activities should be organized in a sequence of systematic, logically related steps driven by a goal. Most assessments follow the general sequence outlined in Figure 3.1.

Receiving and Clarifying the Referral Question

Two related questions must be answered before clinical assessment can begin (McReynolds, 1975): What do we want to know, and how best can we find out about it? Answers to the first question—what do we want to know?—depend on who requested the assessment and for what purpose. The person or agency requesting the psychological assessment is called the *referral source*, and the question or issue to be addressed in the assessment is called the *referral question*. (Information that initiates an assessment is sometimes called the *presenting problem*, but we prefer to begin with a *referral question* because a specific question focuses on the assessment goal, while the presenting problem is often a longer description of the client's difficulties.)

The referral question is very important because it shapes the clinician's choice of assessment instruments and the interpretation and communication of results. Clinicians must therefore understand the context of the referral and often must help referral sources clarify the purpose of the assessment (Harwood, Beutler, & Groth-Marnat, 2011). In doing so, clinicians may need to educate others about what a psychological assessment can and cannot reveal. They may also need to educate them about the practical and ethical constraints involved in conducting assessments.

The referral question is the first step in shaping the ultimate goal of assessment, and, generally, the clearer the goal, the clearer the question. As you can see in Table 3.1, referral questions can be quite varied.

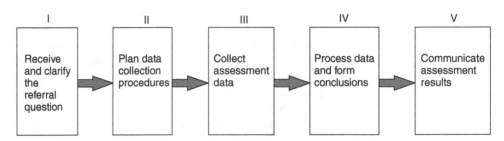

FIGURE 3.1   A Schematic View of the Clinical Assessment Process

TABLE 3.1 Examples of Referral Questions from Various Sources

Source	Referral Question
Therapist	Would this person be a good candidate for group psychotherapy?
	How effective have I been in treating clients with anxiety disorders?
Physician or treatment team	What is the correct psychological diagnosis for this client?
	What cognitive and emotional limitations does this person have following her accident, and what strengths does she have to draw on during rehabilitation?
Client	What, if anything, should we do to salvage this marriage?
	Would I be good at this kind of job?
	How can I worry less and enjoy my life and my family more?
School	What is an appropriate educational placement for this child?
	How should we intervene to help this student better manage violent tendencies and problems in relationships with peers and teachers?
Parent	Is my child suffering from depression and is she in need of counseling?
	How can we help my child cope with the loss of his mother?
	My child becomes very emotional and refuses to go to school: what can I do?
Court	Does this person pose an imminent threat of danger to himself or others?
	Which custody arrangement is in the best interest of this child?
	Is this client mentally able to understand the criminal charges against him and to assist an attorney in mounting a legal defense?
	Has this person sustained psychological injuries that would be relevant to litigation?
Employer, government agency, or other third party	Is this person suffering from a mental illness that would qualify him to receive disability payments?
	What form of treatment would best help this person to resume productive employment, and for which types of employment would the person be best suited?
	Will the survivors of this natural disaster benefit from rapid intervention, and if so, what kind of intervention?

Planning Data Collection Procedures

Answers to the second question—about how best can we find out what we need to know—come into play after the referral question and the clinician's role have been clarified. With a clear goal in mind, the clinician can now begin planning methods to collect data.

There is a vast range of data that might be collected about a client. To illustrate, consider the sheer number of things that can be asked about a person at several interrelated levels, from biological functioning to relationships with other people (see Table 3.2). The enormous diversity of possible assessment data means that we can never learn all there is to know about a client. Of course, clinicians would typically seek more information about the client in categories that are most relevant to the assessment goals.

Although the most important factor in the selection of assessment instruments is the referral question, other factors also affect the selection process. One of these is the quality of the assessment instrument or procedure. Obviously, clinicians would be better off selecting assessment methods whose *psychometric properties* (e.g., reliability, validity, usefulness) are the highest, but they might not always do so. For example, if one test had slightly lower (but still acceptable) reliability than another but provided more relevant information about a particular referral question, the clinician might select the one with slightly lesser reliability but greater relevance to assessment.

TABLE 3.2 Information Used in a Case Study Guide

1. Identifying data, including name, sex, occupation, income (of self or family), marital status, address, date and place of birth, religion, education, cultural identity.

2. Reason for coming to the agency, expectations for service.

3. Present and recent situation, including dwelling place, principal settings, daily round of activities, number and kind of life changes over several months, impending changes.

4. Family constellation (family of origin), including descriptions of parents, siblings, other significant family figures, and respondent's role growing up.

5. Early recollections, descriptions of earliest clear happenings and the situation surrounding them.

6. Birth and development, including age of walking and talking, problems compared with other children, view of effects of early experiences.

7. Health and physical condition, including childhood and later diseases and injuries; current prescribed medications; current use of unprescribed drugs, cigarettes, or alcohol; comparison of own body with others; habits of eating and exercising.

8. Education and training, including subjects of special interest and achievement, out-of-school learning, areas of difficulty and pride, any cultural problems.

9. Work record, including reasons for changing jobs, attitudes toward work.

10. Recreation, interests, and pleasures, including volunteer work, reading, respondent's view of adequacy of self-expression and pleasures.

11. Sexual development, covering first awareness, kinds of sexual activities, and a view of adequacy of current sexual expressions.

12. Marital and family data, covering major events and what led to them, and comparison of present family with family of origin, ethnic or cultural factors.

13. Social supports, communication network, and social interests, including people talked with most frequently, people available for various kinds of help, amount and quality of interactions, sense of contribution to others, and interest in community.

14. Self-description, including strengths, weaknesses, ability to use imagery, creativity, values, and ideas.

15. Choices and turning points in life, a review of the respondent's most important decisions and changes, including the single most important happening.

16. Personal goals and view of the future, including what the subject would like to see happen next year and in 5 or 10 years and what is necessary for these events to happen, realism in time orientation, ability to set priorities.

17. Any further material the respondent may see as omitted from the history.

Source: From Sundberg (1977). Sundberg, N.D., *Assessment of Persons*, 1st Ed., © 1997, pp. 97-98, 207. Reprinted and Electronically reproduced by permission of Pearson Education, Inc., Upper Saddle River, New Jersey.

Clinicians must consider, too, the characteristics of clients when deciding on assessments, selecting instruments that are appropriate for each client in terms of reading level, length, and the like. Similarly, clinicians must explain to clients the procedures and purposes of the assessment using language that clients can understand.

To plan assessments, then, the clinician must think broadly, weighing various features of assessment instruments against practical considerations of time, context, and usefulness to clients and other referral sources (Hunsley & Mash, 2010). The clinician must also plan to combine and integrate the results of assessments into a narrative that serves a specific clinical purpose.

Collecting Assessment Data

Once the referral question has been clarified, the appropriate assessment methods have been selected, and the client's cooperation has been secured, the data-collection stage of assessment can begin.

THE VALUE OF MULTIPLE ASSESSMENT SOURCES   Clinical psychologists collect assessment data from four main sources: interviews, observations, tests, and historical records (case history data). However, they seldom rely on a single assessment source to create a working image of a client. Instead, they use multiple assessment channels to cross-validate information about a wide variety of topics. Thus, hospital records may reveal that a patient has been there for 30 days, thus correcting the patient's self-reported estimate of 2 days. Indeed, the whole story of a client's problems is seldom clear until multiple assessment sources are tapped. For example, people have been observed to be assertive in social situations even though they described themselves in an interview or on a test as generally unassertive (Nietzel & Bernstein, 1976). It often takes multiple sources of assessment to separate those who do not engage in certain behaviors from those who cannot engage in them.

Another benefit of using multiple assessment sources appears when the clinician evaluates the effects of treatment. Suppose a couple enters therapy because they are considering divorce, and then, 3 months later, they do divorce. If the only outcome assessment employed in this case were "marital happiness," as expressed during interviews, the treatment might be seen as having worsened marital distress. However, observations, third-person reports, and life records might show that one or both partners find their newly divorced status liberating and that they are developing new interests and abilities.

Processing Data and Forming Conclusions

After assessment data have been collected, the clinician must determine what those data mean. If the information is to be useful in reaching the clinician's assessment goals, it must be transformed from raw form into interpretations and conclusions that address a referral question. The processing task is formidable because it requires a mental leap from known data to what is assumed to be true on the basis of those data. In general, as the leap from data to assumption gets longer, inference becomes more vulnerable to error.

Consider this: A young boy is sitting on a lawn cutting an earthworm in half. It would be easy to infer from this observational data that the child is cruel and aggressive and that he might become dangerous later in life. These inferences would be off the mark, however, for "what the observer could not see was what the boy, who happened to have few friends, thought as he cut the worm in half: 'There! Now you will have someone to play with'" (Goldfried & Sprafkin, 1974, p. 305). In short, elaborate inference, especially when based on minimal data, can be dangerous.

Processing assessment data is difficult also because information from various sources must be integrated. Unfortunately, there are few empirical guidelines for how best to combine data from interviews, tests, observations, and other sources to reach integrated conclusions. So in forming their conclusions, clinicians often must rely heavily on clinical judgment, a topic we describe in some detail later in this chapter.

Communicating Assessment Results

The final stage in the assessment process is the creation of an organized presentation of results called an *assessment report*. To be of greatest value, assessment reports must be clearly written and clearly related to the goal that prompted the assessment in the first place. If that goal was to classify the client's behavior into a diagnostic category, information relevant to diagnostic classification should be highlighted in the report. If assessment was aimed at determining a client's likely cooperativeness in and responsiveness to psychotherapy, the report should focus on those topics. These simple, self-evident prescriptions are sometimes ignored in assessment reports, especially when assessment goals were never explicitly stated or when clinicians do not fully understand what their assessment instruments can, and cannot, reveal about clients.

SECTION SUMMARY

Assessment progresses in a series of steps that begin with a referral question. The referral question may come from a client, a third party, or the therapist, but the clinician must ensure that the question is clear and can be addressed reasonably by the available assessment instruments. Once the referral question is clarified, planning for assessment begins. Planning involves selection of appropriate instruments—not a simple task given the number of factors affecting clinicians' choices—and preparation of the client. Data collection involves accumulating evidence from historical records, interviews, observations, and tests. Each of these sources has special strengths and limitations. In the data-processing stage, the accumulated data are analyzed and integrated into a coherent assessment. In the final stage, the clinician communicates conclusions and provides recommendations in ways that are clear and useful to the referral source.

THE GOALS OF CLINICAL ASSESSMENT

SECTION PREVIEW

Most referral questions relate to diagnosis, description, treatment planning, or prediction. We first consider diagnostic classification, the labeling of psychological problems. Psychological diagnosis relies primarily on criteria described in the Diagnostic and Statistical Manual of Mental Disorders (DSM) *of the American Psychiatric Association. A diagnosis or label alone seldom tells clinicians all they want to know about a client, so clinicians often assess clients' strengths, weaknesses, and social connections. Diagnoses, descriptions, and other information help clinicians design treatments for each client, which is another goal of assessment. Measuring the outcomes of treatment is yet another assessment goal, an increasingly important one in this era of accountability and evidence-based practice. Finally, clinicians sometimes conduct assessments to make prognoses or predictions, difficult judgments that can be improved if clinicians attend to the lessons provided by years of empirical research on the topic.*

Diagnostic Classification

As discussed in Chapter 2, once clinical psychologists began working with adult clients during and after World War I, they were often asked to perform clinical assessments for the purpose of diagnosing mental disorders in psychiatric patients. This process is variously called diagnostic classification, psychodiagnosis, differential diagnosis, or diagnostic labeling. Today, diagnostic classification remains a significant part of clinical research and practice.

Accurate psychodiagnosis is important for several reasons. First, proper treatment decisions often depend on knowing what, exactly, is wrong with a client (Harwood, Beutler, & Groth-Marnat, 2011; Hays, 2013). Second, research into the causes of psychological disorders requires reliable and valid identification of disorders and accurate differentiation of one disorder from another. Finally, classification allows clinicians to efficiently communicate with one another about disorders in a professional "shorthand" (Sartorius et al., 1996).

The use of a common nomenclature (naming system) is extremely important in any field. Imagine, for example, how confusing it would be if medical patients who developed pharyngitis (a sore throat) because of A-beta-hemolytic *Streptococcus* (a bacterium) received a different diagnosis depending on which state or country they lived in. Fortunately, if you have this condition and are accurately assessed, you will be given the same diagnosis (strep throat) whether you are in New York, Peoria, Hong Kong, or Helsinki. That is because the World Health Organization's (WHO) *International Classification of Diseases* (*ICD*) provides common codes that identify each disease. In clinical psychology and psychiatry, the comparable system is the American Psychiatric Association's *Diagnostic and Statistical Manual of Mental Disorders*, or *DSM*.

A BRIEF HISTORY OF THE *DSM*   Various systems for classifying mental disorders had been used since the early 1900s, but classification of mental disorders became more formalized in 1952 when the American Psychiatric Association published the first *Diagnostic and Statistical Manual of Mental Disorders*. Known as *DSM-I*, it remained in use until 1968, when—to make the *DSM* more similar to the World Health Organization's *ICD*—it was replaced by *DSM-II*.

DSM-I and *DSM-II* provided a uniform terminology for describing and diagnosing abnormal behavior, but they offered no clear rules to guide mental health professionals' diagnostic decisions. Accordingly, when *DSM-III* appeared in 1980, it included a set of criteria for assigning each diagnostic label. These criteria—which referred mainly to specific symptoms and symptom durations rather than inferred causes—were increased in number and specificity in *DSM-III-R*, which was published in 1987. Clients were to be diagnosed with a particular disorder only if they met a pre established number of criteria from the full list of criteria associated with that disorder.

DSM-III and *DSM-III-R* also introduced *multiaxial* diagnoses, allowing clinicians to describe clients along different dimensions, or *axes*, providing a more complete picture of clients' problems and the factors affecting them. Axis I was for disorders that had a noticeable onset and course, such as when a person who is functioning well develops debilitating panic attacks within a relatively short period of time. Axis II disorders included those that are long-standing and resistant to change, such as various pervasive developmental problems (e.g., autistic spectrum disorders) and personality disorders. Axes III through V allowed diagnosticians to identify physical conditions that might affect a person's mental state and functioning (e.g., cancer), the severity of recent psychosocial stressors (e.g., divorce or job loss), and the person's psychological, social, and occupational functioning during the past year. *DSM-III* and *DSM-III-R* improved the reliability of most diagnoses, but they also had shortcomings. So in 1988, only a year after *DSM-III-R* appeared, the American Psychiatric Association established a task force to begin work on *DSM-IV*.

New editions of the *DSM* are always major enterprises; they take years and require coordinating the efforts of thousands of people. To develop *DSM-IV*, planners organized numerous experts into 13 work groups, each of which followed a three-step procedure for studying a different set of disorders and how best to diagnose them (Widiger, Frances, Pincus, Davis, & First, 1991). Each group first reviewed all the clinical and empirical literature relevant to a given disorder and used their findings to guide initial suggestions for changes in diagnostic criteria for that disorder. When literature reviews failed to resolve issues, the work groups sought to conduct analyses on existing patient data sets. Another step involved asking clinicians to use diagnostic criteria in clinical settings with real clients. Conducted at more than 70 sites worldwide, these focused *field trials* examined issues such as how alternate wordings or alternate thresholds (cutoffs) affected reliability, prevalence rates, or concordance with the parallel diagnoses from *ICD-10* (Nathan & Langenbucher, 1999). The *DSM-IV*, with its revised diagnostic criteria, was published in 1994. It was followed in 2000 by a text revision (*DSM-IV-TR*) that did not change its diagnostic criteria, but did update information about the prevalence, onset, course, and other aspects of various disorders (APA, 2000).

The developers of *DSM-IV* and *DSM-IV-TR* sought to extend the improvements in reliability begun with *DSM-III-R*'s use of observable criteria. They hoped to develop categories that relate well to specific outcomes (predictive validity) or specific underlying neurological or genetic constellations (construct validity). But despite its improved empirical foundations, the *DSM-IV* diagnostic system continued to draw criticism. For one thing, although many Axis I disorders showed good to excellent reliability, disorders within the schizophrenic spectrum and some childhood and adolescent disorders did not. And Axis II disorders, particularly the personality disorders, continued to show unacceptably low inter-rater and test-retest reliability (Zanarini et al., 2000).

Critics especially questioned whether the either-or categorizations imposed by *DSM-IV* criteria were the best way to understand psychopathology. If individuals met a certain number of criteria, they were said to "have" a disorder; if not, they do not "have" it. In fact, though, psychological disorders can be present in varying degrees. For example, there is no clear borderline between being depressed and not depressed. Critics contended that diagnoses should be considered as extremes along one or more underlying dimensions (Widiger & Trull, 2007).

Clinicians from various theoretical orientations also criticized the *DSM-IV* for not providing enough useful information about disorders. Behaviorally oriented clinicians were concerned that *DSM-IV* classification ignored the context in which symptoms occur, thus providing no basis for understanding the meaning or function that a particular pattern of disordered behavior might have in different social circumstances (Follette, 1996; Wulfert, Greenway, & Dougher, 1996). Psychodynamically oriented clinicians criticized *DSM-IV*'s strong emphasis on observable symptoms. They were concerned that clinicians think they understand clients once a diagnostic label is applied, when in reality they may not understand the client's *subjective* experience of having the disorder (Packard, 2007). Neurologically oriented clinicians also had criticisms, arguing that emphasizing observable symptoms fails to take into account discoveries about the brain circuitry associated with specific disorders (Bracha, 2006).

Critics also noted that the *DSM* excludes certain conditions. Every version of the *DSM* has been based on, and applied to, North American populations. None included symptom clusters seen in other cultures (Hall, 2005). Also missing from the *DSM* were the many types of *relational disorders*, such as couples conflict, parental discipline problems, child neglect, sibling conflict, domestic abuse, incest, and the like. These conditions produce considerable psychological suffering (First, 2006).

Even the very number of diagnoses in *DSM* has been criticized. The first edition, *DSM-I*, contained 106 diagnoses; in *DSM-IV*, there are 365 (see Figure 3.2). This 300% increase in diagnostic categories over four decades has led some to wonder if that many new disorders have been discovered and scientifically verified, or if the increase is more representative of the expansion of the mental health field and its practitioners' need to identify and treat a wider variety of conditions (see Houts, 2004, for an interesting discussion).

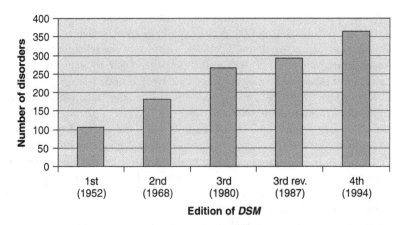

FIGURE 3.2   Number of Diagnoses in the *Diagnostic and Statistical Manual of Mental Disorders (DSM)* Across Editions (DSM-5 did not significantly change the number of possible diagnoses; rather it modified the diagnostic criteria for certain disorders and reorganized disorders into 17 broad categories) *Source:* Houts (2004).

THE *DSM-5*   Like its predecessors, the newest edition of the *DSM, DSM-5*, was designed to be an improvement over previous editions. It too depended on input from numerous work groups, research studies, and field trials. Publication of the *DSM-5* in May of 2013 was preceded by public comment periods, where interested persons expressed their views on proposed changes (see www.dsm5.org). Like its predecessors, this new edition serves as the primary diagnostic system for mental health professionals in North America.

Among the most important changes introduced in *DSM-5* is the new organization of its chapters. Some *DSM-IV* categories have changed, as have some of the diagnoses within those categories. For instance, in *DSM-IV*, bipolar disorders and depressive disorders both appeared in the mood disorders chapter. In *DSM-5*, these disorders appear in separate chapters—one for bipolar and related disorders and one for depressive disorders. Obsessive-compulsive disorder was in the anxiety disorders chapter of *DSM-IV*, but now has its own chapter that also includes body dysmorphic disorder, hoarding disorder, hair-pulling ("trichotillomania") disorder, and skin-picking ("excoriation") disorder (American Psychiatric Association, 2013). The table of contents has also changed (see Table 3.3). The first chapter of *DSM-5* is now the one on neurodevelopmental disorders many of which are diagnosed in infancy or childhood. These include intellectual disability (intellectual developmental disorders; formerly called mental retardation), autism spectrum disorders attention deficit hyperactivity disorder, specific learning disorders, motor disorders, and various communication disorders. Disorders first identified in childhood are also placed first within each of the other chapters. Finally, the multiaxial system has been dropped because the developers concluded that there was not sufficient scientific justification for it.

Consider again the case of Jessie presented at the beginning of this chapter. A tentative *DSM-5* diagnosis for him is presented below. It is based on the information available in the vignette, but the clinician would also investigate further the extent of Jesse's substance use and the "pretty bizarre thoughts" that he reported. The latter would be particularly important because part of the *DSM-5* diagnosis involves determining whether there are psychotic features and whether those features are mood congruent or mood incongruent. In this case, the clinician judged that such features are present, so Jessie's *DSM-5* diagnosis might look like this:

> D 01 Major Depressive Disorder, single episode, with mood-congruent psychotic features
> Severity level: Moderate (based interview and a Patient Health Care Questionnaire)
> Additional concerns: Relational problem, parental divorce

Because of the significant changes in *DSM-5*'s chapter organization, disorder names, and criteria, clinicians who have been using *DSM-IV* will need to retrain themselves to learn the new system, particularly if insurance companies, governmental agencies, and other groups rapidly adopt the changes. Existing psychological tests, structured interviews, and other diagnostic instruments will have to be revised, and new ones will have to be developed so as to conform to

---

TABLE 3.3 Significant Changes in the *Diagnostic and Statistical Manual of Mental Disorders-5 (DSM-5)*

Basic Organization

- Disorders presumed to be more influenced by neurological and neurodevelopmental factors now appear first, a change designed to increase similarity with the *International Classification of Diseases (ICD-11)*
- Disorders with similar features are listed adjacent to each other
- Multi axial categorization of disorders using Axes I-V is discontinued

Disorder Categories

- New disorders such as disruptive mood dysregulation disorder and binge eating disorder are now listed
- Disorders such as Asperger's disorder, childhood disintegrative disorder, and pervasive developmental disorder were dropped as distinct diagnoses; their symptoms are now included in a single diagnosis of autism spectrum disorder
- Depressive disorders and bipolar disorders are placed in separate categories
- Obsessive—compulsive disorder and posttraumatic stress disorder (PTSD) are moved to categories separate from anxiety disorders
- There is a new category of trauma and stressor-related disorders, which includes diagnoses such as PTSD, adjustment disorders, and reactive attachment disorder

Diagnostic Criteria

- The diagnosis of major depressive disorder no longer includes an exemption for bereavement
- Substance abuse and substance dependence categories will be merged

---

changes in *DSM-5* diagnostic criteria. There will no doubt be numerous books, practice manuals, workshops, conferences, seminars, and the like to help mental health professionals make the transition to *DSM-5*.

CRITICISMS AND ALTERNATIVE DIAGNOSTIC PROPOSALS   Like its predecessors, *DSM-5* has generated intense interest and considerable controversy. As you might guess, not everyone is pleased with the development of the new *DSM*. Among the strongest criticisms are those expressed by members of the American Psychological Association's Division 32 (Society for Humanistic Psychology). In an open letter to the developers of *DSM*, they complained about what they perceived as lowered diagnostic standards, the introduction of new disorders, and the lack of empirical grounding for some disorders. Each of these, they contend, increases the "medicalization" of psychological disorders and de emphasizes understanding of the sociocultural factors associated with disorders (Clay, 2012). Others have cautioned that psychiatrists may be inclined to expand certain diagnostic categories, that they may not be entirely objective and evidence based in their decisions (Frances & Widiger, 2011; Miller, 2012). Defenders of *DSM-5* counter that this is an unfair characterization of the motives of honorable professionals who worked hard to create a more effective diagnostic system (Black, 2013).

Clinicians and researchers concerned about the shortcomings in *DSM-IV* and *DSM-5* have proposed alternative diagnostic systems. Several have proposed that rather than assigning diagnoses based on whether or not clients show a specified—some say arbitrary—number of symptoms, clinicians should base diagnoses on measurement of client characteristics on a selected set of dimensions that are relevant for each disorder. Critics contend that such *dimensional approaches* would avoid the *DSM*'s either-or dichotomization.

Arguments for a dimensional approach have been especially persuasive in the diagnosis of personality disorders, where diagnostic reliability has tended to lag. Though *DSM-5* does incorporate some dimensional assessment (American Psychiatric Association, 2013), critics contend that the dimensional approach has not been applied broadly enough. Others (e.g., Westen, 2012) suggest that clinicians should diagnose on the basis of the degree to which a given client's characteristics resemble prototypical examples of particular disorders. So rather than noting the presence or absence of symptoms from a disorder checklist, clinicians could rate, from 1 to 5, the degree to which a client's behavior matched a prototypical description of each disorder.

Other diagnostic proposals call for describing psychopathology in terms of specific theories or contextual principles. For instance, Bornstein (2006) explored how concepts such as ego strength, defense style, and mental representation of the self and others have considerable diagnostic utility. This kind of thinking prompted the publication of an alternative diagnostic system, the *Psychodynamic Diagnostic Manual (PDM)* in 2006. This manual was developed by a task force whose members come from five major psychoanalytic groups. Advocates of this alternative system argue that it promotes more depth-oriented assessment. They claim that it also encourages clinicians to go beyond overt symptoms during the diagnostic process and to generate more complete pictures of clients, which in turn allows for more sophisticated case formulation and better treatment planning (Brabender & Whitehead, 2011; Huprich & Meyer, 2011).

The field of positive psychology has provided another alternative diagnostic approach. Advocates of this approach agree with some other critics that diagnosis based on problematic symptoms alone is insufficient. What is missing, they say, is the systematic assessment of clients' strengths (Ehde, 2010; Joseph & Wood, 2010). In fact, they argue that the "real" psychopathologies, the ones that "cut nature at the joints," might be better understood as the absence of the character strengths, not as the presence of symptoms described by *DSM* (Duckworth, Steen, & Seligman, 2005). One result of this approach is *The Handbook of Positive Psychology Assessment* (Lopez & Snyder, 2003) which describes approaches to assessment based on positive psychology. Another is Peterson's (2006) "*Values in Action (VIA) Classification of Strengths: The un-DSM and the Real DSM.*"

It is no wonder that the diagnostic classification enterprise continues to be a hotbed of controversy. After all, it attempts to differentiate a wide variety of complex, socioculturally defined disorders caused by multiple (often unknown) factors using a relatively small set of shorthand labels organized in a way that will help clinicians make the best possible decisions about their clients. No diagnostic system is likely to ever accomplish all these goals. So although various alternative approaches may each have their advantages, it is unlikely that any of them will replace the current categorical classification system. The categorical system is consistent with the medical model that dominates the health care industry, and it offers an efficient shorthand through which clinicians can communicate with each other. The challenge for competing diagnostic schemes, and for the newest versions of the *DSM,* is to improve upon diagnostic reliability, validity, and utility while still maintaining a system that is efficient.

Description

As just noted, classification should be reliable and valid and serve as an efficient shorthand for communication among clinicians and researchers. But for many clinicians, diagnostic labels are not enough. They want to know more, and consequently, alternative diagnostic proposals often shade over into *descriptive assessment*, which these clinicians see as more important than diagnostic classification.

Descriptive assessment by a cognitive-behavioral therapist, for instance, might focus on outlining factors such as antecedent conditions, environmental incentives and disincentives, alternative sources of reward, cognitive complexity, and attributional style. A psychodynamic therapist might focus descriptive assessment on ego strengths and weaknesses, cognitive functioning, defense mechanisms, quality of family and other relationships, and characteristics of the self (Gabbard, Litowitz, & Williams, 2012). Of course, diagnostic classification and descriptive assessment can go hand in hand. Bertelsen (1999), for instance, suggests that clinical assessment should work at two separate levels: one concerned with diagnostic classification, the other concerned with evaluating multiple factors that influence the course of treatment.

Description-oriented assessment makes it easier for clinicians to pay attention to clients' assets and adaptive functions, not just to their weaknesses and problems. Accordingly, descriptive assessment data are used to provide pretreatment measures of clients' behavior, to guide treatment planning, and to evaluate changes in behavior after treatment. Descriptive assessment can also improve measurement in clinical research. For example, in an investigation of the relative value of two treatments for depression, assessments that describe clients' posttreatment behaviors (e.g., absenteeism, self-reported sadness, and depression test scores) are of greater value than diagnostic labels (e.g., depressive versus nondepressive).

Unfortunately, the movement toward broad description of persons may never dominate clinical assessment, especially in inpatient psychiatric settings and other managed-care facilities.

The reason is time. As skyrocketing health care costs have increased economic pressures to limit hospital stays and to concentrate on focused assessments and short-term treatments, time-consuming and comprehensive patient evaluations are just too expensive. The degree to which descriptive approaches to assessment gain widespread usage will ultimately depend on their empirically demonstrated usefulness—the degree to which clinicians can perform assessments efficiently and use them to design better research and treatments.

Treatment Planning and Treatment Assessment

Diagnostic and descriptive assessment can be used to plan treatments. In the simplest model, a diagnosis (e.g., depression) leads to a preferred treatment (e.g., cognitive-behavioral psychotherapy), just as a given medical illness (e.g., strep throat) might lead to a preferred treatment (e.g., antibiotic). Identifying ideal connections between diagnoses and psychotherapy methods has been a main goal of the empirically supported treatments movement (see our discussions in Chapter 1, "What Is Clinical Psychology," and Chapter 10, "Research on Clinical Intervention").

While efforts to match specific treatments with specific diagnoses have certainly improved the empirical base of psychotherapy, the enterprise has not worked out as cleanly in practice as many had hoped. As the previous discussion on diagnosis implies, diagnostic classification is imprecise, and it is difficult to argue that specific treatments work for specific diagnoses when the diagnoses themselves keep changing. Further, extensive research on psychotherapy effectiveness (discussed in Chapter 10) shows that treatments often have general and overlapping effects, some of which have more to do with characteristics of the persons involved than with the disorders to which they are applied (Beutler & Malik, 2002; Norcross & Lambert, 2011; Singer, 2013). Because of these problems, clinicians have sought to incorporate other factors into treatment-related assessment. The key is to identify which factors, apart from the diagnosis and the "brand" of psychotherapy, best predict how an intervention will work.

In short, treatment planning assessment goes beyond the basic medical-model question: *Which treatments work best for which disorders?* Instead, it addresses the more detailed question, famously stated by Gordon Paul (1967): "*What* treatment, *by whom*, is most effective for *this* individual with *that* specific problem, and under *which* set of circumstances?" (p. 44). In Chapter 6, "Basic Features of Clinical Interventions," and in Chapter 10, "Research on Clinical Intervention," we discuss treatment planning further and we address answers to Paul's important question in much more detail.

Treatment-related assessment can also focus on the question of how well treatment has worked. Indeed, clinicians working in today's accountability-driven climate are increasingly asked to provide evidence of their effectiveness. Generating that evidence requires assessment. As an example, consider a case described by Alan Kazdin (2006).

Gloria, a 39-year-old woman, was self-referred for depression. An initial assessment was conducted, and a treatment plan involving combined cognitive-behavioral and interpersonal therapy, administered on weekly visits, was devised. The therapist also had Gloria come about 20 minutes early each week and complete brief measures designed to track her progress. One measure was a rating on a series of statements developed collaboratively between Gloria and the therapist, which they called the G-Scale. Another was an abbreviated version of the Beck Depression Inventory (BDI; Beck, Steer, & Garbin, 1988), and the last was an abbreviated version of the Quality of Life Inventory (QOLI; Frish, 1998).

Figure 3.3 represents the session-by-session changes in Gloria's scores over several weeks of treatment.

There are many ways to assess the results of treatment. Questionnaires, client self-reports, tests, and a variety of other measures can be used to evaluate treatment progress. For most clinicians, the goal is to record outcomes quickly, efficiently and accurately, and to periodically review the data to assess their treatment's strengths and weaknesses. Having these outcome data is essential even without the pressure applied by third party payers because conscientious self-assessment is part of the professionalism normally expected of clinical psychologists, and indeed of all health care providers.

Assessments can also be used as an explicit component of treatment. There is substantial evidence that discussing assessment methods and results with clients can have great therapeutic value (Finn & Hale, 2013). Imagine, for instance, Gloria and her therapist discussing the assessment results

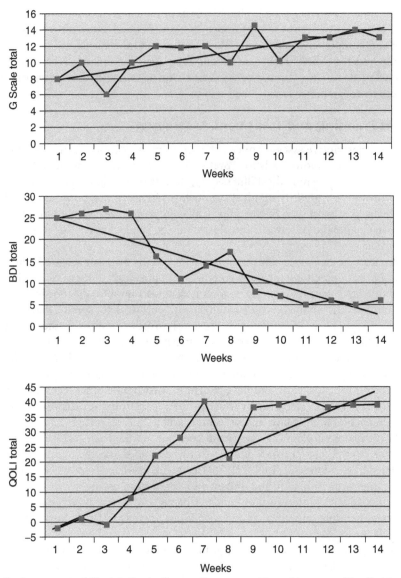

FIGURE 3.3 Assessment of Gloria's Psychotherapy Progress on Three Measures. (The first two weeks can be considered baseline measures. A linear regression line has been fitted to the data points on each graph.)

Note: G Scale is a scale developed by the client, Gloria, and the therapist; BDI is the Beck Depression Inventory (selected items), and QOLI is the Quality of Life Inventory. *Source:* Kazdin, Alan E., Research Design In Clinical Psychology, 4th Ed., © 2003, p. 322. Reprinted and Electronically reproduced by permission of Pearson Education, Inc., Upper Saddle River, NJ 07458.

in Figure 3.3. Greater involvement in assessment might encourage her to be more objective and accurate in her self-monitoring; it might increase her trust in the therapist and in the treatment; it can provide her with another avenue of therapeutic interaction. Assessment expertise is a traditional strength of clinical psychologists, so it makes sense to use this strength to therapeutic advantage (Youngstrom, 2013).

Prediction

A final goal of clinical assessment is to make predictions about human behavior. Such predictions might include forecasts about how the symptoms of a client's disorder might change with or without treatment (prognosis), about future performance (descriptions of how someone will perform in a given job or situation), or about dangerousness (descriptions of the likelihood of someone behaving violently toward the self or others). In any of these predictions, clinicians must have valid information about how the characteristics revealed by assessment relate to the behavior being predicted. Without that link, prediction would be little more than guesswork.

PROGNOSIS   Most often, prognosis refers to a prediction about the outcome of treatment, but it can also refer more generally to predictions about changes in symptoms without treatment or under certain circumstances (e.g., a head injury might change the prognosis for treatment of an anxiety disorder).

DSM diagnoses already contain considerable information about prognosis, including results of long-term studies of the course of a disorder as well as other information related to its typical onset, chronicity, those most at risk, and the like. And although the *DSM* does not provide specific prognostic statements, it is not difficult for clinicians (or students) to recognize that some disorders tend to be more debilitating than others, more chronic or prone to relapses, or more responsive to treatment or to certain positive or negative life circumstances.

So clinicians can build upon the basic information in the *DSM* to improve their prognoses. For example, information about the client's level of social support and subjective distress can alter a prognosis. Relatively high levels of support and moderate, but not debilitating, distress improve prognoses whereas relatively low levels of support and intense distress worsen them. A prognosis can also be influenced by such client factors as impulsivity and coping style, resistance to therapist suggestions, treatment setting (e.g., inpatient versus outpatient), the "fit" between client and therapist (e.g., shared values or cultural background), and the client's beliefs about treatment (Hundt et al., 2013). The degree to which a prognosis should be adjusted by these or other factors should be guided by empirical research evidence about the degree to which each factor has been shown to influence treatment outcomes in similar cases.

PREDICTING FUTURE PERFORMANCE   Clinicians are sometimes asked by businesses, government agencies, police and fire departments, and the military to help them select people who are most likely to perform well in certain jobs. In such cases, the clinician must first collect and/or examine descriptive assessment results to provide data on which to base predictions and selections. This step is critical and often underappreciated by those who believe psychologists should be able to make predictions in any domain simply on the basis of general psychological training. In order to know how someone will perform in a given job or situation, psychologists must have empirical evidence about which characteristics reliably predict which performances. That means that for each job or domain, psychologists have to do their homework; they cannot rely on their assumptions or general clinical judgment. A classic example of how descriptive and predictive assessment can overlap was provided by Henry Murray's use of specialized tests, interviews, and observations to select soldiers who would be the most successful spies, saboteurs, and other behind-enemy-lines operatives during World War II (Office of Strategic Services, 1948). Murray's assessment program was so comprehensive that it took several days to complete and measured everything from intelligence to skill at planning murder.

Similar, though less extensive, prediction-oriented clinical assessment programs also appeared in large-scale postwar screening programs designed to select civilian and military employees (Institute of Personality Assessment and Research, 1970), graduate students in clinical psychology and psychiatry (Holt & Luborsky, 1958; Kelly & Fiske, 1951), and Peace Corps volunteers (Colmen, Kaplan, & Boulger, 1964). Because such assessment programs influence decisions affecting large numbers of people, they must be evaluated not only for their predictive validity but also for their impact on the people being assessed and on the organizations that utilize them.

PREDICTING DANGEROUSNESS   Predictions of dangerousness, long a part of clinical practice and research, are often called forensic evaluations. For instance, a clinician might be asked to evaluate whether an eighth grader who brought a handgun to school represents a continuing homicide risk and should be educated in a secure facility instead of in a regular school (Vincent, 2006). Clinical researchers might develop instruments designed to predict the likelihood that an adult sex offender will commit another offense if released (Langton et al., 2007).

Anna is a 20-year-old university student. Her parents became concerned about her mental state after two phone conversations during which Anna stated she was not leaving her dorm, was not communicating with others, and not attending class. They traveled 200 miles to see her and following a long and sometimes acrimonious discussion, convinced Anna to seek professional help. Anna first went to the university counseling center, where the results of an initial assessment suggested mixed anxiety and depression. Further information revealed, though, that Anna had recently shown signs of mania, so a diagnosis of bipolar I was suggested. During the interview, she was basically cooperative, but poorly groomed and at times agitated or despondent. She said that she probably needed help. Because the university did not have facilities to handle a case as potentially severe as hers, Anna agreed to be transferred to the city hospital's inpatient unit. During an intake interview there, a social worker noticed several scratch marks on her wrists that were of apparently recent origins. She admitted inflicting them, but said they "weren't that big a deal." In addition to finalizing a diagnosis and attempting to engage Anna in planning treatment, the next steps for the clinical staff was to determine Anna's risk of suicide and to take appropriate precautions if it is high.

As in the case of Anna, presented below, predictions become especially harrowing because they involve life-or-death situations, either for the potentially suicidal client or for those whom the client might harm upon release from a mental hospital. How accurate are such predictions?

In fact, clinical psychologists often find it difficult to predict dangerousness accurately (Coid et al., 2011; Fazel, Singh, Doll, & Grann, 2012; Hilton, Harris, & Rice, 2006). One reason is that the *base rate*, or frequency with which dangerous acts are committed in any group of people, is usually very low. The following example shows why this is important.

Assume that a clinician is 80% accurate in predicting homicidal behavior. Assume also that the base rate for homicide in the population the clinician examines is 10 murders per 10,000 people. The accuracy of predictions can be evaluated in terms of the pattern of four possible outcomes. If the clinician predicts dangerousness and the person indeed behaves dangerously, the outcome is called a *true positive*. If the clinician predicts that there is no danger, and the person does not behave dangerously, we have a *true negative* outcome. If the clinician predicts no danger, but the person does act dangerously, a *false negative* outcome occurs. Finally, when the clinician predicts dangerous behavior but dangerous acts do not occur, we call it a *false positive*. As indicated in Table 3.4, the clinician would correctly predict who 8 of the 10 murderers would be. However, if the clinician is 80% accurate, he would incorrectly categorize 20%, or 1,998, of the other 9,990 persons as potential murderers even though none of them would commit violence. So the 8 true positives must be viewed in light of the 1,998 false positives in which the clinician predicted homicides that did not occur.

In this example, then, the clinician's *positive predictive power* to identify murderers would be woefully low (less than 1% of predicted murderers would actually kill someone), while the accuracy of predicting nondangerousness, called *negative predictive power*, would be greater than 99.9%. To maximize true positives, then, the clinician could predict that no one will commit a murder, a prediction that would be correct 99.9% of the time. However, all the errors would be false negatives, and society usually believes that such mistakes (i.e., predicting that dangerous people are safe) are more serious than false positives (i.e., predicting that safe people are dangerous).

To err on the side of caution, then, clinicians tend to overpredict dangerousness. Of course, if there are no serious consequences to false-positive errors, overprediction is not a problem. But typically, errors in either direction can have significant consequences. Imagine, for instance, trying to predict which young adults are likely to engage in school violence, a task that takes on special importance in the wake of the murderous rampages that have taken place at Columbine High School, Sandy Hook Elementary School, and other places. School shootings are extremely low-base-rate events, so trying to identify at-risk individuals will inevitably result in many false-positive

TABLE 3.4 Measuring the Accuracy of Clinical Predictions of Dangerousness

Clinician's Prediction	Ultimate Outcome	
	Homicide	No Homicide
Homicide	8 (true positives)	1,998 (false positives)
No homicide	2 (false negatives)	7,992 (true negatives)

errors. For every correctly identified killer, dozens or hundreds of other youths are at risk of being incorrectly stigmatized with the same label (Cunningham, Sorensen, & Reidy, 2009; Mulvey & Cauffman, 2001).

It is tempting to dismiss the effects of low base rates on prediction—after all, they are "only statistics"—and to cling to the belief that when push comes to shove, the "experts" will be able to accurately predict school violence, suicide, or other violent acts. But experts do not cling to such beliefs. They know that the base-rate statistics reflect how difficult it is for clinicians (and others) to predict dangerousness accurately (Hart & Cooke, 2013). The American Psychiatric Association has taken the position that psychiatrists have no special knowledge or ability that allows them to accurately predict dangerous behavior (1983).

Those who attempt to predict dangerousness do try to minimize errors by following certain guidelines. First, clinicians usually prefer to make predictions about level of risk (e.g., high, moderate, low) rather than about whether a particular individual will or won't commit a particular act. Second, they use validated assessment instruments designed to predict the behaviors in question. There are several instruments for predicting dangerousness, for example, and though none of them have better than a modest predictive accuracy (Yang, Wong, & Coid, 2010), their results appear to be better guides than making guesses on the basis of intuition and limited experience. Researchers seeking to improve prediction of dangerousness increasingly focus on combining assessment evidence from four domains: (a) the defendant's dispositional tendencies, such as anger or impulsiveness; (b) clinical factors, such as evidence of mental or personality disorders; (c) historical factors, especially a record of violence; and (d) contextual factors such as the strength of social support from family and friends (Cassel & Bernstein, 2007).

So in cases like Anna's, a clinician will ask clients about their suicidal thoughts, their desire for death (Baca-Garcia et al., 2011), whether they have already made efforts at suicide, and if so, what kind and how often (Ougrin, et al., 2011). They will also ask clients for their own estimates of their potential for suicide (Peterson, Skeem, & Manchak, 2011). The responses to each of these questions can then be used to adjust upward or downward the estimated risk of suicide derived from a validated suicide screening questionnaire. In addition, clinicians refer to published literature on evidence-based risk assessment and prevention in an effort to improve the accuracy of their predictions of dangerous behavior (e.g., Pompili & Tatarelli, 2011).

SECTION SUMMARY

Clinical assessment goals include diagnostic classification, description, treatment planning and evaluation, and prediction. Diagnosis is typically based on the latest version of the **Diagnostic and Statistical Manual of Mental Disorders,** *the* **DSM-5,** *though alternative diagnostic systems are being considered to remedy perceived shortcomings of the current system. Description involves a fuller characterization of a client than is typically available from a diagnostic classification. Both diagnosis and description can be used to help plan treatments. Assessments can also be used to measure treatment effectiveness and to demonstrate it to others. Finally, clinicians are sometimes asked to make predictions about future behavior, including clients' dangerousness, often a difficult task.*

CLINICAL JUDGMENT AND DECISION MAKING

SECTION PREVIEW

Clinicians make judgments by combining information from different sources. In doing so, they can rely on empirically based methods of decision making, on clinical experience and intuition, or on a combination of the two. While clinical intuition is essential in many situations (e.g., spontaneous events that occur during the course of therapy), research shows that clinical psychologists have no special capacity for intuition: they are prone to the same kinds of error as are other human beings when relying on impressionistic thinking. So wise clinicians incorporate empirically based, actuarial models into their judgments in situations when such models are available (e.g., prediction of dangerousness).

The mass media have long cast clinical psychologists as experts who can astutely translate obscure signs into accurate statements about a person's past, present, or future. As in the case of violence, some events are particularly difficult to predict. But whether a clinician is trying to judge the likelihood of a client attempting suicide, a stalker harming a victim, a child being abused by a parent, a brain-injured client succeeding in a new job, or a particular form of psychotherapy alleviating a sufferer's anxiety, all predictions involve clinical judgment.

Clinical Intuition

As our discussion of prediction of dangerousness suggests, empirical research does not support the idea that clinicians have special inferential capabilities. Donald Peterson made this point forcefully 45 years ago: "The idea that clinicians have or can develop some special kinds of antennae with which they can detect otherwise subliminal interpersonal stimuli and read from these the intrapsychic condition of another person is a myth which ought to be demolished" (Peterson, 1968, p. 105). There is now a large body of research which has addressed the accuracy of clinical intuition by comparing clinical judgments with judgments made by laypersons or with judgments based on statistical or mechanical models. The clear result is that clinical intuition too often underperforms (Ægisdóttir et al., 2006; Goldberg, 1959; Grove, Zald, Lebow, Snitz, & Nelson 2000; Hanson & Morton-Bourgon, 2009; Meehl, 1957, 1965; Spengler et al., 2009).

Why do clinicians not make better clinical judgments, even after years of training and experience? Apparently, being human, clinicians are prone to the same cognitive habits and biases that can lead to error in anyone's information processing. For example, clinicians' judgments, like other humans' judgments, are more prone to error when they rely too heavily on experiences that are recent or remarkable enough to make them especially available to recall. The bias created by this *availability heuristic* can be seen, for example, when people are asked to judge which of the following is more common

> 7-letter English words ending in -*ing* __ __ __ __ i n g
>
> or
>
> 7-letter English words with *n* in the sixth position __ __ __ __ __ n __

People often choose the first option, simply because -*ing* words are much easier to bring to mind than words with *n* in the sixth position, but in fact, words in the latter category are more common. They include all -*ing* words, as well as all 7-letter words that end in *nt* (e.g., *payment*), or *ne* (e.g., *biplane*), and so on. Consider the tragic and highly publicized mass shootings that took place in 2012 at an Aurora, Colorado movie theater and at the Sandy Hook Elementary School in Connecticut. Shocking incidents like these understandably lead people to think that multiple murders are quite common. The truth, though is that while there have been 62 mass shootings since 1983, individual murders are far more frequent. FBI figures show that 8,583 people were shot to death in 2011 alone (Knox, 2013). Nevertheless, judgments about the probability of vivid, highly memorable events can easily become inflated in the minds of the public, clinicians included. In clinical situations, then, a psychologist may overemphasize the likelihood of diagnoses that come most easily to mind and thus misdiagnose (Garb, 1996).

Memorable clinical "folklore" can create *illusory correlations* (Chapman & Chapman, 1967) causing clinicians to draw false inferences from assessment data (Krol, DeBruyn, & van den Bercken, 1995; Lewis, 1991). Thus, some clinicians see paranoid tendencies in clients who draw large eyes on figure-drawing tests, even though there is no firm empirical evidence to support this association (Golding & Rorer, 1972). Like the first impressions all people form, clinicians also tend to display an *anchoring bias* in which they establish their views of a client more on the basis of the first few pieces of assessment information than on any subsequent information (Tutin, 1993). Anchoring bias can also influence clinicians to let assessment information coming from certain sources (e.g., a parent's report of a child's behavior) outweigh any other information they receive (McCoy, 1976). The problem with anchoring bias is that we hold too firmly to first impressions and do not make sufficient adjustments when new data warrants doing so. If anchoring bias combines with *confirmation bias*—the tendency to interpret new information in line with existing beliefs—the clinician may ignore contradictory evidence, discount its validity, or even distort it to fit initial impressions (Strohmer & Shivy, 1994).

Numerous studies also suggest that having larger amounts of assessment information may increase clinicians' confidence about their inferences, but it does not necessarily improve the accuracy of those inferences (Einhorn & Hogarth, 1978; Garb, 1984; Kleinmuntz, 1984; Rock, Bransford, Maisto, & Morey, 1987). That's because additional pieces of information can contribute additional error—the less precise the predictor, the greater the error contributed. Clinicians' judgments may also be prone to error because they misremember information or fail to get important information. Like other people, clinicians tend to remember their successes more clearly than their failures and so may remain wedded to incorrect inference tendencies (or invalid assessment methods) simply because they think of them as valid (Garb, 1989). Indeed, clinicians may not get enough *accurate feedback* about their successes and failures.

CLINICAL AND STATISTICAL PREDICTION   The sobering body of research that has challenged the image of clinicians as experts who can consistently predict future behavior has led some to question whether clinical predictions would be more accurate if they were based upon formal, statistical data-processing methods rather than on expert clinical judgment. *Statistical prediction* (also called *actuarial prediction* or *mechanical prediction*) involves inferences based on probability data and formal procedures for combining information, all usually derived from research. *Clinical prediction*, as we have seen, involves inferences based primarily on a practitioner's training, assumptions, and professional experiences. Which is better? As noted above, there is a large body of research on this question, including numerous meta-analyses that compare clinical and statistical prediction head to head.

When clinicians interpret assessment data informally, make recommendations based on these interpretations, and do research on such activities, it is usually because they believe that they, and perhaps most members of their profession, are good at these tasks. Thus it came as a shock when Paul Meehl's 1954 review of 20 studies comparing formal versus informal inference methods found that, in all but one case, the accuracy of the statistical approach equaled or surpassed that of the clinical approach. Later, even the sole exception to this surprising conclusion was called a tie, and as additional research became available, the superiority of the statistical method of prediction was more firmly established (Dawes, Faust, & Meehl, 1989; Meehl, 1957, 1965; see Table 3.5).

In the years since Meehl's review, numerous published responses have appeared, many of which pointed out methodological defects in some of the studies that could have biased results in favor of statistical procedures. Frederick C. Thorne (1972) put it this way: "The question must not be what naive judges do with inappropriate tasks under questionable conditions of comparability with actual clinical situations, but what the most sophisticated judges can do with appropriate methods under ideal conditions" p. 44. Still, the furor over Meehl's conclusions could not negate the fact that inference based on subjective, clinical methods is not as accurate as it was assumed to be, even on many clinically relevant tasks (Dawes, 1994; Hanson & Morton-Bourgon, 2009). Perhaps the strongest evidence comes

TABLE 3.5 Summary of Outcomes of Studies Comparing Clinical and Statistical Prediction

Source	Number of Studies Reviewed	Variables Predicted	Outcome Clinical Better	Statistical Better	Tie
Meehl (1956)	20	Success in school or military; recidivism or parole violation; recovery from psychosis	1[a]	11	8
Meehl (1957)	27	Same as above, plus personality description; therapy outcome	0	17	10
Meehl (1965)	51	Same as above, plus response to shock treatment; diagnosis label; job success and satisfaction; medical diagnosis	1[a]	33	17
Grove Zald, Lebow, Snitz, and Nelson (2000)	136	Same as above, plus marital satisfaction; success on psychology internship; performance in medical school; and others	8	63	65
Ægisdóttir et al. (2006)	51	Brain impairment; personality; length of hospital stay; diagnosis; adjustment or prognosis; violence or offense; IQ; academic performance; if an MMPI profile was real or fictional; suicide attempt; sexual orientation	5	25	18

[a]Later called a tie.

from meta-analyses comparing clinical and statistical prediction. For example, Grove and colleagues, (Grove, Zald, Lebow, Snitz, & Nelson, 2000) conducted a meta-analysis of 136 studies in which psychologists predicted criteria within their areas of expertise, including psychotherapy outcome, future criminal behavior, fitness for military service, marital satisfaction, psychiatric diagnoses, success on psychology internships, and several others. The results were consistent with previous studies: statistical/mechanical prediction outperformed clinical prediction overall, regardless of the type of judges, judges' experience, type of data being combined, or the design of the study. The advantage for statistical prediction was not large—roughly 10% on average—and in many studies mechanical and statistical prediction were essentially the same. In the small percentage of studies (6 to 16%) where clinical prediction outperformed mechanical prediction, the authors found no pattern of variables that reliably distinguished when or why clinical prediction was superior.

Similar results were obtained in two other meta-analyses, one which examined judgments in a variety of domains, and another which focused on predictions of recidivism among 45,398 sexual offenders (Ægisdóttir et al., 2006; Hanson & Morton-Bourgon, 2009). Both found a larger effect size for statistical prediction. In these studies, the difference in accuracy was not large, about 10–20%, and it varied by type of prediction (e.g., statistical models more clearly outperformed when predictions involved dangerousness; see Hilton, Harris, & Rice, 2006), setting, type of statistical formula used, and amount of information available to clinicians.

In short, there is considerable evidence that too few clinicians have appreciated the limits of clinical intuition. This makes them vulnerable to criticisms from those within and outside their profession (Faust & Ziskin, 1988; Ridley & Shaw-Ridley, 2009; Tavris & Aronson, 2007). Years ago, Thorne (1972) suggested that "clinicians must become much more critical of the types of judgments they attempt to make, the selection of cues upon which judgments are based, and their modes of collecting and combining data" (p. 44). That statement still applies today. Based on years of research on the issue of statistical versus clinical prediction, the following conclusions seem reasonable:

- Statistical/actuarial prediction generally outperforms clinical prediction.
- The superiority of statistical prediction is most evident in predicting violence and other low-base-rate events.
- The overall advantage for statistical prediction is modest, and occasionally clinical prediction does as well or slightly better, though not in any particular pattern of circumstances.
- Practicing clinicians typically underutilize and undervalue actuarial prediction methods.

Improving Clinical Judgment

Clinicians find it discouraging that their inferences, honed by training and experience, are often inferior to mechanical decisions that can be arrived at by anyone who can read and has the relevant assessment data to plug into a formula. Yet, if one takes a broader view, the generally superior performance of actuarial models, particularly for low-base-rate events such as violence, need not be seen as a sign of professional failure. A great deal of clinical experience and research typically goes into the development of useful actuarial models—we have always relied on research to separate the wheat from the chaff in clinicians' favored theories. Further, we don't denigrate meteorologists or stock brokers when they rely on statistical models and computer-generated forecasting. Nor do we distrust physicians who refer to databases and formal decision models to help them diagnose unusual medical conditions. Indeed, though some people are willing to accept intuitive, "from-the-hip" judgments from a doctor, we suspect that most appreciate the thoroughness and professionalism of physicians who take advantage of the latest research and technology in reaching a diagnosis.

At the same time, it is important to recognize that clinical experience and judgment are not invariably error prone. With more years of experience, clinicians' judgments tend to improve, though modestly at best. Spengler et al. (2009) conducted a meta-analysis of 75 judgment studies, involving 4,607 clinicians, and found that accuracy increased by about 13% with experience, regardless of other factors. Just *how* experience improves judgment is not entirely clear. We suspect it is not merely the repeated use of clinical intuition, but rather the repeated use of intuition combined with timely feedback about the accuracy of predictions. More experience may also be associated with more time to learn about research findings on clinical decision processes, including the numerous factors that can bias clinical judgment, which in turn may make clinicians less vulnerable to those factors.

The preceding discussion suggests that clinical psychologists should be familiar with the extensive research literature on clinical judgment and on clinical versus statistical prediction, and that they should be guided by it. What determines whether clinicians incorporate statistical models in their clinical decisions? One survey of 491 members of the American Psychological Association's Division 12 (Clinical Psychology) found that some of them dismissed research on clinical judgment as conceptually misguided or irrelevant to real decisions (Vrieze & Grove, 2009)—an overgeneralization, given the diversity of studies, that risks "throwing the baby out with the bath water." However, the main factor that determined whether clinicians made use of statistical models in their clinical decisions was simply the extent to which that topic was discussed when they were in graduate school.

A number of proposals have been made to make clinical reasoning a more explicit, rather than implicit, part of training in the hopes of teaching health professions to avoid the more common sources of inference errors (Ridley & Shaw-Ridley, 2009; Spengler et al., 2009). By most counts, this change is needed. In accredited clinical psychology programs, issues related to decision making are more likely to be covered in non required courses, such as cognitive psychology, and only 9% of programs required courses that contained a significant component on decision making (Harding, 2007).

Clinical decisions can be difficult. Whether they involve anticipating a client's response to treatment, predicting dangerousness, determining competency to stand trial, or something else, such judgments require envisioning distant events that can be affected by numerous and often unforeseen variables. With experience, clinicians might improve their judgment, but because clinicians are not blessed with special intuitive powers, and because they often receive limited formal instruction in clinical decision making, experience-based improvements alone are likely to be small. Greater improvements in judgment are likely to occur if clinicians develop, through graduate training and/or continuing education, an appreciation of the common errors of judgment to which humans are prone. The appropriate use of formal models can improve specific kinds of decision making.

SECTION SUMMARY

Clinicians are often asked to make inferences that go well beyond observable behavior. When they rely on their beliefs about unobserved phenomena associated with behavior, or about presumed underlying mechanisms or psychic structures that cause behavior, their inferences can appear rich and insightful. However, those same inferences are also more prone to bias and inaccuracy. Years of research suggest that clinicians should be especially aware of the limitations of clinical judgments and employ assessment instruments and decision-making procedures that have the best track records—doing so is the only reliable way to improve one's "clinical intuition." Although prediction is often a difficult task, accuracy can be improved if clinicians seek out the best available evidence and follow established guidelines.

PSYCHOMETRIC PROPERTIES OF ASSESSMENT INSTRUMENTS

SECTION PREVIEW

The assessment goal is the most important factor in determining a clinician's choice of assessment tools, but a number of other factors also affect selection. Among the most important of these are the psychometric properties of instruments. Reliability, validity, standardization, utility, and the like are the "credentials" of assessment instruments. When deciding what tools to use in assessment or research, clinical psychologists must consider these credentials carefully.

Sound clinical judgments depend on the soundness of the measures used to help make those judgments (Ayearst & Bagby, 2010). Assessment instruments of higher quality are those that carefully conducted research has shown to be reliable, valid, and useful. Below we briefly consider the dimensions that determine an instrument's psychometric quality. In the next two chapters, we summarize psychometric information on several of the more popular assessment instruments.

Reliability

Reliability refers to consistency in measurement or to agreement among different judges or raters. It can be evaluated in several ways. If the results of repeated measurements of the same client are very similar, the assessment procedures are said to have high *test-retest* reliability, analogous to a bathroom scale that shows the same weight when someone steps off and back on again.

Another way to evaluate reliability is to examine internal consistency. If data from one part of an assessment, such as odd-numbered test items, are similar to data from other parts, such as even-numbered items, that assessment is said to be *internally consistent*. This dimension has sometimes been called split-half reliability. Finally, *interrater* reliability is measured by comparing the conclusions drawn by different clinicians using a particular assessment system to diagnose, rate, or observe the same client. When clinicians judging the same set of assessment results arrive at significantly differing conclusions, interrater reliability is low. The more they agree, the higher the interrater reliability of the instrument.

Interrater reliability tends to be higher when clinicians make judgments about a diagnosis that has relatively clear diagnostic criteria (e.g., panic disorder). In such cases, they are all using the same interpretive rules. Interrater reliability tends to be lower when clinicians make judgments about a diagnosis with less precise criteria (e.g., antisocial personality disorder) and use unstructured interviews and projective tests—assessments with ambiguity in the possible meanings of information obtained. What about the interrater reliability of *DSM-5* disorders? Preliminary studies suggest that, as with previous *DSMs*, some are very high (e.g., posttraumatic stress disorder) and some unacceptably low (e.g., generalized anxiety disorder) (Freedman et al., 2013).

To make the best use of reliability data, clinicians must examine the published research on specific assessment methods or instruments. They can also consult books or manuals that address assessment issues. In Chapters 4 and 5, we present reliability information on a number of the more common assessment instruments that clinicians use.

Validity

The *validity* of an assessment method reflects the degree to which it measures what it is supposed to measure. Like reliability, validity can be evaluated in several ways. The *content* validity of an assessment method is determined by how well it taps all the relevant dimensions of its target. An interview-based assessment of depression that includes questions about sad feelings but not about their duration or cause would have low content validity. *Predictive* validity is measured by evaluating how well an assessment forecasts events, such as violent behavior or suicide attempts. When two assessment devices agree about the measurement of the same quality, they are said to have *concurrent* validity. Predictive and concurrent validity are subtypes of *criterion* validity, which measures how strongly an assessment result correlates with important independent criteria of interest.

Finally, there is *construct* validity (Cronbach & Meehl, 1955). To oversimplify somewhat, an assessment device has good construct validity when its results are shown to be systematically related to the construct it is supposed to be measuring. Psychologists evaluate construct validity by determining whether a test or other assessment method yields results that make sense in light of some theory about human behavior and mental processes. For example, scores on a measure of anxiety should increase under circumstances thought to increase anxiety (e.g., facing major surgery). If no change occurs, the measure's construct validity is suspect. Fully evaluating construct validity requires numerous studies and an elaborate set of statistical analyses (Campbell & Fiske, 1959).

Validity is related to reliability because an assessment device cannot be any more valid than it is reliable. However, the validity of an instrument is not guaranteed just because the instrument is reliable. Consider a situation in which 50 people use their eyes to assess the gender of a man skilled in female impersonation. All 50 observers might agree on their judgment that the man is a female, but they would all be wrong. In this case, visual assessment had high interrater reliability but very poor criterion validity.

It is important to remember that reliability and validity are matters of degree, not all-or-none propositions. The question is always how much imprecision is tolerable in an assessment. For instance, if a bathroom scale varied by only a few ounces in test-retest procedures, we would likely consider the instrument reliable for our purposes, but if a postal scale varied by that much, we would consider it unreliable. How much error one tolerates depends on the goals and potential uses of the assessment, on the availability of alternative measurement instruments, and on practical constraints such as time and resources.

Remember, too, that the validity of an instrument must always be viewed in relation to the purposes for which the assessment instrument is to be used. For example, a test might be a valid measure of typing skill but an invalid measure of aggressiveness. Test validity can reasonably be assessed only when tests are used for the purposes for which they were designed. So clinicians should compare reliability and validity data only across tests designed for the same purpose and then select the better-performing instrument, all other considerations being equal.

Standardization

When we say that a test or other assessment instrument is standardized, we mean that the designers of the test have given it to a large, representative sample of persons and analyzed the scores. Doing so gives the designers information about what the average score is in a population—the average mathematics score for 7-year-old children, for instance. It also gives information about the variance of scores on individual items or subtests. Without that information, there would be no way to determine whether a particular score on a test was average, below average, or above average.

Key considerations for a clinician are whether the size of the standardization sample was large enough and representative enough. If it wasn't, clinicians should have limited confidence in a test. Another key consideration is whether the particular client being tested is similar enough to the sample on which that test was standardized. Suppose, for instance, a clinician suspects a client might have a somatoform disorder and wants to conduct a structured interview—a series of prescribed questions—to help make a diagnosis. However, the client is an immigrant from China. If the structured interview has not been validated on Chinese or other Asian populations, the client's responses might not be interpretable on the basis of the standardization of the test.

Bandwidth–Fidelity Issues

Clinicians' assessment choices are further guided by their attempts to resolve the *bandwidth–fidelity* dilemma (Shannon & Weaver, 1949). Just as greater bandwidth is associated with lower fidelity in broadcasting, clinicians have found that, given limited time and resources, the more extensively they explore a client's behavior, the less intensive each aspect of that exploration becomes (and vice versa). The breadth of an assessment device is thus referred to as its *bandwidth* and the depth or exhaustiveness of the device as its *fidelity* (Cronbach & Glesser, 1964). This issue is also called the depth–breadth issue. If, during a 2-hour interview, for example, a clinician tries to cover a long list of questions, the result would be superficial information about a wide range of topics (broad bandwidth, low fidelity). If the time is spent exploring the client's early childhood memories, the result would be a lot of detailed information about only one part of the client's life (narrow bandwidth, high fidelity).

Accordingly, clinicians must seek assessment strategies and measurement tools that result in an optimum balance of bandwidth and fidelity. The questions, levels of inquiry, and assessment techniques that will be useful in identifying stress-resistant executives differ substantially from those that will help detect brain damage in a 4-year-old child.

OTHER FACTORS AFFECTING ASSESSMENT CHOICES

SECTION PREVIEW

A variety of other factors affect assessment choices, including the clinician's theoretical orientation and experience with various assessment instruments, as well as the assessment context, and cultural factors.

Clinicians' Experience and Theoretical Orientation

Clinical psychologists may tend to use, or avoid, particular assessment methods because those methods were either emphasized or criticized by faculty in their graduate training programs. Similarly, those who find certain measurement tactics tedious or unrewarding tend to seek answers to assessment questions through other procedures with which they are more comfortable. Ideally, a clinician's comfort with an instrument should not be the primary criteria on for selection, but sometimes clinicians become comfortable—too comfortable, probably—with certain methods of assessments that are not optimal for the task. Such clinician-specific factors help explain why some assessment methods continue to be used by some clinicians even when research evidence fails to support their reliability or validity.

As just described, clinicians' differing theoretical orientations direct them to pursue certain questions and concerns; in effect, orientation provides an outline for assessment. Thus, psychodynamically oriented case study outlines tend to include questions about unconscious motives and fantasies, ego functions, early developmental periods, object relations, and character structure (e.g., Gabbard, 2010). Cognitive-behavioral case study outlines (e.g., Beck, 2011) focus on clients' skills, habitual thought patterns, and the stimuli that precede and follow problematic behaviors. Humanistically oriented clinicians are less likely to follow a specific assessment outline; indeed, they are likely to see assessment as a collaborative process in which they seek to understand with each client how that client perceives himself or herself and the world (Fischer, 2001; Gorske, 2008).

Ideally, a clinician's assessment outline will be broad enough to provide a general overview of the client yet focused enough to allow coverage of all the more specific questions that the clinician wishes to address. The outline guides production of the assessment report—the organized presentation of assessment results. Let's consider two sample assessment outlines representing two theoretical approaches to clinical psychology.

Psychodynamic Assessment Outline

Patient information
    Personal
    Demographic
Presenting problem(s)
History
    Attachment, early family relations
    Medical and psychiatric
    Interpersonal, social, cultural
Psychological testing
    Projective tests
    Objective tests
Mental status
DSM diagnosis
Ego strengths
Defense mechanisms
Relationship boundaries
Self-concept and self-esteem

Cognitive–Behavioral Assessment Outline

Client information
   Personal
   Demographic
Presenting problem(s)
History of presenting problems
Client understanding of problems
Coping responses
   Behavioral
   Cognitive
Psychiatric history
Family, social, educational history
Psychological testing
   Objective
Daily activities
   Mood
   Work and social functioning
Client goals, motivation, and expectations of treatment

Humanistically Oriented Assessment

Humanistically oriented clinicians have suggested assessment alternatives that differ substantially from those of the cognitive-behavioral approach (e.g., Fischer, 2001; Gorske, 2008). Some of them have argued against assessment on the grounds that such procedures are dehumanizing, take responsibility away from clients, and threaten the quality of clinician–client relations (Rogers, 1951). Other humanistic psychologists raise the possibility that assessment data collected through traditional means can be useful if they are processed in line with humanistic principles (Fischer, 1989). For example, test results can be viewed as clues to how a client looks at the world, and conducting those tests can provide opportunities for the clinician and client to build their relationship (Dana & Leech, 1974). Fischer, for instance, argues that assessments using standardized, empirically validated instruments can be both scientific and therapeutic when assessments are conducted interactively between therapist and client. She gives examples of discussing *DSM-IV* criteria and possible interpretations of MMPI-2 profiles with clients, arguing that such collaboration not only provides additional data for assessments but avoids objectifying the client (Fischer, 2001; see also Finn, 1996).

The Assessment Context

The assessment choices that clinicians make are dictated not only by their goals, the quality of their instruments, and the time and resources available, but also by the contexts, or settings, in which assessments are conducted. Common settings include general medical and psychiatric facilities, private or community psychological clinics, jails, prisons, forensic (legal) situations, schools and other educational institutions, and the like. Each type of setting influences the nature of the referral questions asked, the kinds of assessment instruments expected or preferred, and the style of reporting that is most appropriate or most often requested (Groth-Marnat, 2009). For instance, clinicians who are unfamiliar with legal settings may initially find it disconcerting to have their clinical judgments, and even their professional qualifications, challenged. The language used in legal contexts is also different from that used in psychological contexts, and it is incumbent on the clinician to translate psychological terms that may not be understood by non psychologists into terms that those in the legal profession can understand. Similarly, educational settings bring with them their own preferred theories, terms, and methods of practice. So, as mentioned earlier, clinicians must not only clarify the referral question before conducting assessment, they must also select context-appropriate instruments and present their conclusions in ways that are the most useful to the referral source.

Cultural Factors

A European American clinician employed by a community mental health system greets a Mexican American family referred by a school counselor. The daughter has been having difficulties in school—social isolation, academic difficulties, and signs of depression—and there are concerns that the father might be suffering from a mental illness. The family was reluctant, but they agreed to an intake visit. They are now sitting somewhat nervously as the clinician asks them to describe their understanding of why they are there. Their English is poor, and the clinician, anxiously holding a standard multi page assessment form in her hands, does not speak Spanish.

What should the clinician do in a situation like this? What steps could have been taken ahead of time to make the situation less awkward and more productive? What should the goals of this assessment be and what assessment instruments would best accomplish those goals? Will the assessment instruments be understood by the clients? Will the results be valid?

Multicultural competence is increasingly necessary for mental health professionals (Rosenberg, Almeida, & Mcdonald, 2012). With ever more diversity in the U.S. population, there is a much greater chance that clinicians will encounter clients whose cultural backgrounds and world views are significantly different from their own. In such cases, the initial challenge is quite basic: establish lines of communication and trust (Comas-Diaz, 2012). In the case example above, even if the language barrier is overcome—either by hard work on the part of all participants or by referral to a clinician who speaks Spanish—there still may be problems related to trust. Members of minority groups may differ from other clients in their expectations and beliefs about the goals of assessment and the extent to which clinical interventions might help them. So clinicians must take care to assure that assessment goals are not socially or culturally biased in a way that would make the process less valid for minority clients (Mitchell, Patterson, & Boyd-Franklin, 2011).

A good deal of multicultural assessment research is devoted to exploring whether assessment instruments (questionnaires, tests, structured interviews, etc.) are equally valid for different populations. This research is important because many psychological assessments were originally developed and normed on U.S. samples. Psychological tests that are not applicable for other groups—a finding that can only be established by careful cross-cultural research—may not only be inappropriate, but may lead to court decisions prohibiting their use for educational placement and other purposes (see Lambert, 1985, for discussion of the landmark Larry P. *v.* Wilson Riles case in California). When conducting assessments on clients from different cultures, clinicians must therefore be knowledgeable about how sociocultural factors can affect assessment results, as well as diagnosis and treatment (Lopez & Guarnaccia, 2000). We discuss cultural factors and cultural competencies in assessment further in Chapter 4, "Interviewing and Observation in Clinical Psychology," and in Chapter 5, "Testing in Clinical Psychology."

Core Competencies in Clinical Psychology Assessment

There are so many types of assessment that no clinician can be expected to have mastered them all. However, every clinical psychologist should possess a set of core competencies in assessment. While no single formal set of competencies is universally agreed upon, those suggested by professional organizations, employers, educational institutions, and clinical internship sites have many similarities (Krishnamurthy et al., 2004). We have drawn upon those similarities to construct the following list. Some competencies relate to the empirical and theoretical foundations of assessment (e.g., an understanding of personality or cognitive variables that tests measure, an ability to judge reliability and validity), while others relate to the use of specific assessments (e.g., interview formats, intellectual tests, personality tests, diagnostic assessment). Psychologists trained in assessment should be able to

- understand the theoretical, empirical, and contextual bases of assessment.
- evaluate the psychometric properties of assessment instruments.
- successfully administer and interpret instruments designed to assess cognitive functioning, behavioral functioning, and personality.
- conduct and interpret clinical interviews and behavioral observations.
- formulate appropriate *DSM* diagnoses.
- recognize the limitations and appropriate uses of assessment instruments for special populations (cultural and linguistic groups, physically challenged, etc.).

- integrate data from multiple assessment sources into empirically grounded conclusions.
- effectively communicate the results of assessments to others in written and spoken reports.
- understand and follow APA Ethics Code guidelines for assessment.

SECTION SUMMARY

The psychometric properties of various instruments such as reliability, validity, and bandwidth can affect a clinician's assessment choices. The clinician's theoretical orientation and personal experiences with various instruments can also affect choices. While theoretical approaches can be biasing if too rigidly held, they also provide useful guidelines for clinicians by directing data collection efforts toward discovery of selected, clinically relevant information. The settings in which an assessment takes place can affect how assessment is conducted and perceived, and cultural factors can play a significant role in assessment, especially when the clinician and client(s) do not share the same set of assumptions and understandings. Assessment involves numerous skills, and clinical competency in assessment is an ongoing process.

COMMUNICATING ASSESSMENT RESULTS

SECTION PREVIEW

Assessment results are communicated in an assessment report. Although it seems obvious, it is important to remember that reports should be clear, relevant to the goals of the assessment, and conveyed using language that will make them maximally useful to the consumers of the report.

If assessment results are to have maximum value, they must be presented in reports that are clear, relevant to the assessment goals, and useful to the intended consumer. Accordingly, clinicians must guard against problems that can make reports vague, irrelevant, and useless. Table 3.6 illustrates how an assessment outline—in this case, a cognitive-behavioral outline—is translated into an assessment report. Notice that it is sufficiently problem oriented to be used with clients seeking help, while also reminding the assessor to consider broader and less problematic aspects of a person's life.

Report Clarity

The first criterion for an assessment report is clarity. Without this basic attribute, relevance and usefulness cannot be evaluated. Lack of clarity in psychological reports is troublesome because misinterpretation of a report can lead to misguided decisions. Here is a case in point:

A young girl, mentally defective, was seen for testing by the psychologist, who reported to the social agency that the girl's test performance indicated moderate success and happiness for her in "doing things with her hands." Three months later, however, the social agency reported to the psychologist that the girl was not responding well. Although the social agency had followed the psychologist's recommendation, the girl was neither happy nor successful doing things with her hands. When the psychologist inquired what kinds of things, specifically, the girl had been given to do, he was told "We gave her music lessons—on the saxophone." (Hammond & Allen, 1953, p. v)

A related problem exists when the assessor uses jargon that may be meaningless to the reader. Consider the following excerpt from a report on a 36-year-old man:

Test results emphasize a basically characterological problem with currently hysteroid defenses. Impairment of his ability to make adequate use of independent and creative fantasy, associated with emotional lability and naivete, are characteristic of him. Due to markedly passive-aggressive character make up, in which the infantile dependency needs are continually warring with his hostile tendencies, it is not difficult to understand this current conflict over sexual expression. (Mischel, 1968, p. 105)

TABLE 3.6 An Assessment Report Based on a Cognitive-Behavioral Outline

Behavior During Interview and Physical Description

Phil is a 20-year-old college student. At the first interview he seemed shy, soft spoken, and obviously uncomfortable about seeking therapy. Still he seemed willing and able to describe his problems and his feelings.

Presenting Problem:

A. *Nature of problem:*   Anxiety in social situations, especially those involving public speaking, in which he feels that others are evaluating him.

B. *History:*   Phil reports "always" being shy when in social situations and overly concerned with performance. He attributes the latter problem to his father, whom he describes as being harshly critical of him and who would "grade" the quality of his homework before he turned it in and would sometimes make him redo it until it met his exacting standards. He described his mother, too, as overly controlling, though more overtly affectionate than his father. Both parents compared him unfavorably to his younger brother, who was always a good student.

C. *Specific problematic situations:*   Interaction with his parents, academic examinations, family gatherings, class discussions, meeting new people.

D. *Cognitive factors:*   Phil's descriptions suggest that he has adopted unreasonably high standards, expecting himself to achieve perfection in academic and social situations, and believing that he must attain approval from everyone in order to be worthwhile.

E. *Dimensions of problem:*   The client's social and evaluative anxiety are long-standing and occur in a wide variety of day-to-day situations.

F. *Consequences of problem:*   In addition to creating social isolation and underperformance in academic exams, Phil's anxiety may be related to a history of gastrointestinal distress that requires him to take antacids on a regular basis.

Other Problems:

A. *Assertiveness.*   Although obviously shy, Phil said that lack of assertiveness is no longer a problem with him. He feels that he

can stand up for himself better now than in the past, but this is something to explore further to determine if his assertiveness skills are adequate.

B. *Forgetfulness:*   Phil describes himself as "scatterbrained" because he often forgets appointments, loses keys and other items, and even misses exams.

Personal Strengths:

Phil is intelligent, and appeared in the interview to be sensitive, friendly, and to have a good sense of humor.

Targets for Treatment:

Irrational expectations and self-statements in social-evaluative situations; possibly assertiveness.

Recommended Treatment Approach:

Progressive relaxation training to reduce and control anxiety, followed by cognitive restructuring, role-playing, and homework assignments to practice new self-talk and other cognitive skills.

Motivation for Treatment:

High.

Prognosis:

Very good.

Priority for Treatment:

High.

Client's Expectancies:

Phil says he wants to learn to eliminate his anxiety, and it appears he is sincere about this. He will probably be cooperative with the treatment plan.

The writer may understand the client, but will the reader understand the writer? Anyone not well versed in psychoanalytic terminology would find such a report mystifying. Even professionals may not agree on the meaning of the terms employed. Factors such as excessive length (or cryptic brevity), excessively technical information (statistics or esoteric test scores), and lack of coherent organization also contribute to lack of clarity in assessment reports (Olive, 1972; Wright, 2011).

Relevance to Goals

Although far less common today than in the past, clinicians may still be asked for "psychologicals" (usually a standard test battery and interview) without being told why assessment is being done. Under such circumstances, the chances of writing a relevant report are minimal. Unfortunately, there are other cases in which a report's lack of relevance is due mainly to the clinician's failure to keep established assessment objectives in mind.

Usefulness of Reports

Finally, one must ask if an assessment report is useful. Does the information it contains add anything important to what we already know about the client? Reports that present clear, relevant information that is already available through other sources may appear useful but have little real value. Such reports tend to be written when the assessor has either failed to collect new information or has not made useful statements about new data. In the former case, the clinician may have employed techniques that have low incremental validity (Sechrest, 1963). For example, a clinician may use psychological tests to conclude that a client has strong hostile tendencies, but if police records show that the client repeatedly has been arrested for assault, this conclusion doesn't add much to the clinical picture. In other instances, the assessor's report may have limited usefulness because it says nothing beyond what would be expected on the basis of base-rate information, past experience, and common sense.

Consider the following edited version of a report written entirely on the basis of two pieces of information: (a) the client is a new admission to a Veterans Administration (VA) hospital, and (b) the case was to be discussed at a convention session entitled "A Case Study of Schizophrenia."

> This veteran approached the testing situation with some reluctance. He was cooperative with the clinician but mildly evasive on some of the material. Both the tests and the past history suggest considerable inadequacy in interpersonal relations, particularly with members of his family. It is doubtful whether he has ever had very many close relationships with anyone. He has never been able to sink his roots deeply. He is immature, egocentric, and irritable, and often he misperceives the good intentions of the people around him. He tends to be basically passive and dependent, though there are occasional periods of resistance and rebellion against others. Vocationally, his adjustment has been very poor. Mostly he has drifted from one job to another. His interests are shallow, and he tends to have poor motivation for his work. Also, he has had a hard time keeping his jobs because of difficulty in getting along with fellow employees. Although he has had some relations with women, his sex life has been unsatisfactory to him. At present, he is mildly depressed. His intelligence is close to average, but he is functioning below his potential. Test results and case history suggest the diagnosis of schizophrenic reaction, chronic undifferentiated type. Prognosis for response to treatment appears to be poor. (Sundberg, Tyler, & Taplin, 1973, pp. 577–579)

In generating this impressive but utterly generic report, the clinician relied heavily on knowledge of VA hospital residents and familiarity with hospital procedures. For example, as the case was to be discussed at a meeting on schizophrenia, and since schizophrenia diagnoses are common for VA residents, it was easy to surmise the correct diagnosis. Also, because it fits the "average" VA resident, the report was likely to be at least partially accurate. This bogus document exemplifies a feature of assessment reports that reduces their usefulness: overgenerality, or the tendency to write in terms that are so ambiguous they can be true of almost anyone. Documents laden with overly general statements have been dubbed "Barnum reports" (in honor of P. T. Barnum's maxim that there is a sucker born every minute), "Aunt Fanny reports" (because the statements could also be true of "my aunt Fanny"), or "Madison Avenue reports" (given that they "sell" well) (Klopfer, 1983; Meehl, 1956; Tallent, 1992). Such overly general material has the dual disadvantages of spuriously increasing the impressiveness of a report while actually decreasing its usefulness.

SECTION SUMMARY

While there is no universally "right" way to organize assessment data, the criteria of clarity, relevance, and usefulness may be more easily achieved by using an outline organized around the goals of assessment, the clinician's theoretical approach, and the assessment context. It is also worth repeating that the information sought in an outline, and the instruments used to gain that information, should be based on empirical research.

ETHICAL CONSIDERATIONS IN ASSESSMENT

SECTION PREVIEW

A number of ethical issues confront clinicians who perform assessments, especially when they become embroiled in acrimonious divorce or child custody cases, when they help to determine whether clients are eligible for disability based on mental illness, or when they must decide what information to reveal about a client to third-party payers (e.g., insurance companies). Clinicians must know the limitations of the assessments they perform, and they must be clear in advance how those assessments are to be used. They should also be knowledgeable about how federal and state laws and the APA Ethical Principles of Psychologists and Code of Conduct govern their behavior.

The process of collecting, processing, and communicating assessment data obviously gives clinicians access to sensitive information that the client might not ordinarily reveal to others. This places a heavy responsibility on the assessor to use and report this privileged information in a fashion that safeguards the client's welfare and dignity and shows concern for (a) how psychological assessment data are being used; (b) who should have access to confidential material; and (c) the possibility that improper or irresponsible interpretation of assessment information will have negative consequences for clients.

With these concerns in mind, clinicians must first be sure that their inquiries do not constitute an unauthorized invasion of a client's privacy. In order to know what constitutes authorized and unauthorized disclosure of information, clinicians must be familiar with more than the details of individual cases. They must also wrestle with the problem of who may have access to assessment data if they do not maintain sole control over them. When test scores, conclusions, predictions, and other information are communicated in a report, they may be misused by persons who see the report but are not qualified to interpret it. In such cases, not only is the client's privacy invaded, but the assessment data may create harmful outcomes for the client. Minimizing these problems is a major concern of public officials, government agencies, citizens groups, and private individuals.

Perhaps the best way to ensure that clinicians follow ethical assessment practices is for them to know the American Psychological Association's *Ethical Principles of Psychologists and Code of Conduct* (APA, 2000b), particularly Section 9, which deals with assessment. In addition, the APA offers guidelines for certain specialized assessment practices, such as the *Guidelines for Psychological Evaluations in Child Protection Matters* (APA, 1998). Psychologists should also know the *General Guidelines for Providers of Psychological Services* (APA, 1987) and *Standards for Educational and Psychological Testing* (APA, 1985). These guidelines reflect federal legislation, including the Equal Employment Opportunity Act (part of the Civil Rights Act of 1964), which prohibits discriminatory use of tests that have adverse impact on the selection of minority group job candidates, and the Civil Rights Act of 1991, which bans adjustment of test scores on the basis of race, color, religion, sex, or national origin (Sackett & Wilk, 1994). The guidelines must also be implemented in accordance with the regulations of the Individuals with Disabilities Education Act and the Americans with Disabilities Act.

Care should also be taken to assure that assessment goals are not socially or culturally biased such that certain clients (e.g., members of ethnic or racial minorities) are placed at a disadvantage (Malgady, 1996). For example, some psychological tests are alleged to be inappropriate for use with minority groups, leading to court decisions prohibiting their use for educational placement and other purposes (see Lambert, 1985, for discussion of the landmark Larry P. *v.* Wilson Riles case in California). When conducting assessments on clients from different cultures, clinicians must be knowledgeable about how sociocultural factors can affect diagnosis, assessment, and treatment (Lopez & Guarnaccia, 2000).

The guidelines for assessors are often just that—guidelines; they do not clearly tell psychologists what they should or should not do. Ethical decision making often involves taking into account various federal, state, and local laws as well as professional codes and individual concerns. Clinicians faced with difficult decisions can also consult with colleagues and seek guidance from the American Psychological Association about the best course of action. Ethical problems and standards associated with clinical psychology are considered in greater detail in Chapter 15, "Professional Issues in Clinical Psychology."

Chapter Summary

Clinical assessment is the process of collecting information to be used as the basis for informed decisions by the assessor or by those to whom results are communicated. Interviews, tests, observations, and life records serve as the main sources of assessment data in clinical psychology. The clinical assessment process includes five stages: clarifying the referral, planning data collection, collecting data, processing data, and communicating results. The methods and levels of inquiry in assessment tend to follow a case study guide that is shaped by assessment goals, clinicians' theoretical preferences and experience, and contexts. Selection of assessment methods is also guided by research on their reliability (consistency) and validity (ability to measure what they are supposed to measure), and depth versus breadth.

The goals of clinical assessment typically involve diagnostic classification, description, treatment planning, and prediction. Diagnostic classification normally employs the *DSM*. Description involves broader assessments of clients' personalities by looking at person–environment interactions. Assessment for treatment planning involves collecting information about how clients might respond to various treatment approaches. Predictions often involve personnel selection but sometimes focus on a client's potential for violence or suicide.

Unfortunately, clinicians have no unique intuitive power or special information-processing capacity, so the quality of their judgments and decisions about clients can be threatened by the same cognitive biases and errors that affect all human beings. Indeed, research on clinical judgment suggests that in many situations, clinicians can make their greatest contribution to assessment as collectors of information that is then processed by computer-based statistical formulae.

Assessments are driven primarily by the assessment goals, but other factors can also influence how assessments are conducted. The reliability, validity, and generality of assessment instruments should play an important role in a clinician's selection. The clinician's theoretical orientation and prior experience with instruments affect assessment choices, too, as does the context in which assessments are made (i.e., legal, educational, psychiatric hospital, psychological clinic).

The results of clinical assessment are presented in an organized assessment report, which should be clear, relevant to assessment goals, and useful to the intended consumer. These reports often reflect the theoretical approach taken by each clinician, but they should be constructed in a way that is maximally useful to the referral source and consistent with ethical practices.

Study Questions

1. What core competencies in assessment should clinical psychologists possess?
2. What are the steps involved in a psychological assessment?
3. What are the most common data collection techniques?
4. What are the general goals of assessment?
5. How do clinical psychologists make diagnoses?
6. What is the basic structure of the *DSM-IV-R* and how might it differ in *DSM-5*?
7. Discuss the major changes to the *DSM-5*.
8. What are some criticisms of the *DSM* and alternate proposals for clinical diagnosis?
9. What has research revealed about clinical psychologists' abilities to predict future violence?
10. What are clinical judgment and clinical intuition, and how can they be improved?
11. Why are reliability, validity, and bandwidth important considerations in selecting assessment instruments?
12. How does a clinician's theoretical orientation influence assessment?
13. How does the clinical context or setting influence assessment data collection and reporting?
14. What are the basic requirements for a good psychological report?
15. How might clients' cultural or ethnic backgrounds influence the results of assessments?
16. What types of ethical concerns and dilemmas can be raised when clinicians conduct assessments?

Web Sites

- APA Rights and Responsibilities of Test Takers: http://www.apa.org/science/programs/testing/rights.aspx
- APA Report of the Task Force on Test User Qualifications: http://www.apa.org/science/programs/testing/qualifications.pdf
- APA Strategies for Private Practitioners Coping With Subpoenas Compelling Testimony for Client Records or Test Data: http://www.apa.org/about/offices/ogc/private-practitioners.pdf
- For official updates on DSM-5: http://www.dsm5.org/Pages/Default.aspx

MOVIES

A Beautiful Mind (2001): Based on the real life of a gifted mathematician, this film shows the challenges of distinguishing between brilliance and mental illness.

Monster (2003): In a graphic film that depicts a prostitute who tortures and kills many of her clients, this film highlights the questions of dangerousness, responses to childhood trauma, and the fine line between psychological issues versus forensic issues.

MEMOIRS

Hurry Down Sunshine: A Father's Story of Love and Madness by Michael Greenberg (2008; New York: Vintage Books). This father's powerful account of his daughter's symptoms of schizophrenia brings the *DSM* alive.

Manic: A Memoir by Terri Cheney (2009; New York: Harper). In her detailed account of bipolar disorder, this author shows that many other comorbid disorders, such as substance abuse, can compound the challenges of treatment.

References

Ægisdóttir, S., White, M. J., Spengler, P. M., Maugrman, A. S., Anderson, L., et al. (2006). The meta-analysis of clinical judgment project: Fifty-six years of accumulated research on clinical versus statistical prediction. *Counseling Psychologist, 34*, 341–382.

American Psychiatric Association. (1983). *Statement on prediction of dangerousness*. Washington, DC: Author.

American Psychiatric Association. (2000). *Diagnostic and statistical manual of mental disorders (4th ed.): Text revision (DSM-IV-TR)*. Washington, DC: Author.

American Psychiatric Association. (2013). *Diagnostic and statistical manual of mental disorders (5th ed.): DSM-5*. Washington, DC: Author.

American Psychological Association. (1985). *Standards for educational and psychological tests*. Washington, DC: Author.

American Psychological Association. (1987). *General guidelines for providers of psychological services*. Washington, DC: Author.

American Psychological Association. (1998). *Guidelines for psychological evaluations in child protection matters*. Washington, DC: Author.

American Psychological Association. (2000b). *Current major field of APA members by membership status* (Table 3). Retrieved Dec 13, 2001, from http://research.apa.org/member.

Antony, M. M., & Barlow, D. H. (Eds.). (2011). *Handbook of assessment and treatment planning for psychological disorders* (2nd ed.). New York, NY: Guilford.

Ayearst, L. E., & Bagby, R. M. (2010). Evaluating the psychometric properties of psychological measures. In M. M. Antony & D. H. Barlow (Eds.). *Handbook of assessment and treatment planning for psychological disorders* (2nd ed., pp. 23–61) New York, NY: Guilford.

Baca-Garcia, E., Perez-Rodriguez, M. M., Oquendo, M. A., Keyes, M., Hasin, D. S., et al. (2011). "Estimating risk for suicide attempt: Are we asking the right questions?" Passive suicidal ideation as a marker for suicidal behavior. *Journal of Affective Disorders, 134*, 327–332.

Beck, J. S. (2011). *Cognitive behavior therapy* (2nd ed.). New York, NY: Guilford Press.

Beck, A. T., Steer, R. A., & Garbin, M. G. (1988). Psychometric properties of the Beck Depression Inventory: Twenty-five years of evaluation. *Clinical Psychology Review, 8*, 77–100.

Bertelsen, A. (1999). Reflections on the clinical utility of the ICD-10 and DSM-IV classifications and their diagnostic criteria. *Australian & New Zealand Journal of Psychiatry, 32*, 166–173.

Beutler, L. E., & Malik M. L., (2002). *Rethinking the DSM: A psychological perspective*. Washington, DC: American Psychological Association.

Black, D. W. (2013). DSM-5 is approved, but personality disorders criteria have not changed. *Annals of Clinical Psychiatry, 25*, 1.

Bornstein, R. F. (2006). A psychoanalytic construct lost and reclaimed: The psychodynamics of personality psychology. *Psychoanalytic Psychology, 23*, 339–353.

Brabender, V., & Whitehead, M. L. (2011). Using the Psychodynamic Diagnostic Manual in the training of the competent assessor. *Journal of Personality Assessment, 93*, 185–193.

Bracha, H. S. (2006). Human brain evolution and the "neuroevolutionary time-depth principle:" Implications for the reclassification of fear-circuitry-related traits in DSM-V and for studying resilience to warzone-related posttraumatic stress disorder. *Progress in Neuro-Psychopharmacology & Biological Psychiatry, 30*, 827–853.

Campbell, D. T., & Fiske, D. W. (1959). Convergent and discriminant validation by the multitrait-multimethod matrix. *Psychological Bulletin, 56*, 81–105.

Cassel, E., & Bernstein, D. A. (2007). *Criminal behavior* (2nd ed.). Mahwah, NJ: Erlbaum.

Chapman, L. J., & Chapman, J. P. (1967). The genesis of popular but erroneous psychodiagnostic observations. *Journal of Abnormal Psychology, 72*, 193–204.

Clay, R. A. (2012). Protesting proposed changes to the DSM. *Monitor on Psychology*, Jan. 42–43.

Coid, J. W., Yang, M., Ullrich, S., Zhang, T., Sizmur, S., et al. (2011). Most items in structured risk assessment instruments do not predict violence. *The Journal of Forensic Psychiatry and Psychology, 22*, 3–21.

Colmen, J. G., Kaplan, S. J., & Boulger, J. R. (1964, August). *Selection and selecting research in the Peace Corps*. (Peace Corps Research Note No. 7).

Comas-Diaz, L. (2012). *Multicultural care: A clinician's guide to cultural competence*. Washington, DC; American Psychological Association.

Cronbach, L. J., & Glesser, G. C. (1964). *Psychological tests and personnel decisions*. Urbana, IL: University of Illinois Press.

Cronbach, L. J., & Meehl, P. E. (1955). Construct validity in psychology tests. *Psychological Bulletin, 52*, 281–302.

Cunningham, M. D., Sorensen, J. R., & Reidy, T. J. (2009). Capital jury decision making: The limitations of predictions of future violence. *Psychology, Public Policy, and Law, 15*, 223–256.

Dana, R. H., & Leech, S. (1974). Existential assessment. *Journal of Personality Assessment, 38*, 428–435.

Dawes, R. M. (1994). *House of cards*. New York, NY: The Free Press.

Dawes, R. M., Faust, D., & Meehl, P. E. (1989). Clinical versus actuarial judgment. *Science, 243*, 1668–1674.

Duckworth, A. L., Steen, T. A., & Seligman, M. E. P. (2005). Positive psychology in clinical practice. *Annual Review of Clinical Psychology, 1*, 629–651.

Ehde, D. M. (2010). Application of positive psychology to rehabilitation psychology. *Handbook of rehabilitation psychology* (2nd ed., pp. 417–424). Washington, DC: American Psychological Association.

Einhorn, H. J., & Hogarth, R. M. (1978). Confidence in judgment: Persistence of the illusion of validity. *Psychological Review, 85*, 395–416.

Faust, D., & Ziskin, J. (1988). The expert witness in psychology and psychiatry. *Science, 242*, 31–35.

Fazel, S., Singh, J. P., Doll, H., Grann, M. (2012). Use of risk assessment instruments ot predict violence and antisocial behaviour in73 samples involving 24,827 people: Systematic review and meta-analysis. *BMJ, 345*, e4692. doi: 10.1136bmj.e4692.

Finn, S. E. (1996). *Manual for using the MMPI-2 for a therapeutic intervention*. Minneapolis, MN: University of Minnesota Press.

Finn, S. E., & Hale, M. (2013). Therapeutic assessment: Using psychological testing as brief therapy. In K. F. Geisinger, B. A. Bracken, J. F. Carlson, et al. (Eds), *APA handbook of testing and assessment in psychology*, (Vol. 2, pp. 453–465): Washington, DC: American Psychological Association.

First, M. B. (2006). Relational processes in the DSM-V revision process: Comment on the special section. *Journal of Family Psychology, 20*, 356–358.

Fischer, C. T. (1989). A life-centered approach to psychodiagnostics: Attending to lifeworld, ambiguity, and possibility. *Person-Centered Review, 4*, 163–170.

Fischer, C. T. (2001). Psychological assessment: From objectification back to the life world. In B. D. Slife, R. N. Williams, & S. H. Barlow (Eds.), *Critical issues in psychotherapy* (pp. 29–44). Thousand Oaks, CA: Sage.

Follette, W. C. (1996). Introduction to the special section on the development of theoretically coherent alternatives to the DSM system. *Journal of Consulting and Clinical Psychology, 64*, 1117–1119.

Frances, A. J., & Widiger, T. (2011). Psychiatric diagnosis: Lessons from the DSM-IV past and cautions for the DSM-5 future. *Annual Reveiw of Clinical Psychology, 8*, 109–130.

Freedman, R., Lewis, D. A., Michels, R., Pine, D. S., Schultz, S. K., et al. (2013). The initial field trials of DSM-5: New blooms and old thorns. *American Journal of Psychiatry, 170*, 1–5.

Frish, M. B. (1998). Quality of life therapy and assessment in health care. *Clinical Psychology: Science and Practice, 5*, 19–40.

Gabbard, G. O. (2010). *Long-term psychodynamic psychotherapy: A basic text.* Washington, DC: American Psychiatric Publishers.

Gabbard, G. O., Litowitz, B. E., & Williams, P. (Eds.), (2012). *Textbook of psychoanalysis.* Arlington, VA: American Psychiatric Publishing.

Garb, H. N. (1984). The incremental validity of information used in personality assessment. *Clinical Psychology Review, 4*, 641–656.

Garb, H. N. (1989). Clinical judgment, clinical training, and professional experience. *Psychological Bulletin, 105*, 387–396.

Garb, H. N. (1996). The representativeness and past-behavior heuristics in clinical judgment. *Professional Psychology: Theory and Practice, 27*, 272–277.

Goldberg, L. R. (1959). The effectiveness of clinicians' judgments: The diagnosis of organic brain damage from the Bender-Gestalt test. *Journal of Consulting Psychology, 23*, 25–33.

Goldfried, M. R., & Davison, G. C. (1976). *Clinical behavior therapy* (pp. 52–53). New York, NY: Holt, Rinehart, and Winston.

Goldfried, M. R., & Sprafkin, J. N. (1974). *Behavioral personality assessment.* Morristown, NJ: General Learning Press.

Golding, S. L., & Rorer, L. G. (1972). Illusory correlation and subjective judgment. *Journal of Abnormal Psychology, 80*, 249–260.

Gorske, T. T. (2008). Therapeutic neuropsychological assessment: A humanistic model and case example. *Journal of Humanistic Psychology, 48*, 320–339.

Groth-Marnat, G. (2009). *Handbook of psychological assessment* (5th ed.). New York, NY: Wiley.

Grove, W. M., Zald, D. H., Lebow, B. S., Snitz, B. E., & Nelson, C. (2000). Clinical versus mechanical prediction: A meta-analysis. *Psychological Assessment, 12*, 19–30.

Hall, G. C. N. (2005). Introduction to the special section on multicultural and community psychology: Clinical psychology in context. *Journal of Consulting and Clinical Psychology, 73*, 787–789.

Hammond, K. R., & Allen, J. M. (1953). *Writing clinical reports.* Englewood Cliffs, NJ: Prentice-Hall.

Hanson, R. K., & Morton-Bourgon, K. E. (2009). The accuracy of recidivism risk assessments for sexual offenders: A meta-analysis of 118 prediction studies. *Psychological Assessment, 21*, 1–21.

Harding, T. P. (2007). Clinical decision-making: How prepared are we? *Training and Education in Professional Psychology, 1*, 95–104.

Hart, S. D., & Cooke, D. J. (2013). Another look at the (im-)precision of individual risk estimates made using actuarial risk assessment instruments. *Behavioral Science and the Law, 31*, 81–102. doi: 10.1002/bsl.2049.

Harwood, T. M., Beutler, L. E., & Groth-Marnat, G. (Eds.). (2011). *Integrative assessment of adult personality.* New York, NY: Guilford Press.

Hays, D. G. (2013). *Assessment in counseling: A guide to the use of psychological assessment procedures* (5th ed.). Alexandria, VA: American Counseling Association.

Hilton, N. Z., Harris, G. T., & Rice, M. E. (2006). Sixty-six years of research on clinical versus actuarial prediction of violence. *Counseling Psychologist, 34*, 400–409.

Holt, R. R., & Luborsky, L. (1958). *Personality patterns of psychiatrists: A study of methods for selecting residents* (Vol. 1). New York, NY: Basic Books.

Houts, A. C. (2004). Discovery, invention, and the expansion of the modern Diagnostic and Statistical Manuals of Mental Disorders. In L. E. Beutler & M. L. Malik (Eds.), *Rethinking the DSM: A psychological perspective* (pp. 17–68). Washington, DC: American Psychological Association.

Hundt, N. E., Armento, M. E. A., Porter, B., Cully, J. A., Kunik, M. E., et al. (2013). Predictors of treatment satisfaction among older adults with anxiety in a primary care psychology program. *Evaluation and Program Planning, 37*, 58–63.

Hunsley, J., & Mash, E. J. (2010). The role of assessment in evidence-based practice. In M. M. Antony & D. H. Barlow (Eds.), *Handbook of assessment and treatment planning for psychological disorders* (2nd ed., pp. 3–22). New York, NY: Guilford.

Huprich, S. K., & Meyer, G. J. (2011) Introduction to the JPA special issue: Can the Psychodynamic Diagnostic Manual put the complex person back at the center-stage of personality assessment? *Journal of Personality Assessment, 93*, 109–111.

Institute of Personality Assessment and Research. (1970). *Annual report: 1969–1970.* Berkeley, CA: University of California.

Joseph, S., & Wood, A. (2010). Assessment of positive functioning in clinical psychology: Theoretical and practical issues. *Clinical Psychology Review, 30*, 830–838.

Kazdin, A. E. (2003). *Research design in clinical psychology* (4th ed., p. 322). Boston, MA: Allyn & Bacon.

Kazdin, A. E. (2006). Assessment and evaluation in clinical practice. In C. D. Goodhart, A. E. Kazdin, & R. J. Sternberg (Eds.), *Evidence-based psychotherapy* (pp. 153–177). Washington, DC: American Psychological Association.

Kelly, E. L., & Fiske, D. W. (1951). *The prediction of performance in clinical psychology.* Ann Arbor, MI: University of Michigan Press.

Kleinmuntz, B. (1984). The scientific study of clinical judgment in psychology and medicine. *Clinical Psychology Review, 4*, 111–126.

Klopfer, W. G. (1983). Writing psychological reports. In C. E. Walker (Ed.), *The handbook of clinical psychology* (Vol. 1, pp. 501–527). Homewood, IL: Dow Jones-Irwin.

Knox, O. (2013). 547 dead, 475 hurt in mass shootings since 1983. Retrieved March 20 from Yahoo! News at http://news.yahoo.com/blogs/ticket/547-dead-476-hurt-mass-shootings-since-1983-182605303--politics.html.

Krishnamurthy, R., VandeCreek, L., Kaslow, N. J., Tazeau, Y. N., Miville, N. L., et al. (2004). Achieving competency in psychological assessment: Directions for education and training. *Journal of Clinical Psychology, 60*, 725–739.

Krol, N., DeBruyn, E., & van den Bercken, J. (1995). Intuitive and empirical prototypes in childhood psychopathology. *Psychological Assessment, 7*, 533–537.

Lambert, D. (1985). Political and economic determinants of mental health regulations. Unpublished doctoral dissertation, Brandeis University.

Langton, C. M., Barbaree, H. E., Seto, M. C., Peacock, E. J., Harkings, L., et al. (2007). Actuarial assessment of risk for reoffense among adult sex offenders: Evaluating the predictive accuracy of the Static-2002 and five other instruments. *Criminal Justice and Behavior, 34*, 37–59.

Lewis, G. (1991). Observer bias in the assessment of anxiety and depression. *Social Psychiatry and Psychiatric Epidemiology, 26*, 265–272.

Lopez, S., & Snyder, C. R. (Eds.). (2003). *Handbook of positive psychology assessment.* Washington, DC: American Psychological Association.

Lopez, S. R., & Guarnaccia, P. J. (2000). Cultural psychopathology: Uncovering the social world of mental illness. *Annual Review of Psychology, 51,* 571–598.

Malgady, R. G. (1996). The question of cultural bias in assessment and diagnosis of ethnic minority clients: Let's reject the null hypothesis. *Professional Psychology: Research and Practice, 27,* 73–77.

McCoy, S. A. (1976). Clinical judgments of normal childhood behavior. *Journal of Consulting and Clinical Psychology, 44,* 710–714.

McReynolds, P. (1975). Historical antecedents of personality assessment. In P. McReynolds (Ed.), *Advances in psychological assessment* (Vol. 3, pp. 477–532). San Francisco, CA: Jossey-Bass.

Meehl, P. E. (1954). *Clinical versus statistical prediction.* Minneapolis, MN: University of Minnesota Press.

Meehl, P. E. (1956). Wanted—A good cookbook. *American Psychologist, 11,* 263–272.

Meehl, P. E. (1957). When shall we use our heads instead of the formula? *Journal of Consulting Psychology, 4,* 268–273.

Meehl, P. E. (1965). Seer over sign: The first good example. *Journal of Experimental Research in Personality, 1,* 27–32.

Miller, G. (2012). Criticism continues to dog psychiatric manual as deadline approaches. *Science, 336,* 1088–1089.

Mischel, W. (1968). *Personality and assessment.* New York, NY: Wiley.

Mitchell, M. J., Patterson, C. A., & Boyd-Franklin, N. (2011). Commentary: Increasing cultural diversity in pediatric psychology family assessment research. *Journal of Pediatric Psychology, 36,* 634–641.

Mulvey, E. P., & Cauffman, E. (2001). The inherent limits of predicting school violence. *American Psychologist, 56,* 797–802.

Nathan, P. E., & Langenbucher, J. W. (1999). Psychopathology: Description and classification. *Annual Review of Psychology, 50,* 79–107.

Nietzel, M. T., & Bernstein, D. A. (1976). The effects of instructionally mediated demand upon the behavioral assessment of assertiveness. *Journal of Consulting and Clinical Psychology, 44,* 500.

Norcross, J. C., & Lambert, M. J. (2011) Psychotherapy relationships that work II. *Psychotherapy, 48,* 4–8.

Office of Strategic Services Assessment Staff. (1948). *Assessment of men.* New York, NY: Rinehart.

Olive, H. (1972). Psychoanalysts' opinions of psychologists' reports: 1952 and 1970. *Journal of Clinical Psychology, 28,* 50–54.

Ougrin, D., Zundel, T., Kyriakopoulos, M., Banarsee, R., Stahl, D., & Taylor, E. (2011). Adolescents with suicidal and nonsuicidal self-harm: Clinical characteristics and response to therapeutic assessment *Psychological Assessment.* Advance online publication. doi: 10.1037/a0025043.

Packard, E. (2007). A new tool for psychotherapists. *Monitor on Psychology, 38,* 30–31.

Paul, G. L. (1967). Strategy of outcome research in psychotherapy. *Journal of Consulting Psychology, 31,* 109–118.

Peterson, C. (2006). The Values in Action (VIA) Classification of Strengths: The un-DSM and the real DSM. In M. Csikszentmihalyi & I. Csikszentmihalyi (Eds.), *A life worth living: Contributions to positive psychology* (pp. 29–48). New York, NY: Oxford University Press.

Peterson, D. R. (1968). *The clinical style of social behavior.* New York, NY: Appleton-Century-Crofts.

Peterson, J., Skeem, J., & Manchak, S. (2011). If you want to know, consider asking: How likely is it that patients will hurt themselves in the future? *Psychological Assessment.,* doi: 10.1037/a0022971

Pompili, M., & Taraelli, R. (Eds.). (2011). *Evidence-based suicidology: A source book.* Cambridge, MA: Hogrefe Publishing.

Ridley, C. R., & Shaw-Ridley, M. (2009). Clinical judgment accuracy: From meta-analysis to metatheory. *The Counseling Psychologist, 37,* 400–409.

Rock, D. L., Bransford, J. D., Maisto, S. A., & Morey, L. (1987). The study of clinical judgment: An ecological approach. *Clinical Psychology Review, 7,* 645–661.

Rogers, C. R. (1951). *Client-centered therapy.* Boston, MA: Houghton Mifflin.

Rosenberg, A., Almeida, A., & Macdonald, H. (2012). Crossing the cultural divide: Issues in translation, mistrust, and cocreation of meaning in cross-cultural therapeutic assessment. *Journal of Personality Assessment,* Advance online publication doi: 10.1080/00223891.2011.648293.

Sackett, P. R., & Wilk, S. L. (1994). Within-group norming and other forms of score adjustment in preemployment testing. *American Psychologist, 49,* 929–954.

Sartorius, N., Kaelber, C. T., Cooper, J. E., Roper, M. T., Rae, D. S., et al. (1996). Progress toward achieving a common language in psychiatry: Results from the field trial of the clinical guidelines accompanying the WHO classification of mental and behavioral disorders in ICD-10. *Archives of General Psychiatry, 50,* 115–124.

Secrest, L. (1963). Incremental validity: A recommendation. *Educational and Psychological Measurement, 23,* 153-158.

Shannon, D., & Weaver, W. (1949). *The mathematical theory of communication.* Urbana, IL: University of Illinois Press.

Singer, J. A. (2013). Lost in translation? Finding the person in the emerging paradigm of clinical science: Introduction to a special issue on personality psychology and psychotherapy. *Journal of Personality,* online, doi: 10.1111/jopy.12017.

Spengler, P. M., White, M. J., Ægisdóttir, S., Maugherman, A. S., Anderson, L. A., et al. (2009). The meta-analysis of clinical judgment accuracy: Effects of experience on judgment accuracy. *The Counseling Psychologist, 37,* 350–399.

Strohmer, D. C. & Shivy, V. A., (1994). Bias in counselor hypothesis testing: Testing the robustness of counselor confirmatory bias. *Journal of Counseling and Development, 73,* 191–197.

Sundberg, N. D. (1977). *Assessment of persons* (pp. 97–98). New York, NY: Prentice Hall.

Sundberg, N. D., Tyler, L. E., & Taplin, J. R. (1973). *Clinical psychology: Expanding horizons* (2nd ed.). Englewood Cliffs, NJ: Prentice-Hall.

Tallent, N. (1992). *The practice of psychological assessment.* Englewood Cliffs, NJ: Prentice-Hall.

Tavris, C., & Aronson, E. (2007). *Mistakes were made (but not by me).* New York, NY: Harcourt.

Thorne, F. C. (1972). Clinical judgment. In R. H. Woody & J. D. Woody (Eds.), *Clinical assessment in counseling and psychotherapy* (pp. 30–85). Englewood Cliffs, NJ: Prentice-Hall.

Tutin, J. (1993). The persistence of initial beliefs in clinical judgment. *Journal of Social and Clinical Psychology, 12,* 319–335.

Vincent, G. M. (2006). Psychopathy and violence risk assessment in youth. *Child and Adolescent Psychiatric Clinics of North America, 15,* 407–428.

Vrieze, S. I., & Grove, W. M. (2009). Survey on the use of clincal and mechanical prediction methods in clinical psychology. *Professional Psychology: Research and Practice, 40,* 525–531.

Westen, D. (2012). Prototype diagnosis of psychiatric syndromes. *World Psychiatry, 11,* 16–21.

Widiger, T. A., Frances, A. J., Pincus, H. A., Davis, W. W., & First, M. B. (1991). Toward an empirical classification for the DSM-IV. *Journal of Abnormal Psychology, 100,* 280–288.

Widiger, T. A., & Trull, T. J. (2007). Plate tectonics in the classification of personality disorder: Shifting to a dimensional model. *American Psychologist, 62,* 71–83.

Wright, A. J. (2011). *Conducting psychological assessment.* New York, NY: John Wiley & Sons.

Wright, J. W. (2010). *Conducting psychological assessment.* Hoboken, NJ: John Wiley & Sons.

Wulfert, E., Greenway, D. E., & Dougher, M. J. (1996). A logical functional analysis of reinforcement-based disorders: Alcoholism and pedophilia. *Journal of Consulting and Clinical Psychology, 64,* 1140–1151.

Yang, M., Wong, S. C. P., & Coid, J. (2010). The efficacy of violence prediction: A meta-analytic comparison of nine risk assessment tools. *Psychological Bulletin, 136,* 740–767.

Youngstrom, E. A. (2013). Future directions in psychological assessment: Combining evidence-based medicine innovations with psychology's historical strengths to enhance utility. *Journal of Clinical Child and Adolescent Psychology, 42,* 139–159.

Zanarini, M. C., Skodol, A. E., Bender, D., Dolan, R., & Sanislow, C., et al. (2000). The collaborative longitudinal personality disorders study: Reliability of axis I and II diagnoses. *Journal of Personality Disorders, 14,* 291–299.

4 | INTERVIEWING AND OBSERVATION IN CLINICAL PSYCHOLOGY

Chapter Preview

In this chapter, we describe a variety of interview and observation techniques. We begin with interviews, categorized first by their goals and then by their structure. We also address stages of the interview process and what research has revealed about the reliability and validity of interviews. We treat observations in much the same manner: discussing goals and types of observations as well as research on the strengths and limitations of observations. Throughout, we discuss how various factors—particularly interview/observation structure, client diversity, and clinician bias—can affect the results of interviews and observations.

Interviews and observations are the most widely employed tools in clinical psychology. They are central to clinical assessment and also play prominent roles in psychological treatment. Indeed, much of what we have to say in this chapter about interviews and observations also applies to treatment because treatment usually begins with—and is based on—the relationship established through the interview process.

In simplest terms, an interview is a conversation with a purpose or goal (Matarazzo, 1965). That interviews resemble other forms of conversation makes them a natural source of clinical information about clients, an easy means of communicating with them, and a convenient context for attempting to help them. Interviews are flexible, relatively inexpensive, and, perhaps most importantly, provide the clinician with simultaneous samples of clients' verbal and nonverbal behavior. These advantages make the interview useful in a variety of clinical situations.

This chapter does not attempt to teach you how to conduct specific types of interviews or observations; it offers, instead, an introduction to interviewing and observation as assessment data sources. Interview and observation techniques for various situations are detailed in a number of sources (e.g., Cormier, Nurius, & Osborn, 2012; Craig, 2009; Hersen & Beidel, 2012; MacKinnon, Michels, & Buckley, 2009; Othmer & Othmer, 2002; Rogers, 2001; Saklofske, Schwean, & Reynolds, 2013; Segal, Mueller, & Coolidge, 2012; Sommers-Flanagan & Sommers-Flanagan, 2008), but learning how to use these techniques effectively requires more than reading (Bogels, 1994). Clinicians must also engage in carefully supervised interview practice as part of their professional training.

CLINICAL INTERVIEW SITUATIONS

SECTION PREVIEW

There are interviews for a variety of clinical situations: intake interviews to establish the nature of someone's problems and assign a DSM diagnosis, orientation interviews to prepare a client for treatment or research, problem-referral interviews to address a specific referral question, termination or debriefing interviews to end treatment or research, and crisis intervention interviews to offer support through a crisis and to decide what, if any, intervention should be offered next. Although we address these situations separately, they often overlap in practice. A final situation we discuss involves cultural or ethnic differences between interviewer and interviewee and the importance of clinician sensitivity to cultural factors when interviewing.

Intake Interviews

The most common type of clinical interview occurs when a client first comes to the clinician because of some problem in living. *Intake interviews* are designed mainly to establish the nature of the problem. Often, intake interviewers are asked for a classification or assessment of the problem in the form of a DSM diagnosis (e.g., major depressive disorder). They may also be asked to develop broader descriptions of clients and the environmental context in which their behavior occurs.

Information gathered in this situation may also help the clinician decide whether the client has come to the right place. If, on the basis of one or more intake interviews, the answer to the question is no, the clinician will refer the client to another professional or agency for alternative services. If further contact is seen as desirable, additional assessment or treatment sessions are scheduled. Most clinicians conduct their own intake interviews, but in some agencies and group practices, social workers or other personnel perform this function.

Some intake interviews are structured according to a sequence of important topics suggested by the case study outlines described in Chapter 3, "Basic Features of Clinical Assessment." Originally patterned after the question-and-answer format of medical history taking, many psychiatric interviews also include a *mental status examination* (MSE), a planned sequence of questions designed to assess a client's basic mental functioning in a number of important areas (see Table 4.1). The MSE is analogous to the physical examination that makes up part of the assessment of medical problems.

Intake interviews may also lay the groundwork for subsequent therapy efforts by establishing a productive working relationship and organizing the clinician's hypotheses about the origins and development of the client's problems (MacKinnon, Michels, & Buckley, 2009). The

TABLE 4.1 The Mental Status Examination

Here is a typical MSE topic outline (Siassi, 1984), followed by a short excerpt from an MSE interview:

i. General appearance and behavior: Client's level of activity, reaction to interviewer, grooming and clothing are assessed.

ii. Speech and thought: Is client's speech coherent and understandable? Are delusions present?

iii. Consciousness: Is the sensorium clear or clouded?

iv. Mood and affect: Is client depressed, anxious, restless? Is affect appropriate to situation?

v. Perception: Does client experience hallucinations, depersonalization?

vi. Obsessions and compulsions: Amount and quality of these behaviors are noted.

vii. Orientation: Is client aware of correct time, place, and personal identity?

viii. Memory: What is condition of short- and long-term memory?

ix. Attention and concentration: Asking client to count backwards by 7s is a common strategy.

x. Fund of general information: Questions like "Who is the President?" or "What are some big cities in the United States?" are asked.

xi. Intelligence: Estimated from educational achievement, reasoning ability, and fund of information.

xii. Insight and judgment: Does client understand probable outcomes of behavior?

xiii. Higher intellectual functioning: What is the quality of client's form of thinking? Is client able to deal with abstraction?

CLINICIAN: Good morning. What is your name?
CLIENT: Randolph S.
CLINICIAN: Well, Mr. S, I would like to ask you some questions this morning. Is that all right?
CLIENT: Fine.
CLINICIAN: How long have you been here?
CLIENT: Since yesterday morning.
CLINICIAN: Why are you here?
CLIENT: I don't know. I think my wife called the police and here I am.
CLINICIAN: Well, what did you do to make her call the police?
CLIENT: I don't know.
CLINICIAN: What day is today?
CLIENT: Tuesday, the twelfth.
CLINICIAN: What year is it?
CLIENT: 2009.
CLINICIAN: What city are we in?
CLIENT: Chicago.
CLINICIAN: Who is the mayor of Chicago?

intake interview is important to successful treatment because almost half the clients who attend an intake interview fail to return for scheduled treatment (Morton, 1995). The clients' initial perception of their intake interviewer appears to affect this pattern. Clients are more likely to return for subsequent treatment after talking to an interviewer whom they feel treated them with warm friendliness as opposed to businesslike professionalism, who expressed correct understandings of the client's concerns, whose nonverbal behaviors (e.g., facial expressions) were well matched to the clients' nonverbal behaviors, and whose social and cultural backgrounds were more similar (Dimatteo & Taranta, 1976; Patterson, 1989; Rasting & Beutel, 2005; Rosen, Miller, Nakash, Halperin, & Alegria 2012; Tryon, 1990). In some situations, one psychologist conducts the initial intake interview and a different one begins psychotherapy at the next session. This change can be problematic even when clients know about it beforehand. In fact, one study found that clients who experienced this kind of therapist discontinuity were twice as likely to terminate therapy by missing the first treatment appointment (Nielsen et al., 2009).

Problem-Referral Interviews

Clinicians sometimes serve as diagnostic consultants to physicians, psychiatrists, courts, schools, employers, social service agencies, and other organizations. In these circumstances, the client is often referred in order to answer a specific question, such as *Is Mr. P. competent to stand trial? Is Jimmy G. intellectually disabled?* or *Will such-and-such a custody arrangement with Ms. M. and Mr. O be in the best interest of this child?*

In these circumstances, the central goal of the interview is to address the referral question. For this reason, it is important that the referral question be stated clearly. Questions such as *Give me a profile on Mr. Q,* or *Will Ms. Y. make a good parent, or is she disturbed?* are too general or vague. And referral requests such as *Please test my child's IQ so I can prove to the schools that he should be in the gifted class* should raise red flags about the appropriateness of conducting the assessment without further clarification of the parent's motives and needs. As discussed in Chapter 3, the referral question, once clarified, determines the type of assessment conducted.

Orientation Interviews

People receiving psychological assessment or treatment often do not know what to expect, let alone what is expected of them. This is especially true if they have had no previous contact with mental health professionals. To make these new experiences less mysterious and more comfortable, many clinicians conduct special interviews (or reserve segments of interviews) to acquaint the client with the assessment, treatment, or research procedures to come (Prochaska & Norcross, 1994).

Such *orientation interviews* are beneficial in at least two ways. First, because the client is encouraged to ask questions and make comments, misconceptions that might obstruct subsequent treatment progress can be discussed and corrected. Second, orientation interviews can help clients understand upcoming assessment and treatment procedures and what their role in these procedures will be (Couch, 1995). Thus, the clinician might point out that the clients who benefit most from treatment are those who are candid, cooperative, serious, and willing to work to solve their problems. Good orientation interviews, then, can help focus clinicians' efforts on those clients who are most willing to be full partners in the assessment or treatment enterprise.

Orientation interviews are also important for research participants. Although clinicians or researchers might not want to reveal every detail of the research design in order to avoid biasing participants, they are ethically required to assure that each participant understands the nature of the tasks to be performed and any risks associated with them. Research orientation interviews not only satisfy the requirement for informed consent, but they also help ensure motivated cooperation from the participants, something especially important in long-term clinical trials and longitudinal research.

Debriefing and Termination Interviews

Debriefing interviews, designed to provide clients with information and assess their understanding of that information after an event, can occur in a number of situations. For example, people who have just completed a series of assessment sessions involving extensive interviews, tests, and observations are understandably anxious to know "what the doctor found," how the information will be used, and who will have access to it. These concerns are particularly acute when the assessor has acted as consultant to a school or a court. A debriefing interview can help alleviate clients' anxiety about the assessment enterprise by explaining the procedures and protections involved in the transmission of privileged information and by providing a summary and interpretation of the assessment results. Debriefing interviews can also occur with soldiers following battlefield experiences (Adler, Bilese, McGurk, Hoge, & Castro 2011), with clients who attempted suicide or self-injury (Kleespies et al., 2011), or with clinicians in training following realistic simulation exercises (Morse, 2012). In all these situations, debriefings are designed to help people who have experienced a significant event better understand it, ideally ensuring that potential gains are maximized and potential harms minimized.

As their name suggests *termination interviews*, occur when it is time to end a clinical relationship. When psychological treatment has ended successfully, many loose ends must be tied up: There is gratitude to be expressed and accepted, reminders to be given about the handling of future problems, plans to be made for follow-up contacts, and reassurance given to clients about their ability to do it alone. Termination interviews help make the transition from treatment to posttreatment as smooth and productive as possible. When treatment is less successful, as when clients drop out early, termination interviews can inform clinicians or researchers about the dynamics leading to drop-out and suggest ways to more effectively structure treatment in the future (Hummelen, Wilberg, & Karterud, 2007; Rosen et al., 2012).

Debriefing and termination interviews can also occur following participation in research. Typically, the *debriefing* of research participants involves simply providing them with more information about the study, but sometimes researchers may interview participants to better understand how various aspects of the study were perceived.

Crisis Interviews

When people in crisis appear at clinical facilities or call a hotline, suicide prevention center, or other agency, interviewers do not have the luxury of scheduling a series of assessment and treatment sessions. Instead, they conduct *crisis interviews* in which they attempt to provide support, collect assessment data, and provide help, all in a very short time (Sommers-Flanagan & Sommers-Flanagan, 2008).

The interviewer must deal with the client in a calm and accepting fashion, ask relevant questions (e.g., "Have you ever tried to kill yourself?" "What kinds of pills do you have in the house?"), and work on the immediate problem directly or put the client in touch with other services. One or two well-handled interviews during a crisis may be the beginning and the end of contact with a client whose need for assistance was temporary and situation-specific. For others, the crisis interview leads to subsequent assessment and treatment sessions.

Ethnic and Cultural Issues in the Clinical Interview

As the U.S. population becomes increasingly diverse, the number of persons from different ethnic and cultural backgrounds seeking mental health treatment increases (Li, Jenkins, & Grewal, 2012; Sue & Sue, 2007). Cultural differences between clients and interviewers can be problematic, particularly when clients' cultural assumptions, values, and practices do not fit well with the assumptions, values, and practices of the mental health services offered.

UNDERUTILIZATION OF MENTAL HEALTH CARE   The importance of cultural factors is suggested by mental health utilization rates. Members of racial and ethnic minority groups generally receive less mental health care and lower-quality mental health care than does the general population (Nevid, Rathus, & Greene, 2006). Table 4.2 presents key reasons for this underutilization. Some of these relate to access to services while others relate to cultural norms and misunderstandings that can derail the interview process (Iskandarsyah et al., 2013).

The concerns that many members of minority groups have about bias in the mental health system are not entirely unfounded. For instance, clinicians tend to diagnose African American and Hispanic American clients with schizophrenia at higher rates than they diagnose that disorder among European Americans (Aklin & Turner, 2006). At the same time, mood and anxiety disorders are diagnosed less often in African American children than in European American children

TABLE 4.2 Reasons for Underutilization of Mental Health Care Among Ethnic Minorities in the United States

Failures of access	Poverty leaves clients uninsured or underinsured
	Clients lack transportation to mental health facilities
	Language differences impede communication between clients and interviewers
Failures of beliefs and attitudes	Clients are unaware of available mental health services
	Cultural norms prohibit disclosure of problems and emotions to strangers or dictate that they be discussed only with spiritual leaders, medical personnel, or trusted family members
	Clients fear that failure to understand procedures, remedies, or red tape will make them feel ashamed or stupid in the eyes of mental health professionals
	Previous discrimination against or oppression of clients' ethnic group creates fear and mistrust about being mistreated or improperly labeled by mental health professionals

(Aklin & Turner, 2006). Such differences appear to be attributable to biases of clinicians more than to differences in objective criteria.

CULTURAL SENSITIVITY AND CULTURAL COMPETENCE   There can be several possible reasons that clinical interviewers might overdiagnose or underdiagnose psychological disorders among persons from different ethnic groups, but one of them is certainly lack of knowledge. If unaware of cultural variations, a clinician might misinterpret an African American client's reluctance to reveal symptoms as evidence of paranoid ideation rather than as caution or suspiciousness about the mental health system. A clinician might mistakenly assume that an Asian client's reluctance to disclose is evidence of resistance or lack of insight rather than a cultural prohibition against immediate self-disclosure to strangers.

In Chapter 3, we introduced the idea of culture-bound syndromes—those that do not fit neatly into DSM diagnoses. A specific example is *ataque de nervios*, a syndrome that occurs largely among Hispanic groups and is characterized by anxiety and somatic symptoms. Although it is similar to some DSM diagnoses, it is not identical (Tolin et al., 2007). It is important that interviewers and therapists-in-training recognize cultural variations in the expression of distress. Misunderstanding of the meaning of spoken and body language seems to be an especially important problem. For instance, compared to European Americans, Asian clients are more likely to express psychological complaints in terms of somatic symptoms such as nausea, faint vision, and vertigo (Hsu & Folstein, 1997). Such culture-specific symptoms may not be attributable to significantly higher rates of somatoform disorder among Asian people but rather to their cultural belief that it is more acceptable to use somatic terms to convey emotional distress. In short, cultural differences in how symptoms are displayed can easily lead clinicians to misinterpret or misdiagnose (Li, Jenkins, & Grewal 2012; Ross, Schroeder, & Ness, 2013).

Cultural values such as independence versus interdependence also can affect interviews. Among persons from Hispanic and Asian cultures, independence may not be as strongly valued as it is among those from Western European cultures. Interdependence and family obligations may be assigned greater value instead. So interviewers who pursue questioning that seems to imply the value of emotional or psychological independence may unwittingly be alienating their interviewees who sense that the interviewer disapproves of one of their core values.

What should interviewers do when faced with possible cultural issues? It is unrealistic for interviewers to be familiar with *all* the possible cultural variations in interview behavior (and discussion of these is beyond the scope of this text), but it is possible for clinicians to have a reasonably thorough understanding of how interview conclusions can be distorted by ethnic and cultural misunderstandings. Interviewers can improve their cultural competency and avoid bias by educating themselves about the more common cultural variations in interviewing behaviors and those related to the specific ethnic backgrounds of clients they interview. When confronted with situations that might involve cultural misunderstanding, interviewers should openly explore cultural concerns with the client, thereby conveying a sincere desire to understand, rather than just classify, the client. They should also recognize their own limitations and seek consultation and assistance from colleagues with more expertise in working with particular kinds of clients. The American Psychological Association's (2002) *Guidelines on Multicultural Education, Training, Research, Practice, and Organizational Change for Psychologists* and other readings (e.g., Sue & Sue, 2008) are designed to guide psychologists' training in, and practice of, cultural sensitivity as well as to develop a core understanding of the challenges raised by cultural diversity.

Research on multicultural issues in clinical assessment is growing rapidly. The professional literature now contains studies of such topics as: is the borderline personality disorder subscale of the Structured Clinical Interview for *DSM-IV* Axis II Personality disorders valid for Cantonese-speaking Chinese? (Wong & Chow, 2011); what criteria should be used by people who are responsible for assessing the adequacy of trainee's cross-cultural training? (Lanik & Mitchell-Gibbons, 2011); and how might psychological service delivery be improved for refugee populations? (Kaczorowski et al., 2011). Again, practicing clinicians are not expected to have an encyclopedic knowledge of every culture-specific situation, but they are expected to know when their knowledge of multicultural assessment is sufficient to establish competency, and if not, what steps to take to enhance it.

SECTION SUMMARY

Clinical interviews are undertaken to establish the nature of someone's problem, assign a DSM diagnosis, prepare interviewees to participate in treatment or research, address a specific referral question, debrief after a significant event, or at termination of treatment or research, and offer support and intervention in a crisis. Often, several of these goals are combined in an interview. As the U.S. population becomes more diverse, clinicians should be especially sensitive to how cultural or ethnic factors can bias interviews. Doing so involves both didactic education and supervised training.

INTERVIEW STRUCTURE

SECTION PREVIEW

The most fundamental feature of clinical interviews is their structure: the degree to which the interviewer determines the content and course of the conversation. At one end of the structure continuum are open-ended, nondirective, *or* unstructured interviews *in which the clinician does as little as possible to interfere with the natural flow of the client's speech and choice of topics. At the other end are* structured interviews, *which involve a carefully planned question-and-answer format. In between are many blends, usually called* guided *or* semistructured interviews. *While structured interviews are increasingly popular, partly because of their greater reliability and validity, they also have some disadvantages.*

Several factors influence the degree of structure in an interview; among them are the theoretical orientation and personal preferences of the interviewer. In general, humanistic clinicians tend to establish the least interview structure. Psychodynamically oriented clinicians usually provide more, while cognitive-behavioral clinicians are likely to be the most verbally active and directive. Structure may also change during an interview—many interviewers begin in a nondirective way and become more structured as the interview continues. The interview situation also strongly affects the degree of structure. For instance, by their nature, crises demand more structure than might be desirable during a routine intake interview.

Nondirective Interviews

Consider first this segment from a nondirective intake interview.

CLINICIAN: [Your relative] didn't go into much detail about what you wanted to talk about, so I wonder if you'd just start in at whatever you want to start in with, and tell me what kind of nervousness you have.

CLIENT: Well, it's, uh, I think if I were to put it in, in a few words, it seems to be a, a, a complete lack of self-confidence in, and an extreme degree of self-consciousness. Now, I have always been a very self-conscious person. I mean ever, just about, since I was probably 14 years old the first I remember of it. But for a long time I've realized that I was sort of using people as crutches. I mean I, a lot of things I felt I couldn't do myself I did all right if someone was along.

CLINICIAN: Um-hm.

CLIENT: And it's just progressed to the point where I'm actually using the four walls of the house as an escape from reality. I mean I don't, I don't care to go out. I, I certainly can't go out alone. It's sort of a vicious circle. I find out I can't do it, and then I'm sure the next time I can't do it.

CLINICIAN: Um-hm.

CLIENT: And it just gets progressively worse. I think the first that I ever noticed it. . . . (Wallen, 1956, p. 146)

The client continued a narrative about the onset and duration of her problems, her occupation and marriage, her father's death, and other topics. Notice that the clinician hardly says a word, although as we shall see later, there are things he could have done to nondirectively encourage the client to talk had it been necessary. The nondirective interviewer uses direct questions sparingly and relies instead on responses designed to facilitate the client's talking about his or her concerns.

Semistructured Interviews

Compare this nondirective approach to the following semistructured interview in which an organized set of topics is explored in a way that gives the interviewer flexibility in wording questions, interpreting answers, and guiding decisions about what to address next.

CLINICIAN: You're telling me that you get mad all of a sudden, that anger just seems to explode out of you without warning.

CLIENT: Well yeah, it seems so sudden. It scares me, and I know it scares other people too 'cause I can see how they react.

CLINICIAN: You don't want to frighten other people, have them walk on egg shells, but you know they do.

CLIENT: It's like I'm a child at times. I hate it, hate how it pushes people away.

CLINICIAN: What is your idea of how you should feel in those situations?

CLIENT: I don't know. I should be in control. I guess there's reasons for it, after all the stress and all, but a man should be able to control his temper. I even tell my kids that. . . I'm such a hypocrite.

CLINICIAN: So you've got a few things going on at once. You get angry easily, it comes on suddenly. After it comes out, you feel ashamed because you think you ought to be able to control it. And then you're concerned about scaring the people you're close to, pushing those people away.

CLIENT: Yeah, I want to be able to relax, take things in stride, but I'm not that person now.

Notice the nondirective features in this excerpt—the clinician's responses conveyed an understanding of the client's experience and encouraged further talk but did not dictate what the client talked about by requesting specific information. However, the interviewer also placed limits on the topic by asking a specific question. The more specific questions the interviewer asks, the more structure he or she imposes on the interview.

Semistructured interviews have been developed for a variety of clinical purposes, most of them involving assessment of specific conditions or situations. For example, the *Crisis Intervention Semistructured Interview* was developed to help trained clinicians and novices interview clients in crisis situations. Information from the interview is used to provide a standardized method of arriving at intervention decisions (Kulic, 2005). A second example is the *Clinician Home-based Interview to Assess Function* (CHIF), a semistructured interview used to assess functioning in the elderly who show signs of dementia (Hendrie et al., 2006).

Structured Interviews

In structured interviews, the interviewer asks a series of specific questions phrased in a standardized fashion and presented in an established order. Consistent rules are also provided for coding or scoring the clients' answers or for using additional probes to elicit further scoreable responses. Thus, while structured interviews do not outlaw open-ended questions or prohibit interviewers from formulating their own questions to clarify ambiguous responses, they do provide detailed rules (sometimes called *decision trees* or *branching rules*) that tell the interviewer what to do in certain situations (e.g., "if the respondent answers no, skip to question 32; if the respondent answers yes, inquire as to how many times it happened and continue to the next question").

As an example of a fully structured interview, consider the Diagnostic Interview Schedule for *DSM-IV* (DIS-IV; Robins et al., 2000). Designed for use by professionals or nonprofessionals, this interview specifies all the questions and probes (i.e., follow-up questions in response to client statements). The interviewer is not supposed to deviate from the prescribed structure. As a result, this interview can be administered by a person or a computer. The interviewer asks whether respondents have experienced each of a variety of psychological symptoms, and if so, for how long and how recently. Because this is a fairly broad assessment (i.e., wide bandwidth) originally designed for use in epidemiological research, it can take from 90 to 150 minutes to complete (Segal, Mueller, & Coolidge, 2012). There are many other structured and semistructured interviews that, like the DIS-IV, are designed to help clinicians arrive at psychiatric diagnoses by asking questions relevant to specific *DSM* diagnostic criteria. Some examples are shown in Table 4.3. To stay current, the DIS-IV and other structured interviews that rely on *DSM* classification will have to be updated to accommodate the changes made in *DSM-5*.

Advantages and Disadvantages of Structured Interviews

In recent years, structured and semistructured interviews have been used increasingly in a variety of clinical situations (Machado, Beutler, Harwood, Mohr, & Lenore 2011; Segal, Mueller, & Coolidge 2012). This proliferation has occurred even though structured interviews eliminate much of the flexibility of open-ended interviews; they prescribe conversation topics and constrain client answers. So why are structured interviews so popular?

The answer comes largely from the fact that structured interviews provide a systematic way of assessing the variables that interviews are designed to explore. In other words, though they may not be as flexible, they are less prone to error. To understand why, you must understand the sources of error that can affect interviews (Ward, Beck, Mendelson, Mock, & Erbaugh 1962).

One source of error, *client variance*, occurs when the same client provides different answers or displays different behaviors in response to the same questions asked by different clinicians. A second source of error, *information variance*, refers to differences in the way clinicians ask questions or make observations. For instance, if two clinicians do not ask questions the same way, they might receive different answers from a client. Consider these two questions: "Do you get anxious whenever you are in crowded places such as malls?" and "What situations seem to make you the most anxious?" Finally, there is *criterion variance*, which refers to disagreements that occur if clinicians apply different standards of judgment to the same set of client responses. For instance, different clinicians might use different cutoff points or inference rules for what a response means (e.g., what types of responses indicate "significant impairment"). In short, it appears that much of clinicians' disagreements come not from inconsistencies in client responses but from inconsistencies in clinicians' collection and use of those responses (Ward, Beck, Mendelson, Mock, & Erbaugh 1962).

Structured interviews are a mainstay in clinical research because they help reduce variance in clinicians' information gathering, recall, and judgment. The increasing use of structured interviews by clinicians parallels other trends in the history of clinical assessment. As noted in Chapter 3, for

TABLE 4.3 Structured Interviews Frequently Used in Clinical Psychology

Name of Interview	Reference	Purpose
The Schedule for Affective Disorders & Schizophrenia (SADS)	Endicott & Spitzer (1978)	Semistructured interview for differential diagnosis of mood and psychotic mental disorder
Diagnostic Interview Schedule (DIS-IV)	Robins, Wing, Wittchen, Helzer, Babor, et al. (1998)	Extensive structured interview with several modules used in large-scale epidemiological studies; Chinese and Spanish versions available
Structured Clinical Interview for *DSM-IV* Axis I Disorders (SCID)	First, Spitzer, Gibbon, & Williams (1997)	Semistructured interview covering broad-scale differential diagnoses tied to *DSM-IV* criteria; versions for clinical and for research use
Diagnostic Interview Schedule for Children, Revised (DISC-R)	Shaffer, Fisher, Lucas, Dulcan, & Schwab-Stone (2000)	Parallel formats for children and parents for making differential diagnoses of disorders of childhood and adolescence
Composite International Diagnostic Interview (CIDI-2)	World Health Organization— Alcohol, Drug, and Mental Health Administration (1997)	Many of the same items as the DIS but with modifications to improve cross-cultural use
International Personality Disorder Examination (IPDE)	Loranger & Cloninger (1999)	Differential diagnoses among *DSM III* personality disorders; module available for *DSM-IV*
Structured Clinical Interview for Axis II Personality Disorders (SCID-II)	First, Gibbon, Spitzer, Williams, & Benjamin (1997)	Semistructured interview for *DSM-IV* personality disorders; combined SCID and SCID-II are designed to provide a comprehensive diagnostic assessment interview
Psychopathy Checklist (PCL-R)	Hare (2003)	Semistructured interview consisting of structured questions and optional probes for evaluating antisocial functioning
Rogers Criminal Responsibility Assessment Scale (RCRAS)	Rogers, Wasyliw, & Cavanaugh (1984)	Assesses criminal responsibility against specific legal criteria

example, using formal, statistical rules for combining assessment data is usually more effective than relying on clinicians' subjective judgments. Structured interviews are designed to make the data collection process more consistent by standardizing how information is gathered. Empirically driven decision rules can also replace, or at least improve, clinicians' judgments.

At the same time, however, there are limitations to structured interviews. Clinicians who depend too much on structured interviews risk becoming so "protocol bound" that they miss important information that the interview script did not explore. This is another example of the "bandwidth versus fidelity" trade-off described in Chapter 3. Training in a variety of interview techniques combined with a careful analysis of the goals of the assessment can help clinicians remain open to information that was not obvious at initial referral.

The most frequently voiced complaint about structured interviews is that their routinized nature can alienate clients (Segal, Mueller, & Coolidge, 2012). This is especially likely if the clinician does not first establish rapport, fails to explain fully the rationale behind the use of the structured format, or becomes so focused on structured interview assessment that the client feels the interview is more problem-centered than person-centered. So just as in the old medical joke ("the operation was successful but the patient died"), it is possible that in psychological assessment "the diagnosis was impeccable but the client fled treatment" (Segal, Mueller, & Coolidge, 2012, p. 97).

To avoid this situation, clinicians must remember to enhance rapport by using their interaction skills before, during, and after structured interviews. For instance, early in an interview, a clinician might preview the structured interview segment by saying something like, "I want to make sure we clarify your major concerns today, so to begin with, I'd like you to tell me what brought you here. Later, if we get into an area that is particularly important or troubling for you, I might ask a series of questions designed to get a more detailed picture of that problem. OK?" When the time comes for the structured or semistructured interview format, the clinician might introduce it by saying something like, "It seems that depression has been a major problem for you lately, so I'd like to ask you some questions to help us better understand the depth of this problem and how we might plan to fix it."

A final limitation is that, like all other interviews, structured interviews depend heavily on the memory, candor, and descriptive abilities of respondents. So while the reliability of clients' reports (or of different clinicians' inferences from those reports) might be excellent, the validity or meaning of structured interview data can be threatened if the client misunderstands questions, is not motivated to answer truthfully, or cannot recall relevant information.

Because both the questions and the inference rules of structured interviews are scripted, they can be conducted by professional clinicians, trained nonprofessionals, or as noted earlier, by computers (Groth-Marnat, 2003; Peters, Clark, & Carroll, 1998; Pilkonis et al., 1995; Reich, Cottler, McCallum, & Corwin, 1995). Researchers have also investigated whether structured and semistructured interviews can be effectively conducted using (a) experienced interviewers with no formal clinical training (Brugha, Nienhuis, Bagchi, Smith, & Meltzer, 1999); (b) the telephone (Cacciola, Alterman, Rutheford, McKay, & May, 1999; Lyneham & Rapee, 2005); and (c) self-administered questionnaires (Erickson & Kaplan, 2000). Some clinicians worry, though, that interview quality might be compromised by permitting less well-trained interviewers or automated administrations. As a general rule, the less structured the interview, the more training and experience are required to obtain reliable and valid results.

However structured interviews are administered, it is important to remember that they are most easily applied to clinical tasks that have well-defined decision-making criteria, such as diagnosis. There are no structured interviews available for most face-to-face clinical contact hours, such as therapy interviews. As a result, the unstructured interview remains the most common tool used by clinical psychologists on a day-to-day basis (Garb, 2007). So despite trends toward increasing the structure of many clinical interactions, clinicians still need a broad base of skills to manage the various stages of all types of interviews.

SECTION SUMMARY

Nondirective or open-ended interviews are those in which the clinician and client jointly determine the content and flow of the interview. At the other extreme are structured interviews, which involve a carefully planned question-and-answer format. In between are blends, usually called semistructured interviews. Structured and semistructured interviews have higher reliability and validity when the purpose of the interview involves judgments that have relatively clear-cut decision criteria, such as making a diagnosis. The disadvantages associated with structured interviews include the restrictions in the interview format that may result in failure to identify important content. If not handled appropriately by the clinician, the use of highly structured interviews can also inhibit rapport.

STAGES IN THE INTERVIEW

SECTION PREVIEW

In the following sections, we examine techniques commonly employed by clinical psychologists during the beginning, middle, and end stages of interviews. Certain features, such as establishing and maintaining rapport, communicating the goals or purpose of the interview, demonstrating good listening skills, and providing emotional support, are common to most interviews. Others, such as whether to use a structured or unstructured format, for instance, depend on the goals of the interview. Both clinicians and clients must interpret verbal and nonverbal behavior during an interview, so it is important that clinicians are sensitive to various ways in which their communication can be misinterpreted. Sensitivity to differences of interpretation is especially important when clients come from cultural or ethnic backgrounds that differ from the interviewer's.

Interviews usually begin with efforts at making the client comfortable and ready to speak freely (stage 1), continue into a central information-gathering stage (stage 2), and end with summary statements, client questions, and, if appropriate, plans for additional assessment sessions (stage 3). Stage 2, generally the longest one, can often be further subdivided into different stages or phases. Although not all clinical interviews are organized around a beginning–middle–end framework (Craig, 2009), the three-stage model offers a convenient guide for our discussion of typical clinical interviews. There is no single "right" way to conduct an interview, but certain strategies have proven valuable in practice and have thus been adopted by skilled clinicians representing every theoretical approach (Goldfried, 1980).

Stage 1: Beginning the Interview

In one sense, the interview begins prior to meeting the client as the clinician processes the referral. Sometimes, the clinician has only a client's general complaint, perhaps voiced to a secretary at the time of a self-referral. Other times, medical, school, court, or other mental health records may be available. Such information can help the clinician to decide whether specific interviewing or testing materials might be needed (e.g., structured interview or unstructured interview formats).

THE SETTING   Certain settings are especially conducive to building rapport. Except for clients whose cultural background might cause such surroundings to be threatening, interviews are best conducted in a comfortable, private office because most people find it easier to relax when they are physically comfortable. Also, privacy makes it easier to assure the client of the interview's confidential nature.

Several other office characteristics can aid rapport. A reassuring equality is established when two people sit a few feet apart on similar chairs of equal height. If the clinician sits in a massive, high-backed chair behind a huge desk placed 6 feet from the client's smaller, lower seat, rapport may be impaired. A desk cleared of other work, along with precautions to hold phone calls and prevent other intrusions, makes it clear that the clinician is fully attentive and sincerely interested in what the client has to say. Personal effects, such as pictures of family and favored vacation spots, add personal warmth. Interviewers should probably avoid decorations that make bold statements about views because these might alienate some clients (e.g., a big poster or life-size cutout of your favorite celebrity). It is the client's self-expression, not the interviewer's, that should have priority. The list of rapport-building techniques could be extended almost indefinitely; the point is that from the beginning, the clinician should try to create a warm, comfortable environment that encourages the client to speak freely and honestly about whatever topics are relevant to the interview.

THE OPENING   It is important that clinicians handle the first few minutes of initial interviews carefully. This early stage is important because clients may not be ready to talk candidly about personal matters yet, preferring instead to take a wait-and-see approach in which they carefully control what they say and don't say. If this reserved attitude prevails throughout the interview, the clinician is unlikely to gather very much valuable assessment information.

Accordingly, most clinicians see establishing rapport as their main task during the first part of initial interviews. Rapport can be built in several ways, many of which involve common sense and courtesy. A client's anxiety and uncertainty can be eased by demystifying the interview. Upon greeting, a warm smile, a friendly hello, an introduction (e.g., "I'm Doctor Jenkins"), and a handshake are excellent beginnings to an interview. Small talk about the weather or difficulty in finding the office also eases the client's transition into the interview. The skilled interviewer relaxes the client by appearing warm and approachable. But this informal rapport building should not go on so long that the interview loses its distinctive quality or the client begins to suspect that the interviewer might wish to avoid the topics that prompted the interview. The interviewer should get down to business within the first few minutes, thereby communicating that the client's time and problems are important. Skilled clinicians can establish remarkable rapport during the first stage of an initial interview, but even for them, the process continues into the second and third stages and into subsequent sessions as well.

FRAME SETTING AND TRANSITION   Another task that typically accompanies the opening of an interview is called *frame setting*. The frame refers to the norms and expectations that surround an interview, consultation, or therapy session (Walter, Bundy, & Dornan, 2005). When clinicians set the frame, they explain to the client the basic ground rules for the interaction. For example, after introductions and a brief period of small talk, the clinician might say something like the following (items in brackets would be replaced by mention of client's specific symptoms or complaints or with case-specific elaboration):

> We'll have an hour and a half to work together today. During that time, I hope we can talk about [the problems you've been having], maybe get a better handle on how and when these problems began, and how they are affecting you now. My job is mostly to listen at this point, to try to understand [your situation]. As we continue, I might also ask you a set of questions and write some things down to study later. This information should help us understand and also develop a plan of action for [addressing your symptoms]. Our conversation is confidential—what we talk about stays in this room. The exceptions to this are [here the interviewer might elaborate on limits of confidentiality such as if the client is an imminent threat of harm to himself or others, what information will go to third parties such as insurance companies or referral sources, etc.]. Please feel free to ask any questions you like; I'll do my best to answer them. If we don't complete all that we hope to today—that happens sometimes—we can continue during the next appointment.

Setting the frame clarifies time boundaries for the interview session, expresses an expectation about what will be covered and what basic roles the participants will take, and briefly introduces the idea of a structure. It also provides assurances of confidentiality as well as its limits and conveys information about the interviewer's commitment. Notice also the interviewer's use of "we," which is designed to enlist the interviewee as an ally in exploring the problem. This introduction of the frame could occur before or after discussion of the client's troubles has begun in earnest, but it should occur relatively early in the interview. Not all aspects of the frame need be introduced at once. Some topics might be discussed more fully later in the interview or during subsequent meetings as framework issues reemerge, as they frequently do in therapy (especially with clients diagnosed with particular disorders, such as borderline personality disorder for example).

In most cases, interviewers begin the transition into the second stage of the interview with nondirective, *open-ended* questions. Common examples are "So what brings you here today?" or "Would you like to tell me something about the problems you referred to on the phone?" A major advantage of this approach is that it allows a client to begin in his or her own way. An open-ended invitation to talk allows the client to ease into painful or embarrassing topics without feeling coerced and lets clients know that the clinician is ready to listen. Clients often begin with a "ticket of admission" problem that may not be the one of greatest concern to them. The real reason for the visit may appear only after they have "tested the water" with varying amounts of diversionary conversation.

Stage 2: The Middle of the Interview

Transition to the middle of an interview should be as smooth as possible. In the transition and frame setting, the therapist signals whether the therapist or the client will be the main director of the interview topics. These signals continue as the interview progresses. At one extreme are open-ended or nondirective techniques, which allow the client great freedom to direct the conversation. At the other extreme are close-ended or directive techniques, which signal that it will be the therapist who largely directs the conversation. As our previous discussion implies, directive techniques are used extensively in structured interviews. Accordingly, the following information refers mainly to clinical interviews that do not use structured instruments. Here are some ways in which the interviewer provides signals about who will lead the conversation.

NONDIRECTIVE TECHNIQUES   Open-ended questions are used whenever the clinician wishes to prompt clients to speak while exerting as little influence as possible over what they say. Classic remarks like "Tell me more about that" and "How did you feel about that?" exemplify nondirective strategies. These strategies are supplemented by tactics designed to help clients express themselves fully and to enhance rapport by communicating the clinician's understanding and acceptance. The most general of these tactics is called *active listening*, which involves responding to the client's speech in ways that indicate understanding and encourage further elaboration. Active listening was represented in the clinician's "um-hms" in the nondirective interview excerpt presented earlier.

Other signs of active listening include comments such as "I see," "I'm with you," "Right," or even just a nodding of the head.

A related nondirective strategy is called *paraphrasing* in which clinicians restate what their clients say in order to (a) show that they are listening closely and (b) give the clients a chance to correct the remark if it was misinterpreted. Carl Rogers called this strategy *reflection* and emphasized the importance of not only restating content but also highlighting client feelings. Consider these examples.

Example A

CLIENT: Sometimes, I could just kill my husband.

CLINICIAN: You would just like to get rid of him altogether.

Example B

CLIENT: Sometimes, I could just kill my husband.

CLINICIAN: He really upsets you sometimes.

Both are reflective responses, but notice that in example A, the clinician merely reworded the client's remark, and in example B, the clinician reflected the feeling contained in the remark. Most clients respond to paraphrasing by continuing to talk, usually along the same lines as before, often in greater detail. Paraphrasing often is preferable to direct questioning because such questioning tends to change or restrict the conversation, as illustrated in the following interaction.

CLIENT: What it comes down to is that life just doesn't seem worth living sometimes.

CLINICIAN: How often do you feel that way?

CLIENT: Oh, off and on.

There is a place for questions like this one, but unless the clinician knows enough about the general scope of a problem to start pinpointing specifics, interrupting with such questions is likely to limit, and even distort, the assessment picture. Clients who are hit with direct queries early in a nondirective interview may conclude that they should wait for the next question rather than spontaneously tell their story. For many clients, this experience can be frustrating and damaging to rapport. In effect, such behavior invokes the common *doctor–patient interview schema:* The doctor (psychologist) asks questions and the patient (interviewee) answers and then passively waits for the next question. While this format is appropriate for some situations, such as structured interviews, it is not as effective in drawing clients out and encouraging them to be active participants/explorers in solving their own problems.

Paraphrasing can also be helpful when the clinician is confused about what a client has said. Consider the following:

CLIENT: I told my husband that I didn't want to live with him anymore, so he said "fine" and left. Well, when I got back, I found out that the son of a bitch kept all our furniture!

Most clinicians would have a hard time deciphering the sequence of events described here, but if they say "What?" the client might be put off or assume that the clinician is a dunce. Instead, a combination of paraphrase and request for clarification serves nicely:

CLINICIAN: Okay, let's see if I've got this straight. You told your husband you didn't want to live with him, so he left. You later came back to your house from somewhere else and found he had taken the furniture. Is that right?

Ideally, the client will either confirm this interpretation or fill in the missing pieces. If not, the clinician may wish to use more direct questioning.

DIRECTIVE TECHNIQUES   Most interviewers supplement nondirective tactics with more directive questions whose form, wording, and content are often the result of careful (though often on-the-spot) planning. Consider the following illustrative questions:

A.   Do you feel better or worse when your husband is out of town?

B.   How do you feel when your husband is out of town?

Example A offers a clear, but possibly irrelevant, two-choice situation. This is a version of the "Do you walk to work or carry your lunch?" question for which the most valid answer may be "Neither." Some clients are not assertive enough in an interview to ignore the choice, so they settle for one unsatisfactory response or the other. Unless there is a special reason for offering clients only a few response alternatives, skilled interviewers ask direct questions in a form that gets at specific information but also leaves clients free to choose their own words.

Along the same lines, experienced clinicians also avoid asking questions that suggest their own answers. Notice the implications contained in this query: "You've suffered with this problem a long time?" Such questions communicate what the interviewer expects to hear, and some clients will oblige by biasing their response. "How long have you had this problem?" is a better alternative.

NONVERBAL COMMUNICATION   As in all human communication, a constant stream of nonverbal behavior accompanies clients' and interviewers' verbal behavior. Indeed, the nonverbal communication channel usually remains open even when the verbal channel shuts down. Since both members of an interview dyad are sending and receiving nonverbal messages, clinicians must be sensitive not only to incoming signals but also to those they transmit. Table 4.4 presents aspects of clients' nonverbal communication that tend to be of greatest interest to clinicians during interviews.

In addition to noting nonverbal client behaviors, clinicians look for inconsistencies between the verbal and nonverbal channels. The statement "I feel pretty good today" will be viewed differently if the client is on the verge of tears than if the client is showing a happy smile.

Interviewers also try to coordinate their own verbal and nonverbal behavior to convey unambiguous messages to their clients. A client will perceive the message to "take your time" in talking about a sensitive topic as more genuine if the clinician says it slowly and quietly than if it is accompanied by a glance at the clock. Similarly, friendly eye contact, some head nodding, an occasional smile, and an attentive posture let the client know that the interviewer is listening closely. Overdoing it may backfire, however. A plastered-on smile, a continuously knitted brow, sidelong glances, and other theatrics are more likely to convey interviewer anxiety or inexperience than concern.

Clinicians differ as to what they think their clients' nonverbal behavior means. For example, a behaviorist's interpretation of increased respiration, perspiration, and fidgeting while a client talks about sex would probably be that emotional arousal is associated with that topic. Psychodynamic interviewers may infer more, postulating perhaps that nonverbal behaviors (e.g., twirling a ring on a finger) are symbolic representations of sexual activity. Gestalt therapists might suspect that the client is avoiding awareness of unpleasant feelings associated with the belief that he or she is just "going round in circles." Alfred Adler interpreted where clients choose to sit: "One moves toward the desk; that is favorable. Another moves away; that is unfavorable" (Adler, 1933). Whatever they might infer from it, most clinicians believe that nonverbal behavior serves as a powerful communication channel and a valuable source of interview data.

TABLE 4.4 Channels of Nonverbal Communications

1. Physical appearance—height, weight, grooming, style and condition of clothing, unusual characteristics, muscular development, hairstyle
2. Movements—gestures; repetitive arm, hand, head, leg, or foot motions; tics or other apparently involuntary movements; pacing; handling of cigarettes, matches, or other objects
3. Posture—slouching, rigidity, crossed or uncrossed arms or legs, head in hands
4. Eye contact—constant, fleeting, none
5. Facial expressions—smiles, frowns, grimaces, raised eyebrows
6. Emotional arousal—tears, wet eyes, sweating, dryness of lips, frequent swallowing, blushing or paling, voice or hand tremor, rapid respiration, frequent shifts in body position, startle reactions, inappropriate laughter
7. Speech variables—tone of voice, speed, slurring, lisp, stuttering, blocking, accent, clarity, style, sudden shifts or omissions

In addition to concerns about aspects of interviewing that we have covered in this chapter, clinicians face many other interview-related challenges. Dealing with silences, how to address the client, handling personal questions from clients, note taking and recording, and confronting a client's inconsistencies are just a few of these. If you are interested in a more detailed exploration of interviewing issues and techniques, consult the sources cited in the introduction of this chapter.

COMBINING INTERVIEW TACTICS   Because interviews can be flexible, clinicians are usually free to combine the tactics we have described. They may facilitate the client's speech with open-ended requests, paraphrasing, prompts, and other active listening techniques, and then use more directive questions to "zoom in" on topics of special importance. However, directive procedures do not take over completely as interviews progress. They continue to be mixed with less directive tactics. An example of this blending is provided by the concept of *repeated scanning and focusing* in which interviewers first scan a topic nondirectively, then focus on it in a more directive fashion:

CLINICIAN: You mentioned that you tend to avoid crowds. Can you tell me more about that?

CLIENT: Well, I don't like to be in crowds, like at Christmas in a mall or something. And I tend to avoid parties, even though I sometimes make myself go.

CLINICIAN: So being around a lot of people makes you uncomfortable?

CLIENT: Yeah, I sometimes get this worried, panicky feeling, and I'm afraid that I'll say something stupid, make a fool myself.

CLINICIAN: So can you describe that worry for me, what happens in your body, what you think about, what you do?

CLIENT: It just comes over me, I get nervous and think that I should get out of that situation. If I'm in a crowd, I'll just leave, maybe go to my car and sit by myself for a while. If I'm at a party, I'll find a bathroom or something and hide out for a while, maybe slip out and go for a walk. I don't know how other people do it; I just don't know how else to act.

CLINICIAN: How would you compare social situations when you are required to interact with people to those when you are with people but don't have to interact with them, like in a crowd?

The interviewer might go on to explore several specific aspects of the client's anxiety in social situations then move on to another topic, again beginning with scanning procedures and later moving on to more direct questions. Clinicians can accomplish a lot by periodically summarizing their impressions. Consider the following example:

CLINICIAN: I wonder if you could say a little more about what your binge eating episodes are like.

CLIENT: You mean, like what I'm thinking about, what I feel?

CLINICIAN: That's right.

CLIENT: Well, it's like a movie, only I'm in it and I have to play this part. Unfortunately, the part I play is this pathetic, ugly person who keeps shoving food in her face. I know that people will think I'm fat, but I can't stop myself.

CLINICIAN: Does this feeling last after the binge episode as well?

CLIENT: Well, yeah. It goes a long time after, even if I take laxatives or something. Like a day after the last one, I went out with my roommate and this guy seemed to be interested in me, but all I can think is that he can't possibly be.

CLINICIAN: And so while you are binge-eating, it's almost like there is a part of you outside yourself, watching it all happen, but helpless to stop it. And afterward, you feel ashamed, you hate yourself, and you're even more convinced that you are ugly. And if a man seems to find you attractive, it puzzles you more than anything because you see yourself as so unattractive.

CLIENT: Yes, that's just how I feel.

Stage 3: Closing the Interview

The last stage of an interview can provide valuable assessment data as well as an opportunity to enhance rapport. The interviewer may initiate the third stage with a statement like this:

> We have been covering some very valuable information here, and I appreciate your willingness to tell me about it. I know our session hasn't been easy for you. Since we're running out of time for today, I thought we could look back over what we've covered and then give you a chance to ask *me* some questions.

The clinician accomplishes several things here. First, the impending conclusion of the interview is signaled (frame setting). Second, the client is praised for cooperativeness and reassured that the clinician recognized how stressful the interview was (emotional support). Third, the suggested plan for the final minutes invites the client to ask questions or make comments that may be important but had not been put into words.

Sometimes, the last stage of an interview evokes clinically significant behavior or information. For example, suppose that a client said, "Oh gosh, look at the time. I have to hurry to my lawyer's office or I won't be able to find out until Monday whether I get custody of my son." Some clients wait until the end of the interview to reveal this kind of information because they want the clinician to know about it, but they were not yet ready to discuss it. Others might just let such information slip out because the interview "feels" over and they let down the defenses they had been using earlier. Some simply don't want the interview to end. For these reasons, the clinician attaches as much importance to the final stage of the interview as to the stages that precede it. However, because the clinician is responsible for monitoring the boundaries—in this case, time constraints—a comment such as the following might be in order:

> You must be on pins and needles waiting to find out. That seems so important—custody of your son. We didn't talk about that today, but maybe next time we can, or we can make another appointment if you like. I hope things turn out well for you.

Through such a response, the therapist expresses empathy, points out in a nonpunitive way that the client omitted this information from discussion, and invites further discussion later.

SECTION SUMMARY

Interview techniques commonly employed by clinical psychologists during the beginning, middle, and end stages of the interview include nondirective and directive communication. The former is particularly helpful early on in establishing rapport, while the latter, similar to that used in structured interviews, can help elicit and clarify specific areas the interviewer wishes to explore. Rapport can also be enhanced by a number of clinical behaviors such as compassionate and reflective responding, frame setting, and attention to verbal and nonverbal cues. It is important that clinicians are sensitive to various ways their communication can be misinterpreted, particularly when clients come from cultural or ethnic backgrounds different from their own.

RESEARCH ON THE INTERVIEW

SECTION PREVIEW

As the primary tool of clinicians, interviews are often rich sources of data. They are also complex social interactions that can be interpreted in a variety of ways. Therefore, clinicians need to be aware of all potential sources of interview error, including their own biases. Overall, the reliability and validity of unstructured interviews suffer compared with the reliability and validity of more structured interviews, but proper training and sensitivity to sources of error can maximize the value of interviews as a rich source of clinical assessment information.

The fundamental objective in interview communication—as in all human communication—is to encode, transmit, and decode messages accurately. Speakers must encode what they want to convey into transmittable messages made up of words and gestures, which listeners must receive and decode (interpret) within their personal and cultural frame of reference. Lapses in both verbal and nonverbal communication can occur at many points in this process. To take just the simplest of examples, giving the "thumbs up" sign signals approval to people in the United States, but it says "up yours" in Australia.

Communication and Miscommunication in the Interview

Clinicians attempt to avoid the much more subtle communication problems that can plague interviews by maximizing the clarity of the messages they send to their clients and by clarifying the meaning of the messages received from them. Circumventing such problems in clinical interviews can be facilitated by attention to certain guidelines. Skilled interviewers avoid jargon, ask questions in a straightforward way ("What experiences have you had with masturbation?" not "Do you ever touch yourself?"), and request feedback from their client ("Is all this making sense to you?" or "Did I understand you correctly that . . . ?"). They also try to assure that their verbal behavior conveys patience, concern, and acceptance. Expressing impatience or being judgmental is usually not desirable.

Especially worrisome is the possibility that personal biases might affect interviewers' perceptions and color their inferences and conclusions about what clients say during interviews. The role of such biases was noted nearly 70 years ago in a study showing that social workers' judgments of why "skid-row bums" had become destitute were related to the interviewers' personal agendas, not just to what respondents said (Rice, 1929). Thus, an anti-alcohol interviewer saw drinking as the cause of poverty, while a socialist interviewer concluded that interviewees' plights stemmed from capitalist-generated economic conditions. Similarly, as discussed in Chapter 2, "Clinical Psychology's Past and Present," psychoanalysts and behavior therapists tend to draw different causal conclusions about the behavior problems clients describe during interviews. Indeed, interview-based psychodiagnoses, job interview decisions, and the outcome of medical school–admissions interviews may all be prejudiced by information that interviewers receive about interviewees before the interview (Dipboye, Stramler, & Fontenelle, 1984; Shaw, Martz, Lancaster, & Sade, 1995; Temerlin, 1968).

Other studies conducted in mental health, employment, and other settings have shown that interviewers' judgments can also be affected by clients' ethnicity, the clinician's theoretical orientation, or even the clinician's age (Li, Jenkins, & Grewal 2012; Pottick, Kirk, Hsieh, & Tian 2007). As noted in Chapter 3, clinicians are like other human beings in their tendency to seek and recall information that confirms their preexisting biases. Fortunately, the impact of these factors can be reduced to some extent through training programs that sensitize interviewers to the potential effects of personal biases in interviews.

Reliability and Validity of Interview Data

In the context of interviews, reliability refers to the degree to which clients give the same information on different occasions or to different interviewers, while validity relates to the degree to which interview data or conclusions are accurate. The impact of these factors is of special interest to researchers trying to establish the value of interview data.

RELIABILITY   Researchers study the reliability of interviews by examining the consistency of clients' responses across repeated interview occasions. This procedure measures *test-retest reliability*. They also examine the degree to which different judges agree on the inferences (ratings, diagnoses, or personality trait descriptions) they draw from interviews with the same client, a procedure that measures *interrater reliability*.

One particularly useful research strategy to assess interrater reliability is to have several clinicians view interview videos and then make ratings or draw other inferences from them. This approach has been widely used to establish the reliability of clinicians' judgments about *DSM* diagnoses (Widiger, Frances, Pincus, Davis, & First 1991), therapists' evaluations of clients' progress in therapy (Goins, Strauss, & Martin, 1995), therapists' ratings of the quality of client–therapist alliances following intake interviews with immigrants (Shechtman & Tsegahun, 2004), and in a variety of other situations. A general statement about the reliability or validity of interviews is unwarranted because interviews vary so much in their formats and purposes (Craig, 2009). However, as you might expect, test-retest reliability tends to be highest when the interval between interviews is short and when adult clients are asked for innocuous information such as age and other demographic data (e.g., Ross, Stowe, Wodak, & Gold, 1995). Lower reliability coefficients tend to appear when test-retest intervals are longer, when clients are young children, and when interviewers explore sensitive topics such as illegal drug use, sexual practices, or traumatic experiences (Schwab-Stone, Fallon, & Briggs, 1994; Weiss, Najavits, Muenz, & Hufford 1995; Whitehouse, Orne, & Dinges, 2010).

Of course, it is sensitive rather than innocuous information that is often of greatest interest to clinicians. For this reason, structured interviews are often preferred for eliciting reliable data about more sensitive topics. Overall, the test-retest reliability of the commonly used structured interviews tends to be satisfactory to excellent, even when the most sensitive information is requested for diagnostic or other purposes. For example, test-retest reliability of the Diagnostic Interview Schedule for Children (DISC) is satisfactory (Flisher, Sorsdahl, & Lund, 2012), and the inter rater reliabilities of the scales in the Structured Clinical Interview for *DSM-IV* Axis I and Axis II disorders are moderate to excellent (Lobbestael, Leugrans, & Arntz, 2011).

Reliability also depends on the population on which the instrument was standardized. In other words, an interview method having acceptable reliability with one group (e.g., English-speaking European Americans) might not have acceptable reliability with another group (e.g., Spanish-speaking Hispanic Americans). Fortunately, researchers frequently study and measure the degree to which specific instruments apply to diverse groups. As a result, practicing clinicians can have some confidence that, for example, the DISC can be used reliably with South African children (Flisher, Sorsdahl, & Lund 2012) or that a Spanish-language version of the Eating Disorder Examination Interview has reliability comparable to the version for English-speakers (Grilo, Lorzano, & Elder, 2005). Clinicians should always seek out information about cross-cultural reliability and validity when considering using interview formats or psychological tests with clients from different ethnic and cultural backgrounds.

VALIDITY   The most obvious threats to interview validity occur if clients misremember or purposely distort information. The probability of error or distortion increases when clients are intellectually disabled (e.g., Heal & Sigelman, 1995), suffer from various brain disorders (e.g., West, Bondy, & Hutchinson, 1991), or would prefer not to reveal the truth about their behavior problems, drug use, sexual behavior, criminal activity, or previous hospitalizations (e.g., Morrison, McCusker, Stoddard, & Bigelow, 1995). At the other extreme, clients motivated to appear mentally disturbed may give inaccurate interview responses aimed at suggesting the existence of a mental disorder. Concern about such *malingering* led to the creation of special interview methods aimed at detecting it (Rogers, Gillis, Dickens, & Bagby, 1991). In short, the desire to present oneself in a particular light to a mental health professional—called *impression management* (Braginsky, Braginsky, & Ring, 1969)—can undermine the validity of interview data.

As stated in Chapter 3, validity is established in several ways, such as by including all of the relevant aspects of a target domain (content validity), by comparing interview results with other valid measures of the same concept (concurrent validity), or by evaluating an interview's ability to predict expected future outcomes (predictive validity). The latter two involve selecting an external criterion as the standard against which interview conclusions are measured. That external criterion is sometimes called the *gold standard* (Komiti et al., 2001).

When structured diagnostic interview outlines are first developed, they are often validated against this gold standard of clinical judgment (e.g., Zetin & Glenn, 1999). Sometimes, however, it works the other way around: clinical judgments are validated against the gold standard of established structured interviews (e.g., Komiti et al., 2001). How can we evaluate interviews if they are sometimes validated against clinical judgment and sometimes used as a standard for evaluating clinical judgment?

Data on predictive validity can help. Greater confidence in the value of any assessment tool is warranted when it can reliably predict certain outcomes. Thus, an interview designed to assess clients' responses to therapy can demonstrate predictive validity when it clearly distinguishes those who later drop out of therapy from those who do not. Validity is also enhanced when instruments correlate with several conceptually similar indices *(convergent validity)* or are uncorrelated with measures of conceptually different phenomena *(discriminant validity)*. For example, scores on a structured interview for hypochondriasis should not correlate highly with scores on measures of antisocial personality disorder.

Because there are so many kinds of interviews, no blanket statement about interview validity is warranted. As one distinguished researcher put it, "The interview has been used in so many different ways for various purposes, by individuals with varying skills, that it is a difficult matter to make a final judgment concerning its values" (Garfield, 1974, p. 90). However, in general, the interview formats that have the highest validity are those that are more structured and have been cross-validated using multiple indices, such as those in Table 4.3. In addition, concurrent validity tends to be higher for interviews in which there is evidence of good rapport and clients feel they are being listened to (Nakash & Alegria, 2013).

SECTION SUMMARY

Research on the interview as an assessment tool does not justify all-encompassing conclusions, with the exception that structured interviews generally have higher reliability and validity than unstructured ones and that clinicians should not automatically assume that their interview impressions are valid. Clinicians should be aware of the limitations of interviews especially when working with persons from different backgrounds. Any tendency to view interviews as primarily an art form practiced by gifted clinicians and therefore exempt from scientifically rigorous examinations of reliability and validity will ultimately result in the loss of the interview's utility as an assessment tool.

OBSERVATIONAL ASSESSMENT: GOALS AND BENEFITS

SECTION PREVIEW

Observations occur during interviews, so some of what needs to be said about observation has already been said. But there are also more formal observational assessment techniques that differ from interviews. Clinicians can observe client behaviors that occur naturally in hospitals, schools, homes, and other settings. They can also assess clients by developing contrived situations designed to elicit or assess particular kinds of responses. These techniques can often provide information not otherwise available, especially information about situational determinants of behavior and ecological validity.

Observational methods have been defined as "the *selection, provocation, recording,* and *encoding* of behaviors" (Weick, 1968; italics added). This definition highlights the fundamental elements of nearly every type of observational system. The observer first *selects* people, classes of behavior, events, situations, or time periods to be the focus of attention. Second, a decision is made about whether to *provoke* (i.e., artificially bring about) behaviors and situations of interest or to wait for them to happen on their own. Third, plans are made to *record* observations using observer memory, record sheets, audio or video recording, physiological monitoring systems, timers, counters, or other means. Finally, a system for *encoding* raw observations into usable form must be developed. Encoding is often the most difficult aspect of any observational procedure.

Observational assessment systems are used to (a) collect information that is not available in other ways and/or (b) supplement other data as part of a multiple-assessment approach. For example, if a teacher and a pupil give different reports of why they fail to get along ("He's a brat," "She's mean"), a less biased picture of the relationship will probably emerge from observations by neutral parties of relevant classroom interactions. In other instances, knowing what a person can or will do is so important that only observation can suffice. Thus, knowing that a mentally disturbed person feels better and wishes to leave the hospital may be less valuable than observing that person's ability to hold a job, manage their finances, use the bus system, and meet other demands of everyday life.

Clinicians who place greater emphasis on overt behavior have improved on informal observation methods in at least two ways. First, they developed more accurate and systematic methods for observing and quantifying behavior. Second, they demonstrated the feasibility of collecting observational data in situations beyond the testing or interview room. Together, these developments have made it possible for clinicians and researchers to observe scientifically a wide range of human behavior in a multitude of settings.

Goals of Observational Assessment

Observational methods of assessment developed in parallel with interview methods of assessment. Both were recognized early as rich sources of data about clients, but it became clear that the meaning of observations were too often in the eye of the beholder—different observers saw different things, or they interpreted the meaning of the same observation differently. To remedy this problem, observational assessment methods have become more structured, much as happened with interviews. Most observational techniques now define observational targets (i.e., specific behaviors are to be observed) and specify how those behaviors should be recorded, combined, and interpreted. Many of these *structured observations* were first developed for use in research, but as their reliability, validity, and ease of use has improved, so has their prevalence in clinical practice.

SUPPLEMENTING SELF-REPORTS   Self-reports gathered from interviews and some tests may be inaccurate. It is very difficult for most people to provide objective and dispassionate reports on their own behavior, especially in relation to highly charged emotional events. It is questionable, for example, whether a distressed couple can accurately and objectively describe their own behavior in the relationship, especially behavior that occurs during arguments. Other clients, such as those with dementia, are sometimes unable to give accurate self-reports despite their best efforts to do so. Observational data are likely to provide much more valid information in these situations (Larner, 2005; Lints-Martindale, Hadjistavropoulos, Lix, & Thorpe 2012; Miltenberger & Weil, 2013).

In some cases, clients purposely distort their self-reports, usually by offering an overly positive portrayal of their behavior. Such distortions are particularly common in the self-reports by participants in smoking, drug, or alcohol treatment programs, which is the main reason such reports are often supplemented by family members' observations or by biological measures that can detect target substances. Intentional distortions on personality tests such as the MMPI-2 are so widely recognized that special indicators have been devised to detect when clients do not respond honestly (see Chapter 5, "Testing in Clinical Psychology"). Observational assessment helps correct for self-report errors.

HIGHLIGHTING SITUATIONAL DETERMINANTS OF BEHAVIOR   Much of traditional assessment is guided by the assumption that responses to interviews and tests are adequate for understanding clients' personalities and problems because responses reflect general traits that control behavior. For clinicians adopting this view, observations are seen as *signs* of more fundamental, unobservable constructs. In contrast, clinicians who take a behavioral or cognitive-behavioral view tend to regard observational data as *samples* of behavior that help them understand important *person–situation interactions*. They are less likely to draw inferences about hypothesized personality characteristics or problems presumed to be stable across differing situations and over relatively long time periods. Conducting observation-driven functional analyses allows clinicians to avoid the relatively high levels of inference associated with sign-oriented testing and interviewing approaches. Observational procedures are designed to collect "just the facts," thereby minimizing the likelihood of drawing incorrect inferences about clients. Observational assessments allow the clinician to determine the circumstances under which problematic behaviors are most likely to occur, what situational stimuli tend to trigger the behaviors, and what reinforcing consequences in the situation serve to maintain the unwanted actions (Patterson, 1982). Traditional tests and interviews are not designed to accomplish this kind of functional analysis (Miltenberger & Weil, 2013).

ENHANCING ECOLOGICAL VALIDITY   Because observations can occur in the physical and social environments where clients actually live, observational assessment can provide the clearest possible picture of people and their problems. Not only are these observations likely to be *ecologically valid*, they often provide situational details that help clinicians design treatment programs that can be most easily implemented in the home, school, or work environments. This custom-tailoring of interventions may increase the chances for treatment success.

Limitations of Observational Assessment

Early forms of clinical observation required observers to make decisions and draw inferences about what certain behaviors mean and which behaviors should or should not be recorded. As a result, the inter-observer reliability of observation suffered. Lee Cronbach (1960, p. 535) summarized the problem well: "Observers interpret what they see. When they make an interpretation, they tend to overlook facts which do not fit the interpretation, and they may even invent facts needed to complete the event as interpreted."

To reduce unsystematic reporting of observations, most modern observation schemes focus the observer's attention on specific behaviors. The frequency and intensity of these behaviors are then recorded on a checklist or rating scale. The more specific the observations to be made, the fewer judgment calls needed by the observer (for example, "physically striking another child with the hand" is more specific than "violence"). The observers are also trained to use these methods consistently so that inter-observer reliability is as high as possible. Sometimes clinicians or researchers practice applying the same observational assessment form or scale to the same clients' behaviors. Often the clients have been videotaped (so there is no variability in what actually happened). This practice, designed to standardize clinicians' understanding and application of an observational assessment measure, is called *calibrating*.

Even when observational measures can be obtained more easily and reliably using structured observation systems, some clinicians resist using them out of concern that focusing on a few specific observational targets might cause them to miss other client behaviors of interest. These clinicians are less concerned about the potential unreliability of unstructured observations than they are about the possibility of failing to notice clinically significant information while focused on a restricted observational range.

However, as with interviews, the choice between less-structured versus more-structured observations need not be considered an "either-or" decision. Structured observations typically take place within the context of less-structured observations; indeed, interviews, tests, and other forms of assessment all provide opportunities to observe client behaviors. So clinicians may be able to make some general inferences about personality or functioning on the basis of a structured observation that was designed to help in diagnosis, treatment planning, cross-validating self-reports or reports from parents, teachers, and so forth.

Of course, collecting observational data can also be a difficult, time-consuming, and expensive procedure, and the problems associated with this type of assessment discourage some clinicians from attempting to use it (Mash & Foster, 2001). But as you will see in the next section, not all observational approaches require large investments of time and effort, so clinicians should remain mindful of both the strengths and limitations of various forms of observation.

SECTION SUMMARY

Observational assessment focuses on specific client behaviors, the goal being to obtain information not available from interviews or psychological tests. Observations of clients' behaviors can supplement or correct self-reports, reveal situational determinants of behavior, and establish ecological validity. At the same time, observations can be time consuming, and they may constrain observers, possibly causing them to miss significant client behaviors. It is to be hoped that these disadvantages may be outweighed by the advantages of increased reliability and validity of carefully constructed, empirically tested observational methods.

OBSERVATIONAL ASSESSMENT: APPROACHES

SECTION PREVIEW

Observational assessments can be categorized along a few basic dimensions. We have already mentioned one of these, the degree of structure involved. Another involves the settings in which observations take place: these can range from naturalistic to controlled. The former involves observing client behavior in the settings where they normally occur, such as homes, schools, hospitals, malls, airplanes, and the like. Controlled observations involve placing clients in purposely constructed situations that will elicit behaviors of clinical interest. Examples include simulations of airplanes, mock job interviews or other role-playing scenarios, and computer-generated virtual reality environments. In all observational assessments, clinicians must select specific behaviors to pay attention to and have a system to record observations. Ideally, the recording system will limit the biases and errors that can impair the accuracy of observations.

In *naturalistic observation*, the assessor looks at behavior as it occurs in its natural context (e.g., at home or school). *Controlled* observation lies at the other extreme, as the clinician or researcher sets up a special situation in which to observe behavior. Between these extremes are approaches that blend elements of both to handle specific assessment needs, thus creating many subtypes of both naturalistic and controlled observation. In some assessment situations, observers may be *participants* who are visible to the clients being watched and who may even interact with them (as when parents record their child's behavior). *Nonparticipant* observers are not visible, although in most cases the clients are aware that observation is taking place. In all observation, a key goal is to reduce observer bias (Haro et al., 2006). More comprehensive coverage of this material is available in a number of sources (e.g., Antony & Barlow, 2010; Haynes & O'Brien, 2000; Hersen & Beidel, 2012; Madden et al., 2013; Miller & Leffard, 2007; Repp & Horner, 2000).

Naturalistic Observation

Natural settings, such as home, school, or work, provide a background that is realistic and relevant for understanding the client's behavior and the factors influencing that behavior. In addition, naturalistic observation can be done in ways that are subtle enough to provide a picture of behavior that is not distorted by client self-consciousness or motivation to convey a particular impression to an interviewer. In naturalistic observation, the primary focus is on assessing the nature of, and changes in, problems that clinicians are asked to solve—everything from eating disorders, intrusive thoughts, maladaptive social interactions, parenting behaviors, and psychotic behavior to problems such as classroom disruptions and littering (Haynes, 1990).

OBSERVATION BY PARTICIPANT OBSERVERS The classic case of naturalistic observation is the anthropological field study in which a scientist joins a tribe, subculture, or other social organization to observe its characteristics and the behavior of its members (e.g., Mead, 1928; Williams, 1967). In such cases, the observer is a participant in every sense of the term, and observations are usually recorded in anecdotal notes, which later appear as a detailed account called an *ethnography*.

Because some researchers question whether these outsiders can do their job without inadvertently influencing the behavior they are to watch, observations are sometimes conducted by people who are part of the client's day-to-day world. In the following sections, we consider naturalistic observation systems that, while not entirely unobtrusive, do allow for recording the frequency, intensity, duration, or form of specific categories of behaviors by those who are both familiar to clients and in a position to observe them in a minimally intrusive way.

Numerous other observational tools are available to measure clinically relevant behaviors in clients' homes. As was the case in other areas, early home-based clinical observations allowed much inference and rather unsystematic selection of target behaviors (e.g., Ackerman, 1958). More reliable home observation systems have now evolved. One of the first of these was designed by Gerald Patterson (Patterson, Ray, Shaw, & Cobb, 1969) for use in the homes of conduct-disordered children. A more recent example is the Home Observation for Measurement of the Environment (HOME), which was designed to assess characteristics of the home environment that affect child development (Glad, Jergeby, Gustafsson, & Sonnander 2012).

The desire to observe children's behavior for clinical and educational purposes has spawned a number of systems for use in schools, playgrounds, and similar settings (Bunte et al., 2013; Nock & Kurtz, 2005; Ollendick & Greene, 1990). Classroom observation may focus on a single child and those with whom the child interacts, or an observer can sequentially attend to and assess the behavior of several target children or even of a whole class (Milich & Fitzgerald, 1985). We have more to say about the observational assessment of children and the instruments designed for this purpose in Chapter 11, on "Clinical Child psychology."

Observation of hospitalized patients is an important component of their assessment. For example, there is a scale that includes as many as six different observational measures intended to assess the amount of pain experienced by dementia patients, who often have difficulty communicating their pain (Lints-Martindale Hadjistavropoulos, Lix, & Thorpe 2012).

Hospitals and clinics are also excellent places to observe the developing skills of trainees who are learning to conduct interviews and other assessments. Psychologists-in-training, medical interns, and others who will eventually need to conduct these procedures can be observed by supervising faculty; this observation is a critical part of training. As with other observations, however, supervising faculty must have clear measures of the specific behaviors that they observe in order to provide useful and unbiased feedback to trainees (Holmboe, 2004).

SELF-OBSERVATION   *Self-monitoring* requires clients to record the frequency, location, duration, or intensity of events such as exercise, headaches, pleasant thoughts, hair pulling, smoking, eating habits, stress, sleep disorders, anxiety, health-promoting behaviors, or the like. Often, a client and therapist agree on target behaviors, and the client maintains a record or diary of when those behaviors occur, recording the instances, the conditions under which they occurred, and, often, thoughts associated with the instances. Unfortunately, self-monitoring for concerns such as drug use can involve underreporting or occasionally overreporting (Clark & Winters, 2002), but numerous brief self-report measures of symptoms and behaviors are now used with clinical populations (see Table 4.5).

UNOBTRUSIVE AND CORROBORATING MEASURES   The use of insiders as observers of adult behavior for clinical purposes is less common but not unknown. For example, in helping clients quit smoking, a clinician may ask for corroborative reports of success or failure from family members or friends (e.g., Mermelstein, Lichtenstein, & McIntyre, 1983). Such reports may also be solicited as part of the assessment of alcoholism or drug use (e.g., Frank et al., 2005), sexual activity (e.g., Rosen & Kopel, 1977), marital interactions (Johnson, 2002; Jouriles & O'Leary, 1985), and other adult behaviors.

Another approach to naturalistic observation is to inspect the by-products of behavior. For example, school grades, arrest records, and court files have been used to evaluate the treatment of delinquent youth and adult offenders (Davidson, Redner, Blakely, Mitchell, & Emshoff, 1987; Rice, 1997); changes in academic grade point averages have served as indices of improvement in test anxiety (Allen, 1971). Life records, also called *institutional* or *product-of-behavior* measures (Haynes, 1990), are actually part of a broader observational approach, called *nonreactive* or *unobtrusive* measurement, that clinical psychologists and other behavioral scientists use to learn about people's behavior without altering it in the process (Kelly & Agnew, 2012).

In clinical research, unobtrusive measures may be used to test theories about the causes of behavior problems. A creative use of unobtrusive measures in identifying the precursors of

TABLE 4.5 Examples of Self-Report and Observational Measures

Assessment	Approximate Administration Time	Content
Treatment Outcome Package (TOP) (Kraus, Seligman, & Jordan 2005)	5–10 minutes	Assesses a variety of treatment domains; brief measure of treatment outcome
Holden Psychological Screening Inventory (HPSI) (Holden, 1991)	5–7 minutes	General measure of psychopathology; measures social, as well as psychiatric symptoms
Hospital Anxiety and Depression Scale (HADS) (Zigmond & Snaith, 1983)	5 minutes	Measures psychological but not physical symptoms of anxiety and depression
Laboratory Parenting Assessment Battery (Lab-PAB) (Wilson & Durbin, 2012)	2 hours	A rating system covering a broad range of behaviors used to assess parenting behaviors during the early childhood years
Direct Observation Form (DOF) (McConaughy & Achenbach, 2009)	10 minutes	An observational tool for the assessment of conduct problems often seen in school settings

Sources: Bufka, L. F., & Camp, N. (2010) Brief measures for screening and measuring mental health outcomes. In M. M. Antony & D. H. Barlow (Eds.) *Handbook of assessment and treatment planning for psychological disorders* (pp. 62–94). New York, NY: The Guilford Press. McConaughy, S. H., & Achenbach, T. M. (2009). *Manual for the Direct Observation Form.* Burlington, VT: University of Vermont, Center for Children, Youth, & Families. Wilson, S., & Durbin, C. E. (2012). The Laboratory Parenting Assessment Battery: Development and preliminary validation of an observational parenting rating system. *Psychological Assessment.* Advance online publication. doi: 10.1037/a0028352.

schizophrenia is seen in a study that took advantage of the fact that many families today make videos of their children as they grow (Walker, Grimes, Davis, & Smith, 1993). In this study, trained observers analyzed childhood videos of individuals who later became schizophrenic as well as of their same-sex siblings who did not. The results revealed that long before they were diagnosed, the schizophrenics-to-be showed significantly more negative facial expressions than the other children (some of the differences appeared before the children were 4 years old).

Controlled Observation

Because naturalistic observation usually takes place in an uncontrolled environment, unanticipated events can interfere with the assessment. For example, the client may move out of the observer's line of vision or might get help from someone else in dealing with a stressor. How would the client have reacted without help? Another limitation of naturalistic observation involves the long waits that sometimes must occur before low-probability events occur (e.g., a child's tantrum or a family argument).

One way of getting around some of the difficulties associated with naturalistic observation is to set up special circumstances under which clients can be observed as they react to planned, standardized events. This approach is usually called *controlled observation* because it allows clinicians to maintain control over the assessment stimuli in much the same way as they do when giving the psychological tests described in Chapter 5. Controlled observations are also known as *analog behavior observation* (ABO), *situation tests*, and *contrived observations*.

During World War II, military psychologists devised controlled observations for assessing personality traits as well as behavioral capabilities. In the Operational Stress Test, for example, would-be pilots were asked to manipulate the controls of an aircraft flight simulator. The candidates did not know that the tester was purposely trying to frustrate them by giving increasingly complicated instructions accompanied by negative feedback (e.g., "You're making too many errors"; Melton, 1947). During the test, the assessor rated the candidate's reaction to criticism and stress, and these ratings supplemented objective data on skill with the simulator.

The Office of Strategic Services Assessment Staff (OSS, later to become the CIA; 1948) used observational assessment to infer traits of initiative, dominance, cooperation, and group leadership among potential espionage agents and other special personnel. Candidates were assigned to build a 5-foot cube-shaped frame out of large wooden poles and blocks resembling a giant Tinker Toy set, and they were given two "assistants" (actually, psychologists) who called themselves Kippy and Buster. Kippy acted in a passive, sluggish manner. He did nothing at all unless specifically ordered to, but stood around, often getting in the way. Buster, on the other hand, was aggressive, forward in offering impractical suggestions, ready to express dissatisfaction, and quick to criticize what he suspected were the candidate's weakest points. It was their function to present the candidate with as many obstructions and annoyances as possible in 10 minutes. As it turned out, they succeeded in frustrating the candidates so thoroughly that the construction was never completed in the allotted time (OSS, 1948). Since World War II, milder versions of the OSS situational tests have been used for personnel selection.

PERFORMANCE MEASURES   In current clinical and research settings, controlled observations take many forms. In some cases, the "control" consists of asking clients—usually couples, families, or parent–child pairs—to come to a clinic or laboratory and have a discussion or attempt to solve a problem. In controlled observations of performance, clinicians observe clients as they face a clinically relevant situation. For example, during marital therapy, a couple might be asked to discuss an area of conflict between them as the therapist makes audio or video recordings for later analysis (Heyman, 2001). The eating style (amount, speed, preferences) of individuals in a weight loss program might be recorded during a meal or snack in a controlled setting (Spiegel, Wadden, & Foster, 1991). Alcoholic and nonalcoholic drinkers might be observed in specially constructed cocktail lounges located in hospitals or in real bars (Collins, Parks, & Marlatt, 1985; Larsen, Overbeek, Granic, & Engels 2012).

ROLE PLAYING TESTS   Psychologists sometimes create make-believe situations in which the client is asked to *role-play* his or her typical behavior. Role-playing has been advocated by clinicians for many years and serves as the cornerstone for several group, psychodynamic, and humanistic treatments (e.g., Moreno, 1946; Perls, 1969). However, it was not until the late 1960s that role-playing became part of systematic clinical assessment. Since then, role-playing tests have become a standard ingredient in the observational assessment of children's social and safety skills (Harbeck, Peterson, & Starr, 1992), parent–child interactions (Carneiro, Corboz-Warney, & Fivaz-Depeursinge, 2006), depressive behavior (Bellack, Hersen, & Himmelhoch, 1983), responses to threatening situations (Jouriles, Rowe, McDonald, Platt, & Gomez 2010), the social competence and conversational skills of socially anxious or chronically mentally ill persons (Norton & Hope, 2001), therapists' competence in delivering treatment (Fairburn & Cooper, 2011), and many others.

In most role-plays, the clients' or trainees' responses are recorded and then rated by observers on any of dozens of criteria such as appropriateness of content, level of positive and refusal assertiveness, anxiety, latency to respond, response duration, speech dysfluencies, posture, eye contact, gaze, hand gestures, head movements, and voice volume. For example, the Extended Interaction Test assesses the generality and robustness of clients' assertiveness skills by presenting a recorded antagonist who makes a series of gradually escalating unreasonable requests and demands (McFall & Lillesand, 1971). Here is an excerpt from the test:

> Narrator: You are feeling really pressed for study time because you have an exam on Friday afternoon. Now, you are studying at your desk, when a close friend comes in and says, "Hi. Guess what. My parents just called and offered to pay for a plane ticket so I can fly home this weekend. Great, huh!? The only problem is, I'll have to skip my Friday morning class, and I hate to miss out on those notes; I'm barely making it in there as it is. Look, I know you aren't in that class, but it'd really be a big help if you'd go to the class Friday and take notes for me so I could go home. Would you do that for me?"
>
> If the participant refuses, the recorded voice continues:
>
> "I guess it is kinda crazy to expect you to do it, but, gee, I've got so many things to do if I'm gonna get ready to leave, and I don't want to waste the time asking around. Come on, will you do it for me this once?"
>
> If the participant refuses, the recording continues:
>
> "Look, what're friends for if they don't help each other out of a bind? I'd do it for you if you asked. What do you say, will you?"
>
> If the participant refuses, the recording continues:
>
> "But I was counting on you to do it. I'd hate to have to call my folks back and tell them I'm not coming. Can't you spare just one hour to help me out?"
>
> If the participant refuses, the recorded voice continues (sarcastically):
>
> "Now look, I don't want to impose on your precious time. Just tell me. Will you do it or do I have to call my folks back?"

Presumably, a person who withstands repeated requests is more assertive than one who gives in after an initial refusal.

Sometimes, clinicians or researchers use a *staged naturalistic event*. The idea is to look at behavior in a controlled setting that appears naturalistic to the client (Gottman, Markman, & Notarius, 1977). For example, unobtrusive role-playing tests have been used to measure social skills in psychiatric inpatients (Goldsmith & McFall, 1975). In these tests, the client is asked to meet and carry on a conversation with a stranger (actually an assistant to the clinician) who has been instructed to confront the client with three "critical moments": not catching the client's name, responding to a lunch invitation with an excuse that left open the possibility of lunch at another time, and saying "Tell me about yourself" at the first convenient pause in the conversation. Similar contrived situations—such as presenting prospective parents with a doll and instructing them to role play a situation or having parents respond to a video of an incident of child misbehavior—have been used to assess parenting skills (Carneiro, Corboz-Warney, & Fivaz-Depeursinge, 2006; Hawes & Dadds, 2006) and social behaviors (Kern, 1982).

Of course, observations involving deception and possible invasion of privacy must be set up with care and with regard for clients' welfare and dignity. Proponents of unobtrusive controlled observation try to avoid its potential dangers and point out that its value may be limited to measuring specific behaviors (such as refusal) rather than more complex interactive social skills.

PHYSIOLOGICAL MEASURES   Other performance tests measure physiological activity, such as heart rate, respiration, blood pressure, galvanic skin response, muscle tension, and brain functioning, that appears in relation to various stimuli. A classic example was Gordon Paul's (1966) use of measures of heart rate and sweating taken just before giving a talk to help identify speech-anxious clients. These measures were repeated following various anxiety-reduction treatments to aid in the evaluation of their effects (see also Nietzel, Bernstein, & Russell, 1988).

In recent years, clinical psychologists have increased their use of such physiological measures because they have become much more involved in studying insomnia, headache, chronic pain, sexual dysfunctions, gastrointestinal disorders, HIV/AIDS, diabetes, and many other disorders that have clear psychological components (see Chapter 12, "Health Psychology"). For instance, consider physiological measures in the assessment of sexual arousal and sexual dysfunctions. In one such performance assessment system, male subjects listen to audios or watch videos that present various types of erotic behavior involving appropriate and inappropriate sexual stimuli. All the while, a strain gauge attached to the participant's penis records changes in its circumference (called *phallometric measurement*). Greater erectile responses to the recorded material are assumed to signal higher levels of sexual arousal. Some studies have shown that among child pornography offenders, those with higher levels of erectile response are also more likely to engage in pedophilia (Seto, Cantor, & Blanchard, 2006). Unfortunately, patterns of arousal to specific kinds of stimuli have not been identified for each of the various kinds of sex offenses (Blanchard & Barbaree, 2005; Looman & Marshall, 2005), but there is hope that this or other technology, such as measures of pupil dilation (Rieger, 2012), will eventually be able to do so.

With increased interest in the role of psychological factors in health and illness (see Chapter 12), the use of physiological recording devices in clinical assessment will likely continue to increase as well, especially now that many companies are able to market relatively inexpensive, portable devices—including virtual reality systems—that present stimuli and record responses.

VIRTUAL REALITY ASSESSMENT In *virtual reality assessment*, a client is exposed to a realistic simulation run by a computer. Sometimes, the client views a computer screen, but often the simulation is presented via a headset, helmet, and gloves that provide visual, auditory, and sometimes tactile stimuli. This technology allows for the precise presentation and control of stimuli that appears three dimensional; the experience is usually highly realistic for clients. During the presentation, clinicians can obtain self-report measures, conduct behavioral observations, and collect physiological measures or other assessment indices. The collection of such measures has helped establish the value of virtual reality both as an assessment tool and in the administration of treatments (Côtè & Bouchard, 2005; Gorman, 2006; Llobera et al., 2013).

Concerns that assessments based on simulations or virtual reality may not carry over to real situations appear to be largely unfounded. Flight simulation training has long been an established and effective method of assessment and training among civilian and military pilots. Except perhaps for some clients with autistic spectrum disorders, virtual reality assessments and treatment applications appear to transfer to real-world settings quite well (Standen & Brown, 2005). For example, Lew and his colleagues (2005) used a driving simulator to assess the long-term driving performance of clients who had suffered from traumatic brain injury. In this case, the virtual reality assessment was better at predicting future performance than was an actual road test. Another study (Jouriles, Rowe, McDonald, Platt, & Gomez 2010) found that role playing supplemented by virtual reality stimuli elicited stronger and more differentiated responses than role playing alone. We will have more to say about virtual reality when we cover psychological treatment in Chapters 6 through 10.

BEHAVIORAL AVOIDANCE TESTS Another popular performance measure in controlled observation is the behavioral avoidance test, or BAT, which is designed to assess overt anxiety in relation to specific objects and situations. In BATs, clients are confronted with a stimulus they fear while observers record the type and degree of avoidance displayed. Informal BATs were conducted with children as early as the 1920s (e.g., Jones, 1924a,b), but it was not until the early 1960s that systematic avoidance testing procedures became a common form of controlled observational assessment.

In a study of systematic desensitization (see Chapter 8, "Behavioral and Cognitive-Behavioral Therapies") for snake phobia, Peter Lang and David Lazovik (1963) asked clients to enter a room containing a harmless caged snake and to approach, touch, and pick up the animal. Observers gave the clients avoidance scores on the basis of whether they were able to look at, touch, or hold the snake. Many other fear stimuli, including rats, spiders, cockroaches, and dogs have been used in other versions of the BAT, and the "look–touch–hold" coding system for scoring responses has been replaced by more sophisticated measures. In BATs, too, virtual reality technology has made it possible to produce simulated environments to which clients react.

SECTION SUMMARY

Observational assessment can be classified as naturalistic or controlled, though some observational techniques combine elements of both. Naturalistic observations of clients in schools, homes, clinics, and other settings provide ecological validity and can reveal valuable information about clients' responses to specific triggers. In some naturalistic observations, the clinician or researcher is unobtrusive and observes invisibly. In other situations, the clinician is a participant-observer. Controlled observations allow clinicians to target situations that elicit behaviors of greatest clinical interest. Certain techniques such as physiological measurements and virtual reality exposure continue to show promise as focused methods of observational assessment.

RESEARCH ON OBSERVATIONAL ASSESSMENT

SECTION PREVIEW

Although they have face (ecological) validity, observational assessments do have limitations. Observers are more likely to disagree when they are not looking for the same sets of behaviors and coding them in the same way. It is therefore important for behavioral targets to be specified and coded/recorded clearly. As with interviews, reliability is also improved when there are clear inference rules on what recorded observations mean. Of particular concern in observational assessment are clinician biases, often unrecognized because observations seem to be so objective. Clinicians should cross-validate conclusions on the basis of observations with those drawn from other assessment data. In clinical practice, controlled observational assessments are frequently not done as much because of the time and effort required to conduct them; brief structured observations are often preferred in today's health care environment.

Behaviorally oriented clinicians, the most enthusiastic proponents of observational assessment, have argued that observations provide the most accurate and relevant source of assessment data. Observations have even been likened to photographs in that they are thought to provide a clear and dispassionate view of human behavior. But as any photographer knows, a photograph is not just a rendering of a scene, but a combined product of scene elements, the photographer's choices about equipment and framing, and judgments made during the photo editing process. Similarly, a number of factors can influence the reliability and validity of observational assessment.

Defining Observational Targets

A fundamental requirement for establishing both the reliability and validity of observational assessment is clarifying the target to be measured. Thus, decisions about what aspects of behavior to look for and code, and how these targets are defined, reflect the assessor's view of the presence and meaning of an observation. Consider assertiveness for instance. One clinician might assess assertiveness by observing clients' ability to refuse unreasonable requests, while another might focus on the direct expression of positive affect. This problem of definition may never be resolved to everyone's satisfaction, but evaluating the reliability and validity of an observational system begins with questions about what behavioral features are to be coded.

Representativeness of Observed Behavior

Clinicians using observational assessment must be concerned about the possibility that clients under observation will intentionally or unintentionally alter the behaviors that are of greatest clinical interest. The observation situation itself can exert an influence on client behavior through social cues, or *demand characteristics* (Orne, 1962), that suggest what actions are, or are not, appropriate and expected. Thus, if a clinician observes a couple in a setting that contains strong social cues about how the clients should behave (e.g., "We would like to measure just how much fighting you two actually do"), the observation may reveal a degree of conflict that is unusually high (or low) for that couple. For example, in a study designed to measure assertiveness, college students were asked to respond to audio recordings that portrayed social situations similar to those described earlier (Nietzel & Bernstein, 1976). The assertiveness of their responses was scored on a 5-point scale. All subjects heard the tape twice, under either the same or differing demand situations. The "low-demand" situation asked participants for their "natural reactions," but in the "high-demand" situation, they were told to be "as assertive as you think the most assertive and forceful person could be." The results showed that participants on the first test behaved more assertively if they heard high demand instructions than if they heard low demand instructions. And as you might expect, if instructions remained the same on the second test, participants remained about as assertive as they were the first time. However, if the instructions encouraged more assertiveness on the second test than on the first, participants behaved more assertively. Similarly, participants who heard high demand instructions the first time behaved less assertively if they heard low demand instructions on the second test. In short, participants' assertiveness was significantly influenced by what they thought they should do in the assessment situation. Other research on observational anxiety assessment has shown that the instructions given, the presence or absence of an experimenter, the characteristics of the physical setting, and other situational variables influence the amount of fear clients display during BATs (e.g., Bernstein, 1973; Bernstein & Nietzel, 1977).

Various strategies have been suggested to minimize situational bias in observational assessment (Bernstein & Nietzel, 1977; Borkovec & O'Brien, 1976), but the problem cannot be entirely eliminated. As long as the stimuli present when the client's behavior is being observed differ from those present when the client is not being observed, we cannot be sure that the behavior displayed during formal observation will generalize to other situations. The best clinicians can do is minimize any cues that might influence client behavior. Utterly naturalistic or unobtrusive observation is theoretically possible, but often not practical. Accordingly, clinicians will continue to rely on contrived, analog observations to assess some behavioral targets.

Reliability of Observational Assessment

To what extent are observational assessments reliable? Test-retest reliability can be difficult to measure if clients' behaviors change substantially over time. For example, if couples show hostility and considerable anger when discussing a topic at one time but show much less of these emotions a week later, measures of hostility repeated on these two weeks may be considerably different (Heyman, 2001). Repeated measures are needed to establish test-retest reliability, and this can be time consuming and expensive. Therefore, interrater reliability may be more important.

Two factors are especially important in interrater reliability: task complexity and rater training. Reducing *task complexity* often increases interrater reliability (e.g., reliability can be increased if the observer uses a 15-category rather than a 100-category coding system). *Observer training* can also affect reliability. If observers intend to record laughter, for instance, but are not given a definition of laughter, one observer might count belly laughs but not giggles, while another might include everything from smiles to violent guffaws. Finally, when people are first trained to use an observation system, they usually work hard during practice sessions and pay close attention to the task, partly because they are being evaluated. Later, when "real" data are being collected, the observers may become careless if they think no one is checking their reliability (Taplin & Reid, 1973). Accordingly, supervision of persons doing observation and coding is sometimes necessary.

As with interviews, modern, empirically derived clinical observation assessment systems that use trained observers have higher reliability, sometimes with coefficients in excess of 0.80 and 0.90 (Antony & Barlow, 2010; Harwood, Beutler, & Groth-Marnat, 2011). Less structured observations tend to have lower reliability.

Validity of Observational Assessment

At first glance, observation of behavior would appear to rank highest in validity among all clinical assessment approaches. After all, if we observe aggression in a married couple, are we not assessing aggression, and is that not enough to establish the validity of our technique? The answer is yes only if we can show that (a) the behaviors coded (e.g., raised voices) constitute a satisfactory definition of aggression, (b) the data faithfully reflect the nature and degree of aggression occurring during observation, and (c) the clients' behaviors while under observation accurately represent their typical behavior in related, but unobserved, situations.

One way to assess the *concurrent validity* of observation is to ask about the extent to which the resulting conclusions correlate with conclusions drawn from other assessment methods. For example, does the ability to refuse unreasonable requests occur more often in people judged to be assertive by their peers? If so, then the peer judgment correlates with the observation, and we can say that the observation has shown convergent validity. The more an observation correlates with other data, such as interviews, physiological measures, self-reports, and others' appraisals, the greater the convergent validity of the observation (e.g., Andersson, Miniscalco, Johnsson, & Gillberg 2013).

If the observational assessment accurately predicts a future behavior, such as whether a client with a brain injury will be able to drive safely (e.g., Lew et al., 2005), we can say that the observational assessment has *predictive validity*. Not surprisingly, observations that involve clearly defined targets and sample repeated instances of behavior under realistic conditions tend to have higher predictive validity. In one study, for example, researchers collected observations of preschool children's behaviors and mothers' reports of their children's behaviors. They found that the observational measures did a better job than the mother's reports at predicting children's behaviors 4 years later (Zaslow et al., 2006).

Clinicians can now choose from a large and rapidly growing array of observational assessment instruments. Many of these instruments are brief, focus on well-defined symptoms or behaviors, and have reasonably well-established reliability and validity; many others have yet to be thoroughly validated. The validation process can be slow because there is no gold standard against which to compare newly developed observational instruments and thereby quickly establish their validity (Lang & Kleijnen, 2010). As a result, clinicians and researchers faced with so many choices can be uncertain about which ones are best for particular assessment purposes.

SECTION SUMMARY

While observational methods have ecological validity (they are real behaviors that occur in real situations), their concurrent and predictive validity often go unexamined. When they are examined, measures that are more explicitly defined and scored tend to have higher validity. Observations tend to be less reliable when the behavioral targets are not clearly specified and when different observers use different decision rules and therefore draw different conclusions from the same set of observations. Clinicians should be especially aware of their own potential biases in making observations, particularly inferring too much from single, limited observations. Clinicians can cross-validate conclusions on the basis of observations with other conclusions from other assessment data. Although still a useful assessment tool, formal observational assessments are not used frequently in clinical practice because of the time and effort required to conduct them.

Chapter Summary

Interviews are defined as conversations with a purpose, and in clinical situations, these purposes include client intake, problem referral, orientation, termination, crisis intervention, and observation. In nondirective interviews, the clinician interferes as little as possible with the client's speech, while structured interviews present planned inquiries in a fixed sequence. Semistructured interviews fall between these extremes.

Most interviews have three main sections. Intake and problem identification interviews, for example, usually begin with efforts at making the client comfortable, enter an information-gathering middle stage, and end with a summary and discussion. Conducting each phase of an interview and moving smoothly from one to the next requires a combination of common sense, active listening skills, well-phrased questions, and tact. If interviews are to have maximum value, communication

between client and interviewer must be as clear as possible in both verbal and nonverbal channels, and minimally affected by personal and cultural biases.

While the reliability of interviews, especially structured interviews, is generally good, it can depend on several variables, including how questions are phrased, the client's comfort with the interviewer, emotional state, memory skills, and motivation. Reliability and validity can both be threatened by interviewer errors or biases, especially those relating to preconceived views of clients with particular characteristics. Eliminating such errors and biases is a major challenge for clinicians.

Observational assessment systems are designed to collect information about clients that is not available in other ways or that corrects for biases inherent in other assessment methods (e.g., biases in self-reports from interviews). Observation can be conducted in naturalistic or controlled settings (or some blend of the two) by participant or nonparticipant observers. Sometimes, clients are asked to observe and record their own behavior, a procedure called self-monitoring.

Naturalistic observation systems have been developed for use in hospitals, schools, and homes. These systems have the advantage of realism and relevance, but they are expensive and time consuming and may be affected by uncontrollable situational factors. To minimize these problems, clinicians often use controlled observations—special circumstances under which clients can be observed as they react to standardized events—including role-played social interactions and performance tests of smoking, eating, drinking, or dealing with a feared object or situation. During controlled observation, clinicians may monitor clients' physiological as well as overt responses.

While observation gets around some of the inference problems that reduce the reliability and validity of many interview and test procedures, it is not a perfect assessment tool. For one thing, data from observational assessments can be influenced by factors other than the behavior of clients. The reliability and validity of observational data depend on the precise definition of observation targets, training and monitoring of observers, efforts to guard against the effects of observer bias, reactivity in the observation process, and situational influences such as demand characteristics that might create unrepresentative samples of client behaviors.

Study Questions

1. What are the various types of interviews?
2. Which factors should clinicians consider when interviewing persons from diverse cultural or ethnic backgrounds?
3. How does the rate of health care utilization by minorities differ from that of the majority?
4. What are examples of nondirective interviewing techniques?
5. What are structured and semistructured interview formats, and what are examples of each?
6. What are advantages and disadvantages of structured interviews?
7. How can clinicians help clients relax during initial stages of an interview?
8. What is frame setting, and what is its purpose?
9. What factors influence the reliability and validity of interviews?
10. What are the advantages and limitations of observational assessment?
11. What are the main kinds of observational assessment?
12. What are virtual reality assessment and behavioral avoidance tests?
13. What factors influence the reliability and validity of observational assessment?

Web Sites

- World Health Organization Web site about the Composite International Diagnostic Interview (CIDI): http://www.hcp.med.harvard.edu/wmhcidi/about.php
- Centers for Disease Control Web site information on the Composite International Diagnostic Interview (CIDI): http://www.cdc.gov/nchs/data/nhanes/cidi_quex.pdf
- Structured Clinical Interview for *DSM-IV* information: http://www.scid4.org/

MOVIES

Harold and Maude (1971): Macabre comedy about a suicidal older teenager who is obsessed with death, and who along with a therapist and an elderly woman, finds meaning in life.

Lars and the Real Girl (2007): In this quirky independent film, Lars (who lost his mother at child-birth and was raised by a despondent father), becomes romantically involved with an anatomically correct blow-up sex doll, and then with the help of a physician/therapist, and a loving brother and sister-and-law, begins to join the real world of relationships with humans.

MEMOIRS

Finding Fish: A Memoir by Antwone Quenton Fisher (2001; New York: Perennial). In addition to recounting a troubled history of poverty, abandonment, and child abuse, the author describes his first helpful interviews with a military therapist who helps him immensely.

The Quiet Room: A Journey Out of the Torment of Madness by Lori Schiller (1994; New York: Warner Books). Thorough account, using observational data and direct statements by many informants (such as the author's parents, siblings, and therapist) during a period of time when the author was hospitalized and being treated for schizophrenia after a suicide attempt.

References

Ackerman, N. W. (1958). *The psychodynamics of family life*. New York, NY: Basic Books.

Adler, A. (1933). *Social interest: A challenge to mankind*. Vienna, Leipzig: Rolf Passer.

Adler, A. B., Bilese, P. D., McGurk, D., Hoge, C.W., & Castro, C. A. (2011). Battlemind debriefing and battlemind training as early interventions with soldiers returning from Iraq: Randomized by platoon. *Sport, Exercise, and Performance Psychology, 1*, 66–83.

Aklin, W. M., NY & Turner, S. M. (2006). Toward understanding ethnic and cultural factors in the interviewing process. *Psychotherapy: Theory, Research Practice, Training, 43*, 50–64.

Allen, G. J. (1971). The effectiveness of study counseling and desensitization in alleviating test anxiety in college students. *Journal of Abnormal Psychology, 77*, 282–289.

American Psychological Association. (2002). Criteria for evaluating treatment guidelines. *American Psychologist, 57*, 1052–1059.

Andersson, G. W., Miniscalco, C., Johansson, U., & Gillberg, C. (2013). Autism in toddlers: Can observation in preschool yield the same information as autism assessment in a specialized clinic? *The Scientific World Journal, 2013*, 38–47.

Antony, M. M., & Barlow, D. H. (Eds.). (2010). *Handbook of assessment and treatment planning for psychological disorders* (2nd ed.). New York, NY: Guilford.

Bellack, A. S., Hersen, M., & Himmelhoch, J. M. (1983). A comparison of social skills training, pharmacotherapy and psychotherapy for depression. *Behaviour Research and Therapy, 21*, 101–107.

Bernstein, D. A. (1973). Behavioral fear assessment: Anxiety or artifact? In H. Adams & P. Unikel (Eds.). *Issues and trends in behavior therapy* (pp. 225–267). Springfield, IL: Charles C. Thomas.

Bernstein, D. A., & Nietzel, M. T. (1977). Demand characteristics in behavior modification: A natural history of a "nuisance." In M. Hersen, R. M. Eisler, & P. M. Miller (Eds.), *Progress in behavior modification* (Vol. 4, pp. 119–162). New York, NY: Academic Press.

Blanchard, R., & Barbaree, H. E. (2005). The strength of sexual arousal as a function of the age of the sex offender: Comparisons among pedophiles, hebephiles, and teleiophiles. Sexual Abuse: Journal of Research and Treatment, 12, 441–456.

Bogels, S. M. (1994). A structured-training approach to teaching diagnostic interviewing. *Teaching of Psychology, 21*, 144–150.

Borkovec, T. D., & O'Brien, G. T. (1976). Methodological and target behavior issues in analogue therapy outcome research. In M. Hersen, R. M. Eisler, & P. M. Miller (Eds.), *Progress in behavior modification* (pp. 133–172). New York, NY: Academic Press.

Braginsky, B. M., Braginsky, D. D., & Ring, K. (1969). *Methods of madness: The mental hospital as a last resort.* New York, NY: Holt, Rinehart & Winston.

Brugha, T. S., Nienhuis, F., Bagchi, D., Smith, J., Meltzer, H. (1999). The survey form of SCAN: The feasibility of using experienced lay survey interviewers to administer a semi-structured systematic clinical assessment of psychotic and non-psychotic disorders. *Psychological Medicine, 29*, 703–711.

Bufka, L., F. & Camp, N. (2010) Brief measures for screening and measuring mental health outcomes. In M. M. Antony & D. H. Barlow (Eds.) *Handbook of assessment and treatment planning for psychological disorders* (pp. 62–94). New York, NY: The Guilford Press.

Bunte, T. L., Laschen, S., Schoemaker, K., Hessen, D. J., van der Heijden, P. G. M., et al. (2013). Clinical usefulness of observational assessment in the diagnosis of DBD and ADHD in preschoolers. *Journal of Clinical Child & Adolescent Psychology*, online access. doi: 10.1007/s10802-013-9732-1.

Cacciola, J. S., Alterman, A. I., Rutheford, M. J., McKay, J. R., & May, D. J. (1999). Comparability of telephone and in-person Structured Clinical Interview for DSM-III-R (SCID) diagnoses. *Assessment, 6*, 235–242.

Carneiro, C., Corboz-Warney, A., & Fivaz-Depeursinge, E. (2006). The prenatal Lausanne Trilogy Play: A new observational assessment tool of the prenatal co-parenting alliance. *Infant Mental Health Journal, 27*, 207–228.

Clark, D. B., & Winters, K. C. (2002). Measuring risks and outcomes in substance use disorders prevention research. *Journal of Consulting and Clinical Psychology, 70*, 1207–1223.

Collins, R. L., Parks, G. A., & Marlatt, G. A. (1985). Social determinants of alcohol consumption: The effects of social interactions and model status on the self-administration of alcohol. *Journal of Consulting and Clinical Psychology, 53*, 189–200.

Cormier, S., Nurius, P. S., & Osborn, C. J. (2012). *Interviewing and change strategies for helpers* (7th ed.). Pacific Grove, CA: Brooks Cole.

Côtè, S. & Bouchard, S. (2005). Documenting the efficacy of virtual reality exposure with psychophysiological and information processing measures. *Applied Psychophysiology and Biofeedback, 30*, 217–232.

Couch, R. D. (1995). Four steps for conducting a pregroup screening interview. *Journal for Specialists in Group Work, 20*, 18–25.

Craig, R. J. (2009). The clinical interview. In J. Butcher (Ed.). *The Oxford handbook of personality assessment* (pp. 201–225). New York, NY: Oxford University Press.

Cronbach, L. J. (1960). *Essentials of psychological testing* (2nd ed.). New York, NY: Harper & Row.

Davidson, W. S., Redner, R., Blakely, C., Mitchell, C. M., & Emshoff, J. G. (1987). Diversion of juvenile offenders: An experimental comparison. *Journal of Consulting and Clinical Psychology, 55*, 68–75.

Dimatteo, M. R., & Taranta, A. (1976). Nonverbal communication and physician-patient rapport: An empirical study. *Professional Psychology, 10*, 540–547.

Dipboye, R. L., Stramler, C. S., & Fontenelle, G. A. (1984). The effects of the application on recall of information from the interview. *Academy of Management Journal, 27*, 561–575.

Endicott, J., & Spitzer, R. L. (1978). A diagnostic interview: The schedule for affective disorders and schizophrenia. *Archives of General Psychiatry, 35, 837-844.*

Erickson, P. I., & Kaplan, C. P. (2000). Maximizing qualitative responses about smoking in structured interviews. *Qualitative Health Research, 10*, 829–840.

Fairburn, C. G., & Cooper, Z. (2011). Therapist competence, therapy quality, and therapist training. *Behavior Research and Therapy, 49*, 373–378.

First, M. B., Gibbon, M., Spitzer, R. L., Williams, J. B. W., & Benjamin, L. S. (1997). *Structured Clinical Interview for DSM-IV Axis II Personality Disorders (SCID-II).* Washington, DC: American Psychiatric Press.

First, M. B., Spitzer, R. L., Gibbon, M., & Williams, J. B. W. (1997). *Structured Clinical Interview for DSM-IV Axis I Disorders: Clinical version (SCID-CV).* Washington, DC: American Psychiatric Press.

Flisher, A. J., Sorsdahl, K. R., & Lund, C. (2012). Test-retest reliability of the Xhosa version of the Diagnostic Interview Schedule for Children. *Child: Care, Health, and Development, 38*, 261–265.

Frank, E., Shear, M. K., Rucci, P., Banti, S., Mauri, M., et al. (2005). Cross-cultural validity of the Structured Clinical Interview for Panic-Agoraphobic spectrum. *Social Psychiatry and Psychiatric Epidemiology, 40*, 283–290.

Garb, H. N. (2007). Computer-administered interviews and rating scales. *Psychological Assessment, 19*, 4–13.

Garfield, S. L. (1974). *Clinical psychology: The study of personality and behavior.* Chicago, IL: Aldine.

Glad, J., Jergeby, U., Gustafsson, C., & Sonnander, K. (2012). Social work practitioner's experience of the clinical utility of the Home Obsevation for Measurement of the Environment (HOME) Inventory. *Child & Family Social Work, 17*, 23–33.

Goins, M. K., Strauss, G. D., & Martin, R. (1995). A change measure for psychodynamic psychotherapy outcome research. *Journal of Psychotherapy Practice and Research, 4*, 319–328.

Goldfried, M. R. (1980). Toward the delineation of therapeutic change principles. *American Psychologist, 35*, 991–999.

Goldsmith, J. B., & McFall, R. M. (1975). Development and evaluation of an interpersonal skill-training program for psychiatric inpatients. *Journal of Abnormal Psychology, 84*, 51–58.

Gottman, J. M., Markman, H. J., & Notarius, C. (1977). The topography of marital conflict: A sequential analysis of verbal and nonverbal behavior. *Journal of Marriage and the Family, 39*, 461–477.

Grilo, C. M., Lozano, C., & Elder, K. A. (2005). Inter-rater and test-retest reliability of the Spanish Language Version of the Eating Disorders Examination Interview: Clinical and research implications. *Journal of Psychiatric Practice, 11*, 231-240.

Groth-Marnat, G. (2003). *Handbook of psychological assessment* (4th ed.). Hoboken, NJ: Wiley.

Harbeck, C., Peterson, L., & Starr, L. (1992). Previously abused child victims' response to a sexual abuse prevention program: A matter of measures. *Behavior Therapy, 23,* 375–388.

Hare, R. D. (2003). *The Psychopathy Checklist—Revised* (2nd ed.). Toronto: Multi-Health Systems.

Haro, J. M., Kontodimas, S., Negrin, M. A., Ratcliffe, M., Saurez, D., et al. (2006). Methodological aspects in the assessment of treatment effects in observational health outcomes studies. *Applied Health Economics and Health Policy, 5,* 11–25.

Harwood, T. M., Beutler, L. E., & Groth-Marnat, G. (Eds.). (2011). *Integrative assessment of adult personality* (3rd ed.). New York, NY: The Guilford Press.

Hawes, D. J., & Dadds, M. R. (2006). Assessing parenting practices through parent-report and direct observation during parent-training. *Journal of Child and Family studies, 15,* 555–568.

Haynes, S. N. (1990). Behavioral assessment of adults. In G. Goldstein & M. Hersen (Eds.), *Handbook of psychological assessment* (2nd ed., pp. 423–463). New York, NY: Pergamon Press.

Haynes, S. N., & O'Brien, W. O. (2000). *Principles of behavioral assessment: A functional approach to psychological assessment.* New York, NY: Plenum/ Kluwer Press.

Heal, L. W., & Sigelman, C. K. (1995). Response biases in interviews of individuals with limited mental ability. *Journal of Intellectual Disability Research, 39,* 331–340.

Hendrie, H. C., Lane, K. A., Ogunniyi, A., Baiyewu, O., Gureje, O., et al. (2006). The development of a semi-structured home interview (CHIF) to directly assess function in cognitively impaired elderly people in two cultures. *International Psychogeriatrics, 18,* 653–666.

Hersen, M., & Beidel, D. C. (Eds.). (2012). *Adult psychopathology and diagnosis* (6th ed.). New York, NY: Wiley.

Heyman, R. E. (2001). Observation of couple conflicts: Clinical assessment applications, stubborn truths, and shaky foundations. *Psychological Assessment, 13,* 5–35.

Holden, R. R. (1991). Psychometric properties of the Holden Psychological Screening Inventory (HPSI). Paper presented at the meeting of the Canadian Psychological Association, Ottawa.

Holmboe, E. S. (2004). Faculty and the observation of trainees clinical skills: Problems and opportunities. *Academic Medicine. 79,* 16–22.

Hsu, L. K., & Folstein, M. F. (1997). Somatoform disorders in Caucasian and Chinese Americans. *Journal of Nervous and Mental Disease, 185,* 382–387.

Hummelen, B., Wilberg, T., & Karterud, S. (2007). Interviews of female patients with borderline personality disorder who dropped out of group psychotherapy. *International Journal of Group Psychotherapy, 57,* 67–91.

Iskandarsyah, A., Klerk, C., Suardi, D. R., Soemitro, M. P., Sadarjoen, S. S., et al. (2013). Psychosocial and cultural reasons for delay in seeking help and nonadherence to treatment in Indonesian women with breast cancer: A qualitative study. *Health Psychology, Jan 21,* 2013, No Pagination Specified.

Johnson, M. D. (2002). The observation of specific affect in marital interactions: Psychometric properties of a coding system and a rating system. *Psychological Assessment, 14,* 423–438.

Jones, M. C. (1924a). The elimination of children's fears. *Journal of Experimental Psychology, 7,* 382–390.

Jones, M. C. (1924b). A laboratory study of fear: The case of Peter. *Pedagogical Seminary and Journal of Genetic Psychology, 31,* 308–315.

Jouriles, E. N. & O'Leary, K. D. (1985). Interspousal reliability of reports of marital violence. *Journal of Consulting and Clinical Psychology, 53,* 419–421.

Jouriles, E. N., Rowe, L. S., McDonald, R., Platt, C. G., & Gomez, G. S. (2010). Assessing women's response to sexual threat: Validity of a virtual role-play procedure. *Behavior Therapy, 42,* 475–484.

Kaczorowski, J. A., Williams, A. S., Smith, T. F., Fallah, N, Mendez, J. L., et al. (2011). Adapting clinical services to accommodate needs of refugee populations. *Professional Psychology: Research and Practice, 42,* 361–367.

Kelly, J. R., & Agnew, C. R. (2012). Behavior and behavioral assessment. In K. Deaux & M. Snyder (Eds.), *The Oxford handbook of personality and social psychology* (pp. 95–110). New York, NY: Oxford University Press.

Kern, J. M. (1982). The comparative external and concurrent validity of three role-plays for assessing heterosocial performance. *Behavior Therapy, 13,* 666–680.

Kleespies, P. M., AhnAllen, C. G., Knight, J. A., Presskreischer, B., Barrs, K. L., et al. (2011). A study of self-injurious and suicidal behavior in a veteran population. *Psychological Services, 8,* 236–250.

Komiti, A. A., Jackson, H. J., Judd, F. K., Cockram, A. M., Kyrios, M., et al. (2001). A comparison of the Composite International Diagnostic Interview (CIDI-Auto) with clinical assessment in diagnosing mood and anxiety disorders. *Australian & New Zealand Journal of Psychiatry, 35,* 224–232.

Kraus, D. R., Seligman, D. A., & Jordan, J. R. (2005) Validation of a behavioral health treatment outcome and assessment tool designed for naturalistic settings: The Treatment Outcome Package. *Journal of Clinical Psychology, 63,* 285–314.

Kulic, K. R. (2005). The crisis intervention semi-structured interview. *Brief Treatment and Crisis Intervention 5,* 143–157.

Lang, P. J., & Lazovik, A. D. (1963). Experimental desensitization of a phobia. *Journal of Abnormal and Social Psychology, 66,* 519–525.

Lang, P. J., & Lazovik, A. D. (1963). Experimental desensitization of a phobia. Journal of Abnormal and Social Psychology, 66, 519–525.

Lang, S., & Kleijnen, J. (2010). Quality assessment tools for observational studies: Lack of consensus. *International Journal of Evidence-Based Healthcare, 8,* 247.

Lanik, M., & Mitchel-Gibbons, A. (2011). Guidelines for cross-cultural assessor training in multicultural assessment centers. *The Psychologist-Manager, 14,* 221–246.

Larner, A. J. (2005). "Who came with you?" A diagnostic observation in patients with memory problems. *Journal of Neurology, Neurosurgery, & Psychiatry, 76,* 1739.

Larsen, H., Overbeek, G., Granic, I., & Engels, R.C. (2012). The strong effect of other people's drinking: Two experimental observational studies in a real bar. *The American Journal on Addictions, 21,* 168–175.

Lew, H. L., Poole, J. H., Ha Lee, E., Jaffe, D. L., Huang, H., et al. (2005). Predictive validity of driving-simulator assessments following traumatic brain injury: A preliminary study. *Brain Injury, 19,* 177–188.

Li, S. T., Jenkins, S., & Grewal, S. (2012). Impact of race and ethnicity on the expression, assessment, and diagnosis of psychopathology. In M. Hersen & D. Beidel (Eds.), *Adult psychopathology and diagnosis* (6th ed., pp. 117–148). New York, NY: Wiley.

Lints-Martindale, A. C., Hadjistavropoulos, T., Lix, L. M., & Thorpe, L. (2012). A comparative investigation of observational pain assessment tools for older adults with dementia. *The Clinical Journal of Pain, 28,* 226–237.

Llobera, J., Gonzalez-Franco, M., Perez-Marcos, D., Valls-Sole, J., Slater, M., et al. (2013). Virtual reality for the assessment of patients suffering chronic pain: A case study. *Experimental Brain Research, 1,* 105–117.

Lobbestael, J., Leurgans, M., & Arntz, A. (2011). Inter-rater reliability of the Structured Clinical Interview for DSM-IV Axis I disorders (SCID I) and Axis II disorders (SCID II). *Clinical Psychology and Psychotherapy, 18,* 75–79.

Looman, J. & Marshall, W. L. (2005). Sexual arousal in rapists. *Criminal Justice and Behavior, 32,* 367–389.

Lyneham, J. J., & Rapee, R. M. (2005). Agreement between telephone and in-person delivery of a structured interview for anxiety disorders in children. *Journal of the American Academy of Child & Adolescent Psychiatry, 44*, 274-282.

Machado, P., Beutler, L. E., Harwood, T. M., Mohr, D., & Lenore, S. (2011). The integrative clinical interview. In T. Harwood, L. Beutler, & G. Groth-Marnat (Eds), *Integrative assessment of adult personality.* New York, NY: Guilford Press.

MacKinnon, R. A., Michels, R., & Buckley, P. J. (2009). *The psychiatric interview in clinical practice.* Washington, DC: American Psychiatric Publishing.

Madden, G. J., Dube, W. V., Hackenberg, T. D., Hanley, G. P., Lattal, K. A., et al. (Eds). (2013). *APA Handbook of behavioral analysis, Vol. 1: Methods and principles.* Washington, DC: American Psychological Association.

Mash, E. J., & Foster, S. L. (2001). Exporting analogue behavioral observation from research to clinical practice: Useful or cost-defective? *Psychological Assessment, 13*, 86–98.

Matarazzo, J. D. (1965). The interview. In B. B. Wolman (Ed.), *Handbook of clinical psychology* (pp. 403–450). New York: McGraw-Hill.

McConaughy, S. H., & Achenbach, T. M. (2009). *Manual for the Direct Observation Form.* Burlington, VT: University of Vermont, Center for Children, Youth, & Families.

McFall, R. M., & Lillesand, D. B. (1971). Behavior rehearsal with modeling and coaching in assertion training. *Journal of Abnormal Psychology, 77*, 313–323.

Mead, M. (1928). *Coming of age in Samoa.* New York, NY: Morrow.

Melton, A. W. (Ed.). (1947). *Apparatus tests.* Washington, DC: Government Printing Office.

Mermelstein, R., Lichtenstein, E., & McIntyre, K. (1983). Partner support and relapse in smoking-cessation programs. *Journal of Consulting and Clinical Psychology, 51*, 331–337.

Milich, R., & Fitzgerald, G. (1985). Validation of inattention/overactivity and aggression ratings with classroom observations. *Journal of Consulting and Clinical Psychology, 53*, 139–140.

Miller, J. A., & Leffard, S. A. (2007). Behavioral assessment. In S. R. Smith & L. Handler (Eds.), *The clinical assessment of children and adolescents: A practitioner's handbook* (pp. 115–137). Mahwah, NJ: Erlbaum.

Miltenberger, R. G., & Weil, T. M. (2013). Observation and measurement in behavior analysis. In G. Madden, W. Dube, T. Hackenberg, G. Hanley et al. (Eds.) *APA Handbook of behavioral analysis, Vol. 1: Methods and principles* (pp. 121–150). Washington, DC: American Psychological Association.

Moreno, J. (1946). *Psychodrama* (Vol. 1). New York, NY: Beacon House.

Morganstern, K. P., & Tevlin, H. E. (1981). Behavioral interviewing. In M. Hersen & A. S. Bellack (Eds.), *Behavioral assessment: A practical handbook* (2nd ed., pp. 71–100). New York, NY: Pergamon Press.

Morrison, C. S., McCusker, J., Stoddard, A. M., & Bigelow, C. (1995). The validity of behavioral data reported by injection drug users on a clinical risk assessment. *International Journal of the Addictions, 30*, 889–899.

Morse, C. J. (2012). Debriefing after simulated patient experiences. In L. Wilson & L. Rockstraw (Eds), *Human simulation for nursing and health professions* (pp. 58–66). New York, NY: Springer Publishing.

Morton, A. (1995). The enigma of non-attendance: A study of clients who do not turn up for their first appointment. *Therapeutic Communities: International Journal for Therapeutic and Supportive Organizations, 16*, 117–133.

Nakash, O., & Alegria, M. (2013). Examination of the role of implicit clinical judgments during the mental health intake. *Qualitative Health Research*, doi:10.1177/1049732312471732. No pagination specified.

Nevid, J. S., Rathus, S. A., & Greene, B. (2006). *Abnormal psychology in a changing world.* Upper Saddle River, NJ: Prentice Hall.

Nielsen, S. L., Okiishi, J., Nielsen, D. L., Hawkins, E. J., Harmon, S. C., et al. (2009). Termination, appointment use, and outcome patterns associated with intake therapist discontinuity. *Professional Psychology: Research and Practice, 40*, 272–278.

Nietzel, M. T., & Bernstein, D. A. (1976). The effects of instructionally mediated demand upon the behavioral assessment of assertiveness. *Journal of Consulting and Clinical Psychology, 44*, 500.

Nietzel, M. T., Bernstein, D. A., & Russell, R. L. (1988). Assessment of anxiety and fear. In A. S. Bellack & M. Hersen (Eds.), *Behavioral assessment: A practical handbook* (3rd ed., pp. 280–312). New York, NY: Pergamon Press.

Nock, M. K., & Kurtz, S. M. S. (2005). Direct behavioral observation in school settings: Bringing science to practice. *Cognitive and Behavioral Practice, 12*, 359–370.

Norton, P. J., & Hope, D. A. (2001). Analogue observational methods in assessment of social functioning in adults. *Psychological Assessment, 13*, 86–98.

Office of Strategic Services Assessment Staff. (1948). *Assessment of men.* New York, NY: Rinehart.

Ollendick, T. H., & Greene, R. (1990). Behavioral assessment of children. In G. Goldstein & M. Hersen (Eds.), *Handbook of psychological assessment* (2nd ed., pp. 403–422). New York, NY: Pergamon Press.

Orne, M. T. (1962). On the social psychology of the psychological experiment: With particular reference to demand characteristics and their implications. *American Psychologist, 17*, 776–783.

Othmer, E. M., & Othmer, S. C. (2002). *The clinical interview using DSM-IV-TR: Fundamentals.* Washington, DC: American Psychiatric Publishing. New York, NY: Brunner/Mazel.

Patterson, C. H. (1989). Foundations for a systematic eclectic psychotherapy. *Psychotherapy, 26*, 427–435.

Patterson, G. R. (1982). *Coercive family process.* Eugene, OR: Castalia.

Patterson, G. R., Ray, R. S., Shaw, D. A., & Cobb, J. A. (1969). *Manual for coding of family interactions* (Document NO. 01234). Available from ASIS/NAPS, c/o Microfiche Publications, 305 East 46th St., New York, NY 10017.

Paul, G. L. (1966). *Insight versus desensitization in psychotherapy: An experiment in anxiety reduction.* Stanford, CA: Stanford University Press.

Perls, F. S. (1969). *Gestalt therapy verbatim.* Lafayette, CA: Real People Press.

Peters, L., Clark, D., & Carroll, F. (1998). Are computerized interviews equivalent to human interviews? CIDI-Auto versus CIDI in anxiety and depressive disorders. *Psychological Medicine, 28*, 893–901.

Pilkonis, P. A., Heape, C. L., Proietti, J. M., Clark, S. W., McDavid, J. D., et al. (1995). The reliability and validity of two structured interviews for personality disorders. *Archives of General Psychiatry, 52*, 1025–1033.

Pottick, K. J., Kirk, S. A., Hsieh, D. K., & Tian, X. (2007). Judging medical disorders in youth: Effects of client, clinician, and contextual differences. *Journal of Consulting and Clinical Psychology, 75*, 1–8.

Prochaska, J. O., & Norcross, J. C. (1994). *Systems of psychotherapy: A transtheoretical analysis* (3rd ed.). Pacific Grove, CA: Brooks/Cole.

Rasting, M., & Beutel, M. E. (2005). Dyadic affective interactive patterns in the intake interview as a predictor of outcome. *Psychotherapy Research, 15*, 188–198.

Reich, W., Cottler, L., McCallum, K., & Corwin, D. (1995). Computerized interviews as a method of assessing psychopathology in children. *Comprehensive Psychiatry, 36*, 40–45.

Repp, A. C., & Horner, R. H. (2000). *Functional analysis of problem behavior: From effective assessment to effective support.* Belmont, CA: Wadsworth.

Rice, M. E. (1997). Violent offender research and implications for the criminal justice system. *American Psychologist, 52*, 414–423.

Rice, S. A. (1929). Contagious bias in the interview: A methodological note. *American Journal of Sociology, 35*, 420–423.

Rieger, G. (2012). The eyes have it: Sex and sexual orientation differences in pupil dilation patterns. Presentation at the May, 2012 Association for Psychological Science Conference, Chicago, IL.

Robins, L. N., Cottler, L. B., Bucholz, K. K., Comptom, W. M., North, C. S., et al. (2000). *Diagnostic Interview Schedule for DSM-IV.* St Louis, MO: Washington University School of Medicine.

Rogers, R. (2001). *Handbook of diagnostic and structured interviewing* (2nd ed.). New York, NY: Guilford.

Rogers, R., Gillis, J. R., Dickens, S. E., & Bagby, R. M. (1991). Standardized assessment of malingering: Validation of the Structured Interview of Reported Symptoms. *Psychological Assessment, 3,* 89–96.

Rogers, R., Wasyliw, O. E., & Cavanaugh, J. L. Jr. (1984). Evaluating insanity: A study of construct validity. *Law and Human Behavior,* 8, 293-303.

Rosen, D. C., Miller, A. B., Nakash, O., Halperin, L., & Alegria, M. (2012). Interpersonal complemntarity in the mental health intake: A mixed-methods study. *Journal of Counseling Psychology, 59,* 185–196.

Rosen, R. C., & Kopel, S. A. (1977). Penile plethysmography and biofeedback in the treatment of a transvestite-exhibitionist. *Journal of Consulting and Clinical Psychology, 45,* 908–916.

Ross, C. A., Schroeder, E., & Ness, L. (2013). Dissociation and symptoms of culture-bound syndromes in North America: A preliminary study. *Journal of Trauma & Dissociation, 14,* 224–235.

Ross, M. W., Stowe, A., Wodak, A., & Gold, J. (1995). Reliability of interview responses of injecting drug users. *Journal of Addictive Diseases, 14,* 1–2.

Saklofske, D. H., Schwean, V. L., & Reynolds, C. R. (Eds.). (2013). *The Oxford handbook of child psychological assessment.* New York, NY: Oxford University Press.

Schwab-Stone, M., Fallon, T., & Briggs, M. (1994). Reliability of diagnostic reporting for children aged 6–11 years: A test-retest study of the Diagnostic Interview Schedule for Children—Revised. *American Journal of Psychiatry, 151,* 1048–1054.

Segal, D. L., Mueller, A. E., & Coolidge, F. L. (Eds.), (2012). Structured and semistructured interviews for differential diagnosis: Fundamentals, applications, and essential features. In M. Hersen & D. Beidel (Eds.) *Adult psychopathology and diagnosis* (6th ed., pp. 91–115). New York, NY: Wiley.

Seto, M. C., Cantor, J. M., & Blanchard, R. (2006). Child pornography offenses are valid diagnostic indicators of pedophilia. *Journal of Abnormal Psychology, 115,* 610–615.

Shaffer, D., Fisher, P., Lucas, C. P., Dulcan, M. K., & Schwab-Stone, M. E. (2000). NIMH Diagnostic Interview Schedule for Children Version IV (NIMH DISC-IV): Description, differences from previous versions, and reliability of some common diagnoses. *Journal of the American Academy of Child & Adolescent Psychiatry, 39,* 28-38.

Shaw, D. L., Martz, D. M., Lancaster, C. J., & Sade, R. M. (1995). Influence of medical school applicants' demographic and cognitive characteristics on interviewers' ratings of noncognitive traits. *Academic Medicine, 70,* 532–536.

Shechtman, Z., & Tsegahun, I. (2004). Phototherapy to enhance self-disclosure and client-therapist alliance in an intake interview with Ethiopian immigrants to Israel. *Psychotherapy Research, 14,* 367–377.

Siassi, I. (1984). *Handbook of psychological assessment.* New York, NY: Pergamon.

Sommers-Flanagan, J., & Sommers-Flanagan, R. (2008). *Clinical interviewing* (4th ed.). New York, NY: Wiley and Sons.

Spiegel, T. A., Wadden, T. A., & Foster, G. D. (1991). Objective measurement of eating rate during behavioral treatment of obesity. *Behavior Therapy, 22,* 61–68.

Standen, P. J., & Brown, D. J. (2005). Virtual reality in the rehabilitation of people with intellectual disabilities: Review. *CyberPsychology and Behavior, 8,* 272–282.

Sue, D. W., & Sue, D. (2007). *Counseling the culturally diverse: Theory and practice* (5th ed.). New York, NY: John Wiley & Sons.

Sue, D. W., & Sue, D. (2008). *Counseling the culturally diverse: Theory and practice* (5th ed.). New York, NY: John Wiley & Sons.

Taplin, P. S., & Reid, J. B. (1973). Effects of instructional set and experimenter influence on observer reliability. *Child Development, 44,* 547–554.

Temerlin, M. K. (1968). Suggestion effects in psychiatric diagnosis. *Journal of Nervous and Mental Disease, 147,* 349–353.

Tolen, D. F., Robinson, J. T., Gaztambide, S., Horowitz, S., & Blank, K. (2007). Ataques de nervios and psychiatric disorders in older Puerto Rican primary care patients. *Journal of Cross-Cultural Psychology, 38,* 659-669.

Tryon, G. S. (1990). Session depth and smoothness in relation to the concept of engagement in counseling. *Journal of Counseling Psychology, 37,* 248–253.

Walker, E. F., Grimes, K. E., Davis, D. M., & Smith, A. J. (1993). Childhood precursors of schizophrenia: Facial expressions of emotion. *American Journal of Psychiatry, 150,* 1654–1660.

Wallen, R. W. (1956). *Clinical psychology: The study of persons.* New York, NY: McGraw-Hill.

Walter, A., Bundy, C., & Dornan, T. (2005). How should trainees be taught to open a clinical interview? *Medical Education, 39,* 492–496.

Ward, C. H., Beck, A. T., Mendelson, M., Mock, J. E., & Erbaugh, J. K. (1962). The psychiatric nomenclature. *Archives of General Psychiatry, 7,* 198–205.

Weick, K. E. (1968). Systematic observational methods. In G. Lindzey & E. Aronson (Eds.), *Handbook of social psychology* (Vol. 2, 2nd ed., pp. 357–451). Reading, MA: Addison-Wesley.

Weiss, R. D., Najavits, L. M., Muenz, L. R., & Hufford, C. (1995). Twelve-month test-retest reliability of the Structured Clinical Interview for DSM-III-R Personality Disorders in cocaine-dependent patients. *Comprehensive Psychiatry, 36,* 384–389.

West, M., Bondy, E., & Hutchinson, S. (1991). Interviewing institutionalized elders: Threats to validity. *Journal of Nursing Scholarship, 23,* 171–176.

Whitehouse, W. G., Orne, E. C., & Dinges, D. F. (2010). Extreme cognitive interviewing: A blueprint for false memories through imagination inflation. *International Journal of Clinical and Experimental Hypnosis, 58,* 29–287.

Widiger, T. A., Frances, A. J., Pincus, H. A., Davis, W. W., & First, M. B. (1991). Toward an empirical classification for the DSM-IV. *Journal of Abnormal Psychology, 100,* 280–288.

Williams, T. R. (1967). *Field methods in the study of culture.* New York, NY: Holt, Rinehart, & Winston.

Wilson, S., & Durbin, C. E. (2012). The laboratory parenting assessment battery: Development and preliminary validation of an observational parenting rating system. *Psychological Assessment.* Advance online publication. doi: 10.1037/a0028352.

Wong, H. M., & Chow, L. Y. (2011). Borderline personality disorder subscale (Chinese version) of the Structured Clinical Interview for DSM-IV Axis II Personality Disorders: A validation study in Cantonese-speaking Hong Kong Chinese. *East Asian Archives of Psychiatry, 21,* 52–57.

Zetin, M., & Glenn, T. (1999). Development of a computerized psychiatric diagnostic interview for use by mental health and primary care clinicians. *CyberPsychology & Behavior, 2,* 223–233.

Zigmond, A. S., & Snaith, R. P. (1983). The Hospital Anxiety and Depression Scale. *Acta Psychiatrica Scandinavica, 67,* 361–370.

5

TESTING IN CLINICAL PSYCHOLOGY

Chapter Preview

In this chapter, we consider the nature of psychological tests, how tests are constructed, and how they are used by clinical psychologists. Most psychological tests can be categorized as measuring (a) intellectual abilities; (b) attitudes, interests, and values; or (c) aspects of personality, including psychopathology. Tests can also be categorized according to the kinds of responses requested—some ask for brief, easily scored responses (e.g., true or false) and some require longer, more difficult-to-score responses (e.g., stories, drawings). We describe several tests commonly used by clinicians and provide information about their psychometric properties and clinical utility. We end by examining recent developments in psychological testing.

The role of testing as an activity in clinical psychology has undergone large shifts in popularity over the years. Beginning in the 1930s and continuing through the mid-1960s, tests were touted as semi-magical pathways to the "truth" about intelligence, personality, and ability (Reisman, 1976). During those years, clinical psychology students were trained intensively in the use of tests. From the late 1960s through the 1970s, however, testing lost much of its appeal and was deemphasized as a training goal and professional activity for clinicians. The decline of testing during this time was brought about by (a) unflattering results of research on the reliability and validity of many tests; (b) awareness of the susceptibility of tests to various biases; (c) recognition that tests, particularly those assessing intelligence, might discriminate unfairly against certain minority groups; (d) fear that the testing process may invade respondents' privacy; and (e) worry that tests are too easily misused or misinterpreted.

Within the last several years, testing has reversed its decline: it is now a regular part of most clinicians' training and professional activities. This resurgence has occurred partly because new and better tests have been designed to address some of the concerns just mentioned. It has resulted, too, because so many of today's educational and health care systems require psychological testing (Youngstrom, 2013).

BASIC CONCEPTS IN PSYCHOLOGICAL TESTING

SECTION PREVIEW

Here we discuss the basic nature of tests and how they resemble and differ from other forms of assessment. We discuss methods of test construction and the basic requirements for a good test: adequate standardization, reliability, and validity. We also consider the need for test developers and users to avoid test bias. The section ends with some information about patterns of test usage among clinicians.

What Is a Test?

A test is a systematic procedure for observing and describing a person's behavior in a standard situation (Cronbach, 1970). Tests present a set of planned stimuli (factual questions, inkblots, or true–false questions, for example) and ask the client to respond in some way. The clinician then scores or interprets the client's responses using objective, empirically derived scoring rules. Usually, the clinician incorporates the test results into an overall assessment that may also include interviews and other sources of information (see Chapter 3, "Basic Features of Clinical Assessment").

Our description of tests highlights two of their most important features. First, tests are designed to be *objective* measures, just as a ruler is designed to be an objective measure of length. Although no test is perfectly objective, objectivity is the goal because tests are designed to measure the differences among clients, not clinicians. Second, our description highlights the importance of *standardization*. All persons taking the same test should be exposed to the same set of stimuli and evaluated with the same scoring criteria. For example, suppose that one 5-year-old taking an IQ test is asked, "What part of your body goes in your shoe?" and another is asked "How many quarters make two dollars?" If one child responded correctly and the other incorrectly, it would be very difficult to determine whether differences in their scores resulted from differences in their knowledge level or from differences in the test administration.

Domino and Domino (2006) have suggested that the principles of objectivity and standardization allow us to view psychological tests with the same logic as that used to view experiments. In both, the idea is to eliminate extraneous variables so that results can be attributed to one source. If we are successful in an experiment, changes in the dependent variable can be attributed to changes in the independent variable, not extraneous variables. If we are successful in developing and using a test, its scores should reliably reflect characteristics of the client, not characteristics of test administration, scoring procedures, or clinicians.

So tests are like experiments, but they are also like the highly structured interviews or observations discussed in Chapter 4, "Interviewing and Observation in Clinical Psychology," in that they ask clients to respond to specific stimuli presented in a predetermined sequence, and their responses are scored on the basis of explicit rules. Tests also share characteristics with observational assessments by providing an opportunity for the clinician to watch the client in the test situation. In some ways, however, tests are distinct from all other assessment techniques. For example,

1. Usually, a client's test responses can be quantitatively compared to statistical norms established by the responses of hundreds or thousands of other people who have taken the same test under standardized conditions. Standardization allows us to compare a particular 5-year-old's performance with the performance of the average 5-year-old.
2. A test can be taken in private, so observational assessment might not supplement test data.
3. Tests can be administered in groups as well as individually. The SAT and other college entrance examinations provide examples of how tests are used to assess large numbers of people at the same time.

What Do Tests Measure?

Tests provide measures of everything from A (anxiety) to Z (z-scores on achievement tests). In fact, there are so many tests that it takes special publications to list them all and review their reliability, validity, and utility. The best known and most authoritative of these is the *Mental Measurements Yearbook*, first published in 1938 (Buros, 1938) and updated frequently (Plake, Geisinger, Spies, & Buros Institute, 2012). At over a thousand pages, this publication reviews thousands of standardized psychological tests. Many of them must be purchased from their publisher and are available only to qualified individuals. (The reasons for such restrictions are obvious if you consider, for instance, what would happen if someone decided to post on the Internet all the questions and answers on a standard intelligence test.) Other tests are available to researchers or other interested people for free. The American Psychological Association recently launched PsychTESTS, the first centralized, searchable database to provide access to over 2,000 downloadable copies of (primarily unpublished) psychological tests (Weir, 2012).

There are tests designed to be used with infants, children, adolescents, adults, senior citizens, students, soldiers, mental patients, office workers, job applicants, prisoners, and every other imaginable group (Plake, Geisinger, Spies, & Buros Institute, 2012). Some of these tests pose direct, specific questions ("Do you ever feel discouraged?"), while others ask for general reactions to less distinct stimuli ("Tell me what you see in this drawing"). Some have correct answers ("Is a chicken a mammal?"), while others probe for opinions or preferences ("I enjoy looking at flowers: true or false?"). Some are presented in paper-and-pencil form, some are given orally. Some require verbal skill ("What does *analogy* mean?"), some ask the client to perform various nonverbal tasks ("Please trace the correct path through this puzzle maze"), and still others combine verbal, numerical, and performance items. Often, there are several different tests designed to measure the same characteristic.

One reason for the proliferation of tests is that testers are forever hoping to measure clinical constructs in ever more reliable, valid, and sophisticated ways. For example, one clinician may feel that a popular anxiety test does not really assess anxiety very well, and so the clinician creates a new, improved instrument. Other psychologists might be dissatisfied with both tests and soon come up with yet other devices. Another factor responsible for the increasing array of tests is that testers' interests are becoming more specific, thus prompting the development of special-purpose tests. Despite their enormous variety, tests can be grouped into three general categories based on whether they seek to measure (a) *intellectual or cognitive abilities*, (b) *attitudes, interests, preferences, and values*, or (c) *personality characteristics* (see Table 5.1). The tests most commonly used by clinical psychologists in the United States and elsewhere are those of intellectual functioning and personality (Camara, Nathan, & Puente, 2000; Harwood, Beutler, & Groth-Marnat, 2011). These variables are especially relevant to most clinicians' treatment and research activities. Also, other people expect clinicians to offer advice on such things.

TABLE 5.1 A Sampling of Tests Used by Clinical Psychologists

Cognition/Intellectual Functioning	*Focused Measures of Emotional Functioning and Tests for Selected Populations*
Stanford-Binet V	Child Development
Wechsler Adult Intelligence Scale (WAIS-IV)	Bayley Scales of Infant Development
Wechsler Intelligence Scale for Children IV (WISC-IV)	Gesell Developmental Scales
Wechsler Preschool and Primary	Personality Inventory for Children (PIC)
Scale of Intelligence (WPPSI-III)	Peabody Picture Vocabulary Test-Revised (PPVT-R)
Kaufman Assessment Battery for Children (K-ABC-II)	Child Behavior Checklist (CBCL)
Woodcock–Johnson Psychoeducational Battery III	Behavior Assessment System for Children-2 (BASC-2)
Mini Mental Status Exam	Marital/Family Disturbance
Bender Visual Motor Gestalt Test	Family Environment Scale
Broad Measures of Personality and Emotional Functioning	Marital Satisfaction Inventory
Minnesota Multiphasic Personality Inventory-2 (MMPI-2)	Beck Depression Inventory II (BDI-II)
Personality Assessment Inventory (PAI)	Hamilton Rating Scale for Depression
Millon Clinical Multiaxial Inventory (MCMI-III)	State-Trait Anxiety Inventory
Psychological Screening Inventory (PSI)	Neurological Assessment/Aging
Symptom Checklist 90-Revised	Halstead–Reitan Neuropsychological Test Battery
Thematic Apperception Test (TAT)	Drug History Questionnaire (DHQ) Miller Hope Scale (MHS)
Rorschach Inkblot Technique	UCLA Loneliness Scale (ULS)
Cattell 16PF	Hassles Scale
California Psychological Inventory (CPI)	Brief Social Phobia Scale (BSPS)
NEO Personality Inventory-Revised (NEO-PI-R)	Binge Eating Scale (BES)
Internal-External Locus of Control (I-E)	*Forensic*
Sentence Completion Tests	Competency Screening Test
Projective Drawings (e.g., House-Tree-Person Test)	Georgia Court Competency Test
Attitudes, Interests, and Values	California F (fascism) Scale
Holland Self-Directed Search (SDS)	Legal Attitudes Questionnaire (LAQ)
Strong Interest Inventory (SII)	
Kuder Occupational Interest Survey (KOIS)	
Rokeach Value Survey (RVS)	
Study of Values (SoV)	

Note: Tests in this table are categorized according to their primary usage. However, some tests used in one category can also be used in another.

How Are Tests Constructed?

The seemingly odd items on some psychological tests, especially on certain personality tests, lead many people to wonder how psychologists come up with these things. The answer is that they usually construct their tests using *analytic* or *empirical* approaches, though often they use a *sequential system* approach, which combines the two (Burisch, 1984).

Psychologists using the analytic approach, sometimes called the rational approach, begin by asking: What are the qualities I want to measure, and how do I define these qualities? They then build a test by creating items that answer these questions. In other words, a developer creates test materials or items by analyzing the content of a domain and matching questions that he or she believes (or that a theory says) tap that content.

To illustrate the simplest analytic approach, suppose that a clinician wanted to develop a test for identifying males and females. The first step would be to ask what kinds of test items are likely to be answered differently by members of the two sexes. The choice of items, then, will be shaped by what the clinician's knowledge, experience, and favorite theories say is different about the genders. If the clinician chooses to focus on variations in physical characteristics, and prefers a true–false format, the test might contain items such as the following:

1. I was born with a prostate gland.
2. I was born with a uterus.
3. I was born with a penis.
4. I was born with a vagina.

Suppose, however, that the clinician's interest in gender differences is not so much biological sex but rather the distribution of traits stereotypically associated with being male or female. The clinician might develop items designed to tap unconscious processes associated with views of masculinity and femininity. Such a test might search for unconscious themes by asking clients to fill in incomplete sentences such as the following:

1. A dependent person is _____.
2. Strength is _____.
3. The trouble with most men is _____.
4. Most women are _____.

This example illustrates the importance of clearly defining the concept to be measured—a tester interested in gender is likely to construct very different instruments depending on whether the goal is to measure biological sex, gender identity, or gender-role stereotypes. In any case, items on an analytically constructed test will strongly reflect the tester's theory of what aspects of certain concepts should be tested, and how.

The main alternative to analytic test construction is the *empirical approach*. Here, instead of deciding ahead of time what test content should be used to measure a particular target, the tester lets the content "choose itself." Thus, in building a sex test, the clinician would amass a large number of self-report test items, performance tasks, inkblots, or other stimuli and then administer all of them to a large group of people *who have already been identified* as males or females using a biological criterion such as chromosome analysis. The clinician would then examine the entire group's responses to all these testing materials to see which items, tasks, or other stimuli were consistently answered differently by men and women.

Any test items that reliably differentiated the sexes would be used to create the initial version of the sex test, *regardless of whether they have any obvious relationship to sex differences*. Thus, if many more males than females answered "true" to items like "I often have trouble sleeping" or "My shoes are too tight," those items would become part of the test. Empirically driven testers are usually willing to employ items that reliably discriminate among target groups even though the conceptual relevance of those items cannot always be explained clearly. *That* is why some tests contain such apparently odd items.

Several factors affect test developers' choice between analytic and empirical procedures. The analytic approach can be faster and less expensive because it does not require initial administration of many items to many people in order to settle on those that will comprise the test. These features make analytic procedures attractive to clinicians who do not have access to a large pool of test material and willing participants or who are forced by circumstances to develop a test on short notice. Analytic procedures also tend to be favored by clinicians evaluating a particular theory. Suppose that theory suggests that people differ in terms of "geekiness," but no test is available to measure it. To explore the geekiness dimension of personality, the researcher will need a test that taps what the theory says geekiness is. The test would also use measurement methods consistent with the theory. Development of a Geek Test would thus likely proceed on analytic grounds.

Clinicians who have time and other resources available often find the empirical approach more desirable, especially when attempting to make specific predictions about people. If the tester's task is to identify individuals likely to graduate from law school, for example, it makes sense to find out if students who graduate respond to specific test items in a way that is reliably different from those who fail or drop out. In short, the analytic method often results in items that appear sensible but may or may not work; the empirical approach often results in items that work but may or not appear sensible.

The *sequential system approach* to test construction combines aspects of the analytic and empirical techniques. The decision about which items to try is usually made on analytic grounds; some items are selected from existing tests, while others are those the clinician believes "ought" to be evaluated. Testers who choose initial test items analytically may then examine results statistically to determine which item responses do and do not discriminate between people who differ on the characteristic of interest. They may also examine which items are correlated with one another. Groups of correlated items are then identified as *scales*, which are thought to be relatively pure measures of certain dimensions of personality, mental ability, or the like (Maloney & Ward, 1976). Regardless of how a test is constructed initially, its value as an assessment instrument ultimately depends on empirical research demonstrating its reliability and validity (see Chapter 3, "Basic Features of Clinical Assessment").

STANDARDIZATION AND SCORE INTERPRETATION   We have already mentioned that standardization refers to consistency in administration and scoring of a test. Ideally, tests are given in the same way to every person taking them, though this ideal can be taken too far. We know of a testing course in which the professor required that his student-examiners place certain stimulus materials for an IQ test directly in front of the client and exactly 7 inches from the edge of the table. He even walked around with a ruler during practice administrations to be sure this practice was followed. Exact consistency in administration is impossible, but within the bounds of reason clinicians do try to maintain high levels of consistency.

In addition to consistency in administration, standardization can also refer to the sample on which the test was originally developed. To illustrate, suppose that Amy, an 8-year-old, gets 14 out of 23 items correct on a memory test. Is that a high score? A low score? In order to know the answer, we must compare Amy's score with a large sample of scores from persons who are similar to her in age. If 1,000 8-year-olds originally took the test, and only the top 8% were able to get 14 or more answers correct, we would know that Amy's score is a high one, at the 92nd percentile to be exact. In this example, the 1,000 children who took the test provide the *standardization sample* for the test. The scores obtained from this sample became the standard against which subsequent scores can be compared. Their scores provide the main interpretive framework for all individual scores on the test.

The numbers that come from the standardization sample—means, variances, percentages, and so on—are called *norms*. These are the benchmarks that allow meaningful interpretation of a test performance. Every decade or so, major tests are *renormed*. This process can be complex and expensive because it involves identifying a large, representative sample of persons willing to take the test; finding examiners to give the test and report results; and compiling and analyzing all the data. The results of this renorming process are then usually published in the instruction manuals that accompany the tests. After giving a test, clinicians compare their client's scores with those contained in the manual. Most of the tests discussed in this chapter are norm-referenced tests.

Test scores can also be interpreted based on a *criterion* established by the tester rather than on a normative sample. For instance, to qualify as a pilot, candidates must meet a predetermined criterion, or level of proficiency; it is not enough simply to score, say, above the average score of other candidates (Domino & Domino, 2006). Finally, test scores can be interpreted by comparing a person's score, not to other people's or to an external criterion, but to the person's own scores. This process is often called *ipsative measurement*. For example, suppose a test asks therapy clients to list their most important goals for the next year or the number of panic attacks they have had in the past month. It can be informative to compare the results of this test at the beginning of therapy and 6 months later. Ipsative measures are becoming increasingly important because they help clinicians measure the outcomes of treatment. Changes in these measures can also be discussed with clients as part of treatment (Finn & Martin, 2013).

Avoiding Distortion in Test Scores

A multitude of factors can alter or distort the outcome of tests. A classic example is provided by a study in which college men who had just seen photographs of nude females gave more sex-related responses to the TAT when it was administered by a young, informally dressed male graduate student than when given by a man who was older and more formal (Mussen & Scodel, 1955). So the circumstances under which a test is given—anything from temperature extremes and noise to crowding and the presence of a stranger—can affect its results (Plante, Goldfarb, & Wadley, 1993). In one case, for example, a child's scores on repeated IQ tests went from 68 to 120 and back to 79 depending on whether or not a particular adult was in the testing room (Handler, 1974). While most variation is not this extreme, the case illustrates that establishing trust and avoiding distraction can affect the validity of certain kinds of tests.

Another source of distortion in test results is the tendency for some clients to respond in particular ways to most items, regardless of what the items are. This tendency has been called *response set* (Cronbach, 1946), *response style* (Jackson & Messick, 1958), and *response bias* (Berg, 1955). For example, clients are said to display an *acquiescent response style* (Jackson & Messick, 1961) if they tend to agree with virtually any self-descriptive test item. Defensive, deviant, and exaggerated response styles have also been postulated (e.g., Isenhart & Silversmith, 1996).

Clients exhibiting a *social desirability bias* will respond to test items in ways that are most socially acceptable, whether or not those responses reflect their true feelings or impulses (Edwards, 1957; Rychtarik, Tarnowski, & St. Lawrence, 1989). This kind of distortion is less like the relatively unconscious response biases described above and more like deliberate faking. Intentionally distorting one's test responses by answering untruthfully is called *malingering*, and it is an ongoing problem, especially in assessments that involve criminal proceedings, custody evaluations, involuntary commitment, personal injury litigation, etc. (Larrabee, 2012). As we will discuss shortly, many tests contain scales designed to assess the likelihood of malingering.

The significance of response styles and bias in determining test scores has been hotly debated, partly because it is unclear whether response tendencies represent stable client characteristics (McCrae & Costa, 1983) or temporary behaviors dictated and reinforced by the testing circumstances (Linehan & Nielsen, 1983; Stewart, Darnold, Zimmerman, Parks, & Dustin, 2010). Whatever the case, the client's point of view while taking a test cannot be ignored in evaluating test results.

It is impossible to eliminate all extraneous sources of variability in test scores, but test designers can minimize them by (a) developing clear, simple instructions for examiners and test takers, (b) extensively pilot-testing and studying response tendencies on items, (c) enlisting the participation of outside experts in test bias during test development, and (d) building indicators of response bias or deliberate distortion into the test so that these things can be identified if they occur. At the same time, those who give tests can reduce distortion by (a) clearly explaining the purposes of the test and answering any questions the client has, thereby enhancing rapport and client motivation; (b) paying careful attention to the circumstances under which testing takes place so that conditions are essentially the same for each client; and (c) noting and reporting (e.g., to referral sources) any circumstances in the testing that might compromise the validity of the test results. Table 5.2 summarizes some important criteria for evaluating a test, some of which were also discussed in the previous two chapters (Ayearst & Bagby, 2011).

TABLE 5.2 Criteria for Judging the Psychometric Quality of a Test

Criterion	What It Is
Norms	Measures of central tendency and variability for the test obtained from a large, representative standardization sample; these allow meaningful interpretation of scores.
Internal consistency reliability	A measure of reliability, usually accomplished by the split-half method.
Test-retest reliability	Similarity of results from repeat testings of the same persons.
Interrater reliability	Similarity of results when multiple raters independently score the same tests.
Content validity	Items on the test adequately sample all the important domains associated with the trait or ability being measured.
Convergent validity	Results of the test correlate with other well-established measures of the same construct.
Discriminant validity	Results of a test do not correlate with measures of constructs that are conceptually different.
Diagnostic or Clinical Utility	The degree to which test results clearly point to specific diagnosis or preferred treatments, or can reliably measure changes that result from treatment.

CULTURAL FAIRNESS AND BIAS IN PSYCHOLOGICAL TESTS

Suppose you are a clinician and find yourself in the following situation:

Mrs. P., a 37-year-old immigrant from Vietnam, is referred to you as a new client. She speaks English reasonably well, and you conclude from the initial interview that she is probably suffering from depression, but it is difficult to determine the severity of the problem. She also voiced some vague somatic complaints, which you suspect indicate other problems, but, again, it is difficult to determine exactly what they might be. Her insurance company wants an accurate *DSM* diagnosis, as do you, and you would also like to have a better understanding of this client and her difficulties. To get a clearer picture, you decide to administer tests for psychological problems in general and depression in particular.

Will the client be able to understand the test items? Will she interpret the items in the same way as native English speakers would? Do the test norms apply to Vietnamese immigrants? This example introduces a broader question: To what extent do psychological tests adequately assess psychopathology, personality, intelligence, or other characteristics in diverse populations?

Concerns about the cultural fairness of tests appeared first and most prominently in relation to measures of intellectual abilities. Investigators consistently found that, on average, African Americans and Hispanic Americans scored lower than European- and Asian Americans on standard intelligence tests. The controversy is not whether the lower scores occur but rather why they occur. Does the fact that different cultural or ethnic groups show different average scores on a test mean that the test is biased?

As Domino and Domino (2006) point out, test-related bias can result from factors occurring *before* the test, such as when certain cultural and ethnic groups are disadvantaged by discrimination, lower-quality education, poverty, stereotyped portrayals, poor role models, and the like. Bias can also occur *during* the test itself, as when, for example, concepts or vocabulary used on the test are more familiar to clients from some cultural backgrounds than others. Either or both could be responsible for the observed gap in test results between cultural groups. Is there any way to detect which of these sources might explain the observed group differences in tests results?

There is, and the easiest to detect is test item bias. If test designers collect information about the gender and ethnic composition of the test's standardization sample, they can analyze responses to each test item. If, because of unfamiliarity with the item's vocabulary or other content, one group responds incorrectly significantly more often than other groups, developers can simply eliminate that item from the test. The courts have often used an "80%" or "four-fifths" rule to label such an item as biased. That is, if there is a difference of 20% or more between the mean scores of majority and minority groups on a particular test item, that item is considered to be biased. Using such procedures during test development, most carefully designed and widely used psychological tests today have greatly reduced or eliminated culturally biased items. They have also addressed other biasing factors such as confusing instructions and cultural-specific testing materials.

What about cultural inequality as an explanation of intergroup score differences? Most persons familiar with test construction procedures view this factor as the best explanation of why certain minorities score differently, on average, on standardized tests when compared to majority group members (Domino & Domino, 2006). To illustrate the point, try this thought experiment: Imagine that researchers were able to construct culture-neutral intelligence tests in which minority and majority groups scored the same, on average. If you accepted *this* test as valid, you would have to argue that factors such as poverty, discrimination, and inferior educational opportunities have *no effect* on cognitive and academic test performance. To most people, that conclusion would make no sense. As Anne Anastasi (1988) put it,

> Tests are designed to show what an individual can do at a given point in time. They cannot tell us *why* he performs as he does. Tests cannot compensate for cultural deprivation by eliminating its effect from their scores. On the contrary, tests should *reveal* such effects, so that appropriate remedial steps can be taken. To conceal the effects of cultural disadvantages by trying to devise tests that are insensitive to such effects is equivalent to breaking a thermometer because it registers a body temperature of 101°. (p. 66)

In short, average test score differences between minority and majority groups are more likely the result of differences in cultural conditions than of bias in the tests. Further support for this idea comes from the fact that attempts to develop "culture-fair" tests have not been very successful. Such tests appear to be influenced just as much as, or more than, standard tests by cultural and environmental factors (Samuda, 1975), and their validity tends to be lower (Humphreys, 1988).

We are not arguing that test bias does not exist, only that test item bias is reasonably well controlled in more well-established and extensively studied tests. The same is not true for all tests—test fairness depends on the care with which standardization samples are chosen and the degree to which cross-cultural generalizability has been investigated and addressed.

Returning to the case of our client from Vietnam, a conscientious clinician would look for empirical evidence that supports the generalization of standard tests of personality and psychopathology to Asian populations. Were Asian American groups adequately represented in the standardization sample? Does the client have language or cultural background factors that could invalidate the test? Is there a validated version of these tests in the client's native language? Better still, the clinician might use the Vietnamese Depression Scale (Kinzie et al., 1982), a test developed specifically for persons from Mrs. P.'s background. The clinician would also be wise to seek out published material and advice from colleagues who could provide insight into how Mrs. P.'s background might affect her assessment and treatment (e.g., Hays & Iwamasa, 2006) and to engage Mrs. P. in further discussion about her health beliefs, as these may differ from those commonly held by Westerners (Okazaki & Tanaka-Matsumi, 2006).

Many clinical researchers are now examining test use across cultural and age groups (Correa, Rogers, & Hoestring, 2010; Crowther, Austing, Scogin, Harwood, & Harrell, 2011). Their goal is to construct tests that will be valid for specific populations. For example, Jia-xi & Guo-peng (2006) investigated the validity and reliability of a Chinese version of the 16PF, a personality test. They found that the Chinese revision has good applicability, though the scale's internal consistency could be improved.

The American Psychological Association has urged its members to reduce the possibility of inappropriate use or interpretation of tests by adhering to the *Standards for Educational and Psychological Tests* (1999; revised in 2013), a document developed by the American Educational Research Association, the American Psychological Association, and the National Council on Measurement in Education. Additionally, the APA's *Guidelines for Test User Qualifications* provides additional information for those considering the use of tests. The *Uniform Guidelines on Employee Selection Procedures* was developed by the Equal Employment Opportunity Commission (EEOC) to regulate the use of tests and other methods as selection techniques. Together, these documents guide test users and help ensure that when developed, evaluated, administered, interpreted, and

TABLE 5.3 Ethical Standards for Psychologists' Use of Tests

Principle	Example of Application
Competence	Clinicians should be experienced in the administration and interpretation of tests that they use to make decisions about a client.
Professional/scientific responsibility	Clinicians should be familiar with the research literature on a test, particularly its reliability, validity, appropriate uses, and limitations.
Integrity	Clinicians should use tests as intended and not make claims about tests or test results unless those claims are supported by empirical evidence.
Respect for rights and dignity	Clinicians should ensure that a test genuinely applies to persons taking the test, such as persons from different cultures.
Concern for others' welfare	First, clinicians should do no harm in using tests with clients; they should recognize the potential for harm, especially if test results are inappropriately applied.
Social responsibility	Clinicians should not disseminate test materials or the protected content of tests to unauthorized personnel; they should take action to prevent the misuse of tests by others (e.g., colleagues, institutions).
Access to test materials	Ethical practice prohibits test developers and users from making public the contents of certain psychological tests (e.g., I.Q. tests); tests are commercially available only to qualified users.

published with due regard for scientific principles and the rights and welfare of clients, psychological tests can make a positive contribution to society (Robertson & Eyde, 1993). Table 5.3 lists the general principles from the APA Ethical standards regarding the use of tests and provides examples of situations that might apply to each.

In the next section, we describe the tests that are most commonly used by clinical psychologists. Further information about these and other tests for individual and group administration to adults and children is available from the technical manuals associated with each test and from numerous other sources on psychological testing (e.g., Antony & Barlow, 2010; Butcher, 2009; Domino & Domino, 2006; Geisinger, 2013; Groth-Marnat, 2009; Hersen & Beidel, 2012; Plake, Geisinger, Spies, & Buros Institute, 2012).

SECTION SUMMARY

Tests present clients with a series of stimuli in a planned sequence. If variables associated with the test construction, administration, and scoring are adequately controlled, differences in test performance should reflect real differences among the persons taking the test. Because eliminating bias is not easy, test developers must pay careful attention to how various groups of persons react to the items. Test users should be professionally qualified, understand what makes a high-quality test, and follow ethical principles in testing.

TESTS OF INTELLECTUAL FUNCTIONING

SECTION PREVIEW

In this section, we outline how theorists have understood and measured intelligence. We then describe the variety of tests clinicians use to measure cognitive abilities. Some focus on a broad range of abilities and some on specific abilities. Prominent among the first are the Stanford–Binet scales and the Wechsler scales. Clinicians also use a variety of other tests to measure achievement and aptitude.

Theories of Intelligence

While everyone would agree that intelligence is a good thing to have, there is far less consensus about what it actually *is* (Davidson & Kemp, 2011). This state of affairs has generated the half-joking suggestion among clinicians that "intelligence is whatever intelligence tests measure." Indeed, the developers of most intelligence tests have initially proceeded on analytical grounds; each of the more than 200 assessment instruments they have produced reflects its creator's theoretical views about the essential nature of intelligence and about how best to measure intellectual functioning. A description of those theories is beyond the scope of this chapter (see Davidson & Kemp, 2011; Rowe, 2013 for reviews), but it is worth noting that various researchers have generally described intelligence in one of three ways, each of which is briefly described below.

GENERAL INTELLIGENCE   One theory, often favored by those employing a mental testing, or *psychometric* approach to intelligence, describes intelligence as a *general* characteristic. Originally proposed by Spearman (1904), the notion of intelligence as a global, general ability has come to be referred to simply as *g*. While everyone has variations in their ability across different domains, *g* is presumed to be an underlying biological or psychological trait that influences all cognitive abilities. This view is supported by the observation that students who are exceptional in math, for instance, also tend to be good in English, biology, and many other areas. It fits also with the robust and well-established finding that test scores on a variety of cognitive tasks are positively correlated (van der Maas et al., 2006). The underlying factor common to the scores is presumed to be *g*.

MULTIPLE SPECIFIC INTELLIGENCES MODELS   Although researchers find that scores on a variety of cognitive tasks are correlated, the correlation is not always strong. As a result, some have argued that intelligence is better understood as a collection of relatively separate abilities. As many as 120 *specific* intellectual functions (called *s*'s) have been proposed, including abilities such as word fluency, short-term memory, and perceptual speed (Carroll, 1993; Domino & Domino, 2006). However, most theories suggest a far more limited number of abilities that are presumed to reflect intelligence.

One multiple intelligence theory that has received considerable attention is Robert Sternberg's *triarchic theory*. Sternberg argues that there are three basic kinds of intelligence—analytical, creative, and practical—and that conventional tests measure only the first kind well (Sternberg, 2004, 2006a, 2013). Along with his colleagues, Sternberg has developed a test designed to measure all three (the *Sternberg Triarchic Abilities Test*, or *STAT*). A key theme in Sternberg's theory is that intelligence should be understood as something that makes a person successful in life generally, not just in academic settings, and that intelligence tests should measure the factors leading to success (Sternberg, 2011).

A second popular multiple intelligence approach is that of Howard Gardner, who lists eight intelligences or frames of mind: verbal, mathematical, spatial, bodily–kinesthetic, musical, intrapersonal, interpersonal, and naturalistic (Gardner, 1993, 2002). His theory has drawn considerable interest, especially in the field of education. Other specific kinds of intelligence have been proposed, including emotional intelligence (Mayer, Salovey, Caruso, & Cherkasskiy, 2011), social intelligence (Kihlstrom & Cantor, 2011), and even mating intelligence (Geher & Kaufman, 2011).

Specific multiple intelligence theories propose that intelligence is better understood as a collection of relatively separate abilities rather than as a single factor. It is noteworthy that both Sternberg's and especially Gardner's theories have expanded the term *intelligence* to include abilities that are not included in its traditional definition (e.g., kinesthetic athletic skill). Some see these theories as valuable; others argue that they overextend the definition of intelligence—not everything a person does should be considered a kind of intelligence.

HIERARCHICAL AND FACTOR ANALYTIC MODELS   A third view of intelligence might be considered a combination of the previous two. In this hybrid view, separate and general cognitive abilities are related in a hierarchical fashion (see Figure 5.1). At the most elemental level, the bottom stratum in Figure 5.1, are specific abilities such as vocabulary knowledge, visual pattern recognition, and the like (represented in Figure 5.1 as a1, a2, a3, b1, b2, etc.). Specific abilities are not entirely independent of each other; certain ones correlate because they share a common factor (e.g., a good memory, verbal knowledge, rapid processing of visual information). The common factors are represented in Figure 5.1 as factors *a* through *d* in the middle stratum. Finally, these

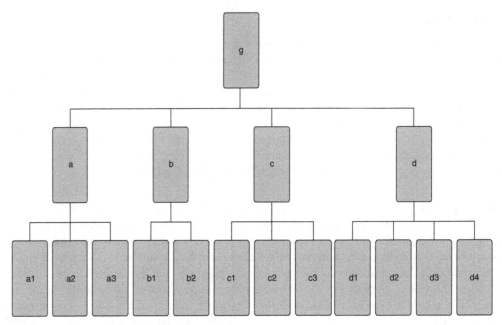

FIGURE 5.1   A Hierarchical Model of Intelligence

higher-order factors are themselves correlated to some degree, and that correlation is represented by the common, top stratum, factor, *g*, that underlies them all.

Is there a way to evaluate these different views of intelligence? For instance, how do we know the degree to which specific abilities cluster together? *Factor analytic studies* measure the degree to which various measures are correlated. Carroll (1993) reviewed earlier work on intelligence by Cattell (1943) and Horn (1965), and then summarized 461 factor analytic studies of intelligence. From this work has emerged a hierarchical model that has, with some modifications, been adopted by most of the major intelligence test developers. Those models continue to evolve in response to empirical research, especially that involving factor analytic studies (Dombrowski, 2013; Urbina, 2011). As we review the various intelligence tests, note the similarities and differences in the factors presumed to be measured by these widely used tests.

The Binet Scales

Alfred Binet was not the first person to develop a measure of intelligence, but his original test and the revisions based on it have been among the most influential means of assessing the mental ability of children. The earliest (1905) form of Binet's test consisted of 30 questions and tasks, including things like unwrapping a piece of candy, following a moving object with the eyes, comparing objects of differing weights, repeating numbers or sentences from memory, and recognizing familiar objects. The child's test score was simply the number of items passed. Beginning with a 1908 revision, the tasks in Binet's test were *age graded*, which means that they were arranged so that younger children were expected to pass only the earlier ones, while older children were expected to pass later ones as well.

The 1908 scale was brought to the United States by Henry Goddard and revised in 1916 by Lewis Terman, a Stanford University psychologist. Terman adopted an idea suggested by German psychologist William Stern for representing numerically the relationship between mental and chronological age: *Stanford–Binet* results were expressed as the *intelligence quotient* (or IQ) that results when mental age (MA) is divided by chronological age (CA) and multiplied by 100. Thus, a 6-year-old whose score on the Stanford–Binet yielded a mental age of 8 would have an IQ of 133 (8/6 × 100). Thus began the tradition of pegging the average IQ score at 100.

The most recent version of the Stanford–Binet, the SB5, was completed in 2003. As happens with all major test revisions, the SB5 went through a pilot phase before its final form was determined. The test was normed on a sample of 4,800 persons who were representative of the U.S. population and stratified on the variables of age, sex, race/ethnicity, geographic region, and socioeconomic level. By recording these variables in a large sample during pilot testing, the

TABLE 5.4 Items of the Type Included in the Stanford-Binet 5	
Vocabulary: Define words like train, wrench, letter, error, and encourage.	*Memory for sentences:* Correctly recall sentences that were presented.
Object Series/Matrices: Choose the right order in which a series of pictures was presented.	*Verbal Relations:* Indicate how three objects or words are alike but different from a fourth. For example, how are dog, cat, and horse alike but different from boy.
Absurdities: Identify the mistakes or "silly" aspects of pictures in which, for example, a man is shown using the wrong end of a rake or a girl is shown putting a piece of clothing on incorrectly.	*Block Span:* Separate blocks into rows coded with yellow and red stripes.
Quantitative Reasoning: Determine which numbers come next in a series of numbers such as the following: 32, 26, 20, 14, ____, ____.	

test developers could determine whether certain items were answered differently, on average, by persons from different ethnic groups or genders. During this phase, numerous items were pilot tested and either kept or discarded (refer to our discussion of test construction earlier in this chapter). Of nearly 1,000 items considered, 293 were selected for the SB5 (Roid, 2003; see Table 5.4).

The SB5 is built around a hierarchical model of intelligence. Examiners can obtain a full-scale IQ score (a measure of *g*), as well as verbal and nonverbal IQ scores and individual subtest scores (each subtest has a mean of 10 and a standard deviation of 3). However, the subtests are now grouped into five factors representing the major domains of intellectual functioning. These factors, comparable to the midlevel stratum in Figure 5.1, were derived from factor analytic studies performed by the authors of the test. In the SB5, those factors are labeled (1) Fluid Reasoning, (2) Knowledge, (3) Quantitative Reasoning, (4) Visual–Spatial Processing, and (5) Working Memory. Other investigators using factor analysis have found similar but not identical factors (Williams, McIntosh, Dixon, Newton, & Youman, 2010).

Research on the reliability of the fifth edition of the Stanford–Binet suggests that it has very high internal consistency, generally above 0.90. The test-retest reliability for the Full-Scale IQ was in the 0.93 to 0.95 range; for factor scores, the median was 0.88. A third measure of reliability, interscorer agreement, yielded a median correlation of 0.90 (Roid, 2003). These numbers suggest high levels of reliability.

One way to judge a test's validity is to compare its results with those obtained from other well-established measures of intelligence (i.e., criterion validity). Full-Scale IQ scores on the SB5 are similar to those obtained from other established intelligence tests (correlations are in the range of 0.78 to 0.84). The test is also able to discriminate among samples of gifted, intellectually disabled, and learning-disordered children (Roid, 2003). In short, the Stanford–Binet remains a highly reliable test widely used for testing of children, diagnosing intellectual disabilities, and predicting and explaining academic achievement (Decker, Brooks, & Allen, 2011; Walsh & Betz, 2001).

The Wechsler Scales

In the 1930s, David Wechsler, chief psychologist at New York's Bellevue Psychiatric Hospital, began developing an intelligence test specifically for adults. The result of his efforts, the *Wechsler–Bellevue (W–B) Intelligence Scale*, was published in 1939. This test differed in several ways from the Stanford–Binet, even though some W–B tasks were borrowed or adapted from it. First, the W–B was aimed at adults age 17 and older. Second, the W–B was a *point* scale in which the client received credit for each correct answer. With this method, IQ does not reflect the relationship between mental age and chronological age but compares the points earned by the client to those earned by persons of equal age in the standardization sample. Although an average IQ is still placed at 100, this method of calculating IQ has become standard for most tests.

Wechsler also developed comparable tests for children: the *Wechsler Intelligence Scale for Children* (WISC, often referred to phonetically as "the Wisk") and the *Wechsler Preschool and Primary Scale of Intelligence* (WPPSI, or "the Whipsee"). Each has gone through several revisions and has become among the most frequently used tests of intelligence.

THE WECHSLER ADULT INTELLIGENCE SCALE (WAIS) In 1955, Wechsler revised his adult test. This revision, called the *Wechsler Adult Intelligence Scale*, or WAIS, soon became the most popular adult intelligence test in the United States. The test was further revised in 1981 (WAIS-II), in 1997 (WAIS-III), and 2008 (WAIS-IV; Wechsler, 2008). As with previous versions of the test, items on the WAIS-IV are arranged and presented in order of increasing difficulty within subtests. The test administrator stops each subtest after a predetermined number of failures and then begins the next subtest. When the test is completed, the administrator can compute a Full-Scale IQ by converting the examinee's point totals to a standardized IQ score with a mean of 100 and standard deviation of 15. Some examples of the types of items included on the WAIS-IV are presented in Table 5.5.

The WAIS-IV contains 15 subtests; 5 are considered supplemental. The subsets can be grouped or combined to create four factor index scores: Verbal Comprehension, Perceptual Reasoning, Working Memory, and Processing Speed. For example, a score on Perceptual Reasoning is derived from subtest scores for Block Design, Matrix Reasoning, and Visual Puzzles (and optionally the supplemental subtests of Figure Weights and Picture Completion). Using exploratory factor analysis on a portion of the WAIS-IV standardization sample, Canivez and Watkins (2010) found that the subtests were properly associated with their factor scales, suggesting the four factors are a reasonable way to represent the mental abilities that this test measures. These index-level scores are comparable to the midlevel factor scores in Figure 5.1. Finally, the four index scores can be further combined to create a General Ability Index score (based on Verbal Comprehension and Perceptual Reasoning scores) or a Full Scale IQ score (based on all four index scores).

TABLE 5.5 Items of the Type Included in the Wechsler Adult Intelligence Scale (WAIS-IV)

Subtest	Simulated Items on the WAIS-III
Information	What does bread come from?
	What did Shakespeare do?
	What is the capital of France?
	What is the malleus malleficarum?
Comprehension	What should you do with a wallet found in the street?
	Why do foreign cars cost more than domestic cars?
	What does "the squeaky wheel gets the grease" mean?
Arithmetic	If you have four apples and give two away, how many do you have left?
	If four people can finish a job in six days, how many people would it take to do the job in two days?
Similarities	Identify similar aspects of pairs like hammer–screwdriver, portrait–short story, dog–flower.
Digit Symbol/Coding	Copy designs that are associated with different numbers as quickly as possible.
Digit Span	Repeat in forward and reverse order two- to nine-digit numbers.
Vocabulary	Define chair, dime, lunch, paragraph, valley, asylum, modal, cutaneous.
Picture Completion	Find missing objects in increasingly complex pictures.
Block Design	Arrange blocks to match increasingly complex standard patterns.
Picture Arrangement	Place increasing numbers of pictures in sequence to make increasingly complex stories.
Symbol Search	Visually scan and recognize a series of symbols.

THE WECHSLER INTELLIGENCE SCALE FOR CHILDREN (WISC) AND WECHSLER PRESCHOOL AND PRIMARY SCALE OF INTELLIGENCE (WPPSI) Appearing in 1949, the WISC was originally designed to be used for children ages 5 to 15. It had 12 subtests (6 verbal, 6 performance) of which only 10 were usually administered. The WPPSI was developed later, for children 4 years old or younger (Wechsler, 1967); its current, third edition covers the age range from 2.5 to 7 years.

The latest version of the WISC, the WISC-IV, covers ages 6 to 17 and retains the basic structure and format of its predecessors. The test provides a Full-Scale IQ and four composite factor scores: Verbal Comprehension, Perceptual Reasoning, Working Memory, and Processing Speed (Wechsler, 2003).

The Wechsler scales have strong psychometric properties. For instance, the WISC-IV was normed on a sample of 2,200 children ages 6 to 17. This sample matched the 2000 U.S. Census data in terms of the distribution of sex, race/ethnicity, parental education level, and geographic region. As with the revised SB5, inclusion of these and other variables allowed experts on cross-cultural research and intelligence testing to scour pilot-tested items for evidence of item bias. Individual items that were responded to differently by specific groups could be discarded in favor of items that did not show such group differences.

The reliability of each of the Wechsler scales is strong. For example, split-half reliabilities for Full-Scale IQ on the WAIS are 0.92 or above, and interscorer agreement ranges from 0.98 to 0.99 (Wechsler, 2003), suggesting that subjective or biased scoring—so often a concern with less structured interviews, observations, or tests—is not a concern. In one study (Watkins & Smith, 2013), test-retest comparisons over a nearly 3-year period found that average subtest scores differed by no more than 1 point, and index scores differed by no more than 2 points. On the other hand, there is some evidence that the best fit scoring structure might change as people get older—a problem for all intelligence tests to the extent that intelligence changes with age (Benson, Hulac, & Kranzler, 2010). Finally, in terms of concurrent and predictive validity, the Wechsler tests correlate well with other established tests such as the Stanford–Binet. There are also appropriately strong correlations with external criteria such as school grades, achievement test scores, and neuropsychological performance (Flanagan & Harrison, 2011). Extensive discussion of standardization, reliability, and validity are provided in the technical manuals published for each test.

CLINICAL INTERPRETATION OF INTELLIGENCE TEST SCORES Using intelligence tests such as the WAIS, WISC, or SB, clinicians can not only obtain a general measure of intellectual functioning (g or Full Scale IQ), but also a multifaceted description of a person's cognitive strengths and weaknesses. The factor scores illustrated as the midlevel stratum II in Figure 5.1 represent potentially useful constructs for clinicians. For example, Wechsler (2003) noted that children with ADHD, learning disorders, or traumatic brain injury show relative weakness on measures of Processing Speed. Others have proposed diagnosing brain damage or impulsivity and other personality characteristics by using the variability or "scatter" of subtest scores (Groth-Marnat, 2003; Ryan, Paolo, & Smith, 1992; Wechsler, 2003). For example, Austin et al. (2011) described links between intellectual skills and personality, affect, risk for psychological disorders, and coping.

However, others suggest that clinicians should use caution when making inferences based on the pattern of intelligence test subtest or factor scores. Unequivocal diagnoses, they say, can rarely be made using the WAIS, SB, or WISC alone because the tests were not designed for neuropsychological assessment. Hunsley and Mash (2007) go further, arguing that the clinical usefulness of interscore comparisons has not been empirically established.

Other Intelligence Tests

Another individually administered intelligence test that has gained popularity in recent years is the *Kaufman Assessment Battery for Children* (Kaufman & Kaufman, 1983, 2004a). Suitable for children 3 to 18 years of age, the test is now in its second edition, the K-ABC-II. This test was based on research and theory in cognitive psychology and neuropsychology (Mays, Kamphaus, & Reynolds, 2009). It defines intelligence as the ability to solve new problems (an ability sometimes referred to as *fluid intelligence*) and also acquired knowledge of facts (which has been termed *crystallized intelligence*). As with the Binet and Wechsler tests, the Kaufman subtests (18 total, 10 core) are grouped into composite scores compatible with a hierarchical model of intelligence. The test's dual theoretical foundation yields two main (higher level) scores: one for Mental Processing and one for the combination of Mental Processing and Acquired Knowledge. With the K-ABC-II, the number of midlevel composite factor scores increases with age; there are three composite scores for children age 3, four for children ages 4 to 6, and five for children ages 7 and older. This arrangement is designed to reflect the increasing complexity of intelligence as children grow.

The standardization sample for the K-ABC-II consisted of 3,025 children who closely matched the U.S. Census on several demographic factors. Internal consistency reliabilities are in the 0.90s range, and test-retest coefficients are in the mid-0.80s to 0.90s. The test shows high correlations with the WISC (McKown, 2011), as well as appropriately strong correlations with criteria such as school grades, achievement test scores, and neuropsychological performance (Braden, 1995; Kaufman & Kaufman, 2004a). A brief version called the *Kaufman Brief Intelligence Test-2* (K-BIT-2) is designed to yield estimates for crystallized and fluid intelligence in about 20 minutes (Kaufman & Kaufman, 2004b).

Several other intelligence tests in use today assess intelligence without emphasis on verbal or vocalization skills. *The Peabody Picture Vocabulary Test–Revised*, the *Porteus Maze Test*, the *Leiter International Performance Scale*, and the *Raven's Progressive Matrices*, for example, allow clinicians to assess intellectual functioning in clients who are very young or have other characteristics that impair their ability at verbal tasks. These tests also provide a backup in cases in which the clinician suspects that a client's performance on a standard IQ test may have been hampered by anxiety, verbal deficits, cultural disadvantages, or other situational factors. Table 5.6 presents basic information for three popular intelligence tests.

Aptitude and Achievement Tests

Intelligence tests can be viewed as general mental ability instruments that measure both aptitude (the capacity to acquire knowledge or skill) and achievement (acquired knowledge or skill). However, there are a number of other tests designed to measure more specific mental abilities. Some aptitude tests are designed to predict success in an occupation or an educational program. They measure the accumulated effects of many different educational and living experiences and attempt to forecast performance on the basis of these effects. Achievement tests measure proficiency at certain tasks; that is, they measure how much people know or how well they can perform in specific areas.

The *Scholastic Aptitude Test* (now simply called the SAT), which is used to predict high school students' potential for college-level work, is familiar to most undergraduates. It yields verbal and quantitative scores, and its recent revision, the SAT-II, now includes scores for an essay in the English section. The specific content of the SAT is revised continuously. The questions change for each administration, and at any given time, some items are being piloted (and subsequently analyzed) for inclusion in a future test. Although the scoring scale stays the same, norms for the test are calculated on the basis of scores of the thousands of persons taking each particular version of the test.

TABLE 5.6 Three Popular Intelligence Tests at a Glance

Test	Age Ranges	Number of Core Subtests	Administration Time Estimates*	Primary Measures Obtained
Stanford–Binet Intelligence Scales (SB5) (Roid, 2003)	2 y–85 y+	10	45–75 min.	Full-scale IQ; Verbal IQ; Nonverbal IQ; five composite scales: Fluid Reasoning, Crystallized Knowledge, Quantitative Knowledge, Visual–Spatial Processing, Working Memory
Wechsler Intelligence Scale for Children—IV (WISC-IV) (Wechsler, 2003)	6 y 0 m–16 y 11 m	10	65–80 min.	Full-scale IQ; four composite scales (indexes): Verbal Comprehension, Perceptual Reasoning, Working Memory, Processing Speed
Kaufman Assessment Battery for Children—II (K-ABC-II) (Kaufman & Kaufman, 2004a)	3 y–18 y	7–11 (varies by age range)	25–75 min.	Mental Processing Index, Fluid-Crystallized Index; five composite scales: Sequential Processing, Simultaneous Processing, Learning Ability, Planning Ability, Knowledge

*Administration time estimates in publishers manuals may be on the conservative side. In practice, times are quite variable and depend on the examinee's age and full-scale IQ, the examiner's experience, and the setting (see Ryan, Glass, & Brown, 2007).

Source: Roid, G. H. (2003). *Stanford-Binet intelligence scales.* Technical manual (5th ed.). Itasca, IL: Riverside Publishing. Wechsler, D. (2003). *WISC-IV technical and interpretive manual.* San Antonio, TX: The Psychological Corporation. Kaufman, A. S., & Kaufman, N. L. (2004a). *KABC-II: Kaufman assessment battery for children* (2nd ed.). Circle Pines, MN: AGS Publishing.

Other popular aptitude or achievement tests include the *Woodcock–Johnson Cognitive Battery III* and its cousin, the *Woodcock–Johnson Achievement Battery III* (Dombrowski, 2013; Woodcock, McGrew, & Mather, 2000). These batteries measure general intellectual ability and specific academic achievement in persons from 2 years old to over 90. The *Wide Range Achievement Test* (WRAT-3) is yet another well-known example (Wilkinson, 1993), as are the *Kaufman Test of Educational Achievement* (K-TEA-II) (Kaufman & Kaufman, 1985) and the *Wechsler Individual Achievement Test* (WIAT). Clinicians and (especially) school psychologists use these tests to assess aptitude and achievement, to help identify learning disorders and to develop educational plans for children and adults (Bardos, Reva, & Leavitt, 2011).

There are numerous other tests measuring achievement and aptitude. The more specific the ability or aptitude being tested, the less familiar the test is likely to be. If you have never heard of the *Seashore Measures of Musical Talents* or the *Crawford Small Parts Dexterity Test*, it is probably because you have never had occasion to be tested on these very specialized abilities. Such ability testing is more often done by human resources staff and educational, vocational, and guidance counselors than by clinical psychologists.

SECTION SUMMARY

The intelligence tests most commonly administered by clinical psychologists are the Stanford–Binet (SB5), the Wechsler Adult Intelligence Scale (WAIS-IV), and the Wechsler Intelligence Scale for Children (WISC-IV). Each of these tests yields full-scale IQ scores (corresponding to g in a hierarchical model), composite factor scores (corresponding to midlevel factors), and specific subtests scores (corresponding to specific abilities). A number of other tests are used for assessing general intelligence and for specific aptitudes or levels of achievement. The more commonly used tests have been revised and renormed periodically, and have high levels of reliability and validity.

TESTS OF ATTITUDES, INTERESTS, PREFERENCES, AND VALUES

Clinical psychologists often find it useful to assess a person's attitudes, interests, preferences, and values. For example, before beginning to work with a distressed couple, the clinician may wish to get some idea about each partner's attitudes about marriage or other committed relationships. Similarly, it may be instructive for the clinician to know that the interests of a client who is in severe conflict about entering the medical profession are utterly unlike those of successful physicians. Finally, assessment of attitudes, interests, preferences, and values can encourage clients to engage in their own self-exploration with respect to career decisions (Holland, 1996).

We do not have room to describe all the many tests available (see Harrington & Long, 2013 for a review), but among those commonly used to assess clients' preferences for various pursuits, occupations, academic subjects, and activities are the *Self-Directed Search* (SDS; Holland, 1994), the *Strong Interest Inventory* (SII) (Hansen & Campbell, 1985), the *Campbell Interest and Skill Survey* (CISS, 2008), and the *Kuder Occupational Interest Survey* (KOIS; Zytowski, 2007).

Tests such as these are widely used by school counselors to help students select college majors and possible occupations. Most of them result in an interest profile that can be compared with composite profiles gathered from members of occupational groups such as biologists, engineers, army officers, carpenters, police, ministers, accountants, salespeople, lawyers, and the like. For example, Holland's Self-Directed Search, a popular and influential assessment, groups people's vocational interests into six dimensions: Realistic, Investigative, Artistic, Social, Enterprising, and Conventional (Hansen, 2011; Wetzel, Hell, & Pässler, 2012). Originally designed as paper-and-pencil tests, most are available from their publishers online. For a fee, interested persons can take the test and, within minutes, receive a detailed report.

Instruments such as the *Study of Values* (SoV) (Allport, Vernon, & Lindzey, 1970) and the *Rokeach Value Survey* (RVS) are designed to measure values or generalized life orientations.

Rokeach (2000) suggested that values are different from attitudes or interests in that values are fewer in number and more central to a person's belief system and psychological functioning. To measure values, the SoV asks the test taker to choose one option in each of 120 pairs of statements representing different values. Results show the relative strength of six basic interests: theoretical ("intellectual"), economic, aesthetic, social, political, and religious. In the RVS, people are asked to rank-order a set of 18 terminal values (e.g., health, social recognition, a comfortable life, a world at peace) and a set of 18 instrumental values (e.g., broad-minded, intellectual, obedient, courageous).

In general, reliability and validity of interest and values instruments is acceptable but not as high as those found with most of the cognitive measures we reviewed earlier. Assessing reliability or validity can be problematic with some of these instruments because they use rankings or forced choices, so when certain items are ranked high, others are necessarily ranked low. Also, test takers often don't have as much confidence in their rankings as they do in more focused items that can be objectively measured (e.g., an item ranked third in one testing might be ranked fifth or sixth a year later). Also, the structure of occupational or vocational interests can differ from one segment of the population or the other (e.g., males vs females, persons high vs low in self-confidence), and this could cause test results to fit some groups better than others (Kantamneni & Fouad, 2010). Despite these psychometric limitations, the tests see relatively wide use, perhaps because of their content validity and their ability to stimulate personal and career exploration.

TESTS OF PSYCHOPATHOLOGY AND PERSONALITY

SECTION PREVIEW

People's attitudes, interests, preferences, and values can be seen as one aspect of their personalities, but the tests designed to measure them were not meant as measures of personality. In this section, we consider prominent examples of psychological tests designed specifically to assess various aspects of personality. Some focus on psychological abnormality; others are designed to measure aspects of normal functioning. There are objective personality tests, which present clients with relatively simple, unambiguous items (e.g., true or false), and projective personality tests, which present clients with more ambiguous stimuli or tasks (e.g., inkblots or storytelling). We discuss the uses, strengths, and weaknesses of tests in both categories.

Personality can be defined as the pattern of behavioral and psychological characteristics by which a person can be compared and contrasted with other people. Some clinicians see personality as an organized collection of traits, while others see it in terms of dynamic relationships among intrapsychic forces, recurring patterns of learned behavior, or perceptions of the world. This theory-driven variation in how clinicians think about personality is reflected in a wide range of methods through which they have attempted to assess it. Indeed, more psychological tests are devoted to personality assessment than to any other clinical target.

There are two major types of personality tests: objective and projective. *Objective tests* present relatively clear, specific stimuli such as questions ("Have you ever wanted to run away from home?") or statements ("I am never depressed") to which the client responds with direct answers, choices, or ratings. Most objective personality tests are of the paper-and-pencil variety and can be scored arithmetically, often by computers, much like the multiple-choice or true–false tests used in many college classes. Some objective tests focus on one aspect of personality, such as anxiety, dependency, or ego strength, while others provide a comprehensive overview of many personality dimensions.

Projective tests ask clients to respond to ambiguous or unstructured stimuli (such as inkblots, drawings, or incomplete sentences). Their responses tend to be complex verbal or graphic productions (e.g., descriptions, stories, drawings). These responses are then scored and interpreted by clinicians, often in terms of both conscious and unconscious aspects of personality structure and dynamics.

Objective Tests of Psychopathology

The first objective personality test developed by a psychologist was the *Personal Data Sheet* used during World War I to screen soldiers with psychological problems (Woodworth, 1920). It asked for yes-or-no answers to questions such as "Did you have a happy childhood?" "Does it make you uneasy to cross a bridge?" These items were selected because they reflected problems and symptoms reported at least twice as often by previously diagnosed "neurotics" as by "normals." No item was retained in the test if more than 25% of a normal sample answered it in an unfavorable manner. Item selection procedures such as these were a prelude to later, more sophisticated empirical test construction procedures (Butcher & Keller, 1984).

MINNESOTA MULTIPHASIC PERSONALITY INVENTORY   Among the hundreds of objective personality measures that have appeared since the Personal Data Sheet, the most influential is the *Minnesota Multiphasic Personality Inventory (MMPI, now the MMPI-2)*. Indeed, the MMPI-2 is the world's most widely used assessment of clinical symptoms and personality (Butcher, 2011; Van Der Heijden, Egger, & Derksen, 2010). This test was first developed during the late 1930s at the University of Minnesota by Starke Hathaway (a psychologist) and J. C. McKinley (a psychiatrist) as an aid to psychiatric diagnosis of clinical patients. Hathaway and McKinley took about 1,000 items from older personality tests and other sources and converted them into statements to which clients could respond "true," "false," or "cannot say." More than half of these items were then presented to thousands of healthy people as well as to people already diagnosed with psychiatric disorders.

Certain response patterns appeared. When compared to people who had not been diagnosed with any disorder, members of various diagnostic groups showed statistically different responses to many items. For example, a particular group of items tended to be answered in the same way by depressed persons, while another group of items was answered in a particular way by persons diagnosed with schizophrenia. Eight of these item groups, or scales, were identified as being associated with a certain diagnostic category and as discriminating between normal individuals and those with disorders. Later, two additional scales were identified as being responded to differently by males and females and by shy, introverted college students. Also included in the MMPI were four *validity scales*. These are groups of items designed to help detect various test-taking attitudes or response distortions. The final version contained 567 items.

Although widely used (it has even been translated into American Sign Language; Brauer, 1993), the original MMPI eventually became outdated (Dahlstrom, 1992). Accordingly, an extensive revision of the MMPI began in 1982 and was completed in 1989 (Butcher, Dahlstrom, Graham, Tellegen, & Kaemmer, 1989). The revision effort focused on gathering new normative data from randomly selected samples of nondisordered adults and adolescents in seven U.S. states, as well as from several clinical populations. Twenty-six hundred people were included in the restandardization sample. Also, 154 items were evaluated for possible inclusion in the test. The names of the clinical scales and the validity scales of the MMPI-2 are listed in Table 5.7.

Paper-and-pencil administration of the MMPI-2 takes about 90 minutes for a person with average or above reading skills (the test is aimed at a sixth-grade reading level). Computer administration is usually somewhat faster. Interpretation of the test involves comparing a client's MMPI profile with those of other clients. This can be done *clinically* by recalling previous clients' patterns, or *statistically* by reference to books containing sample profiles and the characteristics of the people who produced them (e.g., Butcher & Williams, 1992; Dahlstrom, Lachar, & Dahlstrom, 1986; Dahlstrom, Welsh, & Dahlstrom, 1972; Graham, 1990). An example of an MMPI profile appears in Figure 5.2.

The most common method of scoring the MMPI uses the 2-code system, which refers to the client's two highest scores on clinical scales. For example, if those scores were on scales 4 and 9, the clinician would use codes 49 and 94. A 49/94 description in a book of sample profiles would likely include information about the person being impulsive, extraverted, and sensation-seeking; showing antisocial tendencies; and having an unstable family and work history. Sometimes information from additional scales can be used to modify the 2-code description. Hundreds of additional experimental scales have been constructed from the MMPI-2, many of which go well beyond the test's original diagnostic purposes.

Researchers continue to investigate the extent to which the MMPI-2 can yield valid results when used with various ethnic and cultural groups. Knaster and Micucci (2013) found no difference

TABLE 5.7 MMPI-2 Scales

Clinical Scales	Description*
1. Hs (Hypochondriasis)	Items reflect excessive concerns about illness, often those with vague and ill-defined symptoms, such as "I have pains that move from one part of my body to another."
2. D (Depression)	Items reflect feelings of despondency, pessimism, or hopelessness, such as "I frequently feel that nothing good will ever happen to me" (answered true) or "I am an upbeat person" (answered false).
3. Hy (Conversion Hysteria)	Items reflect a strong focus on stress and anxiety, such as "I don't handle stress well."
4. Pd (Psychopathic Deviate)	Items reflect antisocial behavior and conflicts with authority, such as "I hate it when authority figures tell me what to do."
5. Mf (Masculinity–Femininity)	Items reflect those that generally differ between men and women and show traditional or nontraditional gender identity and interests, such as "I like to watch romantic movies."
6. Pa (Paranoia)	Items reflect suspiciousness and beliefs that others intend them harm or ill-will, such as "Most people are trustworthy" (answered false).
7. Pt (Psychasthenia)	Items reflect anxiety, obsessive rumination, and compulsions, such as "I am likely to check 3 or more times to see that my alarm clock is set."
8. Sc (Schizophrenia)	Items reflect irrational, disorganized thinking, delusions, and hallucinations, such as "I hear voices talking to me that no one else hears."
9. Ma (Hypomania)	Items reflect excessive energy combined with irritability, impulsiveness, and poor judgment, such as "Sometimes I have so much energy that I don't need to sleep for days on end."
10. Si (Social Introversion)	Items reflect avoidance of social interactions, such as "In school, I was always one of the most talkative students in class."
Validity Scales	
? (Cannot Say)	Items that go unanswered (total).
L (Lie)	Items that suggest the person is trying to appear excessively good or virtuous, "I treat everyone with great kindness."
F (Frequency or Infrequency)	Items not endorsed by most normals; high endorsement rate suggests confusion or faking, such as "My relatives have been scheming against me."
K (Correction)	Items reflecting unwillingness to admit to problems, such as "I have occasionally felt sad and blue."
VRIN (Variable Response Inconsistency)	Item pairs expected to be answered in the same direction that weren't, such as "I like parties" (true) and "I like social gatherings" (false).
TRIN (True Response Inconsistency)	Item pairs expected to be answered in the opposite direction that weren't, such as "My back often bothers me" (true) and "I am free of aches and pains" (true).
F (Fake Bad)	Items that few people endorse but are endorsed by the testee, such as, "I sometimes become so anxious that I forget my name."

*Note: All quoted items above are for illustration only; none of them appear on the actual test.

Source: Sunberg, N.D., Assessment of Persons, 1st Ed., © 1977, p. 183. Adapted and Electronically reproduced by permission of Pearson Education, Inc. Upper Saddle River, New Jersey.

in clinicians' interpretations of MMPI-2 scores when the ethnicity of the client was randomly assigned as either African American or European American. Similarly, the MMPI-2 produces similar results for Hispanic American and European American populations (Butcher, 2009). Of course, care must be taken when applying any instrument to a population other than the one on which it was normed. Chung, Weed, and Han (2006), for example, examined the cross-cultural equivalence of the MMPI-2 in Korean bilinguals living in the United States. When participants took the test in both languages, the test-retest correlations were lower than same-language correlations except in a subsample of those proficient in English. Questions that contained more complicated English sentences or American expressions were especially problematic. Given findings such as these, clinicians should be cautious in generalizing the interpretation of MMPI-2 scores across cultural groups unless test validity with those groups has been studied (see also Butcher, 2004; Pace et al., 2006).

The MMPI-2 has spawned thousands of research reports, more than any other test. These studies suggest that it has reasonably strong psychometric properties. For instance, test-retest reliability coefficients for the MMPI and MMPI-2 scales range from 0.60 to 0.90 (Pope, Butcher, & Seelen, 1993). A shorter form developed for adolescents, the MMPI-A, consists of 478 items, but

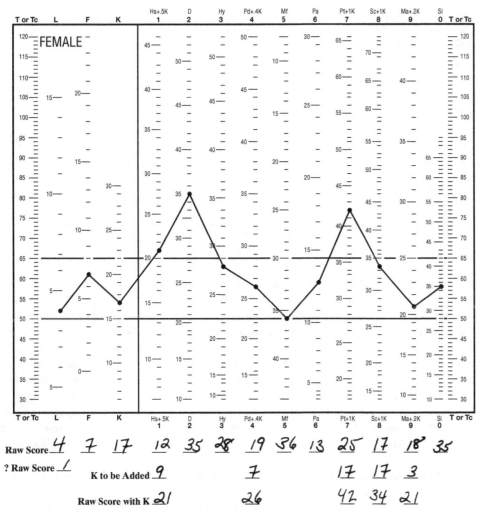

	T or Tc	L	F	K	Hs+.5K 1	D 2	Hy 3	Pd+.4K 4	Mf 5	Pa 6	Pt+1K 7	Sc+1K 8	Ma+.2K 9	Si 0
Raw Score		4	7	17	12	35	28	19	36	13	25	17	18	35
? Raw Score	1													
K to be Added				9				7			17	17	3	
Raw Score with K				21		26				42	34	21		

FIGURE 5.2 An MMPI-2 Profile   *Source:* Minnesota Multiphasic Personality Inventory-2. © by the Regents of the University of Minnesota 1942, 1943 (renewed 1970), 1989. Used by permission of the University of Minnesota Press. All rights reserved. "MMPI" and "Minnesota Multiphasic Personality Inventory" are trademarks owned by the Regents of the University of Minnesota.

it is still long enough to correlate highly with the MMPI-2. This version of the MMPI, designed for persons under the age of 18, has the same validity and clinical scales as on the MMPI-2. It also has similarly strong psychometric properties (Williams & Butcher, 2011).

Because of its popularity, the MMPI continues to be the focus of research, much of it aimed at improving the test. For example, researchers have long known that some MMPI items were used in construction of more than one clinical scale and that such overlap inflated the intercorrelations among scales. In clinical samples, for instance, the correlation between clinical scales 2 and 4 was .60; between scales 7 and 8 it was .90 (Ben-Porath, 2012). Worried that these unacceptably high correlations mean the clinical scales do not measure independent traits, researchers such as Tellegen et al. (2003) have proposed alternative clinical scales, validity scales, and supplemental scales.

Restructured clinical scales are used in an abbreviated test, the MMPI-2-RF for "Restructured Form" (Ben-Porath & Tellegen, 2008; see Table 5.8). This version is made up of 338 items from the original 567 items of the MMPI-2, so it takes less time to administer. This alternative version has generated considerable attention and controversy (Butcher, 2009; Meyer, 2006; Sellbom et al., 2012). Some research finds that the MMPI-2-RF produces scores comparable to the longer version (Van Der Heijdenhas, Egger, & Derksen, 2010), but other studies suggest that the abbreviated form's reconstituted clinical scales and revised supplemental scales do not provide psychometric or clinically useful improvements over the longer MMPI-2 form (Harwood, Beutler, & Groth-Marnat, 2011). For the present, the MMPI-2 remains the dominant form, though clinicians and researchers continue to call for more research on both forms. Ultimately, clinicians' choice of MMPI forms will depend on the goals of assessment and the strength of the empirical support for each version.

TABLE 5.8 MMPI-2 and MMPI-2-Restructured Clinical Scales

MMPI-2 Clinical Scales	MMPI-2 Restructured Clinical Scales
Hs (Hypochondriasis)	RCd (dem: Demoralization)
D (Depression)	RC1(som; Somatic Complaints)
Hy (Conversion Hysteria)	RC2 (lpe; Low Positive Emotions)
Pd (Psychopathic Deviate)	RC3 (cyn;Cynicism)
Mf (Masculinity–Femininity)	RC4 (asb; Antisocial Behavior)
Pa (Paranoia)	RC6 (per; Ideas of Persecution)
Pt (Psychasthenia)	RC7 (dne; Dysfunctional Negative Emotion)
Sc (Schizophrenia)	RC8 (abx; Aberrant Experiences)
Ma (Hypomania)	RC9 (hpm; Hypomanic Activation)
Si (Social Introversion)	

Source: Data from Butcher, J. N. (2009*). Oxford handbook of personality assessment.* New York, NY: Oxford University Press.

PERSONALITY ASSESSMENT INVENTORY   One alternative to the MMPI for assessing psychopathology is the *Personality Assessment Inventory* (PAI). The PAI consists of 344 statements, which clients rate 0, 1, 2, or 3 to reflect the degree to which they agree with each. Designed to assess a broad range of clinical symptoms, the test provides four validity scales (e.g., Inconsistency, Negative Impression), eleven clinical scales (e.g., Somatic Complaints, Anxiety, Borderline Features), and numerous descriptive clinical subscales (e.g., Somatic Complaints-Conversion, Mania-Grandiosity, Antisocial Features-Stimulus Seeking). The test also provides supplemental indexes designed to be used in treatment planning (e.g., Suicide Potential Index, Defensiveness Index) (Morey, 2007). Since its introduction, this instrument has become quite popular in clinical and research settings, no doubt owing partly to the numerous studies examining its reliability and validity (Morey, Lowmaster, Harwood, & Pratt, 2011).

MILLON CLINICAL MULTIAXIAL INVENTORY   Another alternative to the MMPI is the third edition of the Millon Clinical Multiaxial Inventory (MCMI-III). At 175 items, it is shorter than either the MMPI or the PAI. The MCMI was first published in 1982, and revised in 1987 and 1997 (Millon, 2009; Millon, Millon, & Davis, 1997). The MCMI-III yields 28 scales, four of which are designed to assess the test's validity or to modify its clinical interpretation. The test has 10 scales devoted to personality patterns/disorders (e.g., avoidant, antisocial) and was designed to link up with DSM diagnostic criteria, so it will need to be revised to be consistent with the *DSM-5*. Interpretation of the MCMI-III "requires considerable sophistication and knowledge related to psychopathology in general and personality disorders in particular" (Groth-Marnat, 2003, p. 323). As a result, its reliabilities tend to be somewhat lower than those associated with the MMPI. Nevertheless, the test remains one of the more popular in the clinical arsenal; many clinicians find it useful for assessment and for treatment planning (Retzlaff, Dunn, & Harwood, 2011).

PERSONALITY INVENTORY FOR THE *DSM-5* (PID-5)   One of the first tests designed specifically to reflect the *DSM-5* is the Personality Inventory for the *DSM-5* (PID-5). This 220-item self-report test was developed by the *DSM-5* Personality and Personality Disorders Workgroup, and was intended to assess personality disorders as defined in the new *DSM*. Preliminary analyses suggest reasonable convergent validity with measures such as the MMPI-2, but further analyses will be needed on this and all other measures designed to coincide with the new *DSM-5* (Anderson et al., 2013; Ashton, Lee, de Vries, Hendrickse, & Born, 2013).

TESTS MEASURING SPECIFIC ASPECTS OF PSYCHOPATHOLOGY   Clinicians have developed numerous tests that assess specific aspects of psychopathology rather than general profiles. A prominent example is the *Beck Depression Inventory*, now in its second edition, the *BDI-II* (Beck, Steer, & Brown, 1996). At 21 items, the Beck is relatively easy to administer. Clients rate on a 0-to-3 scale the degree to which each item describes them. The test yields scores that are grouped from little or no depression (13 and below) to severe depression (29 and above). The factor structure of this test is reasonably clear, though some studies suggest it measures one factor (a general expression of depression), while others have found two (cognitive and somatic expressions of depression) (Ward, 2006). This test has wide clinical and research appeal, as evidenced by the fact that over 1,000 research studies have used it (Groth-Marnat, 2009). There are several other self-report assessment instruments for measuring depression, including the Center for Epidemiological Studies—Depression Scale, the Hamilton Depression Symptom Questionnaire, and the Profile of Mood States (see Dozois & Dobson, 2010; Feliciano, Renn, & Arean, 2012).

There are also tests aimed at other forms of psychopathology. For example, to assess phobias, a clinician might select the *Fear Survey Schedule* (FSS). It is simply a list of objects, persons, and situations that the client rates in terms of fearsomeness. Different versions of this test contain from 50 to 122 items and use 1-to-5 or 1-to-7 scales for the fear ratings (e.g., Geer, 1965; Lawlis, 1971; Wolpe & Lang, 1969). The FSS-III has been translated into several languages (Abdel, 1994; Johnsen & Hugdahl, 1990) and there are special written and illustrated versions available for use with both cognitively unimpaired and intellectually disabled children (Fleisig, 1993; Gullone & King, 1992; Ramirez & Kratchowill, 1990). Several instruments are available to assess panic disorder, including the Panic Disorder Severity Scale (Shear et al., 1997) and the Anxiety Sensitivity Index-3 (Taylor et al., 2007). Lists and brief descriptions of disorder-specific tests are available in several recent publications (e.g., Antony & Barlow, 2010; Butcher, 2009; Harwood Beutler, & Groth-Marnat, 2011; Hersen & Beidel, 2012).

Objective Tests of Personality

Clinical psychologists are especially interested in assessing psychopathology, but they sometimes assess normal variations in personality, too. They may do so as part of clinical research and also to get a better idea of a client's strengths and weaknesses.

There are numerous tests designed to measure the dimensions of normal personality, each based on various theories of personality and/or on factor analytic research on personality. One of the first personality tests based on factor analytic research was the *Eysenck Personality Questionnaire* (Eysenck & Eysenck, 1975), which measured three basic personality factors: Psychoticism, Introversion–Extraversion, and Emotionality– Stability. Another was Tellegen's (1982) *Multidimensional Personality Questionnaire* (MPQ), which also measured three factors: Positive Emotionality, Negative Emotionality, and Constraint. Other, even broader, tests of normal personality used by clinicians are described below.

THE NEO PERSONALITY INVENTORIES The NEO-PI was originally designed as a measure of three broad personality dimensions—Neuroticism (N), Extraversion (E), and Openness (O)—but it was later expanded to include two other dimensions: Agreeableness (A) and Conscientiousness (C) (Costa & McCrea, 1980, 1985, 1992). This revised edition, known as the NEO-PI-R, has itself been modified recently and is now called the NEO-PI-3 (McCrae, Harwood, & Kelly, 2011).

Though developed as a comprehensive measure of nondisordered adult personality, investigators have found the NEO-PI's Five-Factor Model (FFM) to be helpful in assessing psychological disorders, predicting progress in psychotherapy, and selecting optimal forms of treatment for some clients (Widiger & Presnall, 2013). These uses have been challenged by clinicians who are not convinced that instruments like the NEO-PI add clinically useful information beyond that provided by tests like the MMPI-2 (Ben-Porath & Waller, 1992). Advocates, however, contend that although the NEO-PI-3 is not a stand-alone instrument in clinical settings, it can provide important supplemental information about clients' strengths as well as weaknesses, information that is useful in diagnosis, rapport building, and treatment planning (McCrae, Harwood, & Kelly, 2011). The test takes about 30 minutes to complete, and it has good test-retest reliability and validity. It continues to be an extensively researched test whose clinical applications are still developing.

CALIFORNIA PSYCHOLOGICAL INVENTORY Another example of a broad-range, empirically constructed, objective personality test is the *California Psychological Inventory*. It was introduced in 1957 and revised in 1987 with updated content and reworded items (Gough, 1987). Like the NEO-PI, the CPI was developed specifically for assessing personality in the "normal" population. About half of its 462 true–false items come from the MMPI, but CPI items are grouped into more diverse and positively oriented scales, including sociability, self-acceptance, responsibility, dominance, self-control, and others. There are also three validity scales that serve essentially the same purpose as those on the MMPI. The CPI's strengths include the representativeness of its standardization sample (13,000 males and females from all socioeconomic categories and all parts of the United States) and its relatively high reliability. The test has been used to predict delinquency, parole outcome, academic grades, and the likelihood of dropping out of high school (Anastasi & Urbina, 1997). Computerized scoring and interpretation services are available.

OTHER OBJECTIVE PERSONALITY TESTS   There are numerous other general tests of personality. For example, Raymond B. Cattell used both theory and factor analysis to identify 16 basic factors in personality, and created an instrument to measure them (Cattell, Eber, & Tatsuoka, 1970, 1992). For each of the 187 items on the *16 Personality Factors Questionnaire (16PF)*, test takers select from among three choices (for example, "I would prefer to visit: a museum, a national park, or an art gallery"). Results reveal a person's score on each of the 16 factors, which include dimensions such as intelligence, ego strength, conservative–radical, and schizothymia–affectothymia (Cattell's terms for reserved–outgoing).

The *Myers–Briggs Type Indicator* (MBTI) (Myers & Briggs, 1943) is an analytically derived test based on Jung's psychoanalytic personality-type classification system. The test's 126 forced-choice items are used to sort persons into 16 types based on combinations of four scales: Extraversion/Introversion (E or I), Sensation/Intuition (S or N), Thinking/Feeling (T or F), and Judging/Perceiving (J or P). Although the test provides information about the strength of each dimension, there are significant concerns about its validity (e.g., Domino & Domino, 2006). Among the many other objective personality tests available are the Comrey Personality Scales, the Dimensional Assessment of Personality, and the Guilford–Zimmerman Temperament Survey (Friedman & Schustack, 2011).

Projective Personality Tests

Projective assessment goes back to the 1400s, when Leonardo da Vinci is said to have selected his pupils partly on the basis of the creativity they displayed while attempting to find shapes and patterns in ambiguous forms (Piotrowski, 1972). Projective tests in use today grew out of Freud's notion that people "project," or attribute to others, the unacceptable aspects of their own personality. In other words, the *projective hypothesis* states that each individual's personality will determine, to a significant degree, how he or she interprets and responds to ambiguous stimuli. Tests that encourage clients to display this tendency are called *projective methods* (Frank, 1939). Krishnamurthy, Archer, and Groth-Marnat (2011) suggest that projective tests might also be called indirect, performance-based, or open-ended measures because clients' response options are open, which is not the case in objective tests that allow respondents few options (e.g., true or false). We have space here to consider only a few of the most prominent projective personality tests, but much more detailed coverage of such tests is available in the standard references presented at the beginning of this chapter.

THE RORSCHACH INKBLOT TEST   One of the most widely known and frequently employed projective tests of personality is the *Rorschach Inkblot Test*, a set of 10 colored and black-and-white inkblots created by Swiss psychiatrist Hermann Rorschach between 1911 and 1921. When the test's manual (Rorschach, 1921) was published, European test experts such as William Stern denounced it as "faulty, arbitrary, artificial, and incapable . . . of understanding human personality" (Reisman, 1976). Nevertheless, David Levy, an American psychiatrist studying in Switzerland, brought a copy of the test back to the United States and instructed a psychology trainee named Samuel Beck in its use. In 1937 Beck provided a standardized procedure for administering and scoring the test. Another scoring manual appeared that same year (Klopfer & Kelley, 1937).

The Rorschach became the most commonly used test among clinical psychologists from the 1930s through the 1960s. One prominent clinician noted that "it is hard to conceive of anyone in the field of clinical psychology reaching the postdoctoral level without being thoroughly well-versed in the Rorschach" (Harrower, 1965, p. 398). This is no longer the case. Relative to other tests such as the Wechsler or the MMPI, the Rorschach's popularity declined over the last few decades due to empirical evidence unfavorable to its reliability and validity (Wood et al., 2010).

The test itself is simple. The client is shown 10 cards, one at a time. Each card contains an inkblot similar to that shown in Figure 5.3, and the client is asked what she or he sees or what

FIGURE 5.3 Inkblot Similar to Those Used in the Rorschach.
Source: From Sunberg, N.D., Assessment of Persons, 1st Ed., © 1997, pp. 97-98, 207. Reprinted and Electronically reproduced by permission of Pearson Education, Inc., Upper Saddle River, New Jersey.

the blot could be. The tester records all responses verbatim and takes notes about response times, how the card was held (e.g., upside down, sideways) as responses occurred, noticeable emotional reactions, and other behaviors. After the last card is presented, the tester goes back through them and conducts an *inquiry* or systematic questioning of the client about the characteristics of each blot that prompted the responses.

The client's record of responses, or *protocol*, is later scored and interpreted using a special procedure. Scoring can be complex, but most systems code, at a minimum, the characteristics shown in Table 5.9. For instance, assume that a client responded to Figure 5.3 by saying, "It looks like a bat," and during subsequent inquiry, noted that "I saw the whole blot as a bat because it is black and is just sort of bat shaped." Using one of the available scoring systems, these responses would probably be coded as WFC9 + AP, where W indicates that the whole blot was used (location); F means that the blot's form (F) was the main determinant of the response; and C9 means that achromatic color was also involved. The + shows that the form described corresponded well to the actual form of the blot; A means that there was animal content in the response; and P indicates that bat is a popular response to this particular card.

That responses could be coded somewhat differently by different scoring systems and that each system tends to be used somewhat differently by individual clinicians led to some confusion (it also hurt interrater reliability, as you might imagine). This confusion led John Exner (1974, 1993, 2003; Exner & Erdberg, 2005) to propose what he called a *Comprehensive System* for scoring and interpreting the Rorschach. Using the Comprehensive System, the clinician records the overall number of responses (called *productivity*), categorizes the responses, records the frequency of responses in certain categories, and looks for recurring patterns of responses across cards. For example, because most people tend to use form more often than color in determining their responses, a high proportion of color-dominated determinants may be taken as evidence of weak emotional control.

Exner's Comprehensive System has been widely adopted, becoming the dominant system for administering and scoring the test, but a recent development might change that. The *Rorschach Performance Assessment System* (RPAS; Meyer, Vigloine, Mihura, Erard, & Erdberg, 2010) was intended as an extension of the Comprehensive System, but there are enough differences (e.g., it adds some new indices and excludes others that had poor empirical support) that the RPAS might eventually be seen as a separate scoring system for those who use the Rorschach (Krishnamurthy, Archer, & Groth-Marnat, et al., 2011), depending on the outcome of several lines of ongoing research.

THE THEMATIC APPERCEPTION TEST   The *Thematic Apperception Test* (TAT) consists of 31 cards; 30 show drawings of people, objects, and landscapes and one is blank. In most clinical applications, about 10 of these cards are administered; the clinician chooses a subset based on

TABLE 5.9 Scoring Categories for the Rorschach Inkblot Technique

Scoring Category	Category Refers to
Location	The area of the blot to which the client responds: the whole blot, a common detail, an unusual detail, white space, or some combination of these are location responses.
Determinants	The characteristic of the blot that influenced a response; they include form, color, shading, and "movement." While there is no movement in the blot itself, the respondent's perception of the blot as a moving object is scored in this category.
Content	Subject matter perceived in the blot; content might include human figures, parts of human figures, animal figures, animal details, anatomical features, inanimate objects, art, clothing, clouds, blood, X-rays, sexual objects, and symbols.
Popularity	How often any particular response has been made by previous respondents.
Form Quality	The degree to which the specific content reported fits the blot.

assessment goals and on the client's age and sex. A separate set of cards depicting African Americans is also available. The examiner shows each picture and asks the client to make up a story about it, including what led up to the scene, what is now happening, and what is going to happen. The client is encouraged to say what the people in the drawings are thinking and feeling. For the blank card, the respondent is asked to imagine a drawing, describe it, and then construct a story about it. The TAT was designed in 1935 by Christiana D. Morgan and Henry Murray at the Harvard Psychological Clinic (Murray, 1938, 1943). It was based on the projective hypothesis and the assumption that, in telling a story, the client's needs and conflicts will be reflected in one of the story's characters (Lindzey, 1952).

Analysis of the TAT can focus on both the *content* and the *structure* of TAT stories. Content refers to what clients describe: the people, the feelings, the events, the outcomes. Structure refers to how clients tell their stories: their logic, organization, and use of language, the appearance of speech dysfluencies, the misunderstanding of instructions or stimuli in the drawings, and obvious emotional arousal. As with the Rorschach, however, there is more than one way to score and interpret clients' TAT responses. Those that use elaborate quantitative procedures for scoring TAT stories helped create TAT response norms to which clinicians can compare their clients' responses (Vane, 1981). Others make little use of formal scoring procedures, preferring instead to perform primarily qualitative analyses on the themes in the client's storytelling (Henry, 1956), while still others combine preliminary quantitative analysis with more subjective interpretation (Bellak, 1986; Ronan, Colavito, & Hammontree, 1993). Most clinicians seem to prefer TAT scoring systems that are relatively unstructured and therefore have limited reliability.

OTHER PROJECTIVE TESTS   The *Rosenzweig Picture-Frustration Study* (Rosenzweig, 1949, 1977) is similar to the TAT. It presents 24 cartoons showing one person frustrating another in some way (e.g., "I'm not going to invite you to my party"). The client's task is to say what the frustrated person's response would be. The cards of the *Children's Apperception Test* (CAT) (Bellak, 1992) depict animal characters rather than human beings; those of the *Roberts Apperception Test for Children* (RATC) (McArthur & Roberts, 1982) show children interacting with adults and other children.

Clinicians also use *incomplete sentence tests* as projective measures. As their name implies, these tests ask clients to finish incomplete sentences. The most popular of the sentence completion tests is the *Rotter Incomplete Sentences Blank* (Rotter & Rafferty, 1950). It contains 40 sentence stems such as "I like ___," "My father ___," and "I secretly ___." The client's response to each stem is compared to norms provided in the test manual and is then rated on a 7-point scale of adjustment–maladjustment based on how much the response deviates from those norms. Finally, ratings for all the sentences are summed to provide an overall adjustment score.

Other projective tests whose names describe their nature include the *Draw-a-Person* (DAP) test (Machover, 1949) and the *House-Tree-Person* (HTP) test (Buck, 1948). The client's drawings serve as a basis for the clinician's inferences about various aspects of the client's personality and also as a basis for discussion during an interview. Interpretive inferences are guided by projective assumptions that the inclusion, exclusion, and characteristics of each body part, along with the placement, symmetry, organization, size, and other features of the drawing, are indicative of the client's self-image, conflicts, and perceptions of the world (Machover, 1949).

The *Bender Visual Motor Gestalt Test*, a figure-copying test designed to measure certain aspects of mental ability, particularly neuropsychological functioning, has remained a popular psychological test (Domino & Domino, 2006). Clients are shown geometric shapes on nine cards and asked to draw the shapes as accurately as possible. When used with children, the test is considered a measure of visual–motor development. Some clinicians also use the test as a projective personality measure, assuming that errors and distortions in the copied figures are indicators of a client's personality. Psychometric evidence supports the use of the Bender-Gestalt Test for rough neuropsychological screening and for visual–motor development, but less so for personality assessment (Domino & Domino, 2006).

RELIABILITY AND VALIDITY OF PROJECTIVE TESTS   The Rorschach and other projective tests have generated considerable controversy. From the beginning, skeptics decried these tests for their weak psychometric properties and dependence on psychodynamic personality theory. Advocates championed them as instruments that can yield rich and detailed information about clients' personalities (Gabbard, 2005). How do they actually fare psychometrically?

Test-retest and interrater reliabilities for Rorschach scores have varied considerably. Results from early scoring systems, in particular, fared badly. Using the more recent Comprehensive System to score the Rorschach, advocates point to interrater reliability coefficients that average above 0.80 (Exner & Erdberg, 2005). Research on the Rorschach Performance Assessment System shows higher reliabilities, but certain indices show considerably lower reliabilities (Krishnamurthy, Archer, & Groth-Marnat, 2011). Similarly, Spangler (1992) found certain scores on the TAT reliable, but Rossini and Moretti (1997) argue that the cumulative evidence does not support the value of the test. In short, the evidence for the reliability of projective techniques is mixed (Domino & Domino, 2006; Groth-Marnat, 2009; Hunsley & Mash, 2007; Krishnamurthy, Archer, & Groth-Marnat, 2011).

Concerns about the validity of projective tests have focused on what the tests actually measure and what can be done with those measurements. For many years, clinicians used the Rorschach to help them make DSM diagnoses, but with the exception of diagnoses for schizophrenia, bipolar disorder, and one or two of the personality disorders, diagnoses based on the Rorschach have made a poor showing (Wood, Lilienfeld, Garb, & Nezworski, 2000). Recently accumulating evidence is starting to suggest that the newer scoring systems are associated with improved reliability and validity, but that evidence will have to be more substantial and uniform to overcome years of relatively poor psychometric quality.

What can we conclude about projective (indirect, performance-based) tests? We can certainly say that their use has been, and remains, controversial. Though these tests can provide a great deal of information about clients, it is no easy task to interpret that information accurately. Also, because of the tests' multifaceted scoring systems, clinicians often find it difficult to learn to use the Rorschach, TAT, or other projective techniques effectively. Although almost every senior practitioner knows of at least one TAT or Rorschach "ace" whose reputation shores up general confidence in projective tests, these cases appear to be the exception, not the rule. Perhaps that is one reason the Division of Clinical Psychology of the American Psychological Association recently excluded courses in the Rorschach from its recommendations for a model curriculum in assessment.

SECTION SUMMARY

Among tests of personality and psychopathology, the Minnesota Multiphasic Personality Inventory–2 is the most commonly used. It yields a client profile on a number of scales, revealing which ones, if any, are in the abnormal range. The Personality Assessment Inventory and the Millon Clinical Multiphasic Inventory–III are somewhat briefer alternatives to the MMPI, and the Personality Inventory for the DSM-5 (PID-5) is a new instrument designed to align with the DSM-5. A number of other tests attempt to measure specific problems; the Beck Depression Inventory is a common example. Several tests provide broader descriptions of normal personality traits. Among them are the NEO-PI-R and the California Personality Inventory. Projective tests such as the Rorschach and the Thematic Apperception Test are still widely used, though they are controversial. Advocates point to the rich and varied information available from such tests, while critics point to the tests' relatively weak psychometric properties.

THE CURRENT STATUS OF PSYCHOLOGICAL TESTING
SECTION PREVIEW

Here we take a broader look at psychological testing. First we discuss a study comparing the validity of psychological tests to that of medical tests. Next we discuss how the testing enterprise has developed, and we suggest trends in psychological testing. Prominent among these is the need to focus more on how testing can be used to inform treatment selection and treatment evaluation.

Clinical psychologists are often the toughest critics of psychological tests. Even when a particular test meets acceptable psychometric standards, clinical psychologists are often the first to point out a test's shortcomings. The public, too, has learned to be critical of psychological and educational tests. By the time they have reached college, most students know that tests can be biased and that standardized tests may not do a good job of predicting their intended targets.

Of course, one beneficial effect of focusing attention on the shortcomings of tests has been to stimulate efforts to improve them (Glaser & Bond, 1981). As a result, we have seen ever more careful theorizing about the nature and structure of intelligence, mental abilities, attitudes, and personality. This has led in turn to broader conceptualizations of the construct validity of psychological tests. But testing remains controversial because, even given improvements, every test fails to some degree—none are perfect. But is perfect measurement the standard against which psychological tests should be judged? What makes a test "good enough" to justify its continued use?

Validity of Psychological Testing Versus Medical Testing

Greg Meyer and his colleagues provided an interesting answer to these questions by considering the validity of psychological tests in comparison to the validity of medical tests (Meyer et al., 2001). Most people, psychologists included, have generally assumed that when it comes to accuracy, psychological tests probably lag well behind medical tests. Yet, Meyer and his colleagues found otherwise. Their study was commissioned by the Psychological Assessment Work Group (PAWG), a committee formed by the American Psychological Association's Board of Professional Affairs in 1996. Combining data from more than 125 meta-analyses examining test validity, PAWG found that over a wide range of assessment procedures, the validity of psychological testing is indistinguishable from that of medical testing. Practitioners in both disciplines use tests whose results range from being uninformative to highly informative (see Figure 5.4).

Obviously there is room for improvement in the validity of assessment instruments in both fields, but if the standard by which we judge the adequacy of psychological tests is the validity of medical tests, psychological tests fare reasonably well. Another parallel between psychological tests and medical tests is that both continue to evolve as new research results appear. Intelligence tests are periodically reconstructed to reflect population changes and personality tests undergo similar revisions—scoring methods change, indices are added, dropped, or modified to reflect what empirical research reveals. The same thing happens in medicine: mammograms to test for breast cancer and PSA analysis to test for prostate cancer were routine until research suggested that they may not be sensitive enough assessments.

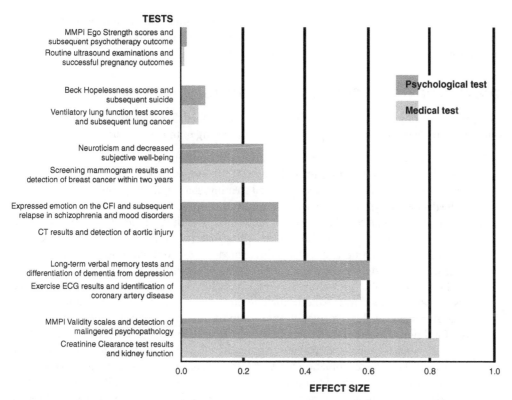

FIGURE 5.4 Sample Effect Sizes for Psychological and Medical Tests. *Source:* Psychological Testing and Psychological Assessment, *American Psychologist*, February 2001, pp. 136–143, Table 2.

Clinical Utility and Evidence-Based Assessment

In the early years of clinical psychology, practitioners used tests mainly to make diagnostic classifications and to select individuals for certain occupations or certain positions in the military. When treatment became a common function of clinical psychologists after World War II, many tests had already been developed, and clinicians used them in much the same way as they always had. In effect, testing and psychotherapy developed on parallel, but separate, paths. Consequently, many authors have noted that "surprisingly little attention has been paid to the treatment utility of commonly used psychological instruments and methods" (Hunsley & Mash, 2007, p. 33). Few tests were developed specifically for making treatment decisions or for measuring treatment results.

Treatment utility (sometimes referred to more broadly as *clinical utility*) refers to the extent to which tests can be used to select specific treatments or to measure treatment outcomes. In an interesting study of treatment utility, numerous clients were asked to take the MMPI prior to treatment (Lima et al., 2005). Half of the treating clinicians were informed about their clients' MMPI results, the other half were not. The researchers found no difference in treatment planning between the two groups of clinicians. Neither were there differences in the improvement ratings of clients nor in the frequency of premature treatment terminations. Apparently, MMPI results had no effect on how therapists planned or conducted psychotherapy. Hunsley and Mash (2007) note that studies such as this one should alert us to the fact that the treatment utility of tests should be empirically assessed, not simply assumed.

Accordingly, they and others argue for testing that more clearly points to specific treatments. The best strategy for doing so may be the reverse of how testing and psychotherapy developed historically. Rather than having tests already developed and adapted to treatment, perhaps researchers should identify the most important treatment variables and *then* develop tests specifically to measure those variables.

A few such tests have already been developed. The *Outcome Questionnaire-45* (OQ-45) and the *Behavior and Symptom Identification Scale* (BASIS-32) are designed to measure treatment outcomes, and both have been shown to be sensitive to client changes over relatively short time periods. Both have also demonstrated convergent, divergent, and concurrent validity (Ellsworth, Lambert, &

Johnson, 2006). These instruments represent attempts to tie testing directly to treatment outcomes. They can also provide therapists with objective feedback about clients' progress. In addition, since these measures are used widely, results of treatment outcome studies can be compared directly.

THE FUTURE OF PSYCHOLOGICAL TESTING

The importance of psychological testing has waxed and waned. Tests continue to evolve. Here we offer (admittedly impressionistic) predictions about testing in the near future.

1. Tests that have survived decades of scrutiny will continue to be used. These include the Wechsler scales, the Binet scales, and the MMPI. However, the "old standby" tests will not simply stand by; under continued empirical scrutiny, changes in the population, and changes in the diagnostic system, these tests will undergo periodic revisions, including renorming.
2. Tests that show unacceptably low levels of reliability, validity, and utility will see diminished use. Projective tests such as the Rorschach (whose materials have not evolved but whose scoring systems have) may never be entirely discredited because some empirical evidence supports some scores derived from them and clinical researchers continue to seek scoring systems that produce more reliable and valid measures. Eventually, however, these tests will be replaced.
3. Testing will continue to expand to include more cross-ethnic and cross-cultural applications. As research yields information about administration and scoring modifications necessary for different cultural groups, more foreign-language versions of tests will be developed.
4. Computers, smart phones, and tablets (e.g., iPads) will play an increasingly important role in assessment. This is a continuation of a trend toward computerizing many paper-and-pencil tests for easier administration and faster, more sophisticated scoring. But beyond that, the increased visual presentation capacities and physiological recording capacities of computers promise to make testing much more dynamic and realistic.
5. Testing designed to aid in treatment planning and treatment outcome measurement will flourish. In this age of accountability, when objective demonstrations of treatment outcomes are critical, such tests will become increasingly important and more of them will be developed.

SECTION SUMMARY

Although psychological testing is often criticized, it is, in general, no less valid than testing in other areas of health care. Because testing developed largely independently from (and earlier than) psychotherapy, testing often does not inform treatment as much as it should. In the future, this shortcoming will likely be addressed, as will cross-cultural testing and quality issues.

Chapter Summary

There are thousands of psychological tests available for use, and more are being developed all the time. Tests are developed using analytic (theoretical) and empirical procedures, often both. An empirical approach is needed to develop test norms, without which test score interpretation is difficult. Norms typically come from a large, representative standardization sample. Even with a representative sample, test developers and clinicians must be cautious to avoid bias that could occur if tests do not "fit" persons from different backgrounds.

Tests commonly used by clinical researchers and practitioners can be categorized by what they measure: cognitive/intellectual abilities, interests/values, and personality/psychopathology. Tests can also be categorized by how they measure. Those that constrain responses to simpler, unambiguous, and easily scored responses (e.g., true or false) are called objective tests. Those that allow complex verbal or graphic responses to ambiguous stimuli (e.g., an inkblot) are called projective tests.

Prominent objective tests of intellectual functioning (whose results are usually expressed as IQ scores) include the Stanford–Binet 5 and the Wechsler scales (e.g., WAIS-IV, WISC-IV). The SAT and the Wide Range Achievement Test (WRAT) exemplify some of the general ability tests in use today. Attitudes, interests, preferences, and values are typically measured through tests such as the Strong Interest Inventory, the Self-Directed Search, the Study of Values, and the Rokeach Values Survey.

The most widely used test of personality/psychopathology in clinical settings is the Minnesota Multiphasic Personality Inventory (MMPI-2). A recent abbreviated form, the MMPI-2-RF, is now available. The Personality Assessment Inventory (PAI) and the Millon Clinical Multiphasic Inventory (MCMI-III) are also commonly used in clinical settings. There are also many tests designed to measure specific areas of difficulty rather than personality broadly conceived. The Beck Depression Inventory (BDI) is a prominent example. Several tests are designed to measure normal personality: the NEO Personality Inventory (NEO-PI-R and NEO-PI-3), the California Psychological Inventory (CPI), the Sixteen Personality Factor Questionnaire (16PF) are examples.

The Rorschach, the Thematic Apperception Test (TAT), sentence-completion tests, and the Draw-a-Person (DAP) test are projective instruments designed to measure aspects of personality and psychopathology. Once the most popular tests used by clinicians, they are used less often now because of concerns about their psychometric properties. However, because many clinicians are convinced of their utility, clinical research designed to improve the reliability and validity of these tests continues.

The testing enterprise continues because tests can be useful and because clinical traditions and societal demands maintain its importance. At present, the overall validity of psychological tests is comparable to the overall validity of tests in other areas of health care, but there is wide variation in each field. With time, those tests that do a poorer job will be replaced, and tests that more clearly translate into treatment planning and evaluation will be more common.

Study Questions

1. Define a test.
2. How are psychological tests similar to, and different from, other forms of assessment?
3. What are standardization samples and test norms?
4. What are the main categories of tests used by clinical psychologists?
5. How are tests constructed using analytic and empirical procedures?
6. How can test developers determine if their test is biased against specific ethnic or cultural groups?
7. What ethical standards and guidelines should clinicians follow in using tests?
8. What are general, specific, and hierarchical models of intelligence?
9. What do intelligence tests used by clinical psychologists actually measure?
10. What is the Stanford–Binet 5, and what scores are derived from it?
11. What are the Wechsler scales, and what scores are derived from them?
12. What other tests of intelligence, achievement, and aptitude do clinicians use commonly?
13. What are the differences between objective and projective personality tests?
14. What is the Minnesota Multiphasic Personality Inventory, and what measures are derived from it?
15. What other tests do clinicians use to measure psychopathology or emotional distress?
16. What tests are commonly used to measure normal personality?
17. How are the Rorschach and the Thematic Apperception Test constructed and administered?
18. Why are projective tests controversial?
19. How do the validities of psychological tests compare with the validities of tests used in other areas of health care?
20. What do clinical utility and treatment utility mean, and why are they significant for testing?

Web Sites

- APA Division 5: Evaluation, Measurement, and Statistics: http://www.apa.org/about/division/div5.html
- Buros Institute of Mental Measurements, publisher of the Mental Measurements Yearbook: http://buros.org/
- Searchable database of tests from Buros Institute of Mental Measurements: http://buros.unl.edu/buros/jsp/search.jsp
- Web site for the Stanford–Binet Intelligence Scales (SB5), fifth edition: http://www.riverpub.com/products/sb5/
- College Board, publishers of the SAT and other tests: http://www.collegeboard.com/testing/
- Web site for the MMPI-2: http://www.pearsonassessments.com/tests/mmpi_2.htm

MOVIES

Forrest Gump (1994): Emotional and amusing drama about a man with below average intelligence, who excels in nearly everything that he does.

I Am Sam (2001): Poignant film about a developmentally delayed father, trying to raise his daughter, who may be taken away by the state for her own well-being.

MEMOIRS

Riding the Bus with My Sister: A True Life Journey by Rachel Simon (2003; New York: Penguin). This poignant memoir shows that limited intelligence does not limit the ability to enjoy life and teach others life lessons.

She's Not There: A Life in Two Genders by Jennifer Finney Boylan (2003; New York: Broadway Books). Along with describing psychological assessment procedures and client-centered therapy, the author eloquently describes her experiences as a transgendered person transitioning from male to female while a professor of English at Colby College.

References

Abdel, K. A. M. (1994). Normative results on the Arabic Fear Survey Schedule III. *Journal of Behavior Therapy and Experimental Psychiatry, 25*, 61–67.

Allport, G. W., Vernon, C. E., & Lindzey, G. (1970). *Study of values* (revised manual). Boston, MA: Houghton-Mifflin.

Anastasi, A. (1988). *Psychological testing* (6th ed.). New York, NY: Macmillan.

Anastasi, A., & Urbina, S. (1997). *Psychological testing* (7th ed.). Upper Saddle River, NJ: Prentice Hall.

Anderson, J. L., Sellbom, M., Bagby, R. M., Quilty, L. C., Veltri, C. O. C., et al. (2013). On the convergence between PSY-5 domains and PID-5 domains and facets: Implications for assessment of DSM-5 personality traits. *Assessment*, first online publication, doi:10.1177/1073191112471141.

Antony, M. M., & Barlow, D. H. (Eds.). (2010). *Handbook of assessment and treatment planning for psychological disorders* (2nd ed.). New York, NY: Guilford.

Ashton, M. C., Lee, K., de Vries, R. E., Hendrickse, J., & Born, M. P. H. (2013). The maladaptive personality traits of the personality inventory for DSM-5 (PID-5) in relation to the HEXACO personality factors and schizotypy/dissociation. *Journal of Personality Disorders, 26*, 641–659.

Austin, E. J., Boyle, G. J., Groth-Marnat, G., Matthews, G., Saklofske, D. H., et al. (2011). Integrating intelligence and personality. In T. M. Harwood, L. E. Beutler, & G. Groth-Marnat (Eds.). *Integrative assessment of adult personality* (pp. 119–151). New York, NY: Guilford.

Ayearst, L. E., & Bagby, R. M. (2011). Evaluating the psychometric properties of psychological tests. In M. M. Antony & D. H. Barlow (Eds.), *Handbook of assessment and treatment for psychological disorders* (pp. 23–61). New York, NY: Guilford Press.

Bardos, A. N., Reva, K. K., & Leavitt, R. (2011) Achievement tests in pediatric neuropsychology. In A. S. Davis (Ed), *Handbook of pediatric neuropsychology* (pp. 235–244). New York, NY: Springer Publishing Co.

Beck, A. T., Steer, R. A., & Brown, G. K. (1996). *Beck Depression Inventory* (2nd ed.). San Antonio, TX: The Psychological Corporation.

Bellak, L. (1986). *The Thematic Apperception Test, the Children's Apperception Test, and the Senior Apperception Technique in clinical use* (4th ed.). New York, NY: Grune & Stratton.

Bellak, L. (1992). *The TAT, CAT, and SAT in clinical use* (5th ed.). Odessa, FL: Psychological Assessment Resources.

Benson, N., Hulac, D. M., & Kranzler, J. H. (2010). Independent examination of the Wechsler Adult Intelligence Scale—Fourth Edition (WAIS-IV): What does the WAIS-IV measure? *Psychological Assessment, 22*, 121–130.

Ben-Porath, Y. (2012). *Interpreting the MMPI-2-RF*. Minneapolis, MN: University of Minnesota Press.

Ben-Porath, Y., & Tellegen, A. (2008). Empirical correlates of the MMPI-2 Restructured Clinical (RC) scales in mental health, forensic, and nonclinical settings: An introduction. *Journal of Personality Assessment, 90*, 119–121.

Ben-Porath, Y. S., & Waller, N. G. (1992). "Normal" personality inventories in clinical assessment: General requirements and potential for using the NEO Personality Inventory. *Psychological Assessment, 4*, 14–19.

Berg, I. A. (1955). Response bias and personality: The deviation hypothesis. *Journal of Psychology, 40*, 61–71.

Braden, J. P. (1995). Review of the Wechsler Intelligence Scale for Children (3rd ed.). In J. C. Conoley & J. C. Impara (Eds.), *Twelfth mental measurements yearbook*. Lincoln, NE: Buros Institute.

Brauer, B. A. (1993). Adequacy of a translation of the MMPI into American Sign Language for use with deaf individuals: Linguistic equivalency issues. *Rehabilitation Psychology, 38*, 247–260.

Buck, J. N. (1948). The H-T-P technique: A qualitative and quantitative scoring manual. *Journal of Clinical Psychology, 4*, 319–396.

Burisch, M. (1984). Approaches to personality inventory construction: A comparison of merits. *American Psychologist, 39*, 214–227.

Buros, O. K. (Ed.). (1938). *The 1940 mental measurements yearbook*. Highland Park, NJ: Gryphon Press.

Butcher, J. N. (2004). Personality assessment without borders: Adaptation of the MMPI-2 across cultures. *Journal of Personality Assessment, 83*, 90–104.

Butcher, J. N. (2009). *Oxford handbook of personality assessment*. New York, NY: Oxford University Press.

Butcher, J. N. (2011). *A beginner's guide to the MMPI-2* (3rd ed.). Washington, DC: American Psychological Association.

Butcher, J. N., Dahlstrom, W. G., Graham, J. R., Tellegen, A., & Kaemmer, B. (1989). *Manual for administration and scoring of the MMPI-2*. Minneapolis, MN: University of Minnesota Press.

Butcher, J. N., & Keller, L. S. (1984). Objective personality assessment. In G. Goldstein & M. Hersen (Eds.), *Handbook of psychological assessment* (pp. 307–331). New York, NY: Pergamon Press.

Butcher, J. N., & Williams, C. L. (1992). *Essentials of MMPI-2 and MMPI-A interpretation*. Minneapolis, MN: University of Minnesota Press.

Camara, W. J., Nathan, J. S., & Puente, A. E. (2000). Psychological test usage: Implications in professional psychology. *Professional Psychology: Research and Practice, 31*, 141–154.

Campbell, D. (1995). The Campbell Interest and Skill Survey (CISS): A product of ninety years of psychometric evolution. *Journal of Career Assessment, 3*, 391–410.

Canivez, G. L., & Watkins, M. W. (2010). Exploratory and higher-order factor analyses of the Wechsler Adult Intelligence Scale—Fourth Edition (WAIS-IV) Adolescent Subsample. *School Psychology Quarterly, 25*, 223–235.

Carroll, J. B. (1993). *Human cognitive abilities: A survey of factor-analytic studies*. Cambridge, UK: University of Cambridge Press.

Cattell, R. B. (1943). The measurement of adult intelligence. *Psychological Bulletin, 40*, 153–193.

Cattell, R. B., Eber, H. W., & Tatsuoka, M. M. (1970). *Handbook for the Sixteen Personality Factor Questionnaire*. Champaign, IL: Institute for Personality and Ability Testing.

Cattell, R. B., Eber, H. W., & Tatsuoka, M. M. (1992). *Handbook for the Sixteen Personality Factor Questionnaire (16PF)*. Champaign, IL: Institute for Personality and Ability Testing.

Chung, J. J., Weed, N. C., & Han, K. (2006). Evaluating cross-cultural equivalence of the Korean MMPI-2 via bilingual test-retest. *International Journal of Intercultural Relations, 30*, 531–543.

Correa, A. A., Rogers, R., & Hoestring, R. (2010). Validation of the Spanish SIRS with monolingual Hispanic outpatients. *Journal of Personality Assessment, 92*, 458–464.

Costa, P. T. Jr., & McCrea, R. R. (1980). Still stable after all these years: Personality as a key to some issues in adulthood and old age. In P. B. Baltes & O. G. Brim, Jr. (Eds.), *Life span development and behavior* (Vol. 3, pp. 65–102). New York, NY: Academic Press.

Costa, P. T. Jr., & McCrae, R. R. (1985). *NEO-Personality Inventory manual*. Odessa, FL: Psychological Assessment Resources.

Costa, P. T., Jr., & McCrae, R. R. (1992). *Manual for the Revised NEO Personality Inventory (NEO-PIR) and the NEO Five-Factor Inventory (BEO-FFI)*. Odessa, FL: Psychological Assessment Resources.

Cronbach, L. J. (1946). Response sets and test validity. *Educational and Psychological Measurement, 6,* 475–494.

Cronbach, L. J. (1970). *Essentials of psychological testing* (3rd ed.). New York, NY: Harper & Row.

Crowther, M. R., Austing, A. L., Scogin, F., Harwood, T. M., & Harrell, S. (2011). Integrative personality assessment with older adults and ethnic minorities. In T. M. Harwood, L. E. Beutler, & G. Groth-Marnat (Eds.), *Integrative assessment of adult personality* (pp. 354–372). New York, NY: Guilford.

Dahlstrom, W. G. (1992). The growth in acceptance of the MMPI. *Professional Psychology: Research and Practice, 23,* 345–348.

Dahlstrom, W. G., Lachar, D., & Dahlstrom, L. E. (1986). *MMPI patterns of American minorities.* Minneapolis, MN: University of Minnesota Press.

Dahlstrom, W. G., Welsh, G. S., & Dahlstrom, L. E. (1972). *An MMPI handbook: Vol. 1. Clinical interpretation* (rev. ed.). Minneapolis, MN: University of Minnesota Press.

Davidson, J. E., & Kemp, I. A. (2011). Contemporary models of intelligence. In R. J. Sternberg & S. B. Kaufman (Eds.), *The Cambridge handbook of intelligence* (pp. 58–84). New York, NY: Cambridge University Press.

Decker, S. L., Brooks, J. H., & Allen, R. A. (2011). Stanford-Binet Intelligence Scales, Fifth Edition. In A. S. Dais (Ed), *Handbook of pediatric neuropsychology* (pp. 389–395). New York, NY: Springer Publishing Co.

Dombrowski, S. C. (2013). Investigating the structure of the WJ-III cognitive at school age. *School Psychology Quarterly*, Advance online publication. doi: 10.1037/spq0000010.

Domino, G., & Domino, M. L. (2006). *Psychological testing* (2nd ed.). New York, NY: Cambridge University Press.

Dozois, D. J. A., & Dobson, K. S. (2010). Depression. In M. M. Anthony & D. H. Barlow (Eds.), *Handbook of assessment and treatment planning for psychological Disorders* (2nd ed., pp. 344–389). New York, NY: Guilford Press.

Edwards, A. L. (1957). *The social desirability variable in personality assessment and research.* New York, NY: Dryden.

Ellsworth, J. R., Lambert, M. J., & Johnson, J. (2006). A comparison of the Outcome Questionnaire-45 and Outcomes Questionnaire-30 in classification and prediction of treatment outcome. *Clinical Psychology and Psychotherapy, 13,* 380–391.

Exner, J. E. (1974). *The Rorschach: A comprehensive system* (Vol. 1). New York: Grune & Stratton.

Exner, J. E. (1993). *The Rorschach: A comprehensive system: Vol. 1. Basic foundations* (3rd ed.). New York, NY: Wiley.

Exner, J. E. Jr., (2003). *Basic foundations and principles of interpretation.* Hoboken, NJ: Wiley.

Exner, J. E. Jr., & Erdberg, P. (2005). *The Rorschach, advanced interpretation.* Hoboken, NJ: Wiley.

Eysenck, H. J., & Eysenck, S. B. G. (1975). *Manual for Eysenck Personality Questionnaire.* San Diego, CA: Educational and Individual Testing Service.

Feliciano, L., Renn, B. N., & Arean, P. A. (2012). Mood disorders: Depressive disorders. In M. Hersen, & D. C. Beidel (Eds.), *Adult psychopathology and diagnosis* (6th ed., pp. 317–356). Hoboken, NJ: Wiley and Sons.

Finn, S. E., & Martin, H. (2013). Therapeutic assessment: Using psychological testing as brief therapy. In K. F. Geisinger, B. A. Bracken, J. F. Carlson, et al. (Eds). *APA handbook of testing and assessment in psychology,* (Vol. 2 pp. 453–465): Washington, DC: American Psychological Association.

Flanagan, D. P., & Harrison, P. L. (2011). *Contemporary intellectual assessment* (2nd ed.). New York, NY: The Guilford Press.

Fleisig, W. E. (1993). The development of the Illustrated Fear Survey Schedule (IFSS) and an examination of its reliability and validity with children with mild mental retardation. *Dissertation Abstracts International, 54,* 17–19.

Frank, L. K. (1939). Projective methods for the study of personality. *Journal of Psychology, 8,* 343–389.

Friedman, H. S., & Schustack, M. W. (2011). *Personality: Classic theories and modern research* (5th ed.). Upper Saddle River, NJ: Prentice-Hall.

Gabbard, G. O. (2005). *Psychodynamic psychiatry in clinical practice* (4th ed.). Washington, DC: American Psychiatric Publishing.

Gardner, H. (1993). *Multiple intelligences.* New York: Basic Books.

Gardner, H. (2002). The pursuit of excellence through education. In M. Ferrari (Ed.), *Learning from extraordinary minds.* Mahwah, NJ: Erlbaum.

Geer, J. H. (1965). The development of a scale to measure fear. *Behaviour Research and Therapy, 3,* 45–53.

Geher, G., & Kaufman, S. K. (2011). Mating intelligence. In R. J. Sternberg & S. B. Kaufman (Eds.), *The Cambridge handbook of intelligence* (pp. 603–620). New York, NY: Cambridge University Press.

Geisinger, K. F. (2013). *APA handbook of testing and assessment in psychology (APA Handbooks in Psychology).* Washington, DC: American Psychological Association.

Glaser, R., & Bond, L. (1981). Introduction to the special issue: Testing: Concepts, policy, practice, and research. *American Psychologist, 36,* 997–1000.

Gough, H. (1987). *California Psychological Inventory: Administrator's guide.* Palo Alto, CA: Consulting Psychologists Press.

Graham, J. R. (1990). *MMPI-2: Assessing personality and psychopathology.* New York, NY: Oxford University Press.

Groth-Marnat, G. (2003). *Handbook of psychological assessment* (4th ed.). Hoboken, NJ: Wiley.

Groth-Marnat, G. (2009). *Handbook of psychological assessment.* New York, NY: Wiley & Sons.

Gullone, E., & King, N. J. (1992). Psychometric evaluation of a revised fear survey schedule for children and adolescents. *Journal of Child Psychology and Psychiatry and Allied Disciplines, 33,* 987–998.

Handler, L. (1974). Psychotherapy, assessment, and clinical research: Parallels and similarities. In A. I. Rabin (Ed.) *Clinical psychology: Issues of the seventies* (pp. 49–62). East Lansing, MI: Michigan State University Press.

Hansen, J. C. (2011). Remembering John L. Holland, PhD. *The Counseling Psychologist, 39,* 1212–1217.

Hansen, J. C., & Campbell, D. P. (1985). *Manual for the SVIB-SCII* (4th ed.). Palo Alto, CA: Consulting Psychologists Press.

Harrington, T., & Long, J. (2013). The history of interest inventories and career assessments in career counseling. *The Career Development Quarterly, 61,* 83–92. doi: 10.1002/j.2161-0045.2013.00039.x

Harrower, M. R. (1965). Clinical psychologists at work. In B. B. Wolman (Ed.), *Handbook of clinical psychology* (pp. 1443–1458). New York, NY: McGraw-Hill.

Harwood, T. M., Beutler, L. E., & Groth-Marnat, G. (Eds., 2011). *Integrative assessment of adult personality* (3rd ed.). New York, NY: The Guilford Press.

Hays, P. A., & Iwamasa, G. Y. (Eds.). (2006). *Culturally responsive cognitive-behavioral therapy.* Washington, DC: American Psychological Association.

Henry, W. E. (1956). *The analysis of fantasy: The thematic apperception technique in the story of personality.* New York, NY: Wiley.

Hersen, M., & Beidel, D. C. (Eds.), (2012). *Adult psychopathology and diagnosis* (6th ed.). New York, NY: Wiley.

Holland, J. L. (1994). *The self-directed search.* Odessa, FL: Psychological Assessment Resources.

Holland, J. L. (1996). Exploring careers with a typology. *American Psychologist, 51,* 397–406.

Horn, J. L. (1965). An empirical comparison of methods for estimating factor scores. *Educational and Psychological Measurement, 25,* 313–322.

Humphreys, L. G. (1988). Trends in levels of academic achievement of blacks and other minorities. *Intelligence, 12,* 231–260.

Hunsley, J., & Mash, E. J. (2007). Evidence-based assessment. *Annual Review of Clinical Psychology, 3,* 29–51.

Isenhart, C. E., & Silversmith, D. J. (1996). MMPI-2 response styles: Generalization to alcoholism assessment. *Psychology of Addictive Behaviors, 10,* 115–123.

Jackson, D. N., & Messick, S. (1958). Content and style in personality assessment. *Psychological Bulletin, 55,* 243–252.

Jackson, D. N., & Messick, S. (1961). Acquiescence and desirability as response determinants on the MMPI. *Educational and Psychological Measurement, 21,* 771–790.

Jia-xi, C., & Guo-peng, C. (2006). The validity and reliability research of 16PF 5th ed. in China. *Chinese Journal of Clinical Psychology, 14,* 13–46.

Johnsen, B. H., & Hugdahl, K. (1990). Fear questionnaires for simple phobias: Psychometric evaluations for a Norwegian sample. *Scandinavian Journal of Psychology, 31,* 42–48.

Kantamneni, N., & Fouad, N. (2010). Structure of vocational interests for diverse groups on the 2005 Strong Interest Inventory. *Journal of Vocational Behavior, 78,* 193–201.

Kaufman, A. S., & Kaufman, N. L. (1983). *KABC: Kaufman Assessment Battery for Children.* Circle Pines, MN: American Guidance Service.

Kaufman, A. S., & Kaufman, N. L. (1985). *Kaufman Test of Educational Achievement.* Circle Pines, MN: American Guidance Service.

Kaufman, A. S., & Kaufman, N. L. (2004a). *KABC-II: Kaufman Assessment Battery for Children* (2nd ed.). Circle Pines, MN: AGS Publishing.

Kaufman, A. S., & Kaufman, N. L. (2004b). *KBIT-2: Kaufman Brief Intelligence Test-2* (2nd ed.). Upper Saddle River, NJ: Pearson Assessments.

Kihlstrom, J.F., & Cantor, N. (2011). Social intelligence. In R. J. Sternberg & S. B. Kaufman (Eds.), *The Cambridge handbook of intelligence:* New York, NY (pp. 564–581). Cambridge University Press.

Kinzie, J. D., Manson, S. M., Vinh, D. H., Nguyen, T. T., Anh, B., et al. (1982). Development and validation of a Vietnamese-language depression rating scale. *American Journal of Psychiatry, 139,* 1276–1281.

Klopfer, B., & Kelley, D. M. (1937). The techniques of the Rorschach performance. *Rorschach Research Exchange, 2,* 1–14.

Knaster, C. A., & Micucci, J. A. (2013). The effect of client ethnicity on clinical interpretation of the MMPI-2. *Assessment, 20,* 143–147.

Krishnamurthy, R., Archer, R. P., & Groth-Marnat, G. (2011). The Rorschach and performance-based assessment. In T. M. Harwood, L. E. Beutler, & G. Groth-Marnat, G. (Eds.), *Integrative assessment of adult personality* (3rd ed., pp. 276–328). New York, NY: The Guilford Press.

Larrabee, G. J. (Ed). (2012). Assessment of malingering. In G. J. Larrabee (Ed.), *Forensic neuropsychology: A scientific approach* (2nd ed., pp. 116–159). New York, NY: Oxford University Press.

Lawlis, G. F. (1971). Response styles of a patient population on the Fear Survey Schedule. *Behaviour Research and Therapy, 9,* 95–102.

Lima, E. N., Stanley, S., Koboski, B., Reitzel, L. R., Richey, J. A., et al. (2005). The incremental validity of the MMPI-2: When does therapist access enhance treatment outcome? *Psychological Assessment, 17,* 462–468.

Lindzey, G. (1952). The thematic apperception test: Interpretive assumptions and related empirical evidence. *Psychological Bulletin, 49,* 1–25.

Linehan, M. M., & Nielsen, S. L. (1983). Social desirability: Its relevance to the measurement of hopelessness and suicidal behavior. *Journal of Consulting and Clinical Psychology, 51,* 141–143.

Machover, K. (1949). *Personality projection in the drawing of the human figure.* Springfield, IL: Charles C. Thomas.

Maloney, M. P., & Ward, M. P. (1976). *Psychological assessment: A conceptual approach.* New York, NY: Oxford University Press.

Mayer, J. D., Salovey, P., Caruso, D. R., & Cherkasskiy, L. (2011). Emotional intelligence. In R. J. Sternberg & S. B. Kaufman (Eds.), *The Cambridge handbook of intelligence* (pp. 528–549). New York, NY: Cambridge University Press.

Mays, K. L., Kamphaus, R. W., & Reynolds, C. R. (2009). Applications of the Kaufman Assessment Battery for Children, in neuropsychological assessment. In C. R. Reynolds, E. Fletcher-Jenson (Eds.), *Handbook of clinical child neuropsychology* (2nd ed., pp. 281–296). New York, NY: Springer.

McArthur, D. S., & Roberts, G. E. (1982). *Roberts Apperception Test for Children: Manual.* Los Angeles, CA: Western Psychological Services.

McCrae, R. R., & Costa, P. T. (1983). Social desirability scales: More substance than style. *Journal of Consulting and Clinical Psychology, 51,* 882–888.

McCrae, R. R., Harwood, T. M., & Kelly, S. L. (2011). The NEO inventories. In T. M. Harwood, L. E. Beutler, & G. Groth-Marnat, G. (Eds.), *Integrative assessment of adult personality* (3rd ed., pp. 252–275). New York, NY: The Guilford Press.

McKown, D. M. (2011). A comparison study: Kaufman Assessment Battery for Children, second edition (IABC-II) and Wechsler Intelligence Scale for Children, fourth edition (WISC-IV) with referred students. *Dissertaion Abstracts International Section A: Humanities and Social Sciences, 71,* 2011–2751.

Meyer, G. J. (2006). MMPI-2 Restructured Clinical Scales [Special Issue]. *Journal of Personality Assessment, 87,* 2.

Meyer, G. J., Finn, S. E., Eyde, L. D., Kay, G. G., Moreland, K. L., et al. (2001). Psychological testing and psychological assessment: A review of evidence and issues. *American Psychologist, 56,* 128–165.

Meyer, G. J., Viglione, D. J., Mihura, J. L., Erard, R. E., & Erdberg, P. (2010, March). *Introducing key features of the Rorschach Performance Assessment System (RPAS).* Workshop presented at the annual meeting of the Society for Personality Assessment, San Jose, CA.

Millon, J., Millon, C., & Davis, R. (1997). *Millon Clinical Multiaxial Inventory: III (MCMI-III) manual* (3rd ed.). Minneapolis, MN: National Computer Systems.

Millon, T. (2009). *The Millon Clinical Multiaxial Inventory-III* (4th ed.). Minneapolis, MN: Pearson.

Morey, L. C. (2007). *The Personality Assessment Inventory professional manual* (2nd ed.). Odessa, FL: Psychological Assessment Resources.

Morey, L. C., Lowmaster, S. E., Harwood, M. T., & Pratt, D. (2011). The Personality Assessment Inventory. In T. M. Harwood, L. E. Beutler, & G. Groth-Marnat (Eds.), *Integrative Assessment of Adult Personality* (pp. 190–218). New York, NY: Guilford.

Murray, H. A. (1938). *Explorations in personality.* Fair Lawn, NJ: Oxford University Press.

Murray, H. A. (1943). *Thematic Apperception Test.* Cambridge, MA: Harvard University Press.

Mussen, P. H., & Scodel, A. (1955). The effects of sexual stimulation under varying conditions on TAT sexual responsiveness. *Journal of Consulting Psychology, 19,* 90.

Myers, I. B., & Briggs, K. C. (1943). *The Myers-Briggs type indicator.* Palo Alto, CA: Consulting Psychologists Press.

Okazaki, S., & Tanaka-Matsumi, J. (2006). Cultural considerations in cognitive-behavioral assessment. In P. A. Hays & G. Y. Iwamasa (Eds.), *Culturally responsive cognitive behavioral therapy* (pp. 247–266). Washington, DC: American Psychological Association.

Pace, T. M., Robbins, R. R., Rockey, R., Choney, S. K., Hill, J. S., et al. (2006). A cultural-contextual perspective on the validity of the MMPI-2 with American Indians. *Cultural Diversity and Ethnic Minority Psychology, 12*, 320–333.

Piotrowski, Z. (1972). Psychological testing of intelligence and personality. In A. M. Freedman & H. I. Kaplan (Eds.), *Diagnosing mental illness: Evaluation in psychiatry and psychology* (pp. 41–85). New York, NY: Atheneum.

Plake, B. S., Geisinger, K. F., Spies, R. A., & Buros Institute. (2012). *The seventeenth mental measurements yearbook*. Lincoln, NE: Buros Institute of Mental Measurement.

Plante, T. G., Goldfarb, L. P., & Wadley, V. (1993). Are stress and coping associated with aptitude and achievement testing performance among children?: A preliminary investigation. *Journal of School Psychology, 31*, 259–266.

Pope, K. S., Butcher, J. N., & Seelen, J. (1993). *The MMPI, MMPI-2, and MMPI in court*. Washington, DC: American Psychological Association.

Ramirez, S. Z., & Kratchowill, T. R. (1990). Development of the Fear Survey for Children With and Without Mental Retardation. *Behavioral Assessment, 12*, 457–470.

Reisman, J. M. (1976). *A history of clinical psychology*. New York, NY: Irvington.

Retzlaff, P. D., Dunn, T., & Harwood, T. M. (2011). The Millon Clinical Multiaxial Inventory-III. In T. M. Harwood, L. E. Beutler, & G. Groth-Marnat (Eds.), *Integrative Assessment of Adult Personality* (pp. 219–251). New York, NY: Guilford.

Robertson, G. J., & Eyde, L. D. (1993). Improving test use in the United States: The development of an interdisciplinary casebook. *European Journal of Psychological Assessment, 9*, 137–146.

Roid, G. H. (2003). *Stanford-Binet Intelligence Scales technical manual* (5th ed.). Itasca, IL: Riverside Publishing.

Rokeach, M. (2000). *Understanding human values*. New York, NY: The Free Press.

Ronan, G. G., Colavito, V. A., & Hammontree, S. R. (1993). Personal problems-solving system for scoring TAT responses: Preliminary validity and reliability data. *Journal of Personality Assessment, 61*, 28–40.

Rorschach, H. (1921). *Psychodynamics: A diagnostic test based on perception*. Oxford, UK: Grune and Stratton.

Rosenzweig, S. (1949). Apperceptive norms for the Thematic Apperception Test. I. The problem of norms in projective methods. *Journal of Personality, 17*, 475–482.

Rosenzweig, S. (1977). *Manual for the Children's Form of the Rosenzweig Picture-Frustration (P-F) Study*. St. Louis, MO: Rana House.

Rossini, E. D., & Moretti, R. J. (1997). Thematic Apperception Test interpretation: Practice recommendations from a survey of clinical psychology doctoral programs accredited by the American Psychological Association. *Professional Psychology: Research and Practice, 28*, 393–398.

Rotter, J. B., & Rafferty, J. E. (1950). *The Rotter Incomplete Sentences Test*. New York, NY: Psychological Corporation.

Rowe, H. A. H. (Ed.). (2013). *Intelligence: Reconceptualization and measurement*. New York, NY: Psychology Press.

Ryan, J. J., Glass, L. A., & Brown, C. N. (2007). Administration time estimates for Wechsler Intelligence Scale for Children-IV subtests, composites, and short forms. *Journal of Clinical Psychology, 63*, 309–318.

Ryan, J. J., Paolo, A. M., & Smith, A. J. (1992). Wechsler Adult Intelligence Scale—Revised intersubtest scatter in brain-damaged patients: A comparison with the standardization sample. *Psychological Assessment, 4*, 63–66.

Rychtarik, R. G., Tarnowski, K. J., & St. Lawrence, J. S. (1989). Impact of social desirability response sets on the self-report of marital adjustment in alcoholics. *Journal of Studies in Alcohol, 50*, 24–29.

Samuda, R. J. (1975). *Psychological testing of American minorities: Issues and consequences*. New York, NY: Dodd, Mead.

Sellbom, M., Ben-Porath, Y. S., Patrick, C. J., Wygant, D. B., Gartland, D. M., et al. (2012). Development and construct validation of MMPI-2-RF indices of global psychopathology, fearless-dominance, and impulsive-antisociality. *Personality Disorders: Theory, Research, and Treatment, 3*, 17–38.

Shear, M. K., Brown, T. A., Sholomskas, D. E., Barlow, D. E., Gorman, J. M., et al. (1997). *Panic Disorder Severity Scale (PDSS)*. Pittsburgh, PA: Department of Psychiatry, University of Pittsburgh School of Medicine.

Spangler, W. D. (1992). Validity of questionnaire and TAT measures of need for achievement: Two meta-analyses. *Psychological Bulletin, 112*, 140–154.

Spearman, C. (1904). "General intelligence" objectively determined and measured. *American Journal of Psychology, 15*, 201–293.

Sternberg, R. J. (2004). Individual differences in cognitive development. In P. Smith & C. Hart (Eds.), *Blackwell handbook of cognitive development*. Malden, MA: Blackwell.

Sternberg, R. J. (2006). *Cognitive psychology* (4th ed.). Belmont, CA: Wadsworth.

Sternberg, R. J. (2011). The theory of successful intelligence. In R. J. Sternberg & S. B. Kaufman (Eds.), *The Cambridge handbook of intelligence*: (pp. 504–526). New York, NY: Cambridge University Press.

Sternberg, R. J. (2013). The intelligence of Nations smart but not wise—a comment on Hunt (2012). *Perspectives on Psychological Science, 8*, 187–189.

Stewart, G. L., Darnold, T. C., Zimmerman, R. D., Parks, L., & Dustin, S. L. (2010). Exploring how response distortion of personality measures affects individuals. *Personality and Individual Differences, 49*, 622–628.

Sunberg, N.D., *Assessment of Persons,* 1st Ed., © 1997, pp. 97-98, 207. Reprinted and Electronically reproduced by permission of Pearson Education, Inc., Upper Saddle River, New Jersey.

Taylor, S., Zvolensky, M. J., Cox, B. J., Deacon, B., Heimberg, R. G., et al. (2007). Robust dimensions of anxiety sensitivity: Development and initial validation of the Anxiety Sensitivity Index—3. *Psychological Assessment, 19*, 176–188.

Tellegen, A. (1982). *Brief manual for the Multidimensional Personality Questionnaire*. Unpublished manuscript, University of Minnesota.

Tellegen, A., Ben-Porath, Y. S., McNulty, J. L., Aribisi, P. A., Grahm, J. R., et al. (2003). *MMPI-2 Restructured Clinical (RC) Scales: Development, validation, and interpretation*. Minneapolis, MN: University of Minnesota Press.

Urbina, S. (2011). Tests of intelligence. In R. J. Sternberg & S. B. Kaufman (Eds.), *The Cambridge handbook of intelligence* (pp. 20–38). New York, NY: Cambridge University Press.

Van Der Heijden, P. T., Egger, J. I. M., & Derksen, J. J. L. (2010). Comparability of scores on the MMPI-2-RF scales generated with the MMPI-2 and MMPI-2-RF booklets. *Journal of Personality Assessment, 92*, 254–259.

Van der Maas, H. L., Dolan, C. V., Grasman, R. P., Wicherts, J. M., Huizenga, H. M., et al. (2006). A dynamical model of general intelligence: The positive manifold of intelligence mutualism. *Psychological Review, 113*, 842–861.

Vane, J. R. (1981). The Thematic Apperception Test: A review. *Clinical Psychology Review, 1*, 319–336.

Walsh, B. W., & Betz, N. E. (2001). *Tests and assessment* (4th ed.). Upper Saddle River, NJ: Prentice Hall.

Ward, L. C. (2006). Comparison of facture structure models for the Beck Depression Inventory-II. *Psychological Assessment, 18*, 81–88.

Watkins, M. W., & Smith, L. G. (2013). Long-term stability of the Weschler Intelligence Scale for Children—Fourth Edition.

Psychological Assessment, No Pagination Specified. doi: 10.1037/a0031653.

Wechsler, D. (1967). *Manual for the WPPSI.* New York, NY: Psychological Corporation.

Wechsler, D. (2003). *WISC-IV technical and interpretive manual.* San Antonio, TX: The Psychological Corporation.

Wechsler, D. (2008). *Wechsler Adult Intelligence Scale—Fourth Edition.* San Antonio, TX: Pearson.

Weir, K. (2012). APA launches a new database of tests and measures. *Monitor on Psychology,* 13.

Wetzel, E., Hell, B., & Pässler, K. (2012). Comparison of different construction strategies in the development of a gender fair interest inventory using verbs. *Journal of Career Assessment, 20,* 88–104.

Widiger, T. A., & Presnall, J. R. (2013). Clinical application of the Five-Factor Model. *Journal of Personality,* first published online, doi: 10.1111/jopy.12004.

Wilkinson, G. S. (1993). *WRAT-3: Wide range achievement test administration manual.* Wilmington, DE: Wide Range, Inc.

Williams, C. L., & Butcher, J. N. (2011). *A beginner's guide to the MMPI-A.* Washington, DC: American Psychological Association.

Williams, T. H., McIntosh, D. E., Dixon, F., Newton, J. H., & Youman, E. (2010). Confirmatory factor analysis of the Stanford-Binet Intelligence Scales, Fifth edition, with a high-achieving sample. *Psychology in the Schools, 47,* 1071–1083. doi: 10.1002/pits.20525.

Wolpe, J., & Lang, P. J. (1969). *Fear Survey Schedule.* San Diego, CA: Educational and Industrial Testing Service.

Wood, J. M., Lilienfeld, S., Garb, H., & Nezworski, M. (2000). The Rorschach Test in clinical diagnoses: A critical review with a backward look at Garfield (1947). *Journal of Clinical Psychology, 56,* 395–430.

Wood, J. M., Lilienfeld, S., Nezworski, M. T., Garb, H. N., Allen, K. H., et al. (2010). Validity of the Rorschach Inkblot scores for discriminating psychopaths from nonpsychopaths in forensic populations: A meta-analysis. *Psychological Assessment, 22,* 336–349.

Woodcock, R. W., McGrew, K. S., & Mather, N. (2000). *Woodcock-Johnson III.* Itasca, IL: Riverside Publishing.

Woodworth, R. S. (1920). *Personal data sheet.* Chicago, IL: Stoelting.

Youngstrom, E. A. (2013). Future directions in psychological assessment: Combining evidence-based medicine innovations with psychology's historical strengths to enhance utility. *Journal of Clinical Child and Adolescent Psychology, 42,* 139–159.

Zytowski, D. G. (2007). Kuder Career Search with Person Match technical manual 1.1. Retrieved 19 June 2007, from http://www.kuder.com/publicweb/kcs_manual.aspx.

6 BASIC FEATURES OF CLINICAL INTERVENTIONS

Chapter Preview

In this chapter, we describe features common to most clinical interventions, focusing primarily on psychotherapy. We begin by examining what psychotherapy is and contrasting it with how it is portrayed in popular media. We describe what research tells us about clients and therapists and which of their characteristics influence therapy outcomes. Next, we examine the goals and basic processes involved in clinical interventions, as well as the professional and ethical codes that help guide practitioners in conducting treatment. Finally, we consider certain practical aspects of treatment such as treatment duration, fees, record keeping, treatment planning, therapist self-disclosure, and termination.

OVERVIEW OF CLINICAL INTERVENTIONS

SECTION PREVIEW

Here we begin to define psychotherapy, first by way of a formal definition and then by way of popular portrayals, which are usually less than accurate. We organize the hundreds of psychotherapy approaches into a handful based on shared assumptions and practices.

Clinical interventions occur when clinicians, acting in a professional capacity, attempt to change a client's behavior, thoughts, emotions, or social circumstances in a desirable direction. Intervention can take many forms, including individual and group psychotherapy, psychosocial rehabilitation, and prevention, but psychotherapy is the intervention activity by which clinical psychologists are best known.

What Is Psychotherapy?

In a nutshell, psychotherapy is treatment offered by trained mental health professionals and administered within the confines of a professional relationship to help clients overcome psychological problems. While no definition of psychotherapy satisfies everyone, this one identifies psychotherapy's participants (clients and therapists), the basic framework (professional relationship), and the treatment's main goal (reduction of suffering). The definition is, however, rather formal and probably not what comes to mind for most people when they hear the word *psychotherapy*.

PUBLIC (MIS)PERCEPTION OF PSYCHOTHERAPY   For many, the ready mental image for psychotherapy goes something like this:

> Two people are in a private office, sitting on comfortable chairs, and talking. Sometimes one of them, the client, is lying on a couch. The client talks about troubling events while the therapist asks probing questions or offers encouragement for the client to say more (e.g., "uh huh," "I see," "Tell me more about that," "And how did that make you feel?"). Over time, the therapist gradually directs the client to focus on emotionally painful events from childhood, events that had been buried in the unconscious. Once the client has fully remembered and discussed these issues, the client improves.

Unfortunately, the popular images of psychologists and other mental health professionals in movies and on television are often inaccurate. Although they may contain elements of truth, the portrayals are often caricatures or stereotypes (much like the popular images of police detectives, medical personnel, attorneys, and judges). In movies and on television, clinical psychologists and psychiatrists are frequently shown as professionals who fail to maintain appropriate professional boundaries, violate ethical codes, or shoot from the hip in treatment rather than conduct evidence-based interventions (Cannon, 2008; Orchowski, Spickard, & McNamara, 2006).

Treatments, too, are often inaccurately portrayed or oversimplified. This can occur because writers and filmmakers formed their impressions of therapy from watching previous media portrayals. That would explain why stereotyped versions of psychoanalysis are repeated with surprising regularity. Gabbard and Gabbard (1999) suggested that "if filmmakers have studied the history of the psychoanalytic movement, it would seem that they stopped reading Freud's work at this particular historical point. Most of the positive portrayals of psychotherapy revolve around the de-repression of a traumatic memory" (p. 28). Table 6.1 describes how psychotherapists are portrayed in several popular movies.

Even print media overgeneralize about psychotherapy. One *Newsweek* article (Begley, 2007) described efforts by psychologist Scott Lilienfeld and others to help distinguish ineffective or harmful psychological treatments from the effective ones (see Lilienfeld, 2007). But the magazine article's title, "Get Shrunk at Your Own Risk," implies that all psychotherapy may be risky (to "get shrunk" is slang for receiving psychotherapy treatment, just as "a shrink" is slang for a psychotherapist). It *is* true that clinical researchers have found that some forms of psychotherapy appear to cause more harm than good (e.g., the article mentions "stress debriefing" to prevent PTSD and using hypnosis to "discover" alternate personalities in persons diagnosed with dissociative identity disorder). It is also true that clinicians and the public would benefit from further efforts to identify ineffective or harmful "fringe" treatments. But the same can be said about medical treatment; researchers periodically discover that commonly used, FDA-approved medical treatments cause harm (for example, the drug Vioxx and hormone replacement therapy for postmenopausal women were both once routinely prescribed until researchers discovered the risks associated with them. Similarly, men were encouraged to undergo regular PSA screenings for prostate cancer until evidence suggested these blood tests may not be as valuable as originally believed). However, a magazine headline that read "Get Medical Treatment at Your Own Risk" would probably be regarded as a gross overgeneralization.

TABLE 6.1 Portrayals of Psychotherapists in Popular Media

Movie or TV Series	Portrayal
Analyze This	Billy Crystal plays a psychotherapist treating a mobster (played by Robert DeNiro). Although seeking to help, the therapist breaks confidentiality numerous times and allows his client to intimidate him.
Good Will Hunting	Robin Williams plays a psychotherapist treating a gifted but troubled young man (played by Matt Damon). The therapist is caring and helpful but at one point assaults and threatens his client and at another visits him at home, behaviors that most would consider well outside the bounds of professionalism.
As Good As It Gets	Psychotherapy portrayals play only a minor part in this movie about a challenging character with obsessive-compulsive disorder, played by Jack Nicholson. At one point, when Nicholson's character, Melvin Udall, barges into his therapist's office demanding to be seen, the therapist (played by Lawrence Kasdan) calmly but firmly explains to Mr. Udall that he needs to make an appointment—a positive portrayal of a therapist setting boundaries with a demanding and difficult client.
Ordinary People	Often regarded as a positive portrayal of psychotherapy, this movie shows Dr. Burger (played by Judd Hirsch) conducting psychotherapy with Conrad, a troubled teenager recently released from a psychiatric hospital after a suicide attempt (played by Timothy Hutton). Dr. Burger helps Conrad understand how the earlier accidental drowning of a beloved older brother and his parents' ineffective attempts to cope were not his fault.
The King's Speech	Colin Firth plays King George VI, who seeks treatment for severe stuttering. Though the focus is speech therapy rather than psychotherapy, the relationship that the therapist, Lionel Logue (played by Geoffrey Rush) maintains with King George is consistently professional and yet deeply personal, as good psychotherapy relationship often are.
The Sopranos	James Gandolfini plays Tony Soprano, a mobster in psychotherapy with Dr. Jennifer Melfi, a psychiatrist played by Lorraine Bracco. The therapy scenes from this series were often discussed among clinicians because the characters were complex and because the psychodynamically oriented sessions avoided cliché. But some sessions, such as one where Dr. Melfi angrily rejects her client, were violations of accepted psychotherapeutic practice.

Common misconceptions and overgeneralizations about psychotherapy and psychotherapists can be explained partly by a lack of *mental health literacy*—people often don't know better. But inaccurate portrayals can have damaging effects. Not only can they mislead the public about the work of mental health professionals, they can also perpetuate stereotypes about the mentally ill and inhibit people from seeking available treatments that could help them.

So what is psychotherapy really like? Let's begin by considering the many kinds of psychotherapy that are available.

How Many Psychotherapy Approaches Are There?

Some investigators have identified as many as 400 "brand name" therapies (Feltham, 2000), and they literally run the gamut from A (Aikido) to Z (Zaraleya psychoenergetic technique) (Herink, 1980). However, there are important similarities among many of these variants, and many of the others are rarely used by, or even known to, most clinicians. Indeed, it has been suggested that only about a dozen "essential" psychotherapies form the core of modern clinical practice (Messer & Gurman, 2011). In short, no one knows exactly how many kinds of psychotherapy there are—the answer depends on how you group them. If arranged according to basic assumptions about personality development, the causes of disorders, and psychotherapy techniques, there are a handful of major approaches.

For example, in Chapter 2, "Clinical Psychology's Past and Present," we noted that five major schools or approaches came to dominate psychotherapy: psychodynamic, humanistic, behavioral, cognitive, and group/systems. To that list we now add alternative and integrative approaches, which include therapies that combine elements of older, more established approaches as well as treatment techniques that do not fit neatly into the other categories. The treatment methods within each major approach do differ from one another, and we point out many examples in Chapter 7, "Psychodynamic and Humanistic Psychotherapies," Chapter 8, "Behavioral and Cognitive-Behavioral Psychotherapies," and Chapter 9, "Alternative Modes of Clinical Intervention."

SECTION SUMMARY

Psychotherapy refers to a variety of psychological treatments that mental health professionals provide to people suffering from various forms of psychopathology. Psychotherapy has captured the public imagination, but its features, methods, and effects are often misunderstood and misrepresented. Although there are numerous kinds of psychotherapy, most of them can be grouped into just a few categories, or approaches.

THE PARTICIPANTS IN PSYCHOTHERAPY

SECTION PREVIEW

Here we discuss clients and therapists, focusing on characteristics of both that are important to successful treatment. We also describe the therapeutic relationship as an important component to treatment and end by describing the settings for clinical interventions.

Psychotherapy involves at least one client and one therapist, though it can involve more than one client at a time (e.g., couples therapy, group therapy) or more than one therapist at a time (e.g., co-therapists, therapeutic teams). Clients and therapists can vary in many ways, including in terms of gender, age, racial or ethnic background, belief systems, personal strengths and weaknesses, communication styles, and so on. Let's first examine the problems and personality characteristics that clients bring to psychotherapy.

The Client

People seek psychological help for a variety of reasons. An unhappy marriage, a lack of self-confidence, a nagging fear, an identity crisis, depression, sexual problems, coping with injury or trauma, and insomnia are just a few of the things that motivate people to enter psychotherapy. In some persons, the disturbance is so great that day-to-day functioning is impaired, there is a risk of suicide or harm to others, and hospitalization may be necessary. In others, the disturbance may be less extreme but still very upsetting. The common essential feature is that the person's usual coping strategies—such as utilizing the support of friends and family or taking a vacation—are no longer sufficient to deal with the problems.

CLIENT PROBLEMS AND TREATMENT UTILIZATION   Mental disorders are found, with only minor variations, in all segments of U.S. society and around the world. Which disorders are the most common? In the United States, when clients are given DSM diagnoses, anxiety disorders top the list, with mood disorders, impulse control disorders, and substance abuse disorders not far behind (National Institute of Mental Health, 2006). Disorders can occur at any point in life, but the more serious disorders usually start early—symptoms often appear by age 14. If untreated, these disorders are more likely to remain, and may worsen (Kessler, Berglund, Demler, Jin, & Walters, 2005).

Of course, not everyone who experiences psychological disorders seeks treatment. In fact, treatment utilization rates are relatively low. Figure 6.1 shows the number of clients per 100, in different demographic categories, who annually used nonhospital outpatient mental health services in the United States. As you can see, those seeking outpatient psychotherapy are more likely to be middle aged, educated, white, female, and divorced or separated, to have public insurance, and to be unemployed. Failure to obtain treatment is more common in minority and lower socioeconomic groups, as are earlier drop-out rates (Olfson & Marcus, 2010).

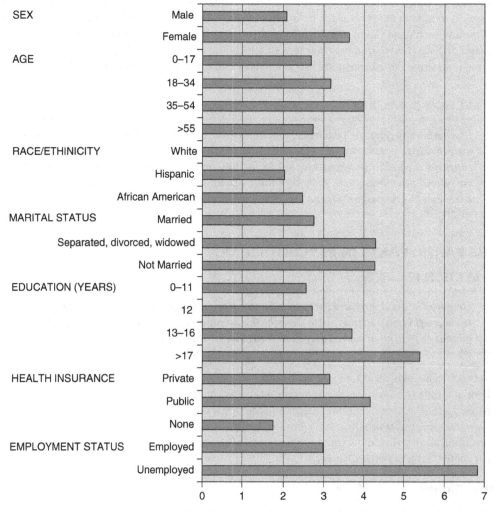

FIGURE 6.1   Percentages of Persons Using Outpatient Psychotherapy in 2007.
Source: Data from Olfson, M., & Marcus, S. C. (2010). National trends in outpatient psychotherapy. *The American Journal of Psychiatry, 167,* 1456–1463.; based on samples of over 29,000 in 2007.

Evidence for the underutilization of psychotherapy comes from several large-scale studies. The National Comorbidity Survey Replication estimated the 12-month prevalence rates for anxiety disorders to be 18%; for any disorder it is 26% (Kessler, Berglund, Demler, Jin, & Walters, 2005). But it is easy to see that no group in Figure 6.1 approaches that rate of treatment seeking. Multi year studies such as those shown in Figure 6.1 suggest that while treatment spending has increased for certain disorders (e.g., depression), that spending is more likely to go for medication than for psychotherapy. For example, Fullerton Busch, Normand, McGuire, and Epstein (2011) found that the use of antidepressant and antipsychotic medications for treating depression increased substantially over a 10-year period, while use of psychotherapy decreased. Unfortunately, this net increase in spending for drug-oriented treatment of depression appears to have resulted in minimal improvements in the quality of care.

CLIENT VARIABLES AND TREATMENT OUTCOMES   Among those who do seek treatment, the client's problem is perhaps the most obvious client-related characteristic. How important is the client's diagnosis in a therapist's selection of specific treatment methods and in the outcome of those treatments? Many clinicians and researchers have sought to match specific treatments to specific diagnoses, but the matching process has not resulted in dramatic gains in treatment effectiveness. Some researchers have even concluded that patient diagnosis has "largely failed as a basis for selecting among treatments" (Beutler & Harwood, 2000, p. 11).

Clinicians and researchers have investigated many other client characteristics with an eye toward finding those that might predict successful treatment outcomes. Broad demographic variables such as the clients' sex, age, ethnicity, socioeconomic status, intelligence, religious attitudes, and dozens of other personality and demographic variables have been considered, but these tend to be relatively poor outcome predictors (Garfield, 1994; Kim & Zane, 2010).

What about clients' personality and attitudes? Conventional wisdom holds that client motivation is directly related to therapeutic outcome. If we think of motivation in behavioral terms, it makes sense that two client variables—*cooperation versus resistance* and *openness versus defensiveness*—consistently show up as important in psychotherapy outcome research (Orlinsky, Grawe, & Parks, 1994; Teasdale & Hill, 2006). Motivation can also be influenced by clients' beliefs and expectations, so it is not surprising that those who have more hope of improvement and less fear of change are more likely to benefit from treatment (Holtforth Krieger, Bochsler, & Mauler, 2011; Messer, 2006). Clients' level of distress and coping style (e.g., externalizing or internalizing) are also important (Harwood, Beutler, & Groth-Marnat, 2011).

Autonomy, a client's freedom and willingness to exercise choices, is also linked to outcomes (Ryan, Lynch, Vansteenkiste, & Deci, 2010; Scheel, 2011). An example of the autonomy variable is clients' preferences about the type of treatment they are to receive. One meta-analysis of 26 outcome studies found that clients who received a preferred treatment had a slightly but significantly, greater chance of showing improvement and were half as likely to drop out of treatment (Swift & Callahan, 2009). Several other client-related variables, including attachment style, previous trauma, tendency toward somatization, and social context have been shown to have small to modest effects on outcome (van Manen et al., 2012). In short, clients vary on many dimensions. Though the clients' presenting problems are often the first targets of clinical attention, other demographic and personality variables, some trait-like (relatively permanent) and some more state-like (changeable), are also important. Indeed, it has been suggested that "it is frequently more important to know what kind of patient has the disorder than what kind of disorder the patient has" (Messer, 2006, p. 39).

The Therapist

Therapists can obviously differ in many ways. Which therapist characteristics are essential and which are less vital to successful therapy? As a general rule, broad demographic variables (e.g., age, sex, ethnicity, or socioeconomic status) play relatively insignificant roles in the overall effectiveness of therapy (Beutler, Machado, & Neufeldt, 1994; Stirman & Crits-Christoph, 2011), but other characteristics can be important.

TRAITS AND SKILLS OF EFFECTIVE THERAPISTS   Many authors (e.g., Brems, 2001; Cormier & Hackney, 2012; Inskipp, 2000; Jennings & Skovholt, 1999; Sommers-Flanagan & Sommers-Flanagan, 2012) have suggested that effective therapists possess a set of basic skills and traits. According to Inskipp, because psychotherapy is an interpersonal activity, psychotherapists must possess strong interpersonal skills, including those related to communication, relationship building, and self-monitoring.

Therapists who can recognize differences and intensities in clients' emotional experiences, and who also have a verbal repertoire capable of putting these shadings into words, are more likely to effectively communicate their understanding to their clients. In addition, therapists with these communication skills are more likely to help clients learn a new psychological vocabulary and new ways of understanding their experiences. This learning can help clients make the behavioral, cognitive, and emotional changes that are the goals of therapy.

As we discuss shortly, the relationship that develops between therapist and client strongly affects therapy outcome. For this reason, a therapist's *relationship-building skills* are critical (see Decker, Nich, Carroll, Martino, 2013). Therapists need to communicate sincerity and to warmly support troubled clients without judging them, and at the same time, they must have the skill to remind clients of their capacity and responsibility for making beneficial changes in their lives. Clinicians often summarize these relationship qualities as *genuineness, empathy*, and *unconditional positive regard*. These are called *Rogerian* qualities because Carl Rogers argued that they are the necessary and sufficient conditions for bringing about therapeutic change. Certain attitudinal variables also appear to differentiate more effective therapists. Those who convey warmth, acceptance, and a positive, hopeful orientation are more effective than those who are challenging or overly confrontational (Sommers-Flanagan & Sommers-Flanagan, 2012).

Finally, therapists need skills in self-awareness or self-management. As in any other line of work, the ability to monitor internal variables that might interfere with performance is important. *Self-monitoring skills* are seldom taught directly in clinical psychology programs, but these skills are learned indirectly as clinical training and supervision proceed.

Different approaches have different ways of developing self-monitoring skills. Psychoanalytically oriented therapists typically undergo analysis as the way to achieve self-monitoring skills. Cognitive or behaviorally oriented therapists are more likely to take an empirical approach, evaluating whether personal issues might be interfering when their interventions seem ineffective (see Burns, 1999, for an interesting discussion of this process). Whatever the approach, a therapist needs some way to monitor his or her contributions to the therapy.

One study (Smith, 2009) used a peer nomination process to identify seven psychologists and two social workers as master therapists. In interviews with those therapists and the individuals who nominated them, three overarching themes emerged: these therapists showed a remarkable commitment to personal development, to professional development, and to relationships. Jennings and Skovholt (1999) used a similar procedure to select 10 master therapists and then attempted to determine what cognitive, emotional, and relational characteristics distinguished these individuals from those who are less effective. Table 6.2 presents the characteristics of effective therapists as suggested by this and other sources.

Broad skills such as communication, relationship building, and self-monitoring can be considered *macroskills*. They are needed regardless of the therapist's theoretical orientation.

TABLE 6.2 Characteristics of Effective Psychotherapists

Characteristics of Master Therapists (adapted from Jennings & Skovholt, 1999)	Selected Traits of Effective Mental Health Professionals (adapted from Brems, 2001)	Helper Qualities and Skills (adapted from Cormier & Hackney, 2012)
Voracious learners who draw heavily on accumulated experience	Sense of ethics and professionalism	Virtue, including making clients' well-being the top priority
Aware of how their emotional health impacts their work	Willingness for introspection and self-reflection	Mindful awareness of one's own internal experiences
Emotionally receptive, valuing cognitive complexity and ambiguity	Cognitive complexity and tolerance for ambiguity	Social justice orientation; appreciation of diversity and multiculturalism
Possess strong relationship skills	Cultural sensitivity and respect for others	Cultural competencies
Mentally healthy, mature, and attend to their own well-being	Personal mental health, self-respect, and appropriate use of power	Resiliency, positive orientation and stamina, especially in the face of adversity
Believe in the working alliance	Empathy and capacity for intimacy with good personal boundaries	

The importance of these skills can be illustrated by paraphrasing Messer (2006): It is frequently more important to know what kind of therapist is offering treatment than to know what kind of treatment the therapist offers. This is also a way of saying that effective psychotherapists are more similar to each other than their varying theoretical orientations might lead you to expect.

THERAPISTS' TRAINING AND EXPERIENCES   It seems obvious that therapists need advanced training, and research partially supports this view. For instance, Machado, Beulter, and Greenberg (1999) found that trained therapists could recognize others' emotions better than untrained novices could. Because emotion recognition is necessary for understanding another person and for expressing empathy with them, it qualifies as a critical psychotherapy skill. Therapists with more training and experience also tend to have lower client drop-out rates (Luborsky, 1989; Swift & Greenberg, 2012).

However, it is not clear exactly what kind of training and what level of experience is best. None of the core mental health professions, which include clinical psychology and psychiatry, for instance, can offer convincing evidence that they produce superior therapy results. Indeed, paraprofessionals or trainees who have only relatively brief and narrowly focused training sometimes produce results equal to those obtained by persons who have had long-term professional training (Forand, Evans, Haglin, & Fishman, 2011).

This result is puzzling to many. Some suggest that methodological problems in the studies have obscured the importance of therapist training and experience (Leon et al., 2005). For example, studies that find trainees to be as effective as more experienced therapists often focus on a narrow range of therapeutic skills (e.g., the use of a specific cognitive-behavioral intervention for anxiety disorders). However, when researchers examine broader outcome variables (e.g., case conceptualization and planning, diagnosis, emotion recognition, need for further evaluation, dropout rates) they often find that more experienced therapists do better than less experienced ones (Eells et al., 2011; Swift & Greenberg, 2012).

Perhaps another reason that level of experience does not clearly translate into improved outcomes is that therapists typically change the nature of their practice and the kinds of problems they encounter as they move through their careers. One survey (Pingitore & Sheffler, 2005) found that clinicians with less than 5 years of experience were more likely to work in public health and/ or mental health settings than were those with more experience. Clinicians with more experience were more likely to be in private practice. Less-experienced psychologists also saw a greater percentage of clients with childhood disorders and substance abuse disorders, and they saw fewer clients per week (about 19 hours per week versus about 25 hours per week for clinicians with 11 to 20 years of experience). If clinicians are more likely to begin their careers in public, community mental health settings before moving into private practice, their clientele and their clients' typical problems change, too. If they take on tougher cases in later years, their success may be adversely affected, but not because experience doesn't help.

CHALLENGES OF THERAPEUTIC WORK   Therapeutic work can be deeply rewarding. For those with a desire to help others, every day presents a new opportunity to make it easier for someone to improve and flourish. However, the work also has its challenges. Some are relatively minor irritations and frustrations, while others are major, causing the clinician to question his or her competence or character. Too often, therapists feel that their graduate training was inadequate in helping them to manage these emotions or to use them therapeutically (Pope, Kieth-Spiegel, & Tabachnick, 2006).

What difficulties do therapists most often face in their work? Schröder and Davis (2004) found that therapists' complaints clustered into three groups:

1. Competency-related difficulties. These difficulties were relatively transient and resulted from situations in which therapists questioned whether they had the knowledge or skills to be effective in a given situation. For example, when a client being treated individually for depression wants to begin marital therapy with her alcoholic husband, the therapist wonders if he is qualified to treat substance abuse and marital problems in addition to the depression.
2. Personality-based difficulties. This category involved therapists questioning the degree to which their own enduring personal characteristics compromised their effectiveness. For example, therapists sometimes wonder if they are deficient in some of the traits listed in Table 6.2.

3. Situational difficulties. These concerns resulted from characteristics of the therapists' client base or work situation. For instance, therapists who work with treatment-resistant violent sex offenders in a prison may have both competence and personal capacity but still find the work very difficult.

How do therapists prepare for and cope with these challenges? The obvious fix for competency-related difficulties is to obtain more training in specified areas. If a therapist struggles with certain clients (e.g., those diagnosed with borderline personality disorder, Asian immigrants, gays/lesbians/bisexuals), it may be because of deficits in the therapist's knowledge and skills. If training for working with such clients was not available during the therapist's graduate school years, it can be obtained afterward through continuing education workshops or seminars offered by professional organizations. Indeed, continuing education is typically a requirement of clinical licensing renewal. Participation in such training also demonstrates the commitment to ongoing professional development that all health-care providers should display.

If a therapist's difficulties are more general, the remedy may have to be more focused on the therapist's own characteristics. As noted earlier, personal therapy has been regarded as an important aspect of psychotherapy training for psychoanalysts and some other psychodynamically oriented therapists (Murdock, 2004). Although few graduate programs specifically require it, approximately 85% of psychotherapists (psychologists, counselors, social workers) have sought psychotherapy for themselves at least once (Bike, Norcross, & Schatz, 2009; Orlinsky, Schofield, Schroder, & Kazantzis, 2011). It is interesting (and encouraging) to note that over 90% of psychotherapists report positive outcomes of their therapy across multiple domains (Bike, Norcross, & Schatz, 2009). Psychotherapists' belief in the value of personal psychotherapy is also suggested by the fact that the percentage of those seeking therapy has gone up over time, from approximately 60% in the 1980s to approximately 70% in the 1990s to the high 80% range currently.

When Pope and Tabachnick (2005) asked a national sample of psychologists whether personal therapy should be required for licensing in clinical psychology, 54.4% said either "absolutely yes" or "probably," while 40.2% said "absolutely not" or "probably not" (the remainder endorsed "don't know"). It is not clear whether undergoing personal psychotherapy makes therapists more effective with clients— Bike and colleagues' (Bike, Norcross, & Schatz, 2009) study found no relationship—but the majority of clinicians believe that it does (Murdock, 2004). Incidentally, the problems therapists present when they go into therapy are much like the problems that other people face: depression, relationship and marital problems, self-esteem concerns, anxiety, and job burnout (Bearse, McMinn, Seegobin, Free, 2013).

The Therapeutic Alliance

In a sense, there is always a "third participant" in any therapeutic encounter: namely, the relationship that develops between client and therapist. From the moment of first contact, each forms impressions, feelings, and cognitions about the other. As they move into extended interaction, these impressions begin to coalesce into a sense of what it is like to be with this other person. The therapeutic relationship, this third participant, is important because research consistently finds that it affects treatment outcomes (Crits-Christoph, Connolly-Gibbons, & Hearon, 2006; Hovarth, Del Re, Fluckiger, & Symonds, 2011).

The therapeutic relationship has many dimensions, but two of them are especially important: (a) the emotional bonds that develop between the therapist and client (liking, trust, etc.), and (b) the shared understanding of what is to be done (tasks) and what is to be achieved (goals). Together, these dimensions are often called the *therapeutic alliance* (see Bohart & Wade, 2013; Martin, Garske, & Davis, 2000).

VIEWS OF THE THERAPEUTIC ALLIANCE No one deserves more credit than Carl Rogers, the founder of client-centered therapy, for drawing attention to the therapeutic alliance. Rogers took the position that the client–therapist relationship is the crucible in which all the necessary and sufficient ingredients for therapeutic change are blended. In a departure from traditional views of therapy, Rogers saw the relationship itself, rather than the technique employed by the therapist, as the main curative factor in psychotherapy. According to Rogers (1951), "the words—of either client or [therapist]—are seen as having minimal importance compared with the present emotional relationship which exists between the two" (pp. 172–173). Rogers did not stress the client's role in creating the therapeutic alliance; it was assumed that if the therapist offered the proper conditions, the relationship would typically develop and clients would benefit (Hovarth, 2000). Humanistically oriented therapists since Rogers have continued to share a similar view of the therapeutic relationship. To them, the alliance is not merely the context for treatment, it *is* the treatment.

Psychoanalysts and psychodynamically oriented clinicians also regard the alliance as critical but are less inclined to believe that the relationship itself is the main ingredient in therapy. According to Meissner (2006), the alliance is essentially a therapeutic pact—a shared understanding about the professional relationship and the kinds of interactions that take place within that pact. In a sense, the alliance provides the context for treatment, but therapeutic techniques are still critical.

Most behavioral and cognitive-behavioral therapists tend to view the therapy relationship as an important but not sufficient condition of therapy (Sweet, 1984). Most see the therapeutic alliance as a useful context in which more specific behavior-change techniques are introduced. In this sense, they are similar to psychoanalytic theorists—both view the relationship as the context for techniques—and different from the humanistically oriented therapists who view the relationship as a treatment in itself. Other behavioral therapists believe that the therapeutic relationship plays a larger role; they see it as the crucial element in bringing about beneficial change because it gives the therapist the opportunity to model new skills and reinforce improvements in the client's behavior (Follette, Naugle, & Callaghan, 1996). In their view, providing contingent reinforcement of clients' appropriate behavior as it occurs in the therapeutic relationship is one of the most powerful intervention tools therapists have (Kohlenberg & Tsai, 1991).

RESEARCH ON THE THERAPEUTIC ALLIANCE   It is clear that the therapeutic alliance has been viewed differently by therapists from different theoretical orientations (Norcross & Lambert, 2011). However, a consensus now appears to be developing. Expanding interest in the therapeutic alliance (see Figure 6.2) has led to the development of instruments for measuring it. These include the *Working Alliance Inventory* (Hovarth & Greenberg, 1989), the *California Psychotherapy Alliance Scales* (Marmar, Gaston, Gallagher, & Thompson, 1989), the *Vanderbilt Psychotherapy Process Scale* (Suh, Strupp, & O'Malley, 1986), and the *Therapeutic Bond Scales* (Saunders, Howard, & Orlinsky, 1989). Some of these scales were designed with specific theoretical views of the alliance in mind (e.g., psychodynamic), while others aim to measure the alliance more generally. Nevertheless, most of these scales are highly intercorrelated, which suggests that they measure essentially the same thing.

Interest in the alliance has spawned much research, and that research has helped create a clearer picture of the topic. For one thing, meta-analytic reviews have clearly established the importance of the alliance to therapy outcomes. These reviews have generally found that the overall effect size for the alliance on therapy outcomes is small to moderate, but the effect size varies considerably depending on a number of variables, including how the alliance is measured (Hovarth, Del Re, Fluckiger, & Symonds, 2011). Crits-Cristoph et al. (2011) suggest that with more careful assessment of the alliance (e.g., using aggregates of alliance measures rather than a single measurement of it), the effect of the alliance on therapy outcomes is larger.

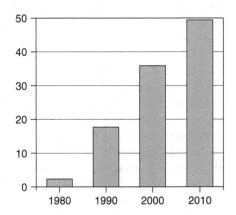

FIGURE 6.2 Frequency of the Term "Therapeutic Alliance" Appearing in APA PsychNet Titles Sampled in Four Years, 1980–2010.

PROMOTING THE THERAPEUTIC ALLIANCE   For clinicians, the key question is how to promote the therapeutic alliance. Orlinsky and Howard (1986) found that the alliance is likely to flourish when both parties are capable of bringing three elements to the situation: role investment (the personal effort both parties devote to therapy), empathic resonance (the degree to which both parties are "on the same wavelength"), and mutual affirmation (the extent to which both parties care for each other's well-being). Still, given that different clients are likely to benefit from different approaches to psychotherapy and that clinicians are typically unable to influence the factors that clients bring to therapy, questions about the therapeutic relationship remain: What variables should be attended to when trying to establish a good therapeutic alliance? Does the alliance matter more for some forms of therapy than others, or for some clients more than others?

One way to promote the therapeutic alliance is to match clients and therapists on one or more characteristics. The idea is that similarity between client and therapist on key characteristics is likely to "jump start" the alliance by making both more comfortable and promoting more agreement on therapy tasks and goals. However, matching clients and therapists on broad demographic variables such as gender or age appears to have little if any effect on therapy outcomes. Matching based on shared ethnicity appears to have benefits, but more in some situations than others. Indeed, Horst et al. (2012) and Rosen, Miller, Nakash, Halperin, and Alegría (2012) suggest that the processes involved in ethnic matching may be driven more by psychological and interpersonal variables than by simple demographic ones. For example, therapists who share a certain ethnicity or background with clients may simply have greater knowledge of the social and interpersonal challenges faced by such persons. In that case, multicultural competency—a learnable skill—rather than demographic similarity, may be what makes particular therapists effective (Chao, Steffen, & Heiby, 2012).

Promising variables for facilitating the therapeutic alliance are discussed in a special issue of the *Journal of Clinical Psychology* (see Norcross & Wampold, 2010). An example of one such variable is the matching of therapy type to client attitude toward therapy. In a meta-analysis of 12 studies, Beutler, Harwood, Michelson, Song, and Holman (2011) found that clients with low levels of resistance had better outcomes with more directive types of treatment, and clients with higher levels of resistance had better outcomes with nondirective treatments. Clinicians may not always have the flexibility to match certain clients with certain therapists or treatments, but with continued research, options for promoting the therapeutic alliance become clearer.

Finally, clinicians should be aware that their perception of the alliance may not be entirely accurate. When researchers measure the therapeutic alliance as seen by clients and therapists, they often find that the two hold differing views (Bachelor, 2011). It is often the case, too, that an observer's assessment of the alliance is more similar to the client's view than to the therapist's. This latter finding suggests that therapists can be biased in their perceptions and should therefore cross-validate their views by periodically assessing clients' views of the alliance or by having measures taken by observers (Decker, Nich, Carroll, & Martino, 2013). We discuss this and other topics related to the therapy relationship further in Chapter 10, "Research on Clinical Intervention."

The Settings for Psychotherapy

The settings for psychotherapy are most easily divided into two categories: *outpatient settings* and *inpatient settings*. The former includes therapists' offices, school counseling centers, spaces in community centers or church basements, or anywhere else clients and therapists agree to meet. The latter includes facilities such as hospitals, prisons, or residential treatment centers, where patients reside for days, months, or rarely, years.

OUTPATIENT SETTINGS   Therapists' offices are by far the most common setting for psychotherapy. The requirements for a therapist's office are minimal, but certain features are important. The first is privacy. Because of the emotional nature of therapy, clients have a right to expect that their communications remain between themselves and their therapists. For this reason, most therapists see clients in rooms that are soundproof, or nearly so. Arrangements should be made to hold calls and other interruptions during therapy sessions. Although it is advisable for offices to be private, to reassure both clients and therapists, they should not be too far removed from other people. Unfortunately, litigation brought by clients for actual or fabricated malpractice is a threat in this society (and one of the causes of skyrocketing malpractice insurance costs), and for therapists who work with potentially aggressive clients, it makes sense to have other persons not too far away from the office.

A psychotherapist's office should be set up to maximize client comfort. Source: alexsokolov - Fotolia

Comfortable places to sit are also essential. With adults, seating should place clients and therapists on approximately equal levels. Office decor should be inviting, orderly, but relatively neutral. That is, therapists' should feel free to have their offices express their tastes and affections, but the personalization of decor should not be so exotic or so expressive as to make clients feel that they don't quite belong there. A study in which students viewed 30 color photographs of therapists' offices found that softness (comfort) and order were most important factors in affecting students' expectations about the quality of care, the expertise of the therapist, and the likelihood of their choosing the therapist based only on their offices (Nasar & Devlin, 2011). If the therapist works with children, the therapy space should have toys and furniture appropriate to the clients' ages. In short, office accommodations should be designed to maximize the treatment goals for the clients with whom a therapist works.

Of course, not all therapy takes place in an office. Group therapy is often conducted in larger spaces in office buildings, hospitals, community centers, senior centers, churches, and the like. As with offices, therapists should try to structure the environment in a way that maximizes therapeutic goals, though they may have less latitude to do so in rented or borrowed spaces.

Some types of treatment can even take place in public settings. For instance, a therapist treating a client with panic disorder might accompany the client to a mall so that the client can practice anxiety management techniques learned in therapy. Similarly, therapists might ride with their elevator-phobic clients in an elevator to help them recognize symptoms, become more aware of cognitions, or practice breathing and relaxation exercises. Therapists may even take client groups on outings where they can practice social and other skills first learned in an office setting (also see Chapter 8, "Behavioral and Cognitive-Behavioral Psychotherapies").

Technology has created a number of "virtual" settings for the delivery of psychotherapy. Some of these involve synchronous communication—where participants interact in real time, but remotely, such as via telephone or streaming video (e.g., Skype). Others involve asynchronous communication—where participants communicate with delays in between responses, such as occurs via email or texting. Telephone, email, and other forms of online therapy have become much more prevalent in practice and in training, and a great deal of research is being devoted to the question of their effectiveness (Harwood et al., 2011; Miller, 2013). We will have more to say about technology-based treatments in Chapter 9 "Alternative Modes of Clinical Intervention."

INPATIENT SETTINGS   Inpatient therapy occurs in public, private, and VA hospitals, residential rehabilitation and treatment centers, prisons, jails, and many other settings. The requirements for therapy here are similar to those for inpatient settings—clients have a right to expect privacy and professional treatment. But there are important differences as well.

For example, in hospitals, the most common inpatient setting, clinicians are likely to be treating clients with severe problems, such as schizophrenia or major depressive disorder. Further, clinicians working in hospitals are often part of a treatment team that includes physicians, psychiatrists, social workers, and other personnel. Psychotherapists must therefore coordinate psychotherapy with other treatments, such as medication, physical therapy, or psychosocial rehabilitation.

SECTION SUMMARY

Psychotherapy is a treatment offered by a trained professional to one or more clients who suffer from a psychological disorder or a social/emotional problem. The key participants in psychotherapy are clients and psychotherapists. Few of the characteristics of either appear to have a large impact on how successful psychotherapy is, but the relationship that develops between them does. Psychotherapy is conducted in both inpatient and outpatient settings.

THE GOALS OF CLINICAL INTERVENTIONS

SECTION PREVIEW

The various approaches to psychotherapy differ in several ways, but they share common therapeutic goals. Those goals include (a) reducing emotional discomfort, (b) fostering insight, (c) providing new information (education) (d) assigning extra therapy tasks (homework), and (e) developing faith, hope, and expectations for change.

Different approaches to psychotherapy differ in their views of personality development and their explanations for the causes of psychological problems. So it is no surprise that they also differ in terms of the changes they are designed to produce. For instance, behavioral therapists are likely to deal directly with the problem as the client initially presents it (along with other difficulties that might contribute to the primary complaint). A mother who reports depression and social isolation and fears that she will harm her children might be assigned a variety of "homework assignments" involving her relationship with her husband, disciplinary methods for her children, or the development of new activities for herself. By contrast, a psychoanalyst would explore the presumed underlying causes of the mother's depression; therapy might be aimed at helping the woman understand how her current symptoms relate to feelings of inadequacy as a mother because of failure to meet her own mother's rigid and unrealistic standards (Cohen Milman, Venturyera, & Falissard, 2011). Finally, a humanistic therapist might deal with the problem by helping the mother discover her potential for creating alternatives that would free her from the one-dimensional life in which she now feels trapped.

Despite their differences, most forms of clinical intervention have a number of common goals. While not every form of psychotherapy strives to maximize each goal, each of the following goals is sought to some degree in all forms of successful treatment.

Reducing Emotional Discomfort

Clients sometimes come to a therapist in such emotional turmoil that it is difficult for them to participate actively in therapy. In such instances, the therapist will try to reduce the client's distress enough to allow the person to begin working on the problem. Therapists recognize that some level of discomfort can be a strong motivator for clients to work on changes, but too much can be debilitating. The challenge is to diminish extreme distress without sapping the client's desire to deal with enduring problems.

A common method for reducing client discomfort is to use the therapeutic relationship to boost the client's emotional strength. Clients gain emotional stability and renewed confidence by knowing that the therapist is a personal ally, a buffer against the onslaughts of a hostile world. Some therapists offer direct reassurances such as "I know things seem hopeless right now, but I think you will be able to make some important changes in your life." Sullivan, Skovholt, and Jennings (2005) found that the ability to provide a safe, collaborative, and supportive atmosphere is one of the key ways that master therapists understand the therapeutic alliance.

Fostering Insight

Insight into psychological problems was a chief objective for Freud, who described it as "re-education in overcoming internal resistances" (Freud, 1904, p. 73). While Freud was interested in a particular type of insight—into unconscious influences—most therapists (even those focused on behavior and cognitive-behavior therapy) aim for more general insight, as in greater self-knowledge. Clients are expected to benefit from learning why they behave in certain ways, because such knowledge is presumed to contribute to the development of new behavior. The psychotherapist's rationale for fostering a client's insight is like the well-known value of studying history: knowing about the errors of the past helps to avoid repeating them.

Therapists of all theoretical persuasions seek to promote self-examination and self-knowledge in their clients, though they may go about it in different ways. Some clinicians focus on a specific type of content, such as dreams. Others try promoting insight by asking their clients to examine the implications of certain behaviors (e.g., "What relationship do you see between your troubles with your boss and the dislike you express for your father?"). Cognitive therapists help clients become more aware of the automatic and maladaptive ways in which they explain events, particularly negative events. Behavioral therapists stress the importance of helping the client understand how behavior is functionally related to past learning and current environmental factors.

A common technique for developing insight is for the therapist to *interpret* the client's behavior. The purpose of interpretation is not to convince clients that the therapist is right about the significance of some event but rather to motivate clients to carefully examine their own behavior and thoughts and draw new and more informed conclusions about them. Although interpretation remains a main technique for many psychotherapists, some clinicians caution against the dangers of interpretations that are too confronting or challenging (Strupp, 1989). Particularly when working with very disturbed clients, therapists who minimize their use of interpretation in favor of being actively supportive, emotionally soothing, and directly reassuring tend to achieve the best outcomes. Conversely, less-disturbed clients benefit more from therapy experiences in which the therapist interprets connections between their behavior in therapy and their relationships outside of therapy (Jones, Cumming, & Horowitz, 1988).

Providing New Information (Education)

Psychotherapy is often educational. Certain areas of a client's adjustment may be plagued by misinformation, about sexual functioning for example, and therapists can often provide valuable information in these areas. Therapists are also educators in the sense that they provide new ways for the client to understand problems. As educators, part of a therapist's skill is in presenting information in ways the client can best understand. When clients understand how their disorders developed, are maintained, and can be overcome, they improve. Some therapists offer direct advice and information to their clients, adopting a teacher like role. Others suggest reading material about a topic, a process known as *bibliotherapy* (Marx, Gyorky, Royalty, & Stern, 1992). Still others rely on less direct methods—a shrug of the shoulder or a skeptical facial expression—to suggest to clients that there are other ways of perceiving the world. New information gives clients an added perspective on their problems that makes the problems seem less unusual as well as more solvable.

Assigning Extratherapy Tasks (Homework)

Therapists often ask clients to perform tasks outside of therapy for the purpose of encouraging the transfer of positive changes to the "real world." A large percentage of therapists assign homework, and the practice appears to be increasing across many psychotherapy approaches (Ronan & Kazantzis, 2006). Homework is typically designed to remind clients of important points from therapy sessions that might otherwise be forgotten and to encourage the practicing of newly learned behaviors (Beck, 2011). Behavioral and cognitive-behavioral therapists have always been advocates of homework assignments, believing them to be an effective way to promote the generalization of new skills learned in the therapist's office (Kazantzis, Daniel, & Simos, 2009). Homework assignments are also often made by psychodynamically oriented practitioners, systems-oriented psychotherapists, and even client-centered therapists (Allen, 2006; Ronan & Kazantzis, 2006). Clients who complete homework assignments appear to fare better in therapy than those who do not (e.g., Burns & Spangler, 2000).

Developing Faith, Hope, and Expectations for Change

Of all the procedures common to all systems of therapy, raising clients' faith, hope, and expectations for change is the ingredient most frequently mentioned as a crucial contributor to therapeutic improvement. The curative power of positive expectations is not restricted to psychotherapy.

It has been said, for example, that the early history of medical treatment is largely the history of the placebo effect (Shapiro, 1971). Some therapy techniques may be particularly potent in raising expectations and creating placebo effects because they appear dramatic or high-tech or because they tap into ingrained cultural norms associated with the best ways to achieve personal change.

Clinicians are so accustomed to thinking about the placebo effect in psychotherapy that many attribute much of psychotherapy's success to it rather than to specific techniques the therapist uses. Recognizing placebo effects in psychotherapy does not eliminate the importance of the specific techniques, nor does it eliminate the need to understand how specific techniques work differently. It does mean, however, that one important element (some might say the most important element) of any effective therapy is that it causes clients to believe that positive changes are attainable (Constantino, Arnkoff, Glass, Amertrano, & Smith, 2011; Orlinsky, Grawe, & Parks, 1994).

Part art and part science, psychotherapy profits from the mystique that surrounds both fields. Clients often begin psychotherapy with the belief that they are about to engage in a unique, powerful experience conducted by an expert who can work miracles. The perceived potency of psychotherapy is further enhanced by the fact that clients usually enter it after having fretted for a long time about whether they really need treatment. By the time this internal debate is resolved, the client has a large emotional investment in making the most of a treatment that is regarded with a mixture of fear, hope, and relief.

For their part, therapists encourage clients' faith in the power of psychotherapy by providing assurance that they understand the problem and that, with hard work and commitment by both partners in the therapeutic relationship, desired changes are possible. The client's perception that "I have been heard and understood and can be helped" can be as important as the soothing effect that physicians create by displaying calm confidence in the face of a patient's mysterious physical symptoms. Most therapists bolster this perception by offering a theory-based *rationale* for why psychotherapy will be effective.

Having structured therapy to increase the client's motivation and expectations for success, the therapist attempts to ensure that the client actually does experience some success as soon as possible. This success might be minor at first—a limited insight after a simple interpretation by the therapist or the successful completion of a not-too-difficult homework assignment. Whatever the means, the objective is to bring about the kind of change the client expects. The cumulative impact of many small changes in the initial stages of therapy helps reinforce clients' confidence that they can control their lives and that their problems are understandable and solvable. As more positive expectancies are confirmed, clients' belief in the possibility of meaningful changes increases. They then pursue changes with even greater determination, which in turn makes further success more likely (Howard, Lueger, Maling, & Martinovich, 1993). All the while, the therapist enhances the client's self-efficacy by pointing out that the changes are the result of the client's own efforts (Bandura, 1982).

SECTION SUMMARY

The different approaches to psychotherapy have similar goals. To varying degrees, they all try to reduce the client's suffering, help the client achieve insight, educate the client, facilitate the transfer of in-session learning, and develop positive expectations.

ETHICAL GUIDELINES FOR CLINICAL INTERVENTIONS

SECTION PREVIEW

Ethical guidelines help define and shape the therapeutic relationship. The primary guidelines for psychologists come from the APA's Ethics Code. The APA also offers a number of other guidelines in publications designed to help practitioners who deal with more specialized situations and client populations.

The practice of psychotherapy is shaped by the therapist's commitment to ethical and professional guidelines. That commitment protects the client and insulates the relationship from the negative influence of outside forces, but ethical guidelines do much more than protect clients and therapists from legal hazards. Ethical principles are intimately tied to the clinician's day-to-day and even moment-to-moment decision making (Nagy, 2011; Sperry, 2007). For example, consider the following examples:

- A depressed client calls a therapist at home and asks for an emergency therapy session that evening. Should she grant the request?
- A therapist considers presenting a case involving one of his clients (using a disguised name) at a convention. Should he do so?
- A 14-year-old client reports that her father occasionally strikes her 12-year-old brother and her mother, but she implores the therapist not to say anything about this during their next biweekly family therapy session. Should the therapist comply with the client's wish?

Each of these clinical situations involves ethical issues, and some involve balancing competing ethical issues (e.g., a duty of care against the requirement to maintain appropriate professional boundaries).

The APA Ethics Code

The main source of ethical guidelines for clinical psychologists is the *APA Ethical Principles of Psychologists and Code of Conduct* (American Psychological Association, 2010). As the name implies, this work consists of two main sections: (a) General Principles and (b) Ethical Standards. There are five General Principles:

1. Beneficence and Nonmaleficence
2. Fidelity and Responsibility
3. Integrity
4. Justice
5. Respect for People's Rights and Dignity

There are 10 Ethical Standards, each of which is divided into sections and subsections, resulting in 151 ethical rules for psychologists. For instance, section 10 covers psychotherapy and has sections on issues such as informed consent, therapy involving couples or families, sexual intimacies with clients, and so on. Table 6.3 describes a number of clinical situations and shows the sections of the Ethics Code that apply.

Four ethical concerns are the most important to psychotherapists (Sperry, 2007). Sometimes called the "four horsemen" of professional ethics, they are confidentiality, competency, informed consent, and conflict of interest.

TABLE 6.3 Examples of Ethical Dilemmas That Therapists May Face

Situation Arousing Ethical Concerns	Applicable Sections of the APA Ethics Code
During therapy, a client says that he has been thinking about killing his girlfriend.	4.01 Maintaining confidentiality 4.02 Discussing the limits of confidentiality
A client who tested positive for HIV reveals to his therapist that he continues to have unprotected sex.	4.01 Maintaining confidentiality 4.02 Discussing the limits of confidentiality
During group therapy, a therapist learns that a group member has broken confidentiality by talking to friends about other group members.	10.03 Group therapy
The court has ordered a client to obtain treatment or face jail time, so the client enters treatment but is unwilling to commit to or invest in it.	3.07 Third-party requests for services
A therapist who has been treating a married couple is now called upon to be a witness for one party in a divorce proceeding.	10.02 Therapy involving couples or families
A therapist would like to present the case of a client at a seminar, but the client wants to remain anonymous.	4.07 Use of confidential information for didactic or other purposes
A therapist considers becoming romantically involved with the ex-husband of a client.	10.06 Sexual intimacies with relatives or significant others of current therapy clients/patients
A therapist learns that a colleague has been using a controversial therapy that research suggests may produce more harm than good.	1.05 Reporting ethical violations 2.04 Bases for scientific and professional judgments

Confidentiality means that the therapist protects the client's privacy and, except in specific circumstances, does not reveal information that the client shares in therapy. (The special circumstances that require a breaching of confidentiality are described in the Ethics Code and discussed in more detail in Chapter 15, "Professional Issues in Clinical Psychology.") Confidentiality obligates clinicians to regard the welfare of their clients as their main priority. With very few exceptions, the therapist's commitment must be directed by a singular concern: *What is best for my client?*

Competency means that clinicians will be professionally responsible and practice only within their areas of expertise. They will maintain high standards of scientific and professional knowledge. Competence is difficult to measure, but it is based on a combination of education, training, experience, and credentialing. In practice, it means that clinicians will not engage in assessment or therapeutic practices unless they have appropriate education, training, and/or supervised experience to do so, nor will they conduct therapy with demographically unfamiliar populations (cultural competency). Competency is probably better thought of as a developmental process than an either–or condition (i.e., competent or not competent). At its most extreme, the competency requirement protects consumers from blatant malpractice, but it is also designed to help motivate clinicians to engage in career-long training and education.

Informed consent obligates therapists to tell clients about the limits of confidentiality, about potential outcomes of treatment, and about anything else that might affect the clients' willingness to enter treatment. For instance, therapists conducting couples therapy typically inform clients that one possible outcome of the therapy is that the couple could decide to separate or divorce.

Conflict of interest refers to the therapist's obligation to maintain therapeutic boundaries or a therapeutic "framework." As discussed in Chapter 4, the framework involves the set of expectations about the roles and interaction patterns that will occur within the therapeutic relationship. A conflict of interest occurs when the therapist's personal interests compete with the best interests of the client. Such conflicts might be minor, as when a therapist must decide whether venting his frustration at a client during a session is good for the client or simply self-indulgent. But conflicts of interest can also be major, such as when a therapist contemplates a sexual relationship with a client or a former client.

Although the Ethics Codes instructs practitioners on what they should or should not do, it is important to note that the code cannot cover every situation that clinicians might face. In fact, as implied by the previous examples, clinical decisions often involve a balancing of ethical concerns. We discuss professional guidelines related to therapeutic relationships in more detail in Chapter 15. There are also a number of books on how ethics affects clinical practice (e.g., Nagy, 2010; Pope & Vasquez, 2011; Sperry, 2007). There are also several guidelines published by the APA for clinicians working in specific areas of practice. The following examples can be found on the APA's Web site.

- APA Guidelines for Child Custody Evaluations in Divorce Proceedings
- APA Guidelines for Psychological Practice with Older Adults
- APA Guidelines for Providers of Psychological Services to Ethnic, Linguistic, and Culturally Diverse Populations
- APA Guidelines for Psychotherapy with Lesbian, Gay, and Bisexual Clients
- APA Statement on Services by Telephone, Teleconferencing, and Internet
- APA Guidelines for Psychological Practice in Health Care Delivery Systems
- APA Specialty Guidelines for Forensic Psychology

Ethics and the Therapist's Values

When clients struggle with value-related issues, therapists struggle as well, particularly if the therapist holds values that are different from those of the client. In fact, it is safe to say that at some point in their careers, all therapists are sure to have their cherished values challenged. Some challenges will be relatively minor, such as when trying to decide whether to try convincing a teenage, court-referred client that watching professional wrestling may not be the most meaningful thing in life. Other challenges can be major, such as when a depressed client with terminal cancer is contemplating suicide; should the therapist try to convince her not to kill herself? Table 6.4 lists a number of other value-laden topics that can come up in therapy.

There is no clear formula for deciding how to handle values conflicts in psychotherapy. Certainly the Ethics Code applies, but exactly how it does so may not be clear in every case. Self-aware

TABLE 6.4 Value-Laden Topics That Can Arise During Psychotherapy

abortion	animal rights	assisted suicide
birth control choices	career choices	child abuse and neglect
criminal activity	death and dying	dietary choices
domestic violence	gang membership	gender roles
health care choices	marriage and cohabitation	medical ethics
politics	premarital sex	racism and sexism
religious beliefs	religious practices	sexual orientation
sexual practices	substance abuse	environmental practices
suicide	use of power in relationships	weight and weight loss

Source: Based on Brems, C. (2001). *Basic skills in psychotherapy and counseling* (p. 46). Belmont, CA: Wadsworth.

therapists must be clear about their own values and how those values can influence treatment, and when confronted with values conflicts, the therapists must make decisions. Should they set their values aside and follow the client's lead, explain to clients how their values are different, endeavor to change the client's perspective, endeavor to change their own perspective, discontinue working with the client, or adopt some other option? Most therapists find it very helpful to discuss the therapeutic and personal implications of values conflicts with supervisors or colleagues. Here again, the APA Ethics Code helps ground the discussion.

SECTION SUMMARY

Clinical practice is guided by the APA Ethics Code, which provides general principles and specific standards in many areas, including psychotherapy. Standards most important to psychotherapy practice involve confidentiality, competency, informed consent, and conflict of interest. Although often thought of as useful only for avoiding malpractice or other hazards, the Ethics Code is an invaluable aid in many areas of clinical decision making, including situations in which a clinician's values conflict with those of their clients. A variety of other codes and guidelines exist to help clinicians navigate the ethical and personal dilemmas that inevitably occur in practice.

SOME PRACTICAL ASPECTS OF CLINICAL INTERVENTION

SECTION PREVIEW

Here we address some practical questions and procedures that apply to all forms of psychotherapy. These topics include treatment duration, fees, record keeping, treatment planning, therapist self-disclosure, and termination. We conclude with discussion of growing trends in clinical intervention.

There are numerous practical questions about psychotherapy: How long does psychotherapy last? How much does it cost? What records do therapists keep? Do therapists talk about themselves during psychotherapy? How do therapists decide what kind of treatment to use? Let's consider each of these questions now.

Treatment Duration and Fees

The duration of treatment can range from one day to several years, depending on the type and severity of the disorder; the motivation and other characteristics of the client; the skill and orientation of the therapist; and the availability of funding for treatment. Traditional psychoanalytic treatment often lasts for years, with clients being seen multiple times per week. Such treatment is rare today, and most clients in individual psychotherapy are seen on a weekly basis (sometimes less, sometimes more) for sessions that average 45 to 55 minutes. Group sessions typically last 90 to 120 minutes. One study that examined 490,000 managed care insurance claims found that the mean number of sessions with psychologists was between 7 and 8, but that this number varied by region and by the client's diagnosis (Crane & Payne, 2011).

Single-session fees charged by psychologists vary substantially, and summary data about fees are hard to come by. However, because clinics and private practitioners now advertise their fees and services online, it is easy to see what they are. A variety of factors, including location (e.g., rural versus urban), clinicians' level of training, funding sources (e.g., private pay versus insurance), and type of disorder, can all affect fees. Further, psychologists or their employing agencies often provide free service or reduced payments on a sliding scale for clients with various levels of financial need. Providers might also accept lower payments from insurance companies who set reimbursement limits for particular services.

Record Keeping

Psychotherapists are ethically bound to keep good records of their services to clients. The *APA Record Keeping Guidelines* (American Psychological Association, 2007) is the primary document outlining this obligation. As with most APA guidelines, they do not mandate exactly what records must be kept. Rather, they outline the basic content of records, control and retention of records, and disclosure of records. Psychologists should keep records of (a) their clients' identifying information, (b) dates and types of service, (c) fees, (d) assessment results, (e) treatment plans, and (f) consultations with others about clients. These records should be presented at a level of detail that would allow another clinician to take over the case should circumstances require it. In short, good record keeping is designed to benefit clients, clinicians, and their institutions. Good records can also be valuable if clinicians are involved in legal proceedings, and reviewing records, especially records of effectiveness, can motivate clinicians to find ways to improve their services.

Case Formulation and Treatment Planning

In Chapter 3, we presented a general model for assessment, which begins when the clinician receives and clarifies the referral question and ends with the communication of assessment results (see Figure 3.1). Psychotherapy also begins with assessment, though it might not involve formal procedures such as structured interviews or psychological tests. Assessment for the purposes of treatment leads to the clinician's *case formulation*, a conceptualization of the client's problems. Case formulations (also called case study guides) may vary depending on the clinician's theoretical orientation (see Chapter 2), but the critical elements in any formulation are facts and impressions about the client that can be used in planning treatment. In short, *treatment planning* depends on case formulation, which in turn depends on assessment.

THREE APPROACHES TO TREATMENT PLANNING   Makover (2004) describes three approaches to treatment planning. The first is *therapist-based treatment planning*, but it could also be called orientation-based or theory-based planning. In this approach, the therapist learns a basic theoretical orientation to psychotherapy (e.g., psychodynamic, behavioral, or whatever) and uses it for every client. Until about the 1950s, psychoanalysis was the dominant form of treatment. Gradually, other approaches emerged, each claiming to be more effective. Therapists and graduate training programs lined up behind one of these major "schools" of psychotherapy and (selectively) pointed to evidence demonstrating that outcomes using that approach were superior. Even today, many clinicians and graduate training programs still ascribe to one main approach to treatment. They acknowledge that clients are different, and their treatment plans vary in accord with those differences, but the treatments offered are still those under the umbrella of one theoretical approach.

Over time, many clinical practitioners and researchers became disenchanted with the "one size fits all" therapist-based approach to treatment planning and adopted *diagnosis-based treatment planning*, in which the client's diagnosis, not the therapist's orientation, determines the mode of treatment selected. Modeled after medical treatment, this approach to treatment planning attempts to link specific diagnoses with the most effective treatment for that diagnosis (see our discussion of evidence-based practices in Chapter 10, "Research on Clinical Intervention"). While most clinicians view diagnosis-based treatment as a more scientific approach to treatment selection than clinician-based treatment, it too has its detractors. As we discussed in Chapter 3, "Basic Features of Clinical Assessment," diagnosis is imprecise. Further, as mentioned earlier in this chapter, a great

TABLE 6.5 Information Sought in Systematic Treatment Selection/InnerLife

Client Dimensions	Therapy/Treatment Dimensions
Level of functional impairment	High versus low treatment intensity
Level of social support	Treatment modality
Problem complexity	Treatment format
Coping style	Skill-building and symptom focus versus insight- and awareness-focused interventions
Level of trait like resistance	
Level of subjective distress	High versus low therapist directiveness
	Relative level of emotional experiencing

Source: Harwood, T. M., Beutler, L. E., Williams, O. B., & Stegman, R. S. (2011). Identifying treatment-relevant assessment: Systematic Treatment Selection/InnerLife. In T. M. Harwood, L. E. Beutler, & G. Groth-Marnat (Eds), *Integrative assessment of adult personality* (pp. 61–79). New York, NY: Guilford.

deal of research has shown that factors other than the client's diagnosis—such as the quality of the therapeutic alliance—are responsible for significant variations in treatment outcomes.

Outcome-based treatment planning is an attempt to base treatment planning on all, or at least the most important, factors that can affect treatment outcome. Some of those factors are related to the client (e.g., diagnosis, personality traits, expectations), some to the therapist (e.g., theoretical orientation, techniques and competencies, personality traits), and some to situational or emergent qualities (e.g., treatment setting, therapeutic alliance).

An example of multifaceted, outcome-based treatment planning is embodied in the *Systematic Treatment Selection/InnerLife* (STS) designed by Beutler and Clarkin (1990) and subsequently refined (see Beutler, Williams, & Norcross, 2008; Harwood Beutler, Williams, & Stegman, 2011). The basic idea is to identify specific client characteristics that research tells us affect therapy outcomes and to match these with specific forms of treatment. The information needed to conduct STS can be obtained by interviews, observations, archival records, or tests. A Web-based program allows both clients and therapists to input key information that could help select which kinds of treatment are most promising. Table 6.5 illustrates some of the information that goes into this approach to treatment planning.

Case Example

The following is an abbreviated version of a case presented in Beutler and Groth-Marnat (2003). It illustrates some of the features of STS.

RW is a 22-year-old Mexican American woman. She has a history of panic attacks, associated with apparent agoraphobia, social phobias, and significant paranoid ideation. She carries a provisional diagnosis of undifferentiated schizophrenia (295.9) and social phobia (300.23). Her history . . . suggests a good deal of social distrust and isolation, largely deriving from her initiation of a long-term but illicit relationship with a high school teacher while she was yet underage (pp. 80–81).

The clinician gathered background information on RW and administered several assessment tools, including the STS Client Rating Form and the Minnesota Multiphasic Personality Inventory-II. These revealed certain client characteristics that were relevant for treatment: a tendency toward externalizing, external fears and anticipation of being harmed, hypersensitivity to others' opinions and criticisms, resistance to authority and concerns about loss of control or autonomy, complex/chronic problems, and moderate levels of distress and adequate social support.

These characteristics in turn suggested long-term treatment that included psychoactive medications and therapy that was instructional, partially client-directed, and not highly charged or confrontational.

The externalizing tendencies suggest the need to focus on discrete symptoms and to utilize a concrete and structured approach that trains the patient in more effective thought and emotion management, effective interpersonal skills, and helps her to test out suspicions of others' motives and behaviors. The high levels of resistance led to the suggestion that self-directed treatments should supplement therapist activities to reduce the degree of confrontation (p. 81).

The STS is neither the first nor the only approach to outcome-based treatment planning. In 1973 Arnold Lazarus suggested that clinicians should gather a range of information about a client when designing interventions. His approach, called *BASIC-ID* (Lazarus, 1973), encouraged clinicians to design treatments based on assessment of clients' Behaviors, Affects, Sensory experiences, Imagery, Cognitions, Interpersonal relationships, and need for Drugs. An increasing number of investigators are working on treatment planning approaches, some of which conform to a particular theoretical approach and some of which attempt to be theory-neutral. A key challenge for outcome-based approaches to treatment planning is to evolve along with the research. Another challenge is for psychological services to be sufficiently flexible to be able to offer multiple options for treatment for clients. This is especially difficult in dealing with clients living in rural areas, for instance.

Therapist Objectivity and Self-Disclosure

Once therapy has begun, clients are expected to disclose a great deal of personal information—indeed, therapy would be impossible without it—but what about therapists? In many instances, therapists must decide whether to share personal information such as their emotional reactions, incidents from their own lives, and the like. Such sharing is called *therapist self-disclosure.* For example, should a therapist reveal feelings of irritation or boredom to a client? Should a therapist reveal that she is mourning a recent death in her family? Should a therapist discuss his former addiction, a divorce, or topics related to his own experience as a client in psychotherapy?

There are potential benefits and risks in both disclosure and nondisclosure. Therapists who never self-disclose risk being perceived as aloof or impersonal, which might damage the therapeutic relationship. Therapists who frequently self-disclose risk being perceived as impulsive, self-focused, or compromising the professional nature of the client–therapist relationship.

There is no firm rule about therapist self-disclosure, and practices vary across therapists and theoretical orientations. Traditional psychoanalytic therapists have advocated strict prohibitions against disclosing personal information—they insist that the focus should always be on the client and the client's problems. Modern psychodynamically oriented clinicians recognize that utter nondisclosure is an impossible ideal because therapists are always revealing something about themselves in their verbal and nonverbal behavior (Gabbard, 2005; Ramseyer & Tschacher, 2011), so minimal self-disclosure is accepted. Cognitive behavioral therapists also tend toward lower levels of self-disclosure (Hansen, 2008). At the other extreme are eclectic and humanistically oriented therapists who favor considerable therapist disclosure; they view it as part of being genuine. Therapists from other orientations fall somewhere in the middle on the acceptability of self-disclosure.

Ethical as well as theoretical guidelines may affect disclosure, too. Therapists must ask themselves (and sometimes make split-second decisions about) whether a disclosure is in the client's best interest. Certainly the intensity of the therapeutic relationship may tempt the therapist to discard a professional orientation in favor of more spontaneous reactions, including pity, frustration, hostility, attraction, or boredom. therapists try to stay alert to these "boundary challenges" (Frankel, Holland, & Currier, 2012) and monitor ways in which their personal needs might intrude upon therapy. The question that always applies is: Whose needs are most being served by a therapist's disclosure?

Termination

Termination of psychotherapy can occur before or after treatment has been completed. The latter case is sometimes called *attrition* or *premature termination.*

Termination that occurs at the end of treatment is likely to bring mixed feelings to both client and clinician. The loss of a meaningful relationship is the most frequently mentioned negative factor for clients (Roe, Dekel, Harel, Fenning, & Fenning, 2006). Therapists, too, often experience a sense of loss. Still, both client and therapist can reflect on their shared efforts and accomplishments. Clients typically experience termination as evidence of their independence and growth. After successful treatment, termination is a positive experience for both.

Two Broad Trends in Clinical Intervention

For many decades, the dominant model for mental health treatment has been individual psychotherapy—a therapist interacts face to face with a client and administers a treatment (psychotherapy) derived from a particular theoretical framework (e.g., psychodynamic, cognitive-behavioral). However, two major trends have emerged that may signal significant changes in the field.

The first is the shift in emphasis from theoretical orientations to clinical utility. For many years, battles over which theories generated the most effective treatments, and what counts as good evidence of effectiveness, have dominated the field (see Chapter 10, "Research on Clinical Intervention"). This has gradually given way to more practical questions about which specific treatments work best for which clients with which disorders. An increasing focus on utility makes everyone more eclectic, and, hopefully, less ideologically committed. Of course, broad theoretical orientations will remain important, still informing training and practice, but the focus on utility is a welcome trend because it can further unify the field and help to expand treatments to an increasingly diverse population (Silverman, 2013).

The second, and closely related, trend is the expansion of methods for delivering mental health services. It has become clear that the majority of persons suffering from mental illness in both developed and developing countries do not receive treatment. The standard delivery method—individual therapy—does not reach most of those in need. As a result, leaders in the field are increasingly advocating alternative modes of mental health delivery. Attempts to think outside the individual psychotherapy box include emphasis on prevention and public health campaigns (similar to those used for smoking or prevention of HIV/AIDS); task shifting in which others in the health system (e.g., doctors, nurses, nonprofessionals) provide certain mental health services and psychologists expand their services to new areas; "disruptive innovations" in which technologies such as cell phones or tablets provide regular opportunities for persons to assess their mental health or to access components of treatment; and other interventions that infuse mental health assessment and treatment more into everyday life (Kazdin & Rabbitt, 2013). The expansion of services beyond the traditional therapy approaches might create new roles for mental health professionals, help further erase the distinction between health care and mental health care, and provide ways to deliver mental health services to many more people.

SECTION SUMMARY

Practical considerations surrounding psychotherapy involve the setting of fees, decisions about the duration of treatment, and keeping of official records. Treatment planning is especially important because it sets the stage for how psychotherapy is conducted. If successfully conducted, the termination of psychotherapy and its aftereffects should be primarily positive for the client. For those who do not or cannot utilize traditional psychotherapy, new models of mental health services are being developed.

Chapter Summary

Clinical intervention involves a deliberate attempt to make desirable changes in clients' behavior, thinking, and social interactions. Treatment is initiated when a client in need of help is seen by a therapist with special training. Therapists can include persons trained in clinical psychology, counseling psychology, psychiatry, psychiatric social work, psychiatric nursing, family counseling, or a variety of other paraprofessional and specialty areas.

The participants in psychotherapy—therapists and clients—bring individual strengths and weaknesses to the situation. Most clinicians agree that effective therapy is facilitated by the development of a supportive yet objective relationship, which in turn is fostered by certain therapist and client

contributions. Effective therapists need advanced training and interpersonal skills in communication, relationship building, and self-monitoring. Characteristics described by Carl Rogers as genuineness, empathy, and unconditional positive regard are especially important in developing a strong therapeutic relationship. Client characteristics such as motivation and openness also contribute to the effectiveness of therapy, but the therapeutic alliance—the bond between therapist and client and their agreement on tasks and goals—remains one of the best predictors of therapeutic outcome.

Psychotherapy is most often conducted in an individual format in an outpatient setting. However, it is also conducted in inpatient settings. Each setting constitutes part of the environment or situation in which therapy takes place.

Although approaches to psychotherapy differ, they all attempt to accomplish a common set of goals (though to varying degrees): reduce suffering, achieve insight, educate the client, facilitate the transfer of in-session learning, and develop positive expectations.

Psychotherapy is guided by the APA Ethics Code. Standards most important to psychotherapy practice involve confidentiality, competency, informed consent, and conflict of interest. The Ethics Code is an invaluable aid in many areas of

clinical decision making. A variety of other codes and guidelines exist to help navigate specific areas of clinical practice.

Psychological treatments involve a number of practical considerations: fees, decisions about the type and length of service, record keeping, and so on. One of the most important practical considerations involves treatment planning. Although treatment planning can be done in a variety of ways, we think that an approach based on psychotherapy outcome research is the most empirically and ethically defensible. Outcomes research will also be critical as psychologists explore new methods of delivering mental health services.

Study Questions

1. How accurate are media portrayals of psychotherapy and psychotherapists?
2. How many kinds of psychotherapy are there?
3. Which are the dominant approaches to psychotherapy?
4. What percentage of persons with psychological disorders seek psychotherapy?
5. What problems are most common among persons seeking psychotherapy?
6. What other client characteristics, besides diagnosis, appear to influence therapy outcomes?
7. What traits and skills do effective psychotherapists exhibit?
8. How is the therapist's training related to psychotherapy outcomes?
9. What are the personal challenges of psychotherapeutic work for therapists?
10. How has the therapeutic relationship been understood?
11. How does the therapeutic relationship influence therapy outcomes?
12. What are the settings of psychotherapy?
13. What are the goals common to most forms of psychotherapy?
14. What are some of the ethical decisions that can confront psychotherapists?
15. What professional guidelines or standards do clinical psychologists use to help them make ethical decisions?
16. What are typical treatment durations for psychotherapeutic services?
17. Why are psychotherapists ethically obligated to keep records?
18. What are commonly used approaches to treatment planning?
19. What positions have therapists taken on therapist self-disclosure?

Web Sites

- APA Help Center: http://www.apa.org/helpcenter/
- National Institutes of Mental Health: http://www.nimh.nih.gov/index.shtml
- Centers for Disease Control and Prevention: http://www.cdc.gov
- Mayo Clinic description of psychotherapy: http://www.mayoclinic.com/health/psychotherapy/MY00186

MOVIES

Girl Interrupted (1999): Based on a memoir of the same name, this film shows what it was like to live on an inpatient ward of a mental hospital in the late 1960s with other troubled adolescent girls.

Moonrise Kingdom (2012): Quirky film about interesting and potentially troubled adolescents who have concerns about being given "shock

treatment," and being placed in an unacceptable residential treatment facility.

MEMOIRS

The Boy With the Thorn in His Side: A Memoir by Keith Fleming (2000; New York: Perrenial). After surviving inpatient hospitalization in his teens, the author describes being rescued by his uncle (writer, Edmund White) and learning to enjoy life again.

Purge: Rehab Diaries by Nicole Johns (2009; Berkeley, CA: Seal Press). This memoir details the author's experiences in a residential treatment facility for eating disorders and includes copies of her hospital records, psychiatrist's notes, and food charts.

References

Allen, D. M. (2006). Use of between-session homework in systems-oriented individual psychotherapy. *Journal of Psychotherapy Integration, 16*, 238–253.

American Psychological Association. (2007). *Record keeping guidelines.* Washington, DC: American Psychological Association.

American Psychological Association, (2010). *Ethical principles of psychologists and code of conduct.* Washington, DC: American Psychological Association.

Bachelor, A. (2011). Clients' and therapists' views of the therapeutic alliance: Similarities, differences and relationship to therapy outcome. *Clinical Psychology and Psychotherapy*, Article first published online: 14 Nov 2011. doi: 10.1002/cpp.792.

Bandura, A. (1982). Self-efficacy mechanism in human agency. *American Psychologist, 33*, 122–147.

Bearse, J. L., McMinn, M. R., Seegobin, W., & Free, K. (2013). Barriers to psychologists seeking mental health care. *Professional Psychology: Research and Practice*, Feb 2013, No Pagination Specified.

Beck, J. S. (2011). *Cognitive behavior therapy: Basics and beyond* (2nd ed.). New York, NY: The Guilford Press.

Begley, S. (2007). Get "shrunk" at your own risk. Newsweek (June 18). Retrieved June 20, 2007, from http://www.newsweek.com/id/34105.

Beutler, L. E., & Clarkin, J. F. (1990). *Systematic treatment selection: Toward targeted therapeutic interventions.* New York, NY: Brunner/Mazel.

Beutler, L. E., & Groth-Marnat, G. (2003). *Integrative assessment of adult personality* (2nd ed.). New York, NY: Guilford.

Beutler, L. E., & Harwood, T. M. (2000). *Prescriptive psychotherapy: A practical guide to systematic treatment selection.* New York, NY: Oxford University Press.

Beutler, L. E., Harwood, T. M., Michelson, A., Song, X., & Holman, J. (2011). Resistance/reactance level. *Journal of clinical Psychology, 67,* 133–142.

Beutler, L. E., Machado, P. P. P., & Neufeldt, S. A. (1994). Therapist variables. In A. Bergin & S. Garfield (Eds.), *Handbook of psychotherapy and behavior change* (4th ed.). New York, NY: Wiley.

Beutler, L. E., Williams, O. B., & Norcross, J. C. (2008). *Innerlife.com.* A copyrighted software package for treatment planning. Available at www.innerlife.com.

Bike, D. H., Norcross, J. C., & Schatz, D. M. (2009). Processes and outcomes of psychotherapists' personal therapy: Replication and extension 20 years later. *Psychotherapy, 46,* 19–41.

Bohart, A. C., & Wade, A. G. (2013). The client in psychotherapy. In M. J. Lambert (Ed.), *Bergin and Garfield's Handbook of psychotherapy and behavior change* (6th ed., pp. 219–257). Hoboken, NJ: Wiley.

Brems, C. (2001). *Basic skills in psychotherapy and counseling.* Belmont, CA: Wadsworth.

Burns, D. D. (1999). *Feeling good: The new mood therapy, Vol. 1* (Rev. ed.). New York, NY: Harper Collins.

Burns, D. D., & Spangler, D. L. (2000). Does psychotherapy homework lead to improvements in depression in cognitive-behavioral therapy or does improvement lead to increased homework compliance? *Journal of Consulting and Clinical Psychology, 68,* 46–56.

Cannon, B. J. (2008). In search of a good psychologist in a good movie: Persisting stereotypes. *The Pennsylvania Psychologist Quarterly,* May/June, 1.

Chao, P. J., Steffen, J. J., & Heiby, E. M. (2012). The effects of working alliance and client-clinician ethnic match on recovery status. *Community Mental Health Journal, 48,* 91–97.

Cohen, D., Milman, D., Venturyera, V., & Falissard, B. (2011). Psychodynamic experience enhances recognition of hidden childhood trauma, *PLoS One, 6,* e18470. Doi: 10:1371journal.pone.0018470.

Constantino, M. J., Arnkoff, D. B., Glass, C. R., Amertrano, R. M., & Smith, J. Z. (2011). Expectations. *Journal of Clinical Psychology, 67,* 184–192.

Cormier, S., & Hackney, H. (2012). *Counseling strategies and interventions* (8th ed.). Boston, MA: Pearson.

Crane, D. R., & Payne, S. H. (2011). Individual versus family psychotherapy in managed care: Comparing the costs of treatment by the mental health professions. *Journal of Marital and Family Therapy, 37,* 273–289.

Crits-Christoph, P., Gibbons, M. B. C., Hamilton, J., Ring-Kurtz, S., & Gallop, R. (2011). The dependability of alliance assessments: The alliance-outcome correlation is larger than you might think. *Journal of Consulting and Clinical Psychology, 79,* 267–278.

Crits-Christoph, P., Gibbons, M. B. C., & Hearon, B. (2006). Does the alliance cause good outcome? Recommendations for future research on the alliance. *Psychotherapy: Theory, Research, Practice, Training, 43,* 280–285.

Decker, S. E., Nich, C., Carroll, K. M., & Martino, S. (2013). Development of the Therapist Empathy Scale. *Behavioral and Cognitive Psychotherapy, 10,* 1–16.

Eells, T. D., Lombart, K. G., Salsman, N., Kendjelic, E. M., Schneiderman, C. T., et al. (2011). Expert reasoning in psychotherapy case formulation. *Psychotherapy Research, 21,* 385–399.

Feltham, C. (2000). What are counselling and psychotherapy? In C. Feltham & I. Horton (Eds.), *Handbook of counselling and psychotherapy.* London, UK: Sage.

Follette, W. C., Naugle, A. E., & Callaghan, G. M. (1996). A radical behavioral understanding of the therapeutic relationship in effecting change. *Behavior Therapy, 27,* 623–642.

Forand, N. R., Evans, S., Haglin, D., & Fishman, B. (2012). Cognitive behavioral therapy in practice: Treatment delivered by trainees at an outpatient clinic is clinically effective. *Behavior Therapy, 42,* 612–623.

Frankel, Z., Holland, J. M., & Currier, J. M. (2012). Encounters with boundary challenges: A preliminary model of experienced psychotherapists' working strategies. *Journal of Contemporary Psychotherapy, 42,* 101–112.

Freud, S. (1904). On psychotherapy. Lecture delivered before the College of Physicians in Vienna. Reprinted in S. Freud, *Therapy and technique.* New York, NY: Collier Books, 1963.

Fullerton, C. A., Busch, A. B., Normand, S. T., McGuire, T. G., & Epstein, A. M. (2011). Ten-year trends in quality of care and spending for depression. *Archives of General Psychiatry, 68,* 1218–1226.

Gabbard, G. O. (2005). *Psychodynamic psychiatry in clinical practice* (4th ed.). Washington, DC: American Psychiatric Publishing.

Gabbard, K., & Gabbard, G. O. (1999). *Psychiatry and the cinema.* Washington, DC: American Psychiatric Press.

Garfield, S. L. (1994). Research on client variables in psychotherapy. In A. Bergin & S. Garfield (Eds.), *Handbook of psychotherapy and behavior change* (4th ed., pp. 190–228). New York, NY: Wiley.

Hansen, J. A. (2008). Therapist self-disclosure: Who and when. Dissertation 69, 1954.

Harwood, T. M., Beutler, L. E., & Groth-Marnat, G. (Eds.). (2011). *Integrative Assessment of Adult Personality* (pp. 354–372). New York, NY: Guilford.

Harwood, T. M., Beutler, L. E., Williams, O. B., & Stegman, R. S. (2011). Identifying treatment-relevant assessment: Systematic Treatment Selection/InnerLife. In T. M. Harwood, L. E. Beutler, & G. Groth-Marnat (Eds), *Integrative assessment of adult personality* (pp. 61–79). New York, NY: Guilford.

Harwood, T. M., Pratt, D., Beutler, L. E., Bongar, B. M., Lenore, S., et al. (2011). Technology, telehealth, treatment enhancement, and selection. *Professional Psychology: Research and Practice, 42,* 448–454.

Herink, R. (Ed.). (1980). *The psychotherapy handbook: The A to Z guide to more than 250 different therapies in use today.* New York, NY: New American Library.

Holtforth, M. G., Krieger, T., Bochsler, K., & Mauler, B. (2011). The prediction of psychotherapy success by outcome expectations in inpatient psychotherapy. *Psychotherapy and Psychosomatics, 80,* 321–322.

Horst, K., Mendez, M., Culver-Turner, R., Amanor-Boadu, Y., Minner, B., et al. (2012). The importance of therapist/client ethnic/racial matching in couples treatment for domestic violence. *Contemporary Family Therapy, 34,* 57–71.

Hovarth, A. O. (2000). The therapeutic relationship: From transference to alliance. *Journal of Clinical Psychology/In Session: Psychotherapy in Practice, 56,* 163–173.

Hovarth, A. O., Del Re, A. C., Fluckiger, C., & Symonds, D. (2011). Alliance in individual psychotherapy. *Psychotherapy, 48,* 9–16.

Hovarth, A. O., & Greenberg, L. S. (1989). Development and validation of the Working Alliance Inventory. *Journal of Counseling Psychology, 36,* 223–233.

Howard, K. I., Lueger, R. J., Maling, M. S., & Martinovich, Z. (1993). A phase model of psychotherapy outcome: Causal mediation of change. *Journal of Consulting and Clinical Psychology, 61,* 678–685.

Inskipp, F. (2000). Generic skills. In C. Feltham & I. Horton (Eds.), *Handbook of counselling and psychotherapy.* London, UK: Sage Publications.

Jennings, L., & Skovholt, T. M. (1999). The cognitive, emotional and relational characteristics of master therapists. *Journal of Counseling Psychology, 46,* 3–11.

Jones, E. E., Cumming, J. D., & Horowitz, M. J. (1988). Another look at the nonspecific hypothesis of therapeutic effectiveness. *Journal of Consulting and Clinical Psychology, 56,* 48–55.

Kazantzis, N., Daniel, J., & Simos, G. (Eds.). (2009). Homework assignment in cognitive behavior therapy. *Cognitive Behavior Therapy: A Guide for the Practicing Clinician* (Vol 2, pp. 165–186). New York, NY: Routledge/Taylor & Francis Group.

Kazdin, A. E., & Rabbitt, S. M. (2013). Novel models of delivering mental health services and reducing the burdens of mental illness. *Clinical Psychological Science, 1,* 170–191.

Kessler, R. C., Berglund, P., Demler, O., Jin, R., & Walters, E. E. (2005). Lifetime prevalence and age-of-onset distributions of DSM-IV disorders in the National Comorbidity Survey Replication. *Archives of General Psychiatry, 62,* 593–602.

Kim, J., & Zane, N. (2010). Client predictors of treatment outcomes in outpatient therapy. Paper presented at the American Psychological Association Convention (August), San Diego, CA.

Kohlenberg, R. J., & Tsai, M. (1991). *Functional analytic psychotherapy: Creating intense and curative therapeutic relationships.* New York, NY: Plenum.

Lazarus, A. A. (1973). Multimodel behavior therapy: Treating the "BASIC-ID." *Journal of Nervous and Mental Diseases, 156,* 404–411.

Leon, S. C., Martinovich, Z., Lutz, W., & Lyons, J. S. (2005). The effect of therapist experience on psychotherapy outcomes. *Clinical Psychology & Psychotherapy, 12,* 417–426.

Lilienfeld, S. O. (2007). Psychological treatments that cause harm. *Perspectives on Psychological Science, 2,* 53–70.

Luborsky, L. (1989). *Who will benefit from psychotherapy?* New York, NY: Basic Books.

Machado, P. P. P., Beutler, L. E., & Greenberg, L. S. (1999). Emotion recognition in psychotherapy: Impact of therapist level of experience and emotional awareness. *Journal of Clinical Psychology, 55,* 39–57.

Makover, R. B. (2004). *Treatment planning for psychotherapists* (2nd ed.). Washington DC: American Psychiatric Publishing.

van Manen, J. G., Kamphuis, J. H., Goossensen, A., Timman, R., Busschbach, J. J. V., et al. (2012). In search of patient characteristics that may guide empirically based treatment selection for personality disorders patients—A concept map approach. *Journal of Personality Disorders, 26,* 481–497.

Marmar, C., Gaston, L., Gallagher, D., & Thompson, L. W. (1989). Alliance and outcome in late-life depression. *Journal of Nervous and Mental Disease, 177,* 464–472.

Martin, D. J., Garske, J. P., & Davis, K. M. (2000). Relation of the therapeutic alliance with outcome and other variables: A meta-analytic review. *Journal of Consulting and Clinical Psychology, 68,* 438–450.

Marx, J. A., Gyorky, Z. K., Royalty, G. M., & Stern, T. E. (1992). Use of self-help books in psychotherapy. *Professional Psychology: Research and Practice, 23,* 300–305.

Meissner, W. W. (2006). The therapeutic alliance—A proteus in disguise. *Psychotherapy: Theory, Research, Practice, Training, 43,* 264–270.

Messer, S. (2006). Patient values and preferences. In J. C. Norcross, L. E. Beutler, & R. F. Levant (Eds.), *Evidence-based practices in mental health* (pp. 31–40). Washington, DC: American Psychological Association.

Messer, S. B., & Gurman, A. S. (Eds.). (2011). *Essential psychotherapies.* New York, NY: The Guilford Press.

Miller, A. (2013). Phone therapy works for mild to moderate disorders, study suggests. *Monitor on Psychology,* Jan 2013, p. 10.

Murdock, N. L. (2004). *Theories of counseling and psychotherapy.* Upper Saddle River, NJ: Pearson.

Nagy, T. F. (2010) *Essential ethics for psychologists: A primer for understanding and mastering core issues.* Washington, DC: American Psychological Association.

Nasar, J. L., & Devlin, A. S. (2011). Impressions of psychotherapists' offices. *Journal of Counseling Psychology, 58,* 310–320.

National Institute of Mental Health. (2006). The numbers count: Mental disorders in America (2006 rev.). Retrieved August 8, 2006, from http://www.nimh.nih.gov.publicat/numbers.cfm.

Norcross, J. C., & Lambert, M. J. (2011) Psychotherapy relationships that work II. *Psychotherapy, 48,* 4–8. doi: 10.1037/a0022180

Norcross, J. C. & Wampold, B. E. (2010). What works for whom: Tailoring psychotherapy to the person. *Journal of Clinical Psychology (Special Issue: Adatpting Psychotherapy to the Individual patient), 67,* 127–132.

Olfson, M., & Marcus, S. C. (2010). National trends in outpatient psychotherapy. *The American Journal of Psychiatry, 167,* 1456–1463.

Orchowski, L. M., Spickard, B. A., & McNamara, J. R. (2006). Cinema and the valuing of psychotherapy: Implications for clinical practice. *Professional Psychology: Research and Practice, 37,* 506–514.

Orlinsky, D. E., Grawe, K., & Parks, B. K. (1994). Process and outcome in psychotherapy—Noch Einmal. In A. E. Bergin & S. L. Garfield (Eds.), *Handbook of psychotherapy and behavior change* (4th ed., pp. 270–276). New York, NY: Wiley.

Orlinsky, D. E., & Howard, K. I. (1986). Process and outcome in psychotherapy. In S. L. Garfield & A. E. Bergin (Eds.), *Handbook of psychotherapy and behavior change* (3rd ed., pp. 311–381). New York, NY: Wiley.

Orlinsky, D. E., Schofield, M. J., Schroder, T., & Kazantzis, N. (2011). Utilization of personal therapy by psychotherapists: A practice-friendly review and a new study. *Journal of Clinical Psychology, 67,* 828–842.

Pingitore, D., & Scheffler, R. M. (2005). Practice patterns across the clinical life span: Results from the California Survey of Psychological Practice. *Professional Psychology: Research and Practice, 36,* 434–440.

Pope, K. S., Kieth-Spiegel, P., & Tabachnick, B. G. (2006). Sexual attraction to clients: The human therapist and the (sometimes) inhumane training system. *Training and Education in Professional Psychology, S,* 96–111.

Pope, K. S., & Tabachnick, B. G. (2005). The therapist as a person. *Professional Psychology: Research and Practice, 25,* Retrieved August 1, 2005, from http:// kspope.com/therapistas/research9.php.

Pope, K. S., & Vasquez, M. J. T. (2011). *Ethics in psychotherapy and counseling* (4th ed.). Hoboken, NJ: John Wiley & Sons.

Ramseyer, F., & Tschacher, W. (2011). Nonverbal synchrony in psychotherapy: Coordinated body movement reflects relationship quality and outcome. *Journal of Consulting and Clinical Psychology, 79,* 284–295.

Roe, D., Dekel, R., Harel, G., Fenning, S., & Fenning, S. (2006). Clients' feelings during termination of psychodynamically oriented psychotherapy. *Bulletin of the Menninger Clinic, 70,* 68–81.

Rogers, C. R. (1951). *Client-centered therapy.* Boston, MA: Houghton Mifflin.

Ronan, K. R., & Kazantzis, N. (2006). The use of between-session (homework) activities in psychotherapy: Conclusions from the Journal of Psychotherapy Integration Special Series. *Journal of Psychotherapy Integration, 16,* 254–259.

Rosen, D. C., Miller, A. B., Nakash, O., Halperin, L., & Alegría, M. (2012). Interpersonal complementarity in the mental health intake: A mixed-methods study. *Journal of Counseling Psychology, 59*, 185–196. doi: 10.1037/a0027045.

Ryan, R. M., Lynch, M. F., Vansteenkiste, M., & Deci, E. L. (2010). Motivation and autonomy in counseling, psychotherapy, and behavior change: A look at theory and practice. *The Counseling Psychologist, 39*, 193–260.

Saunders, S. M., Howard, K. I., & Orlinsky, D. E. (1989). The Therapeutic Bond Scales: Psychometric characteristics and relationship to treatment effectiveness. *Psychological Assessment, 1*, 323–330.

Scheel, M. J. (2011). Client common factors represented by client motivation and autonomy. *The Counseling Psychologist, 39*, 276–285.

Schröder, T. A., & Davis, J. D. (2004). Therapists' experience of difficulty in practice. *Psychotherapy Research, 14*, 328–245.

Shapiro, A. K. (1971). Placebo effects in medicine, psychotherapy, and psychoanalysis. In A. E. Bergin & S. L. Garfield (Eds.), *Handbook of psychotherapy and behavior change: An empirical analysis* (pp. 439–473). New York, NY: Wiley.

Silverman, W. H. (2013). The future of psychotherapy: One editor's perspective. *Psychotherapy*, Feb 11, 2013, doi:10.1037/a0030573

Smith, A. G. (2009). Personal characteristics of master couple therapists. *Dissertation Abstracts, 70* (2-B), 1357.

Sommers-Flanagan, J., & Sommers-Flanagan, R. (2012) *Counseling and psychotherapy theories* (2nd ed.). Hoboken, NJ: John Wiley & Sons.

Sperry, L. (2007). *The ethical and professional practice of counseling and psychotherapy.* Upper Saddle River, NJ: Pearson.

Stirman, S. W., & Crits-Christoph, P. (2011). Psychotherapy research: Implications for optimal therapist personality, training, and development. In R. H. Klein, H. S. Bernard, & V. L. Schermer (Eds), *On becoming a psychotherapist* (pp. 245–268). New York, NY: Oxford University Press.

Strupp, H. H. (1989). Psychotherapy: Can the practitioner learn from the researcher? *American Psychologist, 44*, 717–724.

Suh, C. S., Strupp, H. H., & O'Malley, S. S. (1986). The Vanderbilt process measures: The Psychotherapy Process Scale (VPPS) and the Negative Indicators Scale (VNIS). In L. Greenberg & W. Pinsof (Eds.), *The psychotherapeutic process: A research handbook* (pp. 285–323). New York, NY: Guilford.

Sullivan, M. F., Skovholt, T. M., & Jennings, L. (2005). Master therapists' construction of the therapeutic relationship. *Journal of Mental Health Counseling, 27*, 48–70.

Sweet, A. A. (1984). The therapeutic relationship in behavior therapy. *Clinical Psychology Review, 4*, 253–272.

Swift, J. K., & Callahan, J. L. (2009). The impact of client treatment preferences on outcome: A meta-analysis. *Journal of Clinical Psychology, 65*, 368–381.

Swift, J. K., & Greenberg, R. P. (2012). Premature discontinuation in adult psychotherapy: A meta-analysis. *Journal of Consulting and Clinical Psychology*, April 16, 2012, No Pagination Specified. Doi: 10.1037/a0028226.

Teasdale, A. C., & Hill, C. E. (2006). Preferences of therapists-in-training for client characteristics. *Psychotherapy: Theory, Research, Practice, Training, 43*, 111–118.

7 PSYCHODYNAMIC AND HUMANISTIC PSYCHOTHERAPIES

Chapter Preview

In this and the next two chapters, we focus on specific approaches to psychotherapy. In Chapter 10, we discuss research on the outcomes associated with these approaches, and with psychotherapy in general. Therapy approaches, and variations of them, can be thought of as families whose members are related by certain shared concepts and practices. This chapter describes the psychodynamic and humanistic families, beginning with Freud's traditional psychoanalysis, which stresses the need for clients to develop insight into their primitive drives, unconscious conflicts, and patterns of relating. Next we cover other psychodynamic approaches that share key ideas with traditional psychoanalysis. We then describe the humanistic approaches, including person-centered therapy, Gestalt therapy, and existential treatments. All of these emphasize each client's unique way of experiencing the world. Psychodynamic and humanistic treatments can be considered *relational approaches* because they place strong emphasis on the role of the therapeutic relationship in treatment.

PSYCHOANALYSIS

SECTION PREVIEW

Traditional psychoanalysis stresses the role of unconscious conflict stemming from early childhood relationships and of psychological defenses against anxiety. In therapy, it is assumed that clients will exhibit signs of these conflicts and defenses, such as by reacting to the therapist in ways that reflect relationships with parents and other significant figures from their pasts. By focusing on the transference of old relationship patterns onto the therapeutic relationship, the therapist can interpret the client's maladaptive behaviors and the unconscious causes that motivate them. These interpretations, in turn, help the client to develop insight into the historically grounded conflicts and patterns of behavior related to their symptoms.

Recall from Chapter 2, "Clinical Psychology's Past and Present," that a young Viennese neurologist, Sigmund Freud (1856–1939), often saw patients with neurological symptoms for which no organic cause could be found. Some, for example, complained of paralysis that affected their entire hand but not their arm. Others suffered paralysis of the legs during the day but walked in their sleep. These patients were called *neurotics*, and Freud dealt with the most common type: those displaying hysterical (i.e., nonorganic) paralyses, amnesia, anesthesia, blindness, and speech loss. In Freud's day, treatment for hysteria included wet packs and baths or electrically generated heat. Freud believed that whatever success these methods had were caused by suggestion, so he began experimenting with techniques that maximized the benefits of suggestion, foremost among which was *hypnosis*. Around 1890, Freud began to combine hypnosis with a new technique called the *cathartic method*, which he learned from neurologist Joseph Breuer, who had stumbled on this technique while attempting to relieve the hysterical symptoms of a patient known as Anna O.

Anna O's symptoms, which included headaches, a severe cough, neck and arm paralyses, and other problems, began during her father's illness and intensified following his death. She began to display extremes of mood that went from agitation and hallucinations during the day to calm, trancelike states in the evenings. Breuer was struck by the fact that these "trances" resembled hypnosis.

Breuer discovered that if Anna were permitted, while in the hypnotic state, to recite the contents of all her hallucinations from the day, then she invariably would leave the trance state and enjoy a period of almost normal tranquility and lucidity during the following late night hours. Anna came to refer to the exercise of reciting her hallucinations as the "talking cure" or "chimney sweeping" (Fancher, 1973, p. 48).

This talking cure did not eliminate Anna's daytime disorders, however, and new symptoms began to appear. In attempting to cure one of these, an inability to drink liquids, Breuer made the discovery that would later start Freud on the road to psychoanalysis. During one of Anna's hypnotic states, she began describing to Breuer an Englishwoman whom she knew but did not especially like. The woman had a dog that Anna particularly despised. Anna described how on one occasion she entered the woman's room and observed the dog drinking water from a glass. When the event occurred, Anna was filled with strong feelings of disgust and loathing, but out of politeness she was unable to express them. As she recited this account to Breuer, she for the first time permitted herself the luxury of expressing fully and animatedly her negative feelings about the dog's drinking. When she emerged from the trance, she immediately asked for a glass of water, which she drank without the slightest difficulty (Fancher, 1973, p. 49).

Removal of Anna's fear of drinking was apparently brought about by her vivid recollection of a forgotten event while in a trance. It occurred to Breuer that other hysterical symptoms might be caused by forgotten memories and that their recall might cure them. Breuer found that whenever he could induce Anna to recall those unpleasant scenes and, more importantly, to *express the emotions* they had caused her to feel, the symptoms would disappear (Fancher, 1973, pp. 49–50; italics added).

Freud also found the cathartic method successful, but not all his patients could be hypnotized. To facilitate *conscious* recognition of emotional memories, Freud began asking his patients to relax with their eyes closed and to report whatever thoughts, feelings, or memories came to mind. Recall was often helped by having the patient lie on a couch. This procedure later became known as *free association*, a mainstay among the psychoanalytic techniques to be described later.

Freud also began to pay attention to dreams (his patients' and his own) and concluded that they represented the fulfillment of fantasies and wishes, many of which are socially unacceptable and thus appear—often in disguised form—only when defenses are relaxed during sleep. He suggested that, like dreams, hysterical symptoms could be based on unconscious wishes and fantasies, not just on memories of real events. Thus, a patient's "memory" of childhood sexual abuse by a parent might actually be a *fantasy* or *wish* about sexual intimacy with the parent. Although history scholars have established that there were high rates of actual sexual abuse at that time (DeMause, 1987), the implications of this new theory altered Freud's approach to therapy as well. His *psychoanalytic* treatment of neurosis shifted from the recovery of memories to the broader illumination of the patient's unconscious.

In developing *psychoanalysis*, Freud became the founder of psychotherapy as we know it today, a one-on-one treatment involving frank discussion of a client's thoughts and feelings. Although many more modern treatment approaches are now available, almost all of them reflect one or more of Freud's ideas, including his emphasis on (a) searching for relationships between a person's developmental history and current problems, (b) blockages or dissociations in self-awareness as causes of psychological problems, (c) talking as an approach to treatment, and (d) the therapeutic relationship as a curative factor.

Theoretical Foundations

Freud described mental life as occurring partly at the level of conscious awareness; partly at a preconscious level, which we can become aware of by shifting our attention; and partly at an unconscious level, which we cannot experience without the use of special therapy techniques. This continuum from unconscious, to preconscious, to conscious is called the *topographical model* of the mind, and it is fundamental to understanding Freud's views of personality.

FREUD'S PERSONALITY THEORY AND VIEW OF PSYCHOPATHOLOGY As discussed in Chapter 2, psychodynamic approaches are based on the proposition that mental life is best understood as an interaction among powerful competing forces within the person, some of which are conscious but most of which are unconscious. Those forces are represented in Freud's system as the id, ego, and superego. The *id* is the primitive source of instinctual drives, especially sexual/sensual and aggressive drives. Counterbalancing the id is the *superego*, the mental agency that incorporates

Sigmund Freud (1856–1939).
*Source:*Courtesy of Historical
Pictures Service, Inc., Chicago,
Illinois. Museum/AP Images.
Reprinted by permission.

norms from one's parents, family, and culture. The superego also contains the ego ideal, or how one would like to be. The id and the superego are often in conflict—the id seeks to discharge tension by expressing sexual or aggressive impulses, while the superego seeks to inhibit them or to prescribe more socially appropriate behavior. The *ego* is the part of the personality that tries to mediate between the demands of the id and superego while simultaneously recognizing and responding to external realities. Together, these three agencies—id, ego, and superego—form a *structural model* of the mind; the *topographical model* refers to the level of consciousness associated with these structures (see Figure 7.1).

Freud proposed that dynamic, tension-filled conflict occurs continuously, as seen in many examples of conflicting urges. Imagine sitting through a boring class. One part of you wants to get up and leave, perhaps to do something more exciting. Another part of you urges you to stay and try to pay closer attention, reminding you that you need the class, need to be more mature, need to delay gratification, and the like. While you might be consciously aware of this particular conflict, Freud said that the most important and problematic psychic battles usually occur unconsciously, outside of awareness. To Freud, then, most of mental life is a balancing act involving competing parts of the personality and an ever-changing external reality.

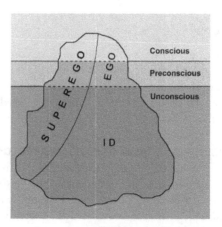

FIGURE 7.1 The Psychoanalytic Structural/Topographical Model of the Mind. Freud proposed that dynamic interaction among psychic structures occurred mostly subconsciously, outside one's awareness.

DEFENSE MECHANISMS Imagine a child who feels strong anger toward a parent but fears that expressing it would result in punishment (a realistic fear if the parent is sometimes verbally or physically abusive). This situation produces anxiety in the child because the child's angry id impulse continues to push for expression. According to psychoanalytic theory, a reasonable adaptation to this conflict would be for the child to adopt defense mechanisms that would help bind up the anxiety and keep it from repeatedly entering consciousness, where it might interfere with functioning. Defense mechanisms are essentially unconscious mental strategies or routines that the ego employs to ward off the anxiety produced by intrapsychic conflict (see Table 7.1).

While Sigmund Freud discussed defense mechanisms, it was his daughter, Anna, who most fully developed the idea. In her book, *Ego and the Mechanisms of Defense* (Freud, 1936/1966), she categorized and described defense mechanisms, stressing their role in everyday life and in psychoanalytic treatment. Anna Freud also applied psychoanalytic concepts to developmental psychology, advancing theories of how psychological problems develop during childhood (Fonagy & Target, 2003).

Defense mechanisms are not always successful or adaptive. People who use denial, repression, projection, or other defense mechanisms may temporarily reduce anxiety, but at the same time, they might distort reality and, over time, jeopardize interpersonal relationships. For instance, return to the child described earlier and imagine that person now grown up. It is not difficult to imagine this person as someone who has developed a habitual way of dealing with aggressive or hostile feelings. Instead of expressing anger when it occurs, he may mistakenly perceive signs of hostility in a relationship partner (an example of the defense mechanism called projection). He may become unable to remember important information (an example of dissociation). He may become extremely nice and solicitous (reaction formation). He might show any of a number of other behavior patterns, all of which are expressions of his attempts to deal with an anxiety-producing conflict. They are the surface disturbances that suggest some historically based emotional conflict lies beneath.

TRANSFERENCE AND COUNTERTRANSFERENCE The psychoanalyst's job is to understand the origins and meaning of clients' symptoms and help clients do the same. Therapists are aided in this work by clients' tendency to repeat patterns of behavior, especially unconsciously motivated behavior. So if a client has developed a maladaptive pattern of relating to other people, characterized by the use of certain defense mechanisms and patterns of relating, those patterns will eventually show up in the way the client relates to the therapist. The client unconsciously brings a maladaptive pattern of relating into the therapy, a phenomenon called *transference*.

Anna Freud was instrumental in developing the concept of defense mechanisms. *Source*: Bettmann/Corbis.

TABLE 7.1 Psychological Defense Mechanisms Ordered Roughly from Less to More Mature

Mechanism	Description	Example
Denial	Simply refusing to recognize or acknowledge threatening experiences	Despite drinking heavily every day for months and recently losing his job, Jim discounts the idea that he has a drinking problem.
Repression	Pushing anxiety-provoking thoughts and memories out of consciousness and into the unconscious; "motivated forgetting"	Pat does not remember anything about the incidents when he was 6 in which his father was physically abusive to his mother.
Regression	Retreating to coping strategies characteristic of earlier stages of development	Following his parents' divorce, 10-year-old Alex begins asking his mother to lay out his clothes in the morning, tuck him in and read to him "like you used to" before bed.
Projection	Attributing one's unacceptable motives and impulses to others	After her husband forgot her birthday (again), Alice perceives him as hurt and angry.
Reaction formation	Adopting thoughts and behaviors that are the opposite of those prompted by one's unacceptable, impulses	Ben has strong hostile feelings toward his boss, but he goes out of his way to defend him when other employees criticize the boss's management style.
Displacement	Directing pent-up impulses toward a safer substitute rather than the target that aroused the feelings	Tracy, reprimanded and embarrassed by her boss at work, comes home and severely punishes her son for a minor infraction.
Rationalization	Providing socially appropriate, but fundamentally untrue, explanations for one's unacceptable behavior	While trying to diet, Paul explains that the pint of ice cream he just ate is high in protein and besides, the calories won't matter because he will exercise tomorrow.
Intellectualization	Approaching upsetting experiences in an overly logical manner, without acceptance of the emotional components	In describing his life since his wife's death last month, Marcus methodically recounts his daily activities and details the contents of books about coping that he has read.
Compensation	Coping with feelings of inferiority in one area by working to become superior in another area	After a brain injury, Ronda has difficulty concentrating and cannot hold her job as an accountant, but she works hard to be an empathic listener and a trusted friend.
Sublimation	Channeling the expression of unacceptable impulses into more socially acceptable activities	Taylor's strong interest in sex is expressed in stylized sculptures of the human body; Tim's aggressive impulses are channeled into football.

In Freud's theory, transference reactions are distortions in the client's reactions to the therapist. These distortions come about because the client's past relationships—especially early, significant relationships such as those with one's parents—create a set of expectations and anticipatory reactions for future relationships. To put it another way, each new relationship is understood by reference to old relationships. For example, a client who is conflicted over aggressive impulses may begin to feel that the therapist is aggressive or punitive (i.e., inclined to punish any negative emotion expressed by the client). Assuming that the therapist is not truly being aggressive, the client's reactions are a demonstration of his or her habitual, internalized, and unconsciously motivated adaptations to relationship conflicts.

The more similar a new relationship is to an old one, the more likely it is that reactions based on the old relationship will occur. The psychotherapy relationship is one in which clients self-disclose intimate details of their mental life while therapists sit in a position of relative power. Emotionally, this situation is not unlike childhood. Therefore, clients are especially likely to replay their earlier emotional "scripts" in therapy. Psychoanalytic treatment is designed to reveal, analyze, and ultimately change those scripts.

Of course, clients are not the only ones whose current relationships are colored by those of the past. Therapists are affected by transference patterns, too. When therapists' reactions toward clients are based on the therapist's personal history and conflicts, those reactions are called *countertransference*. Countertransference can impair the progress of therapy if the therapist begins to distort the therapeutic interaction on the basis of his or her own conflicts and defenses. The inevitability of countertransference reactions is one reason psychoanalytically oriented clinicians believe that therapists themselves should undergo psychoanalysis as part of training. The more a therapist understands and has worked through his or her own conflicts, the less those conflicts will interfere with the treatment of clients.

PSYCHIC DETERMINISM   In psychoanalysis, slips of the tongue and other unexpected verbal associations are presumed to be psychologically meaningful, as are mental images, failures of memory, and a variety of other experiences. If a client suddenly remembers something that seems trivial or unrelated to the topic of discussion during a therapy session (e.g., a family vacation taken when he was 6 years old, or his mother's blue dress), the therapist assumes that there is a reason this material "popped into" the client's head. By asking the client to elaborate, rather than ignoring the material, the therapist looks for clues that might reveal the unconscious connection. The idea that memories, impressions, or experiences that occur together in a client's mind are necessarily related and not random is called *psychic determinism*.

RESISTANCE   As psychoanalytic therapy progresses, and the therapist and client get closer to a client's core unconscious conflicts, the client may begin to experience increasing anxiety. He or she may consequently begin to "forget" appointments, experience panic, become overly intellectual and emotionally detached in discussing topics, or engage in other activities that appear to take the focus away from his or her conflicts. Psychoanalysts expect these or a variety of other *resistance* reactions as treatment focuses more intently on the client's core conflicts. As with transference, the manner in which the client resists is likely to be a reenactment of earlier patterns and therefore may be subject to analysis and interpretation (Gabbard, 2010).

INTERPRETATION, WORKING THROUGH, AND INSIGHT   By offering both emotional support and judicious interpretations, the therapist helps the client understand and *work through* transference reactions and resistance. In so doing, the client develops a new understanding of his or her problems, psychological makeup, and ways of relating to others.

Interpretation involves the analyst suggesting connections between patients' current experiences and their historically based conflicts. In simpler terms, interpretation is a way of pointing out how the past intrudes on the present. Interpretations can be based on material or reactions a client reveals in therapy or on reports of the client's experiences outside the therapy situation. Those that are based on in-session material often involve transference—the client's reactions to the therapist. Optimal psychoanalytic interpretations are interpretations of transference reactions that can be related to the client's current difficulties outside of therapy (e.g., in a relationship) and also to historical forces in the client's past. Wolitzky (2003) describes it this way:

> The optimal interpretation, though not necessarily presented comprehensively at one time, would take the form of "what you are doing (feeling, thinking, fantasizing, etc.) with me now is what you also are doing with your current significant other (spouse, child, boss, etc.), and what you did with your father (and/or mother) for such and such reasons and motives and with such and such consequences." (p. 41)

If this explanation makes cognitive and emotional sense to the client (i.e., if it is accurate *and* the client is ready to process it), he or she may see a particular behavior pattern or problem in a new way. When this happens, it is called *insight*. In psychoanalysis, insight is the basic requirement for, and the beginning of, positive change.

Goals of Psychoanalysis

Freud originally proposed that the goal of psychoanalysis was to make the unconscious conscious, but he later added another goal, namely to replace unconscious id processes with conscious ego processes (Wolitzky, 2011). According to Freud, when patients understand the real, often unconscious, reasons they act in maladaptive ways and see that those reasons are no longer valid, they will not have to continue behaving in those ways.

The process of self-understanding includes *intellectual* recognition of one's innermost wishes and conflicts, *emotional* involvement in discoveries about oneself, and the *systematic tracing* of how unconscious factors have determined past and present behaviors and affected relations with other people.

Thus, the main goals of psychoanalytic treatment are (a) intellectual and emotional *insight* into the underlying causes of the client's problems, (b) *working through* or fully exploring the implications of those insights, and (c) strengthening the ego's control over the id and the superego. Freud saw working through as particularly important because clients need to understand how pervasive their unconscious conflicts and defenses are if they are to be prevented from returning. Thus, it would do little good for a patient to know that she has unconscious feelings of anger toward her mother if she did not also see that she deals with women in the present as if they were her mother and that her problems in relation to these women are based on unconscious hostility and/or attempts to defend against it. Insight provides the outline of a patient's story; working through fills in the details.

Reaching the ambitious goals set by classical psychoanalysis involves dissecting and gradually reconstructing the patient's personality. This process requires a lot of time. In classical Freudian psychoanalysis, three or four sessions each week are standard, and treatment can last for several years. Psychoanalytic psychotherapy, a modified form of psychoanalysis, is often shorter in duration (Wolitzky, 2011). With fees generally well in excess of $100 per hour, the process is expensive.

Case Example

Ellen, a 33-year-old female, sought psychotherapy after having a series of panic attacks over the last year and a half. She also stated that each day was a struggle and she felt little enjoyment of her life, so she had become concerned about depression. Finally, she said that she had questions about her marriage and herself.

At the time of referral, Ellen was employed as a sales representative for a large paper manufacturer, a position she had held for 4 years. She was married to Rick, a radiologist at the local hospital. They had no children but were contemplating them. This too was a source of discomfort, as she reported that she was more in favor of having children than Rick, who said that he was not ready.

Ellen reported having had one panic attack in college—at least she believes that is what it was—but no more until about a year and a half ago. At the time of that more recent incident, she had been attending an industry-related convention in a distant city. After mingling for a while at an evening social hour sponsored by her company, she returned to her room and lay on her hotel bed. While there she noticed her heart racing. It quickly escalated to a rapid, uncontrollable pounding. She had difficulty breathing and was sweating. At one point, she tried getting out of bed but had to lay back down for fear she would faint and fall, possibly injuring herself. By rolling sideways, she was able to reach the phone and call the front desk, and personnel there summoned an ambulance. By the time Ellen arrived at the hospital, her symptoms had subsided, but she still felt shaky and very anxious. After history taking and a number of tests at the hospital, she was given a provisional diagnosis of panic attack. Since that initial attack, she has had others: "some at home, two at work, one while shopping, and one while driving." She said, "They hit me out of the blue. They're terrible, terrifying . . . and embarrassing." She worried frequently about when the next attack might come.

Ellen's concerns about depression had arisen more gradually. During the last year or two, she reported, she had occasionally felt lost and unsure about what she was doing with her life. Despite the fact that she was apparently valued at work—she had been promoted and given a raise twice in the last 2 years—Ellen often felt that there was no point to her daily activities there. These episodes of feeling down and unfulfilled had increased prior to her seeking treatment.

She was also not sure if she loved her husband or if he loved her. She regarded him as a good man, committed to his work, and reasonably pleasant to be around. But she feared that his interest in her had waned because he spent more time in activities with his friends (racquetball, cycling, poker) than ever before. Her satisfaction with their sexual relationship had diminished too. She found herself more inclined to avoid situations that might lead to sex.

Clinical Applications

HISTORY AND CASE FORMULATION As with most treatment, Ellen's psychoanalytic treatment begins with an assessment and case formulation by the therapist. Traditional psychoanalysts do not stress the use of structured assessment instruments. They may use them, especially to make differential diagnostic classifications, but psychoanalysts are more likely to rely on interview data and sometimes on projective tests to develop an understanding of the client. Assessment in psychoanalysis is an ongoing process that occurs over multiple sessions.

In Chapter 3, "Basic Features of Clinical Assessment," we presented a psychoanalytically oriented case study outline. The following would be especially important for psychoanalytic treatment of clients such as Ellen: (a) historical data such as family and developmental history (to identify information related to early conflicts or trauma); (b) mental status, level of distress, ego strengths and deficits, and "psychological mindedness" (to assess the client's intellectual and emotional ability to engage in psychoanalytic treatment); and (c) defense mechanisms, themes, or patterns of attachment difficulties in interpersonal relationships (to identify transference patterns).

Ellen is the older of two children. When she was 12 years old, her father, a physician in a small town, divorced her mother and essentially abandoned the family. This was partly a relief, as there had been numerous fights in which Ellen's mother accused her husband of having affairs. But it also brought difficulties. Ellen's mother maintained a series of service-industry jobs and was barely able to keep the family out of poverty. The mother did not remarry but had a series of boyfriends, none of whom left any lasting impression on Ellen (or, apparently, her mother).

Ellen's father was a particularly important figure in her childhood. A man she described as "dashing," he was outgoing and free-spirited at home. Particularly significant were Ellen's memories of him walking around the house in his underwear, pinching her, and teasing her about being ugly. This behavior continued as Ellen approached early adolescence. His pinching her on the buttocks or on her developing breasts brought her great embarrassment. She denied other forms of sexual abuse but reported strong anger about how his callous behaviors had hurt her self-esteem.

In high school and college, Ellen had a few boyfriends. She said that she was attracted to the rebellious type, but these were often young men she felt to be her intellectual inferiors and the relationships typically did not last more than a few months. She met Rick when she was 27 (he was the same age) and felt that he was an interesting person and a more stable partner. His clear interest in her impressed her, and she agreed to marry him the following year.

FREE ASSOCIATION After formalities of meeting times, payments, assessment procedures, and the like, are completed (important frame-setting procedures), psychoanalysis proper begins with the analyst explaining to the client that therapy requires following a single fundamental rule: The client should say everything that comes to mind without editing or censorship. This is *free association*. As noted earlier, free association evolved from Freud's search for a nonhypnotic way to help his patients recover memories and reveal intrapsychic associations. It is assumed that when the constraints of logic, social amenities, and other rules are removed, unconscious material will surface more easily.

Sometimes, the origins of unconscious conflict are clearly revealed, as when both client and therapist recognize a pattern that is both historical and current. Because of the operation of defense mechanisms, though, it is more common that the unconscious bases for clients' current problems are revealed only gradually and indirectly in the form of memories, feelings, wishes, and impressions arising through free association. It is the therapist's task to try to make sense of these emerging bits and pieces, some of which seem unrelated and even irrelevant.

For example, during one session, Ellen related her reaction to a man she met at a company convention. "He was a jerk. I guess he thought he was hot stuff. I wondered if he was coming on to me, but I think he was like that with several women. Shameless. Greasy. I don't know why he bothered me so, I didn't even really get to know him." After a few moments of silence, Ellen reported, "I don't know why I just thought of this, but I remembered standing in our bathroom when I was growing up, holding my father's comb."

The fact that thoughts about meeting a man at a convention led to memories about holding her father's comb could have significance. In fact, psychoanalysts assume that it does. In Ellen's case, it could mean that characteristics of the man she met reminded her of her father (e.g., greasy black hair, inappropriately flirtatious with women). In therapy, the analyst may engage Ellen in a discussion of the possible connections. One way of doing so would be to encourage more free association around the man, the comb, and her father.

Ellen's psychoanalyst formulated a tentative hypothesis about her problems. He assessed her depression as a secondary symptom arising gradually as she attempted, unsuccessfully, to cope with conflicts that affected her relationships. The analyst believed that her panic attacks were also related to concerns about intimacy, sexuality, and abandonment. Although secondary, the depression was the therapist's initial focus because he needed to determine its severity. After determining that Ellen was not suicidal, that she was motivated for treatment, and that she had sound intellect and adequate ego strength, the analyst and Ellen began a course of psychoanalysis.

THE ROLE OF THE THERAPIST During therapy sessions, traditional psychoanalysts maintain an "analytic incognito," revealing little about themselves during the course of psychotherapy. This orientation is aided by the office arrangements—the client lies on a couch and the therapist sits at its head, largely out of sight. This arrangement makes it easier for clients to focus their attention inward rather than on facial expressions or other visual cues from the therapist (Wolitzky, 2011). In more recent variations of psychoanalytic approaches, chairs are substituted, but the therapist still maintains a relatively neutral attitude. The therapist's likes and dislikes, problems, hopes, and so on, remain unknown to the client. If clients ask personal questions, the therapist usually reminds them that the session is for their benefit and that while the exchange of personal information is appropriate in other circumstances, it does not benefit psychoanalysis. In other words, the therapist remains purposely opaque, much like a blank movie screen, so that clients can be free to *project* onto the therapist the attributes and motives that are unconsciously associated with parents and other important people in their lives. So at various times, the client may see the therapist as a loving caregiver, a vengeful father, a seductive mother, a jealous lover, or others. The therapist may also explore with the client, and perhaps interpret, the motives behind the client's desire to know more about the therapist. Doing so often reveals the client's own concerns, including transference-related concerns.

Of course, the ideal psychoanalyst is not coldly analytical and unresponsive. Psychoanalysts understand the importance of creating emotional safety in the therapeutic relationship, and so they are frequently empathic, supportive, and reflective in their comments (Borden, 2009; Gabbard, 2010; Gastelum, Douglas, & Cabaniss, 2013). They may use direct questions or encouraging phrases to help the client more deeply explore perceptions, emotions, motivations, and the like. The therapist's use of interpretation, when it occurs, can range from the suggestive (e.g., "I wonder if that seems familiar to you?") to the more direct statements that summarize patterns in current and historical conflicts.

ANALYSIS OF EVERYDAY BEHAVIOR Psychoanalysts are as attentive to clients' reports of activities outside of treatment as they are to what happens during treatment sessions. The analyst tries to maintain an "evenly divided" or "free-floating" attention to trivial as well as momentous events, to purposeful acts and accidental happenings, to body language as well as spoken language. Mistakes in speaking or writing (so-called "Freudian slips"), accidents, memory losses, and humor are seen as especially important sources of unconscious material.

ANALYSIS OF DREAMS Because unconscious material is believed to be closer to the surface in dreams than during waking consciousness, great importance is attached to them in psychoanalysis. The client's description of a dream—in which, say, she is running through the woods and suddenly falls into a lake—reveals its *manifest content* or obvious features. Manifest content often contains features associated with the dreamer's recent activities (called "day residue").

For psychoanalytic purposes, though, the most interesting aspect of dreams is their *latent content:* the unconscious ideas and impulses that appear in disguised form. The process of transforming unacceptable material into acceptable manifest content is called *dream work* (Freud, 1900), so most manifest dream content is viewed as being symbolic of something else—the specifics of which differ among people and among dreams. In spite of the popular belief that certain dream symbols (e.g., a snake) always mean the same thing (e.g., a penis), Freud believed dreams must be interpreted more flexibly because each client's unconscious is different.

A common analytic procedure is to ask the client to free associate to a dream's manifest content. In the process, unconscious material may be revealed. Frequently, a series of dreams is explored in analysis as a way of finding patterns of latent content and of not overemphasizing the importance of a single dream. In other words, dreams provide ideas for further probing more often than they provide final answers.

ANALYSIS OF TRANSFERENCE When the patient–therapist relationship creates a miniature version of the causes of the client's problems, it is called the *transference neurosis* and becomes the central focus of analytic work. This reproduction of early unconscious conflicts allows the analyst to deal with important problems from the past as they occur in the present. Transference and transference neuroses must be handled with care as analysts try to decode the meaning of their clients' feelings toward them. If an analyst responded "normally" to a client's loving or hostile comments, the client would not learn much about what those comments reflect. Instead, the goal is to understand the meaning of the client's feelings for the therapist. If this can be done, the transference neurosis will be resolved and, with it, the client's main unconscious conflicts.

Because sensitive handling of the transference is thought so crucial to psychoanalysis, analysts are trained to be keenly alert to their own unconscious feelings, their *countertransference*, so that these feelings do not distort the analytic process. Training, supervision, and peer consultation are also used, as they are in other forms of therapy, to ensure that the therapist consistently responds to the client in helpful ways.

ANALYSIS OF RESISTANCE Client behaviors that interfere with the analytic process are considered signs of resistance against achieving insight. Psychoanalysts try to help clients overcome resistance by pointing out its presence in obstructed free associations, avoidance or sudden changes of topics, feelings of distress upon approaching certain topics, distorted dream reports, missed appointments, lateness for treatment sessions, failure to pay the therapist's bill, or a variety of other behaviors (Fine, 1971; Portuges & Hollander, 2011). Even clients' desire to address troubling symptoms rather than intrapsychic conflicts, or their request for evidence of the value of treatment, might be identified by psychoanalysts as an effort to divert attention from the unconscious causes of their problems.

As Ellen's analysis progressed, she explored her feelings about her childhood, especially her ambivalent feelings about her father and mother. On the one hand, she admired her father and longed to win his affection, but he seemed interested only in himself. On the other hand, Ellen felt rage at her father's selfishness and cruelty.

Being a "psychologically minded" person, Ellen was aware that her father's behavior toward her during her childhood had affected her self-concept and self-esteem. In adulthood, she therefore worked to convince herself that she was attractive and special. She reported that she did this partly by going through some "wild years" during and just after college. During this time, she exerted considerable effort to attract men, and she was typically successful, though with men that she was not that interested in or who were not that interested in her as a person.

Ellen and her therapist considered the possibility that her relationship patterns with men may have multiple causes and meanings (Freud called such situations "overdetermined"). Those patterns were a way to prove her father wrong (she was not ugly), but also they were a symbolic attempt to regain the affection that her father had never given (i.e., if she had been more attractive, more appealing, perhaps he would not have abandoned the family). A fear of abandonment pervaded her relationships.

In one particularly significant session, Ellen was exploring her feelings about her marriage. She discussed imagining herself leaving the relationship or having an affair. She recalled being at a convention and considering having a brief affair with a man who approached her there. Feeling tempted but overwhelmed by the impulse, she went to her hotel room to lie down briefly and consider the matter further. Moments later, a panic attack ensued. Several things seemed to connect in this session—sexual impulses, fears of loss, strivings for autonomy and self-esteem, and the feeling of panic.

MAKING ANALYTIC INTERPRETATIONS   Analysts want clients to gain insight into unconscious conflicts, but they don't want to overwhelm them with potentially frightening material before they are ready to handle it. This is where analytic interpretation comes in. Through questions and comments about the client's behavior, free associations, dreams, and the like, the analyst guides the process of self-exploration. Thus, if the client shows resistance to seeing the potential meaning of some event, the therapist not only points out the resistance but also offers an interpretation of what is going on.

The interpretive process is tentative and continuous, a constant encouragement of clients to consider alternative views, to reject obvious explanations, to search for deeper meanings. As interpretations help clients understand and work through the transference, the therapeutic relationship changes. Clients not only see how defenses and unconscious conflicts caused problems, they learn to deal differently with the world, beginning with the therapist. They also learn that forces from their past no longer need to dictate their behavior in the present. Ideally, this emotional understanding will liberate the client to deal with life in a more realistic and satisfying manner than before.

As Ellen continued in psychoanalysis, she and the therapist began to feel that they better understood many of the complex emotional currents that defined Ellen's relationships. Ellen developed insight into her unconscious concern that her husband's activities "with the guys" foreshadowed his abandonment of the marriage, and she became less worried about his leaving. She recognized that her husband was fundamentally different from her "dashing" but uncommitted father.

Her panic attacks were less frequent but not entirely absent. Her relationship with her mother improved after they were able to have some candid conversations about her father (who had since died). Gradually, however, Ellen began to feel that her therapist was becoming less interested in working with her, though she did not verbalize these feelings.

After Ellen missed an appointment—she said that work required her attention—the therapist explored with Ellen whether her feelings about therapy had changed. She admitted that she had been thinking that maybe she had gone as far as she could go in therapy. Together, she and her analyst explored the possibility of termination. The analyst did not advise it, as he felt that they were working through some important material and talk of termination might be a form of resistance. However, he said that he would support her decision if she chose to terminate.

Ellen missed the next session—again, claiming work commitments. Days later, at the next session, she was cheerful and provocatively dressed but also reported that she had experienced another panic attack. When the therapist commented on her cheerful demeanor and manner of dress, Ellen became angry with him. She felt he did not appreciate her attempts to cheer herself up or to make their interaction more pleasant. She accused him of secretly wanting to terminate the relationship, of probably being bored and uninterested in her "case" any more.

This and the sessions that followed were especially productive because they represented opportunities to analyze Ellen's resistance (suggesting termination, missing appointments) as well as the transference. The therapist suggested that Ellen's feeling that she was about to be abandoned, that the therapist really did not care about her, were a reflection of how she had felt about her husband and about her father. Her attempts to prevent this abandonment by being more attractive, perhaps even seductive (but emotionally inauthentic), and then feeling angry, were also reflections of a historical pattern for her.

Over time, Ellen came to appreciate the repetitive unconscious conflicts that affected her most intimate relationships. In the ensuing sessions, she was able to more clearly differentiate the therapist from her father, as she had begun to do with her husband. Her marriage improved, as did her self-esteem and her relationship with her mother. Symptoms of depression diminished. Although the panic attacks did not disappear entirely, they became much less frequent. Ellen felt that she could now recognize the feelings and behavior patterns that went with her old scripts. This insight allowed her to try out other behaviors in her relationships. In short, by making unconscious conflicts conscious and then working through them in psychoanalysis, she was no longer compelled to repeat them. With insight, she developed greater ego control over her impulses and fears.

Our brief account of classic psychoanalysis techniques has left out many details and simplified others. More complete coverage of the approach is contained in numerous references (e.g., Borden, 2009; Diamond & Christian, 2011; Eagle, 2011; Freud, 1949; Elzer & Gerlach, 2013; Freud, 1949; Gabbard, 2010; Norcross, Vandenbos, & Freedheim, 2011; McWilliams, 2004; Summers & Barber, 2009; Willock, 2007; Wolitzky, 2011).

SECTION SUMMARY

Psychoanalysis, as developed by Freud, rests on a description of personality that involves internal conflict among parts of the personality labeled as id, ego, and superego. When certain of these conflicts develop from early experiences, they are likely to become both habitual (they are repeated in later relationships) and unconscious (they are repeated automatically, without awareness of their origins or effects). Psychoanalysts use free association, dream analysis, and other techniques to understand how the client's past intrudes on the present. They attempt to interpret and lead the client to see similarities in past relationships, current external relationships (e.g., with spouse or children), and especially in the therapy relationship itself (i.e., transference). As clients come to recognize and repeatedly work through these connections, they gain insight and become less impelled to repeat those patterns.

PSYCHODYNAMIC PSYCHOTHERAPY

SECTION PREVIEW

Many theorists have advocated changes in Freudian psychoanalysis, ranging from minor alterations to wholesale rejection of certain fundamental principles. Most of today's psychodynamically oriented clinicians employ treatments that, although based on psychoanalysis, differ from it in that they involve (a) less emphasis on sexual and aggressive id impulses, (b) greater attention to adaptive functioning of the ego, (c) greater attention to the role of close relationships and especially the therapeutic relationship, and (d) flexibility in the degree to which therapists analyze and interpret versus offer empathy and emotional support.

Freud's theories attracted a broad following, but some theorists sought to change certain aspects of psychoanalytic theory while preserving others. Collectively, the therapies that share certain basic assumptions with psychoanalysis but significantly change others are called *psychodynamic psychotherapies*.

These variations were developed by like-minded theorists and practitioners who formed various schools or approaches (Pine, 1990; see Table 7.2). Space limitations prevent us from covering them all, but let's consider some of the most prominent versions of psychodynamic treatment.

Psychoanalytically Oriented Psychotherapy

Therapists whose psychoanalytic procedures depart only slightly from the guidelines set down by Freud are said to employ *psychoanalytically oriented psychotherapy*. For example, during the 1930s and 1940s, Franz Alexander and his colleagues at the Chicago Psychoanalytic Institute questioned the belief that treatment must be intense, extended, and fundamentally similar in all cases (Alexander & French, 1946). They also sought to apply psychoanalysis to "nontraditional" clients such as the young and the severely disturbed.

In psychoanalytically oriented psychotherapy, not every patient is seen for several sessions per week because daily sessions may foster too much dependence on the analyst or may become so routine that the patient pays too little attention to them. The frequency of sessions varies as

TABLE 7.2 Variations on Psychoanalytic Theory and Practice

Approach	Theorists	Emphasis
Early Alternatives to Freudian Psychoanalysis		
Individual psychology	Alfred Adler	Striving to overcome feelings of inferiority; importance of social motives and social behavior
Analytical psychology	Carl Jung	Reconciliation of opposites (e.g., anima, animus) in personality, personality orientations of introversion and extroversion, personal and collective unconscious
Will therapy	Otto Rank	Client choice; therapist humanity rather than technical skill
More Recent Psychodynamic Alternatives		
Ego psychology	Anna Freud, Heinz Hartman, David Rapaport	Focus on adaptive ego functioning and establishment of firm identity and intimacy
Object relations theory	Melanie Klein, Otto Kernberg, David Winnicott, W. R. D. Fairbairn	Modifying mental representations of interpersonal relationships that come from early attachments
Self-psychology	Heinz Kohut	Closely related to object relations theory but stresses development of autonomous self
Interpersonal relations school	Harry Stack Sullivan, Clara Thompson	Interpersonal contexts of disorders and treatment
Relational and postmodern approaches	Steven Mitchell, Robert Stolorow, George Atwood	Strong emphasis on relationships with caretakers and exploration of the "intersubjective space" created jointly by client and therapist
Short-term psychodynamic approaches	Wilhelm Stekel, Hans Strupp	Coping strategies stressed over historical interpretation

Sources: Adapted from Curtis, R. C., & Hirsch, I. (2003). Relational approaches to psychoanalytic psychotherapy. In A. S. Gurman & S. B. Messer (Eds.), *Essential psychotherapies* (2nd ed., pp. 69–106). New York, NY: Guilford; Gabbard, G. O. (2005). *Psychodynamic psychiatry in clinical practice* (4th ed.). Washington, DC: American Psychiatric Publishing; Hergenhahn, B. R. (1994). *An introduction to theories of personality.* Englewood Cliffs, NJ: Prentice Hall; Kutash, I. L. (1976). Psychoanalysis in groups: The primacy of the individual. *Current Issues in Psychoanalytic Practice, 1,* 29–42; Prochaska J. O., & Norcross, J. C. (2002). *Systems of psychotherapy: A trans-theoretical analysis* (5th ed.). Pacific Grove, CA: Brooks Cole; Wolitzky, D. L. (2003). The theory and practice of traditional psychoanalytic treatment. In A. S. Gurman & S. B. Messer (Eds.), *Essential psychotherapies* (2nd ed., pp. 244–68). New York, NY: Guilford Press.

circumstances dictate, but once per week is most common (Alfonso & Olarte, 2011). Early in treatment, the patient may be seen every day; later, sessions may take place less often. Alexander and French (1946) noted as well that while some clients need lengthy psychoanalysis in order to fully explore and work through resistance, insights, and transference, others—especially those whose problems are either relatively mild or especially severe—are candidates for less extensive treatment aimed at support rather than at the uncovering and reconstructing associated with classical analysis (for an example of this approach, see Davanloo, 1994).

Early Alternatives to Classical Psychoanalysis

Alfred Adler was an early follower of Freud who was the first to defect from the ranks of orthodox psychoanalysis. He deemphasized Freud's theory of instincts, infantile sexuality, and the role of the unconscious in determining behavior. His treatment methods focused on exploring and altering misconceptions (or maladaptive lifestyles, as he called them). So where a strict Freudian might see a teenage boy's vomiting before school each morning as a defense of some kind, the Adlerian analyst would view the problem as reflecting tension brought about by a misconception such as "I must do better than everyone else." And where Freudians offer interpretations designed to promote insight into past causes of current problems, Adlerians interpret in order to promote insight into the patient's current lifestyle. Adlerian therapists use modeling, homework assignments, and other techniques to help patients become aware of their lifestyle and to prompt them to change. Another key divergence from Freud is that Adlerians focus more on the social and relational aspects of psychopathology and less on its intrapsychic aspects. Adler's flexibility in treatment methods and his emphasis on relational contexts anticipated important changes in psychoanalytic theory, and in the humanistic therapies described later (Borden, 2009).

Carl Jung, a contemporary of Freud, developed a variation on psychoanalysis called *analytical psychology* that differed from Freud's in a few key ways. Jung stressed the importance of the ego, anticipating the psychodynamic approaches discussed below. He viewed the unconscious not so much as a cauldron of conflicts threatening to boil over with anxiety, but also as a source of creativity and growth. In contrast to classical analysts, Jungian therapists focus more on how clients *create* meaning and construct a life story than on discovering the unconscious meaning of symptoms (Stekel, 2013). This *phenomenological approach* to the self would become central to later psychodynamic approaches and especially to humanistic approaches (Sedgwick, 2013).

Otto Rank and Sándor Ferenczi were among the others who developed variations on Freudian psychoanalysis. As we describe later, Rank's emphasis on will, creativity, and relationship—especially the curative conditions created by the therapeutic relationships—strongly influenced those who later developed humanistic approaches to treatment. Similarly, Ferenczi stressed the importance of the therapeutic relationship and the curative power of empathy. He later collaborated with Rank (see Fogel, 1993) in describing how analysis could help clients by focusing on interactions in the therapy relationship without having to uncover childhood traumas (Borden, 2009).

Ego Psychology

While psychoanalytically oriented psychotherapists mainly revised Freud's procedures, another group of therapists known as *ego analysts* challenged some of his basic principles. They argued, for example, that Freud's preoccupation with sexual and aggressive instincts (the id) as the basis for behavior and behavior disorder is too narrow. Behavior, they said, is determined to a large extent by the ego, which can function not just to combat id impulses or to referee conflicts but also to promote learning and creativity. These ideas led analysts such as Heinz Hartmann (1958), David Rapaport (1951), Erik Erikson (1946), and Freud's daughter, Anna (1936), to use psychoanalytic techniques to explore patients' adaptive ego functions.

Ego-analytic techniques differ from classical analytic techniques in that therapists focus less on working through early childhood experiences and more on working through current problems. Therapists assess and attempt to bolster the client's *ego strengths*, which include reality testing, impulse control, judgment, and the use of more "mature" defense mechanisms such as sublimation. In ego psychology, the therapeutic relationship remains important, but less so for its distorting transferences than for its supportive and trusting functions.

Object Relations and Self-Psychology

Another prominent variation of psychoanalysis has emerged from object relations theory, a movement associated with a group of British analysts including W. R. D. Fairbairn (1952), Donald Winnicott (1965), Melanie Klein (1975), and Margaret Mahler (Mahler, Pine, & Bergman, 1975), as well as Otto Kernberg (1976) and Heinz Kohut (1977, 1983). While ego psychology expanded the role of the ego, object relations theory expanded the role of relationships, especially early relationships, in psychodynamic thought.

Object relations theories, and the therapies based on them, focus on the nature of interpersonal relationships that are built from very early infant–caregiver interactions (Blatt & Lerner, 1983; Eagle, 1984). Because these early relationships act as prototypes for later relationships, disruptions in them can have profound consequences later in life. Therapists working with psychotic or personality-disordered clients, for instance, might find that their client idealizes them at one point and demonizes them at another. With such clients, working through relationship concerns is expected to be especially difficult and time consuming.

Thus, in contrast to classical psychoanalysts, object relations theorists view the therapeutic relationship not as transference to be analyzed but as a "second chance" for the client to obtain in a close relationship the gratification that was absent during infancy. This emphasis on ego support, acceptance, and psychological "holding" of damaged selves has made object relations therapies among the most popular versions of psychoanalysis, largely because they allow a friendly, naturally human stance toward the therapeutic relationship, which many therapists prefer to traditional Freudian neutrality.

Kohut's *self-psychology* focuses more on the self or self-concept but, like object relations approaches, views the analyst's task as providing the type of empathic responding and nurturing that the client is assumed to have missed as an infant. The therapist's role in these approaches is similar to that taken in the humanistic/phenomenological therapies that we discuss later (Kahn, 1985).

Relational Psychodynamic Psychotherapy

The relational psychodynamic approaches blend several theories (Curtis & Hirsch, 2011; DeYoung, 2003), including elements from traditional psychoanalysis, ego psychology, object relations theory, self-psychology, Sullivan's interpersonal therapy, and humanistic, person-centered, and phenomenological approaches (described in the next section). As its name implies, relational psychodynamic theory stresses relationships with caretakers. Like object relations theorists, relational theorists stress the importance of early relationships as templates for later ones. They point out that relationships have an objective dimension (the events that actually happen) and a subjective dimension (the way the relationship is mentally represented, or perceived, by the persons involved). The latter plays an especially important role in relational psychodynamic theory and practice.

In contrast to Freud's intrapsychic approach, relational theorists adopt a strongly interpersonal approach. Harry Stack Sullivan, the father of the interpersonal perspective, played an important role in developing the relational approaches. Sullivan believed that therapists should use their observations of the client's current and past interpersonal relationships to clarify for them how their typical cognitions and behaviors interfere with successful living. However, Sullivan and later relational therapists cautioned against assuming that the therapist's view of the therapeutic relationship was objectively correct. Because the client and the therapist both work from their own subjective viewpoints, relational psychodynamic theorists believe that neither perception can be objectively validated.

The relational psychodynamic approach has achieved considerable popularity in the United States (DeYoung, 2003; Wolitzky, 2011). Part of its popularity comes from its compatibility with the broader intellectual trend variously called *intersubjectivism*, *constructivism*, or *postmodernism* (Neimeyer & Bridges, 2003). Central to this trend is the idea that no objective authority can judge whether one view of reality is "correct," but jointly constructed views are nevertheless highly meaningful. Accordingly, relational psychodynamic therapists view the shared conceptual and interpersonal understanding that develops between client and therapist as a psychological system in its own right, one worthy of analysis (Stolorow, 1993). For this reason, relational psychodynamic therapies are sometimes called "two-person theories" (Gabbard, 2010).

As did the early dissenters of classical psychoanalysis, relational theorists focus on how clients and therapists co-create meaning in therapy. This differs significantly from classical psychoanalysis's emphasis on the client's resistance to gaining full consciousness of the historical roots of unconscious conflicts. The following vignette from Porteuges and Hollander (2011) illustrates the kind of exchange in which therapist and client attempt to understand each other. (Consistent with psychoanalytic practice, the excerpt uses the term "patient," rather than "client.")

The patient is a 39-year-old African American working class woman who came to psychoanalysis as a control case suffering from a depressed mood about not being able to conceive. She has been in psychoanalysis for three years and is now in the second trimester of her first pregnancy, just having learned of the positive results of her amniocentesis. The analyst is a 44-year-old Caucasian woman who is having difficulty getting pregnant. She has just experienced her second failed in vitro fertilization procedure.

PATIENT:	The baby is fine! I am so relieved and happy about the test, I could hardly wait to tell my boss when I got off the phone with the doctor.
ANALYST:	[Audible sigh]
PATIENT:	Um... [pause] I don't know, she didn't seem all that excited. I sure wish she had been a little more enthusiastic... I started to feel irritated and thought "She has three kids and a live-in housekeeper." [pause]. I don't know. She works so hard. She must have been exhausted.
ANALYST:	You paused after sounding so excited about the good news and began speaking critically about your boss's lack of enthusiasm. Then there was a change in your voice and you spoke positively about her. Did you notice something that seemed risky or unsafe about what you were telling me?
PATIENT:	Yes. I was thinking about how I must have seemed to you when I made that crack about her three kids and the support she has that I don't. I sounded too pissed-off and I tried to cover it up and... there is something else. When I said how excited I was to find out about the baby, I heard you sigh and I thought I had upset you.
ANALYST:	I didn't realize that I had sighed. [pause] So you were angry about your boss's reaction to your good news and then you felt distressed about the intensity of your criticism of her. Now you are concerned that I was disturbed by your good news.

As this vignette illustrates, in relational approaches, the principle of analyst neutrality has largely been abandoned. Gabbard (2010) points out that absolute neutrality is probably an unrealistic ideal anyway, because therapists cannot help but self-disclose in a variety of ways all the time through tone of voice, silences, body posture, and the like. Contemporary psychodynamic therapists are therefore more likely to advocate *relative* neutrality. An attitude of restraint, rather than strict anonymity and opacity, governs if or when therapists disclose personal information to clients.

Short-Term Psychodynamic Psychotherapy

Until recently, few people associated short-term treatments with the psychodynamic approach, even though several of Freud's early treatments were brief (Levison & Strupp, 1999). *Short-term dynamic psychotherapy* approaches emphasize pragmatic goals that can be obtained in relatively few sessions, typically 20 or less. Therapists using this approach focus on helping clients cope with a current crisis or problem rather than on helping them work through early relationships or to reconstruct the personality.

Short-term dynamic therapists stress forming a working therapeutic alliance as quickly as possible and then helping clients adopt coping strategies within specific domains. They might focus on anxiety management or coping with a problem relationship at work. Because the pace of therapy is accelerated, therapists are more active than in other forms of psychodynamic therapy. They may use traditional techniques of psychoanalysis, but they also might assign homework, refer clients to self-help groups, or adopt other techniques not typically associated with psychodynamic treatment. There are several models for short-term dynamic therapy, some of which include manuals for treating specific disorders (Binder & Betan, 2013; Levison & Strupp, 1999). Interpersonal psychotherapy (IPT), a treatment typically developed for people with depressive disorders, is an example of a dynamic treatment that can be adapted to short-term therapy (Frank & Levenson, 2011).

Common Features and Key Variations in Psychodynamic Therapies

Although classical psychoanalysis and its variants seem different, and in some ways they are, remember that all of them share core beliefs about the psychological importance of (a) intrapsychic conflict, (b) unconscious processes, (c) early relationships, (d) ego functioning, and (e) the client–therapist relationship. Yet, the approaches differ in important ways.

A useful way of thinking about all the psychodynamic variations we have discussed is to categorize them along a continuum according to their similarity to psychoanalysis. At one end is psychoanalysis itself, and close to it is psychoanalytically oriented psychotherapy. At the other end are the relational and postmodern versions of psychodynamic psychotherapy. In between are treatments based on ego psychology, self-psychology, and interpersonal psychology.

Classical psychoanalysis and its variants also differ on the length of treatment, with the former being longer. Traditional analysis involves sessions lasting 45 to 50 minutes once or twice per week and continuing for several months or years. Psychodynamic psychotherapies vary in length, depending on the client's needs. They can involve weekly individual or group meetings lasting over several weeks or months, or they can be as short as one 25-minute session (Gabbard, 2005).

THE SUPPORTIVE-EXPRESSIVE DIMENSION Another dimension that differentiates the psychodynamic therapies is the degree of emotional support offered by the therapist. Psychoanalysts offer support, but focus more on exploration of emotionally difficult material, hoping that their clients will develop insight. Psychodynamic psychotherapists practice interventions that range from these analytical and interpretive ones to the more supportive and educational interventions stressed by interpersonal and relational approaches. Gabbard (2010) refers to these variations in technique as the *supportive–expressive continuum*.

Therapists offering more supportive interventions typically seek to help clients with coping, stress reduction, and day-to-day functioning; they seek to create an empathic and supportive atmosphere in which clients feel cared for and understood. Many believe that this atmosphere creates a *corrective emotional experience* for the client and is a healing factor independent of insight (Strupp, 1989; Strupp & Blinder, 1984).

How does a clinician decide whether to offer more supportive or more expressive interventions? Several factors influence such a decision, among them the client's level of distress, impulse control, tolerance for frustration, reality testing, motivation, and psychological mindedness. Clients low on these factors will be less able to engage their ego in insight-oriented therapeutic work than will clients who are higher on these factors (Gabbard, 2005).

The Current Status of Psychodynamic Psychotherapy

In comparison to classical psychoanalysis, which is now practiced by only a small minority of clinicians, psychodynamically oriented variations are far more popular. Indeed, the psychodynamic approach is the second most common one, after the cognitive approach, among faculties at accredited graduate and professional schools in clinical psychology (Sayette & Norcross, 2011). Psychodynamically oriented research publications are on the rise, too, though critics argue that the case studies that still dominate the psychodynamic psychotherapy research literature lack scientific rigor. Nevertheless, as described in Chapter 10, recent large-scale reviews and meta-analyses have found that some forms of psychodynamic psychotherapy produce results that are comparable to those of therapies identified as empirically supported (e.g., Gerber et al., 2011; Shedler, 2010). This is especially true of psychodynamic approaches that are shorter in duration or more focused, such as psychodynamic treatments for depression (Sandell, 2012).

It also appears that most psychodynamically oriented clinicians are becoming less ideological in practice. Surveys suggest that though these therapists clearly favor a psychodynamic framework, they are also inclined to endorse features from cognitive-behavioral and other therapy approaches (Alfonso & Olarte, 2011). So despite the tendency of some critics to dismiss all psychodynamic theory because certain aspects of Freud's theory have been discredited, the psychodynamic approach continues to evolve, and it remains a significant force in clinical psychology. More detailed coverage of psychodynamic psychotherapy can be found in the resources listed in the previous section.

SECTION SUMMARY

Psychoanalytic theory and practice has continued to develop beyond Freud's original formulations. Later psychoanalytic theorists moved away from his strong emphasis on id, sex, and aggression. They stressed the role of the ego as an adaptive, creative problem-solving agency. They also greatly expanded consideration of interpersonal relationships in the development of healthy personality, psychopathology, and psychotherapy. Many analytically oriented clinicians continue to analyze transference relationships with the aim of helping clients develop insight into their historically rooted maladaptive patterns. They do so with a view of the therapeutic relationship that differs from Freud's. Relational psychodynamic theorists, in particular, stress the subjective nature of all relationships, including the therapeutic one. This view requires that the process of interpretation and meaning-finding in therapy must be collaborative. Psychodynamic psychotherapists offer a wider range of interventions, from the highly expressive and analytical to the highly supportive.

HUMANISTIC PSYCHOTHERAPY

SECTION PREVIEW

Here we describe humanistic approaches to psychotherapy, which emphasize conscious awareness rather than unconscious conflict. These approaches also stress the need for the therapist to understand the experiential worlds of their clients and to communicate that understanding to clients as a way of creating a favorable climate for psychotherapy. The relationship itself is seen as the primary curative factor in the treatments offered by humanistic therapists.

Humanistic approaches to treatment stress the importance of clients focusing on their immediate, here-and-now experiences. Examples of these approaches include person-centered psychotherapy (Rogers, 1951), Gestalt therapy (Perls, 1969), existential therapy (Frankl, 1967; May, 1981), focusing-oriented psychotherapy (Gendlin, 1996), and several others.

As discussed in Chapter 2, "Clinical Psychology's Past and Pesent," humanistic psychotherapists view humans as creative, growthful beings who, if all goes well, consciously guide their behavior toward realization of their fullest potential as unique individuals. When behavior disorders arise, they are usually seen as stemming from disturbances in awareness or restrictions on existence that can be eliminated through various therapeutic experiences (Fischer, 1989; Greenberg, Elliott, & Lietaer, 1994; Joseph & Murphy, 2013).

Several themes unify the goals and techniques associated with humanistic treatments. First, humanistic therapists assume that their clients' lives can be understood only from the viewpoint of those clients. Second, many humanistic therapists view human beings not as instinct-driven creatures but as naturally good people who are able to make choices about their lives and determine their own destinies. Third, humanistic therapists view the therapeutic relationship as the primary vehicle by which therapy achieves its benefits. It must be a relationship that guarantees honest, emotionally open interpersonal experiences for both client and therapist. This implies that clients are regarded as equals; therapists treat clients as responsible individuals who are experts on their own experiences and who must ultimately be the ones to make decisions about their lives. Finally, many humanistic therapists emphasize the importance of experiencing and exploring emotions that are confusing or painful.

Person-Centered Therapy

By far the most prominent of the humanistic approaches is the *person-centered psychotherapy* developed by Carl Rogers. Rogers originally called his approach *client-centered therapy* but later changed the name as he expanded its applications. First trained in psychodynamic therapy methods in the late 1920s, Rogers eventually became uncomfortable with the idea of therapists as authority figures who searched relentlessly for unconscious conflicts. Rogers felt there had to be a better way to do clinical work, and an alternative began to take shape when he discovered a treatment approach advocated by Otto Rank, whose revision of Freud's ideas was mentioned in Table 7.2. To Rank, the client ". . . is a moving cause, containing constructive forces within, which constitute a will to health. The therapist guides the individual to self-understanding, self-acceptance. It is the therapist *as a human being* who is the remedy, not his technical skill. . . . The spontaneity and uniqueness of therapy lived in the present carry the patient toward health" (Meador & Rogers, 1973, p. 121; italics added).

Rogers believed that people have an innate motive toward growth, which he called the *actualizing tendency:* "the directional trend which is evident in all organic and human life—the urge to expand, extend, develop, mature—the tendency to express and activate all the capacities of the organism" (Rogers, 1961, p. 351). Rogers saw all human behavior—from basic food seeking to artistic creativity, from normal conversation to bizarre delusions—as a reflection of the individual's efforts at *self-actualization* in a uniquely perceived world.

Carl Rogers (1902–1987) by John T. Wood. *Source*: Bettmann/ Corbis.

As Rogers began to incorporate these ideas about growth, nonauthoritarianism, and the value of a good human relationship into his therapy sessions, he came to believe that "it is the client who knows what hurts, what directions to go, what problems are crucial, what experiences have been deeply buried" (Rogers, 1961, pp. 11–12). He also began to see therapy as an "if . . . then" proposition: *If* the correct circumstances are created by the therapist, *then* the client—driven by an innate potential for growth—will spontaneously improve.

Therapists from many different theoretical orientations acknowledge a great debt to Rogers for his focus on therapeutic conditions and the therapeutic relationship (Bohart & Watson, 2011). A survey conducted not long ago found that psychotherapists rated Rogers as the person who had the most influence on their work (Cook & Biyanova, 2009).

ROGERS'S PERSONALITY THEORY AND VIEW OF PSYCHOPATHOLOGY Rogers's person-centered theory proposes a developmental process leading to either more or less healthy personality functioning. Critical to this process is the concept of the self. The *self* represents the experiences the person recognizes as "me" (Murdock, 2004). It includes values, images, memories, behavior patterns, and, especially, current experiences. Two particularly important aspects of the self are the real self and the ideal self. Let's consider how they develop.

THE SELF AND CONDITIONS OF WORTH As children grow, they come to recognize their likes and dislikes, their abilities, emotional states, and the like. In short, their self-concept expands, but not in isolation; it develops in the context of relationships with others, especially parents. The child becomes aware that others regard certain of his or her self-experiences more highly than others.

According to Rogers, the ideal situation is one in which parents are successful at communicating their acceptance (if not approval) of all of the child's behavior and experiences. Rogers called such communication *unconditional positive regard* and considered it as a critical requirement for psychological growth. To the degree that parents communicate acceptance of their child's behavior and experiences, the child naturally incorporates those experiences into his or her *real self-concept*. The child comes to recognize these experiences as part of the self, and because others have valued them, the child values them, too.

However, when parents communicate disapproval or rejection of some of the child's behaviors and experiences, the child may experience love as conditional. This is especially likely to happen if the child feels that the parents' disapproval is of *him or her* rather than of *his or her behavior* (e.g., a parent who says, "You're so stupid!" communicates a different message from one who says, "I love you, but it makes me angry when you do that"). Rogers called this situation *conditions of worth* because the child comes to believe that acceptance, and indeed his or her worth as a person, depends on thinking and acting in certain ways. The more pronounced the conditions of worth, the more the child's real self-concept deviates from his or her *ideal self-concept*. The ideal self is not immediately experienced as "me" but as what the child believes he or she *should* be.

INCONGRUENCE The discrepancy between the real self and the ideal self is called *incongruence*. It is a matter of degree—no parent communicates unconditional positive regard for every behavior and experience a child has. But the more a person experiences his or her positive regard as being dependent upon acting and feeling in ways consistent with what other people value, the more the real self and the ideal self become separated (see Figure 7.2). In short, the conditions of worth force people to distort their real feelings or experiences. When it happens, symptoms of disorder may appear. Thus, if a person really wanted to be an artist but felt those feelings had to be ignored because of family pressure to become an accountant, depression might result. Growth would stop as the person's behavior (e.g., professing satisfaction with accounting) became increasingly discrepant, or incongruent, with real feelings. The distortions and lack of awareness that produce symptoms may not be entirely conscious, but neither are they inaccessible as the psychoanalytic approaches might suggest.

The Goals of Person-Centered Therapy

Because clients know what hurts and what they want to change, person-centered therapists do not set treatment goals for their clients. Instead, clients are free to select their own goals (Bohart & Watson, 2011). From the therapist's point of view, though, a key aim of therapy is to make clients more authentically aware of their moment-to-moment experiences. The therapist promotes such awareness by providing an interpersonal relationship that the client can use to reduce incongruence and foster personal growth. This growth-enhancing relationship can only appear, said Rogers, if the therapist experiences and expresses three interrelated attitudes: unconditional positive regard, empathy, and congruence.

UNCONDITIONAL POSITIVE REGARD The therapeutic attitude Rogers called *unconditional positive regard* conveys that the therapist cares about the client, accepts the client, and trusts the client's ability to change. The ideal form of unconditional positive regard is *nonpossessive caring*, in which genuine positive feelings are expressed in a way that makes clients feel valued but still free to be themselves, not obligated to try to please the therapist. The therapist's *willingness to listen* is an important manifestation of unconditional positive regard. Patient, warm, and interested in what the client has to say, Rogerian therapists do not interrupt the client or change the subject or give other signs that they would rather be doing something else.

The "unconditional" aspect of unconditional positive regard is manifested in the therapist's willingness to accept clients as they are without judging them. Rogers believed that the experience of being prized as a human being, regardless of one's feelings or behaviors, can be a growth-enhancing experience for clients whose development has been hampered by conditions of worth and other evaluative pressures. Fortunately, expressing unconditional positive regard does not require *approving* of all the things a client says or does but merely *accepting* them as part of a person whom the therapist cares about. This ideal is illustrated in the following interaction:

CLIENT: That was the semester my brother died and everything seemed to be going down the tubes. I knew how important it was to my parents that I get into medical

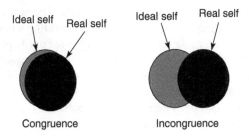

FIGURE 7.2 Congruence and Incongruence

school, but I also knew that my grades would be lousy that year unless I did something. To make a long story short, I bought a term paper and cheated on almost every exam that semester.

THERAPIST: It was a really rough time for you.

Notice that the therapist focuses on the client's feelings in the situation, not on the ethics of the behavior. In other words, to express unconditional positive regard, the therapist must separate a client's worth *as a person* from the worth of the client's *behavior.*

The "positive" component of unconditional positive regard is reflected in the therapist's trust in the client's potential for growth and problem solving. Rogers believed that if clients perceive that their therapist lacks this trust, they will not develop the confidence they need to make changes. So, like other humanistic/experiential therapists, Rogerians try not to give advice, take responsibility for clients, or make decisions for them. Such restraint is sometimes difficult, especially when therapists feel that they know "what's best" for a client. However, the client must be allowed to make bad decisions or experience problems, even if they could have been averted by following the therapist's advice. Advice from a therapist might prevent one problem but could create others: the therapist would become a superior, the client would become more dependent, and, most important, both client and therapist would have less faith in the client's ability to deal independently with problems.

EMPATHY To understand a client's behavior and help the client understand it as well, the therapist must try to see the world as the client sees it. In Rogerian terms, this involves striving for accurate *empathy,* or *empathic understanding.* To illustrate, let's consider an excerpt from the beginning of a therapy session:

CLIENT: My wife was the one who wanted me to come. See, when I made the appointment, we'd just had another big fight over our daughter. At that time, we were both really upset, near the end of our rope, so I agreed. [Pause] Not that it's much better now, but it has cooled down a little. You see, lately our life is a mess because our daughter is skipping school, flunking at least 2 of her classes, fights against everything we say. She, my wife I mean, thinks I'm too hard on our daughter. But I don't think so. I think the kid needs to learn some self-discipline. I always have to be the bad guy, the one grounding her, taking the car away. Sure I get angry at times, maybe say some things I shouldn't, and I drink more than I probably should, especially lately, but it's driving me crazy. I don't know how we're going to make it—it's like everybody is blaming everybody for their unhappiness. I haven't been back from the Middle East that long, and I know some guys who just checked out in one way or another, if you know what I mean. I don't want to go down that road but. . . well, I can see how it happens. It just seems that life shouldn't be this hard. Shit, I feel like I'm just rambling. You must think I'm nuts.

Many therapists would respond to this client using what Rogers called an *external frame of reference.* They would observe the client from the outside and apply their values or psychological theories to what the client says (see the left side of Table 7.3). An empathic therapist, however, would try to adopt an *internal frame of reference* in an effort to understand what it must be like to be this client (see the right side of Table 7.3).

To communicate an empathic attitude to their clients, Rogerian therapists employ the active listening methods described in Chapter 4, "Interviewing and Observation in Clinical Psychology." Of particular value is *reflection,* which serves the dual purposes of (a) communicating the therapist's desire for emotional understanding, and (b) making clients more aware of their own feelings. Reflection is one of the most misunderstood aspects of person-centered therapy because the therapist appears to be stating the obvious or merely repeating what the client has said. But reflection is more than repetition or paraphrasing. As suggested in Chapter 4, it involves distilling and "playing back" the client's feelings. For example, suppose a client says, "This has been such a bad day. I've had to keep myself from crying three or four times. I'm not even sure what's wrong!" The therapist's response could be externally oriented, such as "Well, what exactly happened?" but a more empathic comment might be "You really do feel bad. The tears just well up inside. And it sounds like it is scary to not know why you feel this way."

At first glance, the clinician may seem to be a parrot, but look more closely. The client never *said* she felt bad; the therapist inferred it by taking the client's point of view. Similarly, the client

TABLE 7.3 Therapist Thoughts That Reflect Internal and External Frames of Reference

External	Internal
He's being defensive, denying his problems.	When you made the appointment, you thought you needed help. Now that you're here, you aren't so sure.
The family is really dysfunctional, and he's a big part of the cause.	You're really concerned about your daughter.
He should learn more beneficial parenting techniques.	When you try to be a good parent, it backfires and you end up feeling blamed.
He may be alcoholic; I wonder if I should refer him to AA.	From your perspective, alcohol adds to the problems at home, but it's not the main cause of the problems.
What is meant by this focus on marriage and family?	You're also concerned about how the stressors at home are affecting your marriage
He's a veteran. I wonder if he saw combat action or if he had friends injured or killed. I feel for anybody who spent time in that war.	In addition to the conflicts at home, you're still readjusting to civilian life, and it's not easy.
He's projecting his confusion and negative self-image onto me.	You're concerned that I might think you're screwed up, a lost cause.

never said her sadness frightened her—it was the clinician's ability to put himself in the client's shoes that led to this speculation. If the therapist's inferences are wrong, the client can correct them, but right or wrong, the clinician has let the client know that he wants to understand her experience rather than diagnose it.

CONGRUENCE   Rogers also believed that the more genuine the therapist is in relating to clients, the more helpful the therapist will be. The therapist's feelings and actions, he said, should be *congruent*, or consistent, with one another. "This means that I need to be aware of my own feelings . . . [and willing] to express, in my words and my behavior, the various feelings and attitudes which exist in me" (Rogers, 1961, p. 33). According to Rogers, when the therapist is congruent, a real human relationship occurs in therapy.

To get an idea of how congruence promotes trust, think of a time when a close friend might have told you something that you did not want to hear, perhaps that you looked silly or were wrong about something. Once you know that a friend will say what he or she really feels even if it does not make you happy, it makes it easier to trust whatever else that friend might say. However, if you know that your friend can be incongruent, telling you what you want to hear instead of what he or she genuinely feels, your faith in that person's reactions ("You really look great.") is likely to be undermined.

Here is one way that congruence can be displayed in a therapist–client interaction:

CLIENT: I just feel so hopeless. Tell me what I'm doing wrong in my life.

THERAPIST: I guess when you are feeling this bad, it would be nice if someone could come along and tell you what is going wrong and how you can put everything right again. I wish I could do all that, but I can't. I don't think anyone else can either.

Notice the therapist's reflection of the client's feeling plus the direct expression of (a) a genuine wish to understand and solve the client's problems, and (b) an admission that she is not capable of such a feat.

THE NATURE OF CHANGE IN PERSON-CENTERED THERAPY   Rogers argued that as clients experience empathy, unconditional positive regard, and congruence in a therapeutic relationship, they become more self-aware and self-accepting, more comfortable and less defensive in interpersonal relationships, less rigid in their thinking, more reliant on self-evaluation than on evaluations by others, and better able to function in a wide variety of roles (Rogers, 1951). To many, this is still a surprising claim—that the atmosphere a therapist creates is more important than what is said or what techniques or methods are used.

Case Example

The following description is taken from a person-centered therapy case presented by Murdock (2004, pp. 108–137).

Richard is a 48-year-old Caucasian. He is a high school graduate and has worked as an insurance salesperson for the past 3 years. Prior to this period, he worked at the management level for a telecommunications company but left this job because he found it too stressful.

Richard presents with depressed mood that affects his physical, social, and occupational functioning. He reports experiencing this depression for about the past 2 years. During this period, Richard characterizes himself as often fatigued, socially withdrawn, and ineffective at work. His income has dropped significantly during the last 2 years. Richard feels guilty for having to rely on his wife, Sandy, as the primary income provider. According to Richard, Sandy often expresses disapproval of him nonverbally, such as when she is writing checks for the monthly bills. The couple argues quite frequently about financial matters.

Richard and Sandy have two adult children (Natalie and James) who have completed college within the past 5 years. Richard reports that both children currently earn more than his present income. This situation makes him feel inadequate. As a result, Richard feels emotionally distant from Natalie and James and sees them as closer to Sandy.

Richard's social activities typically involve his wife and are work-related. He spends his spare time with his computer or reading. He reports having no close friends.

During counseling sessions, Richard seems uncomfortable, has difficulty maintaining eye contact, laughs nervously during the shortest periods of silence, and comments on his discomfort with the lack of structure. Although he seems motivated to change, Richard seems to have difficulty discussing his situation.

CASE FORMULATION   A person-centered therapist would not be inclined to seek Richard's personal or family history. Neither would the therapist be inclined to assign a DSM diagnosis unless perhaps insurance reimbursement required it. More important to the person-centered therapist is the client's internal perspective. The therapist would want to discover how Richard experienced his life, including, but not limited to, his symptoms. The therapist's job is to enter into the client's experiential world, to see and feel things he does, while still maintaining some objective perspective (Sommers-Flanagan & Sommers-Flanagan, 2012).

Daryl, Richard's person-centered therapist, begins with the assumption that Richard is inherently a positive, forward-moving individual. . . . Daryl approaches Richard as an equal and encourages him to determine the nature and content of the counseling relationship. He relies on Richard to provide the basic material of counseling. Even though this attitude seems somewhat surprising to Richard and tends to make him a little uncomfortable, Daryl persists in his gentle support of Richard's choices and decisions within the counseling session. In no way does Daryl assess, diagnose, or evaluate Richard. . . .

Richard probably has a negative self-concept. He is able to recognize and reveal "negative" aspects of himself—he is socially withdrawn and ineffective at work. Because he unfavorably compares himself with his children, Richard feels inadequate. Very little in Richard's self-description seems positive, and Daryl also guesses that Richard's ideal self is so close to perfection as to be unobtainable by a human being. . . . Richard's need for positive regard is evident in his reactions to his wife Sandy's disapproval. . . . Daryl knows that Richard's self is conditional. His guilt and depression are likely the result of aspects of his experience that are inconsistent with his internalized conditions of worth. For example, Richard apparently holds the value that to be worthwhile, he should earn a certain amount of money—specifically that he should be the primary provider for his family. He is not fulfilling the conditions that men are strong and provide for their families. . . .

At times Daryl finds himself wanting to mention to Richard something he is not sure Richard has recognized: feelings that Richard has denied or distorted. For instance, Daryl senses Richard's feelings of inadequacy around his role as a husband and provider. Richard becomes anxious if these feelings and their meaning start to surface. In the supportive atmosphere of their relationship, Daryl tries to help Richard move toward experiencing these feelings. He does not, however, push Richard into experiencing these feelings or in any way insist that Richard acknowledge them if Richard is not ready.

THE ROLE OF THE THERAPIST   Daryl's primary responsibility as a therapist is to provide an atmosphere in which Richard can explore his thoughts and feelings about the things that trouble him. The therapist does this by being nondirective—he does not suggest topics, guide the conversation, or interpret Richard's behavior. Instead, the therapist listens empathically, responds reflectively, and models genuineness in his own behavior toward the client.

Empathy is shown in the degree to which the therapist communicates understanding of Richard's experiences, including emotions that he is not fully aware of. For example, when Richard reports that he "feels bad" whenever his wife balances the checkbook and says something such as, "Holy crap, Richard, we're barely squeaking by," the therapist may reply with something like the following:

THERAPIST: When you hear this, you feel negative emotions right away. I'm trying to get a better handle on what that feeling is like for you.

CLIENT: Well, like right away I feel myself tighten up. I know it's my fault. But I hate being reminded, you know. That doesn't help.

THERAPIST: So you feel yourself tighten or close up, then you get angry.

CLIENT: Well, kinda. I don't really *say* I'm angry. I don't know, I just feel bad all over again. It's my fault.

THERAPIST: So when your wife mentions the finances, you feel criticized by her *and* by yourself. You think of yourself as a loser. Another part of you becomes self-protective, and that part tells you that the criticism doesn't help, it only makes things worse.

CLIENT: Yeah, I guess I get all defensive. I'm a loser.

THERAPIST: You don't seem like a loser to me, Richard, and I think that if I felt criticized for being a loser on a regular basis, I'd want to protect myself too.

In these exchanges, the therapist worked to understand the client's feelings, including feelings that the client may not yet fully own. At one point, the therapist suggested Richard felt anger, but Richard's response suggested that this did not fit for him; rather, he felt "like a loser." The therapist later restated Richard's comment about "tightening up" as a self-protective impulse rather than anger. This may be a way of phrasing the experience that Richard can more easily own.

Daryl also demonstrated congruence in reporting his own feeling toward Richard. Congruence requires that the therapist be genuine and not try to maintain a facade of professionalism. However, this does *not* mean that therapists should just say whatever comes to mind, respond reflexively, or always "go with their gut." Nor does it mean that therapists should engage in confessional self-disclosure with the client. Rather, congruence means that therapists should recognize in themselves their genuine and persistent feelings toward their clients and that they may express those feelings to the clients in an appropriate way (Rogers, 1967).

As therapy provides an atmosphere of acceptance, warmth, and genuineness, clients become more accepting of their own experiences. For example, Richard begins to recognize the huge gap between what he thinks he should be and what he is. As he does so, he begins to take a more internal perspective on his emotions and reactions—evaluating them from within his own experiential system rather than from an external perspective. Reactions and behaviors that otherwise seemed irrational from an external perspective (and were the source of self-criticism) make more sense to him from an internal perspective. In short, irrational behavior is often rational from the client's perspective, and so person-centered therapists seek to expand the client's perspective rather than change the client's behavior. Bohart (2003, p. 131) calls the client's growing interest in exploring his internal perspective "mobilizing the client's critical intelligence." This mobilization allows the client to more fully experience emotions that were only vaguely experienced before.

The client's greater recognition and acceptance of internal experience allows him to try out new behaviors because the fear of failure has been reduced. So, for example, when Richard's wife complains about the family finances, Richard more clearly recognizes his automatic tendency to feel criticized, become emotionally defensive, and withdraw from the relationship. But his greater acceptance of himself means that he can tolerate these feelings more—they have less power over him. Because he is less self-defensive, he can try out new behaviors with reduced fear. For example, he may be able to imagine the possibility that Sandy is expressing concern for the family welfare rather than accusing him of being inadequate. Further, because therapy has provided a model for responding to others with empathy, Richard may be able to try out an empathetic response with her (e.g., "It's really frustrating. I'm worried about the money too"). Even if Richard discovered that Sandy really was criticizing him, he might be able to respond without withdrawing or counterattacking (e.g., "I know you're upset, but I'm trying, and criticism doesn't help me").

In short, the process of person-centered therapy is designed to develop a greater sense of self trust. As clients get better at listening to their feelings, they become less likely to misread them, become less self-critical, and their sense of efficacy develops (Bohart & Watson, 2011; Sommers-Flanagan & Sommers-Flanagan, 2012).

SECTION SUMMARY

Carl Rogers's person-centered therapy is based on the idea that persons are basically good and oriented toward growth. His theory assumes that psychological problems develop when conditions of worth lead to incongruence (a divergence between the real self and the ideal self). In therapy, person-centered therapists take a nondirective approach, allowing the client to determine the problems discussed, how they are discussed, and what the goals of treatment should be. Therapists see their job as communicating empathy, unconditional positive regard, and congruence. It is this atmosphere, this genuine relationship, that is assumed to be the principal curative factor in treatment.

OTHER HUMANISTIC APPROACHES

SECTION PREVIEW

Alternative humanistic therapies share with person-centered therapy the belief that awareness and acceptance of immediate emotional experiences is critical for mental health. They also share a strong emphasis on the therapeutic relationship as a curative factor in therapy. Some humanistic alternatives differ in that therapists are more directive than in person-centered therapy. Others differ in the scope of the awareness sought collaboratively by client and therapist; some go beyond awareness of emotional experiences to include awareness of life's meaning and purpose.

Gestalt Therapy

Gestalt therapy, developed by Frederick (Fritz) and Laura Perls, is a variation on humanistic psychology. Like person-centered methods, Gestalt therapy aims at enhancing clients' self awareness in order to free them to grow in their own consciously guided ways (Delisle, 2013). More specifically, the Gestalt therapist seeks to reestablish clients' stalled growth processes by helping them (a) become aware of feelings they have disowned but that are a genuine part of them, and (b) recognize feelings and values they think are a genuine part of themselves but in fact are borrowed from other people.

One of the key differences between person-centered therapy and Gestalt therapy is that Gestalt therapists are much more active and dramatic. Through a variety of therapeutic techniques, the client is encouraged to assimilate or "re-own" the genuine aspects of self that have been rejected and to reject the "phony" features that do not belong. Ideally, when clients assimilate and integrate all aspects of their personality (both the desirable and the undesirable), they start taking responsibility for themselves as they really are instead of being attached to and defensive of a partially phony, internally conflicted self-image.

FOCUS ON THE HERE AND NOW   Gestalt therapists believe that therapeutic progress is made by keeping clients in contact with their feelings as they occur in the here and now. Perls expressed this belief in a conceptual equation where *now = experience = awareness = reality* (Perls, 1970). Any attempt by the client to recount the past or anticipate the future obstructs therapy goals. It is an escape from reality. So instead of reflecting (as a Rogerian might) the client's nostalgia for the past or thoughts about the future, a Gestalt therapist will point out the avoidance and insist that it be terminated.

ROLE PLAYING   Through role-playing or part-taking, clients explore inner conflicts and experience the symptoms, interpersonal games, and psychological defenses they have developed to keep those conflicts—and various other aspects of their genuine selves—out of awareness. By asking clients to "become" their resistance to change, for example, Gestalt therapists help them toward an experiential awareness of what the resistance is doing for and to them.

Gestalt therapists also turn role-playing into extended "conversations" between various parts of the client, including between the client's superego (what Perls called "topdog") and the part that is suppressed by "shoulds" and "oughts" (the "underdog"). Using the *empty chair technique*, therapists encourage clients to "talk" to someone they imagine to be seated in a nearby chair. The person may be a parent, child, spouse, or even an internalized aspect of the self. The client is asked to talk to the imagined person and to express—perhaps for the first time—true feelings about him or her and about events or conflicts in which that person played a part. The client may even respond for the imagined person. Here is an example:

CLIENT: My sister and I used to fight an awful lot when we were kids, but we seemed closer somehow then than we are now.

THERAPIST: Can you put her in that chair and say this to your sister now?

CLIENT: Okay. I feel so far away from you now, Rita. I want to have that feeling of being in a family again.

Clients may also be asked to clarify and release feelings toward significant people in their lives via the *unmailed letter technique:* They write—but do not send—a letter in which they express important but previously unspoken feelings. Role-played *reversals* also are used to enhance awareness of genuine feelings. So the client who conveys an image of cool self-sufficiency and denies feelings of tenderness toward others might be asked to play a warm, loving person. In the process, this client may get in touch with some feelings that have been suppressed for many years.

USE OF NONVERBAL CUES   Gestalt therapists pay special attention to what clients do as they speak, because the nonverbal channel often contradicts the client's words. For example, if a client says that she is nervous and clasps her hands, the therapist might wonder *what* the clasped hands meant. So instead of asking *why* the client clasped them, the therapist might ask her to repeat and exaggerate the hand clasp and to concentrate on the associated feelings. Once the client expressed these feelings, she would be asked to elaborate on them.

FRUSTRATING THE CLIENT   Because it is not always this easy for clients to become aware of hidden feelings, Gestalt therapists use many other methods for self-exploration. To help clients give up their maladaptive interpersonal roles and games, for example, Perls deliberately set out to frustrate their efforts to relate to him as they normally would to others. During individual or group therapy, he put his clients on what he called the "hot seat," where all attention was focused on the client and where his or her symptoms, games, and resistances were pointed out and explored.

Suppose that a client begins a session by saying, "I've really been looking forward to having this session. I hope you can help me." Instead of reflecting this feeling or asking why the client feels this way, a Gestalt therapist would focus on the manipulative aspect of the statement, which seems to contain the message, "I expect you to help me without my having to do much." The therapist might say, "How do you think I could help you?" The client (perhaps taken aback) might respond, "Well, I was hoping you could help me understand why I'm so unhappy." From here, the therapist would continue to frustrate the client's attempt to get the therapist to take responsibility for solving the client's problems and, in the process, would help the client recognize how he avoids responsibility for improving. The therapist might also help the client recognize the unrealistic wish that the therapist would have a magic cure.

As you might imagine, therapeutic techniques that use confrontation and deliberate frustration can be powerful motivators, but they can also drive clients away if the techniques are not implemented properly and carefully. Lilienfeld (2007) found that there is some risk of negative therapy outcomes with Gestalt therapy. For this reason, Sommers-Flanagan and Sommers-Flanagan (2012) caution that therapists, especially relatively inexperienced ones, use caution in applying these techniques.

Existential and Other Humanistic Approaches

Rogers's and Perls's methods of treatment represent two prominent examples of humanistic therapies, but there are others too, many of which blend Rogerian or Gestalt methods with principles from psychodynamic, behavioral, or existential psychology (Ginger & Ginger, 2012; Ladd & Churchill, 2012; Maslow, 1968; May, 1969; Philippson, 2012; Schneider & Krug, 2010; Scholl, McGowan, & Hansen, 2012).

EXISTENTIAL PSYCHOTHERAPIES Existential therapists help clients to explore fully what it means to be alive. These approaches are rooted in existential philosophy, which stresses the immense freedom that human beings have to make sense of their lives. Such freedom can be liberating, but it can also be frightening because it entails exploring questions about the meaning and purpose of one's life and assuming personal responsibility for the answer. In the process, one must confront the possible meaninglessness and finality of one's life. To cope with these questions, many people adopt meanings given to them by others (by parents, religious leaders, etc.). This external frame of reference can be comforting but may not last—at some point, many people find themselves fully facing their freedom.

Existential approaches have a long history, but they developed especially among European thinkers following World Wars I and II. As you might expect, those humanistic therapists committed to European existential philosophies are less likely to argue that all clients naturally strive toward positive goals (Fischer, 1989). Instead, they view humans as having the capacity for extraordinary goodness, extraordinary cruelty, and everything in between.

As in person-centered psychotherapy, existential humanistic therapists try to understand the client's inner world, frames of reference, and flow of experiences. They do not try to formulate diagnoses or objective descriptions. The concept of personality has limited usefulness in existential therapies. Instead, existential humanistic therapists stress freedom, experiential reflection, and responsibility (Schneider, 2003). The client and therapist join in the client's very personal search for meaning.

Therapists use relationship building and empathic responding, as in person-centered therapy, but they may also engage in analysis or interpretation, or they may use techniques from other approaches that focus on the client's ways of experiencing and relating in the here and now. Thus, therapists might comment on client's body postures, tone of voice, use of language, assumptions, and the like (Schneider & Krug, 2010). In short, the method is eclectic or integrative and the focus is on the struggle for the meaning of existence, worked out one client at a time. The therapy may be as brief as a few sessions but is more likely to extend into several months or even up to a few years (Bugental, 1995; Joseph & Murphy, 2013; Schneider 2008).

MOTIVATIONAL INTERVIEWING AND EMOTION-FOCUSED THERAPY Motivational interviewing and emotion-focused therapy are treatment approaches derived explicitly from person-centered therapy (Sommers-Flanagan & Sommers-Flanagan, 2012). In *motivational interviewing*, therapists use reflective listening techniques to call clients' attention to their choices and values (Bohart & Watson, 2011). Often used in substance abuse counseling or in other situations where clients may be resistant to treatment or distrustful of authority, motivational interviewing seeks to meet resistance with reflection rather than with confrontation. The assumption is that if clinicians express empathy and accurately reflect clients' thoughts and feelings, clients will become less defensive. They may also become more aware of discrepancies between their behavior and their deeper values, and that the responsibility for resolving such discrepancies lies with them. The following brief vignettes from Miller and Rollnick (1998) illustrate this approach.

CLIENT: I'm trying! If my probation officer would just get off my back, I could focus on getting my life in order.

INTERVIEWER: It's frustrating to have a probation officer looking over your shoulder.

CLIENT: Who are you to be giving me advice? What do you know about drugs? You've probably never even smoked a joint!

INTERVIEWER: It's hard to imagine how I could possibly understand.

The similarities between reflective responding in client-centered therapy and in motivational interviewing are obvious—both are designed to help clients to see themselves more clearly. But motivational interviewers are inclined to diverge from straight reflection, sometimes purposely overstating or siding with only one side of a client's ambivalence. The purpose of these elaborations is to gently guide the client toward certain problems (i.e., to be subtly directive rather than nondirective).

As its name implies, *emotion-focused therapy* emphasizes the role of emotion in human experience. A prominent example is process-experiential emotion focused therapy (PE-EFT; Greenberg, Rice, & Elliott, 1993). This approach views psychological difficulties as coming from emotional schemes—people's organized patterns of emotional responses. Therapists seek to provide a warm, empathic, and supportive relationship in which clients are better able to fully experience their emotions, particularly emotions of vulnerability. But they are also likely to use a variety of specific tasks to facilitate emotion and emotional integration (Watson, Goldman, & Greenberg, 2011). Emotion regulation is also a focus of the therapy, and so therapists work with clients to become aware of, label, accept, reflect upon, and modify their emotions (Bohart & Watson, 2011).

The Current Status of Humanistic Psychotherapy

Humanistic psychotherapists such as Carl Rogers are often rated by clinicians as highly influential, yet relatively few therapists identify themselves as humanistic (person-centered, Gestalt, existential, etc.). Among counseling programs and free-standing psychology programs, only about 10% claim this orientation; in clinical psychology programs, the percentage is closer to 5% (Bechtoldt Norcross, Wyckoff, Pokrywa, & Campbell, 2001; Sayette & Norcross, 2011).

One reason for the discrepancy may be that humanistic psychotherapy revolves around an insistence on not "pathologizing" clients. It assumes that even bizarre behavior is understandable from the client's point of view. But if clients do not have a "problem," "deficit," "conflict," "illness," or "pathology," and if therapists are not expected to identify, understand, and find solutions to a problem, what is there for the therapist to do? They can passively support clients' efforts to gain the self-awareness presumed necessary to create change, but to many therapists, humanistic approaches do not give them the kind of more active therapeutic role they prefer.

Humanistic approaches may lack appeal also because, generally speaking, empirical support for them is not as strong as it is for other, more popular, therapies. This is not to suggest that humanistic approaches are inherently unscientific. Indeed, Carl Rogers was among the first to recognize the need for scientific research to substantiate the alleged value of any treatment technique, including his own. He was the first to record therapy sessions, and he conducted some of the first empirical research on the relationship between treatment outcome and therapist characteristics such as empathy and warmth. In fact, he was arguably the first modern scientist practitioner (Sommers-Flanagan & Sommers-Flanagan, 2012). But person-centered therapy and related phenomenological treatments can be difficult to study because treatment goals and methods are not clearly articulated ahead of time. Rather, they emerge from the two-person field. It is not surprising that such approaches do not fare as well in empirical outcome studies as highly specified interventions focused on specifically targeted symptoms in targeted populations. Perhaps this is why variations on humanistic therapy that more closely approximate this kind of focus (e.g., motivational interviewing in substance abuse treatment) generally have more positive outcomes.

Despite its shortcomings and apparent lack of popularity, no approach to psychotherapy has done more than the humanistic one to highlight the importance of the therapeutic relationship. As described in Chapter 10, "Research on Clinical Interventions," research on the curative factors in psychotherapy has confirmed that importance. In addition, the collaborative approach to psychotherapy advocated by Rogerians in particular and humanistic clinicians in general has attracted the attention of many therapists, especially those who employ relational psychodynamic methods. And as discussed in the next chapter, even behavioral and cognitive psychotherapists are increasingly attending to the quality of the therapeutic relationship. So humanistic treatment approaches still have considerable impact. Ironically, this is not so much because of their unique identity, but because many therapists from other approaches have adopted humanistic concepts and practices, without fully adopting the humanistic approach (DeRobertis, 2013).

SECTION SUMMARY

Alternatives to person-centered psychotherapy include Gestalt therapy, existential therapy, and other approaches oriented toward fostering awareness. Gestalt therapists use a variety of techniques that are more directive and physically expressive than those used in person-centered therapy. Existential therapists work with clients to help them develop meaning in their lives. They use various techniques to help clients struggle with existential questions and take responsibility for their personal resolution. Motivational interviewing and emotion-focused therapy are newer interventions that are informed by person-centered therapy.

Chapter Summary

Psychodynamic and humanistic psychotherapies share a strong emphasis on the importance of the therapeutic relationship. However, they differ in their assumptions about personality organization, psychopathology, and therapeutic technique.

In Freudian psychoanalysis, clients are helped to explore the unconscious wishes, fantasies, impulses, and conflicts that are presumed to lie at the root of their psychological problems. Psychoanalytic treatment is aimed at helping clients gain insight into the unconscious underlying causes of their conflicts. To get at unconscious material, much of which is based in infancy and childhood, Freud developed a number of treatment techniques, including free association and analysis of the meaning of dreams, of everyday behaviors, of resistance to treatment, and of transference appearing in the therapeutic relationship. Interpretations of the meaning of this material help move clients toward insight and understanding.

Other psychodynamically oriented therapists have developed variations on orthodox Freudian psychoanalysis. Among the most prominent of these methods are psychoanalytically oriented psychotherapy, ego psychology, object relations therapy, and interpersonal therapy. The interpersonal and object relations approaches have blended to form relational psychodynamic approaches. This approach remains fundamentally psychodynamic but shares with the humanistic approaches a belief in the subjective nature of all relationships. The psychodynamic variations tend to be briefer than classical psychoanalysis and to focus more on current problems than on childhood conflicts. They emphasize strengthening ego functions more than analyzing id impulses, actively repairing damage from inadequate early caregiver relationships more than gaining insight into them, and changing maladaptive interpersonal relationships more than delving into their unconscious origins.

Humanistic therapies are based on the assumption that people are inherently growthful and that their progress toward developing their potential will resume when problems that have impaired it are removed by the experience of a supportive therapeutic relationship. These problems are presumed to arise largely from socialization processes that prompt people to distort or suppress genuine feelings and wishes in order to please others, so therapy is aimed at creating a client–therapist relationship in which clients can become more aware and accepting of how they really think and feel.

Therapists using Carl Rogers's person-centered therapy create this relationship by using reflection and other active listening methods to convey empathy, unconditional positive regard, and congruence as they work with clients. The same goals of self-awareness and growth are sought in a more active and direct way through Perls's Gestalt therapy, whose methods include focusing on the present, having clients role-play suppressed or disowned aspects of the self, frustrating their efforts at resistance, attending to their nonverbal behavior, and having them engage in dialogues with imaginary versions of significant people in their lives. Existential humanistic approaches also stress the unique nature of the therapeutic relationship, but they stress helping clients recognize and deal with their most basic needs for meaning, purpose, and connection. More recent treatments, such as motivational interviewing and emotion-focused therapy have been informed by the principles of person-centered therapy.

Psychodynamic approaches have remained popular in clinical psychology. Relatively fewer clinical psychologists identify themselves as humanistic, person-centered, or existential. Nevertheless, some of the basic concepts of these approaches have been increasingly integrated into other more popular therapy approaches.

Study Questions

1. How did psychoanalysis develop?
2. What is the structural model of personality in psychoanalytic theory?
3. What is meant by psychic determinism?
4. What roles do anxiety and defense mechanisms play in the production of psychological problems?
5. What are transference and countertransference? How are they viewed by the various psychodynamic approaches?
6. How do psychodynamic psychotherapies attempt to help clients stop repeating the past?
7. What role do the following play in psychoanalysis: resistance, interpretation, and insight?
8. What major changes or variations in psychoanalytic thought have occurred after Freud?
9. How does the practice of contemporary psychodynamic therapists differ from the practice of psychoanalysts?
10. How do humanistic psychologists view personality and psychological problems?
11. What special role does the self have in humanistic psychotherapy?
12. What are unconditional positive regard, empathy, and congruence, and why are they important in person-centered psychotherapy?
13. What role does the therapeutic relationship play in person-centered and other humanistic psychotherapies?
14. How does Gestalt therapy differ from person-centered therapy?
15. What is the major focus of the existential humanistic psychotherapies?
16. Compared with other major approaches to psychotherapy, how prevalent are the humanistic approaches among practicing clinical and counseling psychologists?

Web Sites

- APA Division 39, Psychoanalysis: http://www.apa.org/about/division/div39.aspx
- APA Division 39, Psychoanalysis, subdivision III: Women, gender, and psychoanalysis: http://www.apadivisions.org/division-39/sections/women/index.aspx
- APA Division 39, Psychoanalysis, subdivision V: Psychoanalytic research society: http://www.sectionfive.org
- Web site of the Freud Museum, London, UK: http://www.freud.org.uk/
- APA Division 32, Humanistic psychology: http://www.apa.org/about/division/div32.aspx
- Web pages devoted to Carl Rogers, created by his daughter, Nancy: http://www.nrogers.com/carlrogers.html
- Web site of the International Society for Existential Psychology and Psychotherapy: http://existentialpsychology.org/

MOVIES

Annie Hall (1977): Classic romantic comedy, with great scenes of therapy—some with a psychoanalyst and some with a client-centered therapist.

Prime (2005): In this light romantic comedy, an unethical situation (in which a therapist continues seeing a client even though the client is dating her son) is played for laughs.

MEMOIRS

Mockingbird Years: A Life In and Out of Therapy by Emily Fox Gordon (2000; New York: Basic Books). By the time the author was 17, she had already had five different therapists and then as a young adult she entered a mental institution where she worked with a psychoanalyst.

Running For My Life: My Journey in the Game of Football and Beyond by Warrick Dunn (2008; New York: Harper Collins). Poignant autobiography by former NFL pro player, who describes how client-centered therapy helped him finally overcome the emotional demeans that plagued him since his mother's murder when he was in high school.

References

Alexander, F., & French, T. M. (1946). *Psychoanalytic therapy: Principles and application.* New York, NY: Ronald Press.

Alfonso, C. A., & Olarte, S. (2011). Contemporary practice patterns of dynamic psychiatrists—survey results. *The Journal of the American Academy of Psychoanalysis and Dynamic Psychiatry, 39,* 7–26.

Bechtoldt, H., Norcross, J. C., Wyckoff, L., Pokrywa, M. L., & Campbell, L. F. (2001). Theoretical orientations and employment settings of clinical and counseling psychologists: A comparative study. *The Clinical Psychologist, 54,* 3–6.

Binder, J. L., & Betan, E. J. (2013). *Core competencies in brief dynamic psychotherapy: Becoming a highly effective and competent brief dynamic psychotherapist.* New York, NY: Routledge/Taylor & Francis Group.

Blatt, S. J., & Lerner, H. (1983). Psychodynamic perspectives on personality theory. In M. Hersen, A. E. Kazdin, & A. S. Bellack (Eds.), *The clinical psychology handbook* (pp. 87–106). New York, NY: Pergamon Press.

Bohart, A. C. (2003). Person-centered psychotherapy and related experiential approaches. In A. S. Gurman & S. B. Messer (Eds.), *Essential psychotherapies* (2nd ed., pp. 107–148). New York, NY: Guilford.

Bohart, A. C., & Watson, J. C. (2011). Person-centered psychotherapy and related experiential approaches. In S. B. Messer, & A. S. Gurman (Eds.), *Essential psychotherapies* (3rd ed., pp. 223–260) New York, NY: The Guilford Press.

Borden, W. (2009). *Contemporary psychodynamic theory and practice.* Chicago, IL: Lyceum Books, Inc.

Bugental, J. F. T. (1995). Preliminary sketches for a short-term existential therapy. In K. J. Schneider & R. May (Eds.), *The psychology of existence: An integrative, clinical perspective* (pp. 261–264). New York, NY: McGraw-Hill.

Cook, J. M., & Biyanova, T. (2009). Influential psychotherapy figures, authors, and books: An internet survey. *Psychotherapy: Theory, Research, Practice, and Training, 46,* 42–51.

Curtis, R. C., & Hirsch, I. (2003). Relational approaches to psychoanalytic psychotherapy. In A. S. Gurman & S. B. Messer (Eds.), *Essential psychotherapies* (2nd ed., pp. 69–106). New York, NY: Guilford.

Curtis, R. C., & Hirsch, I. (2011). Relational psychoanalytic psychotherapy. In S. B. Messer & A. S. Gurman (Eds.), *Essential psychotherapies* (3rd ed., pp. 72–106). New York, NY: The Guilford Press.

Davanloo, H. L. (1994). *Basic principles and techniques in short-term dynamic psychotherapy.* Northdale, NJ: Jason Aronson, Inc.

Delisle, G. (2013). *Object relations in gestalt therapy.* London, UK: Karnac Books.

DeMause, L. (1987). Schreber and the history of childhood. *The Journal of Psychohistory, 15,* 423–430.

DeRobertis, E. M. (2013). Humanistic psychology: Alive in the 21st century? *Journal of Humanistic Psychology, 28,* 20–33.

DeYoung, P. A. (2003). *Relational psychotherapy: A primer.* New York, NY: Burnner-Routledge.

Diamond, M. J., & Christian, C. (Eds.). (2011). *The second century of psychoanalysis: Evolving perspectives on the therapeutic action.* London, UK: Karnac Books.

Eagle, M. N. (1984). *Recent developments in psychoanalysis: A critical evaluation.* Cambridge, MA: Harvard University Press.

Eagle, M. N. (2011). *From classical to contemporary psychoanalysis: A critique and integration.* New York, NY: Routledge.

Elzer, M., & Gerlach, A. (Eds.). (2013). *Psychoanalytic psychotherapy: A handbook.* London, UK: Karnac Books.

Erikson, E. H. (1946). *Ego development and historical change. The psychoanalytic study of the child* (Vol. 2, pp. 359–396). New York, NY: International Universities Press.

Fairbairn, W. R. D. (1952). *Psychoanalytic studies of the personality.* London, UK: Tavistock Publications/ Routledge & Kegan Paul.

Fancher, R. E. (1973). *Psychoanalytic psychology: The development of Freud's thought.* New York, NY: W. W. Norton.

Fine, R. (1971). *The healing of the mind: The technique of psychoanalytic psychotherapy.* New York, NY: David McKay.

Fischer, C. T. (1989). A life-centered approach to psychodiagnostics: Attending to lifeworld, ambiguity, and possibility. *Person-Centered Review, 4,* 163–170.

Fogel, G. I. (1993). A transitional phase in our understanding of the psychoanalytic process: A new look at Ferenszi and Rank. *Journal of the American Psychoanalytic Association, 41,* 585–602.

Fonagy, P., & Target, M. (2003). *Psychoanalytic theories: Perspectives from developmental psychology.* New York, NY: Brunner-Routledge.

Frank, E., & Levenson, J. C. (2011). *Interpersonal psychotherapy.* Washington, DC: American Psychological Association.

Frankl, V. (1967). *Psychotherapy and existentialism: Selected papers on logotherapy.* New York, NY: Washington Square Press.

Freud, A. (1936). *The ego and the mechanisms of defense. In The writings of Anna Freud* (Vol. 2, Revised Edition, 1966). New York: International Universities Press.

Freud, S. (1900). Freud, S. (1900). *The interpretation of dreams.* (Avon Edition, 1965). New York: Avon Books.

Freud, S. (1949). *An outline of psychoanalysis.* (J. Strachey, trans.). New York, NY: W. W. Norton.

Gabbard, G. O. (2005). *Psychodynamic psychiatry in clinical practice* (4th ed.). Washington, DC: American Psychiatric Publishing.

Gabbard, G. O. (2010). *Long-term psychodynamic psychotherapy: A basic text* (2nd ed.). Washington, DC: American Psychiatric Publishing.

Gastelum, E., Douglas, C. J., & Cabaniss, D. L. (2013). Teaching psychodynamic psychotherapy to psychiatric residents: An integrated approach. *Psychodynamic Psychiatry, 41,* 127–140.

Gendlin, E. T. (1996). *Focusing-oriented psychotherapy: A manual of the experiential method.* New York, NY: Guilford.

Gerber, A. J., Kocsis, J. H., Milrod, B. L., Roose, S. P., Barber, J. P., et al. (2011). A quality-based review of randomized controlled trials of psychodynamic psychotherapy. *American Journal of Psychiatry, 168,* 19–28.

Ginger, S., & Ginger, A. (2012). *A practical guide for the humanistic psychotherapist.* London, UK: Karnac Books.

Greenberg, L. S., Elliot, R. K., & Lietaer, G. (1994). Research on experiential psychotherapies. In A. E. Bergin & S. L. Garfield (Eds.), *Handbook of psychotherapy and behavior change* (pp. 509–512). New York, NY: Wiley.

Greenberg, L. S., Rice, L. N., & Elliott, R. (1993). *Facilitating emotional change: The moment-by-moment process.* New York, NY: Guilford Press.

Hartmann, H. (1958). *Ego psychology and the problem of adaptation.* New York, NY: International Universities Press.

Hergenhahn, B. R. (1994). *An introduction to theories of personality.* Englewood Cliffs, NJ: Prentice Hall.

Joseph, S., & Murphy, D. (2013). Person-centered approach, positive psychology, and relational helping. *Journal of Humanistic Psychology, 53,* 26–51.

Kahn, E. (1985). Heinz Kohut and Carl Rogers: A timely comparison. *American Psychologist, 40,* 893–904.

Kernberg, O. (1976). *Object relations, theory and clinical psychoanalysis.* New York, NY: Jason Aronson.

Klein, M. (1975). *The writings of Melanie Klein* (Vol. III). London, UK: Hogarth Press.

Kohut, H. (1977). *The restoration of the self.* New York, NY: International Universities Press.

Kohut, H. (1983). Selected problems of self-psychological theory. In J. D. Lichtenberg & S. Kaplan (Eds.), *Reflections on self psychology* (pp. 387–416). Hillsdale, NJ: Erlbaum.

Kutash, I. L. (1976). Psychoanalysis in groups: The primacy of the individual. *Current Issues in Psychoanalytic Practice, 1,* 29–42.

Ladd, P. D., & Churchill, A. M. (2012). *Person-centered diagnosis and treatment in mental health: A model for empowering clients.* Philadelphia, PA: Jessica Kingsley Publishers.

Levison, H., & Strupp, H. H. (1999). Recommendations for the future of training in brief dynamic psychotherapy. *Journal of Clinical Psychology, 55,* 385–391.

Lilienfeld, S. O. (2007). Psychological treatments that cause harm. *Perspectives on Psychological Science, 2,* 53–70.

Mahler, M. S., Pine, F., & Bergman, A. (1975). *The psychological birth of the human infant.* New York, NY: Basic Books.

Maslow, A. H. (1968). *Toward a psychology of being* (2nd ed.). New York, NY: Van Nostrand Reinhold.

May, R. (1969). *Love and will.* New York, NY: W. W. Norton.

May, R. (1981). *Freedom and destiny.* New York, NY: Norton.

McWilliams, N. (2004). *Psychoanalytic psychotherapy: A practitioner's guide.* New York, NY: Guilford.

Meador, B. D., & Rogers, C. R. (1973). Client-centered therapy. In R. Corsini (Ed.), *Current psychotherapies* (pp. 119–165). Itasca, IL: F. E. Peacock.

Messer, S. B., & Gurman, A. S. (Eds.). (2011). *Essential psychotherapies* (3rd ed.). New York, NY: The Guilford Press.

Miller, W. R., & Rollnick, S. (1998). *Motivational interviewing* (Vols. 1-7). [Video]. Albuquerque, NM: Horizon West Productions.

Murdock, N. L. (2004). *Theories of counseling and psychotherapy*. Upper Saddle River, NJ: Pearson.

Neimeyer, R. A., & Bridges, S. K. (2003). Postmodern approaches to psychotherapy. In A. S. Gurman & S. B. Messer (Eds.), *Essential psychotherapies* (2nd ed., pp. 272–316). New York, NY: Guilford.

Norcross, J. C., Vandenbos, G. R., & Freedheim, D. K. (Eds.). (2011). *History of psychotherapy: Continuity and change*. Washington, DC: American Psychological Association.

Perls, F. S. (1969). *Gestalt therapy verbatim*. Lafayette, CA: Real People Press.

Perls, F. S. (1970). Four lectures. In J. Fagan & I. L. Shepherd (Eds.), *Gestalt therapy now* (pp. 14–38). Palo Alto, CA: Science and Behavior Books.

Philippson, P. (2012). *Gestalt therapy: roots and branches—collected papers*. London, UK: Karnac Books.

Pine, F. (1990). *Drive, ego, object, and self*. New York, NY: Basic Books.

Portuges, S. H., & Hollander, N. C. (2011). The therapeutic action of resistance analysis: Interpersonalizing and socializing Paul Gray's close process attention technique. In M. J. Diamond & C. Christian (Eds.), *The second century of psychoanalysis: Evolving perspectives on the therapeutic action* (pp. 71–96). London, UK: Karnac Books.

Prochaska J. O., & Norcross, J. C. (2002). *Systems of psychotherapy: A trans-theoretical analysis* (5th ed.). Pacific Grove, CA: Brooks Cole.

Rapaport, D. (1951). A conceptual model of psychoanalysis. *Journal of Personality, 20*, 56–81.

Rogers, C. R. (1951). *Client-centered therapy*. Boston, MA: Houghton Mifflin.

Rogers, C. R. (1961). *On becoming a person*. Boston, MA: Houghton Mifflin.

Rogers, C. R. (1967/2003). *Client-centered therapy*. New York, NY: Constable & Robinson.

Sandell, R. (2012). Research on outcomes of psychoanalysis and psychoanalysis-derived psychotherapies. In G. O. Gabbard, B. E. Litowitz, & P. Williams (Eds.), *Textbook of psychoanalysis* (2nd ed., pp. 385–403). Arlington, VA: American Psychiatric Publishing.

Sayette, M. A., & Norcross, J. C. (2011). The heterogeneity of clinical psychology Ph.D. programs and the distinctiveness of APCS programs. *Clinical Psychology: Science and Practice, 18*, 4–11.

Sedgwick, D. (2013). *Introduction to Jungian psychotherapy: The therapeutic relationship*. New York, NY: Routledge.

Schneider, K. J. (2003). Existential-humanistic psychotherapies. In A. S. Gurman & S. B. Messer (Eds.), *Essential psychotherapies* (2nd ed., pp. 149–181). New York, NY: Guilford.

Schneider, K. J. (2008). *Existential-integrative psychotherapy: Guideposts to the core of practice*. New York, NY: Routledge.

Schneider, K. J., & Krug, O. T. (2010). *Existential-humanistic therapy*. Washington, DC: American Psychological Association.

Scholl, M. B., McGowan, A. S., & Hansen, J. T. (2012). *Humanistic perspectives on contemporary counseling issues*. New York, NY: Routledge.

Shedler, J. (2010). The efficacy of psychodynamic psychotherapy. *American Psychologist, 65*, 98–109.

Sommers-Flanagan, J., & Sommers-Flanagan, R. (2012) *Counseling and psychotherapy theories* (2nd ed.). Hoboken, NJ: Wiley & Sons.

Stekel, W. (2013). *Technique of analytical psychotherapy*. New York, NY: Crastre Press.

Stolorow, R. D. (1993). An intersubjective view of the therapeutic process. *Bulletin of the Menninger Clinic, 57*, 450–458.

Strupp, H. H. (1989). Psychotherapy: Can the practitioner learn from the researcher? *American Psychologist, 44*, 717–724.

Strupp, H. H., & Blinder, J. L. (1984). *Psychotherapy in a new key: A guide to time-limited dynamic psychotherapy*. New York, NY: Basic Books.

Summers, R. F., & Barber, J. P. (2009). *Psychodynamic therapy: A guide to evidence-based practice*. New York, NY: The Guilford Press.

Watson, J. C., Goldman, R. N., & Greenberg, L. S. (2011). Humanistic and experiential theories of psychotherapy. In J. C. Norcross, G. R. Vandenbos, & D. K. Freedheim (Eds.), *History of psychotherapy: Continuity and change* (pp. 141–172). Washington, DC: American Psychological Association.

Willock, B. (2007). *Comparative-integrative psychoanalysis: A relational perspective for the discipline's second century*. New York, NY: The Analytic Press.

Winnicott, D. W. (1965). *The maturational processes and the facilitating environment*. New York, NY: International Universities Press.

Wolitzky, D. L. (2003). The theory and practice of traditional psychoanalytic treatment. In A. S. Gurman & S. B. Messer (Eds.), *Essential psychotherapies* (2nd ed., pp. 244– 268). New York, NY: Guilford Press.

Wolitzky, D. L. (2011). Contemporary Freudian psychoanalytic psychotherapy. In S. B. Messer & A. S. Gurman (Eds.), *Essential psychotherapies* (3rd ed., pp. 33–71). New York, NY: The Guilford Press.

8 | BEHAVIORAL AND COGNITIVE-BEHAVIOR PSYCHOTHERAPIES

Chapter Preview

Here we describe a series of approaches to psychotherapy that grew from learning theory and from cognitive psychology. Behavior therapists rely on techniques designed to identify maladaptive behavior and change it. Cognitive therapists view faulty reasoning as the main cause of many disorders, so cognitive therapy is designed to change how clients think about events and about themselves. Despite certain differences, the behavioral and cognitive approaches are highly compatible and are often combined into various forms of cognitive-behavior therapy, one of today's most popular approaches to psychotherapy.

BEHAVIOR THERAPY

SECTION PREVIEW

Here we describe behavior therapy, which developed out of learning theories and research on learning. Applicable to numerous psychological problems, behavior therapy techniques are designed to help clients learn to change their problematic behaviors and/or the environmental circumstances that support those behaviors.

Behavior therapy is not a single method but rather a large collection of techniques designed to address people's psychological problems. Included are systematic desensitization, exposure therapies, relaxation training, biofeedback, assertiveness training, operant conditioning and other reinforcement-based treatments, sensate focus for sexual dysfunction, "bell-and-pad conditioning" to prevent bed-wetting, and many others (Antony & Roemer, 2011a). Some of these techniques, such as relaxation training, are applied in treatment programs for a wide variety of disorders; others, such as bell-and-pad conditioning for bed-wetting, were developed specifically for a particular type of problem. Behavioral techniques are used by theorists from a wide spectrum of clinical orientations to treat both children and adults.

When behavioral treatments began to take shape in the 1950s and 1960s, they relied mainly on the principles of classical and operant conditioning, focusing almost exclusively on clients' overt behaviors and the observable environmental conditions that accompanied them. As cognitive psychologists convincingly showed that people respond more to their perceptions of their environments than to their environments per se, behaviorally oriented clinicians began incorporating mental representations into their theories and practices. This "second wave" of behavior therapy was followed by a "third wave" characterized by a focus on the functional relations between people's internal representations and their overt behaviors (Antony & Roemer, 2011a; Fishman, Rego, Muller, 2011; Hayes, Folette, & Linehan, 2004). In short, behavior therapy has expanded to encompass what psychologists in cognitive, social, and biological psychology have learned about how people think and feel (Norcross, Vandenbos, & Freedheim, 2011). In this chapter we begin by describing the "first wave" of traditional behavioral therapy. Then we describe cognitive approaches, and we end with a discussion of the many variations of cognitive-behavioral approaches being employed today.

Theoretical Foundations

The key assumption underlying behavioral approaches to therapy is that the behaviors seen in psychological problems develop through the same laws of learning that influence the development of other behaviors. So behaviorists see personality, problems in personality development, and most behavior disorders not as "things" that people have but as reflections of how the laws of learning have influenced particular people to behave in particular situations. Our understanding of these laws of learning has emerged from research on classical conditioning, operant conditioning, and observational learning.

Classical conditioning occurs when a neutral stimulus (such as a musical tone) comes just before another stimulus (such as a pin-prick) that automatically triggers a reflexive response (such as a startle reaction). If the two stimuli are paired often enough, the startle reaction begins to occur in response to the previously neutral musical tone. This learning process usually develops gradually, though in some cases, such as when a small child is startled by a large barking dog, a classically conditioned fear response can occur very quickly and even become a phobia. *Operant conditioning* occurs when certain behaviors are strengthened or weakened by the rewards or punishments that follow those behaviors. For instance, a person who has had bad experiences at parties or other social situations will try to avoid such situations or leave them as soon as possible in order to reduce anxiety. These avoidance or escape behaviors are reinforced by the rewarding sense of relief and anxiety reduction that follows them. These behaviors thus become even more likely in the future, and over time the person may become socially crippled by fear, leading to all sorts of problems in dealing with group situations. But perhaps not in all group situations: the same socially anxious person who avoids parties might interact reasonably well with familiar coworkers. This phenomenon illustrates that the adaptive and maladaptive response patterns we learn can be associated with some situations but not others. When two situations are similar enough that they elicit the same response, *stimulus generalization* has occurred. Another way of saying this is that the person does not psychologically *discriminate* (i.e., recognize a difference) between the situations and instead responds to them as if they were the same. Thus, the child who was frightened by a large white dog may later react with fear to all large dogs, or maybe even to all dogs.

People learn many of their behaviors through direct experiences with classical conditioning and operant conditioning, but they also learn a lot by watching how others behave and what happens to them as a result. For example, the phenomena of *observational learning* and *vicarious conditioning* were demonstrated powerfully in Bandura and Ross's (1963) famous "Bobo doll" studies. In these studies, children who watched an adult being rewarded after behaving aggressively toward an inflatable "Bobo" doll were themselves significantly more aggressive when placed in a room with the doll than were children who saw nonaggressive behavior being modeled or saw an aggressive model being punished.

In short, according to the behavioral approach to personality and behavior disorder, normal and abnormal behavior can be explained by the same learning processes. The behavior therapist's task is to help clients learn how to modify problematic behaviors and/or learn new and more adaptive alternatives. As in most other approaches to therapy, the treatment process begins with assessment of the problem to be solved.

ASSESSMENT IN BEHAVIOR THERAPY Behavior therapy assessment is intended to gather detailed information about a client's problematic behaviors, the environmental circumstances under which those behaviors occur, and the reinforcers and other consequences that maintain the behaviors. The assessment process does not typically employ projective personality tests, diagnostic labels, or other traditional methods. Instead, behavior therapists perform a *functional analysis* or a *functional assessment* (Nelson & Hayes, 1986), which examines four key areas: stimulus, organism, response, and consequence (abbreviated SORC). Table 8.1 illustrates the kinds of information that is typically included in such an assessment. Assessment is narrowly focused on relevant problematic behaviors and is integrated with treatment goals (Iwata, DeLeon, & Roscoe, 2013; Spiegler & Guevremont, 2010).

Notice that Table 8.1 includes assessment of cognitions and emotions as well as of observable behaviors. Behaviorally oriented clinicians who adopt a strict behavioral view of disorder do not focus much on cognitive variables, but those who prefer a more comprehensive view of the causes of behavior place greater emphasis on the assessment of those variables (Antony & Roemer, 2011a). As described later, these cognitive and cognitive-behavioral clinicians see their clients'

TABLE 8.1 Areas Assessed in Functional Analysis of Behavior

Area Assessed	General Examples	Specific Examples for a Client Diagnosed with Bulimia (Binging/Purging Type)
Stimulus	Antecedent conditions and environmental triggers that elicit behavior	Watching television, watching commercials about food, selecting clothes to wear, walking by the refrigerator, smelling chocolate
Organism	Internal physiological responses, emotions, and cognitions	Sensation of hunger, anxiety, concern about weight, worry about being fat, anger over being deprived
Response	Overt behavior engaged in by the person	Avoidance of food for a period of minutes to about an hour, followed by binging
Consequences	What happens as a result of the behavior	Satiation, reduction of anxiety, increase in guilt

learned patterns of thinking as important causes of normal and abnormal behavior, causes that must be examined carefully and, if maladaptive, changed.

Behavior therapists are especially likely to use objectively scored quantitative assessment methods such as structured interviews, objective psychological tests, and a variety of behavioral rating forms. These measures are used partly to establish the precise nature of a client's problems and also to establish an empirical baseline level of maladaptive responding. As therapy progresses, the same measures may be administered again in order to assess and document client progress (examples of such repeated assessment are shown in Figure 3.3 in Chapter 3, "Basic Features of Clinical Assessment," and in Figure 11.3 in Chapter 11, "Clinical Child Psychology"). Especially if required for insurance purposes, behavioral clinicians may assign a DSM diagnosis to their clients, but diagnosis is generally not the focus of behavioral assessment.

Because behavioral treatments developed within an empirical tradition, there is a strong commitment to research among behavioral practitioners. Behavior therapists believe that therapy methods should be guided by the results of research on learning. They also place a high value on the evaluation of treatment techniques. Behavior therapists are particularly likely to employ assessment instruments and treatment techniques whose efficacy has been established by the results of controlled research.

THE ROLE OF THE THERAPIST   Behavior therapists recognize the importance of the therapeutic relationship, so they are empathic and supportive in response to clients' feelings of anxiety, shame, hopelessness, distress, or confusion. However, in contrast to humanistic therapists, behavior therapists believe that the client–therapist relationship merely provides the context in which specific techniques can operate to create change. Therapeutic benefits occur when clients make changes in their environments (e.g., by reducing exposure to triggers), internal responses (e.g., by learning relaxation to lower levels of arousal), and overt behaviors (e.g., by practicing conversational skills). Accordingly, behavior therapists focus actively and directively on these factors in therapy (Newman, 2013; Spiegler & Guevremont, 2009). They also play an educational role, explaining the theory behind what they do in ways the client can understand. Ultimately, however, they hope to establish the client as collaborator in a systematic analysis of behavior and its consequences.

The Goals of Behavior Therapy

The primary goal of the behavior therapist is to help the client modify maladaptive overt behaviors as well as the cognitions, physical changes, and emotions that accompany those behaviors. Treatment can proceed without exploring early childhood experiences, unconscious processes, inner conflicts, or the like. In short, in behavior therapy, it is not critical to know how a maladaptive behavior disorder originated; it is enough to know how it is being maintained and how it can be changed.

Clinical Applications

Although built around a general learning model, behavior therapy is applied in a wide variety of treatment packages, each tailored to address particular sets of problematic behaviors. We do not have space to describe all the behavioral treatment techniques that can be combined in these packages, but in the following sections we introduce several of the most prominent and widely used examples.

RELAXATION TRAINING   One of the basic techniques behavior therapists use with anxious clients is *progressive relaxation training* (PRT) (Bernstein, Borkovec, & Hazlett-Stevens, 2000), an abbreviated version of a method pioneered by Edmund Jacobson in 1938 and popularized in the 1960s by Joseph Wolpe (1958). PRT involves tensing and then releasing various groups of muscles while focusing on the sensations of relaxation that follow. (You can get an idea of what the training feels like by clenching your fist for about 5 seconds and then abruptly releasing the tension.) By practicing, many clients can learn to relax themselves and lower their arousal level. As clients become better at relaxing, the process is shortened. Sometimes specific breathing exercises are included as well. This training is occasionally used by itself, but more often it is used in conjunction with other behavioral and cognitive techniques. Relaxation training is effective for several problems seen in behavioral medicine, such as hypertension, headache, insomnia, and negative effects of chemotherapy. When combined with the exposure treatments discussed below, it also contributes to improvement in people with mild to moderate depression, and with several types of phobia (Hazlett & Bernstein, 2012).

In an effort to understand the mechanisms underlying relaxation training, investigators have compared it to mindfulness training (which is discussed below and in Chapter 12). Both techniques encourage nonjudgmental awareness of bodily experiences, and both have few, if any, negative side effects. Early indications suggest that muscle relaxation may work largely by producing decentering and acceptance of one's experiences, but that these cognitive and attitudinal skills are taught more explicitly in mindfulness training. Therefore, though both have beneficial effects, mindfulness might be the preferred form of training for certain disorders (Hayes-Skelton, Usmani, Lee, Roemer, & Orsillo, 2011; Peterson, Hatch, Hryshko-Mullen, & Cigrang, 2012; Roemer, Orsillo, & Salters-Pednaulet, 2008).

SYSTEMATIC DESENSITIZATION   The antianxiety treatment known as *systematic desensitization* (SD) was developed in 1958 by Joseph Wolpe, a South African psychiatrist. SD was based on research with cats that had been repeatedly shocked in a special cage. They resisted being put in that cage and refused to eat while there. Wolpe reasoned that if conditioned anxiety could inhibit eating, perhaps eating might inhibit conditioned anxiety through the principle of *reciprocal inhibition*. According to Wolpe (1958): "If a response antagonistic to anxiety can be made to occur in the presence of anxiety-evoking stimuli so that it is accompanied by a complete or partial suppression of the anxiety responses, the bond between these stimuli and the anxiety responses will be weakened" (p. 71). In fact, when he "counterconditioned" the cats' fear by hand-feeding them in cages that were placed closer and closer to where their anxiety had been learned, most animals showed greatly diminished emotional reactions when placed in the previously feared cage.

Applying these SD methods to persons who suffered phobias, Wolpe used progressive relaxation training instead of food to create responses that are incompatible with anxiety. First, clients are taught progressive relaxation techniques. The next step is to create a *graduated hierarchy* of situations that the client finds increasingly anxiety-provoking. The content and ordering of these items (which are later to be imagined or experienced "live") are guided by the client so that each elicits just a bit more anxiety than the one before it (see Table 8.2). Completion of a hierarchy typically takes three to five sessions, though it is possible to finish a short hierarchy in a single meeting.

After relaxation training and hierarchy construction are complete, desensitization itself begins. Clients first relax and then imagine an item at the bottom of their hierarchy. If anxiety occurs, the item is terminated and client is given time to regain complete relaxation. The same item is then presented again until it no longer creates distress, even after longer presentations. This sequence is continued until the client can calmly imagine all items in the hierarchy. It is now recognized that exposure to real, *in vivo*, stimuli works better than exposure to imagined stimuli, and that it is primarily through the learning process known as *extinction*—the weakening of unreinforced responses—that phobias are reduced in desensitization (Antony & Roemer, 2011b).

TABLE 8.2 A Desensitization Hierarchy

Desensitization hierarchies are lists of increasingly fear-provoking stimuli or situations that clients visualize while using relaxation methods to remain calm. Here are a few items from the beginning and the end of a hierarchy that was used to help a client overcome fear of flying.

1. You are reading a newspaper and notice an ad for an airline.
2. You are watching a television program that shows a group of people boarding a plane.
3. Your boss tells you that you need to take a business trip by air.
4. You are in your bedroom packing your suitcase for your trip.

.
.
.

12. Your plane begins to move as you hear the flight attendant say, "Be sure your seat belt is securely fastened."
13. You look at the runway as the plane is readied for takeoff.
14. You look out the window as the plane rolls down the runway.
15. You look out the window as the plane leaves the ground.

Systematic desensitization can be very effective in the treatment of conditioned maladaptive anxiety. Indeed, Gordon Paul (1969), a pioneer in research on SD, concluded that "for the first time in the history of psychological treatments, a specific therapeutic package reliably produced measurable benefits for clients across a broad range of distressing problems in which anxiety was of fundamental importance" (p. 159). However, SD may be less successful in treating more general and complicated anxiety-related problems, such as panic disorder and obsessive-compulsive disorder. For these more complex problems, behavioral therapists have found that treatments involving directly exposing clients to feared stimuli may be the treatment of choice (Barlow & Wolfe, 1981; Farmer & Chapman, 2008).

EXPOSURE AND RESPONSE PREVENTION TECHNIQUES   *Exposure treatments* entail direct exposure to frightening stimuli, but the idea here is not to prevent anxiety. Instead, exposure to feared stimuli is arranged so that anxiety occurs and continues until—because no harm comes to the client—it eventually disappears through extinction.

In a method called *flooding*, for example, clients who are crippled by fear of dirt or infection might be asked to spend long periods of time touching and holding a variety of everyday items that they are afraid might be "contaminated." Exposure times must be long enough—hours, if necessary—for anxiety to dissipate; exposure should not be terminated while the client is still anxious because the resulting anxiety reduction would reinforce avoidance behavior.

Exposure treatments are especially effective in cases of obsessive-compulsive disorder (in which clients experience *obsessions*—persistently intrusive and fearful thoughts—and engage in *compulsions*, which are repeated behavioral rituals designed to reduce or prevent anxiety stemming from their obsessions). In such cases, exposure is usually accompanied by *response prevention*, meaning that clients are not allowed to perform the rituals they normally use to reduce anxiety (Antony & Roemer, 2011a; Lam & Steketee, 2001). The idea is that with continued exposure to these stimuli without harmful consequences, the stimuli gradually become less anxiety provoking—in other words, the anxiety is gradually extinguished (see Table 8.3).

Exposure techniques are also used extensively with agoraphobia, a severe disorder involving fear of being away from home or some other safe place, or of being in a public place—such as a theater—from which escape might be difficult. Exposure treatments are also used for the panic attacks that often precede the development of agoraphobia, for binge craving in bulimia, and for other problems (see Hersen, 2002; Zalta & Foa, 2012).

Exposure therapies appear to be more effective when certain guidelines are followed. These include making the exposure predictable by putting the intensity and duration of exposure under the client's control, encouraging clients to tolerate somewhat longer and more intense exposure (short of being overwhelming), spacing exposures close together, varying the

TABLE 8.3 Exposure Treatment of Obsessive-Compulsive Disorder

Here is an excerpt from a treatment session in which a client's obsessions about contamination and resulting compulsive cleaning rituals are treated with exposure methods. Notice how the therapist guides and encourages the client to confront a frightening situation (a dead animal by the side of a road) and to stay in contact with it until anxiety begins to subside.

THERAPIST: (Outside the office.) There it is, behind the car. Let's go and touch the curb and street next to it. I won't insist that you touch it directly because it's a bit smelly, but I want you to step next to it and touch it with the sole of your shoe.

CLIENT: Yuck! It's really dead. It's gross!

T: Yeah, it is a bit gross, but it's also just a dead cat if you think about it plainly. What harm can it cause?

C: I don't know. Suppose I got germs on my hand?

T: What sort of germs?

C: Dead cat germs.

T: What kind are they?

C: I don't know. Just germs.

T: Like the bathroom germs that we've already handled?

C: Sort of. People don't go around touching dead cats.

T: They also don't go running home to shower or alcohol the inside of their car. It's time to get over this. Now, come on over and I'll do it first. (*Patient follows.*) OK. Touch the curb and the street, here's a stone you can carry with you and a piece of paper from under its tail. Go ahead, take it.

C: (*Looking quite uncomfortable.*) Ugh!

T: We'll both hold them. Now, touch it to your front and your skirt and your face and hair. Like this. That's good. What's your anxiety level?

C: Ick! Ninety-nine. I'd say 100 but it's just short of panic. If you weren't here, it'd be 100.

T: You know from past experience that this will be much easier in a while. Just stay with it and we'll wait here. You're doing fine.

C: (*A few minutes pass in which she looks very upset.*) Would you do this if it wasn't for me?

T: Yes, if this were my car and I dropped my keys here, I'd just pick them up and go on.

C: You wouldn't have to wash them?

T: No. Dead animals aren't delightful but they're part of the world we live in. What are the odds that we'll get ill from this?

C: Very small I guess . . . I feel a little bit better than at first. It's about 90 now.

T: Good! Just stay with it now.

The session continues for another 45 minutes or until anxiety decreases substantially. During this period, conversation focuses generally on the feared situation and the client's reactions to it. The therapist inquires about the client's anxiety level approximately every 10 minutes.

T: How do you feel now?

C: Well, it is easier, but I sure don't feel great.

T: Can you put a number on it?

C: About 55 or 60 I'd say.

T: You worked hard today. You must be tired. Let's stop now. I want you to take this stick and pebble with you so that you continue to be contaminated. You can keep them in your pocket and touch them frequently during the day. I want you to contaminate your office at work and your apartment with them. Touch them to everything around, including everything in the kitchen, chairs, your bed, and the clothes in your dresser. Oh, also, I'd like you to drive your car past this spot on your way to and from work. Can you do that?

C: I suppose so. The trouble is going home with all this dirt.

T: Why don't you call Ken and plan to get home after he does so he can be around to help you. Remember, you can always call me if you have any trouble.

C: Yeah. That's a good idea. I'll just leave work after he does. OK. See you tomorrow.

Source: From Steketee G., & Foa, E. B. (1985). Obsessive-compulsive disorder. In D. H. Barlow (Ed.), *Clinical handbook of psychological disorders: A step-by-step treatment manual* (pp. 69–144). New York, NY: Guilford. Copyright 1985 by Guilford Press. Adapted with permission.

kinds of exposure (e.g., different snakes), and doing exposures in varied contexts or settings (Antony & Roemer, 2011b).

VIRTUAL REALITY AND ONLINE EXPOSURE   As already noted, exposure treatments are especially effective when clients are carefully exposed to real, rather than imagined, items in their desensitization hierarchies (Chambless, 1990; McGlynn, Moore, Lawyer, & Karg, 1999). However, exposing clients to real situations, such as heights, air travel, or highway situations, can be difficult or expensive, and precise calibration of the desired level of exposure can be difficult to achieve. Computer-generated simulations of feared environments now offer a useful alternative. In *virtual reality (VR) exposure treatments*, clients can be exposed to carefully monitored levels of almost any stimulus situation. Head-mounted displays can now create surprisingly realistic images that respond to wearers' movements, thus immersing them in a virtual reality that can be carefully controlled. For example, clients with fears of heights can experience standing on bridges of gradually increasing heights, on outdoor balconies at higher and higher floors, and in glass elevators as they rise several stories (Meyerbröker & Emmelkamp, 2011; Rothbaum, 2011). Virtual reality treatments also have the advantage of being able to alter the contexts in which exposure to a feared stimulus takes place. By exposing spider phobic clients, for example, to different kinds of spiders in multiple situations, the gains made in phobia treatments generalize and desensitization is more complete (Shiban, Pauli, & Mühleberger, 2013).

VR technology has been helpful in the treatment of a variety of anxiety disorders, and the range of its applications continues to expand. For instance, VR technology has recently been used to help persons with substance abuse problems reduce their responsiveness to external cues or triggers that lead to craving (Rothbaum, 2006). A meta-analysis of 23 studies showed that clients receiving VR treatments did far better than wait-list controls, had results comparable to other exposure treatments, and that the results were stable over time (Opris et al., 2011). While the technology is promising, it is not without extra cost, so many clinicians are awaiting the results of controlled trials to see which applications of VR treatment achieve results that are cost effective when compared with standard *in vivo* exposure treatments (Price & Anderson, 2007).

Exposure treatments can also be delivered online where, as with VR treatments, exposure can be realistic, carefully monitored, and precisely calibrated. Preliminary evidence suggests that such interventions have promise, though, as is the case in many online applications, completion rates may be lower than those seen in face-to-face treatment (Gros, Yoder, Tuerk, Lozano, & Acierno, 2011; Matthews, Scanlan, & Kirby, 2010).

SOCIAL SKILLS TRAINING   Some psychological disorders may develop partly because people lack the social skills necessary for satisfying interpersonal relationships and other social reinforcers. If their skill deficits are severe, these people can become demoralized, anxious, angry, or alienated. Accordingly, behavioral therapists often include *social skills training* in the treatment of adult disorders such as schizophrenia, depression, anxiety, and a variety of childhood disorders, including delinquency, attention deficit hyperactivity disorder, autistic spectrum disorders, and even behavior problems resulting from fetal alcohol syndrome (see Kinnaman & Bellack, 2012).

Social skills training encompasses many techniques, from teaching persons how to shake hands and make eye contact to ordering food in a restaurant and engaging in conversations. *Assertiveness training* is a popular technique, especially with adults whose inability to effectively express their needs and wishes leads to resentment, aggression, or depression. All too often, these people know what they would *like* to say and do in various social situations but, because of thoughts like "I have no right to make a fuss" or "He won't like me if I object," they suffer in silence. Assertiveness training is designed to (a) teach clients how to express themselves appropriately if they do not already have the skills to do so, and/or (b) eliminate cognitive obstacles to clear self-expression. Although initially focused on training in the "refusal skills" many clients need to ward off unreasonable requests, assertiveness training is now also aimed at promoting a broader range of social skills, including making conversation, engaging in interpersonal problem solving, and appropriately responding to emotional provocations (e.g., Tisdell & St. Lawrence, 1988). Because of its demonstrated effectiveness, social skills training has become a standard component of broader treatments for schizophrenia, depression, and several other disorders (Kurtz & Mueser, 2008; Thase, 2012).

MODELING   As already noted, imitation—known in clinical psychology as modeling or observational learning—is a very important mechanism in the development of human behavior (Bandura, 1969). In fact, learning through modeling is usually more efficient than learning through direct reinforcement or punishment. (Imagine if everyone had to be hit by a car before knowing how to cross streets safely!) Observing the consequences of a model's behavior can also inhibit or disinhibit an observer's imitative behavior (e.g., we are unlikely to pet a dog that just bit someone, and we are more likely to cross against a red light after watching someone else do so).

Modeling has been used in the treatment of many clinical problems, including social withdrawal among adults and children, obsessive-compulsive behaviors, unassertiveness, antisocial conduct, physical aggressiveness, and autism spectrum disorders (Rosenthal & Steffek, 1991). It is also commonly used to treat fears. The simplest modeling approach involves having a client observe live or videorecorded models fearlessly and successfully perform behaviors that the client avoids. For example, a dog-phobic client could observe a model interacting happily with a dog; a height-phobic client could watch someone calmly riding an escalator without experiencing any negative consequences. In a common variant of this basic modeling treatment, called *participant modeling*, the client first observes live models, then makes guided, gradual contact with the feared object or situation under controlled and protected circumstances.

BEHAVIORAL ACTIVATION AND BEHAVIORAL REHEARSAL   To help clients develop, solidify, and gain confidence in the new skills they are learning in behavior therapy, behavior therapists establish practice sessions and situations whose demands are minimal, thus maximizing the client's chances of early success. Some clients are pessimistic about these sessions because they believe that their behavior cannot change until their emotions do, but therapists who emphasize behavioral activation contest this belief (Antony & Roemer, 2011b). The idea behind behavioral activation is to help clients recognize their tendency to fear and avoid making changes and then to help them engage in more positive and adaptive behaviors. For instance, if a client is contemplating a behavioral task that seems complex or overwhelming, such as applying for a new job, the behavior therapist will help the client break the task into easier steps (e.g., making a phone call to inquire about openings, driving to pick up an application, filling out the first page of the application, etc.). With properly *graded task assignments*, the client's sense of mastery can grow.

These assignments can be carried out in the client's natural environment, but in cases where clients are not quite ready for "the real thing," the therapist will ask the client to rehearse the new behaviors in the therapy session. These practice sessions, in which client and therapist role-play various kinds of situations and interactions, can help clients fine-tune their approaches, anticipate reactions from others, prepare responses to various scenarios, and receive feedback from the therapist on how they are doing.

AVERSION THERAPY AND PUNISHMENT   *Aversion therapy* is a set of learning-based techniques in which painful or unpleasant stimuli are used to decrease the probability of unwanted behaviors such as drug abuse, alcoholism, overeating, smoking, and disturbing sexual practices. Following classical conditioning principles, most aversion methods pair a noxious stimulus such as electric shock with stimuli that normally elicit problematic behavior. So, for example, an alcoholic is exposed to a foul odor as he sits at a simulated bar, looking at a glass of scotch. Ideally, continued pairings should decrease the attractiveness of the eliciting stimuli until the unwanted behavior is reduced, if not eliminated. The same goal can be sought via the use of punishment in operant conditioning programs. Here, electric shock or some other aversive stimulus is delivered just after the client performs the problematic behavior (e.g., immediately after taking a drink of alcohol).

As you might imagine, there is debate about the ethics of aversion and punishment methods, as well as about their effectiveness. Accordingly, these techniques are used less often than other behavior therapies, and then only as a last resort to control dangerous behavior (such as self-injury) that has not responded to less drastic methods.

TABLE 8.4 A Sampling of Behavior Therapy Techniques

Technique	Description
Progressive relaxation training	Clients learn to lower arousal and reduce stress by tensing and releasing specific muscle groups.
Systematic desensitization	Clients gradually substitute a new learned response (e.g., relaxation) for an old maladaptive response (e.g., fear of an object or situation) by moving stepwise through a hierarchy of situations involving the fear.
Exposure and response prevention	As clients are exposed for long periods to situations that they would normally avoid, the anxiety associated with those situations gradually extinguishes.
Virtual reality exposure	Realistic, computer-based simulations of troublesome situations provide less expensive and better calibrated exposures.
Social skills training	Clients with social skills deficits are trained in specific behaviors such as communication, dating, eating at a restaurant, and assertiveness.
Aversion conditioning and punishment	An aversive stimulus (e.g., shock, nausea) is associated with a stimulus (e.g., alcohol) that currently produces a pleasurable but problematic response (e.g., drunkenness). A problematic response, such as self-injury, is immediately followed by a shock or other unpleasant stimulus.
Acceptance and commitment therapy	A form of therapy that teaches clients to learn to be mindful of, to label, and to accept their thoughts and feelings with the goal of developing more flexible responses based on their values.
Shaping and graded task assignments	When behaviors to be learned are complex, clinicians break those behaviors down into simpler steps that can be successfully accomplished, gradually building to the complex behavioral goal.
Contingency contracting	A form of contingency management, contingency contracting involves a formal, often written agreement between client and therapist regarding the client's behaviors.
Behavioral rehearsal and homework	Clients agree to practice and record behaviors between sessions. The desired behavior(s) is often practiced during a therapy session before the client is given homework.
Response costs	This punishment contingency involves the loss of a reward or privilege following some undesirable behavior.
Token economies	Clients are reinforced with tokens that act as currency to purchase desired rewards (e.g., snacks, television time) when they perform designated behaviors.
Biofeedback	Clients are provided direct feedback of their recorded physiological responses (e.g., heart rate, blood pressure, muscle tension).

There are numerous other techniques that have developed out of the behavioral tradition. Some of them, such as acceptance and commitment therapy and dialectical behavior therapy, are integrative psychotherapy approaches that, though behavioral in origin, borrow liberally from other orientations. These treatments are discussed in more detail in Chapter 9, "Alternative Modes of Clinical Intervention." Others are not therapies in themselves, but rather specific components of behaviorally oriented treatments. Table 8.4 summarizes some of the more commonly employed behavioral techniques.

Case Example

Here is an example of how one team of therapists applied behavior therapy in the case of maladaptive behavior in a child and in the child's family.

As long as he can remember, Robert had problems with being a bit too passive and lacking assertiveness, especially in conflict situations. These challenges were part of what lead to the break-up of his marriage; his wife called him a "wimp" and a "doormat." She left Robert and their then 2-year-old daughter, Ella, and moved out of the country. In order to get help with raising Ella, Robert moved in with his parents. Over the next two years, Ella's behavior became increasingly disturbing. Now 4-years-old, she was refusing to follow directions, screaming if she did not get what she wanted, and breaking toys when she got angry.

As a single father, Robert felt bad that Ella did not have a strong female role model in her life and Robert's parents felt especially bad that Ella no longer had contact with her mother. Robert and his parents tried to compensate for Ella's loss by giving her anything she wanted and they all tended to dote on her. This pattern was especially true of Robert's parents, who were very lenient and who almost never said "no" to Ella. Like any bright child, Ella figured out that if she could not get what she wanted from her father, then she would go to her grandmother and ask. A typical example was when Ella was jumping on the couch and Robert said "No Ella, don't jump on the couch—you might fall down and get hurt." Robert remained firm and did not allow Ella to jump on the couch even when she begged and cried. Later the same day, Robert noticed that his mother let Ella jump on the couch even though his mother knew that he did not allow it. In the past, Robert used to be lenient with Ella too, but he was trying to be more consistent with limits in order to improve Ella's behavior. Robert now realized that he needed his mother to become more consistent, but he was worried about how to share his wishes with her in a way that would not upset her or hurt her feelings, so he did not say anything. Ella continued to get her way with her grandmother and her negative behaviors continued to get worse.

The therapist who worked with the family realized that she needed to help Robert develop assertiveness skills so that he could communicate effectively with his mother. First, the therapist and Robert agreed on that general goal and identified how Robert would like to communicate with his mother. Then they turned this general goal into a clear statement. For example, Robert would make a statement that he would like to say to his mother and the therapist would give feedback on what he was actually communicating. This process continued until both Robert and the therapist felt that Robert's statements would be effective with his mother.

Robert started by saying, "Mom, I would like to speak with you about Ella's behavior and how she keeps pushing us until she gets her way. We shouldn't always give in to her demands." Part of this statement was appropriate (i.e., Robert mentioned a specific aspect of the problem), but part of the statement was not helpful because it did not give Robert's mother direct feedback on what she needed to change. In the past, when Robert tried this strategy, his mother would say "Oh yes, dear. I completely agree," but then would continue to indulge Ella.

Robert ultimately came up with a better plan and practiced the following statements with the therapist, while pretending to speak to his mother. "Thank you for helping me raise Ella. You mean the world to us. With the help of my therapist, I have a new strategy for dealing with Ella's behavior when she tries to get away with things that she knows are wrong. For example, when she jumps on the couch, I say 'No' and even when she begs and cries, I remain firm with this decision. The thing is, I need your help with this plan. So, when you hear limits that I've set with Ella, you need to honor those limits and follow them with Ella—even if you don't agree completely. Do you think you can do that? Because, I really appreciate all of your help with Ella and I know that with both you and me being on the same team—we'll be able to help Ella improve her behavior now and when she is older." The therapist and Robert agreed that these statements would be much more effective than the initial statements because they provide clear and direct guidance for the mother, and also start and end on a positive note—thereby making the mother more likely to "hear" the feedback and not become defensive.

After Robert practiced the statements a few more times with the therapist, he and the therapist role-played the conversation that might ensue in case the mother did not react positively. In this way, the therapist could show the mother's potential negative reactions (such as being defensive or getting angry) and help Robert brainstorm on how to react while he is still in the safe and protected environment of the therapist's office. In fact, the therapist asked Robert to describe the worst, best, and most likely outcome of his upcoming conversation with his mother and they role-played all three possible scenarios (starting with the best outcome in order to build Robert's confidence). Once both Robert and the therapist felt confident about Robert's strategies, he was given the homework assignment of discussing this topic with his mother.

Because he knew that his mother is not very open to discussions when she is hungry or in a hurry, Robert strategically decided to speak with his mother after brunch on Sunday, when she would likely be relaxed and when Ella would likely be taking a nap. If his mother reacted negatively to the initiation of the topic, Robert planned to apologize for bringing up the topic at that time, thank his mother for all of her help, and say that he will speak with her about the issue at another time that is more convenient. With his new-found confidence, you can bet that Robert will follow-through with his mother on this conversation.

Robert's case illustrates several important features of behavior therapy: (a) the focus of therapy is on *specific problems* as opposed to, for instance, personality change or self-concept; (b) *thorough assessment* of problems and their contexts is required for each client; (c) therapists help clients primarily by facilitating *changes in behavior;* (d) behavior change recommendations are *carefully planned in collaboration with clients* to maximize the chances for success. Another feature perhaps not as evident from Robert's case is that (e) behavior therapists *help clients generalize newly learned adaptive behaviors.* For instance, if Robert learns to be appropriately assertive with his mother about Ella, he will have a greater chance of using assertiveness skills with her, and with others, about other issues.

A number of sources provide much more detail about behavior therapy techniques (e.g., Antony & Roemer, 2011a,b; Corey, 2013; Emmelkamp, 2013; Hersen, 2002; Miller, Rathus, Linehan, & Swenson, 2006; Murdock, 2004; O'Donahue & Fisher, 2012; Spiegler & Guveremont, 2011).

SECTION SUMMARY

Behavior therapy developed around the middle of the last century as an application of learning principles to ameliorate psychological problems. Behavior therapists employ behavioral assessment and/or functional analysis to understand problematic behavior and the specific situations under which it occurs. They then employ a wide variety of learning-based treatments, some of which are widely applicable and some of which were developed to address specific disorders or problem behaviors.

COGNITIVE THERAPY

SECTION PREVIEW

Cognitive therapy relies on the assumption that cognitions mediate between environmental events, on one hand, and behavior and emotion on the other. First developed for treating depression, cognitive therapy has grown and been applied to many disorders. The key concept in cognitive therapy is that errors in thinking cause psychological distress. Cognitive therapists work to help clients identify, challenge, and replace those errors.

All therapeutic interventions involve thought processes, but the cognitive therapies are specifically directed toward identifying and changing clients' maladaptive cognitions. These cognitions may include a client's beliefs, causal explanations, expectations, schemas, self-statements, and problem-solving strategies.

Theoretical Foundations

We have seen that behavior therapists originally tended to focus primarily on modifying a client's overt behaviors and/or the environmental situations in which those behaviors occur. By the 1970s, however, many behaviorally oriented theorists had begun to stress the importance of cognitions and "self-statements" as mediators between environmental events and behaviors (Bandura, 1977; A. T. Beck, 1976; Ellis, 1973; Meichenbaum, 1977; Mischel, 1973). At around the same time, cognitive theorists in other areas of psychology were making significant contributions to our understanding of human memory, judgment, problem solving, and social interactions. It became clear that an understanding of psychological functioning that did not include cognitions was incomplete.

As described in Chapter 2, pioneering figures such as Albert Ellis and Aaron Beck advanced many of the key ideas in cognitive therapy. These include the notions that 1) it is not events, but rather our interpretations of events that produce our responses, including maladaptive ones, 2) our interpretations can be accurate or inaccurate, adaptive or maladaptive, 3) inaccurate and maladaptive interpretations result from prior experiences and are often patterned and habitual, and 4) inaccurate and maladaptive thoughts often occur automatically and lead to a variety of negative emotions and problematic behaviors.

COGNITIVE MEDIATION   Perhaps the most basic notion in cognitive therapy is that normal and abnormal behavior is triggered by our cognitive interpretation of events, not by the events themselves. A cognitive model would suggest, then, that every event is followed by an appraisal—a cognitive response—that then shapes our emotional and behavioral responses to that event.

Imagine receiving an invitation to a party where you know there will be lots of strangers. What is your cognitive appraisal of this event? If your first thought is "Great. I'll be able to meet some new people," your emotional response is likely to be positive (anticipation, excitement), and your behavioral response will be to accept the invitation. But if your cognitive appraisal is "Hmm, I won't know a soul there; I'll probably feel awkward and won't know what to say," your emotional response is likely to be negative (e.g., dread, anxiety, shyness), and your behavioral response might be to make up an excuse not to attend. In other words, the same event can produce drastically different reactions depending on what thoughts intervene (see Figure 8.1).

REALISM   It may have occurred to you that cognitive mediation is similar to the idea of constructivism in humanistic and some psychodynamic approaches, both of which stress that the client's reality is what matters most. But there is an important difference. Where constructivism argues that an objective, external reality either does not exist or is not objectively knowable, cognitive therapy is based on a *realist model* of reality. In this model, external events happen whether they are perceived or not, and the various cognitions that mediate between events and emotions can therefore be evaluated as accurate or inaccurate, useful or not useful. As Dobson (2012) says, ". . . human adjustment can also be defined as the extent to which the individual accurately appraises his or her environment and is therefore able to cope with the demands of that environment" (p. 11).

SCHEMAS   With many possible mediating thoughts available to us, what determines which ones we use? According to cognitive psychologists, our thoughts are guided by our *schemas*, also called *schematas*, the organized knowledge structures that influence how we perceive, interpret, and recall information. For instance, the first time a child goes to McDonalds, he or she may not know how to understand the event except at a very basic level (e.g., "mom takes me somewhere to eat"). However, after a few trips, the child will have constructed a fairly detailed understanding that involves knowledge of the setting and of the normal sequences of events and actions that take place there. In effect, the child has internalized a detailed set of beliefs and expectations about how things happen—a "going to McDonalds" schema. Schemas can be built around actions, objects, persons, and situations; they can be helpful guides in everyday life. They tell us that we can expect help from a police officer, that dark alleys can be dangerous, and that you can buy toothpaste at the supermarket. They can also create problems, as when schemas lead to inaccurate stereotypes about particular categories of people or things.

Schemas are of particular interest to cognitive therapists because they serve as filters that influence how persons perceive themselves and their relations to the world. Thus, a depressed person who always feels unworthy is likely to interpret new information in ways consistent with that schema. So, if someone mentions she is going to lunch and follows it with, "Would

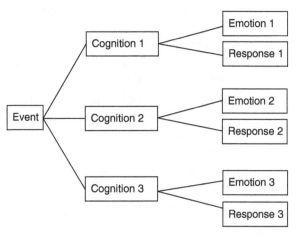

FIGURE 8.1 Cognitive Mediation. Our thoughts about events, rather than the events themselves, shape our feelings and behaviors

you like to come along?" the depressed person is likely to think, "She only asked because she feels sorry for me or because she feels socially obligated—she really doesn't want to have lunch with me. I'll probably sit there and feel awkward, not knowing what to say." People who are guided by such a schemas are typically aware of the negative emotions they feel, but may not be fully aware of having engaged in negative schema-based thinking that led to that emotion. Why should this be?

THE ROLE OF AUTOMATIC THOUGHTS   The cognitive approach strongly emphasizes the habitual nature of some thoughts, including many maladaptive thoughts. Negative schema-driven thoughts can occur so quickly that we are not consciously aware of having them, let alone of being influenced by them. In this respect, the cognitive approach overlaps somewhat with the psychodynamic approach: Both propose that important mental events can take place without the client's conscious awareness. For cognitive therapists, however, these nonconscious cognitions are not deeply buried, nor are they made inaccessible by defense mechanisms. Instead, cognitive therapists view our maladaptive cognitions as learned habits that are near the surface and accessible by simple questioning and conversation. Accordingly, they use the term *automatic* rather than *unconscious* to describe clients' maladaptive and self-defeating cognitions. The list of automatic self-defeating cognitions that characterize psychological problems is potentially endless. Table 8.5 presents some of the most common examples.

As cognitively oriented clinicians worked on identifying clients' automatic thoughts, they noted that persons with certain disorders were inclined to employ some cognitive distortions more than others. For instance, depressed persons have a habitual way of explaining the causes of events, particularly negative events. This is called a *negative attributional style*. Borrowing from theories in social and personality psychology (e.g., Heider, 1958; Weiner, 1974), Abramson, Seligman, and Teasdale (1978) proposed that depressed persons habitually explain negative events in a way that is most damaging to their self-esteem and sense of hope. So when a negative event occurs, depressed persons are more likely than nondepressed ones to attribute the cause of the event to factors that are internal (i.e., something about them), stable (i.e., something relatively permanent), and global (something with widespread effects). This negative attributional style helps create depression and contributes to its maintenance. The idea that characteristic clusters of cognitive errors are associated with specific disorders is called the *cognitive specificity hypothesis*. This hypothesis is an important element of cognitive therapy because it helps clinicians to conceptualize and assess disorders, develop specific treatment methods, and explain elements of the treatment to clients (Reinecke & Freeman, 2003).

TABLE 8.5 Some Automatic, Self-Defeating Thoughts (Cognitive Distortions)

Cognition	Example
Dichotomous (all-or-none) thinking	If I can't be famous I'll be a total failure
Overgeneralization	He unfriended me—that shows that no one likes me
Catastrophizing	They didn't hire me—I'll never get a decent job and I'll never be happy
Personalization	Everyone thinks it's my fault that we lost
Selective Abstraction (Magnification, minimization, disqualifying the positive)	I got one "needs improvement" and ten "goods" in that evaluation—I'm failing
Jumping to conclusions (Mind reading)	When she said, "some people are just clueless" she had me in mind. He just squinted—he must not like me
Fortune-telling error	It's raining today—I know I'm going to blow that test
Emotional reasoning	I feel guilty—I must be a bad person
	I'm scared of airplanes—it must be dangerous to fly
Unrealistic expectations (Should and must statements)	Everyone should like me
	I must act happy all the time;
Labeling	I'm a loser
	I'm an emotional cripple

ASSESSMENT IN COGNITIVE THERAPY   Assessment in cognitive therapy is similar to that in behavior therapy, but cognitive therapists are particularly interested in developing a detailed understanding of the chronicity, intensity, and extent of the client's automatic cognitive distortions. Accordingly, like behavior therapists, they are likely to measure these behaviors at the beginning of therapy and throughout the course of treatment using rating scales, self-reports, and standardized instruments (e.g., the Beck Depression Inventory).

Cognitive therapists also pay particular attention to assessing factors that might support or limit the client's ability to engage in the tasks required in cognitive therapy. These tasks include adopting a "thinking" attitude toward symptoms and emotional experiences, and tolerating the sometimes challenging, or even confrontational, approach adopted by therapists. Clients who are unable to take an objective, rational view of themselves and their experiences, at least occasionally, who are extremely pessimistic, or who are unable to take an active, responsible role in improving their lives may not be the best candidates for cognitive therapy (Wright, Basco, & Thase, 2006).

THE ROLE OF THE THERAPIST   In Chapter 2, "Clinical Psychology's Past and Present," we characterized the role of the cognitive therapist as that of a "scientist" (see Table 2.9) who tries to help clients identify and alter the maladaptive thoughts they hold about themselves and their worlds. Their success in doing so depends in part on having a productive and collaborative therapeutic alliance. In order to foster this alliance, cognitive therapists are empathic and supportive in recognizing the distress associated with the client's emotional experiences, but they also make it clear that the client has an important role to play in treatment. So in addition to support and trust, the alliance is built on *education* about how maladaptive schemas, self-defeating beliefs, negative attributional styles, and other important cognitive factors create and maintain psychological disorders (Newman, 2013). This information is important because it helps clients to better understand the therapist's view of their problems, the techniques that will be used to address the problems, and expectations about the client's role in facilitating the process.

Once a satisfactory working alliance has been achieved and clients understand and accept the basic cognitive model, cognitive therapists engage clients in active examination of their own beliefs, focusing especially on the client's experiences and associated cognitive distortions. This process is called *collaborative empiricism* in recognition of the fact that the therapist and client collaborate to assess problems, determine goals, test hypotheses, develop tasks, and measure progress (Wright, Sudak, Turkington, & Thase, 2012). As already noted, clients are often unaware of the cognitive distortions underlying some of their problems, so cognitive therapists use some of the interviewing techniques described in Chapter 4 "Interviewing and Observation in Clinical Psychology," to help them recognize those distortions. As cognitive therapy continues, therapists also use role-playing, written exercises, self-assessment, and various other forms of homework.

The Goals of Cognitive Therapy

As implied by the theory underlying cognitive therapy, the cognitive therapist's goals in treatment are to (a) educate clients about the role of maladaptive thoughts in behavior and experience, (b) help clients learn to recognize when they engage in those thoughts, and (c) arm them with skills for challenging maladaptive thoughts and for replacing them with more accurate and adaptive ones. Perhaps the simplest formulation of cognitive therapy's goals is this: Identify, Refute, and Replace.

Clinical Applications

Two pioneering forms of cognitive therapy, Aaron "Tim" Beck's *cognitive therapy* and Albert Ellis's *rational-emotive behavior therapy*, illustrate the principles of cognitive therapy we have described. These theories were highly influential in shaping today's cognitive and cognitive-behavioral approaches to treatment.

BECK'S COGNITIVE THERAPY   Beginning in the 1960s, Tim Beck developed an approach to the treatment of depression based on the assumption that depression and other emotions are determined largely by the way people think about their experiences (A. T. Beck, 1963, 1972). He argued that depressive symptoms result from logical errors and distortions that clients make about the events in their lives. For example, they draw conclusions about themselves on the basis of insufficient or irrelevant information, as when a woman believes she is worthless because she was not invited to a party. They also exaggerate the importance of trivial events, as when a man decides that

Aaron "Tim" Beck (1921–), a founder of cognitive therapy, has published numerous works on cognitive therapy, trained many clinicians in cognitive techniques, and developed several widely used assessment scales. *Source*: Aaron T. Beck.

his vintage record collection is ruined because one record has a scratch on it. And they minimize the significance of positive events, as when a student believes that a good test score was the result of luck, not intelligence or hard work.

Beck (1976) proposed that depressed individuals show a characteristic pattern of negative perceptions and conclusions about (a) themselves, (b) their world, and (c) their future. This *cognitive triad* was presumed to distinguish depressive thinking from nondepressive thinking. His version of cognitive therapy has since been applied to anxiety disorders, personality disorders, substance use disorders, and several other problems (J. S. Beck, 2011; Miller, Rathus, Linehan, & Swenson, 2006). Table 8.6 presents an example of the kinds of cognitions characteristic of people with depression.

RATIONAL EMOTIVE BEHAVIOR THERAPY   Another influential and pioneering cognitive therapy is Albert Ellis's *rational-emotive behavior therapy*, or REBT (Ellis, 1995, 2001). As mentioned in Chapter 2, Ellis stated the core principles of REBT as follows:

When a highly charged emotional Consequence (C) follows a significant Activating Event (A), A may seem to but actually does not cause C. Instead, emotional Consequences are largely created by B—the individual's Belief System. When, therefore, an undesirable Consequence occurs, such as severe anxiety, this can usually be quickly traced to the person's

TABLE 8.6 Attributional Tendencies of Depressed Persons

Event	Internal, Stable, Global (Maladaptive) Attributions Characteristic of Depressed Persons	Examples of More Adaptive Attributions Characteristic of Nondepressed Persons
I was home this weekend and no one called me.	It's because of me, it's because I'm not likeable, and it will affect all my relationships.	People are busy right before the holidays (external attribution).
		I often work on weekends, and my friends know this, so they may have chosen not to call (unstable attribution).
		I have a few close friends, so some people like me (specific attribution).
I got a bad grade on a test.	I'm dumb and no good at things.	The test was unfairly difficult (external attribution).
		I didn't study for this test (unstable attribution).
		I'm not so hot in chemistry, but there are other subjects that I do well in (specific attribution).

irrational Beliefs, and when these Beliefs are effectively Disputed (at point D), by challenging them rationally, the disturbed Consequences disappear and eventually cease to reoccur. (p. 167)

In short, Ellis proposed that psychological problems result not from external stress but from the irrational ideas people hold, which lead them to insist that their wishes must be met in order for them to be happy.

The therapist's task in REBT is to attack these irrational, unrealistic, self-defeating beliefs and to instruct clients in more rational or logical thinking patterns that will not upset them (Ellis, 1962; Ellis & Dryden, 1987). The REBT therapist is active, challenging, demonstrative, and often abrasive. Ellis advocated the use of strong, direct communication in order to persuade clients to give up the irrational ideas with which they indoctrinate themselves into misery. Here is an exchange that took place at the beginning of an initial REBT session between a therapist (T) and a young woman (C) who presented several problems, among them the abuse of alcohol.

C: *(After being asked what is wrong.)* . . . my tendency is to say everything. I want to change everything; I'm depressed about everything; et cetera.

T: Give me a couple of things, for example.

C: What I'm depressed about? I, uh, don't know that I have any purpose in life. I don't know what I—what I am. And I don't know in what direction I'm going.

T: Yeah, but that's—so you're saying, "I'm ignorant!" *(Client nods.)* Well, what's so awful about being ignorant? It's too bad you're ignorant. It would be nicer if you weren't—if you had a purpose and knew where you were going. But just let's suppose the worst: For the rest of your life, you didn't have a purpose, and you stayed this way. Let's suppose that. Now why would you be so bad?

C: Because everyone should have a purpose!

T: Where did you get the "should"?

The REBT therapist's frontal assault on the client's irrational beliefs is not restricted to cognitive interventions. Role-playing, sensory-awareness exercises, desensitization, assertion training, and specific homework assignments are also employed in an attempt to provide behavioral complements to cognitive change.

Cognitive therapy today is seldom described apart from behavioral therapy. In theory and practice, the interventions from both perspectives have been so often and closely combined that they are usually described as cognitive-behavior therapy (J. S. Beck, 2011; Craighead, Ritschel, & Zagoloff, 2013). Nevertheless, cognitive therapy has contributed several specific interventions that can best be understood from the cognitive perspective. Let's now consider several techniques that come specifically from the cognitive approach to psychotherapy.

Psychoeducation

Early in therapy, the cognitive therapist begins educating the client about the role of cognitions in disorders. The goal is not to deluge the client with information, so if your "teacher schema" calls to mind someone delivering a long, boring lecture, perhaps try invoking your "independent study project mentor" schema. Therapists seek to socialize clients into a way of thinking about their disorder so that they can quickly become a collaborator and eventually become self-sufficient in identifying, refuting, and replacing cognitive errors. In addition to discussion, the cognitive therapist might use diagrams or charts, recommend videos or books, or assign homework. Some therapists have begun to use computer-based multimedia programs to assist in therapy (Dobson, 2012; Wright, Basco, & Thase, 2006). This kind of "socialization" into treatment is important in all forms of therapy, but it can be especially crucial in cognitive therapy, because if clinicians do not thoroughly explain its rationale, they risk being perceived by their clients as accusatory or insufficiently supportive, and clients are less likely to comply with therapy recommendations (Reinecke & Freeman, 2003). Below is an example provided by Judith Beck (2011), Tim Beck's daughter, illustrating how a therapist might use a client's experience to begin educating the client about automatic thoughts.

THERAPIST: [moving to the first agenda topic]. Should we talk about how upset you were at the park yesterday?

CLIENT: Yes.

T: How were you feeling emotionally: Sad? Anxious? Angry?

C: Sad.

T: What was going through your mind?

C: [further describing the situation instead of relating her automatic thoughts] I was looking at the people in the park, hanging out, playing Frisbee, things like that.

T: What was going through your mind when you saw them?

C: I'll never be like them.

T: Okay. [providing psychoeducation] You just identified what we call an automatic thought. Everyone has them. They are thoughts that just seem to pop into our heads. We're not deliberately trying to think about them; that's why we call them automatic. Most of the time, they're very quick and we're much more aware of the emotion—in this case sadness—than we are of the thoughts. Lots of times the thoughts are distorted in some way. But we react *as if* they're true.

C: Hmmm.

T: What we'll do is teach you to identify your automatic thoughts and then evaluate them to see just how accurate they are. For example, in a minute we'll evaluate the thought, "I'll never be like them." What do you think would happen to your emotions if you discovered that your thought wasn't true—that when your depression lifts you'll realize that you are like the people in the park?

C: I'd feel better.

Socratic Questioning and Guided Discovery

Named after the philosopher Socrates, *Socratic questioning* is a style of discourse in which the therapist pursues a line of questioning until the client's fundamental beliefs and assumptions are laid bare and open to analysis. Judith Beck refers to this as *guided discovery* and maintains that such questioning helps clients gain distance and see their cognitions as ideas rather than certainties. Questions that are commonly asked by therapists (and eventually by clients) as cognitive therapy proceeds include (J. S. Beck, 2011, p. 23):

- What is the evidence? What is the evidence on the other side?
- Is there an alternative way of viewing the situation?
- What is the worst that could happen and how could you cope with it if it did happen? What is the best that could happen? What is the most realistic outcome?
- What is the effect of your/my believing the automatic thought? What could be the effect of changing your/my thinking?
- What advice would you give if your [friend or family member] were in the same situation and had the same automatic thought?

Therapists use a number of variations on these questions, and they also model ways of thinking that provide rational alternative responses. They might also engage in deliberate exaggeration of a client's maladaptive beliefs (e.g., "I should never be late") so that the client can see the unreasonableness of such beliefs. Cognitive therapists commonly ask clients to quantify their statements by rating on a scale from 0 to 100, for example, some experience or emotion. So if a client states "I am the biggest loser in the world," the following exchange might take place:

THERAPIST: Really? In the whole world?

CLIENT: Practically. I feel like the biggest loser.

T: Okay, I understand. You feel pretty incompetent compared with other people.

C: Yeah.

T: In your view, where would you say you fall on a scale of 0 to 100. Say that 0 is absolutely the biggest loser in the world, and 100 is the most competent person in the world. Where would you place yourself?

C: Oh, I don't know, pretty low, maybe . . . 8.

T: Can you think of people who would be near 0, what would they be like?

C: No job, in jail, child molester, no friends, alcoholic, ignorant. . . .

T: Okay, let's look at your situation. How far away from that 0 are you in reality?

C: Well, I still have a job, a family, some friends. I'm not a child molester. . . .

T: And what would someone, say, at about 20 be like? Or 50? Do you have anything in common with them?

In this example, the therapist has encouraged the client to be more explicit about his belief that he is a loser, to quantify it, and then uses Socratic questioning to encourage the client to examine the evidence for his belief. After a review of all the evidence, the client will likely decide to revise upward his evaluation of himself. The exercise is not intended to find the client's "true" standing on the scale but to show him how automatically he produces and accepts an exaggerated negative evaluation of himself. By pursuing exchanges such as this one, phrased in language that clients understand and paced so that they do not feel overwhelmed, clients and therapists in cognitive therapy are gradually able to uncover the clients' maladaptive beliefs about events and themselves.

CHALLENGING AND REPLACING MALADAPTIVE THOUGHTS   The list of cognitive distortions in Table 8.5 presents a challenge for the cognitive therapist because clients are often quite tenacious in holding onto their self-defeating beliefs and attributions. Indeed, clients are like everyone else in seeking to preserve their core beliefs, even including beliefs about themselves that make them anxious, insecure, and unhappy. We discussed this pervasive human tendency, called *confirmation bias*, in Chapter 3, "Basic Features of Clinical Assessment," in the context of biasing factors in psychologists' clinical judgments. As noted there, when it comes to core beliefs, we all tend to pay closer attention to evidence that supports our beliefs than to evidence that undermines them.

To help clients overcome this tendency, cognitive therapists ask them to repeatedly practice challenging maladaptive beliefs. Thus depressed clients whose negative attributional style leads them to interpret events in the most negative way are pushed to consider alternate attributions. This *reattribution training* is illustrated in the following example of a 44-year-old client whose elderly mother lives alone in the same town:

THERAPIST: What went through your mind when your mother said she was unhappy?

CLIENT: That it was my fault, that I don't do enough to help her.

T: And what does that thought mean about you?

C: That I should do more, that I'm . . . lazy . . . an uncaring person. I should take her out more. It's my fault she's unhappy.

T: I understand that you feel concerned when your mother says she's having a bad day, and I understand your empathy for her. But do you think that you *caused* her to have a bad day? Is there any other reason she might have a bad day?

C: Well, her arthritis has been bad lately.

T: Anything else?

C: It's getting close to the time my father died; she always goes through a bad time in February.

T: Okay, maybe you are the cause of her bad day, but it's also possible there could be other causes outside of you.

In this exchange, the therapist has encouraged the client to consider the internal versus external dimension of attributions (see also Table 8.6).

DECATASTROPHIZING   As the name implies, *Decatastrophizing* involves helping clients evaluate their catastrophic predictions. Used particularly with anxious and socially phobic clients, this approach is designed to help them see that there are gradations in discomfort and their most-feared scenarios may in fact be tolerable. For instance, if a socially phobic client fears that standing alone at a party would be the most humiliating thing imaginable, the therapist might ask her to imagine other things (such as standing there naked, or in a chicken suit) that would be more painful. The therapist might ask the client to gauge how long, in minutes and seconds, she thought she could tolerate standing alone. Therapists might also use Socratic questioning to help clients keep problems in perspective (Dienes, Torres-Harding, Reinecke, Freeman, & Sauer, 2011). Exercises such as these help clients to recognize that their capacity to tolerate discomfort—an essential for overcoming their problem—is greater than they realized.

THOUGHT RECORDING AND MULTICOLUMN RECORDS   As in behavior therapy, an important component of treatment is having the client engage in "homework" tasks between therapy sessions. One of the most common techniques for clients in cognitive therapy involves keeping written records of events that have emotional significance. Clients often begin with a *two-column thought record*. In one column, they record the event along with its date and time. In the adjacent column they record their automatic thoughts about the event. This procedure is designed to provide practice in recognizing automatic and often maladaptive cognitions.

Most clients can soon graduate to keeping *three-column records*. The client uses the third column to record emotional reactions and, sometimes, the intensity of those emotions. Eventually, *five-column records* are kept. The fourth column is used to record the name of the cognitive error they made in column two (e.g., overgeneralizing, catastrophizing, personalizing) and propose adaptive alternative behaviors and rational alternatives to the automatic thoughts recorded in column two. The fifth column is used to record the outcome of trying more adaptive thoughts and actions. Table 8.7 shows an example of one client's five-column record sheet.

TABLE 8.7 A Client's Five-Column Thought Record

Event or Situation	Automatic Thoughts	Emotion (Intensity)	Rational Cognitive Alternatives	Outcome and Emotions
At work today, everyone left soon after I came into the lunchroom	Everybody hates me	Anger (70%)	Personalizing	I walked in the lunchroom and asked Joe if I could sit with him. He said yeah. I was anxious (70%) but tolerated it. I asked him about his daughter in college. I guess it went OK
			I came in at 12:40, so people probably had to get back to work	
			The two people who came in after me are best friends who only kinda know me, so maybe they had something to talk about	
			Tomorrow I'll consider sitting with someone when I walk in	
	I'm not a likeable person	Sadness (95%)	Overgeneralizing	
			Only one person there seems to really hate me, and I guess it's his problem. I don't need everyone to like me. I have friends there	

SECTION SUMMARY

Cognitive therapy is based on the idea that cognitions mediate between events and emotional experiences. Certain cognitions, called cognitive distortions, play key roles in creating and maintaining psychological disorders. The primary task of the cognitive therapist is to help clients learn to recognize and challenge these cognitive distortions and replace them with more adaptive modes of thinking, using techniques such as psychoeducation, Socratic dialogue, and thought records.

COGNITIVE-BEHAVIOR THERAPY

SECTION PREVIEW

Cognitive-behavior therapy (CBT) combines the theories and techniques of behavior therapy and cognitive therapy. A systematic and structured approach that stresses empirically tested methods, CBT has gained wide appeal.

As already noted, the behavioral and cognitive approaches have combined to such an extent that it is rare to find contemporary books or articles on behavior therapy that do not give serious consideration to cognition, and it is equally rare to find works on cognitive therapy that do not stress behavior change. Conceptual distinctions between the two therapy approaches can still be made, but in practice the distinctions have virtually disappeared. Reinecke and Freeman (2003) point out that "Behavior therapy associations around the world have added the term 'cognitive' to their name, and the prestigious journal *Behavior Therapy* now carries the subtitle, 'An International Journal Devoted to the Application of Behavioral and Cognitive Sciences to Clinical Problems'" (p. 224). This merger occurred because behaviorally oriented clinicians recognized the importance of cognitions in various disorders, and cognitively oriented clinicians recognized the value of behavior therapy techniques that can help systematically translate cognitive changes into behavioral changes. But there are other reasons these two major approaches have combined (Norcross, Vandenbos, & Freedheim, 2011).

Both behavioral and cognitive approaches come primarily from the empirical tradition in clinical psychology (see Chapter 2, "Clinical Psychology's Past and Present"). As a result, many of the techniques used in both approaches were originally conceived and developed in research settings. Behavioral and cognitive clinicians therefore share a strong belief that clinicians should use methods that have been shown to be effective in carefully controlled research settings. Both approaches also emphasize ongoing collection of data during therapy to track therapeutic effectiveness. Both emphasize assessment of the client's current symptoms and the contexts in which they occur and deemphasize historical factors or global personality variables. Finally, the therapist's role is similar in both. Behavioral and cognitive therapists strive to be genuine and supportive, but they adopt an objective, educational stance toward the client and are quite directive—they aggressively pursue lines of questioning, assign tasks, challenge clients' assumptions, and the like.

Theoretical Foundations

The theoretical foundations of CBT are essentially those of the behavioral and cognitive approaches that we have already described. Most who adopt CBT think that the addition of behavioral principles and practices to the cognitive theoretical framework (or vice versa) leads to a clear, persuasive, and evidence-based description of how normal and abnormal behavior develops and can be changed.

Clinical Applications

In practice, the combination of these two psychotherapy approaches means that cognitive-behavior therapists have at their disposal the full array of interventions that have been developed by behaviorally and cognitively oriented clinicians. How they use these interventions depends on their assessment of each client. As is true of both behavior therapists and cognitive therapists, clinicians who use CBT sometimes use formal, standardized tests, especially if they are required to assign diagnoses, but their therapy-related assessments entail behavioral rating scales, questionnaires, and client self-assessments.

Cognitive-behavior therapists tend to be quite explicit in the way they structure therapy sessions. Each session has an agenda, often a written one, and the sessions generally progress in relatively predictable ways as clients become familiar with the ideas and tasks of therapy. It is common to (a) review the goals and strategies of therapy, (b) review homework progress, (c) identify specific problems and their associated thoughts to which the CBT model is applied, (d) summarize progress, and (e) assign homework for the next session.

Examples of CBT work in the early part of therapy include identifying mood shifts, spotting automatic thoughts, making two- and three-column thought records, identifying cognitive errors, scheduling activities, and conducting behavioral activation. There is an emphasis in the beginning phases of CBT on demonstrating and teaching the basic cognitive model. Feedback is typically given and requested several times during the session and again at the end. Some therapists prefer to set the agenda before performing a symptom check. Homework may be reviewed and/or assigned at multiple points in the session.

As therapy moves toward the middle phases, treatment might focus more on making five-column thought records, providing graded exposure to feared stimuli, and conducting beginning or midlevel work on changing schemas. Later phases of therapy might include identifying and modifying schemas, making five-column thought records, developing action plans to manage problems and/or practice revised schemas, completing exposure protocols, and preparing for termination.

Numerous combinations of specific cognitive-behavioral interventions have been developed for the treatment of specific problems. Detailed coverage of all of them is well beyond the scope of this chapter, so here we mention just two such methods. Additional variations on and applications of CBT are being developed and investigated all the time.

RELAPSE PREVENTION   Alan Marlatt and Judith Gordon's *relapse prevention* treatment is a cognitive-behavioral intervention designed to help clients who are trying to overcome alcoholism or other substance use disorders (Marlatt & Gordon, 1985). Marlatt and Gordon noted that relapse is most likely when clients engage in thoughts (such as "I owe myself a drink") that lead to relapse. Once a relapse episode occurs, guilt and shame tend to generate a cascade of negative self-evaluations ("I've let my family down"; "I'm a complete failure") which increases the probability of continued drinking, an outcome known as the *abstinence violation effect* (Marlatt & Gordon, 1985).

The idea behind relapse prevention is to teach clients to monitor risky cognitions and to replace them with different thinking strategies. For example, instead of thinking about how good it would feel to drink, clients are taught to focus on how miserable it felt to be in jail after a drunk driving arrest. They are also taught to view a relapse episode not as an excuse to resume substance use but as a temporary setback whose recurrence can be prevented by working on better cognitive and behavioral self-control strategies. Relapse prevention techniques have now been adapted for use with other disorders and are a regular part of cognitive-behavior treatment, particularly in helping clients become better at recognizing the particular cognitions or schemas that appear to trigger their symptoms.

DIALECTICAL BEHAVIOR THERAPY   Pioneered by Marsha Linehan (Koerner & Linehan, 2011; Linehan, 1993), *dialectical behavior therapy,* or DBT, is a form of cognitive-behavior therapy often used to help clients who display the impulsive behavior, mood swings, fragile self-image, and stormy interpersonal relationships associated with borderline personality disorder. Many of these clients are adolescents who display multiple disorders; some present risks of suicide or aggressive acting out. DBT has also been applied to eating disorders such as bulimia nervosa (Safer, Telch, & Agras, 2001).

Initially, DBT helps these clients develop skill at containing their erratic behaviors, but after these "containment" goals have been reached, the therapist helps the client confront any traumatic experiences—such as physical or sexual abuse in childhood—that might have contributed to their current emotional difficulties. This phase of treatment concentrates on eliminating self-blame for these traumas, reducing posttraumatic stress symptoms, and resolving questions of who is to blame for the trauma. By consistently helping borderline clients see that almost all events can be thought about from varying perspectives, the dialectical therapist tries to encourage them to see the world in a more integrated or balanced way (Van Dijk, 2013).

A Case Example

The following case of "Carlos," adapted from Gorenstein and Comer (2002, pp. 46–62), illustrates some of the ways in which the combination of behavioral and cognitive techniques can be applied to help a man suffering from depression and somatic concerns.

At the age of 39, Carlos, by now the successful part-owner of his family's plumbing supplies business and the proud father of four children, became increasingly preoccupied with his health. His cousin, who was about 15 years older than Carlos, had recently suffered a fatal heart attack. Carlos was saddened by the loss but didn't think much more of it at the time. However, within a few months, he started to worry about himself and ultimately became convinced that he might also have a heart condition. He began taking his pulse constantly and putting his hand to his chest to decide if his heartbeat was palpable, believing that a pounding heart could be the sign of a heart attack.

Eventually, Carlos went to see his doctor, even though he had just had a checkup a few months before. The doctor performed an electrocardiogram (EKG) in his office; the results were completely normal. Carlos left the doctor's office reassured in a factual sense; but somehow it didn't help his mood. "A heart attack is still possible," he thought to himself.

In the succeeding weeks, he could not get over the idea of disaster striking. On several nights he awoke with an overwhelming sense of despair and sobbed quietly to himself while his wife Sonia lay asleep next to him. At work, Carlos lost all interest in his usual activities and could barely focus his thoughts at times. At home, he just sat and moped. He looked at his children as if they were already orphans, and tears would come to his eyes.

Carlos decided to see his doctor again. This time, the physician told Carlos that his preoccupation with the idea of a heart attack was getting out of hand. "You're fine, my friend, so stop your worrying." As the doctor spoke, Carlos's eyes welled up with tears, and the doctor realized that his patient needed further help in dealing with his fears. The physician recommended that Carlos see a psychologist.

Upon hearing Carlos's recital of his symptoms—feelings of despair, poor concentration, difficulty sleeping, loss of interest in usual activities, and tearfulness—the psychologist told Carlos that she believed he was suffering from depression and would benefit from psychological treatment. The psychologist also recommended that Carlos consult a psychiatrist who could advise him on the benefits of antidepressant medication.

Eventually, Carlos began treatment with Dr. Robert Walden, a psychologist who had trained with Tim Beck at Beck's Center for Cognitive Therapy in Philadelphia. Like other cognitive therapists and researchers, Dr. Walden explained and treated depression largely by focusing on a person's style of thinking. Although a disturbance in mood is the most obvious symptom in this disorder, research suggests that disturbances in cognition have an important—perhaps primary—role in the disorder.

Most of the first therapy session was devoted to a discussion of Carlos's current condition and the events leading up to it. In spite of his obvious distress, Carlos related the events of the past year in a coherent and organized fashion. At the same time, the desperation on his face was almost painful to observe, and his voice trembled with distress . . .

Dr. Walden spent the last 15 minutes of the session giving Carlos a brief overview of the cognitive theory of depression and the implied treatment. . . . The psychologist explained that a major part of therapy would be discovering those aspects of Carlos's thinking and behavior that were undermining his capacity to feel well, and then to help him develop alternative ways of thinking and behaving that would ultimately reduce his depression. To begin, the psychologist explained that Carlos would be asked to monitor his emotional reactions throughout the next week, recording all thoughts or events that produced distress (sadness, anger, anxiety, or whatever) and rating their intensity. In the next session, Dr. Walden explained, they would discuss these matters so as to bring out Carlos's thinking about them. In addition, the psychologist asked him to keep a diary of his activities.

At the next session, Dr. Walden reviewed the records Carlos had kept throughout the week of both his moods and his activities, and these provided the focus of discussion. A distressing thought that Carlos had written down several times each day pertained to the seriousness of his current condition, expressed in several forms: "I'm a basket case." "How did I get so sick?" "I can barely function." These thoughts seemed to arise spontaneously, particularly when Carlos was inactive.

Dr. Walden engaged Carlos in a type of Socratic dialogue that is typical of cognitive therapy.

DR. WALDEN: You say you are a "basket case" and can barely function. What leads you to those conclusions?

CARLOS: Well, I've been hospitalized. That's how bad it's been. I just can't believe it.

DR. WALDEN: I know we discussed it last time, but tell me again what led to that hospitalization.

CARLOS: I sort of got panicked when the medicine didn't help, and I stopped going to work or doing anything else. Dr. Hsu [the psychiatrist] figured that as long as I wasn't working, I might as well go into the hospital where I could try different drugs without having to manage all the side effects on my own. I also was pretty miserable at the time. I told Dr. Hsu that my family would be better off without me.

DR. WALDEN: Do you think they would be better off?

CARLOS: I don't know. I'm not doing them much good.

DR. WALDEN: What would life be like for them without you?

CARLOS: It would be terrible for them. I suppose saying they'd be better off without me is going too far. As bad off as I am, I'm still able to do a few things.

DR. WALDEN: What are you able to do? . . .

With continued discussion, the psychologist helped Carlos to recognize the various capabilities that he did have, and how, in practical terms, he wasn't as compromised as the terms "basket case" and "barely able to function" implied. Dr. Walden also pointed out that Carlos really didn't know the limits of his capabilities because he had deliberately reduced the demands on himself under the questionable assumption that "stress" would worsen his condition. The psychologist suggested that they start testing his assumption by having Carlos make a few simple additions to his activities. After some discussion, it was decided that each day Carlos would make a concerted effort to get up and leave for work at 8:00 A.M., the same time he used to leave before becoming depressed. Second, it was decided that Carlos would read a bedtime story to his two younger children each night; moreover, it was specified that he try hard to attend to the content of the story rather than allow his thoughts to drift into his own concerns. He was to note on his activity record his daily success in carrying out these two assignments.

Finally, Dr. Walden asked Carlos to continue to keep a record of his unpleasant emotions and the thoughts associated with them. This time, however, the client was also to try to produce alternative, more realistic thoughts by considering whether his initial thoughts truly reflected all the evidence. Furthermore, the more realistic thoughts were to be written down.

In subsequent sessions, Dr. Walden asked Carlos first about the behavioral assignments. The client responded that he had continued to read to the children each evening throughout the week and was doing so with a "clear head." On the other hand, he complained that for the rest of the evening, he would just sit around and mope, sometimes sitting in the living room chair for an hour or more worrying about his condition and his inability—or lack of desire—to do anything else, while the rest of the family went about their normal activities. Dr. Walden asked him about his negative thoughts during this period, and the client replied that it was "the same old thing," meaning thoughts about being a basket case and unable to function. The psychologist asked Carlos if he was able to refute such thoughts when they arose. The client replied that he was carrying out the exercise of weighing the evidence and forming alternative thoughts, but that within a few minutes the negative thoughts would return. Then he would carry out the exercise all over again. It was getting repetitive.

On hearing this, Dr. Walden reviewed with Carlos their earlier discussions about the objective extent of Carlos's disability. The client acknowledged that his characterization of his condition as being a basket case was exaggerated, but he seemed to have trouble holding on to this more accurate assessment and had to remind himself constantly that he was in fact functioning reasonably well, all things considered.

Dr. Walden felt that the next step was for Carlos to bring the force of behavior behind his reformulated thoughts. That is, it was time for Carlos to participate more fully in the family's evening routine. . . . A large portion of this session was therefore devoted to working out in detail the appropriate routine for Carlos to follow in the evening at home.

In the next session, Carlos reported that he had been able to follow the prescribed routine at home. He found that keeping his attention focused on the concrete tasks before him—reading the kids a story, asking them questions about school, doing some paperwork—had a way of reducing his pattern of depressive thinking. He told Dr. Walden he was pleased with his ability to do these things and he was even starting to enjoy some activities.

In subsequent sessions, Dr. Walden worked with Carlos to increase his activities at work. Carlos had increased his time at work to 6 hours per day but found himself feeling frequently depressed there. Apparently, he had severely cut down his activities at work under the assumption that stress could exacerbate his condition. As a result, he had a lot of dead time on his hands, which he would spend sitting at his desk, staring at his computer, and brooding over the extent of his disability and his rate of progress. . . .

Dr. Walden pointed out the inconsistency between Carlos's attempts to refute his negative thoughts and his actual behavior in the situation:

DR. WALDEN: It's good that you're challenging the incorrect idea that you're a basket case and can't function. But if you really know that such thinking is wrong, why are you still limiting your activities at work?

CARLOS: I guess I'm afraid that any increased stress might ruin my progress.

DR. WALDEN: What happened when you started taking on more responsibilities at home?

CARLOS: I got less wrapped up in my worries.

DR. WALDEN: What lesson does that seem to teach for the work situation?

CARLOS: That I should start doing more things. I'm not even doing the minimum. And I can't say that I ever had that much stress from work. I mean, I'm one of the owners. I set my own pace. I always put in a good day's work—at least I used to—but I never saw any point in going overboard.

DR. WALDEN: So, getting back to my original question about how to conduct yourself at work. . . .

CARLOS: I know, I know. It makes no sense at this point to be slacking off like I am.

In subsequent sessions, Carlos continued to perform behavioral and cognitive exercises that he and Dr. Walden agreed upon, and he continued to improve. Carlos had returned to full functioning and was in good spirits most of the time. He had even resumed going on overnight business trips. Accordingly, the therapy sessions themselves were now devoted to relapse prevention. The goal was to help Carlos understand the basic beliefs underlying much of his depressive thinking.

It was, for example, apparent that the client's most fundamental depressive belief was a so-called vulnerability to harm and illness schema—a belief that disaster is about to strike at any time and that the client is helpless to protect himself. This particular belief seems to be the basis of Carlos's original preoccupation with heart disease and his preoccupation later on with the prospect of a total mental breakdown.

Session time was spent reviewing the various negative thoughts that had arisen because of this belief. The goal was to improve Carlos's ability to recognize when the belief was active and to take it as a cue to confront the resulting negative thoughts.

SECTION SUMMARY

CBT grew from the merger of the behavioral and cognitive approaches. Because these two approaches derive from the same empirical tradition in psychology, they share many similarities and are quite compatible. Cognitive-behavior therapists conduct carefully planned therapy sessions employing both cognitive and behavioral treatment techniques.

THE CURRENT STATUS OF COGNITIVE-BEHAVIOR THERAPY

As we mentioned in Chapter 2, CBT has surged in popularity in the past several years. Articles and books on CBT have proliferated, and in surveys, an increasing number of clinical psychologists identify themselves as taking a cognitive-behavioral approach (Hollon & DiGuiseppe, 2011; Wade, 2012). In short, the cognitive-behavioral approach to psychotherapy currently enjoys considerable popularity in training programs and in practice.

This popularity seems due not only to empirical evidence for the effectiveness of cognitive-behavioral techniques but also to their straightforward, problem-oriented approach. Most behavioral and cognitive interventions are designed around specific problem behaviors or cognitions, and so the translation from symptom to treatment is relatively clear. Further, the steps to be taken in behavioral and cognitive interventions are usually described in specific terms and in organized sequences, often in highly structured procedure manuals. Manual-based cognitive-behavioral treatments now exist for a wide variety of psychological problems. Compared to other approaches, especially psychodynamic and humanistic approaches, these "scripted" cognitive-behavioral interventions are easier for trainees and practicing clinicians to learn. At the same time, having so many manual-based treatments can pose problems. Practitioners may have to decide whether to become specialists in a few disorders or whether they can be less dependent on manuals and develop effective treatments from principle-based, transdiagnostic methods (Allen, McHugh, & Barlow, 2008; Hollon & DiGuiseppe, 2011).

Finally, it is clear that the cognitive-behavioral approaches continue to evolve. The "first wave" (behavioral approaches) focused on observable behaviors and environmental events and the "second wave" added cognitions. Not long after a comfortable integration of traditional behavioral and cognitive approaches was achieved, there came a "third wave" emphasizing attention, mindfulness, and values. With its emphasis on moment-to-moment experience and the function of symptoms (as opposed to their frequency or validity), these newer contextual approaches appear to share more assumptions with humanistic, existential, and psychodynamic approaches to psychotherapy than had been the case before. Fortunately, because the cognitive-behavioral approaches all share a firm commitment to empirical evidence, the benefits of older and newer approaches will continue to be subjected to scientific tests (Baardseth et al., 2013).

For more information on the cognitive-behavioral approaches to therapy, we recommend that you consult one of several textbooks on the subject (e.g., J. S. Beck, 2011; Craske, 2010; Dobson, 2012; Ledley, Marx, & Heimberg, 2010; Newman, 2013; Van Dijk, 2013; Wright Sudak, Turkington, & Thase, 2010).

Chapter Summary

Behavioral and cognitive-behavioral therapies are based on the principles of learning and on research on cognitive psychology. Their treatment methods are aimed at directly modifying overt maladaptive behaviors as well as the maladaptive thinking patterns that accompany those behaviors. Behavioral methods include various kinds of systematic desensitization, exposure techniques, social skills training (including assertiveness training), behavioral rehearsal, several types of modeling, aversion therapy and punishment, contingency management, and biofeedback (among others).

Cognitive therapy methods were pioneered by Beck's cognitive therapy for depression and Ellis's rational-emotive behavior therapy. These methods, and those that followed, stressed the mediating role of cognitions in behavior, especially the influence of maladaptive cognitions. Such cognitions include dichotomous thinking, personalization, overgeneralization, catastrophizing, and unrealistic expectations (among others).

The cognitive therapist's primary task is to engage the client in identifying these cognitive errors, refuting them, and replacing them with more adaptive thoughts. This is done through the use of Socratic questioning and other directive techniques. As in behavior therapy, homework assignments play a role—clients in cognitive therapy are often asked to maintain a record of events of their automatic thoughts related to the event and themselves, and of their emotions. As they practice with cognitive techniques, clients become more adept at challenging and changing their problematic cognitions.

Cognitive-behavior therapy combines elements of behavior therapy and cognitive therapy whose theoretical and procedural approaches are highly compatible. This compatibility provides cognitive-behavior therapists with a wide array of possible interventions. Cognitive-behavior therapists stress empirical research, preferring interventions that have been validated by controlled studies. Currently, a large percentage of clinical psychologists identify themselves as cognitive-behavioral in orientation.

Study Questions

1. How do behavioral psychologists view personality organization?
2. What are classical conditioning, operant conditioning, observational learning?
3. What information and instruments are behavior therapists likely to favor?
4. How would you describe the role of the therapist in behavior therapy?
5. In what ways are the behavioral concept of stimulus generalization and the psychoanalytic concept of transference similar?
6. What is relaxation training, and what is it used for?
7. What is systematic desensitization, and how is it conducted?
8. Describe other techniques used by behavior therapists.
9. What does it mean to say that cognitions mediate between events and emotions?
10. What are cognitive distortions? Schemas? Give several examples.
11. How are automatic cognitive distortions similar to and different from unconscious processes in psychodynamic theory?
12. What are the main goals of cognitive therapy?
13. What is psychoeducation, and why do cognitive therapists consider it important?
14. What is Socratic questioning? For what purpose do cognitive therapists use it?
15. How do clients use the three-column and the five-column thought records to practice the principles of cognitive therapy?
16. How are cognitive-behavior therapy sessions typically structured?
17. What is relapse prevention, and how do cognitive therapists work with clients on it?
18. How would you describe the status of cognitive-behavior psychotherapy in the United States today?

Web Sites

- APA Behavior Analysis (Division 25): http://www.apa.org/about/division/div25.aspx
- Academy of Cognitive Therapy: http://www.academyofct.org/i4a/pages/index.cfm?pageid$=$1
- Beck Institute for Cognitive Behavior Therapy: http://www.beckinstitute.org/cbt-treatment/
- Association for Behavioral and Cognitive Therapies: http://www.abct.org/Home/

MOVIES

An Unmarried Woman (1978): Intense drama about a woman's life falling apart, and how, with the help of a therapist and friends, she attempts to put it back together.

The Perks of Being a Wallflower (2012): Based on a novel of the same name, this film explores a troubled adolescent who has had to deal with various treatments for his mental health problems and who is trying to regain positive influences in his life.

MEMOIRS

Buzz: A Year of Paying Attention by Katherine Ellison (2010; New York: Hyperion). After her son was diagnosed with attention deficit/hyperactivity disorder, the author realizes that she too has attentional problems, so she begins a journey along with her son to find effective treatments, including cognitive-behavioral therapy.

Rewind, Replay, Repeat: A Memoir of Obsessive-Compulsive Disorder by Jeff Bell (2007; Center City, MN: Hazelden). Detailed account of the daily life of man with OCD, including notes from his cognitive-behavioral therapist.

References

Abramson, L. Y., Seligman, M. E. P., & Teasdale, J. D. (1978). Learned helplessness in humans: Critique and reformulation. *Journal of Abnormal Psychology, 87*, 49–74.

Allen, L. B., McHugh, R. K., & Barlow, D. H. (2008). Emotional disorders: A unified protocol. In D. H. Barlow (Ed), *Clinical handbook of psychological disorders: A step-by-step treatment manual* (4th ed., pp. 216–249). New York, NY: Guilford Press, xiv, 722 pp.

Antony, M. M., & Roemer, L. (2011a). *Behavior therapy*. Washington, DC: APA Books.

Antony, M. M., & Roemer, L. (2011b). Behavior therapy: Traditional approaches. In S. B. Messer & A. S. Gurman (Eds.), *Essential psychotherapies* (3rd ed., pp. 107–142). New York, NY: Springer.

Baardseth, T. P., Goldberg, S. B., Pace, B. T., Wislocki, A. P., Frost, N. D., et al. (2013). Cognitive-behavioral therapy versus other therapies: Redux. *Clinical Psychology Review, 33*, 395–405.

Bandura, A. (1977). Self-efficacy: Towards a unifying theory of behavior change. *Psychological Review, 84*, 191–215.

Barlow, D. H., & Wolfe, B. (1981). Behavioral approaches to anxiety disorders: A report on the NIMH-SUNY, Albany, research conference. *Journal of Consulting and Clinical Psychology, 49*, 448–454.

Beck, A. T. (1963). Thinking and depression: Idiosyncratic content and cognitive distortions. *Archives of General Psychiatry, 9*, 324–333.

Beck, A. T. (1972). *Depression: Causes and treatment*. Philadelphia, PA: University of Pennsylvania Press.

Beck, A. T. (1976). *Cognitive therapy and the emotional disorders*. New York, NY: International Universities Press.

Beck, J. S. (2011). *Cognitive behavior therapy: Basics and beyond*. New York, NY: The Guilford Press.

Bernstein, D. A., Borkovec, T. D., & Hazlette-Stevens, H. (2000). *Progressive relaxation training: A manual for the helping professions* (2nd ed.). New York, NY: Praeger.

Chambless, D. L. (1990). Spacing of exposure sessions in the treatment of agoraphobia and simple phobia. *Behavior Therapy, 21*, 217–229.

Craighead, W. E., Craighead, L. W., Ritschel, L. A., & Zagoloff, A. (2013). Behavior therapy and cognitive-behavioral therapy. In G. Stricker, T. A. Widiger, & E. B. Weiner (Eds.), *Handbook of psychology, Vol. 8: Clinical Psychology* (2nd ed., pp. 291–319). Hoboken, NJ: John Wiley & Sons.

Craske, M. G. (2010). *Cognitive-behavior therapy.* Washington, DC: APA Books.

Dienes, K. A., Torres-Harding, S., Reinecke, M. A., Freeman, A., & Sauer, A. (2011). Cognitive therapy. In S. B. Messer & A. S. Gurman (Eds.), *Essential psychotherapies* (3rd ed, pp. 143–185). New York, NY: Springer.

Dobson, K. S. (2012). *Cognitive therapy.* Washington, DC: APA Books.

Ellis, A. (1962). *Reason and emotion in psychotherapy.* New York, NY: Lyle Stuart.

Ellis, A. (1973). Rational-emotive therapy. In R. Corsini (Ed.), *Current psychotherapies* (pp. 167–206). Itasca, IL: F. E. Peacock.

Ellis, A. (1995). Rational emotive behavior therapy. In R. J. Corsini & D. Wedding (Eds.), *Current psychotherapies* (5th ed., pp. 162–196). Itasca, IL: Peacock Publishers, Inc.

Ellis, A. (2001). Reasons why rational emotive behavior therapy is relatively neglected in the professional and scientific literatures. *Journal of Rational-Emotive and Cognitive Behavior Therapy, 19,* 67–74.

Ellis, A., & Dryden, W. (1987). *The practice of rational-emotive therapy.* New York, NY: Springer.

Emmelkamp, P. M. G. (2013). Behavior therapy with adults. In M. J. Lambert (Ed.), *Bergin and Garfield's handbook of psychotherapy and behavior change* (6th ed., pp. 343–392). Hoboken, NJ: Wiley.

Farmer, R. F., & Chapman, A. L. (2008). Behavioral case formulations. In R. F. Farmer & A. L. Chapman. *Behavioral interventions in cognitive behavior therapy: Practical guidance for putting theory into action* (pp. 71–103). Washington, DC: American Psychological Association.

Fishman, D. B., Rego, S.A., & Muller, K. L. (2011). Behavior theories of psychotherapy. In J. C. Norcross, G. R. Vandenbos, & D. K. Freedheim (Eds.), *History of psychotherapy: Continuity and change* (2nd ed., pp. 101–140). Washington, DC: American Psychological Association.

Geer, J. H. (1965). The development of a scale to measure fear. *Behaviour Research and Therapy, 3,* 45–53.

Gorenstein, E. E., & Comer, R. J. (2002). *Case studies in abnormal psychology.* New York, NY: Worth Publishers.

Gros, D. F., Yoder, M., Tuerk, P. W., Lozano, B. E., & Acierno, R. (2011). Exposure therapy for PTSD delivered to veterans via telehealth: Predictors of treatment completion and outcome comparison to treatment delivered in person. *Behavior Therapy, 42,* 276–283.

Hayes, S. C., Follette, V. M., & Linehan, M. M. (Eds.). (2004). *Mindfulness and acceptance: Expanding the cognitive-behavioral tradition.* New York, NY: Guilford.

Hayes, S. C., Masuda, A., Bissett, R., Luoma, J., & Guerrero, L. F. (2004). DBT, FAP, and ACT: How empirically oriented are the new behavior therapy technologies? *Behavior Therapy, 35,* 35–54.

Hayes, S. C., Villantte, M., Levin, M., & Hildebrandt, M. (2011). Open, aware, and active: Contextual approaches as an emerging trend in the behavioral and cognitive therapies. *Annual Review of Clinical Psychology, 7,* 141–168.

Hayes-Skelton, S. A., Usmani, A., Lee, J. K., Roemer, L., & Orsillo, S. M. (2011). A fresh look at potential mechanisms of change in applied relaxation for generalized anxiety disorder: A case series. *Cognitive and Behavioral Practice, 19,* 451–462.

Hazlett-Stevens, H., & Bernstein, D. A. (2012). Relaxation. In W. T. O'Donahue & J. E. Fisher (Eds.). *Cognitive behavior therapy: Core principles for practice* (pp. 105–132). New York, NY: John Wiley & Sons.

Heider, F. (1958). *The psychology of interpersonal relations.* New York, NY: Wiley.

Hersen, M. (2002). *Clinical behavior therapy.* New York, NY: Wiley.

Hollon, S. D., & DiGuiseppe, R. (2011). Cognitive theories of psychotherapy. In W. T. O'Donahue & J. E. Fisher (Eds.), *Cognitive behavior therapy: Core principles for practice* (pp. 203–241). New York, NY: John Wiley & Sons.

Iwata, B. A., DeLeon, I. G., & Roscoe, E. M. (2013). Reliability and validity of the functional analysis screening tool. *Journal of Applied Behavior Analysis, 46,* 271–284. doi: 10.1002/jaba.31

Jones, M. C. (1924). The elimination of children's fears. *Journal of Experimental Psychology, 7,* 382–390.

Kinnaman, J. E. S., & Bellack, A. S. (2012). Social skills. In W. T. O'Donahue & J. E. Fisher (Eds.), *Cognitive behavior therapy: Core principles for practice* (pp. 251–272). New York, NY: John Wiley & Sons.

Koerner, K., & Linehan, M. M. (2011). *Doing dialectical behavior therapy: A practical guide.* New York, NY: The Guilford Press.

Kurtz, M. M., & Mueser, K. T. (2008). A meta-analysis of controlled research on social skills training for schizophrenia. *Journal of Consulting and Clinical Psychology, 76,* 491–504.

Lam, J. N., & Steketee, G. S. (2001). Reducing obsessions and compulsions through behavior therapy. *Psychoanalytic Inquiry, 21,* 157–182.

Ledley, D. R., Marx, B. P., & Heimbert, R. G. (2010). *Making cognitive-behavioral therapy work* (2nd ed.). New York, NY: The Guilford Press.

Linehan, M. M. (1993). *Cognitive-behavioral treatment of borderline personality disorder.* New York, NY: Guilford.

Marlatt, G. A., & Gordon, J. R. (Eds.). (1985). *Relapse prevention maintenance strategies in the treatment of addictive behaviors.* New York, NY: Guilford.

Matthews, A. J., Scanlan, J. D., & Kirby, K. C. (2010). Online exposure for spider fear: Treatment completion and habituation outcomes. *Behavior Change, 27,* 199–211.

McGlynn, F. D., Moore, P. M., Lawyer, S., & Karg, R. (1999). Relaxation training inhibits fear and arousal during in vivo exposure to phobia-cue stimuli. *Journal of Behavior Therapy and Experimental Psychiatry, 30,* 155–168.

Meichenbaum, D. H. (1977). *Cognitive behavior modification.* New York, NY: Norton.

Meyerbröker, K., & Emmelkamp, P. M. G. (2011). Virtual reality exposure therapy for anxiety disorders: The state of the art. *Studies in Computational Intelligence, 337,* 47–62.

Miller, A. L., Rathus, J. H., Linehan, M. M., & Swenson, C. R. (2006). *Dialectical behavior therapy with suicidal adolescents.* New York, NY: Guilford.

Mischel, W. (1973). Toward a cognitive social learning reconceptualization of personality. *Psychological Review, 80,* 252–283.

Murdock, N. L. (2004). *Theories of counseling and psychotherapy.* Upper Saddle River, NJ: Pearson.

Newman, C. F. (2013). *Core competencies in cognitive-behavioral therapy: Becoming a highly effective and competent cognitive-behavioral therapist.* New York, NY: Routledge/Taylor & Francis Group.

Norcross, J. C., Ellis, J. L., & Sayette, M. A. (2010). Getting in and getting money: A comparative analysis of admission standards, acceptance rates, and financial assistance across the research-practice continuum in clinical psychology programs. *Training and Education in Professional Psychology, 4,* 99–104.

Norcross, J. C., & Sayette, M. A. (2011). *Insider's guide to graduate programs in clinical and counseling psychology: 2012/2013 edition.* New York, NY: The Guilford Press.

Norcross, J. C., Vandenbos, G. R., & Freedheim, D. K. (Eds.). (2011). *History of psychotherapy: Continuity and change.* Washington, DC: American Psychological Association.

O'Donahue, W. T., & Fisher, J. E. (Eds.). (2012). *Cognitive behavior therapy: Core principles for practice.* New York, NY: John Wiley & Sons.

Opris, D., Pintea, S., Garcia-Palacios, A., Botella, C., Szamoskozi, S., et al. (2011). Virtual reality exposure therapy in anxiety disorders: A quantitative meta-analysis. *Brain and Behavior, 29,* 85–93.

Paul, G. L. (1969). Outcome of systematic desensitization II. In C. M. Franks (Ed.), *Behavior therapy: Appraisal and status* (pp. 63–159). New York, NY: McGraw-Hill.

Peterson, A. L., Hatch, J. P., Hryshko-Mullen, A. S., & Cigrang, J. A. (2012). Relaxation training with and without muscle contraction in subjects with psychophysiological disorders. *Journal of Applied Biobehavioral Research, 16,* 138–147.

Price, M., & Anderson, P. (2007). The role of presence in virtual reality exposure therapy. *Journal of Anxiety Disorders, 21,* 724–751.

Reinecke, M. A., & Freeman, A. (2003). Cognitive therapy. In A. S. Gurman & S. B. Messer (Eds.), *Essential psychotherapies* (2nd ed., pp. 224–271). New York, NY: Guilford.

Roemer, L., Orsillo, S. M., & Salters-Pedneault, K. (2008). Efficacy of an acceptance-based therapy for generalized anxiety disorder: Evaluation in a randomized controlled trial. *Journal of Consulting and Clinical Psychology, 76,* 1083–1089.

Rosenthal, T. L., & Steffek, B. D. (1991). Modeling methods. In F. H. Kanfer & A. P. Goldstein (Eds.), *Helping people change* (4th ed., pp. 70–121). New York, NY: Pergamon Press.

Rothbaum, B. O. (2011). Ask the expert: Anxiety disorders virtual reality therapy. *Focus, 9,* 292–293.

Safer, D. L., Telch, C. F., & Agras, W. (2001). Dialectical behavior therapy for bulimia nervosa. *American Journal of Psychiatry, 158,* 632–634.

Shabin, Y., Pauli, P., & Mühleberger, A. (2013). Effect of multiple context exposure on renewal in spider phobia. *Behaviour Research and Therapy, 5* 68–74.

Spiegler, M. D., & Guevremont, D. C. (2010). *Contemporary behavior therapy.* (3rd ed.). Belmont, CA: Wadsworth, Cengage Learning.

Steketee, G., & Foa, E. B. (1985). Obsessive-compulsive disorder. In D. H. Barlow (Ed.), *Clinical handbook of psychological disorders: A step-by-step treatment manual* (pp. 69–144). New York, NY: Guilford Press.

Thase, M. E. (2012). Social skills training for depression and comparative efficacy research: A 30-year retrospective. *Behavior Modification, 36,* 545–557.

Tisdelle, D. A., & St. Lawrence, J. S. (1988). Adolescent interpersonal problem-solving skill training: Social validation and generalization. *Behavior Therapy, 19,* 171–182.

Van Dijk, S. (2013). *DBT made simple: A step-by-step guide to dialectical behavior therapy.* New York, NY: New Harbinger Publications.

Wade, C. J. (2012). Psychotherapeutic skill preferences of clinical psychologists, licensed clinical psychotherapists, licensed specialist clinical social workers, and psychiatrists. Emporia State University unpublished dissertation, URI: http://hdl.handle.net123456789/1077.

Weiner, B. (Ed.). (1974). *Achievement motivation and attribution.* Morristown, NJ: General Learning Press.

Wolpe, J. (1958). *Psychotherapy by reciprocal inhibition.* Stanford, CA: Stanford University Press.

Wright, J. H., Basco, M. R., & Thase, M. E. (2006). *Learning cognitive-behavior therapy.* Washington, DC: American Psychiatric Association.

Wright, J. H., Sudak, D. M., Turkington, D., & Thase, M. E. (2010). *High-yield cognitive-behavior therapy for brief sessions.* Washington, DC: American Psychiatric Publishing.

Zalta, A. K., & Foa, E. B. (2012). Exposure therapy: Promoting emotional processing of pathological anxiety. In W. T. O'Donahue & J. E. Fisher (Eds.), *Cognitive behavior therapy: Core principles for practice* (pp. 75–104). New York, NY: John Wiley & Sons.

9 | OTHER MODES OF CLINICAL INTERVENTION

Chapter Preview

This chapter provides an overview of alternatives to individual clinical treatment, including group, couples, and family therapy; community mental health programs; prevention efforts; and self-help. Also discussed here are new treatment modalities, such as those based on complementary/alternative medicine, spirituality, mindfulness and acceptance, and a variety of new technologies.

The dominant therapy model of the early 20th century, psychodynamic psychotherapy, was originally designed for treating individual clients. Although some clinicians adapted psychoanalytic concepts to group therapy (Bion, 1959), most psychodynamic psychotherapists worked only in a one-on-one format. The behavioral and humanistic approaches that gained recognition during the mid-twentieth century were also originally designed for individuals. Since the middle of the last century, though, there has been a proliferation of therapy modes that involve more than one client at a time and that focus on relationships or relationship systems. Group therapy was the first of these socially oriented therapies, followed somewhat later by the advent of couples and family therapy. The 1960s saw the rise of the self-help movement and of community psychology, which emphasizes the value of treating disorders in local communities as well as of intervening in broader social systems to prevent the development or worsening of mental disorders.

These modes of intervention reflect trends in psychology that view individuals' behavior as a reflection of the relationship systems they inhabit. These approaches assume that psychological problems exist within social contexts; each emphasizes interventions built around these contexts (see Table 9.1).

TABLE 9.1 Socially Oriented Clinical Interventions

Intervention Mode	Emphasis
Group therapy	Understand and alleviate disturbances in interpersonal relationships as revealed in a group setting.
Couples therapy	Help couples in intimate relationships to improve problem-solving and communication skills.
Family therapy	Change harmful family interaction patterns so that the family system functions better.
Community psychology	Create beneficial changes at a community or societal level to prevent disorders or to raise general levels of mental health.
Prevention	Head off the appearance of mental disorders by counteracting risk factors and strengthening protective factors.
Self-help	Encourage people to perform therapeutic functions for themselves, either in groups organized around a specific concern or individually through a course of study.

GROUP THERAPY

SECTION PREVIEW

This section provides an overview of group therapies and discusses their inner workings. In addition to covering traditional supportive and process-oriented groups, we discuss more recent advances in cognitive-behavioral group therapy and psychoeducational groups.

Group therapy was first practiced at the turn of the 20th century in Boston by Joseph Pratt. The increased use of group therapy was later stimulated by the shortage of professional personnel around the time of World War II (Burlingame & Baldwin, 2011). It grew in popularity especially in the 1960s and 1970s and has since progressed to the point that it is now regarded as a valuable intervention in its own right (Burlingame, MacKenzie, & Strauss, 2004).

Every major approach to clinical psychology offers group treatment. There are analytic groups, client-centered and gestalt groups, and behavioral groups. To varying degrees, most group therapists emphasize the importance of interpersonal relationships and assume that personal maladjustment involves difficulties in those relationships. Increasingly, evidence-based practices are being integrated into group therapy formats, with special focus on cognitive-behavioral groups for a number of specific problems and client populations (Crits-Christoph, Johnson, Gibbons, & Gallop, 2013).

Therapeutic Factors in Group Therapy

Group therapies are meant to serve several clients at the same time, with the added benefit of providing support from other group members (Bieling, McCabe, & Antony, 2006). Indeed, group therapy is considered more than the simultaneous treatment of several individuals. Groups provide therapeutic opportunities that cannot be found in individual therapy, and group therapists must learn how to use those opportunities. We summarize these concepts below; a fuller discussion is contained in standard references on traditional group therapy (e.g., Corey, 2011; Yalom & Leszcz, 2005):

- *Sharing New Information.* New information is imparted from two sources in groups: The group leader may offer advice, and advice also comes from other members of the group who share their experiences. Often, feedback from several group members can have more impact on clients than feedback from a single therapist.
- *Instilling Hope.* Not only can confidence be instilled by the therapist, but group members can provide hope and can comment on positive changes that they see in other members.
- *Universality.* By showing that everyone struggles with problems in living, therapy groups help their members learn that they are not alone in their fears, low moods, or other difficulties. Learning about the universality of one's problems also soothes anxiety about "going crazy" or "losing control."
- *Altruism.* Groups give clients a chance to discover that they can help other people. Clinicians refer to the positive emotions that follow altruistic behavior as "feelings of self-worth," an outcome that is promoted by effective group therapy.
- *Interpersonal Learning.* A properly conducted therapy group is an ideal setting to learn new interpersonal skills. It presents repeated opportunities to practice fundamental social skills with various types of people and with immediate feedback on performance.
- *Group Cohesiveness.* Members of cohesive groups accept one another; they are willing to listen to and be influenced by the group. They participate in the group readily, feel secure in it, and are relatively immune to outside disruption of the group's progress. Cohesive groups also permit the expression of hostility, provided such conflicts do not violate the norms of the group. Meta-analytic studies suggest that group cohesion is one of the most important factors underlying the beneficial effects of group therapy (Burlingame, McClendon, & Alonso, 2011).

The Practice of Group Therapy

Therapy groups usually consist of 6 to 12 members. Some leaders of traditional groups believe that their groups should be *homogeneous*, consisting of members who are similar in age, sex, and type of problem. Others prefer to form groups that are *heterogeneous*, meaning that there is a mix of client types. Heterogeneous groups are easier to form. They also have the advantage of exposing members to a wider range of people and perspectives. The major advantage of homogeneous

Therapy groups can often include clients with a diverse array of concerns. *Source*: Richard T. Nowitz/Corbis.

groups is that they facilitate a direct focus on the common problem that motivated each member to enter treatment. In practice, groups will invariably be homogeneous on some dimensions (e.g., diagnosis and problem severity) and heterogeneous on others (e.g., problem duration, personality characteristics, and coping style).

Group meetings usually last about 1 to 2 hours. They are longer than sessions of individual therapy because it often takes more time for all of the clients in a group session to share their experiences and to process the information that is presented.

A Case Example of Group Therapy

Here is a brief description of the fifth session of therapy for a group of five women and three men, all in their late 20s and 30s and all unmarried or separated. The cognitive-behavioral orientation of the group's therapist is evident in that the members are asked to concentrate on helping each other improve their coping skills and interpersonal relationships (Rose & LeCroy, 1991, pp. 422–423).

As the group settled into places on the floor or on chairs, the therapist welcomed them and asked each member to review what he or she had done throughout the week to complete the assignment of the previous week. One at a time, members described their social achievements, their success in coping with anxiety, and the frequency with which they used the relaxation exercise. Several also related unusually stressful situations they had experienced during the week.

After each had summarized her or his experiences, amid a great deal of praise and support from group members for achievements, Delores volunteered to describe in some detail her situation in which her ever-present feelings of helplessness were intensified. Her supervisor at her office, she stated, was always giving her instructions on the least little thing. "It was as if she thought I was stupid and, frankly, I'm beginning to believe it." The other members inquired as to the nature of her job, which was quite complicated. They noted that she did receive good feedback from her peers, who often consulted with her on various problems. She also noted that in a previous job, no one gave her more than the briefest instructions, and she did fine. Charles wondered whether she couldn't conclude that there was a problem between her and her supervisor and not with her as a person. There was just no evidence that she was dumb in any way; in fact, she appeared to be uniquely qualified to do the job. The others agreed.

Delores said she guessed they were right, but she did not know what to do about it, and it was making her miserable. She had thought about quitting, but it was in other ways a good job; and besides, she added, "good jobs were hard to get these days."

> After careful questioning by the other clients in order to have a clear picture of what was going on, they provided her with a number of strategies she could employ to deal with the situation and suggested what she could specifically say to herself and to her supervisor. She evaluated and selected several from among these for practice in the group.

Cognitive-Behavioral Group Therapy

The cognitive-behavioral group therapy illustrated in this example is one of the more common types of group therapy in use today (Crits-Christoph, Johnson, Gibbons, & Gallop, 2013). In fact, cognitive-behavioral techniques are now used five-times more than other techniques in group therapy (Burlingame & Baldwin, 2011). Cognitive-behavioral groups are sometimes known as *psychoeducational groups* because they focus on learning and on sharing information rather than on group process. This approach to group therapy has been used effectively for a number of problems with a number of specific client populations, including

- Depression and anxiety in adults (Oei & Browne, 2006)
- PTSD in veterans living in remote locations; where therapy is provided via video teleconferencing (Greene et al., 2010)
- Alcohol abuse in college students (Michael, Curtin, Kirkley, Jones, & Harris, 2006)
- Coping with cancer (Schnur & Montgomery, 2010)
- Substance abuse in outpatients (Petry, Weinstock, & Alessi, 2011)
- Grief interventions for children who survived traumas (Salloum & Overstreet, 2008)

Table 9.2 provides an outline of the cognitive-behavioral treatment procedure protocol for the first session of group treatment for clients suffering from a combination of depression and social phobia. More information on these procedures and other group therapy approaches is available from several sources (e.g. Corey, 2011; Free, 2007; Wenzel, Liese, Beck, & Friedman-Wheeler, 2012; Yalom & Leszcz, 2005).

TABLE 9.2 Sample Treatment Protocol for First Session of a Group Cognitive-Behavioral Treatment for Comorbid Depression and Social Phobia

Session 1

1. Introduction of therapists and group members
2. Group "rules"
   a. Confidentiality
   b. Check-in and rating scales
   c. Homework
   d. Missing appointments
3. Introducing the CBT approach to depression and social phobia
   a. Behavioral interventions: Activation and exposure
   b. Cognitive interventions
4. Describing the biopsychosocial model of depression and social phobia, and introducing the five components:
   a. Behavior
   b. Thoughts
   c. Emotions
   d. Biology
   e. Environment
5. Overview of social phobia, including
   a. The nature of fear and social anxiety (e.g., occasional social anxiety is normal and has a survival function)
   b. Myths and misconceptions regarding fear and social anxiety
   c. The three components of fear (i.e., physical, cognitive, behavioral)
6. Homework: Complete biopsychosocial model and purchase companion manual

---

Source: From Bieling, P. J., McCabe, R. E., & Antony, M. M. (2006). *Cognitive-behavioral therapy in groups* (p. 382). New York, NY: Guilford Press. Copyright 2006 by Guilford Press. Adapted with permission.

SECTION SUMMARY

Group therapy can be an effective and affordable modality of psychological treatment. There are a number of therapeutic factors in group therapy, including sharing new information, instilling hope, universality, altruism, interpersonal learning, and group cohesiveness. More recent forms of group therapy have included cognitive-behavioral group treatments that focus on teaching clients new skills.

COUPLES AND FAMILY THERAPY

SECTION PREVIEW

In addition to group treatment, therapy can focus on couples and families. This section reviews these therapies, which tend to focus on a disturbance within the relationship, such as conflict between spouses or difficult parent–child interactions.

In *couples therapy* and *family therapy*, the focus is on disturbed relationships rather than on individuals who happen to be in a relationship. Couples therapy used to be referred to as *marital therapy*, but the current term is more descriptive because it includes a wider array of heterosexual and homosexual couples, including spouses, cohabitating partners, romantic partners who do not live together, and any other pair of individuals who consider themselves a couple. Couples therapy focuses on the dyad rather than the individual partners. Family therapy focuses on relationships involving one or more parents (or guardians) and their children. Because both couples and family therapy emphasize communication patterns within close relationships, therapists who work with couples often work with families and vice versa.

Prior to the 1950s, few therapists worked with couples or families (Harway, 2005). However, as other forms of social and multiclient intervention grew, so did family therapy. Since the 1970s, the number of couples and family therapists has increased rapidly (Chabot, 2011). Journals devoted to family psychology first appeared in the United States and Japan during the 1980s, and the Division of Family Psychology was founded within the American Psychological Association in 1985 (Kaslow, 2011). Courses in family psychology are now offered by many psychology, counseling, and social work graduate programs.

Diagnosis in Couples and Family Therapy

One challenge for couples and family therapists is how best to understand relationship difficulties. For individual clients, psychologists use the *Diagnostic and Statistical Manual of Mental Disorders* (DSM) (or the *International Classification of Diseases*, or ICD), to label individual problems. But with couples and family therapy, the client is not so much an individual as a *relationship* or *system of relationships*. How should these relationships and systems be understood and diagnosed? Are there identifiable patterns for dysfunctional relationships that might eventually point the way to effective intervention techniques?

The development of diagnostic categories for interpersonal conflicts has begun. The initial work in this area led to *V-Codes* for relational problems in *DSM-IV*. V-Codes are "Other Conditions That May Be a Focus of Clinical Attention" and include, for instance, Parent–child relational problem (V61.20), Partner relational problem (V61.10), and Sibling relational problem (V61.8). Codes could be listed on Axis I in a DSM IV diagnosis, but most insurance companies did not reimburse for V-Codes. Some clinicians suggested that disorders in relationships and relational processes, such as relationship distress or partner and child maltreatment, should become formal diagnostic categories in the new *DSM-5* (Beach & Kaslow, 2006). That did not happen (Lawrence, Beach, & Doss, 2013), though, partly because clinical scientists have not yet established the reliability, validity, and utility of relational diagnoses. Nevertheless, there is a great deal of interest in conducting the research necessary to do this (Lawrence, Beach, & Doss, 2013).

Couples Therapy

Couples seek therapy for a variety of reasons (see Table 9.3), especially because of problems in affection and communication (Doss, Simpson, & Christensen, 2004). As illustrated in Figure 9.1, these problems tend to occur more frequently at particular stages of a marriage or other relationship,

TABLE 9.3 Reasons Couples Seek Treatment

Reason for Therapy	% of Couples Reporting Problem
Emotional affection (e.g., basic unhappiness, feeling alone)	57
Communication	57
Divorce/separation concerns	46
Improve relationship	46
Arguments/anger	44
Concerns about children	32
Sex/physical affection	28
Spouse critical/demanding	8
Spouse distant/withdrawn	8
Trust issues	8
Social activities/time together	8
Infidelity/flirting	6

Source: Adapted from Doss, B. D., Simpson, L. E., & Christensen, A. (2004). Why do couples seek marital therapy? *Professional Psychology: Research and Practice, 35,* 608–614.

and it is during these stages that couples are most likely to enter treatment. Further, the problems and treatment targets dealt with in couples therapy are similar whether the couple is heterosexual or homosexual (Long & Andrews, 2011). To provide a clearer picture of each partner's communication skills, therapists often ask the clients to complete self-reports on their communication skills before treatment begins (see Figure 9.2).

In most cases, couples therapy focuses mainly on relationship difficulties, but it can sometimes be combined with other methods designed to address other problems. For example, when depression, alcoholism, or severe anxiety disorders affect the quality, and even the existence, of a client's marriage or intimate relationship, some mental health experts recommend couples

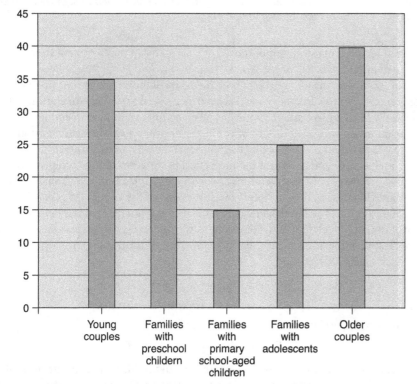

FIGURE 9.1 Marital Satisfaction Across the Lifespan: "Percent of Married Couples Reporting They Experience General Marital Satisfaction All the Time".
Source: Carr, A. (2006). *The handbook of child and adolescent clinical psychology: A contextual approach* (2nd ed., p. 60). New York, NY: Routledge/Taylor & Francis Group.

NAME: _____ DATE: _____

The aim of this form is to identify your strengths and weaknesses in communication and to select goals for improvement. Rate each of the skills below using this code:

    0   Very poor use of skill
    1   Unsatisfactory use of skill
    2   Satisfactory use of skill, but room for improvement
    3   Good use of skill
    N/A Not applicable

Skill	0	1	2	3	N/A
Specific descriptors					
Self-disclosure					
Clear expression of positives					
Assertive expression of negatives					
Attending to partner					
Minimal encouragers (e.g., nods, hm-mm)					
Reserving judgment					
Asking questions					
Summarizing content					
Paraphrasing feelings					
Positive suggestions					

Self-identified strengths in communication: _____

Self-identified weakness in communication: _____

FIGURE 9.2 Communication Skills Self-Evaluation Form.
Source: Halford, W. K., & Moore, E. N., (2002). Relationship education and the prevention of couple relationship problems. In A. S. Gurman & N. S. Jacobson (Eds.), *Clinical handbook of couple therapy* (3rd ed., pp. 400–419). New York, NY: Guilford Press.

therapy—or at least the involvement of the client's partner—in the treatment of these disorders (Baucom, Epstein, Kirby, & Falconier, 2011).

In many instances, the therapist sees both members of the couple at the same time, a procedure called *conjoint therapy.* In other cases, each partner is seen separately for some or all sessions. This is especially likely in *separation counseling,* when couples want help in ending a marriage or long-term relationship with a minimum of conflict over property and/or child custody.

The goals and techniques of couples therapy depend partly on the conflicts that are the most pressing for each couple and partly on the theoretical orientation of the therapist. For example, therapists who prefer systemic interventions and who see couples as interpersonal systems rather than as two individuals would try to intervene at the level of the system (Weeks & Treat, 2001). Systemic therapists usually assume that there is circularity and interrelatedness in each individual's experience of the couple relationship. For example, the following statements alone could be seen as linear, but together they show the circularity of the couples' relationship from a systemic framework (Weeks & Treat, 2001, p. 28):

THERAPIST TO WIFE:	Why do you get so angry?
WIFE:	Because he always withdraws from me.
THERAPIST TO HUSBAND:	Why do you withdraw?
HUSBAND:	Because she is always so angry.

In contrast, a behaviorally oriented couples therapist would be likely to help with a couple's communication problems by teaching the partners to replace hostile, unconstructive criticism with comments that clearly express feelings and directly convey requests for the behaviors that each wants from the other. Cognitive-behavioral couples therapists work to help couples change the way they think about their relationship and modify the attributions they make about each other

(Baucom, Epstein, Kirby, & LaTaillade, 2010). Accordingly, the cognitive-behavioral therapist may teach each member of the couple to recognize, for example, that the other member's anger may reflect anxiety about the future of the relationship, not necessarily an effort to end it.

In general, most couples therapists tend to emphasize problem solving (Baucom, Epstein, Kirby, & Falconier, 2011). The touchstone of problem solving is teaching the couple how to communicate and negotiate more effectively with each other. Among the multiple tasks involved in building better communication are teaching the couple to accept mutual responsibility for working on problems, maintaining focus on current relationship problems rather than old grudges, fostering expression of preferences rather than demands for obedience, and negotiating compromises to problems the couple decide cannot be solved.

The following brief excerpt from a couples therapy session illustrates an attempt by the therapist (T) to help a wife (W) learn new ways of communicating some of her negative feelings to her husband:

T: I do think that what Pete is saying is an important point. There are things that are going to be different about you, and each of you is going to think the things you do maybe make more sense than the other person's, and that's probably going to be pretty much of a reality. You're not going to be able to change all those. You may not be able to change very many of them. And everybody is different. They have their own predilections to do things a certain way, and again what's coming through from you is sort of like damning those and saying those are wrong; they're silly, they don't make sense, I don't understand them or whatever. You may not understand them, but they are a reality of each of you. That's something you have to learn how to deal with in some way. Otherwise, you . . . the reason I'm stressing this is I think it plays a large part in your criticalness.

W: Well, I do find it difficult to cater to, I guess that's the word, cater to some idiosyncrasies that I find or think are totally foolish. I am intolerant. I am, and I find it very difficult. I find it almost impossible to do it agreeably and without coming on as "Oh, you're ridiculous."

T: I guess what would be helpful would be if you could come on honestly enough to say "I don't like them" or "It doesn't sit well with me" without having to add the additional value judgment of whether they're foolish or ridiculous or whatever. That's the part that hurts. It's when you damn him because of these things—that's gonna hurt. I'm sure from Pete's point of view they make sense for his total economy of functioning. There's some sense to why he does things the way he does, just as there is for why you do things the way you do. It's not that they're foolish. They make sense in terms of where you are, what you're struggling with, and what's the best way you can deal with right now. I'm not trying to say that means you have to like them, but when you come across and say "It's ridiculous or foolish"—that's the part that makes it hurt.

W: Well, tell me again how to say it, because I find it hard to say anything except "That's really stupid—that's silly." I know you said it a minute ago, but I lost it.

T: Well, anytime you can say it in terms of how it affects you and stay with it, like "It's hard—I find it hard to take," that doesn't say "I find you're an ass for wanting to do that such and such a way." It's just that, I find it hard to take—I get upset in this circumstance" or whatever. Stay with what your feelings are rather than trying to evaluate Pete. (Ables & Brandsma, 1977, pp. 92–94)

With two clients in the room, couples therapists must take care to avoid becoming *triangulated* by the couple—that is, for example, finding themselves in the middle of their clients' disagreements. Weeks and Treat (2001, pp. 4–8) offer a number of suggestions for preventing triangulation, including these:

- Don't take sides.
- Don't proceed until the problem(s) and goal(s) have been clarified.
- Don't discuss problems abstractly and nonconcretely.
- Don't discount problems, even small problems.
- Don't assume the partners in the couple will perceive the problem in the same way.
- Don't get hooked in the past.
- Don't allow the couple to take charge of the session.

Many of these same suggestions apply when therapists work with families.

Family Therapy

Just as couples therapy is aimed at changing a couple's relationship, family therapy aims to change patterns of family interaction so as to correct disturbances in those interactions (Stanton, 2013). Like couples therapy, family therapy arose from recognition that the problems of individual clients occur in social contexts and have social consequences. It was observed, for example, that clients who showed great improvement during individual therapy while hospitalized often relapsed when they returned to their families. This observation, along with other clinical insights and research, led to several early theories that emphasized the family environment and parent–child interactions as causes of maladaptive behavior (Bateson, Jackson, Haley, & Weakland, 1956; Lidz & Lidz, 1949; Sullivan, 1953).

Family therapy often begins with a focus on a family member who is having particularly noticeable problems. Typically, this *identified client* is a male child whom the parents label as having an unmanageable behavior problem, or a girl who is withdrawn and sad. Soon, however, the therapist will try to reframe the identified problems in terms of disturbed family processes or faulty family communication, to encourage all family members to examine their own contributions to the problem, and to consider the positive changes that each member can make to solve them. As in couples therapy, a common goal of family therapy is improved communication and the elimination of coercion in the family system (Chabot, 2011).

As with individual, group, and couples therapy, there is no single agreed-upon technique for conducting family therapy. Rather, therapists can select from a wide variety of techniques. For example, those operating from a behavioral point of view try to teach family members alternative, noncoercive ways of communicating their needs. They teach parents to be firm and consistent in their child-discipline practices, encourage each family member to communicate clearly with the others, educate family members in behavior-exchange principles, discourage blaming of the identified client for all family problems, and help all members of the family to consider whether their expectations of other members are reasonable. These behavioral methods are also used in *multisystemic therapy*, which conceptualizes families from a systemic, ecological perspective (Henggeler, 2011).

As evidence-based practice becomes more prominent in all forms of therapy, family therapy, too, has tended to focus more closely on behavioral targets and methods. For example, *behavioral parent training* (Briesmeister & Schaefer, 2007), also known as *parent management training* (Kazdin, 2008), has been used to effectively treat a number of externalizing behavior problems in children, such as oppositional defiant disorder and aggression. As in the following case example, behavioral parent training can be modified for use with adolescents as well (Weisz, 2004).

Sal is 13 years old, and he is a "bad dude." Sal is quick to anger and has been expelled from school a number of times for fighting, stealing, and yelling at teachers. Since preschool, his mother has felt that she could not control his behavior, and his father largely ignores the family while he spends most of his time watching television and drinking beer. Due to the repeated suspensions from school, Sal's mother finally tried to get help.

The therapy consisted of many components, including anger management and behavioral parent training. One of the key features of behavioral parent training is to document the child's problematic behavior objectively in order to target behaviors for improvement. Sal's mother comments to the therapist that she feels that Sal is disrespectful and disobedient, but she could not provide specific examples of behaviors that bothered her. Sal's mother also acknowledged that, other than complaining about Sal's behavior, she did little to try to stop him from acting out. Thus, the therapist worked with Sal's mother to identify problematic behaviors and to generate ideas of how to handle the behaviors more effectively. Most important is that the mother must identify just two or three behaviors to start modifying rather than trying to change everything at once (which often backfires on the family). In choosing behaviors to target for intervention, the therapist taught Sal's mother to: (a) be specific, (b) begin with problems you can see, (c) start with fairly neutral behaviors, (d) select behaviors that occur at least two or three times per day, and (e) say what replacement behaviors are needed (Weisz, 2004, pp. 302–303).

Sal's mother chose to target disobeying and disrespect (e.g., smirking, sighing, rolling his eyes). Because using a time-out procedure is not effective with older children, the mother and therapist developed a behavioral contract with Sal whereby there were no positive consequences for unwanted behaviors (e.g., he did not get his way when he complained about something) and there were clear positive consequences for desirable behavior. Based on a point-chart that was posted in the kitchen, Sal would earn points for adaptive behaviors (e.g., getting up on time, doing his chores, obeying his mother) and he would lose points for maladaptive behaviors (e.g., disobeying or disrespecting his mother). At the end of each day, Sal could cash in his points for things like watching television (if his homework was done), playing a computer game, and talking on the phone to his friends.

Both Sal and his mother embraced this program, and with relatively little upheaval, Sal's behavior began to improve rapidly. Since his behavior at school was also tied into the point-chart at home, behavioral improvements were seen both at school and at home (Weisz, 2004).

Interestingly, Sal's behavior improved even without the involvement of the father in treatment. Behavioral parent training can be effective with just one parent, but the effects are more long lasting when both mothers and fathers are involved (Phares, Fields, & Binitie, 2006). Not all cases show such rapid improvement, especially when the clients are adolescents, but this one illustrates that behavioral parent training actually changes both the parent's and the child's behavior (Weisz, 2004).

Another form of family therapy is known as *parent–child interaction therapy* (PCIT). Originally developed by Sheila Eyberg (Eyberg & Matarazzo, 1980), this therapy is based on principles from attachment theory. The therapy allows therapists to work with both parents and children and directly coaches parents about how to interact with their child. PCIT has been found to be very effective with a number of types of problems, especially oppositional defiant disorder (Funderburk & Eyberg, 2011), but more recently it has also been shown to be effective with depression (Luby, Lenze, & Tillman, 2012) and anxiety disorders (Comer et al., 2012) in young children.

The Social Contexts of Couples and Family Therapy

Some of the most important challenges for couple and family therapists come from the changing *social contexts* in which couples and families live (see Figure 9.3). Families are invariably a part of a larger social context, and their functioning is partly dependent on that context. Consider that only about 64.2% of children in the United States live in traditional nuclear families with married, heterosexual parents and one or more biological children (Hofferth, Stueve, Pleck, Bianchi, & Sayer, 2002). The rest are configured as multigenerational, multicultural units; foster families; blended families; gay or lesbian couples with children; or several people living together with no legal ties but with strong mutual commitments (Kaslow, 2011). To be effective in working with such a wide range of family constellations, therapists must understand the special problems each type of family faces and must guard against the influence of bias against family structures that differ from their own.

Our description of couples and family therapy techniques has been brief. Far more information about these techniques is available in a number of authoritative sources (e.g., Becvar, 2013; Carr, 2012; Doherty & McDaniel, 2009; Gottman, 2011; McGoldrick, Giordano, & Garcia-Preto, 2005; McHale & Lindahl, 2011; Nicholes & Minuchin, 2009; Schulz, Pruett, Kerig, & Parke, 2010).

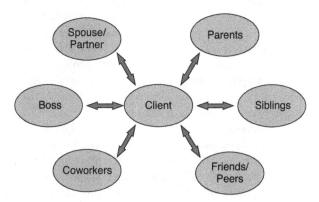

FIGURE 9.3 Families and Couples Have Multiple Influences

SECTION SUMMARY

Couples and family therapy are well-established treatment formats in clinical psychology. Couples therapy often deals with difficulties within the dyad (such as conflict between partners), whereas family therapy deals with problematic relationships in a larger family group. Therapists must be careful not to take sides when working with couples and families and need to remain neutral and open-minded in their role as a therapist.

COMMUNITY PSYCHOLOGY

SECTION PREVIEW

This section covers community psychology, which deals with an even larger scope of problems than couples and family therapy: those that exist on the community level. The history of community psychology and the principles employed by community psychologists are discussed as well.

Despite the dominant status of individual, group, couples, and family therapy, not all clinical psychologists believe that these are the best modes of intervention for psychological problems. To produce truly meaningful improvements in individuals' lives, these critics say, psychologists must employ intervention strategies designed to maximize the "fit" between individuals and specific environments that are likely to promote their adjustment (Moskell & Allred, 2013).

What Is Community Psychology?

One of the primary goals of community psychology is to help individuals adapt to and cope with their environment. Another is to understand the causes of disorders more broadly (e.g., that the cause of individual disorder can lie in larger problems in society, such as poverty), and when possible, to modify community-level causes before they have an opportunity to negatively influence individuals and groups. In short, community psychologists seek to apply psychological principles to (a) understanding individual and social problems, (b) preventing behavioral dysfunction, and (c) creating lasting social change.

Their efforts are based on the *ecological perspective*, which suggests that people's behavior develops out of their interactions with all aspects of their environment: physical, social, political, and economic. Accordingly, community psychologists argue that alleviating individual and social problems requires that we make changes in *both environmental settings and individual competencies*. Along with their emphasis on environmental factors in disorder, community psychologists also focus on the plight of the urban and rural poor and other groups whose problems (a) have tended to be underserved by traditional systems for therapy service delivery and (b) appear more social than psychological and thus require social rather than individual change.

A Brief History of Community Psychology

In the 1950s and 1960s, an array of influences came together to accelerate the development of community psychology. Some of the most prominent of these included disenchantment with the focus on psychodynamic approaches (Rappaport, 1977); skepticism about the reliability and validity of psychological diagnosis of disorders (Rosenhan, 1973) and about the benefits of traditional psychotherapy (Eysenck, 1952); shortages of mental health professionals to deliver individual treatment (Albee, 1959); sociopolitical turmoil over civil rights, gender equality, poverty, and the Vietnam War; and passage of the Community Mental Health Centers Act in 1962, which provided funds for the construction of comprehensive mental health centers.

Today, community psychology is in its sixth decade. It boasts its own division within the American Psychological Association, and there are several journals—including the *American Journal of Community Psychology*, the *Community Mental Health Journal*, and the *Journal of Community Psychology*—devoted to reporting the research and accomplishments of community psychologists. There are also a number of graduate training programs in community psychology, some of which are part of clinical psychology programs.

Principles and Methods of Community Psychology

Unlike traditional clinical psychologists, community psychologists often try to influence local citizens to become active in improving disorder-related conditions in their own communities. Among the other principles and methods that differentiate community psychology from traditional clinical psychology are:

- **Social-System Change.** In accordance with their ecological approach, community psychologists are often more interested in promoting social-system-level changes than in promoting person-oriented changes. Community psychologists emphasize indirect services that have no particular target client but are expected to achieve benefits because the social-system changes they produce radiate to intended target groups (Seidman & Tseng, 2011).
- **Promoting a "Psychological Sense of Community."** Community psychologists attempt to strengthen the ability of a community to plan and implement its own changes by promoting a psychological sense of community (Sarason, 1974). They encourage collective action by individuals with common needs or interests, and they seek to help these coalitions maintain their commitment to mutual problem solving.
- **Paraprofessionals.** Encouraging paraprofessionals (i.e., nonprofessionals) to provide behavior-change functions is a cornerstone of community psychology. Many of these helpers are known as *indigenous paraprofessionals* because they are drawn from the very groups that will receive their services. Indeed, their cultural rootedness in the to-be-served group is one of their fundamental assets.
- **Use of Activism.** Social activism is the use of power to accomplish social reform. This power may be economic, it may be political, or it may be the coercive power of civil disobedience, all of which have pros and cons. Advocates of activist tactics claim that professionals' willingness to provoke, agitate, and confront accounts for a large measure of their effectiveness in promoting change. Opponents of professional social action argue that such activity is incompatible with the objective empiricism that is the defining characteristic of a psychological scientist.
- **Use of Research as a Form of Intervention.** Research as intervention is exemplified by what is called *dissemination research*—experimentation designed to evaluate alternative methods of implementing programs that initial studies have shown to be successful. In the course of finding the most effective means of persuading other communities to adopt a given program, that program is, by necessity, adopted (Maton & Brodsky, 2011).

Despite its innovativeness and obvious good intentions, community psychology has evoked a number of concerns over the years, including about who should make decisions for the community: members of the community or community psychologists. In general, community psychologists try to become integrated into local communities in order make sure that the changes they recommend are consistent with the wishes of the people who live there (Rappaport, 2011).

SECTION SUMMARY

Community psychologists are concerned with the way the social environment influences individual well-being. Through principles of social-system change, promoting psychological sense of community, the use of paraprofessionals, political activism, and research, community psychologists attempt to improve the lives of large groups of individuals.

PREVENTION

SECTION PREVIEW

This section provides an overview of efforts to prevent psychological disorders. These efforts are largely an outgrowth of community psychology. Examples of disorder prevention strategies include improving parenting skills, teaching social skills, changing environments, reducing stress, and increasing empowerment.

A central outgrowth of community psychology is prevention, which is now infused into the entire field of psychology. Decades ago, using principles borrowed from the field of public health, Gerald

Caplan (1964) described three levels at which mental health problems can be prevented: tertiary, secondary, and primary. Later, the Institute of Medicine (1994) suggested other terminology (*indicated prevention interventions, selective mental health prevention,* and *universal mental health prevention,* respectively), which is becoming more common in the field. The following definitions refer to both systems of terminology:

- *Tertiary prevention (indicated prevention intervention)* seeks to lessen the severity of disorders and to reduce short-term and long-term consequences of mental health problems. One example of this type of prevention, *psychosocial rehabilitation,* teaches clients with severe psychopathology how to cope better with the effects of these problems and tries to help the client achieve the highest possible quality of life in the community in order to prevent further negative effects from the psychopathology (Mihalopoulos, Vos, Pirkis, & Carter, 2011).
- *Secondary prevention (selective mental health prevention)* involves interventions for people who are at risk for developing a disorder. Effective secondary prevention requires knowledge of how risk factors culminate in specific disorders. It also usually requires assessment methods that are reliable and valid for detecting the initial signs of a disorder so that attempts can be made to intervene at the earliest possible point. Many secondary prevention programs attempt to increase protective factors for individuals who are at risk for the development of a disorder, a process which is likely to increase the *resilience* of individuals in the program (Mihalopoulos, Vos, Pirkis, & Carter, 2011).
- *Primary prevention (universal mental health prevention)* involves avoiding the development of disorders by either modifying environments or strengthening individuals so that they are not susceptible to those disorders in the first place. Primary prevention programs seek to counteract risk factors and reinforce protective factors (Mihalopoulos, Vos, Pirkis, & Carter, 2011).

These three types of prevention programs differ largely in terms of their target populations. For example, in order to prevent the recurrence of child abuse, a *tertiary* prevention program would identify parents who have abused their children in the past, then arrange for them to attend psychoeducational classes on more effective ways of dealing with children's behavior, along with child development classes, both of which would help them become more informed, competent parents. Anger management classes might be offered as well. A *secondary* prevention program would offer help to a population of parents who are identified as being at risk for abusing their children (e.g., parents who had been physically abused themselves) but who had not yet done so. These parents might be paired with a well-functioning parent in their community who could act as a source of support and helpful information about dealing effectively and nonviolently with children's behavior and misbehavior. *Primary* prevention efforts would involve the entire community population and might include a public-service campaign on radio, television, billboards, and in newspapers in which celebrities, prominent athletes, and other influential figures would discourage child abuse and direct people to get help for child-rearing problems.

The focus of prevention, which is now known as *prevention science,* has been influenced by the development of the National Institute of Mental Health's Prevention Intervention Research Centers (PIRCs), and by recommendations contained in a number of government reports over the years, including recent reports by the National Research Council and Institute of Medicine (2009a; 2009b). Many psychologists continue to pursue primary prevention programs consistent with the PIRC research model, which focused on multidisciplinary research to help prevent the development of psychopathology. Five examples of this type of research are improving parenting skills, teaching social skills, changing environments, reducing stress, and promoting empowerment.

IMPROVING PARENTING SKILLS A number of primary prevention programs are aimed at improving parenting skills in order to reduce the incidence of family violence. Every year, millions of children are victims of physical or sexual abuse or severe neglect or are witnesses to family violence. There is evidence that children reared in violent homes are more likely to become aggressive, abusive, or criminal adults themselves (Dodge, Coie, & Lynam, 2006). Prevention programs attempt to improve parenting skills, reduce the use of corporal punishment, and change parental attitudes (Sandler, Schoenfelder, Wolchik, & MacKinnon, 2011).

TEACHING SOCIAL SKILLS   Another approach to primary prevention of mental disorder involves teaching children and adolescents the interpersonal skills crucial to later development and adjustment. For example, children lacking such skills tend to display, as early as kindergarten, a pattern of behavior that elevates their risk for later delinquency (Welsh & Farrington, 2007). However, there is evidence that if these children can be taught to use effective problem-solving strategies (Shure & Aberson, 2005), they can avoid developing the academic and social problems common in the backgrounds of conduct-disordered youngsters.

CHANGING ENVIRONMENTS   A third approach to primary prevention entails making environments (such as homes, schools, and neighborhoods) more supportive of adaptive behavior. For example, programs such as Head Start that expand preschool opportunities and increase the commitment of parents and children to academic success have been shown to decrease antisocial behavior in the long run, even though this was not their original goal (Ripple & Zigler, 2003). Recently, there has been a call to increase nurturing environments that can allow for the maximum growth of human potential and well-being (Biglan, Flay, Embry, & Sandler, 2012).

REDUCING STRESS   A fourth approach to primary prevention takes the form of reducing environmental stressors. For example, increasing the availability of affordable housing can reduce the frequency of household moves, a major stressor for poor families that has been linked to psychological maladjustment (Rogers et al., 2012; Yoshikawa, Aber, & Beardslee, 2012).

PROMOTING EMPOWERMENT   Finally, there are primary prevention programs designed to empower the powerless, to help those for whom old age, poverty, homelessness, ethnic minority status, physical disability, or other factors have left them without the ability or confidence to take control of their lives. *Empowerment* (Rappaport, 2002) is the development of a belief among formerly dependent and powerless individuals that they can master and control their lives. There is already some evidence that empowering minority-group parents to influence school policies or empowering neighborhoods to control crime can have long-term mental health benefits for the community as a whole (Zimmerman, 2000). One recent trend in empowerment focuses on educating the public about mental health issues and how to deal with them, a concept called *mental health literacy* (Jorm, 2012). This trend is consistent with the attempts by many community psychologists, preventionists, and clinical psychologists to decrease the stigma associated with having mental health problems (Abdullah & Brown, 2011; Corrigan & Shapiro, 2010).

There are a number of other effective prevention programs in a number of different areas, including the prevention of childhood obesity (Haynos & O'Donohue, 2012), eating disorders (Stice, Rohde, Shaw, & Marti, 2013), alcohol abuse (Labbe & Maisto, 2011), criminal behavior (Dekovic et al., 2011), dating violence (Miller et al., 2012), and PTSD (Adler, Bliese, McGurk, Hoge, & Castro, 2009). The title of one recent article states the case boldly: "Major depression can be prevented" (Munoz, Beardslee, & Leykin, 2012). The goal of prevention is not only fully integrated into the field of clinical psychology, but prevention efforts in clinical and community psychology are consistent with and supportive of the growth of positive psychology (Duckworth, Steen, & Seligman, 2005), which focuses on the development of individual strengths and promotes individual well-being (Weisz, Sandler, Durlak, & Anton, 2005). Fueled by both community psychology and prevention, there is renewed emphasis on making changes in neighborhoods and in society (Biglan, Flay, Embry, & Sandler, 2012) as well as on reducing poverty (Yoshikawa, Aber, & Beardslee, 2012). These efforts are designed to enhance well-being and reduce suffering, prevent mental health problems, and thus make health care more cost effective (Mihalopoulos, Vos, Pirkis, & Carter, 2011).

SECTION SUMMARY

Preventive efforts have been integrated into nearly every aspect of clinical psychology. Tertiary prevention (also known as indicated prevention intervention) targets groups of individuals who have already experienced mental health problems, secondary prevention (selective mental health prevention) targets individuals who are at risk for the development of problems, and primary prevention (universal mental health prevention) targets the entire community, whether or not they are at risk for the development of mental health problems.

SELF-HELP

SECTION PREVIEW

This section covers self-help efforts, which can be completed with or without the assistance of a trained professional. These efforts can be guided by self-help books as well as by face-to-face and Internet-based support groups.

Self-help programs have been around for decades, and their popularity seems to be on the rise. Self-help programs were once available mainly via face-to-face support groups, and although such groups still exist, the majority of self-help programs and resources are now accessed online. In fact, nearly 80% of individuals who use the Internet have sought information online for health-related problems, including mental health and relationship difficulties (Norcross, 2006).

If the popularity of an intervention is reflected in the number of books published about it, self-help would clearly be in first place. A recent search of the amazon.com book database yielded 37,271 matches for "psychotherapy," but over seven times that many 268,752 for "self-help." The growing popularity of self-help groups has led some to suggest that self-help interventions may soon rival all other forms of treatment (Harwood & L'Abate, 2010). For many people, self-help is the prime source of psychological advice and treatment (Norcross, Santrock, Zuckerman, Sommer, & Campbell, 2003). For example, applications ("apps") for smart phones and other internet devices allow users to access symptom assessment, treatment support, and other self-help mental health enhancements (Luxton, McCann, Bush, Mishkind, & Reger, 2011). Norcross (2000) has referred to the self-help movement as a "massive, systemic, and yet largely silent revolution" (p. 370).

The self-help movement has its roots in programs such as Alcoholics Anonymous (AA), one of the earliest such interventions. Self-help interventions are similar to psychological treatments in that they provide a structured way of understanding and dealing with a problem. Members assist one another by exchanging information, providing social support, and discussing mutual problems (Coleman, 2005).

With the development of electronic and social media, self-help groups are no longer restricted by geographical boundaries. Many online support groups now operate through social media outlets such as Facebook, where members post comments and replies. One example from the clinical literature describes a therapist-facilitated online support group for Asian American men (Chang & Yeh, 2003). This online group provides information, guidance, and support to these men on issues related to race, culture, gender, and well-being.

As in this example, many self-help groups are not strictly "self-help," because they are conducted or supervised by professionals. In face-to-face groups, the professional might orient new members and act as a consultant to the group. In online groups, the professional might supervise the discussion, suggest links to sources of information, and recommend evidence-based homework exercises for symptom reduction or personal growth.

Self-help interventions are not restricted to support groups. *Bibliotherapy*, that is, reading books about how to deal with psychological problems, is a large component of the self-help movement. A stroll or scroll through your local or online bookstore is all that is needed to get a sense of the prevalence of self-help books. Some of them, such as Burns's (1999) *Feeling Good: The New Mood Therapy*, are based on research in cognitive therapy or other treatment principles. Others were written by leading researchers who chose to disseminate scholarly material in a popular medium. A few examples in the latter category follow:

- Master Your Anxiety and Panic (Barlow & Craske, 2006)
- Taking Charge of Adult ADHD (Barkley & Benton, 2010)
- Overcoming Your Eating Disorder: A Cognitive-Behavioral Treatment for Bulimia Nervosa and Binge-Eating Workbook (Apple & Agras, 2007)
- Your Defiant Teen: Ten Steps to Resolve Conflict and Rebuild Your Relationship (Barkley, Robin, & Benton, 2008)
- Ten Lessons to Transform Your Marriage (Gottman & Gottman, 2006)
- Flourish: A Visionary New Understanding of Happiness and Well-Being (Seligman, 2011)

Although obviously designed for self-help, some of these books are employed by therapists as part of more extensive psychological treatment. One survey found that 82% of therapists recommend high-quality self-help materials to their clients (Norcross, 2006). Bookstore browsers should understand, though, that the vast majority of self-help books are not written by experts in the field and that their publication is no guarantee of their quality. Readers of these books should also recognize that some of the methods described might have proven effective in clinical settings but still need to be validated for use without the help of a trained therapist (Rosen, Glasgow, & Moore, 2003).

Indeed, many psychologists are concerned that some self-help books ignore or distort scientific findings in order to enhance sales. Publishers are typically more concerned with the potential sales of a book than with the empirical support for its recommendations. Accordingly, some self-help books carry a real danger of being misleading and even harmful.

With these considerations in mind, some psychologists have made efforts to help the public evaluate the numerous options of self-help. For example, John Norcross and his colleagues published the *Authoritative Guide to Self-Help Resources in Mental Health, Revised Edition* (Norcross, Santrock, Zuckerman, Sommer, & Campbell, 2003). This book reports the results of surveys of professionals on the value of individual self-help resources (books, groups, Internet sites, etc.) for various disorders. More recently, Mark Harwood and Luciano L'Abate (2010) updated and expanded this information in *Self-Help in Mental Health: A Critical* Review. They focus on self-help programs, online resources, and books that empirical research has shown to be effective. Although, no single resource summarizes all controlled outcome studies of popular self-help books and online resources, there is a growing body of research literature that suggests that bibliotherapy and online resources can be effective for problems such as mild depression, anxiety, eating disorders, gambling, and mild alcohol abuse (Apodaca & Miller, 2003; Carlbring & Smit, 2008; Harwood et al., 2011; Haug, Nordgreen, Ost, & Havik, 2012; Lynch et al., 2010; Mains & Scogin, 2003; Morgan, Jorm, & Mackinnon, 2012; Newman, Szkodny, Llera, & Przeworski, 2011; Varley, Webb, & Sheeran, 2011; Wilson & Zandberg, 2012).

Among professionals, attitudes about self-help are mixed. Some are deeply committed to and involved in assisting the public through self-help ventures, while others are skeptical (Harwood & L'Abate, 2010). The skeptics, in particular, point to the great many precautions that need to be taken before choosing self-help techniques (Rosen, Glasgow, & Moore, 2003). Norcross (2006) argues that psychologists, and the general public, should think about self-help resources with an open mind but also with an eye toward identifying resources that are based on empirical evidence, not just the latest trends popularized in the media.

SECTION SUMMARY

Support groups, online resources and self-help books (known as bibliotherapy) are used extensively throughout the world. Many psychologists worry about people trying to treat themselves, so there is increasing awareness of the need to provide evidence-based material for use in self-help efforts.

OTHER APPROACHES

SECTION PREVIEW

This section covers recent developments in other treatment modalities and methods, including complementary/alternative medicine, spirituality, and mindfulness. Interest in these approaches is strong, but empirical support varies.

No chapter on other treatment approaches would be complete without some discussion of those that are expanding the scope of traditional therapies.

Complementary/Alternative Medicine

Also known as *integrative techniques*, complementary/alternative medicine (CAM) includes herbology (use of over-the-counter herbs for improvement in well-being), chiropractic methods, massage therapy, nutrition (both healthier foods and vitamin supplements), applied kinesiology, and biofeedback (Park, 2013). One study of over 23,000 adults in the United States found that 44.8% had used some type of CAM technique within the past year—either for symptom relief or for health promotion (Davis, West, Weeks, & Sirovich, 2011).

The use of these methods in the hope of alleviating psychological disorders is notable. Kessler and his colleagues (2001) found that 56.7% of individuals with anxiety and 53.6% of individuals with depression were using CAM techniques to help with their symptoms. Among patients in traditional psychological treatment for these disorders, 65.9% with an anxiety disorder and 66.7% with a depressive disorder were also using CAM methods. Thus CAM techniques appear to be commonly used in the general population and even more common among people with mental health problems.

Although many CAM techniques have been around for centuries, researchers have only recently evaluated their effectiveness via controlled experiments. There is now a National Center for Complementary and Alternative Medicine at the National Institutes of Health, and a great deal of federal grant money is being used to investigate a variety of CAM techniques. Some of these studies indicate that some CAM techniques—many of which are used in conjunction with traditional psychological or medical treatments—can indeed be effective (Lake, 2009). Some of the more promising of these are the use of

- Omega-3 essential fatty acids to ameliorate symptoms of depression (Freeman et al., 2010) and to lessen the likelihood of suicide attempts in people who have made previous attempts (Hallahan, Hibbeln, Davis, & Garland, 2007).
- Herbal therapies in conjunction with traditional treatment to reduce the side effects of chemotherapy in the treatment of prostate cancer (Auerbach, 2006).
- Yoga in addition to traditional cognitive-behavioral treatment to treat eating disorders in adolescents (Carei, Fyfe-Johnson, Breuner, & Brown, 2010).
- Sitting meditation in addition to standard treatment for children with a variety of disorders (Black, Milam, & Sussman, 2009).

Many other CAM techniques remain unevaluated, and those that do show promise must still be studied to determine which techniques are helpful for which difficulties.

We already know, though, that some CAM techniques, including a number of "new age" therapies, are not only ineffective but can actually be harmful (Lilienfeld, 2007). Two techniques in this category are recovered memory therapy (in which therapists try to "help" clients recall allegedly repressed experiences of past abuse) and rebirthing and reparenting therapy (in which therapists provide a new "birth experience" for clients by forcing them to spend hours working their way through confined spaces symbolic of the birth canal) (Lynn, Lock, Loftus, Krackow, & Lilienfeld, 2003). Singer and Nievod (2003) warn that although these therapies have been fully discredited, others like them (which also have no empirical support and often have harmful effects) appear on the professional horizon frequently. Empirically oriented clinical psychologists remain open-minded about the possible usefulness of new treatments, including new CAM treatments, but they tend to stick to established interventions whose efficacy and effectiveness have been empirically supported and to demand the same support for new methods before they adopt them.

More information on both promising and discredited CAM methods is available in a number of books, such as *Complementary and Alternative Treatments in Mental Health Care* (Lake & Spiegel, 2006), *How to Use Herbs, Nutrients, and Yoga in Mental Health Care* (Brown, Gerbarg, & Muskin, 2012), and *Complementary and Alternative Medicine for Health Professionas* (Synovitz & Larson, 2012) as well as in the *Journal of Alternative and Complementary Medicine*.

Spirituality

Traditionally, clinical psychologists and clinical researchers have not included spirituality and religiosity in the course of their professional work. For example, early measures of coping methods did not include space for clients to mention that they used prayer or other spiritual methods to deal with stressors, and even the current version of the *Ways of Coping* questionnaire (Folkman & Lazarus, 1988) lists only one religiously oriented option, namely, "I prayed." Yet survey research suggests that 90 to 95% of adults in the United States believe in God or some other higher power. Approximately 90% report that they pray, and about 69% of individuals say that they are members of a church, synagogue, mosque, or other place of worship (Miller & Thoresen, 2003).

As is true of politics or any other value-laden issue, most clinicians are reluctant to mention religion or spirituality during psychological treatment unless the clients bring it up as being an important part of their lives. Indeed, to do so might create relationship problems, especially for nonreligious clients who might start wondering if they are being subjected to some sort of conversion effort, or for gay or lesbian clients who might associate religion with intolerance of their sexual orientations (Yarhouse & Tan, 2005).

Clinicians' appreciation of religious issues in therapy is being enhanced by recent empirical research on the role of spirituality in individuals' lives. For example, the risk and resilience literature has reported that having a guiding faith and having a supportive faith-based community can serve as a protective factor for youth in harsh psychosocial environments (Shaffer, Coffino, Boelcke-Stennes, & Masten, 2007). In adults, prayer and spirituality have been identified as effective mechanisms for coping with cancer (Zaza, Sellick, & Hillier, 2005), HIV and AIDS (Cotton et al., 2006), and the long term effects of cardiac surgery in the elderly (Ai et al., 2010). And in general, the practice of prayer has been associated with higher quality of life and fewer physical and mental health problems (Bantha, Moskowitz, Acree, & Folkman, 2007). Unfortunately, the same cannot be said for intercessory prayer, that is, when one person or group prays for a particular target person (Masters, Spielmans, & Goodson, 2006).

Although we expect that the separation between empirical psychological science and faith-based beliefs will continue, we also expect that more research on topics related to spirituality might give clinicians a broader understanding of religious clients' concerns (such as sin) as well as of their coping resources. As part of their efforts to enhance their own cultural sensitivity, clinicians are also likely to seek out resources that can help them to learn more about how spiritual beliefs might differ across religions and cultures (Raiya & Pargament, 2010).

Mindfulness and Acceptance

The concepts of mindfulness and acceptance are related in some ways to spirituality and CAM methods. These concepts have received a great deal of attention in clinical psychology in recent years, and are even being referred to as "new directions" in cognitive-behavioral therapy (Forman & Herbert, 2009). Research on mindfulness, in particular, has exploded over the past two decades and it continues to grow (see Figure 9.4).

Mindfulness is described as "intentionally bringing one's attention to the internal and external experiences occurring in the present moment" (Baer, 2003, p. 125). It is often taught to clients through meditation exercises designed to help them accept their own thoughts and feelings but also so that they can achieve a certain amount of detachment from those thoughts and feelings (Segal, Williams, & Teasdale, 2002). Mindfulness has been integrated into cognitive-behavioral treatments for depression (Hayes, Follette, & Linehan, 2004) and stress reduction (Bishop, 2007). Mindfulness is usually taught in a nonreligious context in therapy, but it has also been shown to be effective when taught within the context of a spiritual framework such as Buddhism (Ostafin et al., 2006).

Closely related to mindfulness is the concept of *acceptance*, which is defined as "the capacity to remain available to present experience, without attempting to terminate the painful or prolong the pleasant" (Williams & Lynn, 2010, p. 7). Some clinical researchers are now focusing on how

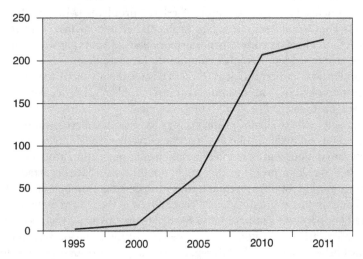

FIGURE 9.4 Number of Articles and Books in PsycINFO on Mindfulness by Year

acceptance and mindfulness can contribute to improvement in symptoms of psychopathology (Herbert, Forman, & England, 2009). Among the evidence-based therapies that feature acceptance, mindfulness, or both, are:

- Acceptance and Commitment Therapy (Levin & Hayes, 2011)
- Mindfulness-Based Stress Reduction (Salmon, Sephton, & Dreeben, 2011)
- Dialectical Behavior Therapy (Dimidjian & Linehan, 2009)
- Integrative Behavioral Couple Therapy (McGinn, Benson, & Christensen, 2011)
- Metacognitive Therapy (Wells, 2011)

More research is needed to identify the mechanisms through which mindfulness and/or acceptance can facilitate treatment (Shapiro, Carlson, Astin, & Freedman, 2006), but they do appear to be promising tools in treating a wide variety of clients for depression, anxiety, and other forms of psychological distress (Hofmann, Sawyer, Witt, & Oh, 2010).

SECTION SUMMARY

Alternative approaches, such as complementary/alternative medicine, spirituality, mindfulness, and acceptance are all becoming more integrated into the traditional practices of clinical psychology. Largely because empirical research has supported their use, these practices are of great interest to clinical psychologists, especially those working within the health and pediatric fields. Care must be taken, however, to focus on methods that are evidence-based, since there are many alternative approaches that do not benefit clients' well-being.

TECHNOLOGICAL INNOVATIONS INFLUENCING PSYCHOLOGICAL TREATMENT

SECTION PREVIEW

This section reviews both the difficulties and promises of new treatment technologies. We review some of the difficulties that have arisen out of online activities and then discuss the ways in which technology has been able to help with psychological assessments and therapy.

Technological advances have changed virtually every aspect of life over the past few decades, and the field of clinical psychology is no exception. As mentioned in previous chapters, technology, and especially the widespread use of the Internet, have led to innovations in assessment and treatment. They have also contributed to new types of problems.

Problems Caused by Technology

In one survey, therapists reported that a significant number of their nearly 1,500 adolescent and adult clients experienced a variety of Internet-related problems (Mitchell, Becker-Blease, & Finkelhor, 2005). For 61% of these clients, the problems had to do with disruptive overuse of the Internet; 20% of those clients reported spending more than 28 hours per week online in activities that were not related to work or to e-mail communications (see Figure 9.5).

The second most common problem (56% of clients, mainly men) was excessive use of the Internet to view pornography. The next most common problem (21% of clients) involved online activities that led, or threatened to lead, to marital infidelity. Of course, as the survey's authors acknowledged, many of these clients' problems may have occurred even without access to computers, but the results do highlight the fact that the pervasive availability of the Internet and its ability to create anonymous and potentially isolating communication around the clock can put some clients at added risk for problems that might not otherwise have occurred.

There are a number of other mental health problems that can be exacerbated by current technologies. For example, approximately 2–7% of adults in the United States have participated in Internet gambling or online gaming and for most of them, this activity has become a significant problem (Gainsbury, 2012). Websites that promote maladaptive behavior, such as eating disorders or sexual contact between adults and children, can be quite dangerous, especially for those especially vulnerable to these behaviors (DeAngelis, 2011; Rouleau & vonRanson, 2011).

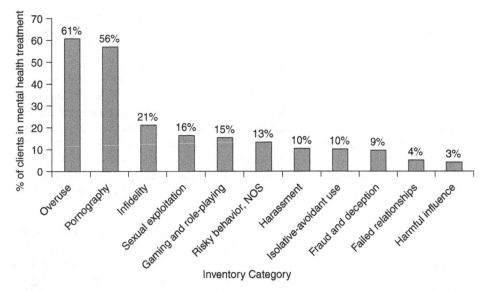

FIGURE 9.5   Percentage Endorsement of Problematic Internet Experiences.   *Source:* Mitchell, K. J., Becker-Blease, K. A., & Finkelhor, D. (2005). Inventory of problematic internet experiences encountered in clinical practice. *Professional Psychology: Research and Practice, 36,* 498–509.

There is also great concern about online "predators" who stalk children for sexual and physical violence. Most of these pedophiles connect with youngsters online in an open way—that is, they meet and befriend them without trying to hide their own age or identity—and then seduce or coerce them into sexual activities in person (Wolak, Findelhor, Mitchell, & Ybarra, 2008).

Another problem receiving increased attention these days is the "cyberbullying" of children and teens. Especially when combined with bullying at school and in the youngster's own neighborhood, cyberbullying leaves victims at elevated risk for internalizing disorders and self-harm (DeAngelis, 2011). Online bullying is a significant problem; one study indicated that 38% of children aged 10 to 15 were being bullied or harassed online and 13% were being both bullied and harassed (DeAngelis, 2011).

In summary, technological advances have allowed new problems in human interactions to develop, but they are also being used in cutting-edge ways by clinical psychologists to assess, treat, and prevent psychological problems.

Technology as a Treatment Tool

Online informational resources; Facebook and other social media; videoconferencing (e.g., Skype); emailing and texting on computers, smartphones, and tablets; virtual reality systems; and even computer gaming systems are all being used in the service of what has become known as *e-health.* Mental health professionals can now assess, diagnose, and sometimes treat clients through remote contact (Glueckauf, Pickett, Ketterson, Loomis, & Rozensky, 2003) which can be especially helpful in geographical areas where clients would not otherwise have access to mental health services.

We discussed the pros and cons of computer-based assessment in Chapter 3. Many of the same pros and cons are evident in the use of the technology for psychological interventions. Various technologies, including the use of online resources, can be especially effective in delivering certain treatments, particularly those involving behavioral packages that target specific, discrete problems (Ritterband et al., 2003). In one randomized study of anxiety treatments, children who received some in-clinic meetings and some interventions delivered online showed improvement comparable to those who received in-clinic treatment alone (Spence, Holmes, March, & Lipp, 2006). A clinical psychologist is usually involved in Internet-based treatment programs, either through an initial face-to-face meeting or at least through regular phone calls, texts, or e-mails to assess the progress of treatment. There has been an explosion of research in this area and here are a few examples of the methods and results of using technology to enhance evidence-based therapies:

- Adolescents were randomly assigned to receive cognitive-behavior therapy for anxiety either online or in person and both groups showed comparable gains, which were significantly better than for a no-treatment group (Spence et al., 2011).

- Standardized text messages were sent to low income adult clients in a cognitive-behavioral therapy program for depression and were found to help the clients remain more engaged in treatment (Aguilera & Munoz, 2011).
- Videoconferencing was used to offer live coaching of parenting skills for parents who were receiving a web-based behavioral therapy program for their children with behavioral problems due to traumatic brain injuries (Wade, Oberjohn, Conaway, Osinska, & Bangert, 2011).
- Virtual reality technology was used to create visual environments associated with cravings for smoking. These virtual cues were used in cue exposure therapy to help smokers quit (Garcia-Rodriguez, Pericot-Valverde, Gutierrez-Maldonado, Ferrer-Garcia, & Secades-Villa, 2012).
- After being treated for eating disorders, women had access to a web-based package (including peer support, self-help, psychoeducational modules, and access to a therapist). Their treatment gains were maintained better than those of a group that did not get the web-based package (Gulec et al., 2011).

Technologically enhanced interventions are unlikely to replace face-to-face interventions for most mental health difficulties, but the use of Internet-based psychological treatments and other technologies is likely to continue to grow (Eonta et al., 2011). As it does, clinicians will have to deal with a number of ethical issues in the delivery of therapy delivered through technology (Perle et al., 2013; we discuss these issues in Chapter 15, "Professional Issues in Clinical Psychology").

SECTION SUMMARY

Many problems have arisen from overreliance on computers and online activities, but through computer-based therapies known as e-health, the Internet also has potential as an effective treatment modality for some circumscribed problems with the use of evidence-based treatment packages.

PSYCHOTHERAPY INTEGRATION

SECTION PREVIEW

This section reviews proposals for how therapists might use approaches from a number of different theoretical orientations. Although there is no consensus on exactly how integration should be accomplished, most in the field regard it as essential.

With all of the focus on different types of therapeutic orientation, it is important to understand that many therapists integrate the best practices across orientations in order to maximize their effectiveness with their clients. As mentioned in Chapter 1, "What Is Clinical Psychology?," *psychotherapy integration* is the process of combining elements of various clinical psychology theories in a systematic manner. Therapists as well as training directors in internships tend to appreciate at least some level of integration of therapies (Lampropoulos & Dixon, 2007).

As you have no doubt noticed, some of the therapies we have described are combinations of two or more "pure" approaches and thus represent at least partial integration. For example, relational psychodynamic approaches combine aspects of psychodynamic and humanistic theory and technique; cognitive-behavioral approaches combine . . . well, that one should be obvious. A number of other integrative therapies are gaining popularity, and their names alone suggest the combination of multiple influences: integrative problem-centered therapy (Pinsof, 2005), cognitive-affective-relational-behavior therapy (Goldfried, 2006), and integrative behavioral couple therapy (McGinn, Benson, & Christensen, 2011).

Integration is a good idea and there are a number of ways to achieve it (Strickler & Gold, 2006). For example, clinicians can select assessment and treatment methods from all those available in the field and apply them to particular clients based on the clinician's understanding of the research support for the various techniques (Goldfried, Glass, & Arnkoff, 2011). Conversely, clinical researchers can try to integrate different psychological theories of change and create a new evidence-based therapy, such as acceptance and commitment therapy, dialectical behavior therapy, and multisystemic therapy (Goldfried, Glass, & Arnkoff, 2011). In addition, researchers and clinicians can seek to focus on *common factors*, such as having a strong and stable therapeutic relationship, that are consistent across many types of therapy and that are found to help make therapy effective (Davis, Lebow, & Sprenkle, 2012).

In short, the predominant theme in psychotherapy integration is to find evidence-based practices that can be applied to specific clients at specific times (Goldfried, Glass, & Arnkoff, 2011). Rarely are there discussions of training in psychotherapy or of psychotherapy integration that do not start with and end with recognizing the need to look closely at the empirical literature. Thus, the focus on evidence-based practices seen in so many aspects of clinical psychology and other fields is also integral to our current understandings of psychotherapy integration (Goldfried, Glass, & Arnkoff, 2011). For more information on psychotherapy integration, consult sources such as the *Journal of Psychotherapy Integration* (Stricker, 2010) or the *Handbook of Psychotherapy Integration* (Norcross & Goldfried, 2005).

Chapter Summary

Psychological treatment can involve modes of intervention that focus on and attempt to use the social contexts in which individuals' problems are embedded. Interventions can be conducted with groups, couples, and families, using methods that combine those employed in individual psychotherapy with specialized techniques unique to these special formats. Group therapy seeks to change the way individuals interact in a wide range of interpersonal relationships, while couples therapy addresses these issues within the context of an intimate dyad. These approaches often rely on systems-theory approaches, so diagnosis and treatment are aimed at changing a system rather than changing individuals. Newer modalities apply cognitive-behavioral or behavioral principles to the group, couple, and family format.

Community psychology is a field that applies psychological principles to understanding individual and social problems and to creating beneficial social changes. Prevention is an outgrowth of community psychology, with a focus on preventing problems before they occur or trying to reduce any exacerbation of problems once they are evident.

Another offshoot of community psychology—self-help groups and resources—have grown into a major therapeutic industry. Professionals' involvement in and attitudes toward the self-help movement are mixed, though it is clear that self-help is widely used.

Other alternative approaches to therapy include those offered by complementary medicine, spirituality, mindfulness, acceptance, and the use of online resources and other technologies to assess and treat mental health problems.

Study Questions

1. What influences led to the growth of interventions that go beyond the individual?
2. When was group therapy first practiced, and by whom?
3. What are the primary therapeutic factors in group therapy?
4. Describe a common group therapy format (such as how many members are involved, what the therapists' role is, how long each session lasts, etc.).
5. How are psychoeducational and cognitive-behavioral therapy groups different from traditional process-oriented group therapies?
6. What are the most common reasons that couples seek treatment?
7. What are some important practices for therapists to keep in mind when working with groups, couples, and families?
8. Discuss the concept of an identified client in the context of family therapy (e.g., theoretical rationale for family therapy, understanding of how problems develop and are treated, etc.).
9. Discuss the use or nonuse of diagnosis within therapeutic work with couples and families.
10. What is community psychology, and how does it differ from other types of clinical psychology?
11. What are the principles and methods of community psychology?
12. What are the three types of prevention programs? Provide an illustrative example of each, along with pros and cons of each method.
13. Take a position either for or against self-help interventions and defend it.
14. Describe current examples of complementary/alternative medicine techniques that are used within clinical psychology. Provide any evidence that supports the use of those techniques.
15. What are the pros and cons of using computers and other technologies for assessment and treatment?

Web Sites

- APA Division 49: Group Psychology and Group Psychotherapy: http://www.apadivisions.org/division-49/index.aspx
- APA Division 43: Family Psychology: http://www.apa.org/divisions/div43/homepage.html
- APA Division 27: Society for Community Research and Action: http://www.scra27.org
- National Center for Complementary and Alternative Medicine: http://nccam.nih.gov/

MOVIES

Hope Springs (2012): The treatment plan for an elderly couple seeking to improve their relationship is not evidence-based, but this film highlights the need for couples to consider seeking professional help for relationship difficulties.

Rabbit Hole (2010): After the loss of their only child, this couple seeks many sources to help them grieve, including a self-help support group with other grieving parents.

MEMOIRS

Blackbird: A Childhood Lost and Found by Jennifer Lauck (2000; New York: Pocket Books). The author describes an idyllic childhood that is torn apart through family tragedies.

The Family Crucible: One Family's Therapy–An Experience That Illuminates All Our Lives by Augustus Y. Napier and Carl A. Whitaker (1978; New York: Bantam Books). First person accounts of co-therapists conducting family therapy with a complicated and interesting family.

References

Abdullah, T., & Brown, T. L. (2011). Mental illness stigma and ethnocultural beliefs, values, and norms: An integrative review. *Clinical Psychology Review, 31*, 934–948.

Ables, B. S., & Brandsma, J. M. (1977). *Therapy for couples.* San Francisco, CA: Jossey-Bass.

Adler, A. B., Bliese, P. D., McGurk, D., Hoge, C. W., & Castro, C. A. (2009). Battlemind debriefing and battlemind training as early interventions with soldiers returning from Iraq: Randomization by platoon. *Journal of Consulting and Clinical Psychology, 77*, 928–940.

Aguilera, A., & Munoz, R. F. (2011). Text messaging as an adjunct to CBT in low-income populations: A usability and feasibility pilot study. *Professional Psychology: Research and Practice, 42*, 472–478.

Ai, A. L., Ladd, K. L., Peterson, C., Cook, C. A., Shearer, M., et al. (2010). Long-term adjustment after surviving open heart surgery: The effect of using prayer for coping replicated in a prospective design. *The Gerontologist, 50*, 798–809.

Albee, G. W. (1959). *Mental health manpower trends.* New York, NY: Basic Books.

Apodaca, T. R., & Miller, W. R. (2003). A meta-analysis of the effectiveness of bibliotherapy for alcohol problems. *Journal of Clinical Psychology, 59*, 289–304.

Apple, R. F., & Agras, W. S. (2007). *Overcoming eating disorders: A cognitive-behavioral treatment for bulimia nervosa and binge-eating workbook.* New York, NY: Oxford University Press.

Auerbach, L. (2006). Complementary and alternative medicine in the treatment of prostate cancer. *Journal of Men's Health and Gender, 3*, 397–403.

Baerger, D. R. (2001). Risk management with the suicidal patient: Lessons from case law. *Professional Psychology: Research and Practice, 32*, 359–366.

Bantha, R., Moskowitz, J. T., Acree, M., & Folkman, S. (2007). Socioeconomic differences in the effects of prayer on physical symptoms and quality of life. *Journal of Health Psychology, 12*, 249–260.

Barkley, R. A., & Benton, C. (2010). *Taking charge of adult ADHD.* New York, NY: Guilford.

Barkley, R. A., Robin, A. L., & Benton, C. M. (2008). *Your defiant teen: Ten steps to resolve conflict and rebuild your relationship.* New York, NY: Guilford.

Barlow, D. H., & Craske, M. G. (2006). *Master your anxiety and panic.* New York, NY: Oxford University Press.

Bateson, C., Jackson, D. D., Haley, J., & Weakland, J. H. (1956). Toward a theory of schizophrenia. *Behavioral Science, 1*, 251–264.

Baucom, D. H., Epstein, N. B., Kirby, J. S., & Falconier, M. K. (2011). Couple therapy: Theoretical perspectives and empirical findings. In D. H. Barlow (Ed.), *The Oxford handbook of clinical psychology* (pp. 789–809). New York, NY: Oxford University Press.

Baucom, D. H., Epstein, N. B., Kirby, J. S., & LaTaillade, J. J. (2010). Cognitive-behavioral couple therapy. In K. S. Dobson (Ed.), *Handbook of cognitive-behavioral therapies* (3rd ed., pp. 411–444). New York, NY: Guilford.

Beach, S. R. H., & Kaslow, N. J. (2006). Relational disorders and relational processes in diagnostic practice: Introduction to the special section. *Journal of Family Psychology, 20*, 353–355.

Becvar, D. S. (Ed.), (2013). *Handbook of family resilience.* New York, NY: Springer.

Bieling, P. J., McCabe, R. E., & Antony, M. M. (2006). *Cognitive-behavioral therapy in groups* (p. 382). New York, NY: Guilford Press.

Biglan, A., Flay, B. R., Embry, D. D., & Sandler, I. N. (2012). The critical role of nurturing environments for promoting human well-being. *American Psychologist, 67*, 257–271.

Black, D. S., Milam, J., & Sussman, S. (2009). Sitting-meditation interventions among youth: A review of treatment efficacy. *Pediatrics, 124*, 532–541.

Briesmeister, J. M., & Schaefer, C. E. (Eds.). (2007). *Handbook of parent training: Helping parents prevent and solve problem behaviors* (3rd ed.). Hoboken, NJ: Wiley.

Brown, R. P., Gerbarg, P. L., & Muskin, P. R. (2012). *How to use herbs, nutrients, and yoga in mental health.* New York, NY: W. W. Norton and Company.

Burlingame, G. M., & Baldwin, S. (2011). Group therapy. In J. C. Norcross, G. R. VandenBos, & D. K. Freedheim (Eds.), *History of psychotherapy: Continuity and change* (2nd ed., pp. 505–515). Washington, DC: American Psychological Association.

Burlingame, G. M., MacKenzie, K. R., & Strauss, B. (2004). Small-group treatment: Evidence for effectiveness and mechanisms of change. In M. J. Lambert (Ed.), *Bergin and Garfield's handbook of psychotherapy and behavior change* (5th ed., pp. 647–696). New York, NY: Wiley.

Burlingame, G. M., McClendon, D. T., & Alonso, J. (2011). Cohesion in group therapy. *Psychotherapy, 48*, 34–42.

Burns, D. D. (1999). *Feeling good: The new mood therapy* (Vol. 1, Rev. ed.). New York, NY: Harper Collins.

Caplan, G. (1964). *Principles of preventive psychiatry.* New York, NY: Basic Books.

Carei, T. R., Fyfe-Johnson, A. L., Breuner, C. C., & Brown, M. A. (2010). Randomized controlled clinical trial of yoga in the treatment of eating disorders. *Journal of Adolescent Health, 46*, 346–351.

Carlbring, P., & Smit, F. (2008). Randomized trial of internet-delivered self-help with telephone support for pathological gamblers. *Journal of Consulting and Clinical Psychology, 76*, 1090–1094.

Carr, A. (2006). *The handbook of child and adolescent clinical psychology: A contextual approach* (2nd ed., p. 60). New York, NY: Routledge/Taylor & Francis Group.

Carr, A. (2012). *Family therapy: Concepts, process, and practice.* Hoboken, NJ: Wiley.

Chabot, D. R. (2011). Family systems theories of psychotherapy. In J. C. Norcross, G. R. VandenBos, & D. K. Freedheim (Eds.), *History of psychotherapy: Continuity and change* (2nd ed., pp. 173–202). Washington, DC: American Psychological Association.

Chang, T., & Yeh, C. J. (2003). Using online groups to provide support to Asian American men: Racial, cultural, gender, and treatment issues. *Professional Psychology: Research and Practice, 34,* 634–643.

Coleman, P. (2005). Privilege and confidentiality in 12-step self-help programs: Believing the promises could be hazardous to an addict's freedom. *Journal of Legal Medicine, 26,* 435–474.

Comer, J. S., Puliafico, A. C., Aschenbrand, S. G., McKnight, K., Robin, J. A., et al. (2012). A pilot feasibility evaluation of the CALM program for anxiety disorders in early childhood. *Journal of Anxiety Disorders, 26,* 40–49.

Corey, G. (2011). *Theory and practice of group counseling* (8th ed.). Belmont, CA: Cengage Learning.

Corrigan, P. W., & Shapiro, J. R. (2010). Measuring the impact of programs that challenge the public stigma of mental illness. *Clinical Psychology Review, 30,* 907–922.

Crits-Christoph, P., Johnson, J. E., Gibbons, M. B. C., & Gallop, R. (2013). Process predictors of the outcome of group drug counseling. *Journal of Consulting and Clinical Psychology, 81,* 23–34.

Davis, M. A., West, A. N., Weeks, W. B., & Sirovich, B. E. (2011). Health behaviors and utilization among users of complementary and alternative medicine for treatment versus health promotion. *Health Services Research, 46,* 1402–1416.

Davis, S. D., Lebow, J. L., & Sprenkle, D. H. (2012). Common factors of change in couple therapy. *Behavior Therapy, 43,* 36–48.

DeAngelis, T. (2011). Is technology ruining our kids? *Monitor on Psychology, 42,* 63–64.

Dekovic, M., Slagt, M. I., Asscher, J. J., Boendrmaker, L., Eichelsheim, V. I., et al. Effects of early prevention programs on adult criminal offending: A meta-analysis. *Clinical Psychology Review, 31,* 532–544.

Dimidjian, S., & Linehan, M. M. (2009). Mindfulness practice. In W. T. O'Donohue & J. E. Fisher (Eds.), *General principles and empirically supported techniques of cognitive behavior therapy* (pp. 425–434). Hoboken, NJ: Wiley.

Dodge, K. A., Coie, J. D., & Lynam, D. (2006). Aggression and antisocial behavior in youth. In N. Eisenberg (Ed.), *Handbook of child psychology* (6th ed., pp. 719–788). Hoboken, NJ: Wiley.

Doherty, W. J., & McDaniel, S. H. (Eds.). (2009). *Family therapy.* Washington, DC: American Psychological Association.

Doss, B. D., Simpson, L. E., & Christensen, A. (2004). Why do couples seek marital therapy? *Professional Psychology: Research and Practice, 35,* 608–614.

Duckworth, A. L., Steen, T. A., & Seligman, M. E. P. (2005). Positive psychology in clinical practice. *Annual Review of Clinical Psychology, 1,* 629–651.

Eonta, A. M., Christon, L. M., Hourigan, S. E., Ravindran, N., Vranan, S. R., et al. (2011). Using everyday technology to enhance evidence-based treatments. *Professional Psychology: Research and Practice, 42,* 513–520.

Eyberg, S. M., & Matarazzo, R. G. (1980). Training parents as therapists: A comparison between individual parent-child interactions training and parent group didactic training. *Journal of Clinical Psychology, 36,* 492–499.

Eysenck, H. J. (1952). The effects of psychotherapy: An evaluation. *Journal of Consulting Psychology, 16,* 319–324.

Folkman, S., & Lazarus, R. S. (1988). *Manual for the ways of coping questionnaire.* Palo Alto, CA: Consulting Psychologists Press.

Forman, E. M., & Herbert, J. D. (2009). New directions in cognitive behavior therapy: Acceptance-based therapies. In W. T. O'Donohue & J. E. Fisher (Eds.), *General principles and empirically supported techniques of cognitive behavior therapy* (pp. 77–101). Hoboken, NJ: Wiley.

Free, M. L. (2007). *Cognitive therapy in groups: Guidelines and resources for practice* (2nd ed.). Hoboken, NJ: Wiley.

Freeman, M. P., Fava, M., Lake, J., Trivedi, M. H., Wisner, K. L., et al. (2010). Complementary and alternative medicine in major depressive disorder: The American Psychiatric Association Task Force Report. *Journal of Clinical Psychiatry, 71,* 669–681.

Funderburk, B. W., & Eyberg, S. (2011). Parent-child interaction therapy. In J. C. Norcross, G. R. VandenBos, & D. K. Freedhaim (Eds.), *History of psychotherapy: Continuity and change* (2nd ed., pp. 415–420). Washington, DC: American Psychological Association.

Gainsbury, S. (2012). *Internet gambling: Current research findings and implications.* New York, NY: Springer.

Garcia-Rodriguez, O., Pericot-Valverde, I., Gutierrez-Maldonado, J., Ferrer-Garcia, M., & Secades-Villa, R. (2012). Validation of smoking-related virtual environments for cue exposure therapy. *Addictive Behaviors, 37,* 703–708.

Glueckauf, R., Pickett, T. C., Ketterson, T. U., Loomis, J. S., & Rozensky, R. H. (2003). Preparation for the delivery of telehealth services: A self-study framework for expansion of practice. *Professional Psychology: Research and Practice, 34,* 159–163.

Goldfried, M. R. (2006). Cognitive-affective-relational-behavior therapy. In G. Stricker & J. Gold (Eds.), *A casebook of psychotherapy integration* (pp. 153–164). Washington, DC: American Psychological Association.

Goldfried, M. R., Glass, C. R., & Arnkoff, D. B. (2011). Integrative approaches to psychotherapy. In J. C. Norcross, G. R. VandenBos, & D. K. Freedheim (Eds.), *History of psychotherapy: Continuity and change* (2nd ed., pp. 269–296). Washington, DC: American Psychological Association.

Gottman, J. M. (2011). *The science of trust: Emotional attunement for couples.* New York, NY: W.W. Norton.

Gottman, J. M., & Gottman, J. S. (2006). *Ten lessons to transform your marriage.* New York, NY: Crown Publishing Group.

Greene, C. J., Morland, L. A., Macdonald, A., Frueh, B. C., Grubbs, K. M., et al. (2010). How does tele-mental health affect group therapy process? Secondary analysis of a noninferiority trial. *Journal of Consulting and Clinical Psychology, 78,* 746–750.

Gulec, H., Moessner, M., Mezei, A., Kohls, E., Tury, F., et al. (2011). Internet-based maintenance treatment for patients with eating disorders. *Professional Psychology, Research and Practice, 42,* 479–486.

Halford, W. K., & Moore, N. E. (2002). Relationship education and the prevention of couple relationship problems. In A. S. Gurman & N. S. Jacobson (Eds.), *Clinical handbook of couple therapy* (3rd ed., pp. 400–419). New York, NY: Guilford Press.

Hallahan, B., Hibbeln, J. R., Davis, J. M., & Garland, M. R. (2007). Omega-3 fatty acid supplementation in patients with recurrent self-harm: Single-centre double-blind randomised controlled trial. *British Journal of Mental Science, 190,* 118–122.

Harway, M. (2005). *Handbook of couples therapy.* Hoboken, NJ: Wiley.

Harwood, T. M., & L'Abate, L. (2010). *Self-help in mental health: A critical review.* New York, NY: Springer.

Harwood, T. M., Pratt, D., Beutler, L. E., Bongar, B. M., Lenore, S., et al. (2011). Technology, telehealth, treatment enhancement, and selection. *Professional Psychology: Research and Practice, 42,* 448–454.

Haug, T., Nordgreen, T., Ost, L. G., & Havik, O. E. (2012). Self-help treatment of anxiety disorders: A meta-analysis and meta-regression of effects and potential moderators. *Clinical Psychology Review, 32,* 425–445.

Hayes, S. C., Follette, V. M., & Linehan, M. M. (Eds). (2004). *Mindfulness and acceptance: Expanding the cognitive-behavioral tradition.* New York, NY: Guilford.

Haynos, A. F., & O'Donohue, W. T. (2012). Universal childhood and adolescent obesity prevention programs: Review and critical analysis. *Clinical Psychology Review, 32,* 383–399.

Henggeler, S. W. (2011). Efficacy studies to large-scale transport: The development and validation of multisystemic therapy programs. *Annual Review of Clinical Psychology, 7,* 351–381.

Herbert, J. D., Forman, E. M., & England, E. L. (2009). Psychological acceptance. In W. T. O'Donohue & J. E. Fisher (Eds.), *General principles and empirically supported techniques of cognitive behavior therapy* (pp. 102–114). Hoboken, NJ: Wiley.

Hofferth, S. L., Stueve, J. L., Pleck, J., Bianchi, S., & Sayer, L. (2002). The demography of fathers: What fathers do. In C. S. Tamis-LeMonda & N. Cabrera (Eds.), *Handbook of father involvement: Multidisciplinary perspectives* (pp. 63–90). Mahwah, NJ: Erlbaum.

Hofmann, S. G., Sawyer, A. T., Witt, A. A., & Oh, D. (2010). The effect of mindfulness-based therapy on anxiety and depression: A meta-analytic review. *Journal of Consulting and Clinical Psychology, 78,* 169–183.

Institute of Medicine. (1994). *Reducing risk for mental disorders: Frontiers for prevention intervention research.* Washington, DC: National Academy Press.

Jorm, A. F. (2012). Mental health literacy: Empowering the community to take action for better mental health. *American Psychologist, 67,* 231–243.

Kaslow, F. W. (2011). Family therapy. In J. C. Norcross, G. R. VandenBos, & D. K. Freedheim (Eds.), *History of psychotherapy: Continuity and change* (2nd ed., pp. 497–504). Washington, DC: American Psychological Association.

Kazdin, A. E. (2008). *Parent management training: Treatment for oppositional, aggressive, and antisocial behavior in children and adolescents.* New York, NY: Oxford University Press.

Kessler, R., Soukup, J., Davis, R., Foster, D., Wilkey, S., et al. (2001). The use of complementary and alternative therapies to treat anxiety and depression in the United States. *American Journal of Psychiatry, 158,* 289–294.

Labbe, A. K. & Maisto, S. A. (2011). Alcohol expectancy challenges for college students: A narrative review. *Clinical Psychology Review, 31,* 673–683.

Lake, J. (2009). *Integrative mental health care: A therapist's handbook.* New York, NY: W. W. Norton and Company.

Lake, J. H., & Spiegel, D. (Eds) (2007). *Complementary and alternative treatments in mental health care.* Washington, DC: American Psychiatric Publishing.

Lampropoulos, G. K., & Dixon, D. N. (2007). Psychotherapy integration in internships and counseling psychology doctoral programs. *Journal of Psychotherapy Integration, 17,* 185–208.

Lawrence, E., Beach, S. R. H., & Doss, B. D. (2013). Couple and family processes in DSM-V: Moving beyond relational disorders. In J. H. Bray & M. Stanton (Eds.), *The Wiley-Blackwell handbook of family psychology* (pp. 165–182). Hoboken, NJ: Wiley.

Levin, M., & Hayes, S. C. (2011). *Mindfulness and acceptance: The perspective of acceptance and commitment therapy. Understanding and applying the new therapies* (pp. 291–316). Hoboken, NJ: Wiley.

Lidz, R. W., & Lidz, T. (1949). The family environment of schizophrenic patients. *American Journal of Psychiatry, 106,* 332–345.

Lilienfild, S. O. (2007). Psychological treatments that cause harm. *Perspectives on Psychological Science, 2,* 53–70.

Long, J. K., & Andrews, B. V. (2011). Fostering strength and resiliency in same-sex couples. In J. L. Wetchler (Ed.), *Handbook of clinical issues in couple therapy* (2nd ed., pp. 225–246). New York, NY: Routledge/Taylor & Francis Group.

Luby, J., Lenze, S., & Tillman, R. (2012). A novel early intervention for preschool depression: Findings from a pilot randomized controlled trial. *Journal of Child Psychology and Psychiatry, 53,* 313–322.

Luxton, D. D., McCann, R. A., Bush, N. E., Mishkind, M. C., & Reger, G. M. (2011). mHealth for mental health: Integrating smartphone technology in behavioral healthcare. *Professional Psychology: Research and Practice, 42,* 505–512.

Lynch, F. L., Striegel-Moore, R., Dickerson, J. F., Perrin, N., DeBar, L., et al. (2010). Cost-effectiveness of guided self-help treatment for recurrent binge eating. *Journal of Consulting and Clinical Psychology, 78,* 322–333.

Lynn, S. J., Lock, T., Loftus, E. F., Krackow, E., & Lilienfeld, S. O. (2003). The remembrance of things past: Problematic memory recovery techniques in psychotherapy. In S. O. Lilienfeld, S. J. Lynn, & J. M. Lohr (Eds.), *Science and pseudoscience in clinical psychology* (pp. 205–239). New York, NY, NY: Guilford.

Masters, K. S., Spielmans, G. I., & Goodson, J. T. (2006). Are there demonstrable effects of distant intercessory prayer? A meta-analytic review. *Annals of Behavioral Medicine, 32,* 21–26.

Maton, K. I., & Brodsky, A. E. (2011). Empowering community settings: Theory, research, and action. In M. S. Aber, K. I. Maton, & E. Seidman (Eds.), *Empowering settings and voices for social change* (pp. 38–64). New York, NY, NY: Oxford University Press.

McGinn, M. M., Benson, L. A., & Christensen, A. (2011). Integrative behavioral couple therapy: An acceptance-based approach to improving relationship functioning. In J. D. Herbert & E. M. Forman (Eds.), *Acceptance and mindfulness in cognitive behavior therapy: Understanding and applying the new therapies* (pp. 210–232). Hoboken, NJ: Wiley.

McGoldrick, M., Giordano, J., & Garcia-Preto, N. (2005). *Ethnicity and family therapy* (3rd ed.). New York, NY: Guilford.

McHale, J. P., & Lindahl, K. M. (2011). *Coparenting: A conceptual and clinical examination of family systems.* Washington, DC: American Psychological Association.

Michael, K. D., Curtin, L., Kirkley, D. E., Jones, D. L., & Harris, R. (2006). Group-based motivational interviewing for alcohol use among college students: An exploratory study. *Professional Psychology: Research and Practice, 37,* 629–634.

Mihalopoulos, C., Vos, T., Pirkis, J., & Carter, R. (2011). The economic analysis of prevention in mental health programs. *Annual Review of Clinical Psychology, 7,* 169–201.

Miller, E., Tancredi, D. J., McCauley, H. L., Decker, M. R., Virata, M. C. D., et al. (2012). "Coaching boys into men": A cluster-randomized controlled trial of a dating violence prevention program. *Journal of Adolescent Health, March 13, 2012.* Early on-line version: 10.1016/j.jadohealth.2012.01.018.

Miller, W. R., & Thoresen, C. E. (2003). Spirituality, religion, and health: An emerging research field. *American Psychologist, 58,* 24–35.

Mitchell, K. J., Becker-Blease, K. A., & Finkelhor, D. (2005). Inventory of problematic internet experiences encountered in clinical practice. *Professional Psychology: Research and Practice, 36,* 498–509.

Morgan, A. J., Jorm, A. F., & Mackinnon, A. J. (2012). Usage and reported helpfulness of self-help strategies by adults with subthreshold depression. *Journal of Affective Disorders, 136,* 393–397.

Moskell, C., & Allred, S. B. (2013). Integrating human and natural systems in community psychology: An ecological model of stewardship behavior. *American Journal of Community Psychology, 51,* 1–14.

Munoz, R. F., Beardslee, W. R., & Leykin, Y. (2012). Major depression can be prevented. *American Psychologist, 67,* 285–295.

National Research Council and Institute of Medicine. (2009a). *Depression in parents, parenting, and children: Opportunities to improve identification, treatment, and prevention.* Washington, DC: National Academies Press.

National Research Council and Institute of Medicine. (2009b). *Preventing mental, emotional, and behavioral disorders among young people: Progress and possibilities.* Washington, DC: National Academies Press.

Newman, M. G., Szkodny, L. E., Llera, S. J., & Przeworski, A. (2011). A review of technology-assisted self-help and minimal contact therapies for anxiety and depression: Is human contact necessary for therapeutic efficacy? *Clinical Psychology Review, 31*, 89–103.

Nichols, M. P., & Minuchin, S. (2009). *Family therapy: Concepts and methods* (9th ed.). Upper Saddle River, NJ: Prentice Hall.

Norcross, J. C. (Ed.). (2002). *Psychotherapy relationships that work: Therapists contributions and responsiveness to patients.* New York, NY: Oxford University Press.

Norcross, J. C. (Ed.). (2006). Integrating self-help into psychotherapy: 16 practical suggestions. *Professional Psychology: Research and Practice, 37*, 683–693.

Norcross, J. C., & Goldfried, M. R. (2005). *Handbook of psychotherapy integration* (2nd ed.). New York, NY: Oxford University Press.

Norcross, J. C., Santrock, J. W., Zuckerman, E. L., Sommer, R., & Campbell, L. F. (2003). *Authoritative guide to self-help resources in mental health* (rev. ed.). New York, NY: Guilford.

Oei, T. P. S., & Browne, A. (2006). Components of group processes: Have they contributed to the outcome of mood and anxiety disorder patients in a group cognitive-behaviour therapy program? *American Journal of Psychotherapy, 60*, 53–70.

Ostafin, B. D., Chawla, N., Bowen, S., Dillworth, T. M., Witkiewitz, K., et al. (2006). Intensive mindfulness training and the reduction of psychological distress: A preliminary study. *Cognitive and Behavioral Practice, 13*, 191–197.

Park, C. (2013). Mind-body CAM interventions: Current status and considerations for integration into clinical health psychology. *Journal of Clinical Psychology, 69*, 45–63.

Perle, J. G., Langsam, L. C., Randel, A., Lutchman, S., Levine, A. B., et al. (2013). Attitudes toward psychological telehealth: Current and future clinical psychologists' opinions of internet-based interventions. *Journal of Clinical Psychology, 69*, 100–113.

Petry, N. M., Weinstock, J., & Alessi, S. M. (2011). A randomized trial of contingency management delivered in the context of group counseling. *Journal of Consulting and Clinical Psychology, 79*, 686–696.

Raiya, H. A., & Pargament, K. I. (2010). Religiously integrated psychotherapy with Muslim clients: From research to practice. *Professional Psychology: Research and Practice, 41*, 181–188.

Rappaport, J. (1977). *Community psychology: Values, research and action.* New York, NY: Holt, Rinehart & Winston.

Rappaport, J. (2002). In praise of paradox: A social policy of empowerment over prevention. In T. A. Revenson, A. R. D'Augelli, S. E. French, D. L. Hughes, & D. Livert (Eds.), *A quarter century of community psychology: Readings from the American Journal of Community Psychology* (pp. 121–145). New York, NY: Kluwer Academic/Plenum Publishers.

Rappaport, J. (2011). Searching for Oz: Empowerment, crossing boundaries, and telling our story. In M. S. Aber, K. I. Maton, & E. Seidman (Eds.), *Empowering settings and voices from social change* (pp. 232–237). New York, NY: Oxford University Press.

Ripple, C. H., & Zigler, E. (2003). Research, policy, and the federal role in prevention initiatives for children. *American Psychologist, 58*, 482–490.

Ritterband, L. M., Gonder-Frederick, L. A., Cox, D. J., Clifton, A. D., West, R. W., et al. (2003). Internet interventions: In review, in use, and into the future. *Professional Psychology: Research and Practice, 34*, 527–534.

Rogers, E. B., Stanford, M. S., Dolan, S. L., Clark, J., Martindale, S. L., et al. (2012). Helping people without homes: Simple steps for psychologists seeking to change lives. *Professional Psychology: Research and Practice, 43*, 86–93.

Rose, S. D., & LeCroy, C. W. (1991). Group methods. In F. H. Kanfer & A. P. Goldstein (Eds.), *Helping people change* (4th ed., pp. 422–453). New York, NY: Pergamon Press.

Rosen, G. M., Glasgow, R. E., & Moore, T. E. (2003). Self-help therapy: The science and business of giving psychology away. In S. O. Lilienfeld, S. J. Lynn, & J. M. Lohr (Eds.), *Science and pseudoscience in clinical psychology* (pp. 399–424). New York, NY: Guilford.

Rosenhan, D. L. (1973). On being sane in insane places. *Science, 179*, 250–258.

Rouleau, C. R., & vonRanson, K. M. (2011). Potential risks for pro-eating disorder websites. *Clinical Psychology Review, 31*, 525–531.

Salloum, A., & Overstreet, S. (2008). Evaluation of individual and group grief and trauma interventions for children post disaster. *Journal of Clinical Child and Adolescent Psychology, 37*, 495–507.

Salmon, P. G., Sephton, S. E., & Dreeben, S. J. (2011). Mindfulness-based stress reduction. In J. D. Herbert & E. M. Forman (Eds.), *Acceptance and mindfulness in cognitive behavior therapy: Understanding and applying the new therapies* (pp. 132–163). Hoboken, NJ: Wiley.

Salovey, P., & Singer, J. A. (1991). Cognitive behavior modification. In F. H. Kanfer & A. P. Goldstein (Eds.), *Helping people change* (4th ed., pp. 361–395). New York, NY: Pergamon Press.

Sandler, I. N., Schoenfelder, E. N., Wolchik, S. A., & MacKinnon, D. P. (2011). Long-term impact of prevention programs to promote effective parenting: Lasting effects but uncertain processes. *Annual Review of Psychology, 62*, 299–329.

Sarason, S. B. (1974). *The psychological sense of community: Prospects for community psychology.* San Francisco, CA: Jossey-Bass.

Schnur, J. B., & Montgomery, G. H. (2010). A systematic review of therapeutic alliance, group cohesion, empathy, and goal consensus/collaboration in psychotherapeutic interventions in cancer: Uncommon factors? *Clinical Psychology Review, 30*, 238–247.

Schulz, M. S., Pruett, M. K., Kerig, P. K., & Parke, R. D. (2010). *Strengthening couple relationships for optimal child development: Lessons from research and intervention.* Washington, DC: American Psychological Association.

Segal, Z. V., Williams, J. M. G., & Teasdale, J. D. (2002). *Mindfulness-based cognitive therapy for depression: A new approach to preventing relapse.* New York, NY: Guilford.

Seidman, E., & Tseng, V. (2011). Changing social settings: A framework for action. In M. S. Aber, K. I. Maton, & E. Seidman (Eds.), *Empowering settings and voices for social change* (pp. 12–37). New York, NY: Oxford University Press

Seligman, M. E. P. (2011). *Flourish: A visionary new understanding of happiness and well-being.* New York, NY: Free Press.

Shaffer, A., Coffino, B., Boelcke-Stennes, K., & Masten, A. S. (2007). From urban girls to resilient women: Studying adaptation across development in the context of adversity. In B. J. R. Leadbeater & N. Way (Eds.), *Urban girls revisited: Building strengths* (pp. 53–72). New York, NY: New York University Press.

Shapiro, S. L., Carlson, L. E., Astin, J. A., & Freedman, B. (2006). Mechanisms of mindfulness. *Journal of Clinical Psychology, 62*, 373–386.

Shure, M. B., & Aberson, B. (2005). Enhancing the process of resilience through effective thinking. In S. Goldstein & R. B. Brooks (Eds.), *Handbook of resilience in children* (pp. 373–394). New York, NY: Kluwer Academic/Plenum Publishers.

Spence, S. H., Donovan, C. L., March, S., Gamble, A., Anderson, R. E., et al. (2011). A randomized controlled trial of online versus clinic-based CBT for adolescent anxiety. *Journal of Consulting and Clinical Psychology, 79*, 629–642.

Spence, S. H., Holmes, J. M., March, S., & Lipp, O. V. (2006). The feasibility and outcome of clinic plus internet delivery of cognitive-behavior therapy for childhood anxiety. *Journal of Consulting and Clinical Psychology, 74*, 614–621.

Stanton, M. (2013). The systemic epistemology of the specialty of family psychology. In J. H. Bray & M. Stanton (Eds.), *The Wiley-Blackwell handbook of family psychology* (pp. 5–20). Hoboken, NJ: Wiley.

Stice, E., Rohde, P., Shaw, H., & Marti, C. N. (2013). Efficacy trial of a selective prevention program targeting both eating disorders and obesity among female college students: 1- and 2-year follow-up effects. *Journal of Consulting and Clinical Psychology, 81*, 183–189.

Stricker, G. (2010). *Psychotherapy integration.* Washington, DC: American Psychological Association.

Strickler, G., & Gold, J. (Eds.). (2006). *A casebook of psychotherapy integration.* Washington, DC: American Psychological Association.

Sullivan, H. S. (1953). *The interpersonal theory of psychiatry.* New York, NY: W. W. Norton.

Synovitz, L. B., & Larson, K. L. (2012). *Complementary and alternative medicine for health professionals.* Burlington, MA: Jones & Bartlett Learning.

Varley, R., Webb, T. L., & Sheeran, P. (2011). Making self-help more helpful: A randomized controlled trial of the impact of augmenting self-help materials with implementation intentions on promoting the effective self-management of anxiety symptoms. *Journal of Consulting and Clinical Psychology, 79*, 123–128.

Wade, S. L., Oberjohn, K., Conaway, K., Osinska, P., & Bangert, L. (2011). Live coaching of parenting skills using the internet: Implications for clinical practice. *Professional Psychology: Research and Practice, 42*, 487–493.

Weeks, G. R., & Treat, S. R. (2001). *Couples in treatment: Techniques and approaches for effective practice* (2nd ed.). New York, NY: Brunner-Routledge.

Weisz, J. R. (2004). *Psychotherapy for children and adolescents: Evidence-based treatments and case examples.* New York, NY: Cambridge University Press.

Weisz, J. R., Sandler, I. N., Durlak, J. A., & Anton, B. S. (2005). Promoting and protecting youth mental health through evidence-based prevention and treatment. *American Psychologist, 60*, 628–648.

Wells, A. (2011). Metacognitive therapy. In J. D. Herbert & E. M. Forman (Eds.), *Acceptance and mindfulness in cognitive behavior therapy: Understanding and applying the new therapies* (pp. 83–108). Hoboken, NJ: Wiley.

Welsh, B. C., & Farrington, D. P. (2007). Saving children from a life of crime: Toward a national strategy for early prevention. *Victims and Offenders, 2*, 1–20.

Wenzel, A., Liese, B. S., Beck, A. T., & Friedman-Wheeler, D. G. (2012). *Group cognitive therapy for addictions.* New York, NY: Guilford.

Williams, J. C., & Lynn, S. J. (2010). Acceptance: An historical and conceptual review. *Imagination, Cognition, and Personality, 30*, 5–56.

Wilson, G. T., & Zandberg, L. J. (2012). Cognitive-behavioral guided self-help for eating disorders: Effectiveness and scalability. *Clinical Psychology Review, 32*, 343–357.

Wolak, J., Finkelhor, D., Mitchell, K. J., & Ybarra, M. L. (2008). Online "predators" and their victims: Myths, realities, and implications for prevention and treatment. *American Psychologist, 63*, 111–128.

Yalom, I. D., & Leszcz, M. (2005). *The theory and practice of group psychotherapy.* New York, NY: Basic Books.

Yarhouse, M. A., & Tan, E. S. N. (2005). Addressing religious conflicts in adolescents who experience sexual identity confusion. *Professional Psychology: Research and Practice, 36*, 530–536.

Yoshikawa, H., Aber, J. L., & Beardslee, W. R. (2012). The effects of poverty on the mental, emotional, and behavioral health of children and youth: Implications for prevention. *American Psychologist, 67*, 272–284.

Zaza, C., Sellick, S. M., & Hillier, L. M. (2005). Coping with cancer: What do patients do? *Journal of Psychosocial oncology, 23*, 55–73.

Zimmerman, M. A. (2000). Empowerment theory: Psychological, organizational and community levels of analysis. In J. Rappaport & E. Seidman (Eds.), *Handbook of community psychology* (pp. 42–63). New York, NY: Kluwer Academic/Plenum Publishers.

10 | RESEARCH ON CLINICAL INTERVENTION

Chapter Preview

This chapter provides an explanation of how we know what works in therapy. Methods of research to establish the usefulness of different therapies are discussed, as are the problems associated with each methodology. The overall findings of therapeutic efficacy and effectiveness are provided for traditional individual treatments as well as for alternative modes of intervention. The chapter closes with a discussion of the use of psychopharmacology in relation to psychological treatments.

A Clinical Case

T.C. is a 26-year-old Chinese American who is experiencing major depressive disorder, generalized anxiety disorder, and anger problems. He lives with his mother in a large city in the United States and is attending graduate school in a technology-related field.

T.C. is the youngest and "least successful" of three children. He was told by his parents that he resulted from an unwanted pregnancy that was almost aborted. There were many stressors in the family while T.C. was growing up, including financial hardship, frequent fights between his parents, his father's gambling problem, and his mother's problem with hoarding items such as used containers. His older sisters were academically gifted, and they both graduated from prestigious universities, which made it all the more difficult when T.C. was not accepted into any colleges. It was at that point, during his senior year in high school, that T.C. experienced his first major depressive episode. He ended up graduating from high school and attending a community college and then transferred to a state university where he earned a Bachelor of Science degree in an engineering-related field. While T.C. was in college, his father's gambling problem intensified, and he had to sell the family grocery store, soon after which T.C.'s parents divorced. T.C. became increasingly depressed and had suicidal ideation, but no specific plan. He commented that he would kill himself if he could find a "fast, secure, and reliable" method.

T.C. sought treatment with Dr. Emily Liu, a Chinese American and who was on an internship in clinical psychology at the time. At the beginning of treatment, T.C. showed noticeably negative interpersonal characteristics, such as rolling his eyes at the therapist, sneering, and being sarcastic. On psychometrically sound assessment measures, he scored in the severe range of depression and in the moderate range of anxiety. He reported poor sleep quality and showed high levels of anger problems. On the positive side, he also showed many strengths, such as honesty, perseverance, and resilience.

T.C. was seen for 41 sessions. In addition to establishing a "no suicide" contract at the outset of treatment, Dr. Liu employed cognitive therapy, cognitive-behavioral case formulation, and cognitive–interpersonal cycle methodologies and also used her knowledge of multicultural techniques to overcome culture-specific challenges to treatment (e.g., T.C. expressed self-defeating thoughts, such as "Keep telling yourself that you are not good enough" and "Don't ever be satisfied with your accomplishments," which were consistent with his culture's values of humility and achievement but were also related to his depressive symptoms). In addition, T.C. received antidepressant medication from a psychiatrist.

By the end of the year-long therapy, T.C. showed decreased symptoms of depression, anxiety, and anger. He had also made some limited improvements in his social skills and he no longer had strong suicidal ideation. When Dr. Liu completed her internship, T.C. was transferred to another therapist to continue to work on improving his social skills and negative cognitions. (Liu, 2007)

This case illustrates the complicated histories that clients can bring to therapy. Luckily, T.C. found a therapist who was culturally competent and who employed the evidence-based practices described later in this chapter. Over the past few decades, no other area of clinical psychology has seen more intense research and debate than efforts to establish which psychological treatments work best. The idea is that clinicians should use only those therapies and assessment techniques that have been shown to be effective on the basis of empirical research evidence. Those that are effective are called *evidence-based therapies* and *evidence-based assessments*, which when combined are known as *evidence-based practices*. Exactly what type of evidence is sufficient to show that a particular method is evidence-based? In this chapter, we explore some of the answers to this complicated question.

STUDYING INDIVIDUAL PSYCHOLOGICAL TREATMENTS

SECTION PREVIEW

We begin by reviewing the history of psychologists' efforts to establish which treatments work best for which problems. Included in the discussion is a summary of the research designs they have used (within-subjects, between-subjects, and randomized clinical trials), the results of their research (based on box score reviews, meta-analytic studies, client satisfaction surveys, outcome studies and the like), and recommendations about how best to translate research knowledge into practice. We also consider research on the impact of common or nonspecific factors in treatment (therapist variables, client variables, and relationship variables).

The modern era of therapy-outcome research began in 1952 when Hans Eysenck, a British psychologist, reviewed several experiments and concluded that the recovery rate seen in patients who receive therapy is about the same as for those who do not. Eysenck argued that the rate of *spontaneous remission* (improvement without any special treatment) was 72% over 2 years compared to improvement rates of 44% for psychoanalysis and 64% for eclectic therapy (Eysenck, 1952). In later reviews, Eysenck (1966) evaluated more studies and, while persisting in his pessimism about the effectiveness of traditional therapy, claimed that behavior therapy produced superior outcomes.

Even after Eysenck's summaries, many clinical researchers continued to ask: *Is psychotherapy effective?* In trying to answer this question, they came to realize that the question was too broad. Starting in the 1970s, therapy-outcome research began to be influenced by Gordon Paul's (1969a) more specific reformulation, sometimes referred to as the "ultimate question" about psychotherapy research: "What treatment, by whom, is most effective for this individual with that specific problem, under which set of circumstances, and how does it come about?" (p. 44).

Alan Kazdin (1982) translated Paul's "ultimate question" into a list of outcome research goals, including to:

- Determine the efficacy of a specific treatment.
- Compare the relative effectiveness of different treatments.
- Assess the specific components of treatment that are responsible for particular changes.

More recently, researchers investigating psychological treatments have sought to:

- Assess the durability of the benefits of particular treatments.
- Identify any negative side effects associated with a treatment.
- Determine how acceptable a treatment is to various kinds of clients.
- Map the cost effectiveness of various treatments.
- Discover whether a treatment's effects are clinically significant and socially meaningful.
- Verify that treatments that work in one setting (such as the research laboratory) are also effective in other settings (such as a community mental health center).
- Establish which delivery method, such as in-person versus online, is associated with the best clinical outcomes.
- Evaluate how treatments lead to changes in behavior (Kazdin & Blasé, 2011; Kendall & Comer, 2011).

The results of their work have led to significant advances in identifying and developing treatments that help decrease some of the most common mental health problems. A look at the history and process of research on clinical interventions will help to highlight how far we have come as a field.

Basic Designs of Outcome Research on Psychological Treatments: Past and Present

For the past few decades, researchers have tried to design and conduct their treatment outcome evaluations in such a way that the results can be interpreted unambiguously. Of all the research designs that can evaluate the presence of a cause–effect relationship between therapy and improvement, the most powerful is the controlled experiment (Greenhoot, 2005). An experiment is an attempt to discover the causes of specific events by making systematic changes in certain factors and then observing changes that occur in other factors. The factors that researchers manipulate are called *independent variables;* the factors in which changes are to be observed are called *dependent variables.* In outcome research, the independent variable is usually the type of therapy that is given (e.g., cognitive-behavioral treatment versus nondirective therapy), and the dependent variable is the amount of change seen in clients (e.g., as measured by tests of depression or anxiety).

Most psychotherapy-outcome experiments employ either within-subjects or between-subjects research designs, both of which allow the researcher to examine the effects of varying treatment conditions (the independent variable) on clients' thinking and behavior (the dependent variables). In *within-subjects designs,* clients get a single kind of treatment, but the experimenter alters it in some way at various points and observes any changes in behavior that might occur. In *between-subjects designs,* different groups of clients are exposed to differing treatments, and the amount and type of changes observed in each group are compared. In *randomized clinical trials,* either within- or between-subjects designs are used to provide a more statistically rigorous research methodology. We discuss each of these in more detail below.

WITHIN-SUBJECTS RESEARCH DESIGNS   Some of the earliest research on clinical interventions was conducted via within-subjects designs (Fishman, Rego, & Muller, 2011). The within-subjects experimental design requires that the dependent variables (client behaviors) be measured on several occasions. The first of these observations usually takes place during a pretreatment, or baseline, period that provides a measure of the nature and intensity of a client's problematic behavior. Once baseline measures have established a stable picture, the intervention phase of the experiment begins. Here, the researcher manipulates the independent variable by introducing some form of treatment and watches the dependent variable for any changes from its baseline level.

Although there are several types of within-subjects experiments used in clinical treatment research, they all allow clinical researchers to conduct fine-grained analyses of the inner workings of therapy in real-world settings (Miltenberger, 2011). A variant on this approach is the *case-study* model in which therapists evaluate their services in clinical settings by developing a specific treatment formulation for each client, then assessing the effects of the therapy for that client using techniques similar to those of single-subject research design (Kazdin, 2011). Figure 10.1 illustrates a within-subjects case-study in a clinical setting. The client was a 6-year-old girl, diagnosed with selective mutism because she would not talk to anyone other than her immediate family. After three days of baseline assessment, treatment was begun by rewarding her with a piece of her favorite sugar-free candy whenever she made any appropriate vocalization to a non-family member.

As this case shows, within-subjects treatment research is usually conducted over time with a single client or sometimes a small number of clients. Indeed, single-subject, or "$N = 1$" research is a popular treatment evaluation strategy when a new treatment is being explored or when a rare disorder is being addressed, and it allows intensive study of the treatment process (Fishman , Rego, & Muller, 2011). However, between-subjects designs have gained in popularity over the past few decades for evaluating most major treatments for most major disorders.

BETWEEN-SUBJECTS RESEARCH DESIGNS   The simplest example of a between-subjects experiment on therapy outcome is one in which the researcher manipulates an independent variable by giving treatment to one group of clients—the *experimental* group—and compares any observed changes to those seen in members of a *control* group, who received no treatment. Measures of the clients' problematic behavior (the dependent variable) are made for both groups before the study (the *pretest*), shortly after the treatment period ends (the *posttest*), and perhaps also at various posttreatment intervals (the *follow-up*).

It is important that clients be *randomly assigned* to experimental or control groups because, given a large enough number of clients, this procedure makes it likely that the treatment and control groups will be approximately equivalent in age, severity of disorder, gender, race/ethnicity,

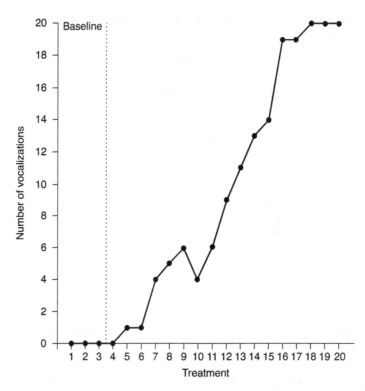

FIGURE 10.1 Number of Vocalizations During Baseline and Intervention

socioeconomic status, and other important variables that might influence treatment outcome. If clients are not randomly assigned to conditions, any between-group differences in behavior seen at the end of the experiment might be attributed to differences that existed between groups before the study ever began.

Statistical comparisons between treatment and no-treatment groups are just a first step in therapy-outcome research. After all, even large and statistically significant differences between a treatment and a no-treatment group tells us only that giving treatment appears to be better than doing nothing. The simple treatment/no-treatment design cannot shed light on the more complex questions that therapy-outcome researchers want to address. In another common design, clients are randomly assigned to one of two treatments whose outcomes are then compared. For example, this type of design was used to compare the effects of motivational interviewing plus cognitive-behavioral therapy with interviewing alone in reducing alcohol abuse in gay men at high risk for HIV transmission (Morgenstern et al., 2007).

Increasingly, researchers have wanted to know which aspects of a therapy are most associated with positive outcomes. In a research design called *dismantling*, researchers can "take apart" treatments that are known to work in order to identify their most helpful components (Dobson & Hamilton, 2009). For example, if a treatment involves, say, relaxation training, education, and homework, a dismantling study would randomly assign some clients to get only the relaxation component, while others would get relaxation and education, and still others would get both of these plus the homework. This type of research design can help clinical scientists understand which aspects of the treatment are most crucial for clients' improvement in an attempt to streamline the treatment in the future (Dobson & Hamilton, 2009).

Between-subjects research designs have become very popular among therapy researchers because they allow manipulation of several independent variables simultaneously rather than sequentially, as required by within-subjects designs. Between-subjects designs are expensive, however. It usually takes many clients and a large research staff to recruit, organize, and treat groups of the size necessary for powerful statistical analyses of results (Greenhoot, 2005).

RANDOMIZED CLINICAL TRIALS Most federally funded research on treatment outcome (including funding from the National Institutes of Health and the Food and Drug Administration) currently focuses on *randomized clinical trials* (RCTs), which can utilize either within- or between-subjects designs. RCTs require homogeneous samples of clients and clinical problems, random assignment of clients to conditions, and carefully monitored treatment regimens (Comer & Kendall, 2013).

The results of RCTs are normally presented in accordance with the *Consolidated Standards of Reporting Trials* (CONSORT Standards), which were updated in 2010 (Schultz, Altman, & Moher, 2010). Researchers who follow these standards present flow charts portraying the progress of clients through each stage of the study, including screening, recruitment, random assignment, treatment, and follow-up.

Figure 10.2 shows an example of a randomized clinical trial in which first-year college students who reported at least two episodes of heavy drinking within the past month were randomly assigned to receive either motivational interviewing along with a substance-free activity session (SFAS) or a control condition of motivational interviewing plus relaxation training (Murphy et al., 2012). This CONSORT flow-chart shows how many participants were screened from the study, how many completed the treatment, and ultimately how many completed the 1-month and semester-long follow-up to the study. The results of this study showed, by the way, that

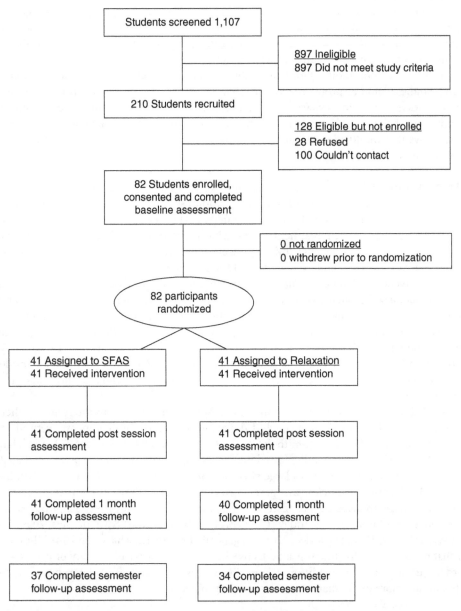

FIGURE 10.2 Flowchart Illustrating Recruitment, Intervention Assignment, and follow-Up assessment.
Source: Murphy, J. G., Dennhardt, A. A., Skidmore, J. R., Borsari, B., Barnett, N. P., et al. (2012). A randomized controlled trial of a behavioral economic supplement to brief motivational interventions for college drinking. *Journal of Consulting and Clinical Psychology, 80,* 876–886.

motivational interviewing plus SFAS (which included an individual therapy session to discuss how to reduce the negative impact of substance abuse on students' academic and career goals) was superior to motivational interviewing plus relaxation training in reducing alcohol problems at both follow-up assessments (Murphy et al., 2012). This study illustrates the importance of following specific steps involved in conducting RCTs and in reporting results in a way that is consistent with the CONSORT guidelines.

Results of Outcome Research on Psychological Treatments: Past and Present

The results of thousands of therapy outcome studies have been summarized and codified in various ways over the last three decades—initially by using box score reviews and more recently by using meta-analytic reviews. Researchers have also used client satisfaction surveys to explore psychological treatments. These efforts have led to the identification of empirically supported treatments, and that knowledge has guided evidence-based practices that are most likely to maximize the benefits of psychological treatments.

BOX SCORE REVIEWS The traditional approach to summarizing outcome research has been the narrative, or *box score*, review (e.g., Lambert & Bergin, 1994; Lambert, Shapiro, & Bergin, 1986; Weisz, Donenberg, Han, & Weiss, 1995). In a box score review, researchers make categorical judgments about whether each outcome study yielded positive or negative results and then tally the number of positive and negative outcomes. Reviewers who use this method have been criticized (including by one another) for being subjective and unsystematic in the way they integrate research studies. Another problem with narrative reviews is that the sheer number of outcome studies makes it difficult for reviewers to weigh properly the merits and results of each study. Disagreements over these results made it clear that an alternative to box score analysis was needed, an alternative that would allow researchers to quantify and statistically summarize the effects of each outcome study, separately and in the aggregate.

META-ANALYTIC STUDIES One such alternative is *meta-analysis*, a quantitative technique that standardizes the outcomes of a large number of studies so they can be compared or combined (Ellis, 2010). In order to quantify the outcome differences between participants who receive treatment and those who do not, a treatment *effect size* is calculated. This is done in the following way: the treatment group mean on a dependent measure minus the control group mean on the same measure is divided by the standard deviation of the control group. In other words, an effect size indicates the average difference in outcome between treated and untreated groups in each study. Effect sizes can also be calculated to compare two different treatment groups rather than just treatment and no-treatment groups. Looking at effect sizes measured immediately after therapy ends, or in some cases, months after treatment, indicates how much better off the average treated client was compared with the average untreated client. Effect sizes begin at 0 and can go above 1, and based on Cohen's (1988) categorizations for comparing two groups, are often considered "small" if they are from .20 to .50, "medium" if they are between .50 and .80, and "large" if they are .80 or above.

Mary Smith and Gene Glass were the first to apply meta-analysis to the results of therapy outcome research. Their 1977 paper concluded that, on average, psychotherapy was very effective, with a medium effect size of .68 (Smith & Glass, 1977). The results of their second, much larger, meta-analysis of 475 outcome studies found that the average treated client was better off than 80% of untreated individuals; there was a large effect size of .85 (Smith, Glass, & Miller, 1980). In the 1980s and 1990s, other research teams performed other meta-analyses using different statistical methods or differently selected sets of studies (e.g., Lambert & Bergin, 1994; Shapiro & Shapiro, 1982), and these efforts continue today (Cuijpers et al., 2012; Stewart & Chambless, 2009; Tolin, 2010; Weisz, Jensen-Doss, & Hawley, 2006). In general, these analyses have confirmed the conclusion that psychological treatment is an effective intervention for a wide variety of psychological disorders (usually showing medium or large effect sizes). As we shall see later, however, some treatments are more useful than others for certain problems.

CLIENT SATISFACTION SURVEYS In the 1990s, while researchers were trying to ascertain whether or not therapy was useful, a huge public survey was undertaken by *Consumer Reports* magazine (Seligman, 1995). Approximately 4,100 respondents who had seen a mental health professional in the previous three years were asked to rate (a) the degree to which formal treatment had helped with the problem that led them to therapy, (b) how satisfied they were with the treatment they received, and (c) how they judged their "overall emotional state" after treatment. Their responses indicated that

- about 90% of clients felt better after treatment.
- there was no difference in the improvement of clients who had psychotherapy alone versus psychotherapy plus medication.
- no particular approach to psychotherapy was rated more highly than others.
- although all types of professionals appeared to help their clients, greater improvements were associated with treatments by psychologists, psychiatrists, and social workers compared to family physicians or marriage counselors.

More recent studies have found comparable ratings of client satisfaction with psychological treatment. For example, one survey of nearly 13,000 adults found that, of those who had received treatment for psychological problems in the past year, 88.5% said that they were satisfied with it (Lippens & Mackenzie, 2011). Although client satisfaction surveys are not as rigorous as randomized clinical trials and meta-analyses of them, these surveys do give clinical researchers evidence about clients' overall views of therapy experiences.

EMPIRICALLY SUPPORTED TREATMENTS (ESTs) AND EVIDENCE-BASED TREATMENTS   Box score reviews, meta-analyses, and client surveys suggest there are no significant differences in the *overall* outcomes of various types of treatment, but that doesn't mean that all treatments have the same effects for all clients with all problems. Accordingly, in 1993, APA Division 12 (now known as the Society of Clinical Psychology, or SCP) convened a special task force to look more closely at the results of psychotherapy-outcome research to determine which specific treatment interventions were most strongly supported by empirical research as being effective for particular kinds of problems. This *Task Force on Promotion and Dissemination of Psychological Procedures* began by establishing a set of criteria for research designs capable of reaching reliable and valid conclusions about the effectiveness of clinical interventions. They then reviewed the massive therapy-outcome literature to determine what such studies said about the effects of various treatments. In 1995, the Task Force published a preliminary list of 25 treatments that high-quality empirical research had identified as *efficacious* (Seligman, 1995). The list was updated in 1996 and again in 1998. The 1998 list included 71 treatments (Chambless et al., 1998). The task force's original 1995 report used the term *empirically validated* to describe those interventions that met its criteria for efficaciousness. However, many clinicians felt that this term was too strong and suggested that there was not a single, final "answer" as to which treatments "worked." Accordingly, the next report of the Task Force referred to *empirically supported* treatments (ESTs).

By 2001, the Task Force, along with seven other work groups using similar methods, had classified 108 treatments for adults and 37 for children as being either:

- *Well-established/efficacious and specific* (i.e., supported by at least two rigorous randomized controlled trials in which treatment showed superiority to placebo–control conditions or another bona fide treatment, or by a large series of rigorous single-case experiments),
- *Probably efficacious/possibly efficacious* (i.e., supported by at least one rigorous randomized controlled trial in which treatment showed superiority to placebo–control conditions or another bona fide treatment, or by a small series of rigorous single-case experiments), or
- *Promising* (i.e., supported by studies whose research designs produced less convincing evidence than those in the first two categories (Chambless & Ollendick, 2001)).

Between 60% and 90% of the treatments on the list of empirically supported treatments (ESTs) are cognitive-behavioral in nature (Chambless & Ollendick, 2001). Since that time, other task forces have come and gone, but there continue to be many concerted efforts to identify treatments that work. The Society of Clinical Psychology now maintains an updated website that lists "Research Supported Psychological Treatments": http://www.div12.org/PsychologicalTreatments/index.html

An APA Presidential Task Force on Evidence-Based Practice (2006) categorized treatments according to whether they have:

- Strong research support (similar to "well established")
- Modest research support (similar to "probably efficacious")

- Controversial research support (meaning that there are conflicting results or that though the treatment is shown to be efficacious, some claims made about the treatment are not based on empirical evidence).

The results presented on the SCP website are too numerous to list here, but Table 10.1 provides some idea about the kinds of treatments that have garnered strong research support for selected clinical problems.

Note that the bulk of the psychological treatments with strong research support continue to fall into the cognitive-behavioral and behavioral categories. These and other findings of the various task forces have been questioned, however, partly because their analyses focused largely on outcome studies in which therapists conducted treatment in accordance with standardized *treatment manuals* rather than on the basis of their own preferences and experiences (Baardseth et al., 2013; Beutler, 2002). This and other criticisms of psychotherapy research are discussed later in this chapter.

These concerns aside, recent treatment outcome task forces have tried not only to understand which therapies are most effective for which problems, but also to identify a broader array of therapeutic practices through which treatment is likely to produce the maximum benefit to clients. Reaching this broader goal, they hope, will allow clinicians to conduct what has become known as *evidence-based practice*.

EVIDENCE-BASED PRACTICE (EBP) The APA Presidential Task Force on Evidence-Based Practice proposed the following Policy Statement, which was officially adopted by the Council of Representatives of APA in August of 2005:

> Evidence-based practice in psychology (EBPP) is the integration of the best available research with clinical expertise in the context of patient characteristics, culture, and preferences. . . . The purpose of EBPP is to promote effective psychological practice and enhance public health by applying empirically supported principles of psychological assessment, case formulation, therapeutic relationship, and intervention. . . . (APA Presidential Task Force on Evidence-Based Practice, 2006, p. 273)

In general, the work of this evidence-based practice task force was an attempt to bring together researchers and clinicians in order to find the many ways that treatments can be shown to be effective in the real world. The policy statement delineates ideas on the best research evidence; clinical expertise; and patients' or clients' characteristics, values, and contexts. It is clear that evidence-based practice has caught on throughout the research and clinical realms. For

TABLE 10.1 Research Supported Psychological Treatments (Selected)

Psychological Treatment	Diagnosis or Clinical Problem
Acceptance and Commitment Therapy	Chronic Pain
Behavior Therapy/Behavioral Activation	Depression
Behavioral Couples Therapy for Alcohol Use Disorders	Alcohol Use Disorders
	Bulimia Nervosa
Cognitive Behavioral Therapy	Depression
	Generalized Anxiety Disorder
Cognitive Therapy	Panic Disorder
Dialectical Behavior Therapy	Depression
Exposure and Response Prevention	Obsessive-Compulsive Disorder
Interpersonal Therapy	Borderline Personality Disorder
Motivational Interviewing/Motivational Enhancement Therapy (MET)/	Obsessive-Compulsive Disorder
	Depression
MET plus CBT	Bulimia Nervosa
Problem Solving Therapy	Substance Abuse/Dependence in General
	Depression

Source: Based on data from http://www.div12.org/PsychologicalTreatments/index.html.

example, there is now a two-volume *Handbook of Evidence-Based Practice in Clinical Psychology* (Sturmey & Hersen, 2012a, 2012b) focused on childhood, adolescent, and adult disorders. There has also been a proliferation of special sections on evidence-based practice in many prominent peer-reviewed journals, including the *Journal of Consulting and Clinical Psychology* (LaGreca, Silverman, & Lochman, 2009), *Clinical Psychology: Science and Practice* (Youngstrom & Kendall, 2009), the *Journal of Clinical Psychology* (Morales & Norcross, 2010), and *Psychotherapy* (Norcross & Lambert, 2011).

With its many specialized terms (effective, efficacious, empirically supported, evidence based, etc.) and multiple task forces emphasizing different aspects of the research literature, psychotherapy outcome research can be confusing. In a nutshell, we can summarize it thus: early research sought to determine if psychotherapy was effective in the lab and efficacious in the community, later research sought to find out which forms of psychotherapy were superior, and recent research has moved even closer to addressing Gordon Paul's (1969a) "ultimate question." The state-of-the-art work in evidence-based practices combines research on specific treatments (e.g., from outcome studies, randomized clinical trials, case-studies, and meta-analyses) with research on the impact of characteristics of clients, therapists, and the therapeutic relationship, and knowledge based on clinicians' professional experiences and expertise.

The hope is to see the dawning of a new era of evidence-based practice in which research evidence and clinical skill can be happily married. Ollendick and Davis (2004) pointed out that clinical science and clinical practice depend on each other and that neither can work productively in isolation. Figure 10.3 shows a schematic model of how clinical expertise, research evidence, and client variables can be combined in integrated clinical decision making (Spring, 2007). For now, though, the marriage is a troubled one. There remains a divide between empirical researchers who

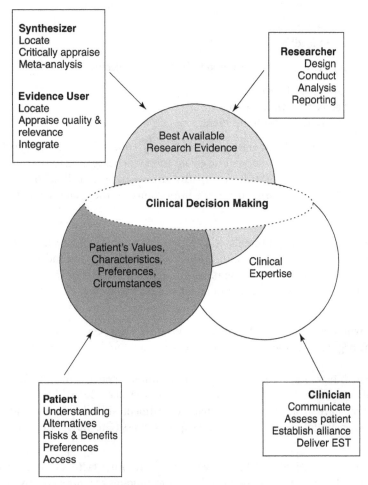

FIGURE 10.3 The Three Circles of Evidence-Based Clinical Practice.
Source: Spring, B. (2007). Evidence-based practice in clinical psychology: What it is, why it matters, what you need to know. *Journal of Clinical Psychology, 63,* 611–631.

cannot understand why clinicians are not jumping at the chance to use empirically supported treatments, and clinicians who cannot understand why researchers keep trying to force them to use treatment techniques with which they are not comfortable, especially because they feel that their current techniques already work.

As meta-analyses suggest, those techniques probably do work, partly because of treatment and therapist characteristics that are common to many therapies. Researchers would like to know more about what those common features are and how they can be maximized to benefit clients.

Research on Common or Nonspecific Factors in Therapy

In Chapter 6, "Basic Features of Clinical Interventions," we introduced the notion that therapist characteristics, client characteristics, and the therapeutic alliance that forms between the client and therapist can be important factors in the outcome of psychotherapy. Here we summarize what researchers have found about how these variables operate to produce their effects.

THERAPIST VARIABLES   What therapist characteristics or behaviors—apart from the therapist's adherence to a specific treatment method—predict positive therapy outcomes? In an attempt to answer this question, a Task Force on Empirically Supported Therapy Relationships was created by the APA Division of Psychotherapy (Division 29). After a thorough review and synthesis of the available research literature, the results were summarized in a book entitled *Psychotherapy Relationships That Work* (Norcross, 2002). This book, which has since been updated (Norcross, 2011) found characteristics of both the therapist and the therapeutic alliance that influence therapy outcomes. Regarding therapist variables, the following were found to be *demonstrably effective* (Norcross & Wampold, 2011):

- Higher levels of empathy
- Collecting client feedback

The following factors were considered to be *probably effective:*

- Positive regard toward the client
- Strong goal consensus with the client
- A sense of collaboration with the client.

These factors were all associated with better outcomes for clients, regardless of what specific treatment technique or therapeutic orientation was being used (Norcross, 2011). Interestingly, many of these factors (such as empathy and positive regard) echo the early work by Carl Rogers (1942) who also argued for the importance of these characteristics in effective therapists.

CLIENT VARIABLES   Although there is less consensus on which client variables are associated with better outcomes, there are some indications about which client attitudes might be the most helpful in gaining benefits from treatment. As discussed in Chapter 6, from the limited studies that exist, the following conclusions about client characteristics that benefit psychotherapy can be drawn.

- Clients who are open and offer higher levels of disclosure and lower levels of resistance from the beginning of therapy tend to have better outcomes (Kahn, Achter, & Shambaugh, 2001).
- Clients with higher symptoms of depression showed greater gains than those with lower levels of depression (Driessen, Cuijpers, Hollon, & Dekker, 2010).
- Clients who have strong expectations that the treatment will be successful tend to have better outcomes than those clients who do not expect success (Greenberg, Constantino, & Bruce, 2006).

Like therapist variables, client variables may interact with other factors to influence outcomes. For example, nondirective and paradoxical therapy techniques are more effective than directive ones for clients entering therapy with high levels of resistance, but directive treatments are more effective for clients with low levels of resistance (Beutler & Harwood, 2000).

RELATIONSHIP VARIABLES In Chapter 6, we discussed various views of the therapeutic relationship, especially the therapeutic alliance, and its measurement. Let's now consider the results of research investigating its influence on therapy outcome.

A large research literature on *therapeutic alliance* now exists, containing thousands of studies, as well as reviews and meta-analyses of those studies. This research shows that better alliance and relationship factors between therapists and clients are associated with better treatment outcomes (Baldwin & Imel, 2013; Horvath, DelRe, Fluckiger, & Symonds, 2011; Shirk, Karver, & Brown, 2011). For example, in a review mentioned earlier (Norcross, 2011; Norcross & Wampold, 2011), a high quality therapeutic alliance with children, adults, and families was repeatedly identified as being *demonstrably effective* in creating positive treatment outcomes across the very large number of studies (Table 10.2 provides example of how a strong therapeutic relationship is manifested).

Note that these therapist, client, and relationship variables are associated with better outcomes for clients, no matter which specific treatment technique or therapeutic orientation is used (Norcross, 2011). There is also research evidence that supports customizing therapy and various aspects of the therapy relationship on the basis of individual client characteristics or behaviors. For example, clients who are not resistant to therapy tend to do better when there is a structured treatment provided by a more directive therapist, whereas clients who are more resistant to therapy appear to do better when the therapist is not too directive and when the therapist provides a treatment related to self-control (reviewed by Norcross & Wampold, 2011).

Tying together what we know about evidence-based treatments and the importance of common factors such as good therapeutic relationships and high client expectations, it seems clear that treatments and therapeutic relationships are both important in offering therapy that works. Norcross and Wampold (2011) put it this way: "Concurrent use of evidence-based therapy relationships *and* evidence-based treatments adapted to the patient is likely to generate the best outcomes" (p. 424). Of course, there is still a need to understand the mechanisms through which treatments work—both in terms of specific treatment techniques and also in terms of common factors across all treatments based on therapist, client, and relationship variables (Kazdin & Blasé, 2011).

SECTION SUMMARY

A number of research designs have been used to try to identify therapies that work (including within subjects and between subjects designs, with a current emphasis on randomized clinical trials). Although early box score reviews and meta-analytic studies showed equivalent results from various forms of treatment, more recent research studies on empirically supported treatments, evidence-based treatments, and evidence-based practices have helped to identify treatments that are the most helpful for certain problems. Research on common or nonspecific factors (therapist variables, client variables, and relationship variables) has identified several characteristics that are associated with treatment gains, with a great deal of support for the importance of the therapeutic relationship.

TABLE 10.2 Excerpt from an Actual Therapy Session Showing Strong Therapeutic Alliance Between Young Adolescent Client and Her Therapist

THERAPIST: So, what is it like when you're feeling really down?

CLIENT: I get like I don't want to talk to anyone. I'm like get away, leave me alone. My Dad asks me how I'm doing and I just say nothing or walk away.

THERAPIST: You just want some space. You don't want to be pushed.

CLIENT: Exactly.

THERAPIST: In here, I'm going to ask you a lot about how you are feeling. If you feel like I'm pushing you, is it possible you will not want to talk with me?

CLIENT: I don't think that'll happen because you're not in my face. Talking gets my stress out. When I'm in a bad mood on the day of our meetings, I look forward to our talking. . . . it helps keep me going because I know you get me.

Source: Shirk, S. R., Karver, M. S., & Brown, R. (2011). The alliance in child and adolescent psychotherapy. *Psychotherapy, 48,* 17–24. (Quote from p. 19).

STUDYING OTHER MODES OF INTERVENTION

SECTION PREVIEW

This section summarizes therapeutic outcome studies of group, couples, and family therapy; preventive interventions; and self-help modalities. The effectiveness of psychopharmacology in relation to psychological treatments is also reviewed.

Compared to research on individual therapies, there is less evidence available about the outcome of group, couple, and family therapies and self-help and preventive techniques. Still, available results suggest that, in general, these other formats are associated with benefits that are at least equal to those of individual treatment.

Findings on Group Therapy

Empirical evidence confirms that group therapy can be an effective form of treatment, especially when there is strong group cohesion and a strong therapeutic alliance (Burlingame & Baldwin, 2011). A number of group therapy interventions have shown strong empirical support, including supportive group therapy for schizophrenia and cognitive behavioral group treatment for depression (Drossel, 2009).

Proponents of group therapy contend that evidence of its effectiveness will lead to its increased use because of the cost savings for clients and insurance companies. And indeed, group cognitive behavioral interventions and group acceptance-based approaches are cost effective and very successful in helping decrease symptoms of depression (Drossel, 2009).

Findings on Couples Therapy

Compared with no-treatment control groups, almost all forms of couples therapy appear to produce significant improvements in couples' relationship satisfaction and psychological adjustment (Baucom, Epstein, Kirby, & Falconier, 2011). There is especially strong research support for behavioral couples therapy. In one review of 30 studies, Shadish and Baldwin (2005) found that 72% of treated couples were better off at the end of treatment than were couples who did not receive treatment. A more recent review suggested that 80% of treated couples were better off than untreated couples (Gurman & Snyder, 2011). Behavioral couples therapy for alcohol use disorders has been shown to be especially effective (Gurman & Snyder, 2011), and integrative behavioral couple therapy, which adds an acceptance-based approach to standard behavioral therapy techniques, also looks very promising (McGinn, Benson, & Christensen, 2011).

There is evidence that two of the key factors in successful couples therapy are communication training and problem-solving skills (Oliver & Margolin, 2009). Still, there is a need to identify the mechanisms in couples therapy that work best with different types of clients and that promote the most durable treatment gains (Gottman & Ryan, 2005; Snyder, Castellani, & Whisman, 2006).

Findings on Family Therapy

Families who complete a course of therapy usually show significant improvements in communication patterns and in the behavior of the family member whose problems prompted therapy in the first place (Kaslow, 2011; Stanton, 2013). This outcome is typically reported in empirical research on family therapy for several kinds of identified client and family problems.

Certain types of family therapy appear more successful than others. Behavioral and structural family therapies have received the strongest empirical support. Treatments such as behavioral parent training or parent management training (Briesmeister & Schaefer, 2007) and parent–child interaction therapy (Funderburk & Eyberg, 2011) are considered very effective practices. Another behaviorally based family therapy, known as multisystemic therapy, is very effective and even works with diverse families from disadvantaged backgrounds (Henggeler, 2011). In addition, family-based treatment for anorexia, family focused therapy for bipolar disorder, and family psychoeducation for schizophrenia all have strong research support (Kaslow, 2011). Note that most of the strongest family therapy procedures include behavioral and psychoeducational components.

Findings on Preventive Interventions

In Chapter 9, we described a number of prevention programs that grew out of the community psychology movement. These programs are often designed to modify social, economic, and environmental risk factors that lead to disorders or to strengthen positive qualities that can protect vulnerable individuals from developing disorders.

Large-scale, well-controlled studies have identified a number of effective prevention programs (Barrera & Sandler, 2006) such as the following:

- Preventing aggression by teaching adolescents anger management and social problem–solving skills as they make the transition from elementary to middle school (Lochman & Wells, 2004)
- Preventing HIV infection by addressing informational, motivational, and behavioral skills competence related to safe-sex methods among inner-city high school students (Fisher, Fisher, Bryan, & Misovich, 2002)
- Preventing binge-drinking on college students' 21st birthday by giving personalized feedback of students' intentions to drink moderately (Neighbors, Lee, Lewis, Fossos, & Walter, 2009)
- Preventing substance abuse by children and adolescents by increasing parenting skills and strengthening healthy connections within families (Kumpfer & Alvarado, 2003).

Overall, there are effective prevention programs for many mental health problems and there is renewed interest in changing communities to make them more consistent with the development of psychological well-being (Biglan, Flay, Embry, & Sandler, 2012).

Findings on Self-Help Resources and Self-Help Groups

The effects of self-help groups and Internet resources are seldom evaluated empirically. Many individuals who use self-help methods are convinced that their groups and/or the resources that they use are valuable and thus see formal outcome research as unnecessary. Evaluation is further complicated because it is not clear who uses which resources and for what problems, especially when the resources are web based.

There has been somewhat more research on using books (i.e., bibliotherapy) and websites for self-help. This research suggests that these resources can be effective for treating mild depression, eating disorders, gambling, anxiety, and mild alcohol abuse (Harwood & L'Abate, 2010). Although it is impossible to develop a complete list of evidence-based self-help books, websites, and apps, a book called *Self-Help That Works: Resouces to Improve Emotional Health and Strengthen Relationships* (Norcross et al., 2013) is an excellent source of information.

Findings on the Combination of Psychotherapy and Medication

Combining prescription medications with psychotherapy can be quite helpful and, in some cases, may be better than either approach alone (e.g., Sammons, 2011). However, most studies have found that, for anxiety disorders and depression, at least, combined treatments do not greatly improve on what either treatment can achieve on its own (Hollon et al., 2005; Hollon, Stewart, & Strunk, 2006). Other studies have found that, for these disorders, psychotherapy can result in benefits that are greater and more enduring than drug treatments (e.g., Hollon, Stewart, & Strunk., 2006; Figure 10.4 shows similar results in the treatment of binge eating).

Despite findings like these, many clients who might once have received psychotherapy alone are now getting drugs, or drugs and psychotherapy, even though they might have done just as well without the drugs. In addition, a number of surveys have found that, given a choice, most clients prefer a psychological intervention to a psychopharmacological intervention (Hazlett-Stevens et al., 2002; Zoellner, Feeny, Cochran, & Pruitt, 2003). Thus, the increasing numbers of clients who are given only psychopharmacological options by their managed care companies may not be receiving the services they want or the ones that are most helpful for their problems (Miller, 2013).

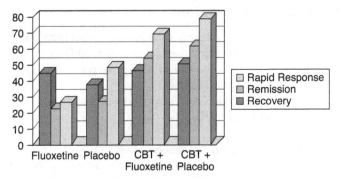

FIGURE 10.4 Results of a Randomized Clinical Trial Comparing the Effects of Fluoxetine (Prozac), a Placebo Pill, Cognitive-Behavioral Treatment (CBT) Plus Fluoxetine, and CBT Plus a Placebo for Treating Binge Eating Disorder. Notice that the highest rates of recovery were associated with CBT with either real or placebo drugs. Rapid response and rates of remission and recovery across treatments: rapid response equals a 65% or greater reduction in frequency of binge eating episodes by the fourth treatment week; remission equals zero binges for the past month; recovery equals less than one binge weekly for the past month.
Source: Grilo, C. M., Masheb, R. M., & Wilson, G. T. (2006). Rapid response to treatment for binge eating disorder. *Journal of Consulting and Clinical Psychology, 74,* 602–613.

SECTION SUMMARY

Although many forms of treatments are helpful, the most effective group, couples, and family therapy as well as preventive interventions tend to utilize cognitive-behavioral or behavioral techniques. There is also evidence that some evidence-based self-help methods are making their way to the popular market. The use of prescription drugs in the treatment of psychological disorders is very common, and can be effective in many cases, but it appears that there are some disorders for which psychological treatment is equal or superior to drug treatment.

ISSUES AND CONCERNS ABOUT RESEARCH ON THERAPY

SECTION PREVIEW

In this section, we review concerns about treatment research, including threats to internal and external validity, and discuss how these concerns are being handled by researchers and clinicians.

We have seen that researchers usually employ within-subjects or between-subjects methods to test how well treatments work. We have also seen that, recently, the main focus has been on randomized clinical trials (RCTs). In all of this research, the primary goal of therapy-outcome researchers is to design experiments whose results have the highest possible levels of both internal and external validity. When they meet this goal, the researchers can be more confident that their studies can serve as useful guides for choosing treatments and charting progress in individual cases (Comer & Kendall, 2013).

Internal and External Validity

An outcome study is said to have high *internal validity* if the design allows the researcher to assert that observed changes in dependent variable(s) were caused by manipulated independent variable(s), not by some unknown, unintended, or uncontrolled confounding factors. The researcher wants to be able to say, for example, that clients' reduced depression was caused by the cognitive therapy they received, not by the confidence they had in the treatment or by a television show they happened to see. Kendall and Comer (2011) argued that the characteristics associated with the highest internal validity in randomized clinical trials include:

- Random assignment to either active treatment and a control group or to one of two active treatments.
- Defining the independent variable (i.e., the treatment) carefully by utilizing a treatment manual that describes how to conduct the therapy.

- *Fidelity checks*, where an independent rater verifies that the treatment is being done properly.
- Carefully selected samples, where client characteristics (such as diagnosis) are carefully screened.
- Multiple evidence-based measures of the dependent variables (e.g., psychological symptoms).

Studies boasting these characteristics have strong internal validity, but would a treatment shown to be effective in such studies work equally well in the real world where such tight experimental controls are often not possible? This is the question of external validity. Outcome studies show strong *external validity* if their results are applicable, or generalizable, to clients, problems, and situations other than those included in the controlled experiment.

External validity does not always follow from internal validity. For example, a study evaluating systematic desensitization for claustrophobia might feature random assignment to groups and include all the control conditions necessary to conclude that desensitization was responsible for clients' improvement. However, suppose this internally valid design employed expert desensitization therapists who treated only European American female college students with mild cases of claustrophobia. These restrictions on therapist and client variables might reduce the external validity of the study because the results might not apply to therapists in general, to clients from varying age or ethnic groups, or to clients who display more disabling phobias.

Most researchers agree that the best way to assess the outcome of psychological treatment is to conduct research on the treatments actually offered by clinicians to clinically disordered clients in real treatment settings. Unfortunately, most large-scale outcome studies are conducted in university research clinics, whereas most clinical services are delivered in the less controlled, and less controllable, world of community mental health centers, hospitals, private practice offices, and other settings. Accordingly, it is important to assure that treatments that are *efficacious* (i.e., work in large-scale studies run under controlled conditions) are also *effective* (i.e., are available and useful in the real world of clinical service delivery) (Kendall & Comer, 2011).

Concerns and Compromises in Therapy Research

By now, you've probably recognized that there is an inherent dilemma in designing valid research on psychological treatments: In order to exert the experimental control necessary to maximize internal validity, researchers may be forced to study clients, therapists, problems, treatments, and treatment settings that may not allow for high external validity. But if the researcher tries to maximize external validity by conducting research on real clients with real problems in community treatment settings, the resulting lack of experimental control may be lethal to internal validity. Given this dilemma, we must recognize that the results of well-controlled experiments can be used to draw only limited conclusions about therapies being conducted in clinical practice (Comer & Kendall, 2013). At the same time, we must be wary of evaluative data coming from less well-controlled research in clinical settings. Indeed, any conclusions drawn from the results of any outcome study must be tempered by awareness of the compromises in research design and methods that were made in an effort to strike a reasonable balance between internal and external validity. Thus, clinical researchers must focus on efficacy (i.e., therapy that works in tightly controlled conditions) as well as effectiveness (i.e., therapy that works in the real world) (Comer & Kendall, 2013).

There are also concerns that randomized clinical trials only focus on comparing different treatments rather than on the common factors (such as therapeutic alliance) that are evident across treatment modalities. As our discussion above shows, the effects of nonspecific and common factors, rather than "active ingredients" in therapy are often responsible for treatment gains (Ahn & Wampold, 2001). Quite often, specific treatment techniques account for only a small proportion of therapy-outcome variance, while therapeutic alliance and other client and therapist factors account for equal or larger proportions of variance (Messer, 2001). Thus, researchers and clinicians currently focus on both treatments that work and therapeutic relationships that work (Nathan & Gorman, 2007; Norcross, 2011).

As mentioned earlier, clinicians have also voiced concerns over the use of *treatment manuals* in research partly because many clinicians have not normally used them or might feel restricted by the structure they impose (Addis & Krasnow, 2000). Recent evidence suggests, however, that

Treatment manuals are used frequently in clinical psychology. *Source*: Renn Valo/ Creative Digital Visions.

practicing clinicians have become far more aware of treatment manuals and that many use them routinely (Safran, Abreu, Ogilvie, & DeMaria, 2011). For example, one study found that 35.9% of clinicians who treat clients with bulimia used treatment manuals (Wallace & vonRanson, 2011). The clinicians most likely to use treatment manuals tend to be younger and to favor cognitive-behavioral techniques. There is increasing evidence that using treatment manuals does not harm the therapeutic alliance and can actually help the therapeutic process (Langer, McLeod, & Weisz, 2011). With such evidence in mind, researchers have tried to make the manuals more user-friendly for practicing clinicians.

In short, answering Paul's (1969a) ultimate outcome question ("What treatment, by whom, is most effective for this individual, with that specific problem, under which set of circumstances, and how does it come about?") requires many researchers to conduct many different kinds of studies over many years.

There are also concerns about how to make information about evidence-based practices available to clinicians and mental health consumers alike. There is growing interest among researchers in *dissemination* of their research results to professionals and the public and in encouraging *implementation* of evidence-based techniques in the real world of clinical practice (Frueh, Ford, Elhai, & Grubaugh, 2012). Here are just a few examples:

- A popular series of treatment manuals and client workbooks has been developed by clinical researchers in conjunction with clinicians. The series is called *Treatments That Work* and it is published by Oxford University Press. The series addresses a number of clinical problems, including anxiety, depression, alcohol use, couples distress, and chronic pain. These workbooks are user-friendly and provide step-by-step details on what works in therapy for these problems (Barlow, 2004).
- Information about state-of-the-art treatments is being disseminated to clinicians and clients online. For example, explanations of evidence-based treatments can be found for adults and youth, respectively at: http://www.div12.org/PsychologicalTreatments/index.html and http://effectivechildtherapy.com/sccap/.
- Information about state-of-the-art evidence-based practices (including treatments that work and relationships that work) can be found at: http://www.EBBP.org.

The need for dissemination and implementation efforts is clear from surveys of practicing clinicians. For example, one study found that the majority of clinicians are not well informed about current research findings on psychotherapy (Boisvert & Faust, 2006). Further, clinicians who were not familiar with evidence-based practices tended to assume that these practices are less valuable than they really are in improving the quality of their clinical work (Boisvert & Faust, 2006). As shown in Figure 10.5, the majority of practicing clinicians appear to rely far more heavily on their own experience than on empirical research findings or treatment manuals (Stewart & Chambless, 2007).

Admittedly, keeping up to date with all the empirical advances in clinical psychology takes time. One study estimated that it would take 627.5 hours each month to read all of the articles related to a particular clinical practice (Alper et al., 2004), so it is not hard to understand why practicing clinicians might be reluctant to try to master all the empirical knowledge pertinent to their area of specialization (Walker & London, 2007). Still, there are indications that clinicians are using and benefiting from various electronic information dissemination efforts. One study of websites

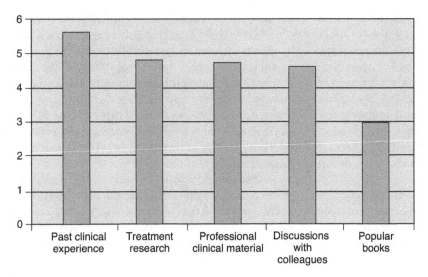

FIGURE 10.5   What Resources Do Clinicians Use to Increase Therapy Skills and Effectiveness? *Source:* From Stewart, R. E. & Chambless, D. L. (2007). Does psychotherapy research inform treatment decisions in private practice? *Journal of Clinical Psychology, 63,* 267–281.

that delineate evidence-based practices found that 60% of clinicians found on-line information to be helpful, that the information increased their awareness of evidence-based practices, and that the information increased their commitment to such practices (Riley et al., 2007). The current focus on evidence-based practices brings together researchers and clinicians who can commit to their shared goals of finding and using treatments that work and relationships that work the best for their clients (Barlow, Bullis, Comer, & Ametaj, 2013).

SECTION SUMMARY

In providing maximally useful evaluations of treatment, clinical researchers must conduct studies that have high internal validity (i.e., reveal genuine cause–effect relationships) and high external validity (i.e., result in outcomes that apply or generalize to clients and problems seen in real-world clinical settings). Researchers and clinicians alike are motivated to find treatments that work and therapeutic relationships that work to improve mental health functioning.

Chapter Summary

Evaluative research on clinical interventions has focused mainly on the effects of various forms of psychological treatment. The goals of this research are to answer questions about the efficacy of specific treatments, the relative effectiveness of different treatments, the components of treatment responsible for improvement, the durability of treatment benefits, and the clinical and social significance of different therapies.

The main method for establishing a causal relationship between therapy and improvement is the controlled experiment in which the researcher makes systematic changes in certain factors (called independent variables) and then observes changes occurring in other factors (called dependent variables). In psychotherapy outcome research, the independent variable is usually the type of therapy given, and the dependent variable is the change seen in clients. Within-subjects studies manipulate a treatment variable and observe its effects on the same

client(s) at different points in time. Between-subjects studies randomly assign clients to different groups, each of which is exposed to differing treatments whose effects are compared. Over the years, therapy outcomes have been investigated and summarized via many techniques (including box scores, meta-analytic techniques, client satisfaction surveys, and randomized clinical trials). Currently, the bulk of the empirically supported, evidence-based treatments falls in the cognitive behavioral and behavioral categories.

There is also a great deal of interest and research into common and nonspecific factors that are associated with the best outcomes. A number of variables of the therapist (such as empathy and asking for client feedback), the client (such as openness and willingness to disclose), and the therapist–client relationship (such as strong therapeutic alliance) are associated with better outcomes for clients.

In addition to the promising treatments and common factors identified in individual therapy, a number of other modes of therapy have been shown to have good outcomes. For example, group therapy seems especially promising when there is strong group cohesion and therapeutic alliance. Certain types of group therapy (such as supportive group therapy for schizophrenia and cognitive behavioral group treatment for depression) have received strong empirical support. Other modes of treatment, such as couples, family, preventive, self-help, and the combination of psychotherapy and medication have also shown promise for certain problems.

There are, however, a number of issues and concerns about psychotherapy research. There is no perfect outcome study and researchers must balance the need for studies that show both internal and external validity. For example, if an outcome study is high on internal validity, the researcher can be confident that observed changes in clients were actually caused by treatment, not by uncontrolled confounding factors. An outcome study is high on external validity if its results are generalizable to clients, problems, and situations other than those included in the experiment. Overall, researchers should try to design outcome studies with the highest levels of both internal and external validity possible. In addition, researchers must consider both the type of therapy as well as the common factors that might be driving the client's progress. Researchers should also try to disseminate research findings widely so that these best-practices can be implemented in the community by clinicians. There is hope that the current focus on evidence-based practices will bring together the strengths of researchers and clinicians for the ultimate improvement of clients' well-being.

Study Questions

1. Describe an example of a within-subjects research design, and discuss the pros and cons of this design.
2. Describe an example of a between-subjects research design, and make note of the independent and dependent variables.
3. What is internal validity, and why are clinical scientists concerned about threats to internal validity?
4. Discuss the importance of external validity, and list the major threats to external validity.
5. What are box scores, and why are they no longer used?
6. Describe the process of meta-analysis, and discuss the strengths and weakness of this approach to investigating which treatments work.
7. What is a randomized clinical trial and what are the pros and cons of this approach?
8. What are some concerns about outcome studies?
9. What are some common factors that are associated with strong outcomes of therapy?
10. What is evidence-based practice?
11. What are dissemination and implementation, and why are they important?
12. Discuss the concerns and challenges for both researchers and clinicians in relation to the definition and use of evidence-based practices.
13. What is therapeutic alliance and why is it important to study?
14. Describe the findings from outcome research on group, couples, and family therapy, prevention programs, and self-help programs.
15. What are the major findings from research on the combination of psychological treatment and drug treatment?

Web Sites

- The Society of Clinical Psychology—APA's Division 12: http://www.div12.org/PsychologicalTreatments/index.html
- The Society of Clinical Child and Adolescent Psychology—APA's Division 53: http://effectivechildtherapy.com/sccap/
- Evidence-based behavioral practices (funded by NIH's Office of Behavioral and Social Sciences Research): http://www.EBBP.org
- Interdisciplinary site for Consolidated Standards of Reporting Trials (CONSORT): http://www.consort-statement.org/home/
- SAMHSA's National Registry of Evidence-Based Programs and Practices: http://www.nrepp.samhsa.gov/

MOVIES

Garden State (2004): Young adult, who has been on antidepressants and other psychoactive medications since childhood, returns home for his mother's funeral and tries to improve his life by confronting issues from his troubled past.

Rachel Getting Married (2008): After being released from a rehabilitation facility to attend her sister's wedding, this movie shows the best and worst of family dynamics that occur at family events such as weddings.

MEMOIRS

Devil in the Details: Scenes From an Obsessive Girlhood by Jennifer Traig (2004; New York: Little, Brown and Company). In addition to describing her symptoms of OCD, this author describes overcoming this disorder through effective treatment.

Unbearable Lightness: A Story of Loss and Gain by Portia De Rossi (2010; New York: Atria Books). Powerful memoir of anorexia disorder and the eventual evidence-based treatment that helps this actress to grow and thrive.

References

Addis, M. E., & Krasnow, A. D. (2000). A national survey of practicing psychologists' attitudes toward psychotherapy treatment manuals. *Journal of Consulting and Clinical Psychology, 68*, 331–339.

Ahn, H., & Wampold, B. E. (2001). Where oh where are the specific ingredients? A meta-analysis of component studies in counseling and psychotherapy. *Journal of Counseling Psychology, 48*, 251–257.

Alper, B. S., Hand, J. A., Elliott, S. G., Kinkade, S., Hauan, M. J., et al. (2004). How much effort is needed to keep up with the literature relevant for primary care? *Journal of the Medical Library Association, 92*, 429–437.

American Psychological Association Presidential Task Force on Evidence-Based Practice. (2006). Evidence-based practice in psychology. *American Psychologist, 61*, 271–285.

Baardseth, T. P., Goldberg, S. B., Pace, B. T., Wislocki, A. P., Frost, N. D., et al. (2013). Cognitive-behavioral therapy versus other therapies: Redux. *Clinical Psychology Review, 33*, 395–405.

Baldwin, S. A., & Imel, Z. E. (2013). Therapist effects: Findings and methods. In M. J. Lambert (Ed.), *Bergin and Garfield's handbook of psychotherapy and behavior change* (6th ed., pp. 258–297). Hoboken, NJ: Wiley.

Barlow, D. H. (2004) Psychological treatments. *American Psychologist, 59*, 869–878.

Barlow, D. H., Bullis, J. R., Comer, J. S., & Ametaj, A. A. (2013). Evidence-based psychological treatments: An update and a way forward. *Annual Review of Clinical Psychology, 9*, 1–27.

Baucom, D. H., Epstein, N. B., Kirby, J. S., & Falconier, M. K. (2011). Couple therapy: Theoretical perspectives and empirical findings. In D. H. Barlow (Ed.), *The Oxford handbook of clinical psychology* (pp. 789–809). New York, NY: Oxford University Press.

Beutler, L. E. (2002). It isn't the size, but the fit. *Clinical Psychology: Science and Practice, 9*, 434–438.

Beutler, L. E., & Harwood, T. M. (2000). *Prescriptive psychotherapy: A practical guide to systematic treatment selection.* New York, NY: Oxford University Press.

Biglan, A., Flay, B. R., Embry, D. D., & Sandler, I. N. (2012). The critical role of nurturing environments for promoting human well-being. *American Psychologist, 67*, 257–271.

Boisvert, C. M., & Faust, D. (2006). Practicing psychologists' knowledge of general psychotherapy research findings: Implications for science-practice relations. *Professional Psychology: Research and Practice, 37*, 708–716.

Briesmeister, J. M., & Schaefer, C. E. (Eds.). (2007). *Handbook of parent training: Helping parents prevent and solve problem behaviors* (3rd ed.). Hoboken, NJ: Wiley.

Burlingame, G. M., & Baldwin, S. (2011). Group therapy. In J. C. Norcross, G. R. VandenBos, & D. K. Freedheim (Eds.), *History of psychotherapy: Continuity and change* (2nd ed., pp. 505–515). Washington, DC: American Psychological Association.

Chambless, D. L., & Ollendick, T. H. (2001). Empirically supported psychological treatments. *Annual Review of Psychology, 52*, 685–716.

Cohen, J. (1988). *Statistical power analysis for the behavioral sciences* (2nd ed.). New York, NY: Taylor and Francis.

Comer, J. S., & Kendall, P. C. (2013). Methodology, design, and evaluation in psychotherapy research. In M. J. Lambert (Ed.), *Bergin and Garfield's handbook of psychotherapy and behavior change* (6th ed., pp. 21–48). Hoboken, NJ: Wiley.

Cuijpers, P., Driessen, E., Hollon, S. D., vanOppen, P., Barth, J., et al. (2012). The efficacy of non-directive supportive therapy for adult depression: A meta-analysis. *Clinical Psychology Review, 32*, 280–291.

Dobson, K. S., & Hamilton, K. E. (2009). Cognitive restructuring: Behavioral tests of negative cognitions. In W. T. O'Donohue & J. E. Fisher (Eds.), *General principles and empirically supported techniques of cognitive behavior therapy* (pp. 194–198). Hoboken, NJ: Wiley.

Driessen, E., Cuijpers, P., Hollon, S. D., & Dekker, J. J. M. (2010). Does pretreatment severity moderate the efficacy of psychological treatment of adult outpatient depression? A meta-analysis. *Journal of Consulting and Clinical Psychology, 78*, 668–680.

Drossel, C. (2009). Group interventions. In W. T. O'Donohue & J. E. Fisher (Eds.), *General principles and empirically supported techniques of cognitive behavior therapy* (pp. 334–342). Hoboken, NJ: Wiley.

Ellis, P. D. (2010). *The essential guide to effect sizes: Statistical power, meta-analysis, and the interpretation of research results.* New York, NY: Cambridge University Press.

Eysenck, H. J. (1952). The effects of psychotherapy: An evaluation. *Journal of Consulting Psychology, 16*, 319–324.

Eysenck, H. J. (1966). *The effects of psychotherapy.* New York, NY: International Science Press.

Fisher, J. D., Fisher, W. A., Bryan, A. D., & Misovich, S. J. (2002). Information-motivation-behavioral skills model-based HIV risk behavior change intervention for inner-city high school youth. *Health Psychology, 21*, 177–186.

Fishman, D. B., Rego, S. A., & Muller, K. L. (2011). Behavioral theories of psychotherapy. In J. C. Norcross, G. R. VandenBos, & D. K. Freedheim (Eds.), *History of psychotherapy: Continuity and change* (2nd ed., pp. 101–140). Washington, DC: American Psychological Association.

Frueh, B. C., Ford, J. D., Elhai, J. D., & Grubaugh, A. L. (2012). Evidence-based practice in adult mental health. In P. Sturmey & M. Hersen (Eds.), *Handbook of evidence-based practice in clinical psychology (Vol. 2): Adult disorders* (pp. 3–14). Hoboken, NJ: Wiley.

Funderburk, B. W., & Eyberg, S. (2011). Parent-child interaction therapy. In J. C. Norcross, G. R. VandenBos, & D. K. Freedheim (Eds.), *History of psychotherapy: Continuity and change* (2nd ed., pp. 415–420). Washington, DC: American Psychological Association.

Gottman, J. M., & Ryan, K. (2005). The mismeasure of therapy: Treatment outcomes in marital therapy research. In W. M. Pinsof & J. L. Lebow (Eds.), *Family psychology: The art of the science* (pp. 65–89). New York, NY: Oxford University Press.

Greenberg, R. P., Constantino, M. J., & Bruce, N. (2006). Are patient expectations still relevant for psychotherapy process and outcome. *Clinical Psychology Review, 26*, 657–678.

Greenhoot, A. F. (2005). Design and analysis of experimental and quasi-experimental investigations. In M. C. Roberts & S. S. Ilardi (Eds.), *Handbook of research methods in clinical psychology* (pp. 92–114). Malden, MA: Blackwell Publishing.

Grilo, C. M., Masheb, R. M., & Wilson, G. T. (2006). Rapid response to treatment for binge eating disorder. *Journal of Consulting and Clinical Psychology, 74*, 602–613.

Gurman, A. S., & Snyder, D. K. (2011). Treatment modalities. In J. C. Norcross, G. R. VandenBos, & D. K. Freedheim (Eds.), *History of psychotherapy: Continuity and change* (2nd ed., pp. 485–496). Washington, DC: American Psychological Association.

Harwood, T. M., & L'Abate, L. (2010). *Self-help in mental health: A critical review.* New York, NY: Springer.

Hazlett-Stevens, H., Craske, M. G., Roy-Birne, P. P., Sherbourne, C. D., Stein, M. B., et al. (2002). Predictors of willingness to consider medication and psychosocial treatment for panic disorder in primary care patients. *General Hospital Psychiatry, 24*, 316–321.

Henggeler, S. W. (2011). Efficacy studies to large-scale transport: The development and validation of multisystemic therapy programs. *Annual Review of Clinical Psychology, 7*, 351–381.

Hollon, S. D., DeRubeis, R. J., Shelton, R. C., Amsterdam, J. D., Salomon, R. M., et al. (2005). Prevention of relapse following cognitive therapy versus medications in moderate to severe depression. *Archives of General Psychiatry, 62*, 417–422.

Hollon, S. D., Stewart, M. O., & Strunk, D. (2006). Enduring effects for cognitive behavior therapy in the treatment of depression and anxiety. *Annual Review of Psychology, 57*, 285–315.

Horvath, A. O., DelRe, A. C., Fluckiger, C., & Symonds, D. (2011). Alliance in individual psychotherapy. *Psychotherapy, 48*, 9–16.

Kahn, J. H., Achter, J. A., & Shambaugh, E. J. (2001). Client distress disclosure, characteristics at intake, and outcomes in brief counseling. *Journal of Counseling Psychology, 48*, 203–211.

Kaslow, F. W. (2011). Family therapy. In J. C. Norcross, G. R. VandenBos, & D. K. Freedheim (Eds.), *History of psychotherapy: Continuity and change* (2nd ed., pp. 497–504). Washington, DC: American Psychological Association.

Kazdin, A. E. (1982). Single-case experimental designs. In P. C. Kendall & J. N. Butcher (Eds.), *Handbook of research methods in clinical psychology* (pp. 461–490). New York, NY: Wiley.

Kazdin, A. E. (2011). *Single-case research designs: Methods for clinical and applied settings* (2nd ed.). New York, NY: Oxford University Press.

Kazdin, A. E., & Blasé, S. L. (2011). Rebooting psychotherapy research and practice to reduce the burden of mental illness. *Perspectives on Psychological Science, 6*, 21–37.

Kendall, P. C., & Comer, J. S. (2011). Research methods in clinical psychology. In D. H. Barlow (Ed.), *The Oxford handbook of clinical psychology* (pp. 52–75). New York: Oxford University Press.

Kumpfer, K. L., & Alvarado, R. (2003). Family-strengthening approaches for the prevention of youth problem behaviors. *American Psychologist, 58*, 457–465.

LaGreca, A. M., Silverman, W. K., & Lochman, J. E. (2009). Moving beyond efficacy and effectiveness in child and adolescent intervention research. *Journal of Consulting and Clinical Psychology, 77*, 373–382.

Lambert, M. J., & Bergin, A. E. (1994). The effectiveness of psychotherapy. In A. E. Bergin & S. L. Garfield (Eds.), *Handbook of psychotherapy and behavior change* (pp. 143–189). New York, NY: Wiley.

Lambert, M. J., Shapiro, D. A., & Bergin, A. E. (1986). The effectiveness of psychotherapy. In S. L. Garfield & A. E. Bergin (Eds.), *Handbook of psychotherapy and behavior change* (3rd ed., pp. 157–211). New York, NY: Wiley.

Langer, D. A., McLeod, B. D., & Weisz, J. R. (2011). Do treatment manuals undermine youth-therapist alliance in community clinical practice? *Journal of Consulting and Clinical Psychology, 79*, 427–432.

Lippens, T., & Mackenzie, C. S. (2011). Treatment satisfaction, perceived treatment effectiveness, and dropout among older users of mental health services. *Journal of Clinical Psychology, 67*, 1197–1209.

Liu, E. T. (2007). Integrating cognitive-behavioral and cognitive-interpersonal case formulations: A case study of a Chinese American male. *Pragmatic Case Studies in Psychotherapy, 3*, 1–33.

Lochman, J. E., & Wells, K. C. (2004). The coping power program for preadolescent aggressive boys and their parents: Outcome effects at the 1-year- follow-up. *Journal of Consulting and Clinical Psychology, 72*, 571–578.

McGinn, M. M., Benson, L. A., & Christensen, A. (2011). Integrative behavioral couple therapy: An acceptance-based approach to improving relationship functioning. In J. D. Herbert & E. M. Forman (Eds.), *Acceptance and mindfulness in cognitive behavior therapy: Understanding and applying the new therapies* (pp. 210–232). Hoboken, NJ: Wiley.

Messer, S. B., & Winokur, M. (1980). Some limits to the integration of psychoanalytic and behavior therapy. *American Psychologist, 35*, 818–827.

Miller, A. (2013). More older adults with depression referred to medication—not psychotherapy—for treatment. *Monitor on Psychology*, Jan, 2013, 12.

Miltenberger, R. G. (2011). *Behavior modification: Principles and procedures* (5th ed.). Belmont, CA: Cenage Learning.

Morales, E., & Norcross, J. C. (2010). Evidence-based practices with ethnic minorities: Strange bedfellows. *Journal of Clinical Psychology, 66*, 821–829.

Morgenstern, J., Irwin, T. W., Wainberg, M. L., Parsons, J. T., Muench, F., et al. (2007). A randomized controlled trial of goal choice interventions for alcohol use disorders among men who have sex with men. *Journal of Consulting and Clinical Psychology, 75*, 72–84.

Murphy, J. G., Dennhardt, A. A., Skidmore, J. R., Borsari, B., Barnett, N. P., et al. (2012). A randomized controlled trial of a behavioral economic supplement to brief motivational interventions for college drinking. *Journal of Consulting and Clinical Psychology, 80*, 876–886.

Nathan, P. E., & Gorman, J. M. (2007). *A guide to treatments that work* (3rd ed.). New York, NY: Oxford University Press.

Neighbors, C., Lee, C. M., Lewis, M. A., Fossos, N., & Walter, T. (2009). Internet-based personalized feedback to reduce 21st-birthday drinking: A randomized controlled trial of an event-specific prevention intervention. *Journal of Consulting and Clinical Psychology, 77*, 51–63.

Norcross, J. C. (2011). *Psychotherapy relationships that work: Evidence-based responsiveness* (2nd ed.). New York, NY: Oxford University Press.

Norcross, J. C. (Ed.). (2002). *Psychotherapy relationships that work: Therapists contributions and responsiveness to patients.* New York, NY: Oxford University Press.

Norcross, J. C., Campbell, L. F., Grohol, J. M., Santrock, J. W., Selagea, F., et al. (2013). *Self-help that works: Resources to improve emotional health and strengthen relationships* (4th ed.). New York, NY: Oxford University Press.

Norcross, J. C., & Lambert, M. J. (2011). Psychotherapy relationships that work II. *Psychotherapy, 48*, 4–8.

Norcross, J. C., & Wampold, B. E. (2011). Evidence-based therapy relationships: Research conclusions and clinical practices. In J. C. Norcross (Ed.), *Psychotherapy relationships that work: Evidence-based responsiveness* (2nd ed., pp. 423–430). New York, NY: Oxford University Press.

Oliver, P. H., & Margolin, G. (2009). Communication/problem-solving skills training. In W. T. O'Donohue & J. E. Fisher (Eds.), *General principles and empirically supported techniques of cognitive behavior therapy* (pp. 199–206). Hoboken, NJ: Wiley.

Ollendick, T. H., & Davis, T. E. (2004). Empirically supported treatments for children and adolescents: Where to from here? *Clinical Psychology: Science and Practice, 11*, 289–294.

Paul, G. L. (1969a). Behavior modification research: Design and tactics. In C. M. Franks (Ed.), *Behavior therapy: Appraisal and status* (pp. 29–62). New York: McGraw-Hill.

Paul, G. L. (1969b). Outcome of systematic desensitization II. In C. M. Franks (Ed.), *Behavior therapy: Appraisal and status* (pp. 63–159). New York: McGraw-Hill.

Riley, W. T., Schumann, M. F., Forman-Hoffman, V. L., Mihm, P., Applegate, B. W., et al. (2007). Responses of practicing psychologists to a Web site developed to promote empirically supported treatments. *Professional Psychology: Research and Practice, 38*, 44–53.

Rogers, C. R. (1942). *Counseling and psychotherapy.* Boston, MA: Houghton Mifflin.

Safran, J. D., Abreu, I., Ogilvie, J., & DeMaria, A. (2011). Does psychotherapy research influence the clinical practice of researcher-clinicians? *Clinical Psychology: Science and Practice, 18*, 357–371.

Sammons, M. T. (2011). Pharmacotheapy. In J. C. Norcross, G. R. VandenBos, & D. K. Freedheim (Eds.), *History of psychotherapy: Continuity and change* (2nd ed., pp. 516–532). Washington, DC: American Psychological Association.

Schulz, K. F., Altman, D. G., & Moher, D. (2010). CONSORT 2010 Statement: Updated guidelines for reporting parallel group randomized trials. *Journal of Clinical Epidemiology, 63*, 834–840.

Seligman, M. E. P. (1995). The effectiveness of psychotherapy: The Consumer Reports study. American Task Force on Promotion and Dissemination of Psychological Procedures (1995). Training in and dissemination of empirically validated psychological treatments: Report and recommendations. *Clinical Psychologist, 48*, 3–23.

Shadish, W. R., & Baldwin, S. A. (2005). Effects of behavioral marital therapy: A meta-analysis of randomized controlled trials. *Journal of Consulting and Clinical Psychology, 73*, 6–14.

Shapiro, D. A., & Shapiro, D. (1982). Meta-analysis of comparative therapy outcome research: A critical appraisal. *Behavioral Psychotherapy, 10*, 4–25.

Shirk, S. R., Karver, M. S., & Brown, R. (2011). The alliance in child and adolescent psychotherapy. *Psychotherapy, 48*, 17–24.

Smith, M. L., & Glass, G. V. (1977). Meta-analysis of psychotherapy outcome studies. *American Psychologist, 32*, 752–777.

Smith, M. L., Glass, G. V., & Miller, T. I. (1980). *The benefits of psychotherapy*. Baltimore, MD: Johns Hopkins University Press.

Snyder, D. K., Castellani, A. M., & Whisman, M. A. (2006). Current status and future directions in couple therapy. *Annual Review of Psychology, 57*, 317–344.

Spring, B. (2007). Evidence-based practice in clinical psychology: What it is, why it matters, what you need to know. *Journal of Clinical Psychology, 63*, 611–631.

Stanton, M. (2013). The systemic epistemology of the specialty of family psychology. In J. H. Bray & M. Stanton (Eds.), *The Wiley-Blackwell handbook of family psychology* (pp. 5–20). Hoboken, NJ: Wiley.

Stewart, R. E., & Chambless, D. L. (2007). Does psychotherapy research inform treatment decisions in private practice? *Journal of Clinical Psychology, 63*, 267–281.

Stewart, R. E., & Chambless, D. L. (2009). Cognitive-behavioral therapy for adult anxiety disorders in clinical practice: A meta-analysis of effectiveness studies. *Journal of Consulting and Clinical Psychology, 77*, 595–606.

Sturmey, P., & Hersen, M. (2012a). *Handbook of evidence-based practice in clinical psychology (Vol 1): Child and adolescent disorders*. Hoboken, NJ: Wiley.

Sturmey, P., & Hersen, M. (2012b). *Handbook of evidence-based practice in clinical psychology (Vol 2): Adult disorders*. Hoboken, NJ: Wiley.

Tolin, D. F. (2010). Is cognitive-behavioral therapy more effective than other therapies? A meta-analytic review. *Clinical Psychology Review, 30*, 710–720.

Walker, B. B., & London, S. (2007). Novel tools and resources for evidence-based practice in psychology. *Journal of Clinical Psychology, 63*, 633–642.

Wallace, L. M., & vonRanson, K. M. (2011). Treatment manuals: Use in the treatment of bulimia nervosa. *Behaviour Therapy Research and Therapy, 49*, 815–820.

Weisz, J. R., Donenberg, G. R., Han, S. S., & Weiss, B. (1995). Bridging the gap between laboratory and clinic in child and adolescent psychotherapy. *Journal of Consulting and Clinical Psychology, 63*, 688–701.

Weisz, J. R., Jensen-Doss, A., & Hawley, K. M. (2006). Evidence-based youth psychotherapies versus usual clinical care: A meta-analysis of direct comparisons. *American Psychologist, 61*, 671–689.

Youngstrom, E. A., & Kendall, P. C. (2009). Psychological science and bipolar disorder. *Clinical Psychology: Science and Practice, 16*, 93–97.

Zoellner, L. A., Feeny, N. C., Cochran, B., & Pruitt, L. (2003). Treatment choice for PTSD. *Behaviour Research and Therapy, 41*, 879–886.

11 | CLINICAL CHILD PSYCHOLOGY

Chapter Preview

This chapter describes the field of clinical child psychology. We begin with a brief history of the field, then we address the unique features of working with children and adolescents as opposed to adults. We describe risk factors that increase the probability of disorders in children, assessment, classification, treatment, and prevention of childhood psychopathology.

Let's assume that you are waiting on tables at a fine-dining establishment, and after a customer learns that you are a psychology major, he asks for your advice. He mentions that his daughter is acting like a bird more and more frequently. She has built herself a "nest" with boxes and blankets in her room, she often chirps rather than talks, and she insists on only eating things that look like worms (e.g., spaghetti, gummy worms). So, other than recommending that he pay his bill before you finish your shift, what is your advice?

Before you run out to check the *DSM* to explore a diagnosis like schizophrenia, it would be crucial to first ask the father the age of his daughter. Imagine the answer is 3, and then imagine the answer is 13. With young children, imaginative play, such as pretending to be a cute animal for short periods of time, is very common and pretty adorable at that. With older children, however, a clinical child psychologist might want to conduct a full evaluation, including exploring the girl's ability to tell reality from fantasy, asking about family history of psychopathology, exploring whether there were any recent traumas such as abuse, assessing any recent substance abuse, and finding out about other aspects of psychosocial functioning such as academic achievement, peer relationships, and sibling relationships. Overall, the most important aspects to establish when considering children's behavior are their age and developmental level. Although most of the information in the previous chapters is relevant to clinical child psychology, you need additional information in order to understand how clinical child psychologists view the functioning of youth and treat problems that exist in children, adolescents, and their families.

Knowing the developmental level of a child will help us understand the child's behavior.

A BRIEF HISTORY OF CLINICAL CHILD PSYCHOLOGY

SECTION PREVIEW

This section highlights the ways that the history of clinical child psychology differs from the history of adult-oriented clinical psychology. Special attention is given to the diagnosis of children's problems.

The history of clinical child psychology reveals something of a paradox. Though clinical psychology has its roots in the assessment and treatment of childhood disorders (see Chapter 2, "Clinical Psychology's Past and Present"), for much of the twentieth century behavior disorders in childhood were largely overlooked in favor of adult disorders (Rubinstein, 1948). Indeed, the study of childhood disorder was, for a long time, simply "a downward extension and extrapolation from the study of psychopathology in adults" (Garber, 1984, p. 30). This adult-oriented perspective on childhood disorders reflects the history of the concept of childhood itself. Not that long ago, children were considered and treated as miniature adults. This "adultomorphic" view was reinforced by psychoanalytic and behavioral approaches to therapy, both of which tended to downplay the unique nature of childhood problems (Gelfand & Peterson, 1985).

During the last five decades, this adult-oriented approach to children's behavior disorders has given way to a more child-centered approach. Clinical child psychologists are discovering that traditional adult-oriented methods of classification, assessment, and intervention may have limited relevance for childhood disorders. For example, the original *DSM*, published in 1952, did not have any disorders specific to childhood or adolescence. When *DSM-II* was published in 1968, there were a handful of disorders that were specific to children and adolescents (e.g., learning disturbances, hyperkinetic reaction, runaway reaction), but most diagnoses were still far more appropriate for adults rather than for youth.

The changing approach to child clients appeared first in *DSM-III*, which included developmental considerations in the diagnostic criteria for childhood disorders. *DSM-IV* contained more than two dozen Axis I disorders specific to infants, children, and adolescents, and *DSM-5* has infused developmentally sensitive criteria into nearly all listed disorders, thereby bringing clinical child psychology into the mainstream. *DSM-5* also contains a new section called "Neurodevelopmental Disorders" that includes disorders that usually appear early in life, such as Autism Spectrum Disorder and Attention Deficit/Hyperactivity Disorder.

In addition, since 1970, several major new journals have appeared, all of which are focused on clinical child issues—including childhood disorders and their treatment (see Table 11.1). By 2000, there were two new divisions of the APA devoted entirely to children's behavioral, learning, and medical problems: Division 53 (Society of Clinical Child and Adolescent Psychology) and Division 54 (Society of Pediatric Psychology). Finally, a relatively new field of study known as *developmental psychopathology* has evolved to study childhood disorders from a developmental perspective (Achenbach, 2008b). Researchers working in this field focus on how various adaptive and maladaptive patterns of behavior are manifested during various stages of development (Achenbach, 2008b). Developmental psychopathologists also study how children develop competencies as well as disorders, and they try to learn about protective factors that prevent some children at risk for disorders from developing them (Sapienza & Masten, 2011).

After so many years of neglect, why is so much attention being devoted to understanding and treating childhood psychopathology? First, psychopathology is relatively common in childhood; approximately 20% of children are diagnosed with a behavioral, emotional, or learning disorder (Houtrow & Okumura, 2011), a figure that has grown over just the past decade (Glied & Frank, 2009). Second, many childhood disorders (e.g., conduct disorders, learning disorders,

---

TABLE 11.1 Selected Clinical Child Psychology Journals

Development and Psychopathology	*Journal of Child Psychology and Psychiatry*
Journal of Abnormal Child Psychology	*Journal of Clinical Child and Adolescent*
Journal of the American Academy of Child and	*Psychology*
Adolescent Psychiatry	*Journal of Family Psychology*

autistic spectrum disorders) have lifelong consequences for the individual, the family, and society at large. Third, most adult disorders have their roots in childhood disorders, many of which go undiagnosed and untreated. One study found that fewer than 25% of children with a diagnosable psychiatric disorder had received any outpatient mental health services in the preceding six months (Jensen et al., 2011). Fourth, by studying the risk factors, causes, and courses of childhood disorders, we may be better able to develop effective early intervention programs that prevent childhood problems from escalating into adult psychopathology. Fifth, media attention devoted to some high-profile, child-related problems—such as bullying, the potential dangers of prescribing psychotropic medications for children, the increase in reported child abuse cases—has caused many individuals to reevaluate the mental health status of children and has led to the development of a number of national task forces, a Surgeon General's report on children's mental health (U.S. Public Health Service, 2000), and White House conferences devoted to understanding and ameliorating childhood mental health problems. Finally, specialized programs have been developed to train clinical child psychologists from the perspective of evidence-based practice (Jackson, Alberts, & Roberts, 2010; Pidano, Kurowski, & McEvoy, 2010). In short, the field of clinical child psychology has grown and is now a well-established specialty within clinical psychology.

SECTION SUMMARY

Historically, children were seen as miniature adults, but more recently, increased professional and cultural focus on the special characteristics of children has raised awareness of their psychological development. The field of clinical child psychology has grown from this focus, especially that related to childhood psychopathology. Clinical child psychology is now an integral part of the field of clinical psychology.

CHARACTERISTICS UNIQUE TO CLINICAL CHILD PSYCHOLOGY

SECTION PREVIEW

Here we review a number of characteristics unique to clinical child psychology, including the referral process, confidentiality, the context of children's behavior, developmental considerations, parent–child interactions, risk factors, and protective factors.

Referral Processes

When adults feel distressed, they can seek professional help, but children must depend on parents, teachers, or other significant people in their lives to determine whether they need the help of a mental health professional. On rare occasions, children are able to find the help they need on their own (e.g., hanging around the office of the guidance counselor at school and finally asking for help), but mostly children rely on their parents and other adults in order to gain access to mental health services. Conversely, children may be referred to a mental health professional for reasons that have more to do with parental or family problems than with the child's emotional or behavioral characteristics (Kaslow, 2011).

Confidentiality

Beginning at the point of referral, working with children is also different from working with adults because of issues related to confidentiality. Clinicians who work with adults know that they cannot share information about their client with anyone else except in cases involving suicidal or homicidal intent or abuse of a child or an elderly, incapacitated person. But what about when the client is a child or an adolescent? Officially, parents or legal guardians are responsible for youth, so the legal commitment to confidentiality does not restrict clinicians from disclosing client information to parents or guardians (Koocher & Daniel, 2012). Of course, working with a young person, especially an adolescent, without being able to promise to keep information secret from the parents will often make the adolescent wary of sharing any information with the therapist. Most often, therapists set ground rules with parents and child or adolescent clients at the outset of treatment. The therapist might say, for example, that all information the adolescent client discloses will be kept private (i.e., not even disclosed to the parents) unless doing so would be potentially harmful to the client or someone else. As discussed in Chapter 3, "Basic Features of Clinical Assessment," Chapter 5, "Testing in Clinical Psychology," and Chapter 6, "Basic Features of Clinical Interventions," therapists are guided by the APA Ethics Code in setting these ground rules.

Contexts of Behavior

When working with children, it is important to consider the context of their behavior. A child's relationship to the environment is quite different from an adult's. For example, adults usually have some amount of control over where they live, what type of job they have, when they go to bed and wake up, with whom they spend their time, what they eat, and how they run their lives. Children and adolescents, for the most part, have less control over these things, and sometimes no control. Especially with younger children, the decisions that their parents make for them are the ones with which they must live (e.g., day care or school settings, activities, food choices, daily routines, access to other children as potential friends). Thus, most clinical work and research has to consider the limited power that children have to structure or change their environments.

Developmental Considerations

As illustrated in the case of the girl who was acting like a bird, knowing a child's age and developmental level are crucial to understanding the child's behavior. For one thing, clinicians must evaluate the appropriateness or inappropriateness of a child's behavior relative to developmental norms in the child's culture. The following list provides a few examples of behaviors considered appropriate at certain developmental stages but less appropriate at other stages (reviewed in Beauchaine & Hinshaw, 2013; Phares, 2013):

- Children aged 2 to 4 years tend to fear imaginary creatures and the dark; children aged 5 to 7 years tend to fear natural disasters (such as fire, flood, thunder), injury, and animals; children aged 8 to 11 tend to fear poor academic and athletic performance; and adolescents aged 12 to 18 tend to fear peer rejection.
- Until the age of 5, some children still wet the bed on occasion. By the age of 5, most children have learned how to control urination, with most children first learning control during the day and later developing control while they sleep.
- Over 50% of boys aged 4 to 5 show excessive demands for attention, and nearly 60% of them show disobedience at home.
- For children between the ages of 6 and 18, nearly 40% of boys and 25% of girls are reported by their parents to have difficulty concentrating.
- The overwhelming majority of adolescent girls experience poor body image, a phenomenon known as *normative discontent*.
- Over half of adolescent girls and boys reported that they had tried alcohol by the age of 16.

In fact, most symptoms of childhood disorders tend to be seen in a notable proportion of the child population at some point in their lives. So, the appropriateness or inappropriateness of children's behavior must be evaluated in light of the developmental stage they are in at the time (Achenbach, 2008b). Thus, a clinician working with children needs a strong background in normal developmental psychology in addition to training in abnormal child psychology.

Parent–Child Interaction Patterns

Many of the advances in understanding and treating childhood behavior disorders that have occurred in the last four decades have been made by theorists who take a *reciprocal* or *bidirectional* view of parent–child interactions. From this perspective, the child's temperament and behavior is seen as influencing the parents' behavior, while parental tolerance and responses alter the child's behavior. An example of this perspective and how it has advanced our understanding of children's behavior problems can be seen in Patterson's (1976, 1982) coercion-escalation hypothesis of aggressive behavior. Patterson's detailed observations in the homes of nonaggressive and aggressive children showed that in both kinds of homes, parents' behavior alters the probability of certain child responses, just as the children's behavior alters the likelihood of certain parental responses (Patterson, Ray, Shaw, & Cobb, 1969). However, Patterson also saw important differences in the family interactions of nonaggressive versus aggressive children. For example, aggressive children were twice as likely as nonaggressive children to persist in their aversive behavior following parental punishment (Patterson, 1976). Rather than seeing this pattern as reflecting parents' ineffective punishment tactics or children's insensitivity to the consequences of their behavior, Patterson looked at how parents and children "teach" each other to adopt and rely on coercive, aversive control tactics that can lead to childhood aggressiveness. Here is a simple case example.

> Suppose that Mrs. Jones has just picked up her 3-year-old son, Billy, from day care and they are now at the grocery store, buying food for dinner. As they pass a freezer case, Billy asks for an ice cream bar, but Mrs. Jones says, "No, you'll spoil your dinner." Billy responds by throwing a temper tantrum, which creates a problem for Mrs. Jones because she needs to finish her shopping, and besides, it is embarrassing to have her child acting out-of-control in public. Mrs. Jones solves the problem by giving Billy an ice cream bar, but with the admonition that this is the last time he will get one this close to dinner. Billy's tantrum stops immediately, and the shopping proceeds.

What do Billy and his mother learn from this interaction? First, Billy learns that if he throws a temper tantrum when his mom says no, he can get his way (tantrum-throwing is positively reinforced). At the same time, Mrs. Jones is reinforced for acceding to Billy's demands—especially when he throws a tantrum in public—because doing so terminates his aversive and humiliating behavior. The principles of operant conditioning outlined in Chapter 8, "Behavioral and Cognitive-Behavioral Psychotherapies," suggest that both Billy and his mother will behave in similar ways when confronted with similar situations in the future. This family dyad has fallen into what Patterson (1982) called the *reinforcement trap*: each obtains a short-term benefit at the expense of undesirable long-term consequences. As Billy becomes harder to manage, his parents may resort to more aversive methods to control him.

Patterson's work on understanding children's aggressive behavior from the perspective of reciprocal interactions between parents and children has led to the development of a systematic and widely employed behavioral intervention program for dealing with such problems, known as Parent Management Training (Forgatch & Patterson, 2010). The program focuses on changing the parents' interactions with their children to decrease the occurrence of coercive exchanges. In general, treatments that are consistent with this conceptualization of aggressive and antisocial behavior have had strong research support and are considered well established (Eyberg, Nelson, & Boggs, 2008).

Risk Factors

Clinicians studying developmental psychopathology have identified a number of *risk factors* for the development of emotional/behavioral problems. Risk factors are characteristics within the child, family, community, culture, or society that are associated with heightened risk that the child will develop some type of emotional/behavioral problem or psychopathology (Cicchetti, 2008; Ingram & Price, 2010; reviewed in Phares, 2013). Let's consider a few of the more salient of these risk factors.

TEMPERAMENT   Children whose temperament in infancy was described as difficult have a higher probability of showing problematic behavior throughout their lives, including stormy peer relationships, academic difficulties when they enter first grade (Calkins & Degnan, 2006), conduct problems from the ages of 4 to 13 (Lahey et al., 2008), increased behavior problems at the age of 15 (Rothbart & Bates, 2006), challenging personality traits at the age of 26 (Caspi et al., 2003), and a greater likelihood of generalized anxiety disorder by the age of 32 (Moffitt et al., 2007). Given that infant temperament is considered to be largely genetically determined (Bijttebier & Roeyers, 2009), these findings suggest that some childhood behavioral problems are partly a function of the child's innate biological characteristics. There are, however, numerous environmental factors (such as family situations and neighborhood conditions) that can increase or decrease the risks posed by difficult temperament (Bijttebier & Roeyers, 2009).

INTERPARENTAL CONFLICT   Decades of research on children's functioning has revealed that when parents argue, children lose. Parents' verbal arguments and fighting are associated with increased emotional and behavioral problems in children and adolescents, especially external-izing problems (Shermerhorn, Chow, & Cummings, 2010). When parents exchange high levels of negative communication and low levels of positive communication, children tend to blame themselves for their parents' conflict and they often feel emotionally insecure (Davies, Martin, & Cicchetti, 2012; DeBoard-Lucas, Fosco, Raynor, & Grych, 2010). When children are put in the middle of their parents' conflicts, a process known as *triangulation*, the effects of those conflicts are even worse (Grych, Raynor, & Fosco, 2004). In fact, evidence suggests that children are better off if their parents divorce, assuming that the interparental conflict then decreases significantly, in comparison with children who remain in intact but highly conflicted families (Schermerhorn, Chow, & Cummings, 2010).

What about early research showing that children who had experienced a parental divorce are much more likely to show emotional and behavioral problems than children who had not experienced a parental divorce (Hetherington, Bridges, & Insabella, 1998)? That pattern does appear, but more recent research has clarified that those group differences tend to be due to other factors, such as continuing interparental conflict and post divorce financial problems, rather than to the divorce itself (Hetherington & Elmore, 2003). Overall, it appears that what goes on in chil-dren's families (e.g., levels of interparental conflict and family functioning) are more important for children's well-being than whether or not they live with both parents (Schermerhorn, Chow, & Cummings 2010).

PHYSICAL ABUSE   Most of us think of child abuse in terms of parental aggression that leaves broken bones, head injuries, and permanent physical scars. But even some forms of harsh disci-plinary actions by parents (such as spanking with a belt) can be considered child physical abuse (Finkelhor, 2011). In fact, in most states, one of the operational definitions of child abuse is an action that leaves a mark of injury on the child's skin.

Estimates suggest that between 5 and 26% of youth in the United States are physically abused each year; many of the more conservative estimates hover around 9 to 10% (Children's Defense Fund, 2012; Finkelhor, Turner, Ormrod, & Hamby, 2009). Physical abuse is associated with a whole host of problems in children, such as conduct disorder, oppositional defiant disor-der, aggression, depression, anxiety disorders, poor social competence, and poor academic per-formance (Wekerle, MacMillan, Leung, & Jamieson, 2008). Given the ramifications of physical abuse, it is not surprising to find that the estimates of physical abuse in child clinical populations are much higher than in nonclinical samples. One study in Los Angeles found that 46.9% of chil-dren receiving services at a community mental health center were victims of abuse (Lau & Weisz, 2003). Further, there is growing evidence that child physical abuse influences children in different ways, partly based on gene and environment interactions as well as the intensity and duration of the abuse (Cicchetti & Rogosch, 2012).

SEXUAL ABUSE   Sexual abuse can also be devastating to children and adolescents. Although there are many definitions of child sexual abuse, most of them focus on sexual exploitation of children by a perpetrator who is older and who has more power than the child (Mannarino & Cohen, 2006). Not all sexual abuse involves sexual intercourse or other forms of sexual contact; it can also include things like exposure to pornography or other sexual material.

It is extraordinarily difficult to get accurate estimates of the prevalence of sexual abuse, given that so much of it goes unreported. However, the high prevalence of this risk factor is suggested by a meta-analysis of 65 scholarly articles covering 22 countries. It found that, overall, 19.7% of women and 7.9% of men had been victims of sexual abuse before the age of 18 (Pereda, Guilera, Forns, & Gomez-Benito, 2009). In the United States, the rates were 25.3% for women and 7.5% for men. Although the media tends to focus on child sexual abuse that is perpetrated by strangers (as in the case of many child abductions), it is estimated that between 75 and 90% of child sexual abuse cases involve a perpetrator who is a family member or who is known to the family, such as a neighbor, caretaker, coach, or family friend (Wekerle, MacMillan, Leung, & Jamieson 2008).

The negative ramifications of child sexual abuse depend somewhat on the nature of the abuse. For example, children are more psychologically harmed by sexual abuse when (a) it was prolonged, (b) the perpetrator was a father or father figure, (c) there was more intrusive sexual contact, such as intercourse, (d) there was coercion or physical force or threats, and (e) the child's report of abuse was not believed (Mannarino & Cohen, 2006; Noll, Trickett, & Putnam, 2003). Sexual abuse is associated with higher risk of depression, a greater risk for suicide attempts, poor coping, health problems, and relationship difficulties in adulthood (Maniglio, 2009, 2011; Mannarino & Cohen, 2006; Nelson, Baldwin, & Taylor, 2012; Wekerle , MacMillan, Leung, & Jamieson, 2008). In short, sexual abuse can have significant damaging and long-lasting effects on children, particularly those who have less psychological resiliency or fewer protective factors, which we discuss later.

POVERTY   Based on the federal definition of the concept, about 21.6% of all U.S. children under the age of 18 are growing up in poverty (Children's Defense Fund, 2012). The percentage varies greatly by ethnicity: 32.4% for Hispanic/Latino/Latina children, 38.2% for African American children, and 13.1% for European American children (Children's Defense Fund, 2012). If you add the 20% of youth whose families are in the "near poverty" category (i.e., family income between 100 and 200% of the poverty line), over 40% of youth under the age of 18 are growing up poor in America (Yoshikawa, Aber, & Beardslee, 2012).

Living in poverty is not just about having too little money. It is also associated with a host of problems, including housing instability, chaotic family environments, exposure to maladaptive peer networks, poorer water quality, fewer parks, and more community violence (Children's Defense Fund, 2012; Yoshikawa, Aber, & Beardslee, 2012). In other words, poverty tends to expose children to several risk factors for behavior disorders. Thus, it is not surprising to learn that growing up in poverty is associated with a number of problems, most of which fall into the externalizing range of behaviors, such as aggression, conduct disorder, and oppositional defiant disorder (Matthews & Gallo, 2011; Santiago, Kaltman, & Miranda, 2013; UNICEF, 2010; vanOort, vanderEnde, Wadsworth, Verhulst, & Achenbach, 2011).

Table 11.2 lists other risk factors for behavior/emotional problems in children. Given the wide range of these risk factors, it is not surprising that many children are exposed to at least one of them. For example, data from the National Longitudinal Study of Adolescent Health (Parra, DuBois, & Sher, 2006) showed that among 11th graders, 43% were exposed to some type of socioeconomic disadvantage (e.g., poverty, inadequate housing, single-parent family), 21% were exposed to interparental conflict, abuse, inadequate schools, and 4% were exposed to parental psychopathology. Only about one-third (32%) of the youth were seen to be at low risk.

Children's harsh surroundings can have a significant impact on their well-being.   *Source:* Joseph Sohm/Visions of America/Corbis.

TABLE 11.2 Examples of Risk Factors for the Development of Psychological Problems in Children

Risk Factors Within the Child	*Risk Factors Within the Community*
Difficult temperament	Poverty
Inadequate coping mechanisms	Inadequate schools
Limited problem-solving skills	Violent neighborhoods
Risk Factors Within the Family	Inadequate opportunities for employment
Parental psychopathology	*Risk Factors Within the Culture and Society*
Interparental conflict	Culture of violence
Harsh parenting	Racial discrimination
Child abuse (physical, sexual, psychological, neglect)	

Protective Factors

Although risk factors can increase the likelihood of problems in children's lives, it is important to recognize that there are also *protective factors* that can lessen or eliminate the ramifications of negative situations (Sapienza & Masten, 2011). Like risk factors, protective factors can exist within the child, family, community, culture, or society (see Table 11.3).

Overall, these protective factors have been well established through research and are relevant for children of all ages and developmental levels (Bonanno, Westphal, & Mancini, 2011; Davydov, Stewart, Ritchie, & Chaudieu, 2010; Masten & Tellegen, 2012; Vanderbilt-Adriance & Shaw, 2008). Figure 11.1 illustrates the process of *resilience* whereby children exposed to one or more risk factors (such as parental psychopathology) can still show positive outcomes when they are also exposed to protective factors (Seifer, 2003).

SECTION SUMMARY

Working with children requires that psychologists understand the many different contexts that influence children's behavior. Because clinical child psychologists usually must inter-act with parents in order to gain access to children and to help them, parental factors are particularly important. Many children are exposed to risk factors that include biological forces (e.g., through predispositions toward certain temperaments), familial forces (e.g., parent–child interactions, interparental conflict, abuse), and social forces (e.g., poverty and violent environments). Protective factors can decrease the likelihood that children will develop psychopathology in the face of harsh forces in their environments.

TABLE 11.3 Examples of Protective Factors that Help Reduce the Risk of Psychological Problems in Children

Protective Factors Within the Child	*Protective Factors Within the Community*
Good cognitive abilities	Connections to caring adult mentors and prosocial peers
Effective behavioral and emotional regulation strategies	High neighborhood quality (e.g., safety, affordable housing, recreation centers)
Perceived efficacy and control	Effective schools (e.g., well-trained and well-paid teachers, after-school programs, sports or arts enrichment activities
Protective Factors Within the Family	*Protective Factors Within the Culture and Society*
Close relationship to caregiver	Value and resources directed at education
Authoritative parenting style (high on warmth, structure/ monitoring, and expectations)	Protective child policies (labor laws, child health, and welfare emphasis)
Faith and spiritual affiliations	Low acceptance of physical violence

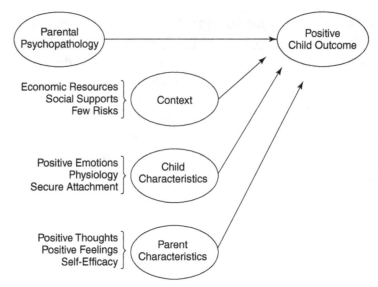

FIGURE 11.1   Resilience Processes in Young Children of Mentally Ill Parents.
Source: Copyright © 2003 Seifer, R. (2003). Young children with mentally ill parents: Resilient developmental systems. In S. S. Luthar (Ed.), *Resilience and vulnerability: Adaptation in the context of childhood adversities* (p. 43). New York, NY: Cambridge University Press. Reprinted with the permission of Cambridge University Press.

CLINICAL ASSESSMENT OF CHILDREN

For both children and adults, the assessment process is designed to serve a number of purposes, including arriving at a diagnosis, making treatment recommendations, offering information about long-term prognosis, and evaluating the progress of therapy. In conducting assessments with children, clinical child psychologists must be especially aware of developmental and contextual factors. Child assessments tend to be more comprehensive than adult assessments; information must be gathered from multiple sources reflecting the child's major life domains, including school, family, and peer group (Achenbach, 2008a).

Clinicians pay careful attention to information supplied by parents and teachers during interviews and on behavior rating scales. Children's emotional and behavioral states depend heavily on the nature of their family life, so assessment often includes exploration of the child's behavior within the family (e.g., observations of parent–child interactions), as well as exploration of parental functioning (e.g., parental depression, interparental conflict).

Because most child referrals pertain in some fashion to school-based problems, the clinical assessment of children routinely includes an evaluation of school performance, including intelligence and achievement testing as well as actual school behavior. Thus, a standard assessment battery for children includes behavior rating scales from multiple informants, clinical interviews, intelligence and achievement testing, structured observations, and an evaluation of family functioning.

SECTION PREVIEW

Clinical child assessment utilizes many techniques to ascertain the strengths and limitations of children who are experiencing difficulties. Common assessment techniques include behavior rating scales, clinical interviews, intellectual and achievement testing, behavioral observations, and measures to assess family functioning.

Behavior Rating Scales

Because they are inexpensive and easy to administer, and usually reliable and valid, behavior rating scales have become a standard part of almost all child assessment batteries. The rating scales generally consist of a list of child behavior problems (e.g., fidgets, easily distracted, shy and withdrawn). The child, parent, or teacher rates each behavior according to how often the behavior occurs. Behavior rating scales differ in their coverage, with some focusing on specific disorders (e.g., the

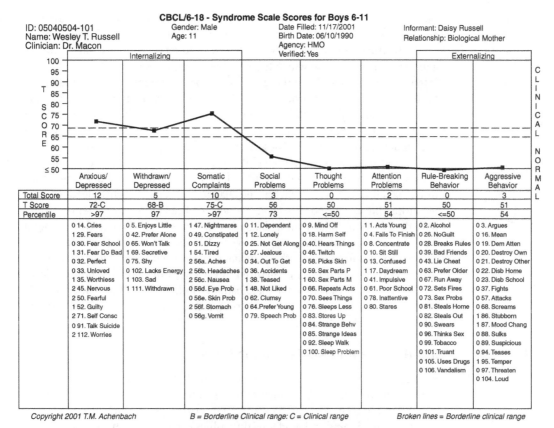

CBCL/6-18 - Syndrome Scale Scores for Boys 6-11

ID: 05040504-101
Name: Wesley T. Russell
Clinician: Dr. Macon

Gender: Male
Age: 11

Date Filled: 11/17/2001
Birth Date: 06/10/1990
Agency: HMO
Verified: Yes

Informant: Daisy Russell
Relationship: Biological Mother

	Anxious/ Depressed	Withdrawn/ Depressed	Somatic Complaints	Social Problems	Thought Problems	Attention Problems	Rule-Breaking Behavior	Aggressive Behavior
Total Score	12	5	10	3	0	2	0	3
T Score	72-C	68-B	75-C	56	50	51	50	51
Percentile	>97	97	>97	73	<=50	54	<=50	54

Anxious/Depressed	Withdrawn/Depressed	Somatic Complaints	Social Problems	Thought Problems	Attention Problems	Rule-Breaking Behavior	Aggressive Behavior
0 14. Cries	0 5. Enjoys Little	1 47. Nightmares	0 11. Dependent	0 9. Mind Off	1 1. Acts Young	0 2. Alcohol	0 3. Argues
1 29. Fears	0 42. Prefer Alone	0 49. Constipated	1 12. Lonely	0 18. Harm Self	0 4. Fails To Finish	0 26. NoGuilt	0 16. Mean
0 30. Fear School	0 65. Won't Talk	0 51. Dizzy	0 25. Not Get Along	0 40. Hears Things	0 8. Concentrate	0 28. Breaks Rules	0 19. Dem Atten
1 31. Fear Do Bad	1 69. Secretive	1 54. Tired	0 27. Jealous	0 46. Twitch	0 10. Sit Still	0 39. Bad Friends	0 20. Destroy Own
0 32. Perfect	0 75. Shy	2 56a. Aches	0 34. Out To Get	0 58. Picks Skin	0 13. Confused	0 43. Lie Cheat	0 21. Destroy Other
0 33. Unloved	0 102. Lacks Energy	2 56b. Headaches	0 36. Accidents	0 59. Sex Parts P	1 17. Daydream	0 63. Prefer Older	0 22. Disb Home
1 35. Worthless	1 103. Sad	2 56c. Nausea	1 38. Teased	1 60. Sex Parts M	0 41. Impulsive	0 67. Run Away	0 23. Disb School
2 45. Nervous	1 111. Withdrawn	0 56d. Eye Prob	1 48. Not Liked	0 66. Repeats Acts	0 61. Poor School	0 72. Sets Fires	0 37. Fights
2 50. Fearful		0 56e. Skin Prob	0 62. Clumsy	0 70. Sees Things	0 78. Inattentive	0 73. Sex Probs	0 57. Attacks
1 52. Guilty		2 56f. Stomach	0 64.Prefer Young	0 76. Sleeps Less	0 80. Stares	0 81. Steals Home	0 68. Screams
2 71. Self Consc		0 56g. Vomit	0 79. Speech Prob	0 83. Stores Up		0 82. Steals Out	1 86. Stubborn
0 91. Talk Suicide				0 84. Strange Behv		0 90. Swears	1 87. Mood Chang
2 112. Worries				0 85. Strange Ideas		0 96. Thinks Sex	0 88. Sulks
				0 92. Sleep Walk		0 99. Tobacco	0 89. Suspicious
				0 100. Sleep Problem		0 101. Truant	0 94. Teases
						0 105. Uses Drugs	1 95. Temper
						0 106. Vandalism	0 97. Threaten
							0 104. Loud

Copyright 2001 T.M. Achenbach   B = Borderline Clinical range: C = Clinical range   Broken lines = Borderline clinical range

FIGURE 11.2   Syndrome Profile from CBCL Completed for "Wesley Russell" by His Mother.
Source: Copyright Achenbach T. M. & Rescorla, L. A. (2001) *Manual for the Achenbach System of Empirically Based Assessment (ASEBA) school-age forms and profiles.* Burlington, VT: University of Vermont, Research Center for Children, Youth, and Families. Copyright 2001 by University of Vermont. P. 65. All names are fictitious. Reproduced by permission.

Child Depression Inventory-2; Kovacs, 2010) whereas others cover most areas of child behavior problems (e.g., the *Child Behavior Checklist* (CBCL); Achenbach & Rescorla, 2001).

Figure 11.2 shows an example of a mother's CBCL report on her 11-year-old son, "Wesley" (not his real name), who was referred for missing school excessively because of asthma and headaches (Achenbach & Rescorla, 2001). The profile shows that, compared to other boys his age, Wesley showed clinically elevated levels of anxious/depressed, withdrawn/depressed, and somatic complaints. The CBCL is an example of an empirically derived measure that is used extensively in clinical practice and there are also parallel measures for teachers and youth to complete.

As already noted, the most frequently used behavior rating scales show high test-retest reliability and good validity (Frick, Kamphaus, & Barry, 2009). For example, measures from the Achenbach System of Empirically Based Assessment (ASEBA) have strong psychometric properties. Similarly, scores on the *Behavior Assessment System for Children*-2 (BASC-2; Reynolds & Kamphaus, 2009) can distinguish between children with higher versus lower levels of behavior problems and can also help identify symptoms of inattention and hyperactivity. Taken together, parent, teacher, and adolescent self-reports can provide reliable, valid, economical, and useful information on children's functioning.

Clinical Interviews

In a survey of clinical child and adolescent psychologists, 71.0% reported that conducting a clinical interview was the most important aspect of their clinical assessment procedure (Cashel, 2002). As they do in adult assessments, child clinicians can use unstructured or structured clinical interviews; most of them use both (see Chapter 4, "Interviewing and Observation in Clinical Psychology," for a discussion of these interview types).

During unstructured interviews, the clinician usually meets with the parents, and depending on the child's age and cognitive maturity, with the child as well. When interviewing the parents, the clinician has the following goals in mind: (a) establish rapport, (b) obtain specific details about the child's problem, (c) chart the course of the problem, (d) gather a developmental history of the child, and (e) explore family factors that may exacerbate the child's problem.

Unstructured interviews with referred children can offer valuable information about them and the environments in which their problems occur (Sattler & Hoge, 2006). The goals of child interviews often differ from those described for the parent interview and include the following: (a) establish rapport; (b) evaluate the child's understanding of the problem that led to referral; (c) evaluate the child's explanations of problematic behavior; (d) obtain a description of the fear, sadness, anxiety, anger, or low self-esteem associated with problems such as childhood depression and anxiety disorders; and (e) observe the child during the interview.

As valuable as unstructured child and parent interviews can be, many clinicians and most clinical researchers use structured clinical interviews to aid in making diagnostic decisions. Structured diagnostic interviews, such as the Diagnostic Interview Schedule for Children (DISC) (Shaffer, Fisher, Lucas, Dulcan, & Schwab-Stone, 2000) can be given to parents as well as children. They have the advantage of providing diagnostic information in a relatively reliable and valid manner. The concern with structured interviews is that they are often very long (e.g., 1 1/2 to 2 hours) and do not usually enhance the clinician's rapport with the child or parent. For these reasons, many clinicians opt for semistructured interviews, which combine the clinical sensitivity of the unstructured interview with the diagnostic reliability of structured interviews. One example of a semistructured interview is the Semistructured Clinical Interview for Children and Adolescents (McConaughy & Achenbach, 2001).

Intelligence and Achievement Tests

Poor school performance, most often in the first year of elementary school, accounts for a large number of child referrals for mental health services. Indeed, behavior problems and academic difficulties are related in complex and reciprocal ways in which behavior problems can impair academic functioning and academic difficulties can worsen behavior problems.

It was once the case that in order for children with behavior or academic difficulties to receive the school support services (e.g., tutoring, special placement) to which they are legally entitled, they had to have received a diagnosis based on standardized and individualized intelligence and achievement testing. Today, this standardized testing is just one part of a more comprehensive assessment.

The most common intellectual assessment in use with children today is the Wechsler Intelligence Scale for Children-Fourth Edition (WISC-IV) (Wechsler, 2003). As described in Chapter 5, "Testing in Clinical Psychology," the WISC-IV can be used with children aged 6 to 17, and yields a full-scale IQ score, four composite (index) scores (verbal comprehension, perceptual reasoning, working memory, and processing speed), and individual subtest scores. The most commonly used measure of academic achievement in the United States is the Woodcock–Johnson Psycho-Educational Battery—Third Edition (WJ-III) (Woodcock, McGrew, & Mather, 2000), also introduced in Chapter 5. The WJ-III is used to measure knowledge that children have acquired in the educational and school environment. Children in different grade levels are assessed on different topics, but the main characteristics assessed at all ages are broad reading, broad mathematics, and written expression.

Projective Tests

Among the projective personality tests used with children and adolescents are the Rorschach inkblot test (Rorschach, 1942), the Children's Apperception Test (CAT) (Bellak, 1954), which is the child version of the Thematic Apperception Test (TAT), drawing techniques such as the Draw-a-Person technique (Koppitz, 1968) and the House-Tree-Person technique (Buck, 1948), and incomplete sentence blanks (Rotter, Lah, & Rafferty, 1992).

As described in Chapter 5, the use of projective testing is controversial, and this is especially true in relation to the assessment of children. Test-retest and interrater reliabilities for these tests are often unacceptably low, especially among child samples (Hunsley, Lee, & Wood, 2003; Wood et al., 2010). In addition, there is no evidence for the incremental validity of projective tests. In other words, even if they did allow valid inferences about children (e.g., that signs of aggression on the CAT predicted aggressive behavior), it is usually the case that this same information is already available through interviews, observations, or other simpler and more reliable and valid means (Hunsley, Lee, & Wood, 2003).

Over three decades ago, one investigator summarized our knowledge in this way: projective tests with children "sometimes . . . tell us poorly something we already know" (Gittelman, 1980, p. 434). This summary remains true today. Nevertheless, some clinicians continue to use such tests, often citing their usefulness for quasi-diagnostic or descriptive purposes (e.g., to get an idea of how children perceive themselves within the family). Other clinicians, however, remain concerned about the poor psychometric properties of these tests and the potential for bias or error that stems from those properties.

Behavioral Observations

Behavioral observations are an integral part of the assessment of childhood disorders. Children's problems usually occur in the home or at school, so observations in these settings give clinicians the opportunity to validate, or get new perspectives on, reports made by parents and teachers through rating scales and interviews.

It is rare these days that clinicians conduct home observations, but they do often set up opportunities to observe parent–child interactions in the clinic office (Frick, Kamphaus, & Barry, 2009). School observation systems focus primarily on classroom behavior, although playground behavior also may be monitored (Lean & Colucci, 2013). Classroom observations often concentrate on behaviors associated with ADHD, including off-task behavior, being disruptive or out-of-seat, and being noncompliant (Lean & Colucci, 2013). Observations can also be used to track the behavioral results after a child begins medication (Brown, Carpenter, & Simerly, 2005; see Figure 11.3).

Family Interaction Measures

A thorough child assessment involves examining the child in the family context. This process is typically accomplished with observations of parent–child interactions in the clinic and on occasion with home observations. Assessment of the family context usually goes beyond simple observations and may include the following areas (Mash & Hunsley, 2007): (a) family history of psychopathology, (b) parental psychopathology, (c) marital relationship and interparental conflict, (d) child-rearing methods and disciplinary patterns, and (e) stress and perceived support.

Sometimes child clinicians have to work hard at explaining why they need to gather this information. Parents may want to talk only about the child's problems and assume that if their parenting behaviors are being assessed, they are being blamed for the child's problems. Child clinicians must take care not to be pejorative or to blame the parents for the child's behavior. They need to explain the nature of a thorough evaluation diplomatically but frankly, emphasizing that the purpose of assessment is not to assign blame. Most parents eventually understand why these aspects of the assessment are important.

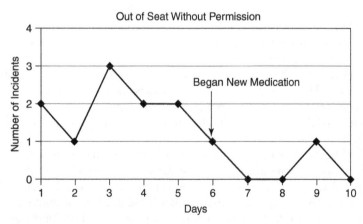

FIGURE 11.3 Examples of Data Collected Using Behavioral Observation.
Source: Brown, R. T., Carpenter, L. A., & Simerly, E. (2005). *Mental health medications for children: A primer* (p. 89). New York, NY: Guilford.

SECTION SUMMARY

Assessing children and adolescents is often more complex than assessing adults because a youth's behaviors are often more dependent on the contexts in which they are embedded. During assessment, a wide range of characteristics must be assessed, including behavior, emotions, cognitions, intellectual and achievement functioning, and family functioning. Different informants (such as mothers, fathers, teachers, and children themselves) often do not see the child's behavior in a similar manner, but integrating the divergent views from multiple informants is important in order to provide a comprehensive understanding of the child's behavior and to provide the most relevant recommendations for intervention, if needed.

SPECIFIC CHILDHOOD DISORDERS

SECTION PREVIEW

This section reviews selected childhood disorders, beginning with the classification of childhood disorders as clinically derived or empirically derived. A review of all childhood diagnoses is beyond the scope of this chapter, but we describe the symptoms, prevalence, and associated features of some of the most common ones, including attention deficit hyperactivity disorder, oppositional defiant disorder, conduct disorder, major depressive disorder, anxiety disorders, autism spectrum disorders, and pediatric problems.

Classification of Childhood Disorders

The classification of childhood disorders has developed somewhat differently from that of adult disorders, although both have the same objectives. Adult disorders have been classified mainly into *clinically derived* diagnostic categories. Clinically derived systems rely on the judgments of experts, who use their clinical and research experience to determine diagnostic criteria. The pros and cons of this approach for the DSM were discussed in Chapter 3; here we only note that these points also relate to diagnoses for children.

As we suggested earlier, the DSM system has improved over the years, especially for diagnosing adult disorders, but it is still of more limited use with children. One improvement in *DSM-IV* was its greater breadth of coverage of childhood disorders; it contained more than four times as many childhood categories as *DSM-II* did. A major goal of the planning committee of *DSM-IV* was to introduce a developmental framework to the classification of the childhood disorders, and this goal remained the same in the development of *DSM-5*.

Unfortunately, the only consistent developmental data offered are age of onset and course of disorders. Further, DSM diagnostic criteria were not adjusted to reflect developmental differences. For example, for several disorders (e.g., depression, generalized anxiety), the clinician is instructed to use the adult criteria, somehow adjusting them to reflect how the symptoms may manifest themselves in childhood. Similarly, the same diagnostic criteria are used for boys and girls, even though there is evidence that for some problems (e.g., aggression), the disorders may be manifested differently for the two sexes (Miller, Malone, Dodge, & Conduct Problems Prevention Research Group, 2010). Finally, the *DSM* offers too little coverage of disorders seen in infancy and early childhood, so many child clinicians use a separate diagnostic system known as *Diagnostic Classification of Mental Health and Developmental Disorders of Infancy and Early Childhood*, Revised Edition (Zero to Three, 2005). It would be ideal, however, to bring disorders at all developmental levels under the umbrella of the DSM system.

Another difficulty in diagnosing children with the *DSM* has to do with *comorbidity*, the co-occurrence of two or more disorders within the same person. Comorbidity is common in adult clinical populations, and it is the rule rather than the exception in child clinical populations (Kessler et al., 2012). For example, a series of studies found that 69% of children and adolescents diagnosed with ADHD also had one or more disorders, such as oppositional defiant disorder, conduct disorder, and anxiety disorders (Nigg, 2013). These high rates of comorbidity have led to questions about the usefulness of the *DSM* for children and adolescents (Jensen, 2003).

Finally, test-retest and interrater reliabilities of DSM diagnoses are much lower for children than for adults, especially in relation to problems such as depression and alcohol abuse (American Psychiatric Association, 2000). Nevertheless, the *DSM* remains the single most-used diagnostic categorization system for children and adolescents in the United States (Mash & Hunsley, 2007).

In contrast to the clinical approach that characterizes *DSM*, empirically derived systems rely on statistical analyses of large amounts of data to determine the symptoms that make up a diagnostic category. The empirical approach to the diagnosis of childhood psychopathology is embodied in the work of Dr. Thomas Achenbach (1978; Achenbach & Edelbrock, 1979, 1981), who developed rating scales for assessing more than 100 of the most common problems of childhood. He asked thousands of parents and teachers to complete these rating scales in relation to both referred and nonreferred boys and girls ranging in age from 4 to 18. Although the results differed somewhat depending on the child's age and sex, several factors emerged that reflect a variety of childhood behavioral problems. Figure 11.2 shows a sample profile of a child who was rated on the CBCL, and Table 11.4 delineates the broadband and narrowband factors on the CBCL, with sample item content (Achenbach & Rescorla, 2001).

Note that the broadband factors of *externalizing* problems and *internalizing* problems are used routinely to conceptualize children's behavior. These conceptualizations have been around for decades (Achenbach & Edelbrock, 1978), and they continue to be useful today (Achenbach, 2008a). The externalizing factor refers to acting-out behavior—such as hyperactivity, aggression, and delinquency—that is aversive to others in the child's environment. The internalizing factor refers to problems in which the child experiences depression, anxiety, somatic problems, and other significant discomfort that may not be evident, let alone disturbing, to others. These two broad factors offer a reliable and valid way of differentiating childhood behavioral problems. Although the broadband factors of externalizing and internalizing problems continue to be helpful in conceptualizing the behavior of youth, most clinicians and researchers also look specifically at narrowband factors (such as anxious/depressed or aggressive). Some clinicians are interested in finding ways to combine the clinical and empirical approaches to diagnosis. *DSM-5* helps those efforts because it offers a more dimensional approach to diagnostic categorizations (Hudziak, Achenbach, Althoff, & Pine, 2008; Ozonoff, 2012).

In the following sections, we offer descriptions of a variety of childhood disorders that clinical child psychologists often encounter in their assessment and treatment activities. These include attention deficit hyperactivity disorder, oppositional defiant disorder, conduct disorder, major depressive disorder, anxiety disorders, autism spectrum disorders, and pediatric health problems. Our descriptions are necessarily brief, but you can learn more about these disorders in a number of textbooks on abnormal child behavior (Mash & Wolfe, 2012; Phares, 2013; Wicks-Nelson & Israel, 2013; Wilmshurst, 2011).

TABLE 11.4 Narrowband and Broadband Factors and Sample Items from the CBCL

Internalizing		Externalizing
Anxious/Depressed	*Social Problems*	*Rule-Breaking Behavior*
feels worthless	lonely	breaks rules
fears	jealous	steals items from home
talks of suicide	not liked by peers	runs away
Withdrawn/Depressed	*Thought Problems*	*Aggressive Behavior*
prefers to be alone	hears or sees nonexistent things	is mean to others
sad	has strange behavior	destroys own things
lacks energy	has strange ideas	attacks others
Somatic Complaints	*Attention Problems*	
tired	fails to finish tasks	
stomach aches	confused	
constipation	inattention	

Attention-Deficit Hyperactivity Disorder

The core features of ADHD are inattention, impulsivity, and overactivity. The attention problems consist primarily of children having difficulty sustaining their focus; they fail to finish school assignments, and they do not stay on task in the classroom (American Psychiatric Association, 2013; Frick & Nigg, 2012). Impulsivity refers to the fact that these children act before they think and that they have difficulty waiting to take turns, they interrupt others, and are impatient. Children with ADHD exhibit overactivity in both gross motor movements (e.g., running around the room, standing on chairs), and fine motor movements, (e.g., fidgeting and squirming, restlessness, and playing with objects).

ADHD is considered one of the most common childhood behavior disorders, affecting approximately 3 to 7% of school-age children (Frick & Nigg, 2012). Although this figure represents, on average, only one child per classroom, it is enough to seriously disrupt the learning environment, as any schoolteacher will confirm. ADHD primarily affects boys (the boy-to-girl ratio ranges from 4:1 to 10:1), and although it appears prior to first grade, the problems it creates are intensified by the demands of the school environment. Approximately one-half to two-thirds of children with ADHD continue to experience ADHD into adulthood (Barkley, Knouse, & Murphy, 2011).

Oppositional Defiant Disorder and Conduct Disorder

Oppositional defiant disorder (ODD) and conduct disorder (CD) are referred to as *disruptive disorders*. ODD is considered less severe than CD, and many children who display ODD during preschool and younger childhood go on to develop CD in adolescence. ODD is characterized by developmentally inappropriate levels of opposition and defiance toward a parent, caretaker, or teacher. Other characteristics of ODD include negative attitude, quick temper, recurrent anger, and deliberate annoyance of others. Prevalence rates of ODD range from 2 to 16%, and the disorder is more common in boys than girls before puberty but is seen about equally often in both sexes afterward (Frick & Nigg, 2012).

Conduct disorder is diagnosed when there is a persistent pattern of violating the rights of others and violating social norms. Examples of CD symptoms include bullying others, initiating physical fights, being physically cruel to other individuals or to animals, forcing sexual activity on an unwilling individual, deliberately setting fires, destroying others' property, being truant from school, and running away. Substance use and abuse is also evident in youth diagnosed with CD, but it is not part of the formal criteria (American Psychiatric Association, 2013; Frick & Nigg, 2012). CD is more common in boys (with a prevalence rate that ranges from 6 to 16%) than in girls (with a prevalence rate from 2 to 9%).

Major Depressive Disorder

Childhood depression is similar to adult depression in terms of its emotional, cognitive, behavioral, and physical manifestations, but the specific symptom picture may differ depending on the child's developmental stage (Garber & Weersing, 2010). Indeed, there is considerable debate over the fact that the *DSM* lists the same criteria for diagnosing depression in both children and adults. Regardless of age, major depressive disorder is diagnosed if the client experiences at least

Depression is more common in girls after puberty. *Source:* Myrleen Pearson/PhotoEdit, Inc.

two weeks of sadness, lethargy, disturbances in energy, disturbed sleeping and eating patterns, possible suicidal ideation, and impairment in social, educational, vocational, or other functioning. In contrast to adults, younger children often show temper tantrums and irritability rather than sad affect (American Psychiatric Association, 2013; Costello, Copeland, & Angold, 2011).

Prevalence rates for depression in childhood and adolescence are often reported to be 2 to 5%, with the lowest rates in the younger years, and rates of 7% and higher in samples of adolescents. As in adults, there is a high degree of comorbidity between depression and anxiety (Garber & Weersing, 2010). Before puberty, depression is approximately equal in boys and girls. After puberty and throughout adulthood, girls and women are much more likely to experience depression, reflected in at least a 2:1 female-to-male ratio.

Anxiety Disorders

Like adults, children and adolescents can be diagnosed with a number of anxiety disorders, including specific phobia, social phobia, obsessive-compulsive disorder, generalized anxiety disorder, and posttraumatic stress disorder. Separation anxiety disorder is particularly interesting from a developmental standpoint, so it is highlighted here.

Separation anxiety disorder is diagnosed when children show developmentally inappropriate and extreme distress when separated from their primary caregiver, usually a parent. It is developmentally normal for infants and toddlers to show distress when separated from their caregiver, so separation anxiety disorder is only considered as a diagnosis when children are quite a bit older than 18 months and when they are terribly distressed when separated from their parent. The symptoms, which must last for at least four weeks, include distress upon separation, concern about future separation, worry about losing the parent permanently, reluctance to be alone, and nightmares about separating from the parent.

Separation anxiety disorder occurs in approximately 4% of the population of youth, with higher rates in younger children than in adolescents (Eisen et al., 2011). Girls are more likely than boys to experience separation anxiety disorder.

Autistic Spectrum Disorder

In the past (including in the previous edition of the *DSM*), *autistic disorder* was considered extremely rare and extremely severe. Children diagnosed with autistic disorder were those who showed severe deficits in their social relationships and communication skills; many could not use language in a meaningful way at all. Many were thought to be severely impaired cognitively and they often showed perseveration (i.e., repeating) of behaviors and peculiar interests and preoccupations (American Psychiatric Association, 2000). Another condition called *Asperger's syndrome* was thought to be a separate, less severe and more common disorder characterized by problems in social interaction (e.g., lack of appropriate eye contact and other social skills, failure to make friends), and the appearance of behaviors, interests, and activities that are unusual, restricted, repetitive, and stereotyped (such as being preoccupied with reading maps). Unlike children with autistic disorder, those with Asperger's disorder typically have adequate language skills and can function relatively well in society (American Psychiatric Association, 2000). In recent years, research in clinical child psychopathology has suggested that these two disorders, along with some other *pervasive developmental disorders*, are actually all related forms of *autistic spectrum disorder* (ASD; see Ozonoff, 2012). Accordingly, in *DSM-5*, the diagnosis of autistic spectrum disorder (often known as "the spectrum") is applied to individuals with severe autistic disorder as well as those whose autistic disorder allows them to function at a level that is high enough that they would previously have been diagnosed with Asperger's syndrome.

The most severe forms of autistic spectrum disorder are extremely rare, affecting only 0.3 to 0.6% of children (Maughan, Iervolino, & Collishaw, 2005). When higher functioning individuals in the spectrum are included, the prevalence rates range from 0.42 to 1.21% (Norbury & Sparks, 2013). For example, a large study conducted by the Centers for Disease Control and Prevention found that, when both low and high functioning youth are included, about one in 88 children (1.1%) showed autistic spectrum disorder (Baio, 2012). Boys are four times more likely than girls to be diagnosed with ASD and non-Hispanic European Americans are more likely than other racial/ethnic groups to meet ASD criteria (Baio, 2012). Although there has been a great deal of media coverage about an "alarming" increase in cases of autistic spectrum disorder, the prevalence has actually risen very little, if at all (Norbury & Sparks, 2013). The perception of a dramatic increase is probably traceable to the change in diagnostic criteria (i.e., combining Asperger's syndrome and autistic disorder in the spectrum), greater public awareness, and increased screenings of youth for ASD (Deisinger, Burkhardt, Wahlberg, Rotatori, & Obiakor, 2012). The fact is that autistic spectrum disorder is far less common than other childhood disorders such as ADHD and oppositional defiant disorder. For an interesting perspective on the sociocultural context of autistic spectrum disorder, such as how language and social skills are valued differently across the world, see Norbury and Sparks' (2013) discussion of whether higher functioning forms of ASD are really disorders or just a variation in human characteristics.

Pediatric Health Problems

Increasingly, clinical child psychologists have been involved in helping understand and treat mental health problems that are related to physical illness in children and adolescents (see Chapter 12, "Health Psychology"). Known as *pediatric psychologists*, these professionals are usually trained as clinical psychologists and receive specialized training in pediatric health problems during graduate school, on internship, and/or on a postdoctoral fellowship. Pediatric psychologists deal with mental health problems associated with a wide array of physical conditions, such as: (a) pediatric asthma, (b) cystic fibrosis, (c) childhood diabetes, (d) sickle cell disease and hemophilia, (e) pediatric oncology (cancer), (f) HIV/AIDS in children and adolescents, (g) pediatric abdominal disorders, and (h) childhood obesity (Roberts & Steele, 2009).

Pediatric psychologists are able to treat the mental health problems related to physical illness, but they are also committed to the prevention of such problems and the promotion of health (Wilson & Lawman, 2009). They often work in hospitals as part of interdisciplinary teams that include pediatricians, medical specialists, pediatric nurses, and social workers. More information on pediatric psychology is available from APA Division 54 (Society of Pediatric Psychology).

A Clinical Case

The disorders we have described might seem abstract and categorical, but the real children encountered by clinical child psychologists present problems that do not always fit neatly into diagnostic categories and for whom clinical assessment data are not always clear. Consider the case of "Megan," for example (Weisz, 2004):

Megan is 13 years old, and she is miserable. She lives with her mother, father, and younger sister. She alternates between seeming depressed and seeming furious with the world. Her grades have plummeted to such an extent that a teacher contacted her parents to express concern. Megan is withdrawn and sullen at home and resents it when her parents try to help her with homework. Recently, she told her mother, "When I'm at home, I feel like a prisoner. All I ever do is work."

Megan's interactions away from home are not much better. She wears black clothes and black lipstick constantly and no longer has any friends. She has recently gained a lot of weight (largely due to late-night snacking), and she skips gym class because she does not want her peers to see how "fat" she is. She is embarrassed by her appearance and feels that her life is "hopeless."

Although Megan has always seemed to be a bit of a pessimist, this most recent bout of depression started when she was not invited to a social event that a number of her friends were having. She became increasingly withdrawn from her friends and in a fit of sobbing, informed her mother that "no one likes me anymore. I'm an outcast."

Although she has not voiced any suicidal ideation directly, Megan has become fascinated by famous people who committed suicide. Her family is worried sick about Megan, and her little sister even asked recently "What's wrong with Megan?"

Given their concerns, Megan's parents take her to a local child psychologist, who uses a wide array of assessment techniques to confirm the diagnosis of depression. The therapist initiates cognitive-behavioral treatment for depression, which can be provided in individual or group sessions. Since Megan is showing negative cognitions, vegetative signs, and family and social stressors, a comprehensive CBT program was selected.

Through therapy, Megan learns to identify her feelings, to understand where they develop, and to identify the consequences of different emotions. The therapist also helps Megan to identify cognitions (i.e., thoughts) that are associated with feeling bad. Figure 11.4 shows the

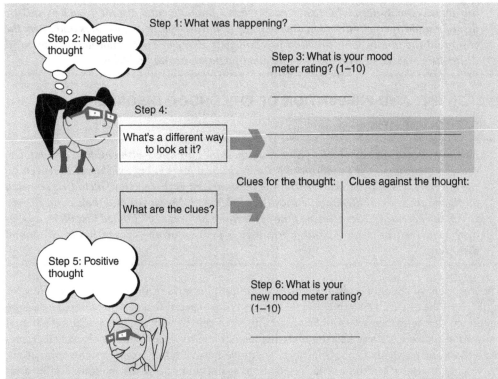

FIGURE 11.4 Cognitive Restructuring Form
Source: Stark, K. D., Hargrave, J., Sander, J., Custer, G., Schnoebelen, S., et al (2006). Treatment of childhood depression: The ACTION treatment program. In P. C. Kendall (Ed.), *Child and adolescent therapy* (3rd ed., p. 204). New York, NY: Guilford.

type of cognitive restructuring form that Megan used to understand the connections between her thoughts and her feelings (Stark et al., 2006). The therapist also helps Megan to identify activities that used to be rewarding to her (e.g., listening to music, reading novels, going to a movie). Megan is helped to see that she can increase these pleasurable activities in order to help elevate her mood. Megan decides that she will "reward" herself with 30-minutes of music each day that she follows a healthy eating and exercise plan.

The therapist also includes Megan's parents in the treatment. Not only do the parents become informed about the skills that Megan has been learning, but they are also invited to engage in these behaviors themselves. For example, Megan and her parents used problem-solving skills to think of ways to help Megan join the family for dinner. Together they generated a number of possible solutions and chose one to try that they all believed would work.

Over the course of treatment, Megan's symptoms of depression decrease and her positive interactions with her family and peers increase. Although no one believes that Megan is "cured" forever, she feels that it is easier to talk with her parents and to use her problem-solving skills in situations that she finds challenging. Likewise, her parents have implemented their new problem-solving skills in order to help their relationship with Megan. Megan and her parents seem to have a renewed sense of hope for the future (Weisz, 2004).

SECTION SUMMARY

Clinically derived classification systems and empirically derived systems are used with children as well as adults. The primary example of a clinically derived system is the DSM, and the most common example of an empirically derived system for children is the ASEBA. Among the many types of disorders in children, ADHD, ODD, and CD are considered examples of externalizing disorders, largely because the behavioral manifestations are external to the child (thereby more noticeable to others, such as parents and teachers). Depressive disorder and anxiety disorders are considered internalizing disorders because the experience is largely within the child's own subjective experience, and mild forms of these disorders are not necessarily noticeable to others. Pervasive developmental disorders, such as autistic disorder and Asperger's disorder, are regarded as autism spectrum disorders and affect the child and the family. Clinical child psychologists also work with emotional/behavioral difficulties associated with asthma and other pediatric health problems.

TREATMENT AND PREVENTION OF CHILDHOOD DISORDERS

SECTION PREVIEW

Different types of psychological and drug therapies are used with children and adolescents, depending on the emotional/behavioral problems being exhibited. Research on the effectiveness of these interventions is summarized in this section, including research on the importance of the therapeutic alliance between therapists and their child clients. Given the potentially devastating long-term consequences of childhood disorders, a great deal of interest in clinical child psychology is focused on the prevention of childhood disorders.

The treatment of childhood disorders differs in important ways from clinical interventions for adults. As is the case with assessment, child therapy poses a special challenge for clinicians because children do not refer themselves for help, and thus, their contact with a therapist requires parental motivation and cooperation. Like the adult therapies discussed earlier in this book, child therapies can be based on psychodynamic, behavioral, cognitive-behavioral, or family-systems approaches. We will not review each of those broad orientations again, but rather focus on more specific interventions that research suggests work best.

Psychological Treatments for Disorders in Children and Adolescents

As has been the case for adult forms of psychotherapy, many task forces, outcome studies, reviews, and meta-analyses have tried to establish which psychological treatments are most effective in helping children and adolescents with internalizing and externalizing disorders and other emotional and behavioral problems (e.g. Chambless & Ollendick, 2001; Harvey & Taylor, 2010; LaGreca, Silverman, & Lochman, 2009; Reynolds, Wilson, Austin, & Hooper, 2012; Silverman & Hinshaw, 2008; Weisz, 2004; Weisz, Doss, & Hawley, 2005; Weisz, Sandler, Durlak, & Anton, 2005). These outcome summaries of child therapy have found that, overall, treatment of children's disorders is beneficial, showing effect sizes ranging from 0.7 to 0.8. These effect sizes are comparable to those found in analyses of adult treatment. Further, the positive outcomes following child treatment tend to be long-lasting and are associated with increased well-being in youthful clients (Kendall, 2012; Weisz, Ng, Rutt, Lau, & Masland, 2013).

Some of these therapies are better than others, though. The ones whose effectiveness in treating children's and adolescents' mental health problems have been "well established" by research evidence are displayed in Table 11.5. As you can see, the majority of these treatments fall into the behavioral, cognitive-behavioral, and family domains.

As with adult therapy, there is intense interest in disseminating these research findings to clinicians in the community and in helping them implement the treatments (Southam-Gerow, Rodriguez, Chorpita, & Daleiden, 2012). These dissemination efforts are aided by the Society of Clinical Child and Adolescent Psychology (Division 53 of APA), whose web site (www.effective-childtherapy.com) for professionals and parents lists evidence-based treatments and also provides free training sessions for practitioners.

Pharmacological Interventions

Many child and adolescent clients are treated with prescription drugs in addition to, or instead of, psychotherapy. For example, stimulant drugs such as methylphenidate (Ritalin, Concerta, Metadate) and amphetamine (Adderall) are prescribed routinely for ADHD (Sinacola & Peters-Strickland, 2012). Hundreds of studies have shown that stimulant medication dramatically improves the behavior of these children (Nigg, 2013). They remain seated longer, finish more academic work, give correct answers more often, and show improved social interactions with peers, parents, and teachers.

TABLE 11.5 Evidence-Based Treatments for Children and Adolescents (Selected)

Psychological Treatment	Diagnosis or Clinical Problem
Behavior Therapy (Lovaas Method)	Severe forms of Autistic Spectrum Disorder
Behavioral Classroom Management	Attention Deficit/Hyperactivity Disorder
Behavioral Parent Management Training	Oppositional Defiant Disorder/Conduct Disorder
Behavioral Parent Training	Attention Deficit/Hyperactivity Disorder
Behavioral Peer Interventions	Attention Deficit/Hyperactivity Disorder
Family Therapy for Anorexia	Anorexia
Family Therapy (Functional Family Therapy)	Adolescent Substance Abuse
Family Therapy (Multidimensional Family Therapy)	Adolescent Substance Abuse
Interpersonal Therapy	Adolescent Depression
Cognitive Behavioral Therapy (Child Group, Plus Parent Component)	Child Depression
Cognitive Behavioral Therapy (Group, Child/Adolescent Only)	Child/Adolescent Depression
Cognitive Behavioral Therapy (Group)	Adolescent Substance Abuse
Cognitive Behavioral Therapy (Trauma Focused CBT)	Child/Adolescent Post-Traumatic Stress Disorder

Source: Based on data from http://effectivechildtherapy.com/.

Nevertheless, controversy continues to surround the use of medication for children's ADHD and other disorders. Peter Breggin, a psychiatrist, is one of the strongest critics of prescribing drugs for children's emotional or behavioral problems. He has summarized his position in books such as *Talking Back to Ritalin: What Doctors Aren't Telling You about Stimulants for Children* (2001), *The War against Children: How the Drugs, Programs, and Theories of the Psychiatric Establishment Are Threatening America's Children with a Medical "Cure" for Violence* (Breggin & Breggin, 1994), and *Medication Madness: The Role of Psychiatric Drugs in Cases of Violence, Suicide, and Crime* (Breggin, 2009). Of particular concern to Breggin is what he sees as the overuse of medication for behaviors that are not necessarily abnormal or that are only abnormal in particular cultures. He fears that we are trying to medicate the childhood out of children. Indeed, a number of medications are contraindicated for children and adolescents or should be prescribed only with extreme caution (Brown, Carpenter, & Simerly, 2005; see Table 11.6).

TABLE 11.6 Medications with Potentially Harmful Side Effects in Children and Adolescents

Medication	Use	Potential Side Effects
Amitriptyline/Elavil Etrafon Limbitrol Triavil	Depression	Can result in cardiac difficulties
Clomipramine/Anafranil	Depression and obsessive-compulsive disorder	Associated with seizures as well as less severe side effects
Clozapine/Clozaril	Schizophrenia	Can cause a potentially fatal drop in bone marrow and white blood cell counts, and seizures
Desipramine/Norpramin	Anxiety disorders, depression, ADHD	Has been associated with cardiac complications leading to death in rare cases
Imipramine/Tofranil	Anxiety disorders, depression, and ADHD	Has been associated with cardiac complications leading to death in rare cases
Nortriptyline/Aventyl Pamelor	ADHD	Can cause cardiac complications and low blood pressure, as well as less severe side effects
Pemoline/Cylert	ADHD	Has been associated with liver failure and other side effects

Sources: Adapted from Brown, R. T., Carpenter, L. A., & Simerly, E. (2005). Mental health medications for children: A primer. New York, NY: Guilford. Richmond, T. K., & Rosen, D. S. (2005). The treatment of adolescent depression in the era of the black box warning. *Current Opinion in Pediatrics, 17,* 466–472.

The most effective treatments for most childhood problems involve cognitive-behavioral or behavioral methods.   *Source:* Lisa F. Young/Shutterstock

The Therapeutic Alliance in Child Therapy

Clinical child researchers are interested not only in determining which treatments are best for which childhood and adolescent problems, but also in exploring common or nonspecific factors that operate to help make those treatments effective. As in adult psychotherapy, researchers want to know if the therapeutic alliance between therapists and their child clients (and with the children's parents) can help strengthen the effectiveness of treatment. This research has lagged behind similar research with adults, but a number of trends are already evident. For example, a strong therapeutic alliance between parents and therapists is associated with fewer canceled appointments, fewer instances of failing to appear for treatment appointments, and greater participation by the family in the therapy sessions (Hawley & Weisz, 2005).

Based on a meta-analysis of 49 treatment studies for child and adolescent emotional/behavioral problems, the following characteristics were found to be related to increased improvement in child and adolescent functioning (Karver, Handelsman, Fields, & Bickman 2005):

- Therapeutic alliance with the parent
- Counselor interpersonal skills
- Therapist direct influence skills
- Child's willingness to participate in treatment
- Parent's willingness to participate in treatment
- Youth participation in treatment
- Parent participation in treatment
- Positive feelings toward the therapist.

A more recent meta-analysis of alliance in child and adolescent therapy also found significant relationships between strong therapeutic alliance and positive outcomes of therapy (Shirk & Karver, 2011). But although a stronger alliance in youth treatment is associated with greater improvements in clients' functioning, the therapeutic alliance may be more meaningful in some treatments than in others. For example, one study of the treatment of troubled adolescents found that the therapeutic alliance was not influential in the effectiveness of cognitive-behavioral treatment but was strongly predictive of success in family therapy (Hogue, Dauber, Stambaugh, Cecero, & Liddle, 2006). Specifically, stronger alliance with family therapists was related to adolescents' decrease in drug use and externalizing behavior problems. This type of research into the specificity of alliance effects is likely to help clarify some of the debate about the importance of specific techniques versus strong relationship skills.

Prevention of Childhood Disorders

No discussion of the treatment of children's emotional/behavioral problems would be complete without a discussion of prevention. A great deal of work has been completed in trying to prevent disorders from occurring in children and adolescents (Institute of Medicine, 2009). A number of effective strategies have been established through prevention programs, including the following:

- Improving parent–child attachment in order to prevent a myriad of emotional/behavioral problems (Van Zeijl et al., 2006).
- Using a television series to teach parents about positive parenting skills in order to increase compliance and decrease aggression in children (Sanders & Murphy-Brennan, 2010).
- Using cognitive-behavioral techniques to provide a primary prevention program to decrease the likelihood of anxiety problems in children (Barrett, Farrell, Ollendick, & Dadds, 2006).
- Educating parents and adolescents about interpersonal skills and cognitive strategies associated with the prevention of depression in adolescents (Shochet et al., 2001).
- Strengthening communication and parental monitoring in African American families in order to prevent adolescents' risky behavior, such as drinking alcohol, using illicit drugs, and having unprotected sex (Brody et al., 2006).
- Bullying can be decreased significantly with large-scale anti bullying programs that help students learn about the problem, develop more empathy for others, and develop strategies to help victims of bullying (Karna et al., 2011).
- Providing additional resources and extensive services to impoverished families and communities in order to prevent a whole host of emotional/behavioral problems in children and adolescents (Brotman et al., 2003).

Ironically, one of the most widely used prevention programs is also one of the least effective. The Drug Abuse Resistance Education (DARE) program is often run by law enforcement groups with the goal of demonstrating the negative consequences of alcohol and drug abuse (West & O'Neal, 2004). The program is used in all 50 states and in a large majority of school districts (West & O'Neal, 2004). Unfortunately, a wealth of well-controlled, long-term studies has shown that the DARE program is not effective in preventing the use of alcohol and drugs. Specifically, when comparing youth who did or did not participate in the DARE program, no differences were found in attitudes toward drugs, the use of drugs, or self-esteem (West & O'Neal, 2004). Other prevention programs, such as the Life Skills Training Program (Botvin & Griffin, 2004), have been shown to be effective in decreasing the likelihood that children will abuse substances, but unfortunately, those programs have not been adopted nearly as widely as the DARE program.

Another line of prevention-oriented research is related to the increasingly popular *positive psychology* movement (Duckworth, Steen, & Seligman, 2005). Specifically, many clinical child psychologists are interested in finding ways to increase *resilience* in children, that is, in finding ways to increase protective factors so as to decrease the likelihood of developing emotional/behavioral problems in children at risk for those problems (Barakat, Pulgaron, & Daniel, 2009; Sapienza & Masten, 2011; Yoshikawa, Aber, & Beardslee 2012).

SECTION SUMMARY

The most effective treatments for childhood disorders generally fall into the cognitive-behavioral, behavioral, and family domains. Although drug treatments can help with some childhood disorders, they also have many drawbacks. There is growing evidence of the importance of the therapeutic alliance in working with children and their families. In addition to the focus on treating problems once they occur, many clinical child psychologists have dedicated their lives to finding ways to prevent childhood problems from ever occurring.

THE FUTURE OF CLINICAL CHILD PSYCHOLOGY

SECTION PREVIEW

This section highlights four factors that are particularly relevant for the future of clinical child psychology: diversity and multiculturalism; increasing access to mental health care; the rise of interdisciplinary research and practice; and the role that technology plays in the mental health of children and adolescents.

Although advances in clinical child psychology have lagged several decades behind developments in adult clinical psychology, the child field is catching up rapidly. In addition to the trends that have already been mentioned elsewhere in relation to clinical psychology in general (e.g., increasing focus on evidence-based assessment and treatment, dissemination of treatments that work so that they can be implemented in the community), a number of other trends are likely to characterize the future of clinical child psychology.

Diversity and Multiculturalism

Because most existing psychological treatments tend to be less effective for youth from single-parent homes, disadvantaged backgrounds, and ethnic minority backgrounds (Huey & Polo, 2010), researchers in clinical child psychology will be seeking to tailor psychological treatments in ways that make them more relevant for youth and families from a wide variety of backgrounds (Yasui & Dishion, 2007). For example, the Familias Unidas program is a family-centered, ecologically and developmentally relevant intervention that works to reduce emotional/behavioral problems in Hispanic/Latino/Latina adolescents (Coatsworth, Pantin, & Szapocznik, 2002). Other efforts have included therapist training in culturally competent practices, altering therapy content to be more culturally sensitive, and matching therapists and clients on culturally meaningful variables (Huey & Polo, 2010). However, when culturally enhanced evidence-based treatments are compared with standard evidence-based treatments for youth, few differences have emerged at outcome (e.g., Huey & Polo, 2010). These findings are in contrast to the effects of culturally adapted treatments for adults, which have shown to be more effective than standard versions for at least some sub groups of clients (Castro, Barrera, & Steiker, 2010). Thus, there is still a way to go in order to make evidence-based treatments even more helpful for culturally diverse young clients.

There is also increasing interest in the commonalities and differences among children and adolescents in various countries around the world. For example, measures from the ASEBA have been translated into 74 languages and have been used in research in 67 different cultures, resulting in over 6,000 publications (Achenbach & Rescorla, 2007; Rescorla et al., 2007). These studies have found that there are more similarities than differences in the psychological functioning and psychological problems of children and adolescents around the globe (Achenbach & Rescorla, 2007; Rescorla et al., 2011) (See Figure 11.5). Perhaps the greater commonalities across youth from different cultures can help us understand the consistency seen in the results of evidence-based treatments across different multicultural groups of youngsters within the United States. Unlike the patterns that are relatively well understood with adult populations, clinical child psychologists still need to ascertain which specific variables influence effective treatment of children from different cultures.

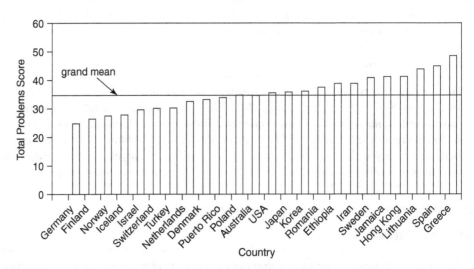

FIGURE 11.5 Youth Self-Report Total Problems Scores in 24 Countries (*N* = 27,206).
Source: Rescorla, L., Achenbach, T. M., Ivanova, M. Y., Dumenci, L., Almqvist, F., et al. (2007). Epidemiological comparisons of problems and positive qualities reported by adolescents in 24 countries. *Journal of Consulting and Clinical Psychology, 75*, 351–358.

Overall, there is a great deal of interest in bringing culturally competent practices to clinical child psychology—both within the United States and around the world (Huey & Polo, 2012; Rescorla et al., 2011; Yoshikawa, Aber, & Beardslee, 2012). Along with the focus on finding more effective treatments for mental health problems in youth, these trends promise to help improve the well-being of children and adolescents both in the short term and the long term.

Access to Care

It appears that as many as 25% of children and adolescents who meet criteria for a psychiatric disorder have never had access to outpatient mental health services (Jensen et al., 2011; Storch & Crisp, 2004). This pattern is particularly true for youth from racial/ethnic minority groups and from impoverished backgrounds (Huey & Polo, 2012). For example, African American parents reported experiencing, or at least perceiving, greater barriers in accessing mental health for themselves and/or their children when compared to European American parents (Thurston & Phares, 2008). Within the Hispanic/Latino/Latina community, unmet need for services appears to be due to a variety of factors, including failure to recognize psychological symptoms, and the perception of a stigma associated with seeking mental health services (Chavez, Shrout, Alegria, Lapatin, & Canino, 2010).

Although we do not yet fully understand all the factors underlying the disparity in service access between ethnic/racial minority and majority groups, clinical child psychologists will be increasingly involved in efforts to make high-quality mental health care services more available to everyone. As with adults, however, these efforts will be complicated by disparities in health care funding across the United States, by reliance on managed care for both physical health and mental health needs, and by the limited funding provided to community mental health centers. One step in the right direction appears to be the delivery of evidence-based treatment programs in the school setting (Adelman & Taylor, 2009). These programs make it possible for youngsters to be treated on a regular basis without the need to rely on (sometimes unmotivated) parents to make appointments and transport children to therapy sessions. On the other hand, when therapy is delivered at school, it may be more difficult to draw parents into the treatment process (Adelman & Taylor, 2009). In addition, parents appear to prefer the idea of taking their child to a private psychologist rather than a psychologist who works in the school system (Raviv, Raviv, Propper, & Fink, 2003). Thus, alternative methods of delivery of services are still being sought.

Interdisciplinary Approaches to Research and Practice

As in clinical psychology generally, the field of clinical child psychology is moving toward an increasingly interdisciplinary view of children's functioning, with special attention to the many interconnections among biological/genetic, cognitive, social, behavioral, and environmental influences on children's functioning, problems, and well-being. For example, one volume in a three-volume book series called *Developmental Psychopathology* was dedicated solely to developmental neuroscience (Cicchetti & Cohen, 2006). Advances in genomics (McGuffin, 2004), genetics (Plomin & Kovas, 2005), behavioral genetics (Moffitt & Caspi, 2007), social neuroscience (Cacioppo, 2006), cognitive-affective neuroscience (Stein, 2006), and research on cortisol reactivity (Davies, Sturge-Apple, Cicchetti, & Cummings, 2007) have all converged toward interdisciplinary understandings of childhood psychopathology. In addition, efforts are being made to identify potential common causes of disorders within the neurodevelopmental arena, such as genetic influences (Beauchaine & Gatzke-Koop, 2013), behavioral inhibition (Kagan, 2013), and emotional dysregulation (Cole, Hall, & Hajal, 2013). Progress in these efforts will depend on cooperation among scientists from various disciplines, including, of course, clinical psychologists.

The cooperation of professionals from many disciplines will be just as important in the successful treatment of children and adolescents. These professionals include teachers, pediatricians, social workers, guidance counselors, child psychiatrists, psychiatric nurses, and the like, and clinical psychologists will increasingly find themselves learning to be comfortable working on interdisciplinary teams (Kazak et al., 2010). In fact, increasing efforts are being made to integrate behavioral health services (such as therapy for mental health issues) into primary care settings, such as pediatricians' offices (Vogel, Kirkpatrick, Collings, Cederna-Meko, & Grey, 2012). Known as *integrated primary care* (IPC), offering mental health services in a primary care setting is thought to improve children's and adolescents' access to the mental health services that they need.

Technology and Youth Mental Health

Technology has dramatically changed the lives of children and adolescents over the last three decades. Surveys suggest that 95% of adolescents aged 12 to 17 use the Internet routinely and 80% of them use social media sites such as Facebook frequently (DeAngelis, 2011). About 87% of 14- to 17-year-olds have cell phones, as do 57% of those aged 12 to 13. A growing number have smart phones (DeAngelis, 2011) that allow them to text, tweet, videochat, and surf the web.

What are the effects of all this technology, and how might it affect the problems faced by clinical child psychologists? What we know so far suggests a mix of outcomes. On the negative side are a number of problems that have been associated with children's and adolescents' use of technology. For example, cyberbullying and sexual exploitation of youth via the internet have been of great concern in recent years. Thankfully these problems are relatively uncommon; only 10% of youth report being bullied online (Ybarra, Boyd, Korchmaros, & Oppenheim, 2012) and only 3.1% report being harassed or receiving unwanted sexual solicitation online (Ybarra, Espelage, & Mitchell, 2007). But even these relatively small numbers are cause for concern because of the potential negative psychological effects, which can range from anxiety and depression to sexual abuse and suicide.

On the positive side, technology has been harnessed to help facilitate children's and adolescents' mental health—both in their everyday lives as well as through improved psychological treatments. For example, texting and social media can help adolescents feel more connected to their friends, and connectedness has been associated with well-being (Valkenburg & Peter, 2009). As with face-to-face interactions, however, young people tend to want to stay connected to their friends who are upbeat and may distance themselves from those who share too many self-critical or negative messages, as in the case of depressed youth. Within the treatment domain, technology has been used to provide online evidence-based treatment to children and adolescents with anxiety disorders (Khanna & Kendall, 2010; Spence et al., 2011), to provide computer-based attention training in inattentive first-graders (Rabiner, Murray, Skinner, & Malone, 2010), and to provide live coaching of parenting skills via videoconferencing (Wade Oberjohn, Conaway, Osinska, & Bangert, 2011).

So though there may be dangers and problems associated with technological advances, those advances have also given child clinical psychologists additional ways to improve the well-being of youth. This trend promises to continue well into the future (DeAngelis, 2011).

SECTION SUMMARY

The field of clinical psychology is increasingly focused on the role of client diversity and on the impact of multiculturalism, and clinical child psychology is no exception. Efforts to increase access to mental health care, especially among impoverished and ethnic minority clients, will be of ever greater concern to clinical child psychologists, and research in the field will be characterized by the integration of various sciences (including biology, genomic studies, cognitive-affective neuroscience, and social neuroscience). The commitment to interdisciplinary research and practice bodes well for improving our understanding of the development, maintenance, and treatment of childhood disorders. Finally, technology can be part of increasing stressors in the lives of youth, but it can also be harnessed to help improve access to evidence-based treatments and prevention programs.

Chapter Summary

The longstanding focus of clinical psychologists on assessing and treating adults has changed over the last four decades to the point that clinical child psychologists have become a prominent subgroup in the field. Clinical psychologists have developed methods of classification, assessment, and intervention that are specialized for use with child and adolescent clients.

In dealing with these clients, clinical child psychologists pay special attention to referral issues, the context of behavior, developmental considerations, the nature of parent–child interactions, and the impact of childhood risk and protective factors.

Taking all these special considerations into account leads clinical child psychologists to ask assessment questions about child clients that they would usually not ask about adults and to use assessment methods (e.g., behavior rating scales, multiple informants during interviews, intelligence and achievement tests, and family and peer interaction measures) that are used less frequently with adult clients.

Unlike the clinically derived classification systems used with adults (which rely on the judgments of experts to determine diagnostic criteria), classification of childhood disorders has tended to emphasize empirically derived systems, which rely on statistical analyses of large amounts of data to determine the symptoms of given diagnostic categories. Empirically derived systems have identified two main types of childhood disorders: externalizing problems such as hyperactivity, aggression, and delinquency and internalizing problems such as depression, anxiety, and somatic problems. Other significant childhood problems include pervasive developmental disorders such as autism spectrum disorder.

Treatment of child clients poses special challenges because children and parents often have different perspectives about a child's behavior and because their presence in therapy requires parental motivation and cooperation. There are a number of evidence-based treatments to help reduce emotional/behavioral problems in children and adolescents, most of which are within the behavioral, cognitive-behavioral, and family domains. Psychoactive medications are being used increasingly to treat childhood disorders, but there are great concerns about the side effects of many medications. Rather than dealing with childhood disorders after the damage has been done, clinical child psychologists would prefer early, comprehensive, and long-term interventions designed to prevent these disorders. Future directions in clinical child psychology include a greater emphasis on diversity, multiculturalism, making mental health services more accessible to clients, interdisciplinary research that includes both biological and environmental factors in understanding the development and treatment of childhood disorders, interdisciplinary practice that helps bring multiple professionals together to help children, and the use of technology to improve the psychological functioning of youth.

Study Questions

1. List the ways in which working clinically with children is different from working with adults.
2. How is the context of children's behavior taken into consideration in evaluating and treating childhood disorders?
3. Provide two examples of developmental issues to consider when working with troubled children.
4. What is infant temperament? How is it related to development over the life span?
5. What are some of the major risk factors linked to emotional/behavioral problems in youth?
6. Discuss the ramifications of childhood physical abuse and childhood sexual abuse.
7. What are protective factors, and how are they associated with children's behavior?
8. What are the pros and cons of using the following assessment techniques: behavior rating scales, unstructured interviews, behavioral observations, and family interaction measures?
9. Describe a thorough assessment protocol for a child who is experiencing academic and behavioral problems in school.
10. What is a clinically derived system of classification? What is an empirically derived system of classification? How are these two systems similar and different?
11. What are the major symptoms of the following disorders: ADHD, ODD, CD, major depressive disorder, and separation anxiety disorder?
12. What points from the research literature did the clinical case of "Billy" (the boy in the grocery store) illustrate?
13. What are some of the evidence-based treatments for childhood disorders?
14. Describe the research findings related to the therapeutic alliance with children, adolescents, and families.
15. Describe a prevention program that works.

Web Sites

- APA Division 53 Society of Clinical Child and Adolescent Psychology https://www.clinicalchildpsychology.org/
- APA Division 54 Society of Pediatric Psychology: https://www.apadivisions.org/division-54/index.aspx
- List of effective child treatments from APA Division 53: https://effectivechildtherapy.com/
- List of effective child treatments from New York University Child Study Center: https://www.aboutourkids.org/
- Children's Defense Fund: https://www.childrensdefense.org/

MOVIES

Bully (2011): Recent documentary that shows actual footage of youth being bullied on busses and at school, with coverage of a funeral of a youngster who took his own life after severe bullying.

56 Up (2012): Documentary film series that shows actual footage of youth, beginning at 7 years old and followed-up every 7 years of their lives until the age of 56.

MEMOIRS

Beautiful Boy: A Father's Journey Through His Son's Addiction by David Sheff (2008; Boston, MA: Mariner Books). Superb account of a father trying to help his son, Nic, overcome addiction.

Tweak: Growing Up on Methamphetamines by Nic Sheff (2008; New York: Atheneum). The author gives his own account of his substance abuse, which was much more serious than his father realized when he wrote *Beautiful Boy*.

References

Achenbach, T. M. (1978). The Child Behavior Profile I: Boys aged 6–11. *Journal of Consulting and Clinical Psychology, 46*, 478–488.

Achenbach, T. M. (2008a). Assessment, diagnosis, nosology, and taxonomy of child and adolescent psychopathology. In M. Hersen & A. M. Gross (Eds.), *Handbook of clinical psychology (Vol. 2): Children and adolescents* (pp. 429–457). Hoboken, NJ: Wiley.

Achenbach, T. M. (2008b). Multicultural perspectives on developmental psychopathology. In J. J. Hudziak (Ed.), *Developmental psychopathology and wellness: Genetic and environmental influences* (pp. 23–47). Arlington, VA: American Psychiatric Publishing.

Achenbach, T. M., & Edelbrock, C. S. (1978). The classification of child psychopathology: A review and analysis of empirical efforts. *Psychological Bulletin, 85*, 1275–1301.

Achenbach, T. M., & Edelbrock, C. S. (1981). Behavioral problems and competencies reported by parents of normal and disturbed children aged four to sixteen. *Monographs of the Society for Research in Child Development, 46* (Serial No. 188).

Achenbach, T. M., & Rescorla, L. A. (2001). *Manual for the Achenbach System of Empirically Based Assessment (ASEBA) school-age forms and profiles.* Burlington, VT: University of Vermont, Research Center for Children, Youth, and Families.

Adelman, H. S., & Taylor, L. (2009). *Mental health in schools: Engaging learners, preventing problems, and improving schools.* Thousand Oaks, CA: Corwin Press.

American Psychiatric Association. (1998). *DSM-IV sourcebook* (Vol. 4). Washington, DC: Author.

American Psychiatric Association. (2000). *Diagnostic and statistical manual of mental disorders-fourth edition; text revision (DSM-IV-TR).* Washington, DC: Author.

American Psychiatric Association. (2013). *Diagnostic and statistical manual of mental disorders-fifth edition (DSM-5).* Washington, DC: Author.

Baio, J. (2012). *Prevalence of autism spectrum disorders: Autism and developmental disabilities monitoring network.* Atlanta, GA: Centers for Disease Control and Prevention.

Barakat, L. P., Pulgaron, E. R., & Daniel, L. C. (2009). Positive psychology in pediatric psychology. In M. C. Roberts & R. G. Steele (Eds.), *Handbook of pediatric psychology* (4th ed., pp. 763–773). New York, NY: Guilford.

Barkley, R. A., Knouse, L. E., & Murphy, K. R. (2011). Correspondence and disparity in the self and other ratings of current and childhood ADHD symptoms and impairment in adults with ADHD. *Psychological Assessment, 23*, 437–446.

Barrett, P. M., Farrell, L. J., Ollendick, T. H., & Dadds, M. (2006). Long-term outcomes of an Australian universal prevention trial of anxiety and depression symptoms in children and youth: An evaluation of the Friends Program. *Journal of Clinical Child and Adolescent Psychology, 35*, 403–411.

Beauchaine, T. P., & Gatzke-Kopp, L. (2013). Genetic and environmental influences on behavior. In T. P. Beauchaine & S. P. Hinshaw (Eds.), *Child and adolescent psychopathology* (2nd ed., pp. 111–140). Hoboken, NJ: Wiley.

Beauchaine, T. P., & Hinshaw, S. P. (Eds.). (2013). *Child and adolescent psychopathology* (2nd ed.). Hoboken, NJ: Wiley.

Bellack, L. (1954). *The thematic apperception test and the children's apperception test in clinical use.* New York, NY: Grune and Straton.

Bijttebier, P., & Roeyers, H. (2009). Temperament and vulnerability to psychopathology: Introduction to the special issue. *Journal of Abnormal Child Psychology, 37*, 305–308.

Bonanno, G. A., Westphal, M., & Mancini, A. D. (2011). Resilience to loss and potential trauma. *Annual Review of Clinical Psychology, 7*, 511–535.

Botvin, G. J., & Griffin, K. W. (2004). Life skills training: Empirical findings and future directions. *Journal of Primary Prevention, 25*, 211–232.

Breggin, P. (2009). *Medication madness: The role of psychiatric drugs in cases of violence, suicide, and crime.* New York, NY: St. Martin's Press.

Breggin, P. R. (2001). *Talking back to Ritalin: What doctors aren't telling you about stimulants for children.* Monroe, ME: Common Courage Press.

Breggin, P. R., & Breggin, G. R. (1994). *The war against children: How the drugs, programs, and theories of the psychiatric establishment are threatening America's children with a medical "cure" for violence.* New York, NY: St. Martin's Press.

Brody, G. H., Murry, V. M., Gerrard, M., Gibbons, F. X., McNair, L., et al. (2006). The Strong African American Families Program: Prevention of youths' high-risk behavior and a test of a model of change. *Journal of Family Psychology, 20*, 1–11.

Brotman, L. M., Klein, R. G., Kamboukos, D., Brown, E. J., Coard, S. I., et al. Preventive intervention for urban, low-income preschoolers at familial risk for conduct problems: A randomized pilot study. *Journal of Clinical Child and Adolescent Psychology, 32*, 246–257.

Brown, R. T., Carpenter, L. A., & Simerly, E. (2005). *Mental health medications for children: A primer.* New York, NY: Guilford.

Buck, J. N. (1948). The H-T-P technique: A qualitative and quantitative scoring manual. *Journal of Clinical Psychology, 4*, 319–396.

Cacioppo, J. T. (2006). Social neuroscience. *American Journal of Psychology, 119*, 664–668.

Calkins, S. D., & Degnan, K. A. (2006). Temperament in early development. In R. T. Ammerman (Ed.), *Comprehensive handbook of personality and psychopathology* (Vol. 3, pp. 64–84). Hoboken, NJ: Wiley.

Cashel, M. L. (2002). Child and adolescent psychological assessment: Current clinical practices and the impact of managed care. *Professional Psychology: Research and Practice, 33*, 446–453.

Caspi, A., Harrington, H., Milne, B., Amell, J. W., Theodore, R. F., et al. (2003). Children's behavioral styles at age 3 are linked to their adult personality traits at age 26. *Journal of Personality, 71*, 495–513.

Castro, F. G., Barrera, M., & Steiker, L. K. H. (2010). Issues and challenges in the design of culturally adapted evidence-based interventions. *Annual Review of Clinical Psychology, 6*, 213–239.

Chambless, D. L., & Ollendick, T. H. (2001). Empirically supported psychological treatments. *Annual Review of Psychology, 52*, 685–716.

Chavez, L. M., Shrout, P. E., Alegria, M., Lapatin, S., & Canino, G. (2010). Ethnic differences in perceived impairment and need for care. *Journal of Abnormal Child Psychology, 38*, 1165–1177.

Children's Defense Fund (2012). *The state of America's children handbook.* Washington, DC: Children's Defense Fund.

Cicchetti, D. (2008). A multiple-levels-of-analysis perspective on research in development and psychopathology. In T. P. Beauchaine & S. P. Hinshaw (Eds.), *Child and adolescent psychopathology* (pp. 27–57). Hoboken, NJ: Wiley.

Cicchetti, D., & Curtis, J. W. (2006). The developing brain and neuroplasticity: Implications for normality, psychopathology, and resilience. In D. Cicchetti & J. W. Curtis (Eds.), *Developmental psychopathology, Vol 2: Developmental neuroscience* (2nd ed., pp. 1–64). Hoboken, NJ: Wiley.

Cicchetti, D., & Rogosch, F. A. (2012). Gene X environment interaction and resilience: Effects of child maltreatment and serotonin, corticotropin releasing hormone, dopamine, and oxytocin genes. *Development and Psychopathology, 24*, 411–427.

Coatsworth, J. D., Pantin, H., & Szapocznik, J. (2002). Familias unidas: A family-centered ecodevelopmental intervention to reduce risk for problem behavior among Hispanic adolescents. *Clinical Child and Family Psychology Review, 5*, 113–132.

Cole, P. M., Hall, S. E., & Hajal, N. J. (2013). Emotion dysregulation as a risk factor for psychopathology. In T. P. Beauchaine & S. P. Hinshaw (Eds.), *Child and adolescent psychopathology* (2nd ed., pp. 341–373). Hoboken, NJ: Wiley.

Costello, E. J., Copeland, W., & Angold, A. (2011). Trends in psychopathology across the adolescent years: What changes when children become adolescents, and when adolescents become adults? *Journal of Child Psychology and Psychiatry, 52*, 1015–1025.

Davies, P. T., Martin, M. J., & Cicchetti, D. (2012). Delineating the sequelae of destructive and constructive interparental conflict for children within an evolutionary framework. *Developmental Psychology, 48*, 939–955.

Davies, P. T., Sturge-Apple, M. L., Cicchetti, D., & Cummings, E. M. (2007). The role of child adrenocortical functioning in pathways between interparental conflict and child maladjustment. *Developmental Psychology, 43*, 918–930.

Davydov, D. M., Stewart, R., Ritchie, K., & Chaudieu, I. (2010). Resilience and mental health. *Clinical Psychology Review, 30*, 479–495.

DeAngelis, T. (2011). Is technology ruining our kids? *Monitor on Psychology, 42*, 63–64.

DeBoard-Lucas, R. L., Fosco, G. M., Raynor, S. R., & Grych, J. H. (2010). Interparental conflict in context: Exploring relations between parenting processes and children's conflict appraisals. *Journal of Clinical Child and Adolescent Psychology, 39*, 163–175.

Deisinger, J., Burkhardt, S., Wahlberg, T., Rotatori, A. F., & Oblakor, F. E. (2012). *Autism spectrum disorders: Inclusive community for the 21st century.* Charlotte, NC: Information Age Publishing.

Duckworth, A. L., Steen, T. A., & Seligman, M. E. P. (2005). Positive psychology in clinical practice. *Annual Review of Clinical Psychology, 1*, 629–651.

Eisen, A. R., Sussman, J. M., Schmidt, T., Mason, L., Hausier, L. A., et al. (2011). Separation anxiety disorder. In D. McKay & E. A. Storch (Eds.), *Handbook of child and adolescent anxiety disorders* (pp. 245–259). New York, NY: Springer.

Eyberg, S. M., Nelson, M. M., & Boggs, S. R. (2008). Evidence-based psychosocial treatments for children and adolescents with disruptive behavior. *Journal of Clinical Child and Adolescent Psychology, 37*, 215–237.

Finkelhor, D. (2011). Prevalence of child victimization, abuse, crime, and violence exposure. In J. W. White, M. P. Koss, & A. E. Kazdin (Eds.), *Violence against women and children* (Vol.1, pp. 9–29). Washington, DC: American Psychological Association.

Finkelhor, D., Turner, H., Omrod, R., & Hamby, S. L. (2009). Violence, abuse, and crime exposure in a national sample of children and youth. *Pediatrics, 124*, 1411–1423.

Forgatch, M. S., & Patterson, G. R. (2010). Parent management training–Oregon model: An intervention for antisocial behavior in children and adolescents. In J. R. Weisz & A. E. Kazdin (Eds.), *Evidence-based psychotherapies for children and adolescents* (2nd ed., pp. 159–178). New York, NY: Guilford.

Frick, P. J., Kamphaus, R. W., & Barry, C. T. (2009). *Clinical assessment of child and adolescent personality and behavior* (3rd ed.). New York, NY: Springer-Verlag.

Frick, P. J., & Nigg, J. T. (2012). Current issues in the diagnosis of attention deficit hyperactivity disorder, oppositional defiant disorder, and conduct disorder. *Annual Review of Clinical Psychology, 8*, 77–107.

Garber, J. (1984). Classification of childhood psychopathology: A developmental perspective. *Child Development, 55*, 30–48.

Garber, J., & Weersing, V. R. (2010). Comorbidity of anxiety and depression in youth: Implications for treatment and prevention. *Clinical Psychology: Science and Practice, 17* 293–306.

Gelfand, D. M., & Peterson, L. (1985). *Child development and psychopathology.* Beverly Hills, CA: Sage.

Gittelman, R. (1980). The role of tests for differential diagnosis in child psychiatry. *Journal of the American Academy of Child Psychiatry, 19*, 413–438.

Glied, S. A., & Frank, R. G. (2009). Better but not best: Recent trends in the well-being of the mentally ill. *Health Affairs, 28*, 637–648.

Harvey, S. T., & Taylor, J. E. (2010). A meta-analysis of the effects of psychotherapy with sexually abuse children and adolescents. *Clinical Psychology Review, 30*, 517–535.

Hawley, K. M., & Weisz, J. R. (2005). Youth versus parent working alliance in usual clinical care: Distinctive associations with retention, satisfaction, and treatment outcome. *Journal of Clinical Child and Adolescent Psychology, 34*, 117–128.

Hetherington, E. M., Bridges, M., & Insabella, G. M. (1998). What matters? What does not? Five perspectives on the association between marital transitions and children's adjustment. *American Psychologist, 53*, 167–184.

Hetherington, E. M., & Elmore, A. M. (2003). Risk and resilience in children coping with their parents' divorce and remarriage. In S. S. Luthar (Ed.), *Resilience and vulnerability: Adaptation in the context of childhood adversities* (pp. 182–212). New York, NY: Cambridge University Press.

Hogue, A., Dauber, S., Stambaugh, L. F., Cecero, J. J., & Liddle, H. A. (2006). Early therapeutic alliance and treatment outcome in individual and family therapy for adolescent behavior problems. *Journal of Consulting and Clinical Psychology, 74*, 121–129.

Houtrow, A. J., & Okumura, M. J. (2011). Pediatric mental health problems and associated burden on families. *Vulnerable Children and youth Studies, 6*, 222–233.

Hudziak, J. J., Achenbach, T. M., Althoff, R. R., & Pine, D. S. (2008). A dimensional approach to developmental psychopathology. In J. E. Helzer, H. C. Kraemer, R. F. Krueger, H. U. Wittchen, P. J. Sirovatka, & D. A. Regier (Eds.), *Dimensional approaches in diagnostic classification: Refining the research agenda for DSM-V* (pp. 101–113). Washington, DC: American Psychiatric Association.

Huey, S. J., & Polo, A. J. (2010). Assessing the effects of evidence-based psychotherapies with ethnic minority youths. In J. R. Weisz & A. E. Kazdin (Eds.), *Evidence-based psychotherapies for children and adolescents* (2nd ed., pp. 451–465). New York: Guilford.

Hunsley, J., Lee, C. M., & Wood, J. M. (2003). Controversy and questionable assessment techniques. In S. O. Lilienfeld, S. J. Lynn, & J. M. Lohr (Eds.), *Science and pseudoscience in clinical psychology* (pp. 39–76). New York: Guilford.

Hunsley, J., & Mash, E. J. (2007). Evidence-based assessment. *Annual Review of Clinical Psychology, 3*, 29–51.

Ingram, R. E., & Price, J. M. (2010). *Vulnerability to psychopathology: Risk across the lifespan* (2nd ed.). New York, NY: Guilford.

Institute of Medicine, (2009). *Preventing mental, emotional, and behavioral disorders among young people: Progress and possibilities.* Washington, DC: National Academies Press.

Jackson, Y., Alberts, F. L., & Roberts, M. C. (2010). Clinical child psychology: A practice specialty serving children, adolescents, and their families. *Professional Psychology: Research and Practice, 41*, 75–81.

Jensen, P. S. (2003). Comorbidity and child psychopathology: Recommendations for the next decade. *Journal of Abnormal Child Psychology, 31,* 293–300.

Jensen, P. S., Goldman, E., Offord, D., Costello, E. J., Friedman, R., et al. (2011). Overlooked and underserved: "Action signs" for identifying children with unmet mental health needs. *Pediatrics, 128,* 970–979.

Kagan, J. (2013). Behavioral inhibition as a temperamental vulnerability to psychopathology. In T. P. Beauchaine & S. P. Hinshaw (Eds.), *Child and adolescent psychopathology* (2nd ed., pp. 227–250). Hoboken, NJ: Wiley.

Karna, A., Voeten, M., Little, T. D., Poskiparta, E., Alanen, E., et al. (2011). Going to scale: A nonrandomized nationwide trial of the KiVa antibullying program for grades 1–9. *Journal of Consulting and Clinical Psychology, 79,* 796–805.

Karver, M. S., Handelsman, J. B., Fields, S., & Bickman, L. (2005). Meta-analysis of therapeutic relationship variables in youth and family therapy: The evidence for different relationship variables in the child and adolescent treatment outcome literature. *Clinical Psychology Review, 26,* 50–65.

Kaslow, F. W. (2011). Family therapy. In J. C. Norcross, G. R. Vanden-Bos, & D. K. Freedheim (Eds.), *History of psychotherapy: Continuity and change* (2nd ed., pp. 497–504). Washington, DC: American Psychological Association.

Kazak, A. E., Hoagwood, K., Weisz, J. R., Hood, K., Kratochwill, T. R., et al. (2010). A meta-systems approach to evidence-based practice for children and adolescents. *American Psychologist, 65,* 85–97.

Kendall, P. C. (2012). *Child and adolescent therapy: Cognitive-behavioral procedures* (4th ed.). New York, NY: Guilford.

Kessler, R. C., Avenevoli, S., Costello, E. J., Georglades, K., Green, J. G. et al. (2012). Prevalence, persistence, and sociodemographic correlates of DSM-IV disorders in the National Comorbidity Survey Replication Adolescent Supplement. *Archives of General Psychiatry, 69,* 372–380.

Khanna, M. S., & Kendall, P. C. (2010). Computer-assisted cognitive behavioral therapy for child anxiety: Results of a randomized clinical trial. *Journal of Consulting and Clinical Psychology, 78,* 737–745.

Koocher, G. P., & Daniel, J. H. (2012). Treating children and adolescents. In S. J. Knapp (Ed.), *APA handbook of ethics in psychology (Vol. 2): Practice, teaching, and research* (pp. 3–14). Washington, DC: American Psychological Association.

Kovacs, M. (2010). *Children's Depression Inventory 2 (CDI-2).* San Antonio, TX: PsychCorp.

LaGreca, A. M., Silverman, W. K., & Lochman, J. E. (2009). Moving beyond efficacy and effectiveness in child and adolescent intervention research. *Journal of Consulting and Clinical Psychology, 77,* 373–382.

Lahey, B. B., VanHulle, C. A., Keenan, K. R., Rathouz, P. J., D'Onofrio, B. M., et al. (2008). Temperament and parenting during the first year of life predict future child conduct problems. *Journal of Abnormal Child Psychology, 36,* 1139–1158.

Lau, A. S., & Weisz, J. R. (2003). Reported maltreatment among clinic-referred children: Implications for presenting problems, treatment attrition, and long-term outcomes. *Journal of the American Academy of Child and Adolescent Psychiatry, 42,* 1327–1334.

Lean, D., & Colucci, V. A. (2013). *School-based mental health: A framework for intervention.* Lanham, MD: Rowman & Littlefield Education.

Maniglio, R. (2009). The impact of child sexual abuse on health: A systematic review of reviews. *Clinical Psychology Review, 29,* 647–657.

Maniglio, R. (2011). The role of child sexual abuse in the etiology of suicide and non-suicidal self-injury. *Acta Psychiatric Scandanavia, 124,* 30–41.

Mannarino, A. P., & Cohen, J. A. (2006). Child sexual abuse. In R. T. Ammerman (Ed.), *Comprehensive handbook of personality and psychopathology* (Vol. 3, pp. 388–402). Hoboken, NJ: Wiley.

Mash, E. J., & Hunsley, J. (2007). Assessment of child and family disturbance: A developmental-systems approach. In E. J. Mash & R. A. Barkley (Eds.), *Assessment of childhood disorders* (4th ed., pp. 3–50). New York, NY: Guilford.

Mash, E. J., & Wolfe, D. A. (2012). *Abnormal child psychology* (5th ed.). Belmont, CA: Cengage Learning.

Masten, A. S., & Tellegen, A. (2012). Resilience in developmental psychopathology: Contributions of the Project Competence Longitudinal Study. *Development and Psychopathology, 24,* 345–361.

Matthews, K. A., & Gallo, L. C. (2011). Psychological perspectives on pathways linking socioeconomic status and physical health. *Annual Review of Psychology, 62,* 501–530.

Maughan, B., Iervolino, A. C., & Collishaw, S. (2005). Time trends in child and adolescent mental disorders. *Current Opinion in Psychiatry, 18,* 381–385.

McConaughy, S. H., & Achenbach, T. M. (2001). *Manual for the semi-structured clinical interview for children and adolescents* (2nd ed.). Burlington, VT: University of Vermont, Center for Children, Youth, and Families.

McGuffin, P. (2004). Behavioral genomics: Where molecular genetics is taking psychiatry and psychology. In L. DiLalla (Ed.), *Behavior genetics principles: Perspectives in development, personality, and psychopathology* (pp. 191–204). Washington, DC: American Psychological Association.

Miller, S., Malone, P. S., Dodge, K. A., & Conduct Problems Prevention Research Group, (2010). Developmental trajectories of boys' and girls' delinquency: Sex differences and links to later adolescent outcomes. *Journal of Abnormal Child Psychology, 38,* 1021–1032.

Moffitt, T. E., Caspi, A., Harrington, H., Milne, B. J., Melchior, M., et al. (2007). Generalized anxiety disorder and depression: Childhood risk factors in a birth cohort followed to age 32. *Psychological Medicine, 37,* 441–452.

Nelson, S., Baldwin, N., & Taylor, J. (2012). Mental health problems and medically unexplained physical symptoms in adult survivors of childhood sexual abuse: An integrative literature review. *Journal of Psychiatric and Mental Health Nursing, 19,* 211–220.

Nigg, J. (2013). Attention-deficit/hyperactivity disorder. In T. P. Beauchaine & S. P. Hinshaw (Eds.), *Child and adolescent psychopathology* (2nd ed., pp. 377–409). Hoboken, NJ: Wiley.

Noll, J. G., Trickett, P. K., & Putnam, F. W. (2003). A prospective investigation of the impact of childhood sexual abuse on the development of sexuality. *Journal of Consulting and Clinical Psychology, 71,* 575–586.

Norbury, C. F., & Sparks, A. (2013). Difference or disorder? Cultural issues in understanding neurodevelopmental disorders. *Developmental Psychology., 49,* 45–58. doi: 10.1037/a0027446.

Ozonoff, S. (2012). Editorial: DSM-5 and autism spectrum disorders–two decades of perspectives from the JCPP. *Journal of Child Psychology and Psychiatry, 53,* e4–e6., doi: 10.1111/j.1469-7610.2012.02587.x

Parra, G. R., DuBois, D. L., & Sher, K. J. (2006). Investigation of profiles of risk factors for adolescent psychopathology: A person-centered approach. *Journal of Clinical Child and Adolescent Psychology, 35,* 386–402.

Patterson, G. R. (1976). The aggressive child: Victim and architect of a coercive system. In L. A. Hamerlynck, L. C. Handy, & E. J. Mash

(Eds.), *Behavior modification and families: Theory and research* (Vol. 1, pp. 267–316). New York, NY: Brunner/Mazel.

Patterson, G. R. (1982). *Coercive family process.* Eugene, OR: Castalia.

Patterson, G. R., Ray, R. S., Shaw, D. A., & Cobb, J. A. (1969). *Manual for coding of family interactions* (Document NO. 01234). Available from ASIS/NAPS, c/o Microfiche Publications, 305 East 46th St., New York, NY 10017.

Pereda, N., Guilera, G., Forns, M., & Gomez-Benito, J. (2009). The prevalence of child sexual abuse in community and student samples: A meta-analysis. *Clinical Psychology Review, 29,* 328–338.

Phares, V. (2013). *Understanding abnormal child psychology* (3rd ed.). Hoboken, NJ: Wiley.

Pidano, A. E., Kurowski, E. C., & McEvoy, K. M. (2010). The next generation: How are clinical child psychologists being trained? *Training and Education in Professional Psychology, 4,* 121–127.

Plomin, R., & Kovas, Y. (2005). Generalist genes and learning disabilities. *Psychological Bulletin, 131,* 592–617.

Rabiner, D. L., Murray, D. W., Skinner, A. T., & Malone, P. S. (2010). A randomized trial of two promising computer-based interventions for students with attention difficulties. *Journal of Abnormal Child Psychology, 38,* 131–142.

Raviv, A., Raviv, A., Propper, A., & Fink, A. S. (2003). Mothers' attitudes toward seeking help for their children from school and private psychologists. *Professional Psychology: Research and Practice, 34,* 95–101.

Rescorla, L., Achenbach, T. M., Ivanova, M. Y., Dumenci, L., Almqvist, F., et al. (2007). Epidemiological comparisons of problems and positive qualities reported by adolescents in 24 countries. *Journal of Consulting and Clinical Psychology, 75,* 351–358.

Rescorla, L. A., Achenbach, T. M., Ivanova, M. Y., Harder, V. S., Otten, L., et al. (2011). International comparisons of behavioral and emotional problems in preschool children: Parents' reports from 24 societies. *Journal of Clinical Child and Adolescent Psychology, 40,* 456–467.

Reynolds, C. R., & Kamphaus, R. W. (2009). *Behavior Assessment System for Children–Second Edition (BASC-2).* Bloomington, MN: Pearson.

Reynolds, S., Wilson, C., Austin, J., & Hooper, L. (2012). Effects of psychotherapy for anxiety in children and adolescents: A meta-analytic review. *Clinical Psychology Review, 32,* 251–262.

Richmond, T. K., & Rosen, D. S. (2005). The treatment of adolescent depression in the era of the black box warning. *Current Opinion in Pediatrics, 17,* 466–472.

Roberts, M. C., & Steele, R. G. (Eds.). (2009). *Handbook of pediatric psychology* (4th ed.). New York, NY: Guilford.

Rorschach, H. (1942). *Psychodiagnostics: A diagnostic test based on perception.* Bern, Switzerland: Hans Huber (Original work published in 1921).

Rothbart, M. K., & Bates, J. E. (2006). Temperament. In N. Eisenberg (Ed.), *Handbook of child psychology* (6th ed., pp. 99–166). Hoboken, NJ: Wiley.

Rotter, J. B., Lah, M. I., & Rafferty, J. E. (1992). *Manual: Rotter Incomplete Sentences Blank* (2nd ed.). Orlando, FL: Psychological Corporation.

Rubinstein, E. (1948). Childhood mental disease in America: A review of the literature before 1900. *American Journal of Orthopsychiatry, 18,* 314–321.

Sanders, M. R., & Murphy-Brennan, M. (2010). The international dissemination of the Triple P–Positive Parenting Program. In J. R. Weisz & A. E. Kazdin (Eds.), *Evidence-based psychotherapies for children and adolescents* (2nd ed., pp. 519–537). New York, NY: Guilford.

Santiago, C. D., Kaltman, S., & Miranda, J. (2012). Poverty and mental health: How do low-income adults and children fare in psychotherapy? *Journal of Clinical Psychology, 69,* 115–126.

Sapienza, J. K., & Masten, A. S. (2011). Understanding and promoting resilience in children and youth. *Current Opinion in Psychiatry, 24,* 267–273.

Sattler, J. M., & Hoge, R. D. (2006). *Assessment of children: Behavioral, social and clinical foundations* (5th ed.). San Diego, CA: Jerome M. Sattler, Publisher.

Schermerhorn, A. C., Chow, S. M., & Cummings, E. M. (2010). Developmental family processes and interparental conflict: Patterns of microlevel influences. *Developmental Psychology, 46,* 869–885.

Seifer, R. (2003). Young children with mentally ill parents: Resilient developmental systems. In S. S. Luthar (Ed.), *Resilience and vulnerability: Adaptation in the context of childhood adversities* (pp. 29–49). New York, NY: Cambridge University Press.

Shaffer, D., Fisher, P., Lucas, C. P., Dulcan, M. K., & Schwab-Stone, M. E. (2000). NIMH Diagnostic Interview Schedule for Children Version IV (NIMH DISC-IV): Description, differences from previous versions, and reliability of some common diagnoses. *Journal of the American Academy of Child and Adolescent Psychiatry, 39,* 28–38.

Shirk, S. R., & Karver, M. S. (2011). Alliance in child and adolescent psychotherapy. In J. C. Norcross (Ed.), *Psychotherapy relationships that work: Evidence-based responsiveness* (2nd ed., pp. 70–91). New York, NY: Oxford University Press.

Shochet, I. M., Dadds, M. R., Holland, D., Whitefield, K., Harnett, P. H., et al. (2001). The efficacy of a universal school-based program to prevent adolescent depression. *Journal of Clinical Child Psychology, 30,* 303–315.

Silverman, W. K., & Hinshaw, S. P. (2008). The second special issue on evidence-based psychosocial treatments for children and adolescents: A 10-year update. *Journal of Clinical Child and Adolescent Psychology, 37,* 1–7.

Sinacola, R. S., & Peters-Strickland, T. (2012). *Basic psychopharmacology for counselors and psychotherapists* (2nd ed.). Boston, MA: Pearson.

Southam-Gerow, M. A., Rodriguez, A., Chorpita, B. F., & Daleiden, E. L. (2012). Dissemination and implementation of evidence based treatments for youth: Challenges and recommendations. *Professional Psychology: Research and Practice, 43,* 527–534.

Spence, S. H., Donovan, C. L., March, S., Gamble, A., Anderson, R. E., et al. (2011). A randomized controlled trial of online versus clinic-based CBT for adolescent anxiety. *Journal of Consulting and Clinical Psychology, 79,* 629–642.

Stark, K. D., Hargrave, J., Sander, J., Custer, G., Schnoebelen, S., et al. (2006). Treatment of childhood depression: The ACTION treatment program. In P. C. Kendall (Ed.), *Child and adolescent therapy* (3rd ed., pp. 169–216). New York, NY: Guilford.

Stein, D. J. (2006). Advances in understanding the anxiety disorders: The cognitive-affective neuroscience of "false alarms." *Annals of Clinical Psychiatry, 18,* 173–182.

Storch, E. A., & Crisp, H. L. (2004). Taking it to the schools: Transporting empirically supported treatments for childhood psychopathology to the school setting. *Clinical Child and Family Psychology Review, 7,* 191–193.

Thurston, I. B., & Phares, V. (2008). Mental health service utilization among African American and Caucasian mothers and fathers. *Journal of Consulting and Clinical Psychology, 76,* 1058–1067.

UNICEF (2010). The children left behind: A league table of inequality in child well-being in the world's rich countries. *Innocenti Report Card 9,* Florence: UNICEF Innocenti Research Centre.

Valkenburg, P. M., & Peter, J. (2009). Social consequences of the internet for adolescents: A decade of research. *Current Directions in Psychological Science, 18,* 1–5.

Van Zeijl, J., Mesman, J., Ijzendoorn, M. H. V., Bakermans-Kranenburg, M. J., Juffer, F., et al. (2006). Attachment-based intervention for enhancing sensitive discipline in mothers of 1- to 3-year-old children at risk for externalizing behavior problems: A randomized controlled trial. *Journal of Consulting and Clinical Psychology, 74,* 994–1005.

Vanderbilt-Adriance, E., & Shaw, D. S. (2008). Protective factors and the development of resilience in the context of neighborhood disadvantage. *Journal of Abnormal child Psychology, 36,* 887–901.

vanOort, F. V. A., vanderEnde, J., Wadsworth, M. E., Verhulst, F. C., & Achenbach, T. M. (2011). Cross-national comparison of the link between socioeconomic status and emotional and behavioral problems in youth. *Social Psychiatry and Psychiatric Epidemiology, 46,* 167–172.

Vogel, M. E., Kirkpatrick, H. A., Collings, A. S., Cederna-Meko, C. L., & Grey, M. J. (2012). Integrated care: Maturing the relationship between psychology and primary care. *Professional Psychology: Research and Practice, 43,* 271–280.

Wade, S., Oberjohn, K., Conaway, K., Osinska, P., & Bangert, L. (2011). Live coaching of parenting skills using the internet: Implications for clinical practice. *Professional Psychology: Research and Practice, 42,* 487–493.

Wechsler, D. (2003). *WISC-IV technical and interpretive manual.* San Antonio, TX: The Psychological Corporation.

Weisz, J. R. (2004). *Psychotherapy for children and adolescents: Evidence-based treatments and case examples.* New York, NY: Cambridge University Press.

Weisz, J. R., Doss, A. J., & Hawley, K. M. (2005). Youth psychotherapy outcome research: A review and critique of the evidence base. *Annual Review of Psychology, 56,* 337–363.

Weisz, J. R., Ng, M. Y, Rutt, C., Lau, N., & Masland, S. (2013). Psychotherapy for children and adolescents. In M. J. Lambert (Ed.), *Bergin and Garfield's handbook of psychotherapy and behavior change* (6th ed., pp. 541–586). Hoboken, NJ: Wiley.

Weisz, J. R., Sandler, I. N., Durlak, J. A., & Anton, B. S. (2005). Promoting and protecting youth mental health through evidence-based prevention and treatment. *American Psychologist, 60,* 628–648.

Wekerle, C., MacMillan, H. L., Leung, E., & Jamieson, E. (2008). Child maltreatment. In M. Hersen & A. M. Gross (Eds.), *Handbook of clinical psychology (Vol. 2): Children and adolescents* (pp. 429–457). Hoboken, NJ: Wiley.

West, S. L., & O'Neal, K. K. (2004). Project D.A.R.E outcome effectiveness revisited. *American Journal of Public Health, 94,* 1027–1029.

Wicks-Nelson, R., & Israel, A. C. (2013). *Abnormal child and adolescent psychology* (8th ed.). Upper Saddle River, NJ: Prentice Hall.

Wilmshurst, L. (2011). *Child and adolescent psychopathology: A casebook* (2nd ed). Thousand Oaks, CA: Sage Publications.

Wilson, D. K., & Lawman, H. G. (2009). Health promotion in children and adolescents: An integration of the biopsychosocial model and ecological approaches to behavior change. In M. C. Roberts & R. G. Steele (Eds.), *Handbook of pediatric psychology* (4th ed., pp. 603–617). New York: Guilford.

Wood, J. M., Lilienfeld, S. O., Nezworski, M. T., Garb, H. N., Allen, K. H., et al. (2010). Validity of Rorschach inblot scores for discriminating psychopaths from nonpsychopaths in forensic populations: A meta-analysis. *Psychological Assessment, 22,* 336–349.

Woodcock, R. W., McGrew, K. S., & Mather, N. (2000). *Woodcock-Johnson III.* Itasca, IL: Riverside Publishing.

Yasui, M., & Dishion, T. J. (2007). The ethnic context of child and adolescent problem behavior: Implications for child and family interventions. *Clinical Child and Family Psychology, 10,* 137–179.

Ybarra, M. L., Boyd, D., Korchmaros, J. D., & Oppenheim, J. K. (2012). Defining and measuring cyberbullying within the larger context of bullying victimization. *Journal of Adolescent Health Care., 51,* 53–58. doi 10.1016/j.jadohealth 2011.12.031.

Ybarra, M. L., Espelage, D. L., & Mitchell, K. J. (2007). The co-occurrence of internet harassment and unwanted sexual solicitation victimization and perpetration: Associations with psychosocial indicators. *Journal of Adolescent Health, 41,* 31–41.

Yoshikawa, H., Aber, J. L., & Beardslee, W. R. (2012). The effects of poverty on the mental, emotional, and behavioral health of children and youth: Implications for prevention. *American Psychologist, 67,* 272–284.

Zero to Three (2005). *Diagnostic classification of mental health and developmental disorders of infancy and early childhood: Revised Edition (DC: 0-3R).* Washington, DC: Zero to Three Press.

12 | HEALTH PSYCHOLOGY

Chapter Preview

In this chapter, we describe how clinical psychologists work with medical professionals to treat disorders, help patients to cope psychologically with medical conditions, and to increase patients' adherence to medical treatment recommendations. We also describe how psychological factors contribute to disease, focusing on relationships among psychosocial variables (e.g., stress, cognitions) and physical functioning (e.g., nervous system activity, circulation, immune system functioning). Next we describe psychological risk factors and treatment interventions for illnesses such as cardiovascular disease, HIV/AIDS, chronic pain, and cancer.

In this chapter and the next, we discuss two specialized areas of clinical psychology—health psychology and neuropsychology—that illustrate how important it is for psychologists to study relationships between psychological and biological factors. We selected these areas because they have been some of clinical psychology's best "growth stocks" in the past 40 years. New research discoveries and expanding professional roles for clinicians have increasingly attracted psychologists to these areas.

WHAT IS HEALTH PSYCHOLOGY?

SECTION PREVIEW

> *In this section, we present some of the theoretical foundations for health psychology. Health psychologists pay special attention to the role of stress on physical and mental health. They also consider how external stressors combine with internal variables such as coping strategies, cognitive habits, and perceived social support to affect vulnerability and resilience to illness.*

Health psychology is a specialty that emerged in the 1970s and is devoted to studying "psychological influences on how people stay healthy, why they become ill, and how they respond when they do get ill" (Taylor, 1995, p. 3). This subfield has enjoyed such rapid growth over the last 40 years that it now has its own division in the APA (Division 38) and its own journal, *Health Psychology*. Health psychology research is also often published in the *Journal of Behavioral Medicine, Psychosomatic Medicine*, and the *Annals of Behavioral Medicine*. Related professional organizations include the Society of Behavioral Medicine and the American Psychosomatic Society. Many clinical psychology training programs now include a "track" that specializes in the training of health psychologists, and some programs have developed health psychology as their major focus.

Health psychology is closely related to the larger field of *behavioral medicine*, which involves the integration of knowledge from the social/behavioral sciences (e.g., psychology, sociology, and anthropology), the biological sciences, and medicine into an interdisciplinary science focused on understanding and treating all types of medical disorders in the broadest possible ways. Health psychology and behavioral medicine follow a *biopsychosocial* model, which holds that physical illness is frequently the result of biological, psychological, and social disruptions. They study how psychological conditions and behavioral processes are linked to illness and health.

Sir William Osler, a physician, is generally considered the father of modern behavioral medicine because he insisted that psychological and emotional factors must be considered in order to

315

Sir William Osler, the father
of modern behavioral
medicine.   *Source*: Science Source.

understand and treat various diseases. In 1910, Osler gave a lecture in which he suggested that many symptoms of heart disease "are brought on by anger, worry, or sudden shock." These ideas are remarkably similar to contemporary proposals about how key psychological factors may be linked to heart disease.

Osler's views were made more relevant by significant changes in the nature of illness in Western cultures during the twentieth century. As recently as 100 years ago, most Americans died of acute infectious diseases such as pneumonia, typhoid fever, and tuberculosis. However, advances in education, sanitation, pharmaceuticals, and vaccination have all but eliminated these diseases, leaving chronic illnesses—heart disease and cancer, for example—as the major threats to life (Currie, 2013; McGrady & Moss, 2013). These diseases are not only chronic in nature but also take years to develop. Further, the major risk factors for developing chronic illnesses include life long health-damaging behaviors such as smoking, unhealthy eating, sedentary lifestyles, and alcohol abuse. Today, nearly half of all deaths that occur in the United States can be attributed to such risky behaviors (Murray, et al., 2013). We now have evidence, for example, that behavioral and psychological factors contribute to the onset or severity of heart disease, ulcers, asthma, stomach disorders, cancer, arthritis, headaches, and hypertension. Reversing this trend will require increased awareness of the problem, changes in public policy, and most importantly, changes in individual health behaviors.

Physicians and other health professionals are becoming increasingly interested in the contributions of health psychologists. Indeed, emotional distress, sometimes as a result of difficulties in coping with an illness, is a factor in up to 60% of all physician office visits (Pallak, Cummings, Dorken, & Henke, 1995). Because physicians are seldom prepared to deal with the emotions accompanying disease, prevention and treatment of emotional distress increasingly fall to persons in the health psychology field. In short, health psychology has grown because evidence strongly shows that it no longer makes sense to treat patients "from either the head up or the neck down" (Dornelas, 2001, p. 1261).

Several books provide more detailed discussions of the history and status of health psychology and behavioral medicine (e.g., Baum, Revenson, & Singer, 2011; Sanderson, 2012; Sarafino, 2010; Straub, 2011; Taylor, 2011).

Stress, Coping, and Health

Stress is the negative emotional and physiological process that occurs as people try to adjust to or deal with circumstances that disrupt, or threaten to disrupt, their daily functioning beyond their ability or perceived ability to cope (Dougall, Wroble-Biglan, Swanson, & Baum, 2013). The circumstances that cause people to make adjustments are collectively called *stressors*. They range in severity from mild to extreme and include a wide array of everyday and unusual experiences such as family and social conflicts, health problems, feeling overwhelmed, losing a loved one, high work demands, academic exams, and suffering abuse or trauma. The physical, psychological, cognitive, and behavioral responses (such as increased heart rate, anger, and impulsiveness) that people display in the face of stressors are called *stress reactions*. Managing stressors and one's own stress reactions are ongoing challenges to health.

Stress and the Nervous System

Physiological reactions to stress include a pattern of responses in the central and autonomic nervous systems. The autonomic nervous system is particularly important because this is the system that normally operates to balance energy and related needs of the body. Under optimal conditions, the two branches of the autonomic system, the sympathetic nervous system and the parasympathetic nervous system, operate in concert to help keep the body in a state of equilibrium.

Many researchers have investigated response patterns of the autonomic nervous system in an effort to understand the biological effects of stressors. For example, Hans Selye (1956) called activation of the sympathetic nervous system during stress the *general adaptation syndrome*, or GAS. The GAS begins with an *alarm reaction*, which is often called the fight-or-flight response because it helps us combat or escape stressors. The alarm reaction releases into the bloodstream a number of "stress hormones," including adrenal corticosteroids, catecholamines (e.g., adrenaline), and endogenous opiates (the body's natural painkillers). These hormones increase heart rate, blood pressure and respiration, pupillary dilation, muscle tension, release of glucose and lipid reserves, and concentration of attention on the stressor. If the stressor persists, or if new ones occur in quick succession, alarm is followed by the *stage of resistance*, during which less dramatic but more continuous biochemical efforts to cope with stress can have harmful consequences. For example, prolonged release of stress hormones can create chronic high blood pressure, damage muscle tissue, and inhibit the body's ability to heal.

If stressors continue long enough, the *stage of exhaustion* appears as various organ systems begin to malfunction or break down. In the stage of exhaustion, people experience physical symptoms ranging from fatigue, weight loss, and indigestion to colds, heart disease, and other more serious problems.

Selye's model was an important contribution to the field of stress and disease research and in particular provided a framework for thinking about how stressors could contribute to physiological changes and, ultimately, disease processes. However, the model fails to account for the importance of cognitive, psychological, and perceptual factors in modifying how and which experiences would be experienced as stressors. In other words, the model does not allow for individual differences in the experience of stress. Thus, more comprehensive models that outline how stressors affect disease progression have been developed.

For example, Barbara Dohrenwend (1978) suggested a four-stage model of how stressors and stress reactions contribute to physical illness and/or psychological disorder. In the first stage, stressful life events occur, followed in the second stage by a set of physical and psychological stress reactions. In the third stage, these stress reactions are mediated by environmental and psychological factors that either amplify or reduce their intensity. Factors likely to reduce stress reactions include things like adequate financial resources, free time to deal with stressors, a full repertoire of effective coping skills, the help and support of friends and family, a strong sense of control over stressors, a tendency to be optimistic, and a view of stressors as challenges. Stress-amplifying factors include things like poverty, lack of social support, inadequate coping skills, pessimism, a sense of helplessness, and seeing stressors as terrifying threats. In stage four, the interaction of particular stressors, particular people, and particular circumstances results in physical and/or psychological problems that may be mild and temporary (some anxiety, a headache, or a few sleepless nights) or severe and persistent (e.g., an anxiety or mood disorder, chronic insomnia, or physical illness).

Today, most health psychologists believe that stress results from interactions between people and their environments, not simply as a function of external events. They recognize, for example, that physical and psychological stress responses may arise not because of obvious external stressors, but because of events and situations that a person *perceives* to be threatening or demanding.

Stress and the Immune System

Another important effect of prolonged stress is suppression of the immune system, the body's first line of defense against disease-causing agents (Dougall, Wroble-Biglan, Swanson, & Baum, 2013). For example, chronic stressors (e.g., taking care of a seriously ill relative) have been shown to lower immune system functioning, and even brief stressors, such as final-exam periods, have been associated with a decline in the activity of immune system cells that fight viruses and tumors (Kiecolt-Glaser & Glaser, 1992). In a series of interesting studies of the relationship between stress and illness, researchers exposed volunteer subjects to cold viruses or a placebo and then measured the amount of stress experienced by the volunteers over a given time period (Cohen et al., 2012; Cohen, Tyrrell, & Smith, 1991). The results showed that the appearance of colds and other infections was correlated with the amount of stress the subjects experienced, thus identifying a physiological mechanism linking stress and the onset of a viral infection. These and many other researchers now suspect that immunosuppression—which is often due to inflammation—is the basis for the association between stressors and increased risk for illnesses, including some forms of cancer (e.g., Cohen et al., 2012; Cohen & Rabin, 1998).

The effects of stress on immune function can also be modified by procedures to reduce stress. An investigation of this phenomenon among married couples examined immune function and the ability of the body to heal minor wounds (Kiecolt-Glaser et al., 2005). On one day, couples discussed an area of marital discord; on another day, they were asked to provide social support to each other and given prompts on how to effectively do so. Measures of wound-healing capacity and other immune system activity were taken during both days. Wound-healing capacity was significantly lower after the couples engaged in a discussion of marital discord, and higher after couples provided social support to each other, and this difference was attributable to the changes in immune function.

This area of research, broadly called *psychoneuroimmunology*, is quite complex. For example, although stressors—especially prolonged stressors—can suppress immune function, short bouts of stress can actually enhance some portions of the immune system (Segerstrom, 2004). These discrete bouts of stress appear to enhance the body's ability to respond to invasions of foreign substances (Atanackovic et al., 2006).

Developmental Aspects of Exposure to Stressors

Health can be affected not only by the type and duration of stressors, but also by when the stressors are experienced. For example, stressors that occur very early in life can have effects on psychological and physical health that echo throughout the life span. So experiencing the stress of poverty, trauma, or other adversities during early childhood is associated with an increased risk of developing heart disease, arthritis, certain cancers, and other health problems in adulthood, even for people who by then had achieved middle or upper class socioeconomic status (Chan Chen, Hibbert, Wong, & Miller, 2011; Lehman et al., 2005). In short, childhood stress can have long-delayed effects.

One line of research has shown that traumatic early life experiences result in fundamental changes in the functioning of the brain and the cardiovascular and immune systems (Taylor, 2010). Even prenatal exposure to stress can alter *telomeres*, protein complexes that ensure stability of chromosomes and that are associated with long-term health and aging (Entringer et al., 2011). Identifying particularly stress-vulnerable times of life, and particularly stress-vulnerable individuals, will ultimately lead to a more complete understanding of how and when health psychologists can intervene to ensure optimal mental and physical health throughout the life span.

Measuring Stressors

To study the relationship between stress and illness, it is necessary to measure stress accurately, and health psychologists have tried to do so in several ways. One example is a questionnaire called the *Schedule of Recent Experiences* (SRE) (Amundson, Hart, & Holmes, 1986), which contains a list of 42 events involving health, family, personal, occupational, and financial matters. Respondents identify the events that have happened to them during the past 6, 12, 24, and 36 months, and then give each event a weight based on the amount of adjustment that was needed to deal with it (1, very little adjustment; 100, maximal adjustment). These weights are summed to give a *Life Change Unit Score.* Although scales that measure life events have the advantage of being standardized, many researchers recognize that a simple listings of life events (even with estimates of how much adjustment is necessary) do not capture the full impact of stressors. Factors such as whether the events have a positive or negative value and how expected or controllable they are also contribute to understanding the true impact of a particular event on particular individuals.

Many health psychologists believe that the most accurate assessment of stress comes not from evaluating environmental experiences but from assessing individual perceptions of stressors, which may be influenced by previous experiences, culture, gender, age, and a variety of other factors (Flores Tschann, Dimas, Pasch, & deGroat, 2010). Thus, some stress inventories ask respondents about the frequency and intensity of perceptions of stress without linking these perceptions to actual events. Cohen's *Perceived Stress Scale* (PSS) is one such commonly used measure (Cohen, Kamarck, & Mermelstein, 1983; Novak et al., 2013).

The results of research with even the best stress assessment scales show that while there is undoubtedly a relationship between stress and illness, the strength of that relationship is relatively weak. In other words, even though people who are exposed to significant stressors are more likely overall to become ill than are those exposed to fewer stressors, most people who experience stressors do not become ill. This realization has led health psychologists to search for variables that might explain how people are protected from the potentially health-harming effects of stress. Among these variables are three particularly important *vulnerability* or *resistance factors* (Kessler, Price, & Wortman, 1985): adaptive coping strategies, stress-hardy personality characteristics, and social support.

Adaptive Coping Strategies

Coping refers to people's cognitive, emotional, and behavioral efforts at modifying, tolerating, or eliminating stressors that threaten them (Carver, 2012; Folkman & Lazarus, 1980). People vary in how they cope with stress. Some try to eliminate or otherwise deal with stressors directly; others attempt to change the way they think about stressors to make them less upsetting; still others concentrate on managing the emotional reactions that stressors cause (Lazarus, 1993).

Richard Lazarus and Susan Folkman developed a *Ways of Coping* checklist consisting of 68 items that describe how 100 middle-aged adults said they coped with stressful events in their lives (Folkman & Lazarus, 1980). These items fall into two broad categories: *problem-focused* and *emotion-focused coping* (see Table 12.1). The 100 respondents reported on a total of 1,332 stressful episodes, and in 98% of them, said they used both coping methods. Their choice was not random, however. Problem-focused coping was favored for stressors related to work, while emotion-focused coping was used more often when the stressors involved health. Men tended to use problem-focused coping more often than women in certain situations, but men and women did not differ in their use of emotion-focused coping. Other researchers using different instruments have reached similar conclusions (Stone & Neale, 1984).

The distinction between problem-focused and emotion-focused coping has been particularly useful, guiding research for the last three decades (Compas, Jaser, Dunn, & Rodriguez, 2012). It is important to note, though, that particular ways of coping are not equally effective for all types of stressors. For example, people who rely entirely on active, problem-focused coping might handle controllable stressors well but find themselves nearly helpless in the face of uncontrollable ones. Health psychologists help individuals under stress understand the range of coping responses possible for specific stressors at hand.

Stress-Hardy Personality Characteristics

Psychologists interested in positive psychology have examined a variety of personality and cognitive characteristics, including optimism (Peterson, 2000; Seligman, 2005; Seligman & Csikszentmihalyi, 2000), resilience (Wright, Masten, & Narayan, 2013), faith and hope (see Myers, 2000), curiosity (Richman, Kubzansky, Maselko, & Kawachi, 2005), subjective well-being (Diener, 2012), and adaptive defense mechanisms (Vaillant, 2000), all of which can contribute to adaptive coping.

TABLE 12.1 Ways of Coping

Problem-focused and emotion-focused coping are two major ways in which people deal with stressors.

Coping Skills	Example
Problem-focused coping	
Confronting	"I stood my ground and fought for what I wanted."
Seeking social support	"I talked to someone to find out more about the situation."
Planful problem solving	"I made a plan of action and I followed it."
Emotion-focused coping	
Self-controlling	"I tried to keep my feelings to myself."
Distancing	"I didn't let it get to me; I tried not to think about it too much."
Positive reappraisal	"I changed my mind about myself."
Accepting responsibility	"I realized I brought the problem on myself."
Escape/avoidance (wishful thinking)	"I wished that the situation would go away or somehow be over with."

Source: From Folkman, S., Lazarus, R. S., Gruen, R. J., & DeLongis, A. (1986). Appraisal, coping, health status, and psychological symptoms. *Journal of Personality and Social Psychology, 50,* 571–579. Copyright 1986. Adapted with permission.

In some cases, the health benefits of positive characteristics can be substantial. For example, one study measured both hope and curiosity in a large group of volunteers, and with their permission, tracked their health status as indicated by medical records. It turned out that those with higher hope and curiosity were less likely to develop high blood pressure, diabetes, and respiratory infections (Richman Kubzansky, Maselko, & Kawachi, 2005). Data such as these support the notion that positive emotional states may play a protective role with regard to health.

Other researchers in this area have investigated the role in physical and mental health of optimistic beliefs, including slightly overoptimistic distortions of reality ("positive illusions"). A review of literature in social psychology and related areas reveals, for example, that positively biased perceptions of reality are more common in people who are not depressed (Taylor, Kemeny, Reed, Bower, & Gruenewald, 2000). Healthy or mature defense mechanisms such as sublimation, altruism, suppression, and humor also appear to safeguard health and lessen the effects of some diseases (Kashdan & Rottenberg, 2010; Vaillant, 2000). A longitudinal study of Catholic nuns found that those who wrote about themselves in a positive emotional style early in life lived significantly longer than those whose early writings contained less positive emotions (Danner, Snowden, & Friesen, 2001).

The benefits of positive attitudes do have their limits, however. For example, it may not be a good idea simply to act happy when you're not. Efforts to inhibit or suppress negative emotions may have some short-term benefits but may be harmful to health in the long run (Salovey, Rothman, Detweiler, & Steward, 2000). One study found that rheumatoid arthritis sufferers who talked about stressful events more tended to have better outcomes than those who talked about such events less (Kelley, Lumley, & Leisen, 1997). And James Pennebaker (1995, 2004) has shown that people who write or talk about extremely stressful experiences (a process known as emotional expression or expressive writing) over successive days have better health outcomes than those who do not. Other research has found that expressing thoughts and feelings about negative experiences can have a positive effect (Snowdon, Greiner, Kemper, Nanayakkara, & Mortimer, 1999; Snowdon, Greiner, & Markesbery, 2000). Findings such as these are consistent with evidence that disclosure of negative emotions (such as in psychotherapy) is related to positive physical health, while inhibition is generally not (Miller & Cohen, 2001).

Of course, certain questions about coping and positive psychology remain unanswered. For example, what is the optimum balance of positive and negative expectations: Is it better to be optimistic or realistic? Optimism can often lead to self-deception and less-careful cognitive processing, but without a certain amount of optimism, people may be more vulnerable to stressors (see Schneider, 2001). Another question relates to how positive and negative experiences aggregate over time to affect health. Finally, we have yet to delineate clearly which features of maladaptive coping are deeply ingrained and therefore difficult to change through therapy (i.e., personality characteristics) and which are less deeply ingrained and are therefore more changable.

Social support enhances psychological *and* physical health.   *Source*: Morgan DDL/ Shutterstock.

Social Support

Social support has been defined in many ways (Schradle & Dougher, 1985), but its essential element appears to be the experience and perception of being cared for, loved, esteemed, and part of a network of communication and mutual obligation (Baumeister & Leary, 1995). Social support, then, involves more than the presence of others. It provides relationships in which emotional support, feedback, guidance, assistance, and values are exchanged.

Several studies have shown that the relationship between stress and illness is weaker among individuals who perceive high levels of social support in their lives (Brannon & Feist, 2009; Sarafino, 2010; Staub, 2011). One explanation is that social support acts as a *buffer* against stress. The buffer model claims that social support enables people who face intense stressors to neutralize those stressors' harmful effects. Social support also provides more opportunities for self-disclosure, and friends are likely to bolster efforts at constructive coping, thereby lessening the chances of self-defeating strategies such as excessive drinking and engaging in other health-damaging behaviors (Myers, 2000; Thoits, 1986). In short, people's perception of social support can strengthen their belief that others care for and value them; it may also enhance their self-esteem and increase feelings of confidence about handling stress in the future.

Another view, sometimes termed the *direct-effect* model, holds that social support is helpful regardless of whether stressful events are experienced because there is a general health benefit to being embedded in supportive relationships (Baumeister & Leary, 1995). A third explanation for the apparent benefits of social support is that high levels of support, good health, and low levels of stress all reflect the influence of some underlying characteristic such as *social competence*, which has positive effects on many areas of functioning.

Of course, some combination of all three models may be operating. It does seem clear that lack of social support, and particularly lack of emotional support, puts people at higher risk for both physical and psychological disorders (Cohen & Wills, 1985; Kessler, Price, & Wortman, 1985) and even premature death (McGrady & Moss, 2013).

Despite its general advantages, social support can carry some risks. For example, having a dense social support network entails increased exposure to large numbers of other people, which increases one's exposure to communicable diseases. Social ties can also create conflicts if others' helping efforts leave the recipient feeling guilty, overly indebted, or dependent. If a recipient is not able to reciprocate helping efforts, she or he may feel disadvantaged in future interactions with the donor. In other instances, potential helpers may behave in misguided ways (giving too much advice or becoming upset when their advice is not followed) that lead the recipient to feel invaded, incompetent, or rejected (Broman, 1993; Cohen, 2004; Malarkey, Kiecolt-Glaser, Pearl, & Glaser, 1994; Wortman & Lehman, 1985). Finally, those with close social ties may be particularly vulnerable to peer pressure to engage in health-damaging behaviors. For example, people whose close friends smoke or are overweight or obese are especially likely than others to smoke or overeat themselves (Christakis & Fowler, 2007, 2008).

SECTION SUMMARY

Health psychologists are concerned with how psychological variables influence people's vulnerability to physical illness and recovery from physical illness. The field of health psychology has grown because more and more diseases are related to psychological factors. One of the most general of these factors is stress, which results from a combination of external events, physiological responses, and individuals' psychological interpretations. A number of psychological variables moderate or affect the degree to which stress compromises health. Among these are coping style, personality characteristics, and perceived social support.

RISK FACTORS FOR ILLNESS

SECTION PREVIEW

In this section, we examine risk factors for two of the most important illnesses that health psychologists study and help treat: cardiovascular disease and HIV/AIDS.

Anything that increases a person's chances of developing an illness is called a *risk factor* for that illness. Some risk factors stem from biological and environmental conditions such as genetic defects or exposure to toxic chemicals (Taylor, Way, & Seeman, 2011). Others come in the form of health-damaging patterns of behavior. For example, smoking, overeating, lack of exercise, poor sleep habits, and consumption of a high-fat, low-fiber diet have all been identified as risk factors for life-threatening illnesses (Smith & Williams, 2013). Conversely, certain behaviors or lifestyles tend to promote health. For example, people who eat breakfast regularly, rarely snack between meals, exercise regularly, do not smoke, get 7 to 8 hours of sleep per night, and do not use alcohol excessively live longer than people who practice none of these behaviors (Smith & Williams, 2013).

Aggressiveness, anxiety, and depression, too, can act as psychological risk factors for illness by increasing physiological arousal, suppressing social support, and interfering with the pursuit of healthy lifestyles. The multifaceted influence of environmental, behavioral, and social risk factors is seen in several serious illnesses, including cardiovascular disease and HIV/AIDS.

Risk Factors for Cardiovascular Disease

About half of the deaths each year in North America result from cardiovascular disease (CVD), high blood pressure, and stroke. That works out to more than 2,600 people per day, or an average of one death every 33 seconds (Centers for Disease Control, 2001a). The list of predisposing risk factors for cardiovascular disease is long, and most of them are of direct relevance to health psychologists. They include family history, ethnicity, depression, anxiety, obesity, sedentary lifestyle, social isolation, hostility, and work-related stress (Schneiderman, Antoni, Saab, & Ironson, 2001). Let's first consider the role of stressors and other psychological factors in CVD.

THE ROLE OF STRESSORS Some of the first strong evidence for the role of stressors in cardiovascular disease came from research on monkeys' responses to various types of stress (Manuck, Kaplan, Adams, & Clarkson, 1988; Manuck, Kaplan, & Clarkson, 1983). Researchers wanted to know whether increases in cardiovascular and endocrine reactivity caused by stressors can, if repeated many times over several years, produce the kinds of changes in the heart or peripheral arteries seen in cardiovascular diseases. The answer appears to be yes; animals showing the greatest increase in heart rate in response to stressors also had significantly more plaque—a build-up of cholesterol and other fatty substances—in their coronary arteries than did animals whose reaction was less extreme. Such an increase in plaque formation makes it more difficult for blood to flow easily through the arteries of the body and is one underlying reason for clinical events like heart attack (lack of blood flow to the heart leading to tissue damage and sometimes death), angina (diminished blood flow leading to pain), and stroke (lack of blood flow to the brain).

As noted earlier, people, too, react to threatening stimuli and other stressors with increases in heart rate, as well as with pronounced changes in blood pressure, and secretion of epinephrine, norepinephrine, and other stress hormones along with lipids (fats) for energy (Anderson, 1989; Krantz & Manuck, 1984; Stoney et al., 2002). In the short run, these changes are biologically adaptive because they provide the short-term increase in energy that is required to respond to many types of physical threats (the fight-or-flight response). Under optimal conditions, such changes in biological functioning return to normal soon after a stressor ends. However, if repeated stressors continually stimulate excessive cardiac activity, these normal biological changes may not be adaptive.

Demographic variables such as ethnicity, education, and poverty are also related to the risk for cardiovascular diseases (Adler & Matthews, 1994), in part, because health-damaging behaviors tend to be inversely related to socioeconomic status (SES). Smoking, for example, is more common among less educated people, as is excessive drinking. Those with lower levels of education are less likely to work and, when they do work, are more likely to find themselves in higher-risk occupations and environments. Residents of poorer neighborhoods also display higher rates of obesity than do residents of higher income neighborhoods (Morland, Diez Roux, & Wing, 2006). Obesity, in turn, significantly increases people's risks for hypertension and coronary heart disease (e.g., Foster & Kendall, 1994).

On the other hand, CVD is about half as common among Chinese and Japanese Americans as among European or African Americans, while high blood pressure is about twice as common among African Americans as European Americans. Males, African Americans of both genders, and older people all suffer higher-than-average rates of heart disease *and* have higher-than-average blood pressure responses to certain stressors. Although the exact mechanisms explaining these differences is not yet clear, physical factors such as diet and cultural factors such as living in stressful environments are almost certainly important contributors.

PSYCHOLOGICAL FACTORS IN CVD As noted earlier, the impact of stressors can be mediated by psychological factors, including whether we think about stressors as threats or challenges and whether we believe we can control them. People who feel helpless in the face of what they see as threats are likely to experience more intense physiological reactivity and emotional upset. On the other hand, those who view stressors as challenges, and feel confident about coping with them, may experience less reactivity and distress (Lazarus & Folkman, 1984).

The relationship between psychological factors and CVD can be complex, as in the case of the *Type-A behavior pattern* (Friedman & Rosenman, 1974). Type-A people are described as displaying (a) explosive, accelerated speech; (b) a heightened pace of living; (c) impatience with slowness; (d) attempts to perform more than one activity at a time; (e) preoccupation with self; (f) dissatisfaction with life; (g) evaluation of accomplishments in terms of numbers; (h) competitiveness; and (i) free-floating hostility (Matthews, 1982). In contrast to Type-A persons, Type-B persons are more relaxed and feel less time pressure. They appear less competitive, controlling, and hostile.

Early research suggested that Type-A behavior is an important risk factor for the development of CVD. Type A individuals in one large study had twice the incidence of heart attacks as Type B individuals (Rosenman et al., 1975). The impact of Type A on CVD risk remained even after the researchers statistically controlled for several other risk factors, including family history of heart disease, high cholesterol, high blood pressure, and cigarette smoking.

However, we now know that the relationship between Type-A behavior and CVD is more complex than was originally believed. For one thing, being a Type-A person does not mean that you are highly likely to suffer a heart attack or other form of CVD. In fact, not all aspects of Type-A behavior are risk factors for CVD (Cohen & Reed, 1985; Eaker, Abbott, & Kannel, 1989; Miller, Turner, Tindale, Posavac, & Dugoni, 1991; Ragland & Brand, 1988). It appears that the most health-risky aspect of the Type-A pattern is *hostility*, a feature that not all Type As display (Birks & Roger, 2000; Williams & Barefoot, 1988; Williams, 2001). Recent research has therefore focused less on the global Type-A pattern and more on hostility and other elements of personality or behavior that are more specifically associated with risk. It turns out that hostile individuals have significantly stronger physiological responses to stress than do less hostile individuals (Rozanski, Blumenthal, & Kaplan, 1999). Specifically, they experience high levels of cardiovascular reactivity most notably in response to interpersonal stressors (Miller et al., 1998; Suls & Wang, 1993).

Depression also plays a role in CVD. Depression among patients with heart disease, and among those who have already had a myocardial infarction (commonly known as a heart attack), is as high as 20%, with an additional 27% showing some symptoms of depression (Burg & Abrams, 2001). After suffering a heart attack, those who are depressed tend to have poorer long-term outcomes, even after controlling for other factors (e.g., cardiac history). Depression also increases the risk of cardiovascular disease among initially healthy individuals (Rugulies, 2003; Wulsin & Singal, 2003). Depression is also associated with lifestyle choices that are associated with additional diseases, so treatment of depression as part of an integrated treatment plan is essential. Still unknown, though, is whether effective treatment of depression can actually reduce the risk for CVD in either healthy individuals or cardiac patients. One large study investigating this question suggests that the timing and type of treatment, as well as the severity of depression, may be important outcome factors (Sheps, Freedland, Golden, & McMahon, 2003).

Risk Factors for HIV/AIDS

It has been estimated that as many as 1 million people in the United States are infected with HIV, the virus that causes acquired immune deficiency syndrome (AIDS). The U. S. Centers for Disease Control (2012) estimates that approximately 50,000 persons are infected with HIV each year in the United States Homosexual males and intravenous drug users are at highest risk, but the incidence of HIV infection is increasing among low-income African Americans and Hispanic American adolescents, and via heterosexual contact. Up to a quarter of those infected in the United States do not know that they are HIV positive (Glynn & Rhodes, 2005). Sadly, the problem is even worse in other parts of the world. Globally, over 34 million persons, 47% of them women, are estimated to be living with HIV/AIDS, and 95% of the cases are in the developing countries of Africa and other third-world regions (World Health Organization, 2013).

Health psychologists have helped focus attention on the fact that most cases of AIDS can be prevented by avoiding several risky behavior patterns: (a) sexual activity without the use of condoms or other protective devices; (b) sexual contact with multiple partners and/or partners with an unknown sexual history; (c) heavy use of alcohol or other drugs that tend to impair judgment about the necessity of using condoms; and (d) for intravenous drug users, sharing injection needles. Stress is also a risk factor for AIDS (as it is for many other diseases) because it not only suppresses the immune system but may distract attention from the need to avoid impulsive and health-damaging behaviors such as drug use or unprotected sex (Perez, Cruess, & Kalichman, 2011).

SECTION SUMMARY

Health psychologists attempt to understand how combinations of risk factors produce specific diseases. Because they affect so many people, cardiovascular disease and HIV/AIDS have been of particular interest. Demographic variables play a significant role in cardiovascular diseases, but psychosocial factors such as perceived social support, hostility, and depression also contribute. Risks for HIV/AIDS are strongly related to behaviors associated with sexual activity and drug use.

ILLNESS PREVENTION AND TREATMENT PROGRAMS

SECTION PREVIEW

In this section, we describe how health psychologists collaborate with physicians, health educators, and other professionals to develop programs for preventing and treating a variety of illnesses. The prevention programs are designed to reduce behavioral and psychological risk factors in specified populations, while treatment programs usually focus on helping medical patients, individually or in small groups, minimize or cope with the symptoms of their illnesses. We highlight health psychology interventions related to cardiovascular diseases, pain, cancer, and HIV/AIDS.

Cardiovascular Diseases

As noted earlier, many people who do not currently have CVD or hypertension are at risk for these diseases because of the health-damaging behaviors they engage in and because of certain cognitive and psychological factors. These people may benefit from preventive interventions designed to reduce their risk.

For example, health psychologists have developed programs aimed at eliminating smoking and other harmful habits and at promoting regular exercise, low fat diets, and other healthy habits (e.g., Azagba & Asbridge, 2013; Jeffery, 1988). Some of these programs focus on a specific risk factor, such as obesity; others address several risk factors at once. Workplace interventions have become popular because corporations believe these interventions reduce the cost of health care and because researchers find that health promotion programs based in work settings permit the control and investigation of several motivational and environmental variables (Glasgow & Terborg, 1988). Community-based and Internet-based interventions are also being tried, with some showing success in assisting patients with behavior change (Bull, Gaglio, Garth, & Glasgow, 2005; Glasgow et al., 2006). A prominent example of multiple-component prevention programs was the Multiple Risk Factor Intervention Trial (MRFIT, 1982), which attempted to lower blood pressure, smoking, and blood cholesterol in thousands of high-risk individuals. Other prevention programs have been based in schools. For instance, the North Karelia, Finland project (Williams, Arnold, & Wynder, 1977), and the Minnesota Heart Health Program (Blackburn et al., 1984) focused on interventions with children and adolescents. Although the North Karelia project was able to demonstrate a 73% reduction in deaths due to coronary heart disease over a 25-year period (Puska, 1999), others have been less successful (Ebrahim, Beswick, Burke, & Smith, 2006).

Pain

Pain may be the single most common physical symptom experienced by medical patients (Turk & Rudy, 1990) and is the most common reason that people visit a health care professional, so pain management is an important objective in psychological interventions with many disorders. Health psychologists have focused their pain research and treatment on chronic pain conditions, headache, and rheumatoid arthritis (Cianfrini, Block, & Doleys, 2013; Keefe, Abernethy, & Campbell, 2005). Their goals are to help patients to perceive less pain, to cope with the psychological distress associated with chronic pain conditions, to decrease impairment of day-to-day functioning, and to develop strategies for more effectively living with chronic pain.

For headache and chronic pain, biofeedback and relaxation training methods have a long record of success, and cognitive-behavioral techniques have also proved effective (e.g., Azar, 1996; Blanchard, 1992). Encouraging healthy behaviors, such as adequate sleep, moderate physical activity when possible, and healthy diets are also an important part of managing chronic pain. And because pain is more severe when people are under stress (Rios and Zautra, 2011), stress management is often effective for many types of pain. For example, arthritis pain has generally been treated effectively via stress management and cognitive-behavioral therapy techniques (Young, 1992). These treatments also have some positive effects on the overall physical impairment associated with arthritis. Clinicians working in health psychology also deal with *phantom pain*, which is sometimes experienced by individuals who have lost a limb. Phantom pain can be

Health psychologists help clients to deal with physical and health challenges, including chronic and phantom pain.   *Source*: Altrendo Images/Getty Images.

extremely difficult to treat, partly because we don't understand its origins. One apparently successful approach is described in a fascinating study using a behavioral treatment called graded motor imagery, in which patients imagine performing motor movements in their missing limb using visual cues provided by mirrors and other devices. Patients in this study experienced a significant reduction in phantom limb pain that had not responded to medications or other pain control methods (Moseley, 2006).

Cancer

Health psychologists have developed a number of interventions designed to address several aspects of cancer (Andersen, 1992; Baum, Reveson, & Singer, 2011). Their goal is to promote an improved quality of life for cancer patients by helping them to (a) understand and confront the disease more actively; (b) cope more effectively with disease-related stressors; and (c) develop emotionally supportive relationships in which they can disclose their fears and other emotions (Andersen, 1992). Behavioral techniques, such as relaxation training, hypnosis, stress management, and cognitive restructuring have proven especially useful. For example, one recent study showed that group therapy for breast cancer patients reduced stress and anxiety, improved perceptions of social support, resulted in decreased smoking and improved dietary habits, and may have improved biological markers of disease as well (Andersen et al., 2004, 2010).

Another aspect of health psychologists' work with cancer patients relates to the severe nausea and vomiting that sometimes results from chemotherapy. After several chemotherapy treatments, some patients develop conditioned responses that cause them to become nauseated even before they receive the drugs. This reaction, known as *anticipatory nausea*, makes some of these patients want to discontinue what can be lifesaving treatment. Thankfully, recent advances in pharmacology have helped alleviate much of the actual nausea and vomiting due to chemotherapy, but health psychologists can continue to help cancer patients with the other common effects of chemotherapy and cancer: fatigue, pain, and depression (Faul & Jacobsen, 2012).

A number of psychological interventions, including relaxation training with guided imagery, progressive muscle relaxation, mindfulness, educational programs and various kinds of supportive individual and group therapy, have been shown to improve the mental and physical well-being of some cancer patients (Andersen et al., 2010; Fawzy, Arndt, & Pasnau, 1995; Goodwin et al., 2001; Helgeson, Cohen, & Fritz, 1998).

HIV/AIDS

Health psychologists are working on AIDS prevention through programs designed to reduce the unprotected sexual contact and needle sharing that are known risk factors for HIV infection (e.g., Bowen & Trotter, 1995; Kalichman, Cherry, & Browne-Sperling, 1999; Taylor, 2011).

In one HIV/AIDS program aimed at African American teenagers at risk for HIV infection, participants were randomly assigned to either a single class on the basic facts about HIV transmission and prevention or to an eight-session program combining the same basic information with behavioral skill training. The behavioral skill training group engaged in role-playing and group activities designed to support sexual abstinence, safer sex practices, and resisting pressure to engage in unsafe sex. Teenagers in the behavioral skills group decreased their rate of unprotected intercourse significantly more than those in the single-class group, and this difference was still evident a year later. Further, among those who had been sexually abstinent when the study began, 88.5% of the teens in the behavioral training program remained so during the follow-up, while only 69% of the one-session information group was still abstinent (St. Lawrence, Brasfield, Jefferson, Alleyne, & O'Bannon, 1995). Success has also been reported following similar programs aimed at adult African American women in inner cities (e.g., Kalichman, Rompa, & Coley, 1996). In another program, gay men participated in twelve group sessions of role-playing, behavioral rehearsal, and problem-solving techniques designed to promote condom use and other safe sex practices. Compared to a control group of gay men who did not receive training, program participants significantly increased their use of condoms, their resistance to sexual coercion, and their knowledge of AIDS risks (Kelly, St. Lawrence, Hood, & Brashfield, 1989).

With the help of health psychologists, many large U.S. cities have established AIDS education programs, clean needle exchanges, condom distributions, and publicity campaigns encouraging safe sex (Kelly & Murphy, 1992; Koester et al., 2007). There are also AIDS prevention

Health psychologists help cancer patients cope with their disease often by teaching progressive relaxation skills. *Source*: Tony Freeman/PhotoEdit, Inc.

programs in many other countries, including those of sub-Saharan Africa, Asia, and parts of the Caribbean where women's AIDS risks have increased dramatically (Canning, 2006). A major goal of AIDS prevention programs in these countries is to empower women to (a) learn about HIV transmission; (b) take greater control of their sexual lives; (c) obtain protective devices such as female condoms or vaginal microbicides; and (d) become less economically dependent on men and therefore less subject to coerced or commercialized sex.

Another important area of research among health psychologists working with HIV/AIDS patients relates to the development of ways to improve these patients' coping skills and quality of life. In one program, 233 men and 99 women infected with HIV/AIDS were randomly assigned to either a five-session group intervention focused on practicing safer sex or a five-session health-maintenance support group (a standard-of-care comparison). The safer sex practices intervention included emphasis on information, motivation, and behavioral skills. At 6-month follow-up, participants in the safe-sex practices intervention engaged in significantly less unprotected intercourse and significantly more condom use (Kalichman et al., 2001; see also Starks, Payton, Golub, Weinberger, & Parsons, 2013).

Other psychological interventions attempt to help patients cope with HIV/AIDS itself. One study of such interventions compared the effectiveness of various kinds of individual psychotherapy for treating depression among HIV-positive patients (Markowitz et al., 1998). In this study, cognitive-behavioral therapists focused on helping clients restructure their appraisals and replace irrational thoughts with more rational ones. Interpersonal therapists focused on mood and helped clients relate moods to environmental events and social roles. Supportive psychotherapy combined client-centered therapy with an educational component about depression. Yet another group received supportive psychotherapy plus imipramine, an antidepressant drug. Reductions in depression appeared in each therapy group, but reductions were significantly better for interpersonal therapy and for supportive psychotherapy plus medication.

Can psychotherapy with HIV-positive patients help to slow the development of full-blown AIDS? In one study on this question, 54 HIV-positive men were randomly assigned to a training program to enhance adherence to medication, while 76 others received the same training program plus a cognitive-behavioral intervention (Antoni et al., 2006). The researchers wanted to know if the psychotherapy intervention might assist patients in adhering to and effectively coping with a complex medical treatment program and thereby improve the patients' immune function. Results indicated that, indeed, the 10-week cognitive-behavior program plus medication adherence program was associated with improved immune function, whereas those in the adherence-only group showed no change.

SECTION SUMMARY

Health psychologists apply their knowledge of risk factors by working to develop disease prevention and treatment programs. The prevention programs often take place in schools, workplaces, or other community settings. Treatment-related programs are typically designed to help patients cope with, and slow the progression of, their illnesses.

A HEALTH PSYCHOLOGY CASE EXAMPLE

Robert E. Feinstein and Marilyn Sommer Feinstein (2001) describe a case example that illustrates many of the conditions encountered by health psychologists. Perhaps the most prominent feature of their work with "Karen" was the co-occurrence of several problems that are of both medical and psychological concern.

Karen's case illustrates another important aspect of health psychology treatment, namely that therapists often must consider conducting interventions outside of the normally defined roles of clinical psychologists. Helping clients to increase exercise is one of these areas (Pollock, 2001). Such nontraditional interventions are indicated because of research evidence that exercise can be as effective as other, more traditional clinical interventions such as cognitive restructuring or emotional support. For instance, Babyak and colleagues (2000) found that exercise was at least as effective as antidepressant medication in reducing the symptoms of mild depression, and more effective in preventing remission. A recent meta-analysis confirmed that physical exercise can have a large overall effect in reducing mild to moderate depression (Josefsson, Lindwall, & Archer, 2013).

Karen, was a 42-year-old married woman with two children (one a stepchild). When she came to the clinic for help with smoking cessation, she was 30 pounds overweight, drank excessively, and had high cholesterol and symptoms of depression. In some areas of her life, she functioned reasonably well, however.

Karen's therapists adopted a transtheoretical model (see Table 12.2) to design her treatment (Prochaska et al., 1994). This model is designed to assess a client's readiness and ability to inhibit certain behaviors (e.g., smoking) or perform others (e.g., exercise), and interventions are shaped accordingly.

The transtheoretical model is one of several models within health psychology that address cognitive factors involved in people's decision to change health-related behaviors (see Rothman, 2000). In this five-step model, the first three involve a person's cognitive readiness to change (Prochaska, DiClemente, & Norcross, 1992).

Karen's treatment planning began with a patient history, then empirical evidence about the health risk for items in that history were collected. Data on success rates for the various methods available to deal with the patient's various problems were also reviewed. These data provided an estimate of how easy or difficult change generally is. Karen and her therapists discussed her personal priorities for treatment and her hopes and expectations about its success. For instance, they considered Karen's motivation and expectations about change in light of the health threats she faced and her probability of achieving change. Through a process known as informed shared decision-making, Karen and her therapists jointly developed an intervention plan.

Karen and her therapists decided to begin a program of once-a-week treatment sessions focused on her depression and lack of exercise. These targets were chosen because, given her history and current situation, efforts at dealing with them appeared to have the greatest chance of success.

TABLE 12.2 A Transtheoretical Model for Assessment and Intervention

Stage	Description
Precontemplation	The person does not perceive a health-related behavior as a problem and has not formed an intention to change.
Contemplation	The person is aware that a health-related behavior should be changed and is thinking about it.
Preparation	The person has formed a strong intention to change.
Action	The person is engaging in behavior change. (Relapse and backsliding are common at this stage.)
Maintenance	After behavior changes have begun, the person must continue performing and/or avoiding specified behaviors.

Source: Based on Prochaska, J. O., Velicer, W. F., Rossi, J. S., Goldstein, M. G., et al. (1994).

IMPROVING ADHERENCE TO MEDICAL TREATMENT REGIMENS

SECTION PREVIEW

In this section, we review a set of behaviors that are essential for health—adherence to medical treatment recommendations. Psychologists help to identify the causes of nonadherence; they also develop various interventions to improve adherence.

Psychological interventions aimed at disease prevention or symptom reduction often result in immediate improvements in healthy behaviors, but unfortunately, these changes may not be maintained long enough to promote a healthier life (Blanchard, 1994). Maintaining behavior change remains one of the most vexing problems in health psychology. For example, smoking cessation programs usually result in significant rates of abstinence, but more than 50% of smokers resume their habit within a year (Jason et al., 1995; Shiffman et al., 1996). Although behavior modification appears to be the most effective psychological intervention for obesity, maintenance of weight loss and learning new eating habits are major difficulties for most people. Most psychologically oriented weight-reduction interventions can achieve reductions of about 1 pound per week, but it is difficult to maintain these reductions beyond 1 or 2 years (Brownell & Wadden, 1992). Similar difficulties are found even when patients try to alter their lifestyles after a heart attack. It would seem reasonable to assume that such a traumatic event might jolt people into permanent lifestyle changes, but as many as 50% of cardiac rehabilitation participants drop out of their programs within 1 year (Burke, Dunbar-Jacob, & Hill, 1997).

The effectiveness of medical treatment, too, depends not only on its being the correct treatment but also on the patient's continued cooperation with it. The extent to which patients adhere to medical advice and treatment regimens is called *compliance* or *adherence* (Rodin & Salovey, 1989). Research on the impact of adherence on medical outcomes makes it clear that adhering to treatment advice is important—clients can even end up worse than when they began if they fail to adhere to treatment. Adherence can be affected by several factors, including the severity and chronicity of the disease, patient age, the quality of the doctor–patient relationship, patients' perceptions of probable outcomes, and the type and complexity of treatment prescribed (DiMatteo, Giordani, Lepper, & Croghan, 2002). Nonadherence in taking prescribed medication may occur in half or more of all patients (Haynes, 1982). A survey among European adults demonstrated that 65% of them failed to complete their full prescribed dose of antibiotics; nearly all of these individuals reported that they did not take the full course of medication because they felt better (Branthwaite & Pechere, 1996). Nonadherence rates among parents who are providing medication for their children tend to be lower, but for some medications taken by adolescents, nonadherence rates can be as high as 80% (Rickert & Jay, 1995). Indeed, adolescents may not take prescribed medications at all, may take it less frequently or more frequently than instructed, or they may ignore rules about the need to take medicine with food or not to consume alcohol while on medication. Nonadherence tends to be especially common in treatments that are complicated, unpleasant, and involve substantial lifestyle changes and long-term consequences. Health psychologists have been involved in efforts to understand the causes of nonadherence and in developing interventions to improve adherence.

Causes of Nonadherence

One cause of nonadherence appears to be miscommunication between physicians and patients. Patients frequently do not understand what physicians tell them about their illnesses or their treatments. As a result, they are confused about what they should do or they forget what they have been told. One study showed that 5 minutes after seeing their physician, general-practice patients had forgotten 50% of what the doctor had told them (Ley, Bradshaw, Eaves, & Walker, 1973).

The emotional aspects of patient–physician communication also are correlated with adherence. A common pattern of troubled communication involves patient antagonism toward the physician, accompanied by physician withdrawal from the patient. Adherence may also be reduced by the sheer complexity, inconvenience, or discomfort associated with some kinds of treatment. In cases where treatments have significant unpleasant side-effects, for example, the effects of following a prescribed treatment regime may feel worse than the effects of the medical condition it is designed to treat. Finally, nonadherence with treatment may appear because patients do not have a good system for reminding themselves about what to do and when to do it.

A psychological theory called the *health belief model* (HBM) (Rosenstock, 1974) has been especially helpful in understanding the reasons for patient nonadherence (Becker & Maiman, 1975). According to the HBM, patients' adherence with treatment depends on factors such as (a) how susceptible to a given illness they perceive themselves to be and how severe the consequences of the illness are thought to be; (b) how effective and feasible versus how costly and difficult the prescribed treatment is perceived to be; (c) the influence of internal cues (physical symptoms) plus external cues (e.g., advice from friends) in triggering health behaviors; and (d) demographic and personality variables that modify the influences of the previous three factors.

Interventions to Improve Adherence

Attempts to improve adherence with treatment can be classified into three general approaches: (a) educating patients about the importance of adherence so that they will take a more active role in maintaining their own health, (b) modifying treatment plans to make adherence easier, and (c) using behavioral and cognitive-behavioral techniques such as self-monitoring, reminder cues, and other tools to increase patients' ability to adhere (Masur, 1981).

EDUCATION One direct and effective intervention for improving adherence with short-term treatments is to give patients clear, explicit, written instructions that supplement oral instructions about how treatment is to proceed. Educating physicians about the causes and management of nonadherence may also be beneficial. In one study (Inui, Yourtee, & Williamson, 1976), physicians who had been educated about the HBM and ways to improve adherence had more adherent patients at a 6-month reassessment. Education can also counteract inaccurate or naive theories of illness that some patients may have.

MODIFICATIONS OF TREATMENT PLANS A second strategy for increasing adherence is to reorganize treatment to make it easier for patients to follow treatment instructions. Examples include timing daily doses of medication to coincide with daily habits (e.g., taking pills right after brushing teeth), giving treatment in one or two injections rather than in several doses per day, packaging medicine in dosage strips or with pill calendars, and scheduling more frequent follow-up visits to supervise adherence. These procedures have shown promise (e.g., Boczkowski, Zeichner, & DeSanto, 1985), but many of them entail additional manufacturing costs and extra time from service providers, two characteristics that tend to limit their usefulness.

BEHAVIOR MODIFICATION Health psychologists have used a number of behavioral techniques, including the use of motivational interviewing, telephone calls, wristwatch alarms, e-mails, text messages, smart phone apps, and other environmental cues to prompt patients to take pills or perform other aspects of treatment plans (Miller, 2012; Rickert & Jay, 1995). They have also set up written *contingency contracts* (described in Chapter 8) between patient and physician that specify what behaviors the patient can perform in order to earn rewards (e.g., more conveniently timed office appointments). Such contracts encourage a more collaborative relationship between patient and physician and have been successful in improving adherence (Swain & Steckel, 1981).

Behavior modification procedures have also been used to reduce nonadherence motivated by the discomfort associated with medical procedures or treatments. The best-known illustration of these methods was described earlier in relation to behavioral treatments for the control of anticipatory nausea in cancer chemotherapy patients. Other examples include teaching children to use breathing exercises and distraction techniques to help them overcome fear of routine vaccinations (Blount et al., 1992), employing hypnosis to reduce pain in burn patients who are undergoing debridement procedures (Patterson, Everett, Burns, & Marvin, 1992), and using relaxation, systematic desensitization, and participant modeling to help fearful patients get the dental work they need but have been avoiding (e.g., Kleinknecht & Bernstein, 1978).

SECTION SUMMARY

Health psychologists help design interventions, but they are also active in trying to find ways to encourage clients to adhere to treatment plans. This can be especially difficult if treatment is extended over weeks or months, which is the case with several of the illnesses described in this chapter. To enhance adherence, clinicians help health care providers modify treatments or communicate with patients; they help educate patients about factors related to adherence and nonadherence; and they employ a number of behavioral techniques.

Chapter Summary

Health psychology is a specialty devoted to studying psychological, behavioral, and social influences on health, illness, and coping with health problems. It is closely related to the larger field of behavioral medicine, which involves the integration of knowledge from many disciplines in understanding and treating medical disorders. Both fields adopt a biopsychosocial model in which physical illness is viewed as involving biological, psychological, and social factors. Health psychologists seek to (a) understand how these factors interact to influence illness and health, (b) identify risk factors for sickness and protective factors for health, (c) promote healthy behaviors and prevent unhealthy ones, and (d) create interventions that contribute to medical treatment of illness.

Stress is the negative emotional and physiological process that occurs as people try to deal with threats, called stressors, that disrupt or threaten to disrupt daily functioning when people do not perceive that they have the ability to cope with those threats. Stress reactions can be physical, psychological, and behavioral. Physical stress reactions include the general adaptation syndrome, which begins with an alarm reaction and, if stressors persist, continues into the stages of resistance and exhaustion. Prolonged stress can result in immunosuppression, impairment of the body's disease-fighting immune system and excessive sympathetic nervous system activation. The impact of stressors tends to be lessened in people with better social support systems. Lack of social support increases risk for physical disorders.

Anything that increases the chances of developing an illness is called a risk factor for that illness. Behaviors associated with risk for cardiovascular disease (CVD) and cancer include smoking, overeating, lack of exercise, and consumption of a high-fat diet. Stressors, hostility, and depression also appear to be risk factors for CVD. Risk factors for HIV/AIDS include unprotected sexual activity and, for intravenous drug users, sharing injection needles.

Illness prevention programs in health psychology seek to reduce risk factors for cardiovascular disease, chronic pain, cancer, AIDS, and other diseases by working with individuals, groups, and whole communities to alter health-risky behaviors. Health psychologists often treat individuals with multiple health problems, and decisions must be made about which conditions have priority. Although many types of interventions are initially successful, long-term behavior change is difficult in some areas, particularly those involving strongly entrenched habits (e.g., smoking, substance abuse, sedentary behaviors, overeating) and behavioral changes that must occur over a long period of time.

Health psychologists' efforts to improve patients' adherence to prescribed medical treatments include education about the importance of adherence, modifying treatment plans to make adherence easier, and using behavioral techniques to increase patients' ability to adhere.

Study Questions

1. What is health psychology?
2. How does stress influence the human nervous system?
3. How does stress influence the immune system?
4. How do health psychologists measure stress?
5. What are problem-focused and emotion-focused coping?
6. Which personality characteristics appear to help people cope with stressors?
7. How does social support influence the experience of stress?
8. What are risk factors for chronic heart disease?
9. What are risk factors for HIV/AIDS?
10. What psychological interventions have been attempted to prevent chronic heart disease?
11. What roles do health psychologists play in the prevention and treatment of chronic pain, cancer, and HIV/AIDS?
12. What are some of the causes of nonadherence to medical treatment?
13. What interventions have psychologists attempted to improve adherence to medical treatment?

Web Sites

- Health Psychology Division of APA (Division 38): http://www.apa.org/about/division/div38.html

- Home page for the journal *Health Psychology:* http://www.apa.org/pubs/journals/hea/index.aspx

- Health Psychology and Rehabilitation home Page: http://www.healthpsych.com

MOVIES

In America (2002): Gripping story that deals with loss of a child and creating a new family, with the help of an artistic neighbor who is living with HIV.

My Sister's Keeper (2009): Strong family drama, which raises ethical questions about having one sibling serve as a required donor for another sibling who is battling leukemia.

MEMOIRS

Blindsided: Lifting a Life Above Illness by Richard M. Cohen (2004; New York: Perennial). This amusing and utterly honest "reluctant" memoir describes the author's 30-year struggle with multiple sclerosis, and the more recent challenges of colon cancer, blindness, and lack of mobility.

The Victoria's Secret Catalog Never Stops Coming—And Other Lessons I Learned from Breast Cancer by Jennie Nash (2001; New York: Plume). This painful yet funny memoir describes the author's battle with breast cancer, with particular emphasis on the impact of illness on the family.

References

Adler, N. E., & Matthews, K. (1994). Health psychology: Why do some people get sick and some stay well. *Annual Review of Psychology, 45*, 229–259.

Amundson, M. E., Hart, C. A., & Holmes, T. H. (1986). *Manual for the schedule of recent experience.* Seattle, WA: University of Washington Press.

Andersen, B. L. (1992). Psychological interventions for cancer patients to enhance the quality of life. *Journal of Consulting & Clinical Psychology, 60*, 552–568.

Andersen, B. L., Farrar, W. B., Golden-Kreutz, D. M., Glaser, R., Emery, C. F., et al. (2004). Psychological, behavioral, and immune changes after a psychological intervention: A clinical trial. *Journal of Clinical Oncology, 22*, 3570–3580.

Andersen, B. L., Thornton, L. M., Shapiro, C. L., Farrar, W. B., Mundy, B. L., et al. (2010). Biobehavioral, immune, and health benefits following recurrence for psychological intervention participants. *Clinical Cancer Research, 16(12)*.

Anderson, N. B. (1989). Racial differences in stress-reduced cardiovascular reactivity and hypertension: Current status and substantive issues. *Psychological Bulletin, 105*, 89–105.

Antoni, M. H., Carrico, A. W., Duran, R. E., Spitzer, S., Penedo, F., et al. (2006). Randomized clinical trial of cognitive behavioral stress management on human immunodeficiency virus load in gay men treated with highly active antiretroviral therapy. *Psychosomatic Medicine, 68*, 143–151.

Atanackovic, D., Schnee, B., Schuch, G., Faltz, C., Schulze, J., et al. (2006). Acute psychological stress alters the adaptive immune response: Stress-induced mobilization of effector T cells. *Journal of Neuroimmunology,176*, 141–152.

Azagba, S., & Asbridge, M. (2013). School connectedness and susceptibility to smoking among adolescents in Canada. Nicotine and Tobacco Research, Online version, 10.1093/ntr/nts340. No pagination specified.

Azar, B. (1996). Behavioral interventions are proven to reduce pain. *APA Monitor* (December), 22.

Babyak, M., Blumenthal, J. A., Herman, S., Khatri, P., Doraiswamy, M., et al. (2000). Exercise treatment for major depression: Maintenance of therapeutic benefit at 10 months. *Psychosomatic Medicine, 62*, 633–638.

Baum, A., Reveson, T. A., & Singer, J. E. (Eds.). (2011). *Handbook of health psychology.* Hillsdale, NJ: Erlbaum.

Baumeister, R. F., & Leary, M. R. (1995). The need to belong: Desire for interpersonal attachments as a fundamental human motivation. *Psychological Bulletin, 117*, 497–529.

Becker, M. H., & Maiman, L. A. (1975). Sociobehavioral determinants of compliance with health and medical care recommendations. *Medical Care, 13*, 10–24.

Birks, Y., & Roger, D. (2000). Identifying components of type-A behavior: "Toxic" and "non-toxic" achieving. *Personality and Individual Differences, 28*, 1093–1105.

Blackburn, H., Luepker, R. V., Kline, F. G., Bracht, N., Carlaw, R., et al. (1984). The Minnesota Heart Health Program: A research and demonstration project in cardiovascular disease prevention. In J. D. Matarazzo et al. (Eds.), *Behavioral health: A handbook of health enhancement and disease prevention* (pp. 1171–1178). New York, NY: Wiley.

Blanchard, E. B. (1992). Psychological treatment of benign headache disorders. *Journal of Consulting and Clinical Psychology, 60*, 537–551.

Blanchard, E. B. (1994). Behavioral medicine and health psychology. In A. E. Bergin & S. L. Garfield (Eds.), *Handbook of psychotherapy and behavior change* (pp. 701–733). New York, NY: Wiley.

Blount, R. L., Bachanas, P. J., Powers, S. W., Cotter, M. C., Franklin, A., et al. (1992). Training children to cope and parents to coach them during routine immunizations: Effects on child, parent, and staff behavior. *Behavior Therapy, 23*, 689–705.

Blumenthal, S. J. (1994). Introductory remarks. In S. J. Blumenthal, K. Matthews, & S. M. Weiss (Eds.), *New research frontiers in behavioral medicine* (pp. 9–15). Washington, DC: National Institute of Mental Health.

Boczkowski, J. A., Zeichner, A., & DeSanto, N. (1985). Neuroleptic compliance among chronic schizophrenic outpatients: An intervention outcome report. *Journal of Consulting and Clinical Psychology, 53*, 666–671.

Bowen, A. M., & Trotter, R. T., II (1995). HIV risk in intravenous drug users and crack cocaine smokers: Predicting stage of change for condom use. *Journal of Consulting and Clinical Psychology, 63*, 238–248.

Brannon, L., & Feist, J. (2009). *Health psychology: An introduction to behavior and health.* Belmont, CA: Wadsworth.

Branthwaite, A., & Pechere, J. C. (1996). Pan-European survey of patients' attitudes to antibiotics and antibiotic use. *Journal of International Medical Research, 24*, 229–238.

Breslow, L. (1979). A positive strategy for the nation's health. *Journal of the American Medical Association, 242*, 2093–2094.

Broman, C. L. (1993). Social relationships and health-related behavior. *Journal of Behavioral Medicine, 16*, 335–350.

Brownell, K. D., & Wadden, T. A. (1992). Etiology and treatment of obesity: Understanding a serious, prevalent, and refractory disorder. *Journal of Consulting and Clinical Psychology, 60*, 505–517.

Bull, S. S., Gaglio, B., Garth, M. H., & Glasgow, R. E. (2005). Harnessing the potential of the Internet to promote chronic illness self-management: Diabetes as an example of how well we are doing. *Chronic Illness, 1*,143–155.

Burg, M. M., & Abrams, D. (2001). Depression in chronic medical illness: The case of coronary heart disease. *Journal of Clinical Psychology/In Session, 57*, 1323–1337.

Burke, L. E., Dunbar-Jacob, J. M., & Hill, M. N. (1997). Compliance with cardiovascular disease prevention strategies: A review of the research. *Annals of Behavioral Medicine, 19*, 239–263.

Canning, D. (2006). The economics of HIV/AIDS in low-income countries: The case for prevention. *Journal of Economic Perspectives, 20*, 121–142.

Carver, C. S. (2011). Coping. In R. J. Contrada & A. Baum (Eds.), *The handbook of stress science: Biology, psychology, and health* (pp. 221–229). New York, NY: Springer.

Centers for Disease Control. (2001a). About cardiovascular disease. Retrieved Dec 3, 2001 from http://www.cdc.gov/nccdphp/cvd/aboutcardio.htm.

Centers for Disease Control. (2001b). Basic statistics—Cumulative AIDS Cases. Retrieved Dec 3, 2001, from http://www.cdc.gov/hiv/stats/cumulati.htm.

Centers for Disease Control. (2001c). Basic statistics—International Statistics. Retrieved Dec 3, 2001, from http://www.cdc.gov/hiv/stats/cumulati.htm.

CDC. Estimated HIV incidence among adults and adolescents in the United States, 2007–2010. HIV Supplemental Report 2012). Available at http://www.cdc.gov/hiv/topics/surveillance/resources/reports/index.htm#supplemental.

Chan, M., Chen, E., Hibbert, A. S., Wong, J. H. K., & Miller, G. E. (2011). Implicit measures of early-life family conditions: Relationships to psychosocial characteristics and cardiovascular disease risk in adulthood. *Health Psychology, 30,* 570–578.

Christakis, N. A., & Fowler, J. H. (2007). The spread of obesity in a large social network over 32 years. *New England Journal of Medicine, 357,* 370–379.

Christakis, N. A., & Fowler, J. H. (2008). The collective dynamics of smoking in a large social network. *New England Journal of Medicine, 358,* 2249–2258.

Cianfrini, L. R., Block, C., & Doleys, D. M. (2013). Comprehensive treatment of chronic pain by medical, interventional, and integrative approaches. *Psychological Therapies, 44,* 827–844.

Cohen, S. (2004). Social relationships and health. *American Psychologist, 59,* 676–684.

Cohen, S., Gottlieb, B., & Underwood, L. (2000). Social relationships and health. In S. Cohen, L. Underwood, & B. Gottlieb (Eds.), *Measuring and intervening in social support* (pp. 3–25). New York, NY: Oxford University Press.

Cohen, S., Janicki-Deverts, D., Doyle, W. J., Miller, G. E., Frank, E., et al. (2012). Chronic stress, glucocorticoid receptor resistance, inflammation, and disease risk. *Proceedings of the National Academy of Sciences,* 109.

Cohen, S., Kamarck, T., & Mermelstein, R. (1983). A global measure of perceived stress. *Journal of Health and Social Behavior, 24,* 385–396.

Cohen, S., & Rabin, B. S. (1998). Psychological stress, immunity, and cancer. *Journal of the National Cancer Institute, 90,* 3–4.

Cohen, J. B., & Reed, D. (1985). Type A behavior and coronary heart disease among Japanese men in Hawaii. *Journal of Behavioral Medicine, 8,* 343–352.

Cohen, S., Tyrrell, D. A., & Smith, A. P. (1991). Psychological stress in humans and susceptibility to the common cold. *New England Journal of Medicine, 325,* 606–612.

Cohen, S., & Wills, T. A. (1985). Stress, social support, and the buffering hypothesis. *Psychological Bulletin, 98,* 310–357.

Compas, B. E., Jaser, S. S., Dunn, M. J., & Rodriguez, E. M. (2012). Coping with chronic illness in childhood and adolescence. *Annual Review of Clinical Psychology, 8,* 455–480.

Currie, D. (2013). Major causes of disability, death, shift around the globe: Chronic diseases now taking the lead. *The Nation's Health, 43,* 1–22.

Danner, D. D., Snowdon, D. A., & Friesen, W. V. (2001). Positive emotions in early life and longevity: Findings from the nun study. *Journal of Personality and Social Psychology, 80,* 804–813.

Diener, E. (2012). New findings and future directions for subjective well-being research. *American Psychologist, 67,* 590–597.

DiMatteo, R., Giordani, P. J., Lepper, H. S., & Croghan, T. W. (2002). Patient adherence and medical treatment outcomes: A meta-analysis. *Medical Care, 40,* 794–811.

Dohrenwend, B. S. (1978). Social stress and community psychology. *American Journal of Community Psychology, 6,* 1–14.

Dornelas, E. A. (2001) Introduction: Integrating health psychology into clinical practice. *Journal of Clinical Psychology/In Session, 57,* 1261–1262.

Dougall, A. L., Wroble-Biglan, M. C., Swanson, J. N., & Baum, A. (2013). Stress, coping, and immune function. In R. J. Nelson, S. J. Y. Mizumori, & I. B. Weiner (Eds), *Handbook of psychology, Vol. 3: Behavioral neuroscience* (2nd ed., pp. 440–460). Hoboken, NJ: Wiley.

Eaker, E. D., Abbott, R. D., & Kannel, W. B. (1989). Frequency of uncomplicated angina pectoris in Type A compared with Type B persons (the Framingham study). *American Journal of Cardiology, 63,* 1042–1045.

Ebrahim, S., Beswick, A., Burke, M., & Davey-Smith, G. (2006). Multiple risk factor interventions for primary prevention of coronary heart disease. *Cochrane Database Systematic Review, 18,* CD001561.

Entringer, S., Epel, E. S., Kumsta, R., Lin, J., Hellhammer, D. H., et al. (2011). Stress exposure in intrauterine life is associated with shorter telomere length in young adulthood. *Proceedings of the National Academy of Sciences, 108,* E513–E518.

Faul, L. A., & Jacobsen, P. B. (2012). Psychosocial interventions for people with cancer. In A. Baum, T. A. Revenson, & J. Singer (Eds.), *Handbook of health psychology* (2nd ed., pp. 697–715). New York, NY: Psychology Press.

Fawzy, F. I., Fawzy, N. W., Arndt, L. A., & Pasnau, R. O. (1995). Critical review of psychosocial interventions in cancer care. *Archives of General Psychiatry, 52,* 100–113.

Feinstein, R. E., & Feinstein, M. S. (2001). Psychotherapy for health and lifestyle change. *Journal of Clinical Psychology/In Session, 57,* 1263–1275.

Flores, E., Tschann, J. M., Dimas, J. M., Pasch, L. A., deGroat, C. L. (2010). Perceived ethnic/racial discrimination, posttraumatic stress symptoms and health risk behaviors among Mexican American adolescents. *Journal of Counseling Psychology, 57,* 264–273.

Folkman, S., & Lazarus, R. S. (1980). An analysis of coping in a middle-aged community sample. *Journal of Health and Social Behavior, 21,* 219–239.

Folkman, S., Lazarus, R. S., Gruen, R. J., & DeLongis, A. (1986). Appraisal, coping, health status, and psychological symptoms, *Journal of Personality and Social Psychology, 50,* 571–579.

Foster, G. D., & Kendall, P. C. (1994). The realistic treatment of obesity: Changing the scales of success. *Clinical Psychology Review, 14,* 701–736.

Friedman, M., & Rosenman, R. H. (1974). *Type A behavior and your heart.* New York, NY: Knopf.

Friedman, M., Thoresen, C. E., Gill, I. J., Ulmer, D., Powell, L.H., et al. (1986). Alteration of Type A behavior and its effect on cardiac recurrences in post-myocardial infarction patients: Summary results of the Recurrent Coronary Prevention Project. *American Heart Journal, 112,* 653–665.

Glasgow, R. E., Nutting, P. A., Toobert, D. J., King, D. K., Strycker, L. A., et al. (2006). Effects of a brief computer-assisted diabetes self-management intervention on dietary, biological and quality-of-life outcomes. *Chronic Illness, 2,* 27–38.

Glasgow, R. E., & Terborg, J. R. (1988). Occupational health promotion programs to reduce cardiovascular risk. *Journal of Consulting and Clinical Psychology, 56,* 365–373.

Glynn, M., & Rhodes, P. (2005). Estimated HIV prevalence in the US at the end of 2003. National HIV Prevention Conference, Atlanta, Georgia.

Goodwin, P. J., Leszcz, M., Ennis, M., Koopmans, J., Vincent, L., et al. (2001). The effect of group psychosocial support on survival in metastatic breast cancer. *The New England Journal of Medicine, 345,* 1719–1726.

Haynes, R. B. (1982). Improving patient compliance: An empirical view. In R. B. Stuart (Ed.), *Adherence, compliance, and generalization in behavioral medicine* (pp. 56–78). New York, NY: Brunner/Mazel.

Helgeson, V. S., Cohen, S., & Fritz, H. (1998). Social ties and the onset and progression of cancer. In J. Holland (Ed.), *Psycho-oncology.* New York, NY: Oxford University Press.

Inui, T., Yourtee, E., & Williamson, J. (1976). Improved outcomes in hypertension after physician tutorials. *Annals of Internal Medicine, 84,* 646–651.

Jason, L. A., McMahon, S. D., Salina, D., Hedeker, D., Stockton, M., et al. (1995). Assessing a smoking cessation intervention involving groups, incentives, and self-help manuals. *Behavior Therapy, 26,* 393–408.

Jeffery, R. W. (1988). Dietary risk factors and their modification in cardiovascular disease. *Journal of Consulting and Clinical Psychology, 56,* 350–357.

Josefsson, T., Lindwall, M., & Archer, T. (2013). Physical exercise intervention in depressive disorder: A meta-analysis and systematic review. *Medicine & Science in Sports,* Article first published online: 30 JAN 2013, doi: 10.1111/sms.12050.

Kalichman, S. C., Cherry, C., & Browne-Sperling, F. (1999). Effectiveness of a video-based motivational skills-building HIV risk-reduction intervention for inner-city African American men. *Journal of Consulting and Clinical Psychology, 67,* 959–966.

Kalichman, S. C., Rompa, D., Cage, M., DiFonzo, K., Simpson, D., et al. (2001). Effectiveness of an intervention to reduce HIV transmission risks in HIV-positive people. *American Journal of Preventive Medicine, 21,* 84–92.

Kalichman, S. C., Rompa, D., & Coley, B. (1996). Experimental component analysis of a behavioral HIV-AIDS prevention for inner-city women. *Journal of Consulting and Clinical Psychology, 64,* 687–693.

Kashdan, T. B., & Rottenberg, J. (2010). Psychological flexibility as a fundamental aspect of health. *Clinical Psyhcological Review, 30,* 467–480.

Keefe, F. J., Abernethy, A. P., & Campbell, L. (2005). Psychological approaches to understanding and treating disease-related pain. *Annual Review of Psychology, 56,* 601–630.

Kelley, J. E., Lumley, M. A., & Leisen, J. C. C. (1997). Health effects of emotional disclosure in rheumatoid arthritis patients. *Health Psychology, 16,* 331–340.

Kelly, J. A., & Murphy, D. A. (1992). Psychological interventions with AIDS and HIV: Prevention and treatment. *Journal of Consulting and Clinical Psychology, 60,* 576–585.

Kelly, J. A., St. Lawrence, J. S., Hood, H. V., & Brashfield, T. L. (1989). Behavioral intervention to reduce AIDS risk activities. *Journal of Consulting and Clinical Psychology, 57,* 60–67.

Kiecolt-Glaser, J. K., & Glaser, R. (1992). Psychoneuroimmunology: Can psychological interventions modulate immunity? *Journal of Consulting and Clinical Psychology, 60,* 569–575.

Kiecolt-Glaser, J. K., Loving, T. J., Stowell, J. R., Malarkey, W. B., Lemeshow, S., et al. (2005). Hostile marital interactions, proinflammatory cytokine production, and wound healing. *Archives of General Psychiatry, 62,* 1377–1384.

Kessler, R. C., Price, R. H., & Wortman, C. B. (1985). Social factors in psychopathology: Stress, social support, and coping processes. *Annual Review of Psychology, 36,* 531–572.

Kleinknecht, R. A., & Bernstein, D. A. (1978). Assessment of dental fear. *Behavior Therapy, 9,* 626–634.

Koester, K. A., Maiorana, A., Vernon, K., Myers, J., Rose, C. D., et al. (2007). Implementation of HIV prevention interventions with people living with HIV/AIDS in clinical settings: Challenges and lessons learned. *AIDS & Behavior, 11(5 Suppl),* S17–S29.

Krantz, D. S., & Manuck, S. B. (1984). Acute psychophysiologic reactivity and risk of cardiovascular disease—A review and methodologic critique. *Psychological Bulletin, 96,* 435–464.

Lazarus, R. S., (1993). From psychological stress to the emotions: A history of changing outlooks. *Annual Review of Psychology, 44,* 1–21.

Lazarus, R. S., & Folkman, S. (1984). *Stress, appraisal, and coping.* New York, NY: Springer.

Ley, P., Bradshaw, P. W., Eaves, D. E., & Walker, C. M. (1973). A method for increasing patient recall of information presented to them. *Psychological Medicine, 3,* 217–220.

Malarkey, W. B., Kiecolt-Glaser, J. K., Pearl, D., & Glaser, R. (1994). Hostile behavior during marital conflict alters pituitary and adrenal hormones. *Psychosomatic Medicine, 56,* 41–51.

Manuck, S. B., Kaplan, J. R., Adams, M. R., & Clarkson, T. B. (1988). Effects of stress and the sympathetic nervous system on coronary artery atheroslerosis in the cynomolgus macaque. *American Heart Journal, 116,* 328–333.

Manuck, S. B., Kaplan, J. R., & Clarkson, T. B. (1983). Behaviorally induced heart rate reactivity and atherosclerosis in cynomolgus monkeys. *Psychosomatic Medicine, 49,* 95–108.

Markowitz, J., Kocsis, M., Fishman, B., Spielman, L., Jacobsberg, L., et al. (1998). Treatment of depressive symptoms in Human Immunodeficiency Virus–positive patients. *Archives of General Psychiatry, 55,* 452–457.

Masur, F. T. (1981). Adherence to health care regimens. In C. K. Prokop & L. A. Bradley (Eds.), *Medical psychology: Contributions to behavioral medicine* (pp. 442–470). New York, NY: Academic Press.

Matthews, K. A. (1982). Psychological perspectives on the Type A behavior pattern. *Psychological Bulletin, 91,* 293–323.

McGrady, A., & Moss, D. (2013). *Pathways to illness, pathways to health.* New York, NY, NY: Springer.

Miller, G. (2012). The smartphone psychology manifesto. *Perspectives on Psychological Science, 7,* 221–237.

Miller, G. E., & Cohen, S. (2001). Psychological interventions and the immune system: A meta-analytic review and critique. *Health Psychology, 20,* 47–63.

Miller, S. B., Freise, M., Dolgoy, L., Sita, A., Lavoie, K., et al. (1998). Hostility, sodium consumption, and cardiovascular response to interpersonal stress. *Psychosomatic Medicine, 60,* 71–77.

Miller, T. Q., Turner, C. W., Tindale, R. S., Posavac, E. J., & Dugoni, B. L. (1991). Reasons for the trend toward null findings in research on Type A behavior. *Psychological Bulletin, 110,* 469–485.

Morland, K., Diez Roux, A. V., & Wing, S. (2006). Supermarkets, other food stores, and obesity. *American Journal of Preventive Medicine, 30,* 333–339.

Moseley G. L. (2006). Graded motor imagery for pathologic pain: A randomized controlled trial. *Neurology, 67,* 2129–2134.

Murray, C. J. L. Vos, T., Lozano, R., Naghavi, M., Flaxman, A., et al. (2013). Disability-adjusted life years (DALYs) for 291 diseases and injuries in 21 regions, 1990–2010: A systematic analysis for the Global Burden of Disease Study 2010. *The Lancet, 380,* 2197–2223.

Myers, D. G. (2000). The funds, friends, and faith of happy people. *American Psychologist, 55,* 56–67.

Norcross, J. C., Krebs, P. M., & Prochaska, J. O. (2011). Stages of change. *Journal of Clinical Psychology, 67,* 143–154.

Novak, M., Björck, L., Giang, K. W., Heden-Stahl, C., Wilhelmsen, L., et al. (2013). Perceived stress and incidence of Type 2 diabetes: A 35-year follow-up study of middle-aged Swedish men. *Diabetic Medicine, 30,* 8–16.

Nunes, E. V., Frank, K. A., & Kornfeld, S. D. (1987). Psychologic treatment for Type A behavior pattern and for coronary heart disease: A meta-analysis of the literature. *Psychosomatic Medicine, 48,* 159–173.

Pallak, M. S., Cummings, N. A., Dorken, H., & Henke, C. J. (1995). Effect of mental health treatment of medical costs. *Mind/Body Medicine, 1,* 7–11.

Patterson, D. R., Everett, J. J., Burns, G. L., & Marvin, J. A. (1992). Hypnosis for the treatment of burn pain. *Journal of Consulting and Clinical Psychology, 60,* 713–717.

Pennebacker, J. W. (1995). *Emotion, disclosure, and health.* Washington, DC: American Psychological Association.

Perez, G. K., Cruess, D. G., & Kalichman, S. C. (2011). Effects of stress on health in HIV/AIDS. In R. J. Contrada & A. Baum (Eds.), *The handbook of stress science: Biology, psychology, and health* (pp. 447–460). New York, NY: Springer.

Peterson, C. (2000). The future of optimism. *American Psychologist, 55,* 44–55.

Petrie, K., Fontanilla, I., Thomas, M., Booth, R., & Pennebaker, J. W. (2004). Effects of written emotional expression on immune function in patients with human immunodeficiency virus infection: A randomized trial. *Psychosomatic Medicine, 66,* 272–275.

Pollock, K. M. (2001). Exercise in treating depression: Broadening the psychotherapist's role. *Journal of Clinical Psychology/In Session, 57,* 1289–1300.

Prochaska,J.O., Velicer,W.F., Rossi,J.S., Goldstein, M. G., et al. (1994). Stages of change and decisional balance for 12 problem behaviors. *Health Psychology, 13,* 39–43.

Puska, P. (1999). The North Karelia Project: From community intervention to national activity in lowering cholesterol levels and CHD risk. *European Heart Journal, 1(Suppl.),* S9–S13.

Ragland, D. R., & Brand, R. J. (1988). Type A behavior and mortality from coronary heart disease. *New England Journal of Medicine, 318,* 65–69.

Richman, L. S., Kubzansky, L., Maselko, J., & Kawachi, I. (2005). Positive emotion and health: Going beyond the negative. *Health Psychology, 24,* 422–429.

Rickert, V., & Jay, S. (1995). The noncompliant adolescent. In S. Parker & B. Zuckerman (Eds.), *Behavioral and developmental pediatrics* (pp. 219–222). Boston, MA: Little, Brown & Company.

Rios, R., & Zautra, A. J. (2011). Socioeconomic disparities in pain: The role of economic hardship and daily financial worry. *Health Psychology, 30,* 58–66.

Rodin, J., & Salovey, P. (1989). Health psychology. *Annual Review of Psychology, 40,* 533–580.

Rosenman, R. H., Brand, R. J., Jenkins, D. D., Friedman, M., Straus, R., et al. (1975). Coronary heart disease in the Western Collaborative Group Study: Final follow-up experience after 8 years. *Journal of the American Medical Association, 233,* 872–877.

Rosenstock, I. M. (1974). Historical origins of the health belief model. *Health Education Monographs, 2,* 328–335.

Rozanski, A., Blumenthal, J. A., & Kaplan, J. (1999). Impact of psychological factors on the pathogenesis of cardiovascular disease and implications for therapy. *Circulation, 99,* 2192–2217.

Rugulies, R. (2003). Depression as a predictor for the development of coronary heart disease: A systematic review and meta-analysis of the literature. *American Journal of Preventive Medicine, 23,* 51–61.

Salovey, P., Rothman, A. J., Detweiler, J. B., & Steward, W. T. (2000). Emotional states and physical health. *American Psychologist, 55,* 110–121.

Sarafino, E. P. (2010). *Health psychology: Biopsychosocial interactions.* Hoboken, NJ: Wiley.

Schneider, S. L. (2001). In search of realistic optimism: Meaning, knowledge, and warm fuzziness. *American Psychologist, 56,* 250–263.

Schneiderman, N., Antoni, M. H., Saab, P. G., & Ironson, G. (2001). Health psychology: Psychosocial and biobehavioral aspects of chronic disease management. *Annual Review of Psychology, 52,* 555–580.

Schradle, S. B., & Dougher, M. J. (1985). Social support as a mediator of stress. Theoretical and empirical issues. *Clinical Psychology Review, 5,* 641–662.

Segerstrom, S., & Miller, G. (2004). Psychological stress and the human immune system: A meta-analytic study of 30 years of inquiry. *Psychological Bulletin, 130,* 601–630.

Seligman, M. E. P. (2008). Positive health. *Applied Psychology, 57,* 3–18.

Seligman, M. E. P., & Csikszentmihali, M. (2000). Positive psychology: An introduction. *American Psychologist, 55,* 5–14.

Selye, H. (1956). *The stress of life.* New York, NY: McGraw-Hill.

Sheps, D. S., Freedland, K. E., Golden, R. N., & McMahon, R. P. (2003). ENRICHD and SADHART: Implications for future biobehavioral intervention efforts. *Psychosocial Medicine, 65,* 1–2.

Shiffman, S., Hickcox, M., Paty, J. A., Gnys, M., Kassel, J. D., et al.. (1996). Progression from a smoking lapse to relapse: Prediction from abstinence violation effects, nicotine dependence, and lapse characteristics. *Journal of Consulting & Clinical Psychology, 64,* 993–1002.

Smith, T. W., & Williams, P. G. (2013). Behavioral medicine and clinical health psychology. In M. J. Lambert (Ed.), *Bergin and Garfield's handbook of psychotherapy and behavior change* (6th ed., pp. 690–734). Hoboken, NJ: Wiley.

Snowdon, D. A., Greiner, L. H., Kemper, S. J., Nanayakkara, N., & Mortimer, J. A. (1999). Linguistic ability in early life and longevity: Findings from the Nun Study. In J.-M. Robine, B. Forette, C. Franceschi, & M. Allard (Eds.), *The paradoxes of longevity* (pp. 103–113). Berlin, Germany: Springer-Verlag.

Snowdon, D. A., Greiner, L. H., & Markesbery, W. R. (2000). Linguistic ability in early life and the neuropathology of Alzheimer's disease and cerebrovascular disease: Findings from the Nun Study. *Annals of the New York, NY Academy of Sciences, 903,* 34–38.

St. Lawrence, J. S., Brasfield, T. L., Jefferson, K. W., Alleyne, E., & O'Bannon, R. E., III (1995). Cognitive-behavioral intervention to reduce African American adolescents' risk for HIV infection. *Journal of Consulting & Clinical Psychology, 63,* 221–237.

Starks, T. J., Payton, G., Golub, S. A., Weinberger, C. L., & Parsons, J. T. (2013). Contextualizing condom use: Intimacy interference, stigma, and unprotected sex. *Journal of Health Psychology,* Published online, doi: 10.1177/1359105313478643.

Staub, R. O. (2011). *Health psychology: A BioPsychoSocial approach.* New York, NY: Worth.

Stone, A. A. & Neale, J. M. (1984). New measures of daily coping: Developments and preliminary results. *Journal of Personality and Social Psychology, 46,* 892–906.

Stoney, C. M., West, S. G., Hughes, J. W., Lentino, L. M., Finney, M. L., et al. (2002). Acute psychological stress reduces plasma triglyceride clearance. *Psychophysiology, 39,* 80–85.

Straub, R. O. (2006). *Health psychology: A biopsychosocial approach* (2nd ed.). New York, NY: Worth Publishers.

Suls, J., & Wang, C. K. (1993). The relationship between trait hostility and cardiovascular reactivity: A quantitative review and analysis. *Psychophysiology, 30,* 1–12.

Swain, M. A., & Steckel, S. B. (1981). Influencing adherence among hypertensives. *Research Nursing and Health, 4,* 213–218.

Taylor, S. E. (1995). *Health psychology.* New York, NY, NY: McGraw-Hill.

Taylor, S. E. (2010). Mechanisms linking early life stress to adult health outcomes. *Proceedings of the National Academy of Sciences, 107,* 8507–8512.

Taylor, S. E. (2011). *Health Psychology*. New York, NY, NY: McGraw-Hill.

Taylor, S. E., Kemeny, M. E., Reed, G. M., Bower, J. E., & Gruenewald, T. L. (2000). Psychological resources, positive illusions, and health. *American Psychologist, 55*, 99–109.

Taylor, S. E., Way, B. M., & Seeman, T. E. (2011). Early adversity and adult health outcomes. *Development and Psychopathology, 23*, 939–954.

Tennen, H., Affleck, G., Armeli, S., & Carney, M. A. (2000). A daily process approach to coping. *American Psychologist, 55*, 626–636.

Testa, M., & Collins, R. L. (1997). Alcohol and risky sexual behavior: Event-based analyses among a sample of high-risk women. *Psychology of Addictive Behaviors, 11*, 190–201.

Thoits, P. A. (1986). Social support as coping assistance. *Journal of Consulting and Clinical Psychology, 54*, 416–423.

Thoresen, C. E., & Powell, L. H. (1992). Type A behavior pattern: New perspectives on theory, assessment, and intervention. *Journal of Consulting and Clinical Psychology, 60*, 595–604.

Turk, D. C., & Rudy, T. E. (1990). Pain. In A. S. Bellack, M. Hersen, & A. E. Kazdin (Eds.), *International handbook of behavior modification and therapy* (2nd ed., pp. 399–413). New York, NY: Plenum Press.

Vaillant, G. E. (2000). Adaptive mental mechanisms: Their role in a positive psychology. *American Psychologist, 55*, 89–98.

Williams, C. L., Arnold, C. B., & Wynder, E. L. (1977). Primary prevention of chronic disease beginning in childhood: The Know Your Body Program: Design of study. *Preventive Medicine, 6*, 344–357.

Williams, R. B., Jr., & Barefoot, J. C. (1988). Coronary-prone behavior: The emerging role of the hostility complex. In B. K. Houston & C. R. Snyder (Eds.), *Type A behavior pattern: Research, theory and intervention* (pp. 189–211). New York, NY: Wiley.

World Health Organization. (2013). HIV/AIDS fact sheet. http://www.who.int/mediacentre/factsheets/fs360/en/index.html

Wortman, C. B., & Lehman, D. R. (1985). Reactions to victims of life crises: Support attempts that fail. In I. G. Sarason & B. R. Sarason (Eds.), *Social support: Theory, research, and applications* (pp. 463–489). Dordrecht, The Netherlands: Martinus Nijhoff.

Wright, M. O., Masten, A. S., & Narayan, A. J. (2013). Resilience processes in development: Four waves of research on positive adaptation in the context of adversity. In S. Goldstein & R. B. Brooks (Eds), *Handbook of resilience in children* (2nd ed., pp. 15–37). New York, NY: Springer.

Wulsin, L. R., & Singal, B. M. (2003). Do depressive symptoms increase the risk for the onset of coronary disease? A systematic quantitative review. *Psychosomatic Medicine, 65*, 201–210.

Yoshimasu, K. (2001). Relation of type A behavior pattern and job-related psychosocial factors to nonfatal myocardial infarction: A case-control study of Japanese male workers and women. *Psychosomatic Medicine, 63*, 797–804.

Young, L. D. (1992). Psychological factors in rheumatoid arthritis. *Journal of Consulting and Clinical Psychology, 60*, 619–627.

Zheng, D., Macera, C. A., Croft, J. B., Giles, W. H., Davis, D., et al. (1997). Major depression and all-cause mortality among white adults in the United States. *Annals of Epidemiology, 7*, 213–218.

13 | CLINICAL NEUROPSYCHOLOGY

Chapter Preview

Clinical neuropsychologists perform assessments and design interventions for persons who experience neurological dysfunction because of brain injury or illness. They also conduct research on both normal and abnormal brain functioning; such research has helped to shed light on psychological disorders such as depression and schizophrenia. Clinical neuropsychology is a relatively new and growing field, and its practitioners must understand brain–behavior relationships and be trained in a variety of assessment and intervention techniques unique to the field.

Muriel was driving her car when she was struck by another vehicle. She hit her head and lost consciousness, and a friend traveling with her was killed. She eventually made a full physical recovery, but she had some new problems. She forgot conversations, missed appointments, failed to meet deadlines, lost things, and asked the same questions again and again. How would you explain these new problems? You could consider several possibilities. For example, you might wonder if she is still upset about the accident, is mourning her lost friend, or perhaps feeling guilty about having survived. Such emotional turmoil could impair concentration and cause forgetfulness. But how could you know whether, instead, brain damage was the cause? You might look at pictures of her brain structure with magnetic resonance imaging to spot areas of gross brain damage. But those pictures can't tell you if damage is fresh or old. Most important, you would still have to decide if the damage is relevant to Muriel's current problems. In other words, you would need to decide if the damaged regions are those which, when injured, could cause memory loss. Further complicating the picture is that brain damage on a microscopic or cellular level can impair psychological functioning but be invisible on an imaging scan. To help sort out all these possibilities, you need a way to assess Muriel psychologically, to test her mental abilities carefully. You must then use a detailed knowledge of psychology and brain function to decide if the pattern of findings suggests brain dysfunction, and if so, where it is. These are some of the tasks that neuropsychologists perform.

Neuropsychology is the field of study that seeks to understand how brain processes make human behavior and psychological functions possible (Heilman & Valenstein, 2011). Neuropsychologists are interested in a wide range of human abilities, including aspects of cognitive functioning (e.g., language, memory, attention, mathematical, and visuospatial skills), motor functioning (e.g., learned skilled movements, gross and fine motor skills), emotional functioning (e.g., motivation, understanding and expressing emotion, anxiety, depression, euphoria), social functioning (e.g., prejudice, social judgment, interpreting social information), and personality traits (e.g., extraversion, neuroticism). Neuropsychologists study how brain operations control such processes and how this control breaks down due to brain dysfunction (e.g., physical trauma, stroke, infection, neurodegeneration) or psychological disorders (e.g., posttraumatic stress disorder, clinical depression, schizophrenia).

Clinical neuropsychologists become involved in the psychological and behavioral evaluation of individuals. By doing careful testing of a person's psychological functions, they can learn whether or not the person shows a pattern of impairments suggestive of brain damage, and if so, to what brain regions.

Clinical neuropsychologists can also help quantify the severity of psychological deficits by comparing a person's performance to the average performance, or norms, established by the previous testing of many other people of similar educational and social backgrounds. The pattern of deficits identified by neuropsychological testing may even offer clues to the cause of brain damage. Clinical neuropsychologists may help to clarify how a person's problems from brain damage are likely to affect that particular individual's ability to function socially, vocationally, and in other aspects of daily living. Finally, clinical neuropsychologists can help formulate a regimen for rehabilitation and recovery from the effects of brain damage.

Clinical neuropsychologists must use several kinds of knowledge and skills in their work. First, as with any clinical psychologist, they make use of the assessment skills described in Chapter 3, "Basic Features of Clinical Assessment," Chapter 4, "Interviewing and Observation in Clinical Psychology," and Chapter 5, "Testing in Clinical Psychology." Thus, neuropsychological assessments consider the entire person, including social and family background, personality dynamics, and emotional reactions to possible brain dysfunction. Second, clinical neuropsychologists must be able to use specialized methods unique to neuropsychological assessment. Third, clinical neuropsychologists must have knowledge of the neurosciences, including neuroanatomy (the study of nervous system structures and the connections between them), neurophysiology (the study of the functioning of the nervous system and its parts, including the chemistry of nerve tissue and the relationship between the nervous system and endocrine functions), and neuropharmacology (the study of how drugs affect nervous system functioning). Fourth, clinical neuropsychologists must know about a wide range of human cognitive abilities, including language and perception, and about how those abilities develop and change over time (e.g., behavioral genetics and life-span psychology). Fifth, neuropsychologists must be able to distinguish behavioral and psychological problems caused by brain dysfunction from those caused by psychopathology in structurally intact brains. Finally, they should be able to design effective rehabilitative programs based on an in-depth understanding of clinical psychology.

A BRIEF HISTORY OF NEUROPSYCHOLOGY

SECTION PREVIEW

Neuropsychology's roots go back to debates in the 1800s about brain organization and function. As case examples and new assessment techniques resolved many of these debates, a clearer understanding of neurological function and dysfunction led to the development of neuropsychology as a specialty within clinical psychology.

Although neuropsychology includes topics that overlap with many areas of psychology, with experimental neuroscience, and with clinical neurology, it has grown into a distinct field with unique investigation methods and treatment approaches. To understand modern neuropsychology, it is important to understand how it developed.

Early Influences

Neuropsychology emerged as a separate field of study during the mid-twentieth century, but its roots lie in two lines of nineteenth-century thinking about the relationship between specific behaviors and specific areas of the brain (Tyler & Malessa, 2000). One view came from anatomists Franz Gall and Johann Spurzheim, who advocated the concept of *localization of function*. According to this then-controversial view, different psychological functions are controlled by different brain areas. This view is largely accepted today, and Gall and Spurzheim would have been more revered figures for proposing it had they not framed their ideas within a larger theory called *phrenology*. Phrenologists reasoned that if certain functions were localized in certain brain areas, and that if a person used particular functions more than others, the corresponding brain region would get larger and raise a bump on the skull above it. As noted in Chapter 1, "What Is Clinical Psychology?," phrenologists claimed that individual differences in personality and intelligence could be assessed by the bumps and indentations on the surface of the skull. Phrenology was very popular with the public but disdained by most scientists because of the lack of evidence to support it. Once phrenology was discredited, the concept of localization of function was stained by association, so it too was seen as misguided (Zola-Morgan, 1995).

An alternative line of thinking about brain and behavior suggested that no particular brain area was more important than any other in the control of psychological function. Pierre Flourens, a widely respected scientist, argued for this view on the basis of careful experiments. For example, he surgically destroyed parts of animals' brains and then observed the behavioral consequences. He concluded that although there was some localization of cortical function, the regions within the cerebral hemispheres functioned more like a single unit than a collection of specialized parts. This view was later supported by the work of Karl Lashley, who emphasized the capacity of one area of the cortex to take over for the functions of a destroyed area, a capacity he called *equipotentiality*.

Eventually, work in behavioral neurology convincingly showed that different areas of the brain, especially in the cerebral cortex, do indeed underlie different specific psychological functions. The pendulum began to swing back toward a localization of function position due to the work of an esteemed French surgeon, Paul Broca (1861, 1865), who discovered that expressive language (e.g., speech) is controlled by a particular part of the brain. Broca had the opportunity to confirm, by autopsy, that a patient with a profound speech problem but otherwise normal intelligence had damage to one small area of cortex in the left frontal lobe. Broca's esteemed reputation brought attention and legitimacy to a localizationist view of brain function (Lorch, 2011). By 1863, he had collected a series of eight cases and had argued so convincingly for localization of function that this view was indisputable. Further support for localization of function came from the work of two Italian ophthalmologists: Antonio Quaglino and Giambattista Borelli. In 1867, they published a paper describing a man who developed *prosopagnoisa*, the inability to recognize familiar faces, after suffering damage to the right hemisphere of his brain. Findings such as these made it clear that particular psychological functions are especially dependent on specific brain areas.

Development of Neuropsychological Assessment Techniques

As part of their evaluation of people, clinical neuropsychologists use standardized tests that assess separate aspects of psychological function. As we described in Chapter 2, "Clinical Psychology's Past and Present," some of this testing tradition dates to the early twentieth century, when French psychologist Alfred Binet had begun assessing children with brain damage. Tests such as his are usually associated with the beginning of modern intelligence testing (see Chapter 5), but they also laid the foundation for neuropsychological assessment. Many of the disorders commonly assessed today with neuropsychological techniques had been identified in Binet's time. These include *aphasia* (disordered language abilities), *apraxia* (impaired abilities to carry out learned purposeful movements), *agnosia* (disorders of perceptual recognition), and *amnesia* (disorders of memory). In Russia, the Psychoneurological Institute was formed in 1907 to study the behavioral effects of brain damage, and throughout the first decade of the 1900s, several people in the United States were using psychological tests to study how brain damage affects behavior.

One of these people was Ward Halstead, who in 1935 founded a neuropsychology laboratory at the University of Chicago. His major contribution was to observe persons with brain damage in natural settings. From these observations, he identified the key characteristics of behavior that should be assessed in any patient undergoing neuropsychological testing. After recording responses in many patients, Halstead compared their performance to control cases and identified 10 measures that could discriminate patients from controls (Reitan & Davison, 1974). His approach was to use a *test battery*, a set of several different tests designed to complement each other to assess all the key categories of psychological function (e.g., language, memory, visual recognition). Halstead's first graduate student, Ralph M. Reitan, started a neuropsychology laboratory in 1951 at the Indiana University Medical Center. Reitan revised Halstead's test battery and included other measures in what came to be known as the *Halstead–Reitan Battery* (HRB). This battery is still widely used today.

Basic research in neuropsychology and advances in assessment methods grew dramatically following World War II, in part because of the need to assess many war-related cases of brain damage. A small number of prominent neuropsychologists developed and validated specific tests and test batteries (Jones & Butters, 1983), some of which were specifically designed to be used in special patient populations, such as people with traumatic brain injury. Others were aimed at assessing certain kinds of deficits, such as the loss of language function.

Split-Brain Research

Another important chapter in the history of neuropsychology is associated with the work of Roger Sperry and his colleagues at the California Institute of Technology (Sperry, 1961, 1982). They studied the psychological effects of cutting the *corpus callosum*, the band of nerve pathways that allow the brain's two hemispheres to communicate directly with each other. This surgical procedure is performed in severe cases of drug-resistant epilepsy in the hope that it will prevent the spread of seizures from one side of the brain to the other in certain cases where drug treatment fails. With the corpus callosum severed, the activity of one cerebral hemisphere proceeds largely isolated from that of the other hemisphere. Although vast sections of brain tissue devoted to complex information processing are rendered incommunicado by this surgery, research methods in the 1940s detected no significant differences between normal people and so-called split-brain patients. Sperry (who won the Nobel Prize in 1981 for his work) and his associates devised new experimental procedures that could show that split brains were indeed different from intact ones and how they differ (e.g., Sperry, 1968).

Research on Normal Brains

Split-brain research, and the innovative testing techniques involved in it, stimulated an increase in studies of the organization of normal brains. Many of these studies used a *tachistoscope*, a device that displays visual stimuli for a very brief period of time. When the eyes are fixated on a central point in the visual field, stimuli briefly flashed to the left of the fixation point are seen only in the left visual field. Similarly, stimuli briefly flashed to the right of the fixation point appear only in the right visual field. Because of the way the eyes are "wired" to the brain, information from the left side of space is sent first to the right cerebral hemisphere and information from the right side goes first to the left hemisphere. The information from each side of space is then normally shared between hemispheres via their connections through the pathways provided by the corpus callosum.

Using tachistoscopic methods, experimenters directed the entry of visual stimuli into one hemisphere or the other and measured a person's accuracy of performance or reaction time in response. By measuring the relative accuracy of responses for the two visual fields, researchers have been able to document and confirm unique hemispheric superiorities for a wide variety of cognitive and perceptual tasks (Hellige, 2001).

SECTION SUMMARY

Clinical neuropsychology emerged as a distinct discipline only in the late twentieth century, but its roots go back to earlier efforts to understand brain organization and function. Key efforts include (a) the finding that specific areas of the brain specialize in specific functions, (b) the development of tests and test batteries to measure intellectual functioning and identify specific areas of normal and abnormal brain function, (c) the discovery of disorders associated with disrupted communication between the brain's hemispheres, and (d) techniques that provided normative information about the functioning of normal brains.

BASIC PRINCIPLES OF NEUROPSYCHOLOGY

SECTION PREVIEW

Here we provide some basic principles about how the brain works. Although various functions are compartmentalized, the various compartments or modules interact with each other in multiple ways. Each hemisphere has its specialties, but both hemispheres are involved in most tasks.

Certain principles of brain–behavior relationships are fundamental to neuropsychology. We review some of them here before describing how clinical neuropsychologists assess brain functioning in patients. In doing so, we refer often to the various regions of the brain presented in Figure 13.1.

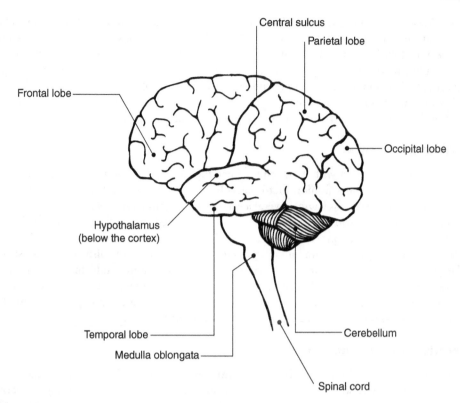

FIGURE 13.1 A Lateral View of the Human Cerebral Cortex and Other Brain Structures

Localization of Function

As already noted, the idea that specific parts of the brain are involved in specific behaviors and psychological functions became the prevailing view of scientists by the end of the nineteenth century (Tyler & Malessa, 2000), and this *localizationist* view is now well established. What is less clear is just what it is that is being localized to a given brain region and how different brain regions interact (Sternberg, 2011).

Theorists who emphasize the interrelatedness of brain areas and who stress the holistic quality of brain functioning are sometimes known as *globalists*. John Hughlings Jackson, Karl Lashley, and Kurt Goldstein are three of the more influential globalists, but it was Alexander Luria who, more than any other scientist, proposed a theory of brain organization that emphasized its integration rather than its specificity (Glozman, 2007). Luria's theory was that the brain is organized into three functional systems: (a) a brain stem system for regulating a person's overall tone or waking state; (b) a system located in the posterior (back) portion of the cortex for obtaining, processing, and storing information received from the outside world; and (c) a system, located mainly in the anterior (front) portion of the cortex, for planning, regulating, and verifying mental operations. So like other globalists, Luria believed that the brain engaged in some specialized "division of labor," but he emphasized the importance of understanding how these different brain areas work together.

Modularity

Today, when neuropsychologists map the brain according to specific functions, they do so in a way that reflects both localizationist and globalist perspectives (Goldberg, 1995; Lezak, Howieson, & Loring, 2004). For example, the influential concept of *modularity* (Fodor, 1983) implies that the brain is divided into regions that are unique in how they receive information, process that information, and then send the processed information to other brain modules. Different brain areas are thus seen as different information-processing modules, something like the many different circuit boards contained in a vast, complex computer. According to the modular view, then, a complicated psychological function such as attention is not "controlled" by a single brain area. Rather, attentional functions are seen to rely on several different brain modules, each adding a different piece to the puzzle, working together in a network distributed widely across many brain regions (Mesulam, 1990; Stam & van Straaten, 2012). Since different aspects of attention will rely more on one brain module than another, it follows that damage to a single module would affect one aspect of attention more than another. It also follows that since a given module may provide a kind of information processing that several psychological functions may each rely on, damage to that particular brain module could have consequences for each of those psychological functions. And because many different modules may be involved in the network of brain areas associated with attention, damage in many different brain areas can affect attention.

Levels of Interaction

Different modules interact with each other to produce a seamless sequence of behaviors. The modules are organized in a fashion that reflects both the structure and function of the brain. Thus, the brain can be seen as having several levels of organization, ranging from the global to the local. For example, the various areas identified in are associated with regions on either side of the central sulcus. These functions can be distinguished by whether they primarily process incoming information (sensory) or program outgoing behavior (motor). They can also be distinguished by modality (for example, whether they primarily process visual or auditory information). In general, brain regions behind the central sulcus are more involved in the reception of sensory information (e.g., touch, pressure, temperature, and body position), whereas brain regions in front of the central sulcus are more involved in programming motor output.

Lateralization of Function

As noted earlier, the cerebral cortex is divided into two hemispheres. The activity of each hemisphere is associated with somewhat different functions. At one time, this difference was described in terms of "cerebral dominance," because the left hemisphere was seen as the "dominant" or "major" one and the right as the "nondominant" or "minor" hemisphere. Over time, this distinction was found to be misleading. Work by Sperry and others showed that different aspects of psychological life may be more dependent on one side of the brain than the other, but in most cases both sides of the brain are involved to some extent in most psychological functions. Thus, it is more appropriate to refer to a psychological function as being left or right "lateralized," but not "dominant."

SPECIALIZATION OF THE LEFT HEMISPHERE   In most right-handed people, the left hemisphere is specialized to handle speech and other aspects of linguistic processing, such as the ability to understand what others say. The ability to speak is very strongly left lateralized in most right-handed people so that the right hemisphere has little or no direct access to speech mechanisms. A similar brain organization is seen in left-handed people, but less consistently so (Strauss & Wada, 1983). Evidence that the left hemisphere is specialized for speech comes from a variety of sources. In addition to studies documenting language deficits in patients with left-hemisphere damage (Rasmussen & Milner, 1975), data from a number of neurosurgical procedures have provided comprehensive evidence for the left hemisphere's special language abilities. For example, before beginning a brain operation, neurosurgeons typically locate, and then try to avoid, regions of the brain that are crucial for language. They do this by electrically stimulating particular areas of the brain to disrupt the usual information processing mechanisms. If this renders the patient unable to speak when instructed to, then those areas may be important for language. Such explorations have shown that stimulation of the left hemisphere, but usually not the right, leads to disruptions in speech production and language processing. Thus, stimulation of the left temporal lobe disrupts verbal memory functions, whereas stimulation of the left frontal lobe disrupts speech production (because it involves complex motor sequences).

Another technique used to investigate language lateralization involves injecting sodium amytal into the internal carotid artery (Wada & Rasmussen, 1960). This procedure temporarily puts one hemisphere "to sleep," during which time the neuropsychologist or neurologist can test the patient. When the left hemisphere is put to sleep, nearly all right-handed people lose their ability to speak (Milner, 1974; Wellmer et al., 2005). Split-brain research has also provided powerful evidence for left lateralization of language functions. For example, a patient with a severed corpus callosum might be asked to sit in front of a screen that makes it impossible to see objects placed in their hands. To identify the object, the patient must depend entirely on tactile information carried by sensory nerves extending from the hand to the brain. Like most nerve pathways, these sensory nerves cross over to the opposite side of the brain before connecting to information processing areas in the cortex. As a result, information from the left hand initially arrives at the right parietal cortex, and information from the right hand arrives at the left parietal cortex. In a normal brain, the corpus callosum transfers this information to the opposite hemisphere in a split second. In split-brain patients, because the corpus callosum is severed, the only way their opposite hemisphere can obtain information about a touched object is if they look at it. What happens when the screen blocks the patient's view? Roger Sperry and his associates (e.g., Sperry, 1974) found that these patients have no difficulty naming objects being held in the right hand (which is connected to their left hemisphere), but when asked to name objects held in the left hand (which is connected to the right hemisphere), the patients could usually not do so. When they were asked to use their left hand to pick out a picture of the object, however, they could do so correctly every time. This finding proved that the right hemisphere "knew" what the object was but could not label it verbally. The obvious conclusion is that the right hemisphere was mute—it had insufficient access to speech mechanisms controlled by the left hemisphere.

More recently, functional imaging studies of the brain have been able to confirm left lateralization of language functions. In these types of studies, an image of the brain shows where nerve cells are most active, or where blood tends to flow (Cheng, 2011; Glover, 2011; Herholz, 2011). The idea is that in brain areas more involved in a task, the nerve cells in those areas will use up more energy. By looking to see where nerve cells are most active, one can infer that the affected brain region may be involved in the information processing demands of the task. Such studies have confirmed what Wada tests would have predicted (Dym, Burns, Freeman, & Lipton 2011): when people are asked to perform linguistic tasks, left hemisphere brain regions become more active and energy demanding (Friederici, 2011).

SPECIALIZATION OF THE RIGHT HEMISPHERE   Right-hemisphere function, too, plays an important role in language and communication, though it usually lacks direct access to the systems that allow people to speak. For example, people with right-hemisphere damage may have difficulty understanding the overall "point" of a paragraph, the plot of a story, or the punch line of a joke (Marini, Carlomagno, Caltagirone, & Nocentini, 2005; Marinkovic et al., 2011). People with right-hemisphere damage also have difficulty understanding linguistic devices such as metaphors. So they might interpret statements like "I cried my eyes out" as if they were literally true (Gardner, Brownell, Wapner, & Michelow, 1983).

In addition to supporting these "supraordinate" levels of language communication, right-hemisphere function is important for social communication. For example, the prosody of language, or the "tone of voice," appears to stem largely from right-hemisphere function. *Aprosodia*, an interruption in normal prosody functions, occurs after right-hemisphere damage more often than after left-hemisphere damage (Schirmer, Alter, Kotz, & Friederici, 2001). A person with expressive aprosodia speaks in a monotone and sometimes must add a phrase such as "I am angry" to allow the listener to understand the intended emotional message. Those with receptive aprosodia, by contrast, may not pick up the sarcasm or anger in another person's voice, which can lead to some rather unfortunate social misinterpretations.

As Sperry and his colleagues showed, if given a nonverbal means of communication, the right hemisphere is able to perform at a level of intelligence equal to that of the left. Indeed, one of the greatest contributions of split-brain research has been to remove the right hemisphere's designation as the "minor" hemisphere and to demonstrate its capacity for high-level information processing. We now know that the right hemisphere is crucial for analyzing many types of spatial and nonverbal information, including the highly complex signals involved in social and emotional communication (Baird et al., 2006; Fournier, Calverley, Wagner, Poock, & Crossley 2008; Najtp & Hausmann, 2013). After all, only part of the most important information in a conversation is carried by the content of the utterances; a great deal of information is conveyed by *how* words are said. The right hemisphere is especially good at perceiving and decoding gestures, tone of voice, facial expressions, body language, and other nonverbal information, and then integrating them into a coherent message. Thus, right-hemisphere damage can sometimes cause dramatic dysfunctions in social communication (Tomkins, 2012).

The difficulties patients with right-brain damage have in judging situations appropriately, in relating to others, and in accurately perceiving social cues is often compounded by another problem—they are often unaware of their deficits. The inability to be aware of neurological problems is called *anosognosia* (Adair & Barrett, 2011; Babinski, 1914). Anosognosia is more common after right sided brain damage than left (Starkstein, Jorge, & Robinson, 2010). It occurs because of damage to the brain areas that allow one to self-monitor one's mental functioning and to know when things have gone wrong. Thus, even some people with severe paralysis caused by a right-hemisphere stroke do not appear to know that they cannot move all or part of their left sides (Heilman, Barrett, & Adair, 1998)! Anosognosia poses a serious obstacle to rehabilitation programs because remedial strategies are less likely to be effective if patients do not perceive that they have a problem (Jenkinson, Preston, & Ellis, 2011).

SECTION SUMMARY

Brain functions are localized in different regions, but those functions are not entirely compartmentalized. Brain regions, or modules, that specialize in certain functions often interact with other modules that may process information differently. The brain's modules are also connected in multiple levels. Because there are multiple connections and multiple layers of organization, damage to one area may result in impairment of certain aspects of a particular mental function (e.g., attention, visual perception) but not others. Damage to one or the other hemisphere often results in specific patterns of psychological or behavioral deficits.

PATTERNS OF NEUROPSYCHOLOGICAL DYSFUNCTION

SECTION PREVIEW

Injuries to specific parts of the brain are associated with particular kinds of psychological problems. Here we describe some behavioral manifestations of brain dysfunction, organized by the regions, or lobes, in which the damage occurred.

Occipital Lobe Dysfunction

Visual information is sent from the retina in each eye to the thalamus and then to the occipital lobes of the cerebral cortex. At each step along the way, this information is represented *topographically*; in other words, neighboring nerve cells respond to neighboring areas of the visual field. A similar arrangement for other types of specific sensory and motor information has given rise to the rather comical maps of the *homunculus* (literally, "little man") which display the relative size of cortical areas representing sensory information or motor output to and from various regions on the opposite side of the body.

The most common problem caused by damage to the occipital lobe is blindness. Because about half of the retinal fibers coming from each eye cross over to the opposite side as they enter the brain, damage to one occipital lobe produces blindness in the opposite visual field. For example, damage to the right occipital lobe causes blindness in the left visual field. Usually, people with blindness due to damage to the occipital lobe have disrupted visual sensations in the affected visual field. But neuropsychologists have shown that some of these people continue to process a certain amount of visual information. This phenomenon, called *blindsight*, can occur because some visual information processing occurs outside of the visual cortex (Cowey, 2010b), but without conscious awareness. So people with blindsight may duck when an object flies rapidly toward their head but not know why they have done so. Or, they may be able to guess the color of an object in front of them, though they are unaware of seeing the object (Cowey, 2010a).

Parietal Lobe Dysfunction

As suggested by the blindsight phenomenon, after visual information is received and processed in the occipital lobes, it is relayed to adjacent cortical areas in the posterior (back) superior (top) parts of the *parietal lobes*. These areas are classified as "association" cortex because they do not receive sensory information directly from sense organs, nor do they directly send movement commands to muscles; instead, they interact mainly with other cortical areas to combine and integrate information from multiple cortical modules.

Parietal association cortex is thus a meeting ground for visual, auditory, and sensory input, making it vital for creating a unified perception of the world. In particular, areas of the parietal lobes help create a map of our environment and the objects in it; they also perform an ongoing analysis of where objects are in our sensory world, and how they are moving. Because of this specialty, cortical parietal regions play a unique role in attention and awareness of spatial location (Ungerleider & Mishkin, 1982). Patients with damage to the parietal lobe on only one side of the brain often display an intriguing deficit called *hemineglect* in which they ignore the side of the body and the side of space opposite the damaged hemisphere (Corbetta & Shulman, 2011). For example, people with damage in the right parietal region might not eat the food on the left side of their plates, or they might forget to comb the hair on the left side of their heads, or fail to button their left shirtsleeve. They might also ignore words on the left side of a page and fail to notice when a doctor or family member approaches from the left. They may even fail to notice the left side of scenes that they imagine in their head (Bisiach, Luzzatti, & Perani, 1979). Hemineglect can be so extreme in some patients that they may believe that parts of their bodies belong to other people. In an anecdote reported by neurologist Oliver Sacks (1990), a patient woke up in the middle of the night and tried to throw his leg out of bed because he thought that it belonged to an invading stranger. The hemineglect syndrome is most common after damage to regions of the right parietal lobe (probably because of the unique specialization of the right hemisphere for processing spatial information), but it can occur after damage to the left parietal lobe as well.

One way in which clinical neuropsychologists test for hemineglect is to ask a patient to draw a clock or a flower. People with hemineglect may draw all the numbers on the clock, or all the details of the flower, on one half of the paper and leave the other half blank. Other tests of hemineglect include tasks in which individuals try to cross out all of the letters or symbols on a page, or try to bisect a line in the middle. People with hemineglect may fail to cross out items on the neglected side, or they may bisect a line off-center, as if part of the neglected side of the line did not exist.

Another possible consequence of parietal lobe dysfunction, especially on the right side of the brain, is *simultanagnosia* (Chechlacz et al., 2012). Patients with this condition can see, but they have difficulty grouping seen items together in space. In essence, they can see the trees, but not the forest. Clinical neuropsychologists typically assess the presence of such parietal lobe deficits by using tests of visuospatial skills. For example, they present patients with "global–local" stimuli (Navon, 1983) such as the one shown in Figure 13.2.

Here is how one simultanagnosia patient responded when she looked at that figure (Shenker, 2005):

EXAMINER: What do you see?

PATIENT: I see T, T, T, T. . . . Do I keep going?

EXAMINER: Anything else?

PATIENT: T, T, T, T . . . lots of Ts.

EXAMINER: Are there any other letters?

PATIENT: No.

EXAMINER: Is there an H?

PATIENT: No, just Ts.

EXAMINER: Is there a big letter?

```
T  T  T         T  T  T
T  T  T         T  T  T
T  T  T         T  T  T
T  T  T  T  T  T  T  T
T  T  T  T  T  T  T  T
T  T  T  T  T  T  T  T
T  T  T         T  T  T
T  T  T         T  T  T
T  T  T         T  T  T
T  T  T         T  T  T
```

FIGURE 13.2 A "Global–Local" Stimulus for Testing Patients for Simultanagnosia

PATIENT: No, I don't see one.

EXAMINER: Is there a big letter H?

PATIENT: No.

EXAMINER: Do the little letters together form the shape of a big letter H?

PATIENT: I don't see how.

EXAMINER: (Outlines the H with finger) Do you see how this is a big H?

PATIENT: I don't see an H.

Temporal Lobe Dysfunction

While incoming visual information is being integrated in the parietal lobes, that same information is also being analyzed in cortical areas of the *temporal lobe* (Barton, 2011). This additional analysis in cortical modules in the posterior and inferior (underneath) temporal lobes allows a person to recognize the identity of seen objects. If these areas are damaged, the person can still see the objects, but might not be able to recognize what they are (Rubens & Benson, 1971). So when people with this problem, called visual *agnosia*, look at an apple, they might describe it as "a rounded smooth spherical object with a thin protrusion at the top" but be unable to name it, say what it is used for, where it can be found, and so on. Because visual agnosia is caused by problems that affect only visual pathways, these patients may instantly recognize and name objects if they are allowed to touch or smell them, for example. In other words, posterior inferior temporal lobe damage disrupts the ability to extract the identity of objects from visual sensations but does not destroy the more general understanding of what those objects are, nor does it impair the ability to recognize those objects via input from other sensory modalities. Some forms of agnosia can be amazingly specific to particular dimensions of the visual world. For example, patients may lose the ability to recognize living things (e.g., a tree or a dog) yet retain the ability to recognize inanimate objects (e.g. a coffee cup or a book) (Wolk, Coslett, & Gloser, 2005). Such dissociations suggest that the brain honors a distinction between highly specific categories of knowledge, a clinical observation that has prompted further study by cognitive scientists.

Parts of the temporal lobes also play roles in other psychological functions, such as processing of auditory information. They are also involved in memory; indeed, the most dramatic effect of temporal lobe damage is the disruption of memory. For example, anterior (front) and medial (toward the inside) temporal lobe structures are critical for the ability to transfer information into long-term memory storage throughout the brain. So when infections like herpes encephalitis damage the medial temporal lobe and its connections to other brain regions, people develop a permanent amnesia syndrome dominated by difficulty forming new memories (Grydeland et al., 2010). And, when medical conditions require surgery to remove the *hippocampus* from both medial temporal lobes, patients become unable to form new long-term memories (Lee, Brodersen, & Rudebeck, 2013; Scoville & Milner, 1957). In such people, every event, no matter how often repeated, seems as if it is happening for the first time. These persons cannot recall previous conversations, nor can they remember the name of someone they met minutes earlier. Interestingly, such memory loss is most evident on a conscious level, because although amnestic patients may not be *explicitly* aware of having seen a particular object in the past, their response to that object sometimes shows an *implicit* memory of having seen it (Dew & Cabeza, 2011). The implicit memory can be detected by improved performance after repeated practice with a puzzle task (Verfaellie & Keane, 1997), patterns of eye movements in searching previously seen versus never seen pictures (Mednick, Makovski, Cai, & Jiang, 2009), or by changes in heart rate or skin conduction in response to familiar stimuli (Gazzaniga, Fendrich, & Wessinger, 1994; Jacoby & Kelley, 1987; Milner & Rugg, 1992).

Other temporal lobe structures are important in attaching emotional or motivational significance to stimuli and events (McGaugh, 2006). People with *temporal lobe epilepsy* (TLE), for example, may display a collection of emotional traits, which some have termed the "TLE personality" (Bear & Fedio, 1977). One of these traits is a tendency to see mundane events as imbued with grand personal emotional significance, a tendency that can lead to magical or sometimes paranoid thinking. Patients with TLE personality also have a tendency to do a lot of writing and take a lot of notes, termed "hypergraphia," and may be slow to pick up on social cues. This last trait can make them socially "sticky," meaning that it is difficult to end a conversation with them.

Clinical neuropsychologists often assess problems associated with temporal lobe pathology by using a variety of memory tests, such as *Benton's Visual Retention Test*, the *Wechsler Memory Scale*, and the *California Verbal Learning Test*. They also compare patients' memory for verbal material, reflective of left temporal lobe function, with their memory for visuospatial material, reflective of right temporal lobe function.

Frontal Lobe Dysfunction

Many areas in the brain's *frontal lobes* are involved in planning behavior. This kind of activity is sometimes called the *executive function* of the brain, because, like the work of a corporate executive, it entails organizing, supervising, sorting, strategizing, anticipating, planning, making judgments and decisions, engaging in self-regulation, assimilating new information, adapting to novel situations, and taking purposeful action (Stuss, 2011). As befits a position of such responsibility, the frontal lobes have lots of association cortex and receive input from almost all other parts of the brain. This input is necessary because making appropriate decisions about responses and actions requires taking into account as much current information as possible from the outside world and from the rest of the body. The frontal lobes can thus compare new information to previous information, assess its motivational and affective significance, and create appropriate sequences of responses.

No wonder, then, that damage to the frontal lobes can profoundly affect social and emotional functioning. A classic case is that of Phineas Gage (Neylan, 1999), a Vermont railroad worker who, in 1848, suffered frontal lobe damage when an explosion sent a steel rod into his skull, creating a hole through his frontal lobes (see Figure 13.3). He not only survived this trauma, but his speech, movements, and overall intelligence seemed unaffected. But his personality changed. Once a responsible, judicious, and socially adept fellow, he became loud and profane, blurted out inappropriate comments, made poor decisions, and did not follow through with plans. Further, he seemed oblivious to these changes (Harlow, 1848). The original report added that Gage had more than just frontal lobe damage—he also had a brain infection and multiple seizures, making interpretation of his personality changes less clear. But the case drew such great attention at the time, and since, that it became a sensational story, and that is part of why it lives on today.

People with frontal lobe damage may show deficits in planning and organizing the various components of a cognitive task, but not necessarily with the components themselves. Eslinger and Damasio (1985) described a patient whose performance on multiple neuropsychological tests was

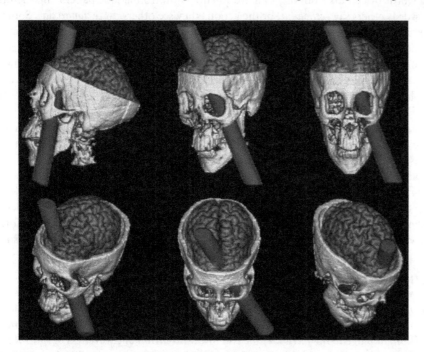

FIGURE 13.3 A Digitally Remastered Image Based on the Skull of Phineas P. Gage. The image suggests the route of transit and extent of brain damage when a 3 foot 7 inch long, 1.25 inch diameter rod shot through Gage's head on September 13, 1848, on a Vermont Railroad. *Source:* Patrick Landmann/Science Source.

TABLE 13.1 A Sampling of Neuropsychological Dysfunctions

Dysfunction	Prominent Symptom
Aphasia	Disordered language abilities
Apraxia	Impaired abilities to carry out learned purposeful movements
Agnosia	Disorders of perceptual recognition
Prosopagnosia	Inability to recognize faces
Amnesia	Disorders of memory
Aprosodia	An interruption in normal prosody (tone of voice) functions
Anosognosia	Inability to be aware of neurological problems
Hemineglect	Ignoring the side of the body and the side of space opposite the damaged hemisphere
Echolalia	Repeating the words someone else has just said
Akinetic mutism	Never moving or speaking
Blindsight	Having no conscious awareness of seeing and yet responding to moving stimuli as if they were seen
Simultanagnosia	Ability to see but difficulty grouping seen items together in space

unimpaired, yet he was unable to hold down a job, do household chores, or even decide what to do next. Despite wholly intact perceptual abilities and intellectual skills, he was unable to integrate all the information available to him and apply it to daily activities in an adaptive fashion. These individuals may also have problems performing goal-directed behavior. For example, when cooking a meal, they may fail to break the task down into its necessary steps, may misplan how to do each step, may mistime each step, or may not make proper adjustments—as when something starts to burn.

The problems in planning and organization created by frontal lobe damage can take curious forms. Consider, for a moment, what would happen if it was hard to plan out what to say, do, feel, or think next? One result might be that one would simply do the same thing over and over, rather than "plan" something new. This is called *perseveration*, and it causes a patient to say or think or do the same thing repeatedly. It is often hard to steer the conversation onto a new topic with such people. Or, if it is hard to plan what to say or do next, one might rely on the convenience of copying words or actions from one's environment. Thus, frontal lobe patients may simply imitate the words others say *(echolalia)* or the actions they see others do *(exhopraxia)*. Some people with executive dysfunction find it so hard to plan out actions and thoughts that they may just not seem to do much at all. These individuals display *abulia*, a reluctance to move, speak, or initiate interactions (Marin & Wilkosz, 2005). Abulic individuals appear withdrawn and unmotivated. In mild cases of abulia, patients show little variety in what they say or do. In extreme cases, they may display *akinetic mutism:* they literally never move or speak. Table 13.1 summarizes some of the many kinds of dysfunction that we have discussed.

It can be difficult to identify deficits in executive functioning using neuropsychological tests. The testing process usually includes tasks requiring a person to identify and act on temporal sequences, to plan and then revise strategies, or to solve problems whose demands change over time (Goldberg & Bougakov, 2005). Two tests commonly used to assess frontal lobe damage are the *Wisconsin Card Sorting Test* and the *Categories Test* from the HRB. Both tests use feedback from the examiner to tell patients whether they were right or wrong on each trial. This feedback is designed to signal when it is time to change unsuccessful strategies when matching or categorizing information. Patients with frontal lobe lesions will often perseverate in the same strategy even if it is unsuccessful.

SECTION SUMMARY

A variety of disordered perception and behavior can occur in association with damage to various kinds of brain damage. Damage to the occipital lobe is likely to affect some aspects of vision; damage to the parietal lobe can affect attention or awareness of spatial location; damage to the temporal lobe can affect recognition, memory, or self-relevant processing; damage to the frontal lobe can affect impulse control, emotionality, and other executive functions.

NEUROPSYCHOLOGICAL ASSESSMENT

SECTION PREVIEW

Clinical neuropsychologists' efforts to identify the symptoms and locations of brain damage and to plan rehabilitative interventions always begin with assessment. It can involve standardized batteries or individual tests specifically selected for individual patients. Because clinical neuropsychologists often work with physicians, they must be familiar with a wide range of medical and neurological assessment techniques.

One of the first steps clinical neuropsychologists take in dealing with patients is to assess their cognitive, emotional, or behavioral functioning. Assessment is designed to (a) establish the nature and severity of a patient's deficits, (b) determine the likelihood that the deficits stem from brain damage, (c) provide an educated guess as to where the damage might be located, and (d) identify the particular disease or the kind of damage responsible for the particular pattern of deficits seen. A deficit is defined as unusually poor task performance in comparison to the norms established by healthy, average people, or if possible, in comparison to the patient's own performance at an earlier time. In addition to using neuropsychological tests, a clinical neuropsychologist will conduct a thorough interview and examine the patient's medical records, including records of previous assessments. Information about *premorbid* (before the onset of the disorder) functioning, demographic, familial, linguistic, and educational history allows the clinician to place the current levels of functioning in a historical context. Repeated testing of the same person can yield information about how rapidly a difficulty is progressing or how general or specific the difficulty is.

Clinical neuropsychologists typically follow one of two approaches to assessment. The first is to use a predetermined, standardized battery of tests with all patients. As described earlier, these test batteries are comprehensive, and their standardization is useful for research. Further, because there is no need for expert judgments about what tests to use, these batteries can be administered by paraprofessionals. Test batteries can be inefficient, though, because they assess many functions that may not be impaired. Batteries may also become obsolete, because it is difficult to revise them to incorporate new and potentially improved tests.

The second approach to neuropsychological assessment is the *individualized method* in which an opening round of tests is routinely given to every patient, but the choice of other tests is based on the results of the first set and is tailored to answer the specific diagnostic questions of greatest interest. Individualized approaches allow in-depth assessment of particular problems, permit the use of new tests as they are developed, and focus more intensely on the specific difficulties that are most relevant for a given patient. One disadvantage of individualized approaches is that they require testers to have the advanced neuropsychology training necessary to know which diagnostic hypotheses to test and which tests will provide the information needed to confirm or disconfirm those hypotheses. Also, because different combinations of tests are used with different people, individualized testing data are less useful to researchers interested in making comparisons across patients.

Neuropsychological Test Batteries

The most widely used battery approach to neuropsychological assessment in the United States is the Halstead–Reitan Battery, or HRB (see Table 13.2 for a description of the tests making up the core of the HRB). It is suitable for persons aged 15 and older, but two other versions can be used for children aged 9 to 14 and for children between 5 and 8. Many examiners who use the HRB also administer a Wechsler Intelligence Scale, tests of memory, and personality tests such as the MMPI-2 (Reitan & Wolfson, 2009). (The Wechsler tests and the MMPI-2 are discussed in Chapter 5.)

The HRB evaluates four aspects of patients' performance. First, *level of performance* is assessed by comparing the patient's performance to that of normative groups; an impairment index is calculated according to the number of tests for which the patient's performance falls into a clinically deficient range. Second, *patterns of performance* are analyzed. Pattern analysis examines variations in performance on different components of a test. Third, emphasis is placed on *comparing right-side to left-side performance* and drawing inferences about hemispheric functioning when large differences appear. Fourth, *pathognomonic signs* are identified. These are deficits that are so strongly and specifically indicative of a disorder that their presence almost always establishes a diagnosis.

TABLE 13.2 The Halstead–Reitan Neurological Test Battery

Test Name	Test is Designed to Measure
Categories Test	Mental efficiency, ability to derive a rule from experience, and ability to form abstract concepts
Tactual Performance Test	Abilities such as motor speed, tactile and kinesthetic perception, and incidental memory
Seashore Rhythm Test	Nonverbal auditory perception, attention, and concentration
Speech-Sounds Perception Test	Language processing, verbal auditory perception, attention, and concentration
Finger Oscillation or Finger Tapping Test	Motor speed
Trail-Making Test	Speed, visual scanning, ability to use different sets, and dysexecutive function
Dynamometer or Strength of Grip Test	Right- versus left-side comparison of physical strength
Sensory-Perceptual Exam	Whether the patient can perceive sensory information separately and with standard variations in the location of the stimulation used
Tactile Perception Tests	Tactile perception
Aphasia Screening Test	Several aspects of language usage and recognition

The HRB has shown good validity in discriminating patients with brain damage from healthy, undamaged people (Loring & Larrabee, 2006). It has also demonstrated good validity in detecting the lateralization and localization (Reitan, 1964) of brain damage, but it does a relatively poor job of discriminating between brain damage and serious psychological disorders such as schizophrenia (Jones & Butters, 1983; Ross, Allen, & Goldstein, 2013).

Strong claims have been made for the value of another set of tests, the Luria-Nebraska battery, in discriminating patients with brain injury from patients with schizophrenia, but this battery has been severely criticized for flawed test construction, improper data analysis, inadequate standardization, and a distortion of Luria's original methods, which simply may not be translatable into items on a battery (see Lezak, Howieson, & Loring, 2004, for a review of these criticisms).

Individualized Approaches to Neuropsychological Testing

One of the most thorough and best-described individualized approaches is that of Muriel D. Lezak, a psychologist at the Oregon Health Sciences University and the Portland, Oregon, Veterans Administration Hospital. Lezak's strategy (Lezak, Howieson, & Loring, 2004) is to give all patients several standard tests that assess major functions in the auditory and visual receptive modalities as well as in the spoken, written, graphic, and constructional response modalities. Following this initial battery, which usually takes 2 to 3 hours, Lezak proceeds with "hypothesis testing," during which she shifts the focus of the assessment from one set of functions to another as the data indicate what abilities may be most impaired.

It is difficult to assess the validity of individualized approaches because they are tailored to each patient's needs and hence are not given in exactly the same form to sufficient numbers of patients to permit large-scale comparisons. And because individualized approaches depend much more than batteries do on the skill of the examiner using them, it becomes difficult to separate the validity of the tests from the clinical acumen of the examiner. Perhaps for these reasons, there is some judicial precedent for using only test battery approaches in court cases (Bigler, 2007).

Despite their limitations, individualized approaches offer good construct validity and may be the best way to get the most personalized assessment of an individual patient. Individualized approaches usually reflect a better theoretical justification for the use of a particular test than does a typical neuropsychological battery. This difference is another example of the distinction between empirical and analytic approaches to test construction that we outlined in Chapter 5.

SECTION SUMMARY

Clinical neuropsychologists use combinations of tests, called batteries, to assess a wide range of functioning in clients. The Halstead–Reitan Battery, consisting of 10 core tests, is one of the best known. An alternative, individualized approach involves clinicians giving a smaller group of tests initially and then selecting additional tests on the basis of the patient's performance.

NEUROPSYCHOLOGICAL APPROACHES TO PSYCHOPATHOLOGY

SECTION PREVIEW

Neuropsychologists study the brain functioning of persons diagnosed with depression, schizophrenia, learning disorders (sometimes called learning disabilities), and other psychological disorders.

Research in neuropsychology has contributed to an understanding of psychological disorders, including depression and schizophrenia. Neuropsychological research has also expanded knowledge of several childhood problems, especially learning disorders.

Depression

Neuropsychologists have been interested in depression ever since Guido Gainotti (1972) documented in a systematic fashion that localized brain damage can produce emotional effects. It is now widely recognized that stroke-induced brain damage commonly produces depression (Robinson & Spalletta, 2010). Interestingly, individuals with right-brain damage may show a rather cheerful, inappropriate, unconcerned reaction to their impairment and hospitalization. This "euphoric" or "indifferent" reaction is often accompanied by anosognosia (unawareness of deficit). In contrast, individuals with left-brain damage more often show a "catastrophic" reaction, which is characterized by tearfulness, despair, and other symptoms of depression. Subsequent studies confirmed that one-third to two-thirds of patients become depressed after experiencing damage to the left side of the brain (Starkstein & Robinson, 1988). These studies have also shown that the probability of depression rises with increasing proximity of the lesion to the front part of the brain. The closer the lesion is to the frontal pole of the left hemisphere, the more severe the depression.

To some degree, these emotional responses stem from the direct effects of losing certain areas of brain function, not simply because people are upset about being impaired. One reason for thinking so is that the degree of depression does not correlate with the severity of disability per se (e.g., Folstein, Maiberger, & McHugh, 1977). The asymmetry findings have been corroborated by EEG, PET, and fMRI measures of brain activity in the left versus the right hemispheres (e.g., Herrington et al., 2005). The left hemisphere in people who are clinically depressed is typically less active than the right; similarly, when people who are not clinically depressed are feeling sad, the left hemisphere is less active than the right hemisphere. These differences in brain activity are most evident over the frontal regions of the brain, confirming their importance for these emotional effects. For example, when both depressed and normal individuals read words that are rated as more pleasant, they all show more activity on fMRI in the left dorsolateral (top and outside part) frontal lobe than the right, but this difference is less strong in depressed patients (Herrington et al., 2010). Such findings suggest that decreases in left frontal brain function could be part of the brain changes that occur in a depressed state.

Tachistoscopic studies have also shown that when visual stimuli are projected to both hemispheres, the left hemisphere typically rates pictures as more positive than the right hemisphere—even though each hemisphere has seen exactly the same images (Heller, 1990). These results suggest that in the healthy brain, regions of the left hemisphere play some role in maintaining a positive perspective on things. It appears that negative mood states result when a lesion or other condition causes these left-side areas to be underactive relative to those in the right hemisphere.

Other studies have found that depression is associated with decreases in right posterior activity (Heller & Nitschke, 1997). People who are depressed show some of the same cognitive deficits displayed by patients with damage to parietal-temporal regions of the brain. They have difficulty with visuospatial information processing and show a number of attentional problems that are similar to patients with right-brain damage. These effects may be caused by the interrelationship of the frontal and posterior regions of the brain. Because frontal regions often inhibit activation in posterior regions, relatively greater activation in the right frontal region compared to the left may be producing too much inhibition of the right posterior regions.

These neuropsychological findings have implications not only for our understanding of depression but also for its diagnosis and treatment after brain damage (Mukherjee, Levin, & Heller, 2006). For example, it is important to consider the possibility that in addition to having problems with impaired language comprehension or expression, a patient with brain injury may also be depressed. Accordingly, neuropsychologists typically ask individuals and family members whether the individual is sleeping and eating normally and recovering as expected. If not, an underlying depression may be present and may require treatment with antidepressant medication and/or psychotherapy. Some people who are depressed, but have no apparent brain damage, also display deficits on neuropsychological assessment measures. Following successful treatment of the depression, these deficits are typically reduced.

Schizophrenia

Neuropsychologists have been deeply involved in studying brain functioning in people with schizophrenia. Early studies, most of which used tachistoscopic methods, suggested the possibility that schizophrenia is characterized by an overactivation of the brain's left hemisphere (Gur, 1978). Current studies continue to look at the differences between left and right hemisphere function, but the picture is now more complicated (Ribolsi et al., 2009).

Both structural (Sapara et al., 2007) and functional (Harrison et al., 2006) abnormalities have been demonstrated in the prefrontal cortex of schizophrenics. Studies measuring regional cerebral blood flow and glucose metabolism suggest that the left prefrontal region of persons with schizophrenia is abnormal because it is not activated during performance on assessments such as the Wisconsin Card Sort Test. In contrast, subcortical regions of the same hemisphere show a hyperactivation compared to controls (Rubin et al., 1991). Studies with functional MRI show that the left prefrontal cortex does not activate normally during a language task, and this brain region also appears to have weaker than usual connections with other brain regions (Bleich-Cohen et al., 2012). Some researchers believe that the results of such neuropsychological and brain imaging studies point to dysfunction of the prefrontal regions, particularly of the left hemisphere, as a fundamental characteristic of brain dysfunction in schizophrenia (Kelly, 2011).

These results are compatible with several observations regarding the symptoms of schizophrenia. Many individuals with schizophrenia display *negative symptoms*, which involve reductions in normal functioning, including "flat" affect, lack of initiative, lack of energy, absence of social engagement, and loss of spontaneity. These same losses are encountered in certain patients with structural lesions to prefrontal regions. Schizophrenia patients can also show *positive symptoms*, in the form of problematic additions to mental life, including nonlinear reasoning, delusions, hallucinations, intrusions into working memory, neologisms (new words), rhyming speech, and other odd language utterances. It is interesting to note that these problems can also be seen after some kind of damage to the specialized regions of the left hemisphere.

Some research suggests that disruptions of right-hemisphere processing may be involved as well, because the right hemisphere has been associated with affective and social functions that are impaired in schizophrenia (Mitchell & Crow, 2005). Other research has raised the possibility that disconnections between frontal and temporal, and perhaps other, brain regions may also be related to the pathology seen in schizophrenia patients (Brambilla et al., 2005; Meyer-Lindenberg et al., 2001). Unfortunately, however, a complete and integrated neuropsychological account of schizophrenia is still lacking.

Learning Disorders

Given neuropsychologists' interest in cognitive abilities, it is not surprising that many of them focus their research, assessment, and intervention efforts on learning disorders. Much of their work focuses on the role of behavioral, environmental, and social factors in these disorders, but they have discovered some fascinating biological correlates, too. Several neuropsychological studies have found, for example, that developmental dyslexia (disruptions in the ability to read) is usually related to dysfunction of the left hemisphere (Shaywitz & Shaywitz, 2005). Brain imaging studies show that variations in children's reading ability across both normal and dyslexic ranges correlate with microstructural variations in left-hemisphere nerve cell pathways (Niogi & McCandliss, 2006). Indeed, even before they learn to read, children who later develop dyslexia show abnormal activity in left hemisphere language regions (Raschle, Zuk, & Gaab, 2012). In children who already have developmental dyslexia, those with greater right hemisphere frontal lobe activation on functional MRI are the ones who seem to respond best to special training and learning to improve their reading performance (Hoeft et al., 2011). This suggests that overcoming the effects of developmental dyslexia depends on being able to use nontraditional right hemisphere brain regions for reading functions.

The results of postmortem examinations of people who were known to have had dyslexia also show that the structure of their left hemispheres differs from that of people without dyslexia. For example, researchers have found evidence for misplaced brain cells, called *ectopias*, in the left hemisphere. Instead of migrating to their proper places during early stages of brain development, these cells appear to have "gotten lost," and some researchers suggest that ectopias can cause developmental delays and deficits in the functioning of the left hemisphere.

Assessments by pediatric clinical neuropsychologists can often help to delineate specific difficulties in left-hemisphere functioning and help design remedial strategies. In fact, children who display school-related attentional difficulties (including attention deficit hyperactivity disorder), memory and language problems, and social and emotional problems (including depression and anxiety) are often referred to a pediatric clinical neuropsychologist. The clinician typically conducts a thorough examination and then consults with teachers and parents on how best to help the child.

Nonverbal Learning Disorders

A different type of learning disorder involves deficits in visuospatial and visuomotor skills, as well as in other abilities that depend on the right hemisphere (Grodzinsky, Forbes, & Bernstein, 2011). This syndrome of *nonverbal learning disorder* (also known as nonverbal disability) was first described in the mid-1970s (Myklebust, 1975), but neuropsychological research has only recently been helping to delineate this disorder (Spreen, 2011). Children with nonverbal learning disorders may have long escaped the notice of professionals because they are often talkative and show high levels of verbal intelligence. Consequently, they sound as though they should be more skillful in the nonverbal realm than they actually are. Children with nonverbal learning disorders often have difficulty keeping up with other children on nonverbal tasks. They are slow to learn such skills as tying shoes, dressing, eating, and organizing their time and their environment. Because their difficulties are relatively subtle, they are likely to be labeled as having an emotional or behavioral problem, not a learning disorder. Unfortunately, if these children are treated as "bad," "uncooperative," or "a problem" long enough, they may end up behaving accordingly. Thus early diagnosis and treatment of nonverbal learning disorders is vital.

Nonverbal learning disorders may result from right-hemisphere deficits early in childhood, which can interfere with normal development (Rourke, 1989). These difficulties inhibit a child from exploring the environment, learning the consequences of actions, and gaining essential experience in coordinated visuomotor skills. They can also interfere with the process of attachment between an infant and its caregivers, a process that depends on nonverbal skills. Because mother–infant interaction predicts the quality of attachment during the toddler phase, and because the quality of attachment predicts social adjustment in early and middle childhood, problems in right-brain functioning not only can create early motoric and cognitive difficulties but also can lead to abnormalities in social relationships that place the children at risk for emotional difficulties later in life.

Some of the social development difficulties seen in these children are probably related to their inability to meet the intense demands for nonverbal information processing in social situations. Overwhelmed by the task of integrating information about other children's facial information, tone of voice, physical activity, and verbal content, they fail to follow even simple exchanges. Over time, their lack of experience and interaction with other children can cause them to feel isolated, lonely, and depressed. It has even been suggested that nonverbal learning disorder may be a risk factor for the development of schizophrenia.

In assessing the possible presence of nonverbal learning disorders, pediatric clinical neuropsychologists look first for a discrepancy between verbal and nonverbal tasks. If the same pattern appears on other tests comparing verbal and visual-spatial/visual-motor skills, a nonverbal learning disorder is likely to be diagnosed. Often, although not always, the pattern of poor performance on right-hemisphere tasks is accompanied by signs on the Halstead–Reitan Battery suggesting impaired right-hemisphere performance.

As they do in relation to other learning disorders, pediatric clinical neuropsychologists work to devise remedial programs for children with nonverbal learning disorders. They encourage parents and teachers to take advantage of the children's verbal skills in ways that can help compensate for lack of understanding in nonverbal domains. They also recommend that these children receive individual attention from a learning disorders specialist or tutor. Without this help, their academic achievement is likely to fall behind that of their classmates as the demands of school increase. The children's impaired social skills can often be addressed by group therapy, social skills workshops, individual therapy, facilitation of structured peer interactions, or participation in after-school programs.

SECTION SUMMARY

Depression appears to be associated with abnormal activity levels in the left frontal and right posterior brain regions. Schizophrenia appears to be associated with structural and functional abnormalities in the prefrontal cortex and regions of the right hemisphere. Left-hemisphere structure and function appears implicated in certain learning disorders. Findings such as these are important not only to help better understand persons diagnosed with these disorders but also to help alert clinical neuropsychologists that persons with damage to these regions may be at higher risks for other disorders.

THE CURRENT STATUS OF CLINICAL NEUROPSYCHOLOGY

The field of clinical neuropsychology has grown tremendously since the mid-twentieth century. In the late 1960s, the *International Neuropsychological Society* (INS) was founded; in the 1970s, clinical neuropsychology emerged as a distinctive professional specialty; and in 1980, the *Division of Clinical Neuropsychology* (Division 40) was formed within the American Psychological Association. Division 40 is now one of the largest divisions of the APA. In 1996, the APA designated clinical neuropsychology as a specialty (similar to clinical, counseling, or health psychology).

In 1997, a group of specialists and educators meeting in Houston, Texas, developed guidelines for the training of clinical neuropsychologists. These guidelines were revised in 2004 (Reitan, Hom, Ven De Voorde, Stanczak, & Wolfson, 2004). They specify core knowledge bases and skills. The core knowledge bases include (a) general psychology (including statistics and methodology, learning, cognition and perception, social psychology, biological bases of behavior, life-span development, history, cultural and individual differences), (b) general clinical psychology (including psychopathology, psychometric theory, interviewing, assessment, intervention, and ethics), (c) foundations for the study of brain–behavior relationships (including neuroanatomy, neurological and related disorders and their etiology, pathology, course and treatment, nonneurological conditions affecting central nervous system functioning, neuroimaging and other neurodiagnostics, neurochemistry of behavior, and neuropsychology of behavior), and (d) foundations for the practice of clinical neuropsychology (specialized assessment, intervention, research design and analysis, ethics and practical implications of neuropsychological conditions). The core skills include (a) assessment, (b) treatment and intervention, (c) consultation, (d) research, and (e) teaching and supervision. Individuals acquire these skills and competencies in graduate school, internship, and postdoctoral residency. Individuals who have undergone the proper training and have had sufficient experience in the practice of clinical neuropsychology can apply to take the examination for diplomate status in clinical neuropsychology.

The Houston Conference guidelines suggest that specialization within clinical neuropsychology will become more common in the future. For instance, one of the most obvious trends in neuropsychological research and practice is an explosion in the use of functional magnetic resonance imaging (fMRI) and other high-tech brain-scanning techniques. Continued development and refinement of these techniques are likely, and they will become more accessible to researchers and clinicians. The growth of interest in fMRI and other measures of brain function has been accompanied by an increasing need for good neuropsychologists (Matarazzo, 1992; Oakes & Lovejoy, 2013). After all, if one wants to watch the activation of a brain region of interest, one must develop testing tasks that require information processing in that brain region (Miller, Elbert, Sutton, & Heller, 2007). Neuropsychologists are in a perfect position to develop and use the tests that neuroscientists need to refine their exploration of brain functioning via imaging methods.

In addition to pursuing their assessment and diagnostic activities, neuropsychologists are also becoming more involved in designing effective interventions to help individual patients (Hunter & Donders, 2011; Ponds & Hendriks, 2006; Winocur et al., 2007). Many of these neuropsychologists work in rehabilitation settings where their efforts to design and implement appropriate services for patients and patients' families take into account the cognitive, social, and emotional consequences of brain damage as well as the long-term needs of people living with such damage. In short, neuropsychologists will continue to provide patients with integrated and comprehensive diagnostic, assessment, and intervention plans.

Chapter Summary

The field of neuropsychology seeks to define the relationship between brain processes and human behavior and psychological functioning, including cognitive and motor abilities, emotional characteristics, personality traits, and mental disorders. Clinical neuropsychologists apply the results of neuropsychological research in their work with children and adults who have had brain trauma or injury or who are experiencing other problems related to brain impairment. Neuropsychology was not defined as a scientific field until the late 1940s, and clinical neuropsychology did not emerge as a distinctive professional specialty until the 1970s.

One of the most important organizational principles underlying brain–behavior relationships is localization of function, which refers to the fact that different parts of the brain are involved in different skills or senses. Lateralization of function is another vital feature of the brain's organization that has important implications for behavior. In most right-handed people, the left hemisphere is particularly specialized to handle speech and other linguistic processing, including the ability to understand and produce spoken language. The right hemisphere is particularly specialized for analyzing spatial and other nonverbal information, including complex signals involved in social communication.

Clinical neuropsychologists use a variety of tools and one of two main approaches to assess patients' cognitive, emotional, or behavioral deficits, and to relate these deficits to specific impairments in brain functioning. In the battery approach, a standardized set of tests is given to all patients, while in the individualized approach, a set of tests is selected depending on the characteristics of each patient. The most widely used assessment battery is the Halstead–Reitan Neuropsychological Test Battery. It consists of ten specific tests and is usually combined with the MMPI-2 and an IQ test. A prominent individualized approach has been developed by Muriel D. Lezak.

Today neuropsychology research is helping clinicians better understand a variety of psychological disorders, including depression, schizophrenia, and verbal and nonverbal learning disorders.

APA's Division of Clinical Neuropsychology has defined the training and educational experiences necessary to become a clinical neuropsychologist and established criteria for demonstrating competence in this specialty.

Study Questions

1. What evidence helped decide debates in the 1800s about localization of function versus equipotentiality?
2. What were some early assessment techniques in clinical neuropsychology?
3. What did split-brain patients and research reveal about lateralization of functioning in the brain?
4. How does the functioning of modules within the brain show both localization and globalism?
5. Which functions appear to be most tied to the right side of the brain, and which to the left side?
6. What are the names and symptoms of some of the neurological dysfunctions clinical neuropsychologists see?
7. Which neurological dysfunctions are likely to be associated with damage to each of the lobes of the cortex?
8. What is the Halstead–Reitan Battery?
9. What is an individualized approach to neuropsychological assessment?
10. What neurological regions appear to be implicated in depression?
11. What neurological regions appear to be implicated in schizophrenia?
12. What professional organizations support clinical neuropsychology?
13. In what ways is clinical neuropsychology likely to continue to grow?

Web Sites

- The International Neurological Society: http://www.the-ins.org
- APA Division of Clinical Neuropsychology (Division 40): http://www.div40.org/
- The American Academy of Clinical Neuropsychology (AACN): http://www.theaacn.org
- The American Board of Clinical Neuropsychology: http://www.theabcn.org

MOVIES

Away From Her (2007). After decades of marriage, a wife with failing memory moves into a rest home and slowly fades away from her husband and reality.

The Iron Lady (2011). Based on the life of Margaret Thatcher, this intense film shows the challenges of growing older, including symptoms of dementia, loss of loved ones, and physical frailty.

MEMOIRS

My Stroke of Insight: A Brain Scientist's Personal Journey by Jill Bolte Taylor (2009; New York: Plume). Detailed memoir by a neuroanatomist who studied brain functioning and who herself experienced a massive stroke, with vivid descriptions of the 8-year process to relearn how to talk, walk, write, read, and function independently.

The Noonday Demon: An Atlas of Depression by Andrew Solomon (2001; New York: Scribner). Detailed account of major depressive disorder, with implications of neuropsychological underpinnings.

References

Abdel, K. A. M. (1994). Normative results on the Arabic Fear Survey Schedule III. *Journal of Behavior Therapy and Experimental Psychiatry, 25*, 61–67.

Adair, J. C., & Barrett, A. M. (2011). Anosognosia. In K. M. Heilman & E. Valenstein (Eds.), *Clinical neuropsychology* (5th ed., pp. 198–213). New York, NY: Oxford.

Babinski, M. J. (1914). Contribiutions a l'etude des troubles mentaux dans l'hemiplegie organique cerebrale (anosognosie). *Review of Neurology, 12*, 845–847.

Baird, A., Dewar, B. K., Critchley, H., Dolan, R., Shallice, T., et al. (2006). Social and emotional functions in three patients with medial frontal lobe damage including the anterior cingulate cortex. *Cognitive Neuropsychiatry, 11*(4), 369–388.

Barton, J. J. (2011). Disorders of higher visual processing. *Handbook of Clinical Neurology, 102*, 223–261.

Bear, D. M., & Fedio, P. (1977). Quantitative analysis of interictal behavior in temporal lobe epilepsy. *Archives of Neurology, 34*, 454–467.

Bigler, E. D. (2007). A motion to exclude and the "fixed" versus "flexible" battery in "forensic" neuropsychology: Challenges to the practice of clinical neuropsychology. *Archives of Clinical Neuropsychology, 22*(1), 45–51. E-pub Dec. 27, 2006.

Bisiach, E., Luzzatti, C., & Perani, D. (1979). Unilateral neglect, representational schema and consciousness. *Brain, 102*(3), 609–618.

Bleich-Cohen, M., Sharon, H., Weizman, R., Poyurovsky, M., Faragian, S., et al. (2012). Diminished language lateralization in schizophrenia corresponds to impaired inter-hemispheric functional connectivity. *Schizophrenia Research, 134*(2–3), 131–136.

Brambilla, P., Cerini, R., Gasparini, A., Versace, A., Andreone, N., et al. (2005). Investigation of corpus callosum in schizophrenia with diffusion imaging. *Schizophrenia Research, 79*(2–3), 201–210.

Broca, P. (1861). Remargues sur le siege de la faculte de la porle articulee, suives d'une observation d'aphemie (perte de parole). *Bulletin Societie Anatomie, 36*, 330–357.

Broca, P. (1865). Sur la faculté du langage articulé. *Bulletin Societe Anthropologie Paris, 6*, 337–393.

Chechlacz, M., Rotshtein, P., Hansen, P. C., Riddoch, J. M., Deb, S., et al. (2012). The neural underpinings of simultanagnosia: Disconnecting the visuospatial attention network. *Journal of Cognitive Neuroscience, 24*(3), 718–735.

Cheng, K. (2011). Recent progress in high-resolution functional MRI. *Current Opinion in Neurology, 24*(4), 401–408.

Corbetta, M., & Shulman, G. L. (2011). Spatial neglect and attention networks. *Annual Review of Neuroscience, 34*, 569–599.

Cowey, A. (2010a). The blindsight saga. *Experimental Brain Research, 200*(1), 3–24.

Cowey A. (2010b). Visual system: How does blindsight arise? *Current Biology, 20*(17), R702–R704.

Dew, I. T., & Cabeza, R. (2011). The porous boundaries between explicit and implicit memory: Behavioral and neural evidence. *Annals of the New York Academy of Sciences, 1224*, 174–190.

Dym, R. J., Burns, J., Freeman, K., & Lipton, M. L. (2011). Is functional MR imaging assessment of hemispheric language dominance as good as the Wada test? A meta-analysis. *Radiology, 261*(2), 446–455.

Eslinger, P. J., & Damasio, A. R. (1985). Severe disturbance of higher cognition after bilateral frontal lobe ablation: Patient EVR. *Neurology, 35*, 1731–1741.

Fodor, J. A. (1983). *Modularity of mind.* Cambridge, MA: MIT Press.

Folstein, M. F., Maiberger, P., & McHugh, P. R. (1977). Mood disorders as a specific complication of stroke. *Journal of Neurology, Neurosurgery & Psychiatry, 40*, 1018–1020.

Fournier, N. M., Calverley, K. L., Wagner, J. P., Poock, J. L., & Crossley, M. (2008). Impaired social cognition 30 years after hemispherectomy for intractable epilepsy: The importance of the right hemisphere in complex social functioning. *Epilepsy and Behavior, 12*(3), 460–471.

Friederici, A. D. (2011). The brain basis of language processing: From structure to function. *Physiological Reviews, 91*(4), 1357–1392.

Gainotti, G. (1972). Emotional behavior and hemispheric side of lesion. *Cortex, 8*, 41–55.

Gardner, H., Brownell, H. H., Wapner, W., & Michelow, D. (1983). Missing the point: The role of the right hemisphere in the processing of complex linguistic materials. In E. Perecman (Ed.), *Cognitive processing in the right hemisphere* (pp. 169–191). New York, NY: Academic.

Gazzaniga, M. S., Fendrich, R., & Wessinger, C. M. (1994). Blindsight reconsidered. *Current Directions in Psychological Science, 3*, 93–95.

Glover, G. H. (2011). Overview of functional magnetic resonance imaging. *Neurosurgery Clinics of North America, 22*(2), 133–139.

Glozman, J. M. (2007). A. R. Luria and the history of Russian neuropsychology. *Journal of the History of Neuroscience, 16*(1–2), 168–180.

Goldberg, E. (1995). Rise and fall of modular orthodoxy. *Journal of Clinical and Experimental Neuropsychology, 17*(2), 193–208.

Goldberg, E., & Bougakov, D. (2005). Neuropsychologic assessment of frontal lobe dysfunction. *Psychiatric Clinics of North America, 28*, 567–580.

Grodzinsky, G. M., Forbes, P. W., & Bernstein, J. H. (2010). A practice-based approach to group identification in nonverbal learning disorders. *Child Neuropsychology, 16*, 433–460.

Grydeland, H., Walhovd, K. B., Westlye, L. T., Due-Tønnessen, P., Ormaasen, V., et al. (2010). Amnesia following herpes simplex encephalitis: Diffusion-tensor imaging uncovers reduced integrity of normal-appearing white matter. *Radiology, 257*(3), 774–781.

Gur, R. E. (1978). Left hemisphere dysfunction and the left hemisphere overactivation in schizophrenia. *Journal of Abnormal Psychology, 87*, 225–238.

Harlow, J. M. (1848). Passage of an iron rod through the head. *Boston Medical and Surgical Journal, 39*, 389–393.

Heilman, K. M., Barrett, A. M., & Adair, J. C. (1998). Possible mechanisms of anosognosia: A defect in self-awareness. *Philosophical Transactions of the Royal Society of London: Series B. Biological Sciences, 353*(1377), 1903–1909.

Heilman, K. M., & Valenstein, E. (Eds.). (2011). *Clinical neuropsychology* (5th ed.) New York, NY: Oxford University Press.

Heller, W. (1990). The neuropsychology of emotion: Developmental patterns and implications for psychopathology. In N. L. Stein, B. L. Leventhal, & T. Trabasso (Eds.), *Psychological and biological approaches to emotion* (pp. 167–211). Hillsdale, NJ: Erlbaum.

Heller, W., & Nitschke, J. B. (1997). Regional brain activity in emotion: A framework for understanding cognition in depression. *Cognition and Emotion, 11*, 637–661.

Hellige, J. B. (2001). *Hemispheric asymmetry: What's right and what's left.* Cambridge, MA: Harvard University Press.

Herholz, K. (2011). Perfusion SPECT and FDG-PET. *International Psychogeriatrics, 23*(Suppl 2), S25–S31.

Herrington, J. D., Heller, W., Mohanty, A., Engels, A. S., Banich, M.T., et al. (2010). Localization of asymmetric brain function in emotion and depression. *Psychophysiology, 47*(3), 442–454.

Herrington, J. D., Mohanty, A., Koven, N. S., Fisher, J. E., Stewart, J. L., et al. (2005). Emotion-modulated performance and activity in left dorsolateral prefrontal cortex. *Emotion, 5*, 200–207.

Hoeft, F., McCandliss, B. D., Black, J. M., Gantman, A., Zakerani, N., et al. (2011). Neural systems predicting long-term outcome in dyslexia. *Proceedings of the National Academy of Sciences USA, 108*(1), 361–366.

Hunter, S. J., & Donders, J. (Eds.). (2011). *Pediatric neuropsychological intervention.* Cambridge, MA: Cambridge University Press.

Jacoby, L. L., & Kelley, C. M. (1987). Unconscious influences of memory for a prior event. *Personality and Social Psychology Bulletin, 13*, 314–336.

Jenkinson, P. M., Preston, C., & Ellis, S. J. (2011). Unawareness after stroke: A review and practical guide to understanding, assessing, and managing anosognosia for hemiplegia. *Journal of Clinical and Experimental Neuropsychology, 33*(10), 1079–1093.

Jones, B. P., & Butters, N. (1983). Neuropsychological assessment. In M. Hersen, A. E. Kazdin, & A. S. Bellack (Eds.), *The clinical psychology handbook* (pp. 377–396). New York, NY: Pergamon Press.

Kelley, M. P. (2011). Schizotypy and hemisphericity. *Psychological Reports, 109*(2), 533–552.

Lee, A. C. H., Brodersen, K. H., & Rudebeck, S. R. (2013). Disentangling spatial perception and spatial memory in the hippocampus: A univariate and multivariate pattern analysis fMRI study. *Journal of Cognitive Neuroscience, 25*, 534–546.

Lezak, M. D., Howieson, D. B., & Loring, D. W. (2004). *Neuropsychological assessment* (4th ed.). New York, NY: Oxford University Press.

Lorch, M. (2011). Re-examining Paul Broca's initial presentation of M. Leborgne: Understanding the impetus for brain and language research. *Cortex, 47*(10), 1228–1235.

Loring, D. W., & Larrabee, G. J. (2006). Sensitivity of the Halstead and Wechsler Test batteries to brain damage: Evidence from Reitan's original validation sample. *Clinical Neuropsychology, 20*, 221–229.

Marin, R. S., & Wilkosz, P. A. (2005). Disorders of diminished motivation. *Journal of Head Trauma Rehabilitation, 20*, 377–388.

Marini, A., Carlomagno, S., Caltagirone, C., & Nocentini. U. (2005). The role played by the right hemisphere in the organization of complex textual structures. *Brain and Language, 93*, 46–54.

Marinkovic, K., Baldwin, S., Courtney, M. G., Witzel, T., Dale, A. M., et al. (2011). Right hemisphere has the last laugh: Neural dynamics of joke appreciation. *Cognitive, Affective, and Behavioral Neuroscience, 11*(1), 113–130.

Matarazzo, J. D. (1992). Psychological testing and assessment in the 21st century. *American Psychologist, 47*, 1007–1018.

McGaugh, J. L.(2006). Make mild moments memorable: Add a little arousal. *Trends in Cognitive Sciences, 10*, 345–347.

Mednick, S. C., Makovski, T., Cai, D. J., & Jiang, Y. V. (2009). Sleep and rest facilitate implicit memory in a visual search task. *Vision Research, 49*(21), 2557–2565.

Mesulam, M. M. (1990). Large-scale neurocognitive networks and distributed processing for attention, language, and memory. *Annals of Neurology, 28*, 597–613.

Meyer-Lindenberg, A., Poline, J-B., Kohn, P. D., Holt, J. L., Egan, M. F., et al. (2001). Evidence for abnormal cortical functional connectivity during working memory in schizophrenia. *American Journal of Psychiatry, 158*, 1809–1817.

Miller, G. A., Elbert, T., Sutton, B. P., & Heller, W. (2007). Innovative clinical assessment technologies: Challenges and opportunities in neuroimaging. *Psychological Assessment, 19*, 58–73.

Milner, B. (1974). Hemispheric specialization: Scope and limits. In F. O. Schmitt & F. G. Worden (Eds.), *The neurosciences: Third study program* (pp. 75–89). Cambridge, MA: MIT Press.

Milner, D. A., & Rugg, M. D. (1992). *The neuropsychology of consciousness.* San Diego, CA: Academic Press, Inc.

Mitchell, R. L., & Crow, T. J. (2005). Right hemisphere language functions and schizophrenia: The forgotten hemisphere? *Brain, 128*(Pt 5), 963–978.

Mukherjee, D., Levin, R. L., & Heller, W. (2006). The cognitive, emotional, and social sequelae of stroke: Psychological and ethical concerns in post-stroke adaptation. *Topics in Stroke Rehabilitation, 13*, 26–35.

Myklebust, H. R. (1975). Nonverbal learning disabilities: Assessment and intervention. In H. R. Myklebust (Ed.), *Progress in learning disabilities* (Vol. 3, pp. 85–121). New York, NY: Grune & Stratton.

Najt, P., Bayer, U., & Hausmann, M. (2013). Models of hemispheric specialization in facial emotion perception—a reevaluation. *Emotion, 13*(1), 159–167.

Navon, D. (1983). How many trees does it take to make a forest? *Perception, 12*, 239–254.

Neylan, T. C. (1999). Frontal lobe function: Mr. Phineas Gage's famous injury. *Journal of Neuropsychiatry and Clinical Neuroscience, 11*, 280.

Niogi, S. N., & McCandliss, B. D. (2006). Left lateralized white matter microstructure accounts for individual differences in reading ability and disability. *Neuropsychologia, 44*(11), 2178–2188.

Oakes, H. J., & Lovejoy, D. W. (2013). Independent neuropsychological evaluations. *Psychological Injury and Law, 6*, 51–62.

Ponds, R. W., & Hendriks, M. (2006). Cognitive rehabilitation of memory problems in patients with epilepsy. *Seizure, 15*, 267–273.

Raschle, N. M., Zuk, J., & Gaab, N. (2012). Functional characteristics of developmental dyslexia in left-hemispheric posterior brain regions predate reading onset. *Proceedings of the National Academy of Sciences USA, 109*(6), 2156–2161.

Rasmussen, T., & Milner, B. (1975). Clinical and surgical studies of the cerebral speech areas in man. In K. J. Zulch, O. Creutzfeldt, & G. C. Galbraith (Eds.), *Cerebral localization.* Berlin & New York: Springer-Verlag.

Reitan, R. M. (1964). Psychological deficits resulting from cerebral lesions in man. In J. M. Warren & K. Akert (Eds.), *The frontal granular cortex and behavior.* New York, NY: McGraw-Hill.

Reitan, R. M., & Davison, L. A. (Eds.). (1974). *Clinical neuropsychology: Current status and applications.* Washington, DC: V. H. Winston.

Reitan, R. M., Hom, J., Ven De Voorde, J., Stanczak, D. E., & Wolfson, D. (2004). The Houston Conference revisited. *Archives of Clinical Neuropsychology, 19*, 375–390.

Reitan, R. M., & Wolfson, D. (2009). The Halstead-Reitan Neuropsychological Test Battery for Adults: Theoretical, methodological, and validational bases. In I. Grant & K. M. Adams (Eds.), *Neuropsychological assessment of neuropsychiatric and neuromedical disorders* (3rd ed., pp. 3–24). New York, NY: Oxford University Press.

Ribolsi, M., Koch, G., Magni, V., Di Lorenzo, G., Rubino, I. A., et al. (2009). Abnormal brain lateralization and connectivity in schizophrenia. *Reviews in Neuroscience, 20*(1), 61–70.

Robinson, R. G., & Spalletta, G. (2010). Poststroke depression: A review. *Canadian Journal of Psychiatry, 55*(6), 341–349.

Ross, S. A., Allen, D. N., & Goldstein, G. (2013). Factor structure of the Halstead-Reitan neuropsychological battery: A review and integration. *Applied Neuropsychology: Adult, 20*, 120–135.

Rourke, B. P. (1989). *Nonverbal learning disabilities: The syndrome and the model.* New York, NY: Guilford.

Rubens, A. B., & Benson, D. F. (1971). Associative visual agnosia. *Archives of Neurology, 24*, 304–316.

Rubin, R., Holm, S., Friberg, L., Videbech, P., Andersen, H. S., et al. (1991). Altered modulation of prefrontal and subcortical brain activity in newly diagnosed schizophrenia and schizophreniform disorder: A regional cerebral blood flow study. *Archives of General Psychiatry, 48*, 987–995.

Sacks, O. (1990). *A leg to stand on.* New York, NY: Summit Books.

Sapara, A., Cooke, M., Fannon, D., Francis, A., Buchanan, R. W., et al. (2007). Prefrontal cortex and insight in schizophrenia: A volumetric MRI study. *Schizophrenia Research, 89*(1–3), 22–34. Epub Nov 13, 2006.

Schirmer, A., Alter, K., Kotz, S. A., & Friederici, A. D. (2001). Lateralization of prosody during language production: A lesion study. *Brain and Language, 76*, 1–17.

Scoville, W. B., & Milner, B. (1957). Loss of recent memory after bilateral hippocampal lesions. *The Journal of Neurology, Neurosurgery, & Psychiatry, 20*, 11–21.

Shaywitz, S. E., & Shaywitz, B. A. (2005). Dyslexia (specific reading disability). *Biological Psychiatry, 57*(11), 1301–1309.

Shenker, J. I. (April 2005). *When you only see trees, is there still a forest?* Paper presented at the American Academy of Neurology Annual Meeting, Miami Beach, FL.

Sperry, R. W. (1961). Cerebral organization and behavior. *Science, 133*, 1749–1757.

Sperry, R. W. (1968). Hemisphere deconnection and unity in conscious awareness. *American Psychologist, 23*, 723–733.

Sperry, R. W. (1974). Lateral specialization in the surgically separated hemispheres. In F. O. Schmitt & F. G. Worden (Eds.), *The neurosciences: Third study program* (pp. 5–20). Cambridge, MA: MIT Press.

Sperry, R. W. (1982). Some effects of disconnecting the cerebral hemispheres. *Science, 217*, 1223–1226.

Spreen, O. (2011). Nonverbal learning disabilities: A critical review. *Child Neuropsychology, 17*(5), 418–443.

Stam, C. J., & van Straaten, E. C. (2012). The organization of physiological brain networks. *Clinical Neurophysiology, 123*,1067–1087

Starkstein, S. E., Jorge, R. E., & Robinson, R. G. (2010). The frequency, clinical correlates, and mechanism of anosognosia after stroke. *Canadian Journal of Psychiatry, 55*(6), 355–361.

Starkstein, S. E., & Robinson, R. G. (1988). Lateralized emotional response following stroke. In M. Kinsbourne (Ed.), *Cerebral hemisphere function in depression.* Washington, DC: American Psychiatric Press.

Sternberg, S. (2011). Modular processes in mind and brain. *Cognitive Neuropsychology, 28*(3–4), 156–208.

Strauss, E., & Wada, J. (1983). Lateral preferences and cerebral speech dominance. *Cortex, 19*, 165–177.

Stuss, D. T. (2011). Functions of the frontal lobes: Relation to executive functions. *Journal of the International Neuropsychological Society, 17*(5), 759–765.

Tompkins, C. A. (2012). Rehabilitation for cognitive-communication disorders in right hemisphere brain damage. *Archives of Physical Medicine and Rehabilitation, 93*(1 Suppl), S61–S69.

Tyler, K. L., & Malessa, R. (2000). The Goltz-Ferrier debates and the triumph of cerebral localizationalist theory. *Neurology, 55*, 1015–1024.

Ungerleider, L. G., & Mishkin, M. (1982). Two cortical visual systems. In D. J. Ingle, M. A. Goodale, & R. J. W. Mansfield (Eds.), *Analysis of visual behavior.* Cambridge, MA: MIT Press.

Verfaellie, M., & Keane, M. M. (1997). The neural basis of aware and unaware forms of memory. *Seminars in Neurology, 17*, 153–161.

Wada, J., & Rasmussen, T. (1960). Intracarotid injection of sodium amytal for the lateralization of cerebral speech dominance. *Journal of Neurosurgery, 17*, 266–282.

Wellmer, J., Fernandez, G., Linke, D. B., Urbach, H., Elger, C. E., et al. (2005). Unilateral intracarotid amobarbital procedure for language lateralization. *Epilepsia, 46*(11), 1764–1772.

Winocur. G., Craik, F. I., Levine, B., Robertson, I. H., Binns, M. A., et al. (2007). Cognitive rehabilitation in the elderly: Overview and future directions. *Journal of the International Neuropsychology Society, 13*, 166–171.

Wolk, D. A., Coslett, H. B., & Glosser, G. (2005). The role of sensory-motor information in object recognition: Evidence from category-specific visual agnosia. *Brain and Language, 94*(2), 131–146.

Zola-Morgan, S. (1995). Localization of brain function: The legacy of Franz Joseph Gall (1758–1828). *Annual Review of Neuroscience, 18*, 359–383.

14 | FORENSIC PSYCHOLOGY

Chapter Preview

This chapter describes a number of ways that clinical psychologists contribute to the legal system and to legal decision making. Forensic psychologists contribute to decisions about whether a defendant is competent to stand trial, whether a defendant was insane at the time he or she committed a crime, and whether specific persons are a threat to others. Clinicians also become involved in civil actions such as determinations about the role of stress or the extent of psychological damages. While activities such as criminal profiling and psychological autopsies are infrequent, other activities such as evaluations in child custody and divorce proceedings are very common for forensic clinical psychologists.

In the fourth edition of this book, published in 1994, we predicted that forensic psychology—a specialty that applies psychological principles and knowledge to legal issues and proceedings—would be a "growth stock" for clinical psychologists. Our prediction was accurate. It is now clear that the demand for psychologists to contribute in various ways to the legal system has grown to the point that forensic psychology has become a major professional activity and a focal point of scholarship among clinical psychologists. Numerous signs indicate this growth surge. For example, the American Psychology-Law Society (Division 41 of the American Psychological Association) now lists over 1,700 members and publishes its own journal, *Law and Human Behavior*; a newsletter, *American Psychology-Law News*; and a book series, *Perspectives in Law and Psychology*. In 1995, APA itself inaugurated the publication of *Psychology, Public Policy, and Law*, another journal devoted to psychology and the law. There are several other journals devoted to legal issues, including *Behavioral Sciences and the Law*; *Law and Psychology Review*; *Journal of Forensic Neuropsychology*; *Journal of Forensic Psychology Practice*; *Psychology, Crime and Law*; *Journal of the American Academy of Psychiatry and the Law*; *International Journal of Law and Psychiatry*; and *Psychiatry, Psychology, and Law*. The popularity of the field is evident in the increasing number of graduate, and even undergraduate, concentrations in forensic psychology. Perhaps the most significant indication of the expansion of the field was the American Psychological Association's approval, in 2001, of forensic psychology as a specialty area of applied psychology, joining clinical, counseling, school, child, health, neuropsychology, and other practice areas.

THE SCOPE OF FORENSIC PSYCHOLOGY

SECTION PREVIEW

Forensic psychologists apply psychological knowledge to a variety of legal contexts and legal decisions. They also research the effects of those decisions and the effectiveness of interventions designed to help people avoid negative contacts with the law.

Forensic psychology (and forensic psychiatry) involves the application of mental health knowledge and expertise to the assessment and treatment of individuals who are in some way involved in the legal process or legal system (Otto, 2013). The term *forensic* comes from the Latin word *forensis*, meaning "of the forum," where the law courts of ancient Rome were held.

Clinical psychologists working in the forensic area may be involved in addressing a wide range of legal issues, including whether (a) an individual is sufficiently mentally ill and potentially dangerous to justify involuntary hospitalization; (b) a person charged with a crime is mentally competent to stand trial; (c) the perpetrator of an illegal act was sane at the time of the offense; and (d) a person suffered psychological harm as the result of an injury or trauma, and if so, how serious it is. Forensic psychologists might also be involved in questions relating to child custody, guardianship, and execution of wills. They answer these and many other questions by applying the skills and techniques of their profession. These include performing assessments, conducting research, and designing interventions based on the results of empirical research. They also offer their expert opinions during testimony at civil and criminal trials or other legal proceedings.

In this chapter, we illustrate the practice of forensic psychology by describing several areas: (a) competence to stand trial and take criminal responsibility; (b) predicting dangerousness of defendants; (c) psychological damages in civil trials; (d) competencies in civil (i.e., noncriminal) areas; (e) psychological autopsies and criminal profiling; and (f) child custody and parental fitness.

Our discussion covers the basic psycholegal questions experts must address in each area, examines the techniques clinicians typically use to evaluate these questions, and summarizes the empirical evidence and legal status associated with psychologists' activities in these areas. Remember, though, that our review of these five areas is merely an introduction to what is going on at the interface of psychology and law. Clinical psychologists play a variety of other roles in the legal system. Although we don't have the space to cover all these other roles in detail, let's consider them briefly.

Law enforcement psychology involves conducting research on the activities of law enforcement agencies and providing direct clinical services in support of these agencies (Shipley & Arrigo, 2012). A clinician working in this area might test candidates for police work to screen out those who are not psychologically fit (e.g., Detrick & Chibnall, 2013), offer crisis intervention to police officers involved in violent encounters, consult with detectives about what kind of individual might have committed a certain type of crime, or help question witnesses in ways that enhance their recollections of crimes (e.g., Cassel, 2000; National Institute of Justice, 1999).

The *psychology of litigation* is concerned with the effects of various legal procedures used in civil or criminal trials. Clinicians working in this area may offer advice to attorneys about jury selection, study the factors that influence jury deliberations and verdicts such as eyewitness testimony (Loftus, 2003), and analyze the effects of specific portions of trials, such as opening statements, examination of witnesses, or closing arguments (Marcus, Lyons, & Guyton, 2000).

Correctional psychology is concerned primarily with the delivery of psychological services to incarcerated criminals (Schwartz, 2003; Van Voorhis & Salisbury, 2013). Most clinicians working as correctional psychologists are employed in prisons, penitentiaries, or juvenile facilities, but they may also operate out of a probation office or be part of a special community-based correctional program.

New research on the interface of psychology and law is constantly being published, and professional psychological services are continually expanding in the legal arena. You can review these advancements in the journals mentioned previously as well as in textbooks on law and psychology (e.g., Brewer & Williams, 2007; Cassel & Bernstein, 2007; Fulero & Wrightsman, 2008; Kapardis, 2010; Monahan & Walker, 2006; Shipley & Arrigo, 2012; Roesch, Zapf, & Hart, 2009; Otto, 2013).

SECTION SUMMARY

Forensic psychologists are involved in a wide variety of research and practice activities. They contribute to cases in which defendants claim or appear to have mental illness; they provide evaluation and treatment services for law enforcement, corrections, and especially the courts; and they study the effects of these interventions as well as other aspects of legal decision making.

CRIMINAL COMPETENCE AND RESPONSIBILITY

SECTION PREVIEW

The law requires that criminal defendants be competent to assist in their own defense. It also requires that to be held responsible for a crime, a defendant must have understood that his or her behavior was wrong. Because these are psychological judgments, forensic psychologists are typically involved in decisions about criminal responsibility.

Courts allow defendants' mental conditions to be considered at trial because our society believes that it is immoral to punish people who, as a result of a mental disorder, either did not know that their actions were wrong or could not control themselves. However, before a verdict is ever reached, courts must determine whether defendants are mentally competent to assist in their defense in court.

Criminal Competence

In January 2011, Jared Lee Loughner, a 22-year-old community college student, walked into a crowd that had gathered on the sidewalk of a Tucson, Arizona strip mall to meet their federal congressional representative, Gabriel Giffords. Firing a semi-automatic weapon, Loughner shot 19 people, killing six and critically injuring Rep. Giffords and others. The dead included a 9-year-old girl and a federal judge. Loughner was charged with 49 offenses, including murder and attempted assassination of a federal official. His attorney claimed he was not mentally competent to stand trial. This argument was supported by testimony from psychologists who had examined Loughner as well as from Loughner's acquaintances and fellow students who recalled his increasingly odd behavior and paranoid rants about the government. This pretrial testimony convinced a judge that Loughner was suffering from a mental illness (paranoid schizophrenia), so instead of scheduling a trial, he sent Loughner to a state hospital for treatment.

In the United States, it is not permissible to continue criminal proceedings against a defendant who is unable to understand the nature and purpose of those proceedings. Forensic psychologists assist in determining a defendant's *competence to stand trial*. The legal standard for competence to stand trial has not changed since the U.S. Supreme Court enunciated it in 1960: "The test will be whether [the defendant] has sufficient present ability to consult with his lawyer with a reasonable degree of rational understanding, and whether he has a rational as well as a factual understanding of the proceedings against him" (*Dusky v. Unites States*, 362 U.S. 402). In short, defendants must be able to understand the proceedings that are taking place and be able to assist their attorneys to prepare their defense.

Competence focuses on the defendant's "present ability" to proceed to adjudication and is to be distinguished from retrospective inquiries regarding criminal responsibility (such as the insanity defense), which focus on the defendant's mental state at the time of the offense. A defendant is considered competent unless and until the defendant convinces the judge otherwise. Defendants must be competent not only at the time of the trial but also at the time of sentencing and, if they received a death sentence, at the time of execution. Clinical psychologists and other mental health experts are also asked to evaluate other kinds of competence in criminal defendants, including competence to confess to a crime, competence to waive the right to an attorney, competence to choose not to invoke the insanity defense, and competence to be sentenced and punished (perhaps by death).

The question of a defendant's competence can be raised by the prosecutor, the defense attorney, or the presiding judge at any point in the criminal process. It is estimated that between 25,000 and 39,000 competency evaluations per year are performed on criminal defendants in the United States (Poythress, Monahan, Bonnie, Otto, & Hoge, 2002). That works out to between 2 and 8% of felony defendants. With the increasing numbers of juveniles now being tried as adults for violent crimes, forensic psychologists are turning their attention to how cognitive immaturity affects the legal competence of juveniles (Cassel & Bernstein, 2007; Grisso et al., 2003).

Assessing Competence

If a question of competence is raised in a particular case, the judge will order a psychological evaluation. Most assessments take place at local community mental health centers, but if the defendant is suffering from a severe disorder such as major depression or schizophrenia, the evaluation may be performed at a state mental hospital or some other inpatient facility. In most states, psychiatrists, psychologists, and social workers are authorized to perform competency evaluations, and they often use special structured interviews to do so (see Table 14.1).

Although the burden of proving incompetence is only by a "preponderance of the evidence" (which is sometimes quantified as at least 51%), 70 to 90% of defendants referred for such evaluations are found competent. The more rigorous the evaluation, the more likely it is that the

---

TABLE 14.1 Assessing Competence to Stand Trial

The assessment of a defendant's competence to participate in criminal proceedings usually begins with a mental status examination, a brief focused interview designed to evaluate the defendant's memory, mood, orientation, thinking, and ability to concentrate. The assessor usually then administers one or more specialized instruments, such as the Competency Screening Test (CST), the Competency Assessment Instrument (CAI), or the MacArthur Competence Assessment Tool–Criminal Adjudication (MacCAT-CA) (Hoge, Bonnie, Poythress, & Monahan, 1997).

The instruments are designed to determine the defendant's ability to

1. Understand the charges filed;
2. Understand the nature and range of possible criminal penalties if convicted;
3. Understand the adversarial nature of the legal process (prosecution versus defense);
4. Disclose to a defense attorney pertinent facts surrounding the alleged offense;
5. Relate to and communicate with the defense attorney;
6. Assist the defense attorney in planning a defense;
7. Realistically challenge the testimony of prosecution witnesses;
8. Behave appropriately in the courtroom;
9. Give relevant testimony in court; and
10. Engage in self-beneficial, as opposed to self-defeating, behaviors throughout the process (Heilbrun & Collins, 1995).

---

defendant will be found to be competent (Heilbrun & Collins, 1995), but most states have a very low threshold for competence. Here is an example of a case in which the question of competence to stand trial was raised (Wrightsman Nietzel, Fortune, & Greene, 2002, p. 297):

Jamie Sullivan was a 24-four-year-old clerk charged with arson, burglary, and murder in connection with a fire he set at a small grocery store in Kentucky. Evidence in the case showed that, after closing time, Sullivan returned to the store where he worked and forced the night manager, Ricky Ford, to open the safe and hand over $800. Sullivan then locked Ford in a small office, doused the store with gasoline, and set it on fire. Ford died in the blaze. Police arrested Sullivan within hours at his grandmother's apartment on the basis of a lead from a motorist who saw him running from the scene.

If convicted on all charges, Jamie Sullivan could have faced the death penalty, but he had an intellectual disability (formally known as mental retardation). He had dropped out of school in the eighth grade, and a psychologist's evaluation at that time reported his IQ to be 68. He could read and write only his name and a few simple phrases. He had a history of drug abuse and at age 15 had spent several months in a juvenile correctional camp after vandalizing five homes in his neighborhood. When he tried to enlist in the Army, he was turned down because of his limited intelligence and drug habit. Jamie's attorney believed that Sullivan's mental problems might render him incompetent to stand trial and therefore asked a psychologist to conduct an evaluation. The psychologist asked Jamie a series of questions about his upcoming trial, to which he gave the following answers:

QUESTION: What are you charged with?

ANSWER: Burning down that store and stealing from Ricky.

Q: Anything else?

A: They say I killed Ricky too.

Q: What could happen to you if a jury found you guilty?

A: Electric chair, but God will watch over me.

Q: What does the judge do at a trial?

A: He tells everybody what to do.

Q: If somebody told a lie about you in court, what would you do?

A: Get mad at him.

Q: Anything else?

A: Tell my lawyer the truth.

Q:	What does your lawyer do if you have a trial?
A:	Show the jury I'm innocent.
Q:	How could he do that best?
A:	Ask questions and have me tell them I wouldn't hurt Ricky. I liked Ricky.
Q:	What does the prosecutor do in your trial?
A:	Try to get me found guilty.
Q:	Who decides if you are guilty or not?
A:	That jury.

After interviewing and testing Sullivan, the psychologist found that his IQ was 65, which fell in the intellectually disabled range, that he did not suffer any hallucinations or delusions, but that he expressed strong religious beliefs that "God watches over his children and won't let nothing happen to them." At a hearing to determine whether Jamie was competent to stand trial, the psychologist testified that the defendant was intellectually disabled and consequently his understanding of the proceedings was not as accurate or thorough as it might otherwise be. However, the psychologist also testified that Sullivan did understand the charges against him as well as the general purpose and nature of his trial. The judge ruled that Jamie Sullivan was competent to stand trial. A jury convicted him on all the charges and sentenced him to life in prison.

What sort of person is usually judged to be incompetent? One large-scale study concluded that most people found incompetent are suffering from a severe mental disorder, such as schizophrenia (Poythress, Monahan, Bonnie, Otto, & Hoge, 2002), but that is far from saying that everyone with a schizophrenia diagnosis is incompetent. Rather, people with a long history of schizophrenia or who are untreated are more likely to be incompetent to assist in their defense.

If a competency evaluation finds a defendant competent, the legal process resumes and the defendant faces trial. If the defendant is found incompetent, the picture becomes more complicated. For crimes that are not serious, the charges might be dropped, sometimes in exchange for requiring the defendant to receive treatment, usually psychotropic medication. If the charges are serious, the defendant usually is returned to an institution for treatment designed to restore competence, which, if successful, will result in the defendant ultimately standing trial. In most states, this mandatory treatment can last up to 6 months (4 months if the defendant is being tried under federal law), after which, if the person is still judged incompetent, the prosecutor may seek a civil commitment by showing that the defendant is a danger to self or others. In the case of a minor, nonviolent offense, the person might be released. Most incompetent defendants are restored to competency through psychotropic medications, at which time they are returned to jail to await trial.

Can a mentally ill defendant be forced to take medication solely to be made competent to stand trial? At least one federal court and several state courts have said yes. Consider the case of Russell Weston Jr., who, on July 24, 1998, stormed the U.S. Capitol building with a .38 caliber handgun. He was looking for the "Ruby Red Satellite System" that he claimed was spreading a deadly disease. During the attack, Weston shot and killed two police officers. Because of a history of schizophrenia and his manifestation of paranoid delusions at the time he was captured, he was sent to the federal prison medical facility in Butner, North Carolina, and evaluated for competency. In interviews with psychiatrists, who diagnosed him as suffering from paranoid schizophrenia, Weston expressed the delusion that the purpose of his trial would be to expose the threat of "cannibalism." When asked if he understood the nature of the death penalty that may be sought against him, he was nonchalant, saying that he could "wake up" whenever he wanted to. Indeed, he said he could "bring back" the victims at will. These statements, and others, indicated that he clearly did not understand the nature of the proceedings nor could he assist his attorneys in his defense.

The judge ordered that Weston receive psychotropic medications so that he could be tried. His attorneys objected to his being medicated because the prosecution might seek the death penalty. Legal wrangling over this issue was not resolved until December 2001, when the U.S. Supreme Court refused to hear the appeal of the court's medication order (Tucker, 2001). As of this writing, Weston remains hospitalized and on medication. It is highly unlikely that he will ever be able to be tried, especially considering that he has been treated for years and has shown no improvement. The time limit on hospitalization for incompetent defendants does not apply to Weston since he has fought efforts to restore his competency.

The Insanity Defense

If Russell Weston ever is found competent to stand trial, he will no doubt plead not guilty by reason of insanity (NGRI). No area of law illustrates the controversies surrounding expert testimony as dramatically as the question of whether a defendant was insane while committing a crime. Proving insanity can result in a defendant's being acquitted, in which case the finding is NGRI. Alternately, the defendant can be found to be guilty but mentally ill (GBMI). If found GBMI, the defendant will be sentenced as any other convicted defendant but ordered to receive such mental health treatment as the correctional institution deems appropriate. In order to understand the legal concept of insanity, it is necessary to understand more about criminal law and how crimes are punished.

A crime is an intentional act (or failure to act) that is a violation of criminal law and committed without a defense or excuse. But even acts that are prohibited by law generally will not rise to the level of criminal conduct unless the accused person possesses *mens rea*, the mental element of culpability. Mens rea literally means "guilty mind," or intent to do wrong.

Criminal defendants are presumed to have mens rea and to be legally responsible for the crimes with which they are charged. Therefore, if defendants plead NGRI, they must present evidence that they lacked the state of mind necessary to be held responsible for a crime. Because insanity is a legal term, not a psychological concept, it is defined by legal standards that have evolved over time.

These standards began to be formalized in 1843, when an Englishman named Daniel McNaughton tried to assassinate the British prime minister, Robert Peel. McNaughton suffered paranoid delusions that Peel was conspiring against him, so he waited outside the prime minister's house at Number 10 Downing Street, where he shot and killed Peel's secretary, whom he mistook for the prime minister. McNaughton was charged with murder but pleaded not guilty by reason of insanity, claiming that he did not know the difference between right and wrong. Nine medical experts testified that McNaughton was insane and, after hearing instructions from the judge, the jury did not even bother to leave the courtroom before deciding that McNaughton was not guilty by reason of insanity. This verdict infuriated the British public, and Queen Victoria was particularly upset because she herself had been the target of several assassination attempts. She demanded that Britain toughen its definition of insanity.

After extended debate in the House of Lords and among the nation's highest judges, a definition of insanity known as the *McNaughton rule* was enacted: ". . . to establish a defense on the grounds of insanity, it must be clearly proved that, at the time of committing the act, the accused was laboring under such a defect of reason, from disease of the mind, as not to know the nature and quality of the act he was doing or, if he did know it, that he did not know what he was doing (was) wrong" (quoted in Post, 1963, p. 113).

In the United States today, the criteria for insanity varies slightly among states. The federal system has its own rule as well, but generally all insanity laws require defendants to prove that, at the time of their crimes, they were suffering from a serious mental disease or defect and (a) lacked substantial capacity to appreciate the criminality or wrongfulness of their conduct or (b) were unable to conform their behavior to the requirements of law. In other words, the defendant has the burden of proving insanity.

MISPERCEPTIONS OF THE INSANITY DEFENSE   At the time that John Hinckley used the insanity defense during his trial for the attempted assassination of President Ronald Reagan, Press Secretary James Brady, and three other people in 1982, federal law did not require his lawyers to prove that he was insane. Instead, it required the prosecution to prove that he was sane, a difficult task since Hinckley had a clear history of disordered behavior (Bonnie, Jeffries, & Low, 2000). After Hinckley was found NGRI, public pressure led to a revision of federal law to require defendants to prove insanity, as is now the case in most state laws.

The uproar over the Hinckley verdict illustrates widespread dissatisfaction with the insanity plea, a dissatisfaction based mostly on misperceptions about the frequency of its use and about its outcomes. Many people believe that criminals routinely claim insanity to evade punishment.

The fact is that insanity pleas occur in only 1 out of every 200 criminal cases and are successful in only 2 of every 1,000 cases (Cassel & Bernstein, 2007). For each successful insanity plea, dozens are unsuccessful, including that of Jack Ruby, killer of Kennedy-assassin Lee Harvey Oswald; Sirhan Sirhan, assassin of Robert Kennedy; and serial killers John Wayne Gacy, Jeffrey Dahmer, David Berkowitz (the "Son of Sam"), and Kenneth Bianchi (the "Hillside Strangler").

The typical defendant who is found not guilty by reason of insanity is similar to the typical defendant who is found incompetent to stand trial. This is not surprising, since most successful insanity pleas involve defendants who at one point were deemed incompetent to be tried. NGRI acquittees are generally seriously mentally ill, unemployed white males in their 20s and 30s, who have a history of hospitalization for mental illness and/or a history of arrest. Few have high school educations. Most are suffering from a serious disorder such as schizophrenia and have been charged with nonviolent crimes. However, even people diagnosed with schizophrenia or other delusional disorders may not convince a jury that they were legally insane at the time of the crime. Take the case of Andrea Yates, the Texas mother who drowned her five children in the bathtub of her Houston, Texas, home in 2001. She had a long history of serious mental illness, including schizophrenia and major depression, yet was found guilty. The jury found that, under Texas law, she knew what she was doing when she committed murder. She was sentenced to serve life in prison, but on appeal, she was retried and in 2006 was found NGRI and confined to a state mental hospital.

DO NGRI ACQUITTEES GET AWAY WITH MURDER?   Many people believe that NGRI acquittees walk free from the courtroom, but like Yates, most of them are immediately confined to a treatment facility. Rarely would an NGRI acquittee be released without any restrictions. The length of time that NGRI acquittees are confined varies with the severity of the crime and the seriousness of the mental illness (Roesch, Zapf, & Hart, 2010). States are required to review the acquittees' mental status periodically, and in accordance with the U.S. Supreme Court judgment in the case of *Foucha v. Louisiana*[1] (1992), defendants judged no longer mentally ill and not dangerous cannot be confined further. But many of the severely mentally ill may never be released and thus are confined longer than others who were convicted of the same types of crimes. It is no surprise then that John Hinckley, having attempted to assassinate a sitting U.S. president, has been confined in St. Elizabeth's hospital in Washington, D.C. since 1982 and that despite his annual efforts to be released, he is unlikely to be allowed out except for supervised visits with his mother (Wilber, 2012). McNaughton himself, whose case gave us the insanity defense, died after 20 years in a mental hospital.

Assessment of Mental Competence. Andrea Yates pleaded not guilty by reason of insanity after drowning her five children. The first legal step in deciding her fate was to confine her in a mental institution to assess her mental competency to stand trial.   *Source*: David J. Phillip, Pool/AP Images.

[1]112 S. Ct. 1780(1992).

THE ROLE OF EXPERT WITNESSES IN THE INSANITY DEFENSE In federal courts and most states, expert witnesses are not allowed to give an opinion as to whether or not a defendant was "sane" or "insane" at the time of committing an offense. Sanity is a legal question that only the judge or jury can answer because there is no diagnosis of "insanity" in the *DSM*. The expert witness can only testify as to the defendant's symptoms, behaviors, and diagnosis. Even before this restriction was codified in state and federal rules of criminal procedure, the American Psychiatric Association took the position that "[No] expert witness testifying with respect to the mental state or condition of a defendant in a criminal case may state an opinion or inference as to whether the defendant did or did not have the mental state or condition constituting an element of the crime charged or a defense thereto. Such ultimate issues are for the trier of fact alone" (APA, 1994).

According to the 1985 U.S. Supreme Court decision in *Ake v. Oklahoma*,[2] indigent (poor) defendants have the right to experts to assist in their insanity defense, but not to the expert of their choice. Absent a showing of some special circumstances or unusual disease or defect, indigents are evaluated by state or federal government-employed mental health professionals, most of whom are highly qualified and competent witnesses. Of course, a person who can afford more than one expert, or the most expensive expert, might mount a more impressive insanity defense than a less affluent defendant, but this economic reality applies to any kind of defense. Having more experts does not necessarily guarantee an insanity verdict, however; even uncontradicted mental health testimony does not always influence juries. Often jurors perceive psychology and psychiatry to be "soft sciences" that are too dependent on subjective interpretations to be used as the basis for decisions about a defendant's guilt or innocence (e.g., Faust, 2011; Rohde, 1999).

This view may change as forensic neuroscience makes its way into the courtroom. These scientists are increasingly recognized as experts who not only can explain how brain structure and function underlies human behavior but also can depict, with real-time, full-color imaging techniques, just what areas of the brain are responsible (Rosen, 2007; Simpson, 2013; also see Chapter 13, "Clinical Neuropsychology"). Of course, jurors still must determine if brain malfunction releases someone from criminal liability, so the essence of the insanity issue has not changed.

Reforming the Insanity Defense

Two major changes have been made over the past 20 years that make it more difficult for mentally ill defendants to obtain the benefit of the insanity defense: Some states (Idaho, Utah, and Montana) have abolished the insanity plea altogether, while others have added the GBMI verdict.

GUILTY BUT MENTALLY ILL AND DIMINISHED CAPACITY DEFENSES For many decades, juries deliberating cases involving the insanity defense could only reach verdicts of guilty, not guilty, or not guilty by reason of insanity. Since 1976, however, 20 states have passed laws allowing juries to find defendants GBMI. This verdict option is available only for defendants who plead NGRI. A defendant found GBMI is usually sentenced to the same period of confinement as any other defendant convicted of the same crime. The order of sentence provides that the mentally ill defendant be treated in the correctional facility. However, such treatment is rarely adequate, if provided at all, because GBMI convicts have no guarantee of medical care beyond the minimal level required by law for other convicts (Shipley, 2013; Slobogin, 1985; Steadman, 1993).

The intent of GBMI laws is to offer a compromise verdict that will decrease the number of defendants found NGRI. Indeed, research on verdicts indicates that when states allow both GBMI and NGRI, jurors usually require stronger proof of insanity before returning the NGRI verdict (Roberts, Sargent, & Chan, 1993) and render GBMI verdicts when they believe defendants may not have been sane enough to be held legally responsible for their actions but were culpable enough to warrant punishment (Sales & Shuman, 1996).

Some states have a defense in which defendants can introduce evidence to show that at the time of a crime they had a "diminished capacity" to know right from wrong or to control behavior. This defense is not designed to absolve the defendant of responsibility but to justify conviction on a lesser charge because of the defendant's incapacity to form meaningful premeditation. Former San Francisco County Supervisor Dan White, who in 1978 shot and wounded the city's mayor and killed another elected official, was found to have had a "diminished" capacity

---

[2]105 S. Ct. 977.

for murder based on the now famous "Twinkie defense." White claimed that his reasoning was clouded by eating too much junk food. The jury found him guilty of manslaughter instead of murder, and he was sentenced to 6 years in prison. In 1982, California abolished the diminished capacity defense.

Assessing Sanity

It is relatively straightforward to assess a defendant's competence, because it requires a determination of the defendant's present mental status. But assessing a defendant's mental condition during a criminal act that took place weeks, months, or even years earlier is a much tougher challenge for mental health professionals. To accomplish this task, a variety of methods are used, including a review of the defendant's family, educational, employment, and medical history; ascertaining if the defendant has a history of prior criminality or mental disorder and treatment; listening to the defendant's version of the crime; and administering a variety of psychological assessment instruments.

Assessments typically used include a structured interview as well as intelligence tests (usually either the Wechsler Adult Intelligence Scale or the Stanford–Binet Intelligence Scale), and several personality assessments such as the Minnesota Multiphasic Personality Inventory (MMPI-2), the Psychopathy Checklist–Revised (PCL-R), the Rorschach Inkblot Test, and the Thematic Apperception Test (TAT). Defendants whose history, observed behavior, or IQ test results suggest the possibility of brain dysfunctions may be given neurological tests like the Halstead–Reitan. If there is a history of head trauma, brain injury, or recent change in personality or behavior, brain imaging procedures (such as an MRI and CT scan) may help determine if brain function or structure are compromised by disease or injury. (These various tests are discussed in more detail in Chapter 4, "Interviewing and Observation in Clinical Psychology," Chapter 5, "Testing in Clinical Psychology," and Chapter 13 "Clinical Neuropsychology.")

Although it is estimated that 20 to 25% of defendants attempt to malinger, or "fake," mental illness, assessment instruments and astute clinicians are very successful in detecting such deception (Rogers, 2012). One famously identified malingerer was Kenneth Bianchi, the "Hillside Strangler," who murdered more than a dozen young women in California and Washington in the 1970s. Although four experts had diagnosed him as having multiple personality disorder (now known as dissociative identity disorder), a savvy prosecution expert detected that Bianchi was faking this condition. His cover blown, Bianchi abandoned his insanity plea and pled guilty to murder in exchange for the opportunity to escape the death penalty (Cassel & Bernstein, 2007).

SECTION SUMMARY

Forensic psychologists help judges determine if defendants are competent to understand the charges against them and to assist in their legal defense. They also help judges and juries determine whether the insanity defense applies—whether, at the time of a crime, a mental disorder prevented defendants from understanding the wrongful nature of their behavior and from controlling their actions. Clinicians use a variety of psychological tests and other assessment data to arrive at their judgments, and then they present the information to judges and juries who make the final determination. Although used much less than is commonly thought, the insanity defense has remained controversial. Some states have abolished it; others have introduced alternatives such as the guilty but mentally ill verdict and allowed for claims of diminished capacity.

PREDICTING DANGEROUSNESS

Russell Weston Jr. had been suffering from paranoid schizophrenia long before his attack on the U.S. Capitol building. Two years earlier, Weston had been involuntarily committed to a Montana mental hospital because of his paranoid delusions and odd behavior, which included claims that President Clinton was his close friend and that he was being spied on by devices planted in television satellite dishes and cable boxes. Weston was released before the term of his court-ordered confinement ended because hospital officials deemed him to be no risk for violent behavior if he took his medications. That was a big "if," to be sure. But could psychologists have known in 1996 that Weston would kill people in 1998?

As we discussed in Chapter 3, "Basic Features of Clinical Assessment," psychologists and other mental health professionals are often called upon by the courts to predict a person's potential for dangerous behavior. For example, psychologists might be asked to determine whether it is safe for someone charged with murder to be freed on bond pending trial or appeal, or whether a person found NGRI can be released from custody without posing a danger to self or society. In civil cases, psychologists might be asked to determine whether someone is likely to commit suicide and should therefore be placed in a mental hospital for his or her own protection.

ASSESSING PSYCHOLOGICAL STATUS IN CIVIL TRIALS

SECTION PREVIEW

Forensic psychologists become involved in civil cases when there are allegations, such as in workers' compensation trials, that a person has suffered psychological harm. Clinicians may also help the courts determine whether someone has sufficient mental capacity to make important decisions, such as making a will or selling property.

Tort law provides a mechanism for individuals to seek redress for the harm they have suffered from the wrongful acts of another party. It thus differs from *criminal law* which—acting on behalf of society as a whole—prosecutes defendants for wrongful behavior and seeks to punish them in an attempt to maintain society's overall sense of justice. When plaintiffs in civil cases sue defendants for causing harm to them and/or to their property, the lawsuits are known as *tort actions*.

Assessing Psychological Damage in Tort Cases

Many kinds of behavior can constitute a tort. Slander and libel are torts, as are cases of medical malpractice, the manufacture of defective products resulting in personal injury, and intentional or negligent behavior producing harm to another person. When clinical psychologists conduct assessments with civil plaintiffs, they typically perform an evaluation that, like most clinical assessments, includes a social history, a clinical interview, psychological testing, interviews with others, and a review of available records. Based on these data, the clinician will reach a decision about what, if any, psychological problems the person might be suffering. This aspect of forensic evaluation is not much different from what a clinician might do with any client, whether or not the client is involved in a lawsuit.

The far more difficult additional question the clinician must answer is whether the psychological problems identified were caused by the tort, were aggravated by the tort, or existed prior to the tort. There is no established procedure for answering this question, so most clinicians try to locate all clinical records and other sources of data that might help establish the point in time at which any diagnosed disorder first appeared. When plaintiffs allege that they were targeted for harassment or some other intentional tort because the defendants knew they had a psychological problem that made them especially vulnerable, the clinician must take this prior condition into account in reaching conclusions about the effects of the tort. Sometimes people allege that a specific kind of mental harm resulted from a defendant's negligence.

Workers' Compensation Cases

When a worker is injured on the job, the law provides for the worker to be compensated, but it does so via a streamlined system that avoids the necessity of proving a tort. This system, known as *workers' compensation law*, is in place in all 50 states and in the federal government. In workers' compensation systems, employers contribute to a fund that provides workers' compensation insurance; they also waive their right to blame the worker or some other individual for the injury. For their part, workers give up their right to pursue a tort against their employers; the award they receive is determined by the type and duration of the injury and the amount of their salary at the time of the injury. Workers can seek compensation for (a) physical and psychological injuries sustained at work, (b) the cost of the treatment they receive for their injuries, (c) lost wages, and (d) the loss of future earning capacity.

Because psychological injuries or mental disorders arising from employment can be compensated, clinical psychologists are often asked to evaluate injured workers and render an opinion about the existence, cause, and implications of any mental disorders that might appear in a given case. Claims for mental disability usually arise in one of three ways.

First, a physical injury or job-related threatening event can cause a mental disorder and psychological disability. A common pattern seen in these *physical–mental* cases is that a worker sustains a serious physical injury—a broken back or severe burns, for example—that results in chronic pain. As the pain continues, the worker begins to experience psychological problems, usually depression and anxiety. These problems worsen until they become full-fledged mental disorders, resulting in further impairments in overall functioning.

The second work-related pathway to mental disability is for an individual to suffer a traumatic incident at work or to undergo a long period of continuous stress that leads to psychological difficulties. The night clerk at a convenience store who is the victim of an armed robbery and subsequently develops posttraumatic stress disorder exemplifies such *mental–mental* cases, as does the clerical worker who, after years of overwork and job pressure, experiences an anxiety disorder, perhaps even posttraumatic stress disorder.

In a third kind of case, known as *mental–physical*, work-related stress is blamed for the onset of a physical disorder such as high blood pressure. Many states have placed special restrictions on these types of claims, and psychologists are seldom asked to evaluate them.

In recent years, the number of psychological claims arising in workers' compensation litigation has increased dramatically. In the 1980s, stress-related mental disorders became the fastest growing occupational disease category in the United States (Hersch & Alexander, 1990), with claims more than doubling from 1985 to 1990. Stress-related workers' compensation claims remain high in both public- and private-sector occupations (Macklin, Smith, & Dollard, 2006).

Clinical psychologists are also heavily involved these days in assessments related to benefits not governed by workers' compensation law. This is because as many as 20% of military veterans are returning from service in Iraq and Afghanistan with posttraumatic stress disorder and/or cognitive injuries (Tanielian & Jaycox, 2008). Military psychologists perform the evaluations necessary in order for these veterans to receive benefits and treatment.

Civil Competencies

In our earlier discussion of competence to stand trial, we focused on the tasks required of defendants during the course of a criminal trial. However, the question of mental competence is raised in several noncriminal situations as well. We refer to these other situations as involving *civil competencies.*

Questions of civil competency focus on whether an individual has the capacity to understand information relevant to making a particular decision and then making an informed choice about what to do. For example, civil competency questions are commonly asked about whether a person is capable of managing personal financial affairs, making decisions about accepting or refusing medical or psychiatric treatment, or executing a will that directs how property should be distributed to heirs or other beneficiaries.

The legal standards used to define competence have evolved over many years, but scholars who have studied this issue agree that four abilities are essential to competent decision making (Appelbaum & Grisso, 1995). A competent individual is expected to be able to (a) understand basic information relevant to making a decision, (b) apply that information to a specific situation in order to anticipate the consequences of various choices that might be made, (c) use logical, rational thinking to evaluate the pros and cons of various strategies and decisions, and (d) communicate a personal decision or choice about the matter under consideration.

The specific abilities associated with each of these general criteria vary, depending on the decision the person must make. Deciding whether to have risky surgery demands different kinds of information and thinking processes than does deciding whether to leave one's estate to one's children or to a charitable organization.

Can persons with serious mental disorders make competent treatment decisions? Do their decision-making abilities differ from persons who do not suffer mental disorders? These questions have been the focus of the MacArthur Treatment Competence Study (Poythress, Monahan, Bonnie, Otto, & Hoge, 2002), which has led to the development of a series of structured interview measures to assess the four basic abilities just discussed. Standardized interviews were conducted with three groups of patients—those with schizophrenia, major depression, or heart disease—and with groups of healthy persons from communities who were demographically matched to the patient groups

(Grisso & Appelbaum, 1995). Only a minority of the persons in all of the groups showed significant impairments in decision making about various treatment options, and patients were capable of significantly better understanding when treatment information was presented to them gradually, one element at a time. However, the patients with schizophrenia and major depression tended to have a poorer understanding of treatment information and used less adequate reasoning in thinking about the consequences of the treatment than did the heart patients or community sample.

In 1990, the Supreme Court decision in *Cruzan v. Director, Missouri Department of Health*[3] recognized that states may allow patients to formalize their desire not to receive life-sustaining medical treatment should they become incapacitated or terminally ill. Accordingly, clinical psychologists and other mental health professionals may be called upon to determine a person's competence to make what are known as *advance medical directives*. The ethical and practical issues involved in determining patients' competence to make prospective end-of-life decisions are enormous, but the trend is to recognize that patients have a high degree of autonomy in accepting or rejecting a variety of treatments and health care provisions (Cantor, 1998; Rich, 1998). The states of Oregon, Washington, and Vermont, which have the only physician-assisted suicide laws in the United States, require that persons must be of sound mind and free of serious mental illness to end their lives.

SECTION SUMMARY

When persons seek legal redress for psychological harm, they take tort action. Examples include claims for workers' compensation based on stress or claims of PTSD based on a traumatic experience. Clinicians gather evidence about the nature and extent of psychological harm using many of the same assessment procedures described in Chapters 3, 4, and 5. They also help courts to judge whether a person is mentally competent to make certain important decisions for themselves.

PSYCHOLOGICAL AUTOPSIES AND CRIMINAL PROFILING

SECTION PREVIEW

Psychological autopsies are often done to help determine whether, for instance, a person's death resulted from suicide, accident, or homicide. Criminal profiling occurs when a crime has been committed but the identity of the person who committed it is unknown. Clinicians acting as profilers use psychological science to describe the most likely categories of suspects.

As already mentioned, most forensic assessments, like most other clinical assessments, include interviewing, observing, and testing living clients. Sometimes, though, clinicians may be called upon to give opinions about a deceased person's state of mind prior to death. In such cases, the clinician obviously must conduct the evaluation without that person's participation. These postmortem psychological evaluations are known as *psychological autopsies* or equivocal death analyses (Botello, Noguchi, Lakshmanan, Weinberger, & Gross, 2013).

Psychological Autopsies

The first psychological autopsies are believed to have been done in the 1950s, when a group of social scientists in Los Angeles began assisting the County Coroner's Office in determining whether suicide, murder, or accident was the most likely cause of death in certain equivocal cases. Since then, psychological autopsies have become commonplace, especially when insurance companies want to know whether their life insurance policyholder committed suicide, in which case death benefits could be denied. Psychological autopsies are also used (a) in workers' compensation cases when an employee's family claims that stressful working conditions or work-related trauma contributed to their relative's suicide or accidental death, (b) to decide whether a deceased individual had the mental capacity necessary to competently execute or modify a will, and (c) to support the argument made by criminal defendants that the person they allegedly killed died by suicide, not homicide.

---

[3]U.S. 261 (1990).

There is no standard format for conducting psychological autopsies, but most clinicians rely heavily on documents and other life records that a person leaves behind, as well as on interviews with those who knew the decedent (Ebert, 1987). Some clinicians concentrate on evidence from the time just before the person's death. What was the person's mood? How was the person doing at work? Were there any pronounced changes in the person's behavior? Clinicians who take a psychodynamic approach look for evidence about family dynamics and personality traits appearing early in the person's life. As a child, how did the person interact with parents or other caregivers? What was the individual's approach to school? To competition with peers?

How valid are psychological autopsies—that is, do they accurately portray a person's state of mind at the time of death? There are certainly reasons to doubt their validity. For one thing, most of the assessment information comes "secondhand," because the person about whom inferences are to be made is not available for interviewing or testing. Further, as noted in Chapter 4, information obtained through third-party interviews may be distorted by memory lapses or by efforts to describe a person in an especially good, or bad, light. There is very little empirical research on the validity of psychological autopsies (Dattilio, 2006), partly because the decedent's "true" state of mind prior to death is unknown and thus cannot be compared to conclusions drawn later by clinicians. This problem may be partially solved if, in future studies, researchers were to assess how well reputed experts do when given psychological autopsy information about cases in which the cause of death appears ambiguous but is actually known. Studying the accuracy of these experts' conclusions, and the reasons behind them, may go a long way toward establishing the validity of psychological autopsies.

In the absence of better research evidence, judges have had mixed reactions to psychological autopsy evidence. In cases involving workers' compensation claims and questions of whether insurance benefits should be paid, the courts have usually admitted psychological autopsy testimony. They have been much more reluctant to do so in criminal cases and in cases involving the question of whether a person had the mental capacity to draft a will (Ogloff & Otto, 1993), because these cases may require psychologists to give testimony about the ultimate issue to be decided in a case. As noted earlier and discussed further later, that sort of testimony is usually not permitted.

Criminal Profiling

In some ways, psychological autopsies resemble a technique known as *criminal profiling*. In both cases, clinicians draw inferences about an individual's motives and state of mind on the basis of life records or other data a person has left behind. In psychological autopsies, however, the identity of the person being assessed is known, and the question is what they did, and why. In criminal profiling, the person's behavior is known, and the question is "who did it?"

One of the first examples of successful criminal profiling came in 1957, with the arrest of George Matesky, the so-called "Mad Bomber" of New York City. After trying for over a decade to identify the person responsible for more than 30 bombings in the New York area, the police consulted Dr. James Brussel, a local psychiatrist. Brussel examined pictures of the bomb scenes and analyzed letters sent to police by the bomber. Based on these data, Brussel advised the police to look for a heavyset, middle-aged, Eastern European, Catholic man who was single and lived with a sibling or an aunt. Brussel also concluded that the man loved his mother and valued neatness. He even predicted that when the man was found, he would be wearing a buttoned double-breasted suit. When the police finally arrested Matesky, this profile turned out to be uncannily accurate, right down to the suit (Brussel, 1968).

Today, the major source of research and development on criminal profiling is the FBI's Behavioral Analysis Unit. This unit includes profilers who have training in behavioral science and who work with a very small number of psychologists and other mental health professionals who are involved in profiling activities. The unit analyzes about 1,000 cases a year (Homant & Kennedy, 1998) and has amassed large amounts of data on the backgrounds, family characteristics, current behaviors, and psychological traits of various types of criminal offenders (Douglas & Olshaker, 1995). The unit has concentrated on the study of violent offenders, especially those who commit bizarre or repeated crimes, including rape, arson, sexual homicides, and mass and serial murders. A key element of the unit's research is the interviewing of various types of known offenders in order to discover how each type selects and approaches their victims, how they react to their crimes, what demographic or family characteristics they share, and what personality features predominate among them. For example, as part of its study of mass and serial killers, the FBI conducted detailed interviews with many notorious killers, including Charles Manson, Richard Speck, and David Berkowitz.

One review of criminal profiling (Homant & Kennedy, 1998) concluded that different kinds of crime scenes can in fact be classified with reasonable reliability and that various kinds of crimes do correlate with certain offender characteristics. At the same time, research on profiling suggests several reasons for caution about its value. For one thing, in contrast to the "mad bomber" case, inaccurate profiles are quite common. Second, many of the evaluation studies have been conducted by FBI profilers themselves and have focused on a rather small number of cases. Finally, the concepts and approaches actually used by profilers have often not been objectively and systematically defined (Bartol & Bartol, 2008). In fact, a survey of 152 police psychologists found that 70% of them had serious questions about the validity of crime scene profiling (Bartol, 1996), and for good reason. To take one example, after a bomb exploded at the 1996 Olympics, Atlanta police almost immediately—and incorrectly, as it turned out—focused their suspicions on Richard Jewell, an Olympic Park security guard. Jewell was singled out because he fit an FBI profile for this kind of bombing; he is a white, single, middle-age male who craves the limelight, sometimes as a police "wannabe." In this case, the profile was wrong; he had nothing to do with the bombing.

SECTION SUMMARY

Psychological autopsies are assessments designed to determine the psychological causes behind a death when those causes are equivocal. Criminal profiling involves attempts to identify the psychological and demographic characteristics associated with people who commit particular types of crimes. Profiling is designed to focus police investigations and locate the guilty party. Although the practice is regarded as important by some, there is a lack of strong empirical evidence to support it.

CHILD CUSTODY AND PARENTAL FITNESS

SECTION PREVIEW

Child custody cases involve more clinical psychologists than any other area of forensic work. Clinicians conduct evaluations of divorcing parents and their children to help the courts decide what courses of action are in the best interests of the children.

One of the fastest growing areas for clinicians in forensic psychology is the assessment of families in crisis.

Child Custody Disputes

Clinical psychologists are often involved in the legal aspects of family crises, especially when parents are separating or divorcing. Here, the clinician is usually asked to conduct a *child custody evaluation* and to offer recommendations to help a court settle disputes over which parent can best meet the children's needs and which, therefore, should retain custody of them. The growth in these assessment activities is attributable, first, to the fact that with half of all marriages in the United States now ending in divorce, child custody questions arise in millions of families; indeed, it is estimated that 40% of children will have experienced parental divorce by the age of 16 (Fabricius, Braver, Diaz, & Velez, 2010). Second, the preference for maternal custody that marked most of the twentieth century gave way in the 1980s to gender-neutral laws that put parents on equal footing, in principle at least. Courts now routinely want to know about the parenting abilities of each parent before making a decision about custody (Fabricius, Braver, Diaz, & Velez, 2010).

Most states permit two kinds of custodial arrangements: joint or sole custody. The law prefers joint custody, in large part because mental health experts have educated the courts about the fact that children's needs are best met when both parents are involved in their lives. But there are two categories of joint custody: legal and physical. Although parents may have joint legal custody, meaning they jointly make decisions about their children's welfare (such as those related to education and health care), generally one parent has sole physical custody; the other has visitation rights. Compared to sole legal custody, joint legal custody distributes the frequency of child contact more evenly between the two parents, leads to more interaction between the divorced parents, generates more demands for cooperation concerning their children, and results in more variation in caregiving arrangements (Clingempeel & Repuccci, 1982).

Clinicians conduct custody evaluations under any of three sets of circumstances. In some cases, a judge appoints a clinician to conduct a custody evaluation that will be available to all the parties. In others, each party retains a different expert to conduct independent evaluations, and in still others, the two sides agree to share the cost of hiring one expert to conduct a single evaluation (Weissman, 1991). Most informed observers, including attorneys, prefer either the first or third option because they minimize the hostilities and adversarial pressures that usually arise when different experts are hired by each side (Keilin & Bloom, 1986).

Although the methods used in custody evaluations vary a great deal depending on the specific issues in each case, the American Psychological Association and the Association of Family and Conciliation Courts have published guidelines for conducting custody evaluations. Most evaluations include clinical and social histories, standardized testing of the parents and the children, observation of parent–child interactions, interviews with individuals who have had opportunities to observe family members, and a review of documents that might be relevant to the case, including medical records of children and parents.

A national survey of mental health professionals who conduct child custody evaluations found that these experts devoted an average of 30 hours to each custody evaluation (Ackerman & Ackerman, 1997). A substantial amount of this time is spent interviewing and observing the parties in various combinations. More than two-thirds of the respondents indicated that they conducted individual interviews with each parent and each child, observed each parent interacting (separately) with each child, and conducted formal psychological testing of the parents and the children. The MMPI was the test most often used with parents; intelligence tests and projective personality tests were the most common instruments used with the children (see Chapter 5). An increasing number of clinicians report using one or two instruments specifically designed for child custody evaluations: the Bricklin Perceptual Scales and the Ackerman–Schoendorf Scales for Parent Evaluation of Custody (ASPECT) (Nicholson, 1999).

The most common recommendation made by these experts was limited joint custody, in which parents share the decision making, but one parent maintains primary physical custody. Single-parent custody without visitation was the least recommended alternative. Do children adapt and function better when raised in joint custody or sole custody arrangements? One might expect it could go either way, because while joint custody allows the child to maintain close ties to both parents, sole custody simplifies custodial arrangements and minimizes children's confusion over where their home is. Indeed, most studies report either no major differences between children in the two types of custody or only somewhat better adjustment by joint-custody children (Pruett & Barker, 2013). However, consistent with the results of earlier research (Emery, 1982; Hetherington & Arasteh, 1988), Crosbie-Burnett (1991) found that continuing hostility and conflicts between the parents, regardless of the type of custody in force, was associated with poorer adjustment on the part of the children. It appears that the quality of the relationship between divorced parents is more important to the adjustment of their children than whether the children are raised in sole-custody or joint-custody arrangements (Pruett & Barker, 2013).

Many mental health professionals believe evaluations regarding child custody and parental fitness are among the most ethically challenging and clinically difficult of all forensic cases. For one thing, the emotional stakes are extremely high, and both parents are often willing to spare no expense or tactic in the battle over who will win custody. Associated with this conflict is the fact that the children are usually forced to live, for months if not years, in an emotional limbo in which they do not know with whom they will eventually live, where they will be going to school, or how often they will see each parent. Second, to conduct a thorough family assessment, the clinician must evaluate the children, both parents, and, when possible, other people who have observed the family's interaction. Often, not all parties agree to such evaluations or do so only under duress, a fact that often creates a lengthy and unfriendly assessment process. Third, to render an expert opinion, the clinician must possess a great deal of knowledge not only about the particular children and parents being evaluated but also about infant–parent attachment, child development, family systems, the effects of divorce on children, adult and childhood mental disorders, and several different kinds of testing (see Chapter 11, "Clinical Child Psychology").

Complicating the situation, too, are changes in traditional definitions of a "family." Increasing tolerance of variability in lifestyles has forced clinical psychologists and legal scholars to confront questions about whether parents' sexual orientation or ethnicity should have any bearing on custody and adoption decisions. For instance, the highest court in New Jersey has given gay men and lesbians the right to adopt children. This is not the case, however, in some other states.

Finally, child custody evaluations are usually highly adversarial processes in which one side challenges the procedures or opinions of any expert with whom it disagrees. Clinicians who conduct custody evaluations must therefore brace themselves for all sorts of attacks on their clinical methods, scholarly competence, personal character, and professional ethics. To guard against these, and to insure that evaluations are done competently and professionally, clinicians follow the APA Guidelines for Child Custody Evaluations in Divorce Proceedings (APA, 2010) (see Table 14.2).

Custody Mediation

Because divorce is such a potent stressor for children and because protracted custody battles tend to leave a trail of emotionally battered family members in their wake, clinicians are devoting increasing attention to helping parents and children cope with these transitions or to finding alternatives to custody battles (Nurse & Thompson, 2013).

Custody mediation services are now often being used in lieu of adversarial court procedures. The job of the mediator is to try to help the parties agree on a resolution of their differences by providing a safe environment for communication and by helping them to explore various options (Emery, 2012). Psychologists can facilitate mediation by helping the parties to emotionally accept the divorce, resolve disputes, and establish a stable coparenting relationship (Nurse & Thompson, 2013). Indeed, a new role is evolving for psychologists in custody disputes. Some psychologists focus on the task of teaching divorced or separated parents how to coparent their

---

TABLE 14.2 Guidelines for Child Custody Evaluations in Family Law Proceedings

  I. Orienting Guidelines: Purpose of a Child Custody Evaluation

    1. The primary purpose of the evaluation is to assess the psychological best interests of the child.

    2. The child's welfare is paramount.

    3. The evaluation focuses on parenting attributes, the child's psychological needs, and the resulting fit.

 II. General Guidelines: Preparing for a Child Custody Evaluation

    1. Psychologists strive to gain and maintain specialized competence.

    2. Psychologists strive to function as impartial evaluators.

    3. Psychologists strive to engage in culturally informed, nondiscriminatory evaluation practices.

    4. Psychologists strive to avoid conflicts of interest and multiple relationships in conducting evaluations.

III. Procedural Guidelines: Conducting the Child Custody Evaluation

    1. Psychologists strive to establish the scope of the evaluation in a timely fashion, consistent with the nature of the referral question.

    2. Psychologists strive to obtain appropriately informed consent.

    3. Psychologists strive to employ multiple methods of data gathering.

    4. Psychologists strive to interpret assessment data in a manner consistent with the context of the evaluation.

    5. Psychologists strive to complement the evaluation with the appropriate combination of examinations.

    6. Psychologists strive to base their recommendations, if any, upon the psychological best interests of the child.

    7. Psychologists create and maintain professional records in accordance with ethical and legal obligations.

children. Known as *parenting coordinators*, these clinicians help clients address parenting issues by focusing on the developmental and emotional needs of the children and to resolve among themselves issues that otherwise would have to be decided by a judge in an adversarial setting (Bailey, 2005).

To assess the impact of mediated versus adversarial child custody procedures, Robert Emery and his colleagues conducted a study in which divorcing couples agreed to be randomly assigned to settle their custody disputes either through mediation or litigation. Emery (2012) found that although mediation took only an average of six hours, it was associated with surprisingly positive results even at 12-year follow-up. For example, in comparison to families who litigated their custody disputes, those who had been assigned to mediation showed less interparental conflict, more involvement with children by the nonresidential parent, and better parenting skills by the nonresidential parent. Given the fact that lower levels of interparental conflict and higher levels of involvement with well-functioning nonresidential parents are generally associated with positive outcomes for children, it is not surprising to find that youngsters in the mediation group did better at long-term follow-up than those in the litigation group (Emery, 2012). Note, however, that mediation may be counterproductive or harmful when domestic violence or substance abuse has led to one partner having more power in the relationship (Emery, 2012).

Termination of Parental Rights

In rare cases, courts may terminate parents' rights to have any contact with a child if the court finds that such contact will be detrimental to the child's mental or physical welfare. Upon such a finding, the child is placed in the custody of the local department of child welfare, which will try to find a permanent home for the child, either permanent foster care or an adoptive home. In most termination of parental rights cases, the agency asking for the termination will provide the court with an evaluation conducted by a clinical psychologist. Clinicians' evaluations address the state's legal requirements (found in statutes and case decisions) for termination. Though the definition of parental unfitness may vary among states (Azar & Benjet, 1994), generally, as in Virginia, a parent must (a) have abandoned the child for more than 6 months, (b) have been convicted of a murder or extreme physical harm to another child, (c) be physically or mentally unfit to care for the child in spite of all efforts of child welfare authorities to keep the child with the parent, or (d) have not remedied the situation that caused the child to first come in contact with child welfare workers (these latter cases typically involve physical or sexual child abuse, gross neglect of the child's physical or medical well-being, and parental drug or alcohol addiction). Parents whose rights are being terminated may introduce their own psychological reports. Since there are usually no juries in parental termination cases, presiding judges give whatever weight they wish to clinicians' reports. In most states, proof of parental unfitness must be "clear and convincing," which is a lower standard than the "beyond a reasonable doubt" that exists in criminal cases, but higher than the civil standard of "a preponderance of the evidence."

As mentioned, evaluations and testimony related to child custody and parental fitness can be complex and contentions. As a result, clinicians involved in them may face a number of practical and ethical dilemmas. How can clinicians be assured that their practices remain professional and in the best interests of the public and the law? One of the key ways is to be familiar with professional guidelines covering clinical practice, including the APA's recently published *Guidelines for Psychological Evaluations in Child Protection Matters* (American Psychological Association, 2013).

SECTION SUMMARY

In child custody evaluations, clinicians provide the courts with evidence about the fitness of parents and about post-separation and divorce arrangements that will most benefit the children involved. Clinicians are also sometimes involved in conducting or arranging custody mediation, a procedure designed to reduce the number of divorce cases that end up in court. Clinicians' involvement in these legal actions is very common, but they can produce a number of practical and ethical dilemmas. Experienced clinicians rely on ethical codes, accepted practices, and professional guidelines to avoid pitfalls.

MENTAL HEALTH EXPERTS IN THE LEGAL SYSTEM

SECTION PREVIEW

Most of the forensic assessment practices we have described require clinicians to testify in court as expert witnesses on a wide range of issues. In doing so, they benefit from knowing how the legal system works and from using empirically validated practices.

Testifying as an expert witness is one of the most visible of clinical psychologists' forensic activities. Clinical psychologists (and psychiatrists) have testified in some of the most notorious criminal proceedings in recent U.S. history, including those of Casey Anthony, O. J. Simpson, Jeffrey Dahmer, John Hinckley, Theodore Kaczynski, and Timothy McVeigh. By legal definition, an expert witness is someone with scientific, technical, or other specialized knowledge acquired by means of experience, training, or education who may testify in the form of an opinion or otherwise if certain requirements are met:

1. An expert testifies at the discretion of the judge when the judge believes that the expert's scientific, technical, or other specialized knowledge will help the trier of fact to understand the evidence or to determine a fact in issue.
2. The expert testimony must be based on sufficient facts or data.
3. The expert's testimony must be based on reliable and accepted principles and methods within the expert's field.
4. The principles and methods used or referred to by the expert must be applicable to the facts or data in the case.

These standards are codified in Federal Rule of Evidence 702, Testimony by Expert Witnesses, which reflects litigation in the 1990s concerning the reliability of scientific expert testimony (*Daubert v. Merrell Dow Pharmaceuticals,*[4] 1993; *General Electric v. Joiner,*[5] 1997; and *Kumho v. Carmichael,*[6] 1999). Although the Federal Rule applies only to trials in federal court, the majority of states also apply its standards. Other states have differing requirements for the admissibility of expert testimony, but require, at the least, that the testimony be based on established and accepted scientific evidence (*Frye v. United States,*[7] 1923; Shuman & Sales, 1999). Table 14.3 describes many situations in which forensic clinical psychologists might testify.

Testimony of experts is limited by law to descriptions of parties' symptoms, behavior, and demeanor; explanation of the evaluation and assessment instruments used; and opinions about the party's mental status, including a diagnosis of mental disorder. Experts are *not* allowed to give an opinion as to whether or not a defendant is competent to stand trial or was sane at the time of an offense, whether a party was competent to make a will, which of two parents would make a better custodian of children, or any other opinion that goes to the ultimate issue before the court. As mentioned earlier, offering "ultimate opinion testimony" would be drawing a legal conclusion that usurps the prerogative of the judge and jury to apply the law to the facts and opinions given by the expert (Cassel & Bernstein, 2007).

Psychological and psychiatric expert testimony has, along with all other types of scientific expert evidence, grown rapidly in recent years. It is estimated that psychologists and psychiatrists testify in approximately 8% of all trials held in federal civil courts, and mental health witnesses participate in as many as a million cases each year (Shuman & Sales, 1999).

Expert testimony is frequent because, as shown in Table 14.3, there are many topics for psychologists to testify about. As scientists learn more about human behavior, attorneys are likely to find their research results helpful in court cases. The press usually focuses on testimony concerning criminal competence and responsibility, but testimony about these topics is actually relatively rare compared to those involving child custody, workers' compensation, tort, and discrimination cases.

---

[4]509 U.S. 579 (1993)

[5]522 U.S. 136 (1997)

[6]526 U.S. 137 (1999)

[7]293 F. 1013 (D.C. CIR. 1923)

TABLE 14.3 Topics for Expert Psychological Testimony

Expert witnesses from psychology testify about topics in criminal trials, civil litigation, and domestic disputes. If fact, expert testimony is given on these topics much more than on claims of insanity. Here are 14 of the more common subjects of expert psychological testimony.

Topic of Testimony	Main Question Addressed in Testimony
1. Insanity	What is the relationship between the defendant's mental condition at the time of the alleged offense and the defendant's responsibility for the crime?
2. Criminal competency	Does the defendant have an adequate understanding of the legal proceeding in which he or she is involved?
3. Sentencing	What are the prospects for the defendant's rehabilitation? What deterrent effects do certain sentences have?
4. Eyewitness identification	What factors affect the accuracy of eyewitness identification?
5. Civil commitment	Does a mentally ill person present a danger, or threat of danger, such that hospitalization is necessary?
6. Psychological damages in civil cases	What psychological consequences has an individual suffered as a result of wrongful conduct? To what extent are the psychological problems attributable to a preexisting condition?
7. Negligence and product liability	How do environmental factors and human perceptual abilities affect an individual's use of a product?
8. Trademark litigation	Is a certain product name or trademark confusingly similar to that of a competitor?
9. Discrimination	What psychological evidence is there that equal treatment is being denied or that certain procedures and decisions discriminate against women and minorities in the schools or in the workplace?
10. Guardianship and conservatorship	Does an individual possess the necessary mental ability to make decisions concerning his or her health and general welfare?
11. Child custody	What psychological factors will affect the best interests of the child whose custody is in dispute?
12. Adoption and termination of parental rights	What psychological factors affect the best interests of a child whose parents' disabilities may render them unfit to raise and care for the child?
13. Professional malpractice	Did a mental health professional's conduct fail to meet the standard of care owed to the client?
14. Mitigating psychosocial factors in litigation	What are the effects of pornography, violence, spouse abuse, and the like on the behavior of litigants who claim that their conduct was affected by one of these influences?

Yet psychological expert testimony has often been criticized as lacking in reliability, validity, propriety, and usefulness. Former federal appellate judge David T. Bazelon, a supporter of legal rights for the mentally ill (1974), once complained that "in no case is it more difficult to elicit productive and reliable testimony than in cases that call on the knowledge and practice of psychiatry." This view was echoed by Warren Burger (1975), a former Chief Justice of the Supreme Court who chided experts for the "uncertainties of psychiatric diagnosis." Sharply worded critiques of psychologists' expert testimony can be found in several other sources (Bonnie & Slobogin, 1980; Ennis & Litwack, 1974; Morse, 1978), and there are well-known guidebooks devoted entirely to the subject of how to cross-examine the expert testimony of psychologists (e.g., Campbell & Lorandos, 2012; Faust, 2011). Such criticism has led to calls for the development of clearer standards of practice in forensic mental health (HeilbrunDeMatteo, Marczyk, & Goldstein, 2008), a call that has been recently answered (American Psychological Association, 2013b).

Tightening the evidentiary standards, as Federal Rule 702 and case decisions have done, forces psychological experts to address some of the concerns lawyers, judges, and appellate courts have had in the past (Smith, 1989), such as the fact that some of their opinions were not based entirely on valid research. Nevertheless, judges and juries still have to contend with the problems that arise when experts do a poor job of testifying and when attorneys who are not knowledgeable enough about psychology as a science fail to properly examine and cross-examine experts. These problems deprive judges and juries of the benefits of a well-presented and effectively challenged opinion; fact-finders cannot be enlightened by testimony they do not understand. Indeed, experts on expert testimony recommend that expert witnesses should take the role of teachers and try to present complex concepts in simple terms, using charts, videos, photographs, and models to help jurors visualize and comprehend the material (Sleek, 1998).

Another problem with psychological expert testimony is that juries are confused and frustrated when opposing sides present experts who directly contradict each other. Faced with this "battle of the experts," jurors tend to ignore them all and base their decision on nonexpert testimony (e.g., Brekke, Enko, Clavet, & Seelau, 1991). Several suggestions have been made that might reduce the overly adversarial nature of all kinds of scientific and technical expert testimony, including that of clinical psychologists. These include (a) limiting the number of experts each side may introduce to testify about a given topic, (b) requiring that the experts be chosen from an approved panel of individuals reputed to be objective and highly competent, and (c) allowing testimony only from experts who have been appointed by a judge, not those hired by opposing attorneys. Published guidelines also help courts determine whether the testimony of experts is based on accepted professional practices (e.g., American Psychological Association, 2013b).

A number of scientific and professional organizations have come forward with proposals to aid the courts in finding skilled experts, an initiative supported by U.S. Supreme Court Justice Stephen Breyer (2000). The National Conference of Lawyers and Scientists, a joint committee of the American Association for the Advancement of Science and the Science and Technology Section of the American Bar Association, has developed a pilot project to test the feasibility of increased use of court-appointed experts in cases that involve technical issues. The project recruited a slate of candidates from scientific and professional organizations to serve as court-appointed experts in cases in which the judge decides that adversarial experts are unlikely to provide the information that is necessary for a well-reasoned resolution of the disputed issues. To further promote the appropriate use of scientific evidence in the courtroom, the National Research Council has compiled a Reference Manual for Scientific Evidence (National Academies of Science, 2011), now in its third edition.

SECTION SUMMARY

Forensic psychologists have testified in a number of high-profile cases. Because the testimony of experts sometimes conflicts, many jurors are skeptical about psychological evidence. The credibility of expert psychological witnesses increases when clinicians follow well-established protocols and provide evidence in clear language.

Chapter Summary

Clinical psychologists are involved in forensic psychology, a specialty that applies mental health knowledge and expertise to questions about individuals involved in legal proceedings. The nature of forensic assessment depends on the questions being asked, but, like most clinical assessments, it often includes a social history, a clinical interview, psychological testing, a review of life records, and perhaps interviews with a variety of third parties.

Evaluating competence to stand trial requires assessment of whether defendants can understand the nature of their trial, participate in their defense, and consult with their attorneys. Most defendants referred for such evaluations are ultimately found competent. Defendants who plead not guilty by reason of insanity (NGRI) must present evidence that they lacked the state of mind necessary to be held responsible for a crime. Psychologists and other mental health experts evaluate these defendants to determine if they meet the legal definition of insanity. This definition has changed over time and can vary from one state to another, but the essence of the laws is that a defendant must be unable, because of a mental disease or defect, to understand the nature of a criminal act or to know that the act was wrong. A variety of reforms—including abolition of the insanity defense,

further changes in the definition of insanity, and the advent of the guilty but mentally ill verdict—have been enacted in order to address criticisms of the insanity defense.

Mental health professionals are called upon to assess the dangerousness of criminal defendants, a task that requires them to look into the future and predict which persons will reoffend.

Psychologists often testify in tort lawsuits, where plaintiffs seek compensatory and punitive damages for wrongful acts they claim caused them psychological harm. The psychologists' testimony concerns the nature, extent, and impact of that harm. Psychologists also conduct assessments designed to determine questions about civil competency, such as whether a person is mentally capable of making decisions about financial affairs, medical or psychiatric treatment, or disposition of assets in a will.

Clinicians involved in conducting psychological autopsies seek to determine the cause of a suspicious death, usually at the behest of courts and insurance companies, and often to rule out suicide. Psychologists with expertise in law enforcement may also be involved in criminal profiling, a practice that seeks to help find the perpetrator of especially heinous or serial crimes.

Psychologists may conduct evaluations in workmen's compensation and other employment-related cases. They are also involved in the assessment of returning war veterans' post-traumatic stress disorder (PTSD) and cognitive impairments that can affect these veterans' ability to return to duty and/or to receive benefits and treatment.

Clinical psychologists who assess families in crisis continue to be in high demand. These psychologists offer opinions about the fitness of divorcing parents to retain custody of their children and whether joint custody, sole custody, or some other arrangement would be best for the children. Many clinicians are also involved in efforts to mediate, rather than litigate, custody battles. Some act as parenting coordinators who help divorced or separated parents agree on parenting issues.

While expert testimony by psychologists is common, critics doubt the reliability, validity, propriety, and usefulness of such testimony. The reputation of psychological expert testimony may be enhanced by a variety of reforms, including setting standards for practice, enactment of procedural rules that govern the type and limits of expert testimony, and creation of registries of experts who will serve the court itself, not individual parties.

Study Questions

1. In what ways do clinical psychologists become involved in legal proceedings?
2. What is criminal competency?
3. How do forensic psychologists assess criminal competency?
4. What is the insanity defense, and how often is it used?
5. How do forensic psychologists contribute to the determination of insanity?
6. What variations of the insanity defense have different states used?
7. What is a tort action?
8. In what ways do clinical psychologists become involved in assessing damages in tort actions?
9. What are psychological autopsies and criminal profiles; how do they differ?
10. How are clinical psychologists usually involved in child custody disputes?
11. What difficulties might clinicians face in conducting child custody and parental fitness assessments?
12. What APA guidelines help clinicians conduct ethically complex evaluations such as those involved in child custody and divorce proceedings?
13. What are some of the roles clinical psychologists assume when providing expert testimony?

Web Sites

- APA's American Psychology Law Society (Division 41): http://www.apa.org/about/division/div41.aspx
- A description of the FBI's Behavioral Analysis Unit: http://www.fbi.gov/about-us/cirg/investigations-and-operations-support/investigations-operations-support
- APA Guidelines for Child Custody Evaluations in Divorce Proceedings: http://www.apa.org/practice/guidelines/index.aspx

MOVIES

American History X (1998). Many forensic issues are dealt with in this compelling drama about a former White supremacist gang leader and his younger brother.

The Girl with the Dragon Tattoo (2011). Multiple examples of Antisocial Personality Disorder and criminality, as well as examples of trauma and triumph, are depicted in this intense film.

MEMOIRS

Makes Me Wanna Holler: A Young Black Man in America by Nathan McCall (1994; New York: Vintage). Powerful memoir of illegal activities during adolescence, prison in young adulthood, and eventual success as a journalist.

Mind Hunter: Inside the FBI's Elite Serial Crime Unit by John Douglas (1995; New York: Pocket Books). This former FBI special agent illustrates many fascinating forensic cases.

References

Ackerman, M. J., & Ackerman, M. (1997). Custody evaluation practices: A survey of experienced professionals (revisited). *Professional Psychology: Research and Practice, 28,* 137–145.

American Psychiatric Association. (1994). *Diagnostic and statistical manual of mental disorders* (4th ed.). Washington, DC: Author.

American Psychological Association. (2010). Guidelines for child custody evaluations in family law proceedings. *American Psychologist, 65,* 863–867.

American Psychological Association. (2013a). Guidelines for Psychological Evaluations in Child Protection Matters. *American Psychologist, 68,* 20–31.

American Psychological Association. (2013b). Specialty Guidelines for Forensic Psychology. *American Psychologist, 68,* 7–19.

Appelbaum, P. S., & Grisso, T. (1995). The MacArthur Treatment Competence Study. I: Mental illness and competence to consent to treatment. *Law and Human Behavior, 19,* 105–126.

Azar, S. T., & Benjet, C. L. (1994). A cognitive perspective on ethnicity, race, and termination of parental rights. *Law and Human Behavior, 18,* 249–267.

Bailey, D. S. (2005, January). A niche that puts children first. *American Psychological Association Monitor* (p. 42). Retrieved 15 March 2007, from http://www.apa.org/monitor/jan05/niche.html.

Bartol, C. (1996). Police psychology: Then, now, and beyond. *Criminal Justice and Behavior, 23*, 70–89.

Bartol, C. R., & Bartol, A. M. (2008). *Criminal behavior: A psychosocial approach* (8th ed.). Upper Saddle River, NJ: Pearson Education, Inc.

Bazelon, D. (1974). Psychiatrists and the adversary process. *Scientific American, 230*, 18–23.

Bonnie, R., & Slobogin, C. (1980). The role of mental health professionals in the criminal process: The case for informed speculation. *Virginia Law Review, 66*, 427–522.

Bonnie, R. J., Jeffries, J. C., Jr., & Low, P. W. (2000). *A case study in the insanity defense: The trial of John W. Hinckley, Jr.* (2nd ed.). New York, NY: Foundation Press.

Botello, T., Noguchi, T., Lakshmanan, S., Weinberger, L. E., & Gross, B. H. (2013). Evolution of the psychological autopsy: Fifty years of experience at the Los Angeles County Chief Medical Examiner-Coroner's Office. *Journal of Forensic Sciences*, Article first published online, doi: 10.1111/1556-4029.12138.

Brekke, N. J., Enko, P. J., Clavet, G., & Seelau, E. (1991). Of juries and court-appointed experts: The impact of nonadversarial expert testimony. *Law and Human Behavior, 15*, 451–477.

Brewer, N., & Williams, K. D. (2007). *Psychology and law: An empirical perspective*. New York, NY: The Guilford Press.

Breyer, S. (2000, Summer). Science in the courtroom. *Issues in Science and Technology*. Retrieved 21 April 2013, from http://www.nap.edu/issues/16.4/breyer.htm.

Brussel, J. A. (1968). *Casebook of a crime psychiatrist*. New York, NY: Bernard Geis Associates.

Burger, W. E. (1975). Dissenting opinion in O'Connor v. Donaldson. *U.S. Law Week, 42*, 4929–4936.

Campbell, T., & Lorandos, D. (2012). *Cross examining experts in the behavioral sciences*. New York, NY: West Thompson Reuters.

Cantor, N. L. (1998). Making advance directives meaningful. *Psychology, Public Policy, and Law, 4*, 629–652.

Cassel, E. (2000). Behavioral science research leads to Department of Justice Guidelines for eyewitness evidence. *Virginia Lawyer, 48*, 35–38.

Cassel, E., & Bernstein, D. A. (2007). *Criminal behavior* (2nd ed.) Mahwah, NJ: Erlbaum.

Clingempeel, W. G., & Reppucci, N. D. (1982). Joint custody after divorce: Major issues and goals for research. *Psychological Bulletin, 91*, 102–127.

Crosbie-Burnett, M. (1991). Impact of joint versus sole custody and quality of co-parental relationship on adjustment of adolescents in remarried families. *Behavioral Sciences and the Law, 9*, 439–449.

Dattilio, F. M. (2006). Equivocal death psychological autopsies in cases of criminal homicide. *American Journal of Forensic Psychology, 24*, 5–22.

Detrick, P., & Chibnall, J. T. (2013). Revised NEO Personality Inventory normative data for police officer selection. *Psychological Services, Feb, 2013*, No pagination specified.

Ebert, B. W. (1987). Guide to conducting a psychological autopsy. *Professional Psychology: Research and Practice, 18*, 52–56.

Emery, R. E. (1982). Interparental conflict and the children of discord and divorce. *Psychological Bulletin, 92*, 310–330.

Emery, R. E. (2012). *Renegotiating family relationships: Divorce, child custody, and mediation* (2nd ed.). New York, NY: Guilford Press.

Ennis, B. J., & Litwack, T. R. (1974). Psychiatry and the presumption of expertise: Flipping coins in the courtroom. *California Law Review, 62*, 693–752.

Fabricius, W. F., Braver, S. L., Diaz, P., & Velez, C. E. (2010). Custody and parenting time: Links to family relationships and well-being after divorce. In M. E. Lamb (Ed.), *The role of the father in child development* (5th ed., pp. 201–240). Hoboken, NJ: Wiley.

Faust, D. (2011). *Coping with psychiatric and psychological testimony*, (6th ed.). New York, NY: Oxford University Press.

Fulero, S. M., & Wrightsman, L. S. (2008). *Forensic psychology*. Belmont, CA: Wadsworth.

Grisso, T., & Appelbaum, P. S. (1995). The MacArthur Treatment Competence Study. III: Abilities of patients to consent to psychiatric and medical treatments. *Law and Human Behavior, 19*, 149–174.

Grisso, T., Steinberg, L., Wollard, J., Cauffman, E., Scott, E., et al. (2003). Juveniles' competence to stand trial: A comparison of adolescents' and adults' capacities as trial defendants. *Law and Human Behavior 27*, 333–363.

Heilbrun, K., & Collins, S. (1995). Evaluations of trial competency and mental state at time of offense: Report characteristics. *Professional Psychology: Research & Practice, 26*, 61–67.

Heilbrun, K., DeMatteo, D., Marczyk, G., & Goldstein, A. (2008). Standards of practice and care in forensic mental health assessment. *Psychology, Public Policy, and Law, 14*, 1–26.

Hersch, P. D., & Alexander, R. W. (1990). MMPI profile patterns of emotional disability claimants. *Journal of Clinical Psychology, 46*, 795–799.

Hetherington, E. M., & Arasteh, J. D. (Eds.). (1988). *Impact of divorce, single parenting, and stepparenting on children*. Hillsdale, NJ: Erlbaum.

Homant, R., & Kennedy, D. B. (1998). Psychological aspects of crime scene profiling. *Criminal Justice and Behavior, 25*, 319–343.

Kapardis, A. (2010). *Psychology and law: A critical introduction*. Boston, MA: Cambridge University Press.

Keilin, W. G., & Bloom, L. J. (1986). Child custody evaluation practices: A survey of experienced professionals. *Professional Psychology: Research and Practice, 17*, 338–346.

Loftus, E. F. (2003). Make-believe memories. *American Psychologist, 58*, 867–873.

Macklin, D. S., Smith, L. A., & Dollard, M. F. (2006). Public and private sector stress: Workers compensation, levels of distress and job satisfaction, and the demand-control-support model. *Australian Journal of Psychology, 58*, 130–143.

Marcus, D. R., Lyons, P. M., & Guyton, M. R. (2000). Studying perceptions of juror influence in vivo: A social relations analysis. *Law and Human Behavior, 24*, 173–186.

Monahan, J., & Walker, L. (2006). *Social science in law* (6th ed.). Minneapolis, MN: Foundation Press.

Morse, S. J. (1978). Law and mental health professionals: The limits of expertise. *Professional Psychology, 9*, 389–399.

National Academies of Science. (2011). *Reference manual for scientific evidence* (3rd ed.). Washington, DC: National Academies Press.

National Institute of Justice. (1999). *Eyewitness evidence: A guide for law enforcement*. Washington, DC: U.S. Department of Justice.

Nicholson, R. A. (1999). Forensic assessment. In R. Roesch, S. D. Hart, & J. R. Ogloff (Eds.), *Psychology and law: The state of the discipline* (pp. 122–173). New York, NY: Kluwer Academic/Plenum.

Nurse, A. R., & Thompson, P. (2013). Collaborative divorce: A family-centered process. In J. H. Bray & M. Stanton (Eds.), *The Wiley-Blackwell handbook of family psychology* (pp. 475–486). Hoboken, NJ: Wiley-Blackwell.

Ogloff, J. R. P., & Otto, R. (1993). Psychological autopsy: Clinical and legal perspectives. *Saint Louis University Law Journal, 37*, 607–646.

Otto, R. K. (Ed.). (2013). *Handbook of psychology: Forensic Psychology* (Vol. 11). Hoboken, NJ: Wiley.

Post, C. G. (1963). *An introduction to the law*. Englewood Cliffs, NJ: Prentice Hall.

Poythress, N., Monahan, J., Bonnie, R., Otto, R. K., & Hoge, S. K. (2002). *Adjudicative competence: The MacArthur Studies*. New York, NY: Kluwer/Plenum.

Pruett, M. K., & Barker, R. (2013). Children of divorce: New trends and ongoing dilemmas. In J. H. Bray & M. Stanton (Eds.), *The Wiley-Blackwell handbook of family psychology* (pp. 463–474). Hoboken, NJ: Wiley-Blackwell.

Rich, B. A. (1998). Personhood, patienthood, and clinical practice: Reassessing advance directives. *Psychology, Public Policy, and Law, 4*, 610–628.

Roberts, C. F., Sargent, E. L., & Chan, A. S. (1993). Verdict selection processes in insanity cases: Juror construals and the effects of guilty but mental ill instructions. *Law and Human Behavior, 17*, 261–275.

Roesch, R., Zapf, P., & Hart, S. (2010). *Forensic psychology and law.* Hoboken, NJ: John Wiley & Sons.

Rogers, R. (2012). *Clinical assessment of malingering and deception* (3rd ed.). New York, NY: Guilford Press.

Rohde, D. (1999, November 7). Juror and courts assailed in subway-killing mistrial. *New York Times*, 32.

Rosen, J. (2007, March 11). The brain on the stand. *New York Times Magazine.* Retrieved 11 March 2007, at http://www.nytimes.com/2007/03/11/magazine/11Neurolaw.t.html?ref=magazine.

Sales, B. D., & Shuman, D. W. (1996). *Law, mental health, and mental disorder.* Pacific Grove, CA: Brooks/Cole.

Schwartz, B. K. (Ed.). (2003). *Correctional psychology: Practice, programming, and administration.* Kingston, NJ: Civil Research Institute.

Shipley, S. L., & Arrigo, B. A. (2012). *Introduction to forensic psychology: Court, law, enforcement, and correctional practices* (3rd ed.). New York, NY: Academic Press.

Shuman, D. W., & Sales, B. D. (1999). The impact of *Daubert* and its progeny on the admissibility of behavioral and social science evidence. *Psychology, Public Policy, and Law, 5*, 3–15.

Simpson, J. R. (2013). Neuroimaging in forensic psychiatry: From the clinic to the courtroom. New York, NY: Oxford University Press.

Sleek, S. (1998, February). Jury tuned out the science in the Nichols trial. *APA Monitor*, 2.

Slobogin, C. (1985). The guilty but mentally ill verdict: An idea whose time should not have come. *George Washington Law Review, 53*, 494–527.

Smith, S. (1989). Mental health expert witnesses: Of science and crystal balls. *Behavioral Sciences and the Law, 7*, 145–180.

Steadman, H. J. (1993). *Reforming the insanity defense: An evaluation of pre- and post-Hinckley reforms.* New York, NY: Guilford.

Tanielian, T., & Jaycox, L. (Eds.). (2008). *Invisible wounds of war: Psychological and cognitive injuries, their consequences, and services to assist recovery.* Santa Monica, CA: Rand Corporation.

Tucker, N. (2001, December 11). High court passes on Capitol suspect. *The Washington Post*, B1.

Van Voorhis, P., & Salisbury, E. (2013). *Correctional counseling and rehabilitation* (8th ed.). New York, NY: Anderson.

Weissman, H. N. (1991). Child custody evaluations: Fair and unfair professional practices. *Behavioral Sciences and the Law, 9*, 469–476.

Wilber, D. Q. (2012, Feb 9). Closing arguments delivered in John Hinckley hearing. *The Washington Post.* Available online at http://www.washingtonpost.com/local/crime/closing-arguments-delivered-in-john-hinckley-hearing/2012/02/09/gIQAr4ZS2Q_story.html.

Wrightsman, L. S., & Fulero, S. M. (2005). *Forensic psychology* (2nd ed.). Belmont, CA: Thomson-Wadsworth.

Wrightsman, L. S., Nietzel, M., Fortune, W., & Greene, E. (2002). *Psychology and the legal system* (5th ed.). Pacific Grove, CA: Brooks/Cole.

15 PROFESSIONAL ISSUES IN CLINICAL PSYCHOLOGY

Chapter Preview

This chapter describes professional issues within clinical psychology, including models for professional training, professional regulation, ethics, professional independence, and multicultural competence. Based on historical and current forces in the field, we also make predictions of where the field of clinical psychology is heading in the future.

As should be obvious from reading the previous chapters, clinical psychologists take professional integrity very seriously. The field has changed significantly over the past 130 years, but the themes of helping people and furthering scientific understanding have remained intact for clinical psychologists worldwide.

The relatively recent changes in the field, including the increasing need for mental health services, the proliferation of managed care systems, the possibility of prescription privileges for psychologists in more states, the focus on multiculturalism and diversity, and the intense focus and debate about evidence-based practice, all suggest that the field of clinical psychology has entered a new era. The discipline of clinical psychology looks very different than it did just 20 years ago, and it is expected to look different again in another 20 years.

The story of the professionalization and current status of clinical psychology is the primary topic of this chapter. It is a story with many subplots because it includes several overlapping developments that have reshaped the identity of the field. We focus on five main issues that have been crucial to the struggle for professional recognition in clinical psychology:

1. *Professional training.* What training does one need to become a clinical psychologist, and what are the options for obtaining it?
2. *Professional regulation.* What are the mechanisms for ensuring that a clinical psychologist possesses requisite skills and meets at least the minimum requirements to function professionally?
3. *Professional ethics.* What principles guide clinicians in determining the ethical standards for their profession? How is unethical behavior handled?
4. *Professional independence.* What is the relationship between clinical psychology and other mental health professions?
5. *Professional multicultural competence.* How has the field changed with regard to diversity and the need for multicultural competence?

Training in clinical psychology involves learning in many venues, including the classroom, mental health clinic, research lab, and community.   *Source*: Auremar/ Shutterstock.

PROFESSIONAL TRAINING

SECTION PREVIEW

In this section, we discuss the historical and current forces that have affected professional training in clinical psychology. These include a number of national conferences on training, the development of the doctor of psychology (PsyD) degree, and the establishment of various training models. The current internship crisis is also discussed.

You may recall from Chapter 2, "Clinical Psychology's Past and Present," that the first four decades of the twentieth century saw little progress in the creation of advanced training for clinical psychologists. For clinicians of that period, experience was not only the best teacher, it was practically the only one. However, during the late 1940s, mental health and social needs brought about by World War II and the financial support provided by the Veterans Administration and the U.S. Public Health Service combined to offer clinical psychology a unique opportunity to establish its identity, expand its functions, and elevate its status. It was then that training became a central concern.

Dr. David Shakow was the most influential psychologist in the development of clinical training programs. Shakow chaired a Committee on Training in Clinical Psychology that was charged with formulating a recommended clinical training program. The committee prepared a report entitled "Recommended Graduate Training in Clinical Psychology," which was accepted by the American Psychological Association in September 1947 and published that same year in the APA's main journal, the *American Psychologist* (Hilgard, Kelly, & Luckey, 1947). The Shakow report set the pattern for clinical training and remains, with surprisingly few exceptions, a standard against which modern clinical programs can be evaluated. There were a great many recommendations in the Shakow report, but the three most important were that

1. A clinical psychologist should be trained first and foremost as a psychologist.
2. Clinical training should be as rigorous as that for nonclinical areas of psychology.
3. Preparation of the clinical psychologist should be broad and directed toward assessment, research, and therapy.

The Shakow report suggested a year-by-year curriculum to achieve these goals within four years. Many of today's clinical training programs are informed by Shakow's prototype, but it now usually takes about 6, rather than 4, years to complete the entire training sequence for a PhD in clinical psychology (Norcross & Sayette, 2012), and the internship is now usually taken in the fifth or sixth year. The major reasons for the extra years are that most programs require a master's thesis (usually in the second year), some universities still retain requirements such as courses in a foreign language or full proficiency in statistics and research methods, and many clinical programs have added required courses in specialty areas such as human diversity, substance abuse, health psychology, clinical child psychology, sexual problems, and neuropsychological disorders.

The greatest impact of the Shakow report was that it prescribed that special mix of scientific and professional preparation that has typified most clinical training programs ever since. This recipe for training—described as the *scientist–professional model*—was officially endorsed at the first major training conference on clinical psychology, which was held in Boulder, Colorado, in 1949 (Raimy, 1950).

The Boulder Conference

The Boulder Conference on Training in Clinical Psychology was convened with the financial support of the Veterans Administration and the U.S. Public Health Service, which asked the APA to (a) name those universities that offered satisfactory training programs and (b) develop acceptable programs in universities that did not have them. The Boulder participants accepted the recommendations of Shakow's committee for a scientist–professional model of training. Shakow's plan thus became known as the *Boulder model*.

Participants at the Boulder Conference further agreed that some mechanism was necessary for monitoring, evaluating, and officially accrediting clinical training programs and internship facilities. As a result, APA formed an Education and Training Board with a Committee on Accreditation, which was charged with these tasks. The most recent version of the APA criteria for accreditation was published in 2009 and is entitled, *Guidelines and Principles for Accreditation of Programs in Professional Psychology* (American Psychological Association, 2009). These new standards apply to areas of "professional psychology," which include clinical, counseling, and school psychology.

Currently, clinical training sites are visited by an APA accreditation team about every 5 years; the longest permissible interval between site visits is 7 years. The results of accreditation site visits are published each year in the *American Psychologist* and can also be found online at the Web site of the APA Commission (formerly "Committee") on Accreditation (www.apa.org/ed/accreditation/programs/clinical.aspx). As of 2013, there were 370 active APA-accredited doctoral programs, 235 (64%) of which were in clinical psychology, 68 (18%) in counseling psychology, 60 (16%) in school psychology, and 7 (2%) in combined programs (American Psychological Association, 2011a, 2012c). Note that almost half the programs in clinical psychology have been accredited since 1980 (McFall, 2006). In addition to these accredited programs, there are many doctoral training programs that operate without APA accreditation, either because the program has not requested a site visit or because approval has not been granted after an accreditation visit (see Chapter 16, "Getting into Graduate School in Clinical Psychology," for information about the importance of APA accreditation).

The Boulder model remains the pivotal point for discussions of clinical psychology training today. However, since its birth in 1949, some clinicians have expressed discontent with it. Accordingly, they explored a number of alternatives in subsequent conferences, including the 1955 *Stanford Conference* (Strother, 1956), the 1958 *Miami Conference* (Roe, Gustad, Moore, Ross, & Skodak, 1959), the 1965 *Chicago Conference*, and, most significantly, the 1973 *Vail Conference*.

The Vail Conference

Held in Vail, Colorado, with grant support from the National Institute of Mental Health (NIMH), the 1973 *Vail Conference* brought together representatives from a wide range of psychological specialties and training orientations, and it included graduate students and psychologists from various ethnic minority groups. The conference officially recognized professional training as an acceptable model for programs that defined their mission as the preparation of students for the delivery of clinical services. These "unambiguously professional" programs were to be given status

A Case Study of a Scientist–Practitioner in Action

Florence Kaslow earned her doctoral degree at Bryn Mawr College in Pennsylvania in 1969 at a time when there were few women leaders in the field of psychology. At the time she was in graduate school, her daughter, Nadine, was 7 years old and her son, Howard, was 4 years old. The children recall her as a "school girl" from 9:00 a.m. to 3:00 p.m. and then as "mommy" from 3:00 p.m. to 9:00 p.m. They also recollect hearing typing late into the night after they were in bed and sometimes when they awoke in the morning while Dr. Kaslow was completing her dissertation. (In case you don't know, typewriters were a lot louder than computer keyboards, which were virtually unknown then.) After graduating, Dr. Kaslow joined the faculty of Hahnemann Medical University in Phila-delphia, where she taught, conducted research, served in administrative roles and saw clients. She was a professor in the Department of Mental Health Sciences and chair of the Forensic Psychiatry/Psychology section as well as codirector of the PhD/JD program, which she initiated.

Dr. Kaslow's work has had a significant impact on the field of clinical psychology, largely because she can speak the same "language" as both clinicians and researchers. She is currently the president of Kaslow Associates in Palm Beach Gardens, Florida, where she continues to practice and write about families, family business, and family research. For example, she is often asked to summarize the history of family psychology and to share her thoughts on the future of the field (Kaslow, 2010, 2011). She is also a distinguished visiting professor at Florida Institute of Technology (F.I.T.) in Melbourne, Florida. She has influenced clinical, family, and forensic psychology not only through her own work, but also by helping to interest her daughter in the field. Dr. Nadine Kaslow is a professor on the faculty at the Emory University School of Medicine and is a leader in the fields of clinical, child, and family psychology. When Nadine became president of APA Division 43 (Family Psychology) in 2002, it was the first time that a mother–daughter team had ever both served as president of the same division of APA (Florence had served as president of Division 43 in 1987). Both also hold Board Certification in three specializations from the American Board of Professional Psychology and have served on the ABPP Board of Trustees. Both Drs. Kaslow serve as impeccable role models for students who wish to integrate science and practice in clinical psychology.

Dr. Florence Kaslow (2011, 2013) has written or edited 31 books and has written more than 250 articles and chapters, mainly focused on family functioning, relationship problems, and international issues such as treating Holocaust survivors. She has conducted workshops in over 50 countries, including presentations on psychotherapy, international and multicultural psychology, family and divorce issues, and family business consultation. She is the epitome of a scientist–practitioner in that she is a scholar–scientist as well as an active coach and clinician. *Source*: Florence Kaslow, Ph.D.

equal to that of their more traditional scientist–professional counterparts. Thus began the new Doctor of Psychology degree, now known as the *PsyD* degree (Stricker, 2011).

One of the most controversial of the Vail recommendations was that people trained at the master's level should be considered professional psychologists. The MA proposal was short-lived, as the APA voted that the title of *psychologist* should be reserved for those who have completed a doctoral training program. This policy remains in effect today, but it has come under intense attack as the number of MA psychology graduates continues to grow and as many states have allowed master's-level clinicians to practice independently. Currently, master's-level clinical, counseling, and school psychology programs accept more applicants than doctoral-level programs do, and three times as many students graduate with master's degrees as with PhDs (Morgan & Korschgen, 2006).

The Salt Lake City Conference

The 6th National Conference on Graduate Education in Psychology was held in 1987, at the University of Utah in Salt Lake City. The conference was convened for several reasons, including the need to evaluate several changes that had taken place in the training of professional psychologists since the Vail conference. There was also a desire to reduce growing tensions between scientists and practitioners over numerous training and organizational issues. There were 67 resolutions passed at the conference, and perhaps the most salient for current training is that in graduate programs seeking accreditation, graduate students must be trained in a core of psychological knowledge that should include research design and methods; statistics; ethics; assessment; history and systems of psychology; biological, social, and cognitive-affective bases of behavior; and individual differences (see also Bickman, 1987, and a special issue of the *American Psychologist*, December 1987).

Clinical Psychology Training Today

What does training in clinical psychology look like after all these national training conferences; several smaller conferences; countless hours of discussion, debate, and argument among clinicians, educators, and students; and periodic revisions of the APA's accreditation guidelines? There is no easy answer to that question, but we can provide a general summary.

The scientist–practitioner model has proven to be a tough competitor and is still reflected in more clinical psychology training programs than any other model (Klonoff, 2011). Many programs that favor the scientist–practitioner model, however, are struggling to find the best way to train clinical psychologists so that their practical skills are well integrated with a solid foundation of scientific knowledge.

Partly in reaction to the continued disconnect between science and practice, Richard McFall (1991) wrote a "Manifesto for a Science of Clinical Psychology," which highlighted the need for all practice to be research based. He argued that "scientific clinical psychology is the only legitimate and acceptable form of clinical psychology" (p. 76). Three years later, in 1994, McFall and other empirically oriented clinical psychologists formed the Academy of Psychological Clinical Science (APCS). Consistent with its empirical research focus, the Academy is housed within the Association for Psychological Science (APS) rather than the more practice-oriented APA. The Academy, which is made up of graduate training programs committed to clinical science, was created in response to concerns that recent developments in health care reform and licensure and accreditation requirements threaten to erode the role of science and empirical research in the education of clinical psychologists. As of 2013, the Academy had 53 doctoral programs and 10 internship sites as members. The current list of Academy programs can be found at: http://acadpsychclinicalscience.org/index.php?page$=$members

Academy programs are committed to training students in interventions and assessment techniques based on empirical research evidence (see Chapter 10, "Research on Clinical Intervention"). Within the ranks of Academy programs and in other research-oriented clinical programs, too, there has been considerable discontent about the perception that the APA accreditation system's standards for clinical research are not kept high enough. For that reason, a subset of Academy members helped to develop a more research-oriented accreditation system: the *Psychological Clinical Science Accreditation System* (21 PCSAS; Baker, McFall, & Shoham, 2009). The first clinical training program was accredited by PCSAS in 2009 and by 2013 there were 21 PCSAS-accredited programs, with five more under review. The current list of programs accredited through the PCSAS can be found at: http://pcsas.org/.

As of this writing, all of the programs accredited by PCSAS have also maintained their APA or CPA (Canadian Psychological Association) accreditation. It remains to be seen whether additional programs will apply for PCSAS accreditation and if so, whether they will forgo their APA accreditation status. Suffice it to say that faculty members of the Academy, its member programs, and the programs accredited by the new PCSAS system are playing critical roles in moving the field of clinical psychology toward a more evidence-based orientation (McFall, 2012).

As implied by the existence of different accreditation systems, the last several decades have seen the creation of graduate programs with differing philosophies about how to train clinicians. Those that are more practice-oriented envision clinicians mainly as health care or human-services professionals and tend to deemphasize empirical research. Many such programs are housed in professional schools of psychology rather than in universities, and they usually offer the PsyD degree rather than the PhD.

Professional Schools and the Doctor of Psychology (PsyD) Degree

In Chapter 2, we noted that proposals to emphasize practice and deemphasize research in clinical psychology training appeared as early as 1917. However, it was 1951 before the first U.S. professional school of psychology, at Adelphi University, was begun; the first freestanding, non–university-based professional school of psychology was established as the California School of Professional Psychology (CSPP), which opened campuses in Los Angeles and San Francisco in 1970 (Benjamin, 2005).

Norcross, Kohout, and Wicherski (2005) argued that "*the* pivotal trend in graduate education in psychology over the past three decades is the emergence of PsyD training" (p. 974). Unlike Boulder model programs, PsyD programs provide training that concentrates on professional skills and clinical services. The emphasis is on the skills necessary for the delivery of a range of assessment, intervention, and consultation services. In most PsyD programs, a master's thesis is not required, nor is a research-oriented dissertation, although most do require a written, doctoral-level report of some type.

The number of APA-accredited PsyD programs continues to grow. As of 2013, there were 62 of them (APA, 2011a, 2012c). They are found in many settings, including university departments of psychology, university-based professional schools, freestanding non–university-based schools, and other sites. PsyD programs enroll more clinical psychology students than practice-oriented or research-practice PhD programs, and research-oriented PhD programs enroll the fewest of all (Norcross, Ellis, & Sayette, 2010). There are still significantly more APA-accredited PhD than PsyD programs in clinical psychology (173 versus 62), but because of the larger class sizes in PsyD programs, there are now more clinical psychology students graduating from PsyD programs than from PhD programs (Sayette, Norcross, & Dimoff, 2011).

Though they enroll the largest number of students, PsyD programs are significantly less likely than PhD programs to offer financial aid (Norcross, Ellis, & Sayette, 2010). There are differences, too, in selection criteria. Compared to PhD programs, PsyD programs tend to admit students with lower mean GPA and GRE scores (McFall, 2006; Templer, 2005). These PsyD graduates are more likely than PhD graduates to be employed in independent practice, managed care, and other health service settings (Norcross & Sayette, 2012).

There is a great deal of heterogeneity among PsyD training programs (Norcross et al., 2004), so it is difficult to make general statements about them. However, there are a number of troubling features associated with freestanding PsyD programs that are not as prevalent in university-based PsyD programs. These features include higher acceptance rates and lower admission criteria. Further, regardless of where the PsyD programs are housed, their students are less likely than those of PhD programs to be accepted into APA-accredited internship programs: 66.0% for PsyD candidates compared to 92.8% for PhD candidates (Graham & Kim, 2011). Graduates of PsyD programs also tend to score lower than PhD program graduates do on the Examination for Professional Practice in Psychology, a licensing exam described later in this chapter. PsyD graduates are also less likely to qualify for a specialty diploma from the American Board of Professional Psychology (also discussed later). In short, graduates of PsyD programs, especially those from programs housed in freestanding professional schools, are less likely overall to have the most distinguished career outcomes.

Training Models within Clinical Psychology

As discussed earlier, various models of training have emerged from conferences such as those held in Boulder and Vail. Currently, there are three predominant training models within clinical psychology (Klonoff, 2011):

- *The clinical scientist model*, which grew out of the Academy of Psychological Clinical Science approach and places heavy emphasis on scientific research (more common in university settings).
- *The scientist–practitioner model*, which follows the Boulder model and provides for approximately equal emphasis on research and application to practice (common in traditional PhD programs and in some professional schools).
- *The practitioner–scholar model*, which follows the Vail model and stresses human-services delivery and places proportionately less emphasis on scientific training (common in professional schools and many PsyD programs).

Cherry, Messenger, and Jacoby (2000) evaluated the training in all three kinds of programs and, as expected, found that graduates of the practitioner–scholar model spent the least time in clinical research, while graduates of clinical scientist programs spent the most time in that activity. More recent reviews have confirmed that this pattern is still widespread (McFall, 2012). These findings raise concerns among those who fear that professional school programs do not offer sufficient training in clinical research.

On the other hand, advocates of the professional school approach have their own concerns about research-oriented training programs. One survey found, for example, that only 51% of clinical faculty in PhD training programs reported current involvement in clinical practice, although the majority of them (74%) held a permanent or provisional license to practice clinical psychology; and an additional 5% reported that they had been licensed at some point in the past (Himelein & Putnam, 2001). Another survey found that senior clinical researchers thought that being clinically active was desirable, especially for researchers focused on psychotherapy outcome studies, but that it was not absolutely necessary (Meyer, 2007). So practice-oriented clinicians fear that research-oriented programs offer too little appreciation of, or training in, the realities of clinical practice.

Ironically, one of the major practice-oriented outcomes of training programs—matching students to internships—is less likely for graduate students in practitioner–scholar programs. A study of over 2,100 internship applicants found that significantly fewer applicants from practitioner–scholar programs were matched to internships compared to applicants from scientist–practitioner programs or from clinical science programs (Neimeyer, Rice, & Keilin, 2007). Thus, practice-oriented graduate programs do not necessarily have stronger practice-oriented outcomes for students.

It is important to note that when practice-oriented or research-oriented clinicians do not conform to the Boulder model's scientist–practitioner ideal, it is not always because they reject it—indeed, most think the scientist–practitioner model is a good one (Grus, McCutcheon, & Berry, 2011). Rather, clinical psychologists often fail to integrate science and practice in their day-to-day work because the incentive systems operating in their work environments do not support it. For instance, university psychology departments seldom offer support or incentives for clinical faculty who wish to work with clients in a part-time private practice or in a nonprofit clinical setting (Overholser, 2007, 2010), and it is increasingly difficult for clinical psychologists without postdoctoral experience to become licensed while holding an academic position (DiLillo, DeGue, Cohen, & Morgan, 2006; Kaslow & Webb, 2011). Conversely, few independent practice clinicians have the resources to conduct the kind of research that is published in scholarly journals (Overholser, 2010). These differing reward structures can reinforce attitudes and behaviors that further split the field into practitioners and researchers. But as Belar (2000) points out, this is a problem with implementation, not a problem with the Boulder model itself. It sometimes seems, then, that the Boulder model is a good idea that has yet to be fully implemented—even after more than 60 years (Grus, McCutcheon, & Berry, 2011).

Evaluating Clinical Psychology Training

Unfortunately, we know relatively little about the comparative clinical effectiveness of graduates from the various training models. Most of the research comparing different training models focuses on the time students or professionals spend in various activities, where they are employed, how much they publish, or how they view the training they received. There is scant information about whether different training models ultimately lead to different outcomes in treating clients. This is unfortunate, but as suggested by meta-analytic and other studies of psychotherapy outcome (see Chapter 10), we would not be surprised if specific training models account for relatively small proportions of the variance in some areas of clinical performance. Does this mean that there are no important differences across models or that it is impossible to evaluate them? We think the answer to both questions is no.

Our view is that clinical training programs can be evaluated in light of whether they produce clinicians and clinical researchers who are competent at performing the professional functions that their work demands. This kind of technical competence is not enough, however. We believe that the single most important goal in training competent clinical psychologists is to teach them to choose and evaluate services in light of research evidence. We think that training programs should emphasize the teaching of those clinical services that have been supported by empirical evidence; they should not offer training in services or roles that have failed to gain research support. We also believe that if clinical training moves too far from its foundation in psychological science and concentrates only on teaching therapy techniques, assessment methods, and other professional skills, clinical psychologists of the twenty-first century will become narrowly specialized practitioners for whom research is of only passing interest. If that happens, clinical psychology will become a poorer science and, ultimately, a weaker profession.

The Internship Crisis

Regardless of their location or training model, almost all graduate programs require their students to complete a full-time, one-year clinical internship. The overwhelming majority of APA-accredited programs require that this internship be one that is APA-accredited.

The coordinating entity for matching graduate students to internships in the United States and Canada is the Association of Psychology Postdoctoral and Internships Centers (APPIC). Graduate students apply for internships through APPIC via a computerized system. These applications are usually submitted in November, and in early December applicants are invited for interviews which take place from mid-December to early February. In the second week of February, the applicants submit a rank-ordered list of their desired internships and the training directors at the internship sites submit their rank-ordered list of their desired applicants. All these rankings are then fed into a computer which is programmed to match applicants to internships in a way that maximizes the desired outcome for both. The results are revealed on a national "match" day, usually in late February. A second round of computerized matching was instituted in 2012 in order to help nonmatched applicants find unfilled slots.

The internship requirement has been in place for decades, but as the numbers of graduate students in clinical psychology has grown and the number of internship slots has shrunk due to funding problems, an internship crisis or "internship imbalance" has arisen (Hatcher, 2011a, 2011b; McCutcheon, 2011). There are just not enough internship slots available to accommodate all the graduate students who are seeking them. For example, in 2012, there were 915 applicants who were not matched to any type of internship. The situation is even more difficult in relation to the APA/CPA-accredited internships that are required by most APA/CPA-accredited graduate programs. The match rate for internship applicants from those programs was only 53.3% in 2012, meaning that an applicant had only a little better than a 50-50 chance of being matched to an APA/CPA-accredited internship (http://appic.org/). Because these students need the internship in order to receive their doctorates, and because the internship application cycle occurs only once a year, failing to be matched is a serious impediment to completing their training.

Various task forces, advocacy groups, and scholarly discussions have addressed the internship crisis (see for example, the special section of the November, 2011 issue of *Training and Education in Professional Psychology* entitled "Struggling to resolve the internship imbalance"). No solution has yet been found, though, and given the still-rising numbers of students in the internship pipeline, the situation is likely to get worse before it gets better (Bieschke et al., 2011).

SECTION SUMMARY

Clinical psychologists have long debated the best way to train members of their discipline. The most influential national conferences have been the Boulder conference (which focused on the scientist–practitioner training model) and the Vail conference (which highlighted the need for professional psychologists and the PsyD degree). The PsyD degree is now well established, but there is a great deal of heterogeneity in the programs offering this degree. Among the more research-oriented programs, are those of the Academy of Psychological Clinical Science, which is dedicated to using empirical methods to enhance psychological practice. A new accreditation system, the Psychological Clinical Science Accreditation System (PCSAS), was developed to provide a sharper focus on research training in clinical psychology doctoral programs. Despite the sometimes vigorous debates about the advantages and disadvantages of different training models, little is known about how graduates from various programs differ in their effectiveness in treating clients. Regardless of training model, the field is currently faced with an internship crisis, with no end in sight.

PROFESSIONAL REGULATION

SECTION PREVIEW

This section highlights the reasons for certification and licensure in clinical psychology and delineates the processes required to obtain both. ABPP certification is also described.

One major responsibility of any health care or human-services profession is to establish standards of competence that members of the profession must meet before they are authorized to practice. The primary purpose of such *professional regulation* is to protect the public from unauthorized or incompetent practice of psychology by impostors, untrained persons, or psychologists who are unable to function at a minimum level of competence. Caveat emptor ("let the buyer beware") is an inadequate protection when buyers such as mental health consumers are not sufficiently informed about what they should be aware of in the services they are seeking. Accordingly, clinical psychology has developed an active system of professional regulation that continues to evolve.

Certification and Licensure

The most important type of regulations are state laws that establish requirements for the practice of psychology and/or restrict the use of the term *psychologist* to persons with certain qualifications. This legislative regulation comes in two kinds of statutes: certification and licensure.

    Certification laws restrict use of the title *psychologist* to people who have met requirements specified in the law. Certification protects only the title of psychologist; it does not regulate the practice of psychology. *Licensure* is a more restrictive type of statute. Licensing laws define the practice of psychology by specifying the services that a psychologist is authorized to offer to the public. The requirements for licensure are usually more comprehensive than for certification. To distinguish between certification and licensure, remember the following rule of thumb: Certification laws dictate who can be called a psychologist, while licensing laws dictate both the title and the activities allowed by psychologists.

    Licensing laws are administered by *state boards of psychology*, which are charged by legislatures to regulate the practice of psychology in each state. State boards of psychology have two major functions:

- determining the standards for admission to the profession and administering procedures for the selection and examination of candidates, and
- regulating professional practice and conducting disciplinary proceedings involving alleged violators of professional standards.

Today, all 50 states, the District of Columbia, and all Canadian provinces have certification or licensure laws. Many states combine their certification and licensure laws into one statute.

    The steps involved in becoming licensed differ somewhat from place to place, but there is enough uniformity in the procedures of most U.S. states to offer a rough sketch of how the aspiring clinical psychologist would approach this task (see Table 15.1).

    Currently, the *Association of State and Provincial Psychology Boards* (ASPPB) coordinates the activities of the state boards of psychology and attempts to bring about uniformity in standards and procedures. ASPPB has developed a standardized, objective test for use by state boards in examining candidates for licensure. First released in 1964 and revised frequently since then, this *Examination for Professional Practice in Psychology* (EPPP) is sometimes called the *national exam*

TABLE 15.1 So You Want to Be a Licensed Psychologist?

Imagine you have just completed a doctoral program in clinical psychology and are now interested in becoming a licensed clinical psychologist. What steps would you have to take? The following hurdles will be encountered in many states. First, you must ask that the state board of psychology review your credentials to determine your eligibility for examination. Their decision is based on several criteria:

1. ***Administrative Requirements.*** You must have reached a certain age and be a U.S. citizen. Not too much can be done about these requirements; you either meet them or you do not. One bit of advice: Don't commit any felonies, engage in treason, or libel your governor. These activities are judged to be indicative of poor moral character and may leave you plenty of time to fantasize about licensure while in prison.

2. ***Education.*** Most states require a doctoral degree in psychology from an accredited university. In most states, accreditation refers to accreditation of the university by a recognized accrediting agency, but many states require that you graduate from an APA-accredited program. Official graduate and undergraduate transcripts are required.

3. ***Experience.*** This requirement usually amounts to multiple years of supervised professional experience in a setting approved by the board. In most states, some of the experience must be postdoctoral; letters of reference will be required from your supervisor(s). If, after scrutinizing your credentials, the board finds that you are eligible for examination, you will be invited to take an examination. Here is what to expect:

Examination Fee. There is a charge for the examination and for having the state board review your credentials. The Examination for Professional Practice in Psychology (EPPP) examination costs $518, and the state board fees range from $50 in Illinois to $765 in Florida, with most falling into the range of $200 to $300 (DiLillo, DeGue, Cohen, & Morgan, 2006; Matthews & Matthews, 2009).

The Examination. Most states use the EPPP national examination, which is a computer-administered multiple choice exam consisting of 225 questions covering general psychology, methodology, applications of psychology, and professional conduct and ethics. Because many candidates want to practice a specialty like clinical, school, or industrial psychology, state boards sometimes provide specialized state tests in these areas or related to state laws and regulations. You may also be required to take an oral examination given by the board in which any material relevant to psychology may be covered. If you pass—congratulations!!! Now you have to pay an annual fee to retain your license, attend continuing education courses, and pay for malpractice insurance. No really, congratulations!!

Reexamination. If you fail any part of the examination, you will be given another chance to take that portion. Most boards feel that twice is enough, however; so if you fail the second time, it might be wise to reconsider the advantages of the family business.

---

because all jurisdictions can use it as a part of their examination procedure. In most states, a person must meet the requirements for licensure before taking the examination, which is available throughout the year at various computer vendor sites (www.asppb.org/).

Candidates' graduate training programs and clinical internship experiences are also evaluated as part of their eligibility for licensure. A number of states, such as Florida, Oklahoma, and Utah, now allow only graduates of APA-accredited doctoral programs to obtain licensure, so a student's choice of a graduate training program may influence his or her ability to obtain a license to practice clinical psychology (see Chapter 16).

After completing the doctoral degree, psychology graduates in most states must complete postdoctoral supervised activities in order to be eligible for licensure. These postdoctoral activities can include direct clinical practice, research, teaching, consulting, and the like, but in most states the work must be closely supervised by a licensed psychologist. Postdoctoral positions can be APA-accredited, but many psychologists receive postdoctoral training within the context of their first job (Matthews & Matthews, 2009). A review of the licensing laws across the United States showed that all the states except Alabama and Washington require some type of postdoctoral supervision of professional experience: Most require between 1,500 and 2,000 hours of such experience although Washington, DC and Michigan require as many as 4,000 hours (Prinstein, 2013).

In most states, psychologists are required to keep their license or certificate up to date by paying a periodic renewal fee and by documenting involvement in *continuing education* (CE). The amount of continuing education hours varies across the United States, with a range of 20 to 40 hours required per 2-year licensing cycle (Neimeyer, Taylor, & Philip, 2010).

Because licensing laws vary among states, there is little *reciprocity* from state to state, meaning that someone licensed as a psychologist in one state cannot automatically transfer licensure to another. Thus, *professional mobility* for licensed psychologists is limited, whether they are just starting their career or wishing to move to another state later on (Matthews & Matthews, 2009). There are even bigger obstacles to retaining one's licensure in other countries (Hall & Lunt, 2005).

There has been enough concern about the lack of reciprocity between states that the American Psychological Association recently updated its Model Act for State Licensure of Psychologists, known as the *model licensure act*, in 2010 (Clay, 2010). Among other things, the revised model licensure act attempts to set consistent standards that would make it easier to move one's license from state to state. The revised model licensure act also suggests that, instead of requiring postdoctoral hours of professional experience, applicants should be required to satisfy the state's required training hours—either in their predoctoral program or through a combination of predoctoral and postdoctoral work (Shaffer, DeMers, & Rodolfa, 2011). We think this act is a step in the right direction for making licenses more manageable and more movable, but in order for it to be of maximum benefit to psychologists wishing to relocate, it would have to be adopted by many, if not all, states (Clay, 2010). APA, the Association of State and Provincial Psychology Boards (ASPPB), and the National Register of Health Service Providers in Psychology (known as the National Register) continue to work toward licensure reciprocity between states, but it is a challenging task (Hall & Boucher, 2008). For now, the best resources available for psychology license applicants are "credential banks" offered through the National Register and programs like the ASPPB's Psychology Licensure Universal System (PLUS), that allow applicants to submit their credentials online and then apply for licensure in multiple states if they wish (Matthews & Matthews, 2009). The licensure mobility challenge will remain significant, though, until more professional mobility options are created, both nationally and internationally.

Licensed psychologists who have at least 5 years of professional experience, who have no professional disciplinary actions filed against them, and who meet certain other requirements can apply for a Certificate of Professional Qualification in Psychology through ASPPB. This certificate can be useful in seeking licensure in a state other than the one in which the person was originally licensed (Robinson & Habben, 2003). Similarly, seeking certification through the National Register of Health Service Providers in Psychology or obtaining diplomate status through the American Board of Professional Psychology (ABPP; see next section) may give practicing psychologists more mobility across state lines (Hall & Boucher, 2008).

A surprisingly large number of graduate students and early career psychologists do not know very much about the licensing processes we have described. For example, one study of nearly 4,000 doctoral psychology graduate students found that although 92% of them planned to apply for licensure, 60% of that group had not yet begun looking into licensure requirements (Hall, Wexelbaum, & Boucher, 2007). In addition, over 75% of those wishing to be licensed were unfamiliar with credentialing organizations such as ASPPB and the National Register (Hall, Wexelbaum, & Boucher, 2007). The same pattern holds true among early career psychologists who were actually seeking licensure! A study of over 1,800 such individuals found that less than 10% reported being very familiar with ASPPB and the National Register (Hall & Boucher, 2008). Obviously, greater efforts are needed within the profession to familiarize graduate students and early career psychologists with the facts about obtaining licensure and improving their chances for professional mobility.

ABPP Certification

As mentioned earlier, licensed clinical psychologists can seek another type of professional recognition, namely certification by the American Board of Professional Psychology (ABPP). ABPP was founded in 1947 as a national organization that certifies the professional competence of psychologists. Its certification is signified by the award of a diploma in one of 14 specialty-specific areas in psychology:

- Clinical
- Clinical child and adolescent
- Clinical health
- Clinical neuropsychology

- Cognitive and behavioral
- Counseling
- Couple and family
- Forensic
- Group
- Organizational and business consulting
- Police and public safety
- Psychoanalysis
- Rehabilitation
- School

Although it carries no special legal authority, an ABPP diploma is considered more prestigious than licensure. While licensure signifies a *minimal* level of competence (and is required before seeking diplomate status), diplomate status is an endorsement of professional expertise, an indication that the person possesses a masterful knowledge of some specialty field. Accordingly, requirements for the ABPP diploma are more rigorous than for licensure. Depending on the specialty-specific area, multiple years of experience are a prerequisite to even take the ABPP examination, which is conducted by a group of diplomates who observe the candidate dealing directly with clinical situations (e.g., giving a test or interacting with a therapy client) and who conduct an oral examination that includes the following related topics: professional knowledge, assessment competence, intervention competence, interpersonal competence with clients, ethical and legal standards and behavior, commitment to the specialty and awareness of current issues, and competence in supervision and consultation (Kaslow, Graves, & Smith, 2012). More information about ABPP diplomate status can be found at www.abpp.org, a Web site that also provides a searchable Directory of Specialists for individuals interested in finding an ABPP professional in their geographic location.

SECTION SUMMARY

In order to protect the public from untrained professionals, states and other regulating bodies have developed certification and licensing laws regarding the practice of psychology. In most states, certification refers to the right to call oneself a psychologist and licensure refers to the activities that clinicians are allowed to perform. Whereas certification and licensure confirm a minimum set of training criteria, the ABPP provides confirmation of excellent skills in the area of clinical practice.

PROFESSIONAL ETHICS

SECTION PREVIEW

In several previous chapters, we discussed the APA Ethical Principles of Psychologists and Code of Conduct, *or* Ethics Code *(American Psychological Association, 2010a, 2010b). Here we describe how the Ethics Code is organized, how standards are implemented, and how ethical violations are reviewed and acted upon. We also discuss malpractice and malpractice litigation.*

Ethical Standards of the American Psychological Association

The Ethical Principles of the APA consist of a Preamble, a set of General Principles, and a large number of specific Ethical Standards. The Preamble and General Principles, are not enforceable rules; they are statements of the aspirations of psychologists to attain their highest ideals, and they provide guidance to psychologists who are evaluating what would be ethically desirable behavior in certain situations. The Preamble provides an overview of the ethics code and the General Principles are as follows:

- ***Principle A: Beneficence and Nonmaleficence.*** The essence of this principle is that psychologists should "do no harm."
- ***Principle B: Fidelity and Responsibility.*** This principle states that psychologists must be trustworthy and uphold the highest ethical standards in their professional relationships.

- *Principle C: Integrity.*   This principle encourages psychologists to remain accurate, honest, and truthful in their professional work.
- *Principle D: Justice.*   This principle focuses on the need to treat all individuals, but especially clients, fairly and justly.
- *Principle E: Respect for People's Rights and Dignity.*   This principle highlights the need for psychologists to treat individuals with the utmost respect for their dignity and individual freedoms.

Although these General Principles are not legally enforceable, they do set the tone for psychologists to maintain the highest ethical standards. The Ethical Standards, however, are enforceable. They apply to members of APA and may be used by other organizations, such as state boards of psychology and the courts, to judge and sanction the behavior of a psychologist, whether or not the psychologist is an APA member.

The Ethical Standards are organized under the following headings:

1. *Resolving Ethical Issues.* This first section contains standards about how psychologists are to resolve ethical questions or complaints.
2. *Competence.* This section states that psychologists must be trained in their specific area of expertise and that they must continue to keep current in their field in order to maintain competence. This section also addresses the issue of when psychologists have personal problems or conflicts that limit their ability to practice in a competent manner.
3. *Human Relations.* These ethical standards deal with such topics as preventing unfair discrimination, sexual or other harassment, multiple relationships, conflict of interest, providing informed consent, and avoiding termination of clinical services when it is not in the best interest of the client.
4. *Privacy and Confidentiality.* These rules cover psychologists' obligations to protect their clients' rights to confidentiality and privacy.
5. *Advertising and Other Public Statements.* Standards that control the way psychologists publicize their services and their professional credentials are presented under this category.
6. *Record Keeping and Fees.* This section provides guidance on documenting professional work, maintaining and disposing of confidential records, fees, referrals, and other financial arrangements.
7. *Education and Training.* This section contains several ethical standards that control psychologists' conduct as they teach and supervise students.
8. *Research and Publication.* Standards that control researchers' activities are included in this section, such as receiving approval from the Institutional Review Board before conducting research, obtaining voluntary informed consent from human research participants, debriefing participants, providing publication credit for coauthors, sharing research data, and conducting reviews of scholarly work.
9. *Assessment.* Rules pertaining to the use and interpretation of tests are listed.
10. *Therapy.* Rules about the structuring, conduct, and termination of therapy are identified here. Specific standards prohibit psychologists from having sexual intimacies with current clients or the relatives and significant others of current clients and from accepting persons as clients if they have had previous sexual intimacies with them. Furthermore, psychologists should not have sexual intimacies with former therapy clients for at least 2 years after the termination of therapy, and even then only if the psychologist can demonstrate that no exploitation of the client has occurred.

Implementation of Ethical Standards

Most psychologists take great pains to deal with complex and ethically ambiguous situations in accordance with the highest standards of professional conduct. But because many situations involve moral and cultural questions and do not match exactly the terminology used in the APA Ethics Code, there is often no clearly best course of action, no obviously right answer.

Consider, for example, the following examples of situations in which the therapist is in both a professional and a nonprofessional role with the client. Multiple relationships are considered unethical because they can harm the therapeutic relationship and they can ultimately harm the client. Do you think that is true in these cases?

A therapist has been seeing a 45-year-old male for over a year for problems related to stress and anxiety. The client recently lost his job as an office administrator because the company went bankrupt, and he is looking for work. At the same time, the therapist is in need of an office assistant/records clerk, and she has had a hard time finding someone who meets her high standards. She knows that the client received rave reviews as an office assistant. She hires him to be her records clerk and continues to see him professionally.

A therapist is seeing a 38-year-old female client who has endured the painful break-up of a long-term relationship. The client mentions that she loves dogs and that she finds great comfort in their company. The therapist happens to be an avid dog lover as well, and she raises and breeds Rottweilers as a hobby. The therapist mentions that she has a new litter of Rottweilers that are ready for new homes, and the client purchases one of them from the therapist.

A cognitive-behavioral therapist in a small town is the only one who specializes in treating clients with anxiety disorders. A 63-year-old male calls this therapist for help with severe agoraphobia, but he has a limited income, no insurance, and he can pay for only one session. In a brief discussion of the client's situation, the therapist learns that the client is an expert carpenter. The therapist offers to treat the client in exchange for carpentry services. The client accepts the offer and builds a set of bookshelves in the den of the therapist's home. (Adapted from Bersoff, 2003.)

How do psychologists manage such ethical problems? They begin with awareness of acceptable and unacceptable practices within their area. Proper informed consent procedures, release of information forms, and case documentation are also important risk-management procedures (Knapp, Bennett, & VandeCreek, 2012). Professionals can also consult books such as the following:

- APA Handbook of Ethics in Psychology—Volume 1: Moral Foundations and Common Themes (Knapp, 2012a)
- APA Handbook of Ethics in Psychology—Volume 2—Practice, Teaching, and Research (Knapp, 2012b)
- Ethics Desk Reference for Psychologists (Barnett & Johnson, 2008)
- Essential Ethics for Psychologists (Nagy, 2011)
- APA Ethics Code Commentary and Case Illustrations (Campbell, Vasquez, Behnke, & Kinscherff, 2010)
- Ethics in Psychotherapy and Counseling: A Practical Guide (Pope & Vasquez, 2011)

Consultation with colleagues and professional organizations is often done, too, as long as confidentiality can be maintained. Finally, many malpractice insurance companies provide consultation to clinician–policyholders who seek clarification on ethical and legal issues. Although these efforts do not provide immunity for psychologists from malpractice suits or other legal actions, they do reflect a conscientious effort to do the right thing, and documentation of such efforts is likely to be looked upon favorably by professional organizations and courts.

Dealing with Ethical Violations

When, as fallible human beings, psychologists behave in an ethically questionable manner, they are subject to censure by local, state, and national organizations whose task it is to deal with violations of ethical practice. Clients or other individuals who believe that a psychologist has been involved in wrongdoing can file a formal complaint with the APA and/or the state licensing board. Fortunately, the number of such complaints against clinical psychologists is relatively small; the vast majority of psychologists never have a formal complaint filed against them (Nagy, 2011). For example, in 2009, the APA Ethics Committee reported only 68 cases in which a formal ethics complaint led to an investigation by the Committee. Given that there are over 150,000 members of APA, the number of active ethics violation cases is small indeed.

Once a complaint of unethical behavior is brought against an APA member and the appropriate committee has decided that the conduct in question was in fact unethical, the question of punishment must be decided. The most severe APA sanction is to dismiss the offender from the association and to inform the membership of this action. Unethical conduct can also cause

TABLE 15.2 Reported Disciplinary Actions Against Psychologists in the United States and Canada, August 1983–December 2009*

Reason for Disciplinary Action	Percent Disciplined
Sexual misconduct	18.1
Unprofessional conduct	18.0
Nonsexual dual relationship or boundary violation	11.2
Negligence	10.8
Conviction of crime	9.1
Failure to maintain adequate or accurate records	7.6
Improper or inadequate supervision or delegation	5.5
Substandard or inadequate care	5.5
Incompetence	5.4
Breach of confidentiality	5.0
Other or unknown	3.7

*$N = 4,397$.

psychologists to have their professional licenses taken away by the board of psychology in the state where they practice. Other actions can include censure, censure with probation, or a decision that no cause for action is warranted. Later, we discuss legal and financial sanctions associated with malpractice litigation.

Formal complaints against psychologists can be made by anybody, including clients and colleagues. The nature of these complaints vary widely, but typically involve allegations of unprofessional/negligent practice, sexual misconduct, dual relationships with clients, being convicted of a crime, improper record keeping, breach of confidentiality, and fraud—especially as related to inappropriate insurance billing (Knapp, Bennett, & VandeCreek, 2012; Pope & Vasquez, 2012). As shown in Table 15.2, the most common disciplinary actions were taken for sexual misconduct and unprofessional conduct.

Other Ethical Standards

In addition to the APA *Ethical Principles of Psychologists and Code of Conduct*, a number of other ethical codes and guidelines are in place. Clinical psychologists are responsible for knowing about other standards that govern their research and psychological services. As mentioned in previous chapters, numerous guidelines must be followed in conducting research, performing assessments and psychotherapy, and working with particular categories of clients. Specialty guidelines, especially, have proliferated. Examples include *Guidelines for Psychological Practice with Lesbian, Gay, and Bisexual Clients* (APA, 2012b), *Guidelines for Assessment of and Intervention with Persons with Disabilities* (2012a), *Guidelines for Psychological Practice with Girls and Women* (2007), and *Guidelines for Psychological Practice in Health Care Delivery Systems* (2013).

Therapists, especially those in medical settings or those who bill insurance companies for their services, have to follow additional rules and regulations. The *Health Insurance Portability and Accountability Act* (HIPAA) was established by the Department of Health and Human Services in order to protect the confidentiality of information about clients and to deal with other issues regarding insurance reimbursement (Nagy, 2011). Therapists who bill insurance companies also must register for a National Provider Identifier, which is another component of the HIPAA regulations (Munsey, 2007a).

Regulation through State Laws

The APA's ethical principles are usually consistent with state laws, but not always, so it is usually best for the psychologist to follow the more stringent of the two (APA, 2010a). For example, whereas the APA ethical standards allow consensual sexual contact between therapists and their former clients two years after termination of the therapeutic relationship (as long as no harm will be done to the client as a result), many states forbid any sexual contact between therapists and their former clients, ever. Psychologists who live in a state that forbids such contact in perpetuity would be well advised to follow the state law rather than to presume that the less stringent APA ethical code would apply. In fact, at least 25 states have developed laws banning therapist–client sexual contact, so psychologists could face criminal prosecution for such behavior (Pope & Vasquez, 2011). In addition to prohibiting sexual contact between therapists and clients, state laws may also mandate particular actions by clinical psychologists in other areas, including *duty to warn*.

DUTY TO WARN   Therapists normally keep clients' information strictly confidential, but should a therapist break confidentiality if clients reveal that they plan to harm someone? This was the question raised in the case of *Tarasoff vs. Regents of the University of California* (reviewed in Nagy, 2011), and the answer has turned out to be yes, at least in some states. Here are the facts of the case.

In 1969, Prosenjit Poddar was a student at the University of California–Berkeley, and he sought therapy through the student mental health services center. During a therapy session, Mr. Poddar told his psychotherapist, Dr. Lawrence Moore, that he intended to kill a young woman, Tatiana Tarasoff, who had apparently rejected his attempts at romantic involvement. The therapist informed his superior, Dr. Harvey Powelson, of this threat. The campus police were called and were also asked, in writing, to confine the client. They did so briefly, but then released him after concluding that he was rational, and they believed his promise that he would stay away from the Tarasoff's home. He did not do so. After terminating his relationship with his therapist, Mr. Poddar killed Ms. Tarasoff. He was later convicted of murder. No one had warned the woman or her parents of the threat. In fact, Dr. Powelson had asked the police to return Dr. Moore's letter and ordered that all copies of the letter and Dr. Moore's therapy notes be destroyed.

Ms. Tarasoff's parents sued the University of California–Berkeley, the psychologists involved in the case, and the campus police to recover damages for the murder of their daughter. Ultimately, the Supreme Court of California found in favor of the parents. Through this ruling, Ms. Tarasoff's parents helped to change mental health laws throughout the United States (Ewing & McCann, 2006).

In reaching its decision, the court weighed the importance of confidential therapy relationships against society's interest in protecting itself from dangerous persons. The balance was struck in favor of society's protection. "The protective privilege ends where the public peril begins."

The *Tarasoff* decision created a *duty to warn* the potential victims of clients whom a therapist believes, or should believe, are dangerous. This duty to warn applies in California and some other U.S. states, but it is not legally binding in all of them—a fact that even many psychologists misunderstand. A total of 37 states have passed laws that specify the conditions under which a therapist is liable for failing to take precautions to protect third parties from the dangerous acts of the therapist's clients (Soulier, Maislen, & Beck, 2010). But state laws can change, so therapists are responsible for keeping up to date about their state requirements regarding protection of third parties.

Regulation through Malpractice Litigation

Civil lawsuits brought by clients who allege they have been harmed by the malpractice of professionals constitute another form of regulating clinical psychologists. If a jury agrees with the client's claim, the clinician may be ordered to pay the client monetary damages to compensate for the harm. To prove a claim of professional malpractice, four elements must be established:

1. A special professional relationship (i.e., service in exchange for a fee) had to exist between the client/plaintiff and the therapist.
2. The clinician was negligent in treating the client. Negligence involves a violation of the standard of care, defined as the treatment that a reasonable practitioner facing circumstances similar to those of the plaintiff's case would be expected to give.
3. The client suffered harm.
4. The therapist's negligence must be the cause of the harm suffered by the client.

TABLE 15.3 Major Areas of Professional Liability Claims Against Psychologists

Source of Loss	Percent of Overall Losses
Ineffective treatment/failure to consult/failure to refer	29%
Failure to diagnose/improper diagnosis	16%
Custody dispute	10%
Sexual intimacy/sexual harassment and/or sexual misconduct	9%
Breach of confidentiality	8%
Suicide	4%
Supervisory issues, conflict of interest or improper multiple relationships	3%
Libel/slander, conflicts in reporting sexual abuse, licensing dispute, no coverage applies	2%
Abandonment, premises liability, repressed memory, failure to monitor, countersuits resulting from fee disputes, client harmed others including homicide, business disputes, miscellaneous liability claims, discrimination/harassment	1% (each)
All other losses	**less than 1 percent**

Source: Adapted from Pope, K. S., & Vasquez, M. J. T. (2011). *Ethics in psychotherapy and counseling: A practical guide* (4th ed.). Hoboken, NJ: Wiley.

Estimates are that less than 2% of clinicians will ever be sued for malpractice during their professional careers. This figure has remained relatively stable for many years (Knapp, Bennett, & VandeCreek, 2012) and is much lower than for medical specialists in obstetrics, emergency medicine, surgery, or radiology (Knapp, Bennett, & VandeCreek, 2012). It used to be that the most common complaint in successful malpractice lawsuits was that the psychologist failed to prevent a client's suicide (Scott & Resnick, 2006). That picture has changed, however. The complaints now most commonly upheld in lawsuits are that the psychologist provided ineffective treatment, failed to consult with other psychologists to better serve their clients, or did not refer clients to other therapists when they were not able to provide effective services (Pope & Vasquez, 2011; see Table 15.3). This pattern underscores the need for therapists to be educated about and competent at providing the types of evidence-based practices that were discussed in Chapter 10.

Although these law suits are rare, a few large malpractice verdicts have been returned in cases in which therapists are accused of influencing clients to falsely recall allegedly *repressed memories* of physical or sexual abuse in childhood. Here is one case example:

Gary Ramona—once a highly paid executive in the California wine industry—sued family counselor Marche Isabella and psychiatrist Richard Rose for planting false memories of trauma in his daughter, Holly, when she was their 19-year-old patient. Ramona claimed that the therapists told Holly that her bulimia and depression were caused by having been repeatedly raped by him when she was a child. They also told her that the memory of this molestation was so traumatic that she had repressed it for years. According to Ramona, Dr. Rose then gave Holly sodium amytal (a so-called truth serum) to confirm her "recovered memory." Finally, Isabella was said to have told Holly's mother that up to 80% of all bulimics had been sexually abused (a statement for which there is no scientific support).

At the trial, the therapists claimed that Holly suffered flashbacks of what seemed to be real sexual abuse. She also became increasingly depressed and bulimic after reporting these frightening images. Holly's mother, Stephanie, who divorced her husband after Holly's allegations came to light, testified that she suspected her husband had abused Holly and listed several pieces of supposedly corroborating evidence. Gary Ramona denied ever sexually abusing his daughter.

Dr. Elizabeth Loftus, a leading critic of aggressive memory therapy, testified that therapists often either suggest the idea of trauma to their clients or are too uncritical in accepting the validity of trauma reports that occur spontaneously. It appeared that Holly's memory had been so distorted by her therapists that she no longer knew what the truth was.

The jury decided that Holly's therapists had planted false memories in her and, in May 1994, awarded damages to Gary Ramona in the amount of $500,000. Since then, according to the False Memory Syndrome Foundation, a group devoted to uncovering abuses associated with memory recovery therapy, several other "false memory" cases have been successfully filed against therapists.

The best way for clinical psychologists and other mental health professionals to decrease their risk of being named in a malpractice lawsuit is to act with the highest level of professional integrity and avoid violating any ethical standards or laws governing mental health treatment (Knapp 2012a, 2012b). This is exactly what the vast majority of clinicians do.

SECTION SUMMARY

The APA ethical standards set the highest expectations for integrity in the field of psychology. These standards are implemented largely through training, self-monitoring, and professional monitoring. Ethical violations that are reported to the APA largely focus on the loss of license at the state level. State boards of psychology most often administer disciplinary action against psychologists for sexual/dual relationships with clients and unprofessional practices. Legal regulations, such as the duty to warn, also are in place. Professional practice is also influenced by malpractice litigation, which arises most often over a therapist's failure to use evidence-based practices.

PROFESSIONAL INDEPENDENCE

SECTION PREVIEW

This section describes how clinical psychologists have sought the right to practice psychotherapy independently and the right to receive insurance coverage for mental health services that are comparable to that given for medical services. This process relates to the changing economics of mental health service delivery and how psychologists can earn a living. The controversy over clinicians' right to prescribe medication is also covered.

Clinical psychologists must consult and collaborate with many other professionals. They often work closely with educators, attorneys, religious leaders, social workers, nurses, physicians, and other psychologists. For the most part, psychology's interprofessional relationships are healthy, profitable, and characterized by goodwill. The most obvious sign of this harmony is the frequency of referrals made across groups.

Interprofessional relationships are not always cordial, however. As described in Chapter 2, clinical psychology's most persistent interprofessional problem has been its wary, often stormy, relationship with the medical profession. Early disputes revolved around the role of psychologists as diagnosticians and treatment providers. More recently, the squabbles have concentrated on psychologists' eligibility for reimbursement under prepaid mental health plans and on psychologists' obtaining privileges to prescribe medication for their clients. Although these controversies are related, we look at them in separate sections that clarify the development of each.

The Economics of Mental Health Care

Having won the battles over licensure and recognition of psychology as an independent profession in the 1970s and 1980s, clinicians turned to struggles involving the economic aspects of mental health care that existed back then. The initial focus of these struggles was whether psychologists should be eligible for insurance reimbursement for their services. Psychologists began lobbying state legislatures to pass *freedom-of-choice* laws, which mandate that services rendered by qualified mental health professionals licensed to practice in a given state shall be reimbursed by insurance plans covering such services regardless of whether the provider is a physician. By 1983, 40 states covering 90% of the U.S. population had passed freedom-of-choice legislation so that licensed psychologists were reimbursable providers of mental health services (Lambert, 1985). Additional legislation at the federal level promoted recognition of psychologists as independent clinicians. The Rehabilitation Act of 1973 (PL 93-112) provided *parity* (i.e., equal coverage) for psychologists and physicians alike in both assessment and treatment services. In 1996, the Mental Health Parity Act was established as a federal law in order to prevent insurance companies from providing lesser coverage for mental health as opposed to physical health services (Munsey, 2007a).

Although that law was a step in the right direction, there were a number of limits to parity for mental health services. Accordingly, after 12 more years of discussions by policy makers, health care administrators, psychologists, and other mental health professionals, Congress approved legislation called the *Paul Wellstone and Pete Domenici Mental Health Parity and Addiction Equity Act* (more commonly known as the Mental Health Parity Act). Signed into law in 2008, this act took effect in October of 2009 (McConnell et al., 2012) and required insurance companies to provide the same coverage for mental health disorders as they do for physical illnesses (Fritz & Kennedy, 2012). It was the Mental Health Parity Act that finally allowed psychologists and other mental health providers to gain professional independence through economic reimbursement equality.

Parity for mental health services applies to all insurance companies and third-party payers, including those that offer *managed care programs* (Gasquoine, 2010). Managed care systems were developed as a method of allocating health services to a group of people in order to provide the most appropriate care while still containing the overall cost of these services. Managed care can be organized in several different ways, including, for example, as employee assistance programs (EAPs), health maintenance organizations (HMOs), preferred provider organizations (PPOs), integrated delivery systems (IDSs), and independent practice associations (IPAs). In general, these organizations provide specific packages of health care services to subscribers for a fixed, prepaid price.

Although the Mental Health Parity Act applies to all these programs, it does not allow payment for unlimited mental health services, or services offered by just any licensed professional. So insurance companies and managed care systems have established *insurance panels*, which are lists of professionals who have been approved to provide services for reimbursement (Goodheart, 2010). In addition, as with medical procedures, mental health services still require *utilization reviews* for both privately and publicly funded systems (Clay, 2011c). Thus, like medical doctors, most therapists still have to follow certain procedures (e.g., only a certain number of therapy sessions are preapproved for the cognitive-behavioral treatment of depression) or request preapproval to deliver some services. Often the approval for these services is based on their effectiveness, so as mentioned in Chapter 10, utilization reviews constitute yet another reason that many mental health providers are focused on learning evidence-based practices.

We see a number of trends in the future of mental health services, including increased use of self-help interventions with clients; the offering of mental health services within easily accessible locations, such as schools, medical clinics, day care centers, and workplaces; expansion of service delivery options such as those made possible by cell phones, tablets, and other personal Internet devices, and public health campaigns; and an increased focus on the improvement of quality of services (Clarke, Lynch, Spofford, & DeBar, 2006). Some observers speculate that the increased focus on providing mental health services in primary care facilities may lead to a greater integration of medical and psychological practice in the future (Clay, 2011a). In addition, there may be a renewed focus on *recovery* (where clients' long-term productivity and personal growth is the goal) rather than merely on the reduction of psychological symptoms (Clay, 2011a).

Independent Practice and the Future of the Profession

It used to be the case that clinical psychologists could finish graduate training, get a license, and open a private practice ("hang out a shingle") with realistic expectations of a six-figure income early in their careers. Sorry, but those days are long gone (Walfish & Barnett, 2009). As discussed in Chapter 1 and shown in Table 1.2, the median income of doctoral-level psychologists in individual private practices with 20–24 years' experience is $89,000, which is notably lower than the median ($104,000) for psychologists in VA Medical Centers with comparable experience. At the low end of the spectrum, doctoral-level clinical psychologists who worked at University Student Counseling Centers with comparable years of experience reported a median salary of $63,500. For the sake of comparison, but not shown in Table 1.2, note that the median salary for full professors

in doctoral departments of psychology with comparable experience was $116,901 (http://www
.apa.org/workforce/publications/11-fac-sal/table-04.pdf). To be sure, all of these salaries provide
a reasonable lifestyle, but our point is that entering into private practice no longer guarantees the
highest salaries within the profession of clinical psychology.

So how do independent practitioners survive these days, and can they continue to do so? A
book called, *Financial Success in Mental Health Practice: Essential Tools and Strategies for Practitioners* (Walfish & Barnett, 2009) describes the following three models of independent practice and
suggests strategies for how to develop these models and make them flourish.

- Solo practice—The clinician owns the entire practice and is responsible for everything,
including renting and decorating office space, purchasing assessment instruments, advertising, billing, and the like;
- Group practice—Two or more clinicians join forces and offer services together, usually sharing the costs of the office, office staff, equipment, and the like. Large group practices often
hire associates, who either work for a set salary or who receive a percentage of the income
they generate from their clients;
- Mixed-model practice—Two or more clinicians work together, as in a group practice, but
they are legally and financially independent. For example, one clinician may simply rent
space in the offices of another clinician.

Deciding which of these models of independent practice is best requires clinicians to consider where their strengths and passions lie. Do they prefer to conduct assessments with young
children, provide preventive interventions for at-risk youth, help couples work through separation
and divorce, deal with adult eating disorders, help the elderly with end-of-life issues, or what?
Which practice model will best allow the clinicians to pursue these interests? The clinician must
also remember that independent practices are small businesses, so in addition to considering
what they are good at and what they enjoy doing, psychologists must also consider whether there
is a market for their services and if so, how to capitalize on being part of that market (Walfish
& Barnett, 2009). Reimbursement rates for clinical services vary widely—depending on whether
the fees are coming from public health care programs (such as Medicare or Medicaid) or private
insurance companies and managed care programs (such as Blue Cross/Blue Shield or Humana).
These rates also depend on geographic region (Gasquoine, 2010), so psychologists must consider
the financial feasibility of opening a practice in their area of specialty and in their location.

Fortunately, as noted in Chapter 1 and on the U.S. Bureau of Labor Statistics website (www
.bls.gov/ooh/life-physical-and-social-science/psychologists.htm), employment rates for psychologists are expected to grow by about 22% between now and 2020. This is a faster rate of expansion
than for many other professions, and it includes psychologists in independent practice.

Prescription Privileges

As some aspects of medical and psychological practices have become more integrated, clinical
psychologists and the medical profession remain at odds over the *prescription privileges* movement.
This movement would allow specially trained clinical psychologists to prescribe psychotropic
medication as well as offer psychotherapy.

Why should clinical psychologists have this *prescriptive authority?* Advocates of that authority point to several reasons. For one thing, surveys indicate that 98% of psychologists have
referred a client to a psychiatrist or physician for psychotropic medication; 75% of psychologists
make such referrals on a monthly basis; and approximately one out of three clients of psychologists is taking psychotropic medication (Meyers, 2006). Thus, medication already is a frequent
consideration in many clinical psychologists' practice. In addition, the knowledge necessary to
competently and safely prescribe medication can apparently be learned in a relatively brief period
and without a full medical education. Finally, many psychologists are worried about clients'
inability to gain access to psychiatrists and qualified primary care physicians, especially in rural
or other geographically isolated regions. In 1996, the APA Council of Representatives voted in
support of seeking prescriptive authority for clinical psychologists. An APA Ad Hoc Task Force
on Psychopharmacology suggested that most of the training necessary for obtaining prescription
privileges could be conducted at the postdoctoral level. The Council also recommended model
legislation to be introduced in states where psychologists are seeking prescriptive authority, as
well as a model postdoctoral curriculum (covering neurosciences, pharmacology, physiology,

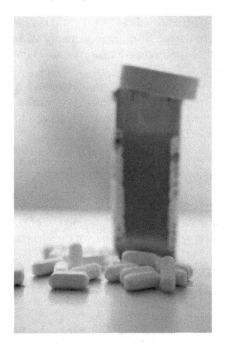

There are mixed opinions as to whether clinical psychologists should seek prescription privileges.   *Source*: Plush Studios/Photodisc/Getty Images.

physical and laboratory assessments, and clinical pharmacotherapeutics) to be used in training prescribers (McGrath, 2010).

The medical profession is not the only faction opposed to these plans. The idea of psychologists prescribing drugs is a controversial one within psychology, too. Although many psychologists support prescription privileges for properly trained clinicians (McGrath & Sammons, 2011), others are worried that existing training for this activity might not be adequate (see Figure 15.1). In particular, they say that training psychologists to prescribe medication could become a health hazard, largely because of inadequate training of psychologists in the medical and physical sciences (see McGrath, 2010). Some argue that psychologists who want to prescribe medication should complete formal medical training, such as obtaining training as a nurse psychologist.

Others are concerned that prescription privileges would lead to an increasingly intense focus on the medical and biomedical aspects of behavior, behavior disorder, and treatment, with a consequent loss of clinical psychology's traditional focus on important psychosocial, environmental,

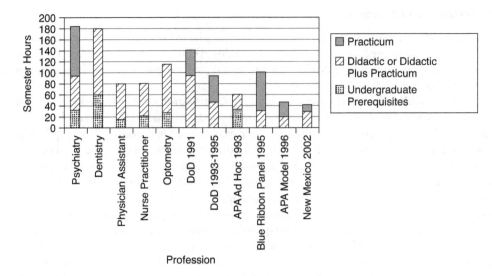

FIGURE 15.1   Comparison of Semester Hour Medical Training by Professions with Prescriptive Authority in all or Most States and Proposal for Medical Training for Psychologists in Order to Obtain Such Authority.   *Source:* Heiby, E. M., DeLeon, P. H., & Anderson, T. (2004). A debate on prescription privileges for psychologists. *Professional Psychology: Research and Practice, 35*(4), 336–344.

cognitive, and behavioral factors in explaining and treating disorders (Levine & Schmelkin, 2006). They say that "if you give someone a hammer, then everything looks like a nail," meaning that if psychologists have prescriptive authority, then every client's problems might seem to require drug treatment rather than psychotherapy.

As of this writing, New Mexico and Louisiana are the only states to have passed laws allowing clinical psychologists to prescribe medications after proper training (Resnick, Ax, Fagan, & Nussbaum, 2012). Prescriptive authority is also allowed for psychologists in the territory of Guam, in the military, and in the Indian Health Service (American Psychological Association, 2011b). Legislators in Hawaii and Oregon passed bills that would allow prescriptive authority for psychologists, but these bills were vetoed and are no longer being considered. So no states have approved prescriptive authority for psychologists since 2004 (Resnick, Ax, Fagan, & Nussbaum, 2012).

Would clinical psychologists in other states apply for prescriptive authority if it were available? The answer is unclear. One survey suggests that clinical interns and training directors who favor prescriptive authority would seek prescriptive authority (Fagan et al., 2004), but another found that only 5% of nurse psychologists chose to seek prescriptive authority and were actually prescribing medications (Wiggins & Wedding, 2004). This same pattern appears to be playing out in New Mexico and Louisiana, where psychologists are eligible for prescriptive authority, but where very few psychologists are seeking the training necessary to attain it (Munsey, 2008). Whether or not prescriptive privileges are gained by psychologists throughout the United States, most professionals agree that psychologists should proceed cautiously as they consider this important option in their training and practice.

SECTION SUMMARY

The field of clinical psychology has gained the right for coverage of mental health services that is comparable to coverage of medical services; psychologists also now have the right to be reimbursed for services through managed care companies. Although independent practice has changed over the years, it remains a viable and expanding professional option. Current battles over prescriptive authority will likely continue into the future, but even when psychologists are given the opportunity to seek advanced training for prescriptive authority, very few do so.

PROFESSIONAL MULTICULTURAL COMPETENCE

SECTION PREVIEW

Clinicians are becoming increasingly aware of how race, ethnicity, gender, sexual orientation, and many other aspects of human diversity can influence clinical practice and outcomes. This section reviews attempts to enhance clinicians' multicultural competence.

As mentioned in Chapter 1, "What Is Clinical Psychology?," the population of the United States is more diverse than ever, and becoming more so. European Americans are still in the majority (63.7%), but other racial/ethnic groups have increased over the past decade. Individuals from a Hispanic/Latino/Latina background represent 16.3% of the population, African Americans represent 12.2%, Asian Americans represent 4.7%, and others (such as Native American Indians, multiracial individuals, and individuals from other racial/ethnic backgrounds) represent 3.1% (Humes, Jones, & Ramirez, 2011). It is expected that half of the U.S. population will be from minority backgrounds by 2050. The field of clinical psychology is responding to these changes in several ways.

One involves attempts to increase diversity within the ranks of professionals. Consider gender; clinical psychology was once a male-dominated profession, but it is less so now. The percentage of women in APA Division 12 (Society for Clinical Psychology) has increased over the last 40 years to reach approximately 32% (see Figure 15.2). Of those under 50 years of age, about 50% of Division 12 members are women (Norcross & Karpiak, 2012). The number of women entering clinical psychology graduate training has increased even more dramatically; over 70% of doctoral degrees in psychology are earned by women.

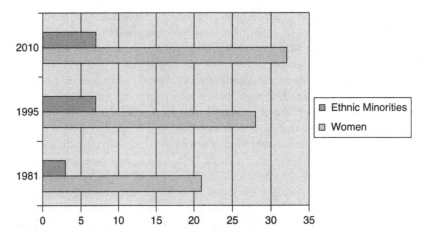

FIGURE 15.2   Percentage of Women and Ethnic Minority Members of APA Division 12 (Society for Clinical Psychology) by Year.   *Source:* Norcross, J. C., & Karpiak, C. P. (2012). Clinical psychologists in the 2010s: 50 years of the APA Division of Clinical Psychology. *Clinical Psychology: Science and Practice, 19*, 1–12.

In terms of ethnic diversity, the field of clinical psychology remains dominated by European Americans (Singh & Dutta, 2010). As can be seen in Figure 15.2, the number of clinicians in Division 12 who are members of racial/ethnic minorities has increased, but it remains relatively low, having grown from 3% in 1981 to about 9% in 2010. However, about 28% of first-year graduate students in psychology are now non-White (Norcross & Karpiak, 2012). This figure is likely to increase further, though, as graduate training programs in clinical psychology continue their efforts to recruit, train, and retain students from diverse backgrounds (Hough & Squires, 2012).

Regardless of their own gender or ethnicity, practicing clinicians are being encouraged to increase their awareness of racial/ethnic/cultural differences and to improve their skills in working with diverse client populations. As we have suggested in previous chapters, growing evidence indicates that psychological treatments and assessments sometimes must be altered in order to be most effective for clients from particular racial/ethnic minority groups (Castro, Barrera, & Steiker, 2010). Clinical training programs are recognizing the need to train graduate students to deal competently with issues of diversity and multiculturalism. There is also a growing awareness that diversity does not begin and end with gender and race/ethnicity. Clinicians are paying increasing attention to adjusting clinical practice to meet the needs of clients who are poor (David & Messer, 2011), who are from various religious and spiritual backgrounds (Saunders, Miller, & Bright, 2010), who are from countries other than the United States (Swierc & Routh, 2003), and who have physical challenges (Williams & Abeles, 2004). Psychologists also need to be sensitive to their clients' sexual orientation (Biaggio, Orchard, Larson, Petrino, & Mihara, 2003) and to develop competence in working with same-sex couples, for example (Riggle & Rostosky, 2005). There is growing awareness of the needs of transgendered clients as well (Mizock & Fleming, 2011). Concern about all of these issues, and the need for training in diversity, led to the development of the APA's *Multicultural Guidelines: Education, Research, and Practice* (American Psychological Association, 2003). The guidelines are as follows:

1. Psychologists are encouraged to recognize that, as cultural beings, they may hold attitudes and beliefs that can detrimentally influence their perceptions of and interactions with individuals who are ethnically and racially different from themselves.
2. Psychologists are encouraged to recognize the importance of multicultural sensitivity/responsiveness to, knowledge of, and understanding about ethnically and racially different individuals.
3. As educators, psychologists are encouraged to employ the constructs of multiculturalism and diversity in psychological education.
4. Culturally sensitive psychological researchers are encouraged to recognize the importance of conducting culture-centered and ethical psychological research among persons from ethnic, linguistic, and racial minority backgrounds.

5. Psychologists are encouraged to apply culturally appropriate skills in clinical and other applied psychological practices.
6. Psychologists are encouraged to use organizational change processes to support culturally informed organizational (policy) development and practices.

Many of these guidelines can be conceptualized by the construct of *openness to the other*, which reflects individuals' ability to remain open to ideas, concepts, thoughts, feelings, and perspectives of others who are different from themselves (Fowers & Davido, 2006). It is all part of efforts in the field of clinical psychology to improve the educational, research, and practice standards of psychologists with attention toward multicultural competence.

Cultural competence makes sense from an ethical and sociopolitical standpoint, and it also helps increase the effectiveness of therapy with clients from diverse backgrounds. A meta-analysis of 65 studies comparing culturally adapted therapy with standard therapy found that culturally adapted therapy was significantly more helpful for clients who are members of minority groups (Smith, Rodriguez, & Bernal, 2011). For example, therapists who used cultural metaphors and culturally consistent expressions were more likely than other therapists to be helpful to their clients. This finding led to the suggestion that clients be allowed to use their preferred language in therapy whenever possible (Smith, Rodriguez, & Bernal, 2011). Of course, not all clients from diverse backgrounds require culturally adapted treatment, especially those who are fully acculturated into the predominant society (Schwartz, Unger, Zamboanga, & Szapocznik, 2010). But understanding and following guidelines for multicultural competence are still a part of the culturally competent clinician's services. Here is a case example:

A Case Study of Culturally Competent Therapy

A client we shall call "Mr. Alvarez" was a 45-year-old Mexican American living in a large Midwestern city with his wife and three children. He was the first in his family to be born in the United States and he was also the first one to graduate from college. He went on to earn a masters in engineering and worked for an auto company for 23 years until he was laid off. For about 9 months, he had been "moping around the house," increasingly withdrawn from family and friends, feeling fatigued, and having a hard time sleeping. At the encouragement of his wife, and thinking he was physically ill, he made an appointment to be evaluated by his primary care physician. The physician diagnosed him with depression and referred him to a psychotherapist.

Although Mr. Alvarez did not agree that he was depressed, he called the therapist to arrange for an appointment. During that initial phone call, the therapist sensed his reluctance about therapy and thus did not probe deeply about any problems. The therapist did ask Mr. Alvarez if he spoke Spanish, at which point Mr. Alvarez shared his sorrow over the fact that his children did not wish to speak his native tongue, even though he tried to speak with them equally in English and Spanish.

During the first treatment session, the therapist ascertained that Mr. Alvarez was equally committed to both the Mexican and the American cultures—including enjoying the food, music, entertainment, and family activities of each. He spoke about the importance of respect and for "doing for the family." The therapist further ascertained that Mr. Alvarez was experiencing major depression in the severe range and anxiety in the moderate range. His thoughts about himself (such as "A good man is a provider—I am not a provider," "I have let my family down—I am useless") were consistent with negative thoughts associated with depression. Mr. Alvarez also had many strengths on which to build, including that he was bright, connected to his family, and motivated to improve. Given Mr. Alvarez's clinical and cultural presentation, the therapist chose to use Beck's cognitive therapy, an evidence-based treatment for major depression, but to modify the treatment to incorporate cultural values that were consistent with Mr. Alvarez's belief system.

Specifically, the therapist chose to focus on three values that are consistent with the Latino culture and that were also meaningful to Mr. Alvarez: *familismo* (the importance of family), *personalismo*, (valuing trust and warmth in interpersonal relationships), and *respeto* (showing genuine respect). At the outset of therapy, the therapist wanted to infuse these cultural values into his work with Mr. Alvarez, so upon greeting him in the lobby for the first appointment, the therapist spoke in Spanish to show personal contact with Mr. Alvarez and he used more formal language (e.g., saying "usted" rather than "tu") to show respect. Once in the consulting room, the therapist honored Mr. Alvarez's family connections by allowing him to discuss the family at length rather than immediately asking for a detailed account of symptoms. Throughout the first session, the therapist showed respect for Mr. Alvarez by asking his permission to address certain topics. For example, the therapist said "May we talk about the 'down' or perhaps depressed feeling that you have been experiencing?" At the end of the first session, the therapist believed that Mr. Alvarez had engaged well with the therapy and that he was committed to working with this therapist.

Treatment lasted 12 sessions, during which time the therapist worked in a culturally competent manner in order to help Mr. Alvarez decrease his negative cognitions ("unhelpful thoughts"), increase his positive experiences, and to help him become reengaged with his family and friends. Although family members are not usually included in CBT treatments with adults, the therapist suggested that Mr. Alvarez invite his wife to treatment in order to further make the connections to the family. She was able to engage in therapy quite successfully and much to her husband's benefit. By the end of treatment, Mr. Alvarez reported almost no depressive symptoms and he showed higher levels of energy than previously. Six months after the final session, Mr. Alvarez called the therapist to report that he had found a new job in the automobile industry and that he felt proud and satisfied at his new accomplishments—largely because the new job meant that he could provide for his family once more. This case shows how evidence-based treatments can be infused with culturally competent practices in order to maximize the therapeutic benefits to the client.

Source: Adapted from Gonzalez-Prendes, A. A., Hindo, C., & Pardo, Y. (2011). Cultural values integration in cognitive-behavioral therapy for a Latino with depression. *Clinical Case Studies, 10,* 376–394.

SECTION SUMMARY

The field of clinical psychology is still not as racially or ethnically diverse as it should be, and efforts are underway to correct this problem. Attention has also been focused in recent years on increasing multicultural competence in training, clinical work, and research, but much more needs to be done. Although much of the work on multicultural competence deals with racial/ethnic diversity, attention is also being paid to other types of diversity, such as sexual orientation, religious background, physical abilities, and country of origin.

THE FUTURE OF CLINICAL PSYCHOLOGY

SECTION PREVIEW

This section highlights a number of trends that we think will occur in the not-too-distant future. Included in this discussion are training, positive psychology, technological advances, dissemination of effective clinical methodology, interdisciplinary science, and outreach to the national and international communities.

We have already discussed some future directions in clinical psychology, such as its increased emphasis on evidence-based practice, the possibility of prescriptive authority for psychologists, and the increasing emphasis on multicultural competence in teaching, research, and practice, but there are other changes on the horizon, too. Let's consider a few of the most important.

Training

Controversy will likely continue over the question of how clinical psychologists should be trained. Differences in the philosophy and training agendas of doctoral training programs based on the clinical scientist, scientist–practitioner, and practitioner–scholar models show no signs of rapid resolution. We expect that some disconnect between PhD and PsyD training programs will continue, but we hope that this gap will close somewhat as programs focus on what is in the best interests of their students and the public in general. In order to do this, and to allow their students to be competitive in the job market, all training programs will need to focus on evidence-based practices (Sturmey, 2012b; Sturmey & Hersen, 2012a), multicultural competence (Castro, Barrera, & Steiker, 2010), and the establishment of competence in practice, teaching, and research (Fauod et al., 2009). McFall (2006) argued that clinical psychology training programs must not allow themselves to become narrowly focused vocational schools, but rather that they need to train students to have a variety of empirical skills that can be applied in a variety of settings. As already noted, the greatest training challenge today relates to the internship crisis, which many professionals are working to solve (Grus, McCutcheon, & Berry, 2011).

Positive Psychology

The *positive psychology* movement, which focuses on understanding and promoting personal growth and human potential, will play an increasingly important role in clinical psychology (McNulty & Fincham, 2012; Wood & Tarrier, 2010). It will appear in research on (a) *posttraumatic growth*, which refers to personal growth that sometimes follows a traumatic event or is associated with surviving a major illness such as HIV/AIDS or cancer (Sawyer, Ayers, & Field, 2010), (b) *resilience* (i.e., the ability to adapt to and overcome challenges such as poverty, racism, abuse; Rutter, 2012), and (c) preventing psychological problems before they occur, especially through social and environmental changes (Biglan, Flay, Embry, & Sandler, 2012; Biswas-Diener, 2011; Munoz, Beardselee, & Leykin, 2012; Yoshikawa, Aber, & Beardslee, 2012). Personal characteristics such as optimism (Carver, Scheier, & Segerstrom, 2010) and gratitude (Wood, Froh, & Geraghty, 2010) are of increasing interest to researchers seeking to understand individuals' well-being. Other aspects of the positive psychology movement will be seen in efforts to decrease the stigma that is still sometimes associated with receiving mental health services (Hinshaw, 2007). The recent focus on recovery, which seeks to improve clients' well-being rather than just decreasing their symptoms is also consistent with the focus on positive psychology.

Technology

As in all other areas of twenty-first century culture, technology will play an increasing role in clinical training, research, and practice. For example, more undergraduate clinical psychology courses will be offered online (Bachman & Stewart, 2011). Although there are currently prohibitions against APA-accredited programs being taught solely online, significant components of graduate training will be provided through distance learning technology (Murphy, Levant, Hall, & Glueckauf, 2007).

Similarly, clinicians will continue to make use of telephones, computers, the Internet, blogs, videoconferencing, smart phones and other hand-held devices, in the delivery of mental health services. Often referred to as *telehealth* or *e-health*, providing services via telephone or the Internet can be especially helpful for individuals in rural areas or other remote locations (Eonta et al., 2011). Technological innovation such as virtual reality–assisted treatments, computer-based assessment, and neuroimaging also expand the possibilities of clinical services. So far, research suggests that enhancing evidence-based practices with new technologies can increase the effectiveness of these practices (Clough & Casey, 2011; Harwood et al., 2011). Given the changing landscape of these new technologies, the field is scrambling to ensure that psychologists continue to use them in accordance with ethical practice. Formal guidelines for the practice of telepsychology are currently under discussion (DeAngelis, 2012).

Dissemination

At various points throughout this book, we have emphasized the importance of mental health literacy—public understanding about mental health issues (Jorm, 2012). Perhaps the most important way to promote this literacy is to have clinicians and clinical researchers communicate with the public more often and more clearly. Known as *dissemination*, the sharing of information with other professionals and with the public is an important aspect of conducting research—especially outcome studies of psychological treatments.

Sommer (2006) argued that researchers should write two parallel papers when they have made important findings—a scholarly article for their colleagues that could be published in a professional journal and an article for the general public that could be published in a popular magazine. A number of APA presidents have encouraged the field to make psychology more accessible to the general public and to "make psychology a household word" (Levant, 2006). In an innovative special series of articles published in *Behavior Therapy*, Santucci, McHugh, and Barlow (2012) argued that we should develop direct-to-consumer marketing plans to share knowledge of evidence-based treatments with consumers and potential clients. It appears that these trends to increase mental health literacy are gaining momentum and will continue in the future. We hope so; scholarly findings can be applied to the larger population more quickly if the points of dissemination are both at the professional and the public levels (Kazdin & Rabbitt, 2013).

Interdisciplinary Science and Practice

A colleague of ours likes to compare the current bickering in the field of psychology (e.g., which training model is best, what "evidence" should be used to support evidence-based practices) with the bickering that blacksmiths must have had in the days just before automobiles came on the scene (e.g., about what size and shape and metal makes the best horseshoe). The point is that clinical psychology is only a small part of the scholarly world that is exploring ways to understand human behavior and that if we do not change with the times, we will go the way of the blacksmiths.

We predict that clinical psychology will become more integrated with other disciplines, such as genomics, genetics, behavioral genetics, social neuroscience, cognitive-affective neuroscience, developmental neuroscience, comparative psychology (studies of nonhuman animals), and other science, technology, engineering, and math (STEM) disciplines (Cacioppo et al., 2007; Price, 2011). For example, a diverse group of scientists, including psychologists, has found that humans and nonhuman primates have what are known as *mirror neurons*, which facilitate learning by watching others and which underlie the expression of empathy, affiliation, and other social behaviors (De Waal, 2012; Winerman, 2005). Mirror neuron systems are being explored in relation to a number of different types of psychopathology, including autistic spectrum disorder and other pervasive developmental disorders (Oberman & Ramachandran, 2007; Werner, Cermak, & Aziz-Zadeh, 2012).

These types of interdisciplinary research projects will likely lead to other discoveries that any discipline alone might not discover. For this and other reasons, federal funding is increasingly supportive of *translational research*, in which the basic sciences are "translated" into applied practices. Increasingly, multidisciplinary teamwork is the only way to conduct research on certain topics.

Like these patterns in interdisciplinary science, there are also growing patterns of interdisciplinary practice—in which clinical psychologists work in conjunction with counseling psychologists, school psychologists, social workers, psychiatrists, educators, primary care physicians, the clergy, and other professionals. Given the complexity of human behavior, it makes a lot of sense for clinical psychologists to reach out to other professions in order to maximize their ability to help clients reach their fullest potential (Bray, 2011).

Outreach to the National and International Communities

There are a great many people in the United States and around the world who need mental health services but do not receive them (Wang et al., 2007). Among many underserved populations are the chronically mentally ill, people in rural areas, substance abusers, and older patients, but the largest *disparities* between those who do and do not receive needed services are seen in ethnic minority groups (Wang et al., 2007). Clinical researchers and practitioners are interested in decreasing these disparities and in increasing access to quality mental health care for everyone. In the United States, NIMH has directed training grant funds toward these "underserved groups" and therefore, services to these groups will probably continue to increase.

Increased attention is also being focused on another underserved population—veterans and military personnel (Gates et al., 2012). Efforts are being made to increase troops' resiliency before they are deployed to combat zones (Casey, 2011), to increase utilization of mental health services for those who need them when they return (Maguen et al., 2010), and to reduce the stigma that some veterans still associate with receiving mental health services (Bryan & Morrow, 2011). These efforts are vital because rates of PTSD are quite high in active-duty, postdeployment, and retired members of the military, and mental health service utilization is often quite low (Bryan & Morrow, 2011; Gates et al., 2012). Consistent with the focus on telehealth, a multimedia wellness program (afterdeployment.org) has been developed for soldiers returning from combat (Bush, Bosmajian, Fairall, McCann, & Ciulla, 2011). All of these efforts are being put into place in hopes of improving the psychological well-being of those in the military.

There is also a great deal of interest in helping individuals and communities in other countries, including by working to reduce human trafficking (Clay, 2011b), engaging in human rights causes (Willyard, 2010), addressing the needs of refugee populations (Kaczorowski et al., 2011), helping to combat global climate change (Swim et al., 2011), and working toward world peace (Chrisite, Tint, Wagner, & Winter, 2008). As the need for these efforts continues to increase, clinical psychologists of the future are increasingly likely to participate in them.

A Final Word

Obviously, clinical psychologists are committed to finding new ways to help people—including through prevention programs and focusing on recovery and personal growth rather than just symptom reduction. As the world has become more interconnected and interdependent, especially given recent technological advances, so too has the field of clinical psychology become more responsive to the world around it. These trends are likely to continue into the foreseeable future. There are a great many talented and dedicated individuals within clinical psychology who sincerely wish to help others and to make a difference. For that reason, we have a great deal of hope for the future of clinical psychology. We hope that this book might play a role in moving you to join in the creation of that future.

SECTION SUMMARY

Clinicians have debated how best to train new clinical psychologists in evidence-based practices, and those debates will continue. Clinicians will become more aware of the growing influence of positive psychology and of technological advances such as online teaching, technologically enhanced delivery of services, and computer-assisted assessment and treatment. To improve mental health literacy in the public (and help ensure a receptive market), clinicians of the future will have to do a better job of dissemination—providing the public with usable information about evidence-based treatments and mental health services. Clinical scientists of the future will need to work with scientists in fields such as biology, genetics, genomics, and other neurosciences. Likewise, clinicians will need to get involved in more collaborative, interdisciplinary practice in order to work in the best interests of their clients.

Chapter Summary

Many professional issues are of prime importance as clinical psychology continues to develop its scientific and professional identity in the twenty-first century. These include training, regulation, ethics, independence, and the need for multicultural competence.

Since the late 1940s, clinical training programs have typically followed some version of the Boulder model, a scientist–practitioner curriculum that emphasizes psychology's scientific foundation more than the development of clinical service skills. Several training conferences since that time have reaffirmed the Boulder model, but training models that emphasize professional skills are also available now. Many of these are Doctor of Psychology (PsyD) programs and practice-oriented PhD programs offered in psychology departments or in freestanding schools of professional psychology. There is also growing interest in programs that are strongly research oriented, and a new accreditation system, the Psychological Clinical Science Accreditation System (PCSAS), now exists to highlight programs that have rigorous research training in conjunction with clinical training. All these training models are being affected by an internship crisis brought about because there are too many applicants for the internships available.

Professional regulation of clinical psychologists comes in several forms, including (a) laws that establish criteria for who may use the title of "psychologist" (certification laws) and perform psychological services (licensing laws), (b) laws establishing therapists' duty to warn, and (c) lawsuits alleging clinical malpractice. In 2010, APA developed a model legislative act to try to standardize licensure across the nation, but for it to have a major impact, all or most states will have to adopt its recommendations.

The code of ethics in psychology is unique because it was developed on the basis of psychologists' experiences with real ethical dilemmas. The current version, called *Ethical Principles of Psychologists and Code of Conduct,* includes a Preamble, General Principles, and a large number of Ethical Standards covering a wide range of specific topics, from advertising services and testing to rules about confidentiality and sexual contact with clients.

The struggle of clinical psychology to gain and retain its status as a profession that is authorized to offer independent services has been long, difficult, and continuing. It first involved the right of clinicians to offer psychotherapy. Later, the issue was whether clinical psychologists could practice independently in hospitals and whether psychologists should be eligible for reimbursement under various public, private, and prepaid mental health insurance plans. The Mental Health Parity Act of 2009 laid many of these issues to rest since mental health services are now covered in the same manner as physical health services. There is growing interest in psychologists gaining prescriptive authority, but there are pros and cons to this venture.

Today, the field of clinical psychology has a greater commitment to understanding diversity, and there is a strong emphasis on developing multicultural competence. The field confronts the formidable challenge of shaping its training programs and service functions to meet needs of diverse client populations.

Study Questions

1. Discuss the different national conferences that led to changes in the training of clinical psychologists, and delineate how these conferences changed the focus of training.
2. What are the differences in terms of qualifications and ultimate outcomes of students who enter PhD versus PsyD programs? What variables are important to consider in the heterogeneity of PsyD programs?
3. List the three primary models of training in clinical psychology currently. Discuss the pros and cons of these models.
4. What is the purpose of licensure, and how is licensure usually obtained?
5. What is an ABPP diploma, and why might it be important in the field of clinical psychology?
6. List four ethical principles and discuss their importance.

7. How are ethical violations dealt with when they arise?
8. What is duty to warn, and what is the case most associated with it?
9. What are the most common reasons for malpractice litigation against clinical psychologists?
10. What does parity mean and how has it changed the landscape of mental health services in recent years?
11. What types of independent practices are common these days?
12. What are the pros and cons of gaining prescriptive authority for clinical psychologists?
13. Provide a rationale for why clinical psychology should be concerned about multicultural competence.
14. Of the primary points we discussed for the future of psychology, which do you think are the most promising for the enhancement of mental health of individuals around the world?

Web Sites

- The Academy of Psychological Clinical Science (APCS): http://www.acadpsychclinicalscience.org/
- Association of Psychology Postdoctoral and Internships Centers (APPIC): http://appic.org/
- APA Ethical Principles: http://www.apa.org/ethics/
- APA Division 42, Psychologists in Independent Practice: http://www.division42.org
- APA Division 55, American Society for the Advancement of Pharmacotherapy (ASAP): http://www.Division55.org
- American Board of Professional Psychology (ABPP): http://www.abpp.org
- Association of State and Provincial Psychology Boards: http://www.asppb.org/
- National Register of Health Service Providers in Psychology: http://www.nationalregister.org/

MOVIES

Prince of Tides (1991). Gripping drama where a therapist helps deal with her suicidal client's past by getting the client's brother involved in treatment (although an unethical romantic relationship ensues).

The Squid and the Whale (2005): Intense family drama that shows, amongst other things, parents meeting with a guidance counselor, a therapy session with an angry adolescent, and unethical behavior between a professor and student.

MEMOIRS

Mixed: My Life in Black and White by Angela Nissel (2006; New York: Villard). With an eye toward achieving multicultural competence, there are many excellent memoirs that psychologists can read such as this one, which describes (with humor and insight) what it's like to live in a biracial world.

The Road of Lost Innocence: The True Story of a Cambodian Heroine by Somaly Mam (2008; New York: Spiegel and Grau). Given the globalization of clinical psychology, it is important for clinical psychologists to learn about issues around the world, such as the human trafficking and child sexual slavery described in this poignant and ultimately uplifting memoir.

References

American Psychological Association. (2003). Guidelines on multicultural education, training, research, practice, and organizational change for psychologists. *American Psychologist, 58*, 377–402.

American Psychological Association. (2007). Guidelines for psychological practice with girls and women. *American Psychologist, 62*, 949–979.

American Psychological Association. (2009). *Guidelines and principles for accreditation of programs in professional psychology*. Washington, DC: Author.

American Psychological Association. (2010a). Amendments to the 2002 Ethical principles of psychologists and code of conduct. *American Psychologist, 65*, 493.

American Psychological Association. (2010b). *Ethical principles of psychologists and code of conduct.* Washington, DC: Author.

American Psychological Association. (2011a). Accredited doctoral programs in professional psychology: 2011. *American Psychologist, 66,* 8834–8898.

American Psychological Association. (2011b). Practice guidelines regarding psychologists' involvement in pharmacological issues. *American Psychologist, 66,* 835–849.

American Psychological Association. (2012a). Guidelines for assessment of and intervention with persons with disabilities. *American Psychologist, 67,* 43–62.

American Psychological Association. (2012b). Guidelines for psychological practice with lesbian, gay, and bisexual clients. *American Psychologist, 67,* 10–42.

American Psychological Association. (2012c). Supplement to listing of accredited doctoral, internship, and postdoctoral training programs in professional psychology. *American Psychologist, 67,* 418–420.

American Psychological Association. (2013). Guidelines for Psychological Practice in Health Care Delivery Systems. *American Psychologist, 68,* 1–6.

Bachman, C. M., & Stewart, C. (2011). Self-determination theory and web-enhanced course template development. *Teaching of Psychology, 38,* 180–188.

Baker, T. B., McFall, R. M., & Shoham, V. (2009). Current status and future prospects of clinical psychology: Toward a scientifically principled approach to mental and behavioral health care. *Psychological Science in the Public Interest, 9,* 67–89.

Barnett, J. E., & Johnson, W. B. (2008). *Ethics desk reference for psychologists.* Washington, DC: American Psychological Association.

Belar, C. D. (2000). Scientist-practitioner =/= science + practice: Boulder is bolder. *American Psychologist, 55,* 249–250.

Benjamin, L. T. (2005). A history of clinical psychology as a profession in America (and a glimpse at the future). *Annual Review of Clinical Psychology, 1,* 1–30.

Biaggio, M., Orchard, S., Larson, J., Petrino, K., & Mihara, R. (2003). Guidelines for gay/lesbian/ bisexual-affirmative educational practices in graduate psychology programs. *Professional Psychology: Research and Practice, 34,* 548–554.

Bickman, L. (1987). Graduate education in psychology. *American Psychologist, 42,* 1041–1047.

Bieschke, K. J., Bell, D., Davis, C., Hatcher, R., Peterson, R., et al. (2011). Forests, grazing areas, water supplies, and the internship imbalance problem: Redefining the paradigm to implement effective change. *Training and Education in Professional Psychology, 5,* 123–125.

Biglan, A., Flay, B. R., Embry, D. D., & Sandler, I. N. (2012). The critical role of nurturing environments for promoting human well-being. *American Psychologist, 67,* 257–271.

Biswas-Diener, R. (Ed.). (2011). *Positive psychology as social change.* New York, NY: Springer Science.

Bray, J. H. (2011). Training for the future of psychology practice. *Training and Education in Professional Psychology, 5,* 69–72.

Bryan, C. J., & Morrow, C. E. (2011). Circumventing mental health stigma by embracing the warrior culture: Lessons learned from the defender's edge program. *Professional Psychology: Research and Practice, 42,* 16–23.

Bush, N. E., Bosmajian, C. P., Fairall, J. M., McCann, R. A., & Ciulla, R. P. (2011). afterdeployment.org: A web-based multimedia wellness resource for the postdeployment military community. *Professional Psychology: Research and Practice, 42,* 455–462.

Cacioppo, J. T., Amaral, D. G., Blanchard, J. J., Cameron, J. L., Carter, C. S., et al. (2007). Social neuroscience: Progress and implications for mental health. *Perspectives on Psychological Science, 2,* 99–123.

Campbell, L., Vasquez, M., Behnke, S., & Kinscherff, R. (2010). *APA ethics code commentary and case illustrations.* Washington, DC: American Psychological Association.

Carver, C. S., Scheier, M. F., & Segerstrom, S. C. (2010). Optimism. *Clinical Psychology Review, 30,* 879–889.

Casey, G. W. (2011). Comprehensive soldier fitness: A vision for psychological resilience in the U. S. Army. *American Psychologist, 66,* 1–3.

Castro, F. G., Barrera, M., & Steiker, L. K. H. (2010). Issues and challenges in the design of culturally adapted evidence-based interventions. *Annual Review of Clinical Psychology, 6,* 213–239.

Cherry, D. K., Messenger, L. C., & Jacoby, A. M. (2000). An examination of training model outcomes in clinical psychology programs. *Professional Psychology: Research & Practice, 31,* 562–568.

Christie, D. J., Tint, B. S., Wagner, R. V., & Winter, D. D. (2008). Peace psychology for a peaceful world. *American Psychologist, 63,* 540–552.

Clarke, G., Lynch, F., Spofford, M., & DeBar, L. (2006). Trends influencing future delivery of mental health services in large healthcare systems. *Clinical Psychology: Science and Practice, 13,* 287–292.

Clay, R. A. (2010). APA updates its model licensure act. *Monitor on Psychology, 41,* 38.

Clay, R. A. (2011a). The future of behavioral health care. *Monitor on Psychology, 42,* 52.

Clay, R. A. (2011b). Modern-day slavery. *Monitor on Psychology, 42,* 72.

Clay, R. A. (2011c). Parity in practice. *Monitor on Psychology, 42,* 54.

Clough, B. A., & Casey, L. M. (2011). Technological adjuncts to enhance current psychotherapy practices: A review. *Clinical Psychology Review, 31,* 279–292.

David, R., & Messer, L. (2011). Reducing disparities: Race, class, and the social determinants of health. *Maternal and Child Health Journal, 15,* 1–3.

De Waal, F. B. M., & Ferari, P. F. (Eds.). (2012). *The primate mind: Built to connect with other minds.* Cambridge, MA: Harvard University Press.

DeAngelis, T. (2012). Practicing distance therapy, legally and ethically. *Monitor on Psychology, 42,* 52.

DiLillo, D., DeGue, S., Cohen, L. M., & Morgan, R. D. (2006). The path to licensure for academic psychologists: How tough is the road? *Professional Psychology: Research and Practice, 37,* 567–586.

Eonta, A. M., Christon, L. M., Hourigan, S. E., Ravindran, N., Vrana, S. R., et al. (2011). Using everyday technology to enhance evidence-based treatments. *Professional Psychology: Research and Practice, 42,* 513–520.

Ewing, C. P., & McCann, J. T. (2006). *Minds on trial: Great cases in law and psychology.* New York, NY: Oxford University Press.

Fagan, T. J., Ax, R. K., Resnick, R. J., Liss, M., Johnson, R. T., et al. (2004). Attitudes among interns and directors of training: Who wants to prescribe, who doesn't, and why? *Professional Psychology: Research and Practice, 35,* 345–356.

Fouad, N. A., Grus, C. L., Hatcher, R. L., Kaslow, N. J., Hutchings, P. S., et al. (2009). Competency benchmarks: A model for understanding and measuring competence in professional psychology across training levels. *Training and Education in Professional Psychology, 3,* S5–S26.

Fowers, B. J., & Davido, B. J. (2006). The virtue of multiculturalism: Personal transformation, character, and openness to the other. *American Psychologist, 61,* 581–594.

Fritz, G. K., & Kennedy, P. J. (2012). The long road ahead to mental health parity. *Journal of the American Academy of Child and Adolescent Psychiatry, 51,* 458–460.

Gaines, L. K., & Falkenberg, S. (1998). An evaluation of the written selection test: Effectiveness and alternatives. *Journal of Criminal Justice, 26,* 175–183.

Gasquoine, P. G. (2010). Comparison of public/private health care insurance parameters for independent psychological practice. *Professional Psychology: Research and Practice, 41*, 319–324.

Gates, M. A., Holowka, D. W., Vasterling, J. J., Keane, T. M., Marx, B. P., et al. (2012). Posttraumatic stress disorder in veterans and military personnel: Epidemiology, screening, and case recognition. *Psychological Services, 9*, 361–382. doi: 10.1037/a0027649.

Gonzalez-Prendes, A. A., Hindo, C., & Pardo, Y. (2011). Cultural values integration in cognitive-behavioral therapy for a Latino with depression. *Clinical Case Studies, 10*, 376–394.

Goodheart, C. D. (2010). Economics and psychology practice: What we need to know and why. *Professional Psychology: Research and Practice, 41*, 189–195.

Graham, J. M., & Kim, Y. H. (2011). Predictors of doctoral student success in professional psychology: Characteristics of students, programs, and universities. *Journal of Clinical Psychology, 67*, 340–354.

Grus, C. L., McCutcheon, S. R., & Berry, S. L. (2011). Actions by professional psychology education and training groups to mitigate the internship imbalance. *Training and Education in Professional Psychology, 5*, 193–201.

Hall, J. E., & Boucher, A. P. (2008). Early career psychologists' knowledge of credentialing in psychology. *Professional Psychology: Research and Practice, 39*, 480–487.

Hall, J. E., & Lunt, I. (2005). Global mobility for psychologists: The role of psychology organizations in the United States, Canada, Europe, and other regions. *American Psychologist, 60*, 712–726.

Hall, J. E., Wexelbaum, S. F., & Boucher, A. P. (2007). Doctoral student awareness of licensure, credentialing, and professional organizations in psychology: The 2005 National Register international survey. *Training and Education in Professional Psychology, 1*, 38–48.

Harwood, T. M., Pratt, D., Beutler, L. E., Bongar, B. M., Lenore, S., et al. (2011). Technology, telehealth, treatment enhancement, and selection. *Professional Psychology: Research and Practice, 42*, 448–454.

Hatcher, R. L. (2011a). The internship supply as a common-pool resource: A pathway to managing the imbalance problem. *Training and Education in Professional Psychology, 5*, 126–140.

Hatcher, R. L. (2011b). Managing the internship imbalance: Response to commentaries. *Training and Education in Professional Psychology, 5*, 217–221.

Heiby, E. M., DeLeon, P. H., & Anderson, T. (2004). A debate on prescription privileges for psychologists. *Professional Psychology: Research and Practice, 35*(4), 336–344.

Hilgard, E. R., Kelly, E. L., Luckey, B., Sanford, R. N., Shaffer, L. F., et al. (1947). Recommended graduate training program in clinical psychology. *American Psychologist, 2*, 539–558.

Himelein, M. J., & Putnam, E. A. (2001). Work activities of academic clinical psychologists: Do they practice what they teach? *Professional Psychology: Research and Practice, 5*, 537–542.

Hinshaw, S. P. (2007). *The mark of shame: Stigma of mental illness and an agenda for change.* New York, NY: Oxford University Press.

Hough, S., & Squires, L. E. (2012). Recruitment, retention and professional development of psychologists in America: Potential issue for training and performance. *Sexual Disability, 30*, 161–170.

Humes, K. R., Jones, N. A., & Ramirez, R. R. (2011). *Overview of race and Hispanic origin: 2010.* Washington, DC: U. S. Census Bureau.

Jorm, A. F. (2012). Mental health literacy: Empowering the community to take action for better mental health. *American Psychologist, 67*, 231–243.

Kaczorowski, J. A., Williams, A. S., Smith, T. F, Fallah, N. Mendez, J. L., et al. (2011). Adapting clinical services to accommodate needs of refugee populations. *Professional Psychology: Research and Practice, 42*, 361–367.

Kaslow, F. W. (2010). A family therapy narrative. *The American Journal of Family Therapy, 38*, 50–62.

Kaslow, F. W. (2011). Family therapy. In J. C. Norcross, G. R. VandenBos, & D. K. Freedheim (Eds.), *History of psychotherapy: Continuity and change* (2nd ed., pp. 497–504). Washington, DC: American Psychological Association.

Kaslow, F. W. (2013). International family psychology. In J. H. Bray & M. Stanton (Eds.), *The Wiley-Blackwell handbook of family psychology* (pp. 684–701). Hoboken, NJ: Wiley-Blackwell.

Kaslow, N. J., Graves, C. C., & Smith, C. O. (2012). Specialization in psychology and health care reform. *Journal of Clinical Psychology in Medical Settings, 19*, 12–21.

Kaslow, N. J., & Webb, C. (2011). Internship and postdoctoral residency. In J. C. Norcross, G. R. VandenBos, & D. K. Freedheim (Eds.), *History of psychotherapy: Continuity and change* (2nd ed., pp. 640–650). Washington, DC: American Psychological Association.

Kazdin, A. E., & Rabbitt, S. M. (2013). Novel models of delivering mental health services and reducing the burdens of mental illness. *Clinical Psychological Science, 1*, 170–191.

Klonoff, E. A. (2011). PhD programs. In J. C. Norcross, G. R. VandenBos, & D. K. Freedheim (Eds.), *History of psychotherapy: Continuity and change* (2nd ed., pp. 615–629). Washington, DC: American Psychological Association.

Knapp, S. J. (Ed.). (2012a). *APA handbook of ethics in psychology— Volume 1: Moral foundations and common themes.* Washington, DC: American Psychological Association.

Knapp, S. J. (Ed.). (2012b). *APA handbook of ethics in psychology— Volume 2: Practice, teaching, and research.* Washington, DC: American Psychological Association.

Knapp, S. J., Bennett, B. E., & VandeCreek, L. (2012). Risk management for psychologists. In S. J. Knapp, M. C. Gottlieb, M. M. Handelsman, & L. D. VandeCreek (Eds.), *APA handbook of ethics in psychology (Vol 1): Moral foundations and common themes* (pp. 483–518). Washington, DC: American Psychological Association.

Lambert, D. (1985). Political and economic determinants of mental health regulations. Unpublished doctoral dissertation, Brandeis University.

Levant, R. F. (2006). Making psychology a household word. *American Psychologist, 61*, 383–395.

Levine, E. S., & Schmelkin, L. P. (2006). The move to prescribe: A change in paradigm? *Professional Psychology: Research and Practice, 37*, 205–209.

Maguen, S., Cohen, G., Cohen, B. E., Lawhon, G. D., Marmar, C. R., et al. (2010). The role of psychologists in the care of Iraq and Afghanistan veterans in primary care settings. *Professional Psychology: Research and Practice, 41*, 135–142.

Matthews, J. R., & Matthews, L. H. (2009). Preparing for licensure. In S. F. Davis, P. J. Giordano, & C. A. Licht (Eds.), *Your career in psychology: Putting your graduate degree to work* (pp. 151–162). Hoboken, NJ: Wiley-Blackwell.

McConnell, K. J., Gast, S. H. N., Ridgely, M. S., Wallace, N., Jacuzzi, N., et al. (2012). Behavioral health insurance parity: Does Oregon's experience presage the national experience with the mental health parity and addiction equity act? *American Journal of Psychiatry, 169*, 31–38.

McCutcheon, S. R. (2011). The internship crisis: An uncommon urgency to build a common solution. *Training and Education in Professional Psychology, 5*, 144–148.

McFall, R. M. (1991). Manifesto for a science of clinical psychology. *The Clinical Psychologist, 44*, 75–88.

McFall, R. M. (2006). Doctoral training in clinical psychology. *Annual Review of Clinical Psychology, 2*, 21–49.

McFall, R. M. (2012). Psychological Clinical Science Accreditation System: FAQs and facts. *The Behavior Therapist, 35,* 11–15.

McGrath, R. E. (2010). Prescriptive authority for psychologists. *Annual Review of Clinical Psychology, 6,* 21–47.

McGrath, R. E., & Sammons, M. (2011). Prescribing and primary care psychology: Complementary paths for professional psychology. *Professional Psychology: Research and Practice, 42,* 113–120.

McNulty, J. K., & Fincham, F. D. (2012). Beyond positive psychology? Toward a contextual view of psychological processes and well-being. *American Psychologist, 67,* 101–110.

Meyer, B. (2007). Do clinical researchers believe they should be clinically active? A survey in the United States and the United Kingdom. *Psychology and Psychotherapy: Theory, Research, and Practice, 80,* 543–561.

Meyers, L. (2006). Psychologists and psychotropic medication. *Monitor on Psychology, 37,* 46–47.

Mizock, L., & Fleming, M. Z. (2011). Transgender and gender variant populations with mental illness: Implications for clinical care. *Professional Psychology: Research and Practice, 42,* 208–213.

Morgan, D. L., & Morgan, R. K. (2001). Single-participant design: Bringing science to managed care. *American Psychologist, 56,* 119–127.

Munoz, R. F., Beardslee, W. R., & Leykin, Y. (2012). Major depression can be prevented. *American Psychologist, 67,* 285–295.

Munsey, C. (2008). Prescriptive authority in the states. *Monitor on Psychology, 39,* 60.

Murphy, M. J., Levant, R. F., Hall, J. E., & Glueckauf, R. L. (2007). Distance education in professional training in psychology. *Professional Psychology: Research and Practice, 38,* 97–103.

Nagy, T. F. (2011). *Essential ethics for psychologists.* Washington, DC: American Psychological Association.

Neimeyer, G. J., Rice, K. G., & Keilin, W. G. (2007). Does the model matter? The relationship between science-practice emphasis in clinical psychology programs and the internship match. *Training and Education in Professional Psychology, 1,* 153–162.

Neimeyer, G. J., Taylor, J. M., & Philip, D. (2010). Continuing education in psychology: Patterns of participation and perceived outcomes among mandated and nonmandated psychologists. *Professional Psychology: Research and Practice, 41,* 435–441.

Norcross, J. C., Ellis, J. L., & Sayette, M. A. (2010). Getting in and getting money: A comparative analysis of admission standards, acceptance rates, and financial assistance across the research-practice continuum in clinical psychology programs. *Training and Education in Professional Psychology, 4,* 99–104.

Norcross, J. C., & Karpiak, C. P. (2012). Clinical psychologists in the 2010s: 50 years of the APA Division of Clinical Psychology. *Clinical Psychology: Science and Practice, 19,* 1–12.

Norcross, J. C., Karpiak, C. P., & Santoro, S. O. (2005). Clinical psychologists across the years: The Division of Clinical Psychology from 1960 to 2003. *Journal of Clinical Psychology, 61,* 1467–1483.

Norcross, J. C., Kohout, J. L., & Wicherski, M. (2005). Graduate study in psychology: 1971 to 2004. *American Psychologist, 60,* 959–975.

Norcross, J. C., & Sayette, M. A. (2012). *Insider's guide to graduate programs in clinical and counseling psychology: 2012/2013 edition.* New York, NY: Guilford.

Oberman, L. M., & Ramachandran, V. S. (2007). The simulating social mind: The role of the mirror neuron system and simulation in the social and communicative deficits of autism spectrum disorders. *Psychological Bulletin, 133,* 310–327.

Overholser, J. C. (2007). The Boulder Model in academia: Struggling to integrate the science and practice of psychology. *Journal of Contemporary Psychotherapy, 37,* 205–211.

Overholser, J. C. (2010). Ten criteria to qualify as a scientist-practitioner in clinical psychology: An immodest proposal for objective standards. *Journal of Contemporary Psychotherapy, 40,* 51–59.

Pope, K. S., & Vasquez, M. J. T. (2011). *Ethics in psychotherapy and counseling: A practical guide* (4th ed.). Hoboken, NJ: John Wiley & Sons.

Price, M. (2011). Promoting psychology as a STEM discipline. *Monitor on Psychology, 42,* 32.

Prinstein, M. J. (2013). *The portable mentor: Expert guide to a successful career in psychology.* New York, NY: Springer.

Raimy, V. C. (1950). *Training in clinical psychology.* New York, NY: Prentice-Hall.

Resnick, R. J., Ax, R. K., Fagan, T. J., & Nussbaum, D. (2012). Predoctoral prescriptive authority curricula: A training option. *Journal of Clinical Psychology, 68,* 246–262.

Riggle, E. D. B., & Rostosky, S. S. (2005). For better or for worse: Psycholegal soft spots and advance planning for same-sex couples. *Professional Psychology: Research and Practice, 36,* 90–96.

Robinson, J. D., & Habben, C. J. (2003). The role of the American Board of Professional Psychology in professional mobility. *Professional Psychology: Research and Practice, 34,* 474–475.

Roe, A., Gustad, J. W., Moore, B. V., Ross, S., & Skodak, M. (Eds.). (1959). *Graduate education in psychology.* Washington, DC: American Psychological Association.

Rutter, M. (2012). Resilience: Causal pathways and social ecology. In M. Ungar (Ed.), *The social ecology of resilience: A handbook of theory and practice* (pp. 33–42). New York, NY: Springer Science.

Santucci, L. C., McHugh, R. K., & Barlow, D. H. (2012). Direct-to-consumer marketing of evidence-based psychological interventions. *Behavior Therapy, 43,* 231–235.

Saunders, S. M., Miller, M. L., & Bright, M. M. (2010). Spiritually conscious psychological care. *Professional Psychology: Research and Practice, 41,* 355–362.

Sawyer, A., Ayers, S., & Field, A. P. (2010). Posttraumatic growth and adjustment among individuals with cancer or HIV/AIDS: A meta-analysis. *Clinical Psychology Review, 30,* 436–447.

Sayette, M. A., Norcross, J. C., & Dimoff, J. D. (2011). The heterogeneity of clinical psychology Ph.D. programs and the distinctiveness of APCS programs. *Clinical Psychology: Science and Practice, 18,* 4–11.

Schaffer, J. B., DeMers, S. T., & Rodolfa, E. (2011). Licensing and credentialing. In J. C. Norcross, G. R. VandenBos, & D. K. Freedheim (Eds.), *History of psychotherapy: Continuity and change* (2nd ed., pp. 651–662). Washington, DC: American Psychological Association.

Schwartz, S. J., Unger, J. B., Zamboanga, B. L., & Szapocznik, J. (2010). Rethinking the concept of acculturation: Implications for theory and research. *American Psychologist, 65,* 237–251.

Scott, C. L., & Resnick, P. J. (2006). Patient suicide and litigation. In R. I. Simon & R. E. Hales (Eds.), *The American Psychiatric Publishing textbook of suicide assessment and management* (pp. 527–544). Washington, DC: American Psychiatric Publishing.

Singh, R., & Dutta, S. (2010). *Race and culture: Tools, techniques and trainings: A manual for professionals.* London, UK: Karnac Books.

Smith, T. B., Rodriguez, M. M. D., & Bernal, G. (2011). Culture. In J. C. Norcross (Ed.), *Psychotherapy relationships that work: Evidence-based responsiveness* (2nd ed.). New York, NY: Oxford University Press.

Sommer, R. (2006). Dual dissemination: Writing for colleagues and the public. *American Psychologist, 61,* 955–958.

Soulier, M. F., Maislen, A., & Beck, J. C. (2010). Status of the psychiatric duty to protect, circa 2006. *Journal of the American Academy of Psychiatry and the Law, 38,* 457–573.

Stricker, G. (2011). PsyD programs. In J. C. Norcross, G. R. VandenBos, & D. K. Freedheim (Eds.), *History of psychotherapy: Continuity and change* (2nd ed., pp. 630–639). Washington, DC: American Psychological Association.

Strother, C. R. (1956). *Psychology and mental health*. Washington, DC: American Psychological Association.

Sturmey, P., & Hersen, M. (2012a). *Handbook of evidence-based practice in clinical psychology (Vol. 1): Child and adolescent disorders*. Hoboken, NJ: Wiley.

Sturmey, P., & Hersen, M. (2012b). *Handbook of evidence-based practice in clinical psychology (Vol. 2): Adult disorders*. Hoboken, NJ: Wiley.

Swim, J. K., Stern, P. C., Doherty, T. J., Clayton, S., Reser, J. P., et al. (2011). Psychology's contributions to understanding and addressing global climate change. *American Psychologist, 66*, 241–250.

Templer, D. I. (2005). Addendum to concerns about professional schools. *Psychological Reports, 97*, 117–118.

Walfish, S., & Barnett, J. E. (2009). *Financial success in mental health practice: Essential tools and strategies for practitioners*. Washington, DC: American Psychological Association.

Wang, P. S., Aguilar-Gaxiola, S., Alonso, J., Angermeyer, M. C., Borges, G., et al. (2007). Use of mental health services for anxiety, mood, and substance disorders in 17 countries in the WHO world mental health surveys. *The Lancet, 370*, 841–850.

Werner, J. M., Cermak, S. A., & Aziz-Zadeh, L. (2010). Neural correlates of developmental coordination disorder. *Journal of Behavioral and Brain Sciences, 2*, 258–268.

Wiggins, J. G., & Wedding, D. (2004). Prescribing, professional identity, and costs. *Professional Psychology: Research and Practice, 35*, 148–150.

Williams, C. R., & Abeles, N. (2004). Issues and implications of deaf culture in therapy. *Professional Psychology: Research and Practice, 35*, 643–648.

Willyard, C. (2010). On-call scientists. *Monitor on Psychology, 41*, 30.

Winerman, L. (2005). The mind's mirror. *Monitor on Psychology, 37*, 48–50.

Wood, A. M., & Tarrier, N. (2010). Positive clinical psychology: A new vision and strategy for integrated research and practice. *Clinical Psychology Review, 30*, 819–829.

Wood, A. M., Froh, J. J., & Geraghty, A. W. A. (2010). Gratitude and well-being: A review and theoretical integration. *Clinical Psychology Review, 30*, 890–905.

Yoshikawa, H., Aber, J. L., & Beardslee, W. R. (2012). The effects of poverty on the mental, emotional, and behavioral health of children and youth: Implications for prevention. *American Psychologist, 67*, 272–284.

16 GETTING INTO GRADUATE SCHOOL IN CLINICAL PSYCHOLOGY

Chapter Preview

Students ask a number of questions when they are thinking of applying to graduate school in clinical psychology. In this chapter, we hope to answer some of those questions and to pose some others that potential applicants need to consider. We begin by addressing questions related to deciding whether to apply to graduate school in clinical psychology, and then discuss the logistics of applying to graduate school. In this chapter we dispense with our usual Section Previews and Section Summaries and present instead a "frequently asked questions" format in which headings provide the questions and the paragraphs that follow provide the answers.

WHAT TYPES OF GRADUATE PROGRAMS WILL HELP ME MEET MY CAREER GOALS?

In thinking about a career in psychology, the first questions you must ask yourself are, "What type of career do I want?" and "What types of graduate programs are available to meet my career goals?" The field of psychology offers many career options so we suggest that you read the APA's free brochure called "Psychology: Scientific Problem Solvers—Careers for the 21st Century." You can find it online at www.apa.org/careers/resources/guides/careers.pdf . There are many options available in clinical psychology itself. Most students know about the possibility of training to become a clinician (psychotherapist) or a psychology professor, but did you know about the following careers in clinical psychology?

> Administrator in a medical setting
>
> Clinical neuropsychologist
>
> Clinician in a university counseling center
>
> Executive coach, consultant, and advisor
>
> Forensic psychologist
>
> Gerontologist
>
> Infant mental health specialist
>
> Mediator
>
> Military psychologist
>
> Program manager in a crisis unit
>
> Public health educator
>
> Research and evaluation consultant
>
> Researcher in a nonprofit organization
>
> Sport psychologist
>
> Trial consultant

Research versus Clinical Emphasis?

All university-based graduate programs in clinical psychology provide training in research as well as in clinical functions, but there are differences in emphasis from one institution to another. It is worth your effort to learn each program's emphasis when you are gathering other information about the program. Subtle differences in a program's description (e.g., scientist–practitioner vs. clinical scientist; see Chapter 15, "Professional Issues in Clinical Psychology") may reveal a great deal about the program's training emphasis.

If your primary career interest is in research on mental health, psychopathology, prevention, and treatment, then a PhD program in clinical psychology is probably your best option. Such programs typically offer the most training in research and widest variety of clinical research options. Clinical researchers find careers in a variety of mental health settings, hospitals, medical schools, government, public, and private agencies. Research-oriented clinical PhD programs also provide training and supervision in clinical work, so graduates of these programs typically have the option of shifting into more clinical work so long as they have kept their licensure requirements up to date.

Certain nonclinical PhD psychology programs may also provide avenues to clinical research. Graduates of developmental psychology, personality psychology, cognitive neuroscience, or social psychology doctoral programs sometimes conduct research with important clinical applications (e.g., childhood psychopathology, positive psychology). Programs that are strictly research oriented make this fact clear in their descriptive information and may even refrain from using "clinical psychology" as a program title. These nonclinical programs tend to attract fewer applicants than clinical programs do, and, though still quite competitive, may be less competitive than clinical programs. However, clinical research options may be more limited in these programs than in clinical PhD programs, and graduates of nonclinical programs will not be eligible for psychotherapy licensure or practice.

If your primary interest is in clinical work, especially therapy, then there are a number of options both inside and outside of clinical psychology. In Chapter 1, "What Is Clinical Psychology?," we described several mental health professions whose graduates engage in assessment, psychotherapy, or counseling. These include counseling psychologists, school psychologists, social workers, rehabilitation counselors, marriage and family therapists, psychiatrists, and psychiatric nurses. We do not have the space here to provide details about the graduate admission requirements for each of these fields, but we do list at the end of the chapter website addresses for some of the main professional organizations in those fields. Also note that the U. S. Government's Bureau of Labor Statistics has a searchable data base on "Occupational Employment Statistics" at www.bls.gov/oes/ that can help you compare incomes earned by people in these various professions.

MA, PhD, or PsyD?

Many students seem to think that if they want to do clinical work, they must enter a PhD program in clinical psychology. In fact, approximately three times as many students get master's degrees in psychology as get doctoral degrees (Morgan & Korschgen, 2006). Many students who are considering clinical PhD programs probably could get their educational and employment needs met in a master's program or in other types of programs that offer training leading to careers in the mental health professions.

The growth of managed care systems has stimulated the job market at the master's-degree level for those seeking a career in direct clinical service. Thus, the master's degree in clinical psychology is a more marketable degree than it had been in the past. Further, what was seen as the biggest drawback to the master's degree—the need for continual supervision from a licensed PhD psychologist—may be changing. The state of Kentucky, for example, allows master's-level psychologists to be licensed to work independently after they meet certain training and professional experience requirements. Other states, such as Florida, allow professionals with a master's degree in a mental health–related field (such as clinical or counseling psychology or rehabilitation counseling) to seek licensure as a Licensed Mental Health Counselor, which ultimately is an independent license. Thus, if you are interested in having a full-time clinical career and if you have limited interest in research training, you may want to consider pursuing a master's degree in clinical psychology or in a related field. It is reasonable to expect that a master's degree in clinical psychology will allow you to secure a full-time job providing mental health services (Martin, 2011).

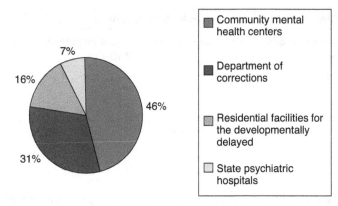

FIGURE 16.1   Work Settings of Individuals with a Master's Degree in Psychology, Based on a Study Conducted in North Carolina. Master's level clinicians known as *Licensed Psychological Associates* (LPAs) can conduct therapy in North Carolina, but must be supervised by a doctoral-level licensed psychologist

The master's degree does carry some limitations, though. In most states, if you want to be licensed as a psychologist (which means that you can actually use the term *psychologist* rather than another term like *counselor*), you have to have either a PhD or a PsyD. Income levels are typically lower for master's-level clinicians, and advancement opportunities are fewer. Certain career opportunities, such as being a professor in a college or university or being awarded program grants from granting agencies, are often unavailable to those without a doctorate. As Figure 16.1 shows, employment settings may be somewhat more restrictive for master's-level clinicians. Thus, the doctoral degree gives you more flexibility, which can be helpful given that your career interests will likely change somewhat over your life span. However, if you are absolutely sure that you only want to do clinical work (as opposed to a combination of research and direct service), then you may want to consider earning a master's degree so that you can seek your desired job in a more timely manner.

At the doctoral level, you have the choice of PhD and PsyD programs. Traditionally, the PhD degree is considered the terminal degree in clinical psychology. As described in Chapter 15, PsyD programs tend to emphasize clinical training while reducing the emphasis on research. However, it is important to remember that PsyD programs themselves vary considerably. Some follow the Boulder model and emphasize research almost as much as some PhD programs do, while others adopt the Vail model and emphasize research considerably less. Programs that deemphasize research still require that students acquire knowledge of statistics and research methods, but students are usually not required to conduct an empirically based thesis or dissertation. Figure 16.2 shows the distribution of how clinical psychologists view their professional roles.

Another difference between PhD and PsyD programs is that the latter are often not affiliated with a specific psychology department or even with a university. Freestanding professional schools

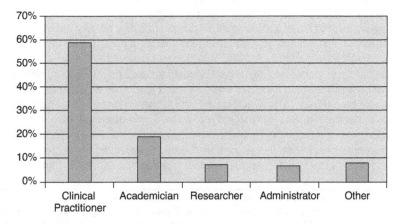

FIGURE 16.2   Clinical Psychologists' Professional Self-Views
Source: Norcross, J. C., Karpiak, C. P., & Santoro, S. O. (2005). Clinical psychologists across the years: The Division of Clinical Psychology from 1960 to 2003. *Journal of Clinical Psychology, 61,* 1467–1483.

TABLE 16.1 Average Acceptance Rates for APA-Accredited Clinical Psychology Programs

	Freestanding PsyD	University-based PsyD	Practice-oriented PhD	Equal-emphasis PhD	Research-oriented PhD
Number of applications	227	163	155	160	183
Number of acceptances	108	58	18	16	12
Acceptance rate	50%	40%	16%	14%	7%

Source: From *Insider's Guide to Graduate Programs in Clinical and Counseling Psychology*, 2012/2013 Edition, by J. C. Norcross and M. A. Sayette, 2012, p. 49 (New York: Guilford Press). Copyright 2012 by Guilford Press. Used with permission.

generally place the least emphasis on research training. These programs are attractive to some students because they so clearly emphasize practice over research and because they generally have considerably lower selection criteria than PhD clinical programs (see Table 16.1). However, some cautionary notes are necessary. First, because these programs are stand-alone institutions, their financial support comes mainly from students' tuition fees. Thus, similar to medical schools and law schools, the fees charged can be quite high and the programs may offer little or no financial aid. In contrast, most clinical PhD programs offer their students some financial support, including tuition fee waivers and research assistant (RA) or teaching assistant (TA) positions. Second, if PsyD programs are to turn a profit, or at least break even, they have to accept a large number of students (e.g., as many as 100) each year. This means that students may not get the same individual attention that they would in a PhD program, where the entering class may include only five to ten students. Finally, the relatively weaker research training in many of these programs means that graduates are less able to move into more research-oriented clinical positions or to combine research with their clinical work. These points are also made in Table 16.2, which presents myths and realities about getting into doctoral degree programs in clinical psychology.

TABLE 16.2 Myths and Realities about Clinical Psychology Graduate Training

Topic	Myth	Reality
Graduate school acceptance rates	Anyone can get into a PsyD program, but it is very difficult to get into a PhD program.	Among APA-accredited programs, PsyD programs accept about 50% of applicants, some higher, some lower. PhD programs accept about 7–16% of applicants, some higher, some lower. PsyD programs typically enroll three to four times the number enrolled in PhD programs, and although there are more PhD programs, the number of PsyD degrees awarded each year exceeds the annual number of PhD degrees awarded.
Financial assistance	You cannot get financial aid if you attend a PsyD program, but you can from a PhD program.	Over 60% of students in university-based PsyD programs received some financial aid, but only 26% of those attending freestanding clinical programs did. For financial assistance, university affiliation probably matters more than the type of degree offered.
Theoretical orientation of clinical faculty	Faculty in traditional PhD programs are mostly cognitive-behavioral, while those in PsyD programs are psychodynamic and humanistic.	A cognitive-behavioral orientation is the most frequently cited one in PhD and PsyD clinical programs. University-based graduate departments tend to have higher percentages of faculty endorsing a CBT perspective. The percentage of faculty endorsing humanistic orientations, though lower than CBT, is highest in freestanding schools.
Training in evidence-based practice	PsyD programs do not train students in empirically tested psychotherapies.	Most programs offer training in treatments that have been defined in manuals and found efficacious in at least two well-controlled randomized clinical studies, but few require both didactic and clinical supervision in them. Professional clinical psychology (PsyD) has the highest percentage of programs (67%) not requiring it.
Performance on national licensing board exam	PsyD students are not well prepared for the Examination for Professional Practice in Psychology (EPPP).	PsyD students score lower on average on the national licensing exam, but there is great variability. Higher exam scores are more reliably associated with smaller-sized clinical programs, better faculty-to-student ratios, and traditional (Boulder model) PhD curricula.

Source: Norcross, J. C., Castle, P. H., Sayette, M. A., & Mayne, T. J. (2004). The PsyD: Heterogeneity in practitioner training. *Professional Psychology: Research and Practice, 35,* 412–419; Norcross, J. C., & Sayette, M. A. (2012). *Insider's guide to graduate programs in clinical and counseling psychology: 2012/2013 edition.* New York, NY: Guilford; Weissman, M. M., Verdell, H., Gameroff, M. J., Bledsoe, S. E., Betts, K., et al. (2006). National survey of psychotherapy training in psychiatry, psychology, and social work. *Archives of General Psychiatry, 63,* 925–934.

AM I READY TO MAKE THE COMMITMENT REQUIRED BY GRADUATE PROGRAMS AT THIS TIME IN MY LIFE?

After exploring the career options available with master's and PhD degrees, and after careful consideration of what you want to achieve, suppose you have decided that a doctoral program in clinical psychology offers you the most career flexibility and the best chance to obtain your research and clinical goals. The next question you have to ask yourself is whether you are prepared to make the major commitments in time, money, and physical and emotional energy that are required to succeed in such a program.

Time Commitments

Typical weekly requirements in graduate school involve a full course load of academic work as well as a 20-hour-per-week job either as a TA, RA, or clinical trainee conducting supervised clinical work (such as completing assessments or conducting therapy). In addition, you will be expected to find time to make continual progress on independent research toward completion of your thesis and dissertation. In more research-oriented programs, you will also be expected to publish and present your independent research as well as research conducted with your major professor. Thus, it is not unusual for graduate students in clinical programs to work 60 hours or more per week, 12 months per year. Unlike many college students, doctoral students know that summer is not a time for rest and relaxation. In fact graduate students and faculty look forward to summers so that they can get more work done.

On average, 5 to 7 years are needed to complete such a program, during which time you will be living on subsistence wages, at best. In addition, new licensing requirements almost guarantee that you will need to take a 1- to 2-year postdoctoral position after you graduate in order to obtain the necessary clinical supervision for licensure. Thus, it may take anywhere from 6 to 9 years after starting graduate school before you are ready to venture fully into the job market. Generally, the more research-oriented a graduate program is, the longer it will take to complete.

Financial Commitments

Given the high cost of graduate education, the majority of graduate students in doctoral programs end up borrowing money. The debt they incur often varies according to the type of program they attend. A survey conducted by the American Psychological Association found that over 75% of recent psychology doctoral graduates had some type of debt after completing their degree (Chamberlin, 2008), and that higher rates of debt were associated with the more practice-oriented programs. The average debt load carried by graduates of PhD psychology programs was nearly $58,000; the figure for graduates of PsyD programs was nearly $103,000. Beginning salaries in clinical psychology are not high enough to make it easy to pay off these debts; it often takes 10–15 years.

Fortunately, many graduate programs offer income opportunities, usually in the form of assistantships or financial aid. Although funding has increased over the years, the median TA or RA stipends continue to be modest for a 20-hour-per-week position. The median graduate pay for either a TA or RA at a public university was between $12,000 and $13,000 for the 9-month academic year of 2009/2010 (Norcross & Sayette, 2012). Many universities also offer fellowships and scholarships on a competitive basis. Fellowships and scholarships are usually given as outright grants to support and encourage students with outstanding academic and research potential (and there is no formal work requirement other than to do well in graduate school). Students can often find out about university-wide fellowships and scholarships by checking the Web site of the graduate school at the university. For example, it is not uncommon for programs to offer fellowships that will increase the diversity of the students accepted into the program. Many programs also provide some form of tuition remission. They may offer complete remission, meaning that the student pays no tuition at all, or they offer some tuition reduction (e.g., 50%). Alternatively, the program may waive the out-of-state tuition and only require that the out of state student pay in-state tuition.

Note that many programs, especially freestanding professional schools, do not offer funding to the large majority of students (Norcross, Castle, Sayette, & Mayne, 2004). One survey of APA-accredited clinical psychology doctoral programs found that approximately 6% of students entering a freestanding PsyD program were offered full financial aid, 57% of students who entered a PhD program with equal emphasis on research and practice were offered full financial aid, and 84% of students who entered a research-oriented PhD program received full funding (Norcross, Castle, Sayette, & Mayne, 2004). Thus, the type of program you are seeking will likely have an impact on your pocketbook.

A relatively new program, called the National Institutes of Health (NIH) Loan Repayment Program, has added some much needed help for psychology graduates with student loan debt (Clay, 2006). If these graduates commit to working at least half time for 2 years in a research-oriented position (e.g., working on nonprofit or government-subsidized research in the areas of clinical, health, or pediatric psychology), they can receive up to $35,000 per year to repay their student loans. Students can apply for more than one year of this funding (Clay, 2006). This federal program is competitive, so the funding is in no way guaranteed, but it has helped a great many research-oriented students to decrease their debt while also adding to the research knowledge needed to help clients. Clinically oriented students also have an option to seek loan repayment through the National Health Service Corps (Clay, 2006). Students who can commit to working for at least 2 years in an underserved area of the United States (such as an impoverished urban area or a rural area that has limited health care services) can apply to have up to $50,000 of their loans repaid. This program is also competitive, but successful applicants can reduce their debt significantly while also helping provide psychological services to individuals who might not otherwise have access to such services.

More information on the NIH Loan Repayment Program can be accessed at www.lrp.nih.gov and more information about the National Health Service Corp program can be found at www.nhsc.bhpr.hrsa.gov. Both of these programs are funded by the federal government and are subject to change, so make sure to access the most up-to-date information when you are close to completing your graduate degree.

Academic and Emotional Commitments

In addition to the financial costs associated with doctoral programs in clinical psychology, you will be expected to make other commitments. For one thing, you will be asked to work harder than you have in previous academic endeavors. In addition, given the competitiveness of clinical psychology PhD programs, the majority of students have to move to attend a program, often uprooting themselves from their friends and family. Another move is likely to take place when students seek a 1-year full time internship toward the end of their graduate program, and perhaps yet another when the time comes to seek a postdoctoral fellowship or a first job.

We are not presenting this admittedly sobering introduction in an effort to discourage you from applying to doctoral programs in clinical psychology. Rather, we are raising these matters to help you better prepare for the initial decision-making process through which all potential applicants should go before they spend the hundreds of dollars and numerous hours needed to apply to graduate programs in clinical psychology.

Contrary to what you might have heard, your application to graduate school in clinical psychology will not be jeopardized if you decide to take some time off after completing your undergraduate studies. In fact, this academic break can enhance your application if you are able to obtain a position in the clinical field, either as a research assistant or as a mental health worker of some kind. Both of these options will help document your commitment to the field as well as give you valuable experience and further insight in helping to decide your future. If you cannot obtain paid research or clinical positions, try to obtain a volunteer position in these areas. If you are located near a university, consider taking one or more graduate courses in psychology or a related discipline. Once again, this will help document your commitment to the field and may help you decide whether graduate school is for you. Although your inclination may be to take clinically related courses, graduate admissions committees will probably be more impressed if you take (and do well in) graduate courses in nonclinical areas, such as statistics, research design, or advanced seminars (e.g., learning theory or cognitive neuroscience). In addition, you may receive credit for these latter courses when you enter a graduate program, while many clinical programs will require that you repeat any clinically related courses you may have taken previously.

We should also mention that for many clinical psychologists, graduate school was an exciting and rewarding time. Despite the work load and relative poverty, there were riches in terms of learning, personal growth, and relationships with friends and colleagues. It is also heartening

TABLE 16.3 Recent PhD Graduates' Satisfaction with Their Current Job

Based on a large survey of students who graduated with a PhD in psychology in 2009, the following numbers reflect the percentage of recent graduates who were either satisfied or very satisfied with these characteristics in their current job:

Income/salary	66.7%
Benefits	75.4%
Opportunities for promotion	62.2%
Opportunities for personal development	77.4%
Opportunities for recognition	75.2%
Supervisor	77.2%
Coworkers	84.6%
Working conditions	81.2%

Source: Data from Table 5c of the APA 2009 Doctorate Employment Survey (www.apa.org/workforce/publications/09-doc-empl/table-5abc.pdf).

to know that graduates tend to be relatively satisfied with their jobs after they complete graduate school (see Table 16.3).

ARE MY CREDENTIALS STRONG ENOUGH FOR GRADUATE SCHOOL IN CLINICAL PSYCHOLOGY?

In order to evaluate your credentials objectively and to be aware of your strengths and weaknesses, it is important to understand the criteria employed by graduate admissions committees in clinical psychology. These include (a) the requisite coursework and undergraduate experiences, especially research experience; (b) Graduate Record Exam (GRE) scores; (c) grade point average (GPA); and (d) letters of recommendation. Each graduate program may weigh these criteria differently, of course, and programs will examine other factors (e.g., personal statements, interviews) as well, but all of these criteria tend to be used, to some extent at least, by all doctoral clinical programs.

Undergraduate Coursework and Experience

Your undergraduate years offer the opportunity not only to take courses but also to gain career-relevant experience in psychology.

COURSEWORK Your undergraduate department will have designed a graduate preparatory major to meet your course needs. It will probably include a core program of introductory psychology, statistics, and experimental psychology (including a laboratory). These are the minimum requirements for most graduate programs, regardless of specialization area. Note that a class in research methods has been identified as the most important class for students who seek training at the doctoral level in a clinical psychology PhD program (Norcross & Sayette, 2012). For careers in clinically oriented fields, you also must consider taking courses like abnormal psychology, abnormal child psychology, behavior modification, clinical research methods, tests and measurement, and other courses that are specific to your area of interest. If they are available, we encourage you to take advanced seminars where you can learn about a topic in depth. Some programs also allow highly motivated undergraduate students, with strong grades, to take a graduate class as a non–degree-seeking student. All of these types of coursework activities should help you come to a better decision as to what type of career you wish to pursue, and they should help you score better on the GRE Subject Test in Psychology.

RESEARCH EXPERIENCE In addition to standard coursework, independent research such as an honors thesis and/or experience as a research assistant is very helpful, in general, and essential for entry into PhD programs. As noted earlier, such research activity not only provides you with desirable experience but also allows faculty supervisors to observe your potential for scholarly endeavors and to include their evaluations and impressions in letters of recommendation.

There are many reasons you should gain research experience prior to applying to doctoral programs in clinical psychology. First, the PhD in clinical psychology is both a research degree and a clinical degree, and you may well spend as much, if not more, of your graduate training on research as on clinical work. Admissions committees want to ensure that applicants understand what is involved in research and that they enjoy participating in such activities. Second, working on several research projects will give you an excellent understanding of what research in graduate school will be like. It is not unusual for undergraduate students to sign up as research assistants simply because they know that the experience will help their application to graduate school, but then find that they truly love being involved in research. Others find that research is really not for them, and so they reconsider their plan to apply to research-oriented PhD programs in clinical psychology. Third, as just noted, working with faculty on their research is an excellent way to obtain letters of recommendation that define more precisely your potential for graduate school. Fourth, working on research projects can help you decide which research areas you would (and would not) like to pursue in graduate school. This information, in turn, will help you apply to those psychology departments whose faculty members are working in the areas of your greatest interest. Finally, research experience serves as an excellent basis for discussion with faculty during any faculty interviews that you might have. In fact, recent years have seen a trend in which an increasing number of interviewees for PhD programs have undertaken independent honors thesis or capstone research experiences. Many successful applicants to research-oriented clinical programs have already presented their research at a conference or have been a coauthor on a published research article. Thus, applicants who do not have research experiences are at a distinct disadvantage during the interview process, because they do not have the depth of knowledge of a specific research project that is associated with having undertaken an honors thesis study.

CLINICAL EXPERIENCE If you think you want to be a clinician, but have never worked with a clinical population, then we encourage you to consider gaining some clinical experience. Often, structured programs (like suicide or crisis hotlines or child advocacy groups like the Guardian ad Litem program) will provide excellent training as well as close supervision for your volunteer work. Working with clients with psychological problems can be very demanding, and it is not for the faint of heart. We know of a number of professors who had planned to become clinicians but changed their minds after volunteering in a clinical facility. Others found that the experience confirmed their belief that the work is both challenging and rewarding.

Although clinical experience can be valuable in helping students decide whether the mental health profession is the field for them, and in knowing which clinical areas (e.g., child, substance use) they are especially interested in, clinical experience appears not to be deemed especially important in the graduate selection process. This is especially true for PhD programs in clinical psychology. Other types of programs (e.g., master's, PsyD, MSW, or counseling psychology), which put more emphasis on clinical training, may value undergraduate clinical experience to a greater degree.

EXTRACURRICULAR ACTIVITIES Participation in extracurricular activities, including psychology clubs and honor societies such as Psi Chi, can help you learn about the field and come into contact with professionals from various specializations. Many psychology clubs or Psi Chi groups provide talks on careers in psychology, how to prepare for the GREs, and how to apply to graduate school. Being a member of these groups will help you learn more about the field, but membership alone will not add significantly to your application for graduate school. Being in a leadership position in one of these organizations, however, will likely strengthen your application because it suggests that you have initiative and leadership skills and it may also lead to a strong and detailed letter of recommendation from the organization's faculty advisor.

Graduate Record Exam (GRE) Scores

Most graduate schools use standardized tests to assist them in evaluating applicants. As already noted, the most common example is the GRE, including both the General Test and the Psychology Subject Test. Students often do not like to hear this, but performance on the GRE is an important predictor of success in graduate school and thus one of the most important selection criteria used by graduate admissions committees. In a summary of multiple meta-analyses, Kuncel and Hezlett (2007) found that, across all disciplines, GRE scores were significant and powerful predictors of performance in graduate school, as measured by a variety of outcome measures (e.g., graduate GPA, publication citation counts, faculty ratings).

Students often ask what scores are necessary on the GREs to get past the initial screenings undertaken by admission committees. This is a difficult question to answer, for several reasons. First, programs vary considerably in the range of GRE scores they expect from their incoming students. Second, graduate programs often do not have strict cutoffs for the GRE scores but instead employ guidelines as to what they are looking for. For example, the minimally acceptable GRE scores reported by schools in the graduate guide books tend to be considerably below the median scores of the entering graduate classes (Morgan & Korschgen, 2006). In other words, if your GRE scores are just at or a little above the minimally acceptable scores reported by a school (e.g., at the 50th percentile on each subtest), you probably will not be admitted to that program. In order to be a serious candidate for admission to an APA-accredited PhD clinical program, it would be ideal for you to score no lower than the 85th percentile on each of the GRE subtests (Norcross & Sayette, 2012). We discuss the GRE in more detail later in this chapter.

Grade Point Average

If the GRE is seen as a reliable and valid predictor of your overall ability, your GPA is seen as an excellent indicator of the effort you have exerted in college and your willingness to work up to or even beyond your predicted potential. Once again, it is impossible to offer absolute guidelines as to what PhD clinical programs are looking for when they examine an applicant's undergraduate GPA. Surveys of entering classes in PhD clinical programs suggest that a psychology GPA of 3.5 or 3.6 (on a 4-point scale) is necessary, at a minimum, to be a strong candidate for admission (Norcross & Sayette, 2012). Thus, if you have obtained a somewhat marginal GPA, seriously consider trying to improve your GPA by repeating those courses in which you did poorly. For example, if you earned a B– in undergraduate statistics, you would be well advised to retake the course to improve your grade. Otherwise, admission committees will be concerned about your ability to handle more difficult graduate statistics courses, where a B– is the minimally acceptable grade.

Letters of Recommendation

When reading letters of recommendation, admissions committee members tend to look for comments relating to the applicant's overall potential for graduate school, willingness to work hard, level of interpersonal skills, and likelihood of success in clinical work. Letter writers are not likely to learn these things about you through classroom contacts alone. Even if you received one of the top grades in the course, if that is the professor's only contact with you, there is not much else he or she can write about you. Thus, it is crucial that you develop means of interacting with faculty outside the classroom. The best way to do this is to get involved as a paid or volunteer member of one or more faculty member's research groups. In addition, make a point of stopping by professors' offices to talk with them about class content that has intrigued you. Most professors welcome students stopping by to talk during office hours, especially if it does not concern complaining about a grade received or explaining why an assignment was missed. A good way to think about letters of recommendation is that, ideally, the professor should be able to write about your motivation, your conscientiousness, your ability to think intelligently about the subject matter, your ability to take on independent responsibility, and your maturity, among other factors. You need to do whatever you can to give the professor enough samples of your behavior in these domains so that he or she can write a positive and knowledgeable letter about you.

GIVEN MY CREDENTIALS, TO WHAT TYPE OF PROGRAM CAN I REALISTICALLY ASPIRE?

One of the most difficult things you need to do when applying to graduate school is to be realistic about evaluating your credentials. Unfortunately, the credentials of many applicants are not strong enough to gain entry to PhD programs in clinical psychology. PhD clinical programs routinely receive anywhere from 100 to 400 applications and these programs generally accept anywhere from five to ten students. Thus, these programs are extremely competitive, and shortcomings in any of the selection criteria described above can undermine your chances of receiving an offer of acceptance. Unless you have pursued other options as well, you may be setting yourself up for failure and disappointment.

Fortunately, several such options are available. For example, master's programs in clinical psychology usually have lower criteria for admission, in terms of expected GRE scores and GPA, than PhD programs. You might want to consider these programs either to earn a terminal master's degree or as the first step toward a PhD program. Counseling psychology, school psychology, and social work programs that offer clinical training also tend to be less competitive than PhD programs in clinical psychology. As noted earlier, students in these programs often receive as much applied training and experience as students in clinical psychology programs, and master's-level job openings, and even potential licensure, appear to be on the rise. Finally, nonclinical PhD programs in psychology (e.g., developmental, social) tend to attract fewer applicants and have lower admission criteria than do clinical programs. If you are committed to the field of psychology and want to remain in a research environment, you may find a nonclinical psychology PhD program more rewarding than a mental health–related doctoral or master's program in another field.

In short, PhD programs in clinical psychology are not for everyone; they are highly competitive, they place great demands on their students, they take 5 to 7 years to complete, and they emphasize research training as much as, if not more than, clinical experience.

Having offered some guidelines to help you assess your credentials and aspirations and to determine whether you should apply to doctoral programs in clinical psychology, we now consider some more general issues that you must address before beginning the application process.

I HAVE DECIDED TO APPLY TO GRADUATE SCHOOL IN CLINICAL PSYCHOLOGY. WHAT SHOULD I DO FIRST?

As already mentioned, the first step in choosing a graduate program is to be sure it will provide the training and professional environment that will meet your needs as determined by your personal goals, objectives, and plans. Are you most interested in research, balanced training in clinical practice and research, or primarily in clinical practice? Are you interested in doctoral-level or master's-level programs? Do you have an interest in a specific client population? These are but a few of the questions you should be asking yourself before the application process begins. The stronger your credentials, the more freedom you will have in deciding to which programs you will apply.

SHOULD I APPLY TO A MASTER'S DEGREE PROGRAM AND COMPLETE IT BEFORE I APPLY TO A DOCTORAL PROGRAM?

As noted earlier, there are various routes you can take to earn the doctorate in clinical psychology. Most PhD clinical programs are designed to prepare doctoral-level clinicians only. They may award the master's degree after a minimum number of credits and a master's thesis have been completed, but it is important to recognize that these departments accept applications for the doctoral degree only. If you earn a terminal master's degree and then wish to pursue a PhD or PsyD degree at a later point, that can be done, but if your ultimate goal is to gain admission into a PhD program in clinical psychology, then your best bet is to apply to those programs directly. If you are not sure that your qualifications are strong enough for admission into a PhD program, then you might consider applying to terminal master's programs as a back-up plan. Many graduates of these programs terminate their formal education at the master's level, but others go on to doctoral programs. In fact, some terminal masters programs focus on preparing students to apply to doctoral programs.

How does earning a master's degree affect your chances for admission to a doctoral program later on? The master's degree itself should neither hurt nor help your chances when applying to a PhD program in clinical psychology, but rather it is what you do with your time in the master's program that will be important for ultimate acceptance into a clinical PhD program. Graduate schools are interested in the best candidates they can find. If your credentials are excellent, your chances for being admitted to a doctoral program are good—but not guaranteed, given the competitive nature of graduate program admissions these days. Some students who feel they need to improve their credentials may find master's degree work helpful in achieving that goal, but doctoral admission committees consider all academic work when making their decision. A mediocre undergraduate academic record is not disregarded because it has been supplemented with a master's degree and good graduate school grades, but these graduate credentials can improve a student's chances for being considered seriously. If accepted into a master's program, you can use the time to strengthen your credentials, such as by studying for and retaking the GRE, excelling in your coursework in order to improve your grades, getting more research experience, and perhaps presenting or publishing your research.

IF I CHOOSE TO TERMINATE MY TRAINING AFTER EARNING A MASTER'S DEGREE, WILL MY OPPORTUNITIES FOR DOING CLINICAL WORK BE LIMITED?

Historically, the doctorate is considered the standard of the profession. You also need to consider that all U.S. states employ some form of licensing or certification for psychologists (see Chapter 15). Although requirements vary among states, an earned doctorate is a prerequisite in most of them. So while the growth of managed care systems has stimulated the job market at the master's degree level for those seeking a career in direct service, be certain that such jobs match your career expectations before deciding to prepare for clinical work by earning a master's degree. This is especially true if your ultimate goal is to have an independent clinical practice. Having said this, the recent change in the licensure law in Kentucky and other states suggests that the future for independent practice for master's-level clinicians may be more promising. Given the impact of managed care systems and the changes in the licensure laws, it is impossible to predict exactly how the job market for master's-level (and even PhD) clinical psychologists will look in 5 to 10 years. If you are considering a terminal master's degree in hopes of practicing clinical psychology when you are finished, you should definitely seek master's programs that train you clinically (rather than solely in research).

APPLICATION PROCEDURES

Let's now review the steps you must take to file admission applications for graduate programs in clinical psychology.

How Do I Get Information about Graduate Schools and Identify "Good" Graduate Programs?

Unlike professions such as law, psychology maintains no widely accepted list of top-ranked programs. To determine whether a particular university, department, and program fits your needs, including whether it offers the mix of "research" versus "clinical" that is right for you, you should gather as much information as possible, not only through the channels described below but also by corresponding with the graduate students and faculty located there. Be sure to learn about the size of the department and the program, whether there are faculty undertaking research in areas of interest to you, the student–faculty ratio, opportunities for a variety of practicum experiences, the size and location of the campus and the community, the type and extent of department resources, and the theoretical orientation(s) or approaches that may exist in or dominate the program.

There are a number of valuable resources available that can help in all stages of the application process. Some are listed in Table 16.4, but three books are highlighted here because they are extremely helpful to students during the application process. The first is *Graduate Study in Psychology* (American Psychological Association, 2013), which lists all master's and doctoral programs in the United States and Canada. This book delineates which programs are APA- or CPA-accredited, but it also lists programs in other areas of psychology (industrial/organizational, behavioral neuroscience, cognitive, etc.). Thus, it can be used for students seeking graduate training in any area of psychology. Note also that APA offers an online version of this book with a searchable database. The cost is approximately $20 for three months of access: www.apa.org/pubs/databases/gradstudy/index.aspx

Similar to the print version of *Graduate Study in Psychology*, a publication called *Getting In: A Step-by-Step Plan for Gaining Admission to Graduate School in Psychology*, 2nd ed. (American Psychological Association, 2007) provides detailed information on the application process for graduate programs in any area of psychology. Many sections of that book focus on specific aspects of the application process (choosing which programs to apply to, preparing a resume, writing a personal statement, etc.), and there is an appendix with a timetable for the application process.

TABLE 16.4 Helpful Resources for Psychology Majors and Those Who Are Considering Applying to Graduate School

Although this is not an exhaustive list, many of these books have been extraordinarily helpful to students who are considering a career in psychology and who plan to apply to graduate school.

Majoring in Psychology and Considering Different Career Options

Careers in Psychology: Opportunities in a Changing World, 4th ed., by Tara L. Kuther and Robert D. Morgan (Belmont, CA: Thomson/ Wadsworth, 2013)

Finding Jobs With a Psychology Bachelor's Degree: Expert Advice for Launching Your Career by R. E. Landrum (Washington, DC: American Psychological Association, 2009)

The Insider's Guide to the Psychology Major: Everything You Need to Know About the Degree and Profession by A. R. Wegenek and W. Buskist (Washington, DC: American Psychological Association, 2010)

The Portable Mentor: Expert Guide to a Successful Career in Psychology (2nd ed.) by M. J. Prinstein (New York: Springer, 2013)

The Psychology Major: Career Options and Strategies for Success (4th ed.) by R. E. Landrum and S. F. Davis (Upper Saddle River, NJ: Prentice Hall, 2009)

Your Career in Psychology: Putting Your Graduate Degree To Work, by S. F. Davis, P. J. Giordano, and C. A. Licht (Malden, MA: Wiley-Blackwell)

Applying to Graduate School

Applying to Graduate School in Psychology: Advice From Successful Students and Prominent Psychologists by A. C. Kracen and I. J. Wallace (Washington, DC: American Psychological Association, 2008)

Getting In: A Step-by-Step Plan for Gaining Admission to Graduate School in Psychology, 2nd ed., by the American, Psychological Association (Washington, DC: American Psychological Association, 2007)

Graduate Study in Psychology, by the American, Psychological Association (Washington, DC: American Psychological Association, 2013)

Insider's Guide to Graduate Programs in Clinical and Counseling Psychology, 2012/2013 Edition, by John C. Norcross and Michael A. Sayette (New York: Guilford, 2012)

Surviving Graduate School and Beyond

The Compleat Academic: A Career Guide, 2nd ed., by John M. Darley, Mark P. Zanna, and Henry L. Roediger (Washington, DC: American Psychological Association, 2004)

Life after Graduate School in Psychology: Insider's Advice from New Psychologists, by Robert D. Morgan, Tara L. Kuther, and Corey J. Habben (New York: Psychology Press, 2005)

You've Earned Your Doctorate in Psychology. . . Now What? Securing a Job as an Academic or Professional Psychologist, by E. M. Morgan and E. Landrum (Washington, DC: American Psychological Association, 2012)

If you already know that you want to apply to a clinical or counseling doctoral program, then an extraordinary resource can be found in the *Insider's Guide to Graduate Programs in Clinical and Counseling Psychology 2012/2013 Edition* (Norcross & Sayette, 2012). This book focuses on the application process and also has a listing of every APA- and CPA-accredited PhD and PsyD program in the United States and Canada, with helpful information about each program. Of particular interest to many applicants, each program is rated on a 1 to 7 scale (where 1 refers to a program that is fully practice oriented, 4 refers to a program with equal emphasis on practice and research skills, and 7 refers to a program that is fully research oriented). This information is usually based on reports by the Director of Clinical Training in each program, so the information can help students find programs that are consistent with their needs and interests.

Additional information can also be accessed online. One valuable resource for gaining information about graduate schools and the application process is the APA Web site (www.apa .org), where students can find out about APA-accredited programs, careers in psychology, and salary information about various jobs in psychology. The Council of University Directors of Clinical Psychology (CUDCP; http://cudcp.us/) also maintains a Web site that provides links to many clinical programs. Note that not all CUDCP programs are APA-accredited, so you must verify the accreditation status of a program through the other resources mentioned above. In an effort to help students learn more about programs as they decide where to apply, CUDCP has a voluntary program through which clinical programs provide "full disclosure" of admissions and outcome data for their program on their Web site. This information is very useful to potential applicants, who can then compare programs directly on the same variables (e.g., number of applicants, number of accepted students, GRE and GPA averages for recently admitted students, number of graduate students who applied for and secured an internship, number of graduating students, average length of time it took for those students to graduate). If you are scanning doctoral programs online, go to the clinical psychology Web page and look for this full disclosure data in a tabular format; it should be labeled "Clinical Student Admissions, Outcomes, and Other Data."

Since January 2007, the American Psychological Association has required all APA-accredited doctoral programs to give applicants the following information:

- Time it takes to complete the program.
- Cost of completing the program (e.g., tuition, fees, financial aid options, etc.).
- Percent of incoming students receiving funding.
- Success of graduate students in obtaining internships.
- Attrition (i.e., how many students enter the program and then drop out each year).
- Number and percentage of graduates from the program who have become licensed in the past decade.

This information is meant to help students compare programs on these variables so that they can make informed decisions when considering their options for graduate training (Munsey, 2007). For example, as noted in Chapter 15, there is a nationwide "internship crisis" that leaves some students without access to an internship site (McCutcheon, 2011). The problem is particularly severe for students in certain training programs (Parent & Williamson, 2010), so be sure to look carefully at the internship "match" rates of all the programs you are considering. Notably, a comparison of APA-accredited clinical psychology programs found that freestanding PsyD programs had significantly lower internship match rates than any other type of program (Norcross, Ellis, & Sayette, 2010). When searching clinical programs' websites, look for the link to "Clinical Student Admissions, Outcomes, and Other Data."

There is also a one-page resource posted on the Web site of CUDCP (http://cudcp.us/files/Reports/CUDCP_2010_Psy_Grad_School_Fact_sheet.pdf). It is a succinct and helpful document written for students who are interested in applying to graduate school in clinical psychology. Much of the information is also relevant to students interested in other aspects of psychology, so it is worth a look.

Another excellent online resource was written by Dr. Mitch Prinstein (2013), who is the director of Clinical Training in the Department of Psychology at the University of North Carolina, Chapel Hill. Titled "Mitch's Uncensored Advice for Applying to Graduate School in Clinical Psychology," this student-friendly document provides up-to-date and reliable advice (www.unc.edu/~mjp1970/Mitch%27s%20Grad%20School%20Advice.pdf).

There is also an impressive blog by Emily Bell, who is a graduate student in clinical psychology at Kent State University. Entitled "How To Apply to Clinical Psychology PhD Programs: Practical advice from someone who's done it . . . three times." A valuable aspect of this blog is its acknowledgement that it often takes multiple tries to get into a PhD program in clinical psychology (http://clinicalpsychgradapp.wordpress.com/).

Finally, there are online message boards for students interested in clinical psychology (Fauber, 2006). Sites such as *The Student Doctor Network* (http://studentdoctor.net/) in clinical psychology receive a great deal of attention from prospective students. Given that the postings are mostly just other students' opinions, you may want to check more formal sites to confirm information that is crucial to your application (e.g., an application date or specific information about a professor), but message boards are yet another way that students can access up-to-date information. With the wealth of information in printed material as well as online, you should have access to plenty of resources during the arduous task of applying to graduate school. But beware. Many websites are run or funded largely by for-profit institutions—so seek information from reputable sources that are not trying to sell you something, and think critically about the information you find.

Obviously, applying to graduate school is a major undertaking, not something to be done on the spur of the moment. Here is a checklist of the tasks you must complete to successfully accomplish this undertaking:

1. Study for and take the GRE General and Subject tests at least once each.
2. Search online for programs to which to apply, and identify at least 10 to 15 appropriate programs.
3. Obtain information on these programs, and fill out the application and financial aid forms for each.
4. Arrange for your transcripts from all of your undergraduate institutions to be sent to each graduate program.
5. Arrange for your GRE scores to be sent to each program.

6. Identify three or four professors who are willing to write letters of recommendation for you, and get them the necessary forms and information about your undergraduate career at least one month prior to the first application deadline.

7. Write a personal statement and revise it as often as necessary based on feedback you have received from one or more faculty members.

Once you have done your "homework" and read these resources and sought information online, you may want to talk with a trusted professor or two to see if they have any suggestions for you during the application process. In preparing for courses, doing research, and keeping current for clinical practice, most faculty members carefully review new ideas and research, attend professional meetings, and participate in continuing education workshops. This exposure to the field helps faculty members learn about various departments, programs, schools, training and research staff, the nature and theoretical orientations of different programs, recent changes in the direction of certain departments, and other pertinent information. Although it is not reasonable to expect faculty members to know about all or even most doctoral programs, they will be able to provide you with good information about many of them. In addition, the faculty may have personal contacts at schools that may help your application. A personal recommendation from a faculty member can be a valuable help in highlighting your credentials and increasing the attention your application receives.

Similarly, graduate students at your undergraduate institution may know a great deal about the application process—they have all been through that process. If you have clinical psychology graduate students as teaching assistants or instructors, make sure to talk with them about their application experiences. They may also have information about programs that you are interested in because they may have also applied to and been interviewed at those programs not long ago.

Professional journals and related publications are additional information sources that many applicants overlook. For example, one way to find programs that meet your needs is to identify faculty who are studying topics that interest you. A thorough search of the literature—using PsycINFO, Google, or other online search engines—will very likely highlight faculty with whom you might like to study and indicate where they can be reached. Using Google or another search engine, you can often find personal websites and/or curriculum vitae (CVs) for faculty members. If you can't, their e-mail addresses are nearly always posted on the university website (check the "People" section for the Psychology Department where the faculty member works); e-mail addresses are also listed on professors' published articles. However, do some "homework" before asking faculty questions about their work or the graduate program that could easily be answered with a quick review of their CV or the departmental website.

What Does It Mean When a Clinical Psychology Graduate Program is Accredited by the American Psychological Association (APA)?

APA accreditation means that a clinical program has met a minimum standard of quality (see Chapter 15). Accreditation applies to educational institutions and programs, not to individuals. It does not guarantee jobs or licensure for individuals, though being a graduate of an accredited program greatly facilitates such achievement. It does speak to the manner and quality by which an educational institution or program conducts its business. It speaks to a sense of public trust, as well as professional quality (APA, 2012).

Thus, graduating with a PhD from any APA-accredited program is seen as a laudatory accomplishment. Further, many APA-approved internships will only accept applicants from APA-approved graduate programs and many states will only grant licensure as a psychologist to applicants from an APA-accredited program. Thus, if you are thinking about a PhD in clinical psychology, there are many reasons to limit your search to APA-approved programs.

A list of APA-accredited programs in clinical psychology is published each year in the December issue of the APA's main journal, *American Psychologist*. The APA also accredits PhD programs in other areas, including counseling and school psychology, as well as a number of PsyD programs. Master's programs are not accredited by APA, so it is more difficult to identify high-quality programs at that level. A complete list of APA accredited programs in clinical, counseling, and school psychology can be found on the APA website at www.apa.org/ed/accreditation/programs/clinical.aspx

What Does it Mean When a Clinical Psychology Graduate Program is Accredited by the Psychological Clinical Science Accreditation System (PCSAS)?

As mentioned in Chapter 15, the new Psychological Clinical Science Accreditation System (PCSAS) was developed by research-oriented clinical scientists who were dissatisfied with the APA accreditation system (Baker, McFall, & Shoaham, 2009). The first clinical psychology program was accredited by PCSAS in 2009, and by 2013, 21 others had been accredited and 5 more were under consideration. The latest list of PCSAS-accredited programs is available at http://pcsas.org/am.

Currently, all of the PCSAS accredited programs are retaining their APA (or CPA) accreditation, so students will probably not have to make a choice among programs that have APA vs. PCSAS accreditation. PCSAS accreditation does, however, highlight these programs' commitment to empirical rigor, so if you are especially interested in a career as a clinical scientist, be sure to look further into these programs.

When Should I Apply, and What Kind of Timeline Should I Expect?

Specific timelines can be found in both *Getting In: A Step-by-Step Plan for Gaining Admission to Graduate School in Psychology*, 2nd ed. (American Psychological Association, 2007) and the *Insider's Guide to Graduate Programs in Clinical and Counseling Psychology* 2012/2013 Edition (Norcross & Sayette, 2012). These guidelines should help to make sure you are accomplishing all of the necessary application tasks in a timely fashion.

In general, it is reasonable to start seeking information in June or July, a little over a year before your desired admission date (e.g., July 2014 for the fall of 2015). Seeking specific information earlier than this can sometimes backfire, because admissions deadlines or requirements might change from year to year, but it is never too early to look for more general information about programs that fit your needs because overall program emphases and training philosophies do not usually change that rapidly.

Nearly all graduate programs post admissions information on their Web sites, most programs also post application forms and related materials, and many have a Frequently Asked Questions section that helps to clarify the application process.

Although department application deadlines vary, most fall between December 1 and January 15. A few come earlier while others (mostly for master's degree programs or professional schools) run later. Some departments with later deadlines select their students continuously as applications arrive for processing. If you apply to programs that use this "rolling admissions" plan, it is to your advantage to submit your application early.

To How Many Programs Should I Apply?

It is difficult to identify a specific number of applications that is appropriate for all students. We are reminded of two cases: One student applied to six schools and was admitted to all of them, while another applied to 27 and was admitted to one. Since competition for admission to PhD programs is keen, the general rule is to apply to as many programs as you can reasonably afford. The larger the number of applications, the better your chances of being accepted.

It is our experience that even students with relatively strong credentials will want to apply to at least 15 programs to ensure at least one offer of acceptance and to increase their chances of receiving funding as well. Norcross and Sayette (2012) suggest that you apply to at least five programs which you might consider "safe" schools where your credentials would be considered to be strong, five "ambitious" programs where your credentials might not be as strong as needed but at least you are in the ball park, and one or two "stretch" programs where your credentials are far below the average but perhaps where you have an especially good fit with the program (e.g., your area of expertise in the research or clinical domain). Note, however, that because of the demand for PhD programs in clinical psychology, there are fewer and fewer programs that can be considered "safe" bets for admission.

As you gather information about potential graduate programs, you should also make a note of how many applications each program receives and how many applicants are admitted to the program. Even among excellent clinical doctoral programs, the percentage of admissions varies significantly, thus affecting your chances of being accepted. For example, in 2011, 80 students applied to the clinical PhD program at the University of South Dakota and 7 (9.2%) entered the program, while 680 students applied to Boston University and 10 (1.2%) entered the program. Both programs are excellent—yet the numbers of applicants varied significantly. Although we know of no formal studies on this issue, it appears that programs in larger cities or programs in more desirable places to live (especially those with mild winters!) tend to receive more applications than comparable programs in smaller towns or in areas with harsher climates.

Thus, if your dream school is in a highly desirable city with perfect weather, you may want to consider looking into equally excellent programs in less popular places because there may well be fewer applicants to those latter programs.

Once you have decided on a final list of schools, ask yourself what you will do if you are not accepted by any of them. If your credentials are somewhat marginal for doctoral programs, you may want to consider applying to a handful of master's programs as a back-up if you do not receive admission into any doctoral programs. Many well-respected psychologists had to first complete a terminal master's program and then reapply to doctoral programs in clinical psychology in order to achieve their goal of the PhD. However, do not apply to programs that are really not acceptable to you. Such applications waste admission committee time, your time, not to mention your money.

How Much Will It Cost to Apply?

Applying to graduate school is an expensive process. Taking both GRE tests (the General and the Subject tests) costs $325. Departmental application fees can be as high as $100, but average about $50 (Norcross & Sayette, 2012). Transcript costs (usually $5 to $10 each) and additional test report fees (e.g., $25 for GRE scores to be sent to each school) can add up very quickly. Someone applying to 10 graduate programs can expect an average cost of over $1,100 during the application process. Note, too, that if you are lucky enough to be invited for an interview, you will also need to cover your own travel costs in most cases.

If you are operating under significant financial constraints, there may be ways for you to lighten the financial burden somewhat. For example, the Educational Testing Service offers a GRE Fee Reduction Program for those who (a) receive financial aid at their university and who receive almost no money from their parents, (b) are involved in certain national programs (such as the McNair Scholars Program or the Gates Millennium Scholars Program), and (c) are unemployed and currently not students. Under this program, GRE fees can be reduced by 50%, but thorough documentation of one's status must be provided and the reductions are awarded on a first-come, first-served basis. In addition, many universities allow you to petition for a reduced or waived application fee—but these reductions and waivers do not come easily. One's financial hardship must be well documented, and in some cases only applicants with certain characteristics (e.g., members of an underrepresented ethnic/minority group) are eligible for a reduced or waived fee. In short, if money is a problem for you, make sure to look for these options—but do not count on them.

What Testing Is Involved in Applying to Graduate School?

As already mentioned, the large majority of graduate schools require the GRE for admission, and most admissions committees weigh GRE scores heavily in their acceptance decisions (Norcross & Sayette, 2012). Here, we review the contents of the GRE, discuss studying for it, and then discuss its role in the graduate school admissions process.

WHAT IS THE GRE? The GRE consists of a general test and a subject test—in this case, the subject is psychology. The General Test is described thoroughly in the *Graduate Record Examinations Information and Registration Bulletin* (www.ets.org/gre/ or for the free downloadable GRE Bulletin: www.ets.org/s/gre/pdf/12_13_gre_info_reg_bulletin.pdf).
The General GRE Test is now called the *GRE revised General Test* due to its new scoring procedures (described later) and has three main components:

- Verbal Reasoning (Vl)
- Quantitative Reasoning (Q)
- Analytical Writing (AW)

The test takes over three hours to complete and is only offered via computer in the United States and most industrialized countries. There are hundreds of official testing sites across the United States and Canada, and students can arrange to take the test at a time that is convenient for them.

The General GRE Test was revised significantly and according to the GRE Bulletin, the ". . . revised test more closely reflects the kind of thinking you will do in graduate or business school and demonstrates that you are ready for graduate-level work." (p. 6). Further, whereas scores on the Verbal and Quantitative sections before August of 2011 could range from 200 to 800 in 10-point increments, these scores can now range from 130–170, in 1-point increments. The scores on Analytical Writing in the revised test range from 0 to 6, in half-point increments.

The Subject Test in Psychology is required by approximately two-thirds of doctoral programs in psychology. It covers the entire field of psychology, including but not limited to: learning, memory, behavioral neuroscience, social, clinical, abnormal, developmental, personality, research methodology, measurement, history, and industrial/organizational psychology. The Subject Test in Psychology takes almost three hours to complete and, unlike the General GRE Test, it can be taken only via the paper-based method, and it is offered only three times a year (usually in October, November, and April). It takes approximately 6 weeks to receive a hard copy of the scores of paper-based tests, so be sure to take the Subject Test on a scheduled date that is at least 6 weeks before your earliest application deadline. For example, if December 1 is the first deadline for the schools to which you are applying, then only the October test date will meet that deadline.

It is obviously important to know the results of your GRE General and Subject Tests before you begin the graduate school application process because the scores will shape your decisions about where to apply. If you score at the 95th percentile it will be reasonable to apply to the most competitive schools, whereas scores at the 50th percentile would require a more conservative strategy.

SHOULD I STUDY FOR THE GRE?   You can, and should, study for the GRE! The GRE Web site describes the types of questions found on the general test, along with a number of strategies you can use in taking the computer-based test. A free full-length sample GRE general test, which includes instructions for evaluating your performance, is available from the GRE program at the Educational Testing Service. ETS also sells practice material, including GRE general tests and GRE subject tests actually administered in previous years. In addition, ETS now sells software that allows you to practice the computer version of the test and receive feedback on your performance. All of this material can help you become familiar with the types and forms of questions you are likely to encounter on the GRE, and it can also give you practice at pacing yourself during the actual examination.

You can also prepare for the GRE general test via test preparation courses (presented live or online by test preparation companies such as Kaplan and Princeton Review) and annually revised test preparation books. Because in-person and online courses can be quite expensive (some cost more than $1,200), most students tend to use the test preparation books. These books usually provide a mathematics and vocabulary review, tips on test taking, and a set of sample test items, and many of them come with computer-based enhancement features. Some of the more frequently used "how to prepare" books are published by Barron's Educational Series, Arco Publishing Company, Kaplan, and Princeton Review. They are readily available at most bookstores (whether online or in the store).

Deciding on test preparation courses versus self-preparation is a matter of individual choice. Some students do not have the time or inclination to design a disciplined preparation study schedule and, for them, the expense of test preparation courses is worth it because the courses provide needed structure. An alternative strategy is to do the self-preparation for the first time you take the test, and then if you are not satisfied with your scores, you can try the more formal test preparation courses. Whether you decide on a formal course or a do-it yourself approach, it is important to prepare for the GRE General Test in some way. The stakes are rather high—whether you receive an offer to a PhD program and/or the type of financial aid you receive depend to a large degree on how well you do on the GRE tests.

As for the Subject Test in Psychology, remember that it covers all areas of the discipline. Names, theories, and definitions are likely to be tested, as will basic concepts. No one is expected to know about every area, so if you have not been exposed to certain aspects of psychology, you will no doubt have trouble with some questions. You can prepare for the Subject Test in psychology by thoroughly reviewing a comprehensive introductory psychology textbook. In addition, books that present the history of psychology and/or systems and theories in psychology provide information that is particularly useful in preparing for the psychology Subject Test. As with the General GRE, there are also in-person, online, and printed materials that can help you prepare for the GRE Subject Test. If you are not a psychology major, then scoring well on the GRE Subject Test is especially important, since it may be the only way for you to show your knowledge of the field. Whether or not you are a psychology major, it is in your best interest to study for both the General and the Subject GRE tests and to prepare extensively for these important exams.

Why is the GRE so important to admission committees? In addition to its predictive validity, the GRE represents the only data for which direct comparisons can be made across all applicants. Everyone takes exactly the same test, so performance is not influenced by differences in collegiate standards, as are letters of recommendation and college grades. A score at the 85th percentile on the verbal subtest for a student at the University of California–San Diego means the same as a score at the 85th percentile for someone at the University of Vermont. Thus, the GRE is widely viewed as providing a valid indicator of a student's potential for successful performance in graduate school. In addition, the GRE and undergraduate GPA together can serve as relatively objective screening instruments that help admission committees reduce several hundred applicants to a more manageable number. With this dramatically smaller pool of applicants, the admissions committee can then give much closer scrutiny to other, more qualitative and time-consuming selection criteria, such as the personal statement, letters of recommendation, and personal interview (Morgan & Korschgen, 2006).

Acceptable GRE scores, however, vary according to the type of program to which you are applying. For example, acceptance into a master's program will likely not require as high a GRE score as acceptance into a doctoral program. Using the old General GRE scoring system, one survey found that students in master's programs averaged 1053 on the GRE (Verbal and Quantitative combined), whereas students in doctoral programs averaged 1183 (Norcross, Karpiak, & Santoro, 2005). Note, however, that this survey included all areas of psychology and also included both PsyD and PhD programs in the category of doctoral programs. In a follow-up to that study, but still using the old GRE scoring system, Norcross, Ellis, and Sayette, (2010) found that across all clinical programs, the average combined score was 1243; the highest average combined score (1283) was found among students in research-oriented PhD programs and the lowest average combined score (1061) was seen among students in freestanding PsyD programs. Overall, the minimum GRE scores reported for PsyD programs are lower than in programs with equal emphasis on research and practice and lower than research-oriented PhD programs (Norcross & Sayette, 2012). Note also that some freestanding, non–university-based PsyD programs do not require the GRE test as part of the admissions process.

Depending on the diversity-related rules and regulations of the university, scores on the GRE and other standardized quantitative tests are sometimes not given as much weight when evaluating applications from members of ethnic minority groups, international students, students with disabilities, and other "nontraditional" or disadvantaged students whose potential might not be captured fully by such tests. When GRE scores or other standardized tests are required by an admissions committee, everyone must submit them, but sometimes the scores are weighted differently depending on the other characteristics of the applicant.

How Important Is My Grade Point Average?

Your GPA is seen as an excellent indicator of the effort you have exerted in college and your willingness to work up to or even beyond your predicted potential. Thus, an outstanding undergraduate GPA may offset to some degree a less than stellar GRE score. Conversely, outstanding GRE scores combined with a mediocre GPA could raise serious concerns about an applicant's motivation for education. This is why the GRE and GPA make such excellent screening instruments— together they offer valid and objective measures of both academic potential and willingness to work hard.

Admissions committees look for several things when examining an applicant's college transcripts. Although your overall GPA is important, admissions committees often focus on your psychology GPA. They also want to make sure you are a serious student and that you did not just "blow off" your other courses because they may have been outside your major. However, the committees tend to be forgiving if you started off in another area of study (e.g., as a premed student) and did poorly in these courses. Admissions committees also consider whether you maintained or improved your GPA as you progressed through college or let your GPA slip as you got closer to graduation. Admissions committees tend to be more forgiving of poorer grades early in your college career than they are of later poorer grades. They also may pay close attention to more rigorous required courses such as statistics and experimental methods. This is why some schools ask that you submit the GPA for only your last two years of college.

Will I Need Letters of Recommendation? If So, How Many and from Whom?

Three letters of recommendation are required by most graduate programs in clinical psychology. Sometimes additional letters of recommendation are allowed, but we do not recommend submitting more than four unless they are requested specifically. Whether you submit three letters or four, at least two of them should be from academic references—that is, from psychology faculty familiar with your academic ability. Ideally, at least one of the letters should be from a faculty member who has supervised you in research-related activities. If faculty from other disciplines can enlarge the picture of your academic achievement and potential for graduate study, feel free to ask them for letters.

A letter from someone who supervised a clinically related experience or relevant job generally is not given much weight by admissions committees. Similarly, letters from "important people" such as senators, governors, and religious leaders do not help your application. Generally, these say nothing more than "I have been asked to write . . . " and "please give this student full consideration." Such letters are likely to leave the impression that you feel incapable of "making it" on your own. Unless the writer is in a position to judge the candidate's potential as a graduate student, researcher, or a clinician, such "prestige" letters should not be submitted. Similarly, if you know a clinical psychologist through social contacts only (e.g., as a friend of the family), then you should not ask him or her to write you a letter of recommendation. Although the psychologist knows what it takes to excel in graduate school, his or her judgment is not considered to be objective because of the personal and social relationships that exist between the psychologist, you, and your family. Most letters of recommendation include a statement as to how the letter writer knows the applicant, and admissions committees do not look kindly on letters that say things like "I have known the applicant for all of her life, and I have watched her grow from a timid toddler into a scintillating senior student."

What Should I Know about Asking for Letters of Recommendation?

When you approach a faculty member to ask for a letter, it is likely that he or she will want you to provide information about yourself as a reminder of what role you played on a research project, what grade you got in a course, what honors you won, and the like. Information about your activities, accomplishments, and job experiences can supplement classroom contacts in a way that enhances the tone and thrust of a recommendation letter.

Here is a list of items you should provide to faculty who are writing letters of recommendation for you (Morgan & Korschgen, 2006, p. 106):

1. Your full name.
2. Major, minor, curriculum, and specialization.
3. A computation of the grade average in your major, in all college work, and in courses taken since the end of your sophomore year.
4. A transcript of your college courses and grades.
5. A list of the psychology laboratory courses you have had.
6. A current resume or curriculum vita.
7. A description of other research experiences, including comments about the full extent of your participation (include a copy of any major research papers you wrote or contributed to).
8. A list of honor societies, clubs, and organizations to which you belong, along with comments on your participation (be sure to mention positions of responsibility you held).

9. A brief discussion of jobs you have held and volunteer work you have done. Some students carry heavy workloads while being enrolled as full-time students in order to pay for their education; this information should be included, too.
10. An outline of your personal and professional plans and goals.
11. Any other information that might be helpful to the person in writing your letter of recommendation.

Be sure to ask for letters and provide all appropriate recommendation information at least one month before the first application is due. Remember, faculty often write letters for many students; give them plenty of time to prepare yours. To reduce the possibility of error and to speed the process, do everything you can to minimize the work the faculty has to do in putting your recommendation material together. So provide your letter writers with a list of the schools to which you are applying, along with the application deadline for each, which specific program you are applying to (e.g., masters in counseling, PhD program in clinical psychology), any additional rating forms to complete, and information about how the letter should be sent (e.g., a hard copy directly to the admission's office, a hard copy in a sealed and signed envelope to be returned to you, or perhaps an e-mail sent to someone or posted to a secure website). If hard copies are required, then you should provide stamped, addressed envelopes for each program. Most programs these days seem to have one of two different application systems:

1. A self-contained application, whereby the applicant has to collect all of the materials (including the letters of recommendation in a sealed envelope signed across the flap by the letter writer) and submit them in one packet, or
2. Completely online (including letters of recommendation that are either sent via e-mail or posted to a secure website in the admissions office).

Will I Be Able to See My Letters of Recommendation?

Because of federal law, letters of reference are not confidential unless you waive your right to see them. We encourage you to do so because many admissions committee members feel that letter writers are more likely to provide candid evaluations when they know that the student will not see the letter. If you are concerned about what the letter might include, ask potential letter writers if they can write in support of your application, not just if they will write a letter of reference. Most faculty are more than willing to indicate whether they can write a favorable letter for you.

What Should I Write about in My Personal Statement?

Most applications require some form of a personal statement, usually two to three pages in length. Good advice on writing a personal statement is provided in *Getting In: A Step-by-Step Plan for Gaining Admission to Graduate School in Psychology*, 2nd ed. (American Psychological Association, 2007) and *Insider's Guide to Graduate Programs in Clinical and Counseling Psychology 2012/2013 Edition* (Norcross & Sayette, 2012). Generally, variations on the same personal statement can be used for all of your applications, but the essay should be revised to reflect how your research and clinical interests mesh with the particular faculty and program to which you are applying. Programs differ in how much weight they give to the personal statement, and although what you write in the personal statement may not help your application a great deal, failure to do a good job can certainly can hurt your chances. Any grammatical or typographical errors will reflect negatively on your writing skills, your conscientiousness, and your attention to details. Therefore, it is absolutely imperative that you ask someone else, preferably a faculty member, to read your statement for coherence and writing style as well as to identify any grammatical or typographical errors.

What should go into a personal statement? Contrary to its title, it should not be too personal. Think of the document as a professional rather than personal statement. In other words, it is not an autobiography, so do not bring up childhood experiences that may have shaped your life. Nor should the statement get into any personal problems that you or family members may have had, even if these experiences ultimately influenced your decision to apply to clinical psychology programs. Instead, the personal statement is your chance to convince the admissions committee that you are a good match for their graduate program. The fact that the committee is reading your personal statement means that you have already passed their initial screening and they feel your credentials are appropriate for their program. Thus, in writing your statement, you need to

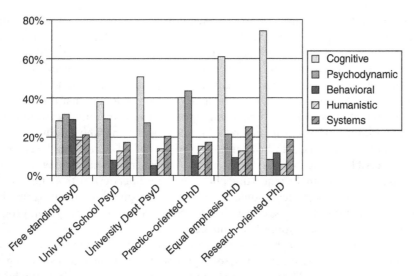

FIGURE 16.3 Faculty Theoretical Orientation by Type of American Psychological Association-Accredited Clinical Program. Univ=university; Dept=department. Source: Norcross, J. C., Ellis, J. L., & Sayette, M. A. (2010). Getting in and getting money: A comparative analysis of admission standards, acceptance rates, and financial assistance across the research-practice continuum in clinical psychology programs. *Training and Education in Professional Psychology, 4*, 99–104.

think about what graduate programs are looking for in their applicants, and then describe how you meet those criteria. As noted earlier, graduate programs generally are looking for students who are intellectually curious, highly motivated, hard working, and have a good familiarity with the science of psychology, especially as it relates to research experience. These are the factors that you should be addressing in some fashion in your personal statement. Bottoms and Nysse (1999) noted that a personal statement should cover four key components: (a) previous research experience, (b) current research interests, (c) other relevant experience, and (d) future career goals. In the section on current research interests, make sure to include some brief discussion of how your interests coincide with ongoing research by the faculty in the program to which you are applying. Once students are accepted, many programs assign students to faculty for research mentoring, so it should be crystal clear how your interests mesh with those of one or more of the faculty in the program. It is quite common, and often expected, that students name faculty members in their personal statement to identify those with whom they would like to work. Listing up to about three faculty members with related interests is considered acceptable, but don't try to list the entire clinical faculty; that will make you seem unfocused and desperate. Ideally, you will have already made contact with some faculty members to express interest in their work and to begin a dialogue that might help at the point of admissions decisions.

In general, then, the personal statement should show how you "fit" with each particular graduate program. As Figure 16.3 shows, clinical theoretical orientations vary widely based on the type of program to which you are applying, so make a case in your personal statement about how you are a good fit for that program—both from a research as well as a clinical perspective.

The section on other relevant experience is the place to include a brief discussion of any clinical volunteer work or extracurricular activities in which you have been involved. Having clinical experience may not be a very important criterion for admission, but admissions committees do like to know if you have had some experience in "helping relationships." Similarly, a long list of extracurricular activities, such as being a member of Psi Chi, will not strengthen your application very much unless you served in a leadership role. So you can include mention of clinical activities and extracurricular activities, but realize that they are not considered strongly in the admissions process except to the extent that they indicate your involvement in psychology, your interpersonal skills, and your willingness to work hard.

Are Personal Interviews Required?

Once applications have been reviewed by admissions committees, it is common for strong candidates to be invited for an in-person interview. The large majority of programs require an interview and most prefer an in-person interview. Offers for interviews usually only come after the admissions committee has considerably narrowed down the number of applicants. Interviews are usually held on campus, which gives the candidate and the department a chance to size each other up. If you are invited to attend an interview, try to do so regardless of the inconvenience or expense involved. If departments have to choose between two equally qualified students, only one of whom interviewed in person, this individual will probably have the advantage. Graduate admissions committees take the lack of an interview as a possible sign that the applicant is not really interested in the program. All things being equal, admissions committees would rather offer acceptance to a student who is clearly interested in the program and who appears ready to attend the program rather than someone who expresses little interest in the program. If it is financially or physically impossible for you to attend the interview, then you may want to show your motivation for admission to the program by requesting phone or Skype interviews with a number of faculty, by contacting a number of graduate students to begin a dialogue about the program, by letting the admissions committee know via e-mail that you remain very interested in their program, and the like. Do not make a pest of yourself, of course.

Programs that require telephone or Skype interviews rather than in-person interviews are the exception rather than the rule. However, some programs conduct an initial screening interview on the phone to gauge the applicant's interest in and appropriateness for the program before actually inviting the candidate for an onsite interview. With this in mind, you might want to try a bit of strategy used by one successful applicant. He created an information sheet about each of the programs to which he had applied (e.g., faculty names, particular emphases and strengths) along with notes about his career interests and goals, and carried the notes with him at all times in case the next cell phone call was from someone on an admissions committee. He felt that if he received a call from a school to which he had applied, having this information handy would reduce his anxiety about the conversation and help him organize his responses so that his emphasis would be appropriate for each institution. This plan also assured that he would include all the points he wanted to make during a call and thus avoid regret over failing to mention something important. He did receive a call and his strategy worked.

The same strategy can be used when you are contacted by e-mail. Increasingly, graduate admissions committees deal with applicants solely electronically, so be sure to check your e-mail frequently throughout the application process. If you have a non–university-based e-mail address with a provocative name (e.g., sexything555), then you should definitely set up an e-mail account with a more formal address well before the application process begins. Also, double check any quotations or images that are sent automatically as part of your e-mail signature, since these sayings or images might not present you in the best light professionally.

Although social norms differ somewhat in the use of e-mail, your e-mail messages during the application in the application process should be very formal. Make sure to use proper grammar, punctuation, and spelling when communicating with a graduate program. Even contact with a graduate student assistant or secretary should be very formal, since these e-mails are often forwarded to the admissions committee. Overall, every contact you have with the university is another opportunity for the admissions committee to make judgments about your intelligence and professionalism. To our knowledge, texting is rarely used for communication between applicants and programs, but if you do receive a text about your application—your response should be as formal and professional as possible.

While we are on the topic of technology, you should be aware that a number of admissions committees look for additional information about applicants by conducting searches on Facebook, MySpace, Twitter, and LinkedIn. They may also locate and read what might be on your personal website or blog. You should do similar searches yourself, review what you find, consider what an admissions committee would think about you after reviewing your online presence, and consider editing your information (Behnke, 2007). This step is important not only to enhance your chances for admission but to burnish your professional image even after you have been accepted by a graduate program. The impression that others have of you online may have professional repercussions. Consider the fact that, for example, once you begin to work with clients as part of your training (and afterward), those clients might well search for information about you online. What impression would their search convey about their therapist? These points relate to many professional issues that were discussed in Chapter 15, but they also are relevant during the application and interview process.

If you did not take part in a face-to-face interview and if you were lucky enough to be admitted into the program, it is appropriate to visit the school and talk with department representatives and graduate students. Make an appointment well ahead of time by e-mailing the admissions coordinator or the director of clinical training and ask to meet with clinical psychology faculty and graduate students. Be prepared to outline briefly the nature of your questions, and have a number of alternative visit dates in mind.

Often, students want to schedule interview appointments before they apply to a school or before they are admitted. Some departments, especially PsyD and master's programs, welcome early interviews. However, other departments have so many applicants that it is impossible to accommodate such requests. Usually, the information you gather through the methods mentioned earlier will be sufficient to help you decide whether or not to apply to a particular program. If the material you accessed is not sufficiently informative to give you a clear picture of a particular program, contact the department for additional details. Before doing so, though, be sure to carefully read the material you have on hand so that you do not ask about things that a department has already covered in its printed or online material. Once you are admitted, however, campus visits and interviews can help you to compare programs and guide your decision about which offer to accept.

How Do I Prepare for an Onsite Interview?

If you are invited for an interview, it means that you are in the final, relatively small (e.g., 25 to 35) pool of applicants to a particular program and thus have a good chance of eventually receiving an offer from that program. So optimize the impact of your interview, both in terms of the information you gather and the impression you make, by engaging in some preparation and practice. Here are some specific suggestions.

1. Gather and read as much information about the program as you can. Read and become familiar with everything the program has sent you, as well as any additional information you can get from the Internet. Nearly all graduate programs use their Web sites for recruitment purposes, so make sure to read everything on the clinical area Web site (including affiliated Web sites or attached documents, if they are provided). It is quite common for programs to show sample course sequences on their Web site (such as the one shown in Table 16.5), so make sure to familiarize yourself with these details before you show up for the interview.
2. Read and become familiar with several published articles by each of the faculty members with whom you are most interested in working. As you read these articles, make notes on topics that interest you and questions that the research raises.
3. Prepare yourself to talk at length about your own research experience. You should be able to describe the purposes of the research, the methodology, the primary results, and the lessons you have learned from this experience. It is a good strategy to prepare in advance a brief description of your research experience and to practice presenting this brief summary. Do not assume you can just show up at the interview and spontaneously describe your research in a coherent and knowledgeable fashion.
4. Plan the questions you will want to ask the faculty. They will assume that you have such questions, and if you are not prepared, the interview will end early on a negative note. Try not to ask questions that can be answered by reading the information on the program's Web site (e.g., what courses will I take in my first year?). In addition, many of the "nuts-and-bolts" issues (e.g., financial support) are handled in group information sessions. Instead, in your faculty interview, you should ask substantive questions that better inform you about what it would be like to be a graduate student in this program. Thus, appropriate topics include the faculty member's mentoring style, the strengths and weaknesses of the program, graduate student–faculty relations, and the types of internships and jobs obtained by graduates from the program.

Some programs offer to have their graduate students provide housing for you during the visit. Take them up on this offer because this is an excellent opportunity for you to spend time asking current graduate students about life in the program. You may want to ask them many of the same questions that you ask the faculty, especially those dealing with mentoring, student–faculty relations, and strengths and weaknesses of the program. A word of caution, however—it is very likely that the graduate students will offer feedback to the faculty regarding the applicants they have met. Therefore, do not let your guard down too much and do not say things that contradict

TABLE 16.5 Sample Schedule for a PhD Program in Clinical Psychology

Although there are many variations in the curricula of APA-accredited clinical training programs, the schedule shown here approximates what students encounter in many of them.

Fall Semester	Spring Semester
First Year	
Psychological Statistics I	Psychological Statistics II
Clinical Assessment I: Cognitive/Intellectual/Achievement	Clinical Assessment II: Clinical and Psychopathology
Psychopathology—Foundations	Advanced Psychopathology
Practicum in Assessment	Practicum in Assessment
Professional Issues: Ethics, Cultural Diversity, and History and Systems of Psychology	Selected Core/Breadth Requirement (Social Psychology, Developmental Psychology, Learning, Physiological Psychology, Cognitive Psychology)
Second Year	
Evidence-Based Treatments I:	Evidence-Based Treatments II:
Interventions Practicum	Interventions Practicum
Selected Core/Breadth (choose one from list above)	Clinical Seminar (Advanced CBT, Behavior Therapy, Child and Family Therapy, Health Psychology, Addictions, Prevention, Dissemination, Group Therapy)
MA Research	MA Research
Third Year	
Psychotherapy Practicum	Psychotherapy Practicum
Clinical Seminar (choose one from list above)	Advanced Nonclinical Seminar
Advanced Clinical Research Seminar (Family Research, Psychopathology Research, Research in Psychotherapy)	Clinical or Nonclinical Research Seminar
Advanced Clinical Seminar	A written qualifying examination is to be taken during the third year of graduate work, but no later than the beginning of the fourth year. Only those students who have completed their master's thesis are permitted to register for the qualifying examination.
Fourth Year	
Clinical or Nonclinical Research Seminar	Same as Fall Semester
Advanced Research Methods	
Research on Dissertation	
Fifth Year	
APA-Accredited Internship	

what you told the faculty members. Further, if the students should happen to take you out on the town after the interview, be very careful about how you behave. The formal interviews may be over, but you will continue to be under scrutiny. So align your behavior—including the amount of alcohol you consume—to match your goal of being admitted. Most faculty can recount instances in which applicants' chances for admission were ruined by things said or done late at night while out with the department's graduate students.

During the interview, you will want to come across as poised, mature, motivated, thoughtful, and interpersonally skilled. Remember that clinical program faculty will not only evaluate you in terms of your potential as a graduate student but also as someone whom they will feel comfortable sending into clinical settings.

A good way to increase your poise and confidence during interviews is to engage in a role-played interview before going on the visit. This mock interview can be with a roommate or, better yet, with a faculty member at your home institution. Make the interview as realistic as possible. Dress appropriately, shake the person's hand, introduce yourself, and in all ways interact as if the interview were the real thing. Address the interviewing faculty members as "Dr." until and unless you are told to do otherwise. If you can arrange to make a video of your practice interview, all the better. Watch the video, ask for feedback from the mock interviewer, and consider doing another role-play so that you can work on correcting any problem areas.

What Kind of Financial Aid Is Available for Graduate Study?

As mentioned earlier, most PhD programs in clinical psychology offer some form of financial aid to their students. PsyD- and master's-level programs are much less likely to do so. Financial aid comes in several forms: loans, fellowships, tuition remission, and work programs. The major source of financial aid for graduate students is the university in which they are enrolled, though aid may also be available through guaranteed loan programs (many of which are government sponsored) and national awards, which are competitive and have specific criteria for application. These awards are given directly to students for use at the school of their choice.

The availability of awards and loans changes regularly, so you should check with the financial aid officer at your college or at the institutions to which you are applying for current information. Because your financial support is most likely to come through the program to which you are admitted, the information you will receive with your application material is very important—read it carefully!

Fellowships and scholarships are given on many campuses as outright grants to support and encourage students with outstanding academic and research potential. These are few in number, and competition for them is fierce. Many fellowships and scholarships are used to encourage applications from people with limited financial resources and from members of racial/ethnic minority groups. Others are designed for applicants who have outstanding academic records or who have distinguished themselves in other ways, such as by conducting or publishing research in a particular topic area.

Assistantships come in two forms: research assistantships (RAs) and teaching assistantships (TAs). As their names imply, both entail working at jobs that require the graduate student to assist faculty in research projects or in teaching responsibilities (e.g., as a discussion leader, laboratory instructor, or grader). Assistantships usually require 10 to 20 hours of work each week. Although RA and TA positions have a work requirement, many graduate programs consider the work requirement to be part of students' training (e.g., learning to conduct research or teach, respectively), so these positions are often helpful to students for what they learn in addition to what they earn.

Loan programs exist on most campuses as a way of assisting students to invest in their own futures. These loans usually carry a low interest rate, and repayment begins only after the student leaves graduate school. Students in PsyD programs are more likely to need loans than those in PhD programs (Norcross & Sayette, 2012). This is because PsyD programs tend to be more expensive and are less likely to offer financial aid or paid teaching or research assistantship positions. Note that, partially due to the increasing rate of defaulting on federal student loans, the rules for these loans are becoming more restrictive. Time and credit limits for completion of masters and graduate programs may apply, and there are more restrictions on who is eligible. So think carefully about enrolling in a program whose cost may leave you with unmanageable debt.

Finally, many programs offer some form of tuition remission. They may offer complete remission, meaning that the student pays no tuition at all, or they offer some portion of remission (e.g., 50%). Alternatively, the program may waive the out-of-state tuition and only require that the student pay in-state tuition, even if the student is coming from out of state.

Not all types of aid are offered at all schools. Again, carefully read the financial aid information you receive to be sure you understand what is available at each school you are considering. Further, tuition costs differ dramatically across schools. If the program does not guarantee tuition remission to its students, then you must factor tuition costs into the equation when deciding to which schools to apply. In addition to consulting the Financial Aid Office website at the universities you are considering, you should explore other resources for information about applying for financial aid. These include, for example, Peterson's (2012), *Scholarships, Grants, and Prizes*. Note too that, as mentioned earlier, APA accredited programs are required to provide information on the percentage of incoming students who received funding, so be sure to look for that information on the programs' websites when you are comparing programs. It will be in the section labeled "Clinical Student Admissions, Outcomes, and Other Data."

ARE THERE ASSISTANTSHIPS AVAILABLE FROM DEPARTMENTS OTHER THAN THE ONE TO WHICH I HAVE APPLIED?   Assistantships of various types may be available on a campus. If you are accepted into a clinical psychology program that offers little or no financial aid, it is well worth your time to check on the availability of assistantships in departments outside psychology. For example, administrators of campus residence halls may hire graduate students to serve as hall counselors. Further, departments offering large undergraduate courses may not have enough graduate students in their programs to fill the teaching assistantships available and thus may "import" assistants from related areas. Identify your skills and experiences and seek out jobs that fit them. Note, however, that many programs require that you receive permission before working outside of the program—so double-check with your mentor or with the Director of Clinical Training before seeking employment on your own.

OTHER IMPORTANT QUESTIONS

Are There Any Last-Minute Things I Need to Do When Applying?

Once you have sent in your applications, check with each department to which you have applied to assure that your application is complete. The large majority of admissions offices now have online tracking systems that allow applicants to verify the status of their applications. Some departments notify students when letters of reference or GRE scores are missing, but many do not. To eliminate this problem, be sure to track your application through the proper channels at the different programs.

When I Am Admitted to a Program, How Long Will I Have to Make a Decision about Whether to Accept?

Most admissions offers include a specific deadline by which the student must accept or reject the offer. For doctoral programs, offers of acceptance and financial aid must be given to applicants by April 1, and applicants must respond by April 15. Realistically, offers from competitive programs often are given well before April 1st, and many offers are made as early as February these days. The April 15th deadline for responding to an offer was adopted by the APA Council of Graduate Departments of Psychology to protect students from being pressured to make decisions before having full information about their alternatives (American Psychological Association, 2013). Once you make a final decision about which offer to accept, you should convey that information to all programs at which you are still being actively considered. Your acceptance decision is considered binding after the April 15th date, although professional courtesy suggests that the decision is binding even if it is made before April 15.

Ideally, applicants will have ranked all their potential programs once they have completed their interviews so that they can provide quick feedback to programs once they begin receiving

Graduate school can be enjoyable and rewarding. *Source*: Ryan McVay/Photodisc/Thinkstock.

offers. For example, students who are lucky enough to get an early offer from their top choice should quickly accept the offer and then also should withdraw their applications from the other programs. Similarly, if applicants receive an offer from their third choice, they could withdraw their applications from their fourth and lower choices but hold onto the acceptance at their third choice while they are waiting to hear from their first and second choices. Overall, if a student has decided not to accept an offer, courtesy dictates informing the department of that decision as soon as possible. This courtesy will be appreciated by the department and may provide space for another student. If you do not receive an acceptance by April 1, you may be the one who appreciates an applicant turning down an offer quickly, since it may free up a space for you.

Will I Be Successful in Gaining Admission?

Obviously, we can't answer this question with certainty, but we hope the information and suggestions presented here will be helpful. A careful examination of your own credentials and the advice of those who have experience with students applying to graduate school in clinical psychology will help you apply to appropriate programs and maximize your chances of admission. We wish you success!

Chapter Summary

This chapter provided information on various career options for the helping professions and reviewed the requirements and procedures for applying to graduate training programs in clinical psychology. There are a number of paths that can lead to a career as a therapist, including earning a master's degree, PhD, or PsyD degree in clinical psychology, a master's or PhD degree in counseling psychology, a PhD degree in school psychology, a specialist degree in education (EDS, EdD), or, a master's or doctorate in social work, a master's degree in rehabilitation counseling, a medical degree in psychiatry or behavioral pediatrics, or a nursing degree in psychiatric nursing.

Depending on which career they are interested in pursuing, students can use coursework, research experience, clinical experience, and extracurricular activities to prepare for their career. Salaries vary across careers, with doctoral-level jobs paying more than master's-level positions.

There are a number of different training options in clinical psychology for students to consider, including a master's, PhD, or PsyD degree. If they are seeking a doctoral program, students are encouraged to seek only APA-accredited programs given potential limitations on licensure from unaccredited programs. In addition, students who are interested in high-level clinical scientist programs are encouraged to seek out programs that are accredited by the Psychological Clinical Science Accreditation System (PCSAS).

Students educated in the process of preparing for and applying to graduate programs should fare better than those who are not. There are significant personal and financial commitments required of persons attending doctoral programs, so students must evaluate their own motivation and goals before proceeding.

If your motivation and energy are strong, then the components of the application process and the process itself should be manageable. The primary components of the application are GRE scores, GPA, letters of recommendation, and personal statements. The process of application is complex but relatively straightforward for students who can keep track of a lot of information. In general, carefulness and conscientiousness are encouraged throughout this process. Good luck!!

Study Questions

1. List the various degrees and career options that lead to the possibility of being a therapist.
2. How might research experience and clinical experience influence your professional life (in terms of career goals and admission to graduate school)?
3. What are the pros and cons of earning a master's versus a PhD in clinical psychology?
4. What are the pros and cons of earning a PhD versus a PsyD in clinical psychology?
5. Describe the APA accreditation process.
6. What is PCSAS?
7. Describe some of the personal costs that exist when in graduate school.
8. In terms of financial costs of graduate school, describe the differences between PhD and PsyD programs. What are the reasons for these differences?
9. Describe the content of the GRE General Test and discuss how the test is administered currently.
10. Describe the content of the GRE Subject Test and discuss how the test is administered currently.
11. What are the different types of GPA calculations that might be requested while applying to graduate programs?
12. What is the process to request letters of recommendation?
13. What should be included in your personal statement?
14. What are the ways to gather information about graduate programs and the application process?
15. What advice do we offer about how many applications to submit?

Web Sites

- APA Committee on Accreditation (with a list of accredited programs): http://www.apa.org/ed/accreditation/
- Academy of Psychological Clinical Science (with a list of programs in the Academy): http://www.psych.arizona.edu/apcs
- Psychological Clinical Science Accreditation System (with a list of accredited programs) http://pcsas.org/
- APA Guide to Getting Into Graduate School: http://www.apa.org/education/grad/applying.aspx
- Graduate Record Exam from the Educational Testing Service: http://www.ets.org/gre
- APA Site for Careers in Psychology: http://www.apa.org/about/students.aspx American Psychiatric Association: http://www.psych.org/
- National Association of Social Workers: http://socialworkers.org/
- American Psychiatric Nurses Association: http://www.apna.org/
- National Association of School Psychologists: http://www.nasponline.org/
- American Association for Marriage and Family Therapy: http://www.aamft.org/

MOVIES

50/50 (2011): In the context of helping treat a young adult dealing with cancer, a beginning therapist shows questionable ethical behavior in this superb drama/comedy.

Five-Year Engagement (2012): Romantic comedy that highlights a recent psychology graduate student who moves across country with her fiancé to complete a postdoctoral fellowship, thereby putting their wedding on hold.

MEMOIRS

Brooklyn Zoo: The Education of a Psychotherapist by Darcy Lockman (2012; New York: Doubleday). Fascinating first-person account by journalist-turned-clinical-psychology-graduate student of her year on internship at Kings Country Hospital near Brooklyn.

Darkness Visible: A Memoir of Madness by William Styron (1990; New York: Vintage Books). Recalling his slide into a major depressive disorder and eventual successful treatment, this well-known writer provides a "must read" memoir for anyone studying to be a clinical psychologist.

References

American Psychological Association. (2007). *Getting in: A step-by-step plan for gaining admission to graduate school in psychology* (2nd ed.). Washington, DC: Author.

American Psychological Association. (2012). *Guidelines and principles for accreditation of programs in professional psychology.* Washington, DC: Author.

American Psychological Association. (2013). *Graduate study in psychology.* Washington, DC: Author.

Baker, T. B., McFall, R. M., & Shoham, V. (2009). Current status and future prospects of clinical psychology: Toward a scientifically principled approach to mental and behavioral health care. *Psychological Science in the Public Interest, 9,* 67–89.

Behnke, S. (2007). Posting on the Internet: An opportunity for self (and other) reflection. *Monitor on Psychology, 38,* 60–61.

Bottoms, B. L., & Nysse, K. L. (1999, Fall). Applying to graduate school: Writing a compelling personal statement. *Eye on Psi Chi, 4,* 20–22.

Chamberlin, J. (2008). Early career concerns. *Monitor on Psychology, 39,* 68–69.

Clay, R. A. (2006). Loan repayment. *GradPSYCH, 4,* 1–3.

Darley, J. M., Zanna, M. P., & Roediger, H. L. (2004). *The compleat academic: A career guide* (2nd ed.). Washington, DC: American Psychological Association.

Davis, S. F., Giordano, P. J., & Licht, C. A. (2009). *Your career in psychology: Putting your graduate degree to work.* Malden, MA: Wiley-Blackwell.

Fauber, R. L. (2006). Graduate admissions in clinical psychology: Observations on the present and thoughts on the future. *Clinical Psychology: Science and Practice, 13,* 227–234.

Kracen, A. C., & Wallace, I. J. (2008). *Applying to graduate school in psychology: Advice from successful students and prominent psychologists.* Washington, DC: American Psychological Association.

Kuncel, N. R., & Hezlett, S. A. (2007). Standardized tests predict graduate students' success. *Science, 315,* 1080–1081.

Kuther, T. L., & Morgan, R. D. (2013). *Careers in psychology: Opportunities in a changing world* (4th ed.). Belmont, CA: Thomson/Wadsworth.

Landrum, R. E. (2009). *Finding jobs with a psychology bachelor's degree: Expert advice for launching your career.* Washington, DC: American Psychological Association.

Landrum, R. E., & Davis, S. F. (2009). *The psychology major: Career options and strategies for success* (4th ed.). Upper Saddle River, NJ: Prentice Hall.

Martin, P. R. (2011). Clinical psychology going forward: The need to promote clinical psychology and to respond to the training crisis. *Clinical Psychologist, 15,* 93–102.

McCutcheon, S. R. (2011). The internship crisis: An uncommon urgency to build a common solution. *Training and Education in Professional Psychology, 5,* 144–148.

Morgan, B. L., & Korschgen, A. J. (2006). *Majoring in psych? Career options for psychology undergraduates* (3rd ed.). Boston, MA: Allyn and Bacon.

Morgan, E. M., & Landrum, R. E. (2012). *You've earned your doctorate in psychology. . . Now what? Securing a job as an academic or professional psychologist.* Washington, DC: American Psychological Association.

Morgan, R. D., Kuther, T. L., & Habben, C. J. (2005). *Life after graduate school in psychology: Insider's advice from new psychologists.* New York, NY: Psychology Press.

Munsey, C. (2007). New disclosure requirements help students compare psychology programs. *GradPSYCH, 5,* 1–2.

Norcross, J. C., Castle, P. H., Sayette, M. A., & Mayne, T. J. (2004). The PsyD: Heterogeneity in practitioner training. *Professional Psychology: Research and Practice, 35,* 412–419.

Norcross, J. C., Ellis, J. L., & Sayette, M. A. (2010). Getting in and getting money: A comparative analysis of admission standards, acceptance rates, and financial assistance across the research-practice continuum in clinical psychology programs. *Training and Education in Professional Psychology, 4,* 99–104.

Norcross, J. C., Karpiak, C. P., & Santoro, S. O. (2005). Clinical psychologists across the years: The Division of Clinical Psychology from 1960 to 2003. *Journal of Clinical Psychology, 61,* 1467–1483.

Norcross, J. C., & Sayette, M. A. (2012). *Insider's guide to graduate programs in clinical and counseling psychology: 2012/2013 edition.* New York, NY: Guilford.

Parent, M. C., & Williamson, J. B. (2010). Program disparities in unmatched internship applicants. *Training and Education in Professional Psychology, 4,* 116–120.

Peterson. (2012). *Scholarships, grants, and prizes.* Lawrenceville, NJ: Peterson's Publishing.

Prinstein, M. J. (2013). *The portable mentor: Expert guide to a successful career in psychology* (2nd ed.). New York, NY: Springer.

Vasquez, M. J. T., & Jones, J. M. (2006). Increasing the number of psychologists of color: Public policy issues for affirmative diversity. *American Psychologist, 61,* 132–142.

Wegenek, A. R., & Buskist, W. (2010). *The insider's guide to the psychology major: Everything you need to know about the degree and profession.* Washington, DC: American Psychological Association.

Weissman, M. M., Verdell, H., Gameroff, M. J., Bledsoe, S. E., Betts, K., et al. (2006). National survey of psychotherapy training in psychiatry, psychology, and social work. *Archives of General Psychiatry, 63,* 925–934.

REFERENCES

Abdel, K. A. M. (1994). Normative results on the Arabic Fear Survey Schedule III. *Journal of Behavior Therapy and Experimental Psychiatry, 25,* 61–67.

Abdullah, T. & Brown, T. L. (2011). Mental illness stigma and ethnocultural beliefs, values, and norms: An integrative review. *Clinical Psychology Review, 31,* 934–948.

Ables, B. S. & Brandsma, J. M. (1977). *Therapy for couples.* San Francisco: Jossey-Bass.

Abood, L. G. (1960). A chemical approach to the problem of mental illness. In D. D. Jackson (Ed.), *The etiology of schizophrenia* (pp. 91–119). New York, NY: Basic Books.

Abramson, L. Y., Seligman, M. E. P., & Teasdale, J. D. (1978). Learned helplessness in humans: Critique and reformulation. *Journal of Abnormal Psychology, 87,* 49–74.

Abt, L. E. (1992). Clinical psychology and the emergence of psychotherapy. *Professional Psychology: Research and Practice, 23,* 176–178.

Achenbach, T. M. (1978). The Child Behavior Profile I: Boys aged 6–11. *Journal of Consulting and Clinical Psychology, 46,* 478–488.

Achenbach, T. M. (2008a). Assessment, diagnosis, nosology, and taxonomy of child and adolescent psychopathology. In M. Hersen & A. M. Gross (Eds.). *Handbook of clinical psychology: Children and adolescents* (Vol. 2, pp. 429–457). Hoboken, NJ: John Wiley & Sons.

Achenbach, T. M. (2008b). Multicultural perspectives on developmental psychopathology. In J. J. Hudziak (Ed.), *Developmental psychopathology and wellness: Genetic and environmental influences* (pp. 23–47). Arlington, VA: American Psychiatric Publishing.

Achenbach, T. M. & Edelbrock, C. S. (1978). The classification of child psychopathology: A review and analysis of empirical efforts. *Psychological Bulletin, 85,* 1275–1301.

Achenbach, T. M. & Edelbrock, C. S. (1981). Behavioral problems and competencies reported by parents of normal and disturbed children aged four to sixteen. Monographs of the Society for Research in Child Development, 46 (Serial No. 188).

Achenbach, T. M. & Rescorla, L. A. (2001). *Manual for the Achenbach System of Empirically Based Assessment (ASEBA) school-age forms and profiles.* Burlington, VT: University of Vermont, Research Center for Children, Youth, and Families.

Ackerman, N. & Sobel, R. (1950). Family diagnosis: An approach to the preschool child. *American Journal of Orthopsychiatry, 20,* 744–753.

Ackerman, N. W. (1958). *The psychodynamics of family life.* New York, NY: Basic Books.

Ackerman, M. J. & Ackerman, M. (1997). Custody evaluation practices: A survey of experienced professionals (revisited). *Professional Psychology: Research and Practice, 28,* 137–145.

Adair, J. C., Schwartz, R., L., & Barrett, A. M. (2003). Anosognosia. In K. M. Heilman & E. Valenstein (Eds.), *Clinical neuropsychology* (4th ed.). New York, NY: Oxford.

Addis, M. E. & Krasnow, A. D. (2000). A national survey of practicing psychologists' attitudes toward psychotherapy treatment manuals. *Journal of Consulting and Clinical Psychology, 68,* 331–339.

Adelman, H. S. & Taylor, L. (2009). *Mental health in schools: Engaging learners, preventing problems, and improving schools.* Thousand Oaks, CA: Corwin Press.

Adler, A. (1933). *Social interest: A challenge to mankind.* Vienna, Leipzig: Rolf Passer.

Adler, A. B., Bliese, P. D., McGurk, D., Hoge, C. W., & Castro, C. A. (2009). Battlemind debriefing and battlemind training as early interventions with soldiers returning from Iraq: Randomization by platoon. *Journal of Consulting and Clinical Psychology, 77,* 928–940.

Adler, A. B., Bilese, P. D., McGurk, D., Hoge, C.W., & Castro, C. A. (2011). Battlemind debriefing and battlemind training as early interventions with soldiers returning from Iraq: Randomized by platoon. *Sport, Exercise, and Performance Psychology, 1,* 66-83.

Adler, N. E. & Matthews, K. (1994). Health psychology: Why do some people get sick and some stay well. *Annual Review of Psychology, 45,* 229–259.

Ægisdóttir, S., White, M. J., Spengler, P. M., Maugrman, A. S., Anderson, L., Cook, R. S., et al. (2006). The meta-analysis of clinical judgment project: Fifty-six years of accumulated research on clinical versus statistical prediction. *Counseling Psychologist, 34,* 341–382.

Aguilera, A. & Munoz, R. F. (2011). Text messaging as an adjunct to CBT in low-income populations: A usability and feasibility pilot study. *Professional Psychology: Research and Practice, 42,* 472–478.

Ahn, H. & Wampold, B. E. (2001). Where oh where are the specific ingredients? A meta-analysis of component studies in counseling and psychotherapy. *Journal of Counseling Psychology, 48,* 251–257.

Ai, A. L., Ladd, K. L., Peterson, C., Cook, C. A., Shearer, M., & Koenig, H. G. (2010). Long-term adjustment after surviving open heart surgery: The effect of using prayer for coping replicated in a prospective design. *The Gerontologist, 50,* 798–809.

Aklin, W. M. & Turner, S. M. (2006). Toward understanding ethnic and cultural factors in the interviewing process. *Psychotherapy: Theory, Research Practice, Training, 43,* 50–64.

Albee, G. W. (1959). *Mental health manpower trends.* New York, NY: Basic Books.

Alexander, F. & French, T.M. (1946). *Psychoanalytic Therapy: Principles and Application.* New York, NY: Ronald Press.

Allen, D. M. (2006). Use of between-session homework in systems-oriented individual psychotherapy. *Journal of Psychotherapy Integration, 16,* 238–253.

Allen, G. J. (1971). The effectiveness of study counseling and desensitization in alleviating test anxiety in college students. *Journal of Abnormal Psychology, 77,* 282–289.

Allen, L. B., McHugh, R. K., & Barlow, D. H. (2008). Emotional disorders: A unified protocol. In D. H. Barlow (Ed), *Clinical handbook of psychological disorders: A step-by-step treatment manual* (4th ed., pp. 216–249). New York, NY: Guilford Press, xiv, 722 pp.

Allport, G. W., Vernon, C. E., & Lindzey, G. (1970). *Study of values* (revised manual). Boston, MA: Houghton-Mifflin.

Alper, B. S., Hand, J. A., Elliott, S. G., Kinkade, S., Hauan, M. J., Onion, D. K., et al. (2004). How much effort is needed to keep up with the literature relevant for primary care? *Journal of the Medical Library Association, 92*, 429–437.

Alphonso, C. A. & Olarte, S. (2011). Contemporary practice patterns of dynamic psychiatrists—survey results. *The Journal of the American Academy of Psychoanalysis and Dynamic Psychiatry, 39*, 7–26.

Ambrosino, R., Heffernan, J., Shuttlesworth, G., & Ambrosino, R. (2012). *Social work and social welfare: An introduction*. Belmont, CA: Brooks/Cole.

American Psychiatric Association. (1983). *Statement on prediction of dangerousness*. Washington, DC: Author.

American Psychiatric Association. (1994). *Diagnostic and statistical manual of mental disorders* (4th ed.). Washington, DC: Author.

American Psychiatric Association. (1998). *DSM-IV sourcebook* (Vol. 4). Washington, DC: Author.

American Psychiatric Association. (2000). *Diagnostic and statistical manual of mental disorders (4th ed.): Text Revision (DSM-IV-TR)*. Washington, DC: Author.

American Psychiatric Association. (2012a). Proposed DSM-5 organizational structure and disorder names. Retrieved February 24, 2012 from http://www.dsm5.org/proposedrevision/Pages/proposed-dsm5-organizational-structure-and-disorder-names.aspx.

American Psychiatric Association (2012b). DSM-5 will not increase the number of mental disorders. Retrieved August 22, 2012 from http://dsmfacts.org/author/apa.

American Psychological Association. (1985). *Standards for educational and psychological tests*. Washington, DC: Author.

American Psychological Association. (1998). *Guidelines for psychological evaluations in child protection matters*. Washington, DC: Author.

American Psychological Association. (2000b). *Current major field of APA members by membership status* (Table 3). Retrieved December 13, 2001, from http://research.apa.org/member.

American Psychological Association. (2002a). Criteria for evaluating treatment guidelines. *American Psychologist, 57*, 1052–1059.

American Psychological Association. (2003). Guidelines on multicultural education, training, research, practice, and organizational change for psychologists. *American Psychologist, 58*, 377–402.

American Psychological Association Presidential Task Force on Evidence-Based Practice. (2006). Evidence-based practice in psychology. *American Psychologist, 61*, 271–285.

American, Psychological Association (2007). *Getting in: A step-by-step plan for gaining admission to graduate school in psychology* (2nd ed.). Washington, DC: Author.

American Psychological Association (2007). Guidelines for psychological practice with girls and women. *American Psychologist, 62*, 949–979.

American Psychological Association (2007). *Record Keeping Guidelines*. Washington, DC: American Psychological Association.

American Psychological Association (2009). *Guidelines and principles for accreditation of programs in professional psychology*. Washington, DC: Author.

American Psychological Association (2010). *Ethical Principles of Psychologists and Codes of Conduct*. American Psychological Association.

American Psychological Association. (2010). Guidelines for child custody evaluations in family law proceedings. *American Psychologist, 65*, 863–867.

American Psychological Association (2011a). Accredited doctoral programs in professional psychology: 2011. *American Psychologist, 66*, 8834–898.

American Psychological Association (2011b). Practice guidelines regarding psychologists' involvement in pharmacological issues. *American Psychologist, 66*, 835–849.

American Psychological Association (2012). *Guidelines and principles for accreditation of programs in professional psychology*. Washington, DC: Author.

American Psychological Association Board of Directors. (2012). APA's statement on the DSM-5 development process. *Monitor on Psychology*, Jan., 10.

American Psychological Association, Division 12 (2012). *About clinical psychology*. Retrieved Jan 1, 2012 from http://www.apa.org/divisions/div12/aboutcp.html.

American Psychological Association, Division 16 (2012). *About school psychology*. Retrieved Jan 1, 2012 from http://www.apa.org/divisions/div12/aboutcp.html.

American Psychological Association, Division 17 (2012). *About counseling psychology*. Retrieved Jan 1, 2012 from http://www.apa.org/divisions/div17/aboutcp.html.

American Psychological Association History and Archives (2012). APA Membership Statistics. Retrieved January 5, 2012 from http://www.apa.org/about/archives/membership/index.aspx.

American Psychological Association (2012a). Guidelines for assessment of and intervention with persons with disabilities. *American Psychologist, 67*, 43–62.

American Psychological Association (2012b). Guidelines for psychological practice with lesbian, gay, and bisexual clients. *American Psychologist, 67*, 10–42.

American Psychological Association (2012c). Supplement to listing of accredited doctoral, internship, and postdoctoral training programs in professional psychology. *American Psychologist, 67*, 418–420.

American Psychological Association (2013). *Graduate study in psychology*. Washington, DC: Author.

Amundson, M. E., Hart, C. A., & Holmes, T. H. (1986). *Manual for the schedule of recent experience*. Seattle, WA: University of Washington Press.

Anastasi, A. (1988). *Psychological testing* (6th ed.). New York, NY: Macmillan.

Anastasi, A. & Urbina, S. (1997). *Psychological testing* (7th ed.). Upper Saddle River, NJ: Prentice Hall.

Andersen, B. L. (1992). Psychological interventions for cancer patients to enhance the quality of life. *Journal of Consulting & Clinical Psychology, 60*, 552–568.

Andersen, B. L., Farrar, W. B., Golden-Kreutz, D. M., Glaser, R., Emery, C. F., Crespin, T. R., et al. (2004). Psychological, behavioral, and immune changes after a psychological intervention: A clinical trial. *Journal of Clinical Oncology, 22*, 3570–3580.

Andersen, B. L., Thornton, L. M., Carson, W. E., III, et al. (2010). Biobehavioral, immune, and health benefits following recurrence for psychological intervention participants. *Clinical Cancer Research, 16(12)*.

Anderson, C. M. & Kim, C. (2005). Evaluating treatment efficacy with single-case designs. In M. C. Roberts & S. S. Ilardi (Eds.), *Handbook of research methods in clinical psychology* (pp. 73–91). Malden, MA: Blackwell Publishing.

Anderson, N. B. (1989). Racial differences in stress-reduced cardiovascular reactivity and hypertension: Current status and substantive issues. *Psychological Bulletin, 105*, 89–105.

Andersson, G. & Asmundson, G. J. G. (2008). Editorial: Should CBT rest on its success? *Cognitive Behavior Therapy, 37*, 1–4.

Antoni, M. H., Carrico, A. W., Duran, R. E., Spitzer, S., Penedo, F., Ironson, G., et al. (2006). Randomized clinical trial of cognitive behavioral stress management on human immunodeficiency virus load in gay men treated with highly active antiretroviral therapy. *Psychosomatic Medicine, 68*, 143–151.

Antony, M. M. & Barlow, D. H. (Eds.) (2011). *Handbook of assessment and treatment planning for psychological disorders* (2nd ed.). New York, NY: Guilford.

Antony, M. M. & Roemer, L. (2011a). *Behavior therapy*. Washington, DC: APA Books.

Antony, M. M. & Roemer, L. (2011b). Behavior therapy: Traditional approaches. In S. B. Messer & A. S. Gurman (Eds.). *Essential Psychotherapies* (3rd ed, pp. 107–142). New York, NY: Springer.

Antony, M. M. & Barlow, D. H. (Eds.) (2011). *Handbook of assessment and treatment planning for psychological disorders* (2nd ed.). New York, NY: Guilford.

Apodaca, T. R. & Miller, W. R. (2003). A meta-analysis of the effectiveness of bibliotherapy for alcohol problems. *Journal of Clinical Psychology, 59*, 289–304.

Appelbaum, P. S. & Grisso, T. (1995). The MacArthur Treatment Competence Study. I: Mental illness and competence to consent to treatment. *Law and Human Behavior, 19*, 105–126.

Apple, R. F. & Agras, W. S. (2007). *Overcoming eating disorders: A cognitive-behavioral treatment for bulimia nervosa and binge-eating workbook*. New York, NY: Oxford University Press.

Arnold, C. (1998). Children and families: A snapshot. Retrieved 12 December 2001, from http://www.clasp.org/pubs/familyformation/stepfamiliesfinal.BK!.htm.

Atanackovic, D., Schnee, B., Schuch, G., Faltz, C., Schulze, J., et al. (2006). Acute psychological stress alters the adaptive immune response: Stress-induced mobilization of effector T cells. *Journal of Neuroimmunology,176*, 141–152.

Atkinson, D. R., Brown, M. T., Parham, T. A., Matthews, L. G., Landrum-Brown, J., & Kim, A. U. (1996). African American client skin tone and clinical judgments of African American and European American psychologists. *Professional Psychology: Research and Practice, 27*, 500–505.

Auerbach, L. (2006). Complementary and alternative medicine in the treatment of prostate cancer. *Journal of Men's Health and Gender, 3*, 397–403.

Austin, E. J., Boyle, G. J., Groth-Marnat, G., Matthews, G., Saklofske, D. H. et al. (2011). Integrating intelligence and personality. In T. M. Harwood, L. E. Beutler, & G. Groth-Marnat (Eds.) *Integrative Assessment of Adult Personality* (pp. 119–151). New York, NY: Guilford.

Ayearst, L. E. & Bagby, R. M. (2010). Evaluating the psychometric properties of psychological measures. . In M. M. Antony & D. H. Barlow (Eds.) *Handbook of Assessment and Treatment Planning for Psychological Disorders* (2nd ed., pp. 23–61). New York, NY: Guilford.

Azar, B. (1996). Behavioral interventions are proven to reduce pain. *APA Monitor* (December), 22.

Azar, S. T. & Benjet, C. L. (1994). A cognitive perspective on ethnicity, race, and termination of parental rights. *Law and Human Behavior, 18*, 249–267.

Babinski, M. J. (1914). Contribiutions a l'etude des troubles mentaux dans l'hemiplegie organique cerebrale (anosognosie). *Review of Neurology, 12*, 845–847.

Babyak, M., Blumenthal, J. A., Herman, S., Khatri, P., Doraiswamy, M., Moore, M., et al. (2000). Exercise treatment for major depression: Maintenance of therapeutic benefit at 10 months. *Psychosomatic Medicine, 62*, 633–638.

Baca-Garcia, E., Perez-Rodriguez, M. M., Oquendo, M. A., et al. (2011). Estimating risk for suicide attempt: Are we asking the right questions?" Passive suicidal ideation as a marker for suicidal behavior. *Journal of Affective Disorders, 134*, 327–332.

Bachelor, A. (2011). Clients' and therapists' views of the therapeutic alliance: Similarities, differences and relationship to therapy outcome. *Clinical Psychology and Psychotherapy*, Article first published online: 14 NOV 2011. DOI: 10.1002/cpp.792.

Bachman, C. M. & Stewart, C. (2011). Self-determination theory and web-enhanced course template development. *Teaching of Psychology, 38*, 180–188.

Baerger, D. R. (2001). Risk management with the suicidal patient: Lessons from case law. *Professional Psychology: Research and Practice, 32*, 359–366.

Bailey, D. S. (2005, January). A niche that puts children first. *American Psychological Association Monitor* (p. 42). Retrieved 15 March 2007, from http://www.apa.org/monitor/jan05/niche.html.

Baio, J. (2012). *Prevalence of autism spectrum disorders: Autism and developmental disabilities monitoring network*. Atlanta, GA: Centers for Disease Control and Prevention.

Baird, A., Dewar, B. K., Critchley, H., Dolan, R., Shallice, T., & Cipolotti, L. (2006). Social and emotional functions in three patients with medial frontal lobe damage including the anterior cingulate cortex. *Cognitive Neuropsychiatry, 11*(4), 369–388.

Baker, T. B., McFall, R. M., & Shoham, V. (2009). Current status and future prospects of clinical psychology: Toward a scientifically principled approach to mental and behavioral health care. *Psychological Science in the Public Interest, 9*, 67–89.

Bandura, A. (1982). Self-efficacy mechanism in human agency. *American Psychologist, 33*, 122–147.

Bantha, R., Moskowitz, J. T., Acree, M., & Folkman, S. (2007). Socioeconomic differences in the effects of prayer on physical symptoms and quality of life. *Journal of Health Psychology, 12*, 249–260.

Barakat, L. P., Pulgaron, E. R., & Daniel, L. C. (2009). Positive psychology in pediatric psychology. In M. C. Roberts & R. G. Steele (Eds.), *Handbook of pediatric psychology* (4th ed., pp. 763–773). New York, NY: Guilford.

Bardos, A. N., Reva, K. K., & Leavitt, R. (2011). Achievement tests in pediatric neuropsychology. In A. S. Davis (Ed), *Handbook of pediatric neuropsychology* (pp. 235–244). New York, NY: Springer Publishing Co, xxi, 1214 pp.

Barkley, R. A., Robin, A. L., & Benton, C. M. (2008). *Your defiant teen: Ten steps to resolve conflict and rebuild your relationship*. New York, NY: Guilford.

Barkley, R. A. & Benton, C. (2010). *Taking charge of adult ADHD*. New York, NY: Guilford.

Barkley, R. A., Knouse, L. E., & Murphy, K. R. (2011). Correspondence and disparity in the self-and other ratings of current and childhood ADHD symptoms and impairment in adults with ADHD. *Psychological Assessment, 23,* 437–446.

Barlow, D. H. (2004). Psychological treatments. *American Psychologist, 59,* 869–878.

Barlow, D. H. & Wolfe, B. (1981). Behavioral approaches to anxiety disorders: A report on the NIMH-SUNY, Albany, research conference. *Journal of Consulting and Clinical Psychology, 49,* 448–454.

Barlow, D. H. & Craske, M. G. (2006). *Master your anxiety and panic*. New York, NY: Oxford University Press.

Barnett, J. E. & Johnson, W. B. (2008). *Ethics desk reference for psychologists*. Washington, DC: American Psychological Association.

Barrett, P. M., Farrell, L. J., Ollendick, T. H., & Dadds, M. (2006). Long-term outcomes of an Australian universal prevention trial of anxiety and depression symptoms in children and youth: An evaluation of the Friends Program. *Journal of Clinical Child and Adolescent Psychology, 35,* 403–411.

Barron, J. W. (Ed.). (1998). *Making diagnosis meaningful: Enhancing evaluation and treatment of psychological disorders*. Washington, DC: American Psychological Association.

Bartol, C. (1996). Police psychology: Then, now, and beyond. *Criminal Justice and Behavior, 23,* 70–89.

Bartol, C. R. & Bartol, A. M. (2008). *Criminal behavior: A psychosocial approach* (8th ed.). Upper Saddle River, NJ: Pearson Education, Inc.

Barton, J. J. (2011). Disorders of higher visual processing. *Handbook of Clinical Neurology, 102,* 223–261.

Bassman, L. E. & Uellendahl, G. (2003). Complementary/alternative medicine: Ethical, professional, and practical challenges for psychologists. *Professional Psychology: Research and Practice, 34,* 264–270.

Bateson, C., Jackson, D. D., Haley, J., & Weakland, J. H. (1956). Toward a theory of schizophrenia. *Behavioral Science, 1,* 251–264.

Baucom, D. H. & Epstein, N. (1990). *Cognitive-behavioral marital therapy*. New York, NY: Bruner/Mazel.

Baucom, D. H., Epstein, N. B., Kirby, J. S., & LaTaillade, J. J. (2010). Cognitive-behavioral couple therapy. In K. S. Dobson (Ed.). *Handbook of cognitive-behavioral therapies* (3rd ed., pp.411–444). New York, NY: Guilford.

Baucom, D. H., Epstein, N. B., Kirby, J. S., & Falconier, M. K. (2011). Couple therapy: Theoretical perspectives and empirical findings. In D. H. Barlow (Ed.), *The Oxford handbook of clinical psychology* (pp. 789–809). New York, NY: Oxford University Press.

Baum, A., Reveson, T. A., & Singer, J. E. (Eds.). (2001). *Handbook of health psychology*. Hillsdale, NJ: Erlbaum.

Baumeister, R. F. & Leary, M. R. (1995). The need to belong: Desire for interpersonal attachments as a fundamental human motivation. *Psychological Bulletin, 117,* 497–529.

Bazelon, D. (1974). Psychiatrists and the adversary process. *Scientific American, 230,* 18–23.

Beach, S. R. H. & Kaslow, N. J. (2006). Relational disorders and relational processes in diagnostic practice: Introduction to the special section. *Journal of Family Psychology, 20,* 353–355.

Bear, D. M. & Fedio, P. (1977). Quantitative analysis of interictal behavior in temporal lobe epilepsy. *Archives of Neurology, 34,* 454–467.

Beaton, E. A. & Simon, T. J. (2011). How might stress contribute to increased risk for schizophrenia in children with chromosome 22q11.2 deletion syndrome? *Journal of neurodevelopmental disorders, 31,* 68–75.

Beauchaine, T. P. & Hinshaw, S. P. (Eds.) (2008). *Child and adolescent psychopathology*. Hoboken, NJ: John Wiley & Sons.

Beauchaine, T. P., Hinshaw, S. P., & Gatzke-Kopp, L. (2008). Genetic and environment in influences on behavior. In T. P. Beauchaine, & S. P. Hinshaw (Eds.), *Child and adolescent psychopathology* (pp. 58–90). Hoboken, NJ: John Wiley & Sons.

Bechtoldt, H., Norcross, J. C., Wyckoff, L., Pokrywa, M. L., & Campbell, L. F. (2001). Theoretical orientations and employment settings of clinical and counseling psychologists: A comparative study. *The Clinical Psychologist, 54,* 3–6.

Beck, A. T. (1963). Thinking and depression: I Idiosyncratic content and cognitive distortions. *Archives of General Psychiatry, 9,* 324–333.

Beck, A. T. (1972). *Depression: Causes and treatment*. Philadelphia, PA: University of Pennsylvania Press.

Beck, A. T. (1976). *Cognitive therapy and the emotional disorders*. New York, NY: International Universities Press.

Beck, A. T., Steer, R. A., & Garbin, M. G. (1988). Psychometric properties of the Beck Depression Inventory: Twenty-five years of evaluation. *Clinical Psychology Review, 8,* 77–100.

Beck, A. T., Steer, R. A., & Brown, G. K. (1996). *Beck Depression Inventory* (2nd ed.). San Antonio, TX: The Psychological Corporation.

Beck, J. S. (2011). *Cognitive behavior therapy*. New York, NY: Guilford Press.

Becker, M. H. & Maiman, L. A. (1975). Sociobehavioral determinants of compliance with health and medical care recommendations. *Medical Care, 13,* 10–24.

Begley, S. (2007). Get "shrunk" at your own risk. Newsweek (June 18). Retrieved June 20, 2007, from http://www.newsweek.com/id/34105.

Behnke, S. (2007). Posting on the Internet: An opportunity for self (and other) reflection. *Monitor on Psychology, 38,* 60–61.

Belar, C. D. (2000). Scientist-practitioner =/= science + practice: Boulder is bolder. *American Psychologist, 55,* 249–250.

Bellack, A. S., Hersen, M., & Himmelhoch, J. M. (1983). A comparison of social skills training, pharmacotherapy and psychotherapy for depression. *Behaviour Research and Therapy, 21,* 101–107.

Bellack, L. (1954). *The thematic apperception test and the children's apperception test in clinical use*. New York, NY: Grune and Straton.

Bellak, L. (1986). *The Thematic Apperception Test, the Children's Apperception Test, and the Senior Apperception Technique in clinical use* (4th ed.). New York, NY: Grune & Stratton.

Bellak, L. (1992). *The TAT, CAT, and SAT in clinical use* (5th ed.). Odessa, FL: Psychological Assessment Resources.

Bender, W. N. (1994). Joint custody: The option of choice. *Journal of Divorce and Remarriage, 21*, 115–131.

Benjamin, L. S. (1997). The origins of psychological species: A history of the beginnings of the divisions of the American Psychological Association. *American Psychologist, 52*, 725–732.

Benjamin, L. T. (2005). A history of clinical psychology as a profession in America (and a glimpse at the future). *Annual review of clinical psychology, 1*, 1–30.

Benson, N., Hulac, D. M., & Kranzler, J. H. (2010). Independent examination of the Wechsler Adult Intelligence Scale—Fourth Edition (WAIS-IV): What does the WAIS-IV measure? *Psychological Assessment, 22*, 121–130.

Ben-Porath, Y. (2012). *Interpreting the MMPI-2-RF*. Minneapolis, MN: University of Minnesota Press.

Ben-Porath, Y. S. & Waller, N. G. (1992). "Normal" personality inventories in clinical assessment: General requirements and potential for using the NEO Personality Inventory. *Psychological Assessment, 4*, 14–19.

Ben-Porath, Y & Tellegen, A. (2008). Empirical correlates of the MMPI-2 Restructured Clinical (RC) scales in mental health, forensic, and nonclinical settings: An introduction. *Journal of Personality Assessment, 90*, 119–121.

Berg, I. A. (1955). Response bias and personality: The deviation hypothesis. *Journal of Psychology, 40*, 61–71.

Bernstein, D., Penner, L. A., Clarke-Stewart, A., & Roy, E. (2011). *Psychology* (9th ed.). Belmont, CA: Wadsworth.

Bernstein, D. A., Borkovec, T. D., & Hazlette-Stevens, H. (2000). *Progressive relaxation training: A manual for the helping professions* (2nd ed.). New York, NY: Praeger.

Bertelsen, A. (1999). Reflections on the clinical utility of the ICD-10 and DSM-IV classifications and their diagnostic criteria. *Australian & New Zealand Journal of Psychiatry, 32*, 166–173.

Beutler, L. E. (2002a). It isn't the size, but the fit. *Clinical Psychology: Science and Practice, 9*, 434–438.

Beutler, L. E. & Malik, (2002). *Rethinking the DSM: A psychological perspective*. Washington, DC: American Psychological Association.

Beutler, L. E. & Clarkin, J. F. (1990). *Systematic treatment selection: Toward targeted therapeutic interventions*. New York, NY: Brunner/Mazel.

Beutler, L. E., Machado, P. P. P., & Neufeldt, S. A. (1994). Therapist variables. In A. Bergin & S. Garfield (Eds.), *Handbook of psychotherapy and behavior change* (4th ed.). New York, NY: John Wiley & Sons.

Beutler, L. E. & Harwood, T. M. (2000). *Prescriptive psychotherapy: A practical guide to systematic treatment selection*. New York, NY: Oxford University Press.

Beutler, L. E. & Groth-Marnat, G. (2003). *Integrative assessment of adult personality* (2nd ed.). New York, NY: Guilford.

Beutler, L. E., Williams, O. B., & Norcross, J. C. (2008). *Innerlife.com*. A copyrighted software package for treatment planning. Available at www.innerlife.com.

Beutler, L. E., Harwood, T. M., Michelson, A., Song, X., & Holman, J. (2011). Resistance/reactance level. *Journal of clinical Psychology, 67*, 133–142.

Bhugra, D. & Bhui, K. (2010). Clinical topics in cultural psychiatry. In R. Bhattacharya, S. Cross, & D. Bhugra (Eds.). *Clinical Topics in Cultural Psychiatry*. London, UK: Royal Colege of Psychiatrists.

Biaggio, M., Orchard, S., Larson, J., Petrino, K., & Mihara, R. (2003). Guidelines for gay/lesbian/ bisexual-affirmative educational practices in graduate psychology programs. *Professional Psychology: Research and Practice, 34*, 548–554.

Bickman, L. (1987). Graduate education in psychology. *American Psychologist, 42*, 1041–1047.

Bieschke, K. J., Bell, D., Davis, C., Hatcher, R., Peterson, R. & Rodolfa, E. R. (2011). Forests, grazing areas, water supplies, and the internship imbalance problem: Redefining the paradigm to implement effective change. *Training and Education in Professional Psychology, 5*, 123–125.

Biglan, A., Flay, B. R., Embry, D. D., & Sandler, I. N. (2012). The critical role of nurturing environments for promoting human well-being. *American Psychologist, 67*, 257–271.

Bigler, E. D. (2007). A motion to exclude and the "fixed" versus "flexible" battery in "forensic" neuropsychology: Challenges to the practice of clinical neuropsychology. *Archives of Clinical Neuropsychology, 22*(1), 45–51. E-pub Dec. 27, 2006.

Bijttebier, P. & Roeyers, H. (2009). Temperament and vulnerability to psychopathology: Introduction to the special issue. *Journal of Abnormal Child Psychology, 37*, 305–308.

Bike, D. H., Norcross, J. C., Schatz, D. M. (2009). Processes and outcomes of psychotherapists' personal therapy: Replication and extension 20 years later. *Psychotherapy, 46*, 19–41.

Birks, Y. & Roger, D. (2000). Identifying components of type-A behavior: "Toxic" and "non-toxic" achieving. *Personality and Individual Differences, 28*, 1093–1105.

Bisiach, E., Luzzatti, C., & Perani, D. (1979). Unilateral neglect, representational schema and consciousness. *Brain, 102*(3), 609–618.

Biswas-Diener, R. (Ed.) (2011). *Positive psychology as social change*. New York, NY: Springer Science.

Black, D. S., Milam, J., & Sussman, S., (2009). Sitting-meditation interventions among youth: A review of treatment efficacy. *Pediatrics, 124*, 532–541.

Blackburn, H., Luepker, R. V., Kline, F. G., Bracht, N., Carlaw, R., Jacobs, B., et al. (1984). The Minnesota Heart Health Program: A research and demonstration project in cardiovascular disease prevention. In J. D. Matarazzo et al. (Eds.), *Behavioral health: A handbook of health enhancement and disease prevention* (pp. 1171–1178). New York, NY: John Wiley & Sons.

Blanchard, E. B. (1992). Psychological treatment of benign headache disorders. *Journal of Consulting and Clinical Psychology, 60*, 537–551.

Blanchard, E. B. (1994). Behavioral medicine and health psychology. In A. E. Bergin & S. L. Garfield (Eds.), *Handbook of psychotherapy and behavior change* (pp. 701–733). New York, NY: John Wiley & Sons.

Blatt, S. J. & Lerner, H. (1983). Psychodynamic perspectives on personality theory. In M. Hersen, A. E. Kazdin, & A. S. Bellack (Eds.), *The clinical psychology handbook* (pp. 87–106). New York, NY: Pergamon Press.

Bleich-Cohen, M., Sharon, H., Weizman, R., Poyurovsky, M., Faragian, S., & Hendler, T. (2012). Diminished language lateralization in schizophrenia corresponds to impaired inter-hemispheric functional connectivity. *Schizophrenia Research, 134*(2-3), 131–136.

Blount, R. L., Bachanas, P. J., Powers, S. W., Cotter, M. C., Franklin, A., Chaplin, W., et al. (1992). Training children to cope and parents to coach them during routine immunizations: Effects on child, parent, and staff behavior. *Behavior Therapy, 23,* 689–705.

Blumenthal, S. J. (1994). Introductory remarks. In S. J. Blumenthal, K. Matthews, & S. M. Weiss (Eds.), *New research frontiers in behavioral medicine* (pp. 9–15). Washington, DC: National Institute of Mental Health.

Bobbitt, B. L. (2006). The importance of professional psychology: A view from managed care. *Professional Psychology: Research and Practice, 37,* 590–597.

Boczkowski, J. A., Zeichner, A., & DeSanto, N. (1985). Neuroleptic compliance among chronic schizophrenic outpatients: An intervention outcome report. *Journal of Consulting and Clinical Psychology, 53,* 666–671.

Bogels, S. M. (1994). A structured-training approach to teaching diagnostic interviewing. *Teaching of Psychology, 21,* 144–150.

Bohart, A. C. (2003). Person-centered psychotherapy and related experiential approaches. In A. S. Gurman & S. B. Messer (Eds.), *Essential psychotherapies* (2nd ed., pp. 107–148). New York, NY: Guilford.

Bohart, A. C. & Watson, J. C. (2011). Person-centered psychotherapy and related experiential approaches. In S. B. Messer, & A. S. Gurman, A. S. (Eds.). *Essential Psychotherapies* (3rd ed., pp. 223–260). New York, NY: The Guilford Press.

Boisvert, C. M. & Faust, D. (2006). Practicing psychologists' knowledge of general psychotherapy research findings: Implications for science-practice relations. *Professional Psychology: Research and Practice, 37,* 708–716.

Bonanno, G. A., Westphal, M. & Mancini, A. D. (2011). Resilience to loss and potential trauma. *Annual Review of Clinical Psychology, 7,* 511–535.

Bonnie, R. & Slobogin, C. (1980). The role of mental health professionals in the criminal process: The case for informed speculation. *Virginia Law Review, 66,* 427–522.

Bonnie, R. J., Jeffries, J. C., Jr., & Low, P. W. (2000). *A case study in the insanity defense: The trial of John W. Hinckley, Jr* (2nd ed.). New York, NY: Foundation Press.

Bordin, E. S. (1979). The generalizability of the psychoanalytic concept of the working alliance. *Psychotherapy: Theory, Research, and Practice, 16,* 252–260.

Borden, W. (2009). *Contemporary psychodynamic theory and practice.* Chicago, IL: Lyceum Books, Inc.

Boring, E. G. (1950). *A history of experimental psychology* (2nd ed.). New York, NY: Appleton-Century-Crofts.

Bornstein, R. F. (2006). A psychoanalytic construct lost and reclaimed: The psychodynamics of personality psychology. *Psychoanalytic Psychology, 23,* 339–353.

Bottoms, B. L. & Nysse, K. L. (1999, Fall). Applying to graduate school: Writing a compelling personal statement. *Eye on Psi Chi, 4,* 20–22.

Botvin, G. J. & Griffin, K. W. (2004). Life skills training: Empirical findings and future directions. *Journal of Primary Prevention, 25,* 211–232.

Bowen, A. M. & Trotter, R. T., II (1995). HIV risk in intravenous drug users and crack cocaine smokers: Predicting stage of change for condom use. *Journal of Consulting and Clinical Psychology, 63,* 238–248.

Brabender, V. & Whitehead, M. L. (2011). Using the Psychodynamic Diagnostic Manual in the training of the competent assessor. *Journal of Personality Assessment, 93,* 185–193.

Bracha, H. S. (2006). Human brain evolution and the "neuroevolutionary time-depth principle:" Implications for the reclassification of fear-circuitry-related traits in DSM-V and for studying resilience to warzone-related posttraumatic stress disorder. *Progress in Neuro-Psychopharmacology & Biological Psychiatry, 30,* 827–853.

Braden, J. P. (1995). Review of the Wechsler Intelligence Scale for Children (3rd ed.). In J. C. Conoley & J. C. Impara (Eds.), *Twelfth mental measurements yearbook.* Lincoln, NE: Buros Institute.

Braginsky, B. M., Braginsky, D. D., & Ring, K. (1969). *Methods of madness: The mental hospital as a last resort.* New York, NY: Holt, Rinehart & Winston.

Brambilla, P., Cerini, R., Gasparini, A., Versace, A., Andreone, N., Nose, N., et al. (2005). Investigation of corpus callosum in schizophrenia with diffusion imaging. *Schizophrenia Research, 79*(2–3), 201–210.

Brannon, L. & Feist, J. (2009). *Health psychology: An introduction to behavior and health.* Belmont, CA: Wadsworth.

Branthwaite, A. & Pechere, J. C. (1996). Pan-European survey of patients' attitudes to antibiotics and antibiotic use. *Journal of International Medical Research, 24,* 229–238.

Bray, J. H. (2011). Training for the future of psychology practice. *Training and Education in Professional Psychology, 5,* 69–72.

Breggin, P. (2009). *Medication madness: The role of psychiatric drugs in cases of violence, suicide, and crime.* New York, NY: St. Martin's Press.

Breggin, P. R. (2001). *Talking back to Ritalin: What doctors aren't telling you about stimulants for children.* Monroe, ME: Common Courage Press.

Breggin, P. R. & Breggin, G. R. (1994). *The war against children: How the drugs, programs, and theories of the psychiatric establishment are threatening America's children with a medical "cure" for violence.* New York, NY: St. Martin's Press.

Brekke, N. J., Enko, P. J., Clavet, G., & Seelau, E. (1991). Of juries and court-appointed experts: The impact of nonadversarial expert testimony. *Law and Human Behavior, 15,* 451–477.

Brems, C. (2001). *Basic skills in psychotherapy and counseling.* Belmont, CA: Wadsworth.

Breslow, L. (1979). A positive strategy for the nation's health. *Journal of the American Medical Association, 242,* 2093–2094.

Brewer, N. & Williams, K. D. (2007). *Psychology and law: An empirical perspective.* New York, NY: The Guilford Press.

Breyer, S. (2000, Summer). Science in the courtroom. *Issues in Science and Technology.* Retrieved 8 December 2001, from http://www.nap.edu/issues/16.4/breyer.htm.

Briesmeister, J. M. & Schaefer, C. E. (Eds.) (2007). *Handbook of parent training: Helping parents prevent and solve problem behaviors (3rd ed.).* Hoboken, NJ: John Wiley & Sons.

Broca, P. (1861). Remargues sur le siege de la faculte de la porle articulee, suives d'une observation d'aphemie (perte de parole). *Bulletin Societie Anatomie, 36,* 330–357.

Broca, P. (1865). Sur la faculté du langage articulé. *Bulletin Societe Anthropologie Paris, 6*, 337–393.

Brody, G. H., Murry, V. M., Gerrard, M., Gibbons, F. X., McNair, L., et al. (2006). The Strong African American Families Program: Prevention of youths' high-risk behavior and a test of a model of change. *Journal of Family Psychology, 20*, 1–11.

Broman, C. L. (1993). Social relationships and health-related behavior. *Journal of Behavioral Medicine, 16*, 335–350.

Brotemarkle, B. A. (1947). Fifty years of clinical psychology: Clinical psychology 1896–1946. *Journal of Consulting Psychology, 11*, 1–4.

Brotman, L. M., Klein, R. G., Kamboukos, D., Brown, E. J., Coard, S. I., & Sosinsky, L. S. (2003). Preventive intervention for urban, low-income preschoolers at familial risk for conduct problems: A randomized pilot study. *Journal of Clinical Child and Adolescent Psychology, 32*, 246–257.

Brown, R. P., Gerbarg, P. L., & Muskin, P. R. (2012). *How to use herbs, nutrients, and yoga in mental health.* New York, NY: W. W. Norton and Company.

Brown, R. T., Carpenter, L. A., & Simerly, E. (2005). *Mental health medications for children: A primer.* New York, NY: Guilford.

Brown, T. A. & Barlow, D. H. (2001). *Casebook in abnormal psychology* (2nd ed.). Belmont, CA: Wadsworth.

Brownell, K. D. & Wadden, T. A. (1992). Etiology and treatment of obesity: Understanding a serious, prevalent, and refractory disorder. *Journal of Consulting and Clinical Psychology, 60*, 505–517.

Breuer, J. & Freud, S. (1895/1955). *Studies on hysteria: Standard Edition* (Vol. 2). London, UK: Hogarth Press.

Brugha, T. S., Nienhuis, F., Bagchi, D., Smith, J., Meltzer, H. (1999). The survey form of SCAN: The feasibility of using experienced lay survey interviewers to administer a semi-structured systematic clinical assessment of psychotic and non-psychotic disorders. *Psychological Medicine, 29*, 703–711.

Brussel, J. A. (1968). *Casebook of a crime psychiatrist.* New York, NY: Bernard Geis Associates.

Bryan, C. J. & Morrow, C. E. (2011). Circumventing mental health stigma by embracing the warrior culture: Lessons learned from the defender's edge program. *Professional Psychology: Research and Practice, 42*, 16–23.

Buck, J. N. (1948). The H-T-P technique: A qualitative and quantitative scoring manual. *Journal of Clinical Psychology, 4*, 319–396.

Buckman, J. R. & Barker, C. (2010). Therapeutic orientation preferences in trainee clinical psychologists: Personality or training? *Psychotherapy Research, 20*, 247–258. Doi: 10.1080/10503300903352693.

Bufka, L. F. & Camp, N. (2010). *Brief measures for screening and measuring mental health outcomes* in M. M. Antony & D. H. Barlow (Eds.) *Handbook of Assessment and Treatment Planning for Psychological Disorders*, pp 62-94. New York, NY: The Guilford Press.

Bugental, J. F. T. (1995). Preliminary sketches for a short-term existential therapy. In K. J. Schneider & R. May (Eds.), *The psychology of existence: An integrative, clinical perspective* (pp. 261–264). New York, NY: McGraw-Hill.

Bull, S. S., Gaglio, B., Garth, M. H., & Glasgow, R. E. (2005). Harnessing the potential of the Internet to promote chronic illness self-management: Diabetes as an example of how well we are doing. *Chronic Illness, 1*,143–155.

Burg, M. M. & Abrams, D. (2001). Depression in chronic medical illness: The case of coronary heart disease. *Journal of Clinical Psychology/In Session, 57*, 1323–1337.

Burger, W. E. (1975). Dissenting opinion in O'Connor v. Donaldson. *U.S. Law Week, 42*, 4929–4936.

Burisch, M. (1984). Approaches to personality inventory construction: A comparison of merits. *American Psychologist, 39*, 214–227.

Burke, L. E., Dunbar-Jacob, J. M., & Hill, M. N. (1997). Compliance with cardiovascular disease prevention strategies: A review of the research. *Annals of Behavioral Medicine, 19*, 239–263.

Burlingame, G. M., MacKenzie, K. R., & Strauss, B. (2004). Small-group treatment: Evidence for effectiveness and mechanisms of change. In M. J. Lambert (Ed.), *Bergin and Garfield's Handbook of Psychotherapy and Behavior Change* (5th ed. pp. 647–696). New York, NY: John Wiley & Sons.

Burlingame, G. M., McClendon, D. T., & Alonso, J. (2011). Cohesion in group therapy. *Psychotherapy, 48*, 34–42.

Burlingame, G. M. & Baldwin, S. (2011). Group therapy. In J. C. Norcross, G. R. VandenBos, & D. K. Freedheim (Eds.), *History of psychotherapy: Continuity and change* (2nd ed., pp. 505–515). Washington, DC: American Psychological Association.

Burns, D. D. (1999). *Feeling good: The new mood therapy, Vol. 1* (Rev. ed.). New York, NY: Harper Collins.

Burns, D. D. & Spangler, D. L. (2000). Does psychotherapy homework lead to improvements in depression in cognitive-behavioral therapy or does improvement lead to increased homework compliance? *Journal of Consulting and Clinical Psychology, 68*, 46–56.

Buros, O. K. (Ed.). (1938). *The 1940 mental measurements yearbook.* Highland Park, NJ: Gryphon Press.

Bush, N. E., Bosmajian, C. P., Fairall, J. M., McCann, R. A., & Ciulla, R. P. (2011). afterdeployment.org: A web-based multimedia wellness resource for the postdeployment military community. *Professional. Psychology: Research and Practice, 42*, 455–462.

Butcher, J. N. (2004). Personality assessment without borders: Adaptation of the MMPI-2 across cultures. *Journal of Personality Assessment, 83*, 90–104.

Butcher, J. N. (2009). *Oxford handbook of personality assessment.* New York, NY: Oxford University Press.

Butcher, J. N. (2011). *A beginner's guide to the MMPI-2 (3rd ed.).* Washington, DC: American Psychological Association.

Butcher, J. N. & Keller, L. S. (1984). Objective personality assessment. In G. Goldstein & M. Hersen (Eds.), *Handbook of psychological assessment* (pp. 307–331). New York, NY: Pergamon Press.

Butcher, J. N., Dahlstrom, W. G., Graham, J. R., Tellegen, A., & Kaemmer, B. (1989). *Manual for administration and scoring of the MMPI-2.* Minneapolis: University of Minnesota Press.

Butcher, J. N. & Williams, C. L. (1992). *Essentials of MMPI-2 and MMPI-A interpretation.* Minneapolis: University of Minnesota Press.

Cacciola, J. S., Alterman, A. I., Rutheford, M. J., McKay, J. R., & May, D. J. (1999). Comparability of telephone and in-person Structured Clinical Interview for DSM-III-R (SCID) diagnoses. *Assessment, 6*, 235–242.

Cacioppo, J. T. (2006). Social neuroscience. *American Journal of Psychology, 119*, 664–668.

Cacioppo, J. T., Amaral, D. G., Blanchard, J. J., Cameron, J. L., Carter, C. S., Crews, D. Et al. (2007). Social neuroscience: Progress and implications for mental health. *Perspectives on Psychological Science, 2,* 99–123.

Cain, D. J. (1990). Celebration, reflection, and renewal: 50 years of client-centered therapy and beyond. *Person-Centered Review, 5,* 357–363.

Cairns, R. B. & Green, J. A. (1979). How to assess personality and social patterns: Observations or ratings? In B. Cairns (Ed.), *The analysis of social interactions: Methods, issues, and illustrations* (pp. 209–226). Hillsdale, NJ: Erlbaum.

Calkins, S. D. & Degnan, K. A. (2006). Temperament in early development. In R. T. Ammerman (Ed.), *Comprehensive handbook of personality and psychopathology* (Vol. 3, pp. 64–84). Hoboken, NJ: John Wiley & Sons.

Camara, W. J., Nathan, J. S., & Puente, A. E. (2000). Psychological test usage: Implications in professional psychology. *Professional Psychology: Research and Practice, 31,* 141–154.

Campbell, D. T. & Fiske, D. W. (1959). Convergent and discriminant validation by the multitrait-multimethod matrix. *Psychological Bulletin, 56,* 81–105.

Campbell, L., Vasquez, M., Behnke, S., & Kinscherff, R. (2010). *APA ethics code commentary and case illustrations.* Washington, DC: American Psychological Association.

Canivez, G. L. & Watkins, M. W. (2010). Exploratory and higher-order factor analyses of the Wechsler Adult Intelligence Scale—Fourth Edition (WAIS-IV) Adolescent Subsample. *School Psychology Quarterly, 25,* 223–235.

Canning, D. (2006). The economics of HIV/AIDS in low-income countries: the case for prevention. *Journal of Economic Perspectives, 20,* 121–142.

Cannon, B. J. (2008). In search of a good psychologist in a good movie: Persisting stereotypes. *The Pennsylvania Psychologist Quarterly,* May/June, 1.

Cantor, N. L. (1998). Making advance directives meaningful. *Psychology, Public Policy, and Law, 4,* 629–652.

Caplan, G. (1964). *Principles of preventive psychiatry.* New York, NY: Basic Books.

Carei, T. R., Fyfe-Johnson, A. L., Breuner, C. C., & Brown, M. A. (2010). Randomized controlled clinical trial of yoga in the treatment of eating disorders. *Journal of Adolescent Health, 46,* 346–351.

Carlbring, P. & Smit, F. (2008). Randomized trial of internet-delivered self-help with telephone support for pathological gamblers. *Journal of Consulting and Clinical Psychology, 76,* 1090–1094.

Carlson, E. T. (1981). Introduction. *Clinical psychiatry* [Facsimile reproduction of the 1907 volume, History of Psychology Series, R. I. Watson (Ed.)]. Delmar, NY: Scholars' Facsimiles & Reprints.

Carniero, C., Corboz-Warney, A., & Fivaz-Depeursinge, E. (2006). The prenatal Lausanne Trilogy Play: A new observational assessment tool of the prenatal co-parenting alliance. *Infant Mental Health Journal, 27,* 207–228.

Carr, A. (2012). *Family therapy: Concepts, process, and practice.* Hoboken, NJ: John Wiley & Sons.

Carroll, J. B. (1993). *Human cognitive abilities: A survey of factor-analytic studies.* Cambridge, UK: University of Cambridge Press.

Carver, C. S., Scheier, M. F., & Segerstrom, S. C. (2010). Optimism. *Clinical Psychology Review, 30,* 879–889.

Casey, G. W. (2011). Comprehensive soldier fitness: A vision for psychological resilience in the U. S. Army. *American Psychologist, 66,* 1–3.

Cashel, M. L. (2002). Child and adolescent psychological assessment: Current clinical practices and the impact of managed care. *Professional Psychology: Research and Practice, 33,* 446–453.

Caspi, A., Harrington, H., Milne, B., Amell, J. W., Theodore, R. F., & Moffitt, T. E. (2003). Children's behavioral styles at age 3 are linked to their adult personality traits at age 26. *Journal of Personality, 71,* 495–513.

Cassel, E. (2000). Behavioral science research leads to Department of Justice Guidelines for eyewitness evidence. *Virginia Lawyer, 48,* 35–38.

Cassel, E. & Bernstein, D. A. (2007). *Criminal behavior* (2nd ed.). Mahwah, NJ: Erlbaum.

Castro, F. G., Barrera, M., & Steiker, L. K. H. (2010). Issues and challenges in the design of culturally adapted evidence-based interventions. *Annual Review of Clinical Psychology, 6,* 213–239.

Cattell, R. B. (1943). The measurement of adult intelligence. *Psychological Bulletin, 40,* 153–193.

Cattell, R. B., Eber, H. W., & Tatusoka, M. M. (1970). *Handbook for the Sixteen Personality Factor Questionnaire.* Champaign, IL: Institute for Personality and Ability Testing.

Cattell, R. B., Eber, H. W., & Tatusoka, M. M. (1992). *Handbook for the Sixteen Personality Factor Questionnaire (16PF).* Champaign, IL: Institute for Personality and Ability Testing.

Cautin, R. L. (2010). A century of psychotherapy, 1860-1960. In J. C. Norcross, G. R. VandenBos, & D. K. Freedheim (Eds). *History of Psychotherapy: Continuity and Change* (2nd ed.). Washington, DC: American Psychological Association.

Cautin, R. L. (2011). A century of psychotherapy, 1860-1960. In J. C. Norcross, G. R. Vandenbos, & D. K. Freedheim (Eds.) *History of Psycotherapy* (2nd ed., pp. 3–38). Washington, DC: American Psychological Association.

Centers for Disease Control (2001a). About cardiovascular disease. Retrieved December 3, 2001 from http://www.cdc.gov/nccdphp/cvd/aboutcardio.htm.

Centers for Disease Control (2001b). Basic statistics—Cumulative AIDS Cases. Retrieved December 3, 2001, from http://www.cdc.gov/hiv/stats/cumulati.htm.

Centers for Disease Control (2001c). Basic statistics—International Statistics. Retrieved December 3, 2001, from http://www.cdc.gov/hiv/stats/cumulati.htm.

Chabot, D. R. (2011). Family systems theories of psychotherapy. In J. C. Norcross, G. R. VandenBos, & D. K. Freedheim (Eds.), *History of psychotherapy: Continuity and change* (2nd ed., pp. 173–202). Washington, DC: American Psychological Association.

Chamberlin, J. (2008). Early career concerns. *Monitor on Psychology, 39,* 68–69.

Chambless, D. L. (1990). Spacing of exposure sessions in the treatment of agoraphobia and simple phobia. *Behavior Therapy, 21,* 217–229.

Chambless, D. L. & Ollendick, T. H. (2001). Empirically supported psychological treatments. *Annual Review of Psychology, 52,* 685–716.

Chan, M., Chen, E., Hibbert, A. S., Wong, J. H. K., Miller, G. E. (2011). Implicit measures of early-life family conditions: relationships to psychosocial characteristics and cardiovascular disease risk in adulthood. *Health Psychology, 30*, 570–578.

Chang, T. & Yeh, C. J. (2003). Using online groups to provide support to Asian American men: Racial, cultural, gender, and treatment issues. *Professional Psychology: Research and Practice, 34*, 634–643.

Chao, P. J., Steffen, J. J., & Heiby, E. M. (2012). The effects of working alliance and client-clinician ethnic match on recovery status. *Community Mental Health Journal, 48*, 91–97.

Chapman, L. J. & Chapman, J. P. (1967). The genesis of popular but erroneous psychodiagnostic observations. *Journal of Abnormal Psychology, 72*, 193–204.

Chavez, L. M., Shrout, P. E., Alegria, M., Lapatin, S., & Canino, G. (2010). Ethnic differences in perceived impairment and need for care. *Journal of Abnormal Child Psychology, 38*, 1165–1177.

Chechlacz, M., Rotshtein, P., Hansen, P. C., Riddoch, J. M., Deb, S., & Humphreys, G. W. (2012). The neural underpinings of simultanagnosia: disconnecting the visuospatial attention network. *Journal of Cognitive Neuroscience, 24*(3), 718–735.

Cheng, K. (2011). Recent progress in high-resolution functional MRI. *Current Opinion in Neurology, 24*(4), 401–408.

Cherry, D. K., Messenger, L. C., & Jacoby, A. M. (2000). An examination of training model outcomes in clinical psychology programs. *Professional Psychology: Research & Practice, 31*, 562–568.

Children's Defense Fund (2012). *The state of America's children handbook.* Washington, DC: Children's Defense Fund.

Christakis, N. A., and Fowler, J. H. (2007). The spread of obesity in a large social network over 32 years. *New England Journal of Medicine, 357*, 370–379.

Christakis, N. A., and Fowler, J. H. (2008). The collective dynamics of smoking in a large social network. *New England Journal of Medicine, 358*, 2249–2258.

Christie, D. J., Tint, B. S., Wagner, R. V., & Winter, D. D. (2008). Peace psychology for a peaceful world. *American Psychologist, 63*, 540–552.

Chung, J. J., Weed, N. C., & Han, K. (2006). Evaluating cross-cultural equivalence of the Korean MMPI-2 via bilingual test-retest. *International Journal of Intercultural Relations, 30*, 531–543.

Cicchetti, D. (2008). A multiple-levels-of-analysis perspective on research in development and psychopathology. In T. P. Beauchaine & S. P. Hinshaw (Eds.), *Child and adolescent psychopathology* (pp. 27–57). Hoboken, NJ: John Wiley & Sons.

Cicchetti, D. & Curtis, J. W. (2006). The developing brain and neuroplasticity: Implications for normality, psychopathology, and resilience. In D. Cicchetti & J. W. Curtis (Eds.), *Developmental psychopathology, Vol 2: Developmental neuroscience* (2nd ed., pp. 1–64). Hoboken, NJ: John Wiley & Sons.

Cicchetti, D. & Rogosch, F. A. (2012). Gene X environment interaction and resilience: Effects of child maltreatment and serotonin, corticotropin releasing hormone, dopamine, and oxytocin genes. *Development and Psychopathology, 24*, 411–427.

Clark, D. B. & Winters, K. C. (2002). Measuring risks and outcomes in substance use disorders prevention research. *Journal of Consulting and Clinical Psychology, 70*, 1207–1223.

Clarke, G., Lynch, F., Spofford, M., & DeBar, L. (2006). Trends influencing future delivery of mental health services in large healthcare systems. *Clinical Psychology: Science and Practice, 13*, 287–292.

Clay, R. A. (2006). Loan repayment. *GradPSYCH, 4*, 1–3.

Clay, R. A. (2010). APA updates its model licensure act. *Monitor on Psychology, 41*, 38.

Clay, R. A. (2011a). The future of behavioral health care. *Monitor on Psychology, 42*, 52.

Clay, R. A. (2011b). Modern-day slavery. *Monitor on Psychology, 42*, 72.

Clay, R. A. (2011c). Parity in practice. *Monitor on Psychology, 42*, 54.

Clay, R. A. (2012). Protesting proposed changes to the DSM. *Monitor on Psychology*, Jan. 42–43.

Clingempeel, W. G. & Reppucci, N. D. (1982). Joint custody after divorce: Major issues and goals for research. *Psychological Bulletin, 91*, 102–127.

Clough, B. A. & Casey, L. M. (2011). Technological adjuncts to enhance current psychotherapy practices: A review. *Clinical Psychology Review, 31*, 279–292.

CNNMoney.com (2012). *Best jobs in America.* Retrieved from http://money.cnn.com/magazines/moneymag/bestjobs/2009/snapshots/23.html.

Coatsworth, J. D., Pantin, H., & Szapocznik, J. (2002). Familias unidas: A family-centered ecodevelopmental intervention to reduce risk for problem behavior among Hispanic adolescents. *Clinical Child and Family Psychology Review, 5*, 113–132.

Cobb, H. C., Reeve, R. E., Shealy, C. N., Norcross, J. C., Schare, M. L., et al. (2004). Overlap among clinical, counseling, and school psychology: Implications for the profession and combined-integrated training. *Journal of Clinical Psychology, 60*, 939–955.

Cohen, D., Milman, D., Venturyera, V., & Falissard, B. (2011). Psychodynamic experience enhances recognition of hidden childhood trauma, *PLoS One 6*, e18470. Doi: 10:1371journal. pone.0018470.

Cohen, J. (1988). *Statistical power analysis for the behavioral sciences* (2nd ed.). New York, NY: Taylor and Francis.

Cohen, J. B. & Reed, D. (1985). Type A behavior and coronary heart disease among Japanese men in Hawaii. *Journal of Behavioral Medicine, 8*, 343–352.

Cohen, J., Marecek, J., & Gillham, J. (2006). Is three a crowd? Clients, clinicians, and managed care. *American Journal of Orthopsychiatry, 76*, 251–259.

Cohen, S. (2004). Social relationships and health. *American Psychologist, 59*, 676–684.

Cohen, S. & Wills, T. A. (1985). Stress, social support, and the buffering hypothesis. *Psychological Bulletin, 98*, 310–357.

Cohen, S., Tyrrell, D. A., & Smith, A. P. (1991). Psychological stress in humans and susceptibility to the common cold. *New England Journal of Medicine, 325*, 606–612.

Cohen, S., Kamarck, T., & Mermelstein, R. (1983). A global measure of perceived stress. *Journal of Health and Social Behavior, 24*, 385–396.

Cohen, S. & Rabin, B. S. (1998). Psychological stress, immunity, and cancer. *Journal of the National Cancer Institute, 90*, 3–4.

Cohen, S., Gottlieb, B., & Underwood, L. (2000). Social relationships and health. In S. Cohen, L. Underwood, & B. Gottlieb (Eds.), *Measuring and intervening in social support* (pp. 3–25). New York, NY: Oxford University Press.

Cohen, S., Janicki-Deverts, D., Doyle, W. J., Miller, G. E., Frank, E., Rabin, B. S., Turner, R. B. (2012). Chronic stress, glucocorticoid receptor resistance, inflammation, and disease risk. *Proceedings of the National Academy of Sciences*, 109.

Coid, J. W., Yang, M., Ullrich, S., Zhang, T., Sizmur, S. et al. (2011). Most items in structured risk assessment instruments do not predict violence. *The Journal of Forensic Psychiatry and Psychology, 22*, 3–21.

Cole, P. M. & Hall, S. E. (2008). Emotion dysregulation as a risk factor for psychopathology. In T. P. Beauchaine & S. P. Hinshaw (Eds.), *Child and adolescent psychopathology* (pp. 265–298). Hoboken, NJ: John Wiley & Sons.

Coleman, P. (2005). Privilege and confidentiality in 12-step self-help programs: Believing the promises could be hazardous to an addict's freedom. *Journal of Legal Medicine, 26*, 435–474.

Collins, R. L., Parks, G. A., & Marlatt, G. A. (1985). Social determinants of alcohol consumption: The effects of social interactions and model status on the self-administration of alcohol. *Journal of Consulting and Clinical Psychology, 53*, 189–200.

Colmen, J. G., Kaplan, S. J., & Boulger, J. R. (1964, August). *Selection and selecting research in the Peace Corps* (Peace Corps Research Note No. 7).

Comas_Diaz, L. (2012). Multicultural care: A clinician's guide to cultural competence. *A clinician's guide to cultural competence Psychologists in Independent practice*. Washington DC: American Psychological Association.

Comer, J. S., Puliafico, A. C., Aschenbrand, S. G., McKnight, K., Robin, J. A., Goldfine, M. E., & Albano, A. M. (2012). A pilot feasibility evaluation of the CALM program for anxiety disorders in early childhood. *Journal of Anxiety Disorders, 26*, 40–49.

Conger, R. D. & Donnellan, M. B. (2007). An interactionist perspective on the socioeconomic context of human development. *Annual Review of Psychology, 58*, 175–199.

Constantino, M. J., Arnkoff, D. B., Glass, C. R., Amertrano, R. M., & Smith, J. Z. (2011). Expectations. *Journal of Clinical Psychology, 67*, 184–192.

Constonguay, L. G., Boswell, J. F., Constantino, M. J., Goldfried, M. R, & Hill, C. E. (2010). Training implications of the harmful effects of psychological treatments. *American Psychologist, 65*, 34–39.

Cook, J. M. & Biyanova, T. (2009). Influential psychotherapy figures, authors, and books: An internet survey. *Psychotherapy: Theory, Research, Practice, and Training, 46*, 42–51.

Coontz, P. D., Lidz, C. W., & Mulvey, E. P. (1994). Gender and the assessment of dangerousness in the psychiatric emergency room. *International Journal of Law and Psychiatry, 17*, 369–376.

Corbetta, M. and Shulman, G. L. (2011). Spatial neglect and attention networks. *Annual Review of Neuroscience, 34*, 569–599.

Corey, G. (2011). *Theory and practice of group counseling* (8th ed.). Belmont, CA: Cengage Learning.

Cormier, S., Nurius, P. S., & Osborn, C. J. (2012*). Interviewing and change strategies for helpers* (7th ed.). Pacific Grove, CA: Brooks Cole.

Cormier, S. & Hackney, H. (2012). *Counseling strategies and interventions* (8th ed.). Boston, MA: Pearson.

Cornblatt, B., & Erlenmeyer-Kimling, L. E. (1985). Global attentional deviance in children at risk for schizophrenia: Specificity and predictive validity. *Journal of Abnormal Psychology, 94*, 470–486.

Correa, A. A., Rogers, R., & Hoestring, R. (2010). Validation of the Spanish SIRS with monolingual Hispanic outpatients. *Journal of Personality Assessment, 92*, 458–464.

Corrigan, P. W & Shapiro, J. R. (2010). Measuring the impact of programs that challenge the public stigma of mental illness. *Clinical Psychology Review, 30*, 907–922.

Costa, P. T. Jr. & McCrea, R. R. (1980). Still stable after all these years: Personality as a key to some issues in adulthood and old age. In P. B. Baltes & O. G. Brim, Jr. (Eds.), *Life span development and behavior* (Vol. 3, pp. 65–102). New York, NY: Academic Press.

Costa, P. T. Jr., & McCrae, R. R. (1985). *NEO-Personality Inventory manual*. Odessa, FL: Psychological Assessment Resources.

Costa, P. T. Jr., & McCrae, R. R. (1992a). *Manual for the Revised NEO Personality Inventory (NEO-PIR) and the NEO Five-Factor Inventory (BEO-FFI)*. Odessa, FL: Psychological Assessment Resources.

Costello, E. J., Copeland, W., & Angold, A. (2011). Trends in psychopathology across the adolescent years: What changes when children become adolescents, and when adolescents become adults? *Journal of Child Psychology and Psychiatry, 52*, 1015–1025.

Couch, R. D. (1995). Four steps for conducting a pregroup screening interview. *Journal for Specialists in Group Work, 20*, 18–25.

Cowey, A. (2010a). The blindsight saga. *Experimental Brain Research, 200*(1), 3–24.

Cowey A. (2010b) Visual system: how does blindsight arise? *Current Biology, 20*(17), R702–R704.

Craig, R. J. (2009). The clinical interview. In J. Butcher (Ed.). *The Oxford Handbook of Personality Assessment*. New York, NY: Oxford University Press, 201–225.

Crane, D. R. & Payne, S. H. (2011). Individual versus family psychotherapy in managed care: Comparing the costs of treatment by the mental health professions. *Journal of Marital and Family Therapy, 37*, 273–289.

Craske, M. G. (2010). *Cognitive-behavior therapy*. Washington, DC: APA Books.

Crits-Christoph, P., Connolly-Gibbons, M. B., & Hearon, B. (2006). Does the alliance cause good outcome? Recommendations for future research on the alliance. *Psychotherapy: Theory, Research, Practice, Training, 43*, 280–285.

Crits-Christoph, P., Connolly Gibbons, M. B., Hamilton, J., Ring_ Kurtz, S., & Gallop, R. (2011). The dependability of alliance assessments: The alliance-outcome correlation is larger than you might think. *Journal of Consulting and Clinical Psychology, 79*, 267–278.

Cronbach, L. J. (1946). Response sets and test validity. *Educational and Psychological Measurement, 6*, 475–494.

Cronbach, L. J. (1960). *Essentials of psychological testing* (2nd ed.). New York, NY: Harper & Row.

Cronbach, L. J. & Glesser, G. C. (1964). *Psychological tests and personnel decisions*. Urbana: University of Illinois Press.

Cronbach, L. J. & Meehl, P. E. (1955). Construct validity in psychology tests. *Psychological Bulletin, 52,* 281–302.

Cronbach, L. J. (1970). *Essentials of psychological testing* (3rd ed.). New York, NY: Harper & Row.

Crosbie-Burnett, M. (1991). Impact of joint versus sole custody and quality of co-parental relationship on adjustment of adolescents in remarried families. *Behavioral Sciences and the Law, 9,* 439–449.

Crowther, M. R., Austing, A. L., Scogin, F., Harwood, T. M., & Harrell, S. (2011). Integrative personality assessment with older adults and ethnic minorities. In T. M. Harwood, L. E. Beutler, & G. Groth-Marnat (Eds.) *Integrative Assessment of Adult Personality* (pp. 354–372). New York, NY: Guilford.

Cuijpers, P., Driessen, E., Hollon, S. D., vanOppen, P., Barth, J., & Andersson, G. (2012). The efficacy of non-directive supportive therapy for adult depression: A meta-analysis. *Clinical Psychology Review, 32,* 280–291.

Cunningham, M. D., Sorensen, J. R., & Reidy, T. J. (2009). Capital jury decision making: The limitations of predictions of future violence. *Psychology, Public Policy, and Law, 15,* 223–256.

Curtis, R. C. & Hirsch, I. (2003). Relational approaches to psychoanalytic psychotherapy. In A. S. Gurman & S. B. Messer (Eds.). *Essential psychotherapies* (2nd ed., pp. 69–106). New York, NY: Guilford.

Curtis, R. C. & Hirsch, I. (2011). Relational Psychoanalytic Psychotherapy. In S. B. Messer & A. S. Gurman (Eds.) *Essential Psychotherapies* (3rd ed., pp. 72–106). New York, NY: The Guilford Press.

Dahlstrom, W. G. (1992). The growth in acceptance of the MMPI. *Professional Psychology: Research and Practice, 23,* 345–348.

Dahlstrom, W. G., Welsh, G. S., & Dahlstrom, L. E. (1972). *An MMPI handbook: Vol. 1. Clinical interpretation* (rev. ed.). Minneapolis: University of Minnesota Press.

Dahlstrom, W. G., Lachar, D., & Dahlstrom, L. E. (1986). *MMPI patterns of American minorities.* Minneapolis: University of Minnesota Press.

Dana, R. H. & Leech, S. (1974). Existential assessment. *Journal of Personality Assessment, 38,* 428–435.

Danner, D. D., Snowdon, D. A., Friesen, W. V. (2001). Positive emotions in early life and longevity: Findings from the nun study. *Journal of Personality and Social Psychology, 80,* 804–813.

Darley, J. M., Zanna, M. P., & Roediger, H. L. (2004). *The compleat academic: A career guide* (2nd ed.). Washington, DC: American Psychological Association.

Dattilio, F. M. (2006). Equivocal death psychological autopsies in cases of criminal homicide. *American Journal of Forensic Psychology, 24,* 5–22.

Davanloo, H. L. (1994). *Basic principles and techniques in short-term dynamic psychotherapy.* Northdale, NJ: Jason Aronson, Inc.

David, R. & Messer, L. (2011). Reducing disparities: Race, class, and the social determinants of health. *Maternal and Child Health Journal, 15,* 1–3.

Davidson, J. E. & I. A. Kemp. (2011). Contemporary models of intelligence. In R. J. Sternberg & S. B. Kaufman (Eds.). *The Cambridge handbook of intelligence* (pp. 58–84). New York, NY: Cambridge University Press.

Davidson, W. S., Redner, R., Blakely, C., Mitchell, C. M., & Emshoff, J. G. (1987). Diversion of juvenile offenders: An experimental comparison. *Journal of Consulting and Clinical Psychology, 55,* 68–75.

Davies, P. T., Sturge-Apple, M. L., Cicchetti, D., & Cummings, E. M. (2007). The role of child adrenocortical functioning in pathways between interparental conflict and child maladjustment. *Developmental Psychology, 43,* 918–930.

Davies, P. T., Martin, M. J., & Cicchetti, D. (2012). Delineating the sequelae of destructive and constructive interparental conflict for children within an evolutionary framework. *Developmental Psychology, 48,* 939–955.

Davis, M. A., West, A. N., Weeks, W. B., & Sirovich, B. E. (2011). Health behaviors and utilization among users of complementary and alternative medicine for treatment versus health promotion. *Health Services Research, 46,* 1402–1416.

Davis, S. D., Lebow, J. L., & Sprenkle, D. H. (2012). Common factors of change in couple therapy. *Behavior Therapy, 43,* 36–48.

Davis, S. F., Giordano, P. J., & Licht, C. A. (2009). *Your career in psychology: Putting your graduate degree to work.* Malden, MA: Wiley-Blackwell.

Davydov, D. M. Stewart, R., Ritchie, K. & Chaudieu, I. (2010). Resilience and mental health. *Clinical Psychology Review, 30,* 479–495.

Dawes, R. M. (1994). *House of cards.* New York, NY: The Free Press.

Dawes, R. M., Faust, D., & Meehl, P. E. (1989). Clinical versus actuarial judgment. *Science, 243,* 1668–1674.

De Waal, F. B. M. & Ferari, P. F. (Eds.). (2012). *The primate mind: Built to connect with other minds.* Cambridge, MA: Harvard University Press.

DeAngelis, T. (2012). Practicing distance therapy, legally and ethically. *Monitor on Psychology, 42,* 52.

DeAngelis, T. (2011). Is technology ruining our kids? *Monitor on Psychology, 42,* 63–64.

DeBoard-Lucas, R. L., Fosco, G. M., Raynor, S. R., & Grych, J. H. (2010). Interparental conflict in context: Exploring relations between parenting processes and children's conflict appraisals. *Journal of Clinical Child and Adolescent Psychology, 39,* 163–175.

Decker, S. L., Brooks, J. H., & Allen, R. A. (2011). Stanford-Binet Intelligence Scales, Fifth Edition. In A. S. Dais (Ed), (2011). *Handbook of pediatric neuropsychology* (pp. 389–395). New York, NY: Springer Publishing Co.

Deisinger, J., Burkhardt, S., Wahlberg, T., Rotatori, A. F., & Oblakor, F. E. (2012). *Autism spectrum disorders: Inclusive community for the 21st century.* Charlotte, NC: Information Age Publishing.

Dekovic, M., Slagt, M. I., Asscher, J. J., Boendrmaker, L., Eichelsheim, V. I., & Prinzie, P. (2011). Effects of early prevention programs on adult criminal offending: A meta-analysis. *Clinical Psychology Review, 31,* 532–544.

DeMause, L. (1987). Schreber and the history of childhood. *The Journal of Psychohistory, 15,* 423–430.

Dennis, W. (1948). *Readings in the history of psychology.* New York, NY: Appleton-Century-Crofts.

Derogatis, L. R. & Melisaratos, N. (1983). The Brief Symptom Inventory: An introductory report. *Psychological Medicine, 13,* 596–605.

Dew, I. T. & Cabeza, R. (2011). The porous boundaries between explicit and implicit memory: Behavioral and neural evidence. *Annals of the New York Academy of Sciences, 1224*, 174–190.

DeYoung, P. A. (2003). *Relational psychotherapy: A primer.* New York, NY: Burnner-Routledge.

Diamond, M. J. & Christian, C. (Eds.). (2011). *The Second Century of Psychoanalysis: Evolving Perspectives on the Therapeutic Action.* London, GB: Karnac Books.

Dienes, K. A., Torres-Harding, S., Reinecke, M. A., Freeman, A., & Sauer, A. (2011). Cognitive therapy. In S. B. Messer & A. S. Gurman (Eds.). *Essential Psychotherapies* (3rd ed., pp. 143–185). New York, NY: Springer.

Dies, R. (2003). Group Psychotherapies. In A. S. Gurman & S. B. Messer (Eds.). *Essential psychotherapies* (2nd ed., pp. 515–550). New York, NY: Guilford.

DiLillo, D., DeGue, S., Cohen, L. M., & Morgan, R. D. (2006). The path to licensure for academic psychologists: How tough is the road? *Professional Psychology: Research and Practice, 37*, 567–586.

Dimatteo, M. R. & Taranta, A. (1976). Nonverbal communication and physician-patient rapport: An empirical study. *Professional Psychology, 10*, 540–547.

DiMatteo, R., Giordani, P. J., Lepper, H. S., & Croghan, T. W. (2002). Patient adherence and medical treatment outcomes: A meta-analysis. *Medical Care, 40*, 794–811.

Dimidjian, S. & Linehan, M. M. (2009). Mindfulness practice. In W. T. O'Donohue & J. E. Fisher (Eds.), *General principles and empirically supported techniques of cognitive behavior therapy* (pp. 425–434). Hoboken, NJ: John Wiley & Sons.

Dipboye, R. L., Stramler, C. S., & Fontenelle, G. A. (1984). The effects of the application on recall of information from the interview. *Academy of Management Journal, 27*, 561–575.

Dobson, K. S. (2012). *Cognitive therapy.* Washington, DC: APA Books.

Dobson, K. S. & Hamilton, K. E. (2009). Cognitive restructuring: Behavioral tests of negative cognitions. In W. T. O'Donohue & J. E. Fisher (Eds.), *General principles and empirically supported techniques of cognitive behavior therapy* (pp. 194–198). Hoboken, NJ: John Wiley & Sons.

Dodge, K. A., Coie, J. D., & Lynam, D. (2006). Aggression and antisocial behavior in youth. In N. Eisenberg (Ed.), *Handbook of child psychology* (6th ed., pp. 719–788). Hoboken, NJ: John Wiley & Sons.

Doherty, W. J., & McDaniel, S. H. (Eds.) (2009). *Family therapy.* Washington, DC: American Psychological Association.

Dohrenwend, B. S. (1978). Social stress and community psychology. *American Journal of Community Psychology, 6*, 1–14.

Domino, G. & Domino, M. L. (2006). *Psychological testing* (2nd ed.). New York, NY: Cambridge University Press.

Donn, J. E., Routh, D. K., & Lunt, I. T. I. (2000). From Leipzig to Luxembourg (via Boulder and Vail): A history of clinical psychology training in Europe and the United States. *Professional Psychology: Research and Practice, 31*, 423–428.

Dornelas, E. A. (2001). Introduction: Integrating health psychology into clinical practice. *Journal of Clinical Psychology/In Session, 57*, 1261–1262.

Doss, B. D., Simpson, L. E., & Christensen, A. (2004). Why do couples seek marital therapy? *Professional Psychology: Research and Practice, 35*, 608–614.

Dozios, D. J. A. & Dobson, K. S. (2010). Depression. In M. M. Anthony & D. H. Barlow (Eds.) *Handbook of Assessment and Treatment Planning for Psychological Disorders* (2nd ed., pp. 344–389). New York, NY: Guilford Press.

Driessen, E., Cuijpers, P., Hollon, S. D., & Dekker, J. J. M. (2010). Does pretreatment severity moderate the efficacy of psychological treatment of adult outpatient depression? A meta-analysis. *Journal of Consulting and Clinical Psychology, 78*, 668–680.

Drossel, C. (2009). Group interventions. In W. T. O'Donohue & J. E. Fisher (Eds.), *General principles and empirically supported techniques of cognitive behavior therapy* (pp. 334–342). Hoboken, NJ: John Wiley & Sons.

DuBois, P. H. (1970). *A history of psychological testing.* Boston: Allyn & Bacon.

Duckworth, A. L., Steen, T. A., & Seligman, M. E. P. (2005). Positive psychology in clinical practice. *Annual Review of Clinical Psychology, 1*, 629–651.

Dym, R. J., Burns, J., Freeman, K., Lipton, M. L. (2011). Is functional MR imaging assessment of hemispheric language dominance as good as the Wada test?: a meta-analysis. *Radiology, 261*(2)), 446–455.

Eagle, M. N. (1984). *Recent developments in psychoanalysis: A critical evaluation.* Cambridge, MA: Harvard University Press.

Eagle, M. N. (2011). *From classical to contemporary psychoanalysis: A critique and integration.* New York, NY: Routledge.

Eagle, N. M. & Wolitzky, D. L. (2011). Systematic empirical research versus clinical case studies: A valid antagonism? *Journal of the American Psychoanalytic Association, 59*, 791–818.

Eaker, E. D., Abbott, R. D., Kannel, W. B. (1989). Frequency of uncomplicated angina pectoris in Type A compared with Type B persons (the Framingham study). *American Journal of Cardiology, 63*, 1042–1045.

Ebert, B. W. (1987). Guide to conducting a psychological autopsy. *Professional Psychology: Research and Practice, 18*, 52–56.

Ebrahim, S., Beswick, A., Burke, M., & Davey-Smith, G. (2006). Multiple risk factor interventions for primary prevention of coronary heart disease. *Cochrane Database Syst Rev., 18*, CD001561.

Edwards, A. L. (1957). *The social desirability variable in personality assessment and research.* New York, NY: Dryden.

Eells, T. D., Lombart, K. G., Salsman, N., Kendjelic, E. M., Schneiderman, C. T., & Lucas, C. P. (2011). Expert reasoning in psychotherapy case formulation. *Psychotherapy Research, 21*, 385–399.

Ehde, D. M. (2010). Application of positive psychology to rehabilitation psychology. *Handbook of rehabilitation psychology* (2nd ed.). Washington, DC: American Psychological Association 417–424.

Eid, M. & Diener, E. (Eds.). (2005). *Handbook of multimethod and measurement in psychology.* Washington, DC: American Psychological Association.

Einhorn, H. J., & Hogarth, R. M. (1978). Confidence in judgment: Persistence of the illusion of validity. *Psychological Review, 85*, 395–416.

Eisen, A. R., Sussman, J. M., Schmidt, T., Mason, L., Hausier, L. A., & Hashim, R. (2011). Separation anxiety disorder. In D. McKay, & E. A. Storch (Eds.), *Handbook of child and adolescent anxiety disorders* (pp. 245–259). New York, NY: Springer.

Ellis, A. (1962). *Reason and emotion in psychotherapy*. New York, NY: Lyle Stuart.

Ellis, A. (1973). Rational-emotive therapy. In R. Corsini (Ed.), *Current psychotherapies* (pp. 167–206). Ithaca, IL: F. E. Peacock.

Ellis, A. (1993). Changing rational-emotive therapy (RET) to rational-emotive behavior therapy (REBT). *The Behavior Therapist, 16,* 257–258.

Ellis, A. (1995). Rational emotive behavior therapy. In R. J. Corsini & D. Wedding (Eds.), *Current psychotherapies* (5th ed., pp. 162–196). Itasca, IL: Peacock Publishers, Inc.

Ellis, A. (2001). Reasons why rational emotive behavior therapy is relatively neglected in the professional and scientific literatures. *Journal of Rational-Emotive and Cognitive Behavior Therapy, 19,* 67–74.

Ellis, A. (2011). *Rational emotive behavior therapy*. Washington, D.C.: American Psychological Association.

Ellis, A. & Dryden, W. (1987). *The practice of rational-emotive therapy*. New York, NY: Springer.

Ellis, A. & Grieger, R. (Eds.). (1977). *Handbook of rational-emotive therapy*. New York, NY: Springer.

Ellis, P. D. (2010). *The essential guide to effect sizes: Statistical power, meta-analysis, and the interpretation of research results*. New York, NY: Cambridge University Press.

Ellsworth, J. R., Lambert, M. J., & Johnson, J. (2006). A comparison of the Outcome Questionnaire-45 and Outcomes Questionnaire-30 in classification and prediction of treatment outcome. *Clinical Psychology and Psychotherapy, 13,* 380–391.

Emery, R. E. (1982). Interparental conflict and the children of discord and divorce. *Psychological Bulletin, 92,* 310–330.

Emery, R. E., Matthews, S. G., & Kitzmann, K. M. (1994). Child custody mediation and litigation: Parents' satisfaction and functioning one year after settlement. *Journal of Consulting and Clinical Psychology, 62,* 124–129.

Emery, R. E., Matthews, S. G., & Wyer, M. M. (1991). Child custody medication and litigation: Further evidence on the differing views of mothers and fathers. *Journal of Consulting and Clinical Psychology, 59,* 410–418.

Ennis, B. J. & Litwack, T. R. (1974). Psychiatry and the presumption of expertise: Flipping coins in the courtroom. *California Law Review, 62,* 693–752.

Entringer, S., Epel, E. S., Kumsta, R., Lin, J., Hellhammer, D. H., Blackburn, E. H., Wust, S., Wadhwa, P. D. (2011). Stress exposure in intrauterine life is associated with shorter telomere length in young adulthood. Proceedings of the National Academy of Sciences, 108, E513–E518.

Eonta, A. M., Christon, L. M. Hourigan, S. E., Ravindran, N., Vranan, S. R., & Southam-Gerow, M. A. (2011). Using everyday technology to enhance evidence-based treatments. *Professional Psychology: Research and Practice, 42,* 513–520.

Epstein, R. (2007). Sexual orientation lies smoothly on a continuum: Verification and extension of Kinsey's hypothesis in a large-scale internet study. *Scientific American*, October, 6.

Erickson, P. I. & Kaplan, C. P. (2000). Maximizing qualitative responses about smoking in structured interviews. *Qualitative Health Research, 10,* 829–840.

Erikson, E. H. (1946). *Ego development and historical change. The psychoanalytic study of the child* (Vol. 2, pp. 359–396). New York, NY: International Universities Press.

Eslinger, P. J. & Damasio, A. R. (1985). Severe disturbance of higher cognition after bilateral frontal lobe ablation: Patient EVR. *Neurology, 35,* 1731–1741.

Ewing, C. P. & McCann, J. T. (2006). *Minds on trial: Great cases in law and psychology*. New York, NY: Oxford University Press.

Exner, J. E. (1974). *The Rorschach: A comprehensive system* (Vol. 1). New York, NY: Grune & Stratton.

Exner, J. E. (1993). *The Rorschach: A comprehensive system: Vol. 1. Basic foundations* (3rd ed.). New York, NY: John Wiley & Sons.

Exner, J. E. Jr. (2003). *Basic foundations and principles of interpretation*. Hoboken, NJ: John Wiley & Sons.

Exner, J. E. Jr. & Erdberg, P. (2005). *The Rorschach, advanced interpretation*. Hoboken, NJ: John Wiley & Sons.

Eyberg, S. M. & Matarazzo, R. G. (1980). Training parents as therapists: A comparison between individual parent-child interactions training and parent group didactic training. *Journal of Clinical Psychology, 36,* 492–499.

Eyberg, S. M., Nelson, M. M., & Boggs, S. R. (2008). Evidence-based psychosocial treatments for children and adolescents with disruptive behavior. *Journal of Clinical Child and Adolescent Psychology, 37,* 215–237.

Eysenck, H. J. (1952). The effects of psychotherapy: An evaluation. *Journal of Consulting Psychology, 16,* 319–324.

Eysenck, H. J. (1966). *The effects of psychotherapy*. New York, NY: International Science Press.

Eysenck, H. J. & Eysenck, S. B. G. (1975). *Manual for Eysenck Personality Questionnaire*. San Diego, CA: Educational and Individual Testing Service.

Fagan, T. K. (1996). Witmer's contribution to school psychological services. *American Psychologist, 51,* 241–243.

Fagan, T. J., Ax, R. K., Resnick, R. J., Liss, M., Johnson, R. T., & Forbes, M. R. (2004). Attitudes among interns and directors of training: Who wants to prescribe, who doesn't, and why? *Professional Psychology: Research and Practice, 35,* 345–356.

Fairbairn, W. R. D. (1952). *Psychoanalytic studies of the personality*. London, UK: Tavistock Publications/ Routledge & Kegan Paul.

Fairburn, C. G. & Cooper, Z. (2011). Therapist competence, therapy quality, and therapist training. *Behavior Research and Therapy, 49,* 373–378.

Fancher, R. E. (1973). *Psychoanalytic psychology: The development of Freud's thought*. New York, NY: W. W. Norton.

Farmer, R. F. & Chapman, A. L. (2008). Behavioral case formulations. In R. F. Farmer & A. L. Chapman *Behavioral interventions in cognitive behavior therapy: Practical guidance for putting theory into action* (pp. 71–103). Washington, DC: American Psychological Association.

Fauber, R. L. (2006). Graduate admissions in clinical psychology: Observations on the present and thoughts on the future. *Clinical Psychology: Science and Practice, 13,* 227–234.

Faust, D. (2012). *Coping with psychiatric and psychological testimony*, (6th ed.). New York, NY: Oxford University Press.

Faust, D. & Ziskin, J. (1988). The expert witness in psychology and psychiatry. *Science, 242*, 31–35.

Fawzy, F. I., Fawzy, N. W., Arndt, L. A., & Pasnau, R. O. (1995). Critical review of psychosocial interventions in cancer care. *Archives of General Psychiatry, 52*, 100–113.

Fazel, S., Singh, J. P., Doll, H., Grann, M. (2012). Use of risk assessment instruments ot predict violence and antisocial behaviour in73 samples involving 24,827 people: Systematic review and meta-analysis. BMJ2012;345:e4692. doi: 10.1136bmj.e4692.

Feinstein, R. E. & Feinstein, M. S. (2001). Psychotherapy for health and lifestyle change. *Journal of Clinical Psychology/In Session, 57*, 1263–1275.

Feliciano, L, Renn, B. N., & Arean, P. A. (2012). Mood disorders: Depressive disorders. In M. Hersen & Beidel, D. C. (Eds.). *Adult Psychopathology and Diagnosis* (6th ed.). (317–356). Hoboken, NJ: John Wiley & Sons.

Feltham, C. (2000). What are counselling and psychotherapy? In C. Feltham & I. Horton (Eds.), *Handbook of counselling and psychotherapy*. London, UK: Sage.

Ferenczi, S. & Rank, O. (1986). *The development of psychoanalysis*. Maddison, CT: International Universities Press. (originally published in 1924).

Figueroa-Moseley, C., Jean-Pierre, P., Roscoe, J. A., Ryan, J. L., Kohli, S., et al. (2007). Behavioral Interventions in Treating Anticipatory Nausea and Vomiting. *Journal of National Comprehensive Cancer Networks, 5*, 44–50.

Fine, R. (1971). *The healing of the mind: The technique of psychoanalytic psychotherapy*. New York, NY: David McKay.

Finger, M. S. & Rand, K. L. (2005). Addressing validity concerns in clinical psychology research. In M. C. Roberts & S. S. Ilardi (Eds.), *Handbook of research methods in clinical psychology* (pp. 13–30). Malden, MA: Blackwell Publishing.

Finkelhor, D. (2011). Prevalence of child victimization, abuse, crime, and violence exposure. In J. W. White, M. P. Koss, & A. E. Kazdin (Eds.), *Violence against women and children* (Vol. 1, pp. 9–29). Washington, DC: American Psychological Association.

Finkelhor, D., Turner, H., Omrod, R., & Hamby, S. L. (2009). Violence, abuse, and crime exposure in a national sample of children and youth. *Pediatrics, 124*, 1411–1423.

Finn, S. E. (1996). *Manual for using the MMPI-2 for a therapeutic intervention*. Minneapolis: University of Minnesota Press.

Finno, A. A., Michalski, M., Hart, B., Wicherski, M., & Kohout, J. L. (2010). Report of the 2009 APA Salary Survey. Retrieved Dec., 28, 2011 from http://www.apa.org/workforce/publications/09-salaries/index.aspx?tab=4.

First, M. B., Gibbon, M., Spitzer, R. L., & Williams, J. B. W., & Benjamin, L. S. (1997). *Structured Clinical Interview for DSM-IV Axis II Personality Disorders (SCID-II)*. Washington, DC: American Psychiatric Press.

First, M. B., Spitzer, R. L., Gibbon, M., & Williams, J. B. W. (1997a). *Structured Clinical Interview for DSM-IV Axis I Disorders: Clinical version (SCID-CV)*. Washington, DC: American Psychiatric Press.

First, M. B. (2006). Relational processes in the DSM-V revision process: Comment on the special section. *Journal of Family Psychology, 20*, 356–358.

Fischer, C. T. (1989). A life-centered approach to psychodiagnostics: Attending to lifeworld, ambiguity, and possibility. *Person-Centered Review, 4*, 163–170.

Fischer, C. T. (2001). Psychological assessment: From objectification back to the life world. In B. D. Slife, R. N. Williams, & S. H. Barlow (Eds.), *Critical issues in psychotherapy* (pp. 29–44). Thousand Oaks, CA: Sage.

Fisher, J. D., Fisher, W. A., Bryan, A. D., & Misovich, S. J. (2002). Information-motivation-behavioral skills model-based HIV risk behavior change intervention for inner-city high school youth. *Health Psychology, 21*, 177–186.

Fishman, D. B., Rego, S.A., & Muller, K. L. (2011). Behavior theories of psychotherapy. In J. C. Norcross, G. R. Vandenbos, & D. K. Freedheim (Eds.) *History of Psychotherapy: Continuity and Change* (2nd ed., pp. 101–140). Washington, DC: American Psychological Association.

Flanagan, D. P. & Harrison, P. L. (2011). *Contemporary intellectual assessment* (2nd ed.). New York, NY: The Guilford Press.

Fleisig, W. E. (1993). The development of the Illustrated Fear Survey Schedule (IFSS) and an examination of its reliability and validity with children with mild mental retardation. *Dissertation Abstracts International, 54*, 1719.

Flisher, A. J., Sorsdahl, K. R., & Lund, C. (2012). Test-retest reliability of the Xhosa version of the Diagnostic Interview Schedule for Children. *Child: Care, Health, and Development, 38*, 261–265.

Flores, E., Tschann, J. M., Dimas, J. M., Pasch, L. A., deGroat, C. L. (2010). Perceived ethnic/racial discrimination, posttraumatic stress symptoms and health risk behaviors among Mexican American adolescents. *J Couns Psychol, 57*, 264–73.

Fodor, J. A. (1983). *Modularity of mind*. Cambridge, MA: MIT Press.

Fogel, G. I. (1993). A transitional phase in our understanding of the psychoanalytic process: A new look at Ferenszi and Rank. *Journal of the American Psychoanalytic Association, 41*, 585–602.

Folkman, S. & Lazarus, R. S. (1988). *Manual for the ways of coping questionnaire*. Palo Alto, CA: Consulting Psychologists Press.

Follette, W. C. (1996). Introduction to the special section on the development of theoretically coherent alternatives to the DSM system. *Journal of Consulting and Clinical Psychology, 64*, 1117–1119.

Follette, W. C., Naugle, A. E., & Callaghan, G. M. (1996). A radical behavioral understanding of the therapeutic relationship in effecting change. *Behavior Therapy, 27*, 623–642.

Folstein, M. F., Maiberger, P., & McHugh, P. R. (1977). Mood disorders as a specific complication of stroke. *Journal of Neurology, Neurosurgery & Psychiatry, 40*, 1018–1020.

Fonagy, P. & Target, M. (2003). *Psychoanalytic theories: Perspectives from developmental psychology*. New York, NY: Brunner-Routledge.

Forand, N. R., Evans, S., Haglin, D., & Fishman, B. (2012). Cognitive behavioral therapy in practice: Treatment delivered by trainees at an outpatient clinic is clinically effective. *Behavior Therapy, 42*, 612–623.

Forgatch, M. S. & Patterson, G. R. (2010). Parent management training–Oregon model: An intervention for antisocial behavior in children and adolescents. In J. R. Weisz & A. E. Kazdin (Eds.), *Evidence-based psychotherapies for children and adolescents* (2nd ed., pp. 159–178). New York, NY: Guilford.

Forman, E. M. & Herbert, J. D. (2009). New directions in cognitive behavior therapy: Acceptance-based therapies. In W. T. O'Donohue & J. E. Fisher (Eds.), *General principles and empirically supported techniques of cognitive behavior therapy* (pp. 77–101). Hoboken, NJ: John Wiley & Sons.

Foster, G. D. & Kendall, P. C. (1994). The realistic treatment of obesity: Changing the scales of success. *Clinical Psychology Review, 14,* 701–736.

Fouad, N. A., Grus, C. L., Hatcher, R. L., Kaslow, N. J., Hutchings, P. S., Madson, M. B., et al. (2009). Competency benchmarks: A model for understanding and measuring competence in professional psychology across training levels. *Training and Education in Professional Psychology, 3,* S5–S26.

Fournier, N. M., Calverley, K. L., Wagner, J. P., Poock, J. L., & Crossley, M. (2008). Impaired social cognition 30 years after hemispherectomy for intractable epilepsy: the importance of the right hemisphere in complex social functioning. *Epilepsy and Behavior, 12*(3), 460–471.

Fowers, B. J. & Davido, B. J. (2006). The virtue of multiculturalism: Personal transformation, character, and openness to the other. *American Psychologist, 61,* 581–594.

Frances, A. J. & Widiger, T. (2011). Psychiatric diagnosis: Lessons from the DSM-IV past and cautions for the DSM-5 future. *Annual Reveiw of Clinical Psychology, 8,* 109–130.

Frank, E., Shear, M. K., Rucci, P., Banti, S., Mauri, M., et al. (2005). Cross-cultural validity of the Structured Clinical Interview for Panic-Agoraphobic spectrum. *Social Psychiatry and Psychiatric Epidemiology, 40,* 283–290.

Frank, E. & Levenson, J. C. (2011). *Interpersonal psychotherapy.* Washington, DC: American Psychological Association.

Frank, L. K. (1939). Projective methods for the study of personality. *Journal of Psychology, 8,* 343–389.

Frankl, V. (1967). *Psychotherapy and existentialism: Selected papers on logotherapy.* New York, NY: Washington Square Press.

Fredrickson, B. L. (2001). The role of positive emotions in positive psychology: The broaden-and-build theory of positive emotions. *American Psychologist, 56,* 218–226.

Free, M. L. (2007). *Cognitive therapy in groups: Guidelines and resources for practice* (2nd ed.). Hoboken, NJ: John Wiley & Sons.

Freeman, M. P., Fava, M., Lake, Trivedi, M. H., Wisner, K. L., & Mischoulon, D. (2010). Complementary and alternative medicine in major depressive disorder: The American Psychiatric Association Task Force Report. *Journal of Clinical Psychiatry, 71,* 669–681.

Freud, A. (1936). *The ego and the mechanisms of defense. In The writings of Anna Freud* (Vol. 2, Revised Edition, 1966). New York, NY: International Universities Press.

Freud, S. (1949). *An outline of psychoanalysis.* (J. Strachey, trans.). New York, NY: W. W. Norton.

Freud, S. (1904). On psychotherapy. Lecture delivered before the College of Physicians in Vienna. Reprinted in S. Freud, *Therapy and technique.* New York, NY: Collier Books, 1963.

Frick, P. J. & Nigg, J. T. (2012). Current issues in the diagnosis of attention deficit hyperactivity disorder, oppositional defiant disorder, and conduct disorder. *Annual Review of Clinical Psychology, 8,* 77–107.

Frick, P. J., Kamphaus, R. W., & Barry, C. T. (2009). *Clinical assessment of child and adolescent personality and behavior* (3rd ed.). New York, NY: Springer-Verlag.

Friederici, A. D. (2011). The brain basis of language processing: from structure to function. *Physiological Reviews, 91*(4), 1357–1392.

Friedman, H. S. & Schustack, M. W. (2011). *Personality: Classic theories and modern research* (5th ed.). Upper Saddle River, NJ: Prentice-Hall.

Friedman, M. & Rosenman, R. H. (1974). *Type A behavior and your heart.* New York, NY: Knopf.

Friedman, M., Thoresen, Gill, Ulmer, Powell, Price, Brown, Thompson, Labin, Breall, et al. (1986). Alteration of Type A behavior and its effect on cardiac recurrences in post-myocardial infarction patients: Summary results of the Recurrent Coronary Prevention Project. *American Heart Journal, 112,* 653–665.

Frish, M. B. (1998). Quality of life therapy and assessment in health care. *Clinical Psychology: Science and Practice, 5,* 19–40.

Fritz, G. K. & Kennedy, P. J. (2012). The long road ahead to mental health parity. *Journal of the American Academy of Child and Adolescent Psychiatry, 51,* 458-460.

Frueh, B. C., Ford, J. D., Elhai, J. D., & Grubaugh, A. L. (2012). Evidence-based practice in adult mental health. In P. Sturmey & M. Hersen (Eds.), *Handbook of Evidence-Based Practice in Clinical Psychology (Vol 2): Adult Disorders* (pp. 3-14). Hoboken, NJ: John Wiley & Sons.

Fulero, S. M. & Wrightsman, L. S. (2008). *Forensic psychology.* Belmont, CA: Wadsworth.

Fullerton, C. A., Busch, A. B., Normand, S. T., McGuire, T. G., & Epstein, A. M. (2011). Ten-year trends in quality of care and spending for depression. *Archives of General Psychiatry. 68,* 1218–1226.

Funder, D. (2001). *The personality puzzle* (2nd ed.). New York, NY: W. W. Norton.

Funderburk, B. W. & Eyberg, S. (2011). Parent-child interaction therapy. In J. C. Norcross, G. R. VandenBos, & D. K. Freedhaim (Eds.), *History of psychotherapy: Continuity and change* (2nd ed., pp. 415–420). Washington, DC: American Psychological Association.

Gabbard, G. O. (2005). *Psychodynamic psychiatry in clinical practice* (4th ed.). Washington, DC: American Psychiatric Publishing.

Gabbard, G. O. (2010). *Long-term psychodynamic psychotherapy: A basic text.* Washington, DC: American Psychiatric Publishers.

Gabbard, G. O., Litowitz, B. E., & Williams, P. (Eds.) (2012). *Textbook of psychoanalysis.* Arlington, VA: American Psychiatric Publishing.

Gabbard, K. & Gabbard, G. O. (1999). Psychiatry and the cinema. Washington, DC: American Psychiatric Press.

Gaines, L. K. & Falkenberg, S. (1998). An evaluation of the written selection test: Effectiveness and alternatives. *Journal of Criminal Justice, 26,* 175–183.

Gainotti, G. (1972). Emotional behavior and hemispheric side of lesion. *Cortex, 8,* 41–55.

Gainsbury, S. (2012). *Internet gambling: Current research findings and implications.* New York, NY: Springer.

Galton, F. (1883). *Inquiries into the human faculty and its development.* London, UK: Macmillan.

Garb, H. N. (1984). The incremental validity of information used in personality assessment. *Clinical Psychology Review, 4,* 641–656.

Garb, H. N. (1989). Clinical judgment, clinical training, and professional experience. *Psychological Bulletin, 105,* 387–396.

Garb, H. N. (1996). The representativeness and past-behavior heuristics in clinical judgment. *Professional Psychology: Theory and Practice, 27,* 272–277.

Garb, H. N. (2007). Computer-administered interviews and rating scales. *Psychological Assessment, 19,* 4–13.

Garber, J. (1984). Classification of childhood psychopathology: A developmental perspective. *Child Development, 55,* 30–48.

Garber, J. & Weersing, V. R. (2010). Comorbidity of anxiety and depression in youth: Implications for treatment and prevention. *Clinical Psychology: Science and Practice, 17* 293–306.

Garcia-Rodriguez, O., Pericot-Valverde, I., Gutierrez-Maldonado, J., Ferrer-Garcia, M. & Secades-Villa, R. (2012). Validation of smoking-related virtual environments for cue exposure therapy. *Addictive Behaviors, 37,* 703–708.

Gardner, H. (1993). *Multiple intelligences.* New York, NY: Basic Books.

Gardner, H. (2002). The pursuit of excellence through education. In M. Ferrari (Ed.), *Learning from extraordinary minds.* Mahwah, NJ: Erlbaum.

Gardner, H., Brownell, H. H., Wapner, W., & Michelow, D. (1983). Missing the point: The role of the right hemisphere in the processing of complex linguistic materials. In E. Perecman (Ed.), *Cognitive processing in the right hemisphere* (pp. 169–191). New York, NY: Academic.

Garfield, S. L. (1974). *Clinical psychology: The study of personality and behavior.* Chicago: Aldine.

Garfield, S. L. (1994). Research on client variables in psychotherapy. In A. Bergin & S. Garfield (Eds.), *Handbook of Psychotherapy and Behavior Change* (4th ed, pp. 190–228). New York, NY: John Wiley & Sons.

Gasquoine, P. G. (2010). Comparison of public/private health care insurance parameters for independent psychological practice. *Professional Psychology: Research and Practice, 41,* 319–324.

Gastelum, E. D., Hyun, A. M., Goldberg, D. A., Stanley, B., Sudak, D. M. et al. (2011). Is that an unconscious fantasy or an automatic thought? Challenges of learning multiple psychotherapies simultaneously. *Journal of the American Academy of Psychoanalysis & Dynamic Psychiatry, 39,* 111–132.

Gates, M. A., Holowka, D. W., Vasterling, J. J., Keane, T. M., Marx, B. P., & Rosen, R. C. (2012). Posttraumatic stress disorder in veterans and military personnel: Epidemiology, screening, and case recognition. *Psychological Services.* Advanced online publication. doi: 10.1037/a0027649.

Gazzaniga, M. (2011). *Who's in charge: Free will and the science of brain.* New York, NY: Harper Collins.

Gazzaniga, M. S., Fendrich, R., & Wessinger, C. M. (1994). Blindsight reconsidered. *Current Directions in Psychological Science, 3,* 93–95.

Geer, J. H. (1965). The development of a scale to measure fear. *Behaviour Research and Therapy, 3,* 45–53.

Geher, G. & Kaufman, S. K. (2011). Mating intelligence. In R. J. Sternberg & S. B. Kaufman (Eds.). *The Cambridge handbook of intelligence* (pp. 603–620). New York, NY: Cambridge University Press.

Gelfand, D. M., & Peterson, L. (1985). *Child development and psychopathology.* Beverly Hills, CA: Sage.

Gendlin, E. T. (1996). *Focusing-oriented psychotherapy: A manual of the experiential method.* New York, NY: Guilford.

Gerber, A. J., Kocsis, J. H., Milrod, B. L., Roose, S. P., Barber, J. P. et al. (2011). A quality-based review of randomized controlled trials of psychodynamic psychotherapy. *American Journal of Psychiatry, 168,* 19–28.

Ginger, S. & Ginger, A. (2012). *A practical guide for the humanistic psychotherapist.* London, GB: Karnac Books.

Gittelman, R. (1980). The role of tests for differential diagnosis in child psychiatry. *Journal of the American Academy of Child Psychiatry, 19,* 413–438.

Glad, J., Jergeby, U., Gustafsson, C., & Sonnander, K. (2012). Social work practitioner's experience of the clinical utility of the Home Obsevation for Measurement of the Environment (HOME) Inventory. Child & Family Social Work, 17, 23–33.

Glaser, R. & Bond, L. (1981). Introduction to the special issue: Testing: Concepts, policy, practice, and research. *American Psychologist, 36,* 997–1000.

Glasgow, R. E., Nutting, P. A., Toobert, D. J., King, D. K., Strycker, L. A., Jex, M., et al. (2006). Effects of a brief computer-assisted diabetes self-management intervention on dietary, biological and quality-of-life outcomes. *Chronic Illness, 2,* 27–38.

Glasgow, R. E. & Terborg, J. R. (1988). Occupational health promotion programs to reduce cardiovascular risk. *Journal of Consulting and Clinical Psychology, 56,* 365–373.

Glied, S. A. & Frank, R. G. (2009). Better but not best: Recent trends in the well-being of the mentally ill. *Health Affairs, 28,* 637–648.

Glover, G. H. (2011). Overview of functional magnetic resonance imaging. *Neurosurgery Clinics of North America, 22*(2), 133–139.

Glozman, J. M. (2007). A. R. Luria and the history of Russian neuropsychology. *Journal of the History of Neuroscience, 16,* (1–2), 168–180.

Glueckauf, R., Pickett, T. C., Ketterson, T. U., Loomis, J. S., & Rozensky, R. H. (2003). Preparation for the delivery of telehealth services: A self-study framework for expansion of practice. *Professional Psychology: Research and Practice, 34,* 159–163.

Glynn, M. & Rhodes, P. (2005). Estimated HIV prevalence in the US at the end of 2003. *National HIV Prevention Conference*, Atlanta, Georgia.

Goins, M. K., Strauss, G. D., & Martin, R. (1995). A change measure for psychodynamic psychotherapy outcome research. *Journal of Psychotherapy Practice and Research, 4,* 319–328.

Gold, J. & Strickler, G. (2006). Introduction: An overview of psychotherapy integration. In G. Strickler & J. Gold (Eds.), *A casebook of psychotherapy integration.* Washington, DC: American Psychological Association.

Goldberg, L. R. (1959). The effectiveness of clinicians' judgments: The diagnosis of organic brain damage from the Bender-Gestalt test. *Journal of Consulting Psychology, 23,* 25–33.

Goldberg, E. (1995). Rise and fall of modular orthodoxy. *Journal of Clinical and Experimental Neuropsychology, 17*(2), 193–208.

Goldberg, E. & Bougakov, D. (2005). Neuropsychologic assessment of frontal lobe dysfunction. *Psychiatric Clinics of North America, 28*, 567–580.

Goldfried, M. R. (1980). Toward the delineation of therapeutic change principles. *American Psychologist, 35*, 991–999.

Goldfried, M. R. (2006). Cognitive-affective-relational-behavior therapy. In G. Stricker & J. Gold (Eds.), *A casebook of psychotherapy integration* (pp. 153–164). Washington, DC: American Psychological Association.

Goldfried, M. R. & Sprafkin, J. N. (1974). *Behavioral personality assessment.* Morristown, NJ: General Learning Press.

Goldfried, M. R., Glass, C. R., & Arnkoff, D. B. (2010). Integrative approaches to psychotherapy. In J. C. Norcross, G. R. Vanden-Bos, & D. K. Freedheim (Eds.) *History of Psychotherapy: Continuity and Change* (2nd ed.). Washington, DC: American Psychological Association.

Goldfried, M. R., Glass, C. R., & Arnkoff, D. B. (2011). Integrative approaches to psychotherapy. In J. C. Norcross, G. R. VandenBos, & D. K. Freedheim (Eds.), *History of psychotherapy: Continuity and change* (2nd ed., pp. 269–296). Washington, DC: American Psychological Association.

Golding, S. L. & Rorer, L. G. (1972). Illusory correlation and subjective judgment. *Journal of Abnormal Psychology, 80*, 249–260.

Goldsmith, J. B. & McFall, R. M. (1975). Development and evaluation of an interpersonal skill-training program for psychiatric inpatients. *Journal of Abnormal Psychology, 84*, 51–58.

Gonzalez-Prendes, A. A., Hindo, C., & Pardo, Y. (2011). Cultural values integration in cognitive-behavioral therapy for a Latino with depression. *Clinical Case Studies, 10*, 376–394.

Goodheart, C. D. (2001). Design for tomorrow. *American Psychologist, 66*, 339–347.

Goodheart, C. D. (2010). Economics and psychology practice: What we need to know and why. *Professional Psychology: Research and Practice, 41*, 189–195.

Goodwin, P. J., Leszcz, M., Ennis, M., Koopmans, J., Vincent, L., Guther, H., et al. (2001). The effect of group psychosocial support on survival in metastatic breast cancer. *The New England Journal of Medicine, 345*, 1719–1726.

Gorenstein, E. E. & Comer, R. J. (2002). *Case studies in abnormal psychology.* New York, NY: Worth.

Gorske, T. T. (2008). Therapeutic neuropsychological assessment: A humanistic model and case example. *Journal of Humanistic Psychology, 48*, 320–339.

Gottman, J. M., Markman, H. J., & Notarius, C. (1977). The topography of marital conflict: A sequential analysis of verbal and nonverbal behavior. *Journal of Marriage and the Family, 39*, 461–477.

Gottman, J. M. (2011). *The science of trust: Emotional attunement for couples.* New York, NY: W.W. Norton.

Gottman, J. M. & Ryan, K. (2005). The mismeasure of therapy: Treatment outcomes in marital therapy research. In W. M. Pinsof & J. L. Lebow (Eds.), *Family psychology: The art of the science* (pp. 65–89). New York, NY: Oxford University Press.

Gottman, J. M. & Gottman, J. S. (2006). *Ten lessons to transform your marriage.* New York, NY: Crown Publishing Group.

Gough, H. (1987). *California Psychological Inventory: Administrator's guide.* Palo Alto, CA: Consulting Psychologists Press.

Graham, J. M. & Kim, Y. H. (2011). Predictors of doctoral student success in professional psychology: Characteristics of students, programs, and universities. *Journal of Clinical Psychology, 67*, 340–354.

Graham, J. R. (1990). *MMPI-2: Assessing personality and psychopathology.* New York, NY: Oxford University Press.

Greenberg, L. S., Elliot, R. K., & Lietaer, G. (1994). Research on experiential psychotherapies. In A. E. Bergin & S. L. Garfield (Eds.), *Handbook of psychotherapy and behavior change* (pp. 509–512). New York, NY: John Wiley & Sons.

Greenberg, L. S., Rice, L. N., & Elliott, R. (1993). *Facilitating emotional change: The moment-by-moment process.* New York, NY: Guilford Press.

Greenberg, R. P., Constantino, M. J., & Bruce, N. (2006). Are patient expectations still relevant for psychotherapy process and outcome. *Clinical Psychology Review, 26*, 657–678.

Greene, C. J., Morland, L. A., Macdonald, A., Frueh, B. C., Grubbs, K. M., & Rosen, C. S. (2010). How does tele-mental health affect group therapy process? Secondary analysis of a noninferiority trial. *Journal of Consulting and Clinical Psychology, 78*, 746–750.

Greenhoot, A. F. (2005). Design and analysis of experimental and quasi-experimental investigations. In M. C. Roberts & S. S. Ilardi (Eds.), *Handbook of research methods in clinical psychology* (pp. 92–114). Malden, MA: Blackwell Publishing.

Grilo, C. M., Masheb, R. M., & Wilson, G. T. (2006). Rapid response to treatment for binge eating disorder. *Journal of Consulting and Clinical Psychology, 74*, 602–613.

Grisso, T. & Appelbaum, P. S. (1995). The MacArthur Treatment Competence Study. III: Abilities of patients to consent to psychiatric and medical treatments. *Law and Human Behavior, 19*, 149–174.

Grisso, T., Steinberg, L., Wollard, J., Cauffman, E., Scott, E., Graham, S., et al. (2003). Juveniles' competence to stand trial: A comparison of adolescents' and adults' capacities as trial defendants. *Law and Human Behavior 27*, 333–363.

Gros, D. F., Yoder, M., Tuerk, P. W., Lozano, B. E., & Acierno, R. (2011). Exposure therapy for PTSD delivered to veterans via telehealth: Predictors of treatment completion and outcome comparison to treatment delivered in person. *Behavior Therapy, 42*, 276–283.

Groth-Marnat, G. (2003). *Handbook of psychological assessment* (4th ed.). Hoboken, NJ: John Wiley & Sons.

Groth-Marnat, G. (2003). *Handbook of psychological assessment* (4th ed.). Hoboken, NJ: John Wiley & Sons.

Groth-Marnat, G. (2009). *Handbook of psychological assessment* (5th ed.). New York, NY: John Wiley & Sons.

Grove, W. M., Zald, D. H., Lebow, B. S., Snitz, B. E., & Nelson, C. (2000). Clinical versus mechanical prediction: A meta-analysis. *Psychological Assessment, 12*, 19–30.

Grus, C. L., McCutcheon, S. R., & Berry, S. L. (2011). Actions by professional psychology education and training groups to mitigate the internship imbalance. *Training and Education in Professional Psychology, 5*, 193–201.

Grych, J. H. & Fincham, F. D. (1992). Interventions for children of divorce: Toward greater integration of research and action. *Psychological Bulletin, 111*, 434–454.

Grydeland, H., Walhovd, K. B., Westlye, L. T., Due-Tønnessen, P., Ormaasen, V., Sundseth, Ø., & Fjell, A. M. (2010). Amnesia following herpes simplex encephalitis: diffusion-tensor imaging uncovers reduced integrity of normal-appearing white matter. *Radiology, 257*(3), 774–781.

Gulec, H., Moessner, M., Mezei, A., Kohls, E., Tury, F., & Bauer, S. (2011). Internet-based maintenance treatment for patients with eating disorders. *Professional Psychology, Research and Practice, 42*, 479–486.

Gullone, E. & King, N. J. (1992). Psychometric evaluation of a revised fear survey schedule for children and adolescents. *Journal of Child Psychology and Psychiatry and Allied Disciplines, 33*, 987–998.

Gur, R. E. (1978). Left hemisphere dysfunction and the left hemisphere overactivation in schizophrenia. *Journal of Abnormal Psychology, 87*, 225–238.

Gurman, A. S. (2003). Marital therapy. In A. S. Gurman & S. B. Messer (Eds.), *Essential Psychotherapies*, (2nd ed., pp 463–514). New York, NY: Guilford.

Gurman, A. S. & Snyder, D. K. (2011). Treatment modalities. In J. C. Norcross, G. R. VandenBos, & D. K. Freedheim (Eds.), *History of psychotherapy: Continuity and change* (2nd ed., pp. 485–496). Washington, DC: American Psychological Association.

Halford, W. K. & Moore, N. E. (2002). Relationship education and the prevention of couple relationship problems. In A. S. Gurman & N. S. Jacobson (Eds.), *Clinical Handbook of Couple Therapy* (3rd ed., pp. 400–419). New York, NY: Guilford Press.

Hall, G. C. N. (2005). Introduction to the special section on multicultural and community psychology: Clinical psychology in context. *Journal of Consulting and Clinical Psychology, 73*, 787–789.

Hall, J. E. & Boucher, A. P. (2008). Early career psychologists' knowledge of credentialing in psychology. *Professional Psychology: Research and Practice, 39*, 480–487.

Hall, J. E. & Lunt, I. (2005). Global mobility for psychologists: The role of psychology organizations in the United States, Canada, Europe, and other regions. *American Psychologist, 60*, 712–726.

Hall, J. E., Wexelbaum, S. F., & Boucher, A. P. (2007). Doctoral student awareness of licensure, credentialing, and professional organizations in psychology: The 2005 National Register international survey. *Training and Education in Professional Psychology, 1*, 38–48.

Hallahan, B., Hibbeln, J. R., Davis, J. M., & Garland, M. R. (2007). Omega-3 fatty acid supplementation in patients with recurrent self-harm: Single-centre double-blind randomised controlled trial. *British Journal of Mental Science, 190*, 118–122.

Hambleton, R. K., Merenda, P. F., & Spielberger, C. D. (Eds.). (2005). *Adapting educational and psychological tests for cross-cultural assessment.* Mahwah, NJ: Erlbaum.

Hammond, K. R. & Allen, J. M. (1953). *Writing clinical reports.* Englewood Cliffs, NJ: Prentice-Hall.

Handler, L. (1974). Psychotherapy, assessment, and clinical research: Parallels and similarities. In A. I. Rabin (Ed.), *Clinical psychology: Issues of the seventies* (pp. 49–62). East Lansing: Michigan State University Press.

Hansen, J. A. (2008). Therapist self-disclosure: Who and when. Dissertation 69, 1954.

Hansen, J. C. (2011). Remembering John L. Holland, PhD. *The Counseling Psychologist, 39*, 1212–1217.

Hanson, R. K. & Morton-Bourgon, K. E. (2009). The accuracy of recidivism risk assessments for sexual offenders: A meta-analysis of 118 prediction studies. *Psychological Assessment, 21*, 1–21.

Harbeck, C., Peterson, L., & Starr, L. (1992). Previously abused child victims' response to a sexual abuse prevention program: A matter of measures. *Behavior Therapy, 23*, 375–388.

Harding, T. P. (2007). Clinical decision-making: How prepared are we? *Training and Education in Professional Psychology, 1*, 95–104.

Harlow, J. M. (1848). Passage of an iron rod through the head. *Boston Medical and Surgical Journal, 39*, 389–393.

Haro, J. M., Kontodimas, S., Negrin, M. A., Ratcliffe, M., Saurez, D., & Windmeijer, F. (2006). Methodological aspects in the assessment of treatment effects in observational health outcomes studies. *Applied Health Economics and Health Policy, 5*, 11–25.

Harrower, M. R. (1965). Clinical psychologists at work. In B. B. Wolman (Ed.), *Handbook of clinical psychology* (pp. 1443–1458). New York, NY: McGraw-Hill.

Hartmann, H. (1958). *Ego psychology and the problem of adaptation.* New York, NY: International Universities Press.

Harvey, S. T. & Taylor, J. E. (2010). A meta-analysis of the effects of psychotherapy with sexually abuse children and adolescents. *Clinical Psychology Review, 30*, 517–535.

Harway, M. (2005). *Handbook of couples therapy.* Hoboken, NJ: John Wiley & Sons.

Harwood, T. M. & L'Abate, L. (2010). *Self-help in mental health: A critical review.* New York, NY: Springer.

Harwood, T. M., Pratt, D., Beutler, L. E., Bongar, B. M., Lenore, S., & Forrester, B. T. (2011). Technology, telehealth, treatment enhancement, and selection. *Professional Psychology: Research and Practice, 42*, 448–454.

Harwood, T. M., Beutler, L. E., & Groth-Marnat, G. (Eds.) (2011a). *Integrative Assessment of Adult Personality* (pp. 354–372). New York, NY: Guilford.

Harwood, T. M., Beutler, L. E., & Williams, O. B., & Stegman, R. S. (2011b). Identifying treatment-relevant assessment: Systematic Treatment Selection/InnerLife. In T. M. Harwood, L. E. Beutler, & G. Groth-Marnat (Eds) *Integrative Assessment of Adult Personality* (pp. 61–79). New York, NY: Guilford.

Harwood, T. M., Pratt, D., Beutler, L. E., Bongar, B. M. Lenore, S., & Forrester, B. T. (2011c). Technology, telehealth, treatment enhancement, and selection. *Professional Psychology: Research and Practice, 42*, 448–454.

Harwood, T. M., Beutler, L. E., & Groth-Marnat, G. (Eds.) (2011). *Integrative assessment of adult personality* (3rd ed.). New York, NY: The Guilford Press.

Hatala, R. & Case, S. M. (2000). Examining the influence of gender on medical students' decision making. *Journal of Women's Health & Gender-Based Medicine, 9*, 617–623.

Hatcher, R. L. (2011a). The internship supply as a common-pool resource: A pathway to managing the imbalance problem. *Training and Education in Professional Psychology, 5*, 126–140.

Hatcher, R. L. (2011b). Managing the internship imbalance: Response to commentaries. *Training and Education in Professional Psychology, 5*, 217–221.

Hatfield, D. R. & Ogles, B. M. (2004). The use of outcome measures by psychologists in clinical practice. *Professional Psychology: Research and Practice, 35*, 485–491.

Haug, T., Nordgreen, T., Ost, L. G., & Havik, O. E. (2012). Self-help treatment of anxiety disorders: A meta-analysis and meta-regression of effects and potential moderators. *Clinical Psychology Review, 32*, 425–445.

Hawes, D. J. & Dadds, M. R. (2006). Assessing parenting practices through parent-report and direct observation during parent-training. *Journal of Child and Family studies, 15*, 555–568.

Hawley, K. M. & Weisz, J. R. (2005). Youth versus parent working alliance in usual clinical care: Distinctive associations with retention, satisfaction, and treatment outcome. *Journal of Clinical Child and Adolescent Psychology, 34*, 117–128.

Hayes, S. C., Follette, V. M., & Linehan, M. M. (Eds.). (2004). *Mindfulness and acceptance: Expanding the cognitive-behavioral tradition.* New York, NY: Guilford.

Hayes, S. C., Masuda, A., Bissett, R., Luoma,J., & Guerrero, L. F. (2004). DBT, FAP, and ACT: How empirically oriented are the new behavior therapy technologies? *Behavior Therapy, 35*, 35–54.

Hayes, S. C., Villantte, M., Levin, M., & Hildebrandt, M. (2011). Open, aware, and active: Contextual approaches as an emerging trend in the behavioral and cognitive therapies. *Annual Review of Clinical Psychology, 7*, 141–168.

Hayes-Skelton, S. A., Usmani, A., Lee, J. K., Roemer, L., & Orsillo, S. M. (2011). A fresh look at potential mechanisms of change in applied relaxation for generalized anxiety disorder: A case series. *Cognitive and Behavioral Practice, 19*, 451–462.

Haynes, R. B. (1982). Improving patient compliance: An empirical view. In R. B. Stuart (Ed.), *Adherence, compliance, and generalization in behavioral medicine* (pp. 56–78). New York, NY: Brunner/Mazel.

Haynes, S. N. (1990). Behavioral assessment of adults. In G. Goldstein & M. Hersen (Eds.), *Handbook of psychological assessment* (2nd ed., pp. 423–463). New York, NY: Pergamon Press.

Haynes, S. N. & O'Brien, W. O. (2000). *Principles of behavioral assessment: A functional approach to psychological assessment.* New York, NY: Plenum/ Kluwer Press.

Haynos, A. F. & O'Donohue, W. T. (2012). Universal childhood and adolescent obesity prevention programs: Review and critical analysis. *Clinical Psychology Review, 32*, 383–399.

Hays, P. A. & Iwamasa, G. Y. (Eds.). (2006). *Culturally responsive cognitive-behavioral therapy.* Washington, DC: American Psychological Association.

Hazlett-Stevens, H. & Bernstein, D. A. (2012). Relaxation. In W. T. O'Donahue & J. E. Fisher (Eds.). (2012). *Cognitive behavior therapy: Core principles for practice* (pp. 105–132). New York, NY: John Wiley & Sons.

Hazlett-Stevens, H., Craske, M. G., Roy-Birne, P. P., Sherbourne, C. D., Stein, M. B., & Bystritsky, A. (2002). Predictors of willingness to consider medication and psychosocial treatment for panic disorder in primary care patients. *General Hospital Psychiatry, 24*, 316–321.

Heal, L. W. & Sigelman, C. K. (1995). Response biases in interviews of individuals with limited mental ability. *Journal of Intellectual Disability Research, 39*, 331–340.

Heiby, E. M., DeLeon, P. H., & Anderson, T. 2004, "A Debate on Prescription Privileges for Psychologists." *Professional Psychology: Research and Practice, 35*(4), 336–344.

Heider, F. (1958). *The psychology of interpersonal relations.* New York, NY: John Wiley & Sons.

Heilbrun, K. & Collins, S. (1995). Evaluations of trial competency and mental state at time of offense: Report characteristics. *Professional Psychology: Research & Practice, 26*, 61–67.

Heilbrun, K. DeMatteo, D., Marczyk, G., & Goldstein, A. (2008). Standards of practice and care in forensic mental health assessment. *Psychology, Public Policy, and Law, 14*, 1–26.

Heilman, K. M., Barrett, A. M., & Adair, J. C. (1998). Possible mechanisms of anosognosia: A defect in self-awareness. *Philosophical Transactions of the Royal Society of London: Series B. Biological Sciences, 353*(1377), 1903–1909.

Heilman, K. M. & Valenstein, E. (Eds.). (2003). *Clinical neuropsychology* (4th ed.). New York, NY: Oxford University Press.

Helgeson, V. S., Cohen, S., & Fritz, H. (1998). Social ties and the onset and progression of cancer. In J. Holland (Ed.), *Psycho-oncology.* New York, NY: Oxford University Press.

Heller, W. (1990). The neuropsychology of emotion: Developmental patterns and implications for psychopathology. In N. L. Stein, B. L. Leventhal, & T. Trabasso (Eds.), *Psychological and biological approaches to emotion* (pp. 167–211). Hillsdale, NJ: Erlbaum.

Heller, W. & Nitschke, J. B. (1997). Regional brain activity in emotion: A framework for understanding cognition in depression. *Cognition and Emotion, 11*, 637–661.

Hellige, J. B. (2001). *Hemispheric asymmetry: What's right and what's left.* Cambridge, MA: Harvard University Press.

Hendrie, H. C., Lane, K. A., Ogunniyi, A., Baiyewu, O., Gureje, O., Evans, R., et al. (2006). The development of a semi-structured home interview (CHIF) to directly assess function in cognitively impaired elderly people in two cultures. *International Psychogeriatrics, 18*, 653–666.

Henggeler, S. W. (2011). Efficacy studies to large-scale transport: The development and validation of multisystemic therapy programs. *Annual Review of Clinical Psychology, 7*, 351–381.

Henry, W. E. (1956). *The analysis of fantasy: The thematic apperception technique in the story of personality.* New York, NY: John Wiley & Sons.

Herbert, J. D., Forman, E. M., & England, E. L. (2009). Psychological acceptance. In W. T. O'Donohue & J. E. Fisher (Eds.), *General principles and empirically supported techniques of cognitive behavior therapy* (pp. 102–114). Hoboken, NJ: John Wiley & Sons.

Herbert, T. B. & Cohen, S. (1993). Stress and immunity in humans: A meta-analytic review. *Psychosomatic Medicine, 55*, 364–379.

Hergenhahn, B. R. (1994). *An introduction to theories of personality.* Englewood Cliffs, NJ: Prentice Hall.

Herholz, K. (2011). Perfusion SPECT and FDG-PET. *International Psychogeriatrics, 23*, Suppl 2, S25–31.

Herink, R. (Ed.). (1980). The psychotherapy handbook: The A to Z guide to more than 250 different therapies in use today. New York, NY: New American Library.

Herrington, J. D., Heller, W., Mohanty, A, Engels, A. S., Banich, M.T., Webb, A. G., & Miller, G. A. (2010). Localization of asymmetric brain function in emotion and depression. *Psychophysiology, 47*(3), 442–454.

Herrington, J. D., Mohanty, A., Koven, N. S., Fisher, J. E., Stewart, J. L., Banich, M. T., et al. (2005). Emotion-modulated performance and activity in left dorsolateral prefrontal cortex. *Emotion, 5*, 200–207.

Hersch, P. D. & Alexander, R. W. (1990). MMPI profile patterns of emotional disability claimants. *Journal of Clinical Psychology, 46*, 795–799.

Hersen, M. (2002). *Clinical behavior therapy*. New York, NY: John Wiley & Sons.

Hersen, M. & Beidel, D. C. (Eds.) (2012). Adult Psychopathology and Diagnosis (6th ed.). New York, NY: John Wiley & Sons.

Hetherington, E. M. & Elmore, A. M. (2003). Risk and resilience in children coping with their parents' divorce and remarriage. In S. S. Luthar (Ed.), *Resilience and vulnerability: Adaptation in the context of childhood adversities* (pp. 182–212). New York, NY: Cambridge University Press.

Hetherington, E. M., Bridges, M., & Insabella, G. M. (1998). What matters? What does not? Five perspectives on the association between marital transitions and children's adjustment. *American Psychologist, 53*, 167–184.

Hetherington, E. M. & Arasteh, J. D. (Eds.). (1988). *Impact of divorce, single parenting, and stepparenting on children*. Hillsdale, NJ: Erlbaum.

Heyman, R. E. (2001). Observation of couple conflicts: Clinical assessment applications, stubborn truths, and shaky foundations. *Psychological Assessment, 13*, 5–35.

Hickling, F. W., McKenzie, K., Mullen, R., & Murray, R. (1999). A Jamaican psychiatrist evaluates diagnoses at a London psychiatric hospital. *British Journal of Psychiatry, 175*, 283–285.

Hilgard, E. R., Kelly, E. L., Luckey, B., Sanford, R. N., Shaffer, L. F., & Shakow, D. (1947). Recommended Graduate Training Program in Clinical Psychology. *American Psychologist, 2*, 539–558.

Hilton, N. Z., Harris, G. T., & Rice, M. E. (2006). Sixty-six years of research on clinical versus actuarial prediction of violence. *Counseling Psychologist, 34*, 400–409.

Himelein, M. J. & Putnam, E. A. (2001). Work activities of academic clinical psychologists: Do they practice what they teach? *Professional Psychology: Research and Practice, 5*, 537–542.

Hinshaw, S. P. (2007). *The mark of shame: Stigma of mental illness and an agenda for change*. New York, NY: Oxford University Press.

Hoeft, F., McCandliss, B. D., Black, J. M., Gantman, A., Zakerani, N., Hulme, C., Lyytinen, H., Whitfield-Gabrieli, S., Glover, G. H., Reiss, A. L., & Gabrieli, J. D. (2011). Neural systems predicting long-term outcome in dyslexia. Proceedings of the National Academy of Sciences USA, 108(1), 361–366.

Hofferth, S. L., Stueve, J. L., Pleck, J., Bianchi, S., & Sayer, L. (2002). The demography of fathers: What fathers do. In C. S. Tamis-LeMonda & N. Cabrera (Eds.), *Handbook of father involvement: Multidisciplinary perspectives* (pp. 63–90). Mahwah, NJ: Erlbaum.

Hofmann, S. G., Sawyer, A. T., Witt, A. A., & Oh, D. (2010). The effect of mindfulness-based therapy on anxiety and depression: A meta-analytic review. *Journal of Consulting and Clinical Psychology, 78*, 169–183.

Hogue, A., Dauber, S., Stambaugh, L. F., Cecero, J. J., & Liddle, H. A. (2006). Early therapeutic alliance and treatment outcome in individual and family therapy for adolescent behavior problems. *Journal of Consulting and Clinical Psychology, 74*, 121–129.

Holden, R. R. (1991). Psychometric properties of the Holden Psychological Screening Inventory (HPSI). Paper presented at the meeting of the Canadian Psychological Association, Ottawa.

Holland, J. L. (1996). Exploring careers with a typology. *American Psychologist, 51*, 397–406.

Hollanders, H. & McLeod, J. (1999). Theoretical orientation and reported practice: A survey of eclecticism among counselors in Britain. *British Journal of Guidance and Counseling, 27*, 405–414.

Hollon, S. D. (2006). Randomized clinical trials. In J. C. Norcross, L. E. Beutler, & R. F. Levant (Eds.), *Evidence-based practice in mental health* (pp. 96–105). Washington, DC: American Psychological Association.

Hollon, S. D., DeRubeis, R. J., Shelton, R. C., Amsterdam, J. D., Salomon, R. M., O'Reardon, J. P., et al. (2005). Prevention of relapse following cognitive therapy versus medications in moderate to severe depression. *Archives of General Psychiatry, 62*, 417–422.

Hollon, S. D. & DiGiuseppe, R. (2010). Cognitive theories of psychotherapy. In J. C. Norcross, G. R. VandenBos, & D. K. Freedheim (Eds.) *History of Psychotherapy: Continuity and Change* (2nd ed.). Washington, DC: American Psychological Association.

Hollon, S. D. & DiGuiseppe, R. (2011). Cognitive theories of psychotherapy. In W. T. O'Donahue & J. E. Fisher (Eds.) *Cognitive behavior therapy: Core principles for practice* (pp. 203–241). New York, NY: John Wiley & Sons.

Hollon, S. D., Stewart, M. O., & Strunk, D. (2006). Enduring effects for cognitive behavior therapy in the treatment of depression and anxiety. *Annual Review of Psychology, 57*, 285–315.

Holmboe, E. S. (2004). Faculty and the observation of trainees clinical skills: Problems and opportunities. *Academic Medicine. 79*, 16–22.

Holt, R. R. & Luborsky, L. (1958). *Personality patterns of psychiatrists: A study of methods for selecting residents* (Vol. 1). New York, NY: Basic Books.

Holtforth, M. G., Krieger, T., Bochsler, K., & Mauler, B. (2011). The prediction of psychotherapy success by outcome expectations in inpatient psychotherapy. *Psychotherapy and Psychosomatics, 80*, 321–322.

Homant, R. & Kennedy, D. B. (1998). Psychological aspects of crime scene profiling. *Criminal Justice and Behavior, 25*, 319–343.

Horn, J. L. (1965). An empirical comparison of methods for estimating factor scores. *Educational and Psychological Measurement, 25*, 313–322.

Horst, K., Mendez, M., Culver-Turner, R., Amanor-Boadu, Y., Minner, B., et al. (2012). The importance of therapist/client ethnic/racial matching in couples treatment for domestic violence. *Contemporary Family Therapy, 34*, 57–71.

Horvath, A. O., DelRe, A. C., Fluckiger, C., & Symonds, D. (2011). Alliance in individual psychotherapy. *Psychotherapy, 48*, 9–16.

Hough, S. & Squires, L. E. (2012). Recruitment, retention and professional development of psychologists in America: Potential issue for training and performance. *Sexual Disability, 30*, 161–170.

House, J. S., Robbins, C., & Metzner, H. L. (1982). The association of social relationships and activities with mortality: Prospective evidence from the Tecumseh Community Health Study. *American Journal of Epidemiology, 116*, 123–140.

Houston, G. (2003). *Brief Gestalt therapy*. Thousand Oaks, CA: Sage.

Houtrow, A. J. & Okumura, M. J. (2011). Pediatric mental health problems and associated burden on families. *Vulnerable Children and youth Studies, 6*, 222–233.

Houts, A. C. (2004). Discovery, invention, and the expansion of the modern Diagnostic and Statistical Manuals of Mental Disorders. In L. E. Beutler & M. L. Malik (Eds.), *Rethinking the DSM: A psychological perspective* (pp. 17–68). Washington, DC: American Psychological Association.

Hovarth, A. O. (2000). The therapeutic relationship: From transference to alliance. *Journal of Clinical Psychology/In Session: Psychotherapy in Practice, 56*, 163–173.

Hovarth, A. O. & Greenberg, L. S. (1989). Development and validation of the Working Alliance Inventory. *Journal of Counseling Psychology, 36*, 223–233.

Hovarth, A. O., Del Re, A. C., Fluckiger, C., & Symonds, D. (2011). Alliance in individual psychotherapy. *Psychotherapy, 48*, 9–16.

Howard, K. I., Lueger, R. J., Maling, M. S., & Martinovich, Z. (1993). A phase model of psychotherapy outcome: Causal mediation of change. *Journal of Consulting and Clinical Psychology, 61*, 678–685.

Hsu, L. K. & Folstein, M. F. (1997). Somatoform disorders in Caucasian and Chinese Americans. *Journal of Nervous and Mental Disease, 185*, 382–387.

Hudziak, J. J., Achenbach, T. M., Althoff, R. R., & Pine, D. S. (2008). A dimensional approach to developmental psychopathology. In J. E. Helzer, H. C. Kraemer, R. F. Krueger, H. U. Wittchen, P. J. Sirovatka, & D. A. Regier (Eds.), *Dimensional approaches in diagnostic classification: Refining the research agenda for DSM-V* (pp. 101–113). Washington, DC: American Psychiatric Association.

Huey, S. J. & Polo, A. J. (2010). Assessing the effects of evidence-based psychotherapies with ethnic minority youths. In J. R. Weisz & A. E. Kazdin (Eds.), *Evidence-based psychotherapies for children and adolescents* (2nd ed., pp. 451–465). New York, NY: Guilford.

Hughes, R., Jr. (1996). The effects of divorce on children. Retrieved 13 December 2001, from http://www.hec.ohio-state.edu/famlife/divorce/index.htm.

Humes, K. R., Jones, N. A., & Ramirez, R. R. (2011). *Overview of race and Hispanic origin: 2010*. Washington, DC: U. S. Census Bureau.

Hummelen, B., Wilberg, T., & Karterud, S. (2007). Interviews of female patients with borderline personality disorder who dropped out of group psychotherapy. *International Journal of Group Psychotherapy, 57*, 67–91.

Humphreys, L. G. (1988). Trends in levels of academic achievement of blacks and other minorities. *Intelligence, 12*, 231–260.

Hunsley, J. & Mash, E. J. (2007). Evidence-based assessment. *Annual Review of Clinical Psychology, 3*, 29–51.

Hunsley, J. & Mash, E. J. (2010). The role of assessment in evidence-based practice. In M. M. Antony & D. H. Barlow (Eds.) *Handbook of Assessment and Treatment Planning for Psychological Disorders* (2nd ed., pp. 3–22). New York, NY: Guilford.

Hunsley, J., Lee, C. M., & Wood, J. M. (2003). Controversy and questionable assessment techniques. In S. O. Lilienfeld, S. J. Lynn, & J. M. Lohr (Eds.), *Science and pseudoscience in clinical psychology* (pp. 39–76). New York, NY: Guilford.

Hunt, M. (1993). *The story of psychology*. New York, NY: Anchor Books.

Hunter, S. J. & Donders, J. (Eds.). (2011). *Pediatric neuropsychological intervention*. Cambridge, MA: Cambridge University Press.

Huprich, S. K. & Meyer, G. J. (2011). Introduction to the JPA special issue: Can the Psychodynamic Diagnostic Manual put the complex person back at the center-stage of personality assessment? *Journal of Personality Assessment, 93*, 109–111.

Ingram, R. E. Price, J. M. (Eds.) (2010). *Vulnerability to psychopathology: Risk across the lifespan* (2nd ed). New York, NY: Guilford Press.

Inskipp, F. (2000). Generic skills. In C. Feltham & I. Horton (Eds.), *Handbook of counselling and psychotherapy*. London, UK: Sage Publications.

Institute of Medicine. (1994). *Reducing risk for mental disorders: Frontiers for prevention intervention research*. Washington, DC: National Academy Press.

Institute of Medicine (2009). *Preventing mental, emotional, and behavioral disorders among young people: Progress and possibilities*. Washington, DC: National Academies Press.

Institute of Personality Assessment and Research. (1970). *Annual report: 1969–1970*. Berkeley: University of California.

Inui, T., Yourtee, E., & Williamson, J. (1976). Improved outcomes in hypertension after physician tutorials. *Annuals of Internal Medicine, 84*, 646–651.

Isenhart, C. E. & Silversmith, D. J. (1996). MMPI-2 response styles: Generalization to alcoholism assessment. *Psychology of Addictive Behaviors, 10*, 115–123.

Jackson, D. N. & Messick, S. (1958). Content and style in personality assessment. *Psychological Bulletin, 55*, 243–252.

Jackson, Y., Alberts, F. L., & Roberts, M. C. (2010). Clinical child psychology: A practice specialty serving children, adolescents, and their families. *Professional Psychology: Research and Practice, 41*, 75–81.

Jacoby, L. L. & Kelley, C. M. (1987). Unconscious influences of memory for a prior event. *Personality and Social Psychology Bulletin, 13*, 314–336.

James, J. W. & Haley, W. E. (1995). Age and health bias in practicing clinical psychologists. *Psychology & Aging, 10*, 610–616.

Jameson, J. P., Blank, M. B., & Chambless, D. L. (2009). If we built it, they will come: An empirical investigation of supply and demand in the recruitment of rural psychologists. *Journal of Clinical Psychology, 65*, 723–735.

Jason, L. A., McMahon, S. D., Salina, D., Hedeker, D., Stockton, M., Dunson, K., & Kimball, P. (1995). Assessing a smoking cessation intervention involving groups, incentives, and self-help manuals. *Behavior Therapy, 26*, 393–408.

Jeffery, R. W. (1988). Dietary risk factors and their modification in cardiovascular disease. *Journal of Consulting and Clinical Psychology, 56*, 350–357.

Jenkinson, P. M., Preston, C., Ellis, S. J. (2011). Unawareness after stroke: a review and practical guide to understanding, assessing, and managing anosognosia for hemiplegia. *Journal of Clinical and Experimental Neuropsychology, 33*(10), 1079–1093.

Jennings, L. & Skovholt, T. M. (1999). The cognitive, emotional and relational characteristics of master therapists. *Journal of Counseling Psychology, 46*, 3–11.

Jensen, P. S. (2003). Comorbidity and child psychopathology: Recommendations for the next decade. *Journal of Abnormal Child Psychology, 31*, 293–300.

Jensen, P. S., Goldman, E., Offord, D., Costello, E. J., Friedman, R., Huff, B., et al. (2011). Overlooked and underserved: "Action signs" for identifying children with unmet mental health needs. *Pediatrics, 128*, 970–979.

Johnsen, B. H. & Hugdahl, K. (1990). Fear questionnaires for simple phobias: Psychometric evaluations for a Norwegian sample. *Scandinavian Journal of Psychology, 31*, 42–48.

Johnson, B. W. & Campbell, C. D. (2004). Character and fitness requirements for professional psychologists: Training directors' perspectives. *Professional Psychology: Research and Practice, 35*, 405–411.

Johnson, M. D. (2002). The observation of specific affect in marital interactions: Psychometric properties of a coding system and a rating system. *Psychological Assessment,14*, 423–438.

Jones, B. P. & Butters, N. (1983). Neuropsychological assessment. In M. Hersen, A. E. Kazdin, & A. S. Bellack (Eds.), *The clinical psychology handbook* (pp. 377–396). New York, NY: Pergamon Press.

Jones, E. E. (1955). *The life and work of Sigmund Freud* (Vol. 2). New York, NY: Basic Books.

Jones, E. E., Cumming, J. D., & Horowitz, M. J. (1988). Another look at the nonspecific hypothesis of therapeutic effectiveness. *Journal of Consulting and Clinical Psychology, 56*, 48–55.

Jones, M. C. (1924). The elimination of children's fears. *Journal of Experimental Psychology, 7*, 382–390.

Jones, M. C. (1924a). The elimination of children's fears. *Journal of Experimental Psychology, 7*, 382–390.

Jones, M. C. (1924b). A laboratory study of fear: The case of Peter. *Pedagogical Seminary and Journal of Genetic Psychology, 31*, 308–315.

Jorm, A. F. (2000). Mental health literacy: Public knowledge and beliefs about mental disorders. *The British Journal of Psychiatry, 177*, 396–401.

Jorm, A. F. (2012). Mental health literacy: Empowering the community to take action for better mental health. *American Psychologist, 67*, 231–243.

Joseph, S. & Wood, A. (2010). Assessment of positive functioning in clinical psychology: Theoretical and practical issues. *Clinical Psychology Review, 30*, 830–838.

Jouriles, E. N. & O'Leary, K. D. (1985). Interspousal reliability of reports of marital violence. *Journal of Consulting and Clinical Psychology, 53*, 419–421.

Jouriles, E. N., Rowe, L. S., McDonald, R., Platt, C. G., & Gomez, G. S. (2010). Assessing women's response to sexual threat: Validity of a virtual role-play procedure. *Behavior Therapy, 42*, 475–484.

Kaczorowski, J. A., Williams, A. S., Smity, T. F., Fallah, N. et al. (2011). Adapting clinical services to accommodate needs of refugee populations. *Professional Psychology: Research and Practice, 42*, 361–367.

Kagan, J. (2008). Behavioral inhibition as a risk factor for psychopathology. In T. P. Beauchaine & S. P. Hinshaw (Eds.), *Child and adolescent psychopathology* (pp. 157–179). Hoboken, NJ: John Wiley & Sons.

Kahn, E. (1985). Heinz Kohut and Carl Rogers: A timely comparison. *American Psychologist, 40*, 893–904.

Kahn, J. H., Achter, J. A., & Shambaugh, E. J. (2001). Client distress disclosure, characteristics at intake, and outcomes in brief counseling. *Journal of Counseling Psychology, 48*, 203–211.

Kalichman, S. C., Cherry, C., & Browne-Sperling, F. (1999). Effectiveness of a video-based motivational skills-building HIV risk-reduction intervention for inner-city African American men. *Journal of Consulting and Clinical Psychology, 67*, 959–966.

Kalichman, S. C., Rompa, D., & Coley, B. (1996). Experimental component analysis of a behavioral HIV-AIDS prevention for inner-city women. *Journal of Consulting and Clinical Psychology, 64*, 687–693.

Kalichman, S. C., Rompa, D., Cage, M., DiFonzo, K., Simpson, D. Austin, J., et al. (2001). Effectiveness of an intervention to reduce HIV transmission risks in HIV-positive people. *American Journal of Preventive Medicine, 21*, 84–92.

Kane, L. (2011). Medscape psychiatry compensation report: 2011 results. Retrieved Dec. 27, 2011 from http://www.medscape.com/features/slideshow/compensation/2011/psychiatry.

Kantamneni, N. & Fouad, N. (2010). Structure of vocational interests for diverse groups on the 2005 Strong Interest Inventory. *Journal of Vocational Behavior, 78*, 193–201.

Kapardis, A. (2010). *Psychology and law: A critical introduction*. Boston, MA: Cambridge University Press.

Kaplan, A. (1964). *The conduct of inquiry*. San Francisco: Chandler.

Karna, A., Voeten, M., Little, T. D., Poskiparta, E., Alanen, E., & Salmivalli, C. (2011). Going to scale: A nonrandomized nationwide trial fo the KiVa antibullying program for grades 1-9. *Journal of Consulting and Clinical Psychology, 79*, 796–805.

Karver, M. S., Handelsman, J. B., Fields, S., & Bickman, L. (2005). Meta-analysis of therapeutic relationship variables in youth and family therapy: The evidence for different relationship variables in the child and adolescent treatment outcome literature. *Clinical Psychology Review, 26*, 50–65.

Kashdan, T. B., Rottenberg, J. (2010). Psychological flexibility as a fundamental aspect of health. Clinical *Psyhcological Review, 30*, 467–480.

Kaslow, F. W. (2010). A family therapy narrative. *The American Journal of Family Therapy, 38*, 50–62.

Kaslow, F. W. (2011). Family therapy. In J. C. Norcross, G. R. VandenBos, & D. K. Freedheim (Eds.), *History of psychotherapy: Continuity and change* (2nd ed., pp. 497–504). Washington, DC: American Psychological Association.

Kaslow, N. J. & Webb, C. (2011). Internship and postdoctoral residency. In J. C. Norcross, G. R. VandenBos, & D. K. Freedheim

(Eds.), *History of psychotherapy: Continuity and change* (2nd ed., pp. 640–650). Washington, DC: American Psychological Association.

Kaslow, N. J., Graves, C. C., & Smith, C. O. (2012). Specialization in psychology and health care reform. *Journal of Clinical Psychology in Medical Settings, 19*, 12–21.

Kaufman, A. S. & Kaufman, N. L. (1983). *KABC: Kaufman Assessment Battery for Children.* Circle Pines, MN: American Guidance Service.

Kaufman, A. S. & Kaufman, N. L. (2004b). *KBIT-2: Kaufman Brief Intelligence Test-2* (2nd ed.). Upper Saddle River, NJ: Pearson Assessments.

Kazak, A. E., Hoagwood, K., Weisz, J. R., Hood, K., Kratochwill, T. R., Vargas, L. A., & Banez, G. A. (2010). A meta-systems approach to evidence-based practice for children and adolescents. *American Psychologist, 65*, 85–97.

Kazantzis, N., Daniel, J., & Simos, G. (Eds.) (2009). Homework assignment in cognitive behavior therapy. *Cognitive Behavior Therapy: A Guide for the Practicing Clinician. Vol 2.,* (pp165–186). New York, NY: Routledge/Taylor & Francis Group.

Kazdin, A. E. (1982). Single-case experimental designs. In P. C. Kendall & J. N. Butcher (Eds.), *Handbook of research methods in clinical psychology* (pp. 461–490). New York, NY: John Wiley & Sons.

Kazdin, A. E. (2006). Assessment and evaluation in clinical practice. In C. D. Goodhart, A. E. Kazdin, & R. J. Sternberg (Eds.), *Evidence-based psychotherapy* (pp. 153–177). Washington, DC: American Psychological Association.

Kazdin, A. E. (2008). *Parent management training: Treatment for oppositional, aggressive, and antisocial behavior in children and adolescents.* New York, NY: Oxford University Press.

Kazdin, A. E. (2011). Evidence-based treatment research: Advancements, limitations, and next steps. *American Psychologist, 66*, 685–698.

Kazdin, A. E. (2011). *Single-case research designs: Methods for clinical and applied settings* (2nd ed.). New York, NY: Oxford University Press.

Kazdin, A. E. & Blase, S. L. (2011). Rebooting psychotherapy research and practice to reduce the burden of mental illness. *Perspectives on Psychological Science, 6*, 21–37.

Keefe, F. J., Abernethy, A. P., & Campbell, L. (2005). Psychological approaches to understanding and treating disease-related pain. *Annual Review of Psychology, 56*, 601–30.

Keilin, W. G. & Bloom, L. J. (1986). Child custody evaluation practices: A survey of experienced professionals. *Professional Psychology: Research and Practice, 17*, 338–346.

Kelley, J. E., Lumley, M. A., & Leisen, J. C. C. (1997). Health effects of emotional disclosure in rheumatoid arthritis patients. *Health Psychology, 16*, 331–340.

Kelly, E. L. & Fiske, D. W. (1951). *The prediction of performance in clinical psychology.* Ann Arbor: University of Michigan Press.

Kelly, G. A. (1955). *The psychology of personal constructs.* New York, NY: W. W. Norton.

Kelly, J. A. & Murphy, D. A. (1992). Psychological interventions with AIDS and HIV: Prevention and treatment. *Journal of Consulting and Clinical Psychology, 60*, 576–585.

Kelly, J. A., St. Lawrence, J. S., Hood, H. V., & Brashfield, T. L. (1989). Behavioral intervention to reduce AIDS risk activities. *Journal of Consulting and Clinical Psychology, 57*, 60–67.

Kelly, J. B. (1991). Parent interaction after divorce: Comparison of medicated and adversarial divorce processes. *Behavioral Sciences and the Law, 9*, 387–398.

Kelly, J. R., Agnew, C. R. (2012). Behavior and behavioral assessment. In K. Deaux & M. Snyder (Eds.), *The Oxford Handbook of Personality and Social Psychology* (pp. 95–110). New York, NY: Oxford University Press.

Kelley, M. P. (2011). Schizotypy and hemisphericity. *Psychological Reports, 109*(2), 533–552.

Kendall, P. C. (2012). *Child and adolescent therapy: Cognitive-behavioral procedures* (4th ed.). New York, NY: Guilford.

Kendall, P. C. & Comer, J. S. (2011). Research methods in clinical psychology. In D. H. Barlow (Ed.), *The Oxford handbook of clinical psychology* (pp. 52–75). New York, NY: Oxford University Press.

Kendall, P. C., Holmbeck, G., & Verduin, T. (2004). Methodology, design, and evaluation in psychotherapy research. In M. J. Lambert (Ed.), *Bergin and Garfield's handbook of psychotherapy and behavior change* (5th ed., pp. 16–43). New York, NY: John Wiley & Sons.

Kern, J. M. (1982). The comparative external and concurrent validity of three role-plays for assessing heterosocial performance. *Behavior Therapy, 13*, 666–680.

Kernberg, O. (1976). *Object relations, theory and clinical psychoanalysis.* New York, NY: Jason Aronson.

Kessler, R. C., Demler, O., Frank, R. G., Olfson, M., Pincus, H. A., et al. (2005). Prevalence and treatment of mental disorders 1990 to 2003. *New England Journal of Medicine, 352*, 2515–2523.

Kessler, R., Soukup, J., Davis, R., Foster, D., Wilkey, S., Van Rompay, M., & Eisenberg, D. (2001). The use of complementary and alternative therapies to treat anxiety and depression in the United States. *American Journal of Psychiatry, 158*, 289–294.

Kessler, R. C., Price, R. H., & Wortman, C. B. (1985). Social factors in psychopathology: Stress, social support, and coping processes. *Annual Review of Psychology, 36*, 531–572.

Kessler, R. C. & Wang, P. S. (2008). The descriptive epidemiology of commonly occurring mental disorders in the United States. *Annual Review of Public Health, 29*, 115–129.

Kessler, R. C., Berglund, P., Demler, O., Jin, R., & Walters, E. E. (2005). Lifetime prevalence and age-of-onset distributions of DSM-IV disorders in the National Comorbidity Survey Replication. *Archives of General Psychiatry, 62*, 593–602.

Kessler, R. C., Avenevoli, S., Costello, E. J., Georglades, K., Green, J. G. Gruber, M. J., et al. (2012). Prevalence, persistence, and sociodemographic correlates of DSM-IV disorders in the National Comorbidity Survey Replication Adolescent Supplement. *Archives of General Psychiatry, 69*, 372–380.

Khanna, M. S. & Kendall, P. C. (2010). Computer-assisted cognitive behavioral therapy for child anxiety: Results of a randomized clinical trial. *Journal of Consulting and Clinical Psychology, 78*, 737–745.

Kiecolt-Glaser, J. K. & Glaser, R. (1992). Psychoneuroimmunology: Can psychological interventions modulate immunity? *Journal of Consulting and Clinical Psychology, 60*, 569–575.

Kiecolt-Glaser, J. K., Loving, T. J., Stowell, J. R., Malarkey, W. B., Lemeshow, S., Dickinson, S. L., & Blaser, R. (2005). Hostile marital interactions, proinflammatory cytokine production, and wound healing. *Archives of General Psychiatry, 62*, 1377–1384.

Kihlstrom, J.F. & Cantor, N. (2011). Social intelligence. In R. J. Sternberg & S. B. Kaufman (Eds.). *The Cambridge handbook of intelligence* (pp. 564–581). New York, NY: Cambridge University Press.

Kim, J. & Zane, N. (2010). *Client predictors of treatment outcomes in outpatient therapy.* Paper presented at the American Psychological Association Convention (August), San Diego, CA.

Kinnaman, J. E. S. & Bellack, A. S. (2012). Social skills. . In W. T. O'Donahue & J. E. Fisher (Eds.). (2012). *Cognitive behavior therapy: Core principles for practice* (pp. 251–272). New York, NY: John Wiley & Sons.

Kinzie, J. D., Manson, S. M., Vinh, D. H., Nguyen, T. T., Anh, B., Tolan, N. T., et al. (1982). Development and validation of a Vietnamese-language depression rating scale. *American Journal of Psychiatry, 139*, 1276–1281.

Kleespies, P. M., AhnAllen, C. G., Knight, J. A., et al. (2011). Self-injury/attempted self-injury debriefing interview. *Psychological Services, 8*, 236-250.

Klein, M. (1975). *The writings of Melanie Klein* (Vol. III). London, UK: Hogarth Press.

Kleinknecht, R. A. & Bernstein, D. A. (1978). Assessment of dental fear. *Behavior Therapy, 9*, 626–634.

Kleinmuntz, B. (1984). The scientific study of clinical judgment in psychology and medicine. *Clinical Psychology Review, 4*, 111–126.

Klonoff, E. A. (2011). PhD programs. In J. C. Norcross, G. R. VandenBos, & D. K. Freedheim (Eds.), *History of psychotherapy: Continuity and change* (2nd ed., pp. 615–629). Washington, DC: American Psychological Association.

Klopfer, W. G. (1983). Writing psychological reports. In C. E. Walker (Ed.), *The handbook of clinical psychology* (Vol. 1, pp. 501–527). Homewood, IL: Dow Jones-Irwin.

Klopfer, B. & Kelley, D. M. (1937). The techniques of the Rorschach performance. *Rorschach Research Exchange, 2*, 1–14.

Knapp, S. J. (Ed.) (2012a). *APA handbook of ethics in psychology—Volume 1: Moral foundations and common themes.* Washington, DC: American Psychological Association.

Knapp, S. J. (Ed.) (2012b). *APA handbook of ethics in psychology—Volume 2: Practice, teaching, and research.* Washington, DC: American Psychological Association.

Knapp, S. J., Bennett, B. E., & VandeCreek, L. (2012). Risk management for psychologists. In S. J. Knapp, M. C. Gottlieb, M. M. Handelsman, & L. D. VandeCreek (Eds.), *APA handbook of ethics in psychology (Vol 1): Moral foundations and common themes* (pp. 483–518). Washington, DC: American Psychological Association.

Koester, K. A., Maiorana, A., Vernon, K., Myers, J., Rose, C. D., & Morin, S. (2007). Implementation of HIV prevention interventions with people living with HIV/AIDS in clinical settings: Challenges and lessons learned. *AIDS & Behavior.* [Epub ahead of print]

Kohlenberg, R. J. & Tsai, M. (1991). *Functional analytic psychotherapy: Creating intense and curative therapeutic relationships.* New York, NY: Plenum.

Kohout, J. & Wicherski, M. (2011). 2011 Graduate Study in Psychology: Applications, acceptances, enrollments, and degrees awarded to master's- and doctoral-level students in the U.S. and Canadian graduate departments of psychology: 2009-2010. *APA Center for Workforce Studies.* Retrieved December 21, 2011 from http://www.apa.org/workforce/publications/11-grad-study/applications.aspx.

Kohut, H. (1977). *The restoration of the self.* New York, NY: International Universities Press.

Kohut, H. (1983). Selected problems of self-psychological theory. In J. D. Lichtenberg & S. Kaplan (Eds.), *Reflections on self psychology* (pp. 387–416). Hillsdale, NJ: Erlbaum.

Komiti, A. A., Jackson, H. J., Judd, F. K., Cockram, A. M., Kyrios, M., Yeatman, R., et al. (2001). A comparison of the Composite International Diagnostic Interview (CIDI-Auto) with clinical assessment in diagnosing mood and anxiety disorders. *Australian & New Zealand Journal of Psychiatry, 35*, 224–232.

Koocher, G. P. & Daniel, J. H. (2012). Treating children and adolescents. In S. J. Knapp (Ed.), *APA handbook of ethics in psychology (Vol. 2): Practice, teaching, and research* (pp. 3–14). Washington, DC: American Psychological Association.

Koerner, K. & Linehan, M. M. (2011). *Doing dialectical behavior therapy: A practical guide.* New York, NY: The Guilford Press.

Korchin, S. J. (1976). *Modern clinical psychology: Principles of intervention in the clinic and community.* New York, NY: Basic Books.

Korman, M. (Ed.). (1976). *Levels and patterns of professional training in psychology.* Washington, DC: American Psychological Association.

Korsch, B. M. & Negrete, V. F. (1972). Doctor-patient communication. *Scientific American, 227*, 66–74.

Kovacs, M. (2010). *Children's Depression Inventory 2 (CDI-2).* San Antonio, TX: PsychCorp.

Kracen, A. C. & Wallace, I. J. (2008). *Applying to graduate school in psychology: Advice from successful students and prominent psychologists.* Washington, DC: American Psychological Association.

Krantz, D. S. & Manuck, S. B. (1984). Acute psychophysiologic reactivity and risk of cardiovascular disease—A review and methodologic critique. *Psychological Bulletin, 96*, 435–464.

Kraus, D. R., Seligman, D. A., & Jordan, J. R. (2005). Validation of a behavioral health treatment outcome and assessment tool designed for naturalistic settings: The Treatment Outcome Package. *Journal of Clinical Psychology, 63*, 285-314.

Krishnamurthy, R., VandeCreek, L., Kaslow, N. J., Tazeau, Y. N., Miville, N. L. et al. (2004). Achieving competency in psychological assessment: Directions for education and training. *Journal of Clinical Psychology, 60*, 725–739.

Krisnamurthy, R., Archer, R. P., & Groth-Marnat, G. (2011). The Rorschach and performance-based assessment. In T. M. Harwood, L. E. Beutler, & G. Groth-Marnat, G. (Eds.) (2011). *Integrative assessment of adult personality* (3rd ed., pp. 276–328). New York, NY: The Guilford Press.

Krol, N., DeBruyn, E., & van den Bercken, J. (1995). Intuitive and empirical prototypes in childhood psychopathology. *Psychological Assessment, 7*, 533–537.

Kulic, K. R. (2005). The Crisis Intervention Semi-Structured Interview. *Brief Treatment and Crisis Intervention 5*, 143–157.

Kumpfer, K. L. & Alvarado, R. (2003). Family-strengthening approaches for the prevention of youth problem behaviors. *American Psychologist, 58*, 457–465.

Kuncel, N. R. & Hezlett, S. A. (2007). Standardized tests predict graduate students' success. *Science, 315*, 1080–1081.

Kurtz, M. M. & Mueser, K. T. (2008). A meta-analysis of controlled research on social skills training for schizophrenia. *Journal of Consulting and Clinical Psychology, 76*, 491–504.

Kurtzman, H. & Bufka, L. (2011). APA moves forward on developing clinical treatment guidelines. Practice update retrieved December 21, 2011 from http://www.apapracticecentral.org/update/2011/07-14/clinical-treatment.aspx.

Kutash, I. L. (1976). Psychoanalysis in groups: The primacy of the individual. *Current Issues in Psychoanalytic Practice, 1*, 29–42.

Kuther, T. L. & Morgan, R. D. (2010). Careers in psychology: *Opportunities in a changing world* (3rd ed.). Belmont, CA: Thomson/Wadsworth.

Labbe, A. K. & Maisto, S. A. (2011). Alcohol expectancy challenges for college students: A narrative review. *Clinical Psychology Review, 31*, 673–683.

Ladd, P. D. & Churchill, A. M. (2012). *Person-centered diagnosis and treatment in mental health: A model for empowering clients.* Philadelphia, PA: Jessica Kingsley Publishers.

LaGreca, A. M., Silverman, W. K., & Lochman, J. E. (2009). Moving beyond efficacy and effectiveness in child and adolescent intervention research. *Journal of Consulting and Clinical Psychology, 77*, 373–382.

Lahey, B. B., VanHulle, C. A., Keenan, K. R., Rathouz, P. J., D'Onofrio, B. M., Rodgers, J. L., & Waldman, I. D. (2008). Temperament and parenting during the first year of life predict future child conduct problems. *Journal of Abnormal Child Psychology, 36*, 1139–1158.

Lake, J. (2009). *Integrative mental health care: A therapist's handbook.* New York, NY: W. W. Norton and Company.

Lake, J. H. & Spiegel, D. (Eds.). (2007). *Complementary and alternative treatments in mental health care.* Washington, DC: American Psychiatric Publishing.

Lam, J. N. & Steketee, G. S. (2001). Reducing obsessions and compulsions through behavior therapy. *Psychoanalytic Inquiry, 21*, 157–182.

Lambert, D. (1985). *Political and economic determinants of mental health regulations.* Unpublished doctoral dissertation, Brandeis University.

Lambert, M. J. & Bergin, A. E. (1994). The effectiveness of psychotherapy. In A. E. Bergin & S. L. Garfield (Eds.), *Handbook of psychotherapy and behavior change* (pp. 143–189). New York, NY: John Wiley & Sons.

Lambert, M. J., Shapiro, D. A. & Bergin, A. E. (1986). The effectiveness of psychotherapy. In S. L. Garfield & A. E. Bergin (Eds.), *Handbook of psychotherapy and behavior change* (3rd ed., pp. 157–211). New York, NY: John Wiley & Sons.

Lampropoulos, G. K. & Dixon, D. N. (2007). Psychotherapy integration in internships and counseling psychology doctoral programs. *Journal of Psychotherapy Integration, 17*, 185–208.

Landrum, R. E. (2009). *Finding jobs with a psychology bachelor's degree: Expert advice for launching your career.* Washington, DC: American Psychological Association.

Landrum, R. E. & Davis, S. F. (2009). *The psychology major: Career options and strategies for success* (4th ed.). Upper Saddle River, NJ: Prentice Hall.

Lang, S. & Kleijnen, J. (2010). Quality assessment tools for observational studies: Lack of consensus. *International Journal of Evidence-Based Healthcare, 8*, 247.

Langeley, D. (2006). *An Introduction to Dramatherapy.* Thousand Oaks, CA: Sage.

Langer, D. A., McLeod, B. D., & Weisz, J. R. (2011). Do treatment manuals undermine youth-therapist alliance in community clinical practice? *Journal of Consulting and Clinical Psychology, 79*, 427–432.

Langton, C. M., Barbaree, H. E., Seto, M. C., Peacock, E. J., Harkings, L., et al. (2007). Actuarial assessment of risk for reoffense among adult sex offenders: Evaluating the predictive accuracy of the Static-2002 and five other instruments. *Criminal Justice and Behavior, 34*, 37–59.

Lanik, M. & Mitchel-Gibbons, A. (2011). Guidelines for cross-cultural assessor training in multicultural assessment centers. *The Psychologist-Manager, 14*, 221-246.

Larner, A. J. (2005). "Who came with you?" A diagnostic observation in patients with memory problems. *Journal of Neurology, Neurosurgery, & Psychiatry, 76*, 1739.

Larrabee, G. J. (Ed), (2012). Assessment of malingering. In G. J. Larrabee (Ed.) *Forensic neuropsychology: A scientific approach* (2nd ed., pp. 116–159). New York, NY: Oxford University Press.

Larsen, H., Overbeek, G., Granic, I., Engels, R.C. (2012). The strong effect of other people's drinking: Two experimental observational studies in a real bar. *The American Journal on Addictions, 21*, 168–175.

Lau, A. S. & Weisz, J. R. (2003). Reported maltreatment among clinic-referred children: Implications for presenting problems, treatment attrition, and long-term outcomes. *Journal of the American Academy of Child and Adolescent Psychiatry, 42*,1327–1334.

Lawlis, G. F. (1971). Response styles of a patient population on the Fear Survey Schedule. *Behaviour Research and Therapy, 9*, 95–102.

Lawrence, E., Beach, S. R. H., & Doss, B. D. (2009). Couple and family processes in DSM-V: Moving beyond relational disorders. In J. H. Bray & M. Standon (Eds.), *The Wiley-Blackwell handbook of family psychology* (pp. 165–182). Hoboken, NJ: Wiley.

Lazarus, A. A. (1973). Multimodel behavior therapy: Treating the "BASIC-ID." *Journal of Nervous and Mental Diseases, 156*, 404–411.

Lazarus, R. S. (1993). From psychological stress to the emotions: A history of changing outlooks. *Annual Review of Psychology, 44*, 1–21.

Lazarus, R. S. & Folkman, S. (1984). *Stress, appraisal, and coping.* New York, NY: Springer.

Leahy, R. L. (Ed.). (2006). *Roadblocks in cognitive-behavioral therapy: Transforming challenges into opportunities for change.* New York, NY: Guilford.

Ledley, D. R., Marx, B. P., & Heimbert, R. G. (2010). *Making cognitive-behavioral therapy work* (2nd ed.). New York, NY: The Guilford Press.

Levant, R. F. (2006). Making psychology a household word. *American Psychologist, 61*, 383–395.

Levin, M. & Hayes, S. C. (2011). *Mindfulness and acceptance: The perspective of acceptance and commitment therapy. Understanding and applying the new therapies* (pp. 291–316). Hoboken, NJ: John Wiley & Sons.

Levine, E. S. & Schmelkin, L. P. (2006). The move to prescribe: A change in paradigm? *Professional Psychology: Research and Practice, 37*, 205–209.

Levison, H. & Strupp, H. H. (1999). Recommendations for the future of training in brief dynamic psychotherapy. *Journal of Clinical Psychology, 55*, 385–391.

Levy, R. A., Ablon, J. S., & Kachele, H. (Eds.) (2011). *Psychodynamic psychotherapy research: Evidence-based practice and practice-based evidence*. New York, NY: Humana Press.

Lewis, G. (1991). Observer bias in the assessment of anxiety and depression. *Social Psychiatry and Psychiatric Epidemiology, 26*, 265–272.

Ley, P., Bradshaw, P. W., Eaves, D. E., & Walker, C. M. (1973). A method for increasing patient recall of information presented to them. *Psychological Medicine, 3*, 217–220.

Lezak, M. D., Howieson, D. B., & Loring, D. W. (2004). *Neuropsychological assessment* (4th ed.). New York, NY: Oxford University Press.

Li, S. T., Jenkins, S., & Grewal, S. (2012). Impact of race and ethnicity on the expression, assessment, and diagnosis of psychopathology. In M. Hersen & D. Beidel (Eds.) *Adult Psychopathology and Diagnosis* (6th ed., pp. 117-148). New York, NY: John Wiley & Sons.

Lidz, R. W. & Lidz, T. (1949). The family environment of schizophrenic patients. *American Journal of Psychiatry, 106*, 332–345.

Lilienfild, S. O. (2007). Psychological treatments that cause harm. Perspectives on Psychological Science, 2, 53–70.

Lima, E. N., Stanley, S., Koboski, B., Reitzel, L. R., Richey, J. A., et al. (2005). The incremental validity of the MMPI-2: When does therapist access enhance treatment outcome? *Psychological Assessment, 17*, 462–468.

Lindsley, O. R., Skinner, B. F., & Solomon, H. C. (1953). *Study of psychotic behavior*. Studies in Behavior Therapy, Harvard Medical School, Department of Psychiatry, Metropolitan State Hospital, Waltham, MA, Office of Naval Research Contract N5-ori-07662, Status Report I, 1 June 1953–31 December 1953.

Lindzey, G. (1952). The thematic apperception test: Interpretive assumptions and related empirical evidence. *Psychological Bulletin, 49*, 1–25.

Linehan, M. M. (1993). *Cognitive-behavioral treatment of borderline personality disorder*. New York, NY: Guilford.

Linehan, M. M. & Nielsen, S. L. (1983). Social desirability: Its relevance to the measurement of hopelessness and suicidal behavior. *Journal of Consulting and Clinical Psychology, 51*, 141–143.

Lints-Martindale, A. C., Hadjistavropoulos, T., Lix, L. M., & Thorpe, L. (2012). A comparative investigation of observational pain assessment tools for older adults with dementia. *The Clinical Journal of Pain. 28*, 226–237.

Lippens, T. & Mackenzie, C. S. (2011). Treatment satisfaction, perceived treatment effectiveness, and dropout among older users of mental health services. *Journal of Clinical Psychology, 67*, 1197–1209.

Liss, M. B. & McKinley-Pace, M. J. (1999). Best interests of the child: New twists on an old theme. In R. Roesch, S. D. Hart, & J. R. Ogloff (Eds.), *Psychology and the law: The state of the discipline* (pp. 339–372). New York, NY: Kluwer Academic/Plenum.

Liu, E. T. (2007). Integrating cognitive-behavioral and cognitive-interpersonal case formulations: A case study of a Chinese American male. *Pragmatic Case Studies in Psychotherapy, 3*, 1–33.

Lobbestael, J., Leurgans, M., & Arntz, A. (2011). Inter-rater reliability of the Structured Clinical Interview for DSM-IV Axis I disorders (SCID I) and Axis II disorders (SCID II). *Clinical Psychology and Psychotherapy, 18*, 75-79.

Lochman, J. E. & Wells, K. C. (2004). The coping power program for preadolescent aggressive boys and their parents: Outcome effects at the 1-year- follow-up. *Journal of Consulting and Clinical Psychology, 72*, 571–578.

Loftus, E. F. (2003). Make-believe memories. *American Psychologist, 58*, 867–873.

Long, J. K. & Andrews, B. V. (2011). Fostering strength and resiliency in same-sex couples. In J. L. Wetchler (Ed.), *Handbook of clinical issues in couple therapy* (2nd ed., pp. 225–246). New York, NY: Routledge/Taylor & Francis Group.

Lopez, S. R. & Guarnaccia, P. J. (2000). Cultural psychopathology: Uncovering the social world of mental illness. *Annual Review of Psychology, 51*, 571–598.

Lopez, S. & Snyder, C. R. (Eds.). (2003). *Handbook of positive psychology assessment*. Washington, DC: American Psychological Association.

Lorch, M. (2011). Re-examining Paul Broca's initial presentation of M. Leborgne: understanding the impetus for brain and language research. *Cortex, 47*(10), 1228–1235.

Loring, D. W. & Larrabee, G. J. (2006). Sensitivity of the Halstead and Wechsler Test batteries to brain damage: Evidence from Reitan's original validation sample. *Clinical Neuropsychology, 20*, 221–229.

Lorr, M., McNair, D. M., & Klett, C. J. (1966). *Inpatient Multidimensional Psychiatric Scale*. Palo Alto, CA: Consulting Psychologists Press.

Luborsky, L. (1989). *Who will benefit from psychotherapy?* New York, NY: Basic Books.

Luby, J., Lenze, S., & Tillman, R. (2012). A novel early intervention for preschool depression: Findings from a pilot randomized controlled trial. *Journal of Child Psychology and Psychiatry, 53*, 313–322.

Luxton, D. D., McCann, R. A., Bush, N. E., Mishkind, M. C., & Reger, G. M. (2011). mHealth for mental health: Integrating smartphone technology in behavioral healthcare. *Professional Psychology: Research and Practice, 42*, 505–512.

Lynch, F. L., Striegel-Moore, R., Dickerson, J. F., Perrin, N., DeBar, L., Wilson, G. T., & Kraemer, H. C. (2010). Cost-effectiveness of guided self-help treatment for recurrent binge eating. *Journal of Consulting and Clinical Psychology, 78*, 322–333.

Lynn, S. J., Lock, T., Loftus, E. F., Krackow, E., & Lilienfeld, S. O. (2003). The remembrance of things past: Problematic memory recovery techniques in psychotherapy. In S. O. Lilienfeld, S. J. Lynn, & J. M. Lohr (Eds.), *Science and pseudoscience in clinical psychology* (pp. 205–239). New York, NY: Guilford.

Machado, P., Beutler, L. E., Harwood, T. M., Mohr, D., & Lenore, S. (2011). The integrative clinical interview. In T. Harwood, L. Beutler, & G. Groth-Marnat, G. (Eds). *Integrative assessment of adult personality*. New York, NY, Guilford Press.

Machover, K. (1949). *Personality projection in the drawing of the human figure*. Springfield, IL: Charles C. Thomas.

MacKinnon, R. A., Michels, R., & Buckley, P. J. (2009). *The psychiatric interview in clinical practice*. Washington, DC: American Psychiatric Publishing.

Macklin, D. S., Smith, L. A., & Dollard, M. F. (2006). Public and private sector stress: Workers compensation, levels of distress and job satisfaction, and the demand-control-support model. *Australian Journal of Psychology, 58*, 130–143.

Maguen, S., Cohen, G., Cohen, B. E., Lawhon, G. D., Marmar, C. R., & Seal, K. H. (2010). The role of psychologists in the care of Iraq and Afghanistan veterans in primary care settings. *Professional Psychology: Research and Practice, 41*, 135–142.

Mahler, M. S., Pine, F., & Bergman, A. (1975). *The psychological birth of the human infant.* New York, NY: Basic Books.

Mahoney, M. J. (1977). Reflections on the cognitive-learning trend in psychotherapy. *American Psychologist, 32*, 5–13.

Maier, S. F. & Watkins, L. R. (1998). Cytokines for psychologists: Implications of bidirectional immune-to-brain communication for understanding behavior, mood, and cognition. *Psychological Review, 105*, 83–107.

Makover, R. B. (2004). *Treatment planning for psychotherapists* (2nd ed.). Washington DC: American Psychiatric Publishing.

Malarkey, W. B., Kiecolt-Glaser, J. K., Pearl, D., & Glaser, R. (1994). Hostile behavior during marital conflict alters pituitary and adrenal hormones. *Psychosomatic Medicine, 56*, 41–51.

Malgady, R. G. (1996). The question of cultural bias in assessment and diagnosis of ethnic minority clients: Let's reject the null hypothesis. *Professional Psychology: Research and Practice, 27*, 73–77.

Maloney, M. P., & Ward, M. P. (1976). *Psychological assessment: A conceptual approach.* New York, NY: Oxford University Press.

van Manen, J. G., Kamphuis, J. H., Goossensen, A., Timman, R., Busschbach, J. J. V. et al. (2012). In search of patient characteristics that may guide empirically based treatment selection for personality disorders patients—A concept map approach. *Journal of Personality Disorders, 26*, 481–497.

Maniglio, R. (2009). The impact of child sexual abuse on health: A systematic review of reviews. *Clinical Psychology Review, 29*, 647–657.

Maniglio, R. (2011). The role of child sexual abuse in the etiology of suicide and non-suicidal self-injury. *Acta Psychiatric Scandanavia, 124*, 30–41.

Mannarino, A. P. & Cohen, J. A. (2006). Child sexual abuse. In R. T. Ammerman (Ed.), *Comprehensive handbook of personality and psychopathology* (Vol. 3, pp. 388–402). Hoboken, NJ: John Wiley & Sons.

Manuck, S. B., Kaplan, J. R., Adams, M. R., & Clarkson, T. B. (1988). Effects of stress and the sympathetic nervous system on coronary artery atheroslerosis in the cynomolgus macaque. *American Heart Journal, 116*, 328–333.

Manuck, S. B., Kaplan, J. R., & Clarkson, T. B. (1983). Behaviorally induced heart rate reactivity and atherosclerosis in cynomolgus monkeys. *Psychosomatic Medicine, 49*, 95–108.

Marcus, D. R., Lyons, P. M., & Guyton, M. R. (2000). Studying perceptions of juror influence in vivo: A social relations analysis. *Law and Human Behavior, 24*, 173–186.

Marin, R. S. & Wilkosz, P. A. (2005). Disorders of diminished motivation. *Journal of Head Trauma Rehabilitation, 20*, 377–388.

Marini, A., Carlomagno, S., Caltagirone, C., & Nocentini. U. (2005). The role played by the right hemisphere in the organization of complex textual structures. *Brain and Language, 93*, 46–54.

Marinkovic, K., Baldwin, S., Courtney, M. G., Witzel, T., Dale, A. M., & Halgren, E. (2011). Right hemisphere has the last laugh: neural dynamics of joke appreciation. *Cognitive, Affective, and Behavioral Neuroscience, 11*(1), 113–130.

Markowitz, J., Kocsis, M., Fishman, B., Spielman, L., Jacobsberg, L., & Francis, A. (1998). Treatment of depressive symptoms in Human Immunodeficiency Virus–positive patients. *Archives of General Psychiatry, 55*, 452–457.

Marlatt, G. A. & Gordon, J. R. (Eds.). (1985). *Relapse prevention maintenance strategies in the treatment of addictive behaviors.* New York, NY: Guilford.

Marmar, C., Gaston, L., Gallagher, D., & Thompson, L. W. (1989). Alliance and outcome in late-life depression. *Journal of Nervous and Mental Disease, 177*, 464–472.

Martin, D. J., Garske, J. P., & Davis, K. M. (2000). Relation of the therapeutic alliance with outcome and other variables: A meta-analytic review. *Journal of Consulting and Clinical Psychology, 68*, 438–450.

Martin, P. R. (2011). Clinical psychology going forward: The need to promote clinical psychology and to respond to the training crisis. *Clinical Psychologist, 15*, 93–102.

Marx, J. A., Gyorky, Z. K., Royalty, G. M., & Stern, T. E. (1992). Use of self-help books in psychotherapy. *Professional Psychology: Research and Practice, 23*, 300–305.

Mash, E. J. & Foster, S. L. (2001). Exporting analogue behavioral observation from research to clinical practice: Useful or cost-defective? *Psychological Assessment, 13*, 86–98.

Mash, E. J., & Hunsley, J. (2007). Assessment of child and family disturbance: A developmental-systems approach. In E. J. Mash & R. A. Barkley (Eds.), *Assessment of childhood disorders* (4th ed., pp. 3–50). New York, NY: Guilford.

Mash, E. J. & Wolfe, D. A. (2012). *Abnormal child psychology* (5th ed.). Belmont, CA: Cengage Learning.

Maslow, A. H. (1968). *Toward a psychology of being* (2nd ed.). New York, NY: Van Nostrand Reinhold.

Masten, A. S. & Tellegen, A. (2012). Resilience in developmental psychopathology: Contributions of the Project Competence Longitudinal Study. *Development and Psychopathology, 24*, 345–361.

Masters, K. S., Spielmans, G. I., & Goodson, J. T. (2006). Are there demonstrable effects of distant intercessory prayer? A meta-analytic review. *Annals of Behavioral Medicine, 32*, 21–26.

Masur, F. T. (1981). Adherence to health care regimens. In C. K. Prokop & L. A. Bradley (Eds.), *Medical psychology: Contributions to behavioral medicine* (pp. 442–470). New York, NY: Academic Press.

Matarazzo, J. D. (1965). The interview. In B. B. Wolman (Ed.), *Handbook of clinical psychology* (pp. 403–450). New York, NY: McGraw-Hill.

Matarazzo, J. D. (1992). Psychological testing and assessment in the 21st century. *American Psychologist, 47*, 1007–1018.

Maton, K. I. & Brodsky, A. E. (2011). Empowering community settings: Theory, research, and action. In M. S. Aber, K. I. Maton, & E. Seidman (Eds.), *Empowering settings and voices for social change* (pp. 38–64). New York, NY: Oxford University Press.

Matthews, K. A. (1982). Psychological perspectives on the Type A behavior pattern. *Psychological Bulletin, 91*, 293–323.

Matthews, K. A. & Gallo, L. C. (2011). Psychological perspectives on pathways linking socioeconomic status and physical health. *Annual Review of Psychology, 62*, 501–530.

Matthews, J. R. & Matthews, L. H. (2009). Preparing for licensure. In S. F. Davis, P. J. Giordano, & C. A. Licht (Eds.), *Your career in psychology: Putting your graduate degree to work* (pp. 151–162). Hoboken, NJ: Wiley-Blackwell.

Matthews, A. J., Scanlan, J. D., & Kirby, K. C. (2010). Online exposure for spider fear: Treatment completion and habituation outcomes. *Behavior Change, 27*, 199–211.

Maughan, B., Iervolino, A. C., & Collishaw, S. (2005). Time trends in child and adolescent mental disorders. *Current Opinion in Psychiatry, 18*, 381–385.

May, R. (1969). *Love and will*. New York, NY: W. W. Norton.

May, R. (1981). *Freedom and destiny*. New York, NY: Norton.

Mayer, J. D., Salovey, P., Caruso, D. R., & Cherkasskiy, L. (2011). Emotional intelligence. In R. J. Sternberg & S. B. Kaufman (Eds.). *The Cambridge handbook of intelligence* (pp. 528–549). New York, NY: Cambridge University Press.

Mays, K. L., Kamphaus, R. W., & Reynolds, C. R. (2009). Applications of the Kaufman Assessment Battery for Children, 2nd Edition, in neuropsychological assessment. In C. R. Reynolds, E. Fletcher-Jenson (Eds.) *Handbook of Clinical Child Neuropsychology* (pp. 281–296). New York, NY: Springer.

McArthur, D. S. & Roberts, G. E. (1982). *Roberts Apperception Test for Children: Manual*. Los Angeles: Western Psychological Services.

McConaughy, S. H. & Achenbach, T. M. (2001). *Manual for the Semistructured Clinical Interview for Children and Adolescents* (2nd ed.). Burlington: University of Vermont, Center for Children, Youth, and Families.

McConaughy, S. H. & Achenbach, T. M. (2009). *Manual for the Direct Observation Form*. Burlington, VT: University of Vermont, Center for Children, Youth, & Families.

McConnell, K. J., Gast, S. H. N., Ridgely, M. S., Wallace, N., Jacuzzi, N., Rieckmann, T. et al. (2012). Behavioral health insurance parity: Does Oregon's experience presage the national experience with the mental health parity and addiction equity act? *American Journal of Psychiatry, 169*, 31–38.

McCoy, S. A. (1976). Clinical judgments of normal childhood behavior. *Journal of Consulting and Clinical Psychology, 44*, 710–714.

McCrae, R. R. & Costa, P. T. (1983). Social desirability scales: More substance than style. *Journal of Consulting and Clinical Psychology, 51*, 882–888.

McCrae, R. R., Harwood, T. M., & Kelly, S. L. (2011). The NEO inventories. In T. M. Harwood, L. E. Beutler, & G. Groth-Marnat, G. (Eds.) (2011). *Integrative assessment of adult personality* (3rd ed., pp. 252–275). New York, NY: The Guilford Press.

McCutcheon, S. R. (2011). The internship crisis: An uncommon urgency to build a common solution. *Training and Education in Professional Psychology, 5*, 144–148.

McFall, R. M. (1991). Manifesto for a science of clinical psychology. *The Clinical Psychologist, 44*, 75–88.

McFall, R. M. (2006). Doctoral training in clinical psychology. *Annual Review of Clinical Psychology, 2*, 21–49.

McFall, R. M. (2012). Psychological Clinical Science Accreditation System: FAQs and facts. *The Behavior Therapist, 35*, 11–15.

McFall, R. M. & Lillesand, D. B. (1971). Behavior rehearsal with modeling and coaching in assertion training. *Journal of Abnormal Psychology, 77*, 313–323.

McGaugh, J. L.(2006). Make mild moments memorable: add a little arousal. *Trends in Cognitive Sciences, 10*, 345–347.

McGinn, M. M., Benson, L. A., & Christensen, A. (2011). Integrative behavioral couple therapy: An acceptance-based approach to improving relationship functioning. In J. D. Herbert & E. M. Forman (Eds.), *Acceptance and mindfulness in cognitive behavior therapy: Understanding and applying the new therapies* (pp. 210–232). Hoboken, NJ: John Wiley & Sons.

McGlynn, F. D., Moore, P. M., Lawyer, S., & Karg, R. (1999). Relaxation training inhibits fear and arousal during in vivo exposure to phobia-cue stimuli. *Journal of Behavior Therapy and Experimental Psychiatry, 30*, 155–168.

McGoldrick, M., Giordano, J., & Garcia-Preto, N. (2005). *Ethnicity and family therapy* (3rd ed.). New York, NY: Guilford.

McGrath, R. E. (2010). Prescriptive authority for psychologists. *Annual Review of Clinical Psychology, 6*, 21–47.

McGrath, R. E. & Sammons, M. (2011). Prescribing and primary care psychology: Complementary paths for professional psychology. *Professional Psychology: Research and Practice, 42*, 113–120.

McGuffin, P. (2004). Behavioral genomics: Where molecular genetics is taking psychiatry and psychology. In L. DiLalla (Ed.), *Behavior genetics principles: Perspectives in development, personality, and psychopathology* (pp. 191–204). Washington, DC: American Psychological Association.

McHale, J. P. & Lindahl, K. M. (2011). *Coparenting: A conceptual and clinical examination of family systems*. Washington, DC: American Psychological Association.

McKown, D. M. (2011). A comparison study: Kaufman Assessment Battery for Children, second edition (IABC-II) and Wechsler Intelligence Scale for Children, fourth edition (WISC-IV) with referred students. *Dissertaion Abstracts International Section A: Humanities and Social Sciences, 71*, 2011–2751.

McMullin, R. E. (2000). *The new handbook of cognitive therapy techniques*. New York, NY: Norton.

McNulty, J. K. & Fincham, F. D. (2012). Beyond positive psychology? Toward a contextual view of psychological processes and well-being. *American Psychologist, 67*, 101–110.

McReynolds, P. (1975). Historical antecedents of personality assessment. In P. McReynolds (Ed.), *Advances in psychological assessment* (Vol. 3, pp. 477–532). San Francisco: Jossey-Bass.

McReynolds, P. (1987). Lightner Witmer: Little-known founder of clinical psychology. *American Psychologist, 42*, 849–858.

McWilliams, N. (2004). *Psychoanalytic psychotherapy: A practitioner's guide*. New York, NY: Guilford.

Mead, M. (1928). *Coming of age in Samoa*. New York, NY: Morrow.

Meador, B. D. & Rogers, C. R. (1973). Client-centered therapy. In R. Corsini (Ed.), *Current psychotherapies* (pp. 119–165). Itasca, IL: F. E. Peacock.

Mednick, S. C., Makovski, T., Cai, D. J., and Jiang, Y. V. (2009). Sleep and rest facilitate implicit memory in a visual search task. *Vision Research, 49*(21), 2557–2565.

Meehl, P. E. (1956). Wanted—A good cookbook. *American Psychologist, 11*, 263–272.

Meehl, P. E. (1957). When shall we use our heads instead of the formula? *Journal of Consulting Psychology, 4*, 268–273.

Meehl, P. E. (1965). Seer over sign: The first good example. *Journal of Experimental Research in Personality, 1*, 27–32.

Meichenbaum, D. H. (1977). *Cognitive behavior modification.* New York, NY: Norton.

Meissner, W. W. (2006). The therapeutic alliance—A proteus in disguise. *Psychotherapy: Theory, Research, Practice, Training, 43*, 264–270.

Melton, G. B., Petrila, J., Poythress, N. G., & Slobogin, C. (1997). *Psychological evaluations for the courts* (2nd ed.). New York, NY: Guilford.

Melchert, T. P. (2011). Foundations of professional psychology: The end of theoretical orientations and the emergence of the biopsychosocial approach. New York, NY: Elsevier Insights.

Melton, A. W. (Ed.). (1947). *Apparatus tests.* Washington, DC: Government Printing Office.

Mermelstein, R., Lichtenstein, E., & McIntyre, K. (1983). Partner support and relapse in smoking-cessation programs. *Journal of Consulting and Clinical Psychology, 51*, 331–337.

Messer, S. (2006). Patient values and preferences. In J. C. Norcross, L. E. Beutler, & R. F. Levant (Eds.). *Evidence-based practices in mental health* (pp. 31–40). Washington, DC: American Psychological Association.

Messer, S. B. & Winokur, M. (1980). Some limits to the integration of psychoanalytic and behavior therapy. *American Psychologist, 35*, 818–827.

Messer, S. B. & Gurman, A. S. (Eds.). (2011). *Essential psychotherapies.* New York, NY: The Guilford Press.

Mesulam, M. M. (1990). Large-scale neurocognitive networks and distributed processing for attention, language, and memory. *Annals of Neurology, 28*, 597–613.

Meyer, B. (2007). Do clinical researchers believe they should be clinically active? A survey in the United States and the United Kingdom. *Psychology and Psychotherapy: Theory, Research, and Practice, 80*, 543–561.

Meyer, G. J. (2006). MMPI-2 Restructured Clinical Scales [Special Issue]. *Journal of Personality Assessment, 87*, 2.

Meyer, G. J., Finn, S. E., Eyde, L. D., Kay, G. G., Moreland, K. L., Dies, R. R., et al. (2001). Psychological testing and psychological assessment: A review of evidence and issues. *American Psychologist, 56*, 128–165.

Meyer, G. J., Viglione, D. J., Mihura, J. L., Erard, R. E., & Erdberg, P. (2010, March). *Introducing key features of the Rorschach Performance Assessment System (RPAS).* Workshop presented at the annual meeting of the Society for Personality Assessment, San Jose, CA.

Meyer-Lindenberg, A., Poline, J-B., Kohn, P. D., Holt, J. L., Egan, M. F., Weinberger, D. R., & Berman, K. F. (2001). Evidence for abnormal cortical functional connectivity during working memory in schizophrenia. *American Journal of Psychiatry, 158*, 1809–1817.

Meyerbröker, K. & Emmelkamp, P. M. G. (2011). Virtual reality exposure therapy for anxiety disorders: The state of the art. *Studies in Computational Intelligence, 337*, 47–62.

Meyers, L. (2006a). Psychologists and psychotropic medication. *Monitor on Psychology, 37*, 46–47.

Michael, K. D., Curtin, L., Kirkley, D. E., Jones, D. L., & Harris, R. (2006). Group-based motivational interviewing for alcohol use among college students: An exploratory study. *Professional Psychology: Research and Practice, 37*, 629–634.

Michaleski, D. S. & Kohout, J. L. (2011). The state of the psychology health service provider workforce. *American Psychologist, 66*, 825–843.

Michalski, D. (2001). Clinical workforce in psychology: Pipeline, employment, challenges, and opportunities. Presentation given at the American Psychological Association Conference, August 6, Toronto, Ontario, Canada.

Mihalopoulos, C., Vos, T., Pirkis, J., & Carter, R. (2011). The economic analysis of prevention n mental health programs. *Annual Review of Clinical Psychology, 7*, 169–201.

Milich, R. & Fitzgerald, G. (1985). Validation of inattention/overactivity and aggression ratings with classroom observations. *Journal of Consulting and Clinical Psychology, 53*, 139–140.

Miller, A. L., Rathus, J. H., Linehan, M. M., & Swenson, C. R. (2006). *Dialectical behavior therapy with suicidal adolescents.* New York, NY: Guilford.

Miller, E., Tancredi, D. J., McCauley, H. L., Decker, M. R., Virata, M. C. D., Anderson, H. A., et al. (2012). "Coaching boys into men": A cluster-randomized controlled trial of a dating violence prevention program. *Journal of Adolescent Health, March 13, 2012.* Early on-line version: 10.1016/j.jadohealth.2012.01.018.

Miller, G. (2012). Criticism continues to dog psychiatric manual as deadline approaches. *Science, 336*, 1088–1089.

Miller, G. A., Elbert, T., Sutton, B. P., & Heller, W. (2007). Innovative clinical assessment technologies: Challenges and opportunities in neuroimaging. *Psychological Assessment, 19*, 58–73.

Miller, G. E. & Cohen, S. (2001). Psychological interventions and the immune system: A meta-analytic review and critique. *Health Psychology, 20*, 47–63.

Miller, J. A. & Leffard, S. A. (2007). Behavioral assessment. In S. R. Smith & L. Handler (Eds.), *The clinical assessment of children and adolescents: A practitioner's handbook* (pp. 115–137). Mahwah, NJ: Erlbaum.

Miller, S., Malone, P. S., Dodge, K. A., & Conduct Problems Prevention Research Group (2010). Developmental trajectories of boys' and girls' delinquency: Sex differences and links to later adolescent outcomes. *Journal of Abnormal Child Psychology, 38*, 1021–1032.

Miller, S. B., Freise, M., Dolgoy, L., Sita, A., Lavoie, K., & Campbell, T. (1998). Hostility, sodium consumption, and cardiovascular response to interpersonal stress. *Psychosomatic Medicine, 60*, 71–77.

Miller, T. Q., Turner, C. W., Tindale, R. S., Posavac, E. J., & Dugoni, B. L. (1991). Reasons for the trend toward null findings in research on Type A behavior. *Psychological Bulletin, 110*, 469–485.

Miller, W. R. & Rollnick, S. (1998). *Motivational interviewing* (Vols. 1-7). [Video]. Albuquerque, NM: Horizon West Productions.

Miller, W. R. & Thoresen, C. E. (2003). Spirituality, religion, and health: An emerging research field. *American Psychologist, 58*, 24–35.

Millon, T. (2009). *The Millon Clinical Multiaxial Inventory-III* (4th ed.). Minneapolis, MN: Pearson.

Millon, J., Millon, C. & Davis, R. (1997). *Millon Clinical Multiaxial Inventory: III (MCMI-III) manual* (3rd ed.). Minneapolis, MN: National Computer Systems.

Milner, B. (1974). Hemispheric specialization: Scope and limits. In F. O. Schmitt & F. G. Worden (Eds.), *The neurosciences: Third study program* (pp. 75–89). Cambridge, MA: MIT Press.

Milner, D. A. & Rugg, M. D. (1992). *The neuropsychology of consciousness.* San Diego: Academic Press, Inc.

Miltenberger, R. G. (2011). *Behavior modification: Principles and procedures* (5th ed.). Belmont, CA: Cenage Learning.

Mischel, W. (1968). *Personality and assessment.* New York, NY: John Wiley & Sons.

Mischel, W. (1973). Toward a cognitive social learning reconceptualization of personality. *Psychological Review, 80*, 252–283.

Mitchell, K. J., Becker-Blease, K. A., & Finkelhor, D. (2005). Inventory of problematic internet experiences encountered in clinical practice. *Professional Psychology: Research and Practice, 36*, 498–509.

Mitchell, M. J., Patterson, C. A., & Boyd-Franklin, N. (2011). Commentary: Increasing cultural diversity in pediatric psychology family assessment research. *Journal of pediatric psychology, 36*, 634–641.

Mitchell, R. L. & Crow, T. J. (2005). Right hemisphere language functions and schizophrenia: The forgotten hemisphere? *Brain, 128* (Pt 5), 963–978.

Mizock, L. & Fleming, M. Z. (2011). Transgender and gender variant populations with mental illness: Implications for clinical care. *Professional Psychology: Research and Practice, 42*, 208–213.

Moffitt, T. E., Caspi, A., Harrington, H., Milne, B. J., Melchior, M., Goldberg, D., & Poulton, R. (2007). Generalized anxiety disorder and depression: Childhood risk factors in a birth cohort followed to age 32. *Psychological Medicine, 37*, 441–452.

Mokdad, A. H., Marks, J. S., Stroup, D. F., & Gerberding, J. L. (2004). Actual causes of death in the United States, 2000. *Journal of the American Medical Association, 291*, 1238–1245.

Monahan, J. & Walker, L. (2006). *Social science in law* (6th ed.). Minneapolis, MN: Foundation Press.

Moodie, W. (1936). Forward. *A guide to mental testing* [au: R. B. Cattell] (pp. vii–viii). London, UK: University of London Press.

Morales, E. & Norcross, J. C. (2010). Evidence-based practices with ethnic minorities: Strange bedfellows. *Journal of Clinical Psychology, 66*, 821–829.

Moreno, J. (1946). *Psychodrama* (Vol. 1). New York, NY: Beacon House.

Morey, L. C., Lowmaster, S. E., Harwood, M. T., & Pratt, D. (2011). The Personality Assessment Inventory. In T. M. Harwood, L. E. Beutler, & G. Groth-Marnat (Eds.) *Integrative Assessment of Adult Personality* (pp. 190–218). New York, NY: Guilford.

Morey, L. C. (2007). *The Personality Assessment Inventory professional manual* (2nd ed.). Odessa, FL: Psychological Assessment Resources.

Morgan, A. J., Jorm, A. F., & Mackinnon, A. J. (2012). Usage and reported helpfulness of self-help strategies by adults with subthreshold depression. *Journal of Affective Disorders, 136*, 393–397.

Morgan, B. L. & Korschgen, A. J. (2006). *Majoring in psych? Career options for psychology undergraduates* (3rd ed.). Boston: Allyn and Bacon.

Morgan, D. L. & Morgan, R. K. (2001). Single-participant design: Bringing science to managed care. *American Psychologist, 56*, 119–127.

Morgan, E. M. & Landrum, R. E. (2012). *You've earned your doctorate in psychology…Now what? Securing a job as an academic or professional psychologist.* Washington, DC: American Psychological Association.

Morgan, R. D., Kuther, T. L., & Habben, C. J. (2005). *Life after graduate school in psychology: Insider's advice from new psychologists.* New York, NY: Psychology Press.

Morganstern, K. P. & Tevlin, H. E. (1981). Behavioral interviewing. In M. Hersen & A. S. Bellack (Eds.), *Behavioral assessment: A practical handbook* (2nd ed., pp. 71–100). New York, NY: Pergamon Press.

Morgenstern, J., Irwin, T. W., Wainberg, M. L., Parsons, J. T., Muench, F., Bux, D. A., et al. (2007). A randomized controlled trail of goal choice interventions for alcohol use disorders among men who have sex with men. *Journal of Consulting and Clinical Psychology, 75*, 72–84.

Morland, K., Diez Roux, A. V., & Wing, S. (2006). Supermarkets, other food stores, and obesity. *American Journal of Preventive Medicine, 30*, 333–339.

Morrison, C. S., McCusker, J., Stoddard, A. M., & Bigelow, C. (1995). The validity of behavioral data reported by injection drug users on a clinical risk assessment. *International Journal of the Addictions, 30*, 889–899.

Morse, S. J. (1978). Law and mental health professionals: The limits of expertise. *Professional Psychology, 9*, 389–399.

Morse, C. J. (2012). Debriefing after simulated patient experiences. In L. Wilson & L. Rockstraw (Eds). *Human simulation for nursing and health professions.* New York, NY: Springer Publishing, 58-66.

Morton, A. (1995). The enigma of non-attendance: A study of clients who do not turn up for their first appointment. *Therapeutic Communities: International Journal for Therapeutic and Supportive Organizations, 16*, 117–133.

Moseley G. L. (2006). Graded motor imagery for pathologic pain: A randomized controlled trial. *Neurology, 67*, 2129–2134.

Mukherjee, D., Levin, R. L., & Heller, W. (2006). The cognitive, emotional, and social sequelae of stroke: Psychological and ethical concerns in post-stroke adaptation. *Topics in Stroke Rehabilitation, 13*, 26–35.

Mulvey, E. P. & Cauffman, E. (2001). The inherent limits of predicting school violence. *American Psychologist, 56*, 797–802.

Munoz, R. F., Beardslee, W. R., & Leykin, Y. (2012). Major depression can be prevented. *American Psychologist, 67*, 285–295.

Munsey, C. (2007). New disclosure requirements help students compare psychology programs. *GradPSYCH, 5*, 1–2.

Munsey, C. (2008). Prescriptive authority in the states. *Monitor on Psychology, 39*, 60.

Murdock, N. L. (2004). *Theories of counseling and psychotherapy.* Upper Saddle River, NJ: Pearson.

Murphy, J. G., Dennhardt, A. A., Skidmore, J. R., Borsari, B., Barnett, N. P., & Colby, S. M. (2012). A randomized controlled trial of a behavioral economic supplement to brief motivational interventions for college drinking. *Journal of Consulting and Clinical Psychology, June 4, 2012, Early on-line edition*: doi: 10.1037/a0028763.

Murphy, M. J., Levant, R. F., Hall, J. E., & Glueckauf, R. L. (2007). Distance education in professional training in psychology. *Professional Psychology: Research and Practice, 38*, 97–103.

Murray, H. A. (1938). *Explorations in personality*. Fair Lawn, NJ: Oxford University Press.

Murray, H. A. (1943). *Thematic Apperception Test*. Cambridge, MA: Harvard University Press.

Mussen, P. H., & Scodel, A. (1955). The effects of sexual stimulation under varying conditions on TAT sexual responsiveness. *Journal of Consulting Psychology, 19*, 90.

Myers, D. G. (2000). The funds, friends, and faith of happy people. *American Psychologist, 55*, 56–67.

Myers, I. B. & Briggs, K. C. (1943). *The Myers-Briggs type indicator*. Palo Alto, CA: Consulting Psychologists Press.

Myklebust, H. R. (1975). Nonverbal learning disabilities: Assessment and intervention. In H. R. Myklebust (Ed.), *Progress in learning disabilities* (Vol. 3, pp. 85–121). New York, NY: Grune & Stratton.

Nagy, T. F. (2011). *Essential ethics for psychologists: A primer for understanding and mastering core issues*. Washington, DC: American Psychological Association.

Nasar, J. L. & Devlin, A. S. (2011). Impressions of psychotherapists' offices. *Journal of Counseling Psychology, 58*, 310–320.

Nathan, P. E. & Langenbucher, J. W. (1999). Psychopathology: Description and classification. *Annual Review of Psychology, 50*, 79–107.

Nathan, P. E. & Gorman, J. M. (2007). *A guide to treatments that work* (3rd ed.). New York, NY: Oxford University Press.

National Association of Social Workers website (2012)

National Center for Education Statistics. (2000). Digest of Education Statistics, 1999. Retrieved December 13, 2001, from http://nces.ed.gov/pubs2000/Digest99/d99t298.htm.

National Institute of Justice. (1999). *Eyewitness evidence: A guide for law enforcement*. Washington, DC: U.S. Department of Justice.

National Institute of Mental Health (2006). The numbers count: Mental disorders in America (2006 rev.). Retrieved August 8, 2006, from http://www.nimh.nih.gov.publicat/numbers.cfm.

National Research Council and Institute of Medicine (2009a). *Depression in parents, parenting, and children: Opportunities to improve identification, treatment, and prevention*. Washington, DC: National Academies Press.

National Research Council and Institute of Medicine (2009b). *Preventing mental, emotional, and behavioral disorders among young people: Progress and possibilities*. Washington, DC: National Academies Press.

Navon, D. (1983). How many trees does it take to make a forest? *Perception, 12*, 239–254.

Neighbors, C., Lee, C. M., Lewis, M. A., Fossos, N., & Walter, T. (2009). Internet-based personalized feedback to reduce 21st-birthday drinking: A randomized controlled trial of an event-specific prevention intervention. *Journal of Consulting and Clinical Psychology, 77*, 51–63.

Neimeyer, G. J., Rice, K. G., & Keilin, W. G. (2007). Does the model matter? The relationship between science-practice emphasis in clinical psychology programs and the internship match. *Training and Education in Professional Psychology, 1*, 153–162.

Neimeyer, G. J., Taylor, J. M., & Philip, D. (2010). Continuing education in psychology: Patterns of participation and perceived outcomes among mandated and nonmandated psychologists. *Professional Psychology: Research and Practice, 41*, 435–441.

Neimeyer, R. A. & Bridges, S. K. (2003). Postmodern approaches to psychotherapy. In A. S. Gurman & S. B. Messer (Eds.), *Essential Psychotherapies* (2nd ed., pp. 272–316). New York, NY: Guilford.

Nelson, S., Baldwin, N., & Taylor, J. (2012). Mental health problems and medically unexplained physical symptoms in adult survivors of childhood sexual abuse: An integrative literature review. *Journal of Psychiatric and Mental Health Nursing, 19*, 211–220.

Nevid, J. S., Rathus, S. A., & Greene, B. (2006). *Abnormal psychology in a changing world*. Upper Saddle River, NJ: Prentice Hall.

Newman, M. G., Szkodny, L. E., Llera, S. J., & Przeworski, A. (2011). A review of technology-assisted self-help and minimal contact therapies for anxiety and depression: Is human contact necessary for therapeutic efficacy? *Clinical Psychology Review, 31*, 89–103.

Neylan, T. C. (1999). Frontal lobe function: Mr. Phineas Gage's famous injury. *Journal of Neuropsychiatry and Clinical Neuroscience, 11*, 280.

Nichols, M. P. & Minuchin, S. (2009). *Family therapy: Concepts and methods* (9th ed.). Upper Saddle River, NJ: Prentice Hall.

Nicholson, R. A. (1999). Forensic assessment. In R. Roesch, S. D. Hart, & J. R. Ogloff (Eds.), *Psychology and law: The state of the discipline* (pp. 122–173). New York, NY: Kluwer Academic/Plenum.

Nielson, S. L., Okiishi, J., Nielsen, D. L., Hawkins, E. J., Harmon, S. C., et al. (2009). Termination, appointment use, and outcome patterns associated with intake therapist discontinuity. Professional Psychology: Research and Practice 40, 272–278.

Nietzel, M. T. & Bernstein, D. A. (1976). The effects of instructionally mediated demand upon the behavioral assessment of assertiveness. *Journal of Consulting and Clinical Psychology, 44*, 500.

Nietzel, M. T., Bernstein, D. A., & Russell, R. L. (1988). Assessment of anxiety and fear. In A. S. Bellack & M. Hersen (Eds.), *Behavioral assessment: A practical handbook* (3rd ed., pp. 280–312). New York, NY: Pergamon Press.

Nigg, J. & Nikolas, M. (2008). Attention-deficit/hyperactivity disorder. In T. P. Beauchaine & S. P. Hinshaw (Eds.), *Child and adolescent psychopathology* (pp. 301–334). Hoboken, NJ: John Wiley & Sons.

Niogi, S. N. & McCandliss, B. D. (2006). Left lateralized white matter microstructure accounts for individual differences in reading ability and disability. *Neuropsychologia, 44*(11), 2178–2188.

Nock, M. K. & Kurtz, S. M. S. (2005). Direct behavioral observation in school settings: Bringing science to practice. *Cognitive and Behavioral Practice, 12*, 359–370.

Nolen-Hoeksema, S., & Watkins, E. R. (2011). A heuristic for developing transdiagnostic models of psychopathology: Explaining multifinality and divergent trajectories. *Perspectives on Psychological Science, 6*, 589–609.

Noll, J. G., Trickett, P. K., & Putnam, F. W. (2003). A prospective investigation of the impact of childhood sexual abuse on the development of sexuality. *Journal of Consulting and Clinical Psychology, 71*, 575–586.

Norbury, C. F. & Sparks, A. (2012). Difference or disorder? Cultural issues in understanding neurodevelopmental disorders. *Developmental Psychology*. Advance online publication. doi: 10.1037/a0027446

Norcross, J. C. (Ed.). (2002). *Psychotherapy relationships that work: Therapists contributions and responsiveness to patients*. New York, NY: Oxford University Press.

Norcross, J. C. (Ed.). (2006). Integrating self-help into psychotherapy: 16 practical suggestions. *Professional Psychology: Research and Practice, 37*, 683–693.

Norcross, J. C. (2011). *Clinical versus counseling psychology What's the diff?* Eye on Psi Chi: Fall, 2000 Retrieved Dec. 27, 2011 from http://www.psichi.org/pubs/articles/article_73.aspx.

Norcross, J. C. & Goldfried, M. R. (2005). *Handbook of psychotherapy integration* (2nd ed.). New York, NY: Oxford University Press.

Norcross, J. C., Santrock, J. W., Zuckerman, E. L., Sommer, R., & Campbell, L. F. (2003). *Authoritative guide to self-help resources in mental health (rev. ed.)*. New York, NY: Guilford.

Norcross, J. C. & Lambert, M. J. (2011). Psychotherapy relationships that work II. *Psychotherapy, 48*, 4–8.

Norcross, J. C., Hedges, M., & Castle, P. H. (2002). Psychologists conducting psychotherapy in 2001: A study of the Division 29 membership. *Psychotherapy: Theory, Research, Practice, Training, 39*, 97–102.

Norcross, J. C., Karg, R. S., & Prochaska, J. O. (1997). Clinical psychologists in the 1990s: Part I. *Clinical Psychologist, 50*, 4–9.

Norcross, J. C., Beutler, L. E., & Levant, R. F. (2006a). *Evidence-based practices in mental health*. Washington, DC: American Psychological Association.

Norcross, J. C., Ellis, J. L., & Sayette, M. A. (2010). Getting in and getting money: A comparative analysis of admission standards, acceptance rates, and financial assistance across the research-practice continuum in clinical psychology programs. *Training and Education in Professional Psychology, 42*, 99–104.

Norcross, J. C., Karpiak, C. P., & Santoro, S. O. (2005). Clinical psychologists across the years: The Division of Clinical Psychology from 1960 to 2003. *Journal of Clinical Psychology, 61*, 1467–1483.

Norcross, J. C., Kohout, J. L., & Wicherski, M. (2005). Graduate study in psychology: 1971 to 2004. *American Psychologist, 60*, 959–975.

Norcross, J. C. & Lambert, M. J. (2011). Psychotherapy relationships that work II. *Psychotherapy, 48*, 4–8. doi: 10.1037/a0022180

Norcross, J. C. & Wampold, B. E. (2010). What works for whom: Tailoring psychotherapy to the person. *Journal of Clinical Psychology (Special Issue: Adatpting Psychotherapy to the Individual patient), 67*, 127–132.

Norcross, J. C., Vandenbos, G. R., & Freedheim, D. K. (Eds.) (2011). *History of Psychotherapy: Continuity and Change*. Washington, DC. American Psychological Association.

Norcross, J. C. & Sayette, M. A. (2011). *Insider's guide to graduate programs in clinical and counseling psychology: 2012/2013 edition*. New York, NY: The Guilford Press.

Nordal, K. C. (2010). Where has all the psychotherapy gone? *Monitor on Psychology, 41*, 10.

Norton, P. J. & Hope, D. A. (2001). Analogue observational methods in assessment of social functioning in adults. *Psychological Assessment, 13*, 86–98.

Nunes, E. V., Frank, K. A., & Kornfeld, S. D. (1987). Psychologic treatment for Type A behavior pattern and for coronary heart disease: A meta-analysis of the literature. *Psychosomatic Medicine, 48*, 159–173.

Oberman, L. M. & Ramachandran, V. S. (2007). The simulating social mind: The role of the mirror neuron system and simulation in the social and communicative deficits of autism spectrum disorders. *Psychological Bulletin, 133*, 310–327.

Occupational Outlook Handbook, 2010-2011 Edition. U.S. Department of Labor Bureau of Labor Statistics. Retrieved Jan. 1, 2012 from http://www.bls.gov/oco/ocos056.htm.

O'Donahue, W. T. & Fisher, J. E. (Eds.). (2012). *Cognitive behavior therapy: Core principles for practice*. New York, NY: John Wiley & Sons.

Oei, T. P. S. & Browne, A. (2006). Components of group processes: Have they contributed to the outcome of mood and anxiety disorder patients in a group cognitive-behaviour therapy program? *American Journal of Psychotherapy, 60*, 53–70.

Office of Strategic Services Assessment Staff. (1948). *Assessment of men*. New York, NY: Rinehart.

Ogloff, J. R. P. & Otto, R. (1993). Psychological autopsy: Clinical and legal perspectives. *Saint Louis University Law Journal, 37*, 607–646.

Okazaki, S. & Tanaka-Matsumi, J. (2006). Cultural considerations in cognitive-behavioral assessment. In P. A. Hays & G. Y Iwamasa (Eds.), *Culturally responsive cognitive behavioral therapy* (pp. 247–266). Washington, DC: American Psychological Association.

Olfson, M. & Marcus, S. C. (2010). National trends in outpatient psychotherapy. *The American Journal of Psychiatry, 167*, 1456–1463.

Olive, H. (1972). Psychoanalysts' opinions of psychologists' reports: 1952 and 1970. *Journal of Clinical Psychology, 28*, 50–54.

Oliver, P. H. & Margolin, G. (2009). Communication/problem-solving skills training. In W. T. O'Donohue & J. E. Fisher (Eds.), *General principles and empirically supported techniques of cognitive behavior therapy* (pp. 199–206). Hoboken, NJ: John Wiley & Sons.

Ollendick, T. H. & Davis, T. E. (2004). Empirically supported treatments for children and adolescents: Where to from here? *Clinical Psychology: Science and Practice, 11*, 289–294.

Ollendick, T. H. & Greene, R. (1990). Behavioral assessment of children. In G. Goldstein & M. Hersen (Eds.), *Handbook of psychological assessment* (2nd ed., pp. 403–422). New York, NY: Pergamon Press.

Olos, L. & Hoff, E. H. (2006). Gender ratios in European psychology. *European Psychologist, 11*, 1–11.

Opris, D., Pintea, S., Garcia-Palacios, A., Botella, C. Szamoskozi, S. et al. (2011). Virtual reality exposure therapy in anxiety disorders: A quantitative meta-analysis. *Brain and Behavior, 29*, 85–93.

Orchowski, L. M., Spickard, B. A., & McNamara, J. R. (2006). Cinema and the valuing of psychotherapy: Implications for clinical practice. *Professional Psychology: Research and Practice, 37*, 506–514.

Orlinsky, D. E. & Howard, K. I. (1986). Process and outcome in psychotherapy. In S. L. Garfield & A. E. Bergin (Eds.), *Handbook of psychotherapy and behavior change* (3rd ed., pp. 311–381). New York, NY: John Wiley & Sons.

Orlinsky, D. E., Grawe, K., & Parks, B. K. (1994). Process and outcome in psychotherapy—Noch Einmal. In A. E. Bergin & S. L. Garfield (Eds.), *Handbook of Psychotherapy and Behavior Change* (4th ed., pp. 270–276). New York, NY: John Wiley & Sons.

Orlinsky, D. E., Schofield, M. J., Schroder, T., & Kazantzis, N. (2011). Utilization of personal therapy by psychotherapists: A practice-friendly review and a new study. *Journal of Clinical Psychology, 67*, 828–842.

Ostafin, B. D., Chawla, N., Bowen, S., Dillworth, T. M., Witkiewitz, K., & Marlatt, G. A. (2006). Intensive mindfulness training and the reduction of psychological distress: A preliminary study. *Cognitive and Behavioral Practice, 13*, 191–197.

Othmer, E. M. & Othmer, S. C. (2002). *The clinical interview using DSM-IV-TR: Fundamentals.* Washington, DC: American Psychiatric Publishing. New York, NY: Brunner/Mazel.

Ougrin, D., Zundel, T., Kyriakopoulos, M., Banarsee, R., Stahl, D., & Taylor, E. (2011). Adolescents With Suicidal and Nonsuicidal Self-Harm: Clinical Characteristics and Response to Therapeutic Assessment. *Psychological Assessment.* Advance online publication. doi: 10.1037/a0025043.

Overholser, J. C. (2007). The Boulder Model in academia: Struggling to integrate the science and practice of psychology. *Journal of Contemporary Psychotherapy, 37*, 205–211.

Overholser, J. C. (2010). Ten criteria to qualify as a scientist-practitioner in clinical psychology: An immodest proposal for objective standards. *Journal of Contemporary Psychotherapy, 40*, 51–59.

Ozonoff, S. (2012). Editorial: DSM-5 and autism spectrum disorders–two decades of perspectives from the JCPP. *Journal of Child Psychology and Psychiatry, July 2012, early online version*, DOI: 10.1111/j.1469-7610.2012.02587.

Pace, T. M., Robbins, R. R., Rockey, R., Choney, S. K., Hill, J. S., et al. (2006). A cultural-contextual perspective on the validity of the MMPI-2 with American Indians. *Cultural Diversity and Ethnic Minority Psychology, 12*, 320–333.

Packard, E. (2007). A new tool for psychotherapists. *Monitor on Psychology, 38*, 30–31.

Pallak, M. S., Cummings, N. A., Dorken, H., & Henke, C. J. (1995). Effect of mental health treatment of medical costs. *Mind/Body Medicine, 1*, 7–11.

Parent, M. C. & Williamson, J. B. (2010). Program disparities in unmatched internship applicants. *Training and Education in Professional Psychology, 4*, 116–120.

Parra, G. R., DuBois, D. L., & Sher, K. J. (2006). Investigation of profiles of risk factors for adolescent psychopathology: A person-centered approach. *Journal of Clinical Child and Adolescent Psychology, 35*, 386–402.

Pate, W. E., II. (2001). Analyses of data from graduate study in psychology: 1999–2000. Retrieved December 12, 2001, from APA Research office, http://research.apa.org/grad00contents.html.

Patterson, C. H. (1989). Foundations for a systematic eclectic psychotherapy. *Psychotherapy, 26*, 427–435.

Patterson, D. R., Everett, J. J., Burns, G. L., & Marvin, J. A. (1992). Hypnosis for the treatment of burn pain. *Journal of Consulting and Clinical Psychology, 60*, 713–717.

Patterson, G. R. (1976). The aggressive child: Victim and architect of a coercive system. In L. A. Hamerlynck, L. C. Handy, & E. J. Mash (Eds.), *Behavior modification and families: Theory and research* (Vol. 1, pp. 267–316). New York, NY: Brunner/Mazel.

Patterson, G. R. (1982). *Coercive family process.* Eugene, OR: Castalia.

Patterson, G. R., Ray, R. S., Shaw, D. A., & Cobb, J. A. (1969). *Manual for coding of family interactions* (Document NO. 01234). Available from ASIS/NAPS, c/o Microfiche Publications, 305 East 46th St., New York, NY 10017.

Paul, G. L. (1966). *Insight versus desensitization in psychotherapy: An experiment in anxiety reduction.* Stanford, CA: Stanford University Press.

Paul, G. L. (1967). Strategy of outcome research in psychotherapy. *Journal of Consulting Psychology, 31*, 109–118.

Paul, G. L. (1969). Outcome of systematic desensitization II. In C. M. Franks (Ed.), *Behavior therapy: Appraisal and status* (pp. 63–159). New York, NY: McGraw-Hill.

Paul, G. L. (1969a). Behavior modification research: Design and tactics. In C. M. Franks (Ed.), *Behavior therapy: Appraisal and status* (pp. 29–62). New York, NY: McGraw-Hill.

Pennebacker, J. W. (1995). *Emotion, disclosure, and health.* Washington, DC: American Psychological Association.

Pereda, N., Guilera, G., Forns, M., & Gomez-Benito, J. (2009). The prevalence of child sexual abuse in communit and student samples: A meta-analysis. *Clinical Psychology Review, 29*, 328–338.

Perls, F. S. (1969). *Gestalt therapy verbatim.* Lafayette, CA: Real People Press.

Perls, F. S. (1970). Four lectures. In J. Fagan & I. L. Shepherd (Eds.), *Gestalt therapy now* (pp. 14–38). Palo Alto, CA: Science and Behavior Books.

Peters, L., Clark, D. & Carroll, F. (1998). Are computerized interviews equivalent to human interviews? CIDI-Auto versus CIDI in anxiety and depressive disorders. *Psychological Medicine, 28*, 893–901.

Peterson, C. (2000). The future of optimism. *American Psychologist, 55*, 44–55.

Peterson, C. (2006). The Values in Action (VIA) Classification of Strengths: The un-DSM and the real DSM. In M. Csikszentmihalyi & I. Csikszentmihalyi (Eds.), *A life worth living: Contributions to positive psychology* (pp. 29–48). New York, NY: Oxford University Press.

Peterson (2012). *Scholarships, grants, and prizes.* Lawrenceville, NJ: Peterson's Publishing.

Peterson, D. R. (1968a). *The clinical style of social behavior.* New York, NY: Appleton-Century-Crofts.

Peterson, J., Skeem, J., & Manchak, S. (2011). If you want to know, consider asking: How likely is it that patients will hurt themselves in the future? *Psychological Assessment,* doi: 10.1037/a0022971.

Peterson, A. L., Hatch, J. P., Hryshko-Mullen, A. S., & Cigrang, J. A. (2012). Relaxation training with and without muscle contraction in subjects with psychophysiological disorders. *Journal of Applied Biobehavioral Research, 16*, 138–147.

Petrie, K., Fontanilla, I., Thomas, M., Booth, R., & Pennebaker, J. W. (2004). Effects of written emotional expression on immune function in patients with human immunodeficiency virus infection: a randomized trial. *Psychosomatic Medicine, 66*, 272–275.

Petry, N. M., Weinstock, J., & Alessi, S. M. (2011). A randomized trial of contingency management delivered in the context of group counseling. *Journal of Consulting and Clinical Psychology, 79*, 686–696.

Philippson, P. (2012). *Gestalt therapy: roots and branches—collected papers.* London, GB: Karnac Books.

Pidano, A. E., Kurowski, E. C., & McEvoy, K. M. (2010). The next generation: How are clinical child psychologists being trained? *Training and Education in Professional Psychology, 4*, 121–127.

Pilkonis, P. A., Heape, C. L., Proietti, J. M., Clark, S. W., McDavid, J. D., et al. (1995). The reliability and validity of two structured interviews for personality disorders. *Archives of General Psychiatry, 52*, 1025–1033.

Pine, F. (1990). *Drive, ego, object, and self.* New York, NY: Basic Books.

Pingitore, D. & Scheffler, R. M. (2005). Practice patterns across the clinical life span: Results from the California Survey of Psychological Practice. *Professional Psychology: Research and Practice, 36*, 434–440.

Piotrowski, Z. (1972). Psychological testing of intelligence and personality. In A. M. Freedman & H. I. Kaplan (Eds.), *Diagnosing mental illness: Evaluation in psychiatry and psychology* (pp. 41–85). New York, NY: Atheneum.

Plake, B. S., Geisinger, K. F., Spies, R. A. & Buros Institute. (2012). *The seventeenth mental measurements yearbook.* Buros Institute of Mental Measurement.

Plante, T. G., Goldfarb, L. P., & Wadley, V. (1993). Are stress and coping associated with aptitude and achievement testing performance among children?: A preliminary investigation. *Journal of School Psychology, 31*, 259–266.

Plomin, R. & Kovas, Y. (2005). Generalist genes and learning disabilities. *Psychological Bulletin, 131*, 592–617.

Pollock, K. M. (2001). Exercise in treating depression: Broadening the psychotherapist's role. *Journal of Clinical Psychology/In Session, 57*, 1289–1300.

Pompili, M. & Taraelli, R. (Eds.). (2011). *Evidence-based suicidology: A source book.* Cambridge, MA: Hogrefe Publishing.

Ponds, R. W,. & Hendriks, M. (2006). Cognitive rehabilitation of memory problems in patients with epilepsy. *Seizure, 15*, 267–273.

Pope, K. S., Butcher, J. N., & Seelen, J. (1993). *The MMPI, MMPI-2, and MMPI in court.* Washington, DC: American Psychological Association.

Pope, K. S., Kieth-Spiegel, P., & Tabachnick, B. G. (2006). Sexual attraction to clients: The human therapist and the (sometimes) inhumane training system. *Training and Education in Professional Psychology, S*, 96–111.

Pope, K. S. & Tabachnick, B. G. (1994). Therapists as patients: A national survey of psychologists' experiences, problems, and beliefs. *Professional Psychology: Research and Practice, 25*, 247–258.

Pope, K. S. & Vasquez, M. J. T. (1998). *Ethics in psychotherapy and counseling* (2nd ed.). San Francisco: Jossey-Bass.

Pope, K. S. & Vasquez, M. J. T. (2011). *Ethics in psychotherapy and counseling: A practical guide* (4th ed.). Hoboken, NJ: John Wiley & Sons.

Popma, A. & Raine, A. (2006). Will future forensic assessment be neurobiologic? *Child and Adolescent Psychiatric clinics of North America, 15*, 429–444.

Portuges, S. H. & Hollander, N. C. (2011). The therapeutic action of resistance analysis: interpersonalizing and socializing Paul Gray's close process attention technique (pp. 71–96). In M. J. Diamond & C. Christian (Eds.). *The Second Century of Psychoanalysis: Evolving Perspectives on the Therapeutic Action.* London, GB: Karnac Books.

Post, C. G. (1963). *An introduction to the law.* Englewood Cliffs, NJ: Prentice Hall.

Pottick, K. J., Kirk, S. A., Hsieh, D. K., & Tian, X. (2007). Judging medical disorders in youth: Effects of client, clinician, and contextual differences. *Journal of Consulting and Clinical Psychology, 75*, 1–8.

Potts, M. K., Burnam, M. A., & Wells, K. B. (1991). Gender differences in depression detection: A comparison of clinician diagnosis and standardized assessment. *Psychological Assessment, 3*, 609–615.

Poythress, N., Monahan, J., Bonnie, R., Otto, R. K., & Hoge, S. K. (2002). *Adjudicative competence: The MacArthur Studies.* New York, NY: Kluwer/Plenum.

Poznanski, J. J. & Mclennan, J. (2003). Becoming a psychologist with a particular theoretical orientation to counseling practice. *Australian Psychologist, 38*, 223–226.

Price, M. (2011). Promoting psychology as a STEM discipline. *Monitor on Psychology, 42*, 32.

Price, M. & Anderson, P. (2007). The role of presence in virtual reality exposure therapy. *Journal of Anxiety Disorders, 21*, 724–751.

Prideaux, D., Roberts, C., Eva, K., Centeno, A., Maccrorie, P. et al. (2011). Assessment for selection for the health care professionals and specialty training: Consensus statement and recommendations from the Ottawa 2010 conference. *Medical Teacher, 33*, 215–223.

Prochaska, J. O. & Norcross, J. C. (1994). *Systems of psychotherapy: A transtheoretical analysis* (3rd ed.). Pacific Grove, CA: Brooks/Cole.

Prochaska J. O. & Norcross, J. C. (2002). *Systems of psychotherapy: A trans-theoretical analysis* (5th ed.). Pacific Grove, CA: Brooks Cole.

Puska, P. (1999). The North Karelia Project: From community intervention to national activity in lowering cholesterol levels and CHD risk. *European Heart Journal, 1(Suppl.)*, S9–13.

Rabiner, D. L., Murray, D. W., Skinner, A. T., & Malone, P. S. (2010). A randomized trial of two promising computer-based interventions for students with attention difficulties. *Journal of Abnormal Child Psychology, 38*, 131–142.

Rabinowitz, J. (1993). Diagnostic reasoning and reliability: A review of the literature and a model of decision-making. *Journal of Mind and Behavior, 14*, 297–315.

Ragland, D. R. & Brand, R. J. (1988). Type A behavior and mortality from coronary heart disease. *New England Journal of Medicine, 318*, 65–69.

Raimy, V. C. (1950). *Training in clinical psychology.* New York, NY: Prentice-Hall.

Raiya, H. A. & Pargament, K. I. (2010). Religiously integrated psychotherapy with Muslim clients: From research to practice. *Professional Psychology: Research and Practice, 41*, 181–188.

Rajecki, D. W. & Borden, V. M. H. (2011). Psychology degrees: employment, wage, and career trajectory consequences. *Perspectives on Psychological Science, 6*, 321–335.

Ramirez, S. Z. & Kratchowill, T. R. (1990). Development of the Fear Survey for Children With and Without Mental Retardation. *Behavioral Assessment, 12*, 457–470.

Ramseyer, F. & Tschacher, W. (2011). Nonverbal synchrony in psychotherapy: Coordinated body movement reflects relationship quality and outcome. *Journal of Consulting and Clinical Psychology, 79*, 284–295.

Rappaport, D. (1951). A conceptual model of psychoanalysis. *Journal of Personality, 20*, 56–81.

Rappaport, J. (1977). *Community psychology: Values, research and action.* New York, NY: Holt, Rinehart & Winston.

Rappaport, J. (2002). In praise of paradox: A social policy of empowerment over prevention. In T. A. Revenson, A. R. D'Augelli, S. E. French, D. L. Hughes, & D. Livert (Eds.), *A quarter century of community psychology: Readings from the American Journal of Community Psychology* (pp. 121–145). New York, NY: Kluwer Academic/Plenum Publishers.

Rappaport, J. (2011). Searching for Oz: Empowerment, crossing boundaries, and telling our story. In M. S. Aber, K. I. Maton, & E. Seidman (Eds.), *Empowering settings and voices from social change* (pp. 232–237). New York, NY: Oxford University Press.

Raschle, N. M., Zuk, J., & Gaab, N. (2012). Functional characteristics of developmental dyslexia in left-hemispheric posterior brain regions predate reading onset. *Proceedings of the National Academy of Sciences USA, 109*(6), 2156–2161.

Rasmussen, T. & Milner, B. (1975). Clinical and surgical studies of the cerebral speech areas in man. In K. J. Zulch, O. Creutzfeldt, & G. C. Galbraith (Eds.), *Cerebral localization.* Berlin & New York, NY: Springer-Verlag.

Rasting, M. & Beutel, M. E. (2005). Dyadic affective interactive patterns in the intake interview as a predictor of outcome. *Psychotherapy Research, 15*, 188–198.

Raviv, A., Raviv, A., Propper, A., & Fink, A. S. (2003). Mothers' attitudes toward seeking help for their children from school and private psychologists. *Professional Psychology: Research and Practice, 34*, 95–101.

Redd, W. H., Jacobsen, P. B., Die-Trill, M., Dermatis, H., McEvoy, M., & Holland, J. C. (1987). Cognitive/attentional distraction in the control of conditioned nausea in pediatric cancer patients receiving chemotherapy. *Journal of Consulting and Clinical Psychology, 55*, 391–395.

Reich, W., Cottler, L., McCallum, K., & Corwin, D. (1995). Computerized interviews as a method of assessing psychopathology in children. *Comprehensive Psychiatry, 36*, 40–45.

Reinecke, M. A. & Freeman, A. (2003). Cognitive therapy. In A. S. Gurman & S. B. Messer (Eds.), *Essential Psychotherapies* (2nd ed., pp. 224–271). New York, NY: Guilford.

Reisman, J. M. (1976). *A history of clinical psychology.* New York, NY: Irvington.

Reitan, R. M. (1964). Psychological deficits resulting from cerebral lesions in man. In J. M. Warren & K. Akert (Eds.), *The frontal granular cortex and behavior.* New York, NY: McGraw-Hill.

Reitan, R. M. & Davison, L. A. (Eds.). (1974). *Clinical neuropsychology: Current status and applications.* Washington, DC: V. H. Winston.

Reitan, R. M., Hom, J., Ven De Voorde, J., Stanczak, D. E., & Wolfson. (2004). The Houston Conference revisited. *Archives of Clinical Neuropsychology, 19*, 375–390.

Reitan, R. M. & Wolfson, D. (1993). *The Halstead-Reitan Neuropsychological Test Battery: Theory and clinical interpretation.* Tucson, AZ: Neuropsychology Press.

Repp, A. C. & Horner, R. H. (2000). *Functional analysis of problem behavior: From effective assessment to effective support.* Belmont, CA: Wadsworth.

Rescorla, L., Achenbach, T. M., Ivanova, M. Y., Dumenci, L., Almqvist, F., Bilenberg, N., et al. (2007). Epidemiological comparisons of problems and positive qualities reported by adolescents in 24 countries. *Journal of Consulting and Clinical Psychology, 75*, 351–358.

Rescorla, L. A., Achenbach, T. M., Ivanova, M. Y, Harder, V. S., Otten, L., Bilenberg, N., et al. (2011). International comparisons of behavioral and emotional problems in preschool children: Parents' reports from 24 societies. *Journal of Clinical Child and Adolescent Psychology, 40*, 456–467.

Resnick, R. J. (1997). A brief history of practice—Expanded. *American Psychologist, 52*, 463–468.

Resnick, R. J., Ax, R. K., Fagan, T. J., & Nussbaum, D. (2012). Predoctoral prescriptive authority curricula: A training option. *Journal of Clinical Psychology, 68*, 246–262.

Retzlaff, P. D., Dunn, T., & Harwood, T. M. (2011). The Millon Clinical Multiaxial Inventory-III. In T. M. Harwood, L. E. Beutler, & G. Groth-Marnat (Eds.) *Integrative Assessment of Adult Personality* (pp. 219–251). New York, NY: Guilford.

Reynolds, C. R. & Kamphaus, R. W. (2009). *Behavior Assessment System for Children-Second Edition (BASC-2).* Bloomington, MN: Pearson.

Reynolds, S., Wilson, C., Austin, J., & Hooper, L. (2012). Effects of psychotherapy for anxiety in children and adolescents: A meta-analytic review. *Clinical Psychology Review, 32*, 251–262.

Ribolsi, M., Koch, G., Magni, V., Di Lorenzo, G., Rubino, I. A., Siracusano, A., & Centonze, D. (2009). Abnormal brain lateralization and connectivity in schizophrenia. *Reviews in Neuroscience, 20*(1), 61–70.

Rice, M. E. (1997). Violent offender research and implications for the criminal justice system. *American Psychologist, 52*, 414–423.

Rice, S. A. (1929). Contagious bias in the interview: A methodological note. *American Journal of Sociology, 35*, 420–423.

Rich, B. A. (1998). Personhood, patienthood, and clinical practice: Reassessing advance directives. *Psychology, Public Policy, and Law, 4*, 610–628.

Richman, L. S., Kubzansky, L., Maselko, J., & Kawachi, I. (2005). Positive emotion and health: Going beyond the negative. *Health Psychology, 24*, 422–429.

Richmond, T. K. & Rosen, D. S. (2005). The treatment of adolescent depression in the era of the black box warning. *Current Opinion in Pediatrics, 17*, 466–472.

Rickert, V. & Jay, S. (1995). The noncompliant adolescent. In S. Parker & B. Zuckerman (Eds.), *Behavioral and developmental pediatrics* (pp. 219–222). Boston: Little, Brown & Company.

Ridley, C. R. & Shaw-Ridley, M. (2009). Clinical judgment accuracy: From meta-analysis to metatheory. *The Counseling Psychologist, 37*, 400–409.

Rieger, G. (2012). The eyes have it: Sex and sexual orientation differences in pupil dilation patterns. Presentation at the May, 2012 Association for Psychological Science Conference, Chicago, IL.

Riggle, E. D. B. & Rostosky, S. S. (2005). For better or for worse: Psycho-legal soft spots and advance planning for same-sex couples. *Professional Psychology: Research and Practice, 36*, 90–96.

Riley, W. T., Schumann, M. F., Forman-Hoffman, V. L., Mihm, P., Applegate, B. W., & Asif, O. (2007). Responses of practicing psychologists to a Web site developed to promote empirically supported treatments. *Professional Psychology: Research and Practice, 38*, 44–53.

Rios, R., Zautra, A. J. (2011). Socioeconomic disparities in pain: the role of economic hardship and daily financial worry. *Health Psychology, 30*, 58–66.

Ripple, C. H. & Zigler, E. (2003). Research, policy, and the federal role in prevention initiatives for children. *American Psychologist, 58*, 482–490.

Ritterband, L. M., Gonder-Frederick, L. A., Cox, D. J., Clifton, A. D., West, R. W., & Borowitz, S. M. (2003). Internet interventions: In review, in use, and into the future. *Professional Psychology: Research and Practice, 34*, 527–534.

Roberts, C. F., Sargent, E. L., & Chan, A. S. (1993). Verdict selection processes in insanity cases: Juror construals and the effects of guilty but mental ill instructions. *Law and Human Behavior, 17*, 261–275.

Roberts, M. C. & Steele, R. G. (Eds.) (2009). *Handbook of pediatric psychology* (4th ed.). New York, NY: Guilford.

Robertson, G. J. & Eyde, L. D. (1993). Improving test use in the United States: The development of an interdisciplinary casebook. *European Journal of Psychological Assessment, 9*, 137–146.

Robins, L. N., Cottler, L. B., Bucholz, K. K., Comptom, W. M., North, C. S., & Rourke, K. (2000). *Diagnostic Interview Schedule for DSM-IV*. St Louis, MO: Washington University School of Medicine.

Robinson, R. G. and Spalletta, G. (2010). Poststroke depression: a review. *Canadian Journal of Psychiatry, 55*(6), 341–349.

Robinson, J. D. & Habben, C. J. (2003). The role of the American Board of Professional Psychology in professional mobility. *Professional Psychology: Research and Practice, 34*, 474–475.

Rochlen, A. B., Zack, J. S., & Speyer, C. (2004). Online therapy: Review of relevant definitions, debates, and current empirical support. *Journal of Clinical Psychology, 60*, 269–283.

Rock, D. L., Bransford, J. D., Maisto, S. A., & Morey, L. (1987). The study of clinical judgment: An ecological approach. *Clinical Psychology Review, 7*, 645–661.

Rodin, J. & Salovey, P. (1989). Health psychology. *Annual Review of Psychology, 40*, 533–580.

Rodriguez, H. & Arnold, C. (1998). Children & divorce: A snapshot. Retrieved 13 December 2001, from http://www.clasp.org/pubs/familyformation/divfinal.htm.

Roe, A., Gustad, J. W., Moore, B. V., Ross, S., & Skodak, M. (Eds.). (1959). *Graduate education in psychology*. Washington, DC: American Psychological Association.

Roe, D., Dekel, R., Harel, G., Fenning, S., & Fenning, S. (2006). Clients' feelings during termination of psychodynamically oriented psychotherapy. *Bulletin of the Menninger Clinic, 70*, 68–81.

Roemer, L., Orsillo, S. M., & Salters-Pedneault, K. (2008). Efficacy of an acceptance-based therapy for generalized anxiety disorder: Evaluation in a randomized controlled trial. *Journal of Consulting and Clinical Psychology, 76*, 1083–1089.

Roesch, R., Zapf, P., & Hart, S. (2010). *Forensic Psychology and Law*. Hoboken, NJ: John Wiley & Sons.

Rogers, C. R. (1951). *Client-centered therapy*. Boston: Houghton Mifflin.

Rogers, C. R. (1942). *Counseling and psychotherapy*. Boston: Houghton Mifflin.

Rogers, C. R. (1946). Significant aspects of client-centered therapy. *American Psychologist, 1*, 415–422.

Rogers, C. R. (1961). *On becoming a person*. Boston: Houghton Mifflin.

Rogers, C. R. (1967/2003). *Client-centered therapy*. New York, NY: Constable & Robinson.

Rogers, E. B., Stanford, M. S., Dolan, S. L., Clark, J., Martindale, S. L., Lake, S. L., et al. (2012). Helping people without homes: Simple steps for psychologists seeking to change lives. *Professional Psychology: Research and Practice, 43*, 86–93.

Rogers, R. (2001). *Handbook of diagnostic and structured interviewing* (2nd ed.). New York, NY: Guilford.

Rogers, R., Gillis, J. R., Dickens, S. E., & Bagby, R. M. (1991). Standardized assessment of malingering: Validation of the Structured Interview of Reported Symptoms. *Psychological Assessment, 3*, 89–96.

Rohde, D. (1999, November 7). Juror and courts assailed in subway-killing mistrial. *New York Times*, 32.

Roid, G. H. (2003). *Stanford-Binet Intelligence Scales (fifth ed.) technical manual*. Itasca, IL: Riverside Publishing.

Ronan, G. G., Colavito, V. A., & Hammontree, S. R. (1993). Personal problems-solving system for scoring TAT responses: Preliminary validity and reliability data. *Journal of Personality Assessment, 61*, 28–40.

Ronan, K. R. & Kazantzis, N. (2006). The use of between-session (homework) activities in psychotherapy: Conclusions from the Journal of Psychotherapy Integration Special Series. *Journal of Psychotherapy Integration, 16*, 254–259.

Rorschach, H. (1921). *Psychodynamics: A diagnostic test based on perception*. Oxford, England: Grune and Stratton.

Rorschach, H. (1942). *Psychodiagnostics: A diagnostic test based on perception*. Bern, Switzerland: Hans Huber (Original work published in 1921).

Rose, S. D. & LeCroy, C. W. (1991). Group methods. In F. H. Kanfer & A. P. Goldstein (Eds.), *Helping people change* (4th ed., pp. 422–453). New York, NY: Pergamon Press.

Rosen, D. C., Miller, A. B., Nakash, O., Halperin, L, & Alegria, M. (2012). Interpersonal complemntarity in the mental health intake: A mixed-methods study. *Journal of Counseling Psychology, 59*, 185–196.

Rosen, G. M., Glasgow, R. E., & Moore, T. E. (2003). Self-help therapy: The science and business of giving psychology away. In S. O. Lilienfeld, S. J. Lynn, & J. M. Lohr (Eds.), *Science and pseudoscience in clinical psychology* (pp. 399–424). New York, NY: Guilford.

Rosen, J. (2007, March 11). The brain on the stand. *New York Times Magazine*. Retrieved 11 March 2007, at http://www.nytimes.com/2007/03/11/magazine/11Neurolaw.t.html?ref=magazine.

Rosen, R. C. & Kopel, S. A. (1977). Penile plethysmography and bio-feedback in the treatment of a transvestite-exhibitionist. *Journal of Consulting and Clinical Psychology, 45,* 908–916.

Rosenberg, A., Almeida, A., & Macdonald, H. (2012). Crossing the cultural divide: Issues in translation, mistrust, and cocreation of meaning in cross-cultural therapeutic assessment. *Journal of Personality Assessment,* Advance online publication DOI: 10.1080/00223891.2011.648293.

Rosenhan, D. L. (1973). On being sane in insane places. *Science, 179,* 250–258.

Rosenman, R. H., Brand, R. J., Jenkins, D. D., Friedman, M., Straus, R., & Wurm, M. (1975). Coronary heart disease in the Western Collaborative Group Study: Final follow-up experience after 8 years. *Journal of the American Medical Association, 233,* 872–877.

Rosenstock, I. M. (1974). Historical origins of the health belief model. *Health Education Monographs, 2,* 328–335.

Rosenthal, T. L. & Steffek, B. D. (1991). Modeling methods. In F. H. Kanfer & A. P. Goldstein (Eds.), *Helping people change* (4th ed., pp. 70–121). New York, NY: Pergamon Press.

Rosenzweig, S. (1949). Apperceptive norms for the Thematic Apperception Test. I. The problem of norms in projective methods. *Journal of Personality, 17,* 475–482.

Rosenzweig, S. (1977). *Manual for the Children's Form of the Rosenzweig Picture-Frustration (P-F) Study.* St. Louis: Rana House.

Rossini, E. D. & Moretti, R. J. (1997). Thematic Apperception Test interpretation: Practice recommendations from a survey of clinical psychology doctoral programs accredited by the American Psychological *Association. Professional Psychology: Research and Practice, 28,* 393–398.

Ross, M. W., Stowe, A., Wodak, A., & Gold, J. (1995). Reliability of interview responses of injecting drug users. *Journal of Addictive Diseases, 14,* 1–2.

Rothbaum, B. O. (2011). Ask the expert: Anxiety disorders virtual reality therapy. *Focus, 9,* 292–293.

Rothbart, M. K. & Bates, J. E. (2006). Temperament. In N. Eisenberg (Ed.) *Handbook of child psychology* (6th ed., pp. 99–166). Hoboken, NJ: John Wiley & Sons.

Rotter, J. B. & Rafferty, J. E. (1950). *The Rotter Incomplete Sentences Test.* New York, NY: Psychological Corporation.

Rotter, J. B., Lah, M. I., & Rafferty, J. E. (1992). *Manual: Rotter Incomplete Sentences Blank* (2nd ed.). Orlando, FL: Psychological Corporation.

Rouleau, C. R. & vonRanson, K. M. (2011). Potential risks for pro-eating disorder websites. *Clinical Psychology Review, 31,* 525–531.

Rourke, B. P. (1989). *Nonverbal learning disabilities: The syndrome and the model.* New York, NY: Guilford.

Routh, D. K. (1994). *Clinical psychology since 1917: Science, practice, organization.* New York, NY: Plenum.

Routh, D. K. (2000). Clinical psychology training: A history of ideas and practices prior to 1946. *American Psychologist, 55,* 236–241.

Routh, D. K. (2011). How clinical psychology linked up with applied behavior analysis. *The Clinical Psychologist, 64,* 10–11.

Rozanski, A., Blumenthal, J. A., & Kaplan, J. (1999). Impact of psychological factors on the pathogenesis of cardiovascular disease and implications for therapy. *Circulation, 99,* 2192–2217.

Rozell, C. A., Berke, D. M., Norcross, J. C., & Karpiak, C. P. (2011). Clinical psychologists in the 2010s: Fifty-year trends in Division 12 membership. Presentation given at 2011 American Psychological Association Convention, August 4, 2011, Washington, DC.

Rozensky, R. H. (2011). The institution of the institutional practice of psychology: Health care reform and psychology's future workforce. *American Psychologist, 66,* 797–808.

Rubens, A. B. & Benson, D. F. (1971). Associative visual agnosia. *Archives of Neurology, 24,* 304–316.

Rubin, R., Holm, S., Friberg, L., Videbech, P., Andersen, H. S., Bendsen, B. B., et al. (1991). Altered modulation of prefrontal and subcortical brain activity in newly diagnosed schizophrenia and schizophreniform disorder: A regional cerebral blood flow study. *Archives of General Psychiatry, 48,* 987–995.

Rubinstein, E. (1948). Childhood mental disease in American: A review of the literature before 1900. *American Journal of Orthopsychiatry, 18,* 314–321.

Rugulies, R. (2003). Depression as a predictor for the development of coronary heart disease: A systematic review and meta-analysis of the literature. *American Journal of Preventive Medicine, 23,* 51–61.

Rutter, M. (2012). Resilience: Causal pathways and social ecology. In M. Ungar (Ed.), *The social ecology of resilience: A handbook of theory and practice* (pp. 33–42). New York, NY: Springer Science.

Ryan, J. J., Paolo, A. M., & Smith, A. J. (1992). Wechsler Adult Intelligence Scale—Revised intersubtest scatter in brain-damaged patients: A comparison with the standardization sample. *Psychological Assessment, 4,* 63–66.

Ryan, R. M., Lynch, M. F., Vansteenkiste, M., & Deci, E. L. (2010). Motivation and autonomy in counseling, psychotherapy, and behavior change: A look at theory and practice. *The Counseling Psychologist, 39,* 193–260.

Rychtarik, R. G., Tarnowski, K. J., & St. Lawrence, J. S. (1989). Impact of social desirability response sets on the self-report of marital adjustment in alcoholics. *Journal of Studies in Alcohol, 50,* 24–29.

Sackett, P. R. & Wilk, S. L. (1994). Within-group norming and other forms of score adjustment in preemployment testing. *American Psychologist, 49,* 929–954.

Sacks, O. (1990). *A leg to stand on.* New York, NY: Summit Books.

Safer, D. L., Telch, C. F., & Agras, W. (2001). Dialectical behavior therapy for bulimia nervosa. *American Journal of Psychiatry, 158,* 632–634.

Safran, J. D., Abreu, I., Ogilvie, J., & DeMaria, A. (2011). Does psychotherapy research influence the clinical practice of researcher-clinicians? *Clinical Psychology: Science and Practice, 18,* 357–371.

Sales, B. D., Miller, M. O., & Hall, S. R. (2005a). Legal credentialing and privileges to practice. In B. D. Sales, M. O. Miller, & S. R. Hall (Eds.), *Laws affecting clinical practice* (pp. 13–22). Washington, DC: American Psychological Association.

Sales, B. D. & Shuman, D. W. (1996). *Law, mental health, and mental disorder.* Pacific Grove, CA: Brooks/Cole.

Salloum, A. & Overstreet, S. (2008). Evaluation of individual and group grief and trauma interventions for children post disaster. *Journal of Clinical Child and Adolescent Psychology, 37*, 495–507.

Salmon, P. G., Sephton, S. E., & Dreeben, S. J. (2011). Mindfulness-based stress reduction. In J. D. Herbert & E. M. Forman (Eds.), *Acceptance and mindfulness in cognitive behavior therapy: Understanding and applying the new therapies* (pp. 132–163). Hoboken, NJ: John Wiley & Sons.

Salovey, P. & Singer, J. A. (1991). Cognitive behavior modification. In F. H. Kanfer & A. P. Goldstein (Eds.), *Helping people change* (4th ed., pp. 361–395). New York, NY: Pergamon Press.

Salovey, P., Rothman, A. J., Detweiler, J. B., & Steward, W. T. (2000). Emotional states and physical health. *American Psychologist, 55*, 110–121.

Sammons, M. T. (2011). Pharmacotheapy. In J. C. Norcross, G. R. VandenBos, & D. K. Freedheim (Eds.), *History of psychotherapy: Continuity and change* (2nd ed., pp. 516–532). Washington, DC: American Psychological Association.

Samuda, R. J. (1975). *Psychological testing of American minorities: Issues and consequences.* New York, NY: Dodd, Mead.

Sandell, R. (2012). Research on outcomes of psychoanalysis and psychoanalysis-derived psychotherapies. In G. O. Gabbard, B. E. Litowitz, & P. Williams (Eds.) *Textbook of psychoanalysis* (2nd ed., pp. 385–403). Arlington, VA: American Psychiatric Publishing.

Sanders, M. R. & Murphy-Brennan, M. (2010). The international dissemination of the Triple P–Positive Parenting Program. In J. R. Weisz & A. E. Kazdin (Eds.), *Evidence-based psychotherapies for children and adolescents* (2nd ed., pp. 519–537). New York, NY: Guilford.

Sandler, I. N., Schoenfelder, E. N., Wolchik, S. A., & MacKinnon, D. P. (2011). Long-term impact of prevention programs to promote effective parenting: Lasting effects but uncertain processes. *Annual Review of Psychology, 62*, 299–329.

Santoro, S. O., Kister, K. M., Karpiak, C. P., & Norcross, J. C. (2004, April). *Clinical psychologists in the 2000s: A national study.* Paper presented at the annual meeting of the Eastern Psychological Association, Washington, DC.

Santucci, L. C., McHugh, R. K., & Barlow, D. H. (2012). Direct-to-consumer marketing of evidence-based psychological interventions. *Behavior Therapy, 43*, 231–235.

Sapienza, J. K. & Masten, A. S. (2011). Understanding and promoting resilience in children and youth. *Current Opinion in Psychiatry, 24*, 267–273.

Sarafino, E. P. (2010). *Health psychology: Biopsychosocial interactions.* Hoboken, NJ: John Wiley & Sons.

Sarason, S. B. (1974). *The psychological sense of community: Prospects for community psychology.* San Francisco: Jossey-Bass.

Sartorius, N., Kaelber, C. T., Cooper, J. E., Roper, M. T., et al. (1996). Progress toward achieving a common language in psychiatry: Results from the field trial of the clinical guidelines accompanying the WHO classification of mental and behavioral disorders in ICD-10. *Archives of General Psychiatry, 50*, 115–124.

Satir, V. (1967). *Conjoint family therapy* (rev. ed.). Palo Alto, CA: Science and Behavior Books.

Sattler, J. M. & Hoge, R. D. (2006). *Assessment of children: Behavioral, social and clinical foundations* (5th ed.). San Diego: Jerome M. Sattler, Publisher.

Saunders, S. M., Howard, K. I., & Orlinsky, D. E. (1989). The Therapeutic Bond Scales: Psychometric characteristics and relationship to treatment effectiveness. *Psychological Assessment, 1*, 323–330.

Saunders, S. M., Miller, M. L., & Bright, M. M. (2010). Spiritually conscious psychological care. *Professional Psychology: Research and Practice, 41*, 355–362.

Sawyer, A., Ayers, S. & Field, A. P. (2010). Posttraumatic growth and adjustment among individuals with cancer or HIV/AIDS: A meta-analysis. *Clinical Psychology Review, 30*, 436–447.

Sayette, M. A. & Norcross, J. C. (2011). The heterogeneity of clinical psychology Ph.D. programs and the distinctiveness of APCS programs. *Clinical Psychology: Science and Practice, 18*, 4–11.

Sayette, M. A., Norcross, J. C., Dimoff, J. D. (2011). The heterogeneity of clinical psychology Ph.D. Programs and the distinctiveness of APCS programs. *Clinical Psychology: Science and Practice, 18*, 4–11.

Schaffer, J. B., DeMers, S. T., & Rodolfa, E. (2011). Licensing and credentialing. In J. C. Norcross, G. R. VandenBos, & D. K. Freedheim (Eds.), *History of psychotherapy: Continuity and change* (2nd ed., pp. 651–662). Washington, DC: American Psychological Association.

Scheel, M. J. (2011). Client common factors represented by client motivation and autonomy. *The Counseling Psychologist, 39*, 276–285.

Schermerhorn, A. C., Chow, S. M., & Cummings, E. M. (2010). Developmental family processes and interparental conflict: Patterns of microlevel influences. *Developmental Psychology, 46*, 869–885.

Schirmer, A., Alter, K., Kotz, S. A., & Friederici, A. D. (2001). Lateralization of prosody during language production: A lesion study. *Brain and Language, 76*, 1–17.

Schneck, J. M. (1975). United States of America in J. G. Howells (Ed.), *World history of psychiatry.* New York, NY: Brunner/Mazel, 432–475.

Schneider, K. J. (2003). Existential-humanistic psychotherapies. In A. S. Gurman & S. B. Messer (Eds.), *Essential psychotherapies* (2nd ed., pp. 149–181). New York, NY: Guilford.

Schneider, K. J. (2008). *Existential-integrative psychotherapy: Guideposts to the core of practice.* New York, NY: Routledge.

Schneider, K. J. & Krug, O. T. (2010). *Existential-Humanistic Therapy.* Washington, DC: American Psychological Association.

Schneider, S. L. (2001). In search of realistic optimism: Meaning, knowledge, and warm fuzziness. *American Psychologist, 56*, 250–263.

Schneiderman, N., Antoni, M. H., Saab, P. G., & Ironson, G. (2001). Health psychology: Psychosocial and biobehavioral aspects of chronic disease management. *Annual Review of Psychology, 52*, 555–580.

Schnur, J. B. & Montgomery, G. H. (2010). A systematic review of therapeutic alliance, group cohesion, empathy, and goal consensus/collaboration in psychotherapeutic interventions in cancer: Uncommon factors? *Clinical Psychology Review, 30*, 238–247.

Scholl, M. B., McGowan, A. S., & Hansen, J. T. (2012). *Humanistic perspectives on contemporary counseling issues.* New York, NY: Routledge.

Schradle, S. B., & Dougher, M. J. (1985). Social support as a mediator of stress. Theoretical and empirical issues. *Clinical Psychology Review, 5*, 641–662.

Schretlen, D., Wilkins, S. S., Van Gorp, W. G., & Bobholz, J. H. (1992). Cross-validation of a psychological test battery to detect faked insanity. *Psychological Assessment, 4*, 77–83.

Schröder, T. A. & Davis, J. D. (2004). Therapists' experience of difficulty in practice. *Psychotherapy Research, 14*, 328–245.

Schulz, K. F., Altman, D. G., & Moher, D. (2010). CONSORT 2010 Statement: Updated guidelines for reporting parallel group randomized trials. *Journal of Clinical Epidemiology, 63*, 834–840.

Schulz, M. S., Pruett, M. K., Kerig, P. K., & Parke, R. D. (2010). *Strengthening couple relationships for optimal child development: Lessons from research and intervention.* Washington, DC: American Psychological Association.

Schwab-Stone, M., Fallon, T., & Briggs, M. (1994). Reliability of diagnostic reporting for children aged 6–11 years: A test-retest study of the Diagnostic Interview Schedule for Children—Revised. *American Journal of Psychiatry, 151*, 1048–1054.

Schwartz, B. K., (Ed.). (2003). *Correctional psychology: Practice, programming, and administration.* Kingston, NJ: Civil Research Institute.

Schwartz, S. J., Unger, J. B., Zamboanga, B. L., & Szapocznik, J. (2010). Rethinking the concept of acculturation: Implications for theory and research. *American Psychologist, 65*, 237–251.

Scott, C. L. & Resnick, P. J. (2006). Patient suicide and litigation. In R. I. Simon & R. E. Hales (Eds.), *The American Psychiatric Publishing textbook of suicide assessment and management* (pp. 527–544). Washington, DC: American Psychiatric Publishing.

Scoville, W. B. & Milner, B. (1957). Loss of recent memory after bilateral hippocampal lesions. *The Journal of Neurology, Neurosurgery, & Psychiatry, 20*, 11–21.

Segal, D. L., Mueller, A. E., & Coolidge, F. L. (Eds.) (2012). Structured and semistructured interviews for differential diagnosis: Fundamentals, applications, and essential features. In M. Hersen & D. Beidel (Eds.) *Adult Psychopathology and Diagnosis* (6th ed., pp. 91–115). New York, NY: John Wiley & Sons.

Segal, Z. V., Williams, J. M. G., & Teasdale, J. D. (2002). *Mindfulness-based cognitive therapy for depression: A new approach to preventing relapse.* New York, NY: Guilford.

Segerstrom, S., Miller, G. (2004). Psychological stress and the human immune system: A meta-analytic study of 30 years of inquiry. *Psychological Bulletin, 130 (4)*, 601–630.

Sehgal, R., Saules, K., Young, A., Grey, M. J., Gillem, A. R., Nabors, N. A. et al. (2011). Practicing what we know: Multicultural counseling competence among clinical psychology trainees and experienced multicultural psychologists. *Cultural Diversity and Ethnic Minority Psychology, 17*, 1–10.

Seidman, E. & Tseng, V. (2011). Changing social settings: A framework for action. In M. S. Aber, K. I. Maton, & E. Seidman (Eds.), *Empowering settings and voices for social change* (pp. 12–37). New York, NY: Oxford University Press.

Seifer, R. (2003). Young children with mentally ill parents: Resilient developmental systems. In S. S. Luthar (Ed.), *Resilience and vulnerability: Adaptation in the context of childhood adversities* (pp. 29–49). New York, NY: Cambridge University Press.

Seligman, M. E. P. (1995). The effectiveness of psychotherapy: The Consumer Reports study. *American Task Force on Promotion and Dissemination of Psychological Procedures (1995). Training in and dissemination of empirically validated psychological treatments: Report and recommendations. Clinical Psychologist, 48*, 3–23.

Seligman, M. E. P. (2008). Positive health. *Applied Psychology, 57*, 3–18.

Seligman, M. E. P. (2011). *Flourish: A visionary new understanding of happiness and well-being.* New York, NY: Free Press.

Seligman, M. E. P. & Csikszentmihali, M. (2000). Positive psychology: An introduction. *American Psychologist, 55*, 5–14.

Sellbom, M., Ben-Porath, Y. S., Patrick, C. J., Wygant, D. B., Gartland, D. M. et al. (2012). Development and construct validation of MMPI-2-RF indices of global psychopathology, fearless-dominance, and impulsive-antisociality. *Personality Disorders: Theory, Research, and Treatment, 3*, 17–38.

Selye, H. (1956). *The stress of life.* New York, NY: McGraw-Hill.

Sexton, T. L., Alexander, J. F., & Mease, A. L. (2004). Levels of evidence for the models and mechanisms of therapeutic change in family and couple therapy. In M. J. Lambert (Ed.), *Bergin and Garfield's handbook of psychotherapy and behavior change* (5th ed., pp. 590–646). New York, NY: John Wiley & Sons.

Shadish, W. R. & Baldwin, S. A. (2005). Effects of behavioral marital therapy: A meta-analysis of randomized controlled trials. *Journal of Consulting and Clinical Psychology, 73*, 6–14.

Shaffer, A., Coffino, B., Boelcke-Stennes, K., & Masten, A. S. (2007). From urban girls to resilient women: Studying adaptation across development in the context of adversity. In B. J. R. Leadbeater & N. Way (Eds.), *Urban girls revisited: Building strengths* (pp. 53–72). New York, NY: New York University Press.

Shaffer, D., Fisher, P., Lucas, C. P., Dulcan, M. K., & Schwab-Stone, M. E. (2000). NIMH Diagnostic Interview Schedule for Children Version IV (NIMH DISC-IV): Description, differences from previous versions, and reliability of some common diagnoses. *Journal of the American Academy of Child and Adolescent Psychiatry, 39*, 28–38.

Shaffer, G. W. & Lazarus, R. S. (1952). *Fundamental concepts in clinical psychology.* New York, NY: McGraw-Hill.

Shamay-Tsoory, S. G., Tomer, R., Berger, B. D., Goldsher, D., & Aharon-Peretz, J. (2005). Impaired "affective theory of mind" is associated with right ventromedial prefrontal damage. *Cognitive and Behavioral Neurology, 18*, 55–67.

Shannon, D. & Weaver, W. (1949). *The mathematical theory of communication.* Urbana: University of Illinois Press.

Shapiro, A. K. (1971). Placebo effects in medicine, psychotherapy, and psychoanalysis. In A. E. Bergin & S. L. Garfield (Eds.), *Handbook of psychotherapy and behavior change: An empirical analysis* (pp. 439–473). New York, NY: John Wiley & Sons.

Shapiro, D. A., & Shapiro, D. (1982). Meta-analysis of comparative therapy outcome research: A critical appraisal. *Behavioral Psychotherapy, 10*, 4–25.

Shapiro, S. L., Carlson, L. E., Astin, J. A., & Freedman, B. (2006). Mechanisms of mindfulness. *Journal of Clinical Psychology, 62*, 373–386.

Shaw, D. L., Martz, D. M., Lancaster, C. J., & Sade, R. M. (1995). Influence of medical school applicants' demographic and cognitive characteristics on interviewers' ratings of noncognitive traits. *Academic Medicine, 70*, 532–536.

Shaywitz, S. E. & Shaywitz, B. A. (2005). Dyslexia (specific reading disability). *Biological Psychiatry, 57*(11), 1301–1309.

Shear, M. K., Brown, T. A., Sholomskas, D. E., Barlow, D. E., Gorman, J. M., et al. (1997). *Panic Disorder Severity Scale (PDSS)*. Pittsburgh, PA: Department of Psychiatry, University of Pittsburgh School of Medicine.

Shechtman, Z. & Tsegahun, I. (2004). Phototherapy to enhance self-disclosure and client-therapist alliance in an intake interview with Ethiopian immigrants to Israel. *Psychotherapy Research, 14*, 367–377.

Shedler, J. (2010). The efficacy of psychodynamic psychotherapy. *American Psychologist*. 65, 98–109.

Shenker, J. I. (April 2005). *When you only see trees, is there still a forest?* Paper presented at the American Academy of Neurology Annual Meeting, Miami Beach, FL.

Sheps, D. S., Freedland, K. E., Golden, R. N., McMahon, R. P. (2003). ENRICHD and SADHART: Implications for future biobehavioral intervention efforts. *Psychosocial Medicine, 65*, 1–2.

Shiffman, S., Hickcox, M., Paty, J. A., Gnys, M., Kassel, J. D., & Richards, T. J. (1996). Progression from a smoking lapse to relapse: Prediction from abstinence violation effects, nicotine dependence, and lapse characteristics. *Journal of Consulting & Clinical Psychology, 64*, 993–1002.

Shirk, S. R., Karver, M. S., & Brown, R. (2011). The alliance in child and adolescent psychotherapy. *Psychotherapy, 48*, 17–24.

Shirk, S. R. & Karver, M. S. (2011). Alliance in child and adolescent psychotherapy. In J. C. Norcross (Ed.), *Psychotherapy relationships that work: Evidence-based responsiveness* (2nd ed., pp. 70–91). New York, NY: Oxford University Press.

Shochet, I. M., Dadds, M. R., Holland, D., Whitefield, K., Harnett, P. H., & Osgarby, S. M. (2001). The efficacy of a universal school-based program to prevent adolescent depression. *Journal of Clinical Child Psychology, 30*, 303–315.

Shuman, D. W. & Sales, B. D. (1999). The impact of *Daubert* and its progeny on the admissibility of behavioral and social science evidence. *Psychology, Public Policy, and Law, 5*, 3–15.

Shure, M. B. & Aberson, B. (2005). Enhancing the process of resilience through effective thinking. In S. Goldstein, & R. B. Brooks (Eds.), *Handbook of resilience in children* (pp. 373–394). New York, NY: Kluwer Academic/Plenum Publishers.

Siassi, I. (1984). *Handbook of psychological assessment.* New York, NY: Pergamon.

Silverman, W. K. & Hinshaw, S. P. (2008). The second special issue on evidence-based psychosocial treatments for children and adolescents: A 10-year update. *Journal of Clinical Child and Adolescent Psychology, 37*, 1–7.

Sinacola, R. S. & Peters-Strickland, T. (2012). *Basic psychopharmacology for counselors and psychotherapists* (2nd ed.). Boston: Pearson.

Singh, R. & Dutta, S. (2010). *Race and culture: Tools, techniques and trainings: A manual for professionals.* London, UK: Karnac Books.

Sleek, S. (1998, February). Jury tuned out the science in the Nichols trial. *APA Monitor*, 2.

Slife, B. D. & Reber, J. S. (2001). Eclecticism in psychotherapy: Is it really the best substitute for traditional theories? In B. D. Slife, R. N. Williams, & S. H. Barlow (Eds.), *Critical issues in psychotherapy* (pp. 213–234). Thousand Oaks, CA: Sage.

Slobogin, C. (1985). The guilty but mentally ill verdict: An idea whose time should not have come. *George Washington Law Review, 53*, 494–527.

Smith, A. G. (2009). Personal characteristics of master couple therapists. *Dissertation Abstracts, 70 (2-B)*, 1357.

Smith, M. L. & Glass, G. V. (1977). Meta-analysis of psychotherapy outcome studies. *American Psychologist, 32*, 752–777.

Smith, M. L., Glass, G. V., & Miller, T. I. (1980). *The benefits of psychotherapy*. Baltimore: Johns Hopkins University Press.

Smith, S. (1989). Mental health expert witnesses: Of science and crystal balls. *Behavioral Sciences and the Law, 7*, 145–180.

Smith, T. B., Rodriguez, M. M. D., & Bernal, G. (2011). Culture. In J. C. Norcross (Ed.), *Psychotherapy relationships that work: Evidence-based responsiveness* (2nd ed.). New York, NY: Oxford University Press.

Snowdon, D. A., Greiner, L. H., Kemper, S. J., Nanayakkara, N., & Mortimer, J. A. (1999). Linguistic ability in early life and longevity: Findings from the Nun Study. In J.-M. Robine, B. Forette, C. Franceschi, & M. Allard (Eds.), *The paradoxes of longevity* (pp. 103–113). Berlin: Springer-Verlag.

Snowdon, D. A., Greiner, L. H., & Markesbery, W. R. (2000). Linguistic ability in early life and the neuropathology of Alzheimer's disease and cerebrovascular disease: Findings from the Nun Study. *Annals of the New York Academy of Sciences, 903*, 34–38.

Snyder, D. K., Castellani, A. M., & Whisman, M. A. (2006). Current status and future directions in couple therapy. *Annual Review of Psychology, 57*, 317–344.

Sommer, R. (2006). Dual dissemination: Writing for colleagues and the public. *American Psychologist, 61*, 955–958.

Sommers-Flanagan, J. & Sommers-Flanagan, R. (2008). *Clinical interviewing* (4th ed.). New York, NY: John Wiley & Sons.

Sommers-Flanagan, J. & Sommers-Flanagan, R. (2012). *Counseling and psychotherapy theories* (2nd ed.). Hoboken, NJ: John Wiley & Sons.

Soulier, M. F., Maislen, A., & Beck, J. C. (2010). Status of the psychiatric duty to protect, circa 2006. *Journal of the American Academy of Psychiatry and the Law, 38*, 457–573.

Southam-Gerow, M. A., Rodriguez, A., Chorpita, B. F., & Daleiden, E. L. (2012). Dissemination and implementation of evidence based treatments for youth: Challenges and recommendations. *Professional Psychology: Research and Practice*.

Spangler, W. D. (1992). Validity of questionnaire and TAT measures of need for achievement: Two meta-analyses. *Psychological Bulletin, 112*, 140–154.

Spearman, C. (1904). "General intelligence" objectively determined and measured. *American Journal of Psychology, 15*, 201–293.

Spence, S. H., Donovan, C. L., March, S., Gamble, A., Anderson, R. E., Prosser, S., & Kenardy, J. (2011). A randomized controlled trial of online versus clinic-based CBT for adolescent anxiety. *Journal of Consulting and Clinical Psychology, 79*, 629–642.

Spence, S. H., Holmes, J. M., March, S., & Lipp, O. V. (2006). The feasibility and outcome of clinic plus internet delivery of cognitive-behavior therapy for childhood anxiety. *Journal of Consulting and Clinical Psychology, 74,* 614–621.

Sperry, L. (2007). *The ethical and professional practice of counseling and psychotherapy.* Upper Saddle River, NJ: Pearson.

Sperry, R. W. (1961). Cerebral organization and behavior. *Science, 133,* 1749–1757.

Sperry, R. W. (1968). Hemisphere deconnection and unity in conscious awareness. *American Psychologist, 23,* 723–733.

Sperry, R. W. (1974). Lateral specialization in the surgically separated hemispheres. In F. O. Schmitt & F. G. Worden (Eds.), *The neurosciences: Third study program* (pp. 5–20). Cambridge, MA: MIT Press.

Sperry, R. W. (1982). Some effects of disconnecting the cerebral hemispheres. *Science, 217,* 1223–1226.

Spiegel, T. A., Wadden, T. A., & Foster, G. D. (1991). Objective measurement of eating rate during behavioral treatment of obesity. *Behavior Therapy, 22,* 61–68.

Spiegler, M. D. & Guevremont, D. C. (2010). *Contemporary behavior therapy* (3rd ed.). Belmont, CA: Wadsworth, Cengage Learning.

Spengler, P. M., White, M. J., Ægisdóttir, S., et al. (2006). The meta-analysis of clinical judgment accuracy: Effects of experience on judgment accuracy. *The Counseling Psychologist, 37,* 350–399.

Spreen, O. (2011). Nonverbal learning disabilities: a critical review. *Child Neuropsychology, 17*(5), 418–443.

Spring, B. (2007). Evidence-based practice in clinical psychology: What it is, why it matters, what you need to know. *Journal of Clinical Psychology, 63,* 611–631.

St. Lawrence, J. S., Brasfield, T. L., Jefferson, K. W., Alleyne, E., & O'Bannon, R. E., III (1995). Cognitive-behavioral intervention to reduce African American adolescents' risk for HIV infection. *Journal of Consulting & Clinical Psychology, 63,* 221–237.

Stahl, P. M. (1994). *Conducting child custody evaluations: A comprehensive guide.* Thousand Oaks, CA: Sage.

Stam, C. J. & van Straaten, E. C. (2012). The organization of physiological brain networks. *Clinical Neurophysiology,* Epub February 20, 2012.

Standen, P. J. & Brown, D. J. (2005). Virtual reality in the rehabilitation of people with intellectual disabilities: Review. *CyberPsychology and Behavior, 8,* 272–282.

Stark, K. D., Hargrave, J., Sander, J., Custer, G., Schnoebelen, S., Simpson, J., & Molnar, J. (2006). Treatment of childhood depression: The ACTION treatment program. In P. C. Kendall (Ed.), *Child and adolescent therapy* (3rd ed., pp. 169–216). New York, NY: Guilford.

Starkstein, S. E., Jorge, R. E., & Robinson, R. G. (2010). The frequency, clinical correlates, and mechanism of anosognosia after stroke. *Canadian Journal of Psychiatry, 55*(6), 355–361.

Starkstein, S. E. & Robinson, R. G. (1988). Lateralized emotional response following stroke. In M. Kinsbourne (Ed.), *Cerebral hemisphere function in depression.* Washington, DC: American Psychiatric Press.

Staub, R. O. (2011). *Health psychology: A BioPsychoSocial approach.* New York, NY: Worth.

Steadman, H. J. (1993). *Reforming the insanity defense: An evaluation of pre- and post-Hinckley reforms.* New York, NY: Guilford.

Stein, D. J. (2006). Advances in understanding the anxiety disorders: The cognitive-affective neuroscience of "false alarms." *Annals of Clinical Psychiatry, 18,* 173–182.

Sternberg, R. J. (2004). Individual differences in cognitive development. In P. Smith & C. Hart (Eds.), *Blackwell handbook of cognitive development.* Malden, MA: Blackwell.

Sternberg, R. J. (2006a). *Cognitive psychology* (4th ed.). Belmont, CA: Wadsworth.

Sternberg, R. J. (2011). The Theory of successful intelligence. In R. J. Sternberg & S. B. Kaufman (Eds.). *The Cambridge handbook of intelligence* (pp. 504–526). New York, NY: Cambridge University Press.

Sternberg, R. J. & Kaufman, S. B. (Eds.). (2011). *The Cambridge handbook of intelligence.* New York, NY: Cambridge University Press.

Sternberg, S. (2011). Modular processes in mind and brain. *Cognitive Neuropsychology, 28*(3-4), 156–208.

Steketee, G. & Foa, E. B. (1985). Obsessive-compulsive disorder," In D. H. Barlow (Ed.), *Clinical Handbook of Psychological Disorders: A Step-by-Step Treatment Manual* (pp. 69–144). New York, NY: Guilford Press.

Stewart, G. L., Darnold, T. C., Zimmerman, R. D., Parks, L., & Dustin, S. L. (2010). Exploring how response distortion of personality measures affects individuals. *Personality and Individual Differences. 49,* 622–628.

Stewart, R. E. & Chambless, D. L. (2007). Does psychotherapy research inform treatment decisions in private practice? *Journal of Clinical Psychology, 63,* 267–281.

Stewart, R. E. & Chambless, D. L. (2009). Cognitive-behavioral therapy for adult anxiety disorders in clinical practice: A meta-analysis of effectiveness studies. *Journal of Consulting and Clinical Psychology, 77,* 595–606.

Stirman, S. W. & Crits-Christoph, P. (2011). Psychotherapy research: Implications for optimal therapist personality, training, and development. In R. H. Klein, H. S. Bernard, & V. L. Schermer (Eds). *On Becoming a Psychotherapist* (245–268). New York, NY: Oxford University Press.

Stokols, D. (1992). Establishing and maintaining healthy environments: Toward a social ecology of health promotion. *American Psychologist, 47,* 6–22.

Stolorow, R. D. (1993). An intersubjective view of the therapeutic process. *Bulletin of the Menninger Clinic, 57,* 450–458.

Stone, A. A. & Neale, J. M. (1984). New measures of daily coping: Developments and preliminary results. *Journal of Personality and Social Psychology, 46,* 892–906.

Stoney, C. M., West, S. G., Hughes, J. W., Lentino, L. M., Finney, M. L., Falko, J., Bausserman. (2002). Acute psychological stress reduces plasma triglyceride clearance. *Psychophysiology, 39,* 80–85.

Storch, E. A. & Crisp, H. L. (2004). Taking it to the schools: Transporting empirically supported treatments for childhood psychopathology to the school setting. *Clinical Child and Family Psychology Review, 7,* 191–193.

Strauss, E. & Wada, J. (1983). Lateral preferences and cerebral speech dominance. *Cortex, 19,* 165–177.

Straub, R. O. (2006). *Health psychology: A biopsychosocial approach* (2nd ed.). New York, NY: Worth Publishers.

Stricker, G. (2010). *Psychotherapy integration.* Washington, DC: American Psychological Association.

Stricker, G. (2011). PsyD programs. In J. C. Norcross, G. R. VandenBos, & D. K. Freedheim (Eds.), *History of psychotherapy: Continuity and change* (2nd ed., pp. 630–639). Washington, DC: American Psychological Association.

Strickler, G. & Gold, J. (Eds.). (2006). *A casebook of psychotherapy integration.* Washington, DC: American Psychological Association.

Strohmer, D. C. & Shivy, V. A. (1994). Bias in counselor hypothesis testing: Testing the robustness of counselor confirmatory bias. *Journal of Counseling and Development, 73,* 191–197.

Strother, C. R. (1956). *Psychology and mental health.* Washington, DC: American Psychological Association.

Strupp, H. H. (1989). Psychotherapy: Can the practitioner learn from the researcher? *American Psychologist, 44,* 717–724.

Stuart, R. B. (1969). Operant-interpersonal treatment of marital discord. *Journal of Consulting and Clinical Psychology, 33,* 675–682.

Sturmey, P. & Hersen, M. (2012a). *Handbook of evidence-based practice in clinical psychology* (Vol 1): *Child and aAdolescent disorders.* Hoboken, NJ: John Wiley & Sons.

Sturmey, P. & Hersen, M. (2012b). *Handbook of evidence-based practice in clinical psychology* (Vol 2): *Adult disorders.* Hoboken, NJ: John Wiley & Sons.

Stuss, D. T. (2011). Functions of the frontal lobes: relation to executive functions. *Journal of the International Neuropsychological Society, 17*(5), 759–765.

Sue, D. W. & Sue, D. (2008). *Counseling the culturally diverse: Theory and practice* (5th ed.). New York, NY: John Wiley & Sons.

Suh, C. S., Strupp, H. H., & O'Malley, S. S. (1986). The Vanderbilt process measures: The Psychotherapy Process Scale (VPPS) and the Negative Indicators Scale (VNIS). In L. Greenberg & W. Pinsof (Eds.), *The psychotherapeutic process: A research handbook* (pp. 285–323). New York, NY: Guilford.

Sullivan, H. S. (1953). *The interpersonal theory of psychiatry.* New York, NY: W. W. Norton.

Sullivan, M. F., Skovholt, T. M., & Jennings, L. (2005). Master therapists' construction of the therapeutic relationship. *Journal of Mental Health Counseling, 27,* 48–70.

Suls, J. & Wang, C. K. (1993). The relationship between trait hostility and cardiovascular reactivity: A quantitative review and analysis. *Psychophysiology, 30,* 1–12.

Summers, R. F. & Barber, J. P. (2009). *Psychodynamic therapy: A guide to evidence-based practice.* New York, NY: The Guilford Press.

Sundberg, N. D. (1977). *Assessment of persons.* New York, NY: Prentice Hall.

Sundberg, N. D., Tyler, L. E., & Taplin, J. R. (1973). *Clinical psychology: Expanding horizons* (2nd ed.). Englewood Cliffs, NJ: Prentice-Hall.

Super, J. T. (1999). Forensic psychology and law enforcement. In A. K. Hess & I. B. Weiner (Eds.), *The handbook of forensic psychology* (2nd ed., pp. 409–439). New York, NY: John Wiley & Sons.

Swain, M. A. & Steckel, S. B. (1981). Influencing adherence among hypertensives. *Research Nursing and Health, 4,* 213–218.

Sweet, A. A. (1984). The therapeutic relationship in behavior therapy. *Clinical Psychology Review, 4,* 253–272.

Swift, J. K. & Greenberg, R. P. (2012). Premature discontinuation in adult psychotherapy: A meta-analysis. *Journal of Consulting and Clinical Psychology,* April 16, 2012, No Pagination Specified. Doi: 10.1037/a0028226.

Swift, J. K., Callahan, J. L. (2009). The impact of client treatment preferences on outcome: a meta-analysis. *Journal of Clinical Psychology, 65,* 368–381.

Swim, J. K., Stern, P. C., Doherty, T. J., Clayton, S., Reser, J. P., Weber, E. U. Et al. (2011). Psychology's contributions to understanding and addressing global climate change. *American Psychologist, 66,* 241–250.

Synovitz, L. B. & Larson, K. L. (2012). *Complementary and alternative medicine for health professionals.* Burlington, MA: Jones & Bartlett Learning.

Tallent, N. (1992). *The practice of psychological assessment.* Englewood Cliffs, NJ: Prentice-Hall.

Tanielian, T. & Jaycox, L. (Eds.). (2008). *Invisible wounds of war: Psychological and cognitive injuries, their consequences, and services to assist recovery.* Santa Monica, CA: Rand Corporation.

Tavris, C. & Aronson, E. (2007). *Mistakes were made (but not by me).* New York, NY: Harcourt.

Taylor, E. (2000). Psychotherapeutics and the problematic origins of clinical psychology in America. *American Psychologist, 55,* 1029–1033.

Taylor, S. E. (1995). *Health psychology.* New York, NY: McGraw-Hill.

Taylor, S. E. (2005). *Health psychology.* New York, NY: McGraw-Hill.

Taylor, S.E. (2010). Mechanisms linking early life stress to adult health outcomes. *Proceedings of the National Academy of Sciences, 107,* 8507–8512.

Taylor, S. E. (2011). *Health Psychology.* New York, NY: McGraw-Hill.

Taylor, S. E., Kemeny, M. E., Reed, G. M., Bower, J. E., & Gruenewald, T. L. (2000). Psychological resources, positive illusions, and health. *American Psychologist, 55,* 99–109.

Taylor, S., Zvolensky, M. J., Cox, B. J., Deacon, B., Heimberg, R. G., et al. (2007). Robust dimensions of anxiety sensitivity: Development and initial validation of the Anxiety Sensitivity Index—3. *Psychological Assessment, 19,* 176–188.

Teasdale, A. C. & Hill, C. E. (2006). Preferences of therapists-in-training for client characteristics. *Psychotherapy: Theory, Research, Practice, Training, 43,* 111–118.

Tellegen, A. (1982). *Brief manual for the Multidimensional Personality Questionnaire.* Unpublished manuscript, University of Minnesota.

Tellegen, A., Ben-Porath, Y. S., McNulty, J. L., Aribisi, P. A., Grahm, J. R. et al. (2003). *MMPI-2 Restructured Clinical (RC) Scales: Development, validation, and interpretation.* Minneapolis: University of Minnesota Press.

Temerlin, M. K. (1968). Suggestion effects in psychiatric diagnosis. *Journal of Nervous and Mental Disease, 147,* 349–353.

Templer, D. I. (2005). Addendum to concerns about professional schools. *Psychological Reports, 97*, 117–118.

Tennen, H., Affleck, G., Armeli, S., & Carney, M. A. (2000). A daily process approach to coping. *American Psychologist, 55*, 626–636.

Testa, M. & Collins, R. L. (1997). Alcohol and risky sexual behavior: Event-based analyses among a sample of high-risk women. *Psychology of Addictive Behaviors, 11*, 190–201.

Thase, M. E. (2012). Social skills training for depression and comparative efficacy research: A 30-year retrospective. *Behavior Modification, 36*, 545–557.

Thoits, P. A. (1986). Social support as coping assistance. *Journal of Consulting and Clinical Psychology, 54*, 416–423.

Thoresen, C. E. & Powell, L. H. (1992). Type A behavior pattern: New perspectives on theory, assessment, and intervention. *Journal of Consulting and Clinical Psychology, 60*, 595–604.

Thorn, B. E. (2007). Evidence-based practice in psychology. *Journal of Clinical Psychology, 63*, 607–609.

Thorne, F. C. (1972). Clinical judgment. In R. H. Woody & J. D. Woody (Eds.), *Clinical assessment in counseling and psychotherapy* (pp. 30–85). Englewood Cliffs, NJ: Prentice-Hall.

Thurston, I. B. & Phares, V. (2008). Mental health service utilization among African American and Caucasian mothers and fathers. *Journal of Consulting and Clinical Psychology, 76*, 1058–1067.

Tisdelle, D. A. & St. Lawrence, J. S. (1988). Adolescent interpersonal problem-solving skill training: Social validation and generalization. *Behavior Therapy, 19*, 171–182.

Tolin, D. F. (2010). Is cognitive-behavioral therapy more effective than other therapies? A meta-analytic review. *Clinical Psychology Review, 30*, 710–720.

Tomlinson-Clarke, S. & Camilli, G. (1995). An exploratory study of counselor judgments in multicultural research. *Journal of Multicultural Counseling and Development, 23*, 237–245.

Tompkins, C. A. (2012). Rehabilitation for cognitive-communication disorders in right hemisphere brain damage. *Archives of Physical Medicine and Rehabilitation, 93*(1 Suppl), S61-69.

Tryon, G. S. (1990). Session depth and smoothness in relation to the concept of engagement in counseling. *Journal of Counseling Psychology, 37*, 248–253.

Tucker, N. (2001, December 11). High court passes on Capitol suspect. *The Washington Post*, B1.

Turk, D. C. & Rudy, T. E. (1990). Pain. In A. S. Bellack, M. Hersen, & A. E. Kazdin (Eds.), *International handbook of behavior modification and therapy* (2nd ed., pp. 399–413). New York, NY: Plenum Press.

Tutin, J. (1993). The persistence of initial beliefs in clinical judgment. *Journal of Social and Clinical Psychology, 12*, 319–335. Vincent, G. M. (2006). Psychopathy and violence risk assessment in youth. *Child and Adolescent Psychiatric Clinics of North America, 15*, 407–428.

Tyler, K. L. & Malessa, R. (2000). The Goltz-Ferrier debates and the triumph of cerebral localizationalist theory. *Neurology, 55*, 1015–1024.

Ullmann, L. P. & Krasner, L. (1975). *A psychological approach to abnormal behavior*. Englewood Cliffs, NJ: Prentice-Hall.

Ungerleider, L. G. & Mishkin, M. (1982). Two cortical visual systems. In D. J. Ingle, M. A. Goodale, & R. J. W. Mansfield (Eds.), *Analysis of visual behavior*. Cambridge, MA: MIT Press.

UNICEF (2010). The children left behind: A league table of inequality in child well-being in the world's rich countries. *Innocenti Report Card 9*, Florence: UNICEF Innocenti Research Centre.

Urbina, S. (2011). Tests of intelligence. In R. J. Sternberg & S. B. Kaufman (Eds.). *The Cambridge handbook of intelligence* (pp. 20–38). New York, NY: Cambridge University Press.

Vaillant, G. E. (2000). Adaptive mental mechanisms: Their role in a positive psychology. *American Psychologist, 55*, 89–98.

Valkenburg, P. M. & Peter, J. (2009). Social consequences of the internet for adolescents: A decade of research. *Current Directions in Psychological Science, 18*, 1–5.

VandenBos, G. R., DeLeon, P. H., & Belar, C. D. (1991). How many psychological practitioners are needed? It's too early to know. *Professional Psychology: Research and Practice, 22*, 441–448.

Vanderbilt-Adriance, E. & Shaw, D. S. (2008). Protective factors and the development of resilience in the context of neighborhood disadvantage. *Journal of Abnormal child Psychology, 36*, 887–901.

Van Der Heijden, P. T., Egger, J. I. M., & Derksen, J. J. L. (2010). Comparability of scores on the MMPI-2-RF scales generated with the MMPI-2 and MMPI-2-RF booklets. *Journal of Personality Assessment, 92*, 254–259.

Van der Maas, H. L. J., Dolan, C. V., Grasman, R. P. P. P., Wicherts, J. M., et al. (2006). A dynamical model of general intelligence: The positive manifold of intelligence mutualism. *Psychological Review, 113*, 842–861.

vanOort, F. V. A., vanderEnde, J., Wadsworth, M. E., Verhulst, F. C., & Achenbach, T. M. (2011). Cross-national comparison of the link between socioeconomic status and emotional and behavioral problems in youth. *Social Psychiatry and Psychiatric Epidemiology, 46*, 167–172.

Van Zeijl, J., Mesman, J., Ijzendoorn, M. H. V., Bakermans-Kranenburg, M. J., Juffer, F., Stolk, M. N., Koot, H. M., & Alink, L. R. A. (2006). Attachment-based intervention for enhancing sensitive discipline in mothers of 1- to 3-year-old children at risk for externalizing behavior problems: A randomized controlled trial. *Journal of Consulting and Clinical Psychology, 74*, 994–1005.

Vane, J. R. (1981). The Thematic Apperception Test: A review. *Clinical Psychology Review, 1*, 319–336.

Varley, R., Webb, T. L., & Sheeran, P. (2011). Making self-help more helpful: A randomized controlled trial of the impact of augmenting self-help materials with implementation intentions on promoting the effective self-management of anxiety symptoms. *Journal of Consulting and Clinical Psychology, 79*, 123–128.

Vasquez, M. J. T. (2011). The internship crisis: Strategies and solutions. *Monitor on Psychology, 42*, 4.

Vasquez, M. J. T. & Jones, J. M. (2006). Increasing the number of psychologists of color: Public policy issues for affirmative diversity. *American Psychologist, 61*, 132–142.

Verfaellie, M. & Keane, M. M. (1997). The neural basis of aware and unaware forms of memory. *Seminars in Neurology, 17*, 153–61.

Vogel, M. E., Kirkpatrick, H. A., Collings, A. S., Cederna-Meko, C. L., & Grey, M. J. (2012). Integrated care: Maturing the relationship between psychology and primary care. *Professional Psychology: Research and Practice, 43*, 271–280.

Vrieze, S. I. & Grove, W. M. (2009). Survey on the use of clinical and mechanical prediction methods in clinical psychology. *Professional Psychology: Research and Practice, 40*, 525–531.

Wachtel, P. L. (2010). *Relational theory and the practice of psychotherapy.* New York, NY: The Guilford Press.

Wada, J. & Rasmussen, T. (1960). Intracarotid injection of sodium amytal for the lateralization of cerebral speech dominance. *Journal of Neurosurgery, 17*, 266–282.

Wade, C. J. (2012). Psychotherapeutic skill preferences of clinical psychologists, licensed clinical psychotherapists, licensed specialist clinical social workers, and psychiatrists. Emporia State University unpublished dissertation, URI: http://hdl.handle .net123456789/1077.

Wade, S. L., Oberjohn, K., Conaway, K., Osinska, P., & Bangert, L. (2011). Live coaching of parenting skills using the internet: Implications for clinical practice. *Professional Psychology: Research and Practice, 42*, 487–493.

Walfish, S. & Barnett, J. E. (2009). *Financial success in mental health practice: Essential tools and strategies for practitioners.* Washington, DC: American Psychological Association.

Walker, B. B. & London, S. (2007). Novel tools and resources for evidence-based practice in psychology. *Journal of Clinical Psychology, 63*, 633–642.

Walker, E. F., Grimes, K. E., Davis, D. M., & Smith, A. J. (1993). Childhood precursors of schizophrenia: Facial expressions of emotion. *American Journal of Psychiatry, 150*, 1654–1660.

Wallace, L. M. & vonRanson, K. M. (2011). Treatment manuals: Use in the treatment of bulimia nervosa. *Behaviour Therapy Research and Therapy, 49*, 815–820.

Wallen, R. W. (1956). *Clinical psychology: The study of persons.* New York, NY: McGraw-Hill.

Walsh, B. W. & Betz, N. E. (2001). *Tests and assessment* (4th ed.). Upper Saddle River, NJ: Prentice Hall.

Walter, A., Bundy, C., & Dornan, T. (2005). How should trainees be taught to open a clinical interview? *Medical Education, 39*, 492–496.

Wampold, B. E., Hollon, S. D., & Hill, C. E. (2010). Unresolved questions and future direction in psychotherapy research. In J. C. Norcross, G. R. VandenBos, & D. K. Freedheim (Eds). *History of Psychotherapy: Continuity and Change* (2nd ed.). Washington, DC: American Psychological Association.

Wang, P. S., Aguilar-Gaxiola, S., Alonso, J., Angermeyer, M. C., Borges, G., Bromet, E. J., et al. (2007). Use of mental health services fro anxiety, mood, and substance disorders in 17 countries in the WHO world mental health surveys. *The Lancet, 370*, 841–850.

Ward, C. H., Beck, A. T., Mendelson, M., Mock, J. E., & Erbaugh, J. K. (1962). The psychiatric nomenclature. *Archives of General Psychiatry, 7*, 198–205.

Ward, L. C. (2006). Comparison of facture structure models for the Beck Depression Inventory-II. *Psychological Assessment, 18*, 81–88.

Watson, J. C., Goldman, R. N., & Greenberg, L. S. (2011). Humanistic and experiential theories of psychotherapy. In J. C., Norcross, G. R. Vandenbos, & D. K. Freedheim, D. K. (Eds.) (2011). *History of Psychotherapy: Continuity and Change* (pp. 141–172). Washington, DC: American Psychological Association.

Watson, R. I. (1953a). A brief history of clinical psychology. *Psychological Bulletin, 50*, 321–346.

Watson, R. I. (1978). *The great psychologists* (2nd ed.). Philadelphia, PA: Lippincott.

Wearden, A. J., Tarrier, N., Barrowclough, C., Zastowny, T. R., & Rahill, A. A. (2000). A review of expressed emotion research in health care. *Clinical Psychology Review, 20*, 633–666.

Wechsler, D. (1967). *Manual for the WPPSI.* New York, NY: Psychological Corporation.

Wechsler, D. (2003). *WISC-IV technical and interpretive manual.* San Antonio, TX: The Psychological Corporation.

Wechsler, D. (2008). Wechsler, D. (2008). *Wechsler Adult Intelligence Scale—Fourth Edition.* San Antonio, TX: Pearson.

Weeks, G. R. & Treat, S. R. (2001). *Couples in treatment: Techniques and approaches for effective practice* (2nd ed.). New York, NY: Brunner-Routledge.

Wegenek, A. R. & Buskist, W. (2010). *The insider's guide to the psychology major: Everything you need to know about the degree and profession.* Washington, DC: American Psychological Association.

Weick, K. E. (1968). Systematic observational methods. In G. Lindzey & E. Aronson (Eds.), *Handbook of social psychology* (Vol. 2, 2nd ed., pp. 357–451). Reading, MA: Addison-Wesley.

Weiner, B. (Ed.). (1974). *Achievement motivation and attribution.* Morristown, NJ: General Learning Press.

Weiner, I. B. & Hess, A. K. (Eds.). (2006). *The handbook of forensic psychology* (3rd ed.). Hoboken, NJ: John Wiley & Sons.

Weir, K. (2012). (2012). APA launches a new database of tests and measures. *Monitor on Psychology*, 13.

Weiss, R. D., Najavits, L. M., Muenz, L. R., & Hufford, C. (1995). Twelve-month test-retest reliability of the Structured Clinical Interview for DSM-III-R Personality Disorders in cocaine-dependent patients. *Comprehensive Psychiatry, 36*, 384–389.

Weissman, H. N. (1991). Child custody evaluations: Fair and unfair professional practices. *Behavioral Sciences and the Law, 9*, 469–476.

Weissman, M. M., Verdell, H., Gameroff, M. J., Bledsoe, S. E., Betts, K., et al. (2006). National survey of psychotherapy training in psychiatry, psychology, and social work. *Archives of General Psychiatry, 63*, 925–934.

Weisz, J. R. (2004). *Psychotherapy for children and adolescents: Evidence-based treatments and case examples.* New York, NY: Cambridge University Press.

Weisz, J. R., Donenberg, G. R., Han, S. S., & Weiss, B. (1995). Bridging the gap between laboratory and clinic in child and adolescent psychotherapy. *Journal of Consulting and Clinical Psychology, 63*, 688–701.

Weisz, J. R., Jensen-Doss, A., & Hawley, K. M. (2006). Evidence-based youth psychotherapies versus usual clinical care: A meta-analysis of direct comparisons. *American Psychologist, 61*, 671–689.

Weisz, J. R., Doss, A. J., & Hawley, K. M. (2005). Youth psychotherapy outcome research: A review and critique of the evidence base. *Annual Review of Psychology, 56,* 337–363.

Weisz, J. R., Sandler, I. N., Durlak, J. A., & Anton, B. S. (2005). Promoting and protecting youth mental health through evidence-based prevention and treatment. *American Psychologist, 60,* 628–648.

Weiten, W. (2011). *Psychology: Themes and variations.* New York, NY, Wadsworth/Cengage.

Wekerle, C., MacMillan, H. L., Leung, E., & Jamieson, E. (2008). Child maltreatment. In M. Hersen & A. M. Gross (Eds.). *Handbook of clinical psychology (Vol. 2): Children and adolescents* (pp. 429–457). Hoboken, NJ: John Wiley & Sons.

Wellmer, J., Fernandez, G., Linke, D. B., Urbach, H., Elger, C. E., & Kurthen, M. (2005). Unilateral intracarotid amobarbital procedure for language lateralization *Epilepsia, 46*(11), 1764–1772.

Wells, A. (2011). Metacognitive therapy. In J. D. Herbert & E. M. Forman (Eds.), *Acceptance and mindfulness in cognitive behavior therapy: Understanding and applying the new therapies* (pp. 83–108). Hoboken, NJ: John Wiley & Sons.

Wells, M. G., Burlingame, G. M., Lambert, M. J., Hoag, M. J., & Hope, C. A. (1996). Conceptualization and measurement of patient change during psychotherapy: Development of the Outcome Questionnaire and Youth Outcome Questionnaire. *Psychotherapy: Theory, Research, Practice and Training, 33,* 275–283.

Welsh, B. C. & Farrington, D. P. (2007). Saving children from a life of crime: Toward a national strategy for early prevention. *Victims and Offenders, 2,* 1–20.

Wenzel, A., Liese, B. S., Beck, A. T., & Friedman-Wheeler, D. G. (2012). *Group cognitive therapy for addictions.* New York, NY: Guilford.

Werner, J. M., Cermak, S. A., & Aziz-Zadeh, L. (2010). Neural correlates of developmental coordination disorder. *Journal of Behavioral and Brain Sciences, 2,* 258–268.

West, M., Bondy, E. & Hutchinson, S. (1991). Interviewing institutionalized elders: Threats to validity. *Journal of Nursing Scholarship, 23,* 171–176.

West, S. L. & O'Neal, K. K. (2004). Project D.A.R.E outcome effectiveness revisited. *American Journal of Public Health, 94,* 1027–1029.

Westen, D. (2012). Prototype diagnosis of psychiatric syndromes. *World Psychiatry, 11,* 16–21.

Wetchler, J. L. (Ed.) (2011). *Handbook of clinical issues in couple therapy* (2nd ed). New York, NY: Routledge/Taylor & Francis Group.

Wetzel, E., Hell, B. & Pässler, K. (2012). Comparison of different construction strategies in the development of a gender fair interest inventory using verbs. *Journal of Career Assessment, 20,* 88–104.

Whitehouse, W. G., Orne, E. C., & Dinges, D. F. (2010). Extreme cognitive interviewing: A blueprint for false memories through imagination inflation. *International Journal of Clinical and Experimental Hypnosis, 58,* 29–287.

Wicks-Nelson, R. & Israel, A. C. (2008). *Abnormal child and adolescent psychology* (7th ed.). Upper Saddle River, NJ: Prentice Hall.

Widiger, T. A., Frances, A. J., Pincus, H. A., Davis, W. W., & First, M. B. (1991). Toward an empirical classification for the DSM-IV. *Journal of Abnormal Psychology, 100,* 280–288.

Widiger, T. A. & Trull, T. J. (2007). Plate tectonics in the classification of personality disorder: Shifting to a dimensional model. *American Psychologist, 62,* 71–83.

Wiggins, J. S. (1973). *Personality and prediction: Principles of personality assessment.* Reading, MA: Addison-Wesley.

Wiggins, J. G. & Wedding, D. (2004). Prescribing, professional identity, and costs. *Professional Psychology: Research and Practice, 35,* 148–150.

Wilber, D. Q. (2012, Feb 9). Closing arguments delivered in John Hinckley hearing. *The Washington Post.* Available online at http://www.washingtonpost.com/local/crime/closing-arguments-delivered-in-john-hinckley-hearing/2012/02/09/gIQAr4ZS2Q_story.html.

Wilkinson, G. S. (1993). *WRAT-3: Wide range achievement test administration manual.* Wilmington, DE: Wide Range, Inc.

Williams, C. L., Arnold, C. B., & Wynder, E. L. (1977). Primary prevention of chronic disease beginning in childhood: The Know Your Body Program: Design of study. *Preventive Medicine, 6,* 344–357.

Williams, C. L. & Butcher, J. N. (2011). *A beginner's guide to the MMPI-A.* Washington, DC: American Psychological Association.

Williams, C. R. & Abeles, N. (2004). Issues and implications of deaf culture in therapy. *Professional Psychology: Research and Practice, 35,* 643–648.

Williams, J. C. & Lynn, S. J. (2010). Acceptance: An historical and conceptual review. *Imagination, Cognition, and Personality, 30,* 5–56.

Williams, R. B., Jr. & Barefoot, J. C. (1988). Coronary-prone behavior: The emerging role of the hostility complex. In B. K. Houston & C. R. Snyder (Eds.), *Type A behavior pattern: Research, theory and intervention* (pp. 189–211). New York, NY: John Wiley & Sons.

Williams, T. H., McIntosh, D. E., Dixon, F., Newton, J. H., & Youman, E. (2010). Confirmatory factor analysis of the Stanford-Binet Intelligence Scales, Fifth edition, with a high-achieving sample. *Psychology in the Schools, 47,* 1071–1083. doi: 10.1002/pits.20525.

Williams, T. R. (1967). *Field methods in the study of culture.* New York, NY: Holt, Rinehart, & Winston.

Willock, B. (2007). *Comparative-integrative psychoanalysis: A relational perspective for the discipline's second century.* New York, NY: The Analytic Press.

Wilmshurst, L. (2008). *Abnormal child psychology: A developmental perspective.* New York, NY: Taylor & Francis, Inc.

Wilson, D. K. & Lawman, H. G. (2009). Health promotion in children and adolescents: An integration of the biopsychosocial model and ecological approaches to behavior change. In M. C. Roberts & R. G. Steele (Eds.), *Handbook of pediatric psychology* (4th ed., pp. 603–617). New York, NY: Guilford.

Wilson, G. T. (2011). Clinical psychology. In *IAPP Handbook of Applied Psychology* (Eds P. R. Martin, F. M. Cheung, M. C., Knowles, et al.), Oxford: Wiley-Blackwell.

Wilson, G. T. & Zandberg, L. J. (2012). Cognitive-behavioral guided self-help for eating disorders: Effectiveness and scalability. *Clinical Psychology Review, 32,* 343–357.

Wilson, S. & Durbin, C. E. (2012). The Laboratory parenting Assessment Battery: Development and preliminary validation of an observational parenting rating system. *Psychological Assessment*. Advance online publication. doi: 10.1037/a0028352.

Willyard, C. (2010). On-call scientists. *Monitor on Psychology, 41*, 30.

Winerman, L. (2005). The mind's mirror. *Monitor on Psychology, 37*, 48–50.

Winnicott, D. W. (1965). *The maturational processes and the facilitating environment*. New York, NY: International Universities Press.

Winocur. G., Craik, F. I., Levine, B., Robertson, I. H., Binns, M. A., Alexander, M., et al. (2007). Cognitive rehabilitation in the elderly: Overview and future directions. *Journal of the International Neuropsychology Society, 13*, 166–171.

Winsor, A. P. (2003). Direct behavioral observation for classrooms. In C. R. Reynolds & R. W. Kamphaus (Eds.), *Handbook of psychological and educational assessment of children: Personality, behavior, and context* (2nd ed., pp. 248–255). New York, NY: Guilford.

Wolak, J., Finkelhor, D., Mitchell, K. J., & Ybarra, M. L. (2008). Online "predators" and their victims: Myths, realities, and implications for prevention and treatment. *American Psychologist, 63*, 111–128.

Wolitzky, D. L. (2003). The theory and practice of traditional psychoanalytic treatment. In A. S. Gurman & S. B. Messer (Eds.), *Essential Psychotherapies* (2nd ed., pp. 244–68). New York, NY: Guilford Press.

Wolitzky, D. L. (2011). Contemporary Freudian Psychoanalytic Psychotherapy. In S. B. Messer & A. S. Gurman (Eds.) *Essential Psychotherapies* (3rd ed., pp. 33–71). New York, NY: The Guilford Press.

Wolk, D. A., Coslett, H. B., & Glosser, G. (2005). The role of sensory-motor information in object recognition: evidence from category-specific visual agnosia. *Brain and Language, 94*(2), 131–146.

Wolpe, J. (1958). *Psychotherapy by reciprocal inhibition*. Stanford, CA: Stanford University Press.

Wolpe, J. & Lang, P. J. (1969). *Fear Survey Schedule*. San Diego: Educational and Industrial Testing Service.

Wong, H. M. & Chow, L. Y. (2011). Borderline personality disorder subscale (Chinese version) of the Structured Clinical Interview for DSM-IV Axis II Personality Disorders: A validation study in Cantonese-speaking Hong Kong Chinese. *East Asian Archives of Psychiatry, 21*, 52–57.

Wood, A. M. & Tarrier, N. (2010). Positive clinical psychology: A new vision and strategy for integrated research and practice. *Clinical Psychology Review, 30*, 819–829.

Wood, A. M., Froh, J. J., & Geraghty, A. W. A. (2010). Gratitude and well-being: A review and theoretical integration. *Clinical Psychology Review, 30*, 890–905.

Wood, J. M., Lilienfeld, S., Garb, H., & Nezworski, M. (2000). The Rorschach Test in clinical diagnoses: A critical review with a backward look at Garfield (1947). *Journal of Clinical Psychology, 56*, 395–430.

Wood, J. M., Lilienfeld, S., Nezworski, M. T., Garb, H. N., Allen, K. H. et al. (2010). Validity of the Rorschach Inkblot scores for discriminating psychopaths from nonpsychopaths in forensic populations: A meta-analysis. *Psychological Assessment, 22*, 336–349.

Woodcock, R. W., McGrew, K. S., & Mather, N. (2000). *Woodcock-Johnson III*. Itasca, IL: Riverside Publishing.

Woodworth, R. S. (1920). *Personal data sheet*. Chicago: Stoelting.

Wortman, C. B. & Lehman, D. R. (1985). Reactions to victims of life crises: Support attempts that fail. In I. G. Sarason & B. R. Sarason (Eds.), *Social support: Theory, research, and applications* (pp. 463–489). Dordrecht, The Netherlands: Martinus Nijhoff.

Wright, J. H., Basco, M. R., & Thase, M. E. (2006). *Learning cognitive-behavior therapy*. Washington, DC: American Psychiatric Association.

Wright, J. H., Sudak, D. M., Turkington, D., & Thase, M. E. (2010). *High-yield cognitive-behavior therapy for brief sessions*. Washington, DC: American Psychiatric Publishing.

Wright, J. W. (2010). *Conducting psychological assessment*. Hoboken, NJ: John Wiley & Sons.

Wrightsman, L. S. & Fulero, S. M. (2005). *Forensic psychology* (2nd ed.). Belmont, CA: Thomson-Wadsworth.

Wrightsman, L. S., Nietzel, M., Fortune, W., & Greene, E. (2002). *Psychology and the legal system* (5th ed.). Pacific Grove, CA: Brooks/Cole.

Wulfert, E., Greenway, D. E., & Dougher, M. J. (1996). A logical functional analysis of reinforcement-based disorders: Alcoholism and pedophilia. *Journal of Consulting and Clinical Psychology, 64*, 1140–1151.

Wulsin, L. R. & Singal, B. M. (2003). Do depressive symptoms increase the risk for the onset of coronary disease? A systematic quantitative review. *Psychosomatic Medicine, 65*, 201–210.

Yalom, I. D. & Leszcz, M. (2005). *The theory and practice of group psychotherapy*. New York, NY: Basic Books.

Yang, M., Wong, S. C. P., & Coid, J. (2010). The efficacy of violence prediction: A meta-analytic comparison of nine risk assessment tools. *Psychological Bulletin, 136*, 740–767.

Yarhouse, M. A. & Tan, E. S. N. (2005). Addressing religious conflicts in adolescents who experience sexual identity confusion. *Professional Psychology: Research and Practice, 36*, 530–536.

Yasui, M. & Dishion, T. J. (2007). The ethnic context of child and adolescent problem behavior: Implications for child and family interventions. *Clinical Child and Family Psychology, 10*, 137–179.

Ybarra, M. L., Boyd, D., Korchmaros, J. D., & Oppenheim, J. K. (2012). Defining and measuring cyberbullying within the larger context of bullying victimization. *Journal of Adolescent Health Care*. Advance online publication: doi 10.1016/j.jadohealth 2011.12.031.

Ybarra, M. L., Espelage, D. L., & Mitchell, K. J. (2007). The co-occurrence of internet harassment and unwanted sexual solicitation victimization and perpetration: Associations with psychosocial indicators. *Journal of Adolescent Health, 41*, 31–41.

Yerkes, R. M. (1921). Psychological examining in the United States army. *Memoirs of the National Academy of Sciences. 15*, 1–890.

Yoshikawa, H., Aber, J. L., & Beardslee, W. R. (2012). The effects of poverty on the mental, emotional, and behavioral health of children and youth: Implications for prevention. *American Psychologist, 67*, 272–284.

Yoshimasu, K. (2001). Relation of type A behavior pattern and job-related psychosocial factors to nonfatal myocardial infarction: A case-control study of Japanese male workers and women. *Psychosomatic Medicine, 63*, 797–804.

Young, L. D. (1992). Psychological factors in rheumatoid arthritis. *Journal of Consulting and Clinical Psychology, 60*, 619–627.

Youngstrom, E. A. & Kendall, P. C. (2009). Psychological science and bipolar disorder. *Clinical Psychology: Science and Practice, 16,* 93–97.

Zalta, A. K. & Foa, E. B. (2012). Exposure therapy: Promoting emotional processing of pathological anxiety. In W. T. O'Donahue & J. E. Fisher (Eds.). *Cognitive behavior therapy: Core principles for practice* (pp. 75–104). New York, NY: John Wiley & Sons.

Zanarini, M. C., Skodol, A. E., Bender, D., Dolan, R., & Sanislow, C. (2000). The collaborative longitudinal personality disorders study: Reliability of axis I and II diagnoses. *Journal of Personality Disorders, 14,* 291–299.

Zapata, A., Kreuch, T., Landers, R. N., Hoyt, T. & Butcher, J. N. (2009). Clinical personality assessment in personnel settings using the MMPI-2: A cross-cultural comparison. *International Journal of Clinical and Health Psychology, 9,* 287–298.

Zaza, C., Sellick, S. M., & Hillier, L. M. (2005). Coping with cancer: What do patients do? *Journal of Psychosocial oncology, 23,* 55–73.

Zero to Three (2005). *Diagnostic classification of mental health and developmental disorders of infancy and early childhood: Revised Edition (DC: 0-3R).* Washington, DC: Zero to Three Press.

Zetin, M. & Glenn, T. (1999). Development of a computerized psychiatric diagnostic interview for use by mental health and primary care clinicians. *CyberPsychology & Behavior, 2,* 223–233.

Zheng, D., Macera, C. A., Croft, J. B., Giles, W. H., Davis, D., Scott, W. K. (1997). Major depression and all-cause mortality among white adults in the United States. *Annals of Epidemiology, 7,* 213–218.

Zigmond, A. S. & Snaith, R. P. (1983). The Hospital Anxiety and Depression Scale. *Acta Psychiatrica Scandinavica, 67,* 361–370.

Zilboorg, G. & Henry, G. W. (1941). *A history of medical psychology.* New York, NY: W. W. Norton.

Zimmerman, M. A. (2000). Empowerment theory: Psychological, organizational and community levels of analysis. In J. Rappaport & E. Seidman (Eds.), *Handbook of community psychology* (pp. 42–63). New York, NY: Kluwer Academic/Plenum Publishers.

Ziskin, J. & Faust, D. (1988). *Coping with psychiatric and psychological testimony* (4th ed., Vols. 1–3). Marina del Rey, CA: Law & Psychology Press.

Zoellner, L. A., Feeny, N. C., Cochran, B., & Pruitt, L. (2003). Treatment choice for PTSD. *Behaviour Research and Therapy, 41,* 879–886.

Zola-Morgan, S. (1995). Localization of brain function: The legacy of Franz Joseph Gall (1758–1828). *Annual Review of Neuroscience, 18,* 359–383.

Zubin, J. & Spring, B. (1977). Vulnerability—A new view of schizophrenia. *Journal of Abnormal Psychology, 86,* 103–126.

Zytowski, D. G. (2007). Kuder Career Search with Person Match technical manual 1.1. Retrieved 19 June 2007, from http://www.kuder .com/publicweb/kcs_manual.aspx.

NAME INDEX

SUBJECT INDEX

CREDITS

TEXT

Chapter 3

Page 75: Sundberg, N. D., Tyler, L. E., & Taplin, J. R. (1973). Clinical psychology: Expanding horizons (2nd ed.). Englewood Cliffs, NJ: Prentice-Hall. (c) Reprinted and Electronically reproduced by permission of Pearson Education, Inc., Upper Saddle River, New Jersey.

Chapter 4

Page 88: Wallen, R. W. (1956). *Clinical psychology: The study of persons.* New York: McGraw-Hill.

Chapter 6

Page 169: Beutler, L. E., & Groth-Marnat, G. (2003). *Integrative assessment of adult personality* (2nd ed.). New York, NY: Guilford.

Chapter 7

Pages 190–191: Some of the material in this book was originally published in The Second Century of Psychoanalysis: Evolving Perspectives on Therapeutic Action, edited by Michael J. Diamond and Christopher Christian (published by Karnac Books in 2011), and is reproduced with kind permission of Karnac Books.

Page 198: (c) Murdock, N. L. (2004). *Theories of counseling and psychotherapy.* Upper Saddle River, NJ: Pearson. Reprint and Electronically reproduced by permission of Pearson Education, Inc., Upper Saddle River, New Jersey.

Page 198: Sommers-Flanagan, J., & Sommers-Flanagan, R. (2012) *Counseling and psychotherapy theories* (2nd ed.). Hoboken, NJ: Wiley & Sons.

Chapter 8

Page 224 (top): Beck, J. S. (2011). *Cognitive behavior therapy: Basics and beyond.* New York, NY: The Guilford Press.

Page 224 (bottom): Beck, J. S. (2011). *Cognitive behavior therapy: Basics and beyond.* New York, NY: The Guilford Press.

Page 229: From: Gorenstein, E. E., & Comer, R. J. (2002). *Case studies in abnormal psychology.* New York, NY: Worth Worth Publishers. Copyright © 2002 by Worth Publishers. Reprinted with permission.

Chapter 9

Page 243: Ables, B. S., & Brandsma, J. M. (1977). *Therapy for couples.* San Francisco, CA: Jossey-Bass.

Page 243: Weeks, G. R., & Treat, S. R. (2001). *Couples in treatment: Techniques and approaches for effective practice* (2nd ed.). New York, NY: Brunner-Routledge.

Page 244: Based on Weisz, J. R. (2004). *Psychotherapy for children and adolescents: Evidence-based treatments and case examples.* New York, NY: Cambridge University Press.

Chapter 10

Page 263 Liu, E. T. (2007). Integrating cognitive-behavioral and cognitive-interpersonal case formulations: A case study of a Chinese American male. *Pragmatic Case Studies in Psychotherapy, 3,* 1–33.

Page 269: Based on data from Chambless, D. L., & Ollendick, T. H. (2001). Empirically supported psychological treatments. *Annual Review of Psychology, 52,* 685–716.

Pages 276–277: Based on data from Kendall, P. C., & Comer, J. S. (2011). Research methods in clinical psychology. In D. H. Barlow (Ed.), *The Oxford handbook of clinical psychology* (pp. 52–75). New York: Oxford University Press.

Chapter 11

Page 300: Based on Weisz, J. R. (2004). *Psychotherapy for children and adolescents: Evidence-based treatments and case examples.* New York, NY: Cambridge University.Press.

Chapter 13

Page 345: Shenker, J. I. (April 2005). *When you only see trees, is there still a forest?* Paper presented at the American Academy of Neurology Annual Meeting, Miami Beach, FL.

Chapter 14

Pages 362–363: From Wrightsman, L. S., Nietzel, M., Fortune, W., & Greene, E. (2002). *Psychology and the legal system* (5th ed.). Pacific Grove, CA: Brooks/Cole. (c) 2002 Wadsworth, a part of Cengage Learning, Inc.

Chapter 15

Pages 405–406: Based on Gonzalez-Prendes, A. A., Hindo, C., & Pardo, Y. (2011). Cultural values integration in cognitive-behavioral therapy for a Latino with depression. *Clinical Case Studies, 10,* 376–394.

Chapter 16

Page 433–434: Based on Morgan, B. L., & Korschgen, A. J. (2006). *Majoring in psych? Career options for psychology undergraduates* (3rd ed.). Boston, MA: Allyn and Bacon.

PHOTOS

Chapter 1

Page 2: Alina Solovyova-Vincent/E+/Getty Images.

Chapter 2

Page 27: Science and Society/Superstock.

Page 30: Bettmann/Corbis.

Page 37: G. Paul Bishop.

Chapter 6

Page 161: Michael Newman/PhotoEdit, Inc.

Chapter 7

Page 178: Courtesy of Historical Pictures Service, Inc., Chicago, Illinois. Museum/AP Images. Reprinted by permission.

Page 179: Bettmann/Corbis

Page 194: Bettmann/Corbis

Chapter 8

Page 222: Aaron T. Beck.

Chapter 9

Page 238: Richard T. Nowitz/Corbis.

Chapter 10

Page 278: Renn Valo/Creative Digital Visions.

Chapter 11

Page 290: Joseph Sohm/Visions of America/Corbis.
Page 298: Myrleen Pearson/PhotoEdit, Inc.
Page 304: Lisa F. Young/Shutterstock

Chapter 12

Page 316: Science Source
Page 321: Morgan DDL/Shutterstock.
Page 325: Altrendo Images/Getty Images.
Page 327: Tony Freeman/PhotoEdit, Inc.

Chapter 14

Page 365: David J. Phillip, Pool/AP Images.

Chapter 15

Page 383: Auremar/Shutterstock.
Page 385: Florence Kaslow, Ph.D.
Page 402: Plush Studios/Photodisc/Getty Images.

Chapter 16

Page 435: Norcross et al. (2010).
Page 440: Ryan McVay/Photodisc/Thinkstock.

FIGURES/TABLES

Chapter 1

Page 5: Figure 1.1 Adapted from Kohout, J., & Wicherski, M. (2011). 2011 Graduate Study in Psychology: Applications, acceptances, enrollments, and degrees awarded to master's- and doctoral-level students in the U.S. and Canadian graduate departments of psychology: 2009–2010. *APA Center for Workforce Studies*. Retrieved Dec 21, 2011 from http://www.apa.org/workforce/publications/11-grad-study/applications.aspx.

Page 8: Figure 1.2 Based on Norcross, J. C., Karpiak, C. P., & Santoro, S. O. (2005). Clinical psychologists across the years: The Division of Clinical Psychology from 1960 to 2003. *Journal of Clinical Psychology, 61*, 1467–1483.

Page 11: Table 1.1 Michalski, D. S., & Kohout, J. L. (2011). The state of the psychology health service provider workforce. *American Psychologist, 66*, 825–843.

Page 12: Table 1.2 Finno, A. A., Michalski, M., Hart, B., Wicherski, M., & Kohout, J. L. (2010). Report of the 2009 APA Salary Survey. Retrieved Dec, 28, 2011 from http://www.apa.org/workforce/publications/09-salaries/index.aspx?tab=4.

Page 13: Figure 1.3 National Center for Education Statistics (2000). Digest of Education Statistics, 1999. Retrieved Dec 13, 2001 from http://nces.ed.gov/pubs2000/Digest99/d99t298.htm. Pate, W. E., II. (2001). Analyses of data from graduate study in psychology: 1999–2000. Retrieved Dec 12, 2001 from APA Research office, http://research.apa.org/grad00contents.html. Rozell, C. A., Berke, D. M., Norcross, J. C., & Karpiak, C. P. (2011). *Clinical psychologists in the 2010s: Fifty-year trends in Division 12 membership.* Presentation given at 2011 American Psychological Association Convention, August 4, 2011, Washington, DC. Sayette, M. A., Norcross, J. C., & Dimoff, J. D. (2011). The heterogeneity

of clinical psychology Ph.D. programs and the distinctiveness of APCS programs. *Clinical Psychology: Science and Practice, 18*, 4–11.

Chapter 2

Page 25: Figure 2.1 Courtesy of the Library of Congress, LC-USZC4-4556.
Page 33: Figure 2.2. American Psychological Association History and Archives, (2012). APA membership statistics. Retrieved January 5, 2012 from http://www.apa.org/about/archives/membership/index.aspx.

Chapter 3

Page 52: Table 3.2 Sundberg, N. D. (1977). *Assessment of persons*, 1st Ed., (c) 1977, pp. 97–98, 207. Reprinted and Electronically reproduced by permission of Pearson Education, Inc., Upper Saddle River, New Jersey.

Page 56: Figure 3.2 Houts, A. C. (2004). Discovery, invention, and the expansion of the modern: Diagnostic and Statistical Manuals of Mental Disorders. In L. E. Beutler & M. L. Malik (Eds.), *Rethinking the DSM: A psychological perspective* (pp. 17–68). Washington, DC: American Psychological Association.

Page 60: Figure 3.3 Kazdin, A. E. (2003). *Research design in clinical psychology* (4th ed., p. 322). Boston, MA: Allyn & Bacon. Reprinted and electronically reproduced by permission of Pearson Education, Inc., Upper Saddle River, NJ.

Chapter 4

Page 104: Table 4.5: Bufka, L., F. & Camp, N. (2010) Brief measures for screening and measuring mental health outcomes. In M. M. Antony & D. H. Barlow (Eds.) *Handbook of assessment and treatment planning for psychological disorders* (pp. 62–94). New York, NY: The Guilford Press.

Chapter 5

Page 130: Table 5.6 Roid, G. H. (2003). *Stanford-Binet Intelligence Scales technical manual* (5th ed.). Itasca, IL: Riverside Publishing., Wechsler, D. (2003). *WISC-IV technical and interpretive manual.* San Antonio, TX: The Psychological Corporation. Kaufman, A. S., & Kaufman, N. L. (2004a). *KABC-II: Kaufman Assessment Battery for Children* (2nd ed.). Circle Pines, MN: AGS Publishing.

Page 134: Table 5.7 Sundberg, N. D. (1977). *Assessment of persons*, 1st Ed., pp. 97–98, 207. (c) (1977) Adapted and Electronically reproduced by permission of Pearson Education, Inc. Upper Saddle River, New Jersey.

Page 135: Figure 5.2 Copyright © by the Regents of the University of Minnesota 1942, 1943 (renewed 1970), 1989.Used by permission of the University of Minnesota Press. All rights reserved. "MMPI" and "Minnesota Multiphasic Personality Inventory" are trademarks owned by the Regents of the University of Minnesota.

Page 136: Table 5.8 Data from Butcher (2009).

Page 139: Figure 5.3 Sundberg, N. D. (1977). *Assessment of persons*, 1st Ed., pp. 97–98, 207. Reprinted and Electronically reproduced by permission of Pearson Education, Inc., Upper Saddle River, New Jersey.

Page 143: Figure 5.4 Psychological Testing and Psychological Assessment, American Psychologist, February 2001, pp. 136–143, Table 2.

Chapter 6

Page 154: Figure 6.1 Data from Olfson, M., & Marcus, S. C. (2010). National trends in outpatient psychotherapy. *The American Journal of Psychiatry, 167*, 1456–1463.

Page 167: Table 6.4 Source: Based on Brems, C. (2001). *Basic skills in psychotherapy and counseling.* Belmont, CA: Wadsworth.

Page 169: Table 6.5 Harwood, T. M., Beutler, L. E., Williams, O. B., & Stegman, R. S. (2011). Identifying treatment-relevant assessment: Systematic Treatment Selection/InnerLife. In T. M. Harwood, L. E. Beutler, & G. Groth-Marnat (Eds), *Integrative assessment of adult personality* (pp. 61–79). New York, NY: Guilford.

Chapter 7

Page 188: Table 7.2 Adapted from Curtis, R. C., & Hirsch, I. (2003). Relational approaches to psychoanalytic psychotherapy. In A. S. Gurman & S. B. Messer (Eds.), *Essential psychotherapies* (2nd ed., pp. 69–106). New York, NY: Guilford Press. Gabbard, G. O. (2005). *Psychodynamic psychiatry in clinical practice* (4th ed.). Washington, DC: American Psychiatric Publishing. Hergenhahn, B. R. (1994). *An introduction to theories of personality*. Englewood Cliffs, NJ: Prentice Hall., Kutash, I. L. (1976). Psychoanalysis in groups: The primacy of the individual. *Current Issues in Psychoanalytic Practice, 1*, 29–42. Prochaska J. O., & Norcross, J. C. (2002). *Systems of psychotherapy: A trans-theoretical analysis* (5th ed.). Pacific Grove, CA: Brooks Cole. Wolitzky, D. L. (2003). The theory and practice of traditional psychoanalytic treatment. In A. S. Gurman & S. B. Messer (Eds.), *Essential psychotherapies* (2nd ed., pp. 244–268). New York, NY: Guilford Press.

Chapter 8

Page 213 Table 8.3 From Steketee, G., & Foa, E. B. (1985). Obsessive-compulsive disorder. In D. H. Barlow (Ed.), *Clinical handbook of psychological disorders: A step-by-step treatment manual* (pp. 69–144). New York, NY: Guilford Press. Adapted with permission.

Chapter 9

Page 239: Table 9.2 From Bieling, P. J., McCabe, R. E., & Antony, M. M. (2006). *Cognitive-behavioral therapy in groups* (p. 382). New York, NY: Guilford Press. Copyright 2006 by Guilford Press. Adapted with permission.

Page 241: Table 9.3 Adapted from Doss, B. D., Simpson, L. E., & Christensen, A. (2004). Why do couples seek marital therapy? *Professional Psychology: Research and Practice, 35*, 608–614.

Page 241 Figure 9.1 Carr, A. (2006). *The handbook of child and adolescent clinical psychology: A contextual approach* (2nd ed., p. 60). New York, NY: Routledge/Taylor & Francis Group.

Page 242: Figure 9.2 Halford, W. K., & Moore, N. E. (2002). Relationship education and the prevention of couple relationship problems. In A. S. Gurman & N. S. Jacobson (Eds.), *Clinical handbook of couple therapy* (3rd ed., pp. 400–419). New York, NY: Guilford Press.

Page 255: Figure 9.5 Mitchell, K. J., Becker-Blease, K. A., & Finkelhor, D. (2005). Inventory of problematic internet experiences encountered in clinical practice. *Professional Psychology: Research and Practice, 36*, 498–509.

Chapter 10

Page 267: Figure 10.2 Murphy, J. G., Dennhardt, A. A., Skidmore, J. R., Borsari, B., Barnett, N. P., et al. (2012). A randomized controlled trial of a behavioral economic supplement to brief motivational interventions for college drinking. *Journal of Consulting and Clinical Psychology, 80*, 876–886.

Page 270: Table 10.1 Based on data from http://www.div12.org/PsychologicalTreatments/index.html

Page 271: Figure 10.3 Spring, B. (2007). Evidence-based practice in clinical psychology: What it is, why it matters, what you need to know. *Journal of Clinical Psychology, 63*, 611–631.

Page 273: Table 10.2 Shirk, S. R., Karver, M. S., & Brown, R. (2011). The alliance in child and adolescent psychotherapy. *Psychotherapy, 48*, 17–24 (Quote from p. 19).

Page 276: Figure 10.4 Grilo, C. M., Masheb, R. M., & Wilson, G. T. (2006). Rapid response to treatment for binge eating disorder. *Journal of Consulting and Clinical Psychology, 74*, 602–613.

Page 279: Figure 10.5 From Stewart, R. E., & Chambless, D. L. (2007). Does psychotherapy research inform treatment decisions in private practice? *Journal of Clinical Psychology, 63*, 267–281.

Chapter 11

Page 292: Figure 11.1 Copyright © 2003 Seifer, R. (2003). Young children with mentally ill parents: Resilient developmental systems. In S. S. Luthar (Ed.), *Resilience and vulnerability: Adaptation in the context of childhood adversities* (pp. 29–49). New York, NY: Cambridge University Press.

Page 293: Figure 11.2 Copyright Achenbach, T. M., & Rescorla, L. A. (2001). *Manual for the Achenbach System of Empirically Based Assessment (ASEBA) school-age forms and profiles*. Burlington, VT: University of Vermont, Research Center for Children, Youth, and Families. Copyright 2001 by University of Vermont. P. 65. All names are fictitious Reproduced by permission.

Page 295: Figure 11.3 Brown, R. T., Carpenter, L. A., & Simerly, E. (2005). *Mental health medications for children: A primer*. New York, NY: Guilford.

Page 301: Figure 11.4 Stark, K. D., Hargrave, J., Sander, J., Custer, G., Schnoebelen, S., et al. (2006). Treatment of childhood depression: The ACTION treatment program. In P. C. Kendall (Ed.), *Child and adolescent therapy* (3rd ed., pp. 169–216). New York, NY: Guilford.

Page 303: Table 11.5 Based on data from http://effectivechildtherapy.com/

Page 303: Table 11.6 Adapted from Brown, R. T., Carpenter, L. A., & Simerly, E. (2005). *Mental health medications for children: A primer*. New York, NY: Guilford. Richmond, T. K., & Rosen, D. S. (2005). The treatment of adolescent depression in the era of the black box warning. *Current Opinion in Pediatrics, 17*, 466–472.

Page 306 Figure 11.5 Rescorla, L., Achenbach, T. M., Ivanova, M. Y., Dumenci, L., Almqvist, F., et al. (2007). Epidemiological comparisons of problems and positive qualities reported by adolescents in 24 countries. *Journal of Consulting and Clinical Psychology, 75*, 351–358.

Chapter 12

Page 320: Table 12.1 From Folkman, S., Lazarus, R. S., Gruen, R. J., & DeLongis, A. (1986). Appraisal, coping, health status, and psychological symptoms, *Journal of Personality and Social Psychology, 50*, 571–579. Copyright 1986. Adapted with permission.

Page 328: Table 12.2 Based on Prochaska, J. O., Velicer, W. F., Rossi, J. S., Goldstein, M. G., et al. (1994). Stages of change and decisional balance for 12 problem behaviors. *Health Psychology, 13*, 39–43.

Chapter 13

Page 347: Figure 13.3 Patrick Landmann/Science Source.

Chapter 15

Page 398: Table 15.3 Adapted from Pope, K. S., & Vasquez, M. J. T. (2011). *Ethics in psychotherapy and counseling: A practical guide* (4th ed.). Hoboken, NJ: John Wiley & Sons.

Page 402: Figure 15.1 Heiby, E. M., DeLeon, P. H., & Anderson, T. (2004). A debate on prescription privileges for psychologists. *Professional Psychology: Research and Practice, 35*(4), 336–344.

Page 404: Figure 15.2 Norcross, J. C., & Karpiak, C. P. (2012). Clinical psychologists in the 2010s: 50 years of the APA Division of Clinical Psychology. *Clinical Psychology: Science and Practice, 19*, 1–12.

Chapter 16

Page 417: Figure 16.2 Norcross, J. C., Karpiak, C. P., & Santoro, S. O. (2005). Clinical psychologists across the years: The Division of Clinical Psychology from 1960 to 2003. *Journal of Clinical Psychology, 61*, 1467–1483.

Page 418: Table 16.1 From Insider's Guide to Graduate Programs in Clinical and Counseling Psychology, 2012/2013 Edition, by J. C. Norcross, J. C., & Sayette, M. A. (2012). *Insider's guide to graduate programs in clinical and counseling psychology: 2012/2013 edition*. New York, NY: Guilford.. Copyright 2012 by Guilford Press. Used with permission.

Page 419: Table 16.2 Norcross, J. C., Castle, P. H., Sayette, M. A., & Mayne, T. J. (2004). The PsyD: Heterogeneity in practitioner training.

Professional Psychology: Research and Practice, 35, 412–419. Norcross, J. C., & Sayette, M. A. (2012). *Insider's guide to graduate programs in clinical and counseling psychology: 2012/2013 edition*. New York, NY: Guilford. Weissman, M. M., Verdell, H., Gameroff, M. J., Bledsoe, S. E., Betts, K., et al. (2006). National survey of psychotherapy training in psychiatry, psychology, and social work. *Archives of General Psychiatry, 63*, 925–934.

Page 421: Table 16.3 Data from Table 5c of the APA 2009 Doctorate Employment Survey (www.apa.org/workforce/publications/09-doc-empl/table-5abc.pdf).

Page 435: Norcross, J. C., Ellis, J. L., & Sayette, M. A. (2010). Getting in and getting money: A comparative analysis of admission standards, acceptance rates, and financial assistance across the research-practice continuum in clinical psychology programs. *Training and Education in Professional Psychology, 4*, 99–104.

Page 440: Ryan McVay/Photodisc/Thinkstock.